D0202959

WITHDRAWN

MAY 1 9 2020

UNBC Library

THE HISTORY OF THE
UNIVERSITY OF OXFORD
VOLUME VIII

THE HISTORY
OF THE
UNIVERSITY OF OXFORD

VOLUME VIII

The Twentieth Century

EDITED BY

BRIAN HARRISON

WITHDRAWN

MAY 1 9 2020

UNBC Library

CLARENDON PRESS · OXFORD

Oxford University Press, Walton Street, Oxford OX2 6DP
Oxford New York
Athens Auckland Bangkok Bogota Bombay
Buenos Aires Calcutta Cape Town Dar es Salaam
Delhi Florence Hong Kong Istanbul Karachi
Kuala Lumpur Madras Madrid Melbourne
Mexico City Nairobi Paris Singapore
Taipei Tokyo Toronto
and associated companies in
Berlin Ibadan

Oxford is a trade mark of Oxford University Press

Published in the United States by
Oxford University Press Inc., New York

© Oxford University Press 1994

All rights reserved. No part of this publication may be reproduced,
stored in a retrieval system, or transmitted, in any form or by any means,
without the prior permission in writing of Oxford University Press.
Within the UK, exceptions are allowed in respect of any fair dealing for the
purpose of research or private study, or criticism or review, as permitted
under the Copyright, Designs and Patents Act, 1988, or in the case of
reprographic reproduction in accordance with the terms of the licences
issued by the Copyright Licensing Agency. Enquiries concerning
reproduction outside these terms and in other countries should be
sent to the Rights Department, Oxford University Press,
at the address above

British Library Cataloguing in Publication Data
Dàta available

Library of Congress Cataloging in Publication Data
Data available
ISBN 0-19-822974-7

3 5 7 9 10 8 6 4

Printed in Great Britain
on acid-free paper by
Ipswich Book Co. Ltd, Suffolk

Preface

Lord Bullock, who launched this multi-volume project, gave the editor of this volume all kinds of help and support, particularly in the early stages when they were most needed. At one time Trevor Aston, the general editor of the series, thought of editing this volume himself, but his tragically early death in 1985 prevented him from seeing more than the sketchiest of plans for it. Nonetheless, the memory of his broad outlook on history and his enthusiasm for linking the past to the present both outlived him and have helped to mould much in this volume. Like its predecessors it owes much to the funding provided from four sources: the university, the colleges, the University's higher studies fund and the Nuffield Foundation.

The prosopographical survey of twentieth-century Oxford's senior and junior members which has informed so many of the chapters, and which has now taken on a life of its own, was generously and most considerately funded first by the Leverhulme Trust and then by the Economic and Social Research Council. The survey could not have succeeded without the colleges' consent to the use of their address-lists or without the willing (and often most painstaking) co-operation from the thousands of old members in our sample who filled in our questionnaires. We are especially grateful to those old members who were at Oxford between 1930 and 1979 who took the trouble to record their experience of Oxford in their own words by completing optional question 20 of the questionnaire. Others responded generously to requests for help published in college magazines. So Oxford's twentieth-century undergraduates have themselves helped to create a uniquely rich archive, which will long outlast this book and will guide our successors on how the University has influenced its junior members. The computerized bibliography of Oxford's history since 1914, which was originally launched as a working bibliography for contributors to this volume, has also taken on a life of its own, and now contains over 12,000 items.

In working on this volume we have been impressed by the goodwill towards it that we have encountered throughout Oxford, and with the trouble that people in all corners of the University have taken to help us. There were the regulars who turned up in fair weather and in foul to the 48 sessions of the seminar on twentieth-century Oxford which Michael Brock and I jointly launched in 1986 and which continued until 1990—not to mention the speakers who addressed them; the transcribed discussions were valuable enough to feature quite often in our footnotes. There were the fellows of Corpus, who were so patient and generous when the editor unscrupulously plundered their specialist knowledge. There were the people who agreed to be interviewed, only a tithe of whose wisdom and experience has been drawn upon in this volume. There were three successive university archivists (Ruth Vyse, Margaret MacDonald and Simon Bailey), who had the patience and understanding to help us get over the special problems posed by the abundance of our raw material, and whose helpfulness went well beyond any call of duty. There were the many college archivists who patiently and considerately handled a demanding editor. The Bodleian Library staff in the catalogue room helped us with tracing books and took special trouble to make material accessible to us.

An attempt has been made in this volume fully to integrate all types of material: text, plates, figures and tables. Figures and tables have deliberately not been consigned to appendices, but appear as far as possible at the point in the text where they are discussed. Likewise with the plates, which have been dispersed as far as possible at the appropriate points in the volume. Here Mr R. L. Wilkins of the Archaeological Institute gave us enormous help. He responded unfailingly and cheerfully to a battery of ill-coordinated requests for copies and enhancements of illustrations, thus performing an important service to the University. Much understanding was also shown by Trevor Langrish of the *Oxford Times and Mail*, whose photographs (Nos. 8.2, 8.4, 8.5, 10.2, 13.10, 14.3, 18.1, 19.13, 25.1, 26.1) appear by kind permission of Oxford and County Newspapers.

The staff of the Development Office, especially Peter Watson and Nick Daisley, gave invaluable help with address-lists. The late John Griffith found the time to translate and amply annotate vice-chancellors' addresses for us from the Latin. Oxford's infallibly knowledgeable and tolerant Head Clerk, Mr P. W. Moss, and his staff (especially Jeremy Drew) gave us crucially important help on numerous occasions, as did David Collins, Students' Record Officer. We owe much to the staff of the Oxford Union, especially to Mr Burden, who allowed the editor to carry off volumes of *Isis*. The staff of Oriel College library gave invaluable help at an early stage by allowing the editor to borrow their *Oxford Magazine*. The University's information officer Anne Lonsdale dug us out of many holes at crucial moments. Professor Fred Lee, when at what was then Leicester Polytechnic, most generously made the typescript of his *Oxford Economics and Oxford Economists* available to us in advance of publication.

The director and staff of the University's Computing Service were ever helpful. In particular, Linda Hayes, Grezyna Cooper, and Christine Windridge remained sympathetic even when our requests for computer resources must have seemed excessive. Lou Burnard gave much thought to technical problems which were no doubt for him tedious, yet he responded to them so cheerfully that we repeatedly came back with more for him to solve. Paul Salotti and later Beth Crutch were particularly helpful with their advice on INGRES, and Paul Griffiths and Glynis Edwards guided us through the intricacies of SAS.

Although he has himself written two chapters in the volume, we must make special mention of Chelly Halsey, who amid his many other commitments always made time to give us friendly help where we badly needed it, help which often he alone was qualified to provide. Many others (including the contributors to this volume) have helped its editor in numerous ways. We can do no more than list those who have helped us alphabetically and hope that we have omitted none who should have been included (all are or were from Oxford University unless otherwise stated): Alan Bell, Belinda Burnard, Brian Campbell, Howard Colvin, Jeremy Catto, Lord Dainton, E. E. East (formerly University Marshal), Jean Floud, Peter Foden, the late Lord Franks, John Goldthorpe, Lucy Howarth, John Jones, Anthony Kenny, David Landau, Jack Lankester, Michael Maclagan, David McKitterick (Trinity College, Cambridge), Jack McManners, Leslie Mitchell, Dennis Nineham, Sir Henry Phelps Brown, Harry Pitt, Bernard Richards, George Richardson, John Roberts, J. S. G. Simmons, Ann Spokes-Symonds, Michael Stansfield (now of Canterbury Cathedral, City and Diocesan Record Office), Richard Symonds, Bryan Ward-Perkins and Bryan Wilson. In the footnotes to their chapters, individual authors have made their special acknowledgements.

Special mention must be made of three people whose dedicated and unselfish labours have enriched all aspects of the volume. Mark Curthoys's commitment to volumes 6 and 7 never prevented him from responding generously when Volume 8 needed to plunder his unrivalled knowledge of Oxford's history since 1800. To crown his services to this volume, he read it through in its entirety and made many valuable suggestions shortly before we sent it to the publishers. Dan Greenstein's success as the volume's first research assistant owed much to qualities which stem from his American origins—energy, resourcefulness and enthusiasm—but it also owed much to rather more personal attributes: to his generosity, versatility, courage, tact and intelligence. Mark Pottle was Dan's ideal successor: self-effacing and efficient, splendidly honest and unfailingly helpful. It is a tribute to these three people that—in a University that has not always encouraged collaborative research in the arts—a small, harmonious and effective team of research assistants came into being. Key members of the group were Sinéad Smith and Daming Wu, whose commitment and resourcefulness were outstanding. They were ably assisted by Mary Heimann, Julie Maldoom, Mike Martin, Christopher Wilkie and by the Clarendon Building's lodge staff, who coped cheerfully with exceptional pressures. The backstage work done by this group involved months of often tedious and repetitive labour, to which this brief acknowledgement cannot begin to do justice. We can only hope that they will find their reward in the volume they did so much to create. Ralph Evans provided invaluable administrative help throughout work on this volume, and did much of the copy-editing for it. When he was unable to continue as copy-editor, Alice Park completed the task with splendid efficiency and resilience. Anne Gelling, who saw this book through the press, displayed to the full the qualities of patience and meticulousness that are so much needed if a volume as complex as this is ever to appear.

The shape of this volume requires brief explanation. The concluding chapters of Volume 7 will provide a broad picture of Oxford as it was at the outbreak of the First World War. Part One of this volume therefore plunges straight into the war in the first of three chapters that set the scene for inter-war Oxford. In Parts Two and Three (chapters 4 to 10) a broadly chronological flow is maintained. Part Two tackles college life first, then developments in teaching and research. Part Three begins with a chapter on the Second World War, and then provides three chapters (symmetrical with those in Part Two) which carry the story forward to 1970. Part Four's ten chapters cover the entire period in the broad areas where continuous treatment seemed desirable. By the end of Chapter 20 the ground is prepared for the three broad survey chapters of Part Five, which investigate Oxford's changing reputation and role in three of its spheres of influence. Part Six analyses the structural and financial implications of much that has so far been discussed, and then rounds off the volume with a discussion of the Franks Commission, whose report itself brilliantly surveys the entire ground covered by this volume. The scale of changes in higher-education policy in the 1980s makes it too early to grasp the full significance of the story told in this volume, but statistical series have wherever possible been carried beyond 1970. Furthermore the Epilogue describes the immediate impact made on Oxford by those changes, and seeks to provide some sort of connecting link between our historical material and Oxford as it is today.

Large as it is, this volume leaves ample scope for further research on the history of twentieth-century Oxford. It is a pity that no section of the Bodleian Library is set aside as a working place for the study of Oxford's history, and that undergraduate historians are not encouraged as a matter of course to submit a thesis for their honours degree. Their immediate environment offers ample scope for such ventures. An undergraduate thesis could, for example, profitably be devoted to the history of the undergraduates' own representative body, the Oxford University Student Union. Furthermore our coverage of individual faculties has been inevitably sketchy, and Oxford needs many more historical studies of its individual faculties along the lines of F. H. Lawson's study of the law school. It is to be hoped that this volume will stimulate rather than stifle the substantial research on Oxford's recent history that still needs to be done.

BRIAN HARRISON

Corpus Christi College, Oxford

Contents

List of plates and line-drawings   xi

List of maps and figures   xx

List of tables   xxii

Abbreviations and conventions   xxvi

List of contributors   xxviii

PART ONE. INTRODUCTION

 1 Oxford and the First World War   J. M. WINTER   3

 2 The Asquith Commission, 1919–1922   JOHN PREST   27

 3 The junior members, 1900–1990: a profile   DANIEL. I. GREENSTEIN   45

PART TWO. OXFORD BETWEEN THE WARS

 4 College life, 1918–1939   BRIAN HARRISON   81

 5 The arts and social studies, 1914–1939   ROBERT CURRIE   109

 6 The non-medical sciences, 1914–1939   J. B. MORRELL   139

PART THREE. OXFORD, 1939–1970

 7 Oxford and the Second World War   PAUL ADDISON   167

 8 College life, 1945–1970   KEITH THOMAS   189

 9 The arts and social sciences, 1939–1970   JOSE HARRIS   217

10 The non-medical sciences, 1939–1970   JOHN ROCHE   251

PART FOUR. LONG-TERM PERSPECTIVES, 1914–1970

11 Religion   F. M. TURNER   293
12 Medicine   CHARLES WEBSTER   317
13 Women   JANET HOWARTH   345
14 Politics   BRIAN HARRISON   377
15 Literary culture   VALENTINE CUNNINGHAM   413
16 Publishing and bookselling   R. A. DENNISTON   451
17 Libraries   GILES BARBER   471
18 Museums and art galleries   CHRISTOPHER WHITE   485
19 Architecture   DIANE KAY   499
20 Sport   D. J. WENDEN   519

PART FIVE. SPHERES OF INFLUENCE, 1914–1970

21 University and locality   RICHARD WHITING   543
22 Oxford and the British universities A. H. HALSEY   577
23 A world university   J. G. DARWIN   607

PART SIX. THE STRUCTURE OF THE UNIVERSITY, 1914–1970

24 Finance since 1914   J. P. D. DUNBABIN   639
25 Government and administration, 1914–1964 BRIAN HARRISON   683
26 The Franks Commission   A. H. HALSEY   721

PART SEVEN. EPILOGUE

27 The University since 1970   MICHAEL BROCK   739

Index of persons   775
General Index   809

List of plates and line-drawings

following p.98

1.1 Balliol freshmen in 1914. From left to right, back row: C. P. Blacker (wounded, twice mentioned in despatches, MC), G. E. Appleby, H. C. Pearson (twice wounded, MC), D. M. Matheson (Acting Major in France, invalided 1918), H. M. Gordon-Clark, W. W. Flint, A. Birnie. Middle row: R. Dutt, W. L. Wood, C. H. Howell, J. P. Shaw (MC, prisoner of war), D. J. Malcolmson, D. W. A. Nicholls (MC), P. M. Jones, J. S. Hickey, T. G. Esmonde. Front row: A. H. Graves (MC and bar, three times wounded, killed in action 1918), E. M. Jenkins, C. F. Hawkins (died of wounds received during experimental work for US Army Chemical Warfare Department, 1918), S. H. Paradise, C. H. Bosanquet, J. A. Byers, J. R. Willis (MC). Reproduced by permission of the Master and fellows of Balliol College.

4.1 Conversation piece of the Master and fellows of University College, 1934 by F. H. S. Shepherd. Under the bust of King Alfred are (back row, left to right) D. L. Keir, E. W. Ainley-Walker, A. D. Gardner, G. D. H. Cole, J. P. R. Maud, A. L. Goodhart, J. H. S. Wild and (front row) E. J. Bowen, A. B. Poynton, Sir Michael Sadler (Master), A. S. L. Farquharson, E. F. Carritt, G. H. Stevenson, K. K. M. Leys. Absent was Professor Sollas. This distinguished group of fellows includes four future masters of University College and one future master of Balliol. Reproduced by permission of the Master and fellows of University College.

4.2 Worcester College senior members at dessert, conversation piece c.1936 by William Rothenstein. Left to right are Paul Roberts (history), W. A. Pickard-Cambridge (philosophy), Col. C. H. Wilkinson (English), A. N. Bryan Brown (classics), Provost Lys. It was painted as a leaving present from a fellow-commoner. The *Times* 17 Aug. 1937, 11 thought Rothenstein had 'caught the essentials of a senior common room—that mixture of learning and comfort, that streak of aloofness between colleague and colleague, and those well-filled, rather large, glasses of port'. We are most grateful to Mr H. G. Pitt for taking much trouble to help us with the caption for this plate and for plates 4.3 and 8.1. These, and plates 4.5, 4.6 and 4.7 are reproduced by permission of the Provost and fellows of Worcester College.

4.3 Worcester College undergraduates in the front quad c.1937 by Edward I. Halliday. The *Times* 17 Aug. 1937, 11 noted that 'hardly any summer game seems unrepresented', from rowing and squash to tennis and rural sports. Drake (JCR Butler) is in the bottom right-hand corner. Also present, receding from foreground, are R. Tullis (with bagpipes), P. M. S. Allen (with gown), M. T. Walker (seated with books), P. Kershaw (seated, with tankard),

B. G. M. Carson (with golf clubs), J. C. Philpot (leaning, with scarf, and talking to G. F. Jarrett), D. Wolfers (V-neck with racquet), P. J. M. Anderson (with tie), T. J. H. Hetherington (with racquet and white trousers), M. E. M. Sandys (reading *Sporting Life*), R. H. More (leaning over him), M. G. R. Nevill (with pipe), E. W. M. Maitland (talking to Nevill), P. R. A. Ford (talking to the Revd G. V. R. Grant, who is in dressing-gown). The bearded man under the arches is the porter, Mr Bryant. The shadow of C. H. Wilkinson, fellow in English, who commissioned the painting, falls on the slope, bottom left.

4.4   Merton College Myrmidons, 1935. This élite club's album in Merton College Library contains many such photographs, and similar dining clubs are to be found in other colleges stuffed with hearties, each with special facings to their jackets. Back row, left to right: W. M. Moore, G. D. Leyland, S. C. Sleeman, R. C. Bewsher, C. L. Hall, A[irey] M. S. Neave. Front row, seated: K. A. Merritt, J. S. Daniel, G. J. Barry, R. A. Lamb, A. F. Johnstone-Wilson. Jeremy Isaacs (by then a prominent power in television) told Merton College's magazine, the *Postmaster*, in 1984 (p. 19) that when he became President of the Union the Myrmidons decided that he was worth knowing and invited him to become a member, but on anti-élitist grounds he politely declined. This photograph was kindly made available by the Librarian of Merton College.

4.5   St John's College Archery Club ladies' day, May 1928. Club members from left to right are Richard Turner (Rugby), Stephen Gatti (Beaumont College), John Blandy (Rugby), Donald Troup (Uppingham), Mervyn Longhurst CBE (Rugby, and owner of the photograph, who kindly supplied it). The man on the right with spectacles was a guest. The women are not undergraduates but mothers and girl friends.

following p. 130
4.6   The river in Eights Week in 1922, from the painting by Evelyn Dunbar. Not a skilful work of art, but excellent for capturing the colour and mood of what was between the wars a major and rather spectacular social event, with college flags flying and teas on the college barge (Worcester College archives).

4.7   Worcester College bump supper, 1929 (Worcester College archives).

6.1   In this photograph from 1924, W. H. Perkin (third from the left, front row) is sitting next to H. J. Stern, who kindly supplied the photograph. On Stern's left is Robert Haworth, whose obituarist in the *Daily Telegraph* 29 May 1990 described him as 'the founding father of the successful chemistry department' at Sheffield. Back row: J. J. Wall (Ch. Ch.), G. Gowring (St J), O. W. Snow (New), W. M. Sedgwick (*sic*, Lincoln), H. S. Pink, L. Rubinstein, F. W. Stoyle. Front row: R. H. Griffith, G. A. Edwards (St J), Perkin, Stern, Haworth, A. W. Bernton (Sweden).

7.1   Trinity College first eight, 1938, head of the river. Photographs of this kind were taken annually for sporting teams in every college. Sport, especially rowing, was very important in Trinity's undergraduate life between the wars, but this photograph is particularly poignant for what happened to its subjects shortly afterwards. From left to right, back row (standing): R. C. Furlong (k-i-a Western Europe Mar. 1945), P. Haig Thomas (coach), D. I. Graham (RAF pilot killed in flying accident Oct. 1941), H. L. O. Stevens (RAF pilot k-i-a Nov. 1940). Seated in front of them is R. H. Hillary (author of *The Last Enemy*, RAF Flt. Lt. shot down Sept. 1940, killed in night-flying training accident Jan. 1943). Seated in the front row are H. M. Young (RAF Flt. Lt. killed on return from the dam busters' raid May 1943), M. W. Rowe (Capt. Scots Guards, fought in North Africa), P. N. Drew-Wilkinson (cox), P. A. L. Waldron (Capt. Scots Guards, twice wounded) and J. S. Stockton (Capt. Scots Guards, k-i-a North Africa Apr. 1943). Photograph is by Gillman and Soame. We are most grateful to the Archivist, Trinity College, for help with this caption. Reproduced by permission of the President and fellows of Trinity College.

7.2 Enid Starkie (then fellow and tutor in modern languages at Somerville) lecturing in the old Bedford House schoolroom at Somerville, taken for an article on 'wartime life at a famous women's college' in the *Sketch*, 12 July 1944. We are most grateful to the Archivist Pauline Adams for help with the captions for this and for plate 13.4, which are reproduced by permission of the Principal and fellows of Somerville College.

8.1 Undergraduates in a (very characteristic undergraduate) room at Worcester, *c*.1952 by Edward I. Halliday. Clockwise from Jeremy Glyn (with tennis racquet, in doorway) are A. E. Harvey (inside window), John Abell (outside window), Lord Nicholas Gordon-Lennox (standing to right), Sir Andrew Cunningham (on sofa), Kerry St Johnston, W. E. Grenville-Grey. C. H. Wilkinson allegedly chose typical Worcester undergraduates for the painting, but his selective eye chose undergraduates drawn entirely from Eton or Winchester, with Cunningham (Wellington) added as an afterthought in response to criticism of his selection.

following p. 322

8.2 Christ Church New Library: north front before and after restoration (*Oxford Mail* 24 Nov. 1962, 4 printed both photographs, the restoration having recently been completed). This was the largest and most costly task hitherto undertaken by the Historic Buildings appeal.

8.3 Corpus Christi College bump supper, 1963. Dons are mingled with junior members. Presiding (with spectacles) is the President, Frank Hardie. The portrait of the founder, Bishop Fox, usually in the centre, has prudently been replaced by a reproduction of the Mona Lisa (Corpus Christi College archives, reproduced by permission of the President and fellows).

8.4 Captioned 'A word from the proctor', this photograph (June 1957) shows some sort of rebuke being delivered outside the Examination Schools by the

Senior Proctor (1957/8) William Holmes in the presence of the University Marshal (Mr W. R. Skinner) and a University policeman. The photograph, an enlarged version of which has long hung in the University Marshal's office, epitomizes disciplinary relationships that soon came to seem antique. The University Marshal Mr E. E. East suspected the undergraduate of being an ex-serviceman because he holds his right arm in approved parade-ground manner (*Oxford Mail* 13 June 1957, 1).

8.5   A. L. Goodhart (Master of University College 1951–63) with ten veteran members of the College staff in 1962. Their combined service totalled 455 years. Back row, left to right: A. Beesley, Gilbert Morse, R. O. Adams, H. A. Cummings, L. Blencowe, G. Mobey. Front row: Lewis Milward (who, with only 40 years' service, was the baby of the gathering), E. A. Heath (with 60 years' service, the longest-serving), the Master, J. H. Wilkins, T. Cox. All were scouts except G. Mobey, who looked after the chapel and Shelley memorial (*Oxford Mail* 29 May 1962, 4).

10.1   William Hume-Rothery (left) with the chief workshop technician, A. P. Fairless, examining (c.1957) a high-temperature arc melting furnace constructed in the department (Department of Materials archive).

10.2   Model (then on show in the Indian Institute) of the proposed zoology department building in the University Parks, 1962 by Chamberlin, Powell and Bon. Its 260-foot tower had 25 floors, and evoked so much controversy that it was never built (*Oxford Mail* 7 June 1962, 3).

following p. 354

10.3   L. R. Wager and colleagues at the Skaergaard base hut in East Greenland, summer 1953. Those present are (from left to right) Charles J. Hughes (research student, later Professor at the Memorial University, St John's, Newfoundland); Geoffrey D. Nicholls (then lecturer at Manchester, later Reader in Geochemistry there); Peter E. Brown (then research student at Manchester, later Professor at Edinburgh); Lawrence Wager (Professor at Oxford, and co-leader of the expedition); G. Malcolm Brown (then university demonstrator at Oxford, later Director of the British Geological Survey, knighted in 1985); William A. Deer (then Professor at Manchester, later Master of Trinity Hall Cambridge and Vice-Chancellor). Professor E. A. Vincent, to whom we owe these identifications, thinks that the photograph was taken by the remaining member of the expedition, Douglas Weedon (then a research student at Oxford, subsequently senior lecturer at Glasgow).

10.4   Members of the Bureau of Animal Population on a field course in Wytham Woods, 11 Sept. 1953. Those present are (from left to right) C. S. Elton, G. Blane, H. N. Southern, A. Macfadyen, M. Todorovic, D. Duckhouse, M. Boyd, T. Myers, T. Bagenall, J. Lock, R. Freeman. Photograph by D. A. Kempson (dept. of zoology). We are grateful to Mr K. T. Marsland for drawing our attention to this photograph and helping with its caption.

10.5 A. R. MacGill, principal technician in the Nuclear Physics Particle Accelerator Group, Clarendon Laboratory, discharging the 1.2 MeV Cockcroft Walton installation after an experimental run, 1954 (Clarendon Laboratory archive).

p. 327

12.1 E. H. Shepard's cartoon in *Punch* for 2 Dec. 1936 shows Lord Nuffield on the left. Lord Nuffield in a letter to the Vice-Chancellor on 15 Oct. 1936 promised to donate £1,250,000 to endow a Medical School Trust. At the meeting of Congregation to welcome this, he unexpectedly increased his offer to £2,000,000. Reproduced by permission of *Punch*.

following p. 354

13.1 Miss Ruth Butler with some home students in 1941 (St Anne's College archives, reproduced by permission of the Principal and fellows).

13.2 Henry Lamb's portrait of the Principal of St Hugh's and four fellows studying plans for the Mary Gray Allen Building in 1936. They are (left to right) Miss Procter (history tutor, and later Principal), Miss Wardale (formerly English language tutor), Miss Francis (French tutor, standing), Miss Gwyer (Principal, with pen) and Miss Ady (historian at the centre of the 'Row' of 1923–4). Reproduced by permission of the Principal and fellows of St Hugh's College.

13.3 Queen Mary's visit to Oxford, 11 Mar. 1921. *Oxford Times* 11 Mar. 1921 said that the main purpose of the visit was to satisfy the Queen's desire to see the work being done by the women students. She was the first woman to receive the Hon. DCL (in the Sheldonian at noon). In her reply to Curzon's address, she said she was 'confident that the women of this University will show themselves worthy of the great victory that they have won' (*Oxford Times* 18 Mar. 1921, 7) and supported the appeal on behalf of the women's colleges, to which she had herself given £500. She then lunched at Balliol and planted a mulberry tree. She visited Barnett House, Lady Margaret Hall and Somerville and had tea in Queen's. Back row, left to right: Miss Moberly (Principal, St Hilda's), Warden Pember (All Souls), Lady Ampthill (Lady-in-Waiting), President Warren (Magdalen), A. L. Smith (Master of Balliol), D. J. White (Dean of Christ Church), Countess Curzon, Miss Jourdain (Principal, St Hugh's), Mr H. Verney (Queen's private secretary). Front row (seated): Princess Mary, L. R. Farnell (Vice-Chancellor), Queen Mary, Earl Curzon (Chancellor), Mrs A. L. Smith, Mrs A. H. Johnson (Principal, Home-Students). Photograph kindly lent by the Dean of Christ Church.

13.4 Miss Darbishire and Miss Farnell with the Somerville JCR committee (all of whom came up in 1929) in a photograph probably taken in 1930–1 and published in the *Graphic*, 5 Mar. 1932. Left to right are Martha Hurst, Margaret Ross, almost certainly Margaret Richards, Diana Bosanquet, Ruth Field, the JCR President (seated), Miss Farnell and Miss Darbishire (Principal). Field later worked for the BBC. Hurst (later a Fellow of Lady

Margaret Hall and Mrs W. C. Kneale) and Ross (later Mrs A. R. W. Harrison) both married prominent Oxford dons (Somerville College archives).

p. 365

13.5 'Trog' responds in a cartoon to the *Observer*'s report on 5 June 1966 of a ruling from the Dean of Somerville, Mrs Mary Proudfoot, that her students should wear skirts 'down to at least knee-length' in their final examinations, so as to avoid distracting other examinees. The paper claimed that 'not one authentic mini-skirt was on display among the Somerville finalists or among girls from any of the other four women's colleges'. In the same issue Charis Frankenburg recalled that in 1913 the Warden of Keble had asked the Principal of Somerville 'that the women should not expose their *ankles* during schools, as it distracted the men'. Reproduced by permission of the *Observer*.

following p. 354

13.6 St Hilda's College eight on Oriel College barge with their coach, Mr Best, in 1921 (St Hilda's College archives, reproduced by permission of the Principal and fellows).

13.7 Oxford University Women's Rowing Crew in 1938 with their coach, Mr J. S. Mills, who is explaining wrist-movement during their final practice for racing against London University (St Anne's College archives, reproduced by permission of the Principal and fellows).

13.8 Menna Prestwich giving a tutorial on the Cromwell special subject to two modern history undergraduates in her room at St Hilda's in 1952. From left to right: Eleanor Brooksbank (now Wooller), Elaine Clement (now Fraser), Menna Prestwich. This was one of a series of publicity photographs taken for the Central Office of Information. We owe it to the late Mrs Wooller, who told us that it was posed: 'as I remember Menna claimed she could "produce the best looking undergraduates in the College". We are all slightly (but only slightly) smarter than usual.'

13.9 Group photograph taken at St Hilda's College ball in Feb. 1955 and owned by Mrs K. M. Baker (née Potter), who read botany at St Hilda's in 1953–6.

13.10 Four principals of St Hilda's College in 1981, celebrating the 90th birthday of Miss Julia de Lacy Mann (seated right, Principal, 1928–55). Seated on her right is Kathleen Major (Principal, 1955–65). Standing are (left) Mary Bennett (Principal, 1965–80) and (right) Mary Moore (Principal, 1980–90). 300 St Hilda's graduates attended the presentation of a brooch with the St Hilda's motif to Miss Mann. On that occasion it was announced that £22,000 had been raised from undergraduates during Miss Mann's time towards an appeal for a research fellowship (*Oxford Mail* 29 Jun. 1981, 8 under the headline 'Top old girls get together').

14.1 The caption 'A Training School for Statesmen: A Remarkable Photograph of an Oxford Union Debate on Victorian Ideals' is misleading because the debate does not seem to be in progress, and all present seem aware that a photograph is being taken. However the photograph (by Hills and Saunders of Oxford) is unusual, and was published in the *Illustrated London News* 9 Dec. 1922, 934–5. It was taken on the occasion of the Oxford Union debate on 30 Nov. 1922 on the motion of J. S. Collis (Balliol) 'that this House would welcome a return to Victorian ideals'. J. Griffith Morgan (St John's) opposed. Principal visiting speaker was Dean Inge, in the front row on the left, next but one to the table. Beverley Nichols also spoke. The motion was lost by 417 votes to 333. Unlike the House of Commons, the Union in 1922 still confined women to the galleries.

following p. 386

14.2 This photograph from the *Tatler* 13 Dec. 1950 shows the Oxford Union debating a verse of Belloc, and portrays five Oxford Union media people in the making. William Rees-Mogg (Librarian) is presiding, with Jeremy Thorpe (Treasurer and President-Elect) on his left. Norman St John-Stevas (mover) is standing on the left, Godfrey Smith (retiring President) is standing on the right. Reclining, centre, is Keith Kyle (Secretary).

14.3 Michael Stewart (Foreign Secretary, and President of the Union Michaelmas term 1929) addressing the Vietnam teach-in at the Oxford Union on 16 June 1965, Christopher Hill (Master of Balliol) in the chair. The teach-in was an innovation based on American precedents, and went on from 3 p.m. to 11.30 p.m. In his autobiography, Stewart says the Foreign Office advised against his going, but 'I decided . . . that I had a good case and knew enough about Oxford student audiences to put it over'. The speech was, he says, 'to the chagrin of the organizers . . . extremely well received, as was my subsequent answering of questions'. The *Oxford Mail* reported the debate on 17 June but does not appear to have used this photograph.

14.4 St Hilda's College undergraduates being presented by the Principal, Miss Mann, to Princess Margaret, who visited the College in 1954 to open a new porter's lodge (St Hilda's College archives, reproduced by permission of the Principal and fellows).

16.1 Water colour of John Johnson with his collection in the last year of his life, by H. A. Freeth, 1956. Johnson is standing in the archway between the third and fourth 'cabins' in which his collection was housed at the University Press before transfer to the Bodleian Library in 1968. These rooms were fitted up for the collection by Constance Meade Johnson. We are grateful to Ms Julie Wilson (of the Bodleian Library) for help with this photograph, which is reproduced by permission of the Freeth family and the John Johnson Collection, Bodleian Library, Oxford.

16.2 The new bindery in the Nagel Building at the Oxford University Press, opened in 1921 at a time of considerable investment in new machinery. At the back can be seen the bobbins of at least three sewing machines. On the left-hand side is a guillotine, and the large machine next to it is a Seybould three-knife trimmer bought in 1922. In the foreground are rounding and backing machines. The old man on the left is gluing by hand (machinery for this did not take over till the 1950s). This photograph was published in the *Clarendonian* for July 1922. We are most grateful to Peter Foden for help with this caption.

16.3   Sir James A. H. Murray (seated, centre) photographed on 10 July 1915 during his last day in the Scriptorium, Banbury Road, where *The Oxford English Dictionary* was created. He died on 26 July. Some of the slips for the *Dictionary*, which he edited from 1879, can be seen at his right elbow. Photographed with him are his daughters Elsie (left) and Rosfrith (right). Behind are (left to right) three helpers with the *Dictionary*: A. T. Maling, F. J. Sweatman and F. A. Yockney. We are grateful to Elizabeth Murray, granddaughter of Sir James, for this photograph.

p. 460
16.4   'Sprod' in *Punch* 17 Aug. 1949 comments on the Oxford English dictionaries. The volumes of the great *Oxford English Dictionary* were completed in 1928, and dates of first publication of its derivatives were: *Concise Oxford Dictionary* (1911), *Pocket Oxford Dictionary* (1924), *Shorter Oxford Dictionary* (1933). Reproduced by permission of *Punch*.

following p. 482
18.1   Queuing for Professor Wind's lecture on Picasso in 1957 at the Taylor Institution. The photograph is interesting not only for its own sake, but for illustrating what male and female undergraduates looked like in the days before jeans (*Oxford Mail* 14 Feb. 1957, 5).

following p. 514
19.1   Rhodes House, north frontage (Copyright A. F. Kersting).

19.2   Campion Hall, interior of chapel looking east (*Architect and Building News* 26 June 1936, 357).

19.3   Lady Margaret Hall chapel (Copyright A. F. Kersting).

19.4   Hubert Worthington's New College library frontage (1939), photographed by John Gibbons Studios on 27 Feb. 1993, with the city wall and bell tower on the left and Longwall Street cottages (now New College accommodation) on the right. (Copyright, New College, Oxford, whose Bursar most kindly arranged for the photograph to be taken for this volume.)

19.5   Merton College: roof of Warden's or Little Hall, after repair (*Architect* June 1975, 39) reproduced by permission.

19.6 St John's 'beehive' building (St John's College Archives, reproduced by permission of the President and fellows).

19.7 The Powell and Moya block at Brasenose, view across rooftops (*Architectural Design* Apr. 1962, 190) reproduced by permission .

19.8 St John's College: Sir Thomas White Building, view from garden (*Arup Journal* Apr. 1979, 4, reference no. AA221/486, reproduced by permission of Arup Associates Architects, Engineers and Quantity Surveyors).

following p. 546

19.9 St Antony's College: interior of dining hall, by courtesy of the British Cement Association.

19.10 St Catherine's College photographed from the air, shortly after completion in 1964. The two long strips are residential blocks. The three central blocks are (from left to right) dining hall (with kitchen attached), library and lecture block. The outlying buildings are (top right, oblong) squash courts, (bottom right, hexagon) music house, (circular structure, bottom left) cycle shed and (immediately above it) Master's Lodging. The Master of St. Catherine's, Dr. E. B. Smith, gave the editor generous help when he was seeking photographs of the College. This photograph, together with 19.11, is in the College's archive, and is reproduced by permission of the Master and fellows.

19.11 St Catherine's College, looking south-east from the north end of the Meadow Block towards (from right to left) the hall, the quad and the Wolfson Library.

19.12 St Cross Building exterior in 1964 (photo: John Donat).

19.13 Professor Nervi's visit to Oxford on 21 Mar. 1968 enabled him to meet the two British architects of the proposed new building for the Pitt Rivers Museum: Philip Powell and (left) Hidalgo Moya. At the lunch, the host, Walter Oakeshott (right), correctly pointed out that it was a long step between design and completion: 'in this case the step is £3,000,000 long'. The plans remained on the drawing-board (*Oxford Mail* 22 Mar. 1968, 9).

20.1 Roger Bannister—later Sir Roger, and Master of Pembroke College, Oxford and then President of the Oxford University Athletics Club—completing the world's first four-minute mile on the Iffley Road track on 6 May 1954, in a match between Oxford University and the Amateur Athletic Association. D. J. ('Charles') Wenden, late author of Chapter 20, was a judge at the event and is holding the scoreboard, clearly overcome with emotion. Bannister had lunched with Wenden and his family earlier that day, and Wenden had known and encouraged Sir Roger for some years (Central Press Photos).

25.1 Students scuffling with bedels, Nov. 1968. The bedel on the right is Alfred Packford, who drew our attention to the photograph. *Oxford Mail* 6 Nov.

1968, 7 reported under the headline 'Students regret scuffles'that Oxford Revolutionary Socialist Students insisted on their right to attend Congregation to present a statement of their demands for a 'transformed' democratic university, incorporating substitution of mixed for single-sex colleges, student participation in electing staff members and abolition of *in loco parentis* rules.

26.1   The Franks Commission's final hearing, 17 June 1965. It was the Commission's deliberate policy to receive all its oral evidence in public. From left to right facing the camera are Maurice Shock, Jean Floud, Sir Lindor Brown, Lord Franks, Sir Robert Hall, Margery Ord and J. Steven Watson, with Miss J. McDonald (shorthand writer) at the end of the table. With backs to the camera are J. B. Bamborough, Sir F. Sandford, Sir K. C. Wheare and J. H. C. Thompson (*Oxford Mail* 18 June 1965, 7).

List of Maps and Figures

1.1   Oxford's war losses, 1914–1919

3.1   Number of Oxford men and women matriculants, 1900–1987

3.2   Oxford's regional recruitment, 1920, 1949, 1970

3.3   Subject-balance of Oxford men and women finalists, 1900–1986

3.4   Norrington scores of Oxford arts and science finalists, and of men and women finalists, 1900–1986

3.5   Distribution of class results, all Oxford finalists, 1900–1986

3.6   Average age of Oxford men and women undergraduates and of postgraduates, 1900/1913 and 1960/1967

10.1   Science undergraduates in Britain, 1937–1989

10.2   Postgraduate students in science at Oxford, 1937–1985

10.3   Postgraduate science students in Britain, 1937–1989

10.4   Oxford scientists holding a university appointment, 1937–1990

10.5   Map showing the growth of the science area, 1914–1970

11.1   Map indicating location of religious institutions in Oxford, 1914–1970

13.1   Percentage of Oxford students 1930–1979 who by 1991 had married, distinguishing men and women

13.2   Percentage of married Oxford students 1930–1979 who married an Oxford spouse, distinguishing men and women

13.3 Percentage of women graduates who described themselves as housewives, voluntary workers or unemployed on leaving Oxford and after 10, 20 and 30 years

16.1 Map showing location of booksellers in Oxford, 1910–1970

16.2 Map showing location of publishers in Oxford, 1910–1970

16.3 Map showing location of printers in Oxford, 1919–1970

19.1 Map showing the main newly-built university and college buildings in Oxford, 1914–1990

20.1 Map showing college and university sports grounds, 1933

21.1 Map showing Oxford's river geography and the growth of Oxford's built-up area, 1918 and 1950

21.2 Map showing Oxford's road and river geography

21.3 Map showing Thomas Sharp's proposed new roads for Oxford

22.1 Number of university teachers in Great Britain by university group, 1910–1964

22.2 Population of Great Britain and number of university students, 1900–1971

22.3 Oxford and Cambridge as a proportion of all students and staff in universities in Great Britain, 1900–1971

23.1 Country of residence of Oxford's junior members, 1948–1973: percentage of total, and of women, from Commonwealth and foreign countries

23.2 Country of residence of Oxford's women junior members, 1948–1973: percentage of women from Commonwealth and foreign countries

24.1 Map showing Oxford's holdings of agricultural land and woodland (acres) in 1871

24.2 Map showing Oxford's holdings of agricultural land and woodland (acres) in 1920

24.3 Map showing Oxford's holdings of agricultural land and woodland (acres) in 1988/9

List of Tables

1.1   Military participation of members of the University of Oxford in all combatant armies in the First World War, distinguishing colleges

1.2   Age-structure of the service and losses of Oxford men in the First World War, distinguishing year of matriculation

3.1   Geographical origins of all Oxford men and women matriculants in 1920/1, 1949/50 and 1970/1, distinguishing British, Commonwealth, European, U.S.A. and other foreign

3.2   Secondary school origins in eight cohorts of Oxford men and women undergraduates in the arts, science and pass schools of the second public examination, 1900–1967

3.3   Father's occupation of Oxford men and women in 1900–1913, 1920–1939, 1946–1967, distinguishing gender

3.4   Career destinations of Oxford male arts finalists, 1900–1967

3.5   Career destinations of Oxford male science finalists, 1900–1967

3.6   Career destinations of Oxford female arts finalists, 1900–1967

3.7   Career destinations of Oxford female science finalists, 1900–1967

6.1   Subjects studied by postgraduates in Oxford at 10-year intervals from 1928/9 to 1964/5, distinguishing arts, social studies, pure science, applied science, agriculture and medicine

6.2   Oxford honour school finalists: individual schools and faculties as a percentage of the year total in 1923, 1928, 1938, 1948, 1958, 1963, 1964

7.1   Oxford undergraduates in residence, 1938–1945, distinguishing gender

7.2   Distribution of full-time students by faculty in Oxford in 1938/9 and 1945/6

10.1   Oxford final honours school scientists by school, and women as a percentage of finalists in those schools, at five-year intervals from 1920/5 to 1965/7

10.2   Fellows of the Royal Society, 1939–1990, showing percentage contributed at five-year intervals by Oxford and by Cambridge

13.1   Careers of Oxford women by cohort, 1900–1967

13.2   Known careers of Oxford women, 1940–1967, on leaving Oxford and 10, 20, 30 and 40 years thereafter

14.1   Election results for Oxford city and University seats, 1918–1970

16.1   The Oxford book trade 1910–1990: numbers of bookselling, printing and publishing firms and their locations

20.1 Academic performance of sample Oxford blues compared with all men, in sample years between 1920 and 1988

20.2 University course taken by sample Oxford blues, 1920–1970, distinguishing honours, pass, research and war degrees and diplomas/certificates

20.3 Norrington score of sample Oxford blues, distinguishing individual sports, 1920–1970

20.4 School of origin of sample Oxford blues, 1920–1970, distinguishing pre-war from post-war

20.5 Results of OUCC first-class matches, 1920–1970

21.1 Shifts in the balance of employment in Oxford at twenty-year intervals, 1911–1971

22.1 Fellows of the Royal Society at twenty-year intervals, 1900–1971/81, specifying the university group where last degree qualification was taken (Oxford/Cambridge, London and others)

22.2 Fellows of the British Academy at twenty-year intervals, 1910–1961/2, specifying the university group where last degree qualification was taken (distinguishing Oxford/Cambridge, London, civic, Scotland, Wales)

22.3 University education of vice-chancellors and principals in 1935, 1967 and 1981, distinguishing Oxford/Cambridge, London, Scotland, civic, other

22.4 Term-time residence of full-time university students in Great Britain, in specified years between 1920/1 and 1979/80, excluding Oxford and Cambridge, distinguishing colleges/halls of residence, lodgings, home

22.5 'Which is the best department in your subject?' Percentage of vote given to institution in each subject, 1976

22.6 Percentage of academic staff in 1976 sample agreeing that Oxford and Cambridge have preserved their predominance in practically everything that counts in academic life

22.7 First preference between university posts, as expressed by sample surveys of university teachers in 1964 and 1976

23.1 Oxford finalists in modern languages at five-year intervals, 1920–1940

23.2 Oxford finalists in geography, modern languages and oriental studies at five-year intervals, 1945–1990, showing their percentage of all finalists

23.3 Overseas students at Oxford in selected years, 1923–1964, showing their percentage of total Oxford students

23.4 Oxford's junior members whose home residence is listed as Commonwealth or foreign: percentage of each college's total, at three-year intervals, 1947–1966

23.5 Country of origin of Oxford's overseas students for each academic year from 1973/4 to 1989/90

24.1   Income or expenditure, and income or expenditure per resident undergraduate or student, for each Oxford college as a multiple of Pembroke's in the 1660s, 1871, 1920, 1954, 1970/1, 1987/8

24.2   Components of Oxford college incomes in 1913, 1920, 1926, 1938, 1948, 1954, 1964, 1970/1

24.3   Oxford college and university holdings of agricultural land and woodland (acres) in 1871, 1920 and 1988/9, distinguishing county, and showing each county's percentage of the total

24.4   Oxford college and university holdings of tithe ['par' or 'gross awarded' value (£)] in 1871 and 1920 in the counties of England and Wales

24.5   Income of Oxford colleges and university from 'houses' and 'non-agricultural land': distribution by county or groups of counties in 1871, 1920 and 1988/9

24.6   Internal expenditure of Oxford colleges (in current £s, constant £s, and constant £s per resident student) in specified years, 1913–1987/8

24.7   Some comparisons of Oxford university and college finances with the equivalents for 'all universities in Great Britain' in 1925/6, 1953/4, 1963/4, 1970/1, 1980/1 and 1987/8.

27.1   Numbers of full-time Oxford students in selected categories in 1968/9 and 1988/9 distinguishing men, women, undergraduates, postgraduates, arts/social studies, maths/science

27.2   Percentage of Oxford men and women in final examinations, 1969 and 1989, obtaining first-, second- and third-class degrees

27.3   Norrington table performances attained by selected Oxford colleges in 1969 and 1989

27.4   Percentage of Oxford finalists gaining class I and class II in 1961/2, 1982 and 1988 by type of school, specifying independent, direct-grant and maintained

27.5   Method of admission of Oxford home undergraduates 1988/9 by type of school, specifying LEA-maintained, independent and other

27.6   Admissions of Oxford home undergraduates by type of school in 1969/70, 1979/80 and 1989/90, specifying percentage from LEA-maintained, direct-grant, independent and other

27.7   Number of Oxford finalists in single-subject, bipartite, and multi-subject courses in 1969 and 1989

27.8   Oxford degree results by type of school in 1989: percentage in each class, specifying single honours, older mixed courses, newer mixed courses

27.9   UK and Oxford staff/student ratios in 1968/9 and 1988/9

27.10 Loss and gain of established academic posts in Oxford, 1981–1990, showing posts at 31 Mar. 1990 abolished or to be abolished, posts created by 31 Mar. 1990, and posts funded or partly funded by the Campaign for Oxford to 31 Mar. 1990

27.11 Ratio of tutors holding CUF lecturerships in arts and social studies to relevant honours students in two Oxford colleges in 1968/9 and 1988/9

Abbreviations and Conventions

The phrase 'junior members' describes the collectivity of undergraduates and postgraduates. 'University' and 'college' are capitalized where a particular institution is under discussion, as in 'University of Oxford', 'Jesus College'. Where it is important to distinguish between spheres of activity *within* Oxford University, both 'university' and 'college' appear in lower case. The term 'graduate' denotes all those who have successfully pursued an undergraduate degree. The term 'postgraduate' denotes all those who are pursuing, but have not yet attained, higher degrees. Academic years and quinquennia are presented in the form 1913/14, whereas other chronological periods are in the form 1914–18. All items abbreviated in footnotes are given in full on their first occurrence in any chapter, except for the following, which apply throughout:

Asquith Report	[H. H. Asquith, chairman] *Report of Royal Commission on Oxford and Cambridge Universities* (PP 1922 x Cmd 1588) and volume of appendices (HMSO 1922)
BCA	Balliol College, Oxford, archives
BMFRS	*Biographical Memoirs of Fellows of the Royal Society* (1954 onward, as continuation of *ONFRS*)
Bodl.	Bodleian Library, Oxford
Calendar	*Oxford University Calendar* (published annually by the University)
CCCA	Corpus Christi College, Oxford, archives
ECA	Exeter College, Oxford, archives
Examination Decrees	*Examination Decrees and Regulations* (published annually by the University)
Franks Report	[Lord Franks, chairman] *Report of Commission of Inquiry* (2 volumes, University of Oxford 1966)
Franks Commission, written evidence	written evidence received by the Commission (14 volumes, Oxford 1964–5)
Franks Commission, oral evidence	transcripts of unpublished oral evidence received by the Commission (103 volumes)
Gazette	*Oxford University Gazette*
Handbook	*Handbook to the University of Oxford* (published annually by the University)

HC Deb.	*House of Commons Debates*
HCP	Hebdomadal Council Papers, University of Oxford
HL Deb.	*House of Lords Debates*
HUA	History of the University archives, now merged with OUA
HUD	History of the University's databases of members of the University 1900–79. The abbreviations HUD/C/CR, HUD/C/MF, HUD/C/ML, HUD/C/RS, HUD/C/SV, HUD/S/REG and HUD/S/UGC refer to sub-sets of the data as explained in footnotes 2, 3, 5, 7, 27, 41 of Chapter 3. The Bodleian Library now holds the confidential questionnaires (HUD/C/SV) completed for the ESRC/Leverhulme projects which are drawn upon in chapters 7, 8 and 13; they are reserved from use for 30 years.
KCA	Keble College, Oxford, archives
MCA	Magdalen College, Oxford, archives
NCA	New College, Oxford, archives
OM	*Oxford Magazine*
ONFRS	*Obituary Notices of Fellows of the Royal Society* (8 volumes 1932–53), continued as *BMFRS*
OUA	Oxford University archives
OUP	Oxford University Press
PP	Parliamentary Papers (followed by date of parliamentary session, volume number and command number)
PRO	Public Record Office
SCA	Somerville College, Oxford, archives
SHCA	St Hilda's College, Oxford, archives
SJM	St John's College, Oxford, muniments
Statutes	*Statuta universitatis oxoniensis*, from 1970 *Statutes, Decrees and Regulations of the University of Oxford* (published annually by the University)
TCA	Trinity College, Oxford, archives
UCA	University College, Oxford, archives

List of Contributors

PAUL ADDISON is a Fellow of Edinburgh University, and former Visiting Fellow of All Souls. His publications include *The Road to 1945* (1975) and *Churchill on the Home Front 1900–1955* (1992).

GILES BARBER is a Fellow of Linacre College, Oxford and Librarian of the Taylor Institution, Oxford.

MICHAEL BROCK was Warden of Nuffield College, Oxford, 1978–88. He is co-editor of volumes 6 and 7 of the *History of the University of Oxford*. His publications include *The Great Reform Act* (1973).

VALENTINE CUNNINGHAM is Fellow and Tutor in English Literature at Corpus Christi College, Oxford. His publications include *Everywhere Spoken Against: Dissent in the Victorian Novel* (1975) and *British Writers of the Thirties* (1988).

ROBERT CURRIE is Fellow and Tutor in Politics at Wadham College, Oxford. His publications include *Methodism Divided* (1968) and *Industrial Politics* (1979).

JOHN DARWIN is a Fellow of Nuffield College, Oxford. His publications include *Britain and Decolonization* (1988).

ROBIN DENNISTON was Oxford Publisher and Senior Deputy Secretary to the Delegates of Oxford University Press 1984–8. He is the co-editor of *Anatomy of Scotland* (1992).

JOHN DUNBABIN is Fellow and Tutor in Politics at St Edmund Hall, Oxford, and has contributed chapters on Oxford finance to volumes 5 and 6 of this *History*. His *History of International Relations since 1945* should be appearing shortly.

DANIEL GREENSTEIN is Senior Lecturer in Modern History at the University of Glasgow.

A. H. HALSEY was Professor of Social and Administrative Studies, University of Oxford, 1978–90. His publications include *The British Academics* (1971, with Martin Trow), *English Ethical Socialism: From Thomas More to R. H. Tawney* (1988), and *The Decline of Donnish Dominion* (1992).

JOSE HARRIS is Fellow and Tutor in Modern History at St Catherine's College and Reader in Modern History at Oxford. Her publications include *Unemployment and Politics* (1972), *William Beveridge* (1977), and *Private Lives, Public Spirit: A Social History of Britain 1870–1914* (1993).

BRIAN HARRISON is Fellow of Corpus Christi College and Reader in Modern British History at Oxford. His publications include *Drink and the Victorians* (1971) and *Prudent Revolutionaries* (1987).

JANET HOWARTH is Fellow and Tutor in Modern History at St Hilda's College, Oxford. Her publications include an edition (1988) of Emily Davies's *The Higher Education of Women*.

DIANE KAY is Inspector, Listing Branch, English Heritage. Her Oxford DPhil thesis was entitled 'University Architecture in Britain, 1950–1975'.

JACK MORRELL was Reader in History of Science in the University of Bradford until 1991 and a Visiting (1985) and Supernumerary Fellow (1987) of Brasenose College, Oxford. His publications include *Gentlemen of Science* (1981, with A. W. Thackray).

JOHN PREST is Fellow and Tutor in Modern History at Balliol College, Oxford. His publications include *Lord John Russell* (1972) and *Politics in the Age of Cobden* (1977).

JOHN ROCHE teaches the history of physics at Linacre College, Oxford and physics at Oxford Brookes University.

SIR KEITH THOMAS has been President of Corpus Christi College, Oxford since 1986. His publications include *Religion and the Decline of Magic* (1971) and *Man and the Natural World* (1983).

FRANK TURNER, Provost of Yale University 1988–1992, is John Hay Whitney Professor of History. His publications include *Between Science and Religion* (1974), *The Greek Heritage in Victorian Britain* (1981) and *Contesting Cultural Authority: Essays in Victorian Intellectual Life* (1993).

CHARLES WEBSTER is Senior Research Fellow of All Souls College, Oxford. His publications include *The Great Instauration* (1975) and *Problems of Health Care* (1988).

CHARLES WENDEN died in 1992. He was an athletics blue, Bursar of St Catherine's College from 1960 to 1970 and of All Souls College from 1970 to 1990, and for 22 years treasurer of the *Fédération Internationale du Sport Universitaire*.

CHRISTOPHER WHITE is Director of the Ashmolean Museum, Professor of the Art of the Netherlands and a Fellow of Worcester College, Oxford. His publications include *Rembrandt as an Etcher* (1969) and *Peter Paul Rubens: Man and Artist* (1987).

RICHARD WHITING is Senior Lecturer in Modern History at the University of Leeds. His publications include *The View from Cowley* (1983), and he is editor of *Oxford: Studies in the History of a University Town since 1800* (Manchester 1993).

JAY WINTER is a Fellow of Pembroke College, Cambridge. His publications include *Socialism and the Challenge of War* (1974) and *The Great War and the British People* (1985).

PART ONE
INTRODUCTION

I

Oxford and the First World War

J. M. WINTER

Honorary degree ceremonies traditionally affirm the international community of learning. Such was the case in June 1914 when Oxford formally celebrated the profound contribution of German culture to European arts and learning. A majority of those receiving honorary doctorates were Germans. Richard Strauss received a doctorate in music. The classical scholar Ludwig Mitteis of the University of Dresden became a doctor of letters. The degree of doctor of civil law was conferred on the German ambassador to the court of St James, Prince Karl Max Furst von Lichnowsky, and on the Duke of Saxe-Coburg and Gotha. In addition the Austrian jurist, Nobel laureate and expert on international arbitration Heinrich Lammasch was honoured by a doctorate in civil law.[1] The First World War severed this Anglo-German cultural tie. Despite attempts after the war, both on a personal and an institutional level, to revive the pre-war mood of Anglo-German friendship in Oxford, the old bonds were never fully restored.

A visible manifestation of the parting of the ways was the disappearance from Oxford of German Rhodes scholars. In a codicil of 1901 to his will of 1897, Cecil Rhodes had provided funds for fifteen German scholars to come to Oxford for three years. Conscription prevented all but a few from staying longer than two years, thus increasing the number of German students appointed.[2] Rhodes believed that such awards would promote international understanding among the great powers to the point that it 'will render war impossible'.[3] Selection was in the Kaiser's personal gift.[4] Most of those who came to Oxford were from the nobility or other prominent families.[5] Count Hélie Talleyrand-Périgord came to Magdalen in 1903; he was not remembered for his academic achievements. Similarly Baron G. G. A. von Diesgardt spent two dilatory years at Christ Church from 1906 to 1908.

[1] *Calendar* 1915, 259.
[2] C. K. Allen (ed.), *The First Fifty Years of the Rhodes Trust and the Rhodes Scholarships 1903–1953* (Oxford 1955), 81.
[3] *Register of Rhodes Scholars* (London 1950), 253.
[4] Oxford, Rhodes House, Rhodes House papers, letter of Trott zu Solz, Minister for Ecclesiastical and Educational Affairs, 14 Apr. 1913, on appointments for that year.
[5] Allen, *First Fifty Years*, 79.

Some came from the political élite. Friedrich von Bethmann-Hollweg, the son of the German Chancellor, arrived at Balliol in 1908 and performed, according to the Oxford Secretary of the Rhodes Trust, in a 'satisfactory' though 'not very strenuous' manner. Since virtually all stayed for less than three years they could not sit for finals. Most chose to study for diplomas, in particular the diploma in economics and political science, and returned to the civil service or teaching professions in Germany.[6]

On the outbreak of war the existence of this small community of German gentlemen-scholars in Oxford embarrassed the Rhodes Trust, the colleges that had welcomed these young men, and presumably the Germans themselves. How was the war to affect these awards? According to some, Rhodes thought the German awards less important than those to scholars from the English-speaking world. According to one confidante of Rhodes, the idea of German scholarships was something of an afterthought. Rhodes 'had been having a "deal" with the Kaiser over East Africa and thought he would like to show his appreciation of his consideration and make him a little present'.[7] What to do about the 'little present' was a headache to the men who oversaw the Rhodes Trust. Lord Rosebery, the chairman, Lord Grey and Viscount Milner were among the trustees. Their views were matters of public record; in the overheated atmosphere of wartime, silence meant acceptance of the status quo.

The administrators of the Trust, Francis (later Sir Francis) Wylie, who looked after the scholars once they arrived in Oxford, and the Organizing Secretary, Dr George (later Sir George) Parkin, initially hoped that no change would be forced on the Rhodes scholarship scheme by the war. In August 1914 a former American Rhodes scholar, Professor Frank Aydelotte of Indiana University, asked Wylie what would become of the German Rhodes scholarships. Wylie answered that it would be unwise to make any 'formal statement' about the issue. He admitted that it would be 'very unlikely that they will now feel like coming to us for some years to come . . . and it will be a half-hearted affair when they did again begin to do so'. Nonetheless, 'the Scholarships will be here for them to take when they want them'.[8]

No such assurance was given to Count Albrecht Theodor von Bernstorff, a German Rhodes scholar at Trinity from 1909 to 1910 and a dedicated Anglophile, when he too raised the question of the future of the scheme. He pointed out in January 1915 that three German Rhodes scholars had already

    [6] Rhodes House papers, lists and reports of German Rhodes scholars 1903–10.
    [7] 'Notes and news', OM 27 Oct. 1916, 14; see also F. Aydelotte, The Vision of Cecil Rhodes (London 1946), 20.
    [8] Rhodes House papers, Wylie to Aydelotte, 31 Aug. 1914, in reply to Aydelotte to Wylie, 18 Aug. 1914.

given their lives for their country and that a fourth was wounded and a prisoner on the eastern front (Bethmann-Hollweg, who later died of his wounds). No dishonour could be attached to such behaviour.[9] Given the growing number of British casualties in the first months of the war, including casualties among Rhodes scholars in allied forces, such news did not resolve the dilemma.

As the war dragged on, aggrieved patriots at home and abroad pressed on the trustees time and again the view that it was absurd to invite Germans to Oxford during the war. The Reverend H. T. F. Duckworth, head of Trinity College, Toronto, wrote that they could not make awards to 'men who are the bitterest, most cruel, most unscrupulous, most barbarous enemies that England has ever had' and who might even put Oxford to the torch as they had Rheims and Ypres.[10] Initially the trustees decided to defer consideration of the future of the German scholarships until after the end of the war.[11] But like the honorary doctorates awarded on the eve of the war, their importance was more symbolic than material. And after 1915, with no end to the war in sight, that symbol of Anglo-German friendship had to be erased. In March 1916 the Rhodes trustees agreed to use the funds previously set aside for Germans to provide scholarships for men in allied countries or dependencies. Three scholarships were given to the Transvaal, the Orange Free State and the South African Union; one each to the Canadian provinces of Alberta and Saskatchewan, which had previously shared an award with the Northwest Territories. One was to be shared in turn by Trinidad, Barbados, British Guiana, the Bahamas and Hong Kong. One award was left to the discretion of the trustees.[12] A parliamentary bill was required to allow the trustees to depart from the terms of Rhodes's will. The Rhodes Estate Act became law in October 1916. Afterwards the 15 additional colonial scholarships replaced the original 12 German scholarships.[13]

This breach with German scholars was repaired temporarily between 1929 and 1939, when the trustees made up to two awards a year to German nationals. But the outbreak of the Second World War buried them once again.[14] The German Rhodes scholar who tried hardest to keep the scheme alive for his countrymen was Bernstorff, who was a diplomat in the German embassy in London in the 1920s. He was also one of those who plotted to kill Hitler in July 1944. Along with other conspirators—including Friedrich

[9] Ibid. note written by Wylie, 22 Jan. 1915.
[10] Ibid. Duckworth to Parkin, 29 Jan. 1915.
[11] Ibid. Wylie to Parkin, 13 Apr. 1915.
[12] Ibid. memorandum of Parkin, 20 Mar. 1916.
[13] Ibid. Milner to H. Hawksley, 7 Feb. 1916; 'Notes and news', *OM* 27 Oct. 1916, 14.
[14] The story of the restoration of Anglo-German ties in recent years goes well beyond the scope of this chapter.

Adam von Trott, a German Rhodes scholar at Balliol from 1931 to 1933—he was tortured and hanged in 1945.[15] The scholarships were not revived till 1970. Some ties between Oxford scholars and their colleagues in Germany and Austria were restored in the 1920s. The first overture was the convening on 23 April 1920 of a general council, with the Warden of Wadham in the chair, to 'send assistance to the Universities of Central Europe—particularly that of Vienna'.[16] In October 1920 Robert Bridges, the Poet Laureate, wrote to 120 Oxford scholars asking them to sign a manifesto of reconciliation. But this appeal to revive the 'fellowship of learning' was turned down by 60 of the 120 to whom it was sent.[17] It was obviously difficult to undo the damage caused by scholars on both sides who denounced the barbarity or inhumanity of the other, or to heal the wounds of many Oxford men who had lost their sons in the war. It was said that Sir William Osler, Regius Professor of Medicine, never recovered from the death of his son in the war.

The loosening of the German ties brought other international connections into prominence. Links with Canadian, Australasian, West Indian, Indian and South African scholars and universities were strengthened. The degree of doctor of philosophy was ratified in 1917, partly in the hope of attracting to Britain—rather than to Germany—Americans in search of higher degrees. The establishment of chairs in Italian and French at Oxford also showed the University's commitment to the study of the cultures of allied nations.[18]

Oxford also showed its support for the allied cause in more material ways. The first was to help the Belgians, which reflected the general tenor of public opinion in 1914. Such measures also caught some of the distress and anger felt by British scholars over damage by German shelling to the library and other buildings of the University of Louvain. Oxford was one of many towns which offered aid to the 200,000 Belgian refugees who fled the fighting and arrived in Britain in 1914 and 1915.[19] In mid-October the Mayor of Oxford welcomed two hundred refugees to Oxford. They were billeted in private lodgings. Ruskin College was put at the disposal of the Belgian refugee aid committee, and thirty working men were lodged there. Work was found for them, with some difficulty, and they took lodgings in the city and in surrounding villages. About fifty Belgian 'refugees of the middle

[15] *Register of Rhodes Scholars*, 258.

[16] 'News', *OM* 30 Apr. 1920, 297.

[17] See *Times* 18 Oct. 1920 for correspondence on this question. See also S. Wallace, *War and the Image of Germany: British Academics 1914–1918* (Edinburgh 1988), 195–6, 241–3 for the list of signatories.

[18] See the note on the first holder of the Marshal Foch chair of French literature, endowed by Sir Basil Zaharoff, *OM* 7 Nov. 1919, 56.

[19] T. Wilson, *The Myriad Faces of War: Britain and the War of 1914–1918* (Cambridge 1986), 775.

classes' were then housed in Ruskin. They were more easily dispersed in University hostels and lodging houses.

Late in 1914 someone had the ingenious idea of opening a toy factory to employ the refugees. In addition an 'Anglo-Belgian Lingerie' was set up to allow the women to carry on their tradition of fine embroidery.[20] The Oxford University Dramatic Society (OUDS), moribund during the war, lent its rooms to house a 'Belgian Club' for refugees. In 1916 a school for Belgian children was opened in St John's College; the teachers were refugees too, and instruction was in French.[21] Approximately twenty Belgian refugees became unmatriculated undergraduates during the war. Balliol allowed her Belgian students to defer payment of college bills until after the end of the war.[22] Another gesture of Oxford's solidarity with the plight of Belgium was perhaps more symbolic than real. In 1916 a 'Belgian relief camp' was built by women undergraduates near Broadway in Gloucestershire to train them and others to help to rebuild Belgium after the war.[23]

The second allied nation that Oxford tried to help was Serbia. Once again the plight of refugees was a central issue. In May 1916 150 Serbian refugees arrived in Oxford and were lodged in Wycliffe Hall. They were among the survivors of the long retreat of the remnants of the Serbian army, joined by thousands of civilians, who in late 1915 walked under appalling conditions through the Albanian mountains to the Adriatic Sea and freedom. Sidney Ball of St John's headed the Oxford Serbian aid committee. Among the refugees were five schoolmasters who (like the Belgians) opened a school for the children among them. Undergraduates of Lady Margaret Hall helped out during the vacations.[24] In 1918 a Serbian theological college was opened at St Stephen's House for refugees training for the priesthood.[25] Serbians, like Belgians, were also admitted as unmatriculated undergraduates. Serbians provided four of the eight successful candidates in 1918 for the diploma in economics, formerly favoured by German Rhodes scholars.[26] Other kinds of assistance were provided too. Queen's College took the unusual step of offering rooms in college to Serbian couples.[27] A number of scholars organized a 'Kosovo day' on 28 June 1916 to celebrate the Serbian

[20] 'Notes and news', *OM* 23 Oct. 1914; SHCA report of City of Oxford Emergency Committee 1914–16, pp. 9, 25.
[21] 'Oxford clubs in war-time', *OM* 31 Oct. 1919, 42 (OUDS); 'Oxford in the war', *OM* 8 Dec. 1916, 96–8 (St John's).
[22] 'Notes and news', *OM* 10 Dec. 1915; BCA college meeting minutes, 15 Jan. 1915, 12 Oct. 1918.
[23] SHCA chronicle of the old students' association 1914–15, 29.
[24] 'Serbians in Oxford', *OM* 26 May 1916, 332; 'Notes and news', *OM* 23 June 1916, 388; SHCA Lady Margaret Hall war work.
[25] 'Notes and news', *OM* 8 Mar. 1918, 204.
[26] BCA college meeting minutes, 13 Oct. 1916; *Calendar* 1919, 202.
[27] 'Oxford in the war', 96–8.

independence day. Lectures were held at Pembroke and the audience was entertained by a Croatian violinist and a Russian tenor.[28]

Most of those associated with the University believed the allied cause to be just, and used their position to say so in whatever way they could. But those engaged in this kind of propaganda also knew the other side of the conflict: its dreariness, its tendency to induce boredom and embarrassment in those barred by age, sex or physical condition from joining the armed forces. Most people not in uniform felt the need to act or to speak out on behalf of the cause, or simply to hold on until the war was over.

Oxford's first way of contributing to the war effort was to facilitate military mobilization, both of its own members and of other soldiers called to the colours in the course of the conflict. As a result, the population of Oxford changed drastically during the war. War broke out in the midst of the long vacation, so most undergraduates and many fellows were away from Oxford during the rush to enlist in August and September 1914. For those still in residence, and for many others too, the simplest way to join up was to apply to the Oxford University Officer Training Corps (OTC) headquarters at 9 Alfred Street. On 2 August the OTC wrote to all its past and present members advising them to come to Oxford in the event of war. The Vice-Chancellor, T. B. Strong, Dean of Christ Church, by-passed the University's delegacy for military instruction, a cumbersome body unused to dealing with a flood of recruits, and set up an *ad hoc* committee to process applications. Strong chaired the board, on which the pro-proctor and the Assistant Registrar also sat. On 4 August they began what was to be a long stint of interviewing. By late September they had processed around two thousand applications for commissions.[29]

Over the next three months most current undergraduates joined up. Of the 132 Oriel men in residence in 1913, 116 were in uniform by Christmas. The only colleges where half the resident undergraduates were still civilians at the end of 1914 were Queen's, Pembroke, Lincoln and Jesus. The rest rapidly emptied as students joined up, alongside one million other British men, before the new year. Fellows too followed the flag. A total of 42 fellows of Oxford colleges enlisted in the first three months of the war. Of the 31 fellows of Magdalen 7 joined up in the first phase of the war. Four each came forward from New College, Hertford and St John's, and three each from University College, Christ Church, Balliol and Wadham.[30] College staff and servants were also among the recruits. Balliol agreed as early as 20 August to pay college servants the difference between their

[28] 'Notes and news', *OM* 16 June 1916, 372.
[29] H. Anson, *T. B. Strong: Bishop, Musician, Dean, Vice-Chancellor* (London 1949), 36–7.
[30] 'Notes and news', *OM* 4 Dec. 1914, 121.

ordinary wages and army pay. Such men were reassured that their jobs would be kept open for them, and that the College would 'make equitable provision' for their dependants.[31] Like other employers throughout Britain, Oxford's colleges created a scheme of separation allowances before the War Office initiated a national plan for the families of enlisted men.

In 1915 the flow of undergraduates and fellows into the armed forces continued, though at a reduced pace. Award-holders were conspicuous by their absence from Oxford. By the beginning of the academic year 1915/16 approximately half the scholars of most colleges were listed as away on military service; by 1918 virtually all were in uniform.[32] The University housed approximately three thousand undergraduates and about a hundred postgraduate students before the war. By 1915 that total had been reduced by two thirds. A year later only 550 students were on the books, a reduction of 72 per cent. By 1917 there were only about 15 per cent and in 1918 12 per cent of the pre-war population in residence.[33]

Fellows also disappeared into many theatres of military operations. The age-structure of fellowships accounts for different patterns of enlistment. Seven of the nine fellows of University College were relieved of their duties for the duration of the war, whereas only two of the fourteen fellows of Corpus Christi, two of the four fellows of Wadham and none of the four fellows of Worcester were away on war service.[34] Fellows of Oxford's colleges contributed to the war effort in a host of ways. H. T. Tizard of Oriel was one of the first test pilots. R. G. Collingwood of Pembroke served in the Admiralty's intelligence department. Bertram Lambert of Merton designed a respirator for soldiers exposed to gas attacks. Harold (later Sir Harold) Hartley worked in the same area. Ernest Dunlop (later Sir Ernest Dunlop) Swinton, elected Chichele Professor of Military History in 1925, was a key figure in the development of the tank. Sir William Osler of Christ Church helped to organize medical services in Malta. Others in the medical field include G. R. Girdlestone in orthopaedic surgery and Sir Arthur Hurst, a specialist in the treatment of shell-shocked soldiers. Those in the arts were also useful, sometimes in unexpected ways. The war in the eastern Mediterranean enabled classicists like Stanley Casson and Sir John Myres to put their knowledge of ancient history to patriotic use. T. E. Lawrence of Magdalen became Lawrence of Arabia, and so on. Most Oxford graduates and undergraduates served in less celebrated but at times equally demanding or nerve-racking corners of the war.

---

[31] BCA college meeting minutes, 20 Aug. 1914, 30 Sept. 1914.
[32] *Handbook* 1915, 1918. Among those who did not join up were R. Palme Dutt, scholar of Balliol [see plate 1.1], and Raymond Postgate, scholar of St John's.
[33] *OM* 1914–18; cf below 46, figure 3.1.
[34] *Handbook* for years from 1914 to 1919.

The University they left behind was a shadow of its former self. Some students were still in residence and had to be taught by some fellows. Women students were still there, as were foreign students, including the non-German Rhodes scholars. A trickle of candidates presented themselves for final honours schools. But by and large both the university and the colleges were left with substantial over-capacity. In the place of the normal residents of Oxford came the soldiers. For the first time since the 1640s Oxford became a military camp. The fourth battalion of the Oxfordshire and Buckinghamshire Light Infantry was billeted in various colleges from 5 August 1914 until barracks were ready for them in Cowley. New College took in 200 members of the seventh service battalion of the same regiment in November. In the following year Brasenose and Christ Church took cadets of the Royal Flying Corps. American cadets and soldiers flooded into Oxford in 1918.[35] The War Office negotiated a flat fee for room and board for these men. Given the shortfall in fees, most colleges were grateful for the income.[36] Occasionally the War Office was faced with bills for damage to college property which had been subjected to soldiers' high spirits.[37]

Oxford in wartime was also a centre of treatment for disabled and wounded soldiers. The Examination Schools were converted into a military hospital and housed both British and German wounded men. Later in the war additional beds were found in University College and the Masonic Hall. Somerville, adjacent to the Radcliffe Infirmary, was turned into a hospital, from 1916 for officers only.[38] Siegfried Sassoon was one of its convalescents. Oriel provided temporary accommodation for Somerville in St Mary Hall quadrangle. Merton's new quad housed nurses, and the gardens of New College were restricted to recuperating servicemen.[39]

With soldiers billeted everywhere in the town, and with a constant stream of the wounded to remind everyone of the carnage, it was difficult for people to resume their normal daily affairs. But as soon as it was apparent that the war would last for years and not for months, people all over Europe settled down to the war. In Oxford too there was a *banalisation de la guerre*.[40] And necessarily so: to retain a belief in the cause, or indeed to push aside natural feelings of horror and despair, required an enormous effort. Those who supported the war tried to keep their hold of the faith that it was justified and the hope that the killing would stop some day soon. Most did so by

[35] H. W. B. Joseph, 'Oxford in the last war', *OM* 22 May 1941, 96–8.

[36] BCA college meeting minutes, 4 Nov. 1914, 3 Dec. 1914, 15 Jan. 1915.

[37] Ibid. 15 Jan. 1915; cf ibid. 19 Jan. 1918, claims to the War Office for 'dilapidation and depreciation of furniture' for soldiers in residence from Mar. 1916 to Nov. 1917.

[38] See the *Rattler*, the undergraduate publication produced in 1917 at the Somerville war hospital.

[39] 'Oxford in the war', 96–8; Joseph, 308.

[40] Cf J. J. Becker, *Les Français dans la grande guerre* (Paris 1980), 99 ff.

resuming their daily routine and preparing the ground for those who would return. In Oxford this meant primarily attending to the daily business of university and college. The issues certainly paled into insignificance beside the slaughter on the western front, but for those responsible for educational institutions these matters had to be faced.

One such was finance. The departure or deferment of the matriculation of thousands of students substantially reduced the income of both the university and the colleges. The university received on average about £40,000 annually in fees for matriculation, degrees and examinations, and in quarterly dues. In the academic year 1914/15 the war-related shortfall in the university's income was estimated to be £10,500.[41] One way of cutting this deficit was taken by readers and professors in the University. In November 1914 they agreed to return part of their emoluments to the university. This act of generosity and other similar donations reduced the deficit by half.[42] Of equal importance was the lifting of restrictions on the use of trust funds administered by the university. To provide maximum flexibility in meeting the deficit the universities sought and received relief in the form of the Universities and Colleges (Emergency Powers) Act of 1915. Henceforth trust funds could be used for general or capital purposes. Finally the freezing of appointments—seventeen chairs were vacant in 1918—and the postponement or elimination of annual payments for prizes and other services helped to reduce the university's overdraft to modest proportions in the latter years of the war.[43]

The same difficulties were faced and met by colleges. Balliol, for example, enforced austerity at home. The Master and fellows reduced their emoluments by 25 per cent and lowered the regular wages of college servants by the same amount in September 1914. Other measures soon followed: only cold baths were supplied in late 1914. In March 1915 Balliol (among other colleges) exercised the financial freedom just granted by parliament to both the university and the colleges. The fellows deferred until after the war the awarding of prizes and agreed to use the money for general purposes. Pension-fund incomes were to be similarly redirected. In addition the stipends of tutorial fellows were fixed at the level of 1914.[44] These expedients kept the College's deficit for 1914/15 to about £800.

A year later the College accounts were out of the red, for three reasons. First, the College did not pay scholars and exhibitioners on military service and thereby saved around £3,000. Secondly, three tutorial fellows were

[41] 'The war budget of the university', *OM* 30 Oct. 1914, 40–1.

[42] W. T. S. Stallybrass, 'Oxford in 1914–1918', *Oxford* winter 1939, 34, 42.

[43] 'The communiqué of Council', *OM* 12 Mar. 1915, 257–8; 'The Vice-Chancellor's speech', *OM* 20 Oct. 1916, 6–8; 'Notes and news', *OM* 2 Feb. 1917, 126–7; 'Notes and news', *OM* 30 May 1919, 317; Stallybrass, 35.

[44] BCA college meeting minutes, 30 Sept. 1914, 11 Mar. 1915.

absent and their emoluments were used for general purposes. Thirdly, the War Office paid Balliol £5,734 to accommodate about fifty officers in that year. In 1917 the College felt secure enough financially to subscribe £4,000 in war loans and to give each college servant a £5 war-loan certificate 'as a bonus'. At the end of 1917 the fellows ended the self-denying ordinance of a 25 per cent reduction in pay. This once again produced a deficit—of £253—though only for the academic year 1917/18. The College had set aside the quarter of each fellow's income forgone for the duration of the war. This sum, totalling £3,000, was donated in 1919 as the fellows' contribution to the College's war-memorial fund.[45]

These day-to-day financial problems of college life were faced throughout the University. In addition fellows worried about air raids and about whether to insure or remove their college's valuable property.[46] This was a reasonable fear, as there had been Zeppelin attacks on London, and Oxford was indeed an armed camp and therefore a legitimate military target. The need to dim lights brought a general gloom to the town, and some missed the reassurance of Great Tom's 101 strokes. Shortages of coal in 1918 made a cold winter colder still, and closed restaurants and theatres earlier than usual.[47] Those who stayed behind occasionally felt that each term in wartime had 'an unbroken tenor of sad monotony'.[48]

All they could do was to try to continue the normal pattern of instruction for a much reduced student population. University College had 148 undergraduates in residence in 1914; 7 in 1917.[49] Sparsely attended lectures were still held and a handful of candidates sat for examinations. Occasionally examination questions reflected contemporary issues. The French translation set in the modern history examination of 1918 was taken from the *Revue des deux mondes*. It began 'Rupert Brooke eut le bonheur envié de mourir dans l'action'. Most other examination questions, both in the history schools and elsewhere, had the musty air of irrelevance to the upheaval of the war. Class-lists were duly published. A kind of academic life still went on.

The very existence of women's colleges and women undergraduates was of great importance to Oxford during the war. Their presence helped to preserve the rhythm of the academic year and gave the impression that not everything was being consumed by the war. Some women found this sheltered atmosphere increasingly difficult to accept. Vera Brittain's description of the non-political ambience of Somerville in 1914 is well known.

[45] BCA college meeting minutes, 20 Mar. 1916, 20 Jan. 1917, 17 Mar. 1917, 13 Oct. 1917, 15 May 1919.
[46] Ibid. 10 Feb. 1915, 17 Feb. 1916.
[47] Stallybrass, 37.
[48] 'Notes and news', *OM* 23 June 1916, 386.
[49] 'Notes and news', *OM* 16 Feb. 1917, 154. For numbers in the University in this period see below, 46, figure 3.1; cf below, 60, figure 3.3.

Greek examinations and daydreams of an all-consuming love-affair filled her life, as it had done for many before the war. Slowly the war and the danger it posed for her lover eroded her interest in academic work and her patience with her female peers. She sat her pass moderations in Greek in the Codrington Library of All Souls and then decided to leave Oxford and become a nurse.[50] Her sense of the inwardness of Oxford had become oppressive and she sought its diametrical opposite in a Voluntary Aid Detachment.

Vera Brittain's solution was but one of many. Some women tried to justify their life of educated—though arduous—leisure in Oxford by volunteering for hard work in the holidays. An Oxford women's war service committee was formed and directed undergraduates and other 'leisured' ladies to farms in need of labour. In this way a small number of students became farmhands, with a varying degree of success.[51] Other women dealt with the ambiguities of undergraduate life through their religious faith. Some joined a 'pilgrimage of prayer' in which women undergraduates went on foot from village to village holding 'simple services' of prayer in rural Oxfordshire.[52] Some joined committees for relief-work on behalf of refugees or the poor. Others stood in for male teachers who had enlisted. Medical students worked in dispensaries or hospitals. Many joined government departments to do clerical work in the vacations.[53] Some were approached to work in munition factories. Vickers wanted factory workers of British stock, 'so that we should not be importing spies'.[54] Within the University, academic excellence had more of a feminine aspect in wartime than ever before. In the modern history examinations in each year from 1910 to 1914, for example, one woman was placed in the first class, with a dozen or more men. In 1915, 1916 and 1918 three women got firsts, in 1917 four. In 1916 no male candidate reached the first class.[55]

The integration of women into the University moved forward during the war. In 1916 women were admitted to read medicine on the same basis as men. In 1917 the University accepted financial responsibility for women's examinations as a whole instead of charging per capita fees for individual

[50] V. Brittain, *Testament of Youth: An Autobiographical Study of the Years 1900–1925* (London 1933), 94–163.

[51] SHCA Oxford women's war service committee report 1915–16. After a stretch on a Northamptonshire farm one St Hilda's undergraduate replied to a suggestion of further chores: 'we'd rather work in the Bod or the Rad for months and months and months': SHCA 'Farming song' to Miss Burrows 'with love from some of the farmers', 1916 (a photograph of seven 'lady farmers' is attached).

[52] SHCA undated printed notice of a pilgrimage.

[53] SHCA Society of Oxford Home-Students, manuscript on war work.

[54] SHCA F. E. Gardner, London officer for labour exchanges and unemployment insurance, to Miss Dewar, 6 Dec. 1915.

[55] *Handbook* 1919.

women students.[56] And fewer voices were raised openly against granting
women degrees and accepting women as voting members of Congregation.[57]
After the war the return to 'normality' certainly meant reconstructing many
unreconstructed prejudices, but the political atmosphere undoubtedly aided
those prepared to admit women to full membership in the University. The
link with the franchise was decisive. The war had made the general reform of
the parliamentary franchise inevitable, and within that reform the limited
enfranchisement of women was a relatively non-controversial step. The
Oxford Magazine reasoned that 'the War has made a peaceable change in the
status of women', leading many to conclude 'that it is absurd for women to
be eligible for Parliament and to be excluded from membership of
University bodies for which they possess academic qualifications'.[58] This
view prevailed, and on 17 February 1920 the 'women's statute' was passed
without significant opposition. Some grumblers grumbled, but they had
clearly lost the day.[59] The fact that this measure was considered formally
only fifteen months after the armistice was probably decisive in assuring its
relatively uncontested passage. The momentum of reform created by the war
faded throughout British life in the early 1920s. Oxford struck while the iron
was hot. Cambridge waited, and in the more sombre mid–1920s declined to
follow Oxford's lead. It took a second world war to bring Cambridge to the
decision Oxford had taken in the shadow of the first.

Other academic developments were also related to the war. The war gave a
significant boost to the standing of scientific work in Oxford—as indeed in
the other British universities.[60] Some subjects were relatively unaffected by
the war. Much depended on the specific needs of the war effort. In Oxford
itself there was much scientific research for government departments during
the war. The Royal Flying Corps and later the Royal Air Force occupied the
department of chemistry, the zoological laboratories and the department of
human anatomy. Georges Dreyer, who held the chair of pathology, showed
that 'enteric' fever at the front was not typhoid but rather paratyphoid fever,
and convinced the War Office to launch a campaign of inoculation against
this disease. He also got a 'standards laboratory' established in Oxford for
foolproof and rapid haematological analysis. C. G. Douglas, an expert on
the physiology of respiration who later held the chair of physiology in
Oxford, worked on respirators and other means of counteracting poison

[56] 'Notes and news', *OM* 2 Feb. 1917, 142.
[57] Stallybrass, 'Oxford in 1914–1918', 45.
[58] 'The admission of women to membership of the university', *OM* 30 Jan. 1920, 185.
[59] 'Notes', *OM* 20 Feb. 1920, 224. Among the grumblers was Percy Gardner, whose letter to
the *Oxford Magazine* suggested that the war had widened, not narrowed, the divide between
the sexes: *OM* 27 Feb. 1920, 250–1.
[60] H. A. L. Fisher, *The Place of the University in National Life* (Barnett House paper 4
London 1920), 6. See also below, 139–40. For the high proportion of scientists among resident
students in these years see below, 60, figure 3.3.

gas.[61] Chemistry was the subject most closely related to the daily requirements of the army. In the newly built Dyson Perrins Laboratory scientists worked on dyes, drugs and the components of gas warfare.[62] In other areas Oxford's scientists were important in streamlining the processes of munition-production.[63] This contribution helped to change the University's approach to the study of chemistry at the undergraduate level. The syllabus was so changed that fully half the part II honours course was devoted to a research project. The intention was to use undergraduate laboratory research to prepare chemists for further study, as well as better to meet the needs of industry and the state.[64] This emphasis on the University's responsibility for encouraging research extended to other subjects as well. The war was the occasion for a general revision of requirements for higher degrees. In 1917 the degree of doctor of philosophy was officially sanctioned by statute and a committee for advanced studies was set up.[65]

The University contributed to the war effort in many other ways. Among them was the lending of its name and prestige to statements justifying the British decision to go to war. The war of words included learned words, and Oxford men were not slow to add to the rhetoric of self-justification. In 1914 'members of the Oxford faculty of modern history' jointly published a study of diplomatic documents which showed the need to resist German militarism and to defend international law.[66] The Oxford University Press issued a series of pamphlets by Oxford academics arguing the moral case for war. Among them was a rebuttal by twenty-five Oxford theologians of a similar collective message from German theologians that their country had been compelled to protect itself 'from being ravaged by Asiatic barbarism'.[67] Such unofficial propaganda appeared throughout the war. Much of this literature was officially distributed, though not formally sponsored. The Oxford theologians' pamphlet, for instance, was one of the first circulated widely by the organization set up at Wellington House under C. F. G. Masterman in 1914 to put the British case for war.[68] Arnold Toynbee, Lewis

[61] 'Obituary: Georges Dreyer', *OM* 18 Oct. 1934, 13; 'Professor C. G. Douglas', *OM* 12 Feb. 1942, 178.

[62] Stallybrass, 32.

[63] M. Sanderson, *The Universities and British Industry 1850–1970* (London 1972), 217 ff.

[64] 'The Vice-Chancellor's speech', *OM* 20 Oct. 1916, 6–8.

[65] 'Notes and news', *OM* 23 Feb. 1917, 168; 'The organization of advanced studies', *OM* 26 Oct. 1917, 23–4.

[66] *Why We Are at War: Great Britain's Case* (Oxford 1914). The authors were E. Barker, H. W. C. Davis, C. R. L. Fletcher, Arthur Hassall, L. G. Wickham Legg and F. Morgan.

[67] *To the Christian Scholars of Europe and America: A Reply from Oxford to the German Address to Evangelical Christians* (Oxford pamphlet no. 2 Oxford 1914). The series also included G. Murray, *How can War ever be Right?* (no. 18), E. Barker, *Nietzsche and Treitschke: The Worship of Power in Modern Germany* (no. 20) and W. Osler, *Bacilli and Bullets* (no. 30). All were published by Oxford University Press in 1914. Cf below, 456.

[68] Wallace, *War and the Image of Germany*, 171.

Namier and A. E. Zimmern were Oxford men who moved easily from Wellington House to the Foreign Office in the course of the propaganda war.

Great War propaganda used reason and demonology in equal measure, and some Oxford dons were adept at both. L. R. Farnell, Rector of Exeter College, recounted to Northumbrian miners stories of Germans burying Belgians alive. He accepted the assurances of a Belgian refugee-scholar that the incident had indeed taken place.[69] Farnell's distaste for Germans was shared by others in Oxford. Professor H. G. Fiedler, an authority on eighteenth-century German literature, had to bear the brunt of such xenophobia.[70] In February 1915 he was invited by the undergraduate magazine *Varsity* to sign a letter condemning German atrocities. In March the magazine took Fiedler's failure to reply as a sign of disloyalty which justified a boycott of examinations in German. Over one hundred signatories protested to the *Oxford Magazine* against this 'petty persecution'.[71] And though Fiedler later explicitly condemned German actions in sinking the *Lusitania* and in using poison gas at Ypres, his loyalty and that of other German academics remained a matter of suspicion to some in Oxford.[72]

Some voices were raised against the coarsening of academic attitudes. As early as November 1914 Charles Gore, Bishop of Oxford, warned his diocese of the dangers of war-enthusiasm, which was 'absorbing, contagious and all devouring' and was 'therefore, very dangerous'.[73] The dangers were visible in Oxford as elsewhere in Britain throughout the war. Not all Oxford men and women were dedicated to the war effort. Despite overwhelming peer-pressure and propaganda, some University members, past and present, stood out against the war. Others fought against conscription or protested against the persecution of those who refused to serve. The two campaigns—against the war and against conscription—were by no means identical. Some puzzled over the allies' war aims and wondered if all the blame for the outbreak of hostilities really lay on one side. Others by-passed the question of war guilt and concentrated on what they took to be the authoritarian theory and practice of state power. This led G. D. H. Cole of Magdalen, among others, to formulate the Guild Socialist ideas which attracted so many dissenters during the war.[74]

[69] L. R. Farnell, *An Oxonian Looks Back* (London 1934), 327–31.

[70] H. G. Fiedler, *Memories of Fifty Years of the English Goethe Society* (Cambridge 1936).

[71] *Varsity* 16 Feb. 1915, 2; 2 Mar. 1915, 5; 9 Mar. 1915, 11–12; *OM* 5 Mar. 1915, 235; 12 Mar. 1915, 253, 263.

[72] Note the uneasiness of A. E. W. Hazel (later Principal of Jesus College) about the loyalty of Germans living in England: *OM* 21 May 1915, 328.

[73] [C. Gore], 'The enthusiasm of the war and the need of a counterpoise', *Oxford Diocesan Magazine* no. 153 (Nov. 1914), 167.

[74] J. M. Winter, *Socialism and the Challenge of War* (London 1974), ch. 5.

Much more important was the debate over conscription, introduced in 1916. No substantial body of opinion within the University opposed conscription, but reactions to the workings of the military service acts illustrate vividly the concerns of many Oxford men and women in wartime. The thorniest problems arose over conscientious objection. With the lists of the fallen lengthening by the day, it is not surprising that some in Oxford had little sympathy for those unable to accept military service on grounds of conscience. Others tried to protect the rights of dissenters by appealing to acquaintances in high office. The Bishop of Oxford intervened on behalf of an Oxford theology student whose appeal for exemption on grounds of conscience had been turned down by the Oxford tribunal on flimsy grounds. Bishop Gore urged tribunals to be 'more respectful' of the views of dissenters.[75] In 1916 Gilbert Murray, Regius Professor of Greek, lunched with the Prime Minister and told Asquith that military-service tribunals were restricting their exemptions to combatant duties only, rather than to all facets of military service. Consequently some men whose objection to conscription was partially accepted were then ordered to perform non-combatant work. If they refused, they were tried by court martial, and were imprisoned for breach of discipline.

One such individual was Stephen Hobhouse of Balliol.[76] The Hobhouse family knew just about everyone who mattered in Whitehall and lost no time in pressing the case for Stephen's release from a term of imprisonment during which he had become seriously ill. Lord Milner had been a friend of Henry Hobhouse, Stephen's father, and pressed his cabinet colleagues to release 'absolutist' conscientious objectors from prison. The War Office blocked this move, but the redoubtable Margaret Hobhouse (sister of Beatrice Webb) then applied pressure to the Home Office, and Gilbert Murray pressed H. A. L. Fisher, President of the Board of Education. Murray supported the war, but acted in this and other cases to defend conscientious objectors.[77] Jan Christiaan Smuts, South African member of the war cabinet and a friend of Emily Hobhouse, also spoke out for Stephen's release. On 8 October 1917 the war cabinet set up a committee to consider the treatment of conscientious objectors. Then a compromise was struck. The release of 'genuine' conscientious objectors was countenanced, along with their disenfranchisement for five years after the end of the war. Within a week a petition over many notable names, lay and ecclesiastical, for

---

[75] *Tribunal* 23 Mar. 1916. The Labour MP Fred Jowett also raised the matter in the House of Commons: *HC Deb.* 15 Mar. 1916, 2070.

[76] See S. Hobhouse, 'Fourteen months' service with the colours' in J. Bell (ed.), *We Did Not Fight: 1914–18 Experiences of War Resisters* (London 1935).

[77] Murray also acted on behalf of Palme Dutt and Clive Bell: F. West, *Gilbert Murray: A Life* (London 1984), 161.

the release of Stephen Hobhouse was sent to the Home Secretary. On 4 December Lord Curzon told the House of Lords that absolutists in poor health would be released from prison, and four days later Stephen Hobhouse was freed from Exeter prison.[78] This incident shows one strategy open to those of social position and political influence, originating in Oxford but extending into Whitehall. Others without Oxford connections were unable to secure what one Liberal MP called 'release by favouritism'.[79] But the Hobhouse case suggests that intolerance in wartime had some limits and that when a personal problem arose, those limits were vigilantly guarded by many, both within the University and among its most distinguished graduates. The politics of conscience, so active in the pre-war years, did not disappear from wartime Oxford.[80]

The sheer scale of the slaughter made it impossible after the armistice to return to the world of 1914. It was not only that the promise of talented men was thrown away; it was also that the war gave a powerful shock to an élite whose self-confidence was based on continuity and their supposed mastery of domestic and world affairs. Such confidence could not be restored immediately after the war; for some it never returned. Furthermore the war destroyed the lives not of the masters, but of the apprentices, and those who took their place were acutely aware of stepping into the shoes of dead men.

From the beginning the Registrar kept lists of Oxford men who died in the war. The University *Gazette* presented obituaries of the fallen in black borders, and cumulative lists were periodically published. In 1920 the *Oxford University Roll of Service* appeared. This is the best source for an analysis of Oxford's losses in the war, although it is flawed in several respects.[81] Its most important defect for our purposes is its incompleteness, which is not surprising, given that the collators were trying to keep track of roughly fifteen thousand Oxford men, past and present, who had served in the war. One omission was deliberate. Of the 56 German Rhodes scholars who had come to Oxford between 1903 and 1914, 49 served in the German army. Of these men 8 were killed; this was in line with the proportion of losses in the German forces as a whole.[82] The war service of these men is not

---

[78] J. Rae, *Conscience and Politics: The British Government and the Conscientious Objector to Military Service 1916–1919* (London 1970), ch. 10; M. Ceadel, *Pacifism in Britain 1914–1945: The Defining of a Faith* (Oxford 1980), ch. 2; T. Kennedy, *The Hound of Conscience: A History of the No-Conscription Fellowship 1914–1919* (Fayetteville Ark. 1981), 187 ff.

[79] Rae, 225 (comments of Joseph King MP in parliament on 28 Feb. 1918).

[80] M. Richter, *The Politics of Conscience: T. H. Green and his Age* (London 1964).

[81] There are also problems of double counting and other inaccuracies. For a discussion of some of these problems see J. M. Winter, 'Balliol's "lost generation" of the first world war', *Balliol College Record* 1975, 1–11.

[82] *Register of Rhodes Scholars*; J. M. Winter, *The Great War and the British People* (London 1986), 75.

recorded in the *Roll of Service*, but the record of Rhodes scholars serving in allied forces is tabulated: 61 fell during the war.[83]

Table 1.1 provides full statistics of the staggering losses of Oxford men in the First World War.[84] Roughly one in five of those who served were killed or died in the war [plate 1.1]. This proportion is significantly above that for Britain as a whole, and also for the allied forces as a whole, in which about 12 per cent of the men who served were killed.[85] There was some variation between the colleges. Jesus College lost 14 per cent of its old members and undergraduates on active service; Corpus Christi College lost 25 per cent. This difference may be explained in part by comparing rates of enlistment early in the war by college. Fully 70 per cent of the junior members of Corpus Christi who were in residence in 1913 had enlisted by December 1914; the figure for Jesus is 35 per cent.[86] In addition, fully 15 per cent of Jesus men who served in the war were not commissioned; only 5 per cent of the Corpus Christi men who served were in the ranks. Death-rates among officers substantially exceeded those among men in the ranks: hence the disparity between the losses of the two colleges.

The social composition of colleges probably lies behind differential rates of casualty. The higher the public-school intake of a college the greater the rush to the colours, and consequently the higher the casualty-rate in the war. There are exceptions to this rule, but the greater preponderance of public schoolboys among Corpus Christi undergraduates as compared to Jesus men in the pre-war period bears out this point.[87] Other variations were probably related to the number of undergraduates reading science. Jesus College had its own laboratory, and among its graduates were men in occupations exempted from military service. Corpus Christi men who had read Greats were not so lucky. We must also note differences in the number of chaplains provided by each college. Some chaplains were killed in the war, and others died of disease, but their rate of survival was much higher than that of the army as a whole. These variations, however, were slight and probably of no great significance in determining the burden of mourning which touched every corner of the University, as it did every home in Britain.

Oxford's losses in the war were roughly the same as those of Cambridge, and higher than those of most other British universities. This disparity stems partly from the propensity of Oxford and Cambridge men to join up early, to receive a commission from an early date and to serve in the infantry rather

---

[83] *Register of Rhodes Scholars*, obituaries.

[84] These corrected figures improve upon those published in Winter, *Great War*, which was concerned primarily with British losses.

[85] See the discussion ibid. ch. 3.

[86] 'Numbers on active service', *OM* 4 Dec. 1914, 121.

[87] I owe this last point to Mark Curthoys and Daniel Greenstein.

TABLE 1.1

MILITARY PARTICIPATION OF
MEMBERS OF THE UNIVERSITY OF
OXFORD IN ALL COMBATANT ARMIES
IN THE FIRST WORLD WAR

colleges	no. served	no. killed	% killed
All Souls	41	9	21.95
Balliol	968	195	20.14
Brasenose	665	116	17.44
Christ Church	1,425	225	15.79
Corpus Christi	350	89	25.43
Exeter	771	141	18.29
Hertford	507	98	19.33
Jesus	442	64	14.48
Keble	966	172	17.81
Lincoln	397	61	15.37
Magdalen	930	187	20.11
Merton	537	98	18.25
New	1,265	258	20.40
Oriel	725	162	22.34
Pembroke	387	60	15.50
Queen's	619	106	17.12
St Edmund Hall	213	21	9.86
St John's	702	119	16.95
Trinity	820	152	10.54
University	770	175	22.73
Wadham	470	68	14.47
Worcester	401	84	20.95
non-collegiate	351	47	13.39
private halls	70	9	12.86
total	14,792	2,716	18.36

Note: Double counting produces larger totals than
in table 1.2 below.

Sources: E. S. Craig and W. M. Gibson (eds),
Oxford University Roll of Service; Register of
Rhodes Scholars.

than in specialist units, where some scientifically trained undergraduates and
graduates of other universities were directed.[88] The privileges enjoyed by
Oxford and Cambridge men in 1914 were paid for by higher than average
losses in the First World War.

The slaughter of junior officers was well known both to the army at the
time and to the authors of war memoirs in subsequent years. It is reflected in

[88] See the discussion in Winter, Great War, 96–9.

the age of the Oxford men who died in the war. Table 1.2 and figure 1.1 present the distribution by age of the war service of Oxford men, including those who served in the German army. Those matriculating in 1882 or before were roughly 50 years old in 1914. About 6 per cent of them died or were killed in the war. The younger the cohort the greater the risk of death, which rises from 9 per cent for those aged 40 in 1914 to 19 per cent of those aged 30 and to 31 per cent of those aged 19 or 20 at the outbreak of the war. The disproportionately heavy losses at younger ages is the distinctive feature of Oxford's lost generation. The location, rank and length of service of Oxford men account for the disproportionately heavy burden they bore during the war. The youngest paid the highest price. Whereas 60 per cent of all British war-dead were younger than 30, fully 70 per cent of the Oxford men who died were under that age.[89]

TABLE 1.2

AGE-STRUCTURE OF THE SERVICE AND LOSSES OF OXFORD MEN IN THE FIRST WORLD WAR

year of matriculation	total served	total killed	% killed
1858–82	359	23	6.41
1883	65	3	4.62
1884	70	2	2.86
1885	86	6	6.98
1886	89	3	3.37
1887	100	4	4.00
1888	142	6	4.23
1889	114	8	7.02
1890	135	10	7.41
1891	142	13	9.15
1892	148	13	8.78
1893	190	11	5.79
1894	224	27	12.05
1895	275	37	13.45
1896	276	42	15.22
1897	348	48	13.79
1898	352	57	16.19
1899	379	65	17.15
1900	382	71	18.59
1901	386	71	18.39
1902	414	75	18.12
1903	476	78	16.39

[89] Ibid. table 3.7. The age-structure of all Oxford men was roughly that of the population as a whole. If anything, there may have been a greater proportion of long-lived Oxford men than in the population, thus understating Oxford's youthful 'lost generation'.

TABLE 1.2 (cont.)

AGE-STRUCTURE OF THE SERVICE AND
LOSSES OF OXFORD MEN IN THE FIRST WORLD
WAR

1904	465	80	17.20
1905	493	103	20.89
1906	511	107	20.94
1907	581	127	21.86
1908	644	138	21.43
1909	574	129	22.47
1910	683	187	27.38
1911	784	220	28.06
1912	760	210	27.63
1913	785	225	28.66
1914	495	121	24.44
1915	178	27	15.17
1916	100	11	11.00
1917	110	4	3.64
1918	114	2	1.75
unmatriculated 1914–18*	347		
total	12,776	2,364	18.50

* students admitted between 1914 and 1918 but matriculated
after the war

Sources: As for table 1.1.

War memorials grace all Oxford colleges of the time. Most display lists of
old members inscribed in stone on a wall in the college. Some contain the
names of choristers or college servants. Some stand in the chapel, some in the
antechapel, cloisters or other part of the college. In front of the west door of
Magdalen's chapel stood a cross bearing the dates 1914 in front and 1918
behind.[90] All provide an enduring reminder of the price Oxford men paid
for allied victory in the war. There is no university war memorial: each
college mourned its own. Most college memorials were erected in the early
1920s, when it was still too early to admit German names to the lists of the
fallen.[91] At Balliol, as elsewhere, old members joined fellows in the planning
and funding of the College's memorial, placed in the approach to the

[90] 'Oxford war memorials', *OM* 21 June 1923, 455–8. The cross at Magdalen was apparently
removed during the Second World War and in 1971 was placed at Wheatley, near Oxford: D.
Boorman, *At the Going Down of the Sun* (Oxford 1988), 54. The most profound commentary
on this phenomenon is A. Prost, 'Monuments aux morts' in P. Nora (ed.), *Les Lieux de
mémoire: la république* (Paris 1986).

[91] In 1930 a tablet commemorating the College's German war-dead was erected in the
antechapel of New College. See F. W. Steer, 'Memorials at New College' in J. Buxton and P. H.
Williams (eds), *New College, Oxford, 1379–1979* (Oxford 1979), 350–1.

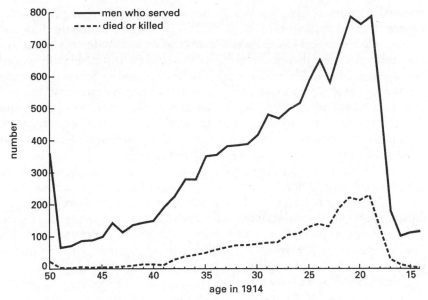

FIGURE I.I OXFORD'S WAR LOSSES, 1914–1919

chapel.[92] Presumably such groups of old members also shared with the families of the fallen the decision to exclude German names from those honoured.

Other forms of commemoration were planned in Oxford after the war. Memorial scholarships and exhibitions were set up in many colleges: Balliol created a war-memorial fellowship; New College and Trinity built libraries; Christ Church has a war-memorial garden.[93] Memorial sermons, recollections, broadcasts and speeches proliferated. Many spoke of gratitude and duty; most were ephemeral. Longer-lasting have been the memoirs of ex-soldiers about the war and the men who did not return. Edmund Blunden and Robert Graves were among the many ex-soldiers who came to Oxford slightly older than other undergraduates in 1919. Their memoirs, *Undertones of War* (1930) and *Goodbye to All That* (1929), are among the most powerful evocations of the world the soldiers knew.

Post-war Oxford was flooded with ex-servicemen. Over 1,800 ex-soldiers either matriculated or resumed their studies in the first year after the war. They were recognized as a unique generation and were given the privilege of counting military service against the residence requirements for their degrees. Within three years most had passed through the University, which

[92] BCA college meeting minutes, 12 Oct. 1918, 15 Feb. 1919, 15 May 1919, 13 Oct. 1921, 13 Dec. 1921, 24 May 1921.
[93] 'Oxford war memorials', 455–8.

resumed its normal life. We should not underestimate, though, how far veterans formed an 'invisible college' of their own. Both among the dons and among old members there were many who spoke of the bond of brotherhood among the men of 1914–18 that was evident long after the end of hostilities. Harold Macmillan was one of the many who believed fervently that the men who went to war had been initiated into mysteries that they and only they could really understand. Whenever they met, in Oxford and elsewhere, they renewed this bond through reminiscence, conversation, regimental reunions, battlefield tours and the like. Those who didn't go, and those too young to have served, were outside this circle.

Oxford bore the mark of the experience of war at other levels too. All are complex and must be seen against the backdrop of changes which had been set in motion long before 1914. The first is financial. In the short term, war-inflation substantially reduced the real value of landed property. This forced some colleges to join other landowners in the greatest transfer of landed property since the Reformation.[94] This process, together with the uncertainty of other forms of investment after the war, undermined the real value of the endowments of Oxford's colleges.

Secondly, the war drew the University, the civil service and industry more closely together. Perhaps the University Grants Committee (founded 1919) or the Committee of Vice-Chancellors and Principals (meeting informally from 1918) would have been established even without the war; perhaps the Department of Scientific and Industrial Research (which dates from 1915) would have been set up anyway. What the war did was to make the logic behind such ventures plain and powerful. The independence of the University and the autonomy of the colleges survived the war intact. But a new dialogue between the University and the state had begun in the Great War, and in the succeeding years the University had no choice but to continue it.

Thirdly, the war was a constant theme in inter-war political debates. Within a few years what the war had really meant and whether it had been 'worth the price' became frequent refrains in debates of many kinds. Many Oxford men and women believed fervently in the League of Nations and worked to help it defuse international tensions. Others remained cynical. Some undergraduates between the wars absorbed the patriotism and uncritical belief in 'England, Right or Wrong' of their fathers without the slightest difficulty. Others rejected it root and branch. This contrast is what the 'King and Country' debate of 1933 in the Oxford Union was all about. Of course the debate was about the Great War. But the Union Society did not vote against war, as so much of the popular press claimed at the time. Instead they voted against the shrill patriotism of the popular press of 1914,

[94] F. M. L. Thompson, *English Landed Society in the Nineteenth Century* (London 1963), 332.

against the language of 'dulce et decorum est pro patria mori', against the persecution of conscientious objectors: in sum against the stance of an earlier generation which spoke an older language about honour, duty and empire.[95]

The language of 1914 was indeed compromised by the Great War, but in Oxford as elsewhere it was far from dead. What the war had done was to force people to think anew about the meaning of patriotism. Some who thought about it came up with the same answers as Rupert Brooke; others echoed Wilfred Owen. In 1936 proctors acted to stop the University Peace Council from laying a wreath on the city's war memorial on armistice day. The dispute showed how sensitive the subject of the commemoration of the war still was.[96] But others forgot about the subject as quickly as possible. In the 1920s and 1930s Oxford was like the rest of Britain: not pacifist, but uneasy about embarking on another war. So when Hitler made war unavoidable in 1939, stoicism, not enthusiasm, was the response of Oxford and of the nation.

[95] One commentator spoke of the emergence of a new attitude to war, in which any 'romantic presentation' had been 'discredited': 'The Union Society and War', *OM* 16 Feb. 1933, 426. See also M. Ceadel, 'The King and Country debate, 1933: student politics, pacifism and the dictators', *Historical Jl* xxii (1979).

[96] See the letter of G. D. H. Cole, Richard Crossman and P. C. Gordon Walker on the incident in *OM* 19 Nov. 1936, 184.

2

The Asquith Commission, 1919–1922

JOHN PREST

The Oxford and Cambridge reformers of the early twentieth century concentrated, in each case, upon the government of the University and the relations between the university and the colleges. In Cambridge, legislation was at the mercy of non-resident MAs. In Oxford, Convocation could still be overrun with non-residents, and the result of a division in Congregation—which was limited to residents—might be determined by persons not engaged in the work of the University. In both universities there was a struggle between the university, with its negligible resources and its desire to raise the status of its professors and its faculties, and the colleges, with their endowments, their monopoly over entrance, their cult of 'the good college man' who might often be a pass man, their stranglehold over teaching and their separatism.

In both universities 'attempts to reform from within' made little progress.[1] In 1907 Charles Gore, Bishop of Birmingham, asked the government to appoint a new commission of inquiry. Gore knew that since 1877 new universities had been founded at Birmingham, Bristol, Leeds, Liverpool, Manchester and Sheffield. Whether one called these institutions 'civic' universities or 'modern' universities, the effect was to bracket Oxford and Cambridge together as 'national' or 'ancient' universities and to expose them to new forms of scrutiny. Their entrance procedures favoured applications from the expensive public schools. The passage of the Education Act of 1902, and the establishment of secondary schools in every area, meant that more and more pupils from the state-aided sector would be seeking access to higher education. Oxford and Cambridge must adjust to this development.[2]

There was scarcely a year between 1908 and 1914 in which the Prime Minister, Herbert Asquith, was not pressed to appoint a royal commission. His instinctive response was to leave reform to Oxford's energetic new Chancellor, Lord Curzon. In his *Principles and Methods of University Reform* Curzon fathomed the government of the University, and rehearsed the arguments for and against change.[3] His initiative led to the establishment of a University Finance Board and to a restriction upon the right of voting in

---

[1] *Times* 24 July 1907, 10. [2] *HL Deb.* 24 July 1907, 1526–33.
[3] Lord Curzon, *Principles and Methods of University Reform* (Oxford 1909).

Congregation to residents engaged in the work of the University. But contact between Oxford and the working classes already took place in extra-mural tutorial classes for adults arranged by the Workers' Educational Association, and Curzon's proposed poor men's college was not acceptable to the labour movement. Congregation was in no hurry to adopt Curzon's suggestion that the time had come to admit women to degrees.

Up to this point the claims of labour had come first, followed by those of women, and Curzon had not foreseen a need to expand the natural sciences. But the war exposed the shortcomings of British industry. In 1914–15 the heavy chemical industry lacked the capacity to manufacture both propellants and explosives on the scale required, and the pharmaceutical industry was virtually non-existent. The war made the recruitment of natural scientists a necessity. 'Practically every chemical technologist and every academic chemist in the country' was put on to war work, the government promoted a new company (now ICI) and in two years the country was able 'to remedy all its former deficiencies'.[4]

The chemists were the heroes of the hour. In March 1915 Professor Perkin looked forward to the day when the 'scientific staffs of our universities and technical schools' would be encouraged by those in authority to undertake industrial research.[5] A few months later Arthur Henderson, the President of the Board of Education, said that if overseas markets lost to Germany between 1870 and 1914 were to be recovered, 'our scientific resources' would have to be 'enlarged and organised'. 'The average manufacturer' being impressed 'with the importance of quick returns', the government would have to take over the encouragement of research and insist, for the dissemination of the results, upon a more co-operative organization of industry.[6] Hence the promotion of the Committee (later Department) for Scientific and Industrial Research. In 1916 a new pressure group, the Science Reorganization Committee, was formed, with Whitehall and the universities as its targets. 'Not only are our highest Ministers of State ignorant of science, but the same defect runs through almost all the public departments of the Civil Service . . . at Cambridge but four colleges are presided over by men of scientific training; at Oxford, not one. Of the 35 largest and best known public schools 34 have classical men as headmasters.'[7] The remedy would be for the civil-service examiners to give more weight to attainment in natural science. Lloyd George responded by appointing a committee to inquire into the position of natural science in the educational system of Great Britain,

[4] W. J. Pope, 'The national importance of chemistry' in A. C. Seward (ed.), *Science and the Nation* (Cambridge 1917), 14.

[5] W. H. Perkin, 'The position of the organic chemical industry', *Jl Chemical Soc.* cvii (1915, transactions), 564.

[6] Board of Education, *Scheme of Organization and Development of Scientific and Industrial Research* (PP 1914–16 l Cd 8005), 352; *Report of the Committee of the Privy Council for Scientific and Industrial Research for the Year 1915–16* (PP 1916 viii Cd 8336), 478.

[7] *Times* 2 Feb. 1916, 10.

and in 1918 the committee recommended that 'Greek should not be retained as a necessary subject in Responsions at Oxford or the Previous Examination at Cambridge', that 'large expenditure of public money is necessary to equip the universities for their work in pure and in applied science' and that 'grants from public funds to the universities should be increased to allow the universities to make a substantial reduction in their fees'.[8]

The President of the Board of Education to whom this report was sent was H. A. L. Fisher (1865–1940) who had read Greats at New College and then taught modern history. In 1907 Fisher signed the Oxford reformers' letter to the *Times* which was published to coincide with Gore's speech.[9] When he became Vice-Chancellor of Sheffield University in 1912 he inspired workmen with 'a vision of what education may do'; but he was warned that whenever education was mentioned, businessmen would 'shake their heads' and say 'think of the rates'.[10] Nothing daunted, he set up a committee to direct manufacturers 'to the technical literature bearing on their problems' and won increased local support for the applied sciences.[11] During the war, Fisher's brother William worked upon anti-submarine warfare, and Fisher understood the peril in which the shortage of scientists had placed the British state.[12]

In 1916, when Lloyd George invited him to succeed Henderson as Minister for Education, Fisher became MP for the Hallam division of Sheffield. He championed the board schools, and believed that the state which valued harmony 'should begin by making its teachers happy'.[13] In 1917 he increased teachers' salaries. In 1918 he exploited 'the prospective enfranchisement of several million new voters' and passed an Education Act which made schooling compulsory up to the age of 14 and introduced state scholarships to the universities.[14] The Act did not make secondary schooling compulsory, but in order to meet the competition of the United States of America it provided for 320 hours a year of day-release training for those who left school at 14.[15] At the general election of 1918 Fisher became member for the combined English universities. He accompanied the peace delegation to Versailles and returned to find that he was losing the battle to convince 'the people of this country' that education was not 'one of those troublesome ailments of childhood which must be got through as quickly as

---

[8] *Report of the Committee appointed by the Prime Minister to Enquire into the Position of Natural Science in the Educational System of Great Britain* (PP 1918 ix Cd 9011), 548.

[9] *Times* 24 July 1907, 10.

[10] Bodl. Fisher papers, box 63, fo 50, M. Trout, nd; ibid. fos 2–3, Rector of Edinburgh Academy, 23 Dec. 1916.

[11] D. Ogg, *Herbert Fisher, 1865–1940* (London 1947), 50.

[12] H. A. L. Fisher, *An Unfinished Autobiography* (London 1940), 93.

[13] Ibid. 105.

[14] H. A. L. Fisher, *Educational Reform: Speeches* (Oxford 1918), pp. xv–xvi.

[15] Ibid. 82.

possible'.[16] The scheme for day-release training was never implemented. Fisher went out with the ministry in 1922, and gave up his seat in parliament in 1926. A year later, when he delivered the centenary oration at London University, he spoke warmly of the chairs of the chemistry of brewing, of reinforced concrete and of glass technology, and noted how easily practical studies were being absorbed into British universities.[17]

From 1916 to 1918 Fisher was overhauling the whole educational system, and as the war drew to a close he told Virginia Woolf that he wanted 'to reform the Universities next, and then I shall have done'.[18] Fisher had become convinced 'that Oxford and Cambridge could not continue to discharge their functions or to cope with the developing requirements of applied science without help from the State'.[19] The vice-chancellors of Oxford and Cambridge were invited to join a deputation from the English universities which would plead impoverishment caused by inflation and ask the Treasury for increased funding. Oxford was 'much more reluctant in the matter than Cambridge'.[20] But the science departments, led by chemistry and medicine, knew what they wanted, and Council gave its blessing to applications by individual departments. Fisher waited until he knew that the various departments would require annual grants of £17,175 just to maintain their activities at the pre-war level and that—led by chemistry, which asked for £100,000—they would need a capital sum of £163,000 for extension. Then he announced that no more applications from separate departments would be received. Future subventions to the universities would take the form of block grants. Before Oxford could receive public funds, parliament would have to be satisfied that the government and administration of the University were in good shape. If the university and college authorities would agree to co-operate with a third commission of inquiry, the government would make an interim grant of £30,000, while holding out the hope of much larger sums being made available in the future.[21]

The *Oxford Magazine* asked whether 'we' were to 'sacrifice our independence' to save 'ourselves the trouble of finding elsewhere the necessary funds for the equipment of our laboratories'.[22] But there would never be a more favourable moment for an inquiry. German universities had lost their attractiveness as a model, Oxford and Cambridge had served the country well during the war, and victory appeared to have vindicated the collegiate system. Council and Congregation accepted Fisher's terms.

[16] H. A. L. Fisher, *Educational Reform: Speeches* p. ix.
[17] H. A. L. Fisher, *Our Universities* (London 1927), 18.
[18] *The Diary of Virginia Woolf*, ed. A. O. Bell (5 vols 1977–84) i. 204.
[19] Fisher, *Unfinished Autobiography*, 115.
[20] A. Mansbridge, *The Older Universities of England* (London 1923), 202.
[21] *Asquith Report*, appx 4.
[22] *OM* 6 June 1919, 332.

Circumstances had already marked out the course that a commission must follow. The life of the state was bound up with the expansion of science. National security told in favour of concentrating some aspects of research in separate establishments dealing with aviation and wireless telegraphy. But these institutions would need to recruit university-trained staff. This, and the belief that university science departments could regenerate British industry, meant that whatever form the inquiry took, the natural sciences would come off best. The rise of the Labour Party necessitated that the working classes too should not be sent away empty-handed. Women, like scientists and working men, had contributed to the war effort, but inevitably they were going to be pushed down to third place. ·

When Fisher decided there was to be a single commission which would consider both Oxford and Cambridge, the form which its recommendations would take was already more than half shaped. Contrasts with other British universities would not be pursued, and the commission would compare Oxford with Cambridge. Or, as Sir John Simon said, every Cambridge man would detect in it 'an unpleasant smell of the Isis' and every Oxford man would allege that 'it smells of the Cam'.[23] In natural sciences Oxford's record, and in extra-mural tutorial classes that of Cambridge, would appear defective. Oxford's Congregation would show to advantage in Cambridge, where there was as yet no equivalent house of residents; Oxford's graduated scale of taxation levied by the university upon the colleges would appear preferable to Cambridge's flat rate; and Oxford would be advised to adopt the Cambridge long vacation term. As for the equality of the sexes, soon after the Commission was appointed Oxford resolved to admit women to degrees, and Cambridge's continuing refusal to follow suit made it certain that attention would be drawn away from Oxford's residual anti-feminism.

Fisher envisaged a commission composed of members of the Privy Council and representatives of Oxford, Cambridge and the great institutions of estate-management. The Commission was to be divided into three sections, for Oxford, for Cambridge and for estates. Towards the end of August Fisher invited the former prime minister Herbert Asquith to head the Commission and to assume command of the Oxford section. After consulting Gilbert Murray, Asquith replied that he was 'keenly interested'. He thought the list of names supplied by Fisher would provide a strong team, but added that he would avoid judges, who 'almost always make a mess of commissions'. 'I am told', he continued, referring to two of the Cambridge names in front of him, 'that Fletcher and Anderson are physiologists: a dangerous type of man'.[24] Fisher's second step was to ask Gerald Balfour to head the Cambridge section and to act as vice-chairman.[25]

[23] J. A. Simon, Viscount Simon, *Retrospect* (London 1952), 283–4.
[24] Bodl. Fisher papers, box 63, fos 254–7.
[25] Ibid. fo 259.

His third was to place in charge of the estates section Rowland Prothero, Lord Ernle, who had been Conservative MP for Oxford University between 1914 and 1919 and President of the Board of Agriculture (with statutory responsibilities for university estates) between 1916 and 1919.

The commission was issued on 14 November 1919. In addition to Asquith, Balfour and Ernle, the Privy Council was represented by Lord Chalmers, who had just retired from the Treasury and was assigned to the Oxford section, where there were going to be anxieties about the conditions attached to grants of public money; by Arthur Henderson, who represented the Labour Party and was directed to the Cambridge section, which needed prodding about its tutorial classes; and by Sir John Simon, who was allotted to the Oxford section, presumably in order to represent All Souls College, of which he was a fellow. Before the Commission proceeded very far, Henderson resigned and was replaced by Willie Graham, the Labour MP for Edinburgh Central. The full Commission was: Oxford section, Asquith, W. G. S. Adams, W. H. Bragg, Chalmers, A. Mansbridge, H. A. Miers, E. Penrose, Simon, T. B. Strong; Cambridge section, Balfour, H. K. Anderson, B. A. Clough, H. Darwin, W. M. Fletcher, Graham, M. R. James, A. Schuster, G. M. Trevelyan; estates section, Ernle, H. M. Cobb, H. Frank, J. H. Oakley, E. G. Strutt.

The Privy Council contingent contained two Conservatives, Balfour and Ernle, and one Labour representative, Graham. But Graham did not attend many of the formal sessions of the Commission (though he volunteered most of the published reservations at the end of the report) and the weight lay with the Liberals, Asquith himself and Simon. To them one must add Chalmers, who had attended the same school as Asquith (City of London School) and who for ten years or more had 'enjoyed at all times the confidence and esteem' of the former prime minister.[26] When Chalmers appeared in Cambridge his manner reminded Maisie Anderson of 'the ponderous gait and crafty watchfulness of a ceremonial elephant'. From the store of his wisdom this sagacious animal offered her a piece of advice upon which, he said, he had based his own career: 'never work between meals!'[27]

Among the members of the Oxford section Bragg and Miers were the representatives of science. Bragg held a chair at University College, London. He and his son together founded the science of crystallography and during the war he worked upon the development of hydrophones for detecting submarines. He was interested in 'Physical science and its applications to industry' (1916) and contributed to A. C. Seward's *Science and the Nation* (1917); he was a brilliant popularizer, writing for example on 'Why people

[26] See obituary of Chalmers by P. E. Matheson in *Proc. British Academy* xxv (1939), 325.
[27] Maisie Anderson, 'Time to the sound of bells', typescript, Gonville and Caius College, Cambridge, p. 151.

sing in bathrooms' (1920).[28] Miers had switched from classics to natural science while still an undergraduate at Oxford and had been appointed to the Waynflete chair, with a fellowship at Magdalen, in 1895. He was now Vice-Chancellor of Manchester University with a special chair in crystallography. He served on the civil-service examinations committee and in 1919 he became a member of the Department for Scientific and Industrial Research. Two days after he accepted Fisher's invitation to join the Asquith Commission he received a request from Sir Auckland Geddes to chair the Commission on coal output, which he declined; Lord Sankey then accepted the post.[29]

Mansbridge, who was the son of a carpenter in Battersea, was the workers' representative and the most direct link between the Commission and Bishop Gore, whom he met in 1894.[30] Gore officiated at Mansbridge's wedding to a fellow Sunday school teacher.[31] Mansbridge believed that 'it was because of the principles' which Gore expressed 'in his lectures on the Epistle to the Ephesians that I conceived the idea which eventuated in the Workers' Educational Association', which was founded in 1903.[32] Oxford had made the WEA welcome, and Mansbridge regarded Oxford as a holy city.[33]

Emily Penrose was the women's representative in the Oxford section. As a student at Somerville she had been the first woman to achieve a first in literae humaniores. She became Principal of Bedford and Royal Holloway colleges before returning to Oxford in 1907 as Principal of Somerville. In 1911 she joined the advisory committee on university grants, and in 1916 she served on the Royal Commission of inquiry into the University of Wales. Now she had to represent the views of the four women's colleges and the home-students. She was deeply religious, as were the other members of the Oxford section identified with the three interest groups—Bragg who was reverent in the face of nature, Miers who addressed the Christian Union, and Mansbridge.[34] Fisher appears to have made this a criterion for selection.

There were two others, Adams and Strong. W. G. S. Adams was the Gladstone Professor and a fellow of All Souls. During the war he served in the Ministry of Munitions and as a member of Lloyd George's secretariat. In 1918 he joined the civil-service examinations committee, and when he returned to Oxford he contributed to the foundation of 'modern Greats'. He was closely connected with the Carnegie Trust, and in 1915 he published a report on library provision in the United Kingdom. He said there that he

[28] *William Henry Bragg and William Lawrence Bragg: A Bibliography of their Non-Technical Writings* (Berkeley Calif. 1978).

[29] Miers's diary, Bodl. MS Eng. misc. d. 661, 22 Sept. 1919.

[30] A. Mansbridge, *Fellow Men* (London 1948), 61.

[31] B. Jennings, *Albert Mansbridge and English Adult Education* (Hull 1976), 7.

[32] A. Mansbridge, *The Trodden Road* (London 1940), 139.

[33] Jennings, 17.

[34] W. H. Bragg, *Science and Faith* (London 1941); Miers's diary, 5 Feb. 1922.

had been in close touch with the development of the WEA, which he described as a body 'destined to exercise a far-reaching influence on the whole well-being of the community'.[35] He was the only member of the Asquith Commission still alive when the Franks Commission was appointed in 1964.

T. B. Strong was the Dean of Christ Church. As a young man he had fallen under the spell of Gore's *Lux Mundi* theology. He is said to have absented himself from Christ Church whenever the bloods were burning the furniture, and to have hated public occasions. He was a dull preacher, but he was lenient about sexual offences, and made a point of visiting clergymen who had been sent to prison. He was a member of the committee which produced *Oxford and Working-Class Education*, published at Oxford in 1908. He was no friend to women's education, but now that women had been allowed into the University, he advocated admitting them to degrees ('I am never in favour of taking two bites at a cherry, especially if it is a sour one'). He was Vice-Chancellor during the war, and when he accepted Fisher's invitation he stipulated that if he became a bishop he was to retain his place on the Commission—as indeed he did when he was appointed Bishop of Ripon in 1920.[36]

Among the Cambridge section Anderson was the Master of Caius, and Fletcher like Anderson was a physiologist who had close links with the Sir William Dunn trustees and the Rockefeller Foundation. Schuster had held chairs in mathematics and physics at Manchester University, and Darwin designed instruments for the natural science laboratories. There was nobody from within the University to represent the working classes, but Miss Clough, the Vice-Principal of Newnham, took the women's part. James, the Provost of Eton and a former provost of King's, appears to have contributed little to the Commission beyond introducing Mansbridge to the pleasures of reading Bulldog Drummond.[37] Trevelyan, like Darwin and Fletcher—and indeed Bragg—was a Trinity man and was known in Caius as 'the great George'.[38] He was a 'whig' historian, and in 1917 he wrote to Fisher to say that what with the (February) revolution in Russia, President Wilson's proclamation, the prospect of another Reform Act and Fisher's new education estimates, he felt ground for hope that 'the world's great age begins anew'.[39] For Fisher, having Trevelyan on the Commission, and having Trevelyan write the Commission's report, was almost like being there himself.

[35] W. G. S. Adams, *A Report on Library Provision and Policy* (Edinburgh 1915), 20–1.
[36] H. Anson, *T. B. Strong: Bishop, Musician, Dean, Vice-Chancellor* (London 1949), 22, 35, 38, 45, 48, 73.
[37] Mansbridge, *Fellow Men*, 29.
[38] Anderson, 'Sound of bells', 152.
[39] Fisher papers, box 63, fo 300.

Upon the estates committee Ernle was a link to the first commission of 1850, through his life of A. P. Stanley, its secretary.[40] Cobb worked for the land agents Clutton's and Frank was a partner in Knight, Frank and Rutley. Oakley was a former president of the Surveyors' Institution. Strutt was a partner in Strutt and Parker; his brother, the third Baron Rayleigh, had been head of the Cavendish Laboratory and from 1908 to 1919 was Chancellor of Cambridge University.

The Commission's terms of reference were 'to enquire into the financial resources of the universities and of the colleges and Halls therein, into the administration and application of those resources, into the Government of the universities, and into the relations of the colleges and Halls to the universities and to each other, and to make recommendations'.[41] There was no mention of the curriculum. The members met for the first time on 27 November 1919 and decided to proceed by questionnaires addressed to the universities and to each college.[42] In addition the Oxford Reform Committee, the Committee of Younger Cambridge Graduates and the Committee of Oxford Heads and Fellows made representations (and rehearsed arguments which had already been aired before 1914). Evidence also came from several outside bodies: the Headmasters' Conference, the Association of Headmasters, the Association of Headmistresses, the Labour Party, the WEA, the Co-operative Union and the National Union of Teachers.[43] On Fridays in June and July 1920 the Commission met in London to interrogate the authors of these submissions. The headmasters and headmistresses complained about the confusion caused by there being so many different entrance examinations. Representatives of labour argued for continuous state control over Oxford and Cambridge; they also developed a case for making all university education, like primary school education, free, because 'a great stream of talent, especially among the children of the working classes, runs to waste every year'.[44] The NUT wanted teaching to be raised into a graduate profession.

From 3 August to 11 August the full Commission sat at Cambridge and interviewed the Vice-Chancellor (Giles) and 'many Professors and officers of the University' in the hall of Emmanuel College. From 18 September to 30 September it met in Oxford, in 'Oriel, All Souls and elsewhere'. It was in Oxford again from 29 March to 4 April 1921. Further meetings took place in London throughout 1921 while the report was being put together, and the last meeting was on 10 February 1922.[45] There were sixty-six meetings in all,

[40] R. E. Prothero, first Baron Ernle, *The Life and Correspondence of Arthur Penrhyn Stanley* (2 vols London 1893).
[41] *Asquith Report*, 3.
[42] Miers's diary, 27 Nov. 1919.
[43] *Asquith Report*, appx 1.ii.
[44] Ibid. p. 61.
[45] Miers's diary.

and the members examined over ninety witnesses.[46] Throughout its deliberations the Commission considered Oxford and Cambridge simultaneously. Asquith found he had 'a strong and on the whole a manageable team', and those 'who contributed the most were the Bishop of Ripon and the Master of Caius'.[47] According to the secretary, C. L. Stocks, all agreed that the Master of Caius was 'the outstanding member'.[48]

The estates section was required to satisfy the Treasury and the taxpayer that the two institutions, most of whose colleges were endowed, were making full use of their own resources. Ernle and his four-man crew worked on their own. First they rejected proposals, emanating mainly from the labour movement, for the landed property of the colleges to be concentrated in a single locality and be managed by the Board of Agriculture and for the colleges' investments to be thrown into a common University pool. Next they justified the existing arrangements on the ground that, amateur as the colleges' administration was, it cost between a third and a half of the likely fees for professional management. They did, however, recommend that the Ministry of Agriculture should be empowered to make provisional orders conferring on either university 'compulsory powers of acquiring from Colleges and outside owners land which can be shown to be essential to its development for educational purposes'.[49] The members of the estates section signed a separate report, which was tacked on to the main one.[50] Ernle apart, they do not appear to have participated in the remainder of the Commission's work.

The members of the Commission understood that their task was to give 'the two Universities a proper place in a world system of Universities'.[51] They agreed, almost without discussion, that teachers and administrators should be entitled to something like the civil-service conditions of employment which many of them had enjoyed during the war. University staffs should be enlarged in order to release tutors from excessive routine teaching of undergraduates and to give them time for advanced teaching and research. Stipends should be raised to compare with 'those of other professional families' and university teachers should be entitled to pensions. In due course, salaries and pensions became the first of the 'principal purposes for which we recommend a grant of public money'. Nor was there any difficulty in deciding straight away that there were 'grave objections to State money being paid to Colleges' and that public funds should be channelled through the universities.[52]

[46] *Asquith Report*, 5.
[47] Fisher papers, box 64, fos 14–15.
[48] C. L. Stocks, *People and Places in Prose and Verse* (np 1970), 47.
[49] *Asquith Report*, 226.
[50] Ibid. 217–26.
[51] Mansbridge, *Older Universities*, 198.
[52] Ibid. 48–53, 57, 55.

Turning to the government of the universities, the Commission noticed that at Oxford Convocation had at last agreed to drop compulsory Greek. But in Cambridge the Senate was still being obstreperous, and the Commission recommended that the powers of both Convocation and Senate should be rendered vestigial. The Commission took the view that resident teachers and administrators should be placed in sole charge of the universities and it rejected every proposal for outside nominees to be placed upon the governing bodies. In both universities professors and heads of house should no longer be treated as separate orders or classes in elections to the Hebdomadal Council. In Oxford the existing General Board of the faculties and the curators of the University Chest should be abolished and replaced by a board of studies and research and a new finance board.[53]

Next the Commission had to consider the demands of the three great interests. At an early stage they set up a committee upon science (Bragg, Miers, Schuster and probably Darwin). Mansbridge was encouraged, in full commission, to speak up for labour. Miss Clough and Miss Penrose were formally constituted into a committee upon the needs of the women's colleges.

In science the present position was summarized in the preamble to the Commission's report, where the passage upon Oxford's studies began with literae humaniores and ended with natural science, while that upon Cambridge's began with science, whose growth 'since the era of the [first and second] Royal Commissions has been perhaps the greatest fact in the history of the University since its foundation'. The commissioners recognized that 'for a long time' Oxford had been unable 'to play her full part in scientific teaching and research'. But 'there could be no greater or more disastrous mistake than for the State to encourage or permit the development of Oxford as a "Humanities" and Cambridge as a "Science" university' and 'a great opportunity' had arrived for Oxford science.[54] It was imperative, as Mansbridge said, 'that every effort should be made to place the laboratories . . . of Oxford in the forefront of their time'.[55] Thanks to the generosity of Dyson Perrins, a new organic chemistry laboratory had already been built. Now fifteen acres in the Parks should be allocated for new buildings, and the next step should be to build a modern laboratory for inorganic chemistry. All practical instruction in chemistry and physics should then be supplied in well organized laboratories belonging to the University, as it was in Cambridge.[56]

When they began to consider the claims of labour, the members of the Commission lost no time in agreeing that extra-mural instruction, which

[53] Ibid. 58–79.
[54] Ibid. 28–33, 114, 45, 114.
[55] Mansbridge, *Older Universities*, 234.
[56] *Asquith Report*, 116–17.

had already been considered by Lloyd George's adult education committee, should be accepted as an established part of 'the normal work of a University'.[57] Next they came to the problem of the 'accessibility of the Universities and Colleges'. This fell into two parts, how to exclude the idle rich and how to include the industrious poor. The first seemed easy, and they agreed to recommend the institution of a University entrance examination, and a means whereby the University, like the colleges, could send men down for idleness.[58] The second was much more intractable. They recommended that—the right to rooms apart—the receipt of the emoluments attached to a college's scholarships should be limited to those in financial need.[59] This would enable the income from the college's endowments to be spread more widely.

The commissioners had to face the fact that living in a college was expensive.[60] Were poor students coming up from state secondary schools to be given outsize grants to enable them to enjoy the traditional standard of living, or were costs in the colleges to be reduced, or were the colleges to continue to provide a high-cost service for the rich while the poorer students were directed towards an expanded non-collegiate sector of the University? The first found advocates in Oxford itself ('the alternative to levelling down is levelling up') and the Commission did recommend an increase in the number of state studentships and local authority awards.[61] But this line of approach was not likely to attract the Treasury during a period of retrenchment. The second was an ideal to which they could all subscribe, and they engaged A. E. Towle, manager of the Midland Railway hotels and refreshment rooms, to carry out an inquiry into college catering arrangements.[62] But they shied away from all the more puritanical arguments in favour of simple living for young males, and when R. H. Tawney made a late submission on 21 September 1921 Asquith was agitated. Abandoning his impassivity as chairman, he interrupted repeatedly and loweringly.[63] The Commission did agree to recommend the adoption of bed-sitting rooms, but that apart, they felt powerless to alter the high cost of living in the men's colleges and they were driven into championing the non-collegiate system as the best solution for the poor. They pointed out that 'to a far greater extent than is commonly realised, provision is already made at Oxford and Cambridge for University education at a moderate cost by the Non-Collegiate organisations [St Catherine's and Fitzwilliam]'. They added,

[57] *Asquith Report*, 123.
[58] Ibid. 165–8.
[59] Ibid. 135.
[60] Ibid. 140–6.
[61] Ibid. 164–5 and appx 1, p. 29 ('levelling up').
[62] Ibid. 146–55.
[63] Asquith Commission papers, Bodl. MS top. Oxon. b. 109, fos 524–42 (R. H. Tawney).

unconvincingly, that there was 'no foundation' for the supposition that non-collegiate students were 'in some way inferior' to students in colleges.[64]

Turning finally to the problem of the women's colleges, they noted the heavy burden of debt afflicting the women's colleges of Oxford, the failure of their appeal—which had raised but £31,300 when Somerville alone, the most secure, needed £80,000—and the low salaries paid to women tutors.[65] The Commission had already decided that public money should not be paid to colleges, and Balfour and others drew attention to the special difficulties attending any grant of public money to a denominational foundation like Lady Margaret Hall or St Hugh's.[66] But the Commission decided to recommend a special grant of £4,000 a year for ten years to help the women's colleges of Oxford. Taking into account the fact that a majority of Cambridge residents had voted in favour of giving degrees to women, they concluded that it would be unfair to deny the Cambridge colleges an equal benefit. They then capitulated to male fears: they expressed themselves strongly in favour of the view 'that Cambridge should remain mainly and predominantly a men's University', recommended that the number of women undergraduates should be limited by University statute to five hundred, and issued an open invitation to Oxford to adopt a similar restriction.[67]

The one topic which brought the Commission close to a crisis was the relation of teaching in the university to that in the colleges. Members started with a clear intention of strengthening the faculties, and on 4 June 1920 Asquith appointed a co-ordinating committee to formulate proposals. It consisted of Anderson, Strong, Chalmers, Bragg and Trevelyan—that is, three members of the Oxford section and two of the Cambridge, but three Cambridge and two Oxford men.[68] The committee's report was considered by the whole Commission on 23 July 1920. The Commission decided that the principal system of lectures should be organized by the University, but already there was a hint of trouble to come when the words 'in a broad sense' were added.[69] Next it decided that tuition and supervision should be left to the colleges. But then came the problem: should the faculties be given power over the selection of college tutors, or should colleges retain the power to appoint their members as inter-collegiate (university) lecturers?

In Cambridge the role of the faculty was already much more widely accepted, and the problem there was the relationship between the different

[64] *Asquith Report*, 145, 155, 156.
[65] Ibid. 169–70.
[66] Somerville College, Penrose papers, notes of discussion on report of sub-committee on women's colleges, 21 Jan. 1921.
[67] *Asquith Report*, 171, 173–4.
[68] Bodl. Asquith papers, box 138, fo 134.
[69] Ibid. box 139, fos 178–83.

parts of the University. But alas for Oxford reformers, Odling, the Professor of Chemistry from 1872 to 1912, had carried out no research.[70] Where the university had failed, the colleges had stepped in. Balliol and Trinity jointly, Christ Church and Magdalen all possessed laboratories dating from before Odling's time; Queen's had opened a new laboratory in 1900 and Jesus furnished another in 1907. H. B. Baker had then arranged that 'each College laboratory should undertake responsibility for one branch of practical work and thus gain the experience and techniques needed for a research group'. As Vernon Harcourt put it upon the occasion of the jubilee of the University Museum in 1910, when the university fails 'the College laboratories with young and eager teachers are prepared to supply any deficiency'.[71] In Cambridge the college laboratories performed more elementary functions than the departments of the university, and science had freed the university from the grip of the colleges. In Oxford, science was not so immediately serviceable an instrument. The reformers were unable to satisfy the colleges on what was to happen under a system of university teaching if there was a bad professor. The drive for faculty-based teaching was weakened by a breakdown in the very discipline whose usefulness to the state had given rise to the Commission.

When the Commission met on 23 July 1920 Ernle said that 'everyone wants the Faculty to be supreme' and Chalmers pronounced 'that the College should subserve the University'. Bragg thought university require-ments should have priority. But Miers, who knew Oxford better, suggested it would be sufficient if colleges continued to make appointments and the faculty reserved the right to withhold recognition from the persons so appointed. Anderson spotted a way through the impasse and proposed that colleges should be allowed to appoint lecturers on probation for between three and five years. If successful the lecturers could be adopted by the appropriate faculty. Strong was torn two ways. As a member of the Commission he gave a cautious welcome to Anderson's proposal. But he had a constituency, and he made it clear that in the eyes of the Oxford colleges the powers of the faculty ought to be limited to the right to draw the attention of a college with a vacancy to the needs of the faculty. Balfour summarized the discussion by saying that 'there appeared to be considerable differences of opinion', and no conclusion was reached.[72]

According to Farnell, the Vice-Chancellor, Asquith was himself a 'college-man'.[73] The colleges of Oxford were given plenty of time to rally. Strong, while conceding that faculty teaching must, despite the college laboratories, predominate in science, mustered support in favour of the

[70] E. J. Bowen, H. Hartley and H. M. Powell, *Chemistry in Oxford* (Cambridge 1966), 5.
[71] Ibid. 10. Cf below, 88, 157–8.
[72] Asquith papers, box 139, fos 178–83.
[73] L. R. Farnell, *An Oxonian Looks Back* (London 1934), 309.

colleges' traditional ascendancy in literae humaniores, law, modern history and theology. Going over to the offensive, he attempted to wrest teaching in the infant faculties of English literature and modern languages from the university and transfer it to the colleges. In March and April 1921 he tried to persuade the members of the Oxford section that what was required was 'a further extension both of the Tutorial system and of the Faculty organization'.[74] The question was left open as long as it could be, until the end of May, when the science committee was putting the final touches to its part of the report.

On 27 May the Oxford section was reconvened in Oxford. Bragg (the only Cambridge man present) repeated that 'Faculty was the proper body to administer' public funds given to support teaching. Chalmers said that 'Oxford would be in a very awkward position' if it held aloof 'in respect of a few subjects from the system followed, or to be adopted, at Cambridge and every other University'. But Sir John Simon 'insisted upon the important differences between teaching in Science and in other subjects' and averred that 'on the literary side it was of great value to a man to be taught by one definitely connected with his own College'. Finally, Asquith himself 'felt that there was a danger of exaggerating the importance of lecturing as compared with tuition'.[75] Strong had carried the day, and the Commission never did insist, as the vast majority of its members had originally intended, upon a real shift of power in all disciplines from the colleges to the relevant faculty boards. In this respect the two universities were in effect allowed to go their own ways.

The Asquith Commission avoided taking hard decisions. It was in the state's interest to pay for a huge expansion of science at Oxford, but by the time the report was published, people had lost sight of the original reason for the Commission's appointment. Public money was not earmarked for the natural sciences and the Commission took the view that the two universities had to be treated even-handedly and receive the same grant. Upon the question of co-ordination the Commission was unwilling to decide between faculties and colleges. The answer, which was expensive, was to have two systems. Every professor appointed by the university was to be found a place in a college and every tutor appointed by a college would (in Oxford) or might (in Cambridge) receive an appointment as a university lecturer. It was not, one may say, a very brave commission. The influx of scientists was concealed behind a further expansion of the arts. Working-class children were to be encouraged provided they did not challenge Oxford's expensive lifestyle, and women must pose no threat to a male society. As Mansbridge expressed it in a very downbeat summary, 'the Commissioners have faced

---

[74] Penrose papers, 'Co-ordination of teaching', 31 Mar. 1921.
[75] Ibid. notes of discussion on 27 May 1921.

big problems and made tentative steps towards their solution'. But then should they ever have attempted to do more? They had taken the view that 'the proper bodies to reform the Universities are the Universities themselves', and they had nudged the colleges 'in the direction of a common University organization'.[76]

This, we may suppose, was the view of Asquith himself. The members of the Commission never quite knew what Asquith was thinking, and when they met at Cambridge from 3 August to 11 August 1920 'Asquith only stayed till the 5th, and played whist all the evening while the rest of us conferred'.[77] But Asquith never intended the Commission to attempt great schemes of reconstruction. In 1923 he wrote that Rome's genius 'was not to originate but to adapt; and not unfrequently, in the process of adaptation, to transmute'.[78] Asquith sought to make sufficient changes to ensure that there would be no need for another royal commission, and no necessity either for 'some kind of continuous control' as suggested by the Master of Caius—who was of course a physiologist and thus in Asquith's estimation 'a dangerous sort of man'.[79] For Asquith it was sufficient that statutory commissioners should be appointed for a fixed term 'to carry out the changes recommended in University and College Statutes and, where necessary, to revise trusts'.[80] In 1923 eleven commissioners were named, headed by F. J. N. Thesiger, Viscount Chelmsford, who had been Viceroy of India from 1916 to 1921.[81] Strong, Mansbridge and Penrose were included to ensure continuity between the Commission of Inquiry and the Statutory Commission. With these three should perhaps be coupled Sidney Peel, who had experience on Curzon's Board of Finance, and P. E. Matheson of New College, who was a leading supporter of Curzon's pre-war reform programme. F. W. Pember was the Warden of All Souls, a college in need of reform. F. J. Lys, the Provost of Worcester (a reactionary who would have liked to undo the work of the previous commissions) and C. R. M. F. Cruttwell of Hertford (the historian of the Great War) took the part of the smaller colleges. Sir Archibald Garrod represented medicine and the Curator of the Ashmolean Museum, D. G. Hogarth, represented the University's galleries and art collections.

1924 was set aside for the university and colleges themselves to frame new statutes.[82] In 1925 the commissioners set up an office in the Examination Schools in Oxford and for two years they negotiated upon the basis of the drafts handed to them. The 'nearest part' of 'paradise' (the University Parks)

[76] Mansbridge, *Older Universities*, 202, 204.
[77] Miers's diary.
[78] C. Bailey (ed.), *The Legacy of Rome* (Oxford 1923), 2.
[79] Asquith papers, box 139, fo 160, summary of proceedings on 16 July 1920.
[80] *Asquith Report*, 227.
[81] 13 and 14 George 5, c. 33.
[82] Ibid. schedule to the Act, p. 11.

was handed over for 'the massive buildings of Science'.[83] A new responsions examination tightened the requirements for admission to the University. The commissioners laid down statutory retirement-ages for professors and for heads and fellows of colleges. Chelmsford himself coerced the colleges into admitting professors (in whose appointment they received only a minority voice) as full (rather than supernumerary) members of their governing bodies.[84] This was the crucial measure which broke the obduracy of the colleges. But then, as Pember expressed it, the commissioners had to go round *handselling the yoke* of the New Statutes'.[85] Chelmsford's commissioners, a majority of whom were working dons exposed to lobbying, never did find the resolve to strengthen the structure and afforce the powers of the university to the extent envisaged by Asquith's Commission. Council was reformed, but the General Board of the faculties and the University Chest were not reconstituted and remained independent bodies outside Council's control. When the commissioners completed their work in 1927, the colleges were weaker and the backwoodsmen had lost their veto in Convocation, but the University was no more able to take decisions than it had been before. The indigenous reform movement was in retreat, and in 1925 Asquith had failed in his bid to succeed Curzon as chancellor.

The radical, observing that Chalmers was elected Master of Peterhouse and that Chelmsford and Adams became successive wardens of All Souls, may be inclined to suppose that the Commission of inquiry and the statutory commissioners were tame and timid. The alternative is to say that Britain paid a high price to expand Oxford's science from about one hundred to nearly two hundred finalists a year, but that within a generation the reputation of Oxford's departments had been transformed. As Fisher lay dying in 1940, he could have reflected that British science was now stronger than it had been during the First World War. It might not be strong enough to enable British businessmen to regain Britain's former place in world trade, but there were just enough graduates available in 1939 to ensure that when British industry passed under the control of the civil service between 1939 and 1945, optimum use could be made of the resources available and that Britain would survive the war.

[83] J. Wells, *Gazette* 9 Oct. 1924, 26.
[84] HCP 128 (1924), 45–8.
[85] *Gazette* 13 Oct. 1927, 23.

3

The Junior Members, 1900–1990: A Profile

DANIEL I. GREENSTEIN

Perhaps the most important influence for change in twentieth-century Oxford is the growth in the number of its junior members.[1] Between 1900 and 1987 the annual number of men and women matriculating as members of the University increased nearly fivefold, to just over 4,500 [figure 3.1].[2] The pattern of growth is strikingly different for men and women. The number of women junior members, virtually unaffected by the First World War, increased steadily until 1927, when a quota was imposed on the number of women allowed in residence. The peak around 1920 reflects the fact that nearly 1,000 women in the three years from 1920 to 1922 retrospectively received the degrees for which they had been examined earlier. The women's societies' slow rate of growth resumed after the quota was lifted in 1957, but rapid growth did not occur until 1974, when five men's colleges admitted women. Thereafter, the University's proportion of women junior members grew fast.

Whereas men's numbers reflected external constraints, women's numbers were moulded by constraints that came primarily from within the University. The First World War virtually denuded Oxford of its men matriculants, and its immediate aftermath saw their numbers swelled by servicemen who had deferred matriculation until after the war, some of whom became eligible for government grants. Male numbers were also swollen by the fact that more than a third of the 1,719 men who were

[1] 'Junior members' denotes undergraduates and postgraduates.

[2] Matriculation figures from a computerized record (HUD/C/ML) of the names of all male (1900–70) and female (1920–70) matriculants listed annually in *Gazette*. This gives a slightly inflated impression of junior-member numbers because the matriculation lists include people who matriculated to take an honorary degree or a degree by incorporation. These figures were supplemented with estimates of the annual intake of women 1900–19 based on a sample of all women coming up to Somerville and the Society of Oxford Home-Students (later St Anne's) every six years, and to Lady Margaret Hall, St Hilda's and St Hugh's every three years from 1900 to 1918 inclusive, and whose names appear in their college's register. Matriculation figures 1971–87 were drawn from aggregate figures published in *Gazette*.

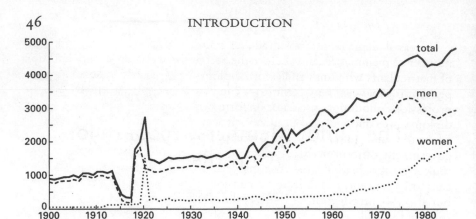

FIGURE 3.1   NUMBER OF MEN AND WOMEN MATRICULANTS, 1900–1987

examined for an honours degree between 1919 and 1922 took shortened honour schools.[3] The pressure on male places was maintained between the wars by the rising number of secondary school-leavers in England (from 100,000 in 1895 to 560,000 in 1937), and by extended financial aid.[4] From 1902 Local Education Authorities (LEAs) offered grants to able students, and by 1937 nearly 1,100 Oxford men and women (about a quarter of those in residence) held such awards.[5] In addition, the Board of Education annually awarded 220 state scholarships to boys and girls from assisted schools, and the lion's share of these were taken up at Oxbridge.[6] College scholarships and exhibitions were a more important source of financial aid for intending Oxford undergraduates; between a quarter and a third of all men matriculants held such awards between 1900 and 1939.[7] By that time, some 53 per cent of all Oxford men and women in residence were receiving some form of financial assistance.[8]

[3] From a computerized version (HUD/C/CR) of a ledger of men's and women's class results in full and shortened honours examinations by subject, 1913–70, kindly made available by Mr Philip Moss at the Registry Office. The series was extended to 1986 with data gathered from a manual count of the men's and women's schools results published annually as class lists by the examiners.

[4] D. V. Glass, 'Education and social change in modern England' in A. H. Halsey, J. E. Floud and C. A. Anderson (eds), *Education, Economy and Society: A Reader in the Sociology of Education* (New York 1961), 392.

[5] I am grateful to Dr Mark Pottle for compiling a computerized record of awards listed in *Gazette* 1938–57, and a computerized record of numbers in residence from the University's manuscript UGC returns (HUD/S/UGC).

[6] In 1936 these were opened up to all candidates from assisted and independent schools and in 1938 the number of awards was increased to 360: R. Davis, *The Grammar School* (London 1967), 240.

[7] From a computerized database (HUD/C/RS and SV) comprising biographical information on a stratified 10 per cent sample of all men matriculants 1900–67 and all women matriculants 1920–67. The sample of Oxford's women members 1900–19 consists of all women who came up to Somerville and the Society of Oxford Home-Students every six years, and to Lady Margaret Hall, St Hilda's and St Hugh's every three years from 1900 to 1918 inclusive. Biographical data were gathered from the published record for individuals up between 1900 and 1939 and through survey questionnaires for those up between 1940 and 1967.   [8] *OM* 20 Oct. 1938, 4.

Increased demand for postgraduate training also helped to inflate the number of men matriculants before the Second World War. The proportion of matriculants who took an Oxford diploma or certificate increased from 1 per cent to 8 per cent between 1900–13 and 1930–9. Oxford's response to the professions' mounting insistence on formal entry qualifications included the diploma in economics and political science, and certificates or diplomas in education and (after the Hadow report on the recruitment of local government officers in 1934) in social administration.[9] Matriculants who took a postgraduate degree rose between 1900–13 and 1930–9 from 7 per cent to 15 per cent; this reflected expansion in the number of part II chemists but also the introduction of the DPhil degree, which attracted to Oxford a small but steadily growing number of graduates from other universities.[10]

Several factors moderated the pressure on places between the wars. One was the Latin entry requirement, which grammar schools could not always satisfy. Between 1900 and 1913 the nine 'Clarendon' schools—Charterhouse, Eton, Harrow, Merchant Taylors', Rugby, St Paul's, Shrewsbury, Westminster and Winchester—supplied 28 per cent of Oxford's men. Between 1920 and 1939 the Clarendon schools were still supplying a fifth of Oxford's men, and another 54 per cent was accounted for by other schools in the Headmasters' Conference (HMC), an organization established in 1869 to represent the most important of the 'endowed' schools.[11] Limited college accommodation also kept the number of men down. Colleges increased their reliance on lodgings between the wars—in 1935 nearly as many men lived in lodgings as matriculated—though dons feared that this might erode their colleges' corporate life.[12]

The cost of an Oxford education also restricted the undergraduate intake. Even in those men's colleges which recruited boys from assisted grammar schools, most junior members were privately funded. A higher proportion of boys from assisted schools (40 per cent) relied on college awards than boys from fee-paying independent schools (29 per cent). Yet boys from fee-paying independent schools in the 1930s took nearly 60 per cent of all college awards, correspondingly reducing the number available for boys from assisted schools.[13] LEA grants and state scholarships were another important source of funding for boys from assisted schools, but these too

[9] HUD/C/RS–SV; HCP 110 (1918), 71–81; 130 (1925), 113–16, 177; 151 (1932), 25–6; 152 (1932), 19–28; 161 (1935), 141–52; P. Hutchinson, 'University men in local government', Oxford winter 1935, 63–75; P. M. Stevenson, 'Graduates in local government', Oxford winter 1937, 85–93; spring 1938, 49–61.

[10] HUD/C/RS–SV.

[11] HUD/C/RS–SV. Based on the total number of male matriculants who, immediately before coming up to Oxford, attended a British secondary school which could be positively identified in school directories (see above, 46 n.7).

[12] Figures from OUA LHD/RP/5. The annual number for men in lodgings was compared with that for men matriculants because figures for men in residence are not available before 1938. On the basis of this comparison it is reasonable to assume that between a quarter and a third of all men in residence were living outside their colleges. On fears for colleges' corporate life see L. R. Phelps, 'Oxford since 1910', OM 9 May 1935, 566–8.

[13] HUD/C/RS–SV.

were limited in number, and the value of LEA awards varied considerably from one authority to another. In the 1930s three-fifths of Oxford's male matriculants who came from assisted schools held nearly all the LEA grants and state scholarships awarded to Oxford men, sometimes in conjunction with college awards, compared to less than 3 per cent of Oxford's male matriculants from fee-paying independent schools. College awards and government grants undoubtedly enabled some boys from humbler origins to come to Oxford, but such opportunities were strictly limited. As many as half a sample of male matriculants in the 1930s known to have attended an assisted school before coming to Oxford funded their education at least in part through money raised from parents, relatives or friends, compared to almost 90 per cent of boys from fee-paying independent schools.[14] Postgraduates were in an even worse financial position. At the discretion of the Board of Education, grants might be given to state scholars who stayed on to do a postgraduate degree, but there were only a few university awards and prizes for postgraduates. College awards, a most important source of funding for undergraduates, were virtually non-existent for postgraduates.[15]

During the Second World War, unlike the first, Oxford's male undergraduate population kept up well, partly because the need for conscripts to serve overseas was less pressing and partly because the University agreed to host special courses for probationers in the Royal Signals and for army and air-force cadets; 3,000 probationers and cadets had matriculated in the University by 1942.[16] The post-war boom in male undergraduate numbers after 1945 was therefore less striking than after 1918. Still more was this so because the compulsory peacetime national service which ended in 1959 postponed until the late 1950s the bunching of school-leavers and ex-servicemen into a single year. Even then, the effects [figure 3.1] may have been mitigated somewhat by the colleges' temporarily reducing their intake of foreign men.[17] So the growth in the number of men matriculants soon after 1945 stems almost entirely from a flood of ex-servicemen who took advantage of the government's Further Education and Training Scheme grants. Between 1945 and 1950 the government provided ex-servicemen with 83,000 of these grants, more than half of which were taken up at universities.[18] At the peak of the scheme in 1947, more than half Oxford's

[14] Based on a preliminary analysis of 556 survey questionnaires collected from men who matriculated in the 1930s. The figure of 556 represents about 4% of the total number of men who matriculated between 1930 and 1939 inclusive.

[15] OUA UR/SF/SCC/5/file 3, Committee of Vice-Chancellors and Principals (CVCP), 'Supplementation of postgraduate awards', 18 Dec. 1953, 1–2 with appended list of University awards; CVCP, 'Awards to postgraduates', 30 Sept. 1955, 1–4.

[16] HCP 170 (1940), 13–14; 183 (1942), 147–8.

[17] Anticipated in 'The ending of national service and its implications for Oxford colleges', *OM* 20 June 1957, 545–6.

[18] R. Lowe, *Education in the Post-War Years* (London 1988), 62.

students in residence held such an award, whereas LEA grants and college awards were held respectively by a tenth and a third of Oxford's junior members.[19] Oxford made it easier for ex-servicemen to get in by relaxing its admissions requirements and by making shortened honours schools available; more shortened honours examinations were created than after the First World War. Between 1941 and 1951 shortened honours schools were taken by 27 per cent of the men and 18 per cent of the women who sat for a final honour school examination.[20]

Thereafter, growth in the number of men junior members was sustained by successive governments' expansionist education policies. The Education Act of 1944 removed financial obstacles to secondary education and expanded the pool of school-leavers. The Barlow report on scientific manpower (1946) envisaged a doubling of graduate numbers, and this was reinforced after 1946 with greatly enhanced university grants. In the four years from 1947/8 to 1950/1 the University Grants Committee (UGC) funded ninety-seven new academic posts to enable Oxford to teach its growing population of junior members.[21] Post-war UGC grants also enabled the colleges to expand accommodation, and Oxford's dependence on government funding grew sharply. By 1951 82 per cent of Oxford's undergraduate members in residence were receiving some form of financial assistance.[22] The growth-rate in the number of male junior members persisted throughout the 1960s with the ending of national service, the incursion into universities of the post-war baby-boom, and yet more increases in government funding urged on by the Robbins Committee, which reported in 1963 on the future pattern of full-time higher education in Great Britain.[23]

Postgraduates, too, were increasing in number after 1945, again with help from increased government funding. In 1955 the Ministry of Education agreed to supplement existing university awards and to fund deserving graduates irrespective of whether they had once been state scholars; hence the dramatic increase in the number of Oxford's postgraduate degrees available.[24] At least 40 new postgraduate degrees were introduced between 1941 and 1968—including 21 diplomas, 14 BPhils, 3 certificates, the BEd and the BMus. This compares with only 7 postgraduate degrees introduced between 1911 and 1940, including the DPhil.[25] Between 1960 and 1967

[19] Dr Mark Pottle's data on awards, 1938–57.
[20] 'When the men come back', OM 1 Feb. 1945, 122; HCP 183 (1942), 147–8; HUD/C/CR.
[21] 'Vice-Chancellor's oration and annual report', Gazette 11 Oct. 1951, 95.
[22] C. Mackenzie, 'Undergraduate finance', Isis 31 Oct. 1951, 22–3.
[23] As predicted in 'Vice-Chancellor's oration and annual report', Gazette 16 Oct. 1956, 112; W. H. G. Armytage, Four Hundred Years of English Education (2nd edn Cambridge 1970), 249; Oxford University Appointments Committee (OUAC), Annual Report (1970–1), 6.
[24] OUA UR/SF/SCC/5/file 3, CVCP, 'Awards to postgraduates', 1–4.
[25] From 'Vice-Chancellor's oration and annual report', Gazette 1911–68.

nearly a quarter of all matriculants went on to obtain a postgraduate degree, a diploma or a certificate.[26]

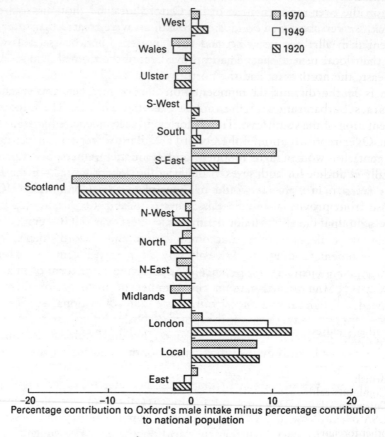

FIGURE 3.2   OXFORD'S REGIONAL RECRUITMENT, 1920, 1949, 1970

How did all this affect the social composition of Oxford's junior members? Geographically, not much [figure 3.2].[27] In 1970, as in 1920 and

[26] HUD/C/RS–SV.

[27] From a computerized record (HUD/C/MF) of the matriculation forms completed by the entire male and female intake in 1920/1, 1949/50 and 1970/1. The forms provide information on matriculants' place and date of birth (by 1970/1 place of birth had been omitted), pre-Oxford education, and fathers' occupation and address at the time of matriculation. The data on father's address at time of matriculation were used in combination with UK census returns for 1921, 1951 and 1971. Regions were composed by grouping counties together following L. Stone, 'The size and composition of the Oxford student body 1580–1910' in L. Stone (ed.), *The University in Society* (2 vols Princeton NJ 1975) i. 102. The measure subtracts the percentage of matriculants at Oxford from each region from the percentage contributed by that region to the national population.

1949, Scotland remained grossly under-represented, no doubt partly because it had an excellent higher education system of its own. The over-representation of the south-east actually increased, and there was little change in the over-representation of the Oxford area. By the standards of the civic universities, however, the Oxford area was decidedly under-represented in all three years because the University aimed at a national rather than local recruitment. The improved representation of Wales, the north-east, the north-west and the north was but small. The only marked change is in the diminished representation of London, but this merely reflects a suburbanization of the middle class, which inflated the over-representation of the south-east. Trends for men and women are remarkably similar. Over-representation of the Oxford area was slightly higher (by 2 or 3 per cent) for women than for men, and London's over-representation (generally in decline for both sexes throughout the period) actually increased for the women in 1949. It would be interesting to know whether one response from provincial middle-class parents during the depression had been to send their daughters to local universities rather than to Oxford.

TABLE 3.1

GEOGRAPHICAL ORIGINS OF ALL OXFORD MEN AND
WOMEN MATRICULANTS IN 1920/1, 1949/50 AND 1970/1
(%)

Father's address	men			women		
	1920/1	1949/50	1970/1	1920/1	1949/50	1970/1
British	70	85	82	94	90	90
Commonwealth	16	7	6	2	5	5
European	2	2	3	3	1	2
USA	9	5	6	1	3	2
other foreign	3	1	3	0	1	1
number in sample 893		2,013	2,523	125	308	574

Geographical contrasts between the sexes were more significant in recruitment from overseas. The proportion of male junior members whose father resided outside the British Isles at the time of matriculation declined between 1920 and 1970, almost entirely because the intake from Common-wealth countries fell [table 3.1].[28] The fall is less marked among graduates of other universities who came to Oxford to read for an advanced degree; 60 per cent of them came from foreign and Commonwealth countries between the wars, 40 per cent by 1960–7.[29] This group, however, made up no more

[28] HUD/C/MF.
[29] HUD/C/RS–SV.

than 10 per cent of all matriculants who went on to take postgraduate degrees. The reverse was true for women junior members. Their non-British intake in 1949 was nearly double that of 1918, largely as the result of growth in the proportion of women from the Commonwealth and from the USA. The picture had hardly changed in 1970.

Oxford became less attractive to male junior members from the Commonwealth after the Second World War because decolonization entailed the development of universities in the newly independent nations, which preferred a local training for their civil servants and professional people.[30] The declining proportion of North American junior members is more puzzling, especially since Oxford's DPhil degree was established in 1917 to attract them. But the DPhil had never been dominated by North American postgraduates. By 1943 approximately 1,000 people had successfully qualified for the degree. Among these, British candidates outnumbered North Americans by nearly four to one.[31] By 1960–7 the proportion of American and Canadian candidates for postgraduate degrees had hardly changed at all;[32] postgraduate teaching at Oxford had expanded in the intervening years to meet the national demand in industry and higher education. Furthermore Oxford found itself under increasing pressure to produce more British graduates. Oxford's intake of foreigners increased only from the 1970s, perhaps partly because foreign students, who by that time paid higher fees than home students, became increasingly attractive when government support for higher education was in decline. The trend was especially apparent among postgraduates, of whom 42 per cent were born outside the UK in 1989, 14 per cent in the USA.[33]

In social class background, Oxford's junior members broadened out between 1900 and 1970. Before the First World War Oxford accommodated the sons but not the daughters of the nation's élites. 80 per cent of male undergraduates who took the second public examination in arts subjects or in the pass school had attended an independent or fee-paying public school [table 3.2].[34] Boys who took the second public examination in science were

[30] 'Vice-Chancellor's oration and annual report', *Gazette* 11 Oct. 1940, 39 discusses developments at Makerere College, Uganda, for example; cf below, 635.

[31] 'Vice-Chancellor's oration and annual report', *Gazette* 8 Oct. 1943, 43, which does not distinguish USA from Canada.

[32] HUD/C/RS–SV.

[33] University of Oxford, 'Fact sheet' (1989/90), 2.

[34] HUD/C/RS–SV. The data refer only to men and women matriculants who came to Oxford from British secondary schools which could be located in school directories. The categories refer to how the schools' fees were met. Independent schools took mostly fee-paying pupils. Maintained schools were wholly financed by local authorities. Direct-grant schools were centrally funded but independently governed schools which reserved at least 25% of their places for pupils from locally assisted primary schools. The category 'other assisted' refers to voluntary-aided and voluntary-controlled schools which also received some funding from government authorities but reserved a degree of independent control over their governance. After 1945 the category also included transitionally assisted schools which were in transition from being privately or centrally funded schools to locally assisted ones. The 'private tuition'

TABLE 3.2

SECONDARY SCHOOL ORIGINS IN EIGHT COHORTS OF OXFORD MEN AND WOMEN UNDERGRADUATES IN THE ARTS, SCIENCE AND PASS SCHOOLS OF THE SECOND PUBLIC EXAMINATION, 1900–1967 (%)

subject area	years	men						women					
		independent	maintained	direct grant	other assisted	private tuition	N	independent	maintained	direct grant	other assisted	private tuition	N
arts school	1900–13	79	5	12	1	2	601	48	4	41	2	5	113
	1914–19	68	11	16	3	2	174	51	6	39	0	4	71
	1920–29	68	13	15	4	0	456	58	10	28	2	2	158
	1930–39	69	12	12	6	1	374	49	17	25	8	1	166
	1940–45	58	21	14	8	0	160	51	19	27	3	0	95
	1946–52	65	18	10	8	0	351	57	14	24	4	0	135
	1953–59	61	16	17	7	0	318	55	11	31	2	0	121
	1960–67	58	13	20	9	0	362	39	22	35	4	0	135
pass school	1900–13	80	5	10	1	4	370	53	5	42	0	0	19
	1914–19	73	13	5	8	1	78	36	14	50	0	0	14
	1920–29	83	6	7	2	2	101	50	8	42	0	0	36
	1930–39	88	5	3	3	0	60	72	6	17	6	0	18
	1940–45	67	13	10	10	0	39	53	16	32	0	0	19
	1946–52	81	5	10	5	0	21	82	0	18	0	0	11
	1953–59	71	14	0	14	0	7	75	0	25	0	0	8
	1960–67	100	0	0	0	0	1	50	0	0	50	0	2
science school	1900–13	61	11	19	8	1	265	40	20	40	0	0	10
	1914–19	52	19	19	8	2	96	0	20	80	0	0	5
	1920–29	64	16	16	4	0	164	47	12	36	1	3	74
	1930–39	63	9	19	9	0	139	55	13	28	4	0	104
	1940–45	54	21	14	11	0	180	68	12	20	4	0	41
	1946–52	55	20	14	11	0	309	53	19	24	4	0	124
	1953–59	53	16	20	10	0	308	45	13	36	5	0	99
	1960–67	53	18	24	5	0	372	47	18	32	3	0	128

much less likely to come from the independent schools. This reflects the Board of Education's emphasis on developing modern subjects in the schools assisted by itself or by LEAs. After the First World War this science/arts contrast in school background steadily diminished, as modern subjects were gradually introduced into independent schools' curricula. Only the pass school continued to attract disproportionate numbers of boys from independent schools, but after 1945 the numbers in the school dwindled away. Perhaps more importantly, the proportion of male undergraduates from independent schools also declined by comparison with those drawn from locally and nationally assisted schools. The greatest change occurred between 1940 and 1945, as the admission of military cadets and probationers brought to Oxford a higher proportion of boys from assisted schools than ever before. After the Second World War, recruitment from the independent schools revived. But government grants for university students were now increasingly available, and this helped to reverse the trend, despite the growth from the late 1960s in the number of independent schools. By 1975 men were recruited in roughly equal proportions from independent and assisted schools.[35]

The proportion of women arts finalists drawn from independent schools also fell between 1920–9 and 1960–7 but only slightly, and the trend is considerably more erratic than that for the men. The proportion of women science finalists from independent schools actually increased before 1945, after which it too began to fall back to the level of 1920–9 [table 3.2]. Still more striking, before the Second World War women undergraduates were far more likely than men to come from assisted schools, especially from the centrally funded direct-grant grammar schools. Between 1921–9 and 1960–7 this contrast moderated steadily as the intake of men from assisted schools increased. Behind this change there no doubt lies an increasing social-class approximation between Oxford's men and women. The same trend emerges from data on fathers' jobs [table 3.3].[36] From 1900 to 1913 more than a third

category includes those matriculants who indicated on their matriculation forms that they had received some private tuition immediately before coming up to Oxford. These categories are not entirely water-tight for those matriculants who attended secondary schools before 1926, the year in which centrally funded (or direct-grant) schools were differentiated from locally funded ones. Schools were placed in the direct-grant category for the first two cohorts if they were on the first list of direct-grant schools published in 1927 and if they appeared on the government grant list before then. Furthermore before 1926, secondary schools could qualify for some government assistance so long as they reserved 25% of their places for pupils whose fees were met by local or central authorities. Consequently schools classified as assisted before 1930 may have given a majority of their places to fee-paying boys. For a brief history of secondary school funding see [D. V. Donnison, chairman] *Second Report of the Public Schools Commission* (London 1970), 5–49; Davis, *Grammar School*; Armytage, *Four Hundred Years*, 182–209.

[35] I am grateful to Mr Richard Little of the University's Undergraduate Admissions Office for providing these figures from 'Oxford colleges statistics for 1975 entry', *Gazette* 21 Jan. 1976, 389.

[36] HUD/C/RS–SV. Table 3.3 is based on the jobs of the fathers of junior members at the time they matriculated. For junior members in the sample who matriculated between 1900 and 1939 the information was taken from the matriculation forms completed by all matriculants.

of Oxford men came from professional and nearly a third from business backgrounds, while nearly one in five described their fathers as landowners or as 'gentlemen'.[37] Sons of clerks, blue-collar workers and small shop-keepers were between 5 per cent and 10 per cent better represented among the candidates for diplomas and certificates throughout the period from 1900 to 1967.[38] For such men a one-year diploma or certificate for which no classical languages were required was far more accessible and less daunting than a full Oxford honours degree.

Socially, Oxford's women junior members were worlds apart from the men before the First World War. Women came overwhelmingly from middle-class families, and there were more daughters of businessmen and professionals and far fewer daughters of landowners and gentlemen. Furthermore the women's colleges could not fund many scholarships, so whereas nearly a third of Oxford's men finalists between 1900 and 1913 held college awards, only a fifth of women finalists did so. The women's colleges therefore drew even fewer entrants than the men's colleges from lower-middle and working-class origins. There was some variation among the five women's societies. In 1900–13 clergymen's daughters comprised nearly a third of the women at Lady Margaret Hall and St Hugh's (societies founded with religious aims) whereas non-denominational Somerville attracted a disproportionate number of businessmen's daughters.[39] Yet what stands out is not the contrast between the women's societies but how their shared characteristics differed from those of the men's colleges.

For junior members who matriculated after 1939 the information was gathered from survey questionnaires. Occupational information was categorized according to three criteria: sector of employment (e.g. commerce, armed services, medical profession); the type of work one did within each sector (e.g. executive, consultant, architect); and geographical location of job (Britain, Commonwealth country, overseas). Sectoral categories were used to create table 3.3 as well as tables 3.4–3.7 on men's and women's career destinations, with two important exceptions. First, wherever occupational information indicated that the person was in blue-collar clerical work it was placed in these residual categories irrespective of the sector in which the job was held. A janitor in an LEA school and a warehouseman working for Cowley Motors would both be categorized as 'unskilled workers' rather than as 'local government' and 'industry', respectively. Similarly a clerk working for an export company and a clerk working for British Steel would both be categorized as 'clerks, skilled workers and small shopkeepers' rather than as 'commerce' and 'industry' respectively. Consequently jobs in the several business categories ('industry', 'commerce' and so on) are at or above the managerial level (including technicians and consultants). Secondly, wherever the first two categories (sectoral and type of work) conflicted and the possession of professional qualifications was implied in the job title—for example, in the case of army surgeons, local government educationalists or company solicitors—the occupations were placed in the appropriate professional category. See D. I. Greenstein, 'Standard, meta-standard: a framework for coding occupational data', *Historical Social Research* 16 (1991), 3–22.

[37] HUD/C/RS–SV. The term 'gentleman' is usually taken to indicate a man of independent means but must be interpreted with some care. Men at Queen's College and at St Edmund Hall, for example, often gave their father's occupation as 'gentleman' by college tradition, irrespective of how they may have been employed.

[38] HUD/C/RS–SV.   [39] Ibid.

TABLE 3.3

FATHER'S OCCUPATION OF OXFORD MEN AND WOMEN IN 1900–1913, 1920–1939, 1946–1967 (%)

Occupational categories	men			women		
	1900–13	1920–39	1946–67	1900–13	1920–39	1946–67
accountant	1.30	1.50	2.30	2.40	2.00	1.80
commerce	10.10	9.80	8.80	13.10	8.10	6.50
finance	3.90	5.30	5.10	2.70	3.50	4.60
industry	10.40	11.80	18.80	10.40	14.00	19.00
publishing, media, leisure	1.70	2.30	2.60	1.50	1.80	2.60
unspecified business	1.40	4.50	2.10	1.80	3.90	1.50
total	28.80	35.20	39.70	31.90	33.30	36.00
gentleman	12.10	2.30	0.20	0.90	0.50	0.10
armed forces and police	3.00	4.30	4.30	1.20	5.30	4.40
land	4.20	5.90	3.70	4.80	2.30	3.70
total	19.30	12.50	8.20	6.90	8.10	8.20
colonial civil service	1.20	1.30	0.90	0.60	1.30	0.80
civil service	4.40	6.50	7.40	4.20	5.30	9.60
local govt	0.20	0.40	1.50	0.00	0.70	1.70
total	5.80	8.20	9.80	4.80	7.30	12.10
clerks, skilled workers and small shopkeepers	2.90	4.80	10.30	3.00	3.40	7.30
semi- and unskilled workers	2.70	5.20	9.10	1.20	4.90	5.50
total	5.60	10.00	19.40	4.20	8.30	12.80
school teacher	4.30	5.30	5.80	4.50	10.00	10.30
university teacher	1.90	2.40	3.40	5.40	5.50	6.40
education related	0.30	0.30	0.60	0.00	0.10	0.90
total	6.50	8.00	9.80	9.90	15.60	17.60
all clergy	17.90	11.40	3.80	20.50	11.10	4.00
doctor	5.60	7.10	6.30	8.60	9.60	6.00
social work and related	0.20	0.20	0.30	0.60	0.10	0.10
lawyer	10.20	7.40	2.80	12.80	6.70	3.10
total	33.90	26.10	13.20	42.50	27.50	13.20
number in sample	1,948	1,840	3,012	336	742	1,171

The social class distinctions between the sexes and (to a lesser extent) between the colleges gradually diminished after the First World War as the pressure to expand the University's male intake increased. Between the wars the proportion of landowners' and gentlemen's sons among the male junior members fell away sharply [table 3.3] while the proportion whose fathers were blue-collar workers, clerks and small shopkeepers simultaneously grew. Working men, clerks and small shopkeepers also contributed more women junior members after the First World War. The proportion of Oxford's male and female junior members whose fathers were in religious callings also declined sharply between the wars, while the proportion whose fathers worked in industry rose slightly. Still, an Oxford education remained relatively expensive and its classical entrance requirements still relatively stringent. So the so-called 'redbrick' universities and London absorbed a disproportionately larger share than Oxford of the growing number of secondary school-leavers.[40] During and immediately after the Second World War the intake of army and air-force cadets—together with ex-servicemen who benefited from Further Education and Training Scheme grants and relaxed admissions standards—helped to sustain inter-war trends. The data on fathers' occupations after 1945 show a continued increase in the proportion of men and women who described their fathers as blue-collar workers, small shopkeepers or clerks, or as working in industry, and this complements a decline in recruitment from landowners and gentlemen and from the professions [table 3.3].

The disappearance of the 'passman' or gentleman commoner between the wars also reflects the broadening social class composition of Oxford's junior members. The proportion of all male matriculants who took only the pass school decreased between 1900–9 and 1930–5 from one-fifth to about one-tenth.[41] The pass school particularly attracted the sons of professional soldiers (27 per cent of whom took pass-school examinations), financiers (29 per cent), 'gentlemen' (34 per cent) and industrialists (25 per cent).[42] Other evidence suggests that the passmen did not so much disappear between the wars as migrate. They moved into what were then the softer honour schools like PPE, jurisprudence and forestry, which produced a high proportion of third- and fourth-class men—or into the bottom of the class lists elsewhere.[43] The proportion of low performers (third- and fourth-class

[40] F. K. Ringer, *Education and Society in Modern Europe* (London 1979), 230.

[41] From a computerized record of the second public examination's class and pass lists annually published and indexed in *Gazette* 1900–70 (HUD/S/REG). Here the data were grouped in the years 1900–9 and 1930–5 to exclude undergraduates whose courses might have been interrupted by military service.

[42] HUD/C/RS-SV.

[43] PPE's growth was said to have occurred at the expense of the pass school, HCP 159 (1934), 171–82. Law's principal weakness was its relatively undemanding first public examination: W. S. Holdsworth, 'The Oxford law school', *OM* 30 Jan. 1930, 386–7.

honours finalists plus those who were examined in the pass school) among men who took the second public examination declined only slightly from about 62 per cent per year between 1900 and 1913 to about 55 per cent per year between 1920 and 1939.[44] Women on the other hand were relatively reluctant to embark on the pass school, if only because the women's societies included few of the well-born in search of a finishing school, though for some the pass school provided a quick and inexpensive way of qualifying for a teaching post, often in conjunction with a diploma. Between the wars women's entry into the pass school all but disappeared.

For some male undergraduates, however, Oxford was a finishing school. Of all male matriculants who came up to Oxford between 1900 and 1909, the names of 26 per cent are not found on class or pass lists of the second public examination.[45] Of this 26 per cent, less than 3 per cent were absent from these lists because they took a diploma or postgraduate degree, while 3–5 per cent can be attributed to mistakes in matching the names on matriculation lists with those on class and pass lists, and a small number who matriculated in order to take an honorary degree or a degree by incorporation.[46] For the remainder, absence from the class list can be explained only by failure to take the exam or failure in the exam. It seems that between 15 per cent and 20 per cent of all matriculants between 1900 and 1909 either took no final examination or failed it, and between 10 and 15 per cent of all male matriculants between 1930 and 1935.

These estimates, based on computerized records of the matriculation and class lists, were borne out by a case-study of all men who matriculated at Balliol in the periods 1900–9 and 1930–5; nearly 20 per cent of all matriculants in the period 1900–9 failed to take the second public examination. Only a quarter of these were graduates from other universities who came to Balliol as probationers in one of the colonial services or to take a postgraduate degree or diploma. The rest—15 per cent of the College's

[44] HUD/S/REG.

[45] Indicating that 26% of the names recorded on computerized matriculation lists could not be linked with corresponding names on the computerized class and pass lists.

[46] People whose names appeared on matriculation lists but not on class or pass lists formed part of the sample of Oxford's members for whom more extensive biographical information was collected and recorded in HUD/C/RS–SV. Only 3% of these in the period 1900–9 went on to take postgraduate degrees or diplomas. There are two types of record-linkage error: names which should have been linked but weren't, and names which were linked incorrectly. The first type is easily identified since everyone whose name appeared on a class list must have also matriculated at some point. In a sample of 110,581 examination records taken for the period 1927–70 (to mitigate the effect of retrospective women matriculants and of women who examined without matriculating before 1920) only 2,341 or 2.1% were not linked. The second type of error can be checked by sampling from among the linked names and referring to college registers or to Registry files held for all matriculants to see whether the matriculating individual was linked to the correct examination record(s). Several such exercises were conducted with small random samples of classified finalists whose names had been linked to the matriculation lists and proved that linked records were at least 98% accurate.

entire intake—appear to have been undergraduates who left Balliol without taking the second public examination. By 1930–5 21 per cent of the College's intake failed to appear on the pass or class lists. Of this group, slightly more than half came from other universities to take a postgraduate course, while slightly less than half—nearly 9 per cent of all matriculants listed in the register—still seem to have taken no examination whatsoever. This group, which had not come to Oxford for narrowly academic reasons, vanished only after the Second World War. As for the women, before 1920, the year when women were first allowed to matriculate in the University, only a self-selected few took honours. All women who came up to Somerville and the Society of Oxford Home-Students every six years and to Lady Margaret Hall, St Hilda's and St Hugh's every three years have been analysed from 1900 to 1918 inclusive; 57 per cent of them did not take honours examinations.[47] After 1920 the proportion of women not taking honours exams dropped—to only 12 per cent by 1930–5. By the 1960s about a fifth of the men and a tenth of the women matriculants were still not appearing in the class and pass lists, but the lion's share of these were graduates of other universities coming to Oxford to do postgraduate work.

There have been marked changes in the relative size of the arts and science schools since 1900. In that year 90 per cent of men finalists and 95 per cent of women finalists took examinations in arts schools, whereas in 1985 more than 40 per cent of men and women finalists took a science subject [figure 3.3].[48] Several factors explain the low proportion of undergraduates before the Second World War who took natural science degrees: Oxford's insistence on a Latin admissions requirement, a relatively high fee for science undergraduates until 1947, and the sheer cost of expanding science facilities, especially during the depression.[49] In 1935 Oxford and Cambridge decided to cut costs by demarcating the expanding areas of the natural sciences in which each university would henceforth specialize.[50] A more important constraint was the colleges' reluctance to alter the subject-balance by offering more awards to scientists. Science finalists were more dependent upon college awards than intending arts finalists—between 1900 and 1939 some 44 per cent of all science finalists held a college award compared to

[47] The majority of these were at the Society of Oxford Home-Students, where nearly 90% of the Society's members did not take the second public examination. Balliol information from I. Elliott, *The Balliol College Register 1833–1933* (Oxford 1934); J. Jones and S. Viney, *Balliol College Register 1930–1980* (Oxford 1983).

[48] HUD/S/REG for 1900–70 data and HUD/C/CR for 1971–86 data.

[49] HCP 132 (1925), 327–44; 193 (1947), 15–16. Science fees were 10% higher than arts fees in the 1920s, and by 1949 science undergraduates' tuition and battels combined could be as much as £50 more than that of arts undergraduates or half the value of many open college scholarships. OUA UR/SF/SCC/2, 'Summary of replies from colleges about present charges, January 1949'.

[50] HCP 161 (1935), 139–40; 'Vice-Chancellor's oration and annual report', *Gazette* 8 Oct. 1936, 24.

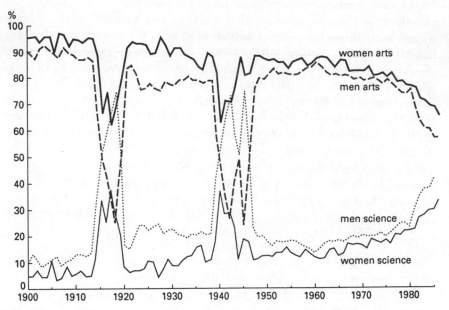

FIGURE 3.3   SUBJECT-BALANCE OF MEN AND WOMEN FINALISTS, 1900–1986

only about 32 per cent of all arts finalists—yet the men's colleges gave
between two-thirds and three-quarters of their awards to arts finalists.[51]
Oxford's non-vocational bias and its justified concern about the limited
career opportunities for scientists before 1945 also limited the science
schools' growth. The arts/science subject-balance of men undergraduates
shifted markedly towards science only during the first and second world
wars. This reflected the national demands being made of the universities'
scientific establishments and (during the Second World War) government
conscription policy, which exempted some male science undergraduates
from military service.

With the exception of the war years, women's choice of degree-subject
slanted the balance still further towards the arts, with 10 per cent of men
between 1910 and 1913 reading for science subjects but only 5 per cent of
women. Furthermore the women students were more likely than the men to
choose the life sciences, botany and zoology, and less likely to choose the
physical sciences. In arts schools too, women finalists concentrated before
the First World War in the so-called 'modern' schools of modern languages,

[51] HUD/C/RS–SV; *OM* 13 May 1943, 272–3; OUA UR/SF/SCC/5/file 1, 'Open scholarships and exhibitions', 1–4. These data were compiled by the University in the 1940s when
negotiating with the UGC about supplementing college awards with government funding. They
represent the most comprehensive account available of the number and type of college awards.

English and modern history; these taken together accounted for between two-thirds and three-quarters of all women finalists. Oxford's five women's societies contributed more than half all finalists in the English and modern languages schools before 1914.[52] This distribution reflects patterns of secondary education for women and also the continuing subordination of women in Oxford, given that these new schools relied heavily on university lecturers, many of whom lacked fellowships.[53] Contrasts in subject-balance at the men's and women's colleges were still pronounced in 1960–9. Women made up about 20 per cent of all matriculants, yet contributed 26 per cent of the finalists in modern languages and 31 per cent of the finalists in English. On the other hand women's proportion of the finalists in what had hitherto been predominantly men's arts subjects was rising in the 1960s—in law, for example. And by the early 1950s the proportion of women reading for natural science degrees almost equalled that of the men [figure 3.3], though since 1977 (when the members of mixed colleges were first examined) the gap has once more opened out.[54]

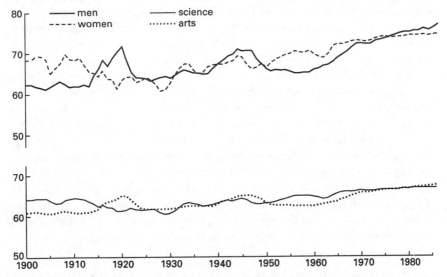

FIGURE 3.4   NORRINGTON SCORES OF ARTS AND SCIENCE FINALISTS, AND OF MEN AND WOMEN FINALISTS, 1900–1986

There have been significant changes since 1900 in undergraduate examination performance. Before 1947 science finalists outperformed arts finalists

[52] HUD/C/CR.
[53] HCP 132 (1925), 285–90; W. J. Entwistle, 'Modern language studies in Oxford', OM 16 Feb. 1933, 427–9.
[54] HUD/S/REG.

[figure 3.4], partly because a higher proportion of scientists held awards.[55] Between 1955 and 1965 the performance of arts and science finalists converged, and both rose slowly thereafter. The distribution of college awards again helps to explain the pattern. After 1947 the numbers reading science degrees increased faster than the number of college awards available to scientists; about 35 per cent of those in both camps were award-holders in 1946–52, falling to 15 per cent in 1960–7.[56] Comparison of men's with women's examination performance shows rather more fluctuation.[57] Before the First World War the women who took honours examinations did better than the men. This perhaps reflects women dons' eagerness in their admissions policy to prove women's academic potential. During the First World War the men overtook the women, perhaps reflecting the much greater preponderance among the male finalists of scientists who tended anyway to do better than arts finalists in the schools. Between the wars the declining overall performance of women and the improving overall performance of men brought the groups broadly into line. An anonymous contributor to the *Oxford Magazine* in 1928 explained that women's examination performance was declining because men and women undergraduates were mixing more, and because women were now more likely to be taught by women dons who lacked experience of examining in the schools.[58] The Second World War again pushed up the male performance; once more the final examinations were denuded of men except for capable scientists who were exempted from military service because engaged in work of national importance. Women did better than men in the 1950s for two, or perhaps three, main reasons: because the quota prevented the women's colleges from dipping as low as the men's colleges in the ability range; because the women's colleges pooled their candidates in a common entrance examination and were probably more efficient at identifying and rewarding talent; and perhaps also because women dons brought pressure to bear on women candidates out of a persisting desire to 'prove themselves' to the men.

From 1977, when candidates from the first mixed colleges took the second public examination, men's aggregate performance in the schools overtook

[55] HUD/S/REG for 1900–70 data and HUD/C/CR for 1971–86 data. The Norrington score used in figure 3.4 is calculated by expressing the total points gained as a percentage of the maximum possible in final examinations. Four points are assigned for each first class, three for each second, two for each third and one for each fourth. The top score of 100 indicates that all classified candidates achieved a first-class mark. Results were divided into the four categories represented on figure 3.4 (all men finalists, all women finalists, all finalists—men and women—in arts schools, all finalists—men and women—in science schools). Annual Norrington scores were then calculated for each category according to the formula:

$$\frac{100 \times (4 \times \text{firsts} + 3 \times \text{seconds} + 2 \times \text{thirds} + \text{fourths})}{4 \times (\text{firsts} + \text{seconds} + \text{thirds} + \text{fourths})}.$$

[56] HUD/C/RS–SV.
[57] HUD/S/REG for 1900–70 data and HUD/C/CR for 1971–86 data.
[58] OM 25 Oct. 1928, 60; 1 Nov. 1928, 86.

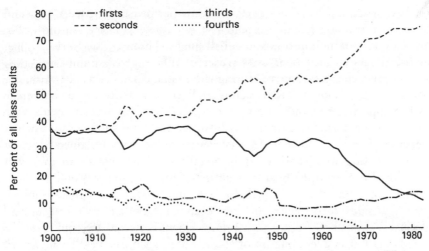

FIGURE 3.5   DISTRIBUTION OF CLASS RESULTS, ALL FINALISTS, 1900–1986

that of the women. What seems to have happened is that women were recruited into the former men's colleges at the expense of less promising male applicants. This is also one reason why the proportion of firsts and seconds registered a marked increase after 1977 [figure 3.5].[59] All this harmed the women's colleges, especially Somerville and Lady Margaret Hall. In league tables showing performance in the final examination during each of the seven decades between 1900–9 and 1960–9, both colleges had been among the top ten.[60] After 1977 all the women's colleges moved towards the bottom of the league.[61] After the second class was divided in 1986 the relative decline in women's final examination results became even more apparent. A comparison of men's and women's results for 1989 shows the men obtaining proportionately more firsts (20 per cent) than the women finalists (12 per cent), slightly more thirds (6 per cent compared to the women's 5 per cent), fewer lower seconds (24 per cent compared to the women's 28 per cent), and also fewer upper seconds (50 per cent compared to the women's 55 per cent). The figures also suggest that women in mixed colleges do slightly better in their final examinations than women in single-sex colleges, getting proportionately more firsts and fewer lower seconds.[62]

[59]   HUD/S/REG for 1900–70 data and HUD/C/CR for 1971–86 data.
[60]   HUD/S/REG.
[61]   D. I. Greenstein, 'Gender results: men and women in the schools 1913–1986', *OM* Hilary 1987, no. 19, 4–6. I am also grateful to Dr Pottle for preparing data from schools results published in *Times* 13 Aug. 1969, 10; 3 Aug. 1985, 4; 22 July 1989, 4, which show the five one-time women's societies moving from the centre to the bottom of the league.
[62]   Dr Pottle's data from *Times* 22 July 1989, 4.

These small-scale contrasts in examination performance between men and women or arts and sciences should not be allowed to obscure the rather dramatic long-term improvements in all finalists' examination performance. Figure 3.5 shows the second class growing at the expense of the third class. The greatest changes occurred during the first and second world wars, the 1930s, and the 1960s. The fourth class declined steadily from 1900 and made its last appearance in 1967. Rather unexpectedly, the first class contracted steadily from 1900 to 1950 (except for two short-lived revivals during wartime, after which there was a very sharp decline) with sustained but slow growth setting in thereafter. Improvements in the overall examination performance of wartime finalists stem from the wartime preponderance in Oxford of women and of male science undergraduates—groups which anyway tended to do better in final examinations than male arts undergraduates at this time [figure 3.4]. Improvement between 1945 and the early 1960s may reflect a levelling-up of student abilities occasioned by increased competition for college places, while improvement after 1963 may reflect the meritocratic emphasis of the men's colleges' reorganized entrance examinations. But other more subjective influences may also be at work. It is clear from the *Oxford Magazine* that dons after 1945 were becoming much more self-conscious about undergraduates' examination performance. Only two articles before 1944 gave any detailed account of how different groups of undergraduates performed in the schools. Thereafter, examination performance seemed to attract more than a passing interest, and the preoccupation became almost obsessional in the late 1950s, when the subjects and the colleges which produced the most failures and the most third- and fourth-class finalists were identified.[63] And in 1962 A. L. P. Norrington created the statistical measure which annually preoccupied every senior common room from the late 1960s.[64] There is also some evidence that the growth of the first and second classes from the early 1960s reflected a collective concern that Oxford's high standards were disadvantaging its undergraduates by comparison with those in universities which awarded proportionately fewer thirds and more firsts and seconds.[65]

One characteristic of Oxford's junior members which has changed very little since 1900 is the age at which they matriculated. Before 1914 the average age was about 19 [figure 3.6], but this fell slightly between the wars.[66] This decline partly reflects Oxford's acceptance for exemption from responsions of school certificates after they were introduced in 1917. Schools encouraged their scholarship candidates to take the school certificate

---

[63] *OM* 15 Oct. 1959, 4; 12 Nov. 1959, 78.
[64] *OM* 1 Nov. 1962, 40; see also *OM* Michaelmas 1966, no. 2, 26.
[65] *OM* 2 Feb. 1968, 160.
[66] HUD/C/RS–SV.

examination as early as possible, thus freeing more time to prepare for
Oxford scholarship examinations.[67] During the Second World War the
average age of men matriculants fell further because male undergraduates
under 18 were allowed up to six months at university before their military
service.[68] After 1945 this trend reversed because most did their military
service before coming up to Oxford.[69] During the 1960s, however, here as so
often elsewhere men and women moved into closer conformity. As for
postgraduates, there has been a long-term decline in the age at matriculation,
perhaps reflecting the increasing tendency to embark on a graduate degree
immediately after completing the second public examination, but also in
response to the ending of national service.

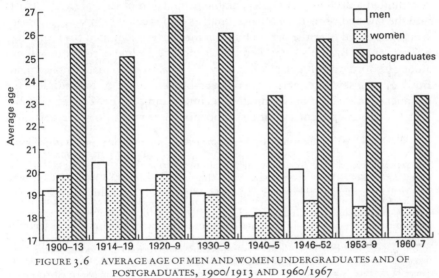

FIGURE 3.6   AVERAGE AGE OF MEN AND WOMEN UNDERGRADUATES AND OF
POSTGRADUATES, 1900/1913 AND 1960/1967

How have the careers pursued by Oxford undergraduates changed since
1900? The many 'inflow' studies which show Oxford's substantial contribution to British élite groups are concerned with only a tiny proportion of
Oxford graduates. They can now be complemented by an 'outflow' study
which analyses the careers of the nearly 120,000 junior members who passed
through Oxford between 1900 and 1967 and compares them with careers in
the nation as a whole over the same period.[70] The careers of Oxford's male
arts and science finalists in a 10 per cent sample of the total intake between

[67] T. F. Higham, 'Latin', *OM* 5 May 1938, 570–5; Armytage, *Four Hundred Years*, 204.
[68] 'Vice-Chancellor's oration and annual report', *Gazette* 8 Oct. 1943, 36.
[69] 'The ending of national service and its implications for the colleges', *OM* 20 June 1957,
545–7.
[70] Figure for all matriculants based on data underlying figure 3.1 (see above, 46).

1900 and 1967 are shown in tables 3.4 and 3.5.[71] Only 3 per cent of Oxford's male arts and science finalists entered occupations as modest as those of clerk, shopkeeper and blue-collar worker between 1900–13 and 1960–7, whereas national censuses record about half of all Britain's employed men in these occupations between 1911 and 1971.[72] A disproportionately large number of Oxford men went into the professions. The proportion of Oxford's male finalists who embarked on some form of teaching declined between 1900–13 and 1960–7—after 1940–5 for arts finalists and after 1900–13 for science finalists—but never fell below a quarter, whereas the proportion of Britain's employed men entering the teaching profession rose between 1911 and 1971 from 0.6 per cent to 2 per cent.[73] Oxford also contributed a declining but considerable proportion of its male arts finalists into the law and of its male science finalists into medicine—two professions which expanded over the period but together never accounted for more than 0.6 per cent of Britain's employed men. Only the decline in religious callings among Oxford's arts finalists follows the national trend in male employment. But here as elsewhere there is a considerable difference of magnitude—the national figures show only a modest decline, from 0.35 per cent to 0.26 per cent.[74] Oxford also sent a great disproportion of its men into managerial jobs

[71] HUD/C/RS–SV. Information on junior members' career destinations from published sources for pre–1940 matriculants and from survey questionnaires for post–1939 matriculants. The questionnaire asked respondents to indicate the first job they held after leaving Oxford, and then the jobs they held 10, 20, 30 and 40 years after leaving Oxford. Tables 3.4 and 3.5 show respectively the career destinations of post–1939 male arts and science finalists 10 years after they left Oxford; this particular job was chosen in order to exclude references to postgraduate research and training posts. For men who matriculated before 1940 the published record revealed rich career histories for some and sparse ones for others. Some attempt was made to structure the variance by structuring careers in up to three distinct phases. Where the published record showed that individuals held two or more distinctive careers, the second of these was taken for the pre–1940 portions of tables 3.4 and 3.5. In most instances, however, only one career destination was available, and in such cases this was used. The tables ignore junior members in the sample whose career destinations are unknown. The occupational categories are identical to those used for fathers' occupations (see above, 54 n.36).

[72] HUD/C/RS–SV. The Registrar General's occupational classification was not used to categorize the occupations of Oxford's junior members since the scheme would have shown the vast majority in categories 1A, 1B (higher and lower professions), and 2B (managerial and administrative). Consequently comparisons between the Oxford data and national census data are based on recombinations of census categories and are nowhere exact (though see Greenstein, 'Standard, meta-standard'). Estimates of national employment patterns are based on 1911, 1921, 1931, 1951 and 1971 census figures in G. Routh, *Occupation and Pay in Great Britain, 1906–79* (London 1980). Figures for low-grade occupations are derived from Routh's table 1.1, which shows proportions of employed men and women in clerical and blue-collar work for each of the five census years. Rough estimates for small proprietors are based on Routh's table 1.1 which gives aggregate figures for the category 'employers and proprietors', and table 1.7 which gives detailed information about that category's composition. There it was assumed that Routh's categories 'distributive trades' (including privately held retailing establishments), 'personal services', and 'catering' consist entirely of small proprietors.

[73] Routh, *Occupation and Pay*, table 1.6.

[74] Routh, *Occupation and Pay*. Estimates are based on tables 1.1 and 1.5 which analyse more closely the composition of Routh's occupational category 1A ('higher professions').

in business and public administration, again contrary to national trends. The proportion of Oxford's male finalists who went into public administration remained consistently high but declined, whereas it attracted 0.7 per cent of Britain's employed men in 1911 and 1.2 per cent in 1971. The proportion of Oxford's male arts and science finalists entering into a wide range of business careers at or above the managerial level (including technicians), nearly tripled between 1900–13 and 1960–7.[75] Although census data are not directly comparable, only about 4 per cent of the nation's employed men in 1966 were occupied at or above the managerial level (excluding technicians) in business careers and public administration combined.[76]

The changing career patterns of Oxford men can be explained partly by the broadening social composition of Oxford's male intake between 1900 and 1967, but changes in graduates' job opportunities and in the formal mechanisms of job recruitment and training within Oxford also need to be considered. Before the First World War, Oxford was a staging post for the sons of Britain's wealthiest families who were travelling from their public schools to their fathers' estates or professions [tables 3.4 and 3.5]. Following in their fathers' footsteps were over a third of the men whose occupations involved the armed services, the law, religion, medicine, business (broadly construed), or the land.[77] Their subjects of study and levels of performance had little impact on their careers. Before the First World War a greater proportion of male honours finalists, especially those in the first and second classes, went into the home civil service and university teaching. Proportionately more passmen and third- and fourth-class male finalists went into business (broadly construed), the armed services, forestry, estate management, the colonial civil services, the law and religious callings.[78]

Before the First World War, a man's social background probably had more influence than his educational achievements on his choice of career. Men from humbler backgrounds used examination success as their route into meritocratic middle-class professions, and were disproportionately represented in the first and second classes. Men from wealthier backgrounds were more reliant on family connections for their careers, and were more

[75] Occupations in the employment sectors indicated in rows 2 to 5 and 12 to 14 of tables 3.3 to 3.7 are at or above the managerial level (including technicians). All jobs in the four business and three public sectors which involve clerical and blue-collar work and the ownership of small shops are included in rows 16 and 17. Only the level of employment indicated in row 6 of the tables ('unspecified business') is unknown, as the category comprises ambiguous occupational references such as 'businessman'. See above, 54 n.36.

[76] Department of Employment, *British Labour Statistics: Historical Abstract 1886–1968* (London 1968), 199.

[77] The data do not show how far sons entered their fathers' firms or professional practices. They merely reproduce one of Glass's tests of élite recruitment which measures how far sons took up their fathers' occupation. D. V. Glass (ed.), *Social Mobility in Britain* (London 1954), 2–28.

[78] HUD/C/RS–SV.

TABLE 3.4

CAREER DESTINATIONS OF OXFORD MALE ARTS FINALISTS, 1900–1967 (%)

Occupational categories	1900–13	1914–19	1920–29	1930–9	1940–5	1946–52	1953–9	1960–7
accountant	0.20	1.29	0.81	1.13	0.54	2.39	3.38	2.29
commerce	2.02	1.28	1.90	1.13	4.32	5.23	5.56	4.79
finance	1.82	3.84	3.54	2.64	2.70	3.70	3.87	5.42
industry	2.42	0.00	4.63	4.91	8.11	13.51	13.77	8.54
publishing, media, leisure	3.20	1.92	5.45	4.91	4.32	4.79	6.76	7.71
unspecified business	4.23	5.76	5.72	3.02	0.54	0.87	2.90	2.71
total	13.89	14.09	22.05	17.74	20.53	30.49	36.24	31.46
gentleman	0.20	0.00	0.27	0.00	0.00	0.00	0.00	0.00
armed forces and police	0.00	0.64	0.55	1.13	2.16	1.74	0.97	1.25
land	1.61	1.92	1.91	0.76	1.62	0.22	0.48	0.42
total	1.81	2.56	2.73	1.89	3.78	1.96	1.45	1.67
colonial civil service	10.89	7.10	5.99	6.79	0.54	1.53	0.00	0.21
civil service	14.92	9.61	10.08	12.83	9.73	10.46	7.01	11.67
local govt	0.20	0.00	0.00	0.00	0.54	2.40	0.73	1.46
total	26.01	16.71	16.07	19.62	10.81	14.39	7.74	13.34
clerks, skilled workers and small shopkeepers	0.00	1.92	0.82	0.00	3.78	1.09	1.45	1.88
semi- and unskilled workers	0.20	0.00	0.27	0.38	0.54	0.44	0.00	0.42
total	0.20	1.92	1.09	0.38	4.32	1.53	1.45	2.30
school teacher	17.14	21.15	23.43	24.15	27.57	20.48	17.39	11.25
university teacher	7.46	13.46	12.53	7.54	15.68	11.11	18.36	19.38
education related	2.02	2.56	1.36	2.64	3.78	3.49	2.66	2.60
total	26.62	37.17	37.32	34.33	47.03	35.08	38.41	33.13
religion	20.70	14.74	10.35	16.98	7.03	6.75	5.07	3.33
doctor	0.00	1.28	0.00	0.76	0.54	0.87	0.73	0.42
social work and related	0.00	0.64	0.27	0.38	0.00	0.44	1.93	1.46
lawyer	10.69	10.89	10.08	7.93	5.95	8.50	7.01	12.92
total	31.39	27.55	20.70	26.05	13.52	16.56	14.74	18.13

CAREER DESTINATIONS OF OXFORD MALE SCIENCE FINALISTS, 1900–1967 (%)

Occupational categories	1900–13	1914–19	1920–29	1930–9	1940–5	1946–52	1953–9	1960–7
accountant	1.33	0.00	0.67	0.00	0.00	0.80	0.79	3.50
commerce	0.89	0.00	0.67	1.82	2.53	1.59	4.72	7.20
finance	0.89	2.17	0.00	0.00	0.00	1.86	1.58	4.32
industry	8.00	9.88	12.00	10.91	29.80	21.75	23.10	22.63
publishing, media, leisure	0.44	1.24	0.67	1.82	0.51	0.53	1.58	2.26
unspecified business	4.44	4.94	2.67	4.55	2.53	1.33	1.05	1.85
total	15.99	18.23	16.68	19.10	35.37	27.86	32.82	41.76
gentleman	0.00	1.24	0.00	0.00	0.00	0.00	0.00	0.00
armed forces and police	0.00	1.24	1.33	3.64	3.54	0.53	0.00	0.62
land	1.78	0.00	1.33	0.00	2.02	4.51	2.10	1.24
total	1.78	2.48	2.66	3.64	5.56	5.04	2.10	1.86
colonial civil service	6.22	1.24	6.00	3.64	3.03	0.80	0.26	0.00
civil service	8.44	7.41	3.33	5.46	7.58	5.57	5.77	6.17
local govt	0.00	2.47	1.33	0.91	2.53	0.80	1.58	3.09
total	14.66	11.12	10.66	10.01	13.14	7.17	7.61	9.26
clerks, skilled workers and small shopkeepers	0.00	0.00	0.00	0.00	0.51	0.53	0.79	0.62
semi- and unskilled workers	0.00	0.00	0.67	0.00	2.02	0.00	0.00	0.21
total	0.00	0.00	0.67	0.00	2.53	0.53	0.79	0.83
school teacher	24.44	18.52	22.00	10.00	10.61	10.61	9.19	6.58
university teacher	14.22	16.05	10.67	20.91	16.16	17.24	25.46	18.52
education related	0.44	1.24	1.33	1.82	3.03	1.86	1.58	1.24
total	39.10	35.81	34.00	32.73	29.80	29.71	36.23	26.34
all clergy	3.56	2.47	2.00	3.64	1.52	2.12	1.05	0.82
doctor	20.44	29.63	33.33	29.09	12.12	27.32	18.64	17.08
social work and related	0.00	0.00	0.00	0.91	0.00	0.27	0.53	0.82
lawyer	4.44	0.00	0.00	0.91	0.00	0.00	0.26	1.24
total	28.44	32.10	35.33	34.55	13.64	29.71	20.48	19.96
number in sample	225	81	150	110	198	377	381	486

likely to appear in the third and fourth classes and in the pass school, whence they moved into their fathers' estates and callings. There were also differences between male arts and science finalists. The teaching and medical professions claimed a greater proportion of male finalists in science than in the arts, while the law and religious callings claimed a greater proportion of male arts finalists. These trends may also reflect contrasts in the social composition of arts and science finalists: the scholarship boys from humbler backgrounds clustered in the science schools, and rose in society often through entering the teaching profession.

Change in the pattern of men's careers was slow. Recruitment to the colonial and home civil services fell away slightly between the wars, whereas more embarked on teaching and medicine. Although there was no significant inter-war change in recruitment to business occupations, the University was growing more interested in this area. It was keen to enlarge its access to talent and wanted to convince middle-class parents that their sons' careers would not suffer from a spell at Oxford.[79] Before 1914 the Appointments Committee's function was mostly to 'distribute dons' surplus patronage in the public and grammar schools',[80] but between the wars the Secretary increased the number of business vacancies notified, extended his contacts with Oxford dons, and got the University to fund his work. By 1939 a third of the men in residence were on the Committee's register. This was a marked improvement over the 1920s, when undergraduates spoke of it as the 'Disappointments Committee'.[81] By 1936 the work of the Committee, 'once regarded as a regrettable necessity', was at last 'recognized as an integral part of the University'.[82]

The University between the wars worked in the same direction with its curricular changes. A two-part chemistry school was introduced in 1919, partly to provide industry with scientists trained in research; the faculty claimed (unsuccessfully) the right of chemistry graduates to accreditation by the Institute of Chemistry.[83] Oxford's emphasis on modern subjects—on PPE in particular—was partly a response to the civil service's need for men trained in politics and economics, partly an attempt to give the University a 'modern' image and to provide a course attractive to foreign students.[84] Oxford did not always respond to the needs of the teaching profession,

[79] HCP 157 (1934), 113–23; D. Milne-Watson, 'University Men in Industry', *Oxford* winter 1934, 43–50.

[80] OUA WPΓ/5/2a–2c, 'OUAC informal discussion', 22 May 1970; OUA WPΓ/5/2b, 'OUAC, 1890–1970'.

[81] OUA WPΓ/5/2b, 'OUAC, 1890–1970', 1–2.

[82] *OM* 22 Oct. 1936, 40.

[83] *OM* 20 Oct. 1916, 7; HCP 149 (1931), 5–6; 161 (1935), 193–4; 163 (1936), 105–7; 167 (1937), 19–20.

[84] HCP 108 (1917), 129–30, 145–6; 109 (1918), 33–5; 145 (1930), 197–203; 'The proposed school of philosophy, politics, and economics', *OM* 22 Oct. 1920, 25.

however; it considered but rejected a new diploma in biology for would-be science teachers,[85] and till 1986 it rejected the divided second class favoured by the Burnham Committee, the body which maintained standardized pay scales for teachers in state-supported schools from 1921.[86] The needs of local government were met to some extent with new diplomas and certificates, but the impact of curricular reforms on recruitment was limited. As the professions demanded more rigorous and specialized qualifications, an Oxford BA became vocationally less useful.[87] So in the 1930s more than a third of Oxford's graduates felt the need to take up further training, not including postgraduate research degrees, after they went down.[88] Despite these changes, inter-war career choice differed little from the situation before 1914; the scientists continued to look after their own, and most arts men who took up jobs in commercial and industrial firms did so through family connections.[89] The Appointments Committee was seen as only a last resort.[90] Law and medicine recruited through their own professional associations, and the civil service framed its own entrance examinations after consulting the universities about their content. Dons could still help to place pupils in teaching posts, but there the Appointments Committee's role was advancing.

In the 1940s the situation changed markedly, partly because meritocratic attitudes gained ground both in the selection of undergraduates at Oxford and in appointments to posts in society at large. The proportion of all male matriculants between 1940 and 1952 who took up careers in industry and commerce virtually doubled and by the late 1940s the Appointments Committee, which now nearly monopolized recruitment into industry and commerce, was seeing as many as half the men in residence and even more of the women.[91] The growing importance of business (broadly construed) as a career owes much to the Education Act of 1944, after which business firms found themselves competing with universities for the best school-leavers and therefore aiming to attract university graduates.[92] It also reflects the lowering of Oxford's social-class base and hence of undergraduate career aspirations, together with the business firm's rising demand for formal qualifications. Between 1945 and 1967 twice as many Oxford men took up a career in business than did so before the Second World War, more than half of them in industry. Partly in consequence, recruitment to other occupations—especially to religious and educational posts—declined. Salaries and

[85] HCP 131 (1925), 249.
[86] HCP 122 (1922), 43, 91, 209; 153 (1932), 11.
[87] Armytage, Four Hundred Years, 209 ff.
[88] OUAC, Annual Report (1958), 10.
[89] OUAC, Annual Report (1929), 1–2.
[90] HCP 163 (1936), 75–7.
[91] OUAC, Annual Report (1950) for women and (1948) for men.
[92] OUA WPΓ/5/2b, 'OUAC, 1890–1970', 16.

status in both areas were in decline, and the relatively high salaries in the private sector may also explain why the proportion of Oxford's science graduates going into the civil service also declined slightly after the Second World War.

There was little change after 1945 in the proportion going into the traditional professions, but posts in higher education attracted a far higher proportion of Oxford men. Growth was most dramatic in the sciences, where by 1961 44.6 per cent of all finalists went on to do postgraduate research—twice as many as among UK science graduates as a whole. As for arts graduates, the proportion who went on to postgraduate research rose from 10 per cent to 20 per cent between 1961 and 1965. This reflected enhanced government funding and the rapid expansion in higher education.[93] These high figures could not survive the contraction in higher education in the 1970s, and by 1982–3 only a tenth of arts finalists and a quarter of science finalists embarked on research degrees.[94] Scientists who would once have gone on to postgraduate research flooded the market for industrial employment at a time when industry's recruitment of postgraduates was declining. Industrial appointments peaked at 14 per cent of all Oxford men in the late 1970s, but fell away by more than half in the 1980s. This forced down the proportion of arts candidates and weaker science finalists who took up industrial appointments. The expanding commercial sector moved in to fill the gap, and by 1986 was attracting nearly one in five of all Oxford finalists.[95] The narrowing opportunities in industry also redirected Oxford scientists into banking, law and accounting—areas which had once been much more attractive to Oxford arts men[96]—and renewed the pressure on arts and science graduates to pursue postgraduate vocational training. From the mid-1970s as many as 40 per cent went on to some form of professional or vocational training.[97]

Differences persisted after 1945 in the career patterns of men who achieved first- and second-class results in finals, and of those who achieved third- and fourth-class results. High achievers were substantially over-represented in university teaching and in the home civil service, while low achievers were over-represented in finance, commerce, industry and schoolteaching.[98] But the different career patterns of male arts and science

[93] OUAC, *Annual Report* (1961); (1964), 12–13; (1965), 5.
[94] Ibid. (1982–3), 5. All figures on men's and women's employment after 1967 are based on surveys conducted annually by OUAC of the first employment destinations of all Oxford graduates six months after their final honours examinations. Response-rates were 85% or better and a follow-up survey of non-respondents conducted in 1970–1 showed a career distribution similar to that of respondents: ibid. (1970–1), 3.
[95] Ibid. (1977–8), 4; 1986–7; OUA WPΓ/5/2b, 'OUAC, 1890–1970', 24.
[96] OUAC, *Annual Report* (1971–2), 4; (1977–8), 6.
[97] OUAC, *Annual Report* (1972–3), 4
[98] HUD/C/RS–SV.

finalists and of male high and low performers can no longer be attributed to contrasting social background. As the social composition of the University's entire male intake broadened between 1900 and 1967, the social background of male arts and science finalists and of men in the top and bottom half of the class lists grew more similar. After the Second World War, educational experience was becoming at least as important as social background in influencing Oxford men's career choices.

The careers of Oxford's female arts and science finalists between 1900 and 1967 contrast sharply with those of Britain's employed women over the same period. In 1911 53 per cent of Britain's gainfully employed women were occupied in blue-collar jobs and another 12 per cent as clerical workers, shopkeepers, shop assistants and in the catering trade. By 1971 the figures were 27 per cent and 47 per cent respectively; the proportion of women in clerical work alone grew from 3 per cent to 26 per cent over the period.[99] In our sample of all Oxford matriculants from 1900 to 1967 the proportion of female arts and science finalists in equivalent forms of employment was far lower [tables 3.6 & 3.7], though clerical work seems to have attracted many of Oxford's female arts finalists, particularly those who were up during and immediately after the Second World War.[100] Like Oxford men, Oxford's women were much more prone to embark on professional or managerial employment than women in the nation as a whole. The proportion of Britain's employed women entering into the teaching profession, for example, increased slightly from 3.7 per cent in 1911 to 4.2 per cent in 1971,[101] yet in these years teaching never absorbed fewer than half Oxford's female arts and science finalists, although its overall importance as a career for Oxford women was declining somewhat. Whereas the medical profession recruited a relatively high proportion of Oxford's female scientists and the legal profession took on a small but not inconsiderable proportion of female arts graduates, neither medicine nor law ever accounted for more than 0.1 per cent of Britain's employed women between 1911 and 1971.[102] Jobs at or above the managerial level (including technicians) in a wide variety of businesses also increased in their importance as careers for Oxford's female arts and science finalists, as did similarly graded jobs in public administration for Oxford's female arts finalists. No

[99] Estimate based on Routh, *Occupation and Pay* (see above, 66–7 nn. 72, 74–5) and K. Gales and P. Marks, 'Twentieth century trends in the work of women in England and Wales', *Journal of the Royal Statistical Society*, Series A (1937), pt 1, 64.

[100] HUD/C/RS–SV. Tables 3.6 and 3.7 are identical in their construction to tables 3.4 and 3.5 with one exception: the post-1939 figures refer to the jobs that the surveyed women held immediately after leaving Oxford and not 10 years after leaving Oxford. This reflects the need to include women who held jobs immediately after leaving Oxford but who gave them up to become full-time mothers sometime thereafter. Women whose career destinations are unknown or who gave their occupations as housewife and/or mother are excluded from the tables.

[101] See above, 66 n. 73.

[102] See above, 66 n. 74.

TABLE 3.6

CAREER DESTINATIONS OF OXFORD FEMALE ARTS FINALISTS, 1900–1967 (%)

Occupational categories	1900–13	1914–19	1920–29	1930–9	1940–5	1946–52	1953–9	1960–7
accountant	1.70	0.00	0.00	0.00	0.90	0.00	0.00	0.00
commerce	0.00	0.00	0.00	2.42	3.60	4.28	3.53	4.15
finance	0.85	0.00	1.33	0.00	0.90	0.00	0.00	0.52
industry	0.00	2.53	1.33	1.21	1.80	2.67	2.94	4.15
publishing, media, leisure	2.54	7.60	3.97	4.85	1.80	9.63	9.41	6.22
unspecified business	1.70	0.00	1.99	1.82	0.90	0.54	0.00	0.52
total	6.79	10.13	8.62	10.30	9.90	17.12	15.88	15.56
gentleman	0.00	0.00	0.00	0.00	0.00	0.00	0.00	0.00
armed forces and police	0.00	0.00	0.00	0.00	3.60	2.14	0.00	0.00
land	0.00	1.27	0.66	0.61	0.90	0.00	0.00	0.00
total	0.00	1.27	0.66	0.61	4.50	2.14	0.00	0.00
colonial civil service	0.00	0.00	0.00	0.00	0.00	1.60	0.00	0.00
civil service	4.24	6.33	2.65	7.27	6.31	10.70	7.06	10.88
local govt	0.85	0.00	0.00	2.42	3.60	1.07	2.35	1.55
total	5.09	6.33	2.65	9.69	9.91	13.37	9.41	12.43
clerks, skilled workers and small shopkeepers	5.93	8.86	7.95	7.27	10.81	16.58	9.41	8.29
semi- and unskilled workers	0.85	0.00	0.66	0.00	0.00	1.07	0.59	0.00
total	6.78	8.86	8.61	7.27	10.81	17.65	10.00	8.29
school teacher	42.37	49.37	42.38	36.97	46.85	34.23	42.35	26.43
university teacher	20.34	10.13	15.89	13.94	11.71	5.35	13.53	17.62
education related	6.78	1.27	5.30	4.24	6.31	3.74	2.94	7.77
total	69.49	60.77	63.57	55.15	64.87	43.32	58.82	51.82
religion	1.70	6.33	1.33	4.24	0.00	0.54	0.59	1.04
doctor	0.85	0.00	1.99	0.61	0.00	0.54	0.00	0.52
social work and related	9.32	6.33	5.30	6.06	0.00	3.21	4.71	5.18
lawyer	0.00	0.00	7.29	5.46	0.00	2.14	0.59	5.18
total	11.87	12.66	15.91	16.37	0.00	6.43	5.89	11.92

CAREER DESTINATIONS OF OXFORD FEMALE SCIENCE FINALISTS, 1900–1967 (%)

Occupational categories	1900–13	1914–19	1920–29	1930–9	1940–5	1946–52	1953–9	1960–7
accountant	0.00	0.00	0.00	0.00	0.00	0.00	0.00	0.00
commerce	0.00	0.00	0.00	0.00	0.00	0.64	0.74	1.71
finance	0.00	0.00	0.00	0.00	0.00	0.64	0.00	0.00
industry	0.00	14.29	1.35	1.11	12.25	10.90	11.03	10.29
publishing, media, leisure	0.00	0.00	0.00	3.33	2.04	1.28	4.41	2.29
unspecified business	0.00	0.00	0.00	1.11	0.00	0.00	1.47	0.00
total	0.00	14.29	1.35	5.55	14.29	13.46	17.65	14.29
gentleman	0.00	0.00	0.00	1.11	0.00	0.00	0.00	0.00
armed forces and police	0.00	0.00	0.00	0.00	4.08	0.64	0.00	0.00
land	0.00	0.00	1.35	0.00	0.00	1.28	0.00	0.00
total	0.00	0.00	1.35	1.11	4.08	1.92	0.00	0.00
colonial civil service	0.00	0.00	0.00	0.00	0.00	0.00	0.00	0.00
civil service	9.09	0.00	2.70	4.44	4.08	3.21	1.47	3.43
local govt	0.00	0.00	4.05	0.00	0.00	3.21	2.94	2.29
total	9.09	0.00	6.75	4.44	4.08	6.42	4.41	5.72
clerks, skilled workers and small shopkeepers	0.00	0.00	1.35	2.22	0.00	3.21	0.74	3.43
semi- and unskilled workers	0.00	0.00	0.00	1.11	2.04	3.85	0.00	1.71
total	0.00	0.00	1.35	3.33	2.04	7.06	0.74	5.14
school teacher	45.46	28.57	37.84	41.11	32.65	32.69	40.44	30.86
university teacher	18.18	28.57	21.62	25.56	16.33	14.10	13.97	25.14
education related	0.00	0.00	4.05	3.33	0.00	2.56	2.21	1.71
total	63.64	57.14	63.51	70.00	48.98	49.35	56.62	57.71
religion	18.18	0.00	0.00	2.22	0.00	0.00	0.00	0.00
doctor	9.09	28.57	20.27	10.00	26.53	19.87	17.65	14.29
social work and related	0.00	0.00	5.41	3.33	0.00	1.28	2.94	2.86
lawyer	0.00	0.00	0.00	0.00	0.00	0.00	0.00	0.00
total	27.27	28.57	25.68	15.55	26.53	21.15	20.59	17.15
number in sample	11	7	74	90	49	156	136	175

directly comparable national series exists, but in the 1960s only about 0.6 per cent of the nation's women were occupied at or above the managerial level (excluding technicians) in private business and in public administration combined.[103]

The career pattern of Oxford women contrasts markedly with that of Oxford men. Female undergraduates were from 1900 onwards socially more homogeneous than male undergraduates. Socially, women arts finalists resemble women science finalists, and women with first- and second-class degrees resemble women who took third- and fourth-class or pass degrees. Women's job opportunities were far more limited than men's, and from an earlier date relied more heavily on accreditation. For both reasons, the career patterns of women arts and science finalists were broadly similar from 1900 onwards. Examination success in arts or science subjects was a gateway to teaching careers, and entry became increasingly competitive between the wars.[104] This is one reason why women disappeared from the pass school after 1920 and did better in the second public examination than the men. Two of the women's societies, Lady Margaret Hall and Somerville, were in the top ten when the colleges are ranked on inter-war finals examinations, and were joined there by St Hugh's College in the 1930s.[105] The pattern of Oxford women's careers also reflects job opportunities available to women, which slowly broadened after 1945. Business appointments increased, as did appointments to the civil service, which predictably grew most during the Second World War. University teaching gained while schoolteaching declined. Elsewhere women's advance was less certain. The percentage of female arts finalists going into the legal profession grew between the wars, but declined again after the Second World War [table 3.6]. Meanwhile the high proportion of women science graduates going into the medical profession [table 3.7] reflects not so much opportunities for women in medicine as the very limited career prospects for women scientists elsewhere, and the disproportionately small number of women under- graduates reading science subjects. As the proportion of women science undergraduates increased, the percentage going into medicine declined.

Women's career patterns may also reflect slight changes in the function of an Oxford education for women. Before the Second World War a university education was necessary for women from humble backgrounds who aimed at teaching posts. Marriage kept only a third of female matriculants who were up in the 1930s from seeking employment immediately after finals.[106] After 1945 marriage proved a greater obstacle to women's careers because

---

[103] See above, 67 n. 76 and 66 n. 75; A. Myrdal and V. Klein, *Women's Two Roles: Home and Work* (2nd edn London 1968), 57.
[104] OUAC, *Annual Report* (1936), 2.
[105] HUD/S/REG.
[106] HUD/C/RS–SV; HCP 152 (1932), 223–5.

there were insufficient part-time or short-term jobs to go round among an increasing proportion of women who needed employment between graduation and marriage. Furthermore married and engaged women felt the need to seek work wherever their husbands or fiancés settled.[107] These problems were not entirely new, and had earlier been used as an argument against amalgamating the men's and women's appointments committees, but were nonetheless more significant after 1945. The change also reflects the fact that the proportion of all Oxford women who married increased from around two-thirds in 1930–9 to four-fifths in 1960–7.[108] It may also owe something to the long-term decline in social-class differences between male and female undergraduates—a change which fostered social mixing and inter-marriage. Of Oxford women up between 1930 and 1939, 46 per cent married Oxford men—a figure which by 1960–7 had risen to 63 per cent.[109]

Throughout the numerous and striking changes in Oxford life between 1900 and 1990 that have been recorded in this chapter, one theme recurs: the gradual erosion of contrasts in both the representation and the experience of different types of junior member—whether scholar or commoner, male or female, rich or poor, student of the arts or of the sciences. Here as so often elsewhere, changes in twentieth-century Oxford reflect changes in the wider society—changes made in response to meritocratic, feminist, political and economic pressures. Underlying them all was a further move towards uniformity that has yet to be discussed: the coming together of the colleges. In 1900 their vitality owed much to their diversity. By 1990 their greatest assets—their distinctive tone and their corporate loyalties—were less secure than at any time during the period under discussion.

[107] OUAC, *Annual Report* (1960), 18–19.
[108] HUD/C/RS–SV.
[109] HUD/C/RS–SV.

PART TWO
OXFORD BETWEEN THE WARS

4

College life, 1918–1939

BRIAN HARRISON

'I did not go back to Oxford after the war', Harold Macmillan recalled in old age. 'I just could not face it. To me it was a city of ghosts.'[1] Nonetheless by Michaelmas term 1919 the University had almost got back into its stride. The men's colleges faced challenges which the war had postponed but in some ways sharpened: from natural science, with its centralizing technology; from academic professionalism, with its intellectually fragmenting tendency; and from political radicalism, with its intrusive pressures for equal opportunity and public accountability. On the other hand the colleges, like so many established British institutions, were in some ways reinforced by the war, which sent Germanic principles of university organization into temporary eclipse. Harvard between the wars acquired houses modelled on the Oxford and Cambridge colleges, and the many American university buildings mimicking English Gothic collegiate styles introduced something of the collegiate reality: the well-rounded and unspecialized training of an élite drawn from first-degree students within a residential setting.[2] The war also gave Oxford's colleges many excuses for building upon their greatest strengths: a sense of place, a preoccupation with tradition, an attachment to personal connections. These substitute-families savoured the successes of their sons past and present, and carefully celebrated and chronicled births, marriages, anniversaries and deaths. On armistice day the Bursar of Keble stood all junior members a glass of port at dinner, Queen's undergraduates set off sky-rockets and ground-flares, and for many months afterwards solemn little ceremonies were held throughout Oxford as each community commemorated its dead.[3]

[1] Sir Harold Macmillan, 'Oxford before the deluge', History of the University seminar, 14 Mar. 1973, HUA tape-recording. This chapter owes a special debt to the many former undergraduates who took the trouble to respond to my request, published in their college magazines, for information on Oxford college life before 1950. I am also grateful for helpful comments on earlier drafts from Dr M. C. Curthoys, Mr Derek Hudson and Sir Keith Thomas.
[2] K. Martin, *Harold Laski (1893–1950): A Biographical Memoir* (London 1953), 30; D. O. Levine, *The American College and the Culture of Aspiration, 1915–1940* (Ithaca NY 1986), 102, 106–7; R. L. Geiger, *To Advance Knowledge; The Growth of American Research Universities 1900–1940* (Oxford 1986), 115. I owe these references to Dr Curthoys.
[3] For Keble see KCA diary of H. R. H. Coney, 11 Nov. 1919; for Queen's, *OM* 14 Nov. 1919, 90.

Presiding at each was the head of house, who needed dignity, presence and a sense of history, and was rarely in post before his 50s. Addressing his undergraduates during the General Strike, M. T. Sadler, Master of University College, referred to the many crises the College had survived: 'our front quad', he said, 'looks all of a piece but was interrupted in building by the Civil War'. Celebrating two years later the quatercentenary of its founder's death, Corpus put its plate on display; its President, the distinguished scholar P. S. Allen, presided at a dinner in hall and gave a speech in praise of the founder, whose big sapphire ring he wore. Celebrating the coronation in 1937, New College held a special dinner that was memorable for the entry into the hall of Warden Fisher, a former minister of education, in the robes of a privy councillor.[4]

Heads could lend personal distinction to their colleges. In one respect their background was limited: all but one of the 69 in post between 1914 and 1945 had studied for first degrees at Oxford, 53 of their 79 degrees came from the classical final honour school and only 6 took a first degree in science or mathematics. But they were intellectually distinguished, and included a Fellow of the Royal Society and eleven Fellows of the British Academy. Twelve took a second undergraduate degree, and between them they won 64 firsts. Of the 66 eligible, 33 got into the *Dictionary of National Biography*. Fisher was the best-known among them, and he knew it. Asked whether he would take the post if offered, he allegedly replied: 'it may come to that'.[5] Links with the Church of England and the public schools persisted: 17 of the 69 were ordained and 3 (Norwood and James of St John's and A. T. P. Williams of Christ Church) were distinguished public-school headmasters. Prominence in university administration was easily acquired because heads of house had the leisure and often the inclination to assume university office. Until 1926 6 of the elected places on Hebdomadal Council were reserved for them, and they contributed nearly half Council's 73 elected members between 1914 and 1939. Not till 1989 was a vice-chancellor drawn from outside their ranks.

His lodgings gave the head an ample and impressive setting in which to entertain with splendid formality, for, as President Warren of Magdalen pointed out, he must 'keep his College up to the mark—and to the fore'.[6] By moving among distinguished outsiders, he could attract the undergraduate talent and the benefactions which, in the absence of state funding, had to be pursued. Fisher was well able to invite three couples to stay overnight and to hold Saturday night dinner-parties and Sunday lunches for eighteen in the lodgings. His weekend dinner-parties are to this day gratefully remembered

---

[4] UCA red box marked 'college history', file endorsed 'General Strike May 1926, papers re Univ', Sadler's typescript diary, p. 12; P. S. Allen, *Letters*, ed. H. M. Allen (London 1939), 262; Bodl. MS Fisher 217, fo 71, D. Balsdon to Mrs Fisher, 27 Apr. 1940. The age of heads of house on accession is conveniently listed in *OM* 17 Oct. 1957, 1; 31 Oct. 1957, 57; 7 Nov. 1957, 82.

[5] Author's tape-recorded interview with Sir Isaiah Berlin, 25 Apr. 1988.

[6] Asquith Commission, written evidence, Bodl. MS top. Oxon. b. 104, fo 202 (undated).

in Oxford. The head's diplomatic arts were likewise integral to the success of All Souls under Adams and Sumner as a meeting-point for dons with the wider world, just as their absence in Beveridge made it easier for University College to part with him in 1945. It was Warden Bowman's seclusion in his lodgings that inspired the unsuccessful attempt by the fellows of Merton to oust him in 1920.[7] Although some shy heads of house—Blakiston of Trinity or Munro of Lincoln for example—found themselves being put at ease by their undergraduate guests rather than the other way round, they did at least make the gesture. To judge from President Allen's letters, a friendly intimacy with junior members was then possible which would now be unusual: evening parties were supplemented by walks in the country, toasts in hall and even the exchange of gifts.

Heads held their colleges together and represented them before the outside world. In the early 1920s President Case of Corpus stood foursquare against all comers in refusing to supply information about his College to outsiders, whoever they might be. Some heads came almost to symbolize their college, as Bowra at Wadham and Stallybrass at Brasenose. Leadership was essential at moments of crisis. Early in the General Strike, Sadler at University College and Stallybrass at Brasenose both summoned a meeting of their junior members and college employees in hall to explain the situation and invite questions. 'All th[r]ough', Sadler recalled, 'I tried to keep the men and the Servants and the dons as one body'.[8] President Gordon gave an annual address to Magdalen freshmen on the first Sunday of Michaelmas term, and at Balliol A. D. Lindsay gave sermons in chapel and 'lay sermons' in hall after Sunday dinner. He more than most heads of house inspired the young, many of whom he got to know through continuing Jowett's tradition of hearing their essays on general topics. And like A. L. Smith, Lindsay used his headship as a platform for wider social and educational purposes. Uniquely among heads of house, his success in the role gained him a peerage.

Heads built up their portfolio of junior members through running the annual admissions exercise. Although the tutors appointed the scholars, the head of house strongly influenced the choice of commoners, often through long and complicated negotiations with schoolteachers and relatives. At Worcester under Lys, or at Trinity under Blakiston, the head also took on many bursarial duties. This was feasible only because much business could be conducted informally; in those days, colleges and governing bodies were smaller and less entangled with outside bodies. Many years later, Lord Franks recalled seeing Walker handing over the *arcana imperii* of Queen's to Streeter in 1934; these, he said, consisted of two brown envelopes, one of them empty, and the other containing a bill from Blackwells for two pounds and ten shillings. Efficiency with paperwork was desirable but not essential.

[7] Merton College, MS Q.2.9 is a remarkable collection of fellows' letters discussing in 1920 how best to oust Warden Bowman.
[8] Sadler's diary, p. 32.

J. R. H. Weaver was so 'totally unbusinesslike' that his secretary burst into tears on hearing that his presidency of Trinity was unexpectedly to be prolonged for two years, yet he held the post for sixteen years.[9] Colleges' informal administration left wide discretion to heads of house, some of whom exploited it. In many colleges the governing body's minutes, elaborately bound and often locked, were written out by the head himself and not circulated. They were in themselves instruments of power. The Corpus tutors in the early 1920s had to band together in self-defence against what they saw as President Case's encroachments on their powers. The fellows of Merton, conspiring in holes and corners against Bowman during 1920, could not bring themselves to the point. He kept a firm hand on the College's purse-strings and endured for another sixteen years.

Still, the heads' long-term decline had already begun. By the 1930s more and more commoners were admitted on their performance in the separately organized scholarship examinations which tutors controlled, and the scientists were moving towards a centralized system of admission by groups of colleges. Tutors rebelled against the head's discretion on admissions—most notably in Magdalen under T. D. Weldon. A college could run well enough with no head: Jesus had no principal from 1915 to 1921, New College no warden from 1940 to 1944. J. R. Magrath, Provost of Queen's from 1878 to 1930, was so rarely seen in his extreme old age that a distant glimpse of him in his bath-chair produced quite a stir among his undergraduates.[10] In 1936 G. D. H. Cole, then a fellow of University College, even suggested rotating the College's mastership among the fellows, using the savings for scholarships and the lodgings for College purposes. Candidates for head of house were more than once required to accept reduced accommodation as the price of election—in Lincoln College in 1918, for example, at University College in 1935 and at Exeter College in 1943. Yet the post was more demanding than Cole imagined: 'one has to be "on call" like a Doctor', A. B. Poynton, the Master, told him, 'and never knows when the work is done'. The slow formalization of business was simultaneously eroding the head's powers and increasing his commitments. On becoming Master in 1937 Beveridge was assigned a secretary to share with the Dean and Senior Tutor—a necessary change, because the new Master 'applied to the small world of the College the organizing abilities which he previously exercised in a wider sphere'. His miniature Beveridge reports were as significant for his College as his report on social insurance was later to be for his country.[11]

[9] Lord Franks in discussion after Sir Folliott Sandford's paper to History of the University seminar, 20 Feb. 1973, HUA tape-recording. For Weaver see TCA DD 20 add 2, J. D. Lambert to B. Ward-Perkins, 19 Feb. 1987.

[10] Walter Eytan to author, 29 May 1989.

[11] UCA file 'mastership 1934–1942', Cole's memorandum with covering letter dated 13 June 1936; ibid. Poynton to Cole 15 June 1936; *University College Record* 1938, 4 (Beveridge).

The preoccupations of governing bodies were then much as they are now: investments, housekeeping, bequests, appointments, undergraduate discipline, commemoration of past events. Only occasionally did outside happenings (the General Strike, coronations, jubilees and world wars) impinge on the minutes. Domestic issues mattered intensely to fellows who then often resided in college and lived more directly off the college's endowments: in 1922 214 of the University's 357 academic staff were fellows of colleges with no university post.[12] H. H. Cox, Lincoln College's philosopher, saw attendance at meetings of the governing body as 'an exacting duty' requiring him to 'spend a whole morning, pacing up and down his room, pondering on the business to be discussed'. In a leisured community of intelligent and often ambitious people, many of them bachelors and devoted to the college, trouble often bubbled beneath the surface. And at a time when research was less salient, when the head's prestige was greater and when the college's hold on loyalties was stronger, there was unobtrusive but recurrent competition for the succession. Dons' preoccupation with research has subsequently directed their ambitions outwards, and so has rendered colleges less fractious. 'If your object is power the more you get the less there is for other people', said the Registrar Sir Douglas Veale, 'but if your object is knowledge, it is almost true to say that the more you get the more there is for other people'.[13]

The mood of decision-making by governing bodies between the wars reflects the fact that if anything, fellows knew each other too well. Governing bodies were small and to a large extent self-selected; their median size in men's colleges other than All Souls and St Catherine's in 1923 was 11, rising to 14 in 1939. Christ Church, New College and Magdalen had by far the largest governing bodies in both years, though Queen's and Exeter were growing fast. A fifth of Oxford's 198 male tutorial fellows in 1937 had been undergraduates at their college, and no less than 14 of Balliol's 26. Only a sixth had not been educated at Oxford, and fellows once appointed tended to stay put: 137 of the 198 spent the rest of their careers in Oxford, 92 of them in the same post.[14]

Oxford's decentralized power-structure fostered loyalty to the college. Fellows readily took college posts and retained them sometimes for years. Rather than tell professional administrators what to do, these dons believed in conducting the administration themselves. The law fellow was a natural for bursar, the historian for librarian, the theologian for chaplain, and so on. Marriage did not exempt deans from being on the spot when needed. Oliver

[12] *Franks Report* ii. 39.

[13] For H. H. Cox see *University College Record* 1974, 400–1; D. Veale, address to Oxford University Lunch Club, *OM* 12 Oct. 1950, 8.

[14] M. C. Curthoys and M. Heimann, 'The Oxford academic community 1937–8', copy in HUA, pp. 6, 8.

Franks as the newly married Dean of Queen's in the 1930s did not question his duty of leaving home at 10 p.m. during term to sleep in College; 'that sort of discipline was absolutely taken for granted', he recalled.[15] Until 1924 Oxford had no fixed age for retirement; to take one example, the average age of Lincoln College's governing body was as high as 50 in both 1914 and 1934. But the tutorial fellows were relatively young: of 207 in 1937, 119 were under 40. Age then expected deference, and scholarship was still widely seen as storing up and preserving wisdom from the past rather than as inquisitively and irreverently pursuing novelty. 'For a junior fellow to speak at a college meeting', Sir Henry Phelps Brown recalled, 'required a certain assertiveness on his part, and might not be well received'.[16]

Fellows could settle much college business informally at the college's many social occasions, and college life subtly blended individuality with conformity. The scholar with unfashionable views or interests (Schiller and Collingwood in philosophy for example) could rest secure within college walls, and individuality—even eccentricity—was accepted and often prized. Social contact was intimate yet circumscribed. Even in full term (which lasted for half the year) the only communal meal was dinner. The fellow could take other meals in his rooms or, if married, at home. College life adjusted only slowly to fellows' marriage. For the many bachelor fellows the college was 'domus' or home. Married fellows were treated as honorary bachelors, and felt a strong obligation to dine regularly. They often lived nearby in houses owned by the college—one-third did so in 1946—so they and their wives were readily drawn into the college family.[17] Nor did the fellows' sociability end with the savoury course. It would have been bad form to eat without going on to converse over port and dessert in the common room afterwards, and the college's guests were seen as a shared responsibility.

The senior common room (SCR), like an officers' mess, was a club within a club. It combined respect for precedent and hierarchy with an almost egalitarian welcome for its newest member [plates 4.1 and 4.2]. Meetings discussed furnishings, the college's employees, food, drink and ceremonial functions. Presiding over them might well be an unmarried senior fellow such as W. N. Stocker, among the last of Oxford's life fellows, who occupied the same rooms in Brasenose for forty-five years and who long exerted in the SCR a 'firm but kindly control of the regular working of that small society in matters of detail'.[18] During term a score of little collegiate theatres put on

[15] Author's tape-recorded interview, 6 July 1985.
[16] Author's tape-recorded interview, 5 June 1987. Sir Henry was fellow of New College in economics, 1930–47. For the age of fellows see V. H. H. Green, *The Commonwealth of Lincoln College 1427–1977* (Oxford 1979), 570 n. 4; Curthoys and Heimann, 13.
[17] The figure for 1946 is from the valuable anonymous article on 'The problem of the married fellow', *OM* 14 Nov. 1946, 81.
[18] *OM* 20 Oct. 1949, 40 (an excellent obituary).

nightly performances of the stylized and much-prized art of conversation. Epigram and repartee were encouraged, and common-room characters sparked off one another in pleasantly predictable routines. Rules, sometimes quite firmly enforced, prescribed conversational content and style. Religion, politics and women were the most likely topics for exclusion, nor could discussion become too earnest, if only because the day's work was thought to be over. Orchestrating, arbitrating, holding back the bore and bringing out the reticent, a score of W. N. Stockers ensured the tasteful display of recondite and usually literary learning, reference books to hand. Later on, the cards came out or the betting-book recorded speculation on politics or on the weights or marital prospects of those present. All Souls SCR regularly conducted sweepstakes on general elections between the wars, and in University College on 8 October 1940 Beveridge bet Wheare 'that there will be no invasion of Britain involving the landing of as much as 5,000 men by Germany in the course of the present war'. In All Souls on 12 May 1942 C. G. Robertson bet Woodward 'that there never was an Eno connected with Eno's Salt', and on 28 February 1943 Faber bet Macartney one shilling that Churchill 'is not less than 5' 7" high (in his socks)'.[19]

Some Oxford conversations were of national importance, especially when (as at All Souls or Christ Church) they included outsiders: leading journalists, churchmen and politicians. All Souls' Saturday night dinners with their complement of bishops, judges, civil servants and politicians were followed next morning by a leisurely and talkative breakfast. Then came the College walk, during which a dozen or more fellows covered fifteen miles of the Oxfordshire countryside, still talking.[20] The distinctive style of twentieth-century Oxford philosophy, world famous for its linguistic facility, flourished in such a climate. SCR conversations spilled over into individual rooms, into the numerous college clubs that drew together senior and junior members, into the less formal after-dinner gatherings in tutors' rooms and into tutorials. They also infiltrated the inter-collegiate salons run by cultivated dons in search of undergraduate talent: Bowra, Boase, Platnauer or their more raffish rivals Kolkhorst and Dawkins. Beverley Nichols's early novel *Patchwork* (1921) assumes throughout that undergraduates strive for the witty remark in the course of formal, rather mannered conversation. All this talk, whether of junior or senior members, was lubricated with alcoholic drinks brought up from a warren of underground college cellars.

Not much fuss was made about research, and there were few postgraduate students. Inter-war Oxford could produce major scholarly achievement, as the career of that convivial and extraordinarily productive legal historian

[19] UCA SCR betting-book 1810–1970; All Souls betting-book 1920–60. I am grateful to Dr Bryan Wilson for enabling me to consult the latter.
[20] Lord [C. J.] Radcliffe, *Censors* (Cambridge 1961), 24–5 gives a fine account.

W. S. Holdsworth shows. Some colleges were well known for research in particular areas: Exeter for social anthropology, Corpus for classics, Queen's for papyrology, not to mention the Balliol–Trinity Laboratory's fame in physical chemistry. Yet for many senior members there was no point in publishing if one already enjoyed the respect of friends close at hand. Still, by the late 1930s sabbatical leave was being more regularly taken, and modern-minded dons began to pursue an international reputation, an FRS or an FBA.[21] The five small college chemistry laboratories in Christ Church, Jesus, Magdalen, Queen's and Balliol–Trinity—vigorously defended in 1930 by Lindemann for devolving power and initiative within the subject—could not possibly satisfy the research needs of science. The Asquith Commission thought the need for them would 'gradually disappear', and two closed between the wars; the completion in 1941 of the centralized physical chemistry laboratory doomed the others.[22] Outside chemistry, college laboratories had scarcely even been tried. In arts subjects the Asquith Commission introduced university lecturerships to promote 'research', hoping that these would help build up the faculty centre. American ideas for a 'research library' had some influence on the design of the Bodleian Library's extension, and a 'higher studies fund' was launched. The non-collegiate research institute crept in, together with the seminar. After 1945, Nuffield College, pioneer of the research-oriented college in Oxford, brought together conversations of the old and the new style. As for professionalism in administration, inter-collegiate meetings of senior tutors, deans and bursars revealed its growth. Donnish eccentricity was on the wane.

The collegiate tutorial structure required college-instructed under-graduates to be assessed by a central examining board on the basis of a statutory university-wide syllabus. This soon became encrusted with vested tutorial interests, and teaching was prised still further from research by colleges' need to concentrate on tutorial appointments in existing mainline subjects. The academic frontiers where research so often grows were not always cultivated, and Oxford's professors often found themselves em-battled against college tutors. The phrasing of Council's committee on anthropology was delicate when it pointed out in 1934 that 'one of the functions of the university has been to foster infant studies and for the Colleges to come to their support when they are mature'.[23] The collegiate structure lay behind several of Oxford's great refusals: the prolonged resistance to psychology, business studies, sociology; the reluctance until the 1960s to widen the range of degrees in combined subjects; the long delays

<hr />

[21] For sabbatical leave see *OM* 17 June 1937, 754.
[22] Nuffield College, Cherwell MSS, B127, fo 1, Lindemann to the Dean of Christ Church, 28 Feb. 1930 (carbon copy); *Asquith Report*, 117.
[23] HCP 157 (1934), 92.

before fellows were appointed in English and modern languages; and the absence of undergraduate degree-courses in subjects for which Oxford was in other respects splendidly equipped—most notably in social anthropology, archaeology and the fine arts.

Nonetheless, academic specialization inevitably advanced, and the colleges could survive it by forming inter-collegiate teaching alliances (quite widely discussed in the period); by appointing a wider range of fellows (slowly being adopted); and, as at Cambridge, by specializing more by subject (not much discussed, but quite widely practised). Between 1921 and 1938 no college approached Jesus in its proportion of finalists (one-seventh) reading chemistry. Likewise no other college approached Keble and St Catherine's in their proportion of theologians, or Corpus in its proportion reading Greats (over a third, the largest concentration on any degree-course within any college). Within the competitive collegiate admission system, colleges that were for some reason unfashionable could often best bump up numbers, funds or talent by cultivating subjects neglected elsewhere—especially through the timely deployment of awards. Partly for this reason geography flourished at Hertford, Jesus and St Edmund Hall and the women's colleges contributed half of those reading English and nearly half of those reading modern languages.[24]

Postgraduate students contributed only a tenth of inter-war Oxford's junior members—in 1938/9 only 536 of its 5,023 matriculated students.[25] There was no graduate college, and despite the advent in 1917 of that transatlantic innovation the DPhil degree, training for higher degrees was informal: one simply 'stayed on for further study' in a predominantly undergraduate college, working with a professor or with a senior member whose prime loyalty lay to his undergraduates. Some senior members rejected the very idea of organized postgraduate research—Oman, for example, and to some extent Lindsay. The Asquith Commission intended its university lecturerships to free arts tutorial fellows for research by reducing their tutorial burden, but by the 1930s the lecturerships were becoming a device for subsidizing college tutorial posts.[26] Furthermore many postgraduates preferred to read for a second undergraduate degree: physics after mathematics, for example, theology after Greats, PPE after history.

The colleges rested secure on the continued primacy of the undergraduate tutorial—the hyphen which joined, the buckle which fastened senior to junior members. The noun 'tutorial' dates from the early 1920s and until the 1960s competed in some colleges with the term 'private hour', but guidance supplied individually or in small groups was much older. Most scientists went along with the tutorial system because they knew it was buttressed by centrally organized demonstrations and lectures. Already by 1937 the men's colleges' 198 tutorial fellows included 14 in chemistry, 7 in physics, 3 in physiology, 3 in medicine and 1 in zoology.[27] Presumed skill in teaching was more important for gaining a fellowship than proved capacity for research; it was better to win a university prize (sometimes entailing research) than to acquire a formal postgraduate qualification. Clever young men were plucked fresh from their final examinations, sent abroad for a year or two, and then swallowed up in tutorial teaching. R. H. S. Crossman got his fellowship at New College in 1930 before his degree result was known. The period abroad could be formative, as was A. J. Ayer's exposure to Viennese philosophy in the early 1930s, but the system made it difficult for a young man to get a major book launched.

Yet from the college's point of view it was sensible to recruit tutorial fellows in this way, given the number of tutorials to be provided, the breadth of the subject-matter taught and the broad span of the inter-war undergraduate's ability and motivation. Furthermore, there were fewer postgraduate students and non-collegiate experts to reinforce tutorial manpower. The tutorial fellow normally taught in the morning, exercised himself in the afternoon, taught again between five and seven and sometimes again after dinner. The introduction of university lecturerships in the mid-1920s began the long-term decline in teaching hours. But it was not thought right to send undergraduates out of college for much of their tuition; in any choice between knowing the subject and knowing the pupil, knowledge of the pupil came first. This is not to say that the pupil received more tutorials then than now: he probably received fewer. Nor were tutorials expected to cover the entire syllabus. The point is that the tutor covered a much larger area of the subject than would now be thought desirable or even possible.

Courses, like tutors, were wide-ranging. Oxford discouraged any narrowly vocational approach to study, and hankered after the earlier ideal of a common culture for all junior members. The new idea of separate preliminary or qualifying examinations for each degree-course only slowly ousted the less specialized pass and natural science moderations. The same non-specialist values moulded Oxford's multi-subject degree-courses— most notably the mods/Greats combination of classical literature, philosophy and ancient history, and the 'modern Greats' combination of philosophy, politics and economics. Unlike Oxford's combined-subject degrees founded in the 1960s, these combinations aimed to provide a broad education rather than to focus attention on the frontier between two single-subject courses. Indeed, the Greats and PPE courses sometimes had the effect of discouraging specialized study within their domain.

[27] Curthoys and Heimann, 'Academic community', 12.

Inter-war Oxford's undergraduate population was intellectually very diverse. Awards (college-funded scholarships and exhibitions) were one of the British social and intellectual élite's numerous devices for drawing up talent from below, and set many sons of smaller professional people on the road to distinction. Male candidates for awards took a special examination, and a college's academic reputation depended heavily on the number and distribution of its awards. Award-holders were distinguished by much more than a long gown: they were 'on the foundation', had special ceremonial duties (saying grace, reading the lesson in chapel), enjoyed special privileges (choice of rooms, the right to stay up in the vacation) and usually sat together in hall. More was expected of them. More often than most of their contemporaries, they would safeguard their working hours by closing the second door (or 'oak') outside their room, and in final examinations they did relatively well.[28]

The college was in a sense educationally comprehensive. Its range of intellectual ability did not diverge markedly from what prevailed at that social level in the world outside. Such an admission policy seemed in the national interest: the industrious scholar was deterred from over-valuing the intellect while the well-to-do commoner acquired a certain intellectual polish. Commoners varied considerably in ability. Responsions (the University's entrance qualification) was not a major hurdle, nor were places in great demand, given the falling middle-class birth-rate and the fact that few families could afford to pay £250 a year for expenses during term. The rich were by no means obliged to send their sons to university; many peers never went there, especially those who chose careers in the armed services, and the offspring of many rich businessmen went straight into the family firm. So senior members—particularly in the colleges that were academically less distinguished, and which took in applicants rejected by their college of first choice—felt a nagging fear that the supply of undergraduates might dry up. Applicants almost exactly matched the number of places available.

Undergraduates between the wars were in no hurry to grow up and felt no need to conceal their immaturity. Hoaxes and horseplay were frequent, nor were bachelor dons living in college immune from a certain childishness in their leisure hours. For the less able undergraduates, Oxford offered a civilizing interval during which the offspring of the well-to-do recovered from adolescence. There in relative privacy they made their mistakes—recorded only in Latin in the minutes of Balliol's governing body—before going off to run the family firm or estate. Their careers had as

[28] Based on an analysis by Dr M. C. Curthoys of the data on 1,424 undergraduates who matriculated in 1921, 1926, 1931 and 1936 collected by Mrs B. N. Clapham and Miss E. Brunner for their unpublished paper, 'A study of Oxford undergraduates: their school and university records' (1944). For an excellent account of the civil service's dependence on the university successes of the scholarship boy, see H. E. Dale, *The Higher Civil Service of Great Britain* (London 1941), 69–70, 74.

much to gain from friendships made at Oxford as from a good degree. It was more important to have been 'up' than to have been examined. 'I had not . . . gone to Oxford to study', Louis MacNeice recalled. 'That was what grammar-school boys did. We products of the English public schools went to Oxford either for sport and beer-drinking . . . or for the aesthetic life and cocktails.' The passmen, reading for a general and unclassified degree, were not necessarily less intelligent than the rest, but from the late Victorian period they were being gradually crowded out by undergraduates seeking honours at ambitious colleges such as Corpus, Balliol and New College. Other colleges followed suit, and the pass degree gradually came to denote someone who had failed or should never have been admitted. The five colleges with fewest passmen between the wars (Balliol, Corpus, Jesus, New and Oriel) were all high up in what came to be known as the Norrington table, which ranked colleges by performance in examinations. The passman's percentage of total first-degree male undergraduates fell from 7.6 in the years 1925–9 to 3.0 in 1935–9. His numbers remained high only in the poorer colleges (Pembroke, Worcester, Keble), which needed his money, or in an aristocratic college such as Christ Church, many of whose undergraduates did not need a degree at all.[29]

In these circumstances, tutors needed to display a schoolmasterly versatility. Unable to take the pupil's motivation for granted, they needed to inspire. Twenty of Oxford's 198 male tutorial fellows in 1937 (11 of them in classics) had themselves been schoolteachers.[30] College tutors had by now supplanted the private tutor or coach, who catered only for the examination failures and passmen. Yet some tutorial fellows were more like the private tutor of an aristocrat; indeed, Evelyn Waugh's Mr Samgrass formally assumed that role in vacations. Friendship between tutor and pupil was the more common because in Oxford, tutors do not examine pupils for their degree. Tutor and pupil conspired in tutorials against an alien and distant band of faculty-appointed examiners. Furthermore, the content of arts courses lent itself as often to moral guidance as to academic instruction. Tutoring could readily become what it was for Kenneth Leys of University College, 'a cure of souls', requiring moral as well as intellectual qualifications. Although fellows now rarely resigned on a question of belief, they were expected to observe conventional moral standards. Moral objections were raised against inviting Roger Fry or Bertrand Russell to lecture, for instance, and A. J. P. Taylor in 1952 was the first fellow to retain his post after divorce.[31]

[29] L. MacNeice, *The Strings are False* (London 1965), 102; I am most grateful to Bernard Richards of Brasenose College for this reference. Figures from HUD.

[30] Curthoys and Heimann, 'Academic community', 7.

[31] For a penetrating obituary of Leys see *OM* 9 Nov. 1950, 108. See also A. J. P. Taylor, *A Personal History* (London 1983), 198; M. Bowra, *Memories 1898–1939* (London 1966), 336 (Fry).

Oxford did not see its education as narrowly academic; it saw college life as educational in itself—cultivating tolerance, articulateness, sociability and qualities of leadership and organization. It was an intimate world, for colleges' median size in 1920 was only 178.[32] The rooms of bachelor dons like Urquhart of Balliol or Garrod of Merton became salons for undergraduates in the evenings, and the cheapness of personal service proliferated lunch-parties, Sunday teas in North Oxford or weekends at hospitable literary homes nearby—with the Masefields and the Murrays at Boars Hill, Lord Berners at Faringdon, or the Morrells at Garsington. The nation's élite was never far away. No 'student culture' had yet emerged which defined itself through excluding the dons, who attended undergraduate club dinners, coached the rowing eight and cheered on the touchline. Dacre Balsdon was not unusual among living-in dons in being 'always conspicuously available'. Kenneth Bell, Balliol's history tutor, took ten or more students on a four- or five-hour walk through the villages round Oxford every Sunday in term, and in the 1920s John Bell, Queen's ancient history tutor, stood in the middle of the front quad and shouted 'drome' when he felt like taking (and paying for) junior members to the cinema. As for the Devon-born Bursar Champernowne of Keble, his renderings of dialect songs at College concerts evoked loud demands for an encore.[33]

Some dons came to know their pupils well, especially if (like Urquhart or Christopher Cox) they organized vacation reading parties at the famous chalet in the French Alps. Symbolic of donnish dedication was the habit of the otherwise unattractive C. T. Atkinson of Exeter, who, when unable to sleep in later life, whiled away the night hours recalling his pupils name by name, year by year and class by class as an alternative to running through the names of unit commanders in the expeditionary force of 1914.[34] Nor did the pupil lose contact on going down. Dedicated college men like Phelps of Oriel, Dundas of Christ Church or Kenneth Bell of Balliol might publish little, but their letters to pupils worldwide were abundant. So also were those of head porters as devoted as Balliol's Esra Hancock and Cyril King. It is from R. W. Raper's wide network of pupil contacts, valuable even to non-Trinity men, that the University's Appointments Committee descends. At a time when so many appointments were made through personal contact, wise employers consulted the tutors who knew their pupils so well.

College life offered strong incentives to achievement. Primed at school to compete in examinations and sport, undergraduates found competitiveness at Oxford carried to a higher power. Oxford was, in Kenneth Tynan's

[32] *Asquith Report*, appx vol., 325.
[33] *Exeter College Association Register 1969*, 11 (Balsdon); W. Crocker, *Travelling Back* (Melbourne 1981), 24 (Kenneth Bell); author's interview with Lord Franks, 6 July 1985 (John Bell); *OM* 9 June 1921, 385 (Champernowne).
[34] *Exeter College Association Register 1964*, 18 (in a fine obituary by Balsdon).

phrase, 'a kind of gymnasium for the personality'.[35] Launching out from success on the college's small stage, talent could manifest itself at the Oxford Union, in the Oxford University Dramatic Society, on the sports field or in *Isis*, which often speculated—most notably in its regular 'Isis Idol' feature—about who would turn out to be the successes of their generation. College and university prizes were significant in both monetary and career terms, and Harold Wilson's undergraduate academic successes caused Jesus College's big sconce to go round the hall on three separate occasions.[36] Famous old members peered down from portraits in hall and dons thirsted for news of Oxford men's achievements. Linking the University into a tight network of public schools and professions, the inter-war *Oxford Magazine* scrutinized honours lists and election results for Oxford men, and took a pride in their successes. C. K. Allen thought Dr Johnson's remark still true in 1932: 'the students are anxious to appear well to their tutors; the tutors are anxious to have their pupils appear well in the college; the colleges are anxious to have their students appear well in the University'.[37]

The tightness of the college community owed much to a shared educational and social background. Inter-war Oxford was overwhelmingly middle-class in its composition.[38] Oxford undergraduates were instantly recognizable by their gowns, accents and clothing: grey flannel trousers, tweed jacket, collar and tie for ordinary occasions, white flannels and blazer for sporting functions [plate 4.3]. Yet within this middle-class collegiate world there were many gradations of status and marked contrasts in income. The thrifty and industrious Harold Wilson, fresh from Wirral Grammar School, was careful to get breakfast and lunch for himself in his rooms when he arrived at Jesus College in 1934. Some colleges designated special areas for different income-levels, and scaled their room-charges accordingly. In Christ Church, for example, Tom, Canterbury and Peckwater quadrangles were respectable, but not the Meadow Buildings.

Public (or as we would now say 'independent') schools contributed four-fifths of the inter-war undergraduates of Lincoln who came from British schools. In Oxford as a whole, 62 per cent of the male non-graduate entrants in the academic year 1938/9 came from independent schools, 13 per cent from direct-grant, 19 per cent from maintained and 5 per cent from other schools in the United Kingdom.[39] Public-school dominance was more than numerical: it was cultural, political, athletic and social. Several colleges had long-standing links with particular public schools—New College with Winchester, Christ Church with Westminster. For many it was important

[35] Interview in *Isis* 2 Nov. 1973, 22.
[36] H. Wilson, *Memoirs: The Making of a Prime Minister 1916–64* (London 1986), 39.
[37] *Handbook* 1932, 123.
[38] See above, 52–6. For the social composition of a single college see Green, *Lincoln College*, 655.
[39] Ibid. 656; *Franks Report* ii. 47.

not simply to have attended a public school, but to have attended the right one. In 1920 a fifth of Christ Church's intake and a sixth of Magdalen's came from Eton alone.[40] Friendships carried forward from school to university, and former schoolfriends were frequently encountered, both casually and at special social functions organized in Oxford for the school's old boys. Boarding-school boys were particularly well prepared for college life, and fashions in clothing, culture and slang spread rapidly from the public schools to Oxford.

Excluded from Oxford's public houses, undergraduates did their drinking in college, where it was closely supervised, and was collectively taken to excess only on recognized occasions. College ales were specially brewed and highly prized, and in some colleges freshmen discovered their limits early when initiated in a 'freshers' blind'. Dining-clubs, often beerily rabelaisian, were occasions when American undergraduates noticed that the Englishman for once lost his disconcerting reserve. Wearing special facings on their dinner jackets, Brasenose's Phoenix Club or Merton's Myrmidons [plate 4.4] would line up for their annual photograph, study their printed menus, dine well and sally forth to terrify some unpopular contemporary. Celebrations would end with an easing of springs at some customary spot within the college—the mulberry tree in Trinity College's outer quad, Corpus's sundial or Exeter's chapel—and the Dean would have to be faced next morning. Less rabelaisian but equally exclusive were the Archery Club at St John's with its annual ladies' meeting in the Groves [plate 4.5] and the Wasps at Corpus, whose president at its twice-yearly dinner held a sweepstake on the number of leaves on the pineapple that was customarily served for dessert.[41]

Public-school and sporting men often ran both the junior common room (JCR) and the junior members' élite dining clubs. JCRs often began as peripatetic debating societies, but by the 1920s usually had their own rooms and articulated undergraduate opinion. Like SCRs they were self-funded, self-governing clubs within a club. Their procedure and ritual were almost masonic in their complexity, and JCR presidents, like captains of boats, sometimes thought it worth compiling confidential guidebooks for their successors. Some JCRs were quite substantial. New College's in 1920 had two dining rooms and two sitting rooms, could let out rooms, invested substantial sums, owned its own silver and employed five servants. Magdalen's, which in the mid–1930s took a pride in its cellar, gave President Gordon wine superior to the wine he himself dispensed.[42]

The JCR's overwhelmingly domestic concerns—food, drink, periodicals, sporting facilities and domestic comforts—kept horizons low. It was wary

[40] HUD.

[41] B. W. Robinson to author, 2 May 1989 (Wasps).

[42] Information about Gordon derived from author's tape-recorded interview with Lord Blake, 25 Aug. 1989.

of outsiders, including all who dreamed of central undergraduate representation, and viewed them as potentially threatening or intrusive. Earnest left-wing causes (shortened halls in aid of the unemployed, help for Basque child refugees) evoked a deflating humour or even indignation from those who viewed high-minded crusading as bad form within the club. The JCR's decidedly ribald humour betokened an all-male, public-school and very private world, whose battered furniture signified how frequently verbal combat degenerated into physical. Its minutes and suggestion-books are rich in *doubles entendres* and dwell at length upon facilities in the baths and lavatories that were then located more communally. JCR suggestion-books are all the same: overflowing with heavy sarcasm, facetious comment, wounded *amour propre*, paradings of misdirected scholarship and fierce pedantry—countered by world-weary JCR officials with crushing brevity and wit.

Through drinking and sport the public-school men periodically asserted their authority in semi-tribal style, culminating in bump-supper saturnalia [plate 4.7] with their mood of licensed excess. Sports club officers were among the freshman's first visitors, pressing him to 'do something for the college'. Refusal risked debagging or the breaking up of rooms, especially when offence was compounded by aesthetic, over-intellectual or left-wing tendencies. A. L. Rowse, at Christ Church in the 1920s, was one of many outsiders who barricaded himself against invaders, 'heart palpitating with fury and indignation as much as fear'. Inter-war bump suppers left a trail of burnt furniture, shattered lavatory seats and elevated chamber-pots behind them. Grammar-school boys could respond to this challenge in very different ways. Norman Brook, a future secretary to the cabinet, arrived at Wadham on a scholarship from Wolverhampton Grammar School in 1921. 'Very quick, Brook', Maurice Bowra recalled. 'Learned the tricks, learned the tricks. Came up with a front pocket stuffed full of pens. Soon disappeared inside. Learned the tricks.' Others nursed a lasting resentment. Larkin's novel *Jill*, set in St John's during the Second World War, shows hard-working grammar-school scholars huddling together in self-protection 'like members of some persecuted sect'.[43] Whitbread's caustic remarks in the novel frequently articulate their resentments, which often gained an outlet in the University's Labour Club; there at least they could find their roots and dream that time was on their side.

College harmony was threatened by nationality as well as by social status. Between the wars 6 per cent of junior members came from the Commonwealth and 5 per cent from elsewhere overseas.[44] Some colleges rejected

---

[43] A. L. Rowse, *A Cornishman at Oxford* (London 1965), 124; Bowra quoted in P. Hennessy, *Whitehall* (Fontana edn. 1990), 145; P. A. Larkin, *Jill* (London 1946), 94.
[44] UGC returns in HUD/S/UGC.

Indians or wanted them assigned a college of their own. The fear of sub-groups forming within the College was Balliol's reason for resisting pressure from the India Office to admit them in 1915.[45] Not for long, though: undergraduates of the 1930s frequently recall the response of cinema audiences, 'well rowed, Balliol!', when black men paddled a canoe in the film *Sanders of the River*. Yet President Gordon in 1934, warding off the possibility of an Indian applicant to Magdalen, told a Harrow schoolmaster in confidence that 'the College is very English in its atmosphere, and, with the best will in the world, seems unable to absorb anything quite so foreign'.[46] For many undergraduates, oriental students were 'black men'—a phrase not meant unkindly, but no doubt helping to push some Indians towards centring their social life on their university society, the Majlis.[47] Scots, Welsh and colonial undergraduates felt the same difficulty in a milder form, and were drawn towards presbyterian chapels, the Dafydd ap Gwilym Society or Rhodes House.

Given these sources of friction, how were colleges held together? Partly through insulation. Morning roll-calls and evening closing hours (9 p.m. in most colleges in the 1920s) insulated undergraduates from the daily timetable of the world outside. The exclusion of women carried insulation further. Women dons shielded their pupils from the men, who in the 1920s tended anyway to regard them as bluestockings, socially somewhat inferior and unsuitable as partners.[48] Among junior members in 1923/4, males outnumbered females by five to one; if only for that reason, female friends were often chosen from the sisters of Oxford male friends or were brought up from home for 'commem balls' or Eights Week [plate 4.7].[49] As Harold Macmillan put it, 'in my day, there were chaps' sisters and cousins in Eights Week, and then there were Gaiety Girls'. Lord Hugh Cecil (MP for Oxford University from 1910 to 1937) was not alone in welcoming the 'nervous intensity' of the all-male community: close male friendships had made Oxford and Cambridge 'the seed-beds of movements of great importance to the community'.[50] Male friendships were often intense enough to cast a golden glow over undergraduate fiction and recollection. In Beverley Nichols's *Patchwork*, male undergraduates regularly walk about arm-in-arm, address one another as 'my dear fellow', and engage in rather intense

[45] BCA minute-book of the Master and fellows, 16 Mar. 1915 (C. Bailey to C. Roberts, 11 Feb. 1915).

[46] MCA CS/33/20, fo 7706, Gordon to R. T. Hughes of Harrow, 10 Oct. 1934; cf CS/33/1, fo 40, Gordon to A. S. Johnson, 30 Aug. 1930 (carbon copies).

[47] On the use of the phrase 'black men' see E. A. St J. Waugh, *A Little Learning* (Harmondsworth 1984), 184.

[48] A. J. Ayer, *Part of My Life* (London 1977), 91.

[49] For the ratio in 1923/4 see *Franks Report* ii. 12.

[50] N. Fisher, *Harold Macmillan: A Biography* (London 1982), 227 (mistranscription corrected); Hatfield House, Lord Robert Cecil papers, CHE 54/17, Lord Hugh to Lady Robert Cecil, 4 Apr. 1918.

heart-to-heart talks. Homosexual conduct may have been fashionable in some Oxford circles in the 1920s, but far more prevalent was an unselfconscious affection between male friends that is readily misinterpreted by more knowing generations.

College paternalism was carried beyond college walls. The lodgings occupied by the two-fifths of undergraduates who lived out were still located in Oxford's more central streets, and so were easily treated as extensions of the college. Official registers of licensed lodging houses—sorted by locality—listed amenities and charges, and landladies supervised their tenants' conduct. Dances in the town were out of bounds and drinking could occur only in college or in private clubs registered with the proctors, who collaborated with deans in keeping undergraduates and prostitutes apart. Those in search of sexual intercourse went to London and returned on the late train from Paddington known as the 'Fornicator'.

Cross-cutting alignments also helped to unite the college. Two undergraduates from divergent background might be assigned a shared set of rooms, like Christopher Warner, the aristocratic playboy, and his admiring grammar-school room-mate John Kemp in Larkin's *Jill*. Wider informal groupings centred on the staircase, which lies at the heart of college life in Oxford novels.[51] Given that lunch and breakfast were then usually served in the undergraduate's rooms, it was natural for those sharing the same scout to eat together. Then there were the college's many more formal academic, sporting, cultural and political groups. Public-school men might dominate the sporting- and dining-clubs, but the agility, intellect, strength or enthusiasm of the shy and impoverished freshman from an obscure grammar school could lend him status. Sporting prowess did much to integrate Rhodes scholars; their age then caused them to stand out more because they took undergraduate courses and postgraduates were rare. Team games were lavishly catered for by Oxford's boathouses and sports grounds [figure 20.1]. The University's collegiate structure was nowhere more extravagant than here, yet the long-term result was a fine green necklace of open space close to the city's heart. In the elaborate and even scholarly 'captain's books', rowing lore was meticulously husbanded for posterity. In 1943 the Undergraduate Representative Council quickly rejected the idea that games should be organized around armed-service structures; college games, it thought, played 'an essential part in retaining the identities of the different colleges'.[52]

Yet friendship could also grow out of shared distaste for sport. For John Betjeman, who arrived at Magdalen in 1925, the division between hearty and aesthete 'overrode all social and college distinctions'. The pejorative term

[51] I. Carter, *Ancient Cultures of Conceit: British University Fiction in the Post-War Years* (London 1990), 93.
[52] OUA Undergraduate Representative Council minutes, 12 Oct. 1943.

1.1 Balliol freshmen, 1914

4.1 University College SCR, 1934

4.2 Worcester College senior members at dessert, *c.*1936

4.3 Worcester College undergraduates *c.*1937

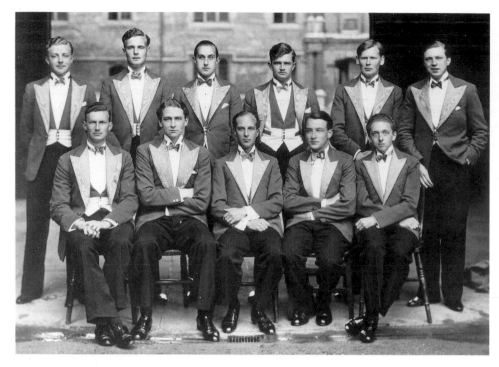

4.4   Merton College Myrmidons, 1935

4.5   St John's College Archery Club ladies' day, May 1928

'hearty' seems to date from the Edwardian period, but the aesthetes became particularly prominent in the early 1920s when Harold Acton imported from Eton his 'escape into the universe of art'.[53] The Anthony Blanches, self-conscious champions of art, set out to startle with their extravagant language, their cosmopolitan culture and fashions, and their affected or genuine homosexuality. Most undergraduates joined neither group, but few failed to join one of the college discussion-groups described in the University's *Handbook* as spending 'magical evenings . . . in the subdued, intimate light of college rooms'.[54] The mass media did not yet compete with recreational self-help, and supreme among educational influences was talk: casual at mealtimes, witty and stylized in college and university societies, ruminative and prolonged in late-night conversations with friends.

In the 1930s Exeter College's undergraduates, not then noted for cultivation, supported a Dialectical (that is, philosophical) Society, Church Society, Essay Club and Lankester (that is, scientific) Society. Keeping quite full minutes, which (together with modest quantities of drink) were often themselves part of the entertainment, these societies sometimes survived for decades. Most gathered to hear witty and not too serious literary papers that resembled the elegant but insubstantial confections often found in the undergraduate journalism of the time. Many of the speakers were famous. St John's Essay Society heard Gilbert Murray, R. G. Collingwood and (in 1929) the sexologist Norman Haire, whose three-hour and comprehensive exposition received 'intense and appreciative attention' from an audience that was 'the largest in the Society's records'. When war required undergraduates to migrate to nearby colleges in 1939, 'each band of exiles, coming into the strange territory of their receiving college, took with it its "Ark" and record, determined at all costs to preserve the ancient traditions, whether of a Junior Common Room or of a Debating Society, or of a Literary Club'.[55]

A more direct route to college unity was through corporate functions: the chapel service with its ecumenical mood and its subtle impact on literary sensibility and musical taste; the pressure to turn out on the touchline to back the college side; above all, the formal dinners in hall. Traditions were readily invented in Oxford, and there were many collegiate and public excuses for assembling the entire college. Exeter planned to celebrate the coronation in 1937 by gathering the whole College, including the servants, in the hall at 12.45 p.m. to drink the health of the King and Queen in champagne, and to install a wireless set in the JCR for the day.[56] The house

[53] B. Hillier, *Young Betjeman* (London 1988), 131; H. Acton, *Memoirs of an Aesthete* (London 1984), 82. For the term 'hearty' see E. M. C. Mackenzie, *My Life and Times* (10 vols London 1963–71) iii (1900–7), 130.

[54] *Handbook* 1932, 110.

[55] SJM H.6.21, Essay Society minute-book, 24 Nov. 1929; Ralph Harry, writing home in Dec. 1939 (xerox copy sent to author in 1989).

[56] ECA A.I.14, order book, fo 291, 22 Apr. 1937.

system, adopted by early nineteenth-century public schools in partial imitation of Oxford and Cambridge colleges, became itself an influence on inter-war collegiate loyalties. There were college scarves, sporting colours, college and club ties. With practical jokes and studied insults, undergraduates at adjacent colleges pursued ancient vendettas, Balliol in its cups hurling its unintelligible Gordouli song over the wall to Trinity, only to encounter Trinity's exhortation to 'bring out your black men'. T. F. Higham drew on twelve years' experience as Dean of Trinity in 1932 to compile a 31-page typescript on 'The Balliol–Trinity frontier'. College loyalties even travelled to Hull in 1926, when strike-breaking undergraduate tram-drivers flew ribbons from their adopted trams in the college colours and engaged in mildly competitive bumpings.[57]

The ultimate reinforcement for college unity was discipline. Paradoxically, it owed much to divisions within the community—divisions of a hierarchical and formal kind. The senior members dined (as now) on a dais; the junior members were often seated hierarchically by year and mode of entry. They were accustomed to strict discipline both at home and at school, and as undergraduates they did not then reach the age of majority until their second or third years. However lax about study, the rules were stringent on conduct. 'Battels which may be considered excessive', say St John's *College Regulations* in 1925, 'are brought to the notice of the President.' Crises of collegiate authority were quite recent memories—in late-Victorian Christ Church and Edwardian New College, for instance—and a firm hand was often required. The dons' hold on junior members was in some ways precarious. Self-funded and socially secure, the junior member by no means always needed formal academic qualifications, and did not necessarily feel much' respect for the dons. The close match between the numbers of applicants and places made it difficult for dons to argue that a delinquent undergraduate was keeping out someone more deserving. Furthermore, colleges depended heavily on the goodwill of old members, whose donations they required.

Some inter-war dons rested their authority on a sarcasm that would not now be acceptable; for most, a delicate balance between familiarity and distance sufficed. They risked their dignity by attending bump suppers in order to monitor behaviour, and in easy-going social exchange they sometimes needed to administer sharp reminders that toleration had its limits. After a memorable bump supper in 1928, Corpus undergraduates were formally warned against hurling bread pellets at high table: the dons thought it 'insulting to be struck, and undignified to attempt to deflect' the missile. The authorities needed to cultivate that subtle understanding of

[57] C. Hopkins and B. Ward-Perkins, 'The Trinity/Balliol Feud', *Trinity College Report* 1989–90, 45–66. P. S. Havens, 'The General Strike of 1926: a reminiscence', *University College Record* 1979, 271–2.

human nature which enables the blind eye occasionally to be turned and discipline thereby to acquire a useful flexibility. The safer routes for climbing in were well known and unobtrusively made safer, punishments were inflicted with a rather elaborate politeness, and each side knew how far it could discreetly go. Oppressive as inter-war college rules might seem today, they were mild indeed by comparison with the boarding-school regulations the undergraduate had left behind. The need to climb in late at night was less an affront to one's dignity than an opportunity for asserting a masculine daring which could be aired at breakfast next morning. As one proctor put it in 1945, 'evading regulations was one of the joys of undergraduate life'.[58] Besides, the dons were not the only rule-makers. The undergraduate educated at a boarding school was no stranger to the initiation ritual, and elaborate self-enforced sconcing rules monitored conduct, dress and topics of low-table dinner-time conversation.

Important aspects of college life were changing between the wars. The opposite sex gradually drew closer. From the early 1920s tea-shops provided what Farnell as Vice-Chancellor denounced as 'unnecessary and unmanly food', and the women's colleges began organizing closely supervised dances. By 1924 'flirtatious and undignified osculation' was being observed in the Radcliffe Camera, and when Barbara Pym (who led a full social life at St Hilda's from 1931 to 1934) heard in 1946 that H. H. E. Craster was writing a history of the Bodleian Library, she told a close friend that she 'could give him plenty of material from the human point of view'.[59] Lectures were another meeting place, and in the Labour Club during the 1930s the presence of the opposite sex added an extra dimension to the excitements that political and international issues could supply. By 1937 motor cars, gramophones, radio and the cinema were so unravelling the tightness of the collegiate community that they provoked an anxious correspondence in the *Times*.[60] Undergraduates were receiving more and more visitors and going off more often at weekends—with bus trips into the country, golf at Frilford and tea at Thame.

Class attitudes too were changing. Many commoners received some type of subsidy, and half the undergraduates at Oxford in the 1930s received aid from one source or another—mainly from Local Education Authorities and school exhibitions.[61] Degree-courses were more likely to be completed. Undergraduates were being more freely admitted to college libraries. Yet by 1939 these trends had not gone very far. Socialists had told the Asquith

[58] OUA Undergraduate Representative Council minutes, 30 Jan. 1946. The Corpus episode comes from the author's tape-recorded interview with Sir Isaiah Berlin, 19 Oct. 1992.

[59] Farnell, *Oxonian Looks Back*, 295; *Isis* 28 May 1924, 22; B. Pym, *A Very Private Eye*, ed. H. Holt and H. Pym (London 1985), 252.

[60] Launched by 'BA' in *Times* 30 July 1937, 15, with leader ibid. 10 Aug. 1937, 11.

[61] *OM* 20 Oct. 1938, 40.

Commission that working-class undergraduates—admitted on merit—would work harder, yet few were admitted between the wars, and the cheaper non-collegiate option so much favoured by the Commission was less frequently taken than had been hoped.[62] Nor has modern Oxford ever witnessed 'the hungry look of the young student who has not had a warm meal for days', so often seen in Europe, 'the man who toils in a workshop all day and sits over his books at night'.[63]

The Oxford college between the wars was far more than a set of buildings: it was a group of people scattered throughout the world. The successes of Magdalen men were closely scanned in President Warren's remarkable scrapbooks of press clippings. 'The Colleges are second families and second homes to their sons', he told the Asquith Commission.[64] The old member was encouraged to leave his name 'on the books', boost college revenue by qualifying for his degree of MA without examination, marry in the college chapel, enter his male children for admission, return occasionally for a gaudy and remember the college in his will. From 1927 the Balliol Society tightened the link with old members, set up an educational trust to help educate their children if orphaned, and inspired imitation elsewhere. At gaudies old members would clamour for a popular don to speak; his characteristic performance, laced with humour and reminiscence, would seldom disappoint. There were also gatherings by subject, such as the annual dinners held by Balliol's Younger Society for Balliol lawyers of all ages. Heads of house made a point of interesting themselves in college sport. Prevented from attending the trial eights in 1930, President Gordon hastened to apologize to Magdalen's ageing rowing stalwart R. P. P. Rowe, who had been training the College's oarsmen in his spare time, for fear that 'you might have put down my absence to indifference'. 'I am in fact very keenly interested in the struggle you are making to recover Magdalen's proficiency on the water.'[65]

James Lees-Milne says that his three years at Magdalen in the late 1920s were 'a complete waste of time, a blank in my life over which I do not now care to linger'. Yet many of his contemporaries treasured the memory of what Evelyn Waugh described as the 'cloistral hush which gave our laughter its resonance, and carried it still, joyously, over the intervening clamour'.[66] For those up before the mid-1920s, there was much about Oxford to delight

---

[62] For the socialist views put to the Commission, see for example Asquith Commission, written evidence, Bodl. MS top. Oxon. b. 104, fo 183 (Ruskin College) and b. 106, fo 12 (R. H. Tawney); cf oral evidence, ibid. b. 109, fos 258, 282 (H. Dalton, 2 July 1920).

[63] The quotation is from A. Schlepegrell's penetrating Anglo-German comparison, 'A German student in Oxford', *University College Record* 1934, 25.

[64] Asquith Commission, written evidence, Bodl. MS top. Oxon. b. 104, fo 200.

[65] MCA CS/33/2, fo 538, carbon copy of Gordon's letter to Rowe dated 24 Nov. 1930.

[66] J. Lees-Milne, *Another Self* (London 1970), 92; E. A. St J. Waugh, *Brideshead Revisited: The Sacred and Profane Memories of Captain Charles Ryder* (London 1945, Harmondsworth 1986 edn), 23.

the ear as well as the eye, and their recollections often dwell upon sounds—the trumpet which summoned Queen's men to dinner, the bells announcing mealtimes and chapel services, Latin graces precisely recalled across half a century. Add to these the memories of the roaring fires in one's room on returning from football, Mr Cross's 'unforgettable' anchovy toast at Jesus, and above all the smallness of the college's architectural scale, the beauty of its buildings, the closeness of its relationships. Such memories gave Oxford men a taste for club-like structures wherever they went in later life. Through A. D. Lindsay and G. D. H. Cole, the collegiate ideal perhaps even contributed something to the political theorist's repertoire of utopias.[67]

This elaborate collegiate structure rested upon the college servants, many of whom worked at the college for longer than the fellows, and for much longer than the junior members. Some even left their names behind them: on Gunner's at Magdalen and Bunce's Hall at Corpus. It was their acute memory that ensured recognition for the long-departed old member on his return, their tact which lubricated Oxford's complex administrative structure, their patience which coped with Oxford's eccentric and often crusty bachelors. Until the advent of motor manufacturing they were an élite in Oxford with their own friendly societies. Their own sporting functions even led to the award of their own blues. Their contacts with a donnish lifestyle—so much more affluent than their own—inspired admiration rather than envy, and many took a pride in their University connection and adopted scholarly hobbies.

Inter-war efforts to unionize college servants never came to much, if only because the servants valued flexibility in their conditions of employment and because their working world was human in scale and subdivided into small departments—each alert to the pay, workload and pretensions of the other, each with its own small hierarchy. A comprehensive survey of college servants' pay and conditions in 1927 placed in the salaried category only the head clerk, head cook, head porter, SCR butler, scouts and junior porter. They were ranked by salary in that order; all the rest—buttery men, clerks, under-cooks, porters, gardeners, waiters, cleaners, charwomen and handymen—were paid weekly or even nightly.[68] Dons were paid far more than any college servant, and in 1927 absorbed 37 per cent of the colleges' net external revenue, whereas the servants took up only 22 per cent. The Second World War so transformed this picture that, despite reduced personal service, the equivalent figures in 1948 were 41 per cent and 46 per cent.[69]

[67] See C. Hill's memoir of Lindsay in E. T. Williams and H. M. Parker (eds), *The Dictionary of National Biography 1951–1960* (London 1971), 643.

[68] CCCA domestic bursars' committee's confidential 'return of wages etc. Michaelmas term, 1927'. I am most grateful to Mr Colin Holmes of Corpus Christi College for drawing this valuable document to my attention.

[69] HCP 205 (1950), 247–8.

The lodge porter was the first college servant the freshman encountered: a formidable person, well able to deliver a rebuke when needed. Balliol's long-serving Cyril King had 'a natural and unforced courtesy and dignity—for no man ever took a liberty with him twice—an unfailing and sensitive tact, and that maturity of judgement which when allied with knowledge becomes true wisdom'. The lodge porter remembers everyone, anticipates many things, sees everything, chooses to ignore some things and acts as 'the centre of the whole nervous system of a College'.[70] The freshman's luggage was taken up to his rooms by his scout, who directed a boy working under him and presided over what now seems an odd combination of luxury and austerity: 'gracious living but with chamber pots'.[71] The freshman found himself with a sitting room and bedroom—bed-sitters were common only in Keble and the women's colleges—and could easily entertain guests to meals. The college's hotel service readily met his individual requirements. For his two years in college he found his clothes laid out, shoes cleaned, beds made, letters delivered, fires lit, fuel and meals brought up, tables laid, plates cleared away, washing water provided, brass polished, grates blacked and chamber-pots emptied. He paid his scout regular tips and something extra for special duties: laying on a lunch party, putting in order a room that had been broken up, cleaning away last night's vomit.

Choosing from a menu, the junior member ordered breakfast and lunch up to his rooms. The kitchen staff had to cater for frequent private parties, culminating in 'the changeless lunch of Eights Week with its salmon mayonnaise and cold chicken' in lunch baskets, complemented by tea on the college barge and dinner-parties in private rooms.[72] The larger JCRs also provided meals; in New College's in 1920, both breakfast and lunch could be ordered up from the kitchens. Inter-war kitchen staff did much of the preparing and preserving of food that is now done commercially, and at Magdalen in the long vacations of the 1930s the kitchen staff harvested and preserved the produce of the College's garden, so that 'by the start of Michaelmas term the far larder was a picture with its shelves covered with large Kilner jars of fruits and vegetables'.[73]

College servants providing personal service on this scale saw themselves as contributing towards the undergraduate's education, and advised him on college customs and social conduct. Fictional servants such as Venner, the JCR steward at St Mary's who seemed to Michael Fane 'the ideal personification of his own most cherished opinions', were drawn from life;

---

[70] *Balliol College Annual Record* 1955, 24; J. P. V. D. B[alsdon], 'Jack Waldron', *Exeter Coll. Assoc. Register* 1966, 8.

[71] R. Massey, *When I Was Young* (Toronto 1976), 226, describing Balliol in 1919–20.

[72] Quotation from E. M. C. Mackenzie, *Sinister Street* (Harmondsworth 1983), 521.

[73] Magdalen College, MS 640, William Jarvis, 'Recollections of the second-chef 1932–1978' [1978], p. 2.

in the 1930s Mr Cross of Corpus before hall, and Mr Mallet of Worcester after hall, presided over little social circles confined to undergraduates whom they approved as 'gentlemen'.[74] Yet here too change was beginning well before 1939. A complex and silent domestic revolution originated in inter-war Oxford and has continued since. Vacation conferences converted college servants into employees paid throughout the year; mechanization and standardized, centralized eating lightened their workload but lowered the undergraduate's living standards and diluted his relationship with his scout. Competition for labour from the Cowley car factory made scouts' boys scarce by the 1930s, but at the same time the advent of electricity and piped water to staircases removed the water-carrying, the gaslights, the fire-grates and the frequent clearings away after meals. Many of these changes come together in Beveridge's memoranda of the late 1930s, which drew heavily on the experience of Merton, Magdalen and St John's. University College's new deal—by installing electric fires and centralizing breakfast—cleared the way for drastic staff cuts, and hence for cuts in charges.

Yet each Oxford college retained its individuality. Contrasts between the colleges—architectural, social and intellectual—lay at the heart of Oxford life. Most obviously, they diverged in date of foundation and in wealth, whether measured in gross terms, in relation to undergraduate numbers or in relation to necessary outgoings—though no Oxford college held the sway of Trinity in Cambridge. Between the wars, contrasts in collegiate wealth profoundly affected the recruitment and living standards of junior members and the salary and perquisites of their seniors. Contrasts in lifestyle were wider between fellows of a poor and a rich college than between university lecturers with and without a fellowship, and an analysis of lodging provision in 1925 shows that it was the poorer colleges (especially St Edmund Hall) which required their junior members to live out of college for the longest period.[75]

The so-called Norrington table of the colleges' performance in examina-tions was not published until 1964, but it can be projected back to the three six-year periods 1921–6, 1927–32 and 1933–8. Balliol was supreme in the first two periods, but was ousted by Queen's (like Magdalen and Wadham, a rising college in the 1930s) in the third. Other high-flying colleges throughout were New College, Merton, Jesus, Somerville, Corpus and St John's. Towards the bottom came the poorer colleges—Pembroke, Trinity, St Hilda's, St Edmund Hall—and the two non-collegiate societies, St Catherine's and St Anne's. The span between top and bottom college widened significantly between the second and third period, but median

[74] Mackenzie, *Sinister Street*, 475; B. W. Robinson to author, 20 July 1989 (Cross); F. B. Hunt to author, 24 June 1989 (Mallet).

[75] OUA LHD/RP/5; I owe this reference to Dr. Greenstein. For college contrasts in wealth, see below, 656–7.

college performance hardly changed, and Balliol's undergraduate reputation made it the prime inter-war exporter of talent to fellowships elsewhere, contributing 59 of the 405 fellows of men's Oxford colleges in 1937.[76]

Regional contrasts in recruitment between colleges were probably declining between the wars, but remained significant, most obviously in Jesus College with its Welsh connection, but also in Queen's, whose Hastings scholarships nourished important links with grammar schools in the north of England. Architectural design—Worcester's loggia and lake, St John's groves—produced marked contrasts in colleges' patterns of social life, just as architectural merit deeply influenced their social standing. The three colleges considered suitable for the Prince of Wales during his residence of 1912—Christ Church, New College and Magdalen—were all architecturally outstanding.[77] Christ Church, with its superb Peckwater and Tom quadrangles, was the special magnet for the landed and titled. By contrast, the architecturally less distinguished but adjacent Pembroke College recruited 'mainly sons of poor professional men', as did the architecturally notorious Keble, with its predilection for the sons of clergymen.[78] Yet the inter-war revolution in road transport was slowly altering the impact made by buildings—diminishing the attraction of colleges on the High, rendering areas in Magdalen unusable for lectures, and destroying privacy in parts of Balliol.[79] In 1934 much publicity attended University College's seismographic tests, which revealed traffic-damage to its older buildings. Changes in colleges' social ranking could be deliberate. Magdalen in the 1930s, for example, chose to join the intelligentsia. Privately discouraging the idea of an undergraduate Austrian prince in 1930, its new President pointed out that 'my colleagues here are at the moment, I suspect, a little tired and shy of princes, archdukes and the like'.[80]

Colleges competed vigorously for sporting talent, most notably Brasenose and Trinity. Sporting success (like embracing an unfashionable academic subject) could get a college known, and to be head of the river was 'a kind of symbol or index of the general prestige of a college'.[81] College loyalty was also exploited by the politically ambitious. Michael Stewart's career in the Oxford Union owed much to 'the tendency of St. John's men to vote solidly . . . for every St. John's name on the ballot paper'. Balliol's head-start, however, gave it no less than a third of the Union's officers between 1919 and 1939—far surpassing the 12 per cent of its nearest rival, Christ Church. Of the 168 British cabinet ministers between 1905 and 1940, 53 were educated at

[76] HUD; Curthoys and Heimann, 'Academic community', 6.
[77] On the choice of college see W. Hayter, *Spooner: A Biography* (London 1977), 120.
[78] Asquith Commission, oral evidence, Bodl. MS top. Oxon. b. 109, fo 482; cf fo 480.
[79] MCA CS/33/2, fo 486, Gordon to Registrar, 14 Nov. 1930 (carbon copy); BCA minutebook of the Master and fellows, 8 Dec. 1930.
[80] MCA CS/33/1, fo 150, Gordon to C. H. C. Pirie-Gordon, 26 Sept. 1930 (carbon copy).
[81] C. K. Allen in *Handbook* 1932, 119.

Oxford, of whom 14 came from Balliol and 9 from Christ Church. Of the successful parliamentary candidates from Oxford colleges at the general election of 1929, however, 17 came from a college (Ruskin) not formally part of the University at all, whereas its nearest rivals (Balliol and New College) each produced only 13.[82] Within a college, the political divide was readily crossed. Presenting portraits of his political opponents Asquith and Loreburn to Balliol in 1912, Curzon said that 'the first thing that strikes me about this function is its purely domestic character. We are all of us past or present Balliol men.' Foreigners, he said, might be surprised at such an occasion, 'but it is our way in this country'.[83]

These collegiate contrasts should not be exaggerated. Inter-war Oxford colleges had already begun their long-term convergence in subject-balance, academic performance, social standing and sporting attainment. They were also supplanting rival structures. The Asquith Commission had wanted to cut costs by expanding Oxford's non-collegiate intake, which in 1919 accounted for only 7.7 per cent of male and female junior members. It pointed out that non-collegiate residence was older than any college, and remained customary in most universities.[84] It was exemplified in Oxford by the Society of Oxford Home-Students (an association of home-based female undergraduates) and by the non-collegiate male undergraduates managed by a delegacy and administered by a censor. Yet by 1920 the male non-collegiates had already appropriated the name of St Catherine for their clubs; they lacked only facilities for eating together. The Asquith Commission opposed converting them into a college because this would only generate pressure for yet another non-collegiate body. But in 1931 Convocation renamed the male non-collegiates the St Catherine's Society and in 1936 the Chancellor opened its new buildings in St Aldate's. Likewise with the Home-Students, who gradually colonized an area of North Oxford in the 1930s and gained incorporation as St Anne's College in 1952. Other colleges adapted to the standard pattern. The women's colleges moved decisively towards it in the 1920s,[85] and in 1937 St Edmund Hall moved further towards independence from Queen's. Together with Keble, it also moved towards the customary Oxford relationship between head of house and fellows.

Between the wars, Oxford's collegiate structure therefore prevailed over its critics and adapted itself to meet new requirements. Containment of the critics began with the Asquith Commission itself, whose chairman believed

[82] M. Stewart, *Life and Labour: An Autobiography* (London 1980), 24; information on Union officers from C. Hollis, *The Oxford Union* (London 1965), 260–5; information on cabinet ministers provided by Dr Curthoys; for Ruskin see *OM* 20 June 1929, 770–1.

[83] *Balliol Record* 1912, 13.

[84] *Asquith Report*, 156–7 and appx vol., 183.

[85] See below, 351–2.

strongly in the college system. It saw 'the strength of the two Universities' as being 'very largely due to the existence of a number of independent Colleges acting in wholesome competition with one another'.[86] Its modest proposals for reform were further toned down by collegiate pressure on its successor, the Statutory Commission. Containment succeeded for reasons transcending the merely local. These include the international reaction after 1918 against German patterns of academic organization and the rapid post-war run-down in reforming enthusiasm in the nation as a whole. Oxford dimensions to the explanation include the inherent attractions of the small self-governing group, especially within a University where such groups were already well established and enjoyed prestige. The colleges' defenders were tightly linked, their enemies were dispersed. In truth, the colleges between the wars controlled Oxford's administrative structure, and there was no critic powerful enough in the country to dislodge them. Still, the challenges already presenting themselves in 1919 did not go away. More and more of the University's talent and resources between the wars were being drawn towards the non-collegiate complex that was growing up in the science area; nor were the arts and social studies untouched by the scientists' professionalism. It remained to be seen whether the colleges could hold their ground as successfully in later decades as they did between the wars.

[86] *Asquith Report*, 200.

5

The Arts and Social Studies, 1914–1939

ROBERT CURRIE

On the eve of the First World War, teaching and research in the arts and social studies at Oxford still presented a largely Victorian picture. New subjects such as anthropology, geography, economics and political science now had their postgraduate diplomas but remained virtually unavailable to candidates for honours degrees. Such degrees had yet to take much notice of the nineteenth century, let alone the twentieth. Despite Napoleon's place in the modern history syllabus, and Balzac's in that of modern languages, these schools continued to lay most emphasis on personalities, events and ideas which would have seemed fairly remote in time even to the twentieth-century students' great-grandfathers. Meanwhile Roman and medieval law still figured prominently in jurisprudence; Old and Middle English were as important to English language and literature as Sanskrit, Assyrian and Old Persian were to oriental studies; theology was almost as devoted to the Old and New Testaments as literae humaniores was to classical antiquity.[1]

The balance of teaching and research in the arts and social studies had not changed much since 1900; nor had recent years seen any very striking structural changes, at least in quantitative terms. Undergraduates still greatly outnumbered postgraduates. During the academic year 1913/14 639 men received the degree of bachelor of arts and 15 were made bachelor of music. Thirteen, already graduates, became bachelors of law. Excluding honorary degrees, a mere 31 men received ordinary or higher research degrees. This total included 8 new doctors of divinity, 3 doctors of letters and 3 of music, 7 bachelors of divinity and 10 bachelors of letters (like the bachelorship of civil law, none of these degrees was open to undergraduates). Undergraduates were now almost exclusively preoccupied with honours degrees. During 1913/14 about 100 men qualified for honours degrees in mathematics and natural sciences; 530 men and women qualified for honours in arts and social studies; only 90 or so qualified (mainly in arts and social studies) for pass degrees. In fact the popularity of pass degrees was steadily declining by 1914, and continued to decline thereafter: by the mid-1920s only about 7 per

[1] Details of courses are drawn from the University's *Examination Statutes*.

cent of male and 4 per cent of female students were working for a pass
degree. In 1913/14 the distribution of students among subjects revealed a
distinct pattern. Of the men newly eligible for honours degrees in arts and
social studies 40 per cent had taken their final schools either in literae
humaniores (31 per cent) or sacred theology (9 per cent). Another 36 per
cent had qualified in modern history, and 17 per cent in jurisprudence. These
four schools therefore produced 93 per cent of the total male honours
graduates in arts and social studies, the rest qualifying in oriental studies or
modern languages or English. The 70 women students who, though
successful in the schools, were as yet still ineligible for degrees, presented a
rather different picture: 42 per cent had qualified in modern history, 36 per
cent in English, 16 per cent in modern languages, and only 6 per cent in
literae humaniores.[2]

The fact that in summer 1914 only 3 per cent of finalists in literae
humaniores were women did nothing to detract from the high status of the
classics, which can be said to have constituted the organizing principle of
pre-war Oxford. Indeed students of classics provided the intellectual élite of
the University in 1914 and for many years afterwards. C. K. Allen calculated
that during the period from 1906 to 1937 scholars and exhibitioners
provided 32 per cent of all finalists, but 70 per cent of first-class finalists. In
1914 73 per cent of all college scholarships and exhibitions were expressly
reserved for classicists.[3]

But whether or not applicants to Oxford aspired to the academic heights,
in 1914 they still had to have some classics even to gain admission to the
University. Unless a musician, any European or American seeking to read
for a first degree in Oxford had to pass responsions, or 'smalls', in various
subjects, including Latin and Greek grammar, Latin prose composition and
unseen translation from both languages. Latin was not very widely taught in
British schools, while not more than 5 per cent of boys in secondary schools
in Britain took Greek to the stage of a first school examination.[4]

Even after responsions, Latin and Greek still occupied the attention of the
non-musical European or American student seeking an Oxford first degree
in arts and social studies. All students had to pass the examination in holy
scripture, or 'divvers', which required them to show, among other things,
their acquaintance either with two gospels in Greek or (if their religion
forbade them that) the original text of a Greek philosopher. The next step
for such students could be the final pass groups in French and German (an
option open in practice only to the very best linguists who were already
certain that they wished to take the final honour school in modern

---

[2] Details of class-lists are drawn from the *Calendar*. I owe these and subsequent statistics on
pass degrees to Mark Curthoys and Mark Pottle.
[3] *OM* 4 Nov. 1937, 126; *Gazette* 4 Nov. 1914, 136–7.
[4] *OM* 10 Nov. 1921, 66–7.

languages) or the preliminary examination in jurisprudence (which included Latin unseens and 235 chapters of Gaius) or some other part of the first public examination, of which 'divvers' was in any event an essential part. Classical scholars and exhibitioners were naturally directed to classical honour moderations, the most searching examination in Latin and Greek in any university in the world. Students who did not attempt any of the foregoing (in other words a very large number of would-be historians and linguists) were entered for pass moderations, that part of the first public examination which was, strictly speaking, designed 'for those who do not seek honours'. Pass moderations was an examination in either logic or mathematics; Latin and Greek books and unseens; and Latin prose composition. It was only after success in pass moderations, which occupied between a tenth and a third of a first-degree course in Oxford, that even the student who did not seek an honours degree could at last stop work on the ancient languages.[5]

This state of affairs may seem odd in hindsight but was all of a piece with the University's public image. The *Oxford University Handbook* for 1914—published by the University Press and, though not actually authorized by the University, most certainly not disowned by it—declared that 'The Final Classical School, or the School of Literae Humaniores, is the oldest and is admitted on all hands the premier School in dignity and importance. It includes the greatest proportion of the ablest students, it covers the widest area of studies, it makes probably the severest demands, both on examiner and candidate, and it carries the most coveted distinction.' But though Oxford might thus still seem to scorn the Greekless, the University was in fact divided: this remarkable passage concealed the true extent not merely of non-classicists' scepticism about the classicists' claims, but the classicists' own doubts about their future.[6]

From 1900 onward the Headmasters' Conference fought an increasingly bitter battle over compulsory Greek against a well organized Greek Defence Committee which was only finally defeated in Congregation in March 1920. Well before 1914, Oxford philosophers were seeking alternative occupations for the day when compulsory Greek did vanish from responsions and the supply of candidates for the philosophy papers in literae humaniores consequently diminished—as Thomas Case, the President of Corpus, predicted. Philosophers had certain advantages when seeking new work in Oxford. Like ancient historians and classical linguists, they had long experience of working with other disciplines. But by contrast with ancient historians and classical linguists, philosophers were unhampered by the need for pupils who knew Latin or Greek. Furthermore, though their partners in literae humaniores might dispute this, philosophy was more prestigious than

[5] Details of courses are drawn from the *Examination Statutes*.
[6] *Handbook* 1914, 135.

either Latin or Greek. Philosophers were therefore uniquely well placed to create new joint schools to supplement or even replace literae humaniores, Oxford's existing joint school in arts or social studies.

The philosophers' understanding of both their problems and their opportunities was indicated by the appearance in 1909 of an anonymous pamphlet, *Wanted! A New School at Oxford*. The author, perhaps J. A. Smith, Waynflete Professor of Moral and Metaphysical Philosophy, briskly cast doubt on the worth of the Greek Defence Committee's efforts by stating that 'even the slight knowledge of Greek hitherto necessary' to study philosophy in literae humaniores would 'in all probability' soon cease to be required of entrants to the University. The author of the pamphlet therefore proposed a Greek-free alternative, 'a modern-side Greats, based on Philosophy', but including other subjects such as economics, a subject which seemed to him 'to stand in particular need of that criticism of assumptions which Philosophy induces', and politics, another subject 'which might benefit by a critical treatment'. With these considerations in mind, the anonymous author set out a scheme of papers which in spread, though not in balance, closely approximated to the scheme of papers eventually adopted for the new school of philosophy, politics and economics in 1920. In the end that school was created by an alliance of philosophers and historians. But despite the anonymous author's sarcasm, he probably intended his pamphlet to appeal not so much to historians as to Oxford's economists, who were then facing a reduced demand for their services since the University had recently decided to dilute the diploma in economics with an element of political science particularly intended to accommodate trade-union students at Ruskin College.[7]

As it happened, the demand for economists did not diminish. But the philosophers continued to worry about the future of their discipline when Greek ceased to be compulsory. In June 1919 they persuaded the literae humaniores board to appoint a committee to pursue the possibility of an honour school of modern philosophy with either natural science or modern history. The committee was very active during the summer of 1919 and on 26 November 1919 the literae humaniores board was in a position to ask Hebdomadal Council to legislate for an 'Honour School of Modern Humanities'. This should cover 'the study of the foundations of nineteenth-century and present-day civilization in its three branches of philosophy, science and political, economic and social development'. Neither literature nor art seemed to belong to civilization; despite the mention of 'science', the proposal for a philosophy and natural sciences school had been hived off into a separate project which was to end in acrimony in 1923; what was left

---

[7] *Wanted! A New School at Oxford* (Oxford 1909), 4–6, 8; *Morning Post* 28 Feb. 1910; A. D. Wilson, *Gilbert Murray OM 1866–1957* (Oxford 1987), 151–3; N. Chester, *Economics, Politics and Social Studies in Oxford, 1900–85* (Basingstoke and London 1986), 14, 20–1.

made 'Modern Humanities' look strikingly like the 'new school' of the 1909 pamphlet, modified so as to give much greater scope for history and to reduce economics to little more than an option.[8]

In February Council also received a letter from Langford Price, the Reader in Economic History, and secretary to the Committee for Economics and Political Science, which managed the diploma in those subjects. Price wanted Council to consider 'a Final Honour School in Economics and Politics', which Ernest Barker and others had just invented and which his committee had not yet had time to approve, but which he apparently hoped might dissuade Council from any hasty decision in favour of 'Modern Humanities'. On 8 March 1920 Council appointed a joint committee to investigate the possibilities of both a school of modern humanities and one in economics and politics.[9]

The historians on the joint committee were in a strong position. They could choose between a course favoured by the many and powerful philosophers, which contained some history, a lot of philosophy but very little economics, and a course favoured by the few and weak economists, which contained a lot of history and a lot of economics but no philosophy at all. The outcome was fairly predictable. The joint committee urged the Committee for Economics and Political Science to refine its ideas and, when that committee failed to make any concession to philosophy, persuaded Council to send the economics and politics scheme to the General Board which, in June 1920, simply abandoned it. Meanwhile the joint committee revised the modern humanities scheme in favour of the historians by dividing what had originally been a single compulsory paper on social, economic and political history into two compulsory papers covering the same ground; and in favour of the economists by making political economy a compulsory paper. On 14 June 1920 Council decided to send the further amended school of modern humanities to Congregation under the name of the 'Honour School of Philosophy, Politics and Economics'. Price and Henry Penson, economics lecturer at Worcester, conducted an unsuccessful campaign for more economics in the new course, and the junior proctor, H. J. Paton, rejected claims that the new school could compare with literae humaniores. On the contrary, he argued, this so-called 'modern Greats' would be 'a soft option for the weaker man'. Yet no one attempted to amend Council's draft statute, which passed Convocation *nemine contradicente* on 30 November 1920.[10]

One obvious charge against philosophy, politics and economics was that, as the *Oxford Magazine* complained, it 'tried to do two quite incompatible

[8] OUA LH/M/1/3, pp. 140, 143, 145; LH/R/1/2, pp. 74, 78; MH/M/1/3, p. 155; *OM* 15 Feb. 1923, 212, 228, 242.

[9] HCP 115 (1920), pp. lxxxi, 83–4.

[10] Chester, 30–8; *OM* 5 Nov. 1920, 56; HCP 116 (1920), pp. lxxiv, xcv, 89–90, 143–5.

things—to provide a School of Modern Humanities and to give opportunities for the development of the new school of Political Economy'.[11]
What the new school lacked, as a school of modern humanities, was a
literary element. That might have been supplied by the honour school of
English language and literature, the development of which had been much
influenced by literae humaniores, and above all by the philological side of
classical studies. In 1914 the English school consisted of nine or ten papers
arranged in a 'language' or philological (overwhelmingly a Germanic-
philological) course A, with three compulsory literary papers, only one of
which covered the period since Shakespeare, and a literary course B, with
three language papers, and two compulsory literary papers on the period
since Shakespeare.[12]

The philosophers' search for a new school passed English by. But the
faculty was not immune from the pressures of the outside world and in
1916/17, when English virtually ceased to attract male candidates, a new
syllabus was devised for examination from 1919. By dint of turning the
existing two courses into three, and adding a paper to each course, philology
was preserved while a new ten- or eleven-paper course, coming up to 1900
and still including only three language papers, was constructed for devotees
of modern literature. In this 'third' course there were four and a half or five
and a half post-Shakespeare literary papers. But this proved to be merely a
temporary expedient. In 1922 another new syllabus was introduced. This
reverted to nine- or ten-paper courses. On the one hand, the philological
options were increased and the new 'second' course (the equivalent of the
'third' course of 1919) was restricted to three and a half or four and a half
post-Shakespeare literary papers. On the other hand, for the first time all
courses offered the option of nineteenth-century literature, as well as a new
list of optional special subjects, including Greek literary criticism, French
classical drama and Italian influences on sixteenth-century English literature.
Since the more philological 'first' and 'third' courses were attempted by only
5 or 10 per cent of candidates, the school remained in practice certainly more
modern, and perhaps more humane, than it had been in 1914.[13]

Yet this venture apart, little interest was shown in alternative versions of
'Modern Humanities' incorporating literary as well as social studies. On the
contrary, the form and content of the philosophy, politics and economics
(PPE) course dominated discussion of educational policy in Oxford during
the first half of the 1920s. When the law board decided, in 1921, to revise the
preliminary examination in jurisprudence, W. M. Geldart persuaded his
colleagues to add a specifically 'PPE' element to the syllabus by introducing a

[11] OM 29 Oct. 1920, 389.
[12] L. R. Farnell, An Oxonian Looks Back (London 1934), 271; Examination Statutes 1917,
395–7.
[13] OUA ML/M/1/1, pp. 45, 54; ML/R/1/1, p. 68; Examination Statutes 1922, 136–8.

paper based on Joseph Barthélemy's *Le Gouvernement de la France*. According to F. H. Lawson, the paper did not 'remain popular' among Geldart's colleagues, possibly because three years after its introduction J. B. Morris, then an undergraduate reading Spanish at Queen's, demonstrated his business acumen by publishing an 'authorized translation' of the text. Nevertheless for most of the 1920s French political institutions remained an integral part of Oxford jurisprudence.[14]

Ernest Barker had less success in his efforts to add 'the working of modern political institutions' to the existing paper in political science in the final honour school of modern history. In February 1921 a committee recommended this innovation to the board, but was ignored. As far as 'politics' was concerned, historians continued to confine themselves to the study of the texts stipulated for the political science paper (then works of Aristotle, Hobbes, Maine and Mill) and to the (optional) special subject on representative government.[15]

Barker left for London, where he was to spend some years as Principal of King's College. Oxford continued to adapt to the new, and often constraining, circumstances of the 1920s, and this process of adaptation involved some striking changes of image. The pre-war *Oxford University Handbook* had been more or less an apologia for classics. By 1932, when the first post-war edition of the *Handbook* belatedly appeared, the University was less interested in the relative merits of 'classical' and 'modern' subjects, and the possibilities of providing a 'humane' education without Greek, and much more interested in the problems raised by political unrest in Europe and Asia and high unemployment in the United Kingdom. It was now admitted on all sides that, with or without Greek, teaching in the arts and social studies could provide a 'general' (if not 'humane') education, but it was felt rather strongly that these subjects must be taught and studied in a thorough, businesslike way and must at least point students in the broad direction of a definite profession or 'calling' which they might follow in later life, whether or not 'a period of special training' was needed 'after completion of the degree course'.[16]

The new *Handbook*'s chapter on 'The Schools', written by P. E. Matheson, formerly classics tutor at New College, did not rehearse the old high claims for literae humaniores. Matheson merely described it as 'the natural continuation and completion of the course followed by students trained on the lines of classical study'. The only mark of special respect shown to these students (who formed but 18 per cent of men and 8 per cent

[14] F. H. Lawson, *The Oxford Law School 1850–1960* (Oxford 1968), 132, 136; J. H. J. B. Barthélemy, *Le Gouvernement de la France* (Paris 1919), trans. J. B. Morris as Joseph-Barthélemy, *The Government of France* (London 1924).

[15] OUA MH/M/1/3, p. 210; MH/R/1/3, p. 2.

[16] *Handbook* 1932, 283 ff.

of women honours finalists in 1932) was the tacit assumption that they need not be told what particular calling suited them. Historians were advised that the school of modern history provided either 'general education' or a training for 'those who intend seriously to pursue historical studies hereafter'. Would-be students of PPE were told that the school offered 'the intellectual discipline of Philosophy' and also a 'training in History and Economics' that prepared people 'for business, the Civil Service, or public life'. The modern history and the PPE schools provided respectively 29 and 12 per cent of men and 27 and 10 per cent of women honours finalists in 1932. Each of the other schools was described by Matheson in terms both of its educational content and the specific career opportunities it afforded: in 'the legal profession', 'the Christian ministry', 'administrative work in the East', 'the teaching profession', 'commerce or manufacture' and so on. In 1932 jurisprudence accounted for 18 per cent, theology for 5 per cent, and all language schools together for 17 per cent of men honours finalists; only 2 per cent of women honours finalists read law, while 31 per cent read English and 23 per cent read modern languages. By comparison with 1914, men had moved out of literae humaniores, theology and modern history into English, modern languages and PPE; women had also moved into PPE and, so far as languages were concerned, they had moved from English to European languages. The pass degree continued to dwindle in all subjects. The 7 per cent of male and 5 per cent of female first degree students studying for pass degrees in the mid-1920s declined to 3 and 1 per cent respectively in 1938.[17]

Literae humaniores exerted significantly less influence on this new Oxford, and the school concentrated on thoughtfully cultivating its own image. Perhaps that image was changing. In 1921 Lewis Farnell recommended classicists to drop 'accents' and take up archaeology, and art as well as archaeology figured more prominently in literae humaniores during the 1920s and 1930s. Yet the careers of young scholars such as Humfrey Payne and Alan Blakeway who, in 1936, both died in post while serving as Director of the British School of Archaeology at Athens, were perhaps imbued as much by a neo-Arnoldian or Gilbert Murray 'Greek spirit' as by dedication to archaeological technique. Both art and archaeology gained a slightly larger place in literae humaniores during the 1920s and 1930s, but the school continued to produce generalists rather than specialists, and the major change to the syllabus in these decades was the abolition in 1935 of the compulsory study of the oratory of Cicero and Demosthenes in classical honour moderations, and the replacement of this essentially political material with a much broader 'anthology' of Greek and Latin literature which was to survive unpruned well into the atomic age.[18]

[17] *Handbook* 1932, 152–62.
[18] *OM* 1 Dec. 1921, 123; 4 June 1936, 660; 22 Oct. 1936, 50; *Examination Statutes* 1935, 37 ff.

This was by no means the most striking change in teaching in the arts and social studies in Oxford between the wars, a period which saw the creation of not one but two new honours schools: PPE in 1920, geography a decade later. Before 1914 the University had offered a diploma in geography following an examination in general, regional, physical, human and historical geography, and surveying. The course thus united the natural sciences, social studies and the arts, and might perhaps have developed as a school of 'Modern Humanities'. However A. J. Herbertson, the Reader in Geography, wanted to establish geography as 'an honour school in natural science', and therefore ignored this possibility, for what it was worth. But the natural scientists did not welcome his ideas while, in 1918, the Treasury committee on the higher civil-service examinations declined to make geography a compulsory subject because it was 'too severe and technical'. Yet the committee reduced the marks allotted to it as an optional subject because the universities had failed to raise it to the status of an honours-degree subject. A dozen British universities then did so, staffing their departments with holders of the Oxford diploma among others. The movement for an Oxford final honour school continued during these years but still appealed neither to the natural scientists nor to the advocates of 'Modern Humanities'. In 1928 jobs in departments of geography were becoming scarcer: the Committee for Geography renewed its plea for an honours degree, emphasizing the advantage Oxford geographers would enjoy in the labour market if they held a degree rather than a diploma. The University responded by founding a chair and creating the new school, which covered more or less the same ground as the diploma. The school grew very fast: first examined in 1933, by 1939 it was attracting 4 per cent of both men and women honours finalists.[19]

Changes also occurred in jurisprudence. By 1927 the *Oxford Magazine* was arguing that the law preliminary was too short (the examination was in fact only two-thirds the length of pass moderations), while the lawyers themselves were embarrassed to find history tutors in the women's colleges putting their pupils into the law preliminary as a quick and easy alternative to the history preliminary. In 1929 the lawyers therefore replaced the two-term preliminary with a three-term moderations. Constitutional history became constitutional law and its history; Barthélemy and unseens went out; criminal law and the history of the judicial system came in. 'In this way', complained R. B. McCallum, 'the narrowest of our honour schools was allowed to become just a little bit narrower still'. The final examination in the school also became at least formally more difficult, because the three-term moderations allowed less time for the second public examination.[20]

[19] C. Firth, *The Oxford School of Geography* (Oxford 1918); OUA SG/M/1/2–4; MH/R/1/6, p. 106.
[20] *OM* 10 Nov. 1927, 96; 23 Oct. 1930, 52; Lawson, *Oxford Law School*, 138–40.

Yet another structural change during these years was the introduction of a residential qualification for the degree of bachelor of music. In 1911 the Professor of Music, Sir Walter Parratt, the Dean of Christ Church, T. B. Strong, and others secured various changes in the statute for this degree. Mere membership of the University, which musicians could obtain through the Greek-free preliminary examination for students in music, had formerly entitled undergraduates to attempt the examinations for the bachelorship of music. From 1911 no one could do so unless he or she had either been admitted to the degree of bachelor of arts or both passed a language group in the final pass school and pursued, either within the University or at an approved institution, a course of musical study consisting of not less than two yearly courses. The new statute enabled a candidate for the degree to prepare for it externally or in Oxford, either exclusively of all other studies or alongside work for the degree of BA in some subject other than music. By the mid-1920s the external option had ceased to satisfy the University's musicians. In 1926/7 only four candidates were allowed this option. On 19 February 1927 Parratt's successor, Sir Hugh Allen, convinced the music board that besides passing the examinations for the bachelorship of music, candidates for that degree should be required to have passed responsions (which were now of course completely Greekless) and either to have been admitted to the degree of BA or to have 'pursued within the University a course of musical study extending over a period of not less than two years', and in any event to have kept six terms' residence. The new scheme preserved the increasingly anachronistic option of preparing for the BA and the BMus simultaneously, eliminated the external option and abandoned the principle that a language group was part of a training in music. Despite a campaign to save the external option, Allen's proposals were accepted by the University, and the new statute operated from 1927.[21]

The residential requirement for music represented a long step towards the establishment of an honour school of music but did little to increase the number of candidates for the degree of bachelor of music in the 1930s. A quantitatively more significant change occurred in modern languages. The board of that faculty had firmly resisted the Prime Minister's Committee on the Position of Modern Languages in the Educational System of Great Britain which, in its report of April 1918, had advocated the integration of languages into a comprehensive 'modern studies' syllabus. The board had good reason not to change its ways, for immediately after the war the future of the school seemed assured. In 1914 there had been 18 men and 11 women honours finalists; in 1921 the honour school and the shortened honours course for ex-servicemen together attracted 59 men and 15 women finalists.

[21] Bodl. GA Oxon. b. 137, p. 155; GA Oxon. b. 140; *Examination Statutes* 1910, 179; 1911, 179; 1927, 193; *Gazette* 5 May 1911, 577; 10 May 1911, 713; 15 June 1927, 672; 29 June 1927, 732; OUA Mus/M/1/1, pp. 92–3; Mus/R/1/1, pp. 63, 65.

However the overall total of 74 finalists was not to be surpassed for another six years and in 1923 the honour school was reduced to 22 men and 18 women.[22]

By 1925 both the size and the standards of the school were subjects of controversy. Delegates of the Parents' Association and the Headmasters' Conference met college representatives at Wadham on 30 January 1926. The parents and the headmasters complained that Oxford was not doing enough for languages; the colleges argued that the candidates coming forward from the schools were not good enough to justify expanding the provision for modern languages; to this the headmasters replied that the best candidates were going to Cambridge, where they could offer two languages in their final examination. This strengthened the hand of H. G. Fiedler, Taylorian Professor of the German Language and Literature, who had long been advocating the introduction of a two-language course as an alternative to the existing one-language course in the final honour school. On 5 March 1926 Fiedler asked the board for a committee on the requirements of the school, and on 27 October 1926 the board resolved to ask the General Board for the change he wanted. The two-language option operated from 1927 onward.[23]

By 1933 modern languages was a larger school than English. The shape of the school changed somewhat as it expanded. In 1926 78 per cent of the 58 finalists offered French, 14 per cent offered German, and the remaining 8 per cent offered Italian, Russian or Spanish. In 1936, when 55 per cent of the 134 classified finalists chose the two-language option, 96 per cent of them offered French, 40 per cent offered German, and 17 per cent offered Italian, Russian or Spanish, with or without another language. The greater flexibility of the course probably appealed to those who planned a career in schoolteaching. The numbers of such candidates gave Cesare Foligno, Serena Professor of Italian Studies, constant cause for complaint. 'The School of Modern Languages is often looked upon as a training school for teachers in modern languages', he wrote in the *Oxford Magazine* in May 1930. Yet, he claimed, the school ought to be regarded as 'one of the humanistic schools'.[24]

Among honour schools in arts and social studies the growth in modern languages between 1923 and 1939 (6.5 per cent per annum) was second only to that of PPE (9.8 per cent per annum). The latter school was decreasingly committed to the 'humanistic' ideals admired by Foligno and by the philosophers who had contributed so much to its creation. By 1925 the PPE examiners were already reporting on the heterogeneity of the school and, in particular, the division between philosophy and the other two branches. From 1926 the philosophers themselves sharpened this division by

---

[22] C. Firth, *Modern Languages at Oxford 1724–1929* (London 1929), 95–6.

[23] *OM* 4 Feb. 1926, 249; 11 Feb. 1926, 290; OUA ML/M/1/1, pp. 197, 207–9; ML/R/1/3, p. 130.

[24] *OM* 15 May 1930, 705–8. Details of finalists are taken from the *Calendar*.

eliminating 'political theory' from the subject-matter of the moral and political philosophy paper. In fact they seemed happy to let the rest of the school go its own way, which was increasingly the way of the economists. The economists' main concern was to increase the element of economic, and especially mathematical economic, theory. From 1926 to 1932 they offered an optional paper in advanced economic theory, including 'modern statistical methods'. This paper partly paralleled the compulsory paper in political economy, which offered a rather old-fashioned and (in some economists' eyes) inferior training in the subject.[25]

On 29 November 1929 A. D. Lindsay, then chairman of the board of studies for philosophy, politics and economics, secured the appointment of a committee to revise the statute and regulations for PPE. This gave the school the opportunity to sharpen its image, or rather the images of its three separate branches. The philosophers renamed the 'history of philosophy from Descartes' paper: it became the 'general philosophy from Descartes' paper. The politicians converted the compulsory social and economic history paper into an alternative to political history 1871–1914, and expanded the politics section of the political and economic organization paper into a political institutions paper. The economists made even more sweeping changes. The further subject in advanced economic theory was replaced by statistical methods, political economy was replaced by economic theory, and an economic organization paper was created from the economics section of political and economic organization. These changes came into effect in 1933, by which time both the new board of the faculty of social studies and the economics sub-faculty were a year old. A separate politics sub-faculty was not created till 1934; the philosophy sub-faculty remained under the literae humaniores board.[26]

During the later 1930s the philosophers remained relatively inactive in PPE; the politicians wavered between the new methodology of political institutions and the document-based approach of the school of modern history, in which almost all of them had been undergraduates; the economists continued the single-minded development of the mathematical side of their subject. In May 1938 they won the board's support for their campaign to add to pass moderations a paper in mathematics preparatory to economics, and in November of that year they created a new further subject in economic theory, including 'mathematical methods'. To avoid confusion, the compulsory paper they had been happy to term 'economic theory' only five years earlier was renamed 'principles of economics'. This taste for innovation expressed their domination of the school, in which they now felt at home. Ideas of a separate economics honour school gained no support

[25] OUA SS/R/1/1, pp. 14–15.
[26] OUA SS/M/1/2, pp. 14–22, 28; SS/R/1/1, pp. 95, 123.

and, heterogeneous as the three branches remained, they were at least occasionally of one mind. In 1937, for instance, they agreed to abolish the school's language requirements, up till then perhaps the most conspicuous survival of the 'School of Modern Humanities' in which philosophy, politics and economics had its origins.[27]

The almost irresistible rise of economics in PPE coincided with a scarcely less resistible rise of philology in English. In 1926 the school finally established its institutional identity by the creation of an English faculty board separate from the modern languages board. When the new board first met, on 5 November, it saw its main task as eradicating what the examiners in the 1926 final honour school called 'an old trouble of ours', namely, 'a widespread and wilful neglect of linguistic study'. Board members thought the school now needed a separate English first public examination, which would preserve the classical training needed for pass moderations, but also provide a course in Old English. The General Board, which disliked the principle as well as the cost of a multiplicity of separate first public examinations, persuaded the English board to produce not a full-scale separate examination but a single paper in Old English which was first set in the enlarged pass moderations of 1930.[28]

Partly because of this innovation, the examiners in the 1933 final honour school felt that 'the general standard of performance in Old English has risen remarkably'. But by that date the final honour school itself had been revised once more. J. R. R. Tolkien appears to have promoted this change. He regarded the philological element in the school as 'a not unworthy offspring of classical discipline'. Though the primarily philological first and third course of 1922 still attracted, at the very most, 10 per cent of English honours finalists, these courses represented what in Tolkien's eyes was the most rigorous part of the school: and the rigorous, he held, need not conflict with the humane. 'The pretence that no "English" curriculum is humane which does not include Shakespeare must naturally be abandoned', he wrote in the *Oxford Magazine* in May 1930.[29]

Two months earlier he had presented the English board with a scheme for two new, overwhelmingly philological and exclusively Germanic final honour courses, in one of which Shakespeare was indeed optional. In the battle to push the school back in time he found something of an ally in H. F. B. Brett-Smith, the Reader in English Literature, who wished to 'avoid the compulsory inclusion of literature after 1800 in the work of all candidates taking the Modern Literature course'. On 22 May 1931 they got more or less

[27] Chester, *Economics, Politics and Social Studies*, 45; OUA MH/R/1/11, p. 58; SS/M/1/2, pp. 121, 131.

[28] *OM* 23 Oct. 1930, 52–3; OUA E/M/1/1, pp. 11, 18; E/R/1/1, pp. 2, 84; *Examination Statutes* 1930, 45–50.

[29] *OM* 29 May 1930, 778–81.

what they wanted. At the price of adding Old French philology to his proposals, Tolkien obtained a medieval philological course covering the period up to Chaucer. There was also to be a modern philological course up to Milton. Post-Milton literature was reserved for the literary course, now renumbered as course three: in this course the literature of the period from 1830 to 1900 was optional. These new courses were first examined in 1933.[30]

Between 1922 and 1928 the number of honours finalists in English had risen by 49 per cent; between 1933 and 1939, under the new syllabus, the number fell by 10 per cent. Meanwhile the proportion of candidates taking the literary course rose towards 95 per cent of the total. But the changes in the syllabus pleased the faculty. The examiners in the 1937 final honour school reported that 'some of the better answers would not have been out of place in a journal of philological research'.[31] But the first public examination still failed to please. The enlarged pass moderations of 1930 had included not only the paper on Old English but also a paper on English history and literature 1603–88. In 1934 the board decided to delete the historical section of this paper, a change which came into force in 1935. However that did not satisfy those who wanted a separate English first public examination, and in October 1937 the board appointed a committee which rapidly produced a scheme for a three-term, five-paper English moderations, covering Old English set texts, Shakespeare set plays, Aristotle's *Poetics* and a Greek or Latin book. The board, disliking the Shakespeare, reduced the scheme to a two-term examination on Sweet's *Anglo-Saxon Reader*, Old English grammar, the *Poetics*, a Greek or Latin book and Greek or Latin unseens. As this might seem an odd way to start an English course, the board noted on 13 June 1938 that 'the general idea underlying our scheme is that some study of the Classics is the best basis for the Honour School'. The proposal also rested on the idea that the honour school was above all philological. The General Board questioned neither of these ideas but inquired whether the proposal was substantial enough to warrant upheaving the recently introduced enlarged pass moderations and creating a separate English first public examination: the point had not been clarified between the two boards by the time war broke out.[32]

Even greater difficulties beset the historians when they attempted to reconstruct their separate first public examination in the late 1930s. These were years of some confusion in modern history. While many tutors turned their attention to PPE, for which they taught the politics papers, the faculty repeatedly avoided any possibility of competition with the new school. Having in 1921 rejected Barker's scheme for incorporating political

[30] OUA E/M/1/1, p. 53; E/R/1/2, p. 136; E/R/1/3, pp. 41, 43; E/R/1/4, p. 47.
[31] OUA E/R/1/6, p. 31.
[32] *Examination Statutes* 1935, 43 ff; OUA E/M/1/1, pp. 150, 157; E/R/1/6, pp. 31, 50, 66, 86, 148.

institutions, the historians abandoned any claim on recent economics eight years later. Henceforth economic theory in modern history was to mean Adam Smith, Mun's *England's Treasure in Forraign Trade* and the *Libelle of Englysche Policye*. The movement to distinguish modern history from PPE reached a climax in the years 1931–3 when, under the guidance of the Regius Professor, F. M. Powicke, the faculty replaced the papers in British 'political' and 'constitutional' history with papers in English history 'as a whole'. A proposal for a paper 'on the study of comparative institutions' aroused 'great difference of opinion', as Powicke put it, and was abandoned: the long-established political science paper was to remain a documentary study of the history of political theory. The revised syllabus was finally adopted on 26 January 1933, when the board resolved to examine the new papers from 1936 onward.[33]

The 1936 syllabus finalized modern history's response to PPE. History was to be understood as a unity to which the study of all times, however remote, equally belonged. Historical method was identified as the study of documents, to which historians were to bring empathy rather than sociology, linguistic rather than mathematical skills. This approach threatened to open up between the 'serious' historian and the run-of-the-mill undergraduate a gap quite as wide and deep as that between mathematical and non-mathematical economists and assumed a knowledge of foreign and dead languages which, as Charles Oman reminded the board in a severe memorandum dated 19 December 1931, few candidates for the modern history final honour school possessed.[34] But even before the new syllabus had been examined in the final honour school, some members of the faculty began pressing for changes in the first public examination. Since 1930 the history preliminary had been merged in the enlarged pass moderations. That change had been expected to achieve two somewhat inconsistent objectives. Weaker candidates would have to do more work for language papers marked at a higher standard by classicists rather than historians, yet stronger candidates could pass the first public examination in one term rather than two, thus obtaining an extra term for schools by taking pass moderations papers thought to require less work than papers set in the modern history preliminary. By the mid-1930s historians had decided that their finalists were as bad at languages as ever, and feared that the reputation of the honour school was beginning to suffer from its association with a pass-standard first public examination.[35]

In June 1936 the modern history board therefore asked the General Board for a separate honours-standard first public examination. The General

[33] OUA MH/M/1/4, pp. 96, 107, 204, 211, 217, 221, 225–7, 229, 233; MH/R/1/5, p. 70; MH/R/1/8, pp. 34, 47, 59, 64, 78, 87, 156.

[34] OUA MH/R/1/8, p. 58.

[35] *OM* 25 May 1933, 698–9; 29 Oct. 1936, 85–6.

Board's dislike of multiplying first public examinations led it to incorporate the historians' proposals in its own scheme for a new general moderations. On 21 October 1937 the modern history board rejected this scheme because the 'normal avenue' to the history final honour school ought to be under the historians' 'complete control'. However, as the General Board was already well aware, historians could not agree how to exercise such control. Some wished to preserve the option of a one-term preliminary for high-flyers; but this the modern history board abandoned on 3 March 1938, apparently hoping thereby to coax the General Board into accepting some less controversial form of separate history first public examination. *En route* to such a new examination, to be taken after two or possibly three terms, the modern history board unfortunately upset some faculty members by deciding to abandon political economy and others by deciding to make medieval history optional in the history moderations, as they were renamed on 9 June 1938. The project thus split the faculty yet again, and scraped through Congregation by 46 votes to 43 on 24 January 1939; it was rejected in the same body by 60 votes to 57 on 28 February, following the circulation two days earlier of a critical flysheet bearing the names of a distinguished cross-section of Oxford historians, from Lord Elton, now a supernumerary fellow of Queen's, to the new medieval history tutor at Lady Margaret Hall, Naomi Hurnard.[36]

By 1939 the development of higher degrees had significantly modified the virtually exclusive concentration on first-degree teaching which had shaped the intellectual life of Oxford before 1914. But this development had been neither rapid nor systematic. McCallum was not far from the truth when, in 1936, he described the University's provision for postgraduate work as 'an unorganised excrescence on our elaborate tutorial and lecturing system'.[37] So far as arts and social studies were concerned, this provision had begun in 1895 when the degree of bachelor of letters (BLitt) was created. By 1914 the degree was open to persons who had either passed the examinations for the degree of bachelor of arts or could otherwise prove to have had 'a good general education', and was being awarded for a suitable dissertation on a subject approved by a board and investigated during 'a course of special study or research'. A board approving a subject might place the candidate under one or more persons 'styled Supervisors', whose duty would be 'to direct and superintend the work' of the candidate but not to give 'systematic instruction'. In 1913/14 8 persons received the degree of BLitt; this number rose to 32 in 1923/4, and to 46 in 1938/9. In any one year the number of persons working for the degree was at least three times the number of those

[36] OUA MH/M/1/5, pp. 79, 88, 91–2, 101–22; MH/R/1/11, pp. 58, 74, 120, 130; MH/R/1/12, pp. 5, 34, 109; Bodl. GA Oxon. b. 141, p. 335; *Gazette* 25 Jan. 1939, 381; 1 Mar. 1939, 464.
[37] *OM* 30 Apr. 1936, 514.

receiving it. About half the candidates' supervisors were professors or readers, about half were college tutors. Between the wars almost half the successful candidates for the BLitt were non-collegiate or women students.[38]

In 1900 the BLitt had been supplemented by the degree of doctor of letters (DLitt) which could be awarded to persons of thirty-four terms' standing if bachelors of letters or thirty-nine terms' if only masters of arts, provided they could produce evidence of 'fitness for the degree' in the form of 'published papers or books, containing an original contribution to the advancement of learning'. Very few persons had received even an honorary DLitt by 1916 when the Reverend E. M. Walker, Senior Tutor of Queen's, proposed, as the *Oxford Magazine* put it, that the University 'should divert the stream' of American aspirants to the German universities' degree of *philosophiae doctor* by opening the degree of DLitt to persons offering a suitable dissertation nine terms after graduation. Apart from a successful move led by Sidney Ball, philosophy tutor at St John's, to distinguish the proposed arrangement from both the DLitt and the German PhD by adopting the English title 'doctor of philosophy' (DPhil), the scheme met with little opposition. There were two routes to the degree. An Oxford graduate or holder of an approved degree from another university might, with the permission of a faculty board, supplicate for the degree of DPhil provided he had been admitted to the status of advanced student by a newly created Committee for Advanced Studies, had completed under the direction and superintendence of a supervisor (whose terms of appointment would be exactly those of a BLitt supervisor) a course of study extending over not less than six terms, and had embodied the results of such study in a suitable published dissertation. This route to the DPhil, which made the degree an accelerated, supervised, lower-status alternative to the DLitt, found few takers and was abolished in 1925. By far the more popular route, following lines along which the degree later developed, was to become an advanced student and offer an unpublished dissertation after five terms if an Oxford BA or if entitled to a BLitt, or after eight terms if a graduate of another university. The candidate who chose this route had to have kept terms as a member of some college, hall or society in the usual way; he had to be publicly examined '*viva voce* in the subject of his dissertation' and both viva voce and in writing 'in matters relevant to the subject of his research'; and his work had both to constitute 'an original contribution to knowledge set forth in such manner as to be fit for publication *in extenso*' and to be 'of a sufficient standard of merit to qualify him for the Degree of Doctor of Philosophy'.[39]

[38] *Examination Statutes* 1915, 196 ff; statistics from *Calendar*.
[39] *Examination Statutes* 1917, 214 ff; 1925, 220 ff; Bodl. GA Oxon. c. 309; *OM* 26 Jan. 1917, 109, 112, 121–2; 2 Feb. 1917, 126, 137; 16 Feb. 1917, 158; 23 Feb. 1917, 168.

By the late 1930s about 100 persons a year held the status of advanced student, and about 20 persons a year received the degree of DPhil, in arts and social studies. Many of these were non-collegiate or women students, and about two-thirds of them were supervised by professors or readers rather than college tutors. The numbers of advanced students, like the numbers of those working for the BLitt, grew more slowly in the 1920s than in the 1930s. The distribution of postgraduate students by faculty was similar to that of undergraduates, though by comparison with the honour schools, English was over- and modern languages and law heavily under-represented among postgraduates. This distribution was at least partly affected by the significant number of Americans among Oxford's postgraduate students.[40]

The absence of systematic instruction for postgraduate students reflected both the colleges' preoccupation with undergraduates and the widespread assumption that a first degree (or at least an Oxford first degree) equipped its holder with all the formal training he needed to make as original a contribution to knowledge as he would ever be capable of making. This assumption was not universal. In 1923/4 a group of professors tried to revise the University's provision for postgraduate work in three ways. They wanted the provision of supervisors for BLitt students to be mandatory (as was the case for advanced students); and they wanted such supervisors to be either professors or readers in an appropriate subject or persons approved by such professors or readers. They also wanted the degree of BLitt to be granted for successful completion of 'a course of special study preparatory to research' which would become 'the necessary avenue to the doctorate'. They gained some concessions. First, a new status of 'Probationer-Student for the Degree of Bachelor of Letters' was created; this would be the necessary avenue to the BLitt; and the probationer would be required both to have a supervisor and 'diligently to pursue any course of study preparatory to research recommended by his Supervisor, and in particular to attend such courses of instruction and classes as his Supervisor may advise' (if any). Secondly, faculty boards were empowered to make transfer to full BLitt studentship conditional on a written test (though the written examination for the DPhil now became optional). Thirdly, the Committee for Advanced Studies began to call the BLitt course 'an apprenticeship in research' and the DPhil course '*advanced* research'; and the BLitt was practically subordinated to the DPhil by granting faculty boards power to permit failed candidates for the latter to supplicate for the former.[41]

Only the English board devised a written test for probationer BLitt students; a course of compulsory classes in such subjects as bibliography and

40 *OM* 30 Apr. 1936, 512–14.
41 OUA LH/R/1/3, pp. 66, 98, 122; MH/R/1/3, pp. 140, 142; MH/R/1/4, pp. 64, 75, 90; *Examination Statutes* 1925, 225; 1926, 208 ff.

Elizabethan handwriting was introduced to prepare probationers for this test. Some members of other boards, notably modern history, wanted to emulate this system. Their discontent led in the early 1930s to renewed demands for changes in the organization of research degrees. But the General Board concluded in 1935 that, while some faculty boards now wanted the BLitt to become 'the *normal* avenue' to the DPhil, most were against the former degree becoming 'an indispensable preliminary' to the latter. Further inquiries indicated that in any event most boards wished to make their own regulations for research degrees, pursuant to existing statute, rather than to promote new statutes, which might meet opposition from other boards. The modern history board therefore persevered with the policy of leaving unaltered or even liberalizing requirements for the DPhil while tightening requirements for the BLitt. During 1937/8 the board decided that a probationer BLitt student in history must, for two terms from admission, spend three hours a week in term-time attending either lectures or classes given under the heading 'Advanced History Teaching' or other lectures approved by his supervisor, and must satisfy the board that this requirement had been fulfilled. The new regulation was introduced in October 1938 but remained controversial. It was difficult to make arrangements which would guide and assist weaker candidates for research degrees while not wasting the time of stronger candidates, some of whom were of course very strong indeed. Perhaps the main problem lay not in want of rules but in the lack of supervision. Powicke wrote rather optimistically in 1932 that 'the supervisor is in the position of a tutor, responsible to the University'. But that was to mistake the position of a tutor and to confuse the university with the colleges.[42]

The tutor's role was shaped by powerful influences which affected all teaching in arts and social studies in Oxford between 1914 and 1939. By 1914 the University had been engaged for seven centuries in a system of teaching which had always included two elements: information (philology, philosophy, theology, law and so on) and a technique for handling information (rhetoric and dialectic). For many generations before the First World War, this teaching had been organized in colleges; by the outbreak of war the University had conducted 113 years of classified examination of those who had been so taught in colleges.

Despite Matthew Arnold's doubts about the virtues of 'uniting the keeping a boarding-house with teaching' and 'cramming and racing little boys for competitive examinations', in 1914 very many fellows of colleges had long been engaged in this way of life.[43] The exigencies of their

---

[42] *Examination Statutes* 1930, 218; 1938, 254; OUA MH/M/1/5, pp. 45, 174; MH/R/1/10, p. 35; *Handbook* 1932, 171, 174.

[43] Matthew Arnold, *Culture and Anarchy* (London 1869), ed. J. D. Wilson (Cambridge 1960), 9–10.

occupations reinforced their loyalty to Greek and Latin. As Robert Birley wrote in 1931, 'the great advantage of the study of Classics was that it provided a system of Education which could be applied to both the clever and the stupid'. Birley and Arnold chiefly had Eton in mind, but their words had much wider application. For Eton and the other leading English schools were linked with Oxford in a highly coherent educational process, based on Greek and Latin, in which grammar and translation forced even the dullest and most recalcitrant scholar to engage at least in what Birley called a 'preliminary wrestling'. From such exercises the better and more dedicated students could progress to 'books'—that is classical texts or portions thereof—and thence to the writing of more or less sophisticated essays or dissertations on literary, historical or philosophical problems.[44] These exercises were admirably suited to prepare candidates for just the sort of 'classification' and 'graduation' by competitive examination which the University provided. Classics thus provided a core-technique for first-degree teaching in arts and social studies.

But by 1914 the attack on classics had already forced Oxford to seek supplementary or alternative methods of teaching. These might have involved mathematics or mathematically based subjects. Birley thought economics could 'provide exactly that quality of hard thinking over a subject, which does not appear simple at first sight', such as had been provided by Greek and Latin. But even in 1939 economics was neither sufficiently acceptable nor widely enough available in Oxford to allow Birley's solution to be adopted. In any event the University had by then developed a new core-technique which, in one form or another, was sustaining every non-classical first-degree course in arts and social studies. This technique combined a certain amount of non-classical language work, exhaustive reading in primary or secondary sources and frequent and regular essay-writing. The quantity and quality of language work varied according to the nature of the course, but the reading was always greater than the student could complete in the time allotted for the essay. In this way the University produced a modern system of education which could indeed 'be applied to both the clever and the stupid'. The latter could show merit by learning and summarizing their material; the former could show extra merit by analysing and assessing theirs. A. L. Rowse complained that he found 'the immense amount of reading for the History School—much of it laboured and dull and ill-written—a fearful burden'; but this burden had to be endured even by the most brilliant intellects if they were to be classified alongside students whose best hope of showing merit in the final honour schools was a demonstration of having at least 'done the reading'.[45]

[44] *OM* 28 May 1931, 751–2.
[45] A. L. Rowse, *A Cornishman at Oxford* (London 1965), 53.

In fact the candidate's natural desire to parade his reading solved all the examiners' problems. On the one hand any reading that had been done would most reliably reveal itself in some form or other, thus enabling examiners to distinguish between candidates with a claim to a third or a fourth and candidates with no claim to any honours class at all. On the other hand the great quantity of reading which serious candidates would have done would generally hinder the slower-witted or more timid of their number from putting their reading to any good purpose in examination conditions. The examiners were thus enabled to distinguish candidates with a claim to a third or a fourth from those with a claim to a second or even a first. Hence the *Oxford Magazine*'s dual criticism of final honour schools: they involved 'an excessively exhausting examination ordeal', that is a searching test of reading and memory; and they encouraged 'the sprinter rather than the long-distance man', namely the candidate who, using such reading as he could remember, could in the few minutes allowed him answer the examiners' questions.[46]

In 1935 the examiners in the final honour school in English discussed the rhetorical and dialectical skills required to answer schools questions: 'many candidates handicapped themselves seriously by entering on an examination with, to all appearances, a large stock of ready-made answers. Instead of trying to think out the new question on the spot, they often seemed to rely on their recollection of old essays. Few candidates seemed to be aware of the heavy penalty which irrelevance invariably carries with it. Direct approach to a question with the support of suitable comment, however meagre, must always secure credit, but evasion of what is asked may throw doubt not only on a candidate's knowledge but also on his qualities of mind, and so may detract from the credit accruing for his better work. These remarks on irrelevance apply equally to all parts of the examination.' They also applied to all other examinations in the arts and social studies.[47]

In these examinations the colleges were competing almost as much as the candidates. Hence the decline of the pass school, which gave neither candidates nor colleges honour; hence too each college's efforts to ensure that its candidates for honours obtained the highest honours. This competitive system produced a characteristic teaching ethos, akin to that of sports-coaching. It is illustrated by the attitudes of men such as A. S. Owen, classics tutor at Keble, of whom Maurice Bowra wrote, 'he genuinely enjoyed teaching, gave unsparingly of his time to it, and was consciously proud of the natural "thirds" whom he turned into "seconds" '.[48] Of course not all fellows of all colleges subscribed unreservedly to this approach.

---

[46] *OM* 23 Jan. 1936, 272.
[47] OUA E/R/1/5, p. 26.
[48] *OM* 23 Jan. 1941, 136.

Critics of the system deplored what they regarded as a waste of intellectual resources. 'We keep our best historians tied to the routine task of giving individual tuition to those unworthy of it', complained Max Beloff in 1937.[49] Yet some very able academics operated the system with undisguised enthusiasm. As an ex-serviceman Robert Boothby was entitled to take a shortened honours course, which he did in 1921. His College, Magdalen, sent him to Lewis Namier, then a lecturer at Balliol, for tuition on the French revolution. Boothby recalled: 'He could bring the whole sweep of it into the compass of a single hour. "You are bound to get a question on Danton," he said. "There are two views about Danton, one orthodox, the other unorthodox. I will give you both." We got the question. I chose the unorthodox view, and I think this was what got me my degree. Anyway, thanks to Namier, I got it.'[50]

Namier's treatment of Danton scholarship exemplifies an Oxford attitude elaborated in R. G. Collingwood's *Autobiography*, perhaps the most sophisticated expression of the Oxford approach to the arts and social studies published between the wars. Collingwood dismissed most historical writing as 'scissors-and-paste', a mere rearrangement of 'the authorities' statements'. The historian ought not to indulge in such futility. Rather he must 'decide exactly what it is he wants to know; and if there is no authority to tell him, as in fact (one learns in time) there never is', he must find 'something that has got the answer hidden in it, and get the answer out by fair means or foul'. And the historian to whom Collingwood addresses himself may be a regius professor or a first-year undergraduate. For as Boothby's encounter with Namier suggests, the Oxford tutor saw his task not as telling his pupil what to think but as forcing him to think for himself, to use his own judgement on the authorities in circumstances in which the results of that exercise really mattered.[51]

Such a relationship between tutor and pupil is, to a degree unusual in education, an equal relationship. Hence Dacre Balsdon's dictum that 'a good tutorial should be a sparring match', not 'a substitute for a lecture'.[52] The same values also created a widespread sense of there being some sort of tutorial contract: as Kenneth Bell said when history tutor at Balliol, 'give me the facts and I will give you the ideas'. Yet Bell by no means assumed his pupils had no ideas of their own, and had merely to absorb his. On the contrary, as Raymond Massey recalled: 'We had to speak up in those tutorials of his. If we were silent, it was evidence of not thinking and that was failure.'[53] In challenging his pupils' silence, Bell was emphasizing the

[49] *OM* 11 Mar. 1937, 503–4.
[50] A. Thwaite (ed.), *My Oxford* (London 1977), 33.
[51] R. G. Collingwood, *An Autobiography* (Oxford 1939), 79–81.
[52] *OM* 7 Feb. 1969, 163.
[53] *OM* 15 Nov. 1951, 80; Thwaite, 43.

4.6 The river in Eights Week, 1922

4.7   Worcester College bump supper, 1929

6.1   W. H. Perkin with his research students, 1924

7.1 Trinity College first eight, 1938, head of the river

7.2 Enid Starkie lecturing in Somerville, 1944

8.1 Undergraduates in a Worcester College room, c.1952

dual imperative of the Oxford system, heavy reading and quick wits. He could not do his pupils' reading for them, but he could sharpen their wits and show them how questions were asked, and answers got out, by one means or another. Arthur Waugh's account of Oman's tutorial on Cicero reveals a formidable Oxonian imparting in a few brisk words 'the whole of Oxford teaching': 'ideas not facts, judgement not an index, life not death'. Waugh had to produce facts to show he had done the reading but his reading still had to be used, not merely regurgitated. Oman insisted his pupil 'get an idea' and 'work it out by illustration to the end', writing nothing 'without first considering construction not mere verbiage'.[54] This is the Oxford tradition.

Yet the institutional embodiment of that tradition was subject to some criticism between 1914 and 1939. Reformers like Farnell wanted a revived and expanded professoriate, the educational services of which would be equally available to all members of the University, and would therefore almost of necessity consist of lecturing to large audiences. Lecturing was also of course the form of instruction best suited from an administrative point of view to the requirements of a university-funded system of teaching such as that favoured by the Asquith Commission. But lectures were not very useful to students. The lecturer who lacked oratorical skills—which fellows of colleges were perhaps rather better at inculcating than practising—was equipped only to perform certain specialized tasks, such as giving commentary on texts, or reporting his reading of foreign-language books, and these tasks were decreasingly in demand as text-based teaching declined and foreign-language books were translated. Meanwhile the inter-war college tutors, demanding ever more reading and writing from their pupils, tended to look askance on any distraction from tasks set for tutorials. Perhaps few tutors went as far as J. O. Prestwich, history tutor at Queen's, who wrote in 1937 that 'the best men will rightly ignore lectures'; but many did little to encourage attendance even at their own lectures, and lectures in general suffered from what McCallum wryly called 'a law of diminishing returns'.[55]

'What, in a university of books and tutors is a poor lecturer to do?' asked a contributor to the *Oxford Magazine* in 1933.[56] One possible answer was to give his university-wide instruction not in lectures but in 'classes': addressing his audience round a table rather than from one end of a hall, using written materials as well as the spoken word, and interrupting his monologue to answer questions. Classes were commonly used in language work, and also in the more popular departments of the pass examinations.

[54] C. W. C. Oman, *Memories of Victorian Oxford and of Some Early Years* (London 1941), 151.
[55] Farnell, *An Oxonian Looks Back*, 271, 344; *OM* 22 June 1931, 323; 4 Mar. 1937, 466–7.
[56] *OM* 25 May 1933, 700.

Such instruction was perhaps rather humdrum, though its efficiency in time and money influenced various inter-war debates, especially those concerning the rival merits of pass moderations and separate honours-standard first public examinations. More prestigious and sophisticated classes (often called 'seminars') were pioneered by Professors Vinogradoff and Firth. Yet these gatherings were highly specialized affairs, usually devoted to the closest study of a particular text, and of little if any use to undergraduates.[57]

The limitations of lectures and classes led, despite some complaints, to a steady expansion of the tutorial teaching which had developed in the nineteenth century. Classics had been taught in two ways: by commentary-lectures and a weekly tutorial hour on composition up to honours moderations, and thereafter by two weekly tutorial hours (one for ancient history, one for philosophy) supplemented by optional lectures. The growth of modern schools, and the shift to essay-writing, made the latter model more influential after the First World War; the *Shorter Oxford English Dictionary* records 1923 as the year in which the handier form 'tutorial' replaced the older 'tutorial hour'. By the 1930s most undergraduates went, for most examination papers, singly or in a pair, for one hour-long tutorial a week (two in literae humaniores and PPE) to a fellow of their own or another college, who would be giving between ten and twenty tutorials a week during the eight weeks of full term. Some colleges did not provide tutorials for some papers in some subjects, and this was partly due to an imbalance between the number of teachers and the number of pupils, with classics at one extreme and modern languages at the other. Gaps in tutorial teaching and indiligence among tutees gave employment to private coaches, such as Bruce Goldie, who sat the final honour school in literae humaniores in 1891, and was still advertising tuition in responsions, honour and pass moderations, the pass school and Latin texts for jurisprudence sixty-two years later.[58] Yet the college tutor continued to be the key figure in Oxford teaching in the arts and social studies.

His maxim was, in T. B. Strong's words, that 'the Tutor should look after his men'.[59] Indeed, so far as the tutor and his college were concerned, it was, as R. R. Marett put it in 1941, 'more important to produce men than books'.[60] However, the production of men meant the dissemination of ideas as well as the development of character and, given the teaching and examining techniques of the period, the former function encouraged even the least-publishing tutor to keep abreast, or even a little ahead, of the latest thinking in his field. His results were unsystematic, perhaps superficial, oral not written, and private not public in character, yet they might well be more

[57] Bodl. GA Oxon. b. 138, p. 84; GA Oxon. b. 141, p. 111.
[58] *OM* 3 Mar. 1932, 525–6; 3 Dec. 1953, 130. I owe this reference to Brian Harrison.
[59] R. Venables, *D: Portrait of a Don* (Oxford 1967), 74–5.
[60] R. R. Marett, *A Jerseyman at Oxford* (London 1941), 226.

original than other people's results as they appeared in the bookshops or the pages of learned journals. K. M. Lea wrote of Janet Spens, English tutor at Lady Margaret Hall from 1911 to 1936: 'Miss Spens had a very subtle mind which expressed itself either in ingenious supposition or by remarkable imaginative penetration. To her pupils this could be immediately exciting, subsequently alarming, occasionally baffling and to many of them ultimately a source of lasting enlightenment. Tutorials were a strenuous mental exercise, one learned a hard way and over the years came to realize that it was unwise to dismiss whatever Miss Spens "had a theory about"; however hard it might be to discern the process by which she arrived at her conclusions her insight was always to be respected.'[61] This judgement could also apply to many of Spens's less prolific Oxford contemporaries.

In fact Oxford published a very great deal between 1914 and 1939. Perhaps the most spectacular category of publishing in the arts and social studies in this period was that comprising the various reports of excavations, among which Arthur Evans's *The Palace of Minos* (1921–36) was probably most famous.[62] K. S. Sandford's studies of palaeolithic man in the Nile Valley (1929–39) received less publicity, but such inquiries were highly regarded among specialists, as was the work of A. M. Blackman at Meir, R. C. Thompson at Abu Shahrain, S. H. Langdon at Kish and others. Archaeology (and collection) supplied materials for other areas of scholarship in which Oxford authors were prominent. The names of Idris Bell, A. E. Cowley and Edgar Lobel were particularly notable in papyrology. J. D. Beazley's *Attic Black Figure* (1928) was but one product of a lifetime's work on Greek vases and vase-painting. Stanley Casson's *The Technique of Early Greek Sculpture* (1933) complemented his work on modern sculpture. Oxford numismatists, as well as archaeologists and art historians, drew on the resources of the Ashmolean Museum: hence, for instance, two notable publications of 1931, J. G. Milne's *Greek Coinage* and Oman's *The Coinage of England*. In 1939 a major impetus was imparted to Oxford Egyptology by the creation of the Griffith Institute in association with the Ashmolean Museum.[63]

The Oxford University Press continued to contribute to the University's research activities, not least by publishing the *Oxford* and *Shorter Oxford* dictionaries, revised editions of which were produced by C. T. Onions in 1933. Henry Fowler's *Modern English Usage* appeared in 1926. *The Dictionary of National Biography* was edited in Oxford between 1914 and 1939: by H. W. C. Davis from 1912, and by Wickham Legg from 1933. Henry Stuart-Jones directed the efforts of many scholars in Oxford and elsewhere in the preparation of the ninth edition of Liddell and Scott's *Greek*

[61] *OM* 30 May 1963, 329.
[62] The *British Library Catalogue* contains bibliographical details of all works cited here.
[63] See below, 491–2.

Lexicon (1925–40)[64]. The University also produced many other reference works, from Thompson's *The Assyrian Herbal* (1924) to F. M. Powicke, C. H. Johnson and W. J. Harte, *The Handbook of British Chronology* (1939) for the Royal Historical Society. Languages, classical and modern, European and Asian, were the subject of a number of grammars, and also of some major surveys: 1934 saw publication of both J. D. Denniston, *The Greek Particles* and M. K. Pope, *From Latin to Modern French*.

Commentaries, editions and translations have long figured prominently among Oxford's publications. Samuel Holmes, *Joshua* appeared in 1914, S. R. Driver, *Job* posthumously in 1921, G. A. Cooke, *Ezekiel* in 1936. New Testament books were studied by such scholars as A. C. Clark (*Acts*, 1933), C. H. Dodd (*Romans*, 1932) and R. H. Charles (*Revelation*, 1920). Several of Euripides' plays were edited; neither Aristophanes nor Aeschylus were neglected.[65] Farnell edited and translated Pindar (1930); W. D. Ross edited Aristotle's *Metaphysics* (1924) and *Physics* (1936); E. C. Marchant edited and translated Xenophon's *Memorabilia* and *Oeconomicus* (1923) and *Scripta minora* (1925). Gilbert Murray's Greek translations were many, various and stimulating. Cicero was more edited than any other Latin author, but A. S. Owen's *Apulei apologia* (with H. E. Butler, 1914) and *Elegies of Propertius* (with E. A. Barber, 1933) and M. Platnauer's *Claudian* (1922) by no means exhaust the list of Oxford Latin texts and translations during the period.[66]

English and modern and oriental language scholars also produced many texts. D. E. Martin Clarke's *Hávamál* appeared in 1923; Tolkien's *Sir Gawain* two years later. R. E. C. Houghton and others edited Shakespeare's plays in the 1930s. Among other editions may be noted Percy Simpson's Jonson texts, Brett-Smith's Peacock and R. W. Chapman's Austen. Hermann Oelsner published an edition of *La divina commedia* in 1933; Gustave Rudler an *Adolphe* in 1935; the edition by E. L. Stahl and others of Rilke's *Duineser Elegien* appeared in 1938; Alfred Ewert's edition of Béroul's *Tristan* in 1939. D. S. Margoliouth's translation of Muhassin ibn Ali's *Table-Talk of a Mesopotamian Judge* (1922), J. G. Woodroffe's *Tibetan Book of the Dead* (1927) and E. H. Johnston's editions of Asvaghosha illustrate Oxford's textual interests in Asia. Meanwhile British historical texts were not neglected. J. G. Edwards's *Flint Pleas 1283–5* appeared in 1922; S. L. Ollard's *Herring's Visitation* in 1928. G. B. Grundy turned his attention from antique battlefields to Saxon charters, publishing a

---

[64] See below, 459–60, 464.
[65] Euripides editions included *Electra* (J. D. Denniston, 1939), *Ion* (A. S. Owen, 1939), *Iphigenia in Tauris* (M. Platnauer, 1938), *Medea* (D. L. Page, 1938). Cf Aristophanes, *Acharnians* (R. T. Elliott, 1914), *The Clouds* (C. Bailey, 1921); Aeschylus, *Persae* (M. R. Ridley, 1922).
[66] Cicero editions and translations included C. Cookson, *Cicero the Advocate* (1928), A. C. Clark's selection of Cicero's *Letters* (1925), W. W. How, *Select Letters* (1925), J. D. Denniston, *Orationes Phillipicae prima et secunda* (1926).

series of volumes on Oxfordshire, Worcestershire, Gloucestershire and Somerset from 1927 onward. Maude Clarke and Noel Denholm-Young's *Kirkstall Chronicle* came out in 1931; 1938 saw publication of both Agnes Leys, *Sandford Cartulary* and C. W. C. Oman, *Second Betting Book of All Souls*.

Oxford made substantial contributions to many kinds of textual and literary criticism between 1914 and 1939. G. R. Driver and D. C. Simpson, *The Psalmists* (1926), B. H. Streeter, *The Four Gospels* (1924), C. F. Burney, *The Poetry of our Lord* (1925) and C. H. Dodd, *The Parables of the Kingdom* (1935) illustrate one aspect of this work. T. W. Allen, *Homer* (1924), A. W. Pickard-Cambridge, *Dithyramb, Tragedy and Comedy* (1927) and D. L. Page, *Actors' Interpolations in Greek Tragedy* (1934) illustrate another. E. K. Chambers dominated English literary criticism in Oxford in these years, with such works as his *Elizabethan Stage* (1933), *Shakespeare: A Survey* (1925), *Shakespeare: A Study of Facts and Problems* (1930) and *Samuel Taylor Coleridge* (1938). Yet C. S. Lewis, *Allegory of Love* (1936), J. Spens, *Spenser's Faerie Queen* (1934), M. M. Lascelles, *Jane Austen and her Art* (1939) and M. R. Ridley, *Keats' Craftsmanship* (1933) further illustrate the English faculty's critical strength during the period. The diversity of criticism in modern languages is exemplified by L. A. Willoughby, *The Classical Age of German Literature 1748–1805* (1926), W. G. Moore, *La Réforme allemande et la littérature française* (1930), E. Starkie, *Baudelaire* (1933) and K. M. Lea, *Italian Popular Comedy* (1934).

Though Oxford had sadly lost the services of Halford Mackinder before 1914, some geography was published between the wars, including J. N. L. Baker's *History of Geographical Discovery and Exploration* (1931). The University was better provided with social anthropologists for most of the period, however. Marett's *Diffusion of Culture* appeared in 1927, and the 1930s saw several major publications: B. M. Blackwood, *Both Sides of Buka Passage* (1935); E. E. Evans-Pritchard, *Witchcraft, Oracles and Magic among the Azande* (1937); A. R. Radcliffe-Brown, *Taboo* (1939).

History made a massive contribution to Oxford's scholarly output in these years. A. W. Pickard-Cambridge's *Demosthenes* (1914) was followed by B. W. Henderson's *Hadrian* (1923) and Balsdon's *Caligula* (1934). G. L. Cheeseman, *Auxilia of the Roman Imperial Army* (1914) had a worthy successor in H. M. D. Parker, *Roman Legions* (1928). The last year of peace saw a remarkable trio of books in ancient history: G. H. Stevenson, *Roman Provincial Administration*; A. N. Sherwin-White, *Roman Citizenship*; Ronald Syme, *Roman Revolution*.

Between the wars Oxford's English historians concentrated on the periods before 1066 and after 1660. P. J. Haverfield, *The Roman Occupation of Britain* (1924), R. G. Collingwood and J. N. L. Myres, *Roman Britain and the English Settlements* (1936) and R. H. Hodgkin, *The History of the Anglo-Saxons* (1935) exemplify work on the earlier period. Perhaps Powicke's *Stephen Langton* (1928) and May McKisack's *Parliamentary Representation of the English Boroughs during the Middle Ages* (1932) can stand for inter-war Oxford's contribution to later medieval history. Post-Restoration England stimulated many studies. G. N. Clark published his *Dutch Alliance* in 1923, his *Later Stuarts* in 1934. Keith Feiling's *Tory Party* appeared in 1924, his *Second Tory Party* in 1938. Lucy Sutherland, *London Merchant* (1933) and David Ogg, *England in the Reign of Charles II* (1934) offer further insights into the seventeenth and eighteenth centuries. Llewellyn Woodward, *Age of Reform* (1938) and R. C. K. Ensor, *England 1870–1914* (1936) were major contributions to Clark's Oxford History of England. Davis's *Age of Grey and Peel* (1929) and Frank Pakenham's *Peace by Ordeal 1921* (1935) illustrate the breadth of inter-war Oxford's interests in recent British history.

But Oxford's interest in European history was slight. Powicke's *Bismarck* (1914), J. A. R. Marriott's *Eastern Question* (1917) and Woodward's *Great Britain and the German Navy* (1935) continued the tradition of Oman's *Peninsular War* (1902–30). The First World War was examined in many Oxford publications besides C. R. M. F. Cruttwell, *The History of the Great War* (1934): Davis's *History of the Blockade* and Arthur Salter's *Allied Shipping Control* (both 1921); Walter Raleigh's volume of *The War in the Air* (1922); C. T. Atkinson's regimental histories;[67] G. D. H. Cole's volumes, notably *Trade Unionism and Munitions* (1923); W. H. Beveridge, *British Food Control* (1928).

International relations attracted Oxford authors, being treated in such works as S. De Madariaga's, *Theory and Practice of International Relations* (1937), Ogg's eight-volume *Texts for Students of International Relations* (1921–7), C. A. W. Manning's *The Policy of the British Dominions in the League of Nations* (1932) and A. E. Zimmern's *The League of Nations and the Rule of Law* (1936). But the University's involvement in the study of contemporary politics was largely confined to the United Kingdom, the British empire and the United States. Marriott's *English Political Institutions* appeared in two inter-war editions and was complemented by R. H. S. Crossman's *Government and the Governed* (1939). H. V. Lovett published his *History of the Indian Nationalist Movement* in 1920; K. C. Wheare, *The Statute of Westminster 1931* first appeared in 1933; J. P. R. Maud, *Johannesburg and the Art of Self-Government* and M. F. Perham, *Native Administration in Nigeria* both appeared in 1937. D. W. Brogan, *The American Political System* (1933) was followed by E. M. Hugh-Jones and

---

[67] These included *The Queen's Own Royal West Kent Regiment 1914–19* (1924), *The Devonshire Regiment 1914–18* (1926), *The Seventh Division 1914–18* (1927), *The South Wales Borderers 1914–18* (1931).

E. A. Radice's book on the New Deal, *An American Experiment* (1936). No less than four Oxford authors—H. W. B. Joseph, A. D. Lindsay, G. D. H. Cole and Isaiah Berlin—published books on Marx.[68]

Oxford economics owed much to the Institute of Agricultural Economics, founded in 1913, and to the Institute of Statistics, set up in 1935 with a grant from the Rockefeller Foundation.[69] C. S. Orwin, *The Determination of Farming Costs* (1917) was followed by such works as D. H. Macgregor, *International Cartels* (1927), E. L. Hargreaves, *The National Debt* (1930), R. P. Harrod, *International Economics* (1933) and *The Trade Cycle* (1936), and R. S. Sayers, *Modern Banking*, which first appeared in 1938. The economic concerns of the 1930s were reflected in such works as K. A. H. Murray's *The Planning of Agriculture* (1933), Cole's *Principles of Economic Planning* (1935) and R. L. Hall's *The Economic System of a Socialist State* (1937).

Though inter-war Oxford had more lawyers than economists, the faculty of law remained small. Yet Oxford lawyers published a wide range of works. W. S. Holdsworth was very prolific, and his *History of English Law* continued through a number of editions under the direction of A. L. Goodhart and H. G. Hanbury. G. C. Cheshire's *Modern Law of Real Property* (1925) and *Private International Law* (1935) were landmarks. Goodhart's *Essays in Jurisprudence and the Common Law* appeared in 1931, Hanbury's *Modern Equity* in 1935. H. F. Jolowicz, *Historical Introduction to the Study of Roman Law* was published in 1932 and R. W. Lee, *An Introduction to Roman-Dutch Law* had appeared in 1915, but apart from Ivy Williams, *The Sources of Law in the Swiss Civil Code* (1922) Oxford showed little further interest in European law. Among many standard works revised by Oxford lawyers were the volumes in the *Stephen's Commentaries* series on *Public Law*, revised by P. A. Landon in 1922 and 1925; *Constitutional and Administrative Law*, revised by F. H. Lawson and others in 1928 and 1938; *The Law of Contracts and Torts*, revised by Cheshire and others in 1928.

For most of the period from 1914 to 1939 Oxford philosophy was largely Aristotelian in inspiration. Despite such works as R. G. Collingwood, *Speculum Mentis* (1924), F. C. S. Schiller, *Logic for Use* (1929) and C. R. Morris, *Idealistic Logic* (1929), the dominant themes were set out in J. C. Wilson's posthumous *Statement and Inference* (1926). H. H. Price, *Perception* (1932) largely continued the Cook Wilson tradition. Oxford's involvement with aesthetics is exemplified by E. F. Carritt's *The Theory of Beauty* (1914) and Collingwood's *Outline of a Philosophy of Art* (1925) and *The Principles of Art* (1938). A renewed interest in Plato (perhaps more

[68] H. W. B. Joseph, *The Labour Theory of Value in Karl Marx* (1923); A. D. Lindsay, *Karl Marx's Capital* (1925); G. D. H. Cole, *What Marx Really Meant* (1934); I. Berlin, *Karl Marx* (1939).

[69] Chester, *Economics, Politics and Social Studies*, 144 ff.

political than epistemological) appeared in the late 1930s.[70] But during these years the wider public came to identify Oxford philosophy with A. J. Ayer's *Language, Truth and Logic*, published in 1936.

[70] H. W. B. Joseph, *Essays on Ancient and Modern Philosophy* (1935); M. B. Foster, *The Political Philosophy of Plato and Hegel* (1935); W. F. R. Hardie, *A Study in Plato* (1936); R. H. S. Crossman, *Plato To-day* (1937); R. W. Livingstone, *Portrait of Socrates* (1938).

6

The Non-Medical Sciences, 1914–1939

J. B. MORRELL

The standard view of Oxford's contribution to the First World War is that brilliant young Oxford graduates such as the physicist H. G. J. Moseley and scientific fellows of colleges like the zoologists J. W. Jenkinson and G. W. Smith were pointlessly sacrificed in the trenches.* This perspective implies that Oxford science had nothing to contribute to the war effort. That was not so. The First World War was the chemists' war which saw H. B. Hartley, science fellow of Balliol, master-minding Britain's chemical warfare programme and W. H. Perkin, Waynflete Professor of Chemistry, doing likewise for the government-formed British Dyes Limited. A third chemist, Andrea Angel, tutor at Christ Church, was killed in an explosion at a munitions factory where he was chief chemist. Physicists—for example H. T. Tizard, science fellow of Oriel—and engineers were drafted into aeronautic research, while W. MacDougall, the Wilde Reader in Mental Philosophy, worked in the army on shell-shock. Able undergraduate scientists who went on to occupy Oxford chairs also served as boffins: A. C. Hardy used his zoological knowledge as a camouflage officer and C. N. Hinshelwood worked on explosives at an ordnance factory.[1]

Oxford's contribution to the war effort through its boffins anticipated the increasing salience of Oxford science from 1918 to 1939. By 1939 Oxford

* The research for this chapter was facilitated by a grant from the Leverhulme Trust, by a supernumerary fellowship at Brasenose College for Michaelmas term 1987 and by the University of Bradford which granted me study-leave for that term. The following sources have been systematically used and specific citations have not been given: Gazette, especially for the annual reports of science departments and institutions; Asquith Report and related papers in Bodl. MSS top. Oxon. b. 104, 107, 109; OUA natural sciences faculty board, minutes and reports 1912–26; OUA physical sciences faculty board, minutes and reports 1926–39; OUA biological sciences faculty board, minutes and reports 1926–39.

[1] J. L. Heilbron, *H. G. J. Moseley: The Life and Letters of an English Physicist, 1887–1915* (Berkeley, Los Angeles and London 1974); A. G. Ogston, 'H. B. Hartley', *BMFRS* xix (1973); L. F. Haber, *The Poisonous Cloud: Chemical Warfare in the First World War* (Oxford 1986); A. J. Greenaway, J. F. Thorpe and R. Robinson, *The Life and Work of Professor William Henry Perkin* (London 1932); W. J. Reader, *Imperial Chemical Industries: A History* (2 vols London 1970–5) i *The Forerunners 1870–1926* (London 1970); R. W. Clark, *Tizard* (London 1965), 23–48; W. Farren, 'H. T. Tizard', *BMFRS* vii (1961); M. Greenwood and M. Smith, 'William MacDougall', *ONFRS* iii (1939–41); N. B. Marshall, 'A. C. Hardy', *BMFRS* xxxii (1986); H. W. Thompson, 'C. N. Hinshelwood', *BMFRS* xix (1973).

housed distinguished individuals with international reputations, especially in chemistry. Its scientists had received honours and held high office in learned societies. Research schools had appeared and awarded the degree of doctor of philosophy, which was available from 1919, and research for many scientists became a self-imposed norm as important as teaching. After protracted and acrimonious controversy a portion of the University Parks, together with the University Museum and the new buildings clustered around it, was in 1934 designated as the science area, and the Keble Road triangle was bought for its future expansion. On this congested site, away from the historic centre of the University [figure 10.5], new buildings funded by the University appeal were completed or begun by 1939. Though money for research was often tight and frustrations abounded, many innovative scientists stayed at Oxford. Those who left had very positive reasons for moving, often to London and the eventual reward of a knighthood: A. C. G. Egerton, Reader in Thermodynamics, assumed the chair of chemical technology at Imperial College, London; G. H. Hardy, Savilian Professor of Geometry, returned to Cambridge; Hartley and M. P. Applebey, chemistry fellow at St John's, were lured into industrial research; F. W. Keeble, Professor of Botany, became the first agricultural adviser to Imperial Chemical Industries (ICI); Tizard went into government administration of science; the zoologist G. R. De Beer left for University College, London; and MacDougall moved to the USA.[2]

TABLE 6.1

SUBJECTS STUDIED BY POSTGRADUATES IN OXFORD, 1928/9–1964/5 (%)

	1928/9	1938/9	1948/9	1958/9	1963/4	1964/5
arts	} 86.6	72.4	66.9	67.6	{ 41.7	41.2
social studies					17.7	18.8
pure science	11.8	23.5	28.5	25.1	33.5	31.9
applied science	—	1.3	0.5	1.0	2.1	3.0
agriculture	1.4	1.7	3.1	3.1	1.5	1.8
medicine	0.3	1.1	1.0	3.2	3.5	3.3
number	357	536	1,071	1,263	1,845	2,153

Source: Franks report ii, 13.

The transformation of Oxford science was made manifest in the quality of individual researchers and the associated growth in postgraduate numbers. As the degree of doctor of philosophy (DPhil) gradually gained in status, the number of postgraduate students in science rose: in the 1930s their number

[2] R. J. Egerton, *Sir Alfred Egerton: A Memoir with Papers* (np 1963); D. M. Newitt, 'A. C. G. Egerton', *BMFRS* vi (1960); E. C. Titchmarsh, 'G. H. Hardy', *ONFRS* vi (1948–9); E. J. W. Barrington, 'G. R. De Beer', *BMFRS* xix (1973).

tripled, thus doubling the percentage of Oxford's postgraduate students in science [table 6.1]. In contrast, at the undergraduate level science was suffering slight losses, confirming the old adage, 'Cambridge for science, Oxford for arts'. By 1938/9 the proportion of undergraduates reading pure science, engineering science, forestry and agriculture was 17 per cent, while that for law or PPE was about 11 per cent and for history 21 per cent [table 6.2]. At Cambridge, however, the corresponding figure for engineering alone was about 11 per cent. About two-thirds of the science undergraduates, predominantly men, read for the final honour schools of chemistry and mathematics. Chemistry and mathematics (or mathematics/physics) were therefore represented in several colleges by two tutorial fellows, but other science subjects were represented either thinly or not at all.

The arts dominance at the undergraduate level was maintained by Oxford's decentralized collegiate structure. The colleges, all autonomous and some wealthy, were ultimately responsible for the teaching of their undergraduates. The university, relatively impoverished, played second fiddle to the colleges: Oxford did not enjoy the decisive shift in power from the colleges to the university which Cambridge experienced in 1926. Attempts to induce the colleges to support the university's science departments were fiercely resisted. Money for science often came from outside—from government, industry and philanthropic bodies—at a time when loyal college fellows saw the university and science as leviathan. For a college, it was sensible to give top priority to fellowships in existing first-degree subjects and not to foster new subjects in which there would be few or no undergraduates; this led to a built-in academic conservatism which was indifferent or hostile to science. Hence the curious case of A. D. Lindsay, who as Vice-Chancellor successfully promoted science in the university but as Master of Balliol presided over the expansion of fellowships in Greats and in PPE; hence the presence in the smaller colleges of only one science tutorial fellow or none at all. No scientist became head of a college until Tizard at Magdalen in 1942. Moreover, the tradition of connoisseurship at high table in fellowship divine sat uneasily with the notion of specialist and allegedly narrow scientific publication. From the college enclave, research could be seen as an ungentlemanly and boorish Germanic notion, and postgraduate supervision as a Yankee device for inserting plebeians into a patrician university. It is significant that scientists who prospered in the college environment shone as connoisseurs: Hinshel-wood, a gastronomic, bibulous and linguistic expert, used to read Dante in the original in his college laboratory. Oxford's academic conservatism led to insularity: the majority of college fellows in science and many laboratory demonstrators were themselves graduates of Oxford. It also meant that science professors were a suppressed class lacking power: if there were college fellows in a subject, they could defy the professor, who could not turn to the colleges by right for staff.

TABLE 6.2

OXFORD HONOUR SCHOOL FINALISTS:
INDIVIDUAL SCHOOLS AND FACULTIES AS A
PERCENTAGE OF THE YEAR TOTAL, 1923–1964

Subject	1923	1928	1938	1948	1958	1964
Greats	14.8	12.1	11.0	7.3	8.2	7.0
Theology	4.8	4.8	5.3	2.5	3.5	2.8
History	29.1	25.6	20.9	26.6	17.0	14.2
English	10.7	10.4	9.7	13.3	11.7	10.3
Languages	6.8	7.7	10.2	11.8	12.1	9.9
Ori. Stud.	0.6	0.2	—	0.7	0.5	0.8
Geography	—	—	3.2	1.5	3.3	3.0
Music	—	—	—	—	0.7	1.0
Arts total	66.8	60.8	60.3	63.7	57.0	49.0
Law	12.6	14.7	11.2	5.3	10.0	8.6
PPE	5.0	8.1	11.3	8.9	10.5	10.3
Soc. Studies total	17.6	22.9	22.6	14.2	20.5	18.9
Mathematics	2.1	2.4	2.5	2.8	4.3	6.1
Physics	2.3	1.9	1.8	3.9	4.3	6.4
Chemistry	4.3	3.5	3.5	4.2	4.7	6.8
Biochemistry	—	—	0.3	—	0.4	0.6
Physiology	3.9	4.4	5.1	3.0	3.1	4.4
Zoology	1.1	0.5	0.6	1.1	0.9	1.4
Botany	0.8	0.6	—	0.4	0.3	0.9
Geology	0.2	0.3	0.2	1.1	0.8	0.4
PPP	—	—	—	0.7	1.0	1.3
Pure Sciences total	14.8	13.5	14.1	17.3	19.8	28.4
Engineering	0.8	1.0	1.2	1.6	2.1	2.3
Metallurgy	—	—	—	—	—	0.3
Applied Sci. total	0.8	1.0	1.2	1.6	2.1	2.6
Agriculture	—	1.3	1.0	2.1	0.2	0.7
Forestry	—	0.6	0.8	1.2	0.4	0.4
Agric. & For. total	—	1.9	1.8	3.3	0.6	1.1

Note: The year cited is the opening calendar year of an academic year (thus 1923 represents 1923–4).

Source: HUD.

Not surprisingly there was little innovation in degree courses. Reorganization and tinkering were the norm, except that natural science moderations were introduced in 1934. Indeed the dominance of literae humaniores was responsible for squashing and deferring two proposals. The first was 'science Greats', originally brought forward in harness with 'modern Greats', that is philosophy, politics and economics (PPE). The latter prospered but the former, which aimed to combine the principles, history and philosophy of science, was rejected by Congregation in 1923.[3] The second concerns the late arrival of experimental psychology, a delay which was the result of a long struggle between ratiocinative and experimental philosophers going back to the row in 1908 between Wilde himself and MacDougall, who set up a laboratory which he lost in the First World War. W. Brown, MacDougall's successor as Wilde Reader in Mental Philosophy, was an equally firm experimentalist who believed in intelligence testing. The philosophers suspected that his unpalatable methods would subvert their approach to mental philosophy and their position in the University, and they succeeded in delaying the introduction of experimental psychology until 1936, when an anonymous endowment of £10,000 from Mrs Hugh Watts led to the establishment of a graduate institute for experimental psychology under Brown's direction.[4]

Given a decentralized collegiate structure which was associated with dominance by certain interests, new departures in science were difficult. When they occurred, they were forced through either by government departments which funded three research institutes, or by entrepreneurs within the University who tried to transform or to add to the existing scientific departments, often with the help of external funding. When there was no external or internal pressure for change, then the status quo was preserved or slow decay set in.

As the colleges were the main vehicles for maintaining the cherished ideal of a liberal education, vocational training for the non-liberal professions was regarded as inferior. Subjects such as engineering, agriculture and forestry, thinly represented in the colleges, were regarded as merely technical, mentally limiting and not ennobling. Oxford took a distancing and cool attitude to industrial and even land-related subjects.

Under the head of industrial studies there were the peculiar cases of Nuffield College and the department of engineering science. In 1937 Lord

[3] D. Scott, *A. D. Lindsay* (Oxford 1971), 49–50; N. Chester, *Economics, Politics and Social Studies in Oxford, 1900–85* (London 1986), 30–40.

[4] The litigious Henry Wilde (1833–1919) wanted psychology to develop within literae humaniores and suspected experimentalists. R. C. Oldfield, 'Psychology in Oxford 1898–1949', *Quarterly Bull. British Psychological Soc.* nos 9 (1950), 345–53 and 10 (1950), 382–7; L. S. Hearnshaw, *The Shaping of Modern Psychology* (London 1987); 'Psychology at Oxford', *Nature* cxxxii (1933), 186. Mrs Hugh Watts was a friend and patient of Brown who practised psychiatry.

Nuffield offered the University about a million pounds for a new college to promote engineering and modern business methods which would bring academic engineering into contact with industrial needs. Eventually £100,000 went towards the building of a new University physical chemistry laboratory, which pleased him, the rest to a college devoted to social studies, which left him feeling cheated.[5] Lacking an expert engineer as an internal adviser, his original aim for an Oxford version of the Massachusetts Institute of Technology was transformed by Lindsay and Douglas Veale, the Registrar. At this time Oxford kept industry and management studies at bay, even though Oxford chemists were becoming powerful as researchers and directors in the bigger chemical firms such as ICI and Albright and Wilson. Finance from industry was crucial for the University as a whole and for particular science departments, the biggest benefactors being Nuffield with four million pounds in the 1930s, Shell and ICI, with a smaller but useful contribution from the British Oxygen Company. Yet engineering was widely scorned, and engineers were seen as men with oily rags stuffed into the pockets of denim overalls, ill suited to enter senior common rooms. Not surprisingly, engineering at Oxford avoided applied science: the formal title of the department was 'engineering science'. Housed in a small building at the north end of the Keble Road triangle, it produced only about ten finalists per year, sometimes with a hefty proportion of fourths. Under the unclubbable and shy Charles Jenkin, the founding professor who resigned to join the Building Research Station, research was undistinguished; but under his amiable and persuasive successor R. V. Southwell it prospered, though always on a small scale. Using staff trained at Cambridge, Southwell's department acquired a research identity, especially in his own field of mathematics for engineering science, in which he built up a small but distinctive school. Even during the depression, Southwell was successful in attracting money and equipment from engineering firms. His greatest coup was in refusing to accept the chair until a readership in electrical engineering, filled by E. B. Moullin, was endowed to widen the scope of teaching and research. Southwell extracted money for this from the Rhodes Trust and then from J. D. Pollock, chairman of both British Oxygen and Metal Industries. Southwell did not try to build up a big department of applied science: he outlawed engineering practice and technical handicraft. His solution—a small but high-quality department focused on the essential scientific equipment of an engineer—was more successfully realized at the postgraduate than at the undergraduate level. In 1939 Southwell was concerned about the poor quality of his undergraduate intake and the total absence of scholarships and fellowships in his subject. He was prescient in his fear that his staff, lacking recognition at Oxford, might be lured

[5] Chester, 63–82; P. S. Andrews and E. Brunner, *The Life of Lord Nuffield: A Study in Enterprise and Benevolence* (Oxford 1955), 309–12.

elsewhere: during the Second World War Southwell himself left for the rectorship of Imperial College, while Moullin and A. M. Binnie, the senior demonstrator, returned to Cambridge.[6]

Agriculture endured a very varied career in its three manifestations of the school of rural economy, the Agricultural Economics Research Institute (founded in 1912) and the Agricultural Engineering Research Institute (founded in 1924), all of which were financially heavily dependent on the Ministry of Agriculture. The problem of the school was that its undergraduates were so low in quality and number in the late 1920s that by 1931 its very existence was in doubt. After a good deal of painful lobbying the Ministry approved the idea of elevating agriculture from a pass to an honour school in the hope of getting value for money from it. The school stopped teaching crop and animal husbandry, eliminated material deemed merely technical, and in the honours scheme established in 1937 made the evolution of agriculture as important as its economic and scientific aspects. These three themes were intended to provide mental discipline for those who would become leaders in the agricultural industry. The school was essentially a teaching department of the University: though J. A. S. Watson was appointed professor in 1925 to promote research, his forte was advice. Research was the prime responsibility of the two agricultural institutes, which received between them about five-sixths of the Ministry's grant to Oxford's agricultural work. Their relations with the school and the University were unclear and in one case disastrous.

The Agricultural Economics Research Institute was the first attempt made in Britain to set up a national centre for research into the economic problems of the land and its use. It was founded in 1912 as a result of an application by the University to the Treasury for a grant to aid agricultural research. In reply the Board of Agriculture asked the University to focus on agricultural economics and the Development Commission provided the money for the Institute. Subsequently it was financed mainly by the Commission, the Ministry of Agriculture and the Agricultural Research Council and by temporary grants from various marketing boards. It published voluminous research reports, acted as a consultant and issued postgraduate diplomas. It specialized in agricultural costing, surveys, marketing and prices and by 1938 had a calculating room for machines, the first of its kind in Oxford for statistical research. Widely recognized as the national institute for agricultural economics, it produced experts in these areas for service in government departments at home and in the colonies and provided staff for agriculture

[6] R. V. Southwell, 'C. F. Jenkin', *ONFRS* iii (1939–41); D. G. Christopherson, 'R. V. Southwell', *BMFRS* xviii (1972); R. V. Southwell, *The Place of Engineering Science in University Studies: An Inaugural Lecture Delivered before the University of Oxford on 7 June 1930* (Oxford 1930); OUA UC/FF/187/2, UDC/M/41/1; personal communications from Sir D. G. Christopherson.

departments in other British universities. It was fortunate in its Director, C. S. Orwin, a prolific publisher, agricultural historian, loyal college man and a dry wit who preferred the title of 'institute' to that of 'institution', which he associated with the poor law and borstal. In a delicate balancing act he usually maintained academic freedom while keeping both the Ministry and the University happy.

That was certainly not the case with the Agricultural Engineering Research Institute, founded in 1924 and funded by the Ministry, which wanted an institute in agricultural machinery. Oxford was chosen because the University already had experience of Orwin's Institute and had departments of agriculture and engineering. The Agricultural Engineering Institute's first Director B. J. Owen, a protégé and former employee of the Ministry, assembled his staff quickly. One of his first successes was the introduction of the combine harvester to Britain. Unfortunately he took advantage of the remoteness of the science departments from the University Chest, 'laundered' money and was imprisoned for forgery and fraud in 1931, leaving his staff confused and demoralized. He had acted in the name of the University, obfuscating the difference between accounts and patents belonging to himself, his Institute and the University. The University was taken to court and was liable from 1931 to 1938 for £750,000, roughly seven times its annual grant from the University Grants Committee. Such paralysing financial uncertainty postponed important developments in the sciences. The Owen affair led to strained relations between the University and the Ministry, which, after 1931, felt it had not received value for money from Owen's Institute and was twice on the point of closing it down. Forbidden by the University to do certain kinds of research, it survived as a tool of the Ministry, which appointed staff and put them on civil-service grades and tenure arrangements. By resorting to short-term contracts (just three months in 1937) and funding—and even sudden cuts in grants already being paid—the Ministry controlled the Institute and the direction and pace of its research. Long-term pure research was discouraged, the emphasis being on short-term applied projects. The Ministry's sudden changes of policy landed the University not only with financial but also with human liabilities, involving 'forced displacements' of staff. For the University, it was a sad experience and a warning about how government interference could accompany government funding in a university institute. Even Veale showed his irritation, telling the Ministry that a university could not engage staff on a monthly basis like domestic servants.[7]

---

[7] This account of the school of agriculture and the two institutes draws on voluminous files in OUA UR/SF/RE/1–1D, 2, 4–4B, 4/1–2, 5/2, U Sol/44/1, MR/7/2/10, UDC/M/15/1–8, UDC/R/8/1; J. A. S. Watson, 'The honour school of agriculture', *OM* 27 May 1937, 668–9; *Agricultural Economics 1913–1938* (University of Oxford Agricultural Economics Research Institute: Oxford 1938).

Forestry resembled agriculture, in that as a pass school it faced a persistent problem of low status. Its relations with the Imperial Forestry Institute (founded in 1924) were strained, and the Institute itself became ungovernable. The low status of forestry was made most manifest in the acrimonious squabble of 1934 about the site for the new forestry building in the congested science area: the study of trees was widely scorned because it was merely technical and vocational, and open-air work was thought to be less scientific than that done inside in a laboratory. After several unsuccessful attempts, forestry was finally elevated to an honour school in 1945, and only in 1950 did it acquire a new building in the science area. Forestry came to Oxford in 1905 when the Indian School of Forestry at Cooper's Hill, and its Director William Schlich, were transferred to Oxford. By 1919 Schlich had raised forestry from a diploma subject to a pass degree and had collected enough money, mainly from colonial governments, to endow a chair, to which his protégé R. S. Troup was elected in 1920. That year and again in 1923, the British Empire Forestry Conference urged the establishment of a central imperial institution for forestry research and postgraduate training. So too did the interdepartmental Committee on Imperial Forestry Education. In 1924 the Imperial Forestry Institute was established with Troup as its Director; it was financed by the Forestry Commission and by overseas governments through the Colonial Office. This arrangement, which involved shared facilities between the school and Institute to reduce cost, raised questions of overlapping functions, of split loyalties of staff and of control. Under pressure from the Forestry Commission, the University agreed in 1934 that there would be a separate director of a permanent institute in exchange for its being brought more under the control of the University. Troup opposed these proposed arrangements: the Institute was not well endowed permanently, its staff were on annual contracts and it was dependent on the school for many facilities such as teaching, buildings, equipment and books; separation would be cripplingly expensive for the Institute, previously carried on the back of the school, and would require some staff to serve two masters. Troup disregarded the fact that in the mid-1930s the Institute, externally funded, was paying three-quarters of the salaries of the four university demonstrators in the school; but the Forestry Commission did not. It threatened to withdraw its grant unless a full-time director of the Institute was appointed. In January 1936 a system of dual control, with Troup heading the school and J. N. Oliphant the Institute, was introduced for three years with dire results: suspicion, distrust and friction were followed by formal complaints and denunciations, the resignation of Ray Bourne, Troup's longest-serving demonstrator, and the transfer of R. N. Chrystal, an expert on woodland insects, to entomology. With an income only a quarter that of the Institute, the school had become subordinate, and its ideology of long-term academic forestry research was temporarily destroyed by Oliphant's insistence on market-led briefing. In 1939 this painful period ended with the merging of the school and the Institute under the exhausted and ill Troup, who died in October, leaving forestry without a new building and with many of its problems unsolved. Overall, the much vaunted prestige of the imperial connection was short-lived in the case of forestry.[8]

Geology, botany, mineralogy, astronomy, zoology and the history of science were subjects which were largely outside the college system but were recognized by the university with a chair or a readership. The professors were supported by departmental and university demonstrators, most of whom never became fellows of colleges or waited a long time for college affiliation. The botanist A. H. Church, for example, was elected a Fellow of the Royal Society (FRS) in 1921 but never became a fellow of a college; J. R. Baker was made departmental demonstrator in 1923, university demonstrator 1927, Reader in Cytology in 1955 and FRS in 1958, but did not become a fellow of New College until 1964, when aged 64. If these subjects were taught, they attracted few undergraduates and did not expand, except zoology which doubled from a small base of six finalists a year to twelve. As research departments, most were quite active and some distinguished, with zoology again the most prominent. Of those who in 1923 were in the zoology department as either staff or students at various levels, nine were or were to become Fellows of the Royal Society. In these small non-vocational subjects a few new senior posts, mainly readerships, were created as rewards for personal research and as a means of conferring responsibility on an individual for all aspects of his subject including teaching. Zoology was the main beneficiary, with readerships in animal ecology (C. S. Elton, 1936) and genetics (E. B. Ford, 1939); the other readerships were in the history of science (R. T. Gunther, 1934), chemical crystallography (T. V. Barker, 1927) and ancient astronomy (J. K. Fotheringham, 1925).[9]

Institutionally, too, zoology was prominent. In 1932 Elton launched the Bureau of Animal Population, the most important centre of research in animal ecology in Britain between the wars, which after a trial period was given limited support by the University. It was devoted to progressively co-ordinated team research on the dynamics of natural populations, especially those of voles and game, and capitalized on Elton's own notions of food

---

[8] OUA UC/FF/584/1; R. S. Troup, 'Forestry at Oxford', *OM* 1 June 1939, 676–8. Troup was a good jungle man: cf *Nature* cxliv (1939), 699–70.

[9] A. G. Tansley, 'A. H. Church', *ONFRS* ii (1936–8); E. N. Willmer and P. C. J. Brunet, 'J. R. Baker', *BMFRS* xxxi (1985); A. V. Simcock, *Robert T. Gunther and the Old Ashmolean* (Oxford 1985); A. E. Gunther, *Robert T. Gunther: A Pioneer in the History of Science 1869–1940* (Oxford 1967); OUA UR/SF/LE/2.

cycles, the pyramid of numbers and ecological niches.[10] In 1935 the Museum
of the History of Science was officially established in the old Ashmolean
building in Broad Street through the endeavours of Gunther. In 1938 the
Edward Grey Institute of Field Ornithology was created as a national centre
for the study of bird behaviour through the efforts primarily of B. W.
Tucker and E. M. Nicholson.[11] These three institutional developments had
several features in common. Each had a persistent, productive and credible
activist: Elton, for example, was the father of animal ecology and from 1932
the first editor of the *Journal of Animal Ecology*. Each exploited a local
pressure group to give visibility to a given project. Elton was a key figure in
the Oxford Exploration Club, established in 1927. Tucker and Nicholson
were prominent in the Oxford Ornithological Society, founded in 1921,
which spawned the Oxford Bird Census in 1927 and in 1932 the British
Ornithological Trust, with Nicholson as secretary. The Friends of the Old
Ashmolean were founded in 1928 to press for the creation of a museum of
the history of science in Oxford in a restored old Ashmolean building and
not just to augment collections in it. All three were heavily dependent on
external endowments, not only before but after they were recognized as
University institutions. In its early years the Bureau of Animal Population
was supported mainly by the Royal Society of London, the New York
Zoological Society, the Agricultural Research Council, ICI and the Carnegie
Corporation; in one year it was financed from sixteen external sources, after
Elton had written over a hundred different begging letters. The Grey
Institute was established with an endowment of £3,000 from the appeal
launched to commemorate Viscount Grey, Chancellor of the University
when he died in 1933. Ornithology had been Grey's favourite hobby; he had
written extensively on it and it was the subject of his final speech in the
House of Lords. The Museum of the History of Science, created from the
Lewis Evans collection in 1924, depended heavily on donations and on
money from the Goldsmiths' Company and other city companies interested
in displays of fine craftsmanship. It was Gunther's ability to lure donations,
to extract financial patronage, to take on his opponents in the Ashmolean
Museum, the Bodleian Library and the University Press, to exploit
anniversaries and to instigate a supporting pressure group which distinguished him from a previous historian of science at Oxford, Charles Singer,
a prolific scholar who left Oxford in disappointment in 1920 for

[10] J. Sheail, *Seventy-Five Years in Ecology: The British Ecological Society* (Oxford 1987),
85–94, 103–5, 115–17; University of Oxford, department of zoology, Elton collection, annual
reports of the Bureau of Animal Population, 1932 onward; C. S. Elton, *Animal Ecology*
(London 1927); OUA UR/SF/Z/2D; personal communications from the late C. S. Elton.

[11] D. E. Allen, *The Naturalist in Britain: A Social History* (Harmondsworth 1978), 252–8;
OUA UR/SF/Z/2B; B. W. Tucker, 'Ornithology in Oxford', *OM* 26 Jan. 1939, 304–6; 2 Feb.
1939, 341–3; F. Pember, 'The national memorial to Viscount Grey of Fallodon', *Oxford* spring
1936, 42–7; personal communications from Mr E. M. Nicholson.

University College, London. Singer's approach had been focused on the history of scientific ideas which he thought best pursued in quiet alcoves of the Radcliffe Library. In contrast Gunther was attached to the study of scientific instruments, and he saw a museum in a venerable building as the most propitious base for the history of science. Again, unlike Singer, he capitalized on local pride and opportunity by popularizing the history of local science as an important branch of what he called the 'archaeology of science' with his multi-volumed *Early Science in Oxford*.[12]

The small non-vocational departments had few undergraduates, and consequently prizes, funds and postgraduate scholarships were disproportionately important in launching research careers. In geology, where there might be only two finalists per year, the Burdett Coutts prize was awarded every other year; in 1925–7 it launched the research career of W. J. Arkell, who soon became the world's specialist in jurassic geology. In entomology J. M. Baldwin endowed the Poulton fund in 1920 to promote the study of natural and social selection; in the 1920s it greatly facilitated the research of the young Ford. The Welch scholarship in biology, established in 1916, enabled several Oxford graduates to launch their research careers. Beneficiaries in the 1920s included A. C. Hardy, G. De Beer, J. R. Baker, J. Z. Young and O. W. Richards, all of whom became Fellows of the Royal Society.[13]

Geology sometimes endured the embarrassment of having fewer finalists than staff. Its problem was to survive, an aim not helped by its professor, W. J. Sollas, the University's oldest science professor, who died in harness in 1936 aged 87. Sollas, who had deserted geology for anthropology, had long been considered dangerously eccentric but he did recognize the great talent of Arkell. Arkell's work was rewarded by New College with a senior research fellowship from 1933, but not by the University: in 1937 J. A. Douglas, who had deputized for Sollas, was preferred for the chair to Arkell who left Oxford in 1940, never to return. Though Douglas's interests in the palaeontology of Persia helped to secure a grant of £25,000 from Shell in 1937 for new geology accommodation, Oxford in losing Arkell lost the opportunity of making its department into a mecca for students of jurassic geology. In one respect the department was unique in the late 1930s: in summer its researchers were constantly disturbed and driven frantic by the ceaseless din emanating from Solly Zuckerman's colony of baboons housed in the anatomy department opposite their windows.[14]

Mineralogy was another very small department under an ageing professor, H. L. Bowman, who had assumed his chair in 1909 at the age of 35. The

[12] R. T. Gunther, *Early Science in Oxford* (14 vols and supplement, Oxford 1920–45).

[13] L. R. Cox, 'W. J. Arkell', *BMFRS* iv (1958); R. Southwood, 'O. W. Richards', *BMFRS* xxxiii (1987). E. B. Poulton (1856–1943) was Hope Professor of Entomology 1893–1933.

[14] Cox, 'Arkell'; OUA UC/FF/500/2 (Sollas, Douglas); OUA UDC/M/41/1 (17 Mar. 1937, Zuckerman).

problems of very low recruitment of undergraduates and the growing importance of crystallography led in 1941 to Bowman's resignation, the abolition of his chair, and the creation of two readerships, one in mineralogy in the department of geology and the other in crystallography in the department of inorganic chemistry. Though Bowman was not himself an active researcher, he encouraged the work of T. V. Barker (a student of Fedorov at St Petersburg in 1908) and R. C. Spiller (a disciple of Barker) on crystal indexes, which involved studying the superficial characteristics of crystals irrespective of their chemical composition and internal structure. From the later 1920s Bowman also recognized the importance—especially after Barker's unexpected death in 1931—of x-ray crystallography as pursued by H. M. ('Tiny') Powell, who had learned the techniques at Leipzig under Schiebold, and by Powell's first undergraduate pupil, Dorothy Hodgkin. In the 1930s Powell and Hodgkin, who worked for her PhD under J. D. Bernal at Cambridge and acquired a fellowship at Somerville in 1936, studied the internal structure and chemical composition of, respectively, inorganic compounds and big organic molecules (steroids, insulin and proteins). Hodgkin's fellowship gave her such intellectual and financial independence that she worked in the mineralogy department unpaid, doing just what she wanted. She was encouraged in her insulin research by Robert Robinson, the Professor of Organic Chemistry, whom she helped with identifications of sterol derivatives. It was Robinson who secured for her external funding from ICI to pay for the extra apparatus, Bowman being deficient in grantsmanship and content with improvised apparatus made from pram wheels and second-hand motorcycle gearboxes. In 1937 she secured her first research student, D. P. Riley, in an unusual way. Even though she was a don, as a woman she was denied membership of the Alembic Club, the University's chemical society. In 1936 she was asked by Riley on behalf of the junior section of the Club to talk about her research at Cambridge; he was so impressed by her account that he asked her to supervise his research. Until the outbreak of war she continued to collaborate with her mentor, Bernal, while developing at Oxford her own independence which was to lead to the award in 1964 of the Nobel prize for chemistry.[15]

[15] D. M. Hodgkin and D. P. Riley, 'Some ancient history of protein X-ray analysis' in A. Rich and N. Davidson (eds), *Structural Chemistry and Molecular Biology* (San Francisco and London 1968); D. P. Riley, 'Oxford: the early years' in G. Dodson, J. P. Glusker and D. Sayre (eds), *Structural Studies on Molecules of Biological Interest: A Volume in Honour of Professor Dorothy Hodgkin* (Oxford 1981); J. Law, 'The formation of specialities in science: the case of X-ray protein crystallography', *Science Studies* iii (1973); D. M. Hodgkin, 'Chemistry at Oxford 1928–60', seminar, Corpus Christi College, 3 Mar. 1989 (Brian Harrison's transcript in HUA), HUA transcript, and in personal communications. The tenacity of the Barkerian approach is shown by R. C. Spiller and M. W. Porter, *The Barker Index of Crystals* (3 vols Cambridge 1951–64).

Botany saw three professors between the wars. The first, F. W. Keeble, was not only at odds with his demonstrator, A. H. Church, but as a horticulturist opposed the application of mathematics to botany, the recently inaugurated DPhil, specialization and the use of experiment, measurement and physical methods in general in the study of plant life. In 1926 he left Oxford to become the first agricultural adviser to ICI, which wanted to boost its sales of fertilizers produced by the continuous and unstoppable Haber-Bosch process at its Billingham works. He was replaced by A. G. Tansley, an ecological botanist of international repute and of independent means, then aged 56. Tansley soon recruited as demonstrators three vigorous researchers, the Oxonian W. H. Wilkins and from outside W. O. James and A. R. Clapham; he also had some success in expanding the numbers of undergraduates and postgraduates. As an editor and writer Tansley led from the front: he edited the *Journal of Ecology* for the British Ecological Society and was hard at work on his monumental (930-page) *British Isles and their Vegetation*. But on one matter he was diffident and on another vacillating. Though he was renowned as an ecological botanist, he did not promote ecology at the expense of what he saw as the even more desirable comprehensive modernization of his department: he fought successfully for laboratories for mycology under Wilkins, an aggressive empire-builder, and for physiological botany under James, leaving only one university demonstrator (Clapham) as an ecologist. It is significant that experimental ecology was begun only in 1937 under Tansley's successor, T. G. B. Osborn. On the issue of where botany should be located, Tansley changed his mind and confused the authorities. The famous Botanic Garden by Magdalen Bridge was of such scientific, aesthetic and historical importance that it was difficult to transform the department there. Two solutions had long been mooted: one was covertly to expand and patch the buildings on the bridge site; the other was to transfer teaching and research to a new building in the science area in order to integrate botany with the other sciences. In 1931 Tansley argued strongly in favour of moving to the science area; then in 1935, realizing that money for a new building was out of the question, he urged that *ad hoc* improvements be made on the bridge site. When Osborn replaced Tansley he immediately made an official complaint about the rambling and piecemeal additions carried out under Tansley, and reported that his own working conditions were the worst of his career. By 1939 the Registrar and Vice-Chancellor had admitted that the laboratory accommodation was shamefully defective and that Osborn simply had no facilities for his own research. At the outbreak of war Oxford's professor of botany endured conditions of work inferior to those he had enjoyed as professor at Adelaide and Sydney universities. In terms of institutional provision, botany remained the cinderella of the sciences in Oxford up to

1939; unsurprisingly the new building for botany and forestry in the science area did not appear until 1950.[16]

The incorporation of the Radcliffe Library into the Bodleian Library in 1927 was relatively peaceful. It enabled the co-ordinated expansion of the Bodleian Library and the Radcliffe Science Library from the mid–1930s.[17] On the other hand the relation between the Radcliffe Observatory (run by the Radcliffe trustees) and the University Observatory became beset by protracted litigation. The University Observatory, opened in 1875, was directed from 1893 by H. H. Turner, Savilian Professor, until his unexpected death at a conference in August 1930. Turner's longest-standing research concerned the distribution and motion of stars as part of an international undertaking concerned with astrographic charts and catalogues. Faced by the increasing obsolescence of his equipment, dating from 1888, Turner began seismological research in 1913 as part of another international undertaking. In the 1920s he developed an interest in the history of astronomy, giving shelter to J. K. Fotheringham, Reader in Ancient Astronomy. From 1924 the Radcliffe Observer was Harold Knox-Shaw who soon became frustrated by Oxford's murky atmosphere and yearned for the clear African skies he had enjoyed for sixteen years. In full collaboration with Turner he proposed a scheme for building a new Radcliffe observatory in cloudless South Africa and for co-operation with the University Observatory. By mid-1930 the Radcliffe trustees were so committed to this scheme that to pay for it they had sold the land and building of their Oxford Observatory to Lord Nuffield for £100,000; but F. A. Lindemann, Lee's Professor of Experimental Philosophy, led the opposition to the scheme on the grounds that it would mean a resource lost and would discourage endowments for Oxford science.[18]

Turner's death and the suspension of his chair for fourteen months enabled Lindemann to keep the subject on the boil. In November 1931 H. H. Plaskett was elected to the chair and immediately announced his wish for a new Radcliffe observatory costing £100,000 and a new solar telescope, both to be in Oxford. With the new Savilian Professor and the Radcliffe Observer at loggerheads, the University foolishly confused statutory right

[16] V. H. Blackman, 'F. W. Keeble', ONFRS viii (1952–3); H. Godwin, 'A. G. Tansley', BMFRS iii (1957); A. G. Tansley, The Future Development and Functions of the Oxford Department of Botany: An Inaugural Lecture Delivered before the University of Oxford on 22 November 1927 (Oxford 1927); A. R. Clapham, 'W. O. James', BMFRS xxv (1979); OUA UR/SF/BG/1, UR/SF/BG/Fl. Cf A. G. Tansley, The British Isles and their Vegetation (Cambridge 1939).

[17] Cf below, 473.

[18] F. A. Bellamy and E. F. B. Bellamy, Herbert Hall Turner: A Notice of his Seismological Work (Oxford and Newport IoW 1931); F. A. Bellamy, 'A plea for astronomy in Oxford', OM 5 Nov. 1931, 126–7; A. D. Thackray, 'Knox-Shaw', Quarterly Jl Royal Astronomical Soc. xii (1971); F. W. F. Smith, second Earl of Birkenhead, The Prof in Two Worlds: The Official Life of Professor F. A. Lindemann, Viscount Cherwell (London 1961).

with custom and took the Radcliffe trustees to court about the removal scheme. After a long action the trustees won in July 1934, to the general acclaim of most British and dominion astronomers, including Plaskett's own father. The Radcliffe Observatory was eventually built near Pretoria, leaving Plaskett with outmoded visual stellar equipment and with a staff expert in astrography and seismology, both of which were embedded in international collaborative schemes and not easily run down. Drawing on his previous experience as Professor of Astrophysics at Harvard University, Plaskett made solar physics the focus of Oxford astronomy, which led to acrimony with the Observatory's old hands. By 1935 Plaskett had secured almost £4,000 from the University for his new solar telescope and spectroscope, which he claimed were perfect, unique and, at 10 per cent of the cost of a stellar telescope, cheap. These resources enabled Plaskett to introduce postgraduate research and to make solar physics the leading research focus, though he shed astrography and seismology only in 1936 and 1946 respectively.[19]

Of the small departments which had few college fellows or none, zoology was the success story. It had the benefit of two chairs: the Linacre chair of zoology and comparative anatomy was occupied by E. S. Goodrich from 1921 to 1945; the Hope chair of entomology was occupied until 1933 by E. B. Poulton and then by his pupil and collaborator G. D. H. Carpenter. Goodrich, who came to his chair with long experience in his department, was widely respected by colleagues and former pupils as a fine researcher who had already built up the department. Faced with the deaths in the First World War of his two senior men, Jenkinson and Smith, he gradually assembled his staff entirely from Oxford graduates taught by himself and often by J. S. Huxley, fellow of New College and senior demonstrator 1919–25. His department was small but brilliant, with an intimate family atmosphere. Goodrich provided the basic morphological training but did not force his staff into his own research mould: the nearest to him was Young, who added an interest in nerves to Goodrich's emphasis on structure. Huxley inspired students with his ideas about the importance of fieldwork, animal behaviour, experimental embryology and population dynamics. Through Huxley and Elton, Oxford zoology became strongly ecological. Goodrich and Huxley were staunch Darwinians, and the department pursued a diversity of work within a Darwinian framework: witness Goodrich's Festschrift produced by Oxford colleagues and pupils with essays on sexual selection by Huxley, ecological genetics by Ford, experimental embryology by De Beer, human evolution by A. M. Carr-

[19] W. H. McCrea, 'H. H. Plaskett', *BMFRS* xxvii (1981); A. D. Thackray, *The Radcliffe Observatory 1772–1972* (London 1972); Bodl. MS DD Radcliffe d. 39; OUA UDC/M/3b/1, UR/SF/AST/1; *Times* 3 July 1934; 'Radcliffe Library extension', *OM* 31 May 1934, 760–1; private communications from Dr M. G. Adam. See also below, 271.

Saunders, animal ecology by Elton, breeding seasons by Baker, the nervous system by Young, dermal bones by J. A. Moy-Thomas and bird evolution by Tucker—all topics on which these past or present demonstrators in Goodrich's department were leading experts. Not surprisingly, pupil–teacher lineages were established over a short time: Huxley taught De Beer who taught Young who taught P. B. Medawar, who was to win a Nobel prize in 1960.[20]

In the Hope department there was an obsessive concern with just one Darwinian topic, namely defensive adaptation and mimicry in insects, to which the overflowing Hope Museum was devoted. With splendid entrepreneurship, Poulton and Carpenter produced the voluminous *Hope Reports*, containing research papers by Poulton and others, which gave the impression of a vast cohort of researchers, but until just before 1939 the Hope department was little more than the professor. Poulton and Carpenter were expert at acquiring large numbers of specimens, especially from the empire, at pulling in motley locals and visitors to work unpaid on them, and then claiming all publications based on such specimens as produced by their department. They cleverly used the Entomological Society as a vehicle of publicity. Though Poulton promoted defensive adaptation in insects *ad nauseam*, his interests did stimulate young zoologists such as Ford, Richards and E. N. Willmer.[21]

After chemistry, the biggest final honour school in science was mathematics, with about twenty-five finalists per year by the outbreak of the Second World War. Though Oxford mathematics was not generally adventurous, it was animated by two mathematicians educated at Cambridge, G. H. Hardy and E. A. Milne. Hardy arrived in Oxford as Savilian Professor of Geometry because he was outraged at the dismissal of Bertrand Russell by Trinity College, Cambridge, for his pacifism. Though under suspicion in Oxford as an anticlerical atheist, and in the mid-1920s President of the Association of Scientific Workers, Hardy was the leading English pure mathematician of his time with an international outlook. A challenging and inspiring teacher and supervisor, he established a flourishing research school of analysis. In 1931, when he returned to Cambridge for

[20] G. R. De Beer, 'E. S. Goodrich', *ONFRS* v (1945–8); A. C. Hardy, 'Goodrich', *Quarterly Jl Microscopical Science* lxxxvii (1947), 317–55; G. R. De Beer (ed.), *Evolution: Essays on Aspects of Evolutionary Biology presented to Professor E. S. Goodrich on his Seventieth Birthday* (Oxford 1938); J. R. Baker, 'J. S. Huxley', *BMFRS* xxii (1976); J. S. Huxley, *Memories* (London 1970), 121–48; M. Ridley, 'Embryology and classical zoology in Great Britain' in T. J. Horder, J. A. Witkowski and C. C. Wylie (eds), *A History of Embryology* (Cambridge 1986); OUA MR/7/1/5, UR/SF/Z/2; V. C. Wynne-Edwards, 'Backstage and upstage with animal dispersion' in D. A. Dewsbury (ed.), *Leaders in the Study of Animal Behaviour: Autobiographical Perspectives* (Lewisburg Pa 1985); personal communications from the late Professor E. B. Ford, Professor V. C. Wynne-Edwards, Professor E. N. Willmer and Professor J. Z. Young.

[21] G. D. H. Carpenter, 'E. B. Poulton', *ONFRS* iv (1942–4); A. Z. Smith, *A History of the Hope Entomological Collections in the University Museum, Oxford* (Oxford 1986).

professional reasons, he was succeeded by his devoted protégé E. C. Titchmarsh. Titchmarsh continued Hardy's field of analysis but not his school. Though Milne came to Oxford in 1929 as the first occupant of the privately endowed Rouse Ball chair of applied mathematics, his field was in fact theoretical astrophysics—which wags called cosmythology. His elevated views of mathematical physics and his suspicions of quantum theory rendered him unhelpful to young experimental physicists and chemists. But in league with Plaskett, the observational astrophysicist, he made Oxford in the 1930s a centre for astrophysics.

Unlike other universities, Oxford had no mathematical institute until 1934 when, after agitation initiated by Hardy, six rooms were set aside in the new extensions to the Radcliffe Science Library as a concession. A mathematical institute appeared in the plan for the science area in 1937 but it was not achieved until the early 1950s—in the form of a former maternity home where mathematicians could divide and multiply. Scholarships and fellowships were far fewer at Oxford than at Cambridge, and as late as the mid-1950s only half the colleges had tutorial fellows in mathematics. In the 1930s most of these were Oxford graduates, appointed on their examination successes, not on their publications, to teach undergraduates in the colleges, not postgraduate students in the university. Naturally they saw no reason to change a system which had rewarded them. Very few of them ever left Oxford to study elsewhere. The obvious exception was J. H. C. Whitehead, who spent a year at Princeton; there Veblen introduced him to topology, which became the speciality of his own research. The insularity of most Oxford mathematicians, many of whom lived on a teaching treadmill, was confirmed by their lack of interest in giving shelter to German refugees from 1933. Though mathematics was an ancient hellenistic and gentlemanly subject, it was tolerated but not encouraged by the colleges and the university, an attitude reinforced by the feeling of inferiority to Cambridge. Crucially, after Hardy's departure nobody replaced him as an activist, and the tendency towards inbred insularity endured.[22]

Chemistry was the largest undergraduate school in science, with about forty-five finalists per year in the 1930s. It was unique among the sciences in that (against the advice of the Asquith Commission) not only did the college laboratories persist in teaching, but one of them, the Balliol–Trinity

[22] G. H. Hardy, A Mathematician's Apology (Cambridge 1967); G. H. Hardy, 'Mathematics', OM 5 June 1930, 819–20; W. H. McCrea, 'E. A. Milne', ONFRS vii (1950–1); E. A. Milne, The Aims of Mathematical Physics: An Inaugural Lecture Delivered before the University of Oxford on 19 November 1929 (Oxford 1929); M. Cartwright, 'E. C. Titchmarsh', BMFRS x (1964); M. H. A. Newman, 'J. H. C. Whitehead', BMFRS vii (1961); OUA UR/SF/BOD/11; M. Rayner, 'Mathematics in Oxford since 1914', seminar, Corpus Christi College, 24 Feb. 1989 (Brian Harrison's transcript in HUA); personal communications from Dame M. Cartwright, the late Professor T. G. Cowling, Professor G. J. Whitrow and Sir Edward Wright.

laboratory, became an important centre of research under Hartley and his pupil Hinshelwood, a Nobel prizewinner in 1956. In order of date of closure they were Magdalen 1923, Queen's 1934, Christ Church 1941, Balliol–Trinity 1941 and Jesus 1947. While physical chemistry prospered in two of the college laboratories using Oxford postgraduates, organic chemistry flourished in the Dyson Perrins Laboratory (opened in 1916) under Perkin and Robinson, successive Waynflete professors, using staff mainly recruited from outside Oxford. The research practices which they imported to Oxford were so successful that in 1947 Robinson was awarded a Nobel prize. A third chemist, Frederick Soddy, had won a Nobel prize in 1921 but was unhappy in his reign as Lee's Professor from 1919 to 1936 over the old inorganic chemistry department in the 'Glastonbury Kitchen' attached to the University Museum. Soddy was at odds with the colleges and most of his colleagues, was averse to compromise, set up no research school and devoted himself to economics. Oxford chemistry was tripartite, but a unifying force was provided by N. V. Sidgwick, fellow of Lincoln, whose synoptic vision was revealed in his publications, his colloquium and his dominance of the Alembic Club and the Dyson Perrins tea club.[23]

Each of the college laboratories had a speciality: quantitative analysis at Magdalen under J. J. Manley; preparative organic chemistry at Queen's under F. D. Chattaway; inorganic chemistry at Christ Church under Angel and A. S. Russell; and physical chemistry at Jesus under D. L. Chapman. Though the Jesus laboratory was purpose-built and occupied three stories, its intellectual range was less than that of Balliol–Trinity, the most important college laboratory. From 1921, under the aegis of Hartley and Hinshelwood, research there received greater emphasis; the former was much indebted to T. W. Richards of Harvard University for experimental procedures and the latter, a true original, began his famous work on kinetics. E. J. Bowen, a pupil of Hartley, branched out into photo-chemistry. In the 1920s the laboratory, rich in improvisation and complicated in its financing, offered a crowded family atmosphere with staff and undergraduates working propitiously at the same bench. On Hartley's departure in 1930 Hinshelwood took charge of the laboratory where he was soon joined by R. P. Bell, another of Hartley's pupils, who developed work on acid-base catalysis. The Balliol–Trinity laboratory was bizarre in that it occupied an endlessly changing suite of converted cellars, outhouses, washrooms and lavatories in

[23] H. Hartley, 'Schools of chemistry of Great Britain and Ireland', pt 16, 'The University of Oxford', Jl Royal Institute of Chemistry lxxix (1955), 116–27, 176–84; H. Hartley, 'The contribution of the college laboratories to the Oxford school of chemistry', Chemistry in Britain i (1965); A. Fleck, 'Frederick Soddy', BMFRS iii (1957); A. D. Cruickshank, 'Soddy at Oxford', British Jl for the History of Science xii (1979); Bodl. MSS Eng. misc. b. 170, Soddy papers; OUA MR/7/2/7, U Sol/6/2; H. T. Tizard, 'N. V. Sidgwick', ONFRS ix (1954); L. Sutton, 'Sidgwick', Proc. Chemical Soc. 1958; Lincoln College Library, Sidgwick papers. Cf below, 267–9.

the two colleges. But such was its success that in 1936 the University restricted Lee's chair to physical chemistry, promptly elected Hinshelwood to it and began planning for its own physical chemistry laboratory, which was paid for mainly by Lord Nuffield and opened in 1941. The case of Hinshelwood suggests that the Oxford tradition of physical chemistry was indigenous, but most Oxford graduates who became fellows of colleges in the 1930s found their fields of research while undertaking postgraduate study in German, American and Danish universities, even during the Third Reich.[24]

Perkin, a disciple of Baeyer of Munich, arrived in Oxford in 1913 with a formidable reputation built up at the University of Manchester as a researcher, leader of a research school, designer of new laboratories and an entrepreneur who could secure external endowments. He was called to Oxford to pep up its chemical research and he obligingly repeated what he had done in Manchester. He soon secured a new laboratory, endowed by C. W. Dyson Perrins, the manufacturer of Worcester sauce. It was designed by himself in collaboration with his trusted Manchester architects, the Waterhouse family, and erected by his Manchester builders in the trusted glazed brown and cream bricks which gave the familiar public-lavatorial appearance. There was a surge of articles published from the Dyson Perrins at Manchester's expense, helped by the importing from Manchester of most of his senior laboratory demonstrators, who from 1922 acted as Perkin's research lieutenants. In 1916 Perkin was largely responsible for introducing the part II in undergraduate chemistry as a fourth year devoted to research, and strongly promoted the introduction of the DPhil to encourage postgraduate research [plate 6.1]. An accomplished host, musician and

[24] Bell studied under Brönsted in Copenhagen 1928–32; H. W. Thompson, fellow of St John's 1930–75, Reader in Infra-Red Spectroscopy 1954–64, Professor of Chemistry 1964–75, worked under Haber in Berlin 1929–30; L. E. Sutton, fellow of Magdalen 1932–73, worked under Debye at Leipzig 1928–9 and under Pauling at the California Institute of Technology 1933–4; J. D. Lambert, fellow of Trinity 1938–76, worked under Euken at Göttingen 1936–7; L. A. K. Staveley, fellow of New College 1939–82, worked under Clusius at Munich 1937–8; L. A. Woodward, fellow of Jesus 1939–70, worked under Debye at Leipzig 1928–31. G. R. Clemo, 'F. D. Chattaway', *ONFRS* iv (1942–4); E. J. Bowen, 'D. L. Chapman', *BMFRS* iv (1958); R. P. Bell, 'E. J. Bowen', *BMFRS* xxvii (1981); K. J. Laidler, 'Chemical kinetics and the Oxford college laboratories', *Archive for History of Exact Sciences* xxxviii (1988); E. J. Bowen, 'The Balliol-Trinity laboratories, Oxford, 1853–1940', *Notes and Records of the Royal Society of London* xxv (1970); T. W. M. Smith, 'The Balliol-Trinity laboratories' in J. Prest (ed.), *Balliol Studies* (London 1982), 185–224; R. T. Gunther, *The Daubeny Laboratory Register 1849–1923* (3 vols Oxford 1904–23); H. Hartley, 'The Theodore William Richards memorial lecture' in *Memorial Lectures Delivered before the Chemical Society 1914–1932* (London 1933); D. A. Long, 'The Sir Leoline Jenkins Laboratories', *Jesus College Record* 1989; K. Hutchison, *High Speed Gas: An Autobiography* (London 1987), 24–42; OUA MR/6/3/34, MR/7/2/7, UR/SF/CHE/1B; personal communications from Sir P. Allen, Professor R. P. Bell, Professor E. F. Caldin, Dr J. Danby, the late Lord Kearton, Professor K. J. Laidler, Dr J. D. Lambert, Professor D. A. Long, Mr D. Murray-Rust, Dr A. G. Ogston, Dr L. A. K. Staveley and the late Dr L. E. Sutton.

gardener, he was the ideal man to introduce Germanic research practices into Oxford. Ironically he created two problems. The introduction of part II increased the grip of the college tutors, mainly physical chemists, on their own pupils, leaving Perkin to recruit researchers mainly externally. Few of his demonstrators were attached to a college; they were helots lacking status and tenure, which frustrated long-term planning.[25]

Robinson was a Manchester pupil of and extensive collaborator with Perkin, in whose family of organic chemists he regarded himself as the chief son, not least as successor to Perkin at Oxford. He continued Perkin's research emphasis but more exclusively, intensely, mercurially and innovatively than his equable chemical father. Research and postgraduate students were such major concerns that he contumaciously ignored the University terms. He explored new fields with new techniques, and with his collaborators produced a paper a fortnight for eight years. Such productivity drew research students like A. R. Todd from many parts of the world—and a few Oxonians, including E. P. Abraham. It engendered considerable industrial consultancies and attracted substantial external endowment for an extension to the laboratory to be begun in 1939. Robinson was used to monolithic departments, and treated his 'unattached' demonstrators autocratically; but he had no control of those college fellows who were physical organic chemists working in his laboratory. They occupied independent fiefdoms. In the 1930s he failed to disturb the dominance of the physical chemists in college fellowships.[26]

Research done in the inorganic chemistry department was humdrum except for the pioneering work in the science of metallurgy undertaken by the totally deaf William Hume-Rothery [plate 10.1], a graduate of Oxford in chemistry, whose research at Oxford was externally endowed for no fewer than twenty-six years. In 1938 he gained some local recognition when he was made a university lecturer, having been elected FRS in 1937. His pioneering work on atomic structure and on the theory of the metallic state with respect to the structure and formation of alloys, initially facilitated by a senior demyship at Magdalen and a grant from the Armourers and Braziers Company, would have ended in 1932 but for the lucky accident of the establishment that year of the Gordon Warren research fund of the Royal

[25] J. C. Smith, *The Development of Organic Chemistry at Oxford* (2 vols Oxford 1968–75); Greenaway, Thorpe and Robinson, *Perkin*; W. H. Perkin, 'The Baeyer memorial lecture' in *Memorial Lectures*; W. H. Perkin, 'The position of the organic chemical industry', *Jl Chemical Soc.* cvii (1915, transactions); R. Robinson, 'Perkin', *Jl Soc. of Chemical Industry* xlviii (1929); OUA UM/F/4/15; personal communications from Professor W. Baker.

[26] A. R. Todd and J. W. Cornforth, 'Robert Robinson', *BMFRS* xxii (1976); Royal Society of London, Robinson papers; Smith, *Organic Chemistry*; OUA UR/SF/CHE/1 and 5; personal communications from Sir E. P. Abraham, Lord Todd and Dr M. Tomlinson. Todd, who was to win a Nobel prize in 1957, had studied in Glasgow and Frankfurt before arriving in Oxford in 1931: A. R. Todd, *A Time to Remember: The Autobiography of a Chemist* (Cambridge 1983), 23–8.

Society of London. Against great competition Hume-Rothery was awarded a Warren fellowship for seven years, and remained dependent on it until 1955. His loyalty to Oxford, his remarkable enthusiasm, his own pocket and the prescience of the Royal Society kept metallurgy alive at Oxford in the 1930s.[27]

In physics the most remarkable event was the transformation of the Clarendon Laboratory by a group of low-temperature physicists from Breslau who came to Oxford in 1933 at the invitation of Lindemann. Unlike many Oxford scientists, Lindemann saw the advent of the Third Reich as an opportunity as well as a tragedy. Though no longer active in research, Lindemann was such a public figure—active in the 1930s as a politician and in air defence—that he has overshadowed his two fellow professors of physics, A. E. H. Love and J. S. E. Townsend, both of whom did their best work before 1914. The former, liked but outmoded, held the Sedley chair of natural philosophy until his death in 1940 at the age of 77; while Townsend, as Wykeham Professor of Physics from 1900 until 1941, ran the electrical laboratory in an increasingly insulated way intellectually and institutionally, so that the electrical and Clarendon laboratories were separate and sometimes competing institutions.

From 1919 Lindemann had three ambitions: to rival the Cavendish Laboratory at Cambridge; to raise the status of science at Oxford relative to classics; and finally, motivated by his long-lasting and deep loyalty to W. H. Nernst under whom he took his PhD in Berlin, to promote low-temperature physics as a vehicle for justifying Nernst's heat theorem. Until 1933 these aims were only partly realized. Lindemann failed to sustain low-temperature research in the early 1920s but he did recruit a mélange of talented physicists, most of whom he had met in Berlin or at Farnborough where he was a boffin in the First World War. Three of these researchers—G. M. B. Dobson (who discovered the ozone layer in the atmosphere), T. R. Merton and the colourful D. A. Jackson (both spectroscopists)—were men of independent means who did not need to beg the University for money. Solo research was the order of the day. Only Egerton, a specialist in combustion, ran a research group—and significantly he was lured in 1936 to Imperial College, London.

From 1931 Lindemann revived his interest in low-temperature physics, using a hydrogen liquifier designed by and bought from Franz Simon, a PhD pupil of Nernst at Berlin, which he had just left for Breslau. In January 1933 Lindemann secured a coup when K. A. G. Mendelssohn, Simon's senior assistant whom he had invited to Oxford, made a Simon helium liquifier work in the Clarendon Laboratory and enabled Lindemann at last to steal a

[27] G. V. Raynor, 'William Hume-Rothery', *BMFRS* xv (1969); Royal Society of London, council minute book 24 (Warren research fund committee). See also below, 272–3.

march on Cambridge. This successful importation of skill and apparatus spurred Lindemann to bring to Oxford later in 1933 not only Mendelssohn but other Breslau low-temperature physicists and their apparatus, namely Simon himself, Nicholas Kurti and Heinz London. Armed with money from ICI, Lindemann even toured Germany in the summer of 1933 and recruited H. G. Kuhn, a Göttingen spectroscopist. The Breslau cohort enabled Lindemann to fulfil his long-cherished aims of establishing a school of low-temperature physics, of rivalling Cambridge and of raising the status of science and his laboratory in Oxford.

The Breslau physicists, supported mainly by short-term grants from ICI, soon became the dominant research sector in the Clarendon Laboratory. Dobson continued solo, while Jackson and Kuhn worked as a pair with no postgraduate students, Jackson himself paying for much of the apparatus. But postgraduate research, by graduates of Oxford and by foreigners, prospered under Simon and Mendelssohn, who were standard-setters and gave an enduring identity to the laboratory. The chief director of research was Simon, with Mendelssohn occupying a subsidiary yet independent role. They relied on T. C. Keeley as the general manager of the laboratory and on Lindemann as the public figure and entrepreneur who dealt with prospective patrons. Simon depended heavily on Kurti, who acted as his lieutenant and was master of the temperamental cryogenic apparatus. It was the success of the Breslau physicists and of Kuhn which enabled Lindemann to press the University for the new laboratory which was completed in autumn 1939 at a cost of £77,000. Yet Lindemann felt unhappy about the lack of money to keep other distinguished refugees in Oxford and he deplored the small size of the contributions made by the colleges and the university towards keeping his researchers in post.[28]

---

[28] This and the preceding three paragraphs are based on B. Bleaney, A. H. Cooke, N. Kurti and K. W. H. Stevens, 'F. A. Lindemann, Viscount Cherwell', *Physics Bull.* xxxvii (1986); Smith, *The Prof*, 81–210; G. Thomson, 'F. A. Lindemann, Viscount Cherwell', *BMFRS* iv (1958); Nuffield College, Lindemann papers; E. A. Milne, 'A. E. H. Love', *ONFRS* iii (1939–41); A. von Engel, 'J. S. E. Townsend', *BMFRS* iii (1957); J. T. Houghton and C. D. Walshaw, 'G. M. B. Dobson', *BMFRS* xvi (1970); H. Hartley and D. Gabor, 'T. R. Merton', *BMFRS* xvi (1970); H. G. Kuhn and C. Hartley, 'D. A. Jackson', *BMFRS* xxix (1983); N. Kurti, 'F. E. Simon', *BMFRS* iv (1958); N. Arms, *A Prophet in Two Countries: The Life of F. E. Simon* (Oxford 1966); Royal Society of London, Simon papers; D. Shoenberg, 'K. A. G. Mendelssohn', *BMFRS* xxix (1983); K. A. G. Mendelssohn, *The World of Walther Nernst: The Rise and Fall of German Science* (London 1973), 71, 164–75; Bodl. Mendelssohn papers; D. Shoenberg, 'Heinz London', *BMFRS* xvii (1971); R. V. Jones, *Most Secret War* (London 1978), 8–42; R. V. Jones, 'Oxford physics in transition: 1929–39' in R. Williamson (ed.), *The Making of Physicists* (Bristol 1987), 113–26; P. Hoch, 'The reception of central European refugee physicists of the 1930s: USSR, UK, USA', *Annals of Science* xl (1983), 217–46; R. E. Rider, 'Alarm and opportunity: emigration of mathematicians and physicists to Britain and the United States, 1933–1945', *Historical Studies in the Physical Sciences* xv (1984); OUA MR/7/1/7, UR/SF/PHE/4; and personal communications from Professor B. Bleaney, the late Dr A. H. Cooke, Professor R. V. Jones, Dr H. G. Kuhn, Professor N. Kurti and Dr H. Megaw.

Between the two world wars Oxford science was not homogeneous. Though each subject faced common structural features, the responses to these varied considerably, showing that each science was also *sui generis*. The variety of aims and perceptions among scientists makes it impossible to indulge in contrasts between them and arts men as a whole. Yet certain trends were apparent. In comparison with the years before 1914, Oxford's scientists between the wars were much more successful as academic entrepreneurs and builders of departments, mainly in research work and rarely by the expansion of undergraduate numbers. Given Oxford's inability or reluctance to siphon much of the aggregate wealth of the colleges to the university's science departments, entrepreneurial scientists had to go round prospective patrons cap in hand seeking external funding, often a gruelling and time-consuming business. Most scientists saw a larger grant from the University Grants Committee as the best source of regular funding to maintain people at work in the new, extended or revamped premises occupied by several departments. A second way, involving the creation of more research and tutorial fellowships in the colleges, seemed a pipedream. Heads of department resented the frittering away of research time in raising and administering small, temporary and *ad hoc* grants. No wonder that there was a poor field for some of the vacant chairs.

External funding for buildings and people came from various sources. Agriculture and forestry relied heavily on the British and colonial governments, especially through the Ministry of Agriculture and Fisheries, the Colonial Office and the Forestry Commission. In the 1930s the Department of Scientific and Industrial Research became increasingly important as a supporter of postgraduate researchers in general. Of industrialists, Lord Nuffield was in a class of his own. Though Oxford disdained industry, industrialists and manufacturers made significant contributions. Of the chemical firms Shell, ICI (through Harry McGowan, its chairman in the years from 1930 to 1950) and British Oxygen (through its chairman J. D. Pollock) were the most prominent. A saucemaker, Dyson Perrins, enabled organic chemistry to shine, while the biscuit firm of Huntley and Palmer of Reading helped entomology by providing for Poulton an affluent wife and dozens of biscuit tins for lepidoptera. Among philanthropic bodies the Rockefeller Foundation was unrivalled, but the contributions made by the Rhodes and Grey trustees were not negligible. It was still possible for important innovations to be endowed by individuals, some of whom were otherwise obscure. Though Rouse Ball was a well-known figure, Mrs Watts and Dr J. E. Crombie were not; yet their financial contributions were essential in experimental psychology and seismology, respectively.

By 1939 research had become a widespread disciplinary and departmental imperative as well as a personal commitment among Oxford scientists. For some of them, especially Perkin and Robinson, personal research and publication overrode all other academic functions. Research schools of varying renown and size had appeared in a number of subjects, the most significant being those led by Southwell (relaxation methods), Goodrich (Darwinian evolutionary biology), Elton (Bureau of Animal Population), Milne and Plaskett (astrophysics), Simon and Mendelssohn (low-temperature physics), Hinshelwood (chemical kinetics), Hume-Rothery (metallurgy), Tansley (botany) and above all Perkin and Robinson (organic chemistry). Innovators in research and its organization had arrived in Oxford in four ways. Those such as Hinshelwood and the Goodrichian Darwinians were graduates of Oxford who had initiated or maintained an indigenous tradition which owed little to other universities. Secondly, young Oxford postgraduates went abroad or elsewhere in Britain to learn about or discover a topic or technique under an acknowledged expert, and on their return to Oxford introduced it and made it their research speciality from a base in either a department or a college. Oxford's high reputation in mineralogical and crystallographic research owed much to the time spent by Barker in St Petersburg, Powell in Leipzig and Hodgkin in Cambridge. Some of the physical chemists were so aware of the benefits to be gained from postgraduate study abroad that they either stayed there a long time or visited various important centres. The best illustration of this indebtedness is H. W. Thompson, who studied under Haber in Berlin, Fowler at Imperial College, London, and Badger at the California Institute of Technology. The third way of promoting research was to import as professors or directors of research established people from such other universities as Cambridge, Manchester, Harvard and Sydney. This was most obviously so in organic chemistry, which was heavily dependent on the University of Manchester through Perkin and Robinson, neither of whom had any connection with Oxford before assuming his chair; as a first-class waiting room, Manchester University was appropriately situated on Oxford Road. Last there were the émigré or refugee scientists who had a disproportionately important effect in physics compared with other sciences. Lindemann saw that the Breslau low-temperature physicists and Kuhn could enable him to realize some long-held ambitions, and he had the pull with industrialists to secure special external funding and materials for them at a time when money and jobs were not readily available for indigenous physicists. These four modes of recruiting researchers ensured that many Oxford scientists made a notable contribution as boffins during the Second World War, and that the expansion of undergraduate teaching in the non-medical sciences in the 1950s would be based on a strong reputation for research.

PART THREE

OXFORD, 1939–1970

7

Oxford and the Second World War

PAUL ADDISON

On 9 February 1933, ten days after Hitler became Chancellor of Germany, the Oxford Union carried by 275 votes to 153 the motion 'that this House will in no circumstances fight for its King and Country'.[1] Traditional Tories were profoundly shocked, and Winston Churchill condemned the resolution as an 'abject, squalid, shameless avowal'.[2] The debate received worldwide publicity and created a lasting impression of Oxford as a nursery of pacifist and Communist youth. But let us turn to a different scene. At the outbreak of war in September 1939 the War Office set up a joint recruiting board in the Clarendon Building. Conscription had been applied only to men aged 20 and 21, most of whom had yet to receive their call-up papers. So it was still possible, as in 1914, to volunteer, and the government was keen to recruit potential officers. The board therefore invited all undergraduates, and resident postgraduates under 25, to offer their services. Of a potential group of 3,000 volunteers, 2,362 came forward.[3]

What had become of the anti-war sentiments of 1933? Evidently their significance had been exaggerated. The youthful politicians of the Oxford Union were doubtless an unrepresentative minority. 'This was probably', wrote Christopher Hollis, 'the period when the Union was most unpopular with undergraduates at large'.[4] Nor did the vote against 'King and Country' indicate unqualified pacifism. From 1931 onward Union debates were dominated by a loosely aligned left consisting of Liberals, Labour and the Communists. None of these groups was opposed on principle to war. On the contrary, they gravitated in the course of the decade from an anti-war position in 1933 to an anti-Fascist position by the time of the Munich agreement of September 1938. In alliance with such Tory critics of the government as Edward Heath, they swung the Union strongly against

[1] *OM* 16 Feb. 1933, 426–7.
[2] M. Gilbert, *Winston S. Churchill* (8 vols and 5 companion vols in 13 pts London 1966–88) v. 456.
[3] *Annual Reports 1939–1945* (University of Oxford 1947), 17.
[4] C. Hollis, *The Oxford Union* (London 1965), 197.

Neville Chamberlain's policies of appeasement. In May 1939 the Union voted in favour of conscription.[5]

In another sense the 'King and Country' debate foreshadowed the future. The pacific sentiments of 1933 signalled a rejection of the heroic interpretation of war. The literature of the western front—the work of Graves, Blunden, Sassoon and others—mingled in the minds of young people with fears of another great war in which whole cities would be destroyed by bombing. In a manifesto of October 1932 calling on the government to adopt a peace policy, five young fellows of Oxford colleges spoke of 'a generation which has learned to see war as it is, stripped of every shred of lustre and romance'.[6] By 1939 there was a widespread acceptance that a war would have to be fought. But the lustre and romance had indeed vanished.

Richard Hillary, later famous as a fighter pilot in the Battle of Britain, was a commoner at Trinity in 1939 and a member of the University Air Squadron. He and his friends were the public-school 'hearties' of their day [plate 7.1]. But their response to the outbreak of war was far from jingoistic. 'It demanded no heroics', wrote Hillary, 'but gave us the opportunity to demonstrate in action our dislike of organized emotion and patriotism'.[7] The historian R. B. McCallum, a fellow of Pembroke, recalled two students who came to say goodbye to him before leaving for their units: 'each of them separately observed that if they had to vote on the notorious Union resolution at that moment, they would vote for it. One of them declared: "I am not going to fight for King and Country, and you will notice that no one, not Chamberlain, nor Halifax, has asked me to".'[8] This was true. The patriotism of 1939 was no less deeply felt than the patriotism of 1914, but it was differently expressed.

The outbreak of war marked the end of a period of intense conflict over foreign policy in British politics. In Oxford the issues had been debated at the Union and argued over at high tables. More remarkably, they had ranged don against don in a public display of division. In the Oxford City by-election of October 1938 ten heads of house and two professors came out in favour of the pro-Munich candidate, Quintin Hogg, while six heads of house and three professors aligned themselves with the Master of Balliol, A. D. Lindsay, in his opposition to appeasement.[9]

In the months following the by-election there appears to have been a quiet closing of the ranks within the University. As hopes for a new and lasting peace faded, preparations for war began to seem more important than the

[5] M. Ceadel, 'The King and Country debate, 1933: student politics, pacifism and the dictators', *Historical Jl* xxii (1979); *OM* 4 May 1939, 566–7.

[6] *OM* 20 Oct. 1932, 52.

[7] R. H. Hillary, *The Last Enemy* (London 1942), 28.

[8] R. B. McCallum, *Public Opinion and the Last Peace* (Oxford 1944), 179.

[9] *Times* 20 Oct. 1938, 15; 21 Oct. 1938, 7.

rights and wrongs of Munich. Though colleges had already made some preparations against air raids, the September crisis revealed that in other respects the University was unready. Serious contingency planning now began under the new Vice-Chancellor, George Gordon, President of Magdalen, who took up his duties in October 1938. On his own authority Gordon conducted negotiations with various government departments for the wartime use of university and college buildings and for converting science departments to government work. Plans were submitted to Council and agreed early in 1939.[10] Shortly after Munich, the historian G. N. Clark, a veteran of the Great War, proposed to the Oxford University Press that following the precedent of 1914–18 a series of pamphlets should be published to explain 'why we are about to be at war again'. The first of the new series, Sir Alfred Zimmern's *The Prospects of Civilization*, was published in July 1939.[11] As war approached, the University was asserting its identity as a national institution and an integral part of the state. There was no one in Oxford to speak up for the lost cause of 1939—peace.

In the Great War the University had been converted into a military camp with colleges serving as barracks. Would history repeat itself? In the academic year 1938/9 81.5 per cent of all students were men and 81 per cent were in the humanities.[12] If the government were to fix the age of conscription at 18, four-fifths of the undergraduate population would disappear. Except for the women's colleges, only the science and medical departments, whose activities were vital to the war effort, would remain. On 21 September the War Office announced that the age of call-up would be 20. Most undergraduates would have to leave before completing their courses, but there was nothing to prevent school-leavers from coming up to university as usual. For the time being, therefore, an abridged version of undergraduate life would continue. At the beginning of Michaelmas term 1939, 2,761 men and 750 women came into residence, compared with 3,750 men and 850 women the previous year.[13]

Meanwhile the joint recruiting board, chaired by A. D. Lindsay, was busy interviewing undergraduate volunteers. Generally speaking, they were either recommended for training at an officer cadet training unit (OCTU) or, in the case of scientific or medical students, instructed to continue with their studies. Gradually, as conscription was extended, the conscripts too appeared before the board and were sorted out into categories as before. Conscientious objectors were directed to 'work of national importance'.[14]

[10] MCG [Mary C. Gordon] *The Life of G. S. Gordon 1881–1942* (London 1945), 153–4; Merton College library, D.1.81, I. D. Jones, 'Merton College 1939–1945' (typescript of a pamphlet published for the College in 1947 under the same title and over the initials IDJ), 2.
[11] P. Sutcliffe, *The Oxford University Press: An Informal History* (Oxford 1978), 249.
[12] *Franks Report* ii. 13, table 5.
[13] *OM* 4 Nov. 1943, 50.
[14] *Annual Reports 1939–1945*, 17–18; *OM* 17 Oct. 1940, 1.

It was government policy to disperse people and institutions from London, a prime target for German bombing, to reception areas in the provinces. University and college buildings were therefore subject to government requisition and conversion, in whole or in part, to other uses. The political intelligence department of the Foreign Office, a subdivision of Chatham House, occupied most of Balliol. Most of Merton was taken over by the Ministry of Transport and half of Queen's by the Ministry of Home Security. Both St Hugh's and the Examination Schools were converted into hospitals, while the Slade School of Fine Art was housed at the Ashmolean Museum. The controllers of fish and potatoes at the Ministry of Food were billeted together at St John's—'the biggest fish and chip shop the world has ever seen'.[15] A concentration of intelligence activities in and around Oxford brought the secretarial staff from MI5 to Keble and the map-making section to the Bodleian Library. By the end of 1940 the War Office's intelligence corps was established at Oriel.[16]

One consequence of requisitioning was the need for greater co-operation between the colleges. When a college lost part of its accommodation, some of its undergraduates had to be put up in another college. There were pairing arrangements whereby, for instance, Exeter housed all the students from Lincoln, Trinity took some from Balliol, and Pembroke some from Christ Church. Some colleges were now in a position to benefit financially while others were liable to be penalized, and since this was evidently unfair, a pooling system was devised to balance gains and losses. Colleges paid in 75 per cent of the income they received from the use of their buildings; the money was then shared out in proportion to the number of students each college had in residence in 1938/9. Sometimes colleges also pooled their tutorial resources.[17]

Dons over the age of 25 belonged to a reserved occupation, but early in 1939 the Ministry of Labour had invited all British academics who were prepared to undertake government service in wartime to place their names on a central register. Most had done so, and at the outbreak of war ministries hastened to recruit the most talented candidates. So great was the flight from Oxford that the University's teaching strength was dangerously impaired. Faculties were therefore asked to fix a minimum teaching strength in each subject, and the Ministry of Labour agreed to consult the University before a civil-service post was offered to a teaching member. By November 1940 it was estimated that 132 senior members of the University were absent on war service, of whom 60 were in the armed forces and 72 in civilian posts.

---

[15] P. Hennessy, *Whitehall* (London 1989), 115.

[16] N. West, *MI5: British Security Operations 1909–1945* (London 1981), 146; C. Andrew, *Secret Service: The Making of the British Intelligence Community* (London 1985, London 1986 edn), 641.

[17] *Annual Reports 1939–1945*, 15; Jones, 'Merton College', 5.

Assuming a total of 504 academic staff in September 1939, more than a quarter were now on leave.[18]

The exodus was matched by an influx of newcomers to Oxford. Apart from the swarm of officials, thousands of working-class mothers and children, evacuees from the East End of London, were temporarily accommodated in colleges or cinemas before dispersing to homes in and around Oxford. The Principal of the Society of Oxford Home-Students, Grace Hadow, described 'seething crowds of excited small people with strong cockney accents . . . and, at first, numbers of obviously East End mothers pushing prams . . . who strolled rather sadly up and down "the Corn" obviously thinking it was not a patch on the Mile End Road'. Nineteen schools had been evacuated from London and relocated in Oxfordshire. The women's colleges each adopted one of the schools and undergraduates devoted weekends to looking after the children.[19]

At night the black-out plunged Oxford into the dark. The Master of Pembroke, Homes Dudden, inquired of Council what action was proposed to protect male undergraduates against the solicitations of prostitutes in the darkened streets.[20] A more poetic effect, depicted by Grace Hadow, was 'the sight of Oxford in the full moon, with no artificial light to disturb its peace, and with Magdalen Tower and St Mary's spire steeped in a radiance infinitely more lovely than flood-lighting'.[21] In the colleges, windows were blacked out at night and air-raid shelters prepared. Scouts doubled as air-raid wardens. College treasures—precious manuscripts and paintings, the college silver, even stained glass windows—were stored away in safe places. The corporate life of the colleges was diminished, with fewer undergraduates living or dining in their own college.[22] And whereas in peacetime undergraduates could look forward to three or four years at Oxford, most would now have to leave after a year or so, before taking their final examinations.

This raised the complex problem of academic qualifications in wartime. The underlying principles, agreed in outline in Michaelmas term 1939, were simple enough. Undergraduates who faced the call-up were to be examined on the basis of a shortened curriculum, and provided they satisfied the examiners would obtain a special certificate. This, together with a period of military service in lieu of residence, would qualify the holder for a war degree. A war degree, however, was not to be confused with a peacetime honours degree. At the end of the war the holders of a war degree would be entitled to return to Oxford and to convert it into a full honours degree. Faculty boards rapidly instituted shortened honours courses based on

[18] OM 14 Nov. 1940, 65; Franks Report ii. 39.
[19] M. Reeves, St Anne's College Oxford: An Informal History (Oxford 1979), 26.
[20] HCP 174 (1939), p. xix (28 Sept.).
[21] Reeves, 26.
[22] Jones, 'Merton College', 4–10 describes the first year of the war at Merton.

'sections'—one-term courses examined at the end of each term. In each section it was possible to obtain either a pass or a distinction. The shortened course consisted of three sections, and students were allowed to count the first public examination ('prelims') as one section. After passing all three sections, which it was expected would occupy three successive terms, the student would obtain the special certificate, or in other words qualify (after a period of national service) for a war degree.

When this was formally proposed, controversy broke out. One school of thought strongly opposed the granting of a war degree on the basis of such a short period of residence. The University, it was argued, was in danger of devaluing its war degree well below the level of other universities: Cambridge was demanding five terms' work and most universities six. The issue was not finally resolved until December 1940, when Congregation voted for a compromise. From those matriculating up to the end of 1940 only three terms of residence and three sections were to be required; those matriculating subsequently would need five terms of residence and four sections. This made it very much more likely that candidates for the war degree would have to leave Oxford with their qualifications incomplete and return after the war to complete the degree.

From Michaelmas term 1940 a further refinement was introduced. Sections were incorporated into a new type of shortened honours school in two parts. Where sections had been examined every term, parts were to be examined at intervals of a year or more and were also to be classified. They varied in the amount of work prescribed, covering one, one and a half or two years' work. Where a part covered one year's work only, a war candidate had to add a further section in order to qualify for a war degree. Where a part covered at least four terms' work, this was sufficient. A student who completed parts 1 and 2 would obtain a classified honours degree, but as a general rule undergraduates would only have time for part 1 and would have to return after the war if they wished to complete the shortened honours course.[23]

By the time the question of war degrees was settled the war had entered a new phase. No account of Britain in the Second World War could fail to stress the transformation which occurred between the spring and summer of 1940 as Hitler's armies conquered western Europe and the British began to prepare themselves for invasion. For A. J. P. Taylor, a fellow of Magdalen, it was a period of high spirits. 'My friends who lived through this time agree with me that we never laughed so much . . . Strangers stopped me in the street and said, "Poor old Hitler. He's done for himself this time now that he's taken us on." '[24] Others were less buoyant. The Warden of Wadham,

[23] OM 19 Oct. 1939, 8–9; 25 Apr. 1940, 261; 5 Dec. 1940, 117–18; HCP 178 (1941), 133–7, report of the committee on war degrees (27 Feb.).
[24] A. J. P. Taylor, A Personal History (London 1983), 153–4.

Maurice Bowra, had served with the Royal Artillery in the First World War and was anxious to play a more active part in the second. 'I find it almost unendurable sitting here when the whole country is in deadly peril', he wrote to Lindemann on 3 June. As Churchill's trusted friend and adviser, Lindemann was now a very powerful man. On 21 June Bowra urged him to get the University closed down altogether, except for the science departments. 'A large number of young men who would make excellent soldiers, sailors and airmen', he wrote, 'are wasting their time on studies which contribute nothing to the national effort'. The current state of affairs, he concluded, was 'not getting a good name for the University and may do us harm later'.[25] Can it be a coincidence that about this time the War Office informed the Vice-Chancellor that men destined for the army would no longer be allowed to go up to university, but would be sent to young soldiers' battalions for training? The Vice-Chancellor firmly resisted the proposal and the War Office decided to abandon it for the time being.[26]

For undergraduates, Trinity term 1940 was a tranquil, sunlit interlude. 'It was good to be alive even if the world was falling about our ears', wrote John Stokes, an Australian at Magdalen. 'While the men were coming back from Dunkirk we sat in the warm twilight on the lawn in front of the Library, listening to the *Water Music*.' But might this be the last of Oxford? In its final issue of the term the *Oxford Magazine* reflected that it took leave of its readers 'in circumstances of grave uncertainty. The question of whether the University will re-open in October can only be determined by the course of the war in the next few months.'[27]

So perilous was Britain's position that signs of panic appeared. Swept by fears that a fifth column was preparing to betray Britain from within, the government capitulated to demands for the mass internment of enemy aliens. Since 1933 a flow of refugee scholars from Nazi Germany had sought asylum and employment in Britain. Oxford had played its part in the work of the Academic Assistance Council, the voluntary organization of British academics set up to assist these victims of Nazism. By February 1939 posts had been found in Britain for 128 academic refugees, of whom 27 were in Oxford.[28] During the first year of the war more refugees arrived and they too were found work if possible. At the Institute of Statistics, for example, most of the senior staff entered government service. The economists who replaced them were mainly refugees.[29] The problem was that although some

[25] Nuffield College, Cherwell MSS, M25/B123, Bowra to Lindemann, 3 June 1940; Bowra to Lindemann, 21 June (incorrectly endorsed in pencil, 1941).
[26] Gordon, *G. S. Gordon*, 155.
[27] 'Oxford yesterday: the university at war', *Oxford Today* Trinity 1989, 56; *OM* 13 June 1940, 377.
[28] *OM* 9 Feb. 1939, 368.
[29] G. D. N. Worswick, 'Kalecki at Oxford, 1940–44', *Oxford Bull. Economics and Statistics* xxxix (1977), 19–20.

refugee scholars had become naturalized, others were still 'enemy aliens'. Douglas Veale, the Registrar, complained to the *Times* that 477 enemy aliens were at large in Oxford: 'aliens are a potential menace and we feel they should be interned'.[30] Among those interned were four economists from the Institute of Statistics and three who were later to be employed there.[31] By contrast with Veale, two Oxford voices were raised against the policy of indiscriminate internment. From his retirement Gilbert Murray condemned public hysteria: 'this is the reaction of the average ignorant and unthinking man, who can see no difference between one German and another'. In Whitehall dissent was vigorously expressed by R. T. E. Latham, a barrister, fellow of All Souls and temporary clerk in the refugee section of the Foreign Office. His protests contributed to the eventual reversal of the policy.[32]

Another symptom of anxiety in the summer of 1940 was the evacuation of children overseas. There were commonsense arguments in favour of transporting them to safety, and the government itself ran a scheme of assisted passages to the dominions. But some ministers, including Churchill, regarded the scheme as bad for morale, and the spectacle of wealthy parents hastening to ship their children overseas raised awkward questions about social privilege. In June 1940 Oxford received an invitation from the University of Toronto to accommodate the children of senior members. Some parents were eager to take up the offer. 'We were less worried about bombing', one parent recalls, 'than the possibility that our children might be brought up under a Nazi regime, and indoctrinated with Nazi beliefs'. On 8 July a party of 125 children, escorted by 25 mothers and a doctor, left Oxford on a special train to Liverpool. On the other side of the Atlantic the party was diverted by an invitation to Yale, where most of the mothers and children decided to stay.[33]

The long-awaited blitz began in September 1940. First London, then the provinces were thrust into the front line. But in spite of the importance of Cowley for munitions and the targeting of cultural centres in the 'Baedeker' raids of 1942, Oxford was never bombed. 'Hitler's keeping Oxford for himself', the Dean of Somerville told Vera Brittain. 'He wants it to look as it always has when he comes for his Honorary Degree.'[34] Yet the blitz felt very close. There were frequent false alarms, and German bombers could be heard throbbing their way through the night skies to the midlands and the north. In Philip Larkin's novel *Jill*, his undergraduate hero is rudely awoken from his daydreams by reports that his home town has suffered heavy raids.

[30] West, *MI5*, 113.

[31] I am grateful to Mr G. D. N. Worswick for this information.

[32] B. Wasserstein, *Britain and the Jews of Europe 1939–1945* (London 1979), 95, 104.

[33] D. Allen, *Sunlight and Shadow* (London 1960), 115–16; *Times Saturday Review* 23 June 1990, 11; see also A. S. Symonds, *Havens Across the Sea* (Oxford 1990).

[34] V. Brittain, *England's Hour* (London 1941), 209–10.

Dashing home in a panic, he discovers to his intense relief that his parents are alive and the street where they live untouched.[35]

The blitz prompted the University to step up its air-raid precautions. A university fire-brigade was formed, with a trailer-pump in every college. Huge static water-tanks were placed in college quadrangles and fire-fighting teams of dons, students and scouts took part in elaborate training exercises in collaboration with other colleges and the city's fire-brigade. The climbing of college roofs, formerly a disciplinary offence, was now a patriotic obligation, with ladders provided. As fire-watching duties had to be carried out for 365 nights a year, colleges offered free residence in the vacations to undergraduates who volunteered for duty. At Merton, a control-centre for the neighbouring group of colleges, the scheme required the continuous presence on duty of about twenty men.[36]

As the war intensified, shortages of manpower became acute and the government whittled away the time available for study at university. The age of call-up fell to 19 in the second half of 1941 and to 18 in the course of 1942. In December 1941 conscription was extended for the first time to women: all unmarried women between the ages of 20 and 30 were to be called up for some form of national service. The effects of the changes at Oxford can be summarized briefly. From May 1941 to December 1942 the government allowed male undergraduates in the humanities to defer their call-up for at least twelve months, thus enabling them to complete part 1 of their examinations. But this was on condition that they accept military instruction in the Senior Training Corps or Air Squadron. As a result they would normally spend about nine months at Oxford with two days a week devoted to military training, which now officially took priority over the timetable for lectures and tutorials. In order to ensure for themselves a period at university, pupils began to leave school earlier, and the University allowed them to matriculate at the beginning of the Hilary or Trinity terms. Courses often ran on into the vacations, and the distinction between term and vacation was rapidly disappearing.[37]

From December 1942 entry was further restricted to those under 18 at the time of matriculation. This would have drastically reduced the number of male undergraduates but for the fact that from 1942 onward the University agreed to introduce six-month short courses, free of the normal entry requirements, for service cadets. Army cadets were confined to science courses, but the navy and the air force allowed their candidates a free choice of subject. Short courses, in which military training was combined with part-time study, bore little relationship to the normal honours curriculum. Nevertheless service cadets were matriculated, housed in college and lived

[35] P. Larkin, Jill (London 1946, London 1975 edn), 203–15.
[36] Jones, 'Merton College', 15.
[37] For the changing regulations see Annual reports 1939–1945, 43, 66–7, 90.

under academic rather than military discipline. A scheme which brought Richard Burton, a miner's son from the Rhondda, to Oxford may have had some effect in broadening the social basis of entrance to the University. Many short-service candidates—though not Burton himself—returned after the war to undertake a full degree-course.[38]

The introduction of national service for women allowed them, at first, to spend up to two years at university, with a further year of study for qualifications leading to 'professions or callings of national importance'. In practice this enabled most women to continue reading for a full honours degree. But in March 1943 the regulations were tightened up to restrict entry to women who could complete at least six terms by the age of 20. The effect of this was to prevent women over 19 from entering university, while most of those under 19 would now be unable to complete a full degree course [plate 7.2]. The result was that from Trinity term 1943 most women switched to sections or parts of the shortened honours curriculum.

Despite the restrictions a few undergraduates continued to pursue a full honours curriculum in the humanities. Among them was the novelist John Wain, a student at St John's from the Hilary term of 1943. 'We were a strange group: a handful of those like myself who had been rejected on medical grounds, reinforced—and, as time went by, outnumbered—by men invalided out of the Services with more or less permanent disabilities. With our artificial legs, our glass eyes, our deflated lungs, our asthma, our heart disease, we limped about, discussing Shakespeare and Milton amid the skirling of huge lorries running in four-wheel drive.'[39]

The various shortened courses ensured a rapid turnover of undergraduates. The number of male undergraduates in residence at any one time was substantially reduced, while female numbers remained remarkably stable. There was thus a sharp increase in the proportion of women students, as shown by table 7.1. This was an aberration from a rising masculine trend. By 1948/9 the percentage of women students had fallen to 15 per cent, below the pre-war level, whence it declined again to 14 per cent in 1958/9.[40]

Over the war years as a whole there was also a marked increase in the proportion of students in the scientific and medical faculties and a corresponding reduction in the humanities, as may be seen from table 7.2. These figures marked the beginning of a long-term trend. The proportion of students in the sciences had risen to 20 per cent by 1948/9, and again to 24 per cent by 1958/9.[41]

[38] H. Carpenter, *OUDS: A Centennial History of the Oxford University Dramatic Society 1885–1985* (Oxford 1985), 147–8; F. H. Lawson, *The Oxford Law School 1850–1965* (Oxford 1968), 149.
[39] J. B. Wain, *Sprightly Running: Part of an Autobiography* (London 1962), 100.
[40] *Franks Report* ii. 13.
[41] Ibid.

TABLE 7.1

OXFORD UNDERGRADUATES IN RESIDENCE, 1938–45

year*	men	women	% women
1938/9	3750	850	18.5
1939	2761	750	21.4
1940	2029	NA	
1941	2059	820	28.5
1942	1799	816	31.2
1943	1813	803	30.7
1944	1735	827	32.3
1945	2538	915	26.5

* figures for Michaelmas term except for 1938/9.

Source: OM 4 Nov. 1943, 50 and 17 Oct. 1946, 6.

TABLE 7.2

DISTRIBUTION OF FULL-TIME STUDENTS BY FACULTY IN OXFORD IN 1938/9 AND 1945/6 (%)

	arts	science	medicine	other
1938/9	81.4	11.4	4.6	2.6
1945/6	74.2	16.1	7.5	2.2

Source: *The Problems Facing British Universities* (Nuffield College 1948), 111–12.

From statistics we must return to experiences and impressions. The Oxford of the later war years was no longer a provincial town but a cosmopolitan crossroads. A. L. Rowse described the scene in 1941: 'the life of the streets, even in the old centre of the town, has ceased to be dominated by the University. So many thousands of evacuees and refugees have flooded into the area, mainly from London: it is said that the population has gone up by some twenty per cent, perhaps twenty thousand people. Then there are all the men in uniform, who crowd into this convenient centre by all the bus routes from round about . . . Pavements are incessantly crowded; shopping has become a nightmare (not that that much concerns dons and under-graduates); theatres are packed with unknown faces—as the war wears on it becomes rarer and rarer to recognise a friend.'[42] Wartime Oxford was a magnet for politicians and academics exiled from Europe. The University

---

[42] A. L. Rowse, 'Oxford in war-time' in his *The English Spirit: Essays in History and Literature* (London 1944), 261.

responded with hospitality and support. Study facilities were granted to three Czech universities; a Polish law faculty, which awarded its own degrees with an Oxford seal attached, was established with the assistance of the law school.[43] The café life of the town, Rowse observed, had become distinctly continental: 'from the languages being spoken all around one, one might be inhabiting a bit of old Vienna or some Central European University town'.[44]

The University also extended its hospitality to members of the allied armed forces. Among the military bases nearby was a Canadian army camp. On the initiative of the Professor of Jurisprudence, Arthur Goodhart, informal arrangements were made in 1942 for part-time courses for Canadian troops. They were put up in the colleges for a week and treated to a mixed programme of lectures, discussions and sightseeing, with a Tuesday evening dance at Rhodes House. So successful was the venture that in 1943 it was formally adopted by the University, housed at Balliol (the staff of Chatham House having returned to London) and extended to troops of other allied powers. Prominent among them were, of course, the Americans. There was an American base at Cowley, and US servicemen were a familiar sight as they strolled around Oxford or gathered at the Red Cross Club in the Cornmarket.[45] During Help for Russia week, the Hammer and Sickle was to be seen flying beside the Union Jack at Carfax. But Russian visitors to Oxford were few and far between, and the University appears to have had no academic or ceremonial connection with the Soviet Union. President Roosevelt, on the other hand, was awarded an honorary degree, as were Dr Salazar of Portugal, Queen Wilhelmina of the Netherlands and King Haakon of Norway.[46] Oxford's mystique was quite unashamedly deployed in the service of diplomacy. The international contacts of undergraduates seem to have been limited to the occasional decorous tea-party for American soldiers at Somerville.[47]

Wartime students led very English lives in spartan surroundings. The majority now undertook military training, while the rest were expected to perform some type of war work. Women students helped out in hospitals or nurseries or worked part-time on munitions. Eleanor Plumer, who succeeded Grace Hadow as Principal of the Society of Oxford Home-Students, was the daughter of a field marshal and determined to do her bit. After a long vacation working as a factory hand at Cowley, she conceived the idea of subcontracting work to her staff and students in North Oxford.

    [43] Lawson, 147.
    [44] Rowse, 262.
    [45] Allen, *Sunlight and Shadow*, 128–30.
    [46] *Annual reports 1939–1945*, 40, 105; *OM* 14 Oct. 1943, 1.
    [47] This section draws on 15 personal recollections contained either in letters to Brian Harrison or in HUD, and on 5 brief recollections in M. Figgis, 'After Armageddon', *Oxford Today* Trinity 1989, 6–8.

Trays of fusecaps were laid out on long tables to be tested, and young and old bent earnestly to the task.[48] Austerity was the common lot of civilians in wartime, and the hardships of undergraduates ought not be exaggerated. A naval cadet at Magdalen in 1943/4 recalled the college servants 'bringing hot water of a morning, polishing shoes, turning down one's bed in the evening, washing up the tea crockery'.[49] In most colleges one of the more depressing aspects of wartime life was the food. Students handed in their ration books at the beginning of term and collected them again at the end. In return they received unappetizing meals in hall, meagre rations of milk, tea and sugar and a pound pot of marmalade per term. A much greater hardship was the bitter cold of draughty rooms in winter, with heating restrictions enforced. 'I was never so cold during fifteen years in the Canadian west', recalled a short-service cadet at University College.[50]

This was no place for the dandies and swells of peacetime. In the new Cromwellian Oxford a more egalitarian tone prevailed. 'The war was a great leveller', according to an ex-grammar-school boy and state scholar who went up to Queen's in 1941. 'High taxation and the fact that practically everything including clothing was rationed meant that I could mix easily with those whose parents were much better off than mine.'[51] 'Perhaps the most difficult thing to convey', wrote Philip Larkin, 'was the almost-complete suspension of concern about the future. There were none of the pressing dilemmas of teaching or Civil Service, industry or America, publishing or journalism; in consequence, there was next to no careerism.'[52]

In spite of austerity, wartime Oxford had much to offer. Junior common rooms, some jointly occupied by the members of two colleges, were usually warm and hospitable. If college food was poor, more appetizing dishes could be found at one of the British Restaurants in town, or perhaps at the Taj Mahal, the Randolph or the Mitre. Queues formed outside Oliver and Gurdens, the 'cake factory' in Summertown. Though social and sporting facilities were undoubtedly curtailed, a great variety of activities continued. One undergraduate at St Edmund Hall from 1940 to 1941 'played soccer in the college XI (badly), tennis in the second VI, attended the essay society, the play reading society, blew a trumpet in the Bach Choir and attended most meetings of the Labour Club'.[53] A number of contemporaries recall thriving college boat clubs; the annual University boat race, though suspended in 1941/2, was resumed from 1943. Students with theatrical ambitions turned to the Friends of the Oxford University Dramatic Society,

---

[48] Reeves, *St Anne's*, 26–8.
[49] HUD/C/SV/M1943422.
[50] C. A. G. Palmer (University College 1944–5, 1949–52) to Brian Harrison, Jan. 1989.
[51] HUD/C/SV/M1941211.
[52] Larkin, *Jill*, 12.
[53] HUD/C/SV/M1940729.

a wartime version of OUDS organized by Nevill Coghill, a fellow of Exeter.[54] Weekly repertory continued throughout the war at the Playhouse, and West End productions were often transferred to the New Theatre. A galaxy of cinemas beckoned: 'the Electra in Queen Street, the New Cinema in Headington, the Regal in Cowley Road, the Ritz in Gloucester Green, the Super in Magdalen Street and the Scala in Walton Street: the latter even offered double seats'.[55]

In the First World War the Oxford Union had been closed down for the duration. In the second it remained open, though motions for debate were subject to censorship by the proctors, who forbade wording directly critical of the conduct of the war. In general, debates were still dominated by the left, an ascendancy that was to last until 1946. One extraordinary moment, transcending the usual divisions of opinion, deserves to be singled out. On 28 January 1943 Victor Gollancz moved that the government should adopt 'a more energetic and practical policy towards the rescue of Jews in Europe'. Little was known at this time of the Holocaust, but as Gollancz spoke he conveyed the magnitude of the tragedy unfolding in Europe. At the conclusion of his speech the opponents of the motion crossed the floor to join him and the motion was carried by 188 votes to 21.[56]

The Union also resolved 'that a return to God through organized religion is essential for the establishment of a new world order'. The revival of Christian practice and belief was a powerful undercurrent in wartime Britain. In the first winter of the war Sir Cyril Norwood observed that 'preachers who have something to say already command congregations of a size to which they have not been accustomed, and all religious societies alike report increased membership and a new attitude'.[57] According to John Wain the removal to Whitehall of left-wing secular dons, and the hunger for a Christian message, enabled Anglican scholars like C. S. Lewis and Charles Williams to dominate the scene. 'Anglicanism, for years regarded as a quaint, intellectually dowdy set of attitudes . . . suddenly became the adventurous spearhead of English intellectual and artistic life.'[58]

But we must turn our attention from the inner life of Oxford to the University's role in the wider war. The military aspect has already been described. From 1941 the University was to a great extent a part-time training ground for officer cadets. Mercifully the casualty rate in the Second World War was lower than it had been in the first and the University's roll of honour was shorter. But it was far from negligible, and the sense of loss was

---

[54] Carpenter, *OUDS*, 142–8.

[55] D. R. Johnston-Jones (New College 1945, 1948–51) to Brian Harrison, Aug. 1989.

[56] *OM* 4 Feb. 1943, 164–5.

[57] H. Carpenter, *The Inklings: C. S. Lewis, J. R. R. Tolkien, Charles Williams, and their Friends* (London 1978), 174; C. Norwood, 'Oxford today', *Oxford* winter 1939, 30.

[58] Wain, *Sprightly Running*, 143.

no less grievous. In September 1940 Maurice Bowra told Marion Frankfurter: 'all my frustrated paternal instincts which have gone into producing undergraduates are perpetually harrowed and the daily casualty lists are a permanent horror'.[59] Afterwards the *Oxford Magazine* calculated the death toll as 2,857 for the First World War and 1,719 for the second. But the latter figure was clearly an underestimate: one college alone had more than a hundred names which had yet to be added to the list.[60] This time there was to be no 'lost generation', but many young men of promise were killed. Collin Dillwyn, a historian and Student of Christ Church, shot himself during the retreat to Dunkirk rather than fall into enemy hands.[61] Of the undergraduate volunteers of 1939, the fighter pilot Richard Hillary wrote a wartime classic, *The Last Enemy*, but was killed on a practice flight in January 1943. Keith Douglas, ex-Merton and ex-Officer Training Corps, enjoyed a growing reputation as a war poet but was killed in the Normandy landings of June 1944.

More typical of the times were the many dons who enjoyed 'a good war' and returned in 1945 as more substantial figures, the coming men of post-war Britain. The recruitment of academics to various branches of cloak-and-dagger warfare is a familiar theme and ought not to be laboured: intellectuals were a transient minority in the world of secret intelligence. Among those employed at Bletchley Park, the wartime home of the government's code and cypher school, were Denys Page of Christ Church, an authority on Greek tragedy, and two philosophers, Gilbert Ryle of Christ Church and Stuart Hampshire of All Souls. MI5 recruited the Christ Church historian J. C. Masterman to chair the Twenty Committee, the body which directed the 'double-cross' system of counter-espionage against Germany. Hugh Trevor-Roper, a research fellow at Merton, was recruited to MI5's radio security service, where his 'irreverent thoughts and dangerous contacts' got him into trouble with the pre-war professionals who ran the organization.[62]

The government was far more dependent on academic expertise in the scientific conduct of the war. When Churchill returned to the Admiralty in September 1939 he took Lindemann with him as his adviser, and Lindemann in turn offered the new Clarendon Laboratory's staff and facilities to the Admiralty. Henceforth the Laboratory's team worked mainly on the design and development of microwave radar for ships and aircraft, with funding from the Department of Scientific and Industrial Research (DSIR). Some of the scientists at the Clarendon Laboratory were, however, of non-British birth and were excluded from the work on security grounds. Their response

---

[59] Washington DC, Library of Congress, Felix Frankfurter MSS, Bowra to Marion Frankfurter, 13 Sept. 1940.

[60] *OM* 19 June 1947, 435; see also above, 18–24, esp. table 1.2.

[61] A. J. Ayer, *Part of My Life* (London 1977, London 1978 edn), 233.

[62] West, *MI5*, 161; Andrew, *Secret Service*, 646, 672–3; J. C. Masterman, *On the Chariot Wheel: An Autobiography* (London 1975), 211–20.

was to devote themselves unofficially to research on atomic energy. Working in collaboration with Frisch and Peierls at Birmingham, Simon, Kurti, Arms and Kuhn laid the groundwork for the separation of U235, the isotope responsible for nuclear fission in uranium. The awesome project of an atomic bomb was strongly backed by Lindemann and endorsed by Churchill in August 1941. After this, the atomic energy team at the Clarendon Laboratory was incorporated in the government's 'tube alloys' research programme and funded by the DSIR.[63]

By a familiar paradox the war also stimulated research into the saving of life. With the aid of physicists from the Clarendon Laboratory the Nuffield Professor of Anaesthetics, Robert Macintosh, developed a portable vaporizer capable of delivering a rapid and even flow of ether to the patient. Production was started at the Morris Motor Works at Cowley, and by 1945 over 4,000 vaporizers had been delivered to British and American field hospitals. The Professor of Surgery, Hugh Cairns, conducted research into the treatment of head injuries at St Hugh's. The most outstanding achievement was that of Howard Florey, the Professor of Pathology, in collaboration with the Jewish refugee, Ernst Chain, who was demonstrator and lecturer in chemical pathology. They were the first to obtain penicillin in a pure and stable form. Produced in the United States, penicillin was then applied to the treatment of wounded servicemen, revolutionizing their chances of survival.[64]

We have yet to examine the migration of academics to Whitehall. By November 1940 some 72 Oxford dons were employed as temporary civil servants. Of these, a handful of eminent experts on foreign countries were on the staff of the political intelligence department of the Foreign Office, and mostly worked at Balliol, to which Chatham House had been evacuated. As the useless and expensive staff of 'Cheatham House', they were lampooned by Gerald Berners in his novel Far From The Madding War (1941). It is difficult to say whether this was a fair judgement: the nature of their work remains obscure. Others played a more active role in foreign policy. Isaiah Berlin's lucid analyses of the course of American politics, dispatched to London from the British embassy in Washington, were highly valued by Churchill. William Deakin, one of Churchill's pre-war research assistants on the History of the English-Speaking Peoples, was head of section for SOE (the Special Operations Executive) in New York, before parachuting into Yugoslavia as leader of the British military mission to Tito. Most of the 'temporaries' were, however, employed in home affairs and in managing the war economy. In October 1939, at Churchill's request, Lindemann set up a

[63] For early post-war accounts see the articles by TCK [Thomas Keeley] and FES [Franz Simon] in OM 16 May 1946, 289 and OM 13 June 1946, 352.
[64] Times 12 Sept. 1989, 13 (Macintosh); ADG [A. D. Gardner] 'Sir Hugh Cairns', OM 23 Oct. 1952, 22; HWF [Hugh Florey] 'Penicillin', OM 29 Nov. 1945, 97–8.

'statistical section' to monitor the economic progress of the war and to brief Churchill in his battles with other departments. On the advice of Roy Harrod, Lindemann recruited a number of economists from the Institute of Statistics, and Harrod himself joined in January 1940. The Prime Minister's statistical section, as it became in May 1940, enabled Churchill to keep in touch with the war economy and to intervene from time to time to impose his own priorities. In particular, Churchill relied on Lindemann and the section to resist further extensions of rationing and austerity, which he regarded as harmful to morale.[65]

Oxford, together with Cambridge and Manchester, supplied most of the economists recruited as temporaries in the wartime civil service. But one overbearing personality whom few in Whitehall were eager to recruit was the Master of University College, William Beveridge. In July 1940 the Minister of Labour, Ernest Bevin, appointed him to conduct a rapid survey of manpower requirements. Bevin, however, distrusted Beveridge and seized the opportunity in 1941 of sidetracking him into chairing the committee on social insurance, where it was expected that his task would be mainly technical.[66] Of the younger generation of economists Robert Hall, a fellow of Trinity, had been recruited to the Ministry of Supply at the outbreak of war, and Harold Wilson, a protégé of Beveridge, entered the economic section of the war cabinet in 1941. Economic administration, however, was never the exclusive preserve of economists. Oliver Franks was Professor of Moral Philosophy at Glasgow when summoned to the Ministry of Supply in September 1939. But in the words of Douglas Jay, Franks possessed 'not merely an outstanding talent for manipulating a large organization, but a rare intuition into the psychology of colleagues, high or low, and not least in the business world'.[67] He proved to be the outstanding temporary civil servant of the period.

Academics might succeed at the nuts and bolts of administration, but they were also important as publicists and manipulators of opinion. Richard Crossman embarked on a career in psychological warfare, or 'black propaganda' as it was called.[68] A. J. P. Taylor was taken on by the Ministry of Information's regional headquarters at Reading to raise morale by lecturing to the public. 'Of course the whole thing was nonsense. The morale of my audiences needed no boosting.'[69] Perhaps so, but many academics felt they must do what they could to assist morale through journalism, broadcasting or lectures to the troops under the army education scheme. In

[65] R. F. Harrod, *The Prof* (London 1959), 180–7; F. W. F. Smith, second Earl of Birkenhead, *The Prof in Two Worlds: The Official Life of Professor F. A. Lindemann, Viscount Cherwell* (London 1961), 212–18.

[66] P. Addison, *The Road to 1945* (London 1975), 168–9.

[67] D. Jay, *Change and Fortune: A Political Record* (London 1980), 93.

[68] T. Dalyell, *Dick Crossman: A Portrait* (London 1989), 50–64.

[69] Taylor, *Personal History*, 159.

so far as academics were the makers of 'public doctrine' in Britain, it was their task to explain the origins and aims of the war. But over and above the generally agreed objective of the defeat of Hitler there was of course a divergence of opinion. All who belonged to the progressive camp, which ranged at this period from Communists on the left to Tory reformers on the right, maintained that social reconstruction was an indispensable war aim. On the other side were the reactionaries who wished to return to the economic and social status quo. The reactionaries, however, were on the defensive and tended to be mute or evasive. Oxford failed to provide them with a spokesman or a platform. At the Treasury, Hubert Henderson of All Souls composed trenchant and pessimistic attacks upon Keynesian policies. But he did so in secret.[70] The 'Inklings'—J. R. R. Tolkien, C. S. Lewis, Charles Williams and their friends—were deeply hostile to modernity, and hence to social reconstruction. But their conservatism took religious and literary forms: politically speaking they were invisible. The most articulate spokesman for conservatism was perhaps the anonymous versifier who wrote in the *Oxford Magazine*:

> I would not build Jerusalem
> In England's pleasant land
> All post-war moralisers
> And prophets should be banned
> I won't be reconstructed
> I don't want to be planned[71]

While conservative Oxford stood by, progressive Oxford laboured to advance the cause of social reform. The University's greatest benefactor, Lord Nuffield, was of strongly right-wing outlook, so there was some irony in the fact that Nuffield College should initiate, under the direction of a socialist, a major inquiry into social reconstruction. In September 1939 Nuffield College consisted of an empty building site, six fellows and a Warden, Sir Harold Butler. The skeleton College appeared at first to lack any useful wartime function. But in June 1940 Council accepted the Warden's view 'that the College could play a valuable part in the investigation of certain cardinal problems of social and economic reconstruction'.[72] In the following November G. D. H. Cole was appointed director of the Nuffield College social reconstruction survey. A grant from the Treasury of £5,000 a year met about a third of the costs and the rest was borne by the College.[73]

[70] A. Booth, 'The "Keynesian revolution" in economic policy-making', *Econ. Hist. Rev.* Feb. 1983, 108, 110–12.
[71] *OM* 29 Oct. 1942, 39.
[72] HCP 176 (1940), p. lxxxi (17 June).
[73] G. D. N. Worswick, 'Cole and Oxford 1938–1958' in A. Briggs and J. Saville (eds), *Essays in Labour History* (London 1967 edn), 30.

The survey began with ambitious terms of reference. It was to inquire into the distribution of industry and population, the future of the social services and the efficiency of democratic institutions. In association with the survey, Cole organized from 1941 onward a series of private conferences dealing with such topics as the post-war export trade, relations between education and industry, the education of girls and the supply and training of teachers. Four of the conferences were devoted to employment policy.[74] The survey proper ended in a débâcle with its work unfinished. In 1943 the Treasury withdrew its grant, the official justification being that the reports were not of the quality Whitehall required.[75] Other motives may be suspected. The Beveridge report of December 1942 had taken Whitehall by surprise. Possibly the Treasury decided not to risk the same thing happening again in the shape of a Cole report. If so, the fact that Cole was a socialist must surely have played into the hands of his opponents. Cole fought hard within the University to keep the survey in being, but lost the battle and resigned from the survey in January 1944. Perhaps University conservatives were not so inert after all.

The most successful aspect of the survey was the series of reconstruction conferences. These were remarkable for bringing together academics, civil servants and industrialists. Post-war reconstruction plans, it has been argued, were the consequence of prolonged bargaining between interest groups and officials. No exclusive significance can be claimed for the Nuffield conferences, which were only rehearsals for a process of negotiation which took place in Whitehall. But they produced an exchange of ideas between socialists like Durbin, Balogh and Kaldor and industrialists like Melchett, Weir and Cadbury—with civil servants listening in. Here was a sounding-board for the politics of a coalition government.[76]

There is no need to repeat the story of the making of the Beveridge report of 1942. No doubt Beveridge could equally well have written the report as Director of the London School of Economics. But the Oxford connection was more than incidental. At the turn of the century Beveridge had studied at Balliol in the company of his brother-in-law and friend R. H. Tawney. His interest in social reform had originated in Oxford and had been re-awakened at University College by his friendship with Cole. Beveridge followed up his report with his own inquiry—financed by progressive businessmen—into full employment. Inclined at first towards a socialist solution, he was partially converted to Keynesianism by the economist E. F. Schumacher of the Institute of Statistics. Beveridge also worked closely with the Nuffield social survey, submitting drafts of his ideas for discussion at three successive

[74] Nuffield College, wartime research committee and social reconstruction survey, private conferences Oct. 1941 to July 1955.
[75] M. Cole, G. D. H. Cole (London 1971), 246–7.
[76] K. Middlemas, Power, Competition and the State i (London 1986), 60–1.

conferences.[77] Shortly after the appearance of Beveridge's *Full Employment in a Free Society*, the Institute of Statistics published its own analysis of the way ahead in *The Economics of Full Employment*. 'In essentials', wrote Cole, 'there is complete agreement between Sir William Beveridge and the six authors of the collective volume, who are in effect underlining Sir William's theoretical analysis'.[78] It would be misleading to suggest that Beveridge or the Institute determined government policy. But they did help to establish the conviction that mass unemployment could and should be avoided.

As might be expected, Oxford influences were also at work in the making of educational policy. The All Souls Group, convened by Warden Adams in June 1941, created a circle of leading educationalists in close touch with R. A. Butler, the President of the Board of Education. Its deliberations, wrote Frank Mitchell, 'were of seminal importance in helping to shape the pattern of wartime educational legislation and postwar educational developments'.[79] Butler also appointed a committee under Sir Cyril Norwood, the classicist and President of St John's, to report on the secondary-school curriculum. The Norwood report of 1943 argued in favour of a tripartite system of grammar, technical and modern schools—a recommendation justified by the unscientific claim that children fall naturally into three different categories of mental ability. The report, though not incorporated in the 1944 Education Act, was important as a victory for continuity. The tripartite system already in place was now to be extended into a world of secondary education for all.

Among the various reconstruction plans there was none for reconstructing the University itself. Perhaps this was the great unthinkable. Or perhaps it was felt that so many changes were already in the making that it would be impractical to look beyond them. It would be no simple task for the colleges to overcome the backlog of repairs and maintenance, or to cope with the impending wave of ex-servicemen. In other parts of the University, major innovations were in progress. The impact of Lord Nuffield was working its way through in the planning of Nuffield College and the transformation of the medical school. The Clarendon Laboratory was a growing empire in which the total number of students, demonstrators and staff grew from 81 in 1939 to 256 in 1946.[80]

External factors were increasing the demand for places and propelling the University towards expansion. The coalition government's further education and training scheme, launched early in 1943, offered grants covering the full costs of a university education, including allowances for dependants, to

[77] J. Harris, *William Beveridge* (Oxford 1977), 433–4; Nuffield College, social reconstruction survey, conferences of 12–13 Dec. 1942, 11–12 Sept. 1943, 18–19 Mar. 1944.
[78] *OM* 7 Dec. 1944, 98.
[79] Quoted in M. Sanderson, *Educational Opportunity and Social Change in England* (London 1987), 109.
[80] Nuffield College, Cherwell MS B42, memorandum on the future of physics at Oxford.

everyone on war service whose post-school education had been interrupted or deferred: the financial barriers to Oxford entry were abruptly removed. For men and women in the services who had never qualified for university, but who now wished to do so, a common services entrance exam, conducted by the civil service commissioners, was instituted. By 1949 45,000 university places had been awarded under the scheme.[81]

One of the coalition government's last decisions was to finance a rapid, two-year programme of expansion for the universities. In the first instance this was part of a deal whereby the universities agreed to reserve 90 per cent of their places for ex-service candidates in 1946 and 1947. But there was also a long-term shift towards a state-funded expansion of higher education. The Attlee government increased the number of state scholarships and local-authority awards. They also accepted the recommendations of the Barlow report of May 1946, which called for the annual output of scientists to be doubled.[82] Between 1945 and 1950 the redbrick universities and colleges increased their total numbers by 130 per cent. In Oxford, where the collegiate system made it physically more difficult to expand, the increase was less but still substantial. The number of undergraduates rose from 4,391 in 1938/9 to 6,159 in 1948/9 and 7,436 in 1958/9.[83]

Dilution of standards at first seemed a danger, yet the ex-servicemen of 1945 proved to be excellent students. John Mabbott, a philosophy tutor at St John's who had also taught the returning soldiers of 1918, was in a position to compare the two post-war generations. After the First World War, he recalled, ex-servicemen had sought to recapture the *douceur de vivre* of the Edwardian years. 'The 1945 generation could not have been more different. They did not look back to "pre-war" as an earthly paradise, but as a period of unease and menace. They were forward-looking and entirely serious. There was no line between workers and playboys; they were a delight to teach because of their maturity and enthusiasm.'[84]

Seen from a distance, the outstanding characteristic of the University in wartime was its adaptability. A new model of college and university administration, a new structure of degrees and a new way of life were improvised between 1939 and 1942. Of course, these were temporary changes, the response to an emergency which ended with the bonfires and fireworks of VE-day. But Oxford also displayed adaptability over the longer run. In the main the University was a whiggish institution in which the active majority of dons and undergraduates believed in moving with the times, but not too fast. After 1945 there was a period of restoration in which the revival of the collegiate system took pride of place. Yet this was a

[81] H. C. Dent, *Growth in English Education 1944–1952* (London 1954), 26–7.
[82] Ibid. 170.
[83] *Franks Report* ii. 12, table 4; Dent, 171–2.
[84] J. Mabbott, *Oxford Memories* (Oxford 1986), 107–8.

restoration subsidized by the Treasury and adapted to the requirements of government policy. In 1965, after a lifetime's experience of Oxford, Maurice Bowra looked back upon the Second World War as a turning-point in the University's fortunes. In his view the 1944 Education Act not only rescued the University from growing financial difficulty, but raised academic standards by multiplying the number of candidates competing for places.[85] The effect of the war, in other words, was the partial incorporation of the University in the welfare state. In the mid–1960s, as Bowra reflected on these developments, there still seemed no reason to doubt that the consequences had been all to the good.

[85] Franks Commission, written evidence iv. 16–17.

8

College Life, 1945–1970

KEITH THOMAS

The end of the war saw a rapid return by the men's colleges to some approximation of normality.* The static water-tanks and air-raid shelters were removed from the gardens. The government departments went back to Whitehall, and colleges which had been temporarily billeted elsewhere, like Brasenose in the Meadow Buildings of Christ Church or St Peter's in Corpus, returned to their former homes. Memorial services were held in the college chapels for those who had fallen in the war, and a determined effort was made to pick up the threads of pre-war existence. Yet the next thirty-five years were to see huge changes in the position of the colleges and the character of Oxford life. The colleges would survive, but only at the price of renouncing many of their former characteristics.

The traditional notion of a college was of an autonomous, residential community, to which all members owed their first allegiance. The Master of Balliol wrote in 1960: 'Every true Oxford man would agree that the essence of Oxford is college life. To have one's own rooms, on one's own staircase, making one's friendships with undergraduates and dons, to have meals together, to drop into one's own J.C.R., read in one's College Library, worship in one's own College chapel, to play on one's own field or row from one's own boathouse—all these, taken together, make up the experience men come to Oxford to get and always treasure. It is on this intimacy of daily life that an Oxford education is based. From this it derives its unique value. A college is more than a hostel; it is more than just a private society of teachers and pupils; it is a household, a very large one, of course, but a household all the same. There is nothing quite like it and its Cambridge counterpart in the whole world.'[1] This was the ideal [plate 8.1]. How did it

---

* Much of this chapter is based upon memories and impressions. I have also made heavy use of the recollections of former members of the University recorded in their confidential returns in HUD/C/SV. I am most grateful to Mark Pottle, who has tirelessly answered queries and supplied indispensable material. For other valuable advice and information I thank Michael Brock, John Dunbabin, Rodney Needham, Harry Pitt, John Prest, Charles Wenden and, above all, Brian Harrison. For life in the women's colleges see below, 361–9.

[1] *Balliol College Record* 1960, 5 (Sir David Lindsay Keir).

compare with the post-war reality and what were the new pressures to which the colleges were forced to respond?

The first and most immediate challenge came from sharply rising numbers. The flood of returning ex-servicemen coincided with new provisions for the public funding of university students. These very soon made it possible for most people with a place at Oxford to secure some form of grant from the state or local education authority which would pay their fees and even, subject to a means test, the cost of their maintenance.[2] Since it was in the colleges' financial interest to maximize the number of their students, the outcome was a spectacular increase in the number of undergraduates admitted. Between the wars the number of students in the University had risen from 4,163 (in 1923/4) to 5,023 (in 1938/9). After 1945 it accelerated sharply to 7,323 in 1949/50. It slackened a little in the early 1950s, but with the ending of national service and consequent doubling-up of the entry in the latter part of the decade it rose again to 8,975 in 1960/1 and to 10,947 in 1970/1.[3] In individual colleges the change was often striking. Brasenose had averaged 140 undergraduates reading for the schools in the 1930s. In 1949 the figure was 340.[4] By the mid-1960s the median size of the men's colleges was 325.[5] In general the post-war colleges were double their pre-war size, and they were under constant pressure to expand.

The number of fellows of colleges also grew, because the public funding of the University made it possible to appoint more university and Common University Fund (CUF) lecturers. Between 1945 and 1970 University College went from 13 to 35 fellows, Balliol from 23 to 57, Keble from 9 to 35. All governing bodies doubled; some virtually trebled, with the biggest growth coming in the 1960s.[6] The growing size and complexity of the colleges also led to an increase in the administrative staff. As Rector of Lincoln, Keith Murray had managed with a college secretary, a steward and one other person.[7] But after 1945 bursarial and secretarial staffs expanded. The domestic bursarship often became a full-time appointment and the colleges recruited a galaxy of retired admirals, generals and colonial civil servants to manage their staff or run their estates.

A great deal of what is distinctive about the development of the colleges after 1945 can be attributed to this sheer rise in numbers and its sometimes unintended consequences. In the first place it created an insatiable demand for more accommodation. The immediate response was to divide existing rooms into smaller units. The late 1940s and 1950s saw the sharing of sitting

---

[2] On changes in methods of funding see below, 672–4.
[3] University of Oxford, general office, returns to UGC 1923–66; *Gazette* xcviii (1967/8) – ci (1970/1).   [4] *Brazen Nose* 1952, 258.
[5] *Franks Report* ii. 33.
[6] Figures extracted from the *Calendar*.
[7] V. H. H. Green at History of the University seminar on 'Changes in college life', Nuffield College, 31 Oct. 1986 (Brian Harrison's transcript, HUA), 14.

rooms and the splitting of sets of rooms into bedsitters, the unit which would ultimately become the norm. In their search for new accommodation, colleges also encroached further upon the head of house's lodgings, taking advantage of every vacancy in the office to slice off rooms and convert attics and cellars to other purposes. The growth of bursaries and college offices, the expansion of libraries and muniment rooms, the increased size of the junior and senior common rooms: all intensified the pressure on space. Attic floors were added to old buildings, and a warren of cubicles was created behind ancient façades. The colleges also moved wherever possible into existing premises adjacent to their site. Lincoln expanded into the Turl, took back the Mitre Hotel and, most spectacularly, when the city church of All Saints was declared redundant in 1971, set about appropriating it as its library. A few years earlier St Edmund Hall had secularized St Peter in the East for a similar purpose.[8] Keble acquired property from St John's in Blackhall Road and Museum Road. Colleges also built on any remaining space within their original site. Substantial building occurred in the 1950s at Wadham, St John's and Brasenose, while the 1960s were a decade of college building on an almost unprecedented scale, with major projects at Balliol, Christ Church, Corpus, Exeter, Jesus, Keble, Magdalen, Merton, New College, Pembroke, Queen's, St Edmund Hall, Trinity, University College and Worcester. The colleges also moved into the city: some bought up houses or erected blocks of flats, like University College in Staverton Road (1967), while others, like Balliol and Jesus, encroached on the fringes of their playing fields. Between 1955 and 1965 1,661 units were added to college accommodation, 85 per cent taking the form of bedsitters.[9]

Parallel to this great wave of new building was the refurbishing and restoration of existing premises. The Oxford Historic Buildings appeal (1957) made possible wholesale cleaning and renovation. The external appearance of the colleges was transformed. Romantic creepers and mouldering walls gave way to spruce machine-cut stone [plate 8.2]. Behind these gleaming façades other changes were occurring. By the winter of 1958 no man in Keble any longer needed to walk in the open air to reach a bath.[10] The shortage of domestic service and the growth of the conference trade encouraged bursars to install washbasins and running water, new bathrooms and lavatories. Coal fires gave way to gas, and in newer buildings to central heating. The opening of the Bulkley-Johnson Building in Balliol in 1968 was followed by complaints, unique in the history of the College, that the rooms were over-heated.[11] Despite all this activity, relatively few undergraduates

---

[8] V. H. H. Green, *The Commonwealth of Lincoln College 1427–1977* (Oxford 1979), 547–8; J. N. D. Kelly, *St Edmund Hall: Almost Seven Hundred Years* (Oxford 1989), 140–1.

[9] *Franks Report* ii. 38. Cf 509–12.

[10] *Keble College Record* 1958, 5; 1959, 4. For a survey of college accommodation and furnishings see *Isis* 3 Nov. 1965, 11–13. On the renovation of buildings see below, 507–9.

[11] *Balliol College Record* 1969, 4.

during these years spent all their time within college accommodation. In 1949/50, at the peak of the post-war bulge, 52 per cent of all students were living in lodgings. The proportion contracted thereafter, but in 1968 there were still 4,664 students (45 per cent) living out—a larger proportion than in many other British universities.[12]

For most people, therefore, life in digs was an integral part of the Oxford experience. At first, undergraduates could hope to find a landlady who would cook them large breakfasts, make their beds and do their washing. Some were much loved Oxford figures with whom men kept in touch long after they had gone down. There was Mrs Richardson of 159 Iffley Road, for example, whose one-hundredth birthday was celebrated in Magdalen College in 1981 by sixty-five of her former lodgers, all of whose names she was able to recall.[13] But the long-term trend was to bedsitters with no service provided. In 1970 the University abandoned its rule that junior members living out should occupy only approved accommodation. This led to the renting of houses and flats by little groups of undergraduates, for whom the experience provided a novel experiment in communal living. It also meant that students would henceforth compete for accommodation with other inhabitants of the city.

The existence of a large number of undergraduates living outside the colleges had always been a direct challenge to the old college system, whose ideal was essentially that of a community whose members dwelt behind the same walls and lived and ate together. Even before the war some 40 per cent of students had lived in digs.[14] After the war the numbers rose and the digs became dearer and more remote. The Oxford regional committee of the National Union of Students (NUS) told the Franks Commission: 'the shift in orientation of undergraduates from college to University is accelerated by the large proportion living in lodgings, many of whom commute to the centre of Oxford in the mornings, and use the libraries as somewhere warm to sit, read, write letters, and meet their friends simply because there is nowhere where they can do these things.'[15] In the late 1950s and early 1960s the Bodleian Upper Reading Room was full of people with newspapers and shopping bags, making their dispositions for the day.

The pressure of increased numbers of applicants also changed the whole character of Oxford admissions. Instead of the weaker colleges having difficulty in filling their places, as had sometimes happened before the war, there were now far more qualified candidates than colleges could take. The effect was a gradual change in the system of admission and the criteria

[12] University of Oxford, general office, returns to UGC 1947–66; HCP 230 (1958), 81.

[13] *Magdalen College Record* 1990, 86; HUD/C/SV. Mrs Richardson remarked that she would remember the occasion for many years to come. She died at the age of 108.

[14] University of Oxford, general office, returns to UGC 1923–64.

[15] Franks Commission, written evidence x. 134.

adopted. The scholarship examination had always been a competitive affair, conducted by the tutors, whereas commoner places were awarded on the basis either of a less demanding examination or no examination at all. Sir Maurice Bowra told the Franks Commission that 'commoners should not be cut all to the same pattern or taken solely on the chance that they will do well in Final Schools'. It was important to accept some candidates who might be academically undistinguished but who would 'plainly benefit by extra-curricular activities and add to the variety of college life'.[16]

In the 1950s the practical working of this distinction between scholars and commoners was a regular source of contention within the colleges. Broadly speaking, on one side in the conflict were the head and the older tutors, who tended to favour the claims of old members' sons and who liked having about the college good-looking sportsmen and people of, as they put it, 'character'; on the other side were the younger tutors, who were more exclusively interested in academic potential and suspicious of anything which looked like nepotism or social injustice. For though there was no necessary correlation between the good commoner and the public school-boy, there was a tendency for the categories to overlap. Hugh Stretton described the divisions among the fellows of Balliol in the 1950s: 'the Left suspected that the Right's idea of a decent commoner was an amiable, well-connected public-school dunce, keen on rugger and beagling but usually too drunk for either, likely to pass without effort (or qualifications) into the upper-middle ranks of government or business, to the ultimate detriment of British power, prosperity, and social justice, but sure to turn up to Gaudies and quite likely to donate silver or endow a trophy or two. The Right suspected that the Left's idea of a decent commoner was a bespectacled black beetle from a nameless secondary school who would speak to nobody, swot his solitary, constipated way to an indifferent degree, then forget the College the day he left it for a job in local government, where his chief effect on the national life would be as a chronic claimant on, and voter for, the National Health.'[17]

In the immediate aftermath of the war many heads seem to have admitted commoners after only the most perfunctory scrutiny, and until the mid-1960s there were still one or two colleges where sporting ability was an easy passport to acceptance. In the 1950s at St Edmund Hall C. W. F. R. Gullick, the Senior Tutor, always welcomed sportsmen and all-rounders. At Keble C. V. Davidge's lawyers in 1962 allegedly comprised eight potential rowing blues and five others of a size which suited them to be coxes. One man recalls having been offered a place at the College by Davidge when, as a schoolboy, he was still sitting in one of the winning

---

[16] Ibid. iv. 20, 18.
[17] H. Stretton, in 'Christopher Hill: some reminiscences' in D. H. Pennington and K. Thomas (eds), *Puritans and Revolutionaries* (Oxford 1978), 14–15.

boats at Henley.[18] But colleges varied greatly in the extent to which they were prepared to condone this sort of thing. At most of them the scholarship and common entrance examinations came increasingly to be regarded as similar operations. Growing competition, both among candidates and between colleges, tended inexorably to make academic criteria the decisive ones. In such circumstances the age-old distinction between scholar and commoner shrank to vanishing point. In response to the Hardie report of 1962 the entrance and scholarship examinations were combined. The three groups into which colleges were divided were adjusted to keep them equipollent and a wholly meritocratic entrance scheme was adopted.[19]

The practical and symbolic consequences of this change were very considerable. By indicating that the essential requirement of the Oxford undergraduate was academic promise, the new procedure implied a radical departure from the older notion that, though Oxford existed to train scholars, it was also there to educate a governing élite of all-rounders. In the late 1940s, for example, W. T. S. Stallybrass, the Principal of Brasenose, was convinced that games-playing helped to build character, and wanted Brasenose to be a place where scholars and commoners would mix to their mutual benefit. 'One of his deepest concerns since the war was that present-day trends were leading to the extermination of the commoner.' At Christ Church Steven Watson argued that the criteria used at college entrance should recognize 'the need to civilize those who are born to great responsibilities' and 'the desire to be tender to claims of loyal old members'. Until 1957 the University's *Handbook* contained C. K. Allen's statement that 'something besides intellectual earnestness is expected of the Oxford man . . . it is felt, and justly felt, that a man who has no interests of the more mundane sort, outside himself and his work, has little *raison d'être* in a collegiate society'.[20]

These voices were becoming untypical of tutorial opinion. The trend was towards the selection of undergraduates by the subject-tutors, no longer responsible to the head or even to a college committee, applying wholly academic criteria and increasingly indifferent to the older ideal of a 'rounded' human being. This process gave increasing offence to old members, whose children had now to compete on equal terms with other candidates, as well as to the many potential employers who associated leadership and enterprise with sporting prowess rather than examination success.[21] To those who

[18] Kelly, *St Edmund Hall*, 134–5; HUD/C/SV.
[19] [W. F. R. Hardie, chairman] *Admissions to Colleges: Report of a Working Party on Admissions* (University of Oxford 1962).
[20] *Brazen Nose* 1949, 19 (Stallybrass); J. S. Watson, 'University admissions', *Oxford* Dec. 1960, 54; *Handbook* 1952, 266.
[21] Sir Ronald Weeks, chairman of Vickers Ltd 1948–56, declared that 'the real danger which faces the universities' was 'studiousness': M. Sanderson, *The Universities and British Industry 1850–1970* (London 1972), 356.

regarded the college system as a means of developing all-round ability, the new tendency seemed dangerous. Russell Meiggs of Balliol told the Franks Commission that 'if the only function of the University is academic, the college system is an extravagant medium. A considerable part of the defence for the college system lies in its contribution to total development.' By this time only a few colleges admitted to giving any places, and then only 2–5 per cent, to candidates 'on the grounds of character or interests rather than on performance in examinations', though nearly all claimed that character and interests were still taken into account.[22]

Undergraduates chosen on purely academic criteria tended inevitably to be harder working. The college libraries expanded and they were much more intensively used. By 1969 the junior members of that one-time athletic camp, Brasenose College, were complaining because the library closed at midnight.[23] In some colleges the weekly essay had turned into the twice-weekly essay.[24] The afternoon between 2 p.m. and 5 p.m., once sacred for games-playing or long walks, was by the late 1960s beginning to become the most crowded period in the libraries and even a possible time for tutorials. In 1968 the fourth class in schools was abolished.

Academic work gained ground partly because few undergraduates now felt assured by family background of a comfortable subsistence in later life. The social composition of the University was changing. In 1948 the percentage of male students from independent schools had dropped from 62 per cent, the figure in 1938, to 45 per cent. After the ex-servicemen had gone, the proportion of public-school boys rose a little to 52 per cent in 1958, but dropped thereafter to 45 per cent in 1964 and 41 per cent in 1965.[25] Reinforcing the trend was the further professionalization of the college tutor. In the 1940s and 1950s there were still a few tutors whose academic qualifications were slender and there were many who made no pretence whatsoever of engaging in research. When appointments were made, youth, sociability, readiness to live in college and take on a college office counted as much as academic distinction, for a college electing a tutor was choosing not a technician but another member of its little family. College fellowships gave security of tenure, and freed their holders from the pressures and ambitions of academic life elsewhere. The typical Oxford don, however, was becoming someone who engaged in both teaching and research; increasingly he tended to regard the former, however necessary and rewarding, as essentially an interruption of the latter—of his 'own work', as he would call it.

During these years it became less frequent for college tutors to be appointed soon after they had taken schools. In the 1950s the average age of

[22] Franks Commission, written evidence iv. 126 (Meiggs); vii, *passim* (answers by colleges to question 4a).   [23] *Brazen Nose* 1969, 5.
[24] *Franks Report* ii. 112 (undergraduates attended on average 1.5 tutorials a week).
[25] Ibid. 47.

election to an established university post was 30.8 in arts and 34.2 for scientists.[26] Such persons had normally taken a doctorate, and had often served a period in another university, where they had acquired habits of living and teaching which did not easily accord with the old collegiate ideal of the resident or semi-resident tutor, available at all hours to his pupils and a ready participant in other aspects of college life. Teaching loads were in general less heavy than before the war, at least once the post-war veterans had passed through, but the norm for arts tutors was still about 13 hours a week during term;[27] and the amount of necessary preparation had greatly increased, with the much enhanced volume of scholarly publication following the post-war expansion of the academic profession. Tutors now took sabbatical leave more frequently. They went to academic conferences and they took advantage of favourable tax laws to make extra money by taking temporary positions in the USA. Heads found the academically ambitious reluctant to assume college office.

Broadly speaking, the new tutors were more businesslike within the tutorial than their predecessors had been, but less ready to devote extra time to their pupils' non-academic activities outside it. The tutorial hour was changing its character, becoming more didactic with a more active input by the tutor, and possibly a more passive and receptive role on the part of the pupil [plate 13.8]. The change was reflected in the increased use of the word 'teaching'. Standard at the end of the period, the word was much less used at the beginning, when a tutor was more likely to say that Mr So and So had been 'reading' with him that term than to say that he had been 'teaching' him.

Tutors raised in an older tradition despised the new attempt to 'cover the course'. Roy Harrod and Robert Blake, both of Christ Church, warned the Franks Commission about the tendency to 'spoonfeeding' which they believed was debasing the tutorial hour, a criticism which Franks endorsed. The colleges, according to his report, were competitive and anxious to do well in final honour schools; long before the Norrington table of 1964 there had been much public discussion of the number of firsts and seconds achieved by different colleges. There was therefore an increase in the number of tutorials and more pre-digestion of the material by the tutors.[28] Everywhere the tutorial was an increasingly conscientious affair, marked by more frequent reference to the questions likely to be set in schools papers and the introduction of such pedagogic devices as the typed reading-list, allegedly the invention of John Morris, the law tutor at Magdalen.[29]

[26] *OM* 15 Mar. 1962, 253. See also Franks Commission, written evidence vii (answers by colleges to question 28a).

[27] *Franks Report* ii. 286.

[28] Ibid. i. 37, 102, 108; Franks Commission, written evidence iv. 9–14 (Blake); xi. 51–3 (Harrod).

[29] P. M. North, 'John Humphrey Carlile Morris 1910–1984', *Proc. British Academy* lxxiv (1988), 445–6.

The tutorial system with its regular deadlines, 'essay crises' as they were known, inculcated useful working habits, taught people to write and gave them the confidence that, when confronted by unfamiliar material, they could quickly master its essentials. All the evidence suggests, however, that the success of the system depended very much upon the personalities involved. At its most intense, as in the teaching of Morris himself or of his Magdalen colleague K. B. McFarlane, the tutorial could be an experience which would mark the pupil's interests and intellectual habits for life. Young men were sometimes so imprinted by their tutors that they even unconsciously copied their gestures, mannerisms and way of walking and speaking. In other cases the chemistry failed to work and relations between a hard-pressed or bored tutor and a nervous or indolent pupil were cool or indifferent. Growing specialization and the subdivision of academic subjects made it harder for a single tutor to see his pupils through all the course, as often used to happen in the past. New tutors taught fewer papers than did old tutors and tended to farm out more of their pupils to colleagues in other colleges.

In some subjects, however, the colleges had no tutorial fellow at all. The post-war expansion of Oxford had seen a widening in the range of subjects on offer. A shift to the sciences, an increase in the numbers reading English, law and modern languages and the growth of new schools like psychology, philosophy and physiology (PPP) posed problems to colleges whose tutorial strength lay in more traditional areas. For colleges could not always afford to expand their fellowships at the rate which the new subjects required. Neither could they stock their libraries accordingly. As a result many undergraduates reading, say, music, botany, zoology, PPP or oriental languages had only a distant relationship with the fellows of their own college.[30] Whether they had a college tutor or not, scientists and medical students spent much of their day in the laboratory, away from the college.

More undergraduates, of more diverse origins, reading for a greater variety of schools, threatened the cohesiveness of the old college community. At the senior level the increase in the size of the governing bodies had the same effect. It reduced personal animosities of the kind which had racked some of the claustrophobic little communities in pre-war colleges. But it also diminished the individual fellow's sense of involvement. Relations between colleagues became more cordial, but they were also more superficial. An increasing proportion of dons lived out. By 1964 only 21 per cent of tutorial fellows in men's colleges were resident.[31] The married don, living in a servantless house further away from the college, and whose wife

[30] Figures in H. G. Reading, 'Deprived students', *OM* 9 Feb. 1973, 5–7, and ensuing correspondence.
[31] *Franks Report* ii. 394.

possibly had a job of her own, was much less able to dine regularly, to attend college societies and to be about in the quad, than his pre-war counterpart.[32] There were still some old-style bachelor dons who regarded themselves as married to the college. They took a keen interest (sometimes too keen an interest) in the young men and their private lives, and they always had time for the old members. Every college depended on devoted individuals of this kind to hold college offices, edit the college *Record* and keep in touch with past generations. There were also a great number of dedicated tutors. They were very different from the increasingly common brand of don who regarded tutorials as more or less irksome interruptions of his time in library or laboratory, or who tore off to London to sit on committees and who might lunch quite often but never dined. It was in the late 1950s that in many colleges lunch came to be part of common table; and it very quickly superseded dinner as the meal of the day when fellows could expect to meet their colleagues.

The normal pattern of life in a senior common room (SCR) became that of regular lunching combined with a weekday guest-night and one on Sunday, when the dress would be black tie. Dinner tended increasingly to be a meal for resident fellows, particularly junior ones, together with those non-resident fellows who had guests whom they did not wish or were unable to entertain at home. At dessert, which was served after dinner on guest nights, and in some colleges more regularly than that, there would be port, fruit and nuts, usually circulated with a good deal of formality. The senior common room was constitutionally distinct from the college. The head of the college did not preside, and if present usually wore a gown to signify his status as a guest. In his place was the steward, a dominating figure who set the tone. He was frequently a bachelor, noted neither for learning nor for the love of women, like W. N. Stocker, who retired as curator of the Brasenose common room in December 1945, after 37 years in the office; he was said to have lost the habit of work after examining in schools in 1904.[33] In St John's, Edwin Slade administered an arcane set of rules at dessert involving a distinction between 'major' and 'minor' fruit and the exact sequence in which a junior fellow should offer them to his seniors. In Keble C. V. Davidge presided over drinking bouts of eighteenth-century proportions; of him it was said euphemistically that he gave Keble 'a reputation for hospitality unequalled in the University'.[34] For these often lonely figures the common room was the centre of their existence, and the increasing tendency of newer fellows to ignore the formalities or to absent themselves altogether seemed an act of almost personal betrayal.

    [32] *OM* 14 Nov. 1946, 81 (66% of fellows in 1946 were married); *Franks Report* ii. 394 (53% of tutorial fellows in men's and graduate colleges lived more than a mile from college).
    [33] *Brazen Nose* 1946, 65; 1949, 47.
    [34] *Keble College Record* 1968, 6.

Even the newest recruits, however, took the government of the college seriously. The fellows were an autonomous community, meeting regularly as the governing body, to take decisions about the management of the endowment, the making of new appointments and the general administration of the college. They were presided over by the head, who could still be a crucially influential figure, particularly if appointed young. At Wadham Maurice Bowra was a dominating presence; at Lincoln Keith Murray after 1946 was both rector and bursar, as well as presiding in common room and controlling admissions; at Brasenose Stallybrass was vice-principal or principal for thirty-seven years. In St Edmund Hall under A. B. Emden the requirement that new fellows should promise to obey the Principal was not dropped until 1951,[35] and at new foundations like St Antony's, St Catherine's and Linacre the first head (or, in the case of Nuffield, the head when the charter was granted) decisively shaped the character of the college. In 1950 nearly half the heads of house were unmarried. Overall, however, the period saw a decline in the status of heads. The end of a separate system of entry for commoners removed their influence on admissions, while the pressure on space reduced the grandeur of their lodgings.[36] After Franks, moreover, heads were no longer automatically in line for the vice-chancellorship.

Yet the heads continued to symbolize the college in the public eye. Their portraits usually hung in hall and their tenure of office provided the periodization into which colleges divided their history. Their styles of government varied considerably. At some colleges they were figureheads who left the real business to a group of experienced and dedicated fellows. In others they were brisk administrators or notable scholars. Occasionally they were fund-raisers and benefactors, like A. L. Goodhart, who brought $1 million into University College during his term of office. One or two were outright eccentrics, like Neville Murphy of Hertford (1939–59) locally known because of his retiring nature as 'the undisclosed principal' after an obscure branch of agency law. Undergraduates brought him watches to mend, not merely because he did it free but because he was much more expert than the college porter, who did such repairs as a business. It is recorded that 'undeterred by modern secretarial methods, Murphy continued to treat much of the college's correspondence with a fine old-fashioned detachment from files, duplicate copies and prompt answers'.[37]

Undergraduates of course knew little of such matters, but all colleges attached importance to their social intermingling with the fellows. 'If a gulf

[35] Kelly, St Edmund Hall, 134.

[36] On admissions see Franks Commission, written evidence vii, passim (answers by colleges to question 4c).

[37] A. Goudie (ed.), Seven Hundred Years of an Oxford College (Hertford College, 1284–1984) (Oxford [1984]), 76; HUD/C/SV.

is fixed between them, except for purely didactic purposes, there will be
something wrong with the "tone" of the college and it will shrink in
efficiency and repute.' Thus C. K. Allen in the University's *Handbook*.[38] In
accordance with this ideal, heads entertained junior members to lunches and
sherry parties of varying degrees of conviviality. Tutors began to receive
entertainment allowances, which made it possible for them to invite pupils
to occasional meals or parties in college or at home, though the very
introduction of the allowance hinted that this was now more of a duty than a
pleasure. A few fellows—usually but not necessarily the unmarried
ones—kept open house in their rooms on regular occasions, like Christopher Hill's Monday-night beer parties for Balliol historians.[39] But
circumstances were now making it unlikely that many fellows would devote
much time to informal relationships of this kind. Marriage, absence all day in
the science laboratories, and the competing claims of research, all got in the
way. As colleges became more departmentalized, offering tuition in a wide
range of wholly distinct subjects, each with its own working location and
routine, undergraduates came to know few fellows of the college other than
their own tutors, and more often than not knew the latter only in an
academic context.

During these decades there were many self-conscious attempts to restore
the intimacy between senior and junior members. In the 1960s several
colleges began to advertise junior research fellowships for young bachelors
who were required to give up some of their time to informal contacts with
undergraduates. The latter often lamented that they did not see enough of
the SCR and contrived devices for closer contact with dons, inviting them to
coffee in the junior common room or encouraging them to eat occasionally
in the body of the hall. Some tutors made well-intentioned but faintly
archaic attempts at organizing vacation reading parties or meetings at which
senior members talked informally about their work. Few of these devices
lasted for very long. The fact was that male camaraderie of a late Victorian or
Edwardian kind conflicted too directly with the mounting pressures of
domesticity and peer group. As the NUS told Franks, genuine, uncontrived
social contact between junior and senior members was very rare. There was 'a
lack of will on both sides'.[40]

Colleges continued to appoint 'moral tutors' who had pastoral charge of
junior members and were expected to exercise benevolent supervision over
all their problems, financial and personal; and some tutors still took seriously
the notion that their job was to oversee the all-round development of their
charges. But most undergraduates no longer welcomed intrusive though
benevolent surveillance of this kind, and they resented highly personal

[38] *Handbook* 1947, 264.
[39] On these see Maurice Keen in 'Christopher Hill: some reminiscences', 18.
[40] Franks Commission, written evidence x. 133–4.

questions about their sex lives of the kind fired at them by R. H. Dundas of Christ Church.[41] Dons were ceasing to regard their role as analogous to that of a public-school housemaster; and the University's Appointments Committee was usurping the responsibility for advising their pupils about employment when they went down. In the 1960s the Student Council Committee told Franks that the system of moral tutors was 'for most undergraduates a dead letter'; and a group of local parents who were hostile to these developments nevertheless conceded that 'a strong school of thought has arisen which maintains that the function of a university is to train the mind alone, and that dons should have nothing to do with the spiritual or moral life of their pupils'.[42] Symbolic of the decline of the don's pastoral role was the rise of semi-professional counselling agencies. In the 1960s the University's *Handbook* declared that there was no formal student counselling service in Oxford because the tutorial system made it unnecessary. But in 1955 the Vicar of St Mary's, R. S. Lee, had started an unofficial one, and thereafter the demand for professional counselling or psychiatric advice grew steadily.[43] Between 1947 and 1966 twenty-six students killed themselves and between 1950 and 1966 more than a thousand were referred by GPs for psychiatric advice at the Warneford Hospital.[44] In most colleges pastoral care came increasingly to be left to the chaplain, the college nurse or some specially constituted panel of sympathetic fellows.

More fundamental was the decline of the colleges' attempt to regulate the personal lives of their junior members. When the ex-servicemen returned after the war they found that the University forbade them to go into public houses and required them to wear gowns if they went out after dinner, even to the cinema. These requirements were soon tacitly relaxed. Similarly, compulsory chapel, which had survived the war at a few colleges, disappeared altogether over the next decade and a half. The colleges, however, continued to enforce strict rules about hours and visitors. All junior members were expected to return to their college or lodgings by midnight, or sooner in some colleges, and visitors, particularly female visitors, were required to leave much earlier. Absence overnight needed special permission. The college walls were fortified with spikes, railings and broken claret bottles to prevent night-time invasion; and porters and scouts were required to report all misdemeanours.

These rules, benevolently administered by long-serving deans, were, of course, successfully evaded. If the college gate was closed, then the

---

[41] On whom see for example E. Williams, *George: An Early Autobiography* (London 1961), 281–2; Lord Boothby in A. Thwaite (ed.), *My Oxford* (London 1977), 30.

[42] Franks Commission, written evidence iii. 87; xi. 115.

[43] *Handbook* 1962, 277; *OM* 3 Nov. 1955, 70, 72.

[44] R. W. Parnell, 'Report of the committee on student health: mental health aspects', *OM* 26 May 1967, 346; R. G. McInnes, 'The Warneford and student mental health', *Isis* 20 Feb. 1963, 10–12.

undergraduate climbed in, usually by a relatively easy route that had been thoughtfully left unimpeded by the college authorities. Entering by a ground-floor window was regarded as unsporting and frowned on by the dean, but more daring methods were generally admired. The attitude to these rules was jocular. For the most part the restrictions were taken for granted [plate 8.4]. There was good-humoured negotiation about visiting hours but concessions were not readily made. 'If you cannot achieve what you wish by 10 p.m., you will be unlikely to achieve it by 11 p.m.,' the Dean of Brasenose told his flock. From the late 1950s, however, gate-fines were abolished and the hours at which visitors were permitted were gradually pushed back from 10.00 to 11.00 to 11.30. Then, in the later 1960s, the barriers collapsed altogether. Somerville was the first college to issue gate-keys to undergraduates, and Brasenose in 1967 the first men's college to follow that example.[45] St Catherine's (1962) was designed as an open college without a gate at all. By 1972 most colleges had gone over to the new system. Junior members and their visitors could come and go. It became more common for undergraduates to go away for the weekend; and the only objection to women spending the night in college would soon become the bursarial one that two were living for the price of one.

This was a revolution in the relationship between the college and its junior members. Only a few years earlier Sir George Pickering had told the Franks Commission that 'the college accepts responsibility for guiding the scholar's conduct scholastically, socially and morally'.[46] The breakdown of the belief that dons were *in loco parentis* was accelerated by the new legal status of young people, made adults at 18 by the Family Reform Act of 1969. It also reflected changing standards of sexual morality. The Student Council Committee told Franks that the 'greater independence and earlier maturity of young people' had weakened the rationale for a paternalistic, familial environment.[47]

Increasingly free from the intervention of their elders, the junior members continued to organize their own forms of entertainment. Every college had its sports ground and regularly fielded teams in rugby, soccer, cricket, tennis and other sports to compete in the inter-college competitions known as 'cuppers'. Rowing provided its devotees with physical exhilaration, companionship and a sense of achievement. Damp and muddy, the crews soaked in hot water in dingy bath rooms in the cellars of colleges, from which raucous singing and steam emerged. Success at 'torpids' or 'eights' led to a 'bump supper' [plate 8.3], an institution in which senior members participated and which sometimes culminated in the burning of a boat in the quadrangle and associated horseplay. The sporting and athletic life of

[45] *Brazen Nose* 1967, 146, 189.
[46] Franks Commission, oral evidence xx. 15 (Pickering, 12 Nov. 1964).
[47] Franks Commission, written evidence iii. 80.

Oxford was the aspect at which many old members looked back with most pleasure.

Within each college there was for much of the period a wide range of undergraduate societies. There was usually a dramatic society which put on a play in the college garden in the summer; a debating society which debated such motions as 'that this house prefers bed to breakfast' or 'that this house prefers masters to principals'; a paper-reading society devoted to literary, philosophical or aesthetic matters; and subject societies, particularly for history and law. Musical societies gave concerts, often produced jointly by a men's and a women's college. Dining clubs—which sometimes wore special facings on their dinner jackets—periodically had to be banned by the dean. Some of these societies were long-lasting, like Tenmantale, Keble's history society, which celebrated its thousandth meeting in 1970.[48] Others were highly ephemeral, founded by a few enthusiasts and disappearing with the minute-book and other records when the enthusiasts went down.

Undergraduate clubs and societies of this kind enjoyed an Indian summer in the 1950s, but their number and popularity dwindled thereafter. The Keble *Record* explained to its readers in 1970 that 'the concept of a "closed", elective society is apparently now found to be less congenial than used to be the case'.[49] It was partly because undergraduates had become harder working and more narrowly academic in their preoccupations. But more important were the competing attractions of cinema, pop concert and pub. Fewer junior members now came from boarding schools, where such societies were familiar, and fewer wanted to spend their evenings in all-male company. College law-moots gradually disappeared, to be reorganized centrally, and by 1970 the old kind of elective society which met in someone's room, listened to a paper and discussed it with some formality to the accompaniment of mulled claret in a silver jug had almost totally gone. To many, its disappearance seemed a further weakening of the whole *raison d'être* of the collegiate system. Bowra told the Franks Commission that 'no college can justify its existence unless its undergraduate members lead a full and vigorous life outside their academic obligations. The essential idea of a college is that of a community in which the members share all kinds of interests and help to educate each other in the widest sense . . . College and University societies . . . provide a highly stimulating and civilizing influence, and enrich an undergraduate's life in ways which lie beyond the scope of his academic work.'[50]

The junior common room (JCR) was also changing its character. Modelled on a gentlemen's club, though in practice somewhat grubbier, it contained large armchairs and newspapers and was a place where people met

[48] *Keble College Record* 1970, 22.
[49] Ibid. 41.
[50] Franks Commission, written evidence iv. 17.

before and after meals. It elected a president and other officers, usually chosen for their popularity within the college, and it maintained a suggestions book in which criticisms of college food and personal insults would be offered and returned in a tone of determined facetiousness. After the war many JCRs patronized contemporary art and built up impressive collections of pictures and prints to be lent out for members' rooms. Some, like Balliol, were famous for their teas, with anchovy toast or Gentleman's Relish. All had a ball committee which planned a triennial 'commem. ball' or annual summer dance. At JCR meetings there were endless debates about whether to take or discontinue the *Daily Worker* or the *Tatler* or some other journal with symbolic resonance. But party politics were largely absent. In the late 1950s this began to change. JCRs financed scholarships for refugee or third-world students and organized War on Want lunches. Officers began to be chosen for their political allegiance and the tone became less flippant.

Colleges were little democracies so far as the fellows were concerned, but the junior members had traditionally played no part in determining the rules to which they were subject. A few colleges had a committee at which undergraduates could complain about the food to the domestic bursar, but in the late 1940s and 1950s there was no demand for any other form of student participation. The old order was accepted more or less unquestioningly. In the 1960s this ceased to be the case. The Principal of Jesus told the old members at the gaudy in June 1969 that there had been a change in the attitudes and assumptions of undergraduates: 'the present generation shows a greater desire to "have a say in things" than was common when we were up'.[51]

The reasons for this change lie in the social history of the period. Growing prosperity had made young people an important consumer group. An international youth culture had developed, based on popular music and distinctive styles of clothing. It was disseminated by the mass media and intensified by the invention of the contraceptive pill. In Oxford the passing of the national-service generation, the arrival of television sets in the JCRs and the increase in the proportion of undergraduates from state schools all helped to make junior members responsive to these wider changes. They felt a new affinity with students in other universities. In the 1940s and 1950s every JCR had regularly debated whether to affiliate to the National Union of Students, and had usually decided not to. In the 1960s, however, junior members ceased to refer to each other as 'undergraduates' or 'gentlemen', and began to speak of themselves as students, with the implication that they were not a special élite, but just another branch of the worldwide student community and indeed of the local student community, which included institutions like Ruskin College and Oxford Polytechnic. An interesting

[51] *Jesus College Record* 1969, 4–5.

transitional case is the Balliol rules book for 1970, which begins by referring to '*gentlemen* admitted to the College', proceeds to say that the key for 'a *man*'s room may be obtained from the Bursary', and describes the JCR as 'the Balliol *Students*' Club'.[52] Undergraduates dressed indistinguishably from the youth of the town, discarding the sports jackets, flannels, polished leather shoes and short-back-and-sides haircuts of the 1950s [plate 18.1] for the long hair, boots and denim worn by their pop-star idols. The college beer-cellars, most of them constructed in the 1950s, replaced the JCRs as the main social centres. Gowns, as a symbol of membership of a separate academic estate, became increasingly unpopular. During the 1960s they ceased to be worn in tutorials and, at some colleges, even at hall dinner. Meanwhile the colleges' retreat from regulating their junior members' personal lives confirmed the notion that students were not a subordinate class, but an important group of consumers entitled to participation and equality.

The college system, with its relatively close relations between tutor and pupil, did something to reduce the impact of these pressures on Oxford. As late as 1969 the Brasenose magazine commented on the absence of 'student unrest' in the College and the general 'satisfaction with the Brasenose way of life'.[53] But elsewhere there was a great deal of hostility to the rituals, formality and hierarchy of college life. The late 1960s saw the formation in most colleges of joint committees of senior and junior members which debated the rules of the college and advanced the claims of junior members to representation at the governing body. Most of the student radicalism in Oxford between 1967 and 1974 was concentrated on the university rather than the colleges. But within the colleges themselves there were some aggressive incidents, as at Oriel, where undergraduates invaded a meeting of the governing body in January 1970, or at Balliol, where a visit by the Prime Minister, Edward Heath, in June 1971 was the occasion of what nearly became a violent collision. The colleges survived these events, usually at the cost of admitting a few junior members to a modest share in their government. But the memory would linger as a reminder that the old unquestioning hierarchy could never be restored.

For senior and junior members alike, the mode of life within the college was evolving. In the past, Oxford had been a place to which the offspring of the well-to-do had come, and they had lived in the style to which they were accustomed. A scout, assisted by a boy, laid fires, brought shaving water, made beds, emptied chamber pots, cleaned rooms and waited at meals. The main meal was dinner in hall, normally of three courses, with silver on the table, a Latin grace, sconcing, and the dons often in evening dress. This was

---

52 *Balliol College Rules and Information* 1970–1 (author's emphasis).
53 *Brazen Nose* 1969, 4.

'la vie aristocratique et un peu monacale', as some French visitors to Keble put it in 1955.[54] To a lower-middle-class youth it was initially disconcerting to be addressed as 'Sir', referred to as a 'gentleman', and equipped with a personal servant. In the 1960s this old style of personal service began to encounter strong ideological objections. Ties ceased to be worn at dinner in hall in some colleges and procedures became less formal. Peter Bayley wrote in the revised (1965) version of the University's *Handbook* that 'college life still patterns a larger society that has almost totally disappeared. It memorializes a society that was split into leaders and led, gentry and servants, and this some progressives find repellent.'[55]

Few qualms, however, were expressed by the older college servants. Many had been in the college longer than either dons or undergraduates [plate 8.5], and they were usually stern supporters of traditional ways. At St Antony's no one did more than the steward, Fred Wheatley—previously a scout at Wadham, Queen's and Christ Church—to ensure that the dining habits of this new and hybrid institution would conform to the traditions of the old order. At Balliol it was said of Edward Nelson, the head scout (who in 1956 was a guest of honour at a dinner of bench and bar at Gray's Inn) that 'his loyalties were simple, transparent and direct: the College, its good name, its best traditions, its high achievements'. As the rhyme had it:

> I'm Steward: N-LS-N is my name.
> Things have never been the same
> Since Nineteen-Twelve, and I aver
> That even then things never were.[56]

Everywhere the college servants exercised a pronounced influence upon the tone of the college. The head porter knew all the secrets of senior and junior members alike. He presided over the lodge, the pivotal point of the college from which visitors were scrutinized as they passed through. He and his assistants sorted the mail which came by post and internal messenger, and maintained the noticeboards by means of which tutors communicated with pupils and undergraduates advertised plays, talks, concerts and other forthcoming attractions. The head porter had to be a good judge of human nature and to display firmness as well as tact, for it was to him that the dean would turn at times of uproar. The SCR butler was accustomed to seeing dons in their cups, and he overheard many indiscretions. His manner might range from poker-faced impassivity to rough and unobsequious candour. The scouts gave their youthful charges tactful advice on how to behave and what to do, particularly in the first few weeks of their arrival at Oxford. Some college servants had a legendary memory for names and faces; and

[54] *Keble College Record* 1956, 24.
[55] *Handbook* 1965, 303.
[56] *Balliol College Record* 1957, 7; *Balliol College Annual Record* 1972, 39.

when old members returned, their first port of call would be 'Dick' in the lodge or 'Tom' in the buttery.

The 1950s, however, saw the retirement of many venerable figures who had joined the college as scouts' boys and spent the rest of their lives in the same institution. At University College in 1955 four college servants retired after respectively forty-five, forty-eight, fifty-four and fifty-eight years' service.[57] Every college had their counterparts. Of the Brasenose groundsman Edmund King it was said in 1963 that he was perhaps the only person whose death could give rise to so universal a sense of personal loss among all Brasenose men. He had joined the College in 1895 and he stayed on in a house on the sports ground when he retired in 1959. 'He loved Brasenose and all Brasenose men,' recorded the College magazine. 'His favourite reading was *The Brazen Nose* . . . Not a little of Brasenose itself died with Edmund King.'[58]

His was the last generation of faithful retainers. After the war there was a marked decline in the amount of domestic service provided for junior members. The pressure of numbers, bursarial economies and the continuance of food-rationing had established that henceforth all meals would be taken in hall, often in two sittings and sometimes on a cafeteria basis. These were years of shortage, with meals in the British Restaurants and queues outside the cake factory in North Oxford. Heating and lighting were in short supply, particularly during the cold winter of 1947, and one old member of Jesus confesses to having been reduced to stealing coal from the SCR.[59] After 1953 undergraduates no longer had to carry their rations of butter and sugar to breakfast, and things grew more plentiful. But running water and gas fires reduced the amount of domestic service needed. Better wages at Cowley meant that college service no longer attracted young men at the outset of their careers. The scouts' boys had already disappeared, and colleges increasingly found themselves drawing upon men who had become unemployed in middle age. More radically, they began to employ women. The move from male scout to female cleaner usually involved a change to a much more limited relationship between employee and college. It also coincided with a steady contraction in the extent of service provided. Cleaners came in only once a day, they no longer cleaned shoes and sometimes they even ceased to make beds. It became too expensive to send clothes to the laundry, and in the early 1960s JCRs began to acquire washing machines. By the 1970s the scout had almost vanished.[60] The undergraduate

---

[57] *University College Record* 1956, 18.

[58] D. L. Stockton, 'Edmund Jesse King 1872-1963', *Brazen Nose* 1964, 251-2.

[59] HUD/C/SV.

[60] C. Platt, *The Most Obliging Man in Europe: The Life and Times of the Oxford Scout* (London 1986), 15. For interesting reflections on the decline of personal service within the college and the need for further economies see TCA Arch C/1: memorandum of 5 Jan. 1966 by Dr R. A. Fletcher.

was no longer a young gentleman with his personal servant; he had become the occupant of a hard-pressed and multi-purpose boarding house, catering for students in term and conference visitors during the vacation. Even so, his was a more comfortable existence than that of his contemporaries in most other British or American universities. So was that of the senior members. Many colleges were enlivened by an annual feast and other convivial occasions, while at All Souls the fellows, undeterred by the reproaches of the Franks Commission, continued to enjoy a style of life reminiscent of an Edwardian country house.[61]

The texture of life within these small and highly distinct communities is not easy to evoke. In the 1950s undergraduates came up to Oxford by train, their trunks sent on ahead and piled high in the college lodge, awaiting their arrival. Once installed, they did not normally leave Oxford or see their parents until term was over. For those accustomed to boarding school or life in the army, the transition was easy. College was a continuation of public-school existence, though with much greater freedom. For those who had not previously left home, the initial experience could involve considerable cultural shock, for college life required independence and self-reliance. Unaccustomed to coping on their own and to devising working routines unaided, young people often felt lonely and adrift. Innumerable old members later said that they came up too young; they were emotionally too immature to take advantage of what Oxford had to offer and a year or two off between school and university would have made all the difference.[62]

Within the colleges the mixture of persons from a wider variety of backgrounds and nationalities did not always cohere very effectively. The immediately post-war juxtaposition of hardened ex-servicemen with callow schoolboys was notably unsuccessful. In Trinity term 1948 the average age of the JCR committee at Queen's was 28.[63] Ex-majors with MCs, wives and moustaches had little in common with 17-year-old boys who carried green ration-books entitling them to extra bananas. As for the effect of class differences, the retrospective evidence of old members is conflicting. Some claim that origins and schooling were irrelevant: people were treated as individuals and judged on their merits. But many comment on the divisive effects of social class. Those who had been officers during their national service looked down upon those who had not; and those who had been in smart regiments remained conscious of the fact. 'Trogs' and 'grey men' (industrious scholars) were despised. The socially mobile had no difficulty in assimilating themselves to a new style of living, often acquiring a new accent and a new style of dressing. Others recoiled from loud and self-confident public schoolboys in their British Warms and cavalry twill trousers. They

[61] Cf *Franks Report* i. 145–51.
[62] HUD/C/SV.
[63] *Queen's College Record* 1948, 7.

equated Oxford with snobbishness and social competition, and some of them left the University with a permanent feeling of inferiority or resentment.[64]

Paradoxically, the more exotic an undergraduate's origins, the easier it was for him to assimilate. Americans were more readily accepted than those whose inferior place in the British class system was immediately obvious. Trinity in the early 1960s is said to have been more welcoming to an ex-miner from Ruskin than to boys from conventional state grammar schools. In the later 1960s, however, the tone began to change. Instead of poor boys copying rich ones, the upper-class boys decked themselves out in a parody of proletarian dress and assumed a demotic accent. In general, colleges tended to be split up into a number of little overlapping groups or sets, united sometimes by class or intellectual affinity, sometimes by a common interest in sport or music or religion. This last was a conspicuous feature of Oxford life and many subsequently recalled their undergraduate time as a decisive period when they either found religious faith or lost it. The Catholic chaplaincy or the John Wesley Society meant as much to them as did their college. Individual experience as an undergraduate was so diverse as to make generalization almost impossible. But for most people, Oxford seems to have offered a broadening of their horizons, an opening to new cultural opportunities, and a sense of intellectual and social liberation. College life enabled most people to make close and often lasting friendships. Hundreds of old members looked back on their undergraduate years as the happiest of their lives. One of them subsequently wrote that 'college life in all its aspects was the greatest thing about being at Oxford'.[65]

The men's colleges, however, remained male societies. Some dons' wives acted as surrogate mothers to their husbands' pupils, and the practice from the late 1940s of inviting wives to occasional dinners in the SCR did something to bring them closer to the life of the college. But for junior members, opportunities for casual conversations with women were not frequent. Some undergraduates had girlfriends back at home. Others went to tea in women's colleges. Many met nurses, occupational therapists and secretaries at dances at the Forum Restaurant or the Arlosh ('Slosh') Hall. To the adventurous, Oxford offered love-affairs and sexual initiation, to which the restricted visiting hours were no obstacle. For them, as Maurice Bowra used to say, the evening was for drinking, the afternoon for fornication. For much of the period, therefore, there was no great pressure to admit women to a fuller part in the life of the men's colleges. When in 1971 Balliol polled its old members on whether the College should become co-residential, the generations who had been up in the 1940s and 1950s were firmly against the

[64] HUD/C/SV.
[65] This paragraph is based on HUD/C/SV.

change. Those who had come up in the 1960s, however, were in favour.[66] And it was in the 1960s that the colleges relaxed their barricades. First, women were allowed as guests at college societies, though this had happened occasionally in the 1950s. Next they were allowed in, from time to time, as guests at dinner in hall. After this came the relaxation of gate-hours and the issue of keys to everyone.

The overall effect of these changes was to give the casual visitor the impression that colleges were already mixed, and that was the background against which the discussions of co-residence took place. Nuffield had been mixed from the beginning and St Antony's admitted women in 1962. So did Linacre House, founded in the same year. But when in 1964 New College announced its desire to become mixed, there ensued a decade of heated discussion. The popular interim solution was an alliance between a men's college and a women's college whereby each could use the other's facilities. Corpus formed a link with Somerville, Brasenose with St Hugh's and St Edmund Hall with the Department of Education. But such schemes were soon swept aside in favour of the inevitable solution: making women full members of the former men's colleges. In 1972 five men's colleges agreed to admit women with effect from the following year. Nothing did more to breathe new life into the old college community. The desire for mixed company had supplied much of the pressure for a central students' union in the 1960s, whereas the shift to co-residence revived the college as a natural focus of social life for most undergraduates.

There was one category of junior member, however, to whom the colleges still offered very little. This was the postgraduate student. In 1938/9 there had been only 536 of them in the whole University, 11 per cent of all students. By 1964/5 there were 2,153 (23 per cent).[67] These postgraduates did not fit easily into the pattern of college life. They were older than the undergraduates and often unaccustomed to the college system. Over a third were married and their supervisors were usually in other colleges. The colleges gave them little more than access to the library, sports facilities and dinner in hall. In 1960 only 22 per cent of the postgraduate population were living in college accommodation.[68] Many felt lonely, isolated and neglected, particularly arts postgraduates, who did not have the companionship and support of the science laboratory. The Franks Commission discovered that only a minority of those postgraduates who had not been undergraduates at Oxford thought that the traditional college system was appropriate for postgraduate studies. Most preferred the graduate colleges of Nuffield and St Antony's. The retrospective testimony of those who were postgraduate

[66] *Balliol College Annual Record* 1972, 7.

[67] *Franks Report* ii. 12.

[68] HCP 236 (1960), 779. The figure of 15% for 1964 in *Franks Report* ii. 232 excludes graduates in their first year.

students in the late 1950s and early 1960s suggests that much bitterness was felt about the lack of personal interest taken in their situation, and the general lack of support afforded them by their colleges.[69]

Only slowly did the colleges begin to make some adjustments. The first middle common room was established at Lincoln in 1958. The model rapidly spread, and the early to mid–1960s saw the foundation of middle or graduate common rooms in over half the colleges. They provided reading rooms with refreshments and newspapers and there were special guest nights or tables at which postgraduates might entertain visitors in hall. By 1970, however, the assimilation of postgraduates into the college structure had a long way to go. To many postgraduates the college still seemed a remote entity.

The greatest threat to the college system was the growth of the university at the centre. Since 1945 the balance of power had shifted decisively. By 1963 the university's annual income was more than £6 million, that of the colleges, excluding board and lodging charges, only £2.5 million.[70] Not even the richest colleges could now support their activities without the common services provided by the university and its contribution to the payment of fellows via university and CUF lecturerships. If the graduate colleges (Nuffield and St Antony's) are excluded, it seems that scarcely any important intellectual innovation was pioneered by the colleges during these years; it was the university which was now the active partner and the function of the colleges was to respond to initiatives from above.

Meanwhile it was becoming increasingly difficult to contain the ever-expanding university within the collegiate system. In principle the university was no more than the colleges. In practice, it had developed at a much faster rate. The growth of new subjects and the expansion of old ones had outstripped the readiness of the colleges to absorb new staff. The so-called 'non-dons', the university lecturers and others holding no college fellowship, found themselves unable to take part in the choice of their own students and greatly resented their inability to earn the higher stipends and allowances which accompanied the greater duties of college fellows. Their pressure led to the election to college fellowships in 1964 of fifty non-dons, the creation in 1965 of the new graduate societies Iffley (later Wolfson) and St Cross, and the decision that all future academic appointments should be made jointly by the university and a college.[71]

In the eyes of many science professors the colleges appeared obstructive bodies, reluctant to absorb their growing staff, antiquated in their time-consuming teaching methods and indifferent to the needs of research.[72] It is

[69] Franks Commission, written evidence xi. 35; iii. 84–5; HUD/C/SV.

[70] *Franks Report* i. 40, 283, 290.

[71] For these developments see below, 713–15, 742–4.

[72] Franks Commission, written evidence iv. 44–8, 106–7, 140–4, 151–3; Franks Commission, oral evidence iii (Jones, 20 Oct. 1964); xxi (Peierls, 12 Nov. 1964); xxviii (Pringle, 19 Nov. 1964); xxxvii (Darlington, 1 Dec. 1964).

not true, of course, that the colleges did nothing for research, since many of them maintained junior research fellows at the critical early period of their careers. But colleges tended to block intellectual innovation by giving priority to their teaching needs when making joint teaching appointments and consequently preferring tutors who professed some supposedly 'mainline', that is to say traditional, branch of their subject as against those who were associated with some newfangled specialism. In the arts faculties, moreover, the complaint was that, though fellows took their college teaching very seriously, they were far too casual about their university duties. Certainly most undergraduates seem to have left Oxford believing that tutorials were often very good and lectures usually very bad.[73] Meanwhile the incorporation of non-dons into the college fellowships increased the size of governing bodies and diminished the proportion of fellows who had any direct dealings with the college's junior members. In this way the cohesion of the college community was further reduced.

That community, however, extended far beyond Oxford, for membership of the college was conceived of as a lifelong affair. Those old members who kept their names on the books were listed each year in the *University Calendar* and regularly invited back to gaudies. Most colleges had societies of old members which held regular reunions and dinners, usually in a London restaurant. During these years colleges laid increasing emphasis on their continuity, commissioning biographical registers and issuing annual reports or newsletters, usually edited by some fellow, who took endless pains to include news of honours and appointments and keep readers in touch with the college. Until his sudden death in 1948 Stallybrass published in the *Brazen Nose* an annual column entitled 'The Principal's Scrap Book', containing news gleaned from the thousands of letters he exchanged with old members. The tone was heavily jocular: 'H. L. Puxley (1919) is in Canada. What he is doing there I cannot imagine.' Matrimony was frequently referred to as a misfortune incurred.[74]

In the early 1960s there was a change in the system. Former members of the University were no longer required to pay dues when out of residence (a system which had discouraged many from taking their MA because of the cost of paying arrears owing over many years). Instead, dues were payable only by those in residence and thereafter life membership was secured. This had the effect of both enlarging and diluting the body of old members. It increased the numbers eligible to be invited to gaudies and consequently slowed down the frequency of invitations. A study of gaudy acceptance-rates would give some indication of the degree of loyalty felt by old members to their colleges. So would an analysis of the response to appeals

73 HUD/C/SV.
74 *Brazen Nose* 1945–8, 165, 191.

for money. The peak seems to have been achieved by Balliol in its seven-hundredth anniversary appeal in 1963, when 60 per cent of all living old members contributed.[75] But in every college, old members made gifts of money, silver, pictures and books for the library.

Changes in the composition of the University inevitably threatened the continuity which colleges did their utmost to maintain. The new criteria for entrance made it harder for old members' children to secure admission. The growth of student radicalism diminished the attachment to their colleges of those affected and evoked the distaste of their predecessors. Nevertheless, the enduring influence of college life during this period is shown by the desire of many old members to keep in touch with their colleges, to contribute to their appeals and to send their own children in their footsteps.

College life between 1945 and 1970 presents a picture of immense vitality and diversity. Of course the differences between colleges were steadily diminishing over these years as the system for admitting undergraduates and electing fellows became standardized and the cost of living in different colleges more equal. Applicants were now more concerned to get into Oxford than to a particular college.[76] Yet differences in academic performance were still very marked, as can be seen if schools results are averaged out over each decade.[77] Balliol was pre-eminent (second in the 1940s; top in the 1950s and 1960s). Magdalen was the next most successful (top in the 1940s, second in the 1950s and fourth in the 1960s). Queen's came third in the 1940s and 1950s, but fell to eighth in the 1960s. By that time Corpus was second and Merton third. The most striking rise was that of Wadham (twenty-first in the 1940s, but seventh in the 1960s). The worst falls were at Christ Church (thirteenth to twenty-sixth), Hertford (fifteenth to twenty-ninth) and Oriel (sixteenth to twenty-fifth). These results reflected the differing abilities of undergraduates admitted, but also the capacity and outlook of the head and fellows. A college could achieve great success by drawing predominantly from grammar schools (as at Queen's and Wadham). It could do even better by a mixture of grammar-school and public-school entrants (as at Balliol, Magdalen and Corpus). But concentrating too heavily on the public schools was always fatal.

The differences between the colleges in size, social composition, sporting reputation and general tone thus remained very considerable; and they were reflected in the notably uneven distribution of blues, bachelor fellows, dining clubs, overseas students, essays twice a week and all the other variables of college existence. The texture of life in Corpus, with only 202 junior members in 1965, was different from that in St Catherine's, with 460.

[75] *Balliol College Record* 1966, 5.
[76] Franks Commission, oral evidence vii. 21 (Fisher and Lee, 22 Oct. 1964).
[77] I draw upon the retrospective Norrington tables compiled for the History of the University by Dr D. I. Greenstein.

In 1964 Balliol had 22 Rhodes scholars, Keble none at all.[78] In 1965 the proportion of undergraduates from independent schools at Queen's was 25 per cent, at Christ Church 71 per cent.[79] In 1959 St Edmund Hall was not just head of the river, but also won rugby cuppers, soccer cuppers and athletic cuppers. At the end of the period there were still disparities in stipends, allowances and teaching hours between the fellows of rich and poor colleges.

During these years the men's colleges more or less successfully withstood the challenges they faced: the increase in numbers; the growth of science, organized on a departmental basis and taking both students and tutors out of college for most of the working day; the expansion of knowledge, which made the old tutorial system much less self-sufficient; the change in the social composition of the junior members, less likely to have experienced boarding-school life, less accustomed to a socially elevated style of living and more susceptible to the appeal of the youth culture outside the college; the increase in the number of postgraduate students, insufficiently integrated into the undergraduate colleges; the greater professionalization and domesticity of the college fellows; the rise in the number of senior members of the University who were not fellows at all; the disappearance of the colleges' relationship to undergraduates *in loco parentis*; the demand of junior members for participation in the government of the college; and the incursion of women.

'One day,' declared a writer in *Isis* in 1958, 'the autonomy of Oxford colleges will probably have to be abolished'. In the 1960s it seemed as if that day might be approaching. In its evidence to the Franks Commission in 1965, the Oxford regional committee of the NUS proposed that admissions should be made by faculties not colleges, that teaching should be more centralized and that college endowments should pass to the university.[80] In fact the 1960s proved to be the decade when the colleges successfully consolidated their position. They maintained their hold on admissions and they defeated the proposal in the Franks report that there should be a council of colleges whose members would be bound by a majority vote.[81] Unobtrusively they created a number of intermediate bodies uniting the various college officers (bursars, deans, senior tutors and domestic bursars) into a network of influential committees. Former 'societies' received full collegiate status, like St Anne's (1959), St Catherine's (1960) and St Peter's (1961). The post-war success of Nuffield (charter 1958, full college 1963) and St Antony's (charter 1953, full college 1963) had shown that the collegiate model could be effectively adopted by institutions comprising fellows and

[78] Franks Commission, written evidence vii. 43.
[79] *Franks Report* ii. 62.
[80] *Isis* 11 June 1958, 28; Franks Commission, written evidence x. 131, 134, 135.
[81] See below, 715, 733–4, 740–2.

postgraduate students only. In the 1960s All Souls decided after much heated debate that it would neither amalgamate with St Antony's nor admit postgraduate students but would continue as a college for fellows only, though with a new programme of visiting fellowships for scholars and distinguished persons from outside Oxford. The non-dons were placated by the foundation of yet more colleges: Linacre, Wolfson and St Cross. The collegiate ideal thus emerged from the tumult of the late 1960s and early 1970s with undiminished vitality.

But the price paid for the continuing survival of the colleges as the basis of the Oxford system was the weakening of their place both in the lives of their members and in the structure of the University. Franks said that Oxford had moved from being a confederation of colleges to a collegiate university.[82] At the end of the period the colleges still retained their traditional autonomy, though the enhanced power of the university and the greater importance of public funding made much of that autonomy a fiction. For the average male undergraduate the college was still the centre of his Oxford life, but its control of his existence had relaxed and its claims upon his loyalty were less intense. In this modified state, the Oxford college would continue to flourish and to provide its members with a living and working environment superior to that yet devised by any other academic institution.

[82] *Franks Report* i. 132.

9

The Arts and Social Sciences, 1939–1970

JOSE HARRIS

Academic life in Oxford on the eve of the Second World War was dominated by a cluster of over-arching and interlocking themes: the pre-eminence of the humanities, the power of the colleges, the priority given to the teaching of undergraduates, the special relationship with the nation's governing and administering élites, and a distinctively 'Anglo-Saxon' style of thought and scholarship in many spheres. More than 75 per cent of dons and more than 85 per cent of undergraduate students were engaged in various branches of humane learning: classics, history, languages, law and theology, supplemented since 1923 by some of the more liberal aspects of the new 'social sciences', gathered together under the umbrella of philosophy, politics and economics (PPE). Greatest prestige still attached to the faculty of literae humaniores and to the study of classical mods and Greats (two years of intensive philological study of Greek and Latin, followed by two years of the history and philosophy of Greece and Rome).

In all arts disciplines, however, the faculties—and indeed the University itself—were remote and shadowy entities, encountered by many students only on the final day of reckoning in the Examination Schools. Material resources and the day-to-day direction of studies were concentrated in the hands not of professors and departments but of colleges and college fellows. Undergraduates (known as *men*) studied (or rather *read*) for their degrees with tutors in their own colleges (in rich colleges with several tutors, in poorer colleges often with a single tutor who might cover every subject in an eight-term honours course). Colleges were overwhelmingly composed of 'arts' dons (all but the most distinguished of scientists being largely confined to the much less prestigeful university departments). The college tutors included among their number many distinguished scholars. But innovatory scholarship was admired as an almost incidental by-product of the tutor's job, not as a *raison d'être*; and in most senior common rooms excellent teaching and general acumen brought far greater respect from a tutor's peers than learned publications. In each faculty there were professors and readers concerned with research and advanced teaching, but in all arts subjects research students and candidates for higher degrees were conspicuous by their rarity. Decades after its introduction, the degree of doctor of philosophy (DPhil) was still viewed by many arts dons as a distasteful medium of dry Teutonic pedantry.[1] The University was peopled overwhelmingly by undergraduates, only a minute proportion of whom would proceed to a life of vocational scholarship; and to most Oxford tutors the passing on of humane learning to young men who would make their careers not in academe but in public and professional life was still the main reason for the University's existence. Except for a tiny minority, Oxford was intended to be neither a medium of vocational training nor a centre of advanced research, but a nursery for citizens and gentlemen. Outside the sphere of classical learning, the focus of Oxford arts studies lay predominantly in courses with a strongly English dimension: in English history, in Anglo-Saxon philology, in the common law, and in the development of an empiricist philosophical style that many deemed peculiarly English. And beyond England lay powerful ties with the British empire. The vision of a peaceful transition from empire to Commonwealth, embodied in the Statute of Westminster in 1931, was a vision conceived in Oxford;[2] and although Oxford tutors no longer saw themselves as nurturing imperial pro-consuls in quite the manner of Benjamin Jowett, there remained nevertheless a widely diffused sense that one of the purposes of an Oxford arts education was to train its recipients to administer the world.

Many aspects of Oxford's pre-war character survived intact into the 1950s and 1960s; and Oxford in 1970 was still recognizably the humane, collegiate, undergraduate and predominantly non-vocational university of thirty years before. In the intervening years, however, changes had occurred on many fronts: changes that to a large extent mirrored wider changes in the structure of British society. The natural sciences now accounted for 35 per cent of the University's undergraduates and nearly 50 per cent of senior members; and, within the humanities, the new social sciences were growing rapidly at the expense of the traditional arts disciplines. Throughout the 1960s pressures and proposals were afoot at many levels to shift the balance of power in university teaching away from the 'generalist' colleges to the more 'specialist' faculties. The number of postgraduate students rose almost fourfold between 1938/9 and 1964/5 to a total of 2,153.[3] In the arts as well as the sciences, college tutors as well as professors were now expected—and indeed aspired—to engage in original research; and the explosion of knowledge in many fields was generating recurrent tension between the demands of 'frontline' scholarship and the demands of day-to-day tutorial teaching. The

[1] OM 23 Jan. 1941, 136; 3 Dec. 1959, 117.
[2] D. Lavin, 'Lionel Curtis and the idea of Commonwealth' in F. Madden and D. K. Fieldhouse (eds), Oxford and the Idea of Commonwealth (London and Canberra 1982).
[3] Franks Report ii. 12.

universalization of secondary education and the introduction of state scholarships and local-authority grants had created a new constituency of potential entrants to Oxford, who at first had been painlessly contained within traditional structures, but who by the 1960s were increasingly in revolt against the content and character of the traditional honours schools. And, after many generations in which sixth-form syllabuses had been virtually dictated by the goal of Oxford scholarships, the University found itself increasingly obliged to tailor its entrance requirements to the democratic realities of mass secondary education. Moreover, from the late 1950s onward Oxford was subject to a series of damaging external attacks: from Sir Charles Snow, who blamed the traditional Oxbridge humanities curricula for the curse of the 'two cultures'; from the Robbins Committee, which saw the Oxford scholarship and entrance system as threatening the growth of the new universities; and from politicians, reformers and businessmen who increasingly linked Britain's economic stagnation and decline to the cultural predominance of an anti-technological, arts-trained Oxbridge dilettante élite.

The debate about the wider impact of Oxford culture upon British economic and political history lies outside the scope of this chapter. An attempt will be made here, however, to trace the internal responses of Oxford's arts and social science faculties to social and intellectual change in Britain after 1939. How did professors and tutors adapt to new developments in thought and scholarship, to the changing social character of the student body, and to changing public expectations about the role of the University in national life? Such responses differed at different times and among different academic groups (one of the few common characteristics of Oxford dons continuing to be their tenacious and sometimes perverse idiosyncrasy). It is possible, however, to detect certain general trends over time, both subjective and statistical. No arts faculty was unaffected by the quantitative growth of academic knowledge that occurred in the post-war era, though the fall-out was most far-reaching in the sphere of the social sciences. No area of academic inquiry was unaffected by the war, the welfare state and the era of student revolution—though again it was the social sciences that most markedly both reflected and mediated wider social change. The tutorial relationship—that mystical relationship 'twixt don and man, seen by many as the quintessence of Oxford life—subtly and controversially evolved over the period, as did the underlying philosophy of an Oxford education in the humanities. The rudiments of classical learning—seen in the 1940s and 1950s as still indispensable for any Oxford matriculant in whatever discipline—were progressively dismantled over the course of the 1960s. Oxford's intellectual life—still in 1939 powerfully hallmarked by classics, Englishness and Christianity—became increasingly secularized and international. This chapter will attempt to map the main contours of change, first across the whole spectrum of the humane disciplines, and then in the context of the different subjects and faculties.

Oxford life between 1939 and 1970 may conveniently be divided into four periods, marked partly by an underlying institutional continuity but partly also by a succession of distinctive moods and styles. These four periods consisted of wartime, the immediately post-war period, the curiously static and somnolent 1950s, and the epoch of intense self-criticism and re-evaluation that set in after 1960. Even before the outbreak of war there were some indications of desire for change. The financial appeal launched in 1937 referred to the need for endowment of humanities research and the liberation of tutors from excessive teaching of undergraduates—though the appeal's report came down firmly against moving towards academic 'specialization'.[4] The war period was necessarily a time of makeshift and compromise, as dons and students were called up, as evacuees were housed in colleges, and as the residuum of under-age and female students was rushed through a system of abbreviated, two-year degrees. Much scholarly research into the humanities came to an abrupt halt in 1940, and many arts dons found themselves either overwhelmed with crash teaching programmes or drafted into counter-espionage, fire-watching and public administration. The war necessarily gave priority to scientific and technological goals, and for the first time in Oxford's history the largely invisible scientific departments and laboratories came into their own as publicly acknowledged centres of theoretical innovation and advanced research. The battle for national survival inevitably modified the somewhat arcane and patrician priorities of a traditional Oxford education.

Yet the shock to Oxford's predominantly humanistic identity—and to the link between that identity and the wider life of the nation—was perhaps less traumatic than might have been supposed. The war gave a great boost to social, economic and psychological studies, and to the aspirations of the group of social scientists headed by G. D. H. Cole who formed the nucleus of the infant Nuffield College. Throughout the war All Souls, Nuffield, Corpus and the recently founded Institute of Statistics were all important centres of social, educational and post-war planning. Moreover, the sense that the war was more than just a battle for survival but a battle for civilization gave a certain enhanced legitimacy to traditional humane studies. The election of Winston Churchill in 1942 to an honorary fellowship at Merton (his father's old College) was interpreted as a symbol of 'the high value which the present Government obviously attaches to the arts and academic studies'.[5] The arrival in Oxford of a number of eminent émigré

[4] *Oxford University: A Programme of Development* (University of Oxford 1938), copy in Bodl. GA Oxon. 8. 1132 (21).
[5] *OM* editorial of 30 Apr. 1942, 257. For Cole, see G. D. N. Worswick, 'Cole and Oxford 1938–58' in A. Briggs and J. Saville (eds), *Essays in Labour History* (London 1967 edn).

European scholars injected a powerful element of continental learning into many traditional arts disciplines. And even in the darkest days of the war there was a surprising degree of institutional growth, sometimes in areas of quite arcane scholarship—a new chair in social and political theory, a new readership in Old Icelandic, a campaign to promote a new degree in archaeology.

The wartime shortage of tutors caused difficulties for all arts subjects; but at the same time it promoted an unprecedented degree of inter-collegiate teaching, some critical reappraisal of the tutorial system, and the setting up for the first time of a permanent, university-wide senior tutors' committee (senior tutors at this time and for several decades thereafter were almost without exception senior arts dons).[6] Constraints on publishing limited the appearance of new academic monographs, but there was a steady trickle of works by Oxford classicists, philosophers and historians (including R. G. Collingwood's *Autobiography* and *The New Leviathan*, which together provoked heated debate on whether the moral collapse of the 1930s had been fostered by the 'realism' and logical positivism espoused by Oxford philosophers). Oxford historians of both older and younger genera-tions—such as R. C. K. Ensor, H. A. L. Fisher, E. H. Carr and A. J. P. Taylor—were in constant demand as lecturers and commentators on the causes of the war and the lessons to be drawn from it; while Professor Neale's 1942 Ford lectures on the Elizabethan parliaments helped to consolidate highbrow national identity in a manner comparable with the impact of Laurence Olivier's *Henry the Fifth* in 1944. Moreover, the successful entry of many arts and social science dons into work of national importance encouraged a widespread feeling in Oxford circles that the war had not undermined but confirmed the intellectual advantages of an Oxford generalist education. The war was proving to be 'a scholar's war', proclaimed one optimistic classics tutor towards the end of 1940: 'For years now students of the ancient world have watched the familiar past stalking to meet them in the thin disguise of the future, and their subject, every year more topical, has renewed itself in the light of current events. Demosthenes has been more often quoted since the rape of Austria than in the half-century preceding it: Catiline and Clodius are no longer the mysterious figures they were even ten years ago. And now Greece is at war with Rome, and British scholarship finds itself mercifully allied on the side on which its sympathies would naturally lie. The Classical Atlas has become a war map . . . Classical education has become a national asset overnight; a year spent in the British School at Athens is worth three months in an OCTU.'[7]

This confident belief in the practical relevance of traditional disciplines, and in their perennial adaptability to changing conditions, survived into the

---

[6] *OM* 25 May 1940, 267; 14 Nov. 1940, 68.
[7] *OM* 21 Nov. 1940, 81.

post-war world. Oxford after 1945 was full of a generation of under-graduates quite different from any that had ever been seen before; mature men, and a sprinkling of women, who had fought in battles, managed government departments, traded in espionage and lived through bombing, but who (in striking contrast with undergraduate veterans of the First World War) seemed remarkably unscathed by their experiences. On average they were nearly three years older than those who had come up to Oxford in the late 1930s; and tutors who remembered the rootless and shell-shocked freshmen of 1919 to 1922 uneasily anticipated several years of academic malaise and maladjustment. But in fact this did not happen. After some initial grumbling in undergraduate newspapers about parochialism and 'memory tests', the class of 1946 threw itself into traditional academic studies with all the vigour and self-discipline of a platoon upon a parade-ground.[8] Post-war Oxford was in many respects an idealistic and socially reformist community, but its constructive zeal was largely directed towards institutions and culture in the wider society (the possibility that Oxford itself might be part and parcel of those wider institutions was curiously ignored).

This is not of course to suggest that there was no post-war innovation of any kind. On the contrary, the brief period of freely flowing government funds at the end of the war encouraged experiment in a number of arts and social science fields, among them the introduction of an honours school of psychology, philosophy and physiology and new diplomas in archaeology and social anthropology.[9] New chairs were created in European archaeology and oriental studies and new lecturerships in Russian and economics. 1947 also brought the introduction of the postgraduate degree of bachelor of philosophy (BPhil) for those wishing to do advanced work in philosophy, politics or economics. The BPhil (later to be extended to other arts subjects) was to be an outstanding academic success and, particularly in the sphere of philosophy, was to lay the foundation of Oxford's claim to be an advanced modern international university. But generous funding for new departures did not survive the international monetary crisis of 1947; and from within Oxford itself during the post-war years there was much nervous resistance to academic change. A proposal for a 'European Greats' degree, which would have combined modern history, philosophy, literature and European languages, 'foundered upon the unchanging rocks which guard the entrance to the Faculty of Modern Languages'; while a proposal for a fully fledged degree in anthropology and archaeology was 'shot down' by those who saw

[8] For the complaints see 'The schools: law', *Isis* 13 Mar. 1946, 18. Cf above, 65, 187, 208.
[9] A witness to the Franks Commission seventeen years later recalled 'the wonderful year of 1947, when everybody got everything': Franks Commission, oral evidence xxxiii. 13 (Professor L. R. Palmer).

it as a dangerous competitor to Greats.[10] In all the major arts schools—Greats, history, English, modern languages and PPE—the curricula of the 1930s were reinstated virtually without revision. Intellectual innovation in certain largely technical spheres (such as 'ordinary language' philosophy and the critical handling of historical documents) co-existed with a widely diffused anti-modernism in many aspects of Oxford's thought and culture. In all colleges the pre-war pedagogic-cum-pastoral relationship between pupil and tutor was resumed (frequently in 1946 with a tutor who might be several years younger and considerably less worldly-wise than his undergraduate charges). No less than in the 1930s the weekly (or twice-weekly) essay and 'private hour' remained for the vast majority of arts students the intellectual spinal cord of their Oxford experience.

Traditional structures continued to dominate University life in the 1950s, in spite of the fact that the advance of the publicly funded grammar-school boy meant that Oxford was slowly undergoing a minor social revolution. There was a gradual expansion in arts and social sciences research, largely financed by private benefactors like Lord Nuffield, Nubar Gulbenkian and Antonin Besse; and 1955 brought an unprecedented experiment in interdisciplinary co-operation in the form of the Oxford Research Laboratory for Archaeology and the History of Art.[11] But the enormous increase in undergraduate applications to Oxford, fuelled by the new system of state grants, kept at bay any serious questioning or reconsideration of Oxford's public and educational role. Far from dwindling in the utilitarian climate of the post-war era, arts faculties continued to maintain and expand their numbers (surveys showed that students from working-class backgrounds were even more inclined to opt for traditional, non-vocational, humanities courses than students from the public schools).[12] Arts graduates of Oxford and Cambridge continued to monopolize entry into the higher ranks of the civil service, the BBC and the learned professions, if anything even more markedly than they had done a generation before. Many Oxford dons were self-consciously defensive about the onward march of 'Americanization', a phenomenon that they identified with the mass-production of PhDs, the psychological assessment of student aptitude, and the growth of such disciplines as 'communication engineering'. The *Oxford Magazine* noted in 1955 that a North American manual on monitoring student progress would 'puzzle and amuse' the English reader, but was 'too far from his ways to challenge detailed criticism'.[13] There was some alarm about the projected

[10] 'The Hayter report', *OM* 22 Feb. 1962, 205; Franks Commission, oral evidence xxxiii. 7 (Professor C. F. C. Hawkes).

[11] C. F. C. Hawkes, 'The research laboratory: its beginning', *Archaeometry* xxviii (1986), 131–2.

[12] *OM* 26 May 1960, 294–6.

[13] *OM* 10 Mar. 1955, 281.

population bulge of the 1960s: Kingsley Amis's 'more means worse' was widely quoted, usually with approval, together with the dictum that 'a faculty should be no bigger than can cheaply attend one sherry party'.[14]

By the late 1950s, however, there were signs of discontent with both the organization and the traditional academic content of Oxford life, often in unexpected quarters. 'Oxford is dull', observed the Master of Pembroke, R. B. McCallum, in an article satirizing recent complaints about Oxford graduates from a prominent industrialist.[15] There was much nervous discussion among Oxford dons about the role of intellectuals in modern British society: some deploring the rise of a tyrannous and trendy 'cultured' intelligentsia, others equally deploring the comfortable retreat of the nation's educated élite into a privatized culture of wine, food, bird-watching, reading Jane Austen and 'the cultivation of personal relations'.[16] The damaging (and historically recent) cultural divisions between arts and science disciplines were spotlighted by the Professor of Thermodynamics, Sir Francis Simon, long before Snow delivered his famous lecture on the 'two cultures'.[17] Snow's lecture of 1959 and its intemperate tone were widely denounced in Oxford, but there can be little doubt that its message struck many uneasy chords in the academic conscience, particularly among those in the traditional humanities fields.[18] Anxiety about cross-cultural illiteracy and premature specialization led to growing disquiet about the nature of the Oxbridge entrance system, which more than any other single factor had traditionally forced English public and grammar schools to turn out pupils who were highly educated within a very narrow range. It was claimed, moreover, that this pressure had begun to invade the advanced-level school certificate, even for pupils who had no intention of applying for admission to the ancient universities.[19]

Discontent with the entrance examination rapidly spilt over into many other spheres. There were increasing complaints among tutors about the endemic tension between primary research and the duty to provide a broad general education for the nation's 'intellectual aristocracy': a tension highlighted when the historian of the Russian revolution, E. H. Carr, decided to abandon his tutorship at Balliol for a research fellowship at

[14] OM 2 June 1955, 377–8.
[15] R. B. McCallum, 'Oxford is dull', Oxford May 1957.
[16] C. S. Lewis, 'Lilies that fester', Twentieth Century Apr. 1955; J. Joll, 'On being an intellectual', ibid. June 1955.
[17] Letter from F. E. Simon, OM 5 May 1955, 304.
[18] See for example F. M. H. Markham, 'Arts and sciences in the university', OM 2 June 1960, 209.
[19] R. S. Stanier, 'The arts and science sides in the sixth form' [review of a report to the Gulbenkian Foundation by the Oxford University department of education], OM 26 May 1960, 294–6; A. D. C. Petersen, 'The sixth form experience of Oxford entrants', OM 6 Feb. 1964, 172–3.

Trinity College, Cambridge.[20] There was rising concern about the fact that the rapid expansion of the number of postgraduate students in the humanities in the late 1950s had been accompanied by an almost total lack of provision for either their social needs or their academic instruction (other than for the small handful reading for the BPhil). There were hints of smouldering discontent with the tutorial system and a growing suspicion in some quarters that, while for some it might be a marriage of true minds, for others it was often an embarrassing and expensive failure.[21] There were frequent complaints by undergraduates about the anarchic character of university lectures, and about the fact that in all arts faculties there was little attempt to cover any agreed syllabus or to avoid duplication in the timetable. There was also increasing debate about the role of compulsory Latin, as more and more schools gave voice to the view that pupils could no longer cope with both the Oxford Latin entrance requirement and the success at A-level required by grant-giving public authorities.

The mounting disquiets of the late 1950s gave rise to a spate of internal and external inquiries that was to last for most of the 1960s: inquiries whose repercussions were in many respects to transform the structure and character of an Oxford education. The first of these inquiries was that carried out in 1959 by a committee on entrance requirements, chaired by Dr Guy Chilver, an ancient history tutor at Queen's. The Chilver Committee addressed itself to the problem of narrow specialization in sixth forms and proposed that, while compulsory Latin should be retained for arts candidates, it should be abolished for candidates in the natural sciences—its place to be taken by a general literacy paper on the 'use of English'. The Chilver report aroused heated debate in Oxford and in the national press; and the case for Latin as an indispensable tool of European civilization was forcefully propounded by two prominent English dons, Dame Helen Gardner and Lord David Cecil. Others defended Latin not for its literary merit, but for its inculcation of logical, linguistic and critical skills: it was 'from Latin that we learnt the discipline of analysis, which we could later apply to the slogans and trash of everyday life', declared the Professor of Semitic Philology. The issue was debated in Congregation in February 1960, resulting in a defeat for the supporters of compulsory Latin for scientists. It was a decision widely and to some extent correctly interpreted by the popular press as a major symbolic turning point in the intellectual history of Oxford.[22]

[20] OM 10 Mar. 1955, 266; 2 June 1955, 378.
[21] A. Quinton, 'The tutorial system', pt 1, OM 19 May 1960, 284–6; G. J. Warnock, 'The tutorial system', pt 2, ibid. 286–7; J. Bayley, 'Tutor's view', Isis 2 June 1966, 5.
[22] OM 4, 11, 18, 25 Feb. and 3 Mar. 1960, passim. Exemption was at first granted only to those with a pass at A-level in mathematics or a science or a comparable college award. The 'Report of the committee to review the requirements for admission into the University', chaired by G. E. F. Chilver, was published as supplement no. 1 to the Gazette 28 Jan. 1960, 535–50.

Other issues explored by the Chilver Committee would not lie down, however, and the debate about Latin proved to be merely the preliminary skirmish in a much more prolonged battle about the internal structure of Oxford's degrees, about methods of teaching, lecturing and supervision, and about the wider relation of Oxford to national secondary education. The undergraduate newspaper, *Isis*, began to publish critical reviews of lectures (a practice that had some support from tutors but was eventually banned by the proctors); and in May 1960 the University Grants Committee announced that it proposed to carry out an inquiry into Oxford's teaching methods, including the role of tutorials.[23] Tutors themselves engaged in often acrimonious controversy over the need for reform. Some, like Lawrence Stone of Wadham, denounced the parochial philistinism of Oxford in particular and of British education in general; while others, like J. M. Kaye of Queen's, defended the excellence of the British education system and dismissed complaints against Oxbridge dominance as 'frivolous and fatuous'.[24] Within all the traditional arts disciplines there were murmurings of discontent about the narrowness of Oxford courses and about the need for a more interdisciplinary approach: a discontent that found an ironic echo within the faculty of social studies, where some at least of the tutors increasingly complained of the opposite problem—that the compulsory union of philosophy, politics and economics within a single undergraduate degree was inhibiting professional standards and advanced research.[25]

The appointment of the Robbins Committee on higher education in 1962 brought many aspects of Oxford life under public scrutiny; and throughout the Robbins inquiry there was widespread apprehension in Oxford that the Committee was fundamentally out of sympathy with the ancient universities (a suspicion not helped by Robbins's publication of misleading statistics suggesting that the average Oxford don taught for only 4.2 hours a week). Robbins made it clear from the outset that he had little patience with the blithe assumption of Oxford colleges that they had a seigneurial right to take their pick of the nation's best sixth-form candidates. He was highly critical of the continuing social bias of Oxford entrance (70 per cent of Oxford places still going to candidates from the public schools); and he continually warned that resource-priorities over the next twenty-five years would have to lie with the newer civic and provincial universities. The opening of several new universities, and in particular the University of Sussex, caused further heart-searching in Oxford circles. The Sussex humanities courses were based not on single subjects but on clusters of interlocking disciplines that focused

[23] *OM* 12 May 1960, 269.

[24] Letter from Lawrence Stone, *OM* 4 Feb. 1960, 172–3; J. M. Kaye, 'Legal education in Oxford', *OM* 2 Nov. 1961, 47–9.

[25] D. L. Munby, 'A new school in economics', *OM* 14 and 21 Nov. 1963, 79–80 and 94–5.

on 'area studies' (rather similar to the 'European Greats' course rejected in Oxford in 1947). Coming at a time when both tutors and students in Oxford were voicing dissatisfaction with the enormous factual content and limited intellectual range of the traditional honours schools, the rivalry of Sussex caused widespread alarm; and there were many rumours of bright sixth-formers deliberately turning their backs upon the outmoded charms of Oxford and flocking to Brighton to work with Asa Briggs.[26]

Oxford's anxieties during the early 1960s coincided with what later became known as the 'rise of the student estate'; and debate on the nature of an Oxford education began for the first time to include the voice of the undergraduate. Undergraduates presented petitions to the history faculty asking for reform of the syllabus in 1961 and again in 1962; and from 1963 onward a new university-based Student Representative Council began to advance the case for systematic reform of the major humanities degrees. Student reformers pressed for more interdisciplinary studies, less exclusive emphasis on the one-to-one tutorial and more opportunity for movement from one course to another.[27] These demands were accompanied by the growth of student activism in other spheres, most notably in resistance to the traditional disciplinary authority of the colleges and the proctors. And at about the same time Oxford began to receive extremely adverse coverage in the popular press, as a debauched and disorderly backwater of aristocratic privilege.[28] In 1963 and 1964 there was a marked decline in sixth-form applications to Oxford, and final honours school results in arts and social science subjects were the poorest of the post-war years. There was widespread pessimism about Oxford's future, and many rumours that the ancient universities were going to be subject to a public commission of inquiry, comparable in scope with the great investigative royal commissions of the mid-Victorian years.

In fact this mood of pessimism did not last, and measures began to be taken to avert Oxford's threatened decline. Several powerful senior academics came to the conclusion that Oxford had to make a serious effort to reform itself: to overhaul its recruitment procedures, to modernize its courses, and to open up the University to a wider range of social backgrounds and intellectual talents.[29] Groups of colleges synchronized their entrance exams, and scholars and commoners were increasingly selected on performance in the same examination. The separate Oxbridge entrance system was forcefully defended, as a device not for enabling

[26] 'Gems from the commission', OM 3 Dec. 1964, 133.

[27] The Proctors and the Student Press (Oxford University Student Council report 3, 1963); College Discipline (Oxford University Student Council report 4, 1964).

[28] R. Meiggs, 'Oxford in the dock again', OM 6 Feb. 1964, 177–8.

[29] D. N. Chester, 'Reform of the university', OM 20 Feb. 1964, 206–7; M. Reeves, 'Reform of the first degree course', OM 27 Feb. 1964, 242–3; G. Pickering, 'Oxford reformed', OM 5 Nov. 1964, 82–5.

Oxford to cream off the élite, but for detecting future promise rather than past performance and as a positive antidote to cramming.[30] For the first time there was serious and concerted discussion of curricular reform, and much support was voiced for the extension of 'mixed' degrees, for a shift to the 'tripos' system of frequent examinations, and for enabling students to switch their courses from one subject to another (proposals that were formally endorsed by the report of the Kneale Committee early in 1965).[31] And finally the determination to avoid yet another royal commission on Oxford led to the setting up of Oxford's own internal public commission of inquiry, under the chairmanship of Sir Oliver Franks, ex-Whitehall mandarin and Provost of Worcester College: an inquiry which in 1964–5 brought under the microscope the whole range of Oxford's administrative, financial, research and teaching procedures in all disciplines.

The full scope of the Franks inquiry will be considered in a later chapter, but something must be said here of its implications for arts and social science subjects.[32] The Committee took written and oral evidence from a wide variety of institutions and individuals, ranging from faculty boards to the Student Representative Council, from regius professors through to individual dons, students and private citizens who wished to air their views on Oxford life. This evidence gave voice to widespread discontents on such topics as the tutorial system, the final honour schools, Oxford's entrance requirements, the relations between colleges and faculties, the gap between arts and sciences and the recurrent tension between undergraduate teaching and pure research. There was much criticism of the Common University Fund (CUF) system of joint college and university posts which led—so it was claimed—to the invariable appointment of teaching 'all-rounders' rather than of scholars working in minority subjects or on the frontiers of research.[33] Several witnesses pressed for the setting up of an institute of 'advanced studies' modelled on that of Princeton; and there were many proposals for the introduction of more 'mixed' degrees, including a revival of the earlier scheme for 'European Greats'.[34] There was also a plan for a degree in 'science Greats' which would combine the history and philosophy of science with social and economic history and the study of public policy;[35] and one self-critical arts tutor proposed that all students who took finals in

---

[30] M. G. Brock, 'Admissions: the state of the case', *OM* 25 Feb. 1965, 238–40.

[31] [W. C. Kneale, chairman] *Report of the Committee on the Structure of the First and Second Public Examinations* (University of Oxford 1965).

[32] Cf below, 726–31.

[33] Franks Commission, oral evidence l (D. N. Chester); written evidence xi, Professor C. F. C. Hawkes.

[34] Franks Commission, written evidence iv, Professor E. L. Stahl; xi, R. Pedley, A. L. C. Bullock and Professor Sir Isaiah Berlin, F. M. H. Markham.

[35] Franks Commission, written evidence xi, S. E. Toulmin, 'Greats for the late twentieth century'.

an arts subject should be compelled to take a two-term preliminary course in natural science.[36] By no means all the evidence, however, was hostile to traditional Oxford subjects and methods. There was much defence of the democratic and egalitarian spirit fostered by Oxford's college-based system, compared with the professorially dominated bureaucratic hierarchies of more departmental universities.[37] Oxford graduates who had left Oxford to teach or study elsewhere were virtually unanimous in their praise of Oxford degrees and in their preference for the Oxford tutorial system over other methods of teaching. Witnesses who had taught in American universities warned of the dangers of the 'spreading of education in ever thinner doses through ever longer periods of time'; and one witness who had studied at a British provincial university claimed that 'nothing could rival the inefficiency of the seminars I attended there'.[38]

This wide diversity of views about Oxford life was reflected in the eventual substance of the Franks report, which laid great emphasis upon reconciling what was unique and valuable in Oxford's traditions with adaptation to change and modernity. The report defended both the college and tutorial systems, and firmly scotched the insinuation of Robbins that Oxford dons did much less work than elsewhere (on the contrary, the statistics produced by Franks suggested that, in both arts and science subjects, academics in Oxford on average both taught for longer hours and produced more scholarly research than their counterparts in other British universities).[39] The report also defended the traditional structure of the Oxford honours schools, in which most students after a minor preliminary exam were not re-examined until the end of their final year. The rationale of such a system, argued Franks, was not mere mindless cramming but a highly sophisticated educational philosophy that allowed students to amass knowledge and to mature their ideas over a long period, so as to arrive at their 'own conception of what it all means'.[40] The report was sympathetic to the predicament of dons torn between teaching and research, but it rejected proposals that Oxford should become purely a research institute or that the faculties should set up a series of specialist postgraduate schools. Oxford, as in the past, was to retain an absolute commitment to deep and highly personalized undergraduate studies.

Nevertheless, the Franks report proved to be something of a watershed for Oxford's traditional arts disciplines. There was nothing in it that could

[36] Franks Commission, written evidence xi, A. G. Rigg.

[37] Franks Commission, written evidence iv, J. R. Lucas; oral evidence xxxvi (J. R. Lucas), lxxxiv (B. G. Mitchell) and written evidence xi (M. J. Gilbert).

[38] Franks Commission, written evidence xi, written submissions of S. Medcalf, Dr R. O. C. Norman, Professor C. H. Wilson, D. R. Thornber.

[39] *Franks Report* ii. 310–11, 339, 351.

[40] Ibid. i, para. 244; this view had been cogently developed and defended a year earlier by I. M. Crombie, 'In defence of honour schools', *OM* 28 May 1964, 334–5.

be construed as specifically hostile to the arts (though there was some questioning of the academic value of much of the arts research currently being carried out by postgraduate students).[41] But there was much comment in the report that was an implied condemnation of existing practice in the various arts subjects. And, more fundamentally, the whole thrust and tenor of Franks's proposals implicitly questioned the centuries-old hegemony of the humanities in Oxford life—and, indirectly, in the public life of the nation. Franks argued strongly that the overall numbers at Oxford should be limited, in order to maintain an intimate academic community; but at the same time the proportions of postgraduate students, scientists, social scientists and women in the University should be greatly increased. This meant inevitably that 'the number of men reading arts must be held stable or reduced', to something like one-third of the total undergraduate body.[42]

The Commission was also highly critical of the casual and spasmodic character of lectures, classes and the supervision of postgraduate students in arts faculties, and it found the college tutorial system to be 'in process of debasement'.[43] Tutorials had ceased to be informal meetings of scholarly minds in which tutor and student discussed problems of logic and method; instead they had become surrogates for formal lectures, in which tutors frantically tried to cover the bloated factual content of entire subjects. Franks proposed not that tutorials should be done away with but that they should be restored to their proper role of training in craftsmanship: the ideal was that 'if a few bore-holes are sunk in different types of territory and the apprentice learns how to manage in the area, he may be left to carry out further exploration on these lines by himself'.[44] More factual instruction should be conveyed by greater use of lectures, seminars and classes, which should be organized not by colleges but by departments and faculties; and the increased teaching role of the university in arts disciplines should be physically embodied (as had always been the case in the natural sciences) in departmental centres, which would house libraries, seminar rooms, and studies for faculty staff. The process of reform was to be rounded off by giving a much more substantial and systematic role to research by arts dons and to the supervision of postgraduate students. Postgraduate supervision was henceforth to have parity of esteem with undergraduate teaching. Tutors in the arts and social sciences were to be encouraged to take sabbatical leave and to apply for research funding like their colleagues in science departments, and senior research posts should be created in colleges with financial support from the faculties. Research in the arts, no less than in

---

[41] *Franks Report* i, para. 108.
[42] Ibid. i, ch. 3.
[43] Ibid. i, para. 65.
[44] Ibid. para. 233.

the natural sciences, was to be seen henceforth by Oxford tutors not as a 'spare-time' occupation, but as 'the first priority in their lives, giving meaning to the rest of their activities'.[45]

The publication of the Franks report in March 1966 marked a major turning point in Oxford's long-drawn-out shift of emphasis from the arts to the natural sciences and from undergraduate teaching to postgraduate research. As already indicated, however, the transition was a slow and piecemeal one, and the Franks Commission itself contained and channelled rather than unleashed the forces of change. The practical impact of Franks was perhaps less immediately noticeable in the purely academic sphere than in university and college finance and administration; and many of Franks's proposals about the organization of teaching and research were still contentious issues within the different arts faculties a quarter of a century later. The response to Franks among Oxford academics was generally favourable (there was much more hostility to the Kneale report, which proposed to replace the final honours schools with something like the annually examined Cambridge tripos system).[46] But the very fact that the Franks Commission had combined its criticisms with much favourable comment on Oxford life was in itself a brake upon rapid change. The recommendation that arts dons should engage in much more extensive supervision of postgraduate students was accompanied by almost no discussion of what such supervision should or should not consist of—apart from the strongly expressed view of two senior professors that arts postgraduate students, unlike their counterparts in the natural sciences, should not be expected to participate in their supervisors' projects.[47] The historian may perhaps detect in the Franks report an underlying reluctance to face the possibility that certain desirable academic goals were ultimately incompatible: a reluctance which mirrored a similar sentiment that was endemic throughout Oxford life and that was particularly strong among professors, tutors and students in arts subjects. Franks put forward a composite ideal of university life which would combine the 'cosmopolitan' with the 'parochial': the don who was at the forefront of international scholarship was still to be based in a college 'small enough to have something of the atmosphere of a family'; and he was to continue to teach 'his own pupils . . . not as the blurred outlines of an audience but as sharply defined characters sitting by his fireplace'.[48] Such a vision exactly pinpointed the polarities of Oxford's academic life, but it heightened rather than resolved

[45] Ibid. para. 281.

[46] Worcester College tutors, 'The Kneale report', *OM* 5 Nov. 1965, 91–6; R. Buxton, 'The Kneale report: further doubts', *OM* 12 Nov. 1965, 112–14.

[47] Franks Commission, written evidence xi, Professor Sir Isaiah Berlin and Professor H. L. A. Hart, 'Postgraduate studies in Oxford'.

[48] *Franks Report* i, paras 208–9.

the tensions between them. The resolution of such tensions varied widely between individual academics and between different colleges and faculties; and, as in earlier periods, different subject areas responded in rather different ways to the pressures of social, scholarly and intellectual change. At this point therefore we must turn from a general overview of the arts and social sciences in Oxford to a more detailed analysis of tradition and change in the different humane disciplines.

As emphasized above, Oxford at the start of the period—and still to some extent at the end—was dominated both numerically and intellectually by the traditional humanities disciplines, supplemented since the 1920s by the school of PPE. Between the different arts faculties, however, there was a distinct hierarchy of academic esteem, and a number of very different and sometimes mutually competing intellectual traditions. At the apex of the hierarchy was the faculty of literae humaniores, devoted to teaching and research in the history, philosophy and languages of ancient Greece and Rome, and commanding proportionately far more professorships, fellowships, endowed scholarships and college and university prizes than any of Oxford's other faculties. Throughout the period a far higher proportion of students who read for classical mods and Greats obtained first-class honours than in any other humanities faculty: a fact which some ascribed to the ample supply of classics scholarships, others to the intellectual rigour and personal commitment required by Latin and Greek.[49] Whichever was the case, however, there can be no doubt that post-war Oxford attracted a particularly vigorous generation of classical scholars and students, many of whom were not mere antiquarians but were convinced of the direct relevance of classics to the understanding of the modern world. Plato in *The Laws* seemed to one Oxford classicist like 'the very model of a modern Colonial Secretary', while another ascribed Nazism to 'the Germans' neglect of Virgil'. And to one distinguished continental scholar it appeared that the current British style of interpreting ancient history 'cannot be explained without the English tradition of Royal Commissions, social surveys, Fabian Society pamphlets'.[50]

Moreover, the influence of Greats extended far beyond the immediate confines of the faculty of literae humaniores. In 1937 more than two-thirds of all Oxford fellows and more than a third of tutors in other arts faculties had originally graduated in Greats, and although these proportions declined in the post-war years the skills and interests acquired in Greats continued to

[49] Alan Ryan, 'Spartacus redivivus', *Isis* 31 May 1961, 15; R. W. B. Burton's letter to Brian Harrison, 9 Feb. 1988.

[50] Obituary of Edward David Mortier Fraenkel, *OM* 13 Mar. 1970, 209–10; A. Momigliano, review of A. H. M. Jones, *The Later Roman Empire* in *OM* 4 Mar. 1965, 264. See also 'Premature specialisation', *OM* 9 June 1960, 319 on 'the strictly utilitarian aspect' of a classical education.

permeate the study of other disciplines.[51] Oxford philosophy in particular continued to be deeply engaged with definitional and linguistic problems initially propounded by the philosophers of fourth-century Athens: J. L. Austin for example tended to write and speak of Aristotle as though he were an interesting but slightly exasperating colleague living on the next staircase. And, at a more diffuse level, a widespread popular latinity played an important role in Oxford's day-to-day culture, a role that was manifest not just in high scholarship but in public ceremonies, donnish wit, literary style and a widespread lingua franca of classical references and themes. 'Nil habet infelix paupertas durius in se / quam quod ridiculos homines facit', declared the University's public orator on the occasion when an honorary degree was conferred on Charlie Chaplin in 1956.[52]

The power and prestige of the classics survived with remarkable tenacity into the post-war world. Indeed, the collapse of humane studies in central Europe under Hitler's regime, and the flight of many mid-European classical scholars to Oxford, meant that in the 1940s and 1950s Oxford was more than ever before the acknowledged international capital of Greek and Latin learning. More finalists took Greats in 1960 than in any previous year of the University's history; and in the following year the new Professor of Greek, Hugh Lloyd-Jones, vigorously defended the cosmopolitan framework of the classics against the carping Cassandras of the two cultures.[53] From the mid-1950s onward, however, there were signs of unease with both the traditional structure of classical studies at Oxford, and with the role of classical learning in the wider life of the University. The growing inability of many schools to cope with the task of preparing pupils for the Oxford Latin entrance requirement has already been discussed. This external popular revolt against Latin coincided with growing internal criticism of the character of mods and Greats and of the detailed and minuscule character of much current classical scholarship. Spasmodic discussion in *Isis* and the *Oxford Magazine* focused upon the increasing incompatibility between a historical approach to ancient thought and the technical requirements of modern analytical philosophy. There was recurrent discontent among the University's archaeologists, who felt that they were denied their fair share of classical posts and at the same time prohibited by the jealousy of the classicists from developing an independent degree.[54] And in 1961 a Lincoln

---

[51] M. C. Curthoys and M. Heimann, 'The Oxford academic community 1937–8', copy in HUA, p. 7 (table 5).

[52] Obituary of A. N. Bryan-Brown (1900–68) in *OM* 16 May 1969, 296–7. The quotation from Juvenal, Satire III. 152–3 may be loosely translated as 'the worst thing about poverty and misfortune is that they turn you into a figure of fun'.

[53] P. H. J. Lloyd-Jones, *Greek Studies in Modern Oxford* (inaugural lecture: Oxford 1961).

[54] Franks Commission, oral evidence xxxiii (Dr E. T. Hall, Professor C. F. C. Hawkes and Professor L. R. Palmer).

classics don, J. P. Sullivan, published a sustained attack upon current approaches to the study of classical literature—condemning in particular the obsession with philological minutiae and the total indifference of classical scholars to modern canons of literary criticism.[55]

These attacks from both without and within began for the first time to challenge the predominant status of classics in Oxford. After 1960 numbers applying from schools began to fall as sixth-form classics dwindled. This trend may be explained partly by changing fashion and declining pupil-demand, but partly also by the self-reinforcing impact of abandoning entrance Latin and—from the mid–1960s onward—by the shift from grammar to comprehensive education. There was also an increasing movement out of classics and into other disciplines among Oxford students who had initially taken classical mods; and many colleges began to divert classical entrance scholarships to less well endowed subjects. Evidence to the Franks Commission gave vent to increasing irritation among philosophers and ancient historians about their compulsory union within a single faculty: irritation which came to a head over the question of whether a new professor of ancient philosophy should be chosen primarily for his skill as a philosopher or for his knowledge of Latin and Greek.[56] Throughout the 1960s the number of students taking Greats continually fell—a decline that was not arrested by a major reform of the Greats syllabus in 1968 and the inclusion for the first time of classical literature and drama. By 1970 classical studies in Oxford still attracted students of the highest quality, and the University remained one of the world's leading centres of classical research. But in terms both of numbers and of influence within the wider academic community, the position of classics was now a mere shadow of what it had been only a short generation before.

Modern history had never enjoyed quite the prestige of Greats, but like the Greats course it had a long tradition both of training a minority of students for academic scholarship and of preparing the majority for a role in public life. It was by far the largest of the long-established arts schools, with over a thousand undergraduates throughout the 1950s; and for that reason if for no other may perhaps be seen as the most representative of Oxford humanities opinion, both old and new. The traditional core of the Oxford history syllabus consisted of continuous English history from the Roman withdrawal down to 1914, together with compulsory papers in constitutional history and 'political science' (the latter, comprising the thought of the great political philosophers, was re-labelled 'political thought' in 1959). In addition students could choose one select period of foreign history, and candidates for first- or second-class honours were required to take one of a

[55] J. P. Sullivan, 'The classics and their critics', *Essays in Criticism* xi (1961).

[56] R. M. Hare, 'Philosophy and its ancient umbrella', *OM* 19 Nov. 1965, 137–9; letter from Professor Hugh Lloyd-Jones, *OM* 26 Nov. 1965, 166.

number of 'special subjects', which introduced them to the study of archival sources. The faculty's research reputation, though not necessarily its teaching strength, was most marked in medieval history, headed by Maurice Powicke, who was Regius Professor from 1928 to 1947; and the archival and bibliographic resources of the Bodleian Library meant that both in 1939 and in 1970 Oxford was perhaps the world's leading centre for historical research in the medieval sphere.

The shape and purpose of the Oxford history school were deeply rooted in its origins in the late nineteenth century, when modern history had been widely viewed, if not exactly as an explicitly vocational subject, at least as a practical and relevant subject peculiarly adapted for training students to cope with public affairs. This meant that history was perhaps more vulnerable than other arts disciplines, not merely to shifts in intellectual fashion, but to changes in domestic social structure and in Britain's role and status within the wider world. However, just as changes in the social and political spheres were not fully visible in the 1940s and 1950s, so for a long time the changing role of history as an academic discipline was not fully perceived or understood. After the interruptions of war, the history school in 1945 resumed its portmanteau role as a training ground for a small handful of outstanding scholars, a nursery for the nation's statesmen, and—in the words of one returning undergraduate veteran—a repository for the 'dead-weight of people for whom history is just the easiest subject to read'.[57] In spite of the recent war and the presence in Oxford of major young European specialists like A. J. P. Taylor and Alan Bullock, foreign history—and particularly twentieth-century foreign history—remained a minority inter-est: the foreign history option in schools being described as a 'dim oil lamp in an even darker street'.[58] The review section of the *Oxford Magazine* in 1954 welcomed a monograph on the late Lancastrian receipt of the Exchequer as a 'major event', but dismissed current interest in American history as a 'fashionable craze' (even though the Rhodes trustees had recently acknowledged the growing importance of American history by recommending the endowment research in this sphere).[59]

Most Oxford historians at the start of the period laid great emphasis on impartiality and precise archival accuracy: an emphasis which many of them managed to combine with an almost Actonian belief in the function of history as a mirror of right opinion. Thus history examination papers were full of questions that invited students to pass judgement on the actions of statesmen; set texts for a special subject on imperial history were chosen at least in part to demonstrate 'the impact on colonial policy of humanitarian principles'; and A. J. P. Taylor's works on European history received a

[57] 'The schools: modern history', *Isis* 8 May 1946, 16.
[58] Ibid. 16.
[59] *OM* 4 Nov. 1954, 73–5.

guarded reception in Oxford because of their 'deep silence' on 'moral implications'.[60] The work of Namier was admired for its documentary thoroughness and dexterity, but not for its attempt to purge English history of liberal triumphalism (the advance of liberty being, for some at least of the Oxford history school, what the academic study of history was all about). Moreover, in spite of the emphasis on archives there was much suspicion of 'research', and some history dons believed (not perhaps without reason) that a second undergraduate degree in subjects such as law or economics was a better preparation for professional scholarship than working for a doctorate.[61] These attitudes co-existed in many cases with high standards of scholarship. But they were not infrequently the complement of parochialism and philistinism—of lack of interest in philosophic, intellectual and aesthetic history, and of indifference or resistance to the relationship of history to archaeology, anthropology, psychology and the new social sciences.

Such attitudes survived in many forms down to 1970; but throughout the period the traditional assumptions and practices of the modern history school were continually being questioned and subverted from many quarters, both by the inner dynamics of intellectual change and by changes in the wider national culture. Even in the 1940s and early 1950s there were recurrent complaints against both the narrowness of the syllabus and the absence of sustained reflection about the underlying purposes of history.[62] A new graduate college, St Antony's, was founded in 1954 specifically to promote a more international approach to research in the humanities; and the College soon began to attract foreign visitors like Fernand Braudel and Charles Morazé—who brought with them new French fashions in historical demography and in the symbiotic relationship of history with the social sciences.[63] In the late 1950s there was widespread discussion in the faculty about the need for reform of the syllabus: discussion that led to the introduction of economic history as an optional alternative to constitutional history in the final honour school, and to the introduction of a historiography paper (based on the works of Gibbon and Macaulay) in the history preliminary examination.[64] The work of Oxford historians like Christopher Hill, Lawrence Stone and (slightly later) Keith Thomas stimulated discussion of Marxian, sociological and anthropological history; and, though such discussion was often critical, it was increasingly difficult for serious historians to ignore these new intellectual currents. The succession of Hugh Trevor-Roper as Regius Professor in 1957 was viewed by some as a personal

[60] OM 3 Dec. 1953, 139; 20 Jan. 1955, 156.
[61] Franks Commission, written evidence iv, R. Lennard.
[62] 'The schools: modern history', Isis 8 May 1946, 16; C. Curley, 'Hidebound history', Isis 11 Mar. 1953, 12; 'Views on four schools: history', Isis 20 Feb. 1957, 19.
[63] OM 5 May 1955, 302; 19 May 1955, 337.
[64] J. Hart, 'Changes in the modern history syllabus', OM 4 June 1959, 438–40.

rebuff to A. J. P. Taylor and his style of history, by others as a hopeful sign of Oxford's awakening interest in the history of culture and European thought.

Concurrently with these changes in intellectual fashion came a more subterranean change in the relationship of history to wider social and political life. As the role of Britain shrank in the world, and as social structure became more complex, more fluid and more porous, it became increasingly difficult to view Oxford history either as an adjunct of British national identity or as a preparatory training course for public administration. The 'idea of history (even English history) as the story of liberty has become suspect', wrote J. P. Cooper of Trinity in 1960; instead, history was increasingly concerned with the study of different cultures for their own sakes, as 'unique' and 'non-comparable' manifestations of human experience.[65] And in the following year Richard Southern's inaugural lecture as Chichele Professor caused a stir by suggesting that the use of history as a 'system of education for practical men' had outlived its purpose: there was a need to reconstitute the subject on a quite different basis, as a broad humane discipline incorporating art, anthropology, science and the history of ideas as well as more conventional historical studies.[66]

This broader and more relativist vision of history soon found an echo in further and more fundamental demands for syllabus reform put forward by both dons and students (the latter including some who were themselves later to become distinguished academic historians). Peter Burke on behalf of postgraduate students attacked the failure of the faculty to offer any conceptual, methodological and linguistic training to those setting out on doctoral research; and at the end of 1961 a petition from undergraduates was presented to the history faculty, demanding a syllabus that was less Anglocentric, more conceptual and less weighted down with chronology and narrative.[67] A joint meeting of the Oxford University History Society and the Stubbs Society at the end of the Michaelmas term was addressed by Asa Briggs, who told them that 'history in English universities was becoming cut off from contemporary interests and living on the capital of its past'.[68] A further more detailed petition was presented in the following year, asking for a reduction of compulsory English history and its extension in time to 1939, the option of presenting a thesis in finals, and the introduction of more courses in social, cultural and intellectual history (including 'sociology', 'the slave trade' and special subjects with texts in foreign

---

[65] J. P. Cooper, review of G. R. Elton's *The Tudor Constitution* in *OM* 8 June 1961, 405–6.

[66] R. W. Southern, *The Shape and Substance of Academic History* (inaugural lecture: Oxford 1961); see also K. V. Thomas, 'Should historians be anthropologists?', *OM* 1 June 1961, 387.

[67] P. Burke, 'Graduate studies in Oxford', *OM* 9 Nov. 1961, 60 and 'The reform of the history syllabus', *OM* 23 Nov. 1961, 90–1; T. Mason, 'The teaching and study of history', *Isis* 31 May 1961, 20–1.

[68] *OM* 23 Nov. 1961, 90.

languages).[69] Controversy over the nature and scope of the history syllabus raged in the donnish and undergraduate press for some years thereafter, and there were many further demands for a contraction in the role of tutorials, for less Anglocentric history, for more specialist university teaching and for greater emphasis on interdisciplinary methods and themes.[70] The degree of discontent is difficult to weigh precisely; but it seems clear that a majority of undergraduates and many individual history tutors favoured some measure of far-reaching change.

Change when it came, however, was more limited than might have been expected, and consisted largely of adding further options to an already overloaded syllabus rather than of change in the underlying structure and philosophy of the history degree. The admission of a wider range of special and further subjects brought more non-British and non-political history into the course, and from 1968 onward candidates for the final honour school were allowed to submit an optional thesis. The introduction from 1969 of joint honours schools (the alternative preferred to the Kneale Committee's recommendation of a tripos system) enabled historians for the first time to study their subject concurrently with modern languages, ancient history or economics. But in the main modern history school there was no reduction in the English history requirement, and little shift in the core papers away from mainstream political history. And though more special and further subject teaching began to take place in faculty classes, there was no reduction in tutorial teaching: if anything, the reverse was the case, as the volume of writing on history continued to burst all bounds and as college tutors desperately tried to keep themselves and their pupils abreast of the tidal wave of new scholarly publications. Moreover, structural change was inhibited by the fact that those who were pressing for reform were very divided among themselves about the kind of changes they desired. Thus dons who favoured change in the syllabus varied from those who wanted to promote a wholly new conception of history, through to those whose main concern was to release more time for research. And, similarly, student reformers ranged from those who simply wanted to write fewer tutorial essays through to those who were systematically opposed to 'the atomization of social phenomena' or who saw debates about the nature of history as part of the 'coming struggle' for social and political power.[71] Against these impassioned but divided groups were ranged those who saw little need for change other than of a gradual and piecemeal kind. The latter were often

[69] T. Mason, 'Reform of the history syllabus', *Isis* 5 Dec. 1962, 15.

[70] T. Mason, 'The history syllabus: the end of the road?', *Isis* 13 Mar. 1963, 11; C. S. L. Davies, 'Reform of the history school', *OM* 30 Apr. 1964, 267; A. F. Thompson, 'The history syllabus', *OM* 11 Mar. 1965, 274–5.

[71] Michael Beloff, 'Looking-glass logic: the history syllabus re-examined', *Isis* 30 Oct. 1963, 22–3; T. Mason, 'Reform of the history syllabus', *Isis* 5 Dec. 1962, 15.

dedicated and highly successful tutors (some of them deeply wounded by the apparent breakdown in pastoral relationships signified by demands for 'student representation') who looked with suspicion upon the vagaries of intellectual fashion. They defended the history school as already embodying a delicate balance between study in depth and study in breadth, between the demands of fine scholarship and the demands of a broad and open-ended liberal education.[72]

Similar pressures and conflicts occurred in other arts disciplines, though with many local variations. The faculty of English throughout the period was dominated by the principle that the evolution of English as both a living and a literary language should be studied from its earliest roots in the Anglo-Saxon period. This principle generated a powerful and fertile school of Old and Middle English scholarship; but it led also to an undergraduate degree course dominated by philology and language studies, within which even the most 'literary' options included no writing after 1830. Moreover, the rise of the powerful new genre of twentieth-century literary criticism was virtually ignored, and examiners in the English school were famous for their jejune and ingenuous questions, like 'what seems to you lastingly delightful in *Paradise Lost?*' or 'give a careful account of what happens to the four lovers in the wood until they are awakened by Theseus'.[73]

As in the modern history school, the belief that the English faculty was archaic and out of touch with vital social forces was constantly at odds with the view that the function of English was to transmit the deepest tap-roots of culture and not the ephemera of fashion. For a long time the traditional view was exemplified and protected by the presence of C. S. Lewis, who combined defence of Old and Middle English with an immense output of literary studies that roamed across many centuries—and who at the same time conducted a fierce and unrelenting polemic against modernity and social change. Lewis's influence was evident in much wartime and post-war Oxford poetry, which frequently linked the blitz, Communism and Fascism to such themes as Arthur, Beowulf and the tramp of the troll kings.[74] Lewis firmly set himself against the view which was becoming fashionable in Cambridge, that the core of an English school was 'criticism', and that the function of criticism was to maintain moral and intellectual standards in an encircling mass society—an élite dominion that Lewis scathingly dismissed as 'Charientocracy . . . the rule of the χαριεντεσ, the *venustiores*, the Hotel de Rambouillet, the Wits, the Polite, the "Souls", the "Apostles", the

---

[72] R. Lennard, 'The modern history school', *OM* 25 Jan. 1962, 142–3; letters from Lennard, *OM* 15 Feb. 1962, 194 and 7 May 1964, 283; letter from J. Prestwich, *OM* 7 May 1964, 283.

[73] 'The English school: John Gross has an *agenbite of inwit*', *Isis* 3 Mar. 1954, 22; A. Pattison, 'Teen-age Beowulf: Oxford English school', *Isis* 6 May 1959, 15.

[74] W. Bell (ed.), *Poetry from Oxford in Wartime* (London 1945).

Sensitive, the *Cultured*, the Integrated, or whatever the latest password may be'.[75]

Lewis's towering personality exerted great influence over colleagues and students alike, but from the start of the post-war period there were murmurings of dissent, partly against the monopoly of philology, partly against the exclusion from the syllabus of any echo of the new criticism, partly against the permeation of the faculty's intellectual life by values that were deemed not literary but religious and moral.[76] Formal criticism flourished not in lectures and tutorials but in dissident undergraduate societies and in the solitary voice of F. W. Bateson of Corpus (himself a religious man, but in a very different mould from Lewis). Bateson, who had spent the war as an eminently practical agricultural civil servant, returned to his Oxford tutorship determined to purge English literary studies of their penchant for 'pastoral pipings' in 'La Belle Sauvage'.[77] The message of *Essays in Criticism*, an annual series edited by Bateson which was first published in 1951, was that literary study should be not archaic or arcadian, but critical, practical and realistic; its aim should be not mere private pleasure but 'the conscious stimulation of a poetry-reading *élite*, who can be the missionaries of poetry in a world of prose'.[78] Bateson gradually gathered around himself a small group of disciples, who over the next twenty years acted as a vocal fifth column for the insemination of critical and 'Leavisite' ideas into the Oxford faculty of English. But the long-term impact of Bateson's mission was not apparent until after the end of the period. Complaints against the dominance of Old and Middle English and the absence of modern criticism continued throughout the 1950s and 1960s, and towards the end of the period English like other arts faculties suffered from stationary and even declining student numbers. The evidence of English dons to the Franks Commission appeared somewhat dispirited—deploring the current lack of confidence in Oxford's teaching methods, the growing obsession with exam results at the expense of wide and adventurous reading, and the lack of facilities in Oxford for advanced literary research.[79]

Similar discontents and tensions may be detected in many other quarters. Modern languages, like English, was under fire throughout the period for excessive concentration on philology and phonology and for a literary syllabus that ended in 1914 (thus enabling specialists in French to study only the first two volumes of what many regarded as the twentieth century's greatest literary work, Proust's *A la recherche du temps perdu*).[80] Moreover,

[75] Lewis, 'Lilies that fester', 336.
[76] Pattison, 'Teen-age Beowulf', 15.
[77] F. W. Bateson, 'The Anti-Romantics', poem printed at the head of Bateson's *English Poetry: A Critical Introduction* (London 1950, 2nd edn London 1966).
[78] Ibid. 201.
[79] Franks Commission, oral evidence xxxviii (Lord David Cecil).
[80] P. Wiles, 'Tayloriana', *Isis* 11 Feb. 1953, 20.

even in the study of language Oxford was dismissed by some as a backwater: an American specialist on linguistics who came to Oxford in the mid-1960s expecting to work with computers found instead 'philosophy, philology and clerks—a complete triumph of the nineteenth century over the twentieth'.[81] Oxford's school of jurisprudence housed an internationally renowned coterie of legal theorists, headed by Arthur Goodhart, A. M. Honoré and H. L. A. Hart, who cross-fertilized English legal thought with insights from linguistic philosophy and from Roman and civil law. The advanced degree of bachelor of civil law was acknowledged worldwide as imposing the most exacting standards of rigorous legal scholarship. But in nearly all Oxford colleges law had the worst student–teacher ratio of any large subject; and at the mundane level of tutors and undergraduates there was increasing concern about rote-learning, syllabus-overloading, and the latent incompatibility between law as a form of liberal education and law as a system of professional skills.[82] The school of geography (which like modern history had close traditional links with empire and public administration) was under recurrent attack from critics who claimed it had no intellectual core that was not reducible to some other subject. Geography was defended, however, by those who argued that it was simultaneously both a 'humane' discipline in its own right and an excellent ancillary to the study of the social sciences.[83] Such a defence highlighted a theme that was of growing importance in postwar Oxford and whose centrality in the Franks report has already been noted: namely, the evolution and increasing prominence of a range of newer disciplines that were broadly classed under the older humanities umbrella. The most important of these new disciplines were psychology, social anthropology, social administration and the cluster of subjects grouped together under the school of PPE.

Oxford had had no undergraduate degree in social-science subjects until the early 1920s, and even in 1939 the status of the social sciences was still a blurred and ambiguous one. It might perhaps have been expected that the increasingly positivist tone of new Oxford philosophical writing in the 1930s would have given rise to a school of positivist social science, but this was not in fact the case (if anything, the underlying tone of the undergraduate school was still one of lingering Edwardian idealism). By 1939 philosophy in the school of PPE was still very secondary to its teaching in Greats; the study of politics had hardly emancipated itself from the study of political history; and the dominant style of Oxford economics was historical, descriptive and institutional. The formal study of sociology was unknown in inter-war

---

[81] Franks Commission, written evidence iv, G. A. Miller, 'Reflections on leaving Oxford'.

[82] 'The schools: law', *Isis* 13 Mar. 1946, 18; J. M. Kaye, 'Legal education in Oxford', *OM* 2 Nov. 1961, 47–8; J. Eekelaar, 'Proposals', *Isis* 2 June 1966, 6.

[83] EWG, 'Geography at Oxford and Cambridge', *OM* 14 Feb. 1957, 274–8; G. Hawthorn, 'Geography', *OM* 4 Mar. 1965, 256–7; letter from Colin Clark, *OM* 29 Apr. 1965, 294.

Oxford, except among the small handful of trainee social workers at Barnett House. Moreover, nearly all social-science tutors were graduates of the older arts disciplines; and the ease with which many of them moved around from one subject to another was indicative of the fact that 'social studies' in Oxford were viewed not as a cluster of discrete exact sciences, but as a sphere of broad humanistic learning. The career of G. D. H. Cole, who for many years was the most prominent figure in the faculty of social studies, was a case in point. Cole had graduated in Greats, wrote books on political thought and social history, tutored in political institutions, was promoted to a readership in economics, and in 1944 became the first Chichele Professor of Social and Political Theory: a personal odyssey that exactly mirrored the underlying academic philosophy of the early days of PPE.

This wide-ranging, humanistic approach to the social sciences persisted well into the post-war era. The contraction of empire coincided with a great flowering of Oxford anthropological studies, headed by Professor E. E. Evans-Pritchard who strongly defended the character of social anthropology as a humane cultural and philosophical discipline. Much original field-work was carried out by a group of ex-colonial administrators who used their practical experience to give the subject a unique historical perspective.[84] Wartime and post-war social change brought a great expansion of interest in the more applied social-science disciplines and in their capacity to solve practical social problems; and many new social-science posts were created in the brief era of post-war academic expansion (including the permanent establishment of the Oxford Institute of Economics and Statistics).[85] In 1947 the new degree in psychology, philosophy and physiology was deliberately designed as an experiment in linking traditional humane concerns to scientific methods. A decade later the humane and philosophical character of Oxford psychology was judged to be one of the outstanding hallmarks of the school (by contrast with more quantitative and behaviourist studies elsewhere);[86] and the same might well have been said of the very much larger school of PPE.

By the 1950s most PPE tutors had ceased to teach more than one of the three constituent disciplines of philosophy, politics and economics. But within those disciplines they still expected to teach all aspects of their subject, both institutional and theoretical, and there was still much doubling up between the teaching of politics and of modern history. At a time of very rapid growth in all areas of the social sciences, such teaching demands soon began to impose a major constraint not merely upon research but upon the capacity of tutors to keep abreast of new knowledge: a conflict that was only

[84] E. E. Evans-Pritchard, 'The Institute of Anthropology', *OM* 26 Apr. 1951, 354–60.

[85] D. N. Chester, *Economics, Politics and Social Studies in Oxford, 1900–85* (Basingstoke and London 1986), 161–84.

[86] O. L. Zangwill, 'Psychology at Oxford and Cambridge', *OM* 10 May 1956, 396–8.

partly relieved by the growth of Nuffield College as a centre for advanced social-science research. The problem was to some extent resolved by the development of the degree of BPhil, which was initially designed as an advanced teaching and research programme for those wishing to specialize in a particular area of PPE, and which rapidly became recognized as an excellent apprenticeship for future university teachers. But throughout the period the problems experienced in the older arts faculties—of overcrowded syllabuses, explosion of knowledge, and chronic tension between specialist excellence and all-round education—were experienced in PPE to an acute degree. Such problems were made worse by the fact that, particularly in economics, technical and theoretical change and the accumulation of new data were much more rapid and far-reaching than in more traditional spheres.

The result, as in other faculties, was recurrent demand from many quarters for change: a demand that often went hand in hand with a desire to preserve the original broad, interdisciplinary philosophy of PPE as a modern counterpart to Greats. From the early 1950s there was pressure to reduce the number of disciplines studied by undergraduates from three to two, in order to allow space for more advanced work; and there was growing criticism of the fact that the three parts of the PPE syllabus no longer interlocked or nourished each other in the way originally envisaged by the school's founding fathers.[87] This latter criticism was particularly levelled at new styles of philosophy in Oxford. Neither the linguistic positivism of the 1930s and 1940s nor the 'ordinary language' philosophy that came to the fore after the war—which together dominated Oxford philosophy from the 1940s down to the 1970s—had much to say about theoretical and moral issues in the social sciences. And where linguistic positivism did have something to say (as in Ian Little's brilliant *A Critique of Welfare Economics* or in T. D. Weldon's much less brilliant *The Vocabulary of Politics*) the effect was negative and largely hostile to further theoretical work (exemplifying Ayer's famous comment on Austin, 'you are like a greyhound that refuses to race but bites the other greyhounds to prevent their racing either').[88] The result for much of the 1950s was a certain disenchantment with moral and political philosophy, and a reinforcement of Oxford's characteristically descriptive and inductive approach to social and political issues (discussion of political ideas being kept alive in the University not by their inherent relevance but by the personal magnetism and rhetorical brilliance of their chief exponent in Oxford, Isaiah Berlin).

The stagnation of the 1950s, however, was of fairly short duration. After some decline in the early 1950s, applications to the faculty of social studies

---

[87] A. Sutherland, 'A practical P.P.E.', *Isis* 9 May 1951, 13–14.

[88] A. Quinton, S. Hampshire, I. Murdoch and I. Berlin, 'Philosophy and beliefs', *Twentieth Century* June 1955; A. J. Ayer, *Part of My Life* (London 1977), 160.

began to rise rapidly in the late 1950s, less in response to changes within Oxford than to changes in wider society; and it seems clear that by the early 1960s some of those who would previously have read Greats or history were now migrating to PPE. Appointments within the faculty of social studies greatly increased between 1955 and 1965, and many of the new posts were either research posts, university lecturerships or fellowships of Nuffield College, all of which allowed more time for advanced teaching and research than college-based tutorships. Moreover, the early 1960s brought a great increase in public demand for the services of social scientists—particularly economists—in government, industry, finance and the new universities. The setting up of national economic planning councils in 1963 and the onset of Harold Wilson's 'hundred days' in 1964 siphoned off large numbers of Oxford economists into Whitehall; and 'expert' knowledge in the social sciences increasingly rivalled 'generalist' education in the humanities as the professional key to the corridors of power. Increasing numbers and public prestige were accompanied by increasing pressure for intellectual and curricular change (though members of the faculty of social studies, which already linked several disciplines, were markedly less enamoured of the rising fashion for interdisciplinary themes than their counterparts in other faculties). In 1961 there were renewed demands for a reduction of PPE subjects from three to two, together with proposals for serious political philosophy and for the liberation of politics from its dependence on 'escaped historians'.[89] Two years later a proposal was put forward for a specialist three-year degree in economics, designed to rival the very concentrated course now available in Cambridge; and although this proposal came to nothing, the introduction in 1965 of a joint degree in engineering science and economics symbolized the gradual separation of technical economics from its traditional chrysalis of all-round political economy.[90]

Much discussion also took place in the early 1960s of the potential role of sociology. Sociology of a speculative kind had attracted some interest in Oxford earlier in the twentieth century, but like other quasi-metaphysical modes of thought it had gone down in the great shipwreck of idealism in the 1920s and 1930s. In the post-war period it was widely derided in Oxford as at best a means of practical training for social workers, at worst a species of authoritarian and linguistically bogus hocus-pocus. By the 1950s, however, there were many sociologists in Oxford working under the guise of other disciplines such as psychology and anthropology, and there was an increasing demand among school-leavers for degrees in sociology. The Herbert Spencer lectures for 1960 were delivered by Noel Annan, who portrayed sociology as the intellectual victim of British positivism and

[89] Ryan, 'Spartacus redivivus', 15–17.
[90] D. L. Munby, 'A new school in economics', OM 14 and 21 Nov. 1963, 79–80 and 94–5.

reinterpreted several major literary figures as nascent 'sociologists'.[91] In the same year a committee was appointed to elect the University's first reader in sociology. This committee reported, however, that no suitable candidate could be found, and recommended deferring the appointment for two years: a recommendation that produced a storm of protest from intellectual radicals, and much heated debate on the nature and role of sociology as an academic discipline.[92] An appointment was eventually made in 1964, and in the same year sociology was examined for the first time as an option for the PPE degree—followed a year later by the introduction of a BPhil in sociology for graduates in other subjects. Such reforms did not satisfy the growing demand for radical reconstruction of Oxford's social sciences; but as one grateful refugee from ordinary language philosophy recalled, the appearance in the PPE syllabus of Marx, Weber and Dahrendorf 'gave me the intellectual means to get outside the society I lived in and see for the first time the stuff of which it was made'.[93]

Oxford no less than other academic institutions was caught in the whirlwind of student revolution that erupted in Britain and elsewhere in the late 1960s. One aspect of that revolution was fierce debate about syllabus and teaching reform among representative student bodies and in the student press: a debate rendered all the more intense by the conviction of many participants that the substance of their academic studies was directly related to revolutionary praxis. Long-standing discontents with the cautious, descriptive character of Oxford politics and history and with linguistic and methodological positivism were catalysed by visits from eminent protagonists of an alternative mode of discourse, most notably Noam Chomsky and Claude Lévi-Strauss. Articles in Isis accused the PPE school of 'systematic devaluation of values'—of triviality, quietism, marginalization of political thought, and exaltation of J. S. Mill at the expense of Karl Marx—while articles on the English school pressed for replacement of philology by structuralist linguistics and for the study of literature not as a mode of cultural escapism but as a living representation of class and ideology.[94] Such attacks coincided with widespread discussion of reform of the syllabus in all faculties, leading in 1969/70 to extensive revision of the scope and character of several of the major honours schools.

Whether these changes came about as a result of student unrest, however, or whether they were the fruit of the previous decade of continuous social, intellectual and administrative debate—of which student revolt was itself a

[91] 'The Herbert Spencer lecture', OM 10 Mar. 1960, 233.

[92] 'Congregation, May 31st, 1960', OM 9 June 1960, 320–1; M. Argyle, L. J. Barnes, P. C. Collison, A. Flanders, G. P. Hirsch and H. Tajfel, 'The position of sociology in Oxford', OM 17 Nov. 1960, 113–14; B. Wilson, 'Sociology', OM 19 Nov. 1964, 105–6.

[93] A. Oakley, Taking It Like a Woman (London 1984), 41.

[94] T. Pateman and J. Birtwhistle, 'The poverty of philosophy, politics and economics', Isis 16 Oct. 1968, 9; M. Rosen, 'MacSweeney versus Beowulf', ibid. 10.

part—remains unclear. Major changes occurred in the structure of the PPE school, where student criticism had been most vociferous. But the changes introduced—which extended the range of optional courses and allowed candidates for the PPE school to take two rather than all three of the main constituent disciplines—reflected the remorseless rise of specialization and decline of the old synoptic vision of the social sciences much more clearly than the voice of student revolution. There were also far-reaching changes in the law degree (involving severe curtailment of Roman law and the introduction of a range of new optional subjects), but these were in train in the faculty long before the onset of student agitation.[95] By contrast, major structural reform of the English and history schools did not come about until much later, long after the eclipse of the era of student unrest. Social anthropology, which was one of the cult disciplines of 1960s radicalism, did not become incorporated in any of the honours schools but remained what it had been over the previous half-century: a highly esteemed but marginal subject available only to students for postgraduate diplomas and research degrees. The same was true of archaeology, which since 1945 had developed as perhaps the most genuinely interdisciplinary of Oxford subjects, yet never managed to acquire the status of an undergraduate degree. It seems reasonable to conclude therefore that student revolution was a symptom rather than a cause of intellectual and curricular change; it highlighted and dramatized a process of debate, self-criticism, conflict, reform and resistance to reform that had been taking place over a much longer period.

What impact, if any, did changes in the structure and content of academic disciplines make to the day-to-day culture of Oxford and to the outlook of dons and students? This is a question with wide implications, for during the period under review the intellectual, scholarly and literary interests of society at large were channelled more and more exclusively into university departments. For better or worse, universities after the Second World War monopolized the life of the mind far more comprehensively than in any earlier period of British history. At the same time, however, universities were much less autonomous than they had been in the past. Their financial dependence on government, reinforced by the encircling moral context of mass democracy, meant that disciplines, departments and individual academics had to respond much more directly than in any previous generation to external pressures for change. The ways in which departments, colleges, dons and students thought and behaved were therefore not merely of local interest but in some sense seminal to the wider life of society.

Throughout the period there was much pouring of new wine into old academic bottles, and it is often difficult to distinguish the semblance from

    [95] F. M. B. Reynolds, 'Changes in the honour school of jurisprudence', *OM* 27 Oct. 1967, 27–30.

the reality of change. The survival of the college tutorial system as the central teaching medium in all arts disciplines (and to a slightly lesser extent in the social sciences as well) gives a sense of underlying continuity to an era of unprecedented change. Even Oxford's severest critics of the 1960s were reluctant to abandon the collegiate system and the peculiar intimacy of the relationship between pupils and their tutors—as one group of students put it, 'the deep sense of sharing with them a certain intellectual style'.[96] But dons, students and tutorials were all in certain important respects different from what they had been in 1939. Many accounts have emphasized the transformation of donnish domestic lifestyles, from genteel bachelordom in college cloisters to washing up and nappy-changing in the outer suburbs; and, although this process had been taking place over a much longer period, examples can still be found in the post-war era of individual tutors who exactly illustrate this change.[97] But for the purposes of this chapter a more important change was the increasing absorption of a younger generation of arts dons in the professional concerns of their disciplines. This was partly expressed in an increasing commitment to research, partly in an attempt to bring undergraduate teaching to the frontiers of knowledge—often to the great scandal of an older generation, who cherished the ideal of 'reading with' their pupils rather than conveying 'the latest news on various bits of the field from a series of experts'.[98] The clash between these two tutorial styles—between what some saw as 'amateur' and 'professional' approaches to the transmission of knowledge[99]—accounted perhaps more directly than any other factor for the departmental and intellectual conflicts outlined above. It was intensified also by the fact that, while public esteem and prospects of promotion increasingly emphasized the need for advanced 'research', the *genius loci* of Oxford continued to reserve its highest palm for the dedicated Socratic tutor who made overall guidance of the young a higher priority than his own or other people's learned publications.[100]

Students also changed, though in diverse and often unpredictable ways. Competition for places in all arts subjects soared after the war; whereas virtually anyone who could afford it could get a commoner's place at Oxford in 1939, by 1970 it was difficult to get accepted by a college without being an examination high-flyer. The standards required of commoners were increasingly assimilated to those required of scholars, and the differences of status between the two groups (once a major feature of Oxford life) rapidly

[96] *Memorandum to the Franks Commission* (Oxford University Student Council 1964).
[97] Cf above, 200–1.
[98] Franks Commission, written evidence iv, R. Lennard.
[99] R. M. Ogilvie, 'When did you last see your tutor?', *OM* 29 Oct. 1965, 74–5.
[100] A priority made abundantly clear in donnish obituaries throughout the period. Compare, for example, the glowing tone of the *Oxford Magazine*'s obituary notices of E. M. Walker (16 Oct. 1941), Neville Ward-Perkins (2 June 1960), A. F. Wells (Oct. 1966) and A. N. Bryan-Brown (16 May 1969) with the somewhat grudging comments on J. H. Jolliffe (12 Mar. 1964).

diminished. Fourth-class degrees ceased after 1967, and the so-called 'pass schools' were in a state of terminal decline.[101] Quite what the dramatic rise in the academic qualifications of students meant in terms of intellectual quality was a matter of continuing discussion. In the 1950s and early 1960s there was much adverse comment among dons in arts disciplines about the deadening treadmill of mass education and A-levels; and students themselves often found the loose structure of the traditional arts degree puzzling and unrewarding. 'An arts student has nothing to do except sit and read or write as he works', complained one young woman, who looked with envy at the more organized and varied programme of students in the natural sciences.[102] In 1964 a disgruntled Balliol economics don complained about the arrival in Oxford of a new breed of students reminiscent of Camus's 'outsider' and Norman Mailer's 'white negroes', whose interest in thought and scholarship appeared to be nil.[103] By contrast a study carried out by the psychology department found a high level of commitment to academic ideals (more than a quarter aspired to become dons). And a sample survey of 1961/2 portrayed Oxford students as 'honest and sincere young men taking their studies very seriously', whose lives were worn down by anxiety about academic work and by a 'complete divorce between learning and pleasure'.[104] But even as this survey was being carried out academic culture was changing; and over the next decade students in the arts and social sciences were actively engaged in debating questions about the content, boundaries, ontological premises and practical application of their disciplines in a way that would have been unthinkable less than a generation before.

For students, no less than for academics, one of the major changes and problems of the period was that the traditional arts subjects were no longer seen as possessing the self-authenticating public utility that they had been believed to possess in earlier generations. Practitioners of those subjects were therefore increasingly forced to define their role and purpose in more intrinsically cultural and intellectual terms. This was brilliantly done by some major Oxford figures such as R. G. Collingwood, E. E. Evans-Pritchard, Richard Southern and Isaiah Berlin, with the result that by the end of the period many arts subjects—though numerically and institutionally weaker than formerly—were conspicuously more rigorous, self-critical

---

[101] See above, 64, 84, 193–5.
[102] Letter from Mary Ruth Fasnacht, OM 5 Nov. 1964, 59.
[103] P. Streeten, 'Teaching the cool', OM 22 Oct. 1964, 33–4.
[104] 'What are you going to do when you grow up?', OM 12 May 1960, 269; F. Zweig, The Student in the Age of Anxiety (London 1963), pp. xiii and 205. I confess to some scepticism about Zweig's survey. Zweig recorded that 40% of his Oxford sample had 'no ambition', the nadir being reached by a Greats finalist who gave as his ultimate aim in life: 'I want to have a comfortable home and mow the lawn on Sundays'. The respondent, who happens to be a personal friend of mine, does indeed have a comfortable home and a lawn. But he is also a senior civil servant commuting between the EC and the Department of Trade and Industry.

and imaginatively fertile than they had been thirty years before. But such re-evaluation was an unsettling and unnerving process, and drove many to migrate to what appeared to be more useful and less problematic spheres. For some, an attractive half-way house was to be found in the social sciences. The social sciences admittedly had their own problems of method and underlying purpose; and throughout the period Oxford's social scientists insisted on the need to retain 'some sense of isolation from contemporary affairs if academic values are to be preserved'.[105] There was much scepticism of purely positivist forms of social analysis: a scepticism that was predictably strongest among anthropologists and social historians, but was also found to a certain extent among practitioners of the newer social disciplines.[106] Such perspectives acted as a partial counterweight to powerful forces that sought to promote the social sciences as a clinical adjunct of management and public administration. Nevertheless the social sciences, particularly economics, were increasingly perceived as providing the kind of semi-vocational link between scholarship and public affairs that had once been offered by history and Greats: a transition symbolized by the numbers graduating in the final honours schools in 1970, when candidates in modern history were for the first time outstripped by those in PPE. Whether this shift in modes of thought was objective and permanent or socially constructed and transient, or a mixture of the two, remains unclear. So too does the question of whether such changes materially affected, for good or ill, the wider life of the British nation.

[105] Anon. review of an essay by Bryan Wilson in M. Reeves (ed.), *Eighteen Plus: Unity and Diversity in Higher Education* (London 1965), *OM* 13 May 1965, 334.

[106] E. E. Evans-Pritchard, *Nuer Religion* (Oxford 1956); B. Wilson, *Religion in Secular Society: A Sociological Comment* (London 1966); A. H. Halsey, *Change in British Society* (Oxford 1978, 3rd edn Oxford 1986).

IO

The Non-Medical Sciences, 1939–1970

JOHN ROCHE

The Second World War brought many changes to the natural sciences in Oxford.* A night patrol of the science area was set up with members drawn from the University Museum's private fire brigade. Air-raid shelters were built between the department of biochemistry and the University Observatory. James Douglas, Professor of Geology, became commander of the Oxford City Home Guard, and most of his department's staff were involved in military or civil defence duties. The more valuable museum exhibits were moved to safer places. Many science professors and senior staff spent much time outside Oxford on war committees or defence projects. Robert Robinson, Professor of Organic Chemistry, served on many bodies concerned with chemical defence, explosives and chemotherapy. The physicist Lord Cherwell, Dr Lee's Professor of Experimental Philosophy, was mostly absent in London as adviser to Churchill. R. V. Southwell, Professor of Engineering Science, was on the Ministry of Supply's advisory council and chaired several committees concerned with wartime engineering research. All the research students of E. B. Moullin, Reader in Electrical Engineering, left with him to work for the Admiralty.[1] In an examiner's note, E. A. Milne, Rouse Ball Professor of Mathematics from 1929 to 1950, wrote of 'war-time conditions . . . necessitating team rather than individual work . . . demanding results rather than principles, and . . . withholding "secret" results'.[2] The effectiveness of team research was among the war's legacies to Oxford.

* I am grateful to Dr T. G. Halsall of Linacre College for many illuminating discussions on the science area and the history of chemistry at Oxford since the war; to Mr A. V. Simcock of the Museum of the History of Science, Oxford, for his most kind assistance in many ways; and to Professor Robert Fox, who jointly ran the Linacre College seminars on the history of the science area in Oxford. Tape-recordings of these are in my possession.

[1] *Gazette* lxxi (1940/1), 246, 248; lxxii (1941/2), 224–7, 231–9; A. R. Todd and J. W. Cornforth, 'Robert Robinson', *BMFRS* xxii (1976); R. Robinson, *Memoirs of a Minor Prophet* (Amsterdam, Oxford and New York 1976); T. I. Williams, *Robert Robinson, Chemist Extraordinary* (Oxford 1990), 117–23; personal communication from Brebis Bleaney, 3 Sept. 1991.

[2] OUA reports of examiners, board of the faculty of physical sciences, vol. ix, 15 Jan. 1942, p. 13.

War lent a new prominence to the natural sciences. Although the number of undergraduates reading for natural science degrees fell sharply early in the war, the number of arts undergraduates fell even more sharply, so that the proportion of science undergraduates at Oxford reached its highest level of modern times [figure 3.3].[3] The war also gave Oxford scientists the prestige that Cherwell had always wanted for them. For security reasons, though, their labours could not be publicized; the wartime *Gazette* ceased to publish details of research being done in the faculty of physical sciences. Cherwell himself, as Churchill's scientific and statistical adviser and subsequently as Privy Counsellor and Paymaster General, was operating at the highest political levels, but lesser known Oxford scientists were undertaking research of the greatest strategic importance in three areas: on the atomic bomb, radar and penicillin.

In 1939 low-temperature research was suspended, and F. E. Simon, a refugee from Nazi Germany who had been shrewdly recruited for Oxford by Cherwell in 1933, began a programme of nuclear weapons research in the new Clarendon Laboratory. This highly secret work, code-named 'tube alloys', was largely concerned with separating the uranium 235 isotope by gaseous diffusion, and was carried out by a team of some thirty scientists and thirty supporting staff.[4] Oxford was soon incorporated into the government's nationally co-ordinated research programme in this area, and it was the Oxford team which demonstrated that it was feasible to separate fissile isotopes. This significantly influenced the American decision to launch the Manhattan project.[5] On radar too, Oxford participated in a large and co-ordinated national war effort involving industrial firms and universities. By summer 1940 a prototype 10 cm radar set had already been built and successfully operated. The famous cavity magnetron generator and transmitter came from Birmingham University, but the first successful prototypes for most of the complex receiving equipment were made at the Clarendon.[6] The success of this research contributed greatly to the victory over the German U-boats.[7]

As for penicillin, its anti-bacterial properties were first discovered by Sir Alexander Fleming,[8] but the first comprehensive investigation of it was

---

[3] See above, 176–7.

[4] 'Physics in Oxford during the war', pt 2, F. E. Simon, 'Atomic energy', *OM* 13 June 1946, 352–4; C. H. Collie, 'Oxford physics and the war', *Oxford* winter 1946–7; N. Kurti, 'F. E. Simon', *BMFRS* iv (1958). See also above, 181–2.

[5] Collie, 57–8.

[6] 'Physics in Oxford during the war', pt 1, T. C. Keeley, 'Radar', *OM* 16 May 1946, 289–91; B. Bleaney, 'Physics at the University of Oxford', *European Jl Physics* ix (1988), 285; Collie, 56; F. W. F. Smith, second Earl of Birkenhead, *The Prof in Two Worlds: The Official Life of Professor F. A. Lindemann, Viscount Cherwell* (London 1961), 239.

[7] A. J. Croft, 'Oxford's Clarendon Laboratory' (typescript, 1986, in Radcliffe Science Library, Oxford); Smith, 233–9.

[8] L. Colebrook, 'Alexander Fleming', *BMFRS* ii (1956), 121–3.

initiated at the Sir William Dunn School of Pathology immediately before the war by its head, H. W. Florey, in collaboration with E. B. Chain, a refugee from Nazi Germany, and others. Because the problem was complex, and because wartime conditions made work in some ways difficult, research proceeded slowly. A chemical trial of very impure penicillin introduced into the bloodstream was carried out at the Radcliffe Infirmary, Oxford, in 1941. This first demonstrated that it was a powerful systemic anti-bacterial agent with potential for use in the war,[9] but it was not until 1943 that Chain and E. P. Abraham finally purified penicillin. Concerned to increase production, Florey in 1941 went to America, where he convinced powerful figures in the academic and research establishment that the drug was important. Forty large organizations—including government, universities and pharmaceutical companies—and perhaps a thousand chemists were eventually involved in classified research on the chemistry and production of penicillin. This led to penicillin being made in the United States on a scale larger than was possible in the United Kingdom, and by 1944 the drug was being used to treat war casualties. In 1945 Fleming, Florey and Chain won the Nobel prize for their work.[10]

These three were only the most outstanding among a host of wartime projects mounted in the science area: on gas-mask charcoal, respirators, signal flares, anti-malarials and aircraft fuels, for example. Oxford physiologists studied British drug plants to replace continental supplies now cut off, and along with his wife, W. O. James of the department of botany set up the 'Oxford medicinal plants scheme'. C. S. Elton's research was diverted to the protection of food supplies through rodent control.[11] A Peripheral Nerve Injuries Centre was set up to study the nerve-surgery required for gunshot wounds, and the geographers produced handbooks for use by the armed services in Africa and the Middle East.[12]

These wartime achievements provided Oxford with a firm base from which to respond to the post-war worldwide expansion in science. The number of Oxford's undergraduates in the natural sciences grew rapidly after the war in every subject. Science undergraduates also rose as a proportion of Oxford's total undergraduate body—from 19 per cent in 1939 to 23 per cent in 1955 to 35 per cent in 1970 [figure 3.3]; their absolute

[9] D. Hodgkin, 'Chemistry at Oxford 1928–60', History of the University seminar, Corpus Christi College, 3 Mar. 1989, Brian Harrison's transcript, HUA, 10; J. Burnet, 'Plant sciences', tape-recorded seminar in Linacre College, 8 May 1990; E. P. Abraham, 'H. W. Florey, Baron Florey of Adelaide and Marston', BMFRS xvii (1971); H. W. Florey, 'Penicillin', OM 29 Nov. 1945, 97–8.

[10] T. I. Williams, Howard Florey (Oxford 1984), 131–42; Abraham, 267.

[11] HCP 174 (1939), 15; Gazette lxxi (1940/1), 257; lxxii (1941/2), 235; Lord Blake and C. S. Nicholls (eds), The Dictionary of National Biography 1971–1980 (Oxford 1986), 450–1 (W. O. James).

[12] Gazette lxxii (1941/2), 235; R. W. Steel, 'The Oxford school of geography since 1930', tape-recorded seminar in Linacre College, 11 May 1989.

TABLE 10.1

OXFORD FINAL HONOURS SCHOOLS SCIENTISTS BY SCHOOL AND (IN BOLD) WOMEN AS PERCENTAGE OF FINALISTS IN THOSE SCHOOLS, 1920–1967

*(In each cell the first figure is the number of scientists; the figure in **bold** is women as a percentage of finalists.)*

	1920–5	1925–30	1930–5	1935–40	1940–5	1945–50	1950–5	1955–60	1960–5	1965–7
chemistry	171 **5**	183 **5**	217 **6**	201 **4**	147 **6**	314 **5**	430 **8**	476 **7**	665 **7**	757 **10**
mathematics	81 **1**	113 **8**	133 **12**	151 **12**	29 **72**	200 **19**	299 **25**	395 **22**	519 **23**	701 **24**
physics	87 **5**	81 **4**	111 **9**	95 **3**	13 **46**	284 **5**	318 **7**	447 **8**	652 **9**	713 **9**
physiology	211 **10**	197 **8**	221 **6**	225 **7**	38 **19**	178 **23**	337 **14**	340 **16**	352 **17**	475 **21**
zoology	26 **23**	24 **38**	58 **6**	46 **41**	20 **75**	51 **52**	90 **38**	115 **43**	143 **38**	183 **42**
geology	28 **0**	11 **0**	12 **0**	11 **0**	4 **25**	45 **4**	41 **3**	64 **6**	73 **7**	45 **7**
botany	26 **27**	23 **61**	40 **43**	30 **50**	10 **50**	27 **37**	45 **36**	53 **32**	54 **30**	64 **22**
engineering	69 **0**	—	46 **0**	40 **3**	60 **0**	114 **1**	111 **2**	176 **1**	242 **1**	294 **2**
geography			27 **37**	140 **35**	43 **75**	113 **37**	256 **19**	347 **13**	351 **15**	355 **16**
agriculture				6 **0**	1 **0**	89 **1**	81 **4**	39 **13**	53 **11**	38 **11**
forestry					7 **0**	65 **0**	42 **0**	56 **0**	42 **0**	21 **0**
psychology, philosophy & physiology						22 **5**	73 **10**	100 **4**	135 **11**	283 **19**
biochemistry							15 **27**	34 **35**	79 **20**	125 **22**
metallurgy									30 **0**	48 **0**
engineering & economics										100 **0**

Source: HUD. Compiled by Dr D. I. Greenstein and Dr M. Postle.

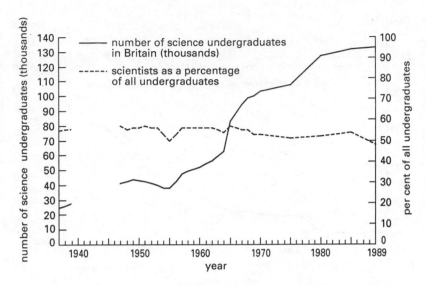

number of science undergraduates (thousands)

per cent of all undergraduates

——— number of science undergraduates in Britain (thousands)

----- scientists as a percentage of all undergraduates

year

FIGURE 10.1   SCIENCE UNDERGRADUATES IN BRITAIN, 1937–1989

number rose much faster than in Britain as a whole [figure 10.1].[13] At Cambridge the proportion of those taking science was 41 per cent in 1938 and 44 per cent in 1955. In both physics and chemistry, Oxford by the 1960s had the largest undergraduate schools in the country.[14] Between 1948 and 1970 the proportion of women undergraduates taking science rose from 10 per cent to 39 per cent [figure 3.3], though women's proportion of all Oxford's science undergraduates remained roughly static at about 15 per cent. In the 1970s this figure rose to about 20 per cent and by 1985 to about 30 per cent.[15] Table 10.1 shows that, with the notable exception of agriculture and forestry, women undergraduates preferred the life sciences to the physical sciences. The reduced percentage of women taking geography after the war reflects, perhaps, women's move into previously 'male' subjects and men's move into 'female' subjects.

The number of postgraduates in science was rising too, but given the even sharper rise in arts in the 1960s the natural sciences' percentage of all postgraduates fell slightly [figure 10.2]. Here the rise in Oxford's numbers roughly followed the national trend [figure 10.3]. Staff numbers rose accordingly [figure 10.4] together with the number of science professors; three new chairs were set up between 1939 and 1955, four from then to 1960,

[13] See above, 59–61.
[14] 'A comparison between Oxford and Cambridge', OM 8 Mar. 1956, 328–30; Bleaney, 'Physics', 288.
[15] Data compiled by Dr. D. I. Greenstein from HUD.

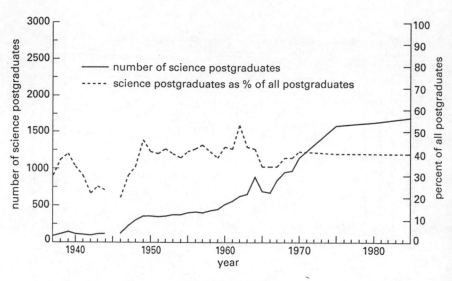

FIGURE 10.2   POSTGRADUATE STUDENTS IN SCIENCE AT OXFORD, 1937–1985

and no less than twenty from then to 1970.[16] A new chair, or a new incumbent of an old chair, often meant new and expensive equipment, an incursion of new personnel, or even a new department.

Expansion on this scale increased the postwar pressure on space in the pre-war science area, which could expand only into Merton sports ground and the so-called 'Keble triangle', where engineering and metallurgy were housed [figure 10.5].[17] The geographical tendency of departments was simultaneously centripetal and centrifugal. Scientific work hitherto done outside the science area—in the college laboratories and in the botany school for example—was gradually drawn into the science area; its usable floor space trebled from about 300,000 square feet in 1939 to 900,000 in 1970, despite being prevented from encroaching on the University Parks. The outcome was an unsightly clustering of large buildings without coherent plan or style, described by Sir Rex Richards in 1986 as an 'architectural slum'.[18] Yet this centripetal tendency brought two major advantages to

[16] *Supplement to the Historical Register of 1900* (University of Oxford 1951) and *Supplement to the Historical Register of 1900* (University of Oxford 1970).

[17] S. G. Plant, 'The university science area' in A. F. Martin and R. W. Steel (eds), *The Oxford Region* (Oxford 1954); 'Future requirements of the science departments: a report of the committee on requirements and sites', *Gazette* xciii (1962/3), 211–19; 'Future requirements of the science departments: report by Sir William Holford', ibid. 1253–66.

[18] *Gazette* xciii (1962/3), 211–12; University Surveyor, 'Return to the University Grants Committee [UGC] of accommodation at 1 October 1967' (I am indebted to the University Surveyor's department for this document, known as the 'Bible'); Sir Rex Richards in History of the University seminar on 'Academic breakthroughs', Nuffield College, 24 Jan. 1986, Brian Harrison's transcript, HUA.

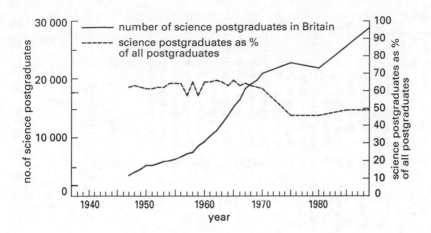

FIGURE 10.3   POSTGRADUATE SCIENCE STUDENTS IN BRITAIN, 1937–1989

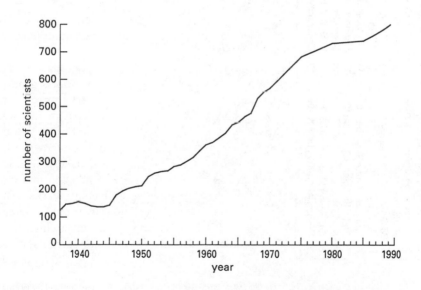

FIGURE 10.4   OXFORD SCIENTISTS HOLDING A UNIVERSITY APPOINTMENT, 1937–1990

Oxford science: research was not geographically separated from teaching, and departments could readily collaborate and share services and resources. One of the great success stories of Oxford science in the late 1960s which continued until 1989—the Enzyme Group, which studied from many

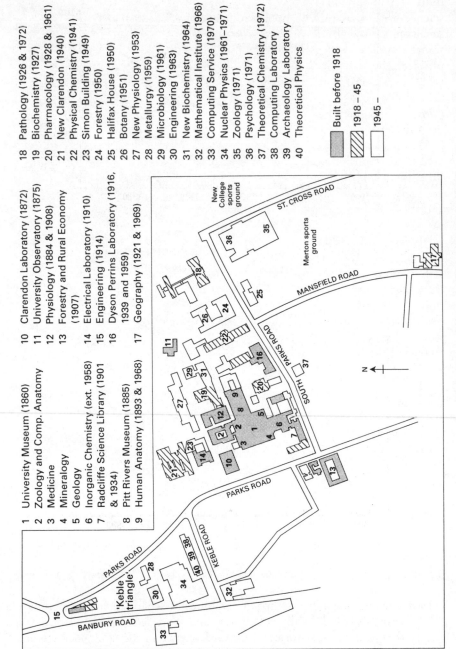

1   University Museum (1860)
2   Zoology and Comp. Anatomy
3   Medicine
4   Mineralogy
5   Geology
6   Inorganic Chemistry (ext. 1958)
7   Radcliffe Science Library (1901 & 1934)
8   Pitt Rivers Museum (1885)
9   Human Anatomy (1893 & 1968)
10 Clarendon Laboratory (1872)
11 University Observatory (1875)
12 Physiology (1884 & 1908)
13 Forestry and Rural Economy (1907)
14 Electrical Laboratory (1910)
15 Engineering (1914)
16 Dyson Perrins Laboratory (1916, 1939 and 1959)
17 Geography (1921 & 1969)

18 Pathology (1926 & 1972)
19 Biochemistry (1927)
20 Pharmacology (1928 & 1961)
21 New Clarendon (1940)
22 Physical Chemistry (1941)
23 Simon Building (1949)
24 Forestry (1950)
25 Halifax House (1950)
26 Botany (1951)
27 New Physiology (1953)
28 Metallurgy (1959)
29 Microbiology (1961)
30 Engineering (1963)
31 New Biochemistry (1964)
32 Mathematical Institute (1966)
33 Computing Service (1970)
34 Nuclear Physics (1961–1971)
35 Zoology (1971)
36 Psychology (1971)
37 Theoretical Chemistry (1972)
38 Computing Laboratory
39 Archaeology Laboratory
40 Theoretical Physics

■ Built before 1918
▨ 1918 – 45
□ 1945 –

FIGURE 10.5   THE GROWTH OF THE SCIENCE AREA, 1914–1970

perspectives the complex proteins which regulate biochemical activity—strikingly illustrates the advantages of this compact but diverse science area. It required close co-operation between some twenty senior scientists from eight departments. Among them were scientists of international standing such as David Phillips from zoology, Rex Richards from physical chemistry and R. J. P. Williams from inorganic chemistry. For more than fifteen years they met fortnightly in college after dinner. Also of critical importance to the Group was the development of superconducting magnets manufactured by the Oxford Instrument Company, which had originated from the Clarendon Laboratory.[19]

Yet this concentration was accompanied by dispersal. Some scientists favoured establishing a second campus, but these ideas came to nothing and the dispersal of Oxford science was in the end uncoordinated. Botanists and zoologists used the Wytham estate after its acquisition in 1942, for example, and the engineers colonized the old Oxford power station in Osney, which the University bought in 1969.[20] The centrifugal tendency was carried still further when national and international scientific projects to the south of Oxford, notably at Harwell and Culham, located the University within an area of major scientific investment. As the *Oxford Magazine* wrote in 1945, 'future historians will point to Harwell as a crucial point in the industrialisation of Oxford science, the nationalisation of learning'.[21] Oxford nuclear physics co-operated closely with the Atomic Energy Research Establishment at Harwell, which generously made available its research facilities, and later with the Rutherford high-energy nuclear physics laboratory which the Science Research Council established near Harwell. By 1966 over thirty academic research staff and postgraduates from the nuclear physics department were doing their high-energy physics experiments on the proton accelerator at the Rutherford Laboratory.[22]

If certain areas of science at Oxford between the wars were somewhat introverted, this situation soon changed dramatically. Oxford after 1945 involved itself fully in the national and international expansion of science through collaborative projects with British and overseas universities and institutions, through hosting international scientific conferences, through publishing and editing many international journals and through its sheer

[19] *Gazette* xciii (1962/3), 211–12; Richards in 'Academic breakthroughs', 7. I am grateful to Professor R. J. P. Williams for help in preparing this and other sections of this chapter.

[20] For ideas on a second campus see HCP 243 (1962), 125; 245 (1963), 243; R. J. P. Williams, 'The science area', *OM* 31 Jan. 1963, 149; P. D. Henderson, 'The Holford report and the resolution', *OM* 6 June 1963, 341. For Wytham see HCP 181 (1942), 71–82; 182 (1942), p. xci; 183 (1942), p. xii; 184 (1943), pp. xxxix–xl; C. Hibbert and E. Hibbert (eds), *The Encyclopaedia of Oxford* (London 1988), 'Wytham'.

[21] *OM* 8 Nov. 1945, 49.

[22] D. H. Perkins, 'The University and the Rutherford Laboratory', *OM* 4 Trinity 1966, 407; B. Bleaney, 'The Clarendon Laboratory', *OM* 8 May 1958, 414–20.

volume of research publications. Perhaps physics has the highest profile in this respect but every other science department played its part. From 1939 onward the Imperial Forestry Institute at Oxford, later the Commonwealth Forestry Institute, built up the world's largest library of forestry publications. In the 1960s, largely as a result of its experience with tropical forestry through its Commonwealth connections, the Institute set up a programme of voluntary international collaboration to explore, evaluate and conserve endangered tropical forest genetic resources. This involved much field work in Latin America and the distribution of collected material to nearly one hundred countries for field trials.[23]

Meteorology, the research area with perhaps the longest tradition at the Clarendon Laboratory, flourished under G. M. B. Dobson (*ad hominem* professor, 1945–55), who won international recognition for his ozone research. In 1948 Oxford became headquarters of the International Ozone Commission under Sir Charles Harman. Oxford's atmospheric physics department co-ordinated international ozone research for the international geophysical year in 1957–8, which meant that, besides many other tasks, all ozone-measuring instruments came to Oxford for final calibration. Subsequently the department collaborated with Reading University and the American National Aeronautics and Space Administration (NASA) in international meteorological research.[24] The engineering and, later, the mathematics departments became involved with national thermonuclear research at Culham and subsequently with the Joint European Torus (JET), the controlled thermonuclear fusion project there; some Oxford postgraduate students carried out their research at Culham.

Oxford's overall growth in the natural sciences, as well as the relative growth of each of its constituent parts, is reflected in its building programmes. Chemistry was the subject best established in Oxford in 1939. The new physical chemistry laboratory was sufficiently complete by July 1941 to allow the transfer of all apparatus from the Balliol–Trinity laboratory, which was then dismantled, and in 1947 the Jesus College laboratory was the last college laboratory to close.[25] After 1945 the three

[23] A. Greaves, 'Fresh woods', *Oxford Today* Trinity 1989, 18–20; *The Oxford Forestry Institute* [publicity brochure] (Oxford 1989). I am grateful to Dr Tony Greaves of the Forestry Institute for his assistance and advice.

[24] G. M. B. Dobson, 'Forty years research on atmospheric ozone at Oxford: a history', *Applied Optics* vii (1968), 400, 401–3; J. T. Houghton, 'Space research at Oxford', *OM* 23 Oct. 1970, 41–2; J. T. Houghton and C. D. Walshaw, 'G. M. B. Dobson', *BMFRS* xxiii (1977); C. D. Walshaw, 'The early history of atmospheric ozone' in J. Roche (ed.) *Physicists Look Back* (Bristol and New York 1990), 316–19.

[25] HCP 166 (1937), 85–6; 168 (1937), 51–2; *Gazette* lxviii (1937/8), 220; lxix (1938/9), 215; lxxi (1940/1), 246, 250; lxxii (1941/2), 224, 228; E. J. Bowen, 'The development of the university laboratories', *Chemistry in Britain* i (1965); K. J. Laidler, 'Chemical kinetics and the Oxford college laboratories', *Archive for History of the Exact Sciences* xxxviii (1988), 218; R. Barrow and C. J. Danby, *The Physical Chemistry Laboratory at Oxford: The First 50 Years* (Oxford 1991).

branches of chemistry (organic, inorganic and physical) continued to demand more space, and the subject helped to generate several new departments: chemical crystallography (1941), metallurgy (1956) and theoretical chemistry (1972).

The spectacular growth in physics also resulted in substantial building projects, most notably the new Clarendon Laboratory (completed in 1939) and the nuclear physics laboratory, built in three stages between 1961 and 1971.[26] By then the floor-space assigned to physics was about the same as that for chemistry: approximately 150,000 square feet.[27] Other major buildings were for forestry (completed in 1950), botany (1951), physiology (1953), metallurgy (1959), engineering (1963), biochemistry (1964), mathematics (1966) and the zoology and psychology complex completed in 1971. Given the unpredictable directions of scientific growth, buildings had to be increasingly flexible. Already by 1935 Council had recommended that laboratory buildings be standardized, with 'easily removable partitions and pipes, wiring and plumbing uncovered'. Sir Hans Krebs's successor as Whitley Professor of Biochemistry benefited considerably from the fact that the biochemistry building's load-bearing walls were on the perimeter and its services either external or between the floors.[28] Whereas the earliest of these buildings were funded largely by Nuffield and the University, post-war building and equipment costs forced the University increasingly to rely on funding from the University Grants Committee; science received the major part of Oxford's share in this between 1950 and 1970.[29] Only in the 1980s did Oxford turn once more to research foundations, industry and charitable bodies for major assistance in this area.

In all science departments laboratory equipment grew in quantity, sophistication and expense, both in undergraduate and postgraduate laboratories; computer data-storage, processing and modelling played a steadily increasing role. Research funding came mainly from government research bodies such as the Department of Scientific and Industrial Research (DSIR), the Medical Research Council (MRC), the Agricultural Research Council (ARC) and the Science Research Council (SRC). Some of these

[26] *Gazette* lxix (1938/9), 215; xcii (1961/2), 812; xciii (1962/3), 824–5; HCP 170 (1938), 33; 173 (1939), 15–16, 225–35; F. A. Lindemann, 'Designing a new physics laboratory', *Oxford* summer 1938; Sir Denys Wilkinson in History of the University seminar on 'Academic breakthroughs', Nuffield College, 5 Dec. 1986, Brian Harrison's transcript, HUA.

[27] University Surveyor, 'Return to UGC 1 Oct. 1967', 6, 36–7.

[28] HCP 160 (1935), 78; M. G. Ord, 'The biochemical explosion', tape-recorded seminar in Linacre College, 15 May 1990.

[29] The UGC provided £104,000 for the forestry building, £190,000 for botany, £397,000 for physiology, £146,000 for metallurgy, £641,000 for engineering (£458,000 of which was for equipment), £629,000 for biochemistry, £283,000 for the Mathematical Institute, £180,000 for nuclear physics (in addition to £750,000 from the Department of Scientific and Industrial Research) and £275,000 for the zoology and psychology building. See the abstracts of accounts in the *Gazette* 1954–76.

bodies set up their own research units or institutes in science departments. These include the Imperial Forestry Institute, funded by the Ministry of Overseas Development and the Commonwealth, the agronomy unit, supported by the ARC, and the MRC units in the departments of human anatomy, biochemistry and zoology. Industry, learned bodies such as the Royal Society, and private donations also played an important part. Between 1939 and 1968 the science departments' annual research publications grew from about 500 to about 1,800.[30] The quality of this research is reflected in the six Nobel prizes won by Oxford scientists during this period: H. W. Florey and E. B. Chain (medicine, 1945), R. Robinson (chemistry, 1947), C. N. Hinshelwood (chemistry, 1956), D. Hodgkin (chemistry, 1964), R. Porter (physiology, 1972), and N. Tinbergen (physiology, 1973). It is also reflected in the significant absolute increase from 1939 to 1970 in Oxford's Fellows of the Royal Society, and in Oxford's modest advance by comparison with Cambridge [table 10.2].

TABLE 10.2

FELLOWS OF THE ROYAL SOCIETY AT OXFORD AND CAMBRIDGE, 1939–1990

	Oxford		Cambridge		all fellows
	no.	%	no.	%	
1939	33	7.3	68	15.1	450
1945	30	6.4	67	14.3	467
1950	34	6.7	68	13.4	509
1955	44	7.9	65	11.6	560
1960	49	8.2	84	14.1	594
1965	58	9.0	86	13.3	647
1970	60	8.4	90	12.6	713
1975	69	8.8	107	13.6	784
1980	80	9.2	108	12.4	874
1985	80	8.2	123	12.6	977
1990	96	9.1	131	12.4	1,060

Source: *Yearbook of the Royal Society of London* 1939–70; the figures for Oxford and Cambridge, which are based on the university addresses given in the yearbook, are approximate.

What went on in the science area besides research? By no means all the undergraduate teaching took place there; tutorials remained central to

---

[30] *Franks Report* i. 128–9. For publications of the science area, see appropriate reports in the *Gazette*.

instruction, and normally took place within the colleges. Oxford scientists sometimes questioned the virtues of the traditional tutorial. For example Michael Atiyah, Professor of Mathematics, told the Franks Commission that colleagues thought university classes would be more efficient. Yet experiments in this direction came to naught, if only because mathematics undergraduates continued to ask their tutors to explain things they had not understood in the classes; hence the reinstatement of tutorials.[31] Also college-based were the entrance examinations and the setting and marking of termly 'collections' (informal examinations to test undergraduate work in progress). Mathematics lectures continued to be given in colleges for longer than lectures in the natural sciences; in Hilary term 1951 17 out of 45 still took place in colleges. Yet even in mathematics, and still more so in the natural and applied sciences, lectures were moving towards the science area. In Hilary term 1939 only 14 of about 200 natural science lecture courses were given in colleges, only 2 in 1951 and none at all in 1970.[32] Natural science lecture courses became both more numerous and more specialized. Taking the lecture and laboratory courses on offer in Oxford's four science faculties in Hilary term, their number rose from 230 in 1946 to 416 in 1950, and to 800 in 1970. In Michaelmas term 1964, science undergraduates attended twice as many lectures as arts undergraduates. When laboratory classes are included, the organizational achievement and teaching load on scientists seem considerable, although the staff–student ratio in science was greater than in arts.[33]

At the heart of the science area lies the Radcliffe Science Library, which by the mid-1960s held some 333,000 items, including 4,700 serials; it had become a major science library of international importance, and a research library for all the sciences at Oxford, including medicine. Until 1974 Balliol and Trinity had a combined science library, a relic from the Balliol–Trinity laboratories; Magdalen maintained the Gerrans Mathematical Library; and there were about forty science departmental libraries. Nevertheless the Radcliffe Science Library was the undergraduate scientist's main resource. With only 334 seats for readers, mounting undergraduate numbers caused it to become intolerably overcrowded by the mid-1960s. The congestion was much eased in 1971 when the Hooke Library (a small lending library) was set up, and in 1974 when the Lankester Room (an underground extension to

[31] *Franks Report* i. 108–9; Franks Commission, oral evidence xlvii. 6; M. Rayner, 'Mathematics in Oxford since 1914', History of the University seminar, Corpus Christi College, 24 Feb. 1989, Brian Harrison's transcript, HUA.

[32] *Gazette* lxix (1938/9), *passim*; lxxxi (1950/1), 284–97; c (1969/70), 424–55.

[33] *Gazette* lxxvi (1945/6), 180–97; lxxxi (1950/1), 267–97; c (1969/70), 393–455; *Franks Report* i. 107; ii. 156, 262; C. Mackenzie, 'Work or play', *Isis* 28 Nov. 1951, 22–3. Staff–student ratios can be roughly determined in 1964/5 from *Franks Report* ii. 14, 39 and figure 10.4. For that year, in arts the staff–student ratio was 1 to 9, in science it was 1 to 7.5.

the Radcliffe Science Library which included a large new area for readers) was built below the forecourt of the University Museum.[34]

It disturbed Oxford scientists that Oxford continued to be seen as best for the arts, Cambridge as best for the natural sciences. In a survey completed in 1966, only 3 per cent of natural science applicants put Oxford as their first choice, whereas Cambridge was first choice for 24 per cent.[35] Yet schoolteachers' misapprehensions were a natural response to Oxford's distribution of its entrance awards; in the mid-1950s there were 316 for arts and only 141 for the natural sciences. Furthermore Oxford's science undergraduates came from a somewhat less affluent background; whereas 65 per cent of entrance awards in classics and history were won by candidates from public schools, the proportion was almost exactly reversed in science and modern languages.[36]

Oxford's scientists, like their contemporaries in the humanities, became increasingly concerned with reform of the syllabus, a reflection not simply of advances in knowledge and changing emphases within subjects, but also of shifting relationships between subjects. The overall trend was steadily towards more rigorous up-to-date science, towards autonomy in departmental and examination structure, and away from older notions of an integrated first stage of the degree course. This led not only to changes in existing courses but to the establishment of more specialized preliminary examinations and to new final honour schools in agriculture (1937), forestry (1944), biochemistry (1949) and the science of metals (metallurgy, 1956).[37] This specialization was a natural working out of the Oxford tradition of single-subject honour schools. Partly as a reaction against this, and partly to acknowledge the growing importance of interdisciplinary studies, joint honour schools appeared in psychology, philosophy and physiology (PPP, 1947), engineering and economics (1963), physics and philosophy (1968), mathematics and philosophy (1968) and agriculture and forestry (1971).[38]

We can turn now to a more detailed survey of research in the natural sciences since 1945, starting with the three large schools: physics, chemistry and mathematics. Its structural context deserves attention because, as Hinshel-

---

[34] [R. Shackleton, chairman] *Report of the Committee on University Libraries* (University of Oxford 1966), 65–75; *Annual Report of the Curators of the Bodleian Library for 1970–71* (supplement 8 to *Gazette* cii, 1971/2), 45–6. I am grateful to Claire Hopkins of Trinity for information on the Balliol-Trinity science library.

[35] D. Hutchins, 'The Oxbridge pull for science', *OM* 6 Michaelmas 1966, 102–3. See also above, 141.

[36] 'Scholarships at Oxford 1955–6', *OM* 17 May 1956, 409–10.

[37] *Gazette* lxvii (1936/7), 733–4; HCP 188 (1944), pp. xli, xlii, 6, 59; *Gazette* lxxix (1948/9), 684; lxxxvi (1955/6), 1112–13.

[38] *Gazette* lxxvii (1946/7), 429–30; xciii (1962/3), 1392–3; lxxviii (1967/8), 1318; *Examination Decrees* 1971, 276–9.

wood pointed out in 1958, 'the kind of society which has now grown up in the larger University laboratories has in many ways its own special character'. This society had a great deal of technical equipment and needed a skilled staff which was not easy to recruit; both these aspects presented problems of management similar to those in modern industry, though without its clear division of labour.[39] Within his department the Oxford professor was powerful, though rather less so than in other universities. This was because fellows of colleges had a power-base of their own, including the power to admit undergraduates, and sometimes even a freedom publicly to criticize their own departments. The professor had statutory power to appoint all junior academic staff, laboratory personnel and technical and auxiliary staff, and sometimes also effective power to appoint senior staff. He negotiated with the General Board, and with private and governmental funding agencies, on financing extensions or alterations to his buildings, on funding new posts or research enterprises, and on purchasing expensive apparatus. He could also 'feed or starve a particular research project at will'.[40]

The power of the science professors evoked criticism from the more egalitarian arts tutors.[41] Devolution of power to colleagues 'would make the running of the department rather closely like the running of a college', argued R. J. P. Williams in 1961; the professor would then be more free to reflect upon the general development of his subject.[42] The Franks Commission noted that departmental committees already existed in some science departments; 'their formalization would remove the possibility of unfair or dictatorial action by professors' and would ease the professors' administrative burden; they should therefore become universal. The Commission envisaged a biennial change in the membership of six or eight, with professors and readers as 'official' members who should not exceed three or four and would include the titular head of department, who would normally act as chairman. It saw them as evolving 'general policy' on teaching, research, junior appointments, building, and allocating resources and facilities. As a result, departmental committees were eventually set up in all science departments—though rather less uniformly than had been envisaged. The committees often had advisory rather than executive powers, but they did at least formalize effective consultation with departmental staff.

[39] *OM* 5 June 1958, 488.
[40] R. J. P. Williams, 'The organization of a science department', *OM* 11 May 1961, 334–5.
[41] Ibid.; Hodgkin 'Chemistry at Oxford', 9; J. Roche, 'The natural sciences in Oxford', History of the University seminar, Corpus Christi College, 23 Feb. 1990, Brian Harrison's transcript, HUA, 7; C. J. Danby, 'The physical chemistry laboratory at Oxford: the first fifty years', tape-recorded seminar in Linacre College, 30 Apr. 1991, pp. 8–9, 13. See also Richards in 'Academic breakthroughs', 7.
[42] Williams, 'Organization', 335; cf J. Wilks, 'The university demonstrator', *OM* 5 Dec. 1957, 176.

A parallel development, influenced perhaps by the style of American science departments but also by social developments in Britain, was the emergence of less formal, less hierarchical relationships between all levels of staff in Oxford science.[43]

Nowhere were professors more powerful, for good or ill, than in physics. Cherwell, who retired as Lee's Professor in 1956, had long been far from the frontiers of research. Not so his successor Sir Francis Simon, for whom a chair of thermodynamics had been specially created in 1949, and who set in train the vast development of nuclear physics at Oxford.[44] Simon held Cherwell's chair for only one month before he died in 1956, and was succeeded by Simon's pupil Brebis Bleaney, who remained in the chair till 1977. As for the Wykeham chair, Sir John Townsend was induced to retire from it in 1941 after he had refused to co-operate in training cadets in scientific subjects.[45] After the war his chair was assigned to theoretical physics, following the pre-war recommendation of W. L. Bragg. There was widespread support for this in the Clarendon Laboratory, although some, most notably Cherwell, felt that since Oxford physics by tradition was heavily experimental there was no need for non-experimental theoreticians.[46] Despite these misgivings the chair was a great success, largely because it had a sequence of distinguished occupants who co-operated closely with the experimentalists: M. H. L. Pryce until 1956, W. E. Lamb until 1963 and Sir Rudolf Peierls until 1974. In the 1960s Oxford's contribution to theoretical physics compared well with the other large national theoretical physics groups. It supported four more or less independent groups in solid state and atomic physics, nuclear structure and elementary particle physics.[47]

Undergraduate numbers rose faster in physics during the 1950s and early 1960s than in any other natural science subject in Oxford, and research at the Clarendon Laboratory expanded greatly in scale and range. Under F. E. Simon, N. Kurti and their collaborators, a high magnetic field laboratory was established; this, together with the extensive low-temperature facilities at Oxford, placed the Clarendon Laboratory at the forefront of research into superconducting magnets and the solid state. It also led the world in the early years of the new field of electron paramagnetic resonance and nuclear

[43] *Franks Report* i. 257; see also DLC [D. L. Chapman], 'The college laboratories', *OM* 13 Nov. 1947, 111–12; R. Cecil, 'Departmental committees', *OM* 7 June 1968, 363–4.

[44] Wilkinson in 'Academic breakthroughs', 3.

[45] E. T. Williams and H. M. Parker (eds), *The Dictionary of National Biography 1951–1960* (London 1971), 983–5 (J. S. E. Townsend); HCP 179 (1941), pp. lxxx, 153–4, 185; A. von Engel, 'J. S. E. Townsend', *BMFRS* iii (1957); P. K. Hoch and E. J. Yoxen, 'Schrödinger at Oxford: a hypothetical national cultural synthesis which failed', *Annals of Science* 1987, 607; Croft, 'Clarendon Laboratory', 132–3.

[46] OUA reports of examiners, board of the faculty of physical science, vol. x, Jan. 1945, p. 60; Croft, 178–84.

[47] Croft, 179–84.

magnetic resonance at low temperatures. A major first was Bleaney's recognition in 1950 of a magnetic method for aligning the nuclei of certain crystals. The first successful experiment was carried out in the Clarendon Laboratory in 1951. This technique became a powerful tool in nuclear and solid state physics and gave rise to a large new field of research.[48]

Major expansion in nuclear physics took place after 1956, when Simon invited Denys Wilkinson from Cambridge to head the nuclear physics research group. With extensive political skills and connections, Wilkinson was able to prevail over major difficulties both inside and outside Oxford in his efforts to build up a large nuclear research laboratory. At one point in the negotiations, late in 1960, the Minister for Science, Lord Hailsham, decided that the whole project should go to Harwell, but Wilkinson managed to marshal sufficient pressure to retain it in Oxford. Two particle-accelerators in tandem were installed on the Keble Road site, together with substantial auxiliary equipment, and staff also used the international facilities of CERN (Conseil Européen pour la Recherche Nucléaire) in Geneva, and the Rutherford Laboratory. The academic staff in nuclear physics rose from 20 in 1957 to 135 in 1963, and postgraduates increased from 10 to 64.[49] By 1971 Oxford had become established as a leading European centre of research in nuclear physics.

In 1939 chemistry was Oxford's largest undergraduate science school and the largest chemistry school in the country: it remained so thereafter. Partly because it was so well established in the colleges through the long history of the college chemical laboratories, undergraduate numbers in chemistry grew very fast in the 1950s and early 1960s, though much more slowly later. By 1966 there were about 360 research workers spread among the various chemistry departments and, if staff and students are added, chemistry's numbers in that year reached about 1,000.[50] By 1970 there were five professors of chemistry in Oxford. After 1941 chemistry occupied three substantial locations within the science area: the physical chemistry laboratory, the Dyson Perrins Laboratory for organic chemistry, and the inorganic chemistry laboratory attached to the University Museum [figure 10.5]. A special strength of Oxford chemistry was part II of the degree course, which undergraduates took in their fourth (research) year. Undergraduates spent diminishing time in laboratory classes, however, because spectroscopic methods were replacing instruction in qualitative methods of analysis, and because of increasing pressures from the theoretical content of the syllabus.

[48] Croft, 162, 187; Kurti, 'Simon'; R. Berman, 'Low temperature physics and cryogenics at the Clarendon' in R. G. Scurlock (ed.), History and Origins of Cryogenics (Oxford 1992).

[49] Wilkinson in 'Academic breakthroughs'.

[50] H. M. Powell, 'Oxford chemistry 1966', Chemistry in Britain i (1965), 557.

Undergraduates, postgraduates and senior members of the chemistry departments met at the weekly evening meetings of the Alembic Club, another vestige of the connection between colleges and chemistry, which met in Jesus College's lecture-theatre. Until the 1960s the Club provided virtually the only regular research seminar for chemists, with lectures from distinguished outside speakers. Until 1950, membership was confined to men, which meant—most notoriously—that Dorothy Hodgkin was not allowed to attend internal meetings. Until he died in 1963 F. M. ('Freddy') Brewer, secretary to the sub-faculty and Mayor of Oxford in 1959, was treasurer and put his wide range of connections to good effect in organizing the Club's annual dinner in the Randolph Hotel. Here former members, often distinguished industrialists and academics, met together with invited guests, and the occasion helped to strengthen links between Oxford science and industry. After Brewer's death the Club's importance declined somewhat, mainly because each chemistry department eventually established its own research seminars for outside speakers.[51]

Oxford chemistry, which owed so much to Manchester, was already world-famous in 1939. Chemists were especially successful in placing graduates in academic and industrial posts. In 1961, for example, several divisions of Imperial Chemical Industries (ICI) had an Oxford chemist as research director, and the atmosphere in at least one of its senior staff rooms was said to resemble that of an Oxford common room. For many decades Oxford chemists held the highest posts both academic and industrial.[52] Oxford chemistry after 1945 reflected in part the rapid world-wide changes in the subject. The best-known work includes the crystallographic studies by H. M. Powell, Dorothy Hodgkin and their colleagues on the structure of vitamin B12, insulin, penicillin, cephalosporin and other substances. This work was done partly in collaboration with the school of pathology, and won Hodgkin the Nobel prize in 1964. In the Dyson Perrins Laboratory, research covered many aspects of organic chemistry including both physical organic chemistry and the structure, synthesis and biosynthesis of natural products.

During the 1960s collaborative work began on the mechanisms of enzyme action, and this developed into the Enzyme Group mentioned above. Work in this field had earlier begun in the inorganic chemistry laboratory in the 1950s, which foreshadowed still wider developments in bio-organic chemistry in Dyson Perrins begun in the 1970s. In 1955 Robinson used his retirement to bring to fulfilment a long-standing project, the founding of

[51] Hodgkin, 'Chemistry at Oxford', 15–16; E. J. W. Whittaker, 'Chemistry teaching in Oxford in 1939–43 through the eyes of an undergraduate', letter to Brian Harrison, 3 Dec. 1989, p. 13; E. J. Bowen, 'Chemistry at Oxford', undated typescript in my collection, pp. 15–16; J. C. Smith, *The Development of Organic Chemistry at Oxford* (2 vols Oxford 1968–75), ii. 56–7.
[52] Bowen, 'University laboratories'.

Tetrahedron, a journal of organic chemistry. He was succeeded in the chair of organic chemistry by E. R. H. Jones, who extended the laboratories and re-equipped them with more modern spectroscopic and other apparatus. Research on inorganic chemistry included the study of explosion and combustion phenomena in gases, Raman spectroscopy, modern analytical methods, chromatography, complex formation and field ion microscopy. From 1963 J. S. Anderson was the first to hold the new chair of inorganic chemistry, and introduced new approaches to analysing solid-state proper- ties of inorganic crystals. In physical chemistry work was done on reaction kinetics, infra-red and ultraviolet spectroscopy, electron-diffraction, nuclear magnetic resonance, the physical chemistry of bacterial growth and the chemical applications of ultra high vacua. In 1964 Hinshelwood was succeeded as Dr Lee's Professor of Chemistry by Rex Richards, one of the first in England to apply nuclear magnetic resonance to chemistry and to build his own NMR spectrometers.

In 1939 mathematics at Oxford was second only to chemistry in the number of its undergraduates. With four professors and ten tutorial fellows, it was a presence in the colleges, but tied very closely to physics. It was quite common for a mathematics tutor to double up as the college's physics tutor, just as the Mathematical Institute doubled up as a school of theoretical physics. From the mid-1940s, however, the number of undergraduate mathematicians rose rapidly [table 10.1], as did the number of college fellowships; by the early 1970s every college had at least one tutor in mathematics.[53] Unlike chemistry, mathematics lacked adequate accom- modation to cope with its growing numbers of undergraduates, postgraduate students and academic staff, and began to press the General Board for more accommodation. In 1952 the Mathematical Institute moved from its rooms in the Radcliffe Science Library to 10 Parks Road [figure 10.5], which had been vacated by the Institute of Social Medicine, and was given statutory recognition in 1953. The Institute did not acquire its own purpose-built centre of operations in St Giles until 1966.[54] Mathematics gradually established its autonomy in other ways. In 1962 a new honour moderations course was set up in physics, mathematics and engineering science which effectively ended the role of the mathematics school as provider of service-teaching for other faculties. In 1963 mathematics broke away from physical sciences to form its own faculty, thus gaining a representative on the General Board.[55]

Oxford's marked individualism in research was especially pronounced in mathematics. The first post-war research group in pure mathematics, in

[53] Rayner, 'Mathematics'.
[54] HCP 145 (1930), 187–90; 235 (1960), 425–35; 247 (1964), 590; 251 (1965), 609; *Statutes* 1953; Rayner, 'Mathematics'.
[55] *Examination Statutes 1962*, 55.

topology, was built up by Henry Whitehead, Waynflete Professor of Pure Mathematics from 1947 to 1960. His impact on Oxford mathematics owed much to his view of his subject as 'essentially a social occupation'. The austere beauty of the subject did not attract him for its own sake—rather he enjoyed talking about it and hearing others talk about it.[56] C. A. Coulson, who was appointed Rouse Ball Professor of Mathematics in 1952, made a deep impact on the Mathematical Institute and on the physical sciences generally at Oxford. He established a research group in theoretical chemistry at the Institute, a group which was in close contact with physical chemistry and which attained independence as a department of theoretical chemistry in 1972, with Coulson as the first professor. Coulson improved the informal contacts between members of the Institute by setting up the first departmental common room in Oxford, a tea club, Tuesday morning coffee parties and an annual summer spree. With extraordinary energy he maintained close contacts with schools through prize-givings and also through the local branch of the Mathematical Association. He also found time to travel the world as a Methodist lay preacher.[57] The international standing of Oxford mathematics rose greatly in the 1950s and 1960s and owed much to Coulson; to George Temple, Sedleian Professor of Natural Philosophy 1953–68, an applied mathematician who became a Benedictine monk in 1982; to Michael Atiyah, Savilian Professor of Geometry 1963–9, who worked in pure and applied mathematics; and to Graham Higman, Waynflete Professor of Pure Mathematics 1960–84, a group theorist.[58]

From 1952 Coulson was a prime mover in the creation of the computing laboratory, which was established in 1957 at 9 South Parks Road. In 1964 it moved reluctantly to the old engineering building at the apex of the Keble triangle. Its first director, Leslie Fox, was appointed in 1957. In 1969 Oxford computing bifurcated into the computing service, established at 15–19 Banbury Road and independent from 1978, and the computing laboratory, which joined the faculty of mathematics in 1968. In 1984 the computing laboratory moved fully into 8–11 Keble Road, after expanding to include a numerical analysis group and a programme research group.[59] From the 1960s the computing service became one of the fastest growing services in the University, and installed computers of ever-growing power and sophistication. It became indispensable not only to scientists but increasingly to libraries, to the university administration, and eventually even to arts departments.

    [56] Obituary by 'GH', OM 2 June 1960, 308; Williams and Parker, DNB 1951–60, 1047–8.
    [57] S. L. Altmann and E. J. Bowen, 'C. A. Coulson', BMFRS xx (1974).
    [58] Rayner, 'Mathematics'.
    [59] HCP 221 (1955), 78–82; 226 (1957), 240–1; 227 (1957), pp. ciii, 28; Gazette lxxxix (1958/9), 742–4, annual report of computing laboratory for 1957/8; OUA Proc. General Board, cv (Michaelmas term 1963), 235–40; Computing Laboratory: Annual Report for 1968–9 (supplement 10 to Gazette c, 1970/1).

So far we have been concerned primarily with Oxford's larger natural science schools. To the smaller scientific schools Oxford's collegiate structure presented special problems. In 1955 64 per cent of chemistry's academic staff held college fellowships, the corresponding figure for physics being 60 per cent, biochemistry 55 per cent, pathology and physiology 50 per cent, pharmacology 20 per cent, botany 17 per cent, human anatomy 13 per cent, zoology 11 per cent. In forestry, agriculture, engineering, geology, entomology, astronomy and several other subjects only the professor held a fellowship.[60] Given the colleges' preoccupation with undergraduate teaching, tutorial appointments in small subjects could seldom be justified. A college without a tutorial fellow in the subject had no incentive to encourage a steady flow of talent into the subject from the schools, and a department which could not offer fellowships was hindered in recruitment and understandably disgruntled. Furthermore the small departments' resultant high staff–student ratio did not win friends among the larger departments. It was a vicious circle, later labelled as the 'entitlement problem'.[61]

Detailed discussion of the smaller natural science schools can conveniently begin with three physical sciences: astronomy, metallurgy and engineering. Oxford's astronomers after 1945 continued the research tradition in solar physics built up under Harry Plaskett, Savilian Professor of Astronomy from 1931 to 1960. In the mid-1950s Plaskett built a reflecting solar telescope with a focal length of 120 feet; in its day it was in certain respects the most powerful instrument in the world.[62] Increased funding enabled Donald Blackwell, his successor as Savilian Professor from 1960 to 1988, rapidly to build up staff and student numbers from a complement of about five to about fifty. He added new areas of research, including laboratory astrophysics, stellar and extra-galactic astronomy and later high-energy astrophysics and cosmology, and established co-operative projects with the observatories being set up by the Science and Engineering Research Council at sites around the world with better viewing conditions. There had been some theoretical astrophysics in Plaskett's time through collaboration with E. A. Milne, but its role was greatly strengthened by the arrival of the group led by D. W. Sciama in 1970.[63] The astronomers had to struggle to ensure that their telescopes' lines of sight were not disrupted by the science buildings being erected nearby. Their need for stable working conditions

[60] 'Fellowships for scientists', *OM* 3 Mar. 1955, 262. These figures omit heads of department, whether professors or readers; they include all other readers, university demonstrators, research officers and departmental demonstrators.
[61] See below, 713–15.
[62] HCP 221 (1955), 368–71; W. H. McCrea, 'H. H. Plaskett', *BMFRS* xxvii (1981); and see above, 153–4.
[63] Letter of D. E. Blackwell to J. Roche, 7 Aug. 1991; cf above, 156.

also enabled them to render sterling service to those who in the 1950s resisted proposals for a ring road through the area of the University Parks. However from 1944 the department was encouraged to search for a new site because its special needs restricted development in an area pressed for space. Pressure to move greatly increased in 1960 when Plaskett retired, but Blackwell struggled to keep the site, and the astronomers lost their battle only after he retired in 1988.[64]

Metallurgy was one of post-war Oxford's success stories. The foundation of a metallurgical department and undergraduate course was due almost entirely to the efforts of William Hume-Rothery [plate 10.1]. He revolutionized his subject by rescuing it from empiricism, placing it on a secure theoretical basis, and slowly persuading industry of the value of scientific metallurgy. In 1945 despite his growing international reputation he and his research group still had only two rooms and a covered yard in the old inorganic chemistry laboratory.[65] Metallurgy remained a postgraduate subject until 1949, when 'metallography' was first taught as a supplementary subject in the honour school of natural science. In 1953 Simon suggested that an institute for metal research, based on the very successful Institute for the Study of Metals in Chicago, be founded under Hume-Rothery's direction. But when an appeal for funds from industry was launched it became obvious that industrial metallurgists wanted an undergraduate degree course, not a research institute. The resultant internal conflict illuminates the attitude of some Oxford scientists to applied science. The physical sciences faculty board resolved in 1951 that a degree in scientific metallurgy should have 'no more technology than is contained in the degree courses in chemistry and physics' and stated that 'the man who has studied pure science at a university can take up technology on entering industry much more easily than one who has studied technology can later take up the pure science which may be required for his work'.[66]

Hume-Rothery himself preferred to concentrate on research and at first doubted whether undergraduates should be taught the subject, though he later became enthusiastic. Eventually it was agreed that the new degree should be a four-year course; the three-year part I would combine two-thirds of the existing chemistry part I with a new course on the science of metals, and part II was to be a research year, following the model of the chemistry school. The title 'science of metals' was soon replaced by 'metallurgy'. In 1955 the Pressed Steel Company of Cowley funded the George Kelley Readership, whose first holder was Hume-Rothery himself (1955–8). The Isaac Wolfson chair was established in 1957, and Hume-

[64] M. G. Adam, 'The changing face of astronomy at Oxford', tape-recorded seminar in Linacre College, 19 May 1992; *Handbook* 1969, 227–8; HCP 221 (1955), 368–71.

[65] G. V. Raynor, 'William Hume-Rothery', *BMFRS* xv (1969); see also above, 159–60.

[66] HCP 208 (1951), 165–7.

Rothery again was the first to occupy it (1958–66). With a degree course set up in the science of metals in 1956 and a metallurgy building completed in 1959 (the first of the new buildings in the Keble triangle) metallurgy was making rapid strides towards autonomy. The link with chemistry was finally severed in 1968, when a new first-year preliminary examination in chemistry and metallurgy was introduced and the department had enough academic staff to teach a full metallurgical course for finals. The number of undergraduates reading for parts I and II rose to 62 by 1973 and has continued to expand in recent years, as have the floor-area and research activities of the department.[67]

No Oxford science subject went through more dramatic change after 1945 than engineering. Its early history illustrates well two traits of Oxford science: its distaste for a narrow vocationalism and its contentment with small numbers if compatible with high quality. During the 1950s, however, government pressure for more engineers combined with suspicions in Oxford that the department was too small to be viable. This led to calls for its expansion, especially since space was at last available in the Keble triangle [figure 10.5]. In 1955 an advisory committee on the future of engineering science was set up which included members drawn from Cambridge (which had a large and successful engineering school), government, research and industry. The committee recommended doubling the size of the department and trebling its floor-area. Opposition to expansion came from Cherwell, who thought engineering better studied in technical colleges; from Hinshelwood; and from Vice-Chancellor A. H. Smith, who feared that expanded technology courses might undermine the college system.[68] Nonetheless the planned expansion went ahead and a new engineering laboratory with eleven floors was completed in 1963, with little benefit to Oxford's skyline. It was, said Bryan Keith-Lucas, senior lecturer in local government and a member of Oxford City Council, 'enough to show the danger and to demonstrate the rightness of the City Council's resolution to prevent any more high buildings'.[69]

Honour moderations in physics, mathematics and engineering science were first introduced in 1962, so for the first time undergraduates could in

[67] *Gazette* lxxxvi (1955/6), 103–4; OUA note by D. Veale headed 'Metallurgy appeal'; HCP 226 (1957), 76, 99–106, 154; *Gazette* xc (1959/60), 864; xcii (1961/2), University of Oxford *Abstract of Accounts*, 174–5; J. W. Christian, 'The history of metallurgy at Oxford 1936–86', tape-recorded seminar in Linacre College, 17 Apr. 1989. I am indebted to Professor Christian for much help with this section.

[68] HCP 222 (1955), 199–200; 223 (1956), 155–6, 249–56; F. A. Lindemann, Viscount Cherwell, 'Technologists', *OM* 2 Feb. 1956, 238; H. Motz, 'Engineering education at Oxford', *OM* 23 Feb. 1956, 292. Motz, who became Professor of Electrical Engineering in 1973, played an important part in developing engineering science at Oxford: A. M. Howatson, 'Aspects of the history of engineering science at Oxford', tape-recorded seminar in Linacre College, 18 May 1989. See also Smith, *The Prof*, 317.

[69] B. Keith-Lucas, 'Academic heights', *OM* 23 May 1963, 311; cf below, 515, 543.

effect be channelled directly from the sixth form into engineering at Oxford. The first college to appoint a tutorial fellow in the subject was St Edmund Hall, where Joseph Todd joined the governing body in 1959. In 1983 honour moderations in engineering science and in physics were separated, which meant that the mathematical content of the two courses no longer had to be identical. By Oxford standards, the engineering department had always had quite close contacts with industry, and this bore further fruit in 1963, when the combined degree course in engineering and economics was set up. When placing the proposal before Council, the sub-faculties of engineering and economics argued that 'a grounding in the principles of engineering science combined with a study of economics would be most useful for potential industrial managers'.[70] Undergraduate numbers in engineering shot up from the late 1950s to the 1980s [table 10.1] and by 1970 there were thirty academic staff and three hundred undergraduates in the school of engineering science. Research under Alexander Thom (Professor from 1945 to 1961) and Douglas Holder (Professor from 1961 to 1977) expanded greatly in its range from the well-known relaxation techniques for solving a wide range of engineering problems pioneered by Professor Richard Southwell to the study of automobile engineering, fluid and plasma dynamics, microwave engineering, advanced electronics, turbomachinery, high-speed photography, biomedical engineering and much else.[71]

Oxford geology, too, long remained small but distinguished. Before 1970 its undergraduate finalists in one year never rose above twenty-four and no tutorial fellow in the subject was appointed until 1964. In 1941 the chair of mineralogy and crystallography was disestablished and converted into separate readerships, reflecting scientific opinion that x-ray and structural crystallography was an important and rapidly growing research field and should become a specialized research department. Mineralogy joined geology as a sub-department and continued its teaching role and its care of the mineralogical collections in the University Museum.[72] In 1984 the department of geology and mineralogy merged with the department of surveying and geodesy to become the department of earth sciences.[73]

By 1937, when James Douglas was appointed to the chair of geology, the department had already established a high reputation in classical field geology. In 1939 the University Gazette listed fourteen research publications by the department, compared with twenty-three from physics, and the University Handbook for that year published an impressive list of geological field researches; these included the geology of remote parts of Peru and Spitzbergen and, nearer home, the glaciation of the Thames valley. The war

[70] 'Proposed honour school of engineering and economics', HCP 245 (1963), 42.
[71] Handbook 1969, 210–11.
[72] HCP 176 (1940), 23–5; Gazette lxxi (1940/1), 534–5. See also above, 150–1.
[73] HCP 308 (1984), 351.

interrupted research as well as the conversion of the old Clarendon Laboratory to the use of geology; Douglas retired in 1950, somewhat thwarted in his efforts to build up the department. His successor in the chair, Lawrence Wager (1950–65), was wide-ranging in his interests and was almost as well known as an explorer and mountaineer [plate 10.3]. War and its aftermath considerably weakened the department, but Wager was a stimulating head and something of a perfectionist; he rapidly built up a vigorous research school in igneous petrology and geochemistry. He was quick to see the significance for geology of more refined methods for the radiometric dating of rocks, and established in Oxford the first laboratory in Britain for this kind of work. This soon achieved international recognition, largely through the efforts of Stephen Moorbath and his associates. There were many delays before the geologists' hopes of better accommodation and facilities were even partially satisfied, but Wager's work was built upon and considerably extended by his successor E. A. Vincent (1967–86), who encouraged several areas of geological research which Wager had somewhat neglected.[74]

Undergraduate finalists in agriculture between the post-war boom and 1970 never rose above eleven in any one year, and the college connection was therefore weak [table 10.1]. Furthermore, by no means all those reading agriculture had any real need for a good degree; the others were either preparing themselves to run the parental estate or making the right contacts in the hope of becoming an agent to a large landowner.[75] It is hardly surprising that Geoffrey Blackman, Sibthorpian Professor from 1945 to 1970, chose to emphasize research, thereby transforming the approach to the subject in Oxford and rendering it more scientific; he promoted both applied agricultural research and fundamental science concerned with the underlying principles of agriculture. The ARC released Blackman to Oxford on condition that he was allowed to bring his wartime team with him and continue its research. Although the original members of the team soon left Oxford, searching perhaps for independence, he was able to recruit distinguished replacements, and in 1950 set up in the department an agronomy research unit completely funded by the ARC. In 1951 he established the University field station at Northfield Farm in Wytham and expanded work on hormone physiology and selective herbicides. Blackman's department also set up the Weed Research Organization and

[74] On Douglas, see above, 150, 251. On Wager, see 'Lawrence Rickard Wager', *University College Record* 1966, 12–16; E. A. Vincent, 'Geology and mineralogy at Oxford', tape-recorded seminar in Linacre College, 4 May 1989. I am very grateful to Professor Vincent for help with this section. J. Hargreaves, *L. R. Wager: A Life 1904–1965* (privately printed 1991); I am most grateful to Mrs Phyllis Wager for presenting me with a copy of this volume, for lending me photographs of her husband and for providing illuminating details about his life.

[75] Sir Roger du Boulay, letter to Brian Harrison, 14 July 1989, p. 24.

Letcombe Laboratory.[76] His achievement was considerable, though perhaps he switched the emphasis rather too far towards research. His successor John Burnett (1970–9) set about building up undergraduate numbers from eight to thirty-five in 1985.[77]

In botany the traditions of research in plant respiration, mycology, ecology, plant growth and metabolism established under the very cramped conditions of the 1930s enjoyed more breathing space in the new building after 1951. Its location made fertilization from related natural sciences more likely, and a fruitful collaboration with biochemists on radio-isotopes was one of the results. Many new fields were opened up under T. G. Osborn, Sherardian Professor of Botany from 1937 to 1953, including taxonomic studies of the African flora and the production of bacteriostatic substances by fungi; in the 1960s under Cyril Darlington plant genetics and cytology studies were included.[78] But botany suffered more seriously than other small departments from the weakness of its college connections, which left one of its most distinguished researchers, W. O. James, permanently embittered.[79]

Also damaging was the succession of Darlington to the chair of botany in 1953. A founder of modern genetics, he was a most distinguished scientist and introduced important new fields of research to Oxford botany. He contributed significantly to the University's collections of plants; the establishment of the University arboretum at Nuneham Courtenay and of the genetic garden, now in the University Parks, was almost entirely due to his efforts. However, his abrasive manner and his virtual obsession with genetics as the basis of biology were hardly likely to conciliate his opponents in the department, several of whom left for posts elsewhere. While he held the chair (1953–71) his department's national reputation suffered, partly because the 'Darlington refugees' were senior, influential and scattered but also because botany was not growing at a time when other science departments were growing fast. The department's annual research publications declined from forty-four in 1958 to twenty-one in 1968, and undergraduate numbers in botany also remained small [table 10.1]. Darlington lacked experience in university organization, for after graduating from London University he had spent much time in a horticultural research institution.[80] The department's standing within Oxford was hardly helped by his much advertised contempt for aspects of the college system.

[76] HCP 200 (1948), 391–3; 206 (1950), p. lxxix; J. R. Harley, 'G. E. Blackman', *BMFRS* xxvii (1981).

[77] Sir John Burnett, 'The plant sciences in twentieth-century Oxford', tape-recorded seminar in Linacre College, 8 May 1990.

[78] *Handbook* 1967, 216–18.

[79] Burnett, 'Plant sciences'.

[80] D. Lewis, 'C. D. Darlington', *BMFRS* xxix (1983).

Postgraduate fees were, he declared in 1960, 'a tax absent-mindedly levied on young gentlemen for the use of an address', and in oral evidence to the Franks Commission he vented his grievances about tutorials and college appointments in the presence of those whom he left to run the system: 'I do not attend committees', he said, 'I let other people exercise the power', and described the colleges as 'corrupt self-perpetuating oligarchies'.[81]

In forestry too, undergraduate numbers were small; between the post-war boom and 1970 the number of finalists in any one year never rose above eighteen. Yet considerable progress had been made by 1970 in bridging the gulf between a rather weak undergraduate school and a distinguished research institute, the Imperial Forestry Institute, which changed its name to the Commonwealth Forestry Institute in 1961. There was little need to boost the prestige of the Institute, whose imperial connections under H. G. Champion, Professor of Forestry from 1940 to 1959, made the professor 'the king-emperor . . . as far as forestry was concerned', with ample postgraduate students from abroad and abundant career opportunities within his patronage.[82] Its library was receiving over three hundred periodicals as early as 1950; it also housed the Commonwealth Forestry Bureau, whose card-index catalogues were then growing at the rate of sixteen thousand a year, and provided the basis for its *Forestry Abstracts*, internationally accepted as the definitive catalogue of the world's forestry literature.[83] The library and journal were reinforced by another of the Institute's international resources, the herbarium and xylarium (wood collection). In Britain the Institute carried out research at Wytham and Bagley woods and at a field station in Yorkshire into silviculture, forest ecology, soils and measurement, forest pathology and economics, tree physiology, microbiology and wood structure. The real need in the Institute was for the mood of natural science to permeate the undergraduate school of forestry. As with agriculture, this aim was substantially advanced in 1971 when the combined honour school of agriculture and forest sciences was set up. The marriage between forestry's preoccupation with perennial crops and agriculture's preoccupation with annual crops was stimulating, and Oxford's one-time unity of the plant sciences was fruitfully restored.[84]

In zoology three distinguished Linacre professors followed one another in succession. E. S. Goodrich remained until 1945. The brilliant academic staff

---

[81] *OM* 11 Feb. 1960, 187, letter from C. D. Darlington; Franks Commission, oral evidence xxxvii. 6. I am greatly indebted to Dr Brian Cox of Linacre College and of the department of plant sciences for his written observations (6 Sept. 1991) on the history of the botany department.

[82] Burnett, 'Plant sciences'.

[83] 'The new Imperial Forestry Institute', *OM* 19 Oct. 1950, 37; see also the annual reports of the Committee for Forestry in the *Gazette* during this period.

[84] Burnett, 'Plant sciences'.

he built up from 1921 included Charles Elton, 'father of animal ecology' [plate 10.3], the cytologist J. R. Baker and the population geneticist E. B. Ford.[85] In teaching and research the emphasis rested on whole-animal biology—that is, on classification, evolution and anatomy. The department under Goodrich showed little interest in animal physiology. Alister Hardy, Professor from 1946 to 1961, broadened the department's intellectual base, expanded field studies in ecology and animal behaviour, and built up the departmental library. In 1948 Hardy united the Bureau of Animal Population and the Edward Grey Institute of Field Ornithology into a single research department of zoological field studies, and in 1949 brought Nikolaas Tinbergen from the Netherlands, an ethologist of world fame who won a Nobel prize in 1973, to set up a centre for the study of animal behaviour. Hardy directed teaching away from comparative anatomy and towards general zoology. He had little sympathy with physico-chemical explanations of life, and after retirement established and directed Manchester College's Religious Experience Research Unit. At Hardy's departure the zoology department was rather conservative, there was little laboratory equipment, and research was still more individualistic than team-based.[86]

Much of this changed with the advent of a Cambridge man, John Pringle, Linacre Professor of Zoology from 1961 to 1979. Keen to launch new areas of research, particularly in molecular biology, he brought in research teams, most notably on muscle physiology and on enzymes. Pringle was also much interested in human biology, was keen to dissolve conventional boundaries between the 'life sciences', and was the main driving force behind the new honour school in human sciences. All these claims on space worsened what was already a difficult situation. Undergraduate numbers in the subject grew fast from the mid-1940s to the 1980s and the old zoology wing of the University Museum was becoming very overcrowded; nor did the University appear in the best light when it came to finding a remedy.

Before he retired, Hardy had persuaded the General Board to commit the University to provide a new zoology building with 100,000 square feet of floor-space. Pringle was forceful and frank, and not always patient with the participatory and roundabout ways of doing academic business in Oxford. 'Mercurius Oxoniensis' satirized him as 'a deep politician of imperious will, very persuasive and not to be gainsaid by our academick governors'.[87] The height and location of the proposed zoology tower [plate 10.2] aroused such controversy that Congregation's debates filled the Examination Schools and the Playhouse. The plans were thrown out by Congregation on 19 June 1962 even though (according to Mercurius) an 'auxiliary army of chymists

[85] See above, 148–9.
[86] N. B. Marshall, 'A. C. Hardy', *BMFRS* xxxii (1986).
[87] HCP 242 (1962), 749; 243 (1962), 299–300; *The Letters of Mercurius Oxoniensis* (London 1970), 50.

marched in, under the command of Sir Hans Krebs, at the goose-step, to vote for the Tower'. With much admired resilience, Pringle persisted and Merton's playing field eventually provided the way out. The new building, completed in 1970 to house both zoology and psychology, was controversial in both size and style, but there was little controversy about the quality of the zoological research it was now required to house.[88] Pringle's new ventures placed the department in the world class, a position consolidated under his successor Sir Richard Southwood.

Almost as controversial were Pringle's efforts to introduce a new broadly based honour school in human sciences. The idea was launched, following an after-dinner conversation in 1963 in Linacre College common room, as an attempt to bridge the science–arts divide. A remarkable collaboration of faculties resulted in the provision of undergraduate teaching for a course which included biology, psychology, geography, sociology, anthropology and statistics. Many thought this betrayed the single-subject honour school's specialist ideal and the new degree course was lampooned as being a 'weak and watery hodge-podge', a fit training only for 'coffee-house oracles'. Yet although the debate in the Sheldonian Theatre on 18 November 1969 was intense, the new honour school was accepted and prospered.[89]

The psychology department's move in 1971 was the culmination of decades of effort to expand into suitable premises. Psychological studies had been established at Oxford in 1936 at the Institute of Experimental Psychology. The Director from 1936 to 1945 was Dr William Brown, Wilde Reader in Mental Philosophy and founder of the Oxford Psychological Society. He took no salary, showing an altruism not uncommon in the world of Oxford science until well after the Second World War. From 1946 the new honour school of PPP greatly increased psychology's teaching responsibilities. Not without opposition, a chair in psychology was created and in 1947 G. Humphrey was the first to occupy it, followed in 1956 by R. C. Oldfield, and in 1967 by L. Weiskrantz. Psychology, which in Oxford covered a wide range of experimental studies, was administered by a board of studies until 1959, when a faculty of psychological studies was created. A single honour school of experimental psychology was added in 1970.[90]

Although the school of geography belongs with the natural sciences, its first two professors—Kenneth Mason (1932–53), explorer-surveyor and

[88] Cf below, 566–7; *Mercurius Oxoniensis*, 52.

[89] *Gazette* xcix (1968/9), 1438–40; V. Wigglesworth, 'J. W. S. Pringle', *BMFRS* xxix (1983); *Mercurius Oxoniensis*, 54; P. C. J. Brunet, 'The history of the zoology department in Oxford', tape-recorded seminar in Linacre College, 1 May 1990.

[90] R. C. Oldfield, 'Psychology in Oxford 1898–1949', *Bull. British Psychological Soc.* 1950; 'A new honour school', *OM* 28 Nov. 1946, 119–20; 'The development of psychological studies at Oxford', *OM* 1 Mar. 1951; 'Psychology at Oxford and Cambridge' *OM* 10 May 1956, 396–7; L. S. Hearnshaw, 'Professor G. Humphrey', *Nature* ccx (1966), 1313–14. See also above, 143.

subsequently Master of the Drapers' Company, and Edmund Gilbert (1953–67)—saw geography in their inaugural lectures primarily as a 'humane study' and history as 'its sister subject'.[91] By 1939 the number of finalists in geography had risen to thirty-nine; this number rose dramatically after 1945, partly as a result of ex-servicemen's zest for 'planning' [table 10.1]. Emphasis was placed somewhat controversially on regional human geography rather than on physical geography, though the latter was well represented in teaching and research.[92] From the early 1960s the quality of undergraduates reading the subject steadily improved, and their choice of options broadened. Academic staff grew in number and new research areas were developed, including geomorphology, urban geography, planning, third-world problems and climatology. By 1967 all tenured staff had college fellowships. The school established a research library which became one of the outstanding departmental libraries of Oxford. Geography at Oxford traditionally had close links with the city in planning traffic routes and in environmental conservation; J. N. L. Baker, Reader in Historical Geography from 1935 to 1949, became Lord Mayor of Oxford in 1974. When J. Gottmann became Professor in 1968, a long overdue modernization was introduced to the department—in undergraduate courses, numbers of teaching staff and laboratory and computing facilities.[93]

Four broad themes emerge from a survey of this vast range of scientific studies. There is, first, the persisting enthusiasm among some Oxford scientists until quite recently for improvisation and individualism, a trait that is closely linked to their belief that 'small is beautiful'. This individualism, which sometimes verged on eccentricity, emerges vividly from the career of John Randal Baker, who strongly contested J. D. Bernal's view that research should be co-ordinated and planned with the aid of the state; in 1940, together with Michael Polanyi and Sir Arthur Tansley he set up the Society for Freedom in Science.[94] The distinguished Oxford geneticist E. B. Ford, Professor of Ecological Genetics from 1963 to 1969, 'was impatient of anything that he could call an engine' and did work of the 'utmost importance with the minimum of resources and with very simple laboratory techniques'.[95] In the 1980s old hands recalled with some nostalgia the dangers almost cavalierly encountered in laboratories forty years earlier, in

[91] 'Geography: a humane study', *OM* 18 Nov. 1954, 97 (reporting Gilbert's inaugural lecture); E. W. Gilbert, *Geography as a Humane Study* (Oxford 1955).
[92] For a scorching denunciation by a former Oxford geographer of the concentration on human geography see G. Hawthorn, 'Geography', *OM* 4 Mar. 1965, 256–7.
[93] R. W. Steel and W. E. Gordon Smith, 'The Oxford school of geography since 1930', tape-recorded seminar in Linacre College, 11 May 1989.
[94] E. N. Willmer and P. C. J. Brunet, 'J. R. Baker', *BMFRS* xxxi (1985), 47–8; J. R. Baker, 'Counterblast to Bernalism', *New Statesman* 29 July 1939, 174–5. For the Society, see below, 395.
[95] *Memorial Addresses of All Souls College, Oxford* (Oxford 1989), 253.

an age without fire-doors and innocent of an awareness of the danger posed by high radioactivity and asbestos insulation. 'For normal purposes goggles and glasses were unknown', wrote E. Whittaker of his experiences as a chemistry undergraduate in the early 1940s; 'we slopped benzene around by the litre and mercury by the dish full'.[96] 'We lived in a sort of miasma of class 1 poisons', Peter Brunet recalled of the zoology laboratories at the same period.[97]

The growing complexity and cost of science gradually eroded Oxford's scientific individualism. Large and expensive co-operative research projects became common, wartime 'big science' at Oxford accelerated the trend, and new professors (Blackman in agriculture, for example, Wilkinson in nuclear physics or Krebs in biochemistry) brought in their research teams. Nor could individualism easily be reconciled with the increasing dominance of powerful and expensive apparatus which required specialized manufacture and skilled technical staff for its installation, operation and maintenance [plate 10.5]. In this context it became less and less necessary for individual senior and junior members to improvise, design and manufacture equipment.

So research in Oxford relied increasingly on the technicians. By November 1955 the 1,616 undergraduates and postgraduates and the 250 senior members who were working in the science area were buttressed by 540 technical and administrative staff.[98] Oxford's scientific achievement since 1945 owes much to a small number of outstanding technicians such as the zoology department's Percy Trotman, who began his career lighting fires at the age of 14 and ended his career with an honorary MA, as did his successor Leonard Small. Trotman was extraordinarily well-informed on where to find terrestrial invertebrates in the local countryside, and both were adept at providing specimens and slides for teaching purposes.[99] Douglas Cook, another honorary MA, came from Pye in Cambridge, and eventually took charge of the physical chemistry laboratory's mechanical and electronic workshops, making major contributions to all aspects of the laboratory's work.[100]

With the advent of nuclear physics in the late 1950s the technicians' contribution to research reached new heights. The vast expense and complexity of such research facilities as the Van de Graaf generator meant that high-grade technologists and engineers on academic salary-scales had to be introduced to maintain and operate them. Teams of professional scientists without academic duties were introduced to design, conduct and publish

[96] Letter from E. J. W. Whittaker to Brian Harrison, 3 Dec. 1989.
[97] Brunet, 'Zoology'.
[98] *OM* 10 Nov. 1955, 90.
[99] Brunet, 'Zoology'.
[100] Danby, 'Physical chemistry laboratory'.

experiments. Clerical staff grew rapidly. Laboratory and departmental administrators were needed to manage what had become a considerable enterprise. With the growing number, professionalism, specialization and unionization of technicians, much effort went into resolving issues of training, grading, wages and demarcation: in 1951, for example, eight grades and subgrades of technician are listed. Anxiety was frequently expressed about the loss of highly trained technicians to industry. Nevertheless in many cases loyalty to the University was strong; for example Thomas and Kenneth Marsland, father and son, between them spent more than seventy years employed by the University, the former in physiology and the latter in zoology.[101]

A second continuing theme is the relationship between Oxford scientists and industry. It was a many-sided relationship and cannot simply be measured by the number of industry's research contracts placed with the University. Nor can it be considered in isolation from the national research organizations already touched upon, not to mention the international agencies such as the United Nations Food and Agriculture Organization (FAO) which became increasingly involved with research in Oxford. As British industry became more science-based after the war and began to recruit more science graduates, their quality became its direct concern. Before the war only chemists and engineers were recruited directly into industry, but after the war graduates in physics, biochemistry, metallurgy, pathology, pharmacology and other sciences were required in industries such as electronics, computing, aviation, pharmaceuticals, defence research and telecommunications. Not only did the research director or his representatives seek recruits from Oxford, they often established permanent contacts with senior members. Not infrequently the recruiters were themselves former graduates of Oxford and exploited local contacts when trying to fill vacancies. Furthermore science professors frequently acted as consultants to large industrial firms.[102] Several science departments arranged annual research conferences and these were frequently over-subscribed by industrial research personnel wishing to attend.

Many Oxford scientists felt a natural interest in business, and moved freely in business circles. Sir Robert Robinson took out thirty-two chemical patents, acted as consultant for many years to ICI, and became a director of Shell Chemicals after his retirement. The geologist James Douglas was for many years adviser to the Anglo-Iranian Oil Company, and we have seen how Pressed Steel of Cowley promoted metallurgy at Oxford and how Oxford responded to the government's call in the 1950s to involve itself

---

[101] HCP 209 pt. ii (1951), 6; 233 (1959), 523–5; 235 (1960), 185–7; private communication from Mr Kenneth Marsland.
[102] Smith, *Organic Chemistry at Oxford* ii. 56.

more deeply in engineering.[103] Through multiple contacts of this sort, industry and the science departments at Oxford learned much about each other. The very large firms such as ICI or General Electric Company had their own research laboratories and during this period did not usually place specific research contracts in Oxford; but there were important exceptions to this, such as the research on gas turbines carried out jointly by the engineering science department and Rolls-Royce, and the large companies sometimes funded research of a more basic nature.

Oxford's discoveries in basic science have sometimes led to important commercial ventures. The research at Oxford on penicillin effectively gave rise to the modern antibiotics industry, but was not patented because leading medical bodies in Britain then thought it was unethical to do so, and also perhaps because it might have been difficult to specify patents of lasting value. Several American firms, by contrast, did take out patents on their own discoveries in penicillin and profited enormously from them. British attitudes to medical patents changed after the war. In 1953 the anti-bacterial substance cephalosporin C was isolated by E. P. Abraham and Guy Newton at the Dunn School. They proceeded to analyse its structure by chemical methods, and early in 1959 Abraham proposed the correct structure while on a skiing vacation in Norway. They then patented this substance and its nucleus through the National Research Development Corporation. Abraham and Newton established an important precedent by setting up charitable trusts which channelled millions of pounds from their royalties into medical, biological and chemical research and the endowment of University posts. In 1990 the cephalosporin and penicillin industries had world sales of £4.7 billion and £1.6 billion, respectively.[104]

Fundamental research on high-field magnets in the Clarendon Laboratory led Martin Wood with his wife Audrey to set up the Oxford Instrument Company, with the Laboratory's encouragement, in 1959. This became the largest manufacturer of specialized superconducting magnets in the world; in 1986 it was exporting about £1 million worth of them per week. Oxford Instruments plc is now perhaps best known for its whole-body magnetic resonance scanners.[105] On a much smaller scale E. T. Hall, director from 1955 of the Research Laboratory for Archaeology and the History of Art, was led by his research on detecting underground archaeological artefacts

[103] Todd and Cornforth, 'Robinson'; Vincent, 'Geology and mineralogy'; 272–4 above.

[104] E. P. Abraham, 'A glimpse of the early history of the cephalosporins', *Review of Infectious Diseases* i (1979); Williams, *Florey*, 307–14; E. P. Abraham in 'Academic breakthroughs', 24 Jan. 1986; E. P. Abraham to J. Roche, 12 May 1992. I am greatly indebted to Professor Abraham for an illuminating account of the history of penicillin and cephalosporin research in Oxford.

[105] Berman, 'Low temperature physics'; Richards in 'Academic breakthroughs'; A. Wood, *Oxford Instruments: Our First 21 Years* (Oxford 1980), 14–15.

into setting up a cottage industry to manufacture metal detectors.[106] On several occasions, far from the scientists failing to respond to the needs of industry, the problem was rather the other way round. Oxford scientists repeatedly found themselves forced into manufacturing equipment that would otherwise have been unobtainable. Florey had to go to the United States for help in the mass production of penicillin;[107] and in the 1960s the Enzyme Group had to go to Germany for magnetic resonance and other electronic equipment which became so essential at a crucial stage in their research. 'I do think it's absolutely pathetic', Rex Richards recalled many years later, 'that there was no manufacturer in this country interested in manufacturing this equipment'.[108] Nonetheless Oxford's wariness of applied scientific research distanced some subjects, notably engineering, from industry; in 1966 the Franks Commission recommended 'a selective, but rapid development in a number of fields of advanced technology' and warned that 'no university has ever remained for long out of touch with the life around it and stayed great'.[109]

A third theme must be the relationship between the departmentally based natural sciences and the college system. In an age of such rapid scientific expansion, tensions between the two were bound to erupt. 'We must continue to doubt if Oxford is the right place for a project of this kind', said the *Oxford Magazine* in 1963, sceptical about whether the new nuclear physics department's stress on research could be reconciled with the collegiate structure.[110] In relation to their overall numbers in Oxford, scientists remained under-represented among the fellows of colleges well into the 1970s, and were therefore under-represented in the government of the University as a whole. Of the twenty-two members of Council (sometimes described by scientists as 'the arts council') in 1964, only seven were scientists. In the same year only six of the General Board's twenty-three members represented the science faculties.[111] The imbalance on the Board was easier to rectify, and following years of energetic discussion a compromise was worked out whereby arts and science faculties were grouped in such a way as to allocate eight representatives to each.[112] Until the 1950s Oxford scientists only rarely made an appearance in the *Oxford Magazine*, and the Oxford University Press showed little of the enterprise in

[106] E. T. Hall, 'The research laboratory for archaeology and the history of art', tape-recorded seminar in Linacre College, 14 May 1991.

[107] Florey, 'Penicillin', 98.

[108] Richards in 'Academic breakthroughs'.

[109] *Franks Report* i. 35; see also i. 49.

[110] *OM* 14 Feb. 1963, 177.

[111] *Statutes* 1964, 189–91; Franks Commission, written evidence v. 71–2; OUA Proc. General Board, cviii (Michaelmas term 1964), [3], 20.

[112] OUA Proc. General Board, cxv (Hilary term 1967), [2–3], 155–69; *Gazette* xcvii (1966/7), 1680–1; *Statutes* 1969, 26.

scientific publication that was displayed during the 1950s and 1960s by Maxwell and Blackwell.[113]

Undoubtedly the topic which aroused strongest feeling among Oxford scientists with respect to the colleges was the problem of 'entitlement' to college fellowships. Some of the most distinguished Oxford scientists—for example David Lack, Nikolaas Tinbergen and Charles Elton—had little taste for a college-based social life, but the entitlement problem was not simply a social one. Not to have a college fellowship meant loss of status and academic autonomy, impoverished relations with pupils, distance from collegiate and university business and therefore isolation from Oxford's centres of corporate life. Some distinguished scientists without fellow-ships—Hugh Blaschko of pharmacology, for example—felt no resentment about being denied a college fellowship, but many saw themselves as second-class citizens. Some were embittered; the enthusiasm of others was perhaps lessened; some even sought employment elsewhere. The subject was hotly debated from the 1950s, with Simon and other distinguished scientists speaking out strongly about it.[114]

As long as the smaller schools remained outside the college system, a rival social life inevitably built up in the science area. It was to protect the colleges from this mounting challenge that the entitlement question had eventually to be tackled. Halifax House became an important lunching place for postgraduates in science without a college and for senior members whose lunch needed to be taken near the science area. In 1946 it moved into the convent building that eventually became St Antony's College, and by February 1947 50 of its 200 members were lunching daily. In 1950 it moved to houses in South Parks Road, and by 1960 it had 558 members and was serving an average of 100 lunches a day.[115] There was less scope for sociability within the laboratories themselves, though in some sub-jects—most notably in mathematics and biochemistry in the 1950s—the exchange of ideas over coffee and tea was intellectually important. And in pharmacology during the Second World War J. H. Burn (Professor 1937–59) introduced what he described as the smallest works canteen in Oxford. He presided at the head of the table, carving the joint and briefing himself on what was going on, after which a piano recital was often provided by Edith Bülbring, the refugee from Hitler who later herself became a professor.[116]

There were signs before 1970 that the colleges were going to respond constructively in the face of these problems. The collegiate structure can prove flexible, especially when collegiate advantage is involved. Some

[113] Cf below, 463–4.

[114] F. E. Simon, 'Scientists in Oxford', *OM* 24 Feb. 1955, 244–6. See also below, 713–15.

[115] *OM* 6 June 1946, 333; 6 Feb. 1947, 186; Franks Commission, written evidence iii. 75–7.

[116] H. Blaschko, 'The department of pharmacology', tape-recorded seminar in Linacre College, 14 Apr. 1990. For a memoir of Burn by W. Paton and P. Phizackerley see *Balliol College Record* 1981, 14–17; for Bülbring see *Independent* 7 July 1990, 14.

colleges (St Edmund Hall with engineering, Jesus with geography) were positively helpful when it came to getting small subjects established. They had a financial interest in attracting inexpensive fellows and boosting the number of their junior members, and there were long-term benefits to be won by stepping in where other colleges feared to tread. More importantly though, the intellectual separation between the arts and sciences, which in some ways lay at the heart of the gulf between the colleges and the science area, was well on the way to resolution.

The final theme must therefore be the changing relationship in Oxford between the arts and the sciences. Jowett in 1884 had seen 'those who, like ourselves, are entrusted with the care of ancient studies' as engaged in 'a hard battle . . . against the physical sciences which are everywhere encroaching and will certainly lower the character of knowledge if they are not counteracted'. He feared that those 'who will only believe what they can hold in their hands will be too much for us'.[117] Fears of this kind may not have been as vigorously expressed after 1914 as they were in late Victorian times, but they survived into the 1960s in covert and occasionally even in explicit forms, and unobtrusively moulded much of the colleges' resistance to 'entitlement' in those years. An editorial attack on 'bespectacled, scruffy laboratory workers' in *Isis* evoked much angry rebuttal during 1952, and in 1964 Lord Murray of Newhaven welcomed the fact that Oxford 'is about the only university in the country where the Humanities have not got an inferiority complex'.[118] More arts tutors than in Cambridge looked on science courses as narrowing, and felt uncomfortable with the hierarchies prevailing within the science area. 'There was a strong sense of the cuckoo in the nest', John Lucas recalled, 'with German-style professors [who] seemed to be . . . barons with territorial ambitions, and with an ever-increasing army of serfs'.[119]

The rapid expansion of science at Oxford after the war alarmed some in the arts. W. T. Stallybrass once allegedly asserted in Council 'that science in Oxford was continuing to expand; that had got to stop and this was where it was going to stop'.[120] Cherwell spent much of his energies in Oxford countering prejudice against science. 'For some reason', he complained in 1954, 'it is considered in many influential circles that technological competence is not really on a par socially or intellectually with a knowledge of the older subjects . . . arts men . . . seem to consider it quite natural and normal not to know how soda is made or how electricity is produced

---

[117] E. Abbott and L. Campbell, *The Life and Letters of Benjamin Jowett* (2 vols London 1897) ii. 268.
[118] *Isis* 23 Jan. 1952, 7; cf 6 Feb. 1952, 10 and 13 Feb. 1952, 16; Franks Commission, oral evidence xxix. 9.
[119] Roche, 'Natural sciences in Oxford'.
[120] Wigglesworth, 'Pringle', 530.

provided they once learned something . . . about the mistresses of Charles II or the divagations of Alcibiades'.[121] Hugh Last, the distinguished ancient historian, warding off from Brasenose potential hordes of scientists as fellows without pupils, began his assault by describing himself as 'one who believes that, whereas research is one duty of Oxford, a large part in the education of the intellectual aristocracy of the country is another'. To which F. E. Simon rejoined that the culture of the colleges was incomplete without adequate representation for science. 'Familiarity with the progress of science was regarded by an educated person as a matter of course up to the times of Humboldt and Darwin. Our present attitude is thus of rather recent origin, and is bound to be a passing phase.'[122]

Nonetheless in retrospect Jowett's views seem unduly alarmist. Two world wars helped to produce mounting recognition on the arts side that the achievements of natural science were necessary to the survival even of humane culture. Privately urging Cherwell to conscript more of the young men then in Oxford, Bowra in June 1940 thought that 'no decent fellow can concentrate on humane studies now . . . the University has no function now except to train scientists'.[123] At several points in Oxford's history between 1914 and 1970 there were moves from the arts side towards setting up courses which would open up links with the sciences—including the schemes of the early 1920s for a 'science Greats', and the philosophers' recurrent enthusiasm for finding ways of collaborating with their science colleagues. The Kneale Committee in 1965 thought undergraduates should be urged to offer mathematics in their first public examination, and that the University should encourage this by giving special help in the subject. 'Mathematics and natural science', it pointed out, 'have now succeeded to the dominant position which the classics used to have in secondary education'.[124]

The scientists too tried to build bridges. The virulence of the late Victorian controversy between science and religion no longer persisted. This was partly because Anglican intellectuals had relaxed their commitment to biblical literalism, and partly because the scientists' claims for their subjects had also moderated. Several of the new courses set up in the 1960s, together with the creation of an honour school in human sciences in 1971, reflected a widespread feeling that the gulf should be bridged between what C. P. Snow had called 'the two cultures' in his Rede lecture of 1959.[125] And far from

[121] R. V. Jones, 'Lindemann beyond the laboratory', *Notes and Records of the Royal Society* xli (1987).

[122] *OM* 10 Mar. 1955, 266, letter from Hugh Last; *OM* 5 May 1955, 304, letter from F. E. Simon.

[123] Nuffield College, Cherwell MSS, B123, fo 2, Bowra to Lindemann, 21 June (endorsed in pencil as 1941, but almost certainly 1940).

[124] [W. C. Kneale, chairman] *Report of the Committee on the Structure of the First and Second Public Examinations* (University of Oxford 1965), 73, 97.

apologizing for colleagues such as Hinshelwood—with his tastes in painting, Chinese porcelain and eastern carpets and his presidency of the Classical Association—Oxford scientists frequently expressed pride in such breadth of cultivation. When undergraduate leisure habits were surveyed in 1952, 93 per cent of all the scientists who replied said they enjoyed reading poetry and 68 per cent had read more than twelve books outside the syllabus during their previous year.[126]

Furthermore scientists were eager to bring what help they could to some of the most difficult problems confronting their colleagues in the arts. A striking illustration of this was E. T. Hall's laboratory, which was conceived in 1950 and established in 1955. It grew out of Hall's childhood taste for self-funded experimenting at home. 'I think we must make an honest woman of science', said Cherwell, launching Hall, who had contributed to the recognition of the Piltdown forgery, on the venture.[127] Cherwell hoped that the laboratory would achieve his lifelong aim of raising the prestige of science in Oxford, and this it gradually helped to do. Its work involved the detection of buried antiquities by the proton magnetometer, their non-destructive analysis by optical and x-ray fluorescent spectroscopy and, later, their dating by the carbon-14 method.[128] In 1958 the laboratory launched the journal *Archaeometry*, which soon achieved international recognition. Its best known piece of subsequent research was its contribution towards dating the Turin shroud in 1988.[129]

The philosophy of science and of mathematics and the history of science also built bridges between the arts and sciences at Oxford. In 1948 senior posts were established in the philosophy of mathematics and in the philosophy of science, filled by Friedrich Waismann and Stephen Toulmin respectively. Frank Sherwood Taylor, Curator of the Museum of the History of Science from 1940 to 1949, promoted teaching in the history of science at Oxford and helped to secure the lectureship filled by Alistair Crombie in 1953. In 1958 a joint committee for the history and philosophy of science was established, directly under the General Board. At Oxford the philosophy of science was attached to the school of philosophy, whereas the history of science was at first more isolated. Between 1957 and 1963 examined options in the history and philosophy of science were introduced into undergraduate and postgraduate courses, and by the 1960s Oxford had

[125] See for example D. L. Munby, 'Engineering and economics', *OM* 16 May 1963, 293. C. P. Snow, *The Two Cultures and the Scientific Revolution* (Cambridge 1959).

[126] H. Hartley, 'Sir Cyril Hinshelwood' in E. T. Williams and C. S. Nicholls (eds), *The Dictionary of National Biography 1961–1970*, 518; Lord Todd, 'Sir Robert Robinson' in Blake and Nicholls, *DNB 1971–80*, 731; *Isis* 5 Mar. 1952, 22–3.

[127] E. T. Hall, 'Quantitative analysis by secondary x-rays for use particularly in archaeology' (Oxford DPhil thesis 1953), 152–68; Hall, 'Research laboratory'; C. F. C. Hawkes, 'The research laboratory: its beginnings', *Archaeometry* xxviii (1986), 131–2.

[128] E. T. Hall, 'Some uses of physics in archaeology', *Year Book of the Physical Society* 1958.

[129] P. E. Damon *et al.*, 'Radiocarbon dating of the shroud of Turin', *Nature* cccxxxvii (1989).

Britain's largest graduate school in the history and philosophy of science. A Wellcome Unit for the History of Medicine was set up in Oxford in 1972, under Charles Webster; and a chair in the history of science in 1973, with Margaret Gowing as the first professor. For structural reasons, however, Cambridge was far more successful in incorporating the history and philosophy of science into its degree courses and in attracting a large body of undergraduates.[130] Although the philosophy of science failed to gain a chair, and like the history of science remained a small subject, it secured its future at Oxford in 1968 when joint honour schools were established in physics and philosophy and in mathematics and philosophy.[131] Thus by the early 1970s Oxford's students had gained—through the archaeology laboratory, the history of science and the various joint schools—opportunities for interdisciplinary study linking the arts and sciences.

With the advent of the tape-recorder in the 1950s and the personal computer in the 1980s, an ultimate technical dependence on the natural scientist became built into the very intimacies of humane scholarship. Indeed, the importance of research at Oxford is now as much emphasized in the arts faculties as in the sciences, and the scientists' long experience of team research is gaining new converts. The gulf between Oxford's two cultures had not been removed by 1970, but it was being bridged more frequently than had seemed conceivable thirty years before.

[130] A. C. Crombie, *Science, Optics and Music in Medieval and Early Modern Thought* (London and Ronceverte WVa 1990), apps b–c, 458–64; OUA Proc. General Board, lxxiv (Trinity term 1953), pp. xxvi, xxviii; lxxxii (Hilary term 1956), 223–4; lxxxix (Trinity term 1958), 120, 124–5; HCP 270 (1971), 196–201.

[131] OUA Proc. General Board, lix (1948), 16.

PART FOUR
LONG-TERM PERSPECTIVES,
1914–1970

I I

Religion

F. M. TURNER

Throughout the twentieth century, despite growing secularization in both the programmes of study and the general intellectual outlook of the University, Oxford religion maintained a significant and noted physical and social as well as spiritual presence in the life of the University. Before motor cars and buses dominated Oxford's streets, the sound of bells from the cathedral, churches and colleges reminded the city and University of their religious institutions. In the college halls grace was recited before and after meals. Indeed in 1932 F. R. Barry observed that 'there is probably no place in the world where such lavish provision is made both officially and unofficially for the teaching and practice of religion' as in Oxford. Only Cambridge among British universities could boast a clerical presence matching that of Oxford. In addition to the college chaplains, significant numbers of clergy were attached to the cathedral, the university church, Pusey House, the Roman Catholic chaplaincy, the Anglican theological colleges, the three nonconformist colleges, the Oxford Pastorate and the various city congregations [figure 11.1]. There were also clergy in the several faculties, as well as visiting preachers in the University. The *Oxford Magazine* once quipped, 'there can surely be no spot in Christendom, with the possible exception of Malta, which is exposed to such a concentration of clerics'.[1]

Oxford's religious character often evoked comment. In Evelyn Waugh's *Brideshead Revisited* Charles Ryder, describing his journey among crowds of Sunday worshippers in Oxford during the 1920s, remarked, 'so through a world of piety I made my way to Sebastian'. And that journey led Ryder into the unfamiliar world of Roman Catholicism. Not a few students acquired a deeper understanding of Christianity at Oxford. Sir John Betjeman recalled:

[1] F. R. Barry, 'Religion', *Handbook* 1932, 278; *OM* 30 May 1946, 322. R. W. Macan, *Religious Changes in Oxford during the Last Fifty Years* (Oxford 1917) and V. H. H. Green, *Religion at Oxford and Cambridge* (London 1964) are important sources for religion at Oxford in this period.

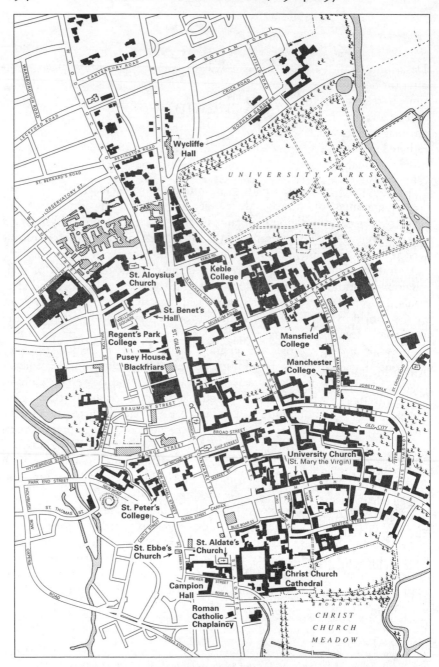

FIGURE 11.1   THE LOCATION OF RELIGIOUS INSTITUTIONS IN
OXFORD, 1914–1970

Despite my frequent lapses into lust,
Despite hypocrisy, revenge and hate,
I learned at Pusey House the Catholic faith.

Describing in the early 1960s his study of literature during and immediately after the Second World War, John Wain observed: 'it was impossible, at that time, to take in "Oxford" without taking in, if not exactly the Christian faith, at least a very considerable respect for Christianity . . . Everybody to whom an imaginative and bookish youth naturally looked up, every figure who radiated intellectual glamour of any kind, was in the Christian camp. I knew more rationalists, atheists, and people who were simply indifferent to religious questions in Stoke-on-Trent than I ever met at Oxford.' In 1952 and again in 1978, polls in *Isis* reported widespread church attendance, though on both occasions the journal insisted that religious ideas played little part in the lives of students.[2] Despite such disclaimers, all polls of religious attendance indicated higher attendance in Oxford than in Great Britain as a whole. Furthermore, observers frequently stood amazed at the continued vitality of evangelical groups bent on actively converting students to the Christian faith.

Within twentieth-century Oxford, religion became one constituent of a pluralistic university and in turn became more pluralistic itself. From the late nineteenth century, Oxford witnessed a renewed gathering of the religious faithful as nonconformists, Roman Catholics, high-church and evangelical Anglicans, and Jews established their own distinctive institutions and societies. Although the Anglican presence remained dominant, there were more varieties of religious devotion in Oxford during this century than at any time in the previous history of the University.

The Congregationalists posed the first challenge to the Anglican academic monopoly in the city by opening Mansfield College in October 1886.[3] The institution, previously known as Spring Hill College and located in Birmingham, trained Congregational ministers. Denominational leaders hoped that locating the College near the University would permit its graduates to enjoy greater academic respect. They also hoped that an alternative religious fellowship would discourage nonconformist undergraduates from drifting towards Anglicanism via the college chapels. Mansfield, which was not part of the University, required its students to matriculate in one of the official Oxford colleges. Consequently Mansfield students became part of the University while the College itself remained

[2] E. A. St J. Waugh, *Brideshead Revisited: The Sacred and Profane Memories of Captain Charles Ryder* (Boston Mass. 1945 edn), 60; John Betjeman, *Summoned by Bells* (Cambridge Mass. 1960), 83; J. B. Wain, *Sprightly Running: Part of an Autobiography* (London 1962), 142; *Isis* 23 Jan. 1952, 21; 2 May 1978, 20.

[3] W. B. Selbie, 'Fifty years at Oxford', *Congregational Quarterly* 1938, 282–90; W. T. P. Davies, *Mansfield College: Its History, Aims and Achievements* (Oxford 1947); *OM* 14 June 1962, 370.

separate. The strains on the University during the First World War allowed Mansfield's senior members to receive greater recognition and to participate in the faculty of theology.

Mansfield College certainly fulfilled its religious and intellectual promise during its first half-century. Its neo-gothic chapel became a major centre for nonconformist worship. Its notable scholars included A. M. Fairbairn, W. B. Selbie, C. H. Dodd, Nathaniel Micklem, C. J. Cadoux, J. S. Whale and George Caird. Furthermore, Mansfield looked intellectually to both Germany and America. Its tutors prided themselves on an open and undogmatic approach to scripture that is best epitomized by Dodd's contribution to Cambridge biblical scholarship after 1935. Mansfield also embodied the spirit of ecumenism throughout this period, most especially under the leadership of Nathaniel Micklem. Not until 1955 however, when it was designated a permanent private hall, did Mansfield become integrated with the University. This allowed the admission of non-theological students and so overcame the financial difficulties occasioned by rising costs and declining numbers of students intending to become ministers.[4] Although Mansfield has subsequently lost much of its early distinctive character, it has moved further in an ecumenical direction and has formed close relations with American Lutherans. Its traditional open approach to religion allowed Mansfield to become the first society to appoint a woman chaplain, Justine Wyatt, in 1980.[5]

In 1893 Manchester College, the major Unitarian institution for the training of ministers, moved to Oxford. Its relationship to the University went through a number of stages. Between 1901 and 1905 it functioned as a permanent private hall. Thereafter it stood for over half a century as an independent entity with insecure finances. In 1960 it tried unsuccessfully to regain its status as a permanent private hall.[6] There were so few students aiming for the Unitarian ministry that in 1965 the College changed its mission from that of training clergy to that of serving 'the Unitarian Movement and Liberal Religion in the field of education, nationally and internationally' and to relating 'religion to other disciplines and studies'.[7] In the same year the University granted the College status as a society or institution for higher study. Two years later it was permitted to grant diplomas but not degrees.

---

[4] M. D. Johnson, *The Dissolution of Dissent, 1850–1918* (New York 1987), 300; *Mansfield College Magazine* July 1955, 272–5.

[5] Mansfield was still a permanent private hall rather than a full college in 1980; Nuffield was to be the first college to appoint a woman as chaplain.

[6] *OM* 31 May 1962, 338–9; *Report of Manchester College, Oxford* 20 June 1949, 9; 24 June 1960, 7; 21 June 1961, 6. The University denied the request on the grounds that it had told the University Grants Committee that it wanted expansion limited to the completion of St Catherine's College.

[7] *Report of Manchester College, Oxford* 22 June 1965, 4.

Despite institutional ambiguity and continued financial uncertainty Manchester College made significant contributions to Oxford's religious life. L. P. Jacks, its Principal from 1915 to 1931, became a major spokesman for liberal religion in Britain. The College sponsored publication of the *Hibbert Journal*, which from its founding in 1902 until at least the middle of the century was one of the major journals of religion and philosophy in the English-speaking world. Manchester College's library housed one of the most important theological collections in Oxford. With the establishment of the Religious Experience Research Unit in 1969, later called the Alister Hardy Centre, the College fostered study of the psychology of religion. The College's chapel, under separate governance, served as the meeting place for the city of Oxford's Unitarian congregation.

Baptists established an institution in Oxford in 1927 when Regent's Park College, a Baptist seminary, moved to St Giles'.[8] The College had previously operated in London, and for ten years it continued to function in both cities. The students at Regent's Park College initially obtained membership of the University by matriculating through St Catherine's Society, but became more fully assimilated in 1957 when the College was designated a permanent private hall. From the beginning there was close co-operation with Mansfield College. Regent's Park College also reached an agreement with the New Road Baptist church that it would not form a distinct congregation.

Regent's Park College brought to Oxford as its Principal Henry Wheeler Robinson, the most outstanding British Old Testament scholar of his generation.[9] He was immediately appointed examiner by the University's faculty of theology and enjoyed the support and friendship of senior members of the University. In 1934 he became Reader in Biblical Criticism and in 1937 served as the first nonconformist chairman of the faculty of theology. He lectured on the Old Testament and was the Old Testament tutor for Mansfield College. Throughout his years at Oxford Robinson published prolifically and established himself as the most important biblical scholar in the University.

By the second half of the twentieth century the nonconformist colleges confronted very considerable difficulties in finance and self-identity. In no small measure these reflected the larger problems of the ministerial vocation and of the Free Churches in British religious life, as well as the difficulties of mainstream denominational protestantism within the larger Christian framework. Despite these difficulties the nonconformist colleges had made a contribution to Oxford that neither their founders nor their critics could

---

[8] R. A. Cooper, *From Stepney to St. Giles': The Story of Regent's Park College, 1810–1960* (London 1960); *OM* 23 May 1957, 457; 21 Nov. 1957, 134–5.
[9] E. A. Payne, *Henry Wheeler Robinson: A Memoir* (London 1946), 80–95; *OM* 24 May 1945, 262–4.

initially have envisaged. They brought to Oxford a deep tradition of theological and biblical scholarship that would otherwise have been missing. There can be no question that after the death of S. R. Driver in 1914 the most important biblical scholarship in Oxford was associated with the nonconformist colleges. Only R. H. Lightfoot and B. H. Streeter among Anglican scholars rivalled the Free Church scholars in the level of biblical scholarship and familiarity with continental theology.[10] Paradoxically the nonconformist colleges, seen at first as culturally provincial, became the most outward-looking and international of Oxford's religious institutions. It was to the nonconformist colleges that the most important theologians and religious commentators from outside the British Isles—such as William James, Josiah Royce, Henri Bergson, Albert Schweitzer and Reinhold Niebuhr—came to lecture. The nonconformist colleges also had the closest contact with the Scottish universities. Without the presence of those colleges, twentieth-century Oxford would have been more remote from developments in the reformed tradition of Germany and the United States.

Roman Catholics officially returned to Oxford after the English bishops and the Holy See removed in 1896 the prohibition of 1867 that had prevented Roman Catholics from attending Oxford and Cambridge.[11] The decision arose in response to pressures from aristocratic and upper middle-class Roman Catholics who wanted their sons to enter the mainstream of English life. Unlike the protestant nonconformists, the Roman Catholics did not look to Oxford as a location for the training of their clergy. Roman Catholic undergraduates entered the University directly through the existing colleges rather than through a distinctly Roman Catholic foundation, as some had advocated during the second half of the nineteenth century. The faith and religious education of Oxford Roman Catholic students were guided by a Roman Catholic chaplaincy under the authority of the Universities' Catholic Education Board, whose brief included Cambridge as well as Oxford.

By appointing Canon Charles Kennard as the first chaplain, the Board indicated its determination to permit no individual Roman Catholic order to dominate the chaplaincy. Nonetheless several orders quickly appeared in Oxford.[12] The Jesuits established a hall in 1896 (designated Campion Hall in 1918), and the Benedictines established theirs in 1897. Both were granted the status of permanent private halls in 1918. Greyfriars received similar status only in 1957, though the Franciscans had returned to Oxford in 1910. Blackfriars was established in 1921 and became an important centre for

---

[10] D. Nineham, 'R. H. Lightfoot and the significance of biblical criticism', *Theology* lxxxviii (1985).

[11] V. A. McClelland, *English Roman Catholics and Higher Education, 1830–1903* (Oxford 1973), 217, 369–87. Roman Catholic sons had attended the University during the years of the ban by receiving special permission from either the Pope or a bishop.

[12] McClelland, 401–5; *OM* 28 May 1936, 628–9; 28 Nov. 1957, 150–2.

Roman Catholic preaching and scholarship, though it did not become a permanent private hall. Each of these halls linked the University with international Roman Catholic scholarship and theological discussion.

The Roman Catholic chaplaincy became a major institution of Oxford religious life. Its earliest chaplains were not especially notable. One, Father Maturin, died on the *Lusitania*. In 1916 his successor 'Mugger' Barnes (1915–26) acquired the property at the corner of Rose Place and St Aldate's known as the Old Palace. The key element in establishing the character of the Roman Catholic chaplaincy was the appointment in 1926 of Ronald Knox. Son of an evangelical Anglican bishop, Knox had been at Eton and Balliol and was a former chaplain of Trinity College, where he had displayed high-church sympathies and antipathy towards modern biblical criticism. He was received into the Roman Catholic Church in September 1917 and was ordained two years later. He then worked for over seven years at St Edmund's, Old Hall, in Hertfordshire. In 1926 through the efforts of F. F. Urquhart, a fellow of Balliol and the first Roman Catholic don at Oxford since the reformation, Knox was appointed to Oxford's Roman Catholic chaplaincy.[13] During his thirteen years his ministerial charges grew from 125 to about 170 and he opened a new chapel which was funded by royalties from his detective stories. Only during the Second World War were female undergraduates admitted to the congregation at the Old Palace.

Knox, like the Roman Catholic chaplains before and after him, saw his duty as providing pastoral care and religious instruction rather than promoting conversions. Although Knox had taught in the University, was a scholarly figure and wrote widely while he was chaplain, he was not admitted to the faculty of theology. The issue seems not even to have arisen. No Roman Catholic chaplain would be so admitted until Father Roderick Strange in 1980. Knox's sharp sense of humour and gift for witty discourse perhaps brought him as much influence in the University as did his faith. His contribution to the 'funny' Eights Week debates at the Oxford Union carried his reputation to parts of the University never touched by his sermons. In 1939 Knox resigned the chaplaincy to undertake the translation of the Vulgate into English. His successor was Father A. De Zulueta.

Between the wars, when Roman Catholicism enjoyed something of a renaissance among intellectuals and upper-class English families, Father Martin C. D'Arcy SJ provided the most vigorous intellectual defence of Roman Catholicism in the University. Educated at Oxford during the First World War, he returned to Campion Hall in 1927 and became its Master in 1933. Unlike the Roman Catholic chaplains he actively received converts, the most famous of whom was Evelyn Waugh. Eager to make the intellectual case for Roman Catholicism, he wrote widely and urged his Jesuit students

---

[13] E. Waugh, *The Life of the Right Reverend Ronald Knox* (London 1959).

towards academic excellence. Determined that the Jesuits should study in a proper architectural setting, he commissioned Sir Edwin Lutyens to design the new buildings of Campion Hall in Brewer Street.[14] By the mid-1930s D'Arcy had achieved an international reputation and was widely honoured by Roman Catholics in the United States. Yet D'Arcy, like Knox, represented an older kind of English Roman Catholicism that was associated with the traditional élite Catholic schools and was attached to the older liturgies, much of which was to change after the Second World War.

The increased diversity of post-war students markedly transformed the mission of the chaplaincy, which like other Oxford religious institutions prospered in the middle of the century. The admission of women to mass, in addition to the general expansion in the number of undergraduates, helped to increase numbers of Roman Catholic undergraduates being served to over eight hundred. Beginning in 1947 with the appointment of Valentine Elwes, Roman Catholic chaplains were no longer converts. Elwes had served in the war and identified easily with those undergraduates who had also seen wartime action. In 1966, under the leadership of Father Michael Hollings, the chaplaincy opened new buildings designed not only for church services but also for a whole array of student activity.[15] Hollings brought a wider variety of preaching and liturgical innovation to the chaplaincy.

The Roman Catholic chaplaincy experienced competition from other Catholic bodies. Some Roman Catholic students attended mass at the church of St Aloysius. Others sought out the preaching at Blackfriars. The most serious challenge occurred in 1961 when representatives of the Spanish Roman Catholic organization Opus Dei arrived in Oxford and informed Father Hollings that they had come to minister to Roman Catholics. This group represented an extremely conservative mode of Roman Catholicism and intended to establish a Roman Catholic college. The Vice-Chancellor consulted Hollings and the plan was rejected. However, Opus Dei purchased Grandpont House and retained a presence in Oxford.[16]

The Roman Catholic chaplaincy was the most successful religious institution of twentieth-century Oxford. Roman Catholic students, unlike their Anglican counterparts, usually arrived at Oxford with some religious training; the chaplaincy could build on this and help students to interrelate their religious and university experiences. Furthermore the chaplaincy was the single major centre of Roman Catholic life in the University; it provided an alternative community to that of the colleges but did not compete directly with them. After the Second Vatican Council the Roman Catholic chaplains,

[14] A. Oswald, 'Campion Hall, Oxford', *Country Life* 27 June 1936, 676–91; 'Campion Hall, Oxford', *Architect and Building News* 26 June 1936.
[15] B. Nicholas, 'The new Roman Catholic chaplaincy building', *OM* 3 Hilary 1966, 237–9.
[16] *Times* 6 Feb. 1961, 10; 7 Feb. 1961, 9; *OM* 4 Mar. 1965, 258–9.

such as Walter Drumm, Crispian Hollis and Roderick Strange, became much more involved with the colleges. By the middle of the 1980s a Roman Catholic mass had been celebrated in virtually every college chapel. From the standpoint of the Roman Catholic Church, no doubt the most important achievement of the Oxford chaplaincy was its contribution of more vocations to the priesthood than any British diocese.

The Jewish Society was founded in 1904, succeeding various Jewish organizations of the previous ten or more years. Jewish students worshipped in the synagogue in Richmond Road.[17] Apart from one brief period there was no resident Jewish chaplain. Various senior members of the University who gave instruction in rabbinics or Hebrew literature provided some pastoral care for Jewish students. The most notable of these was Herbert Loewe, who held a lecturership in rabbinics during the 1920s, and Cecil Roth, who was appointed to the readership in post-biblical Jewish studies established in 1938. In 1953 the Hillel Foundation made available funds to expand the premises to provide facilities for kosher meals. In 1974, through a national appeal, the Oxford Jewish Centre was erected and used jointly by the Oxford University Jewish Society and Oxford's Jewish congregation. During the late 1980s the American Lubavitch movement sponsored the establishment of a Chabad House on the Cowley Road with the student group known as the L'Chaim Society, now based in St Aldates.

Exogenous religious movements with little or no denominational base also added to the pluralism of Oxford religious life. The most significant of these was the Oxford Group movement, founded by the American Lutheran evangelist Frank Buchman and later known as Moral Re-Armament.[18] Buchman first appeared in Oxford in 1921. By the middle of the decade his message had attracted a significant following among undergraduates and local clergy. In 1928 a small number of such Oxford undergraduates visited South Africa where they bore witness to their faith. It was the press coverage of this trip that first used the description 'Oxford Group', a name that was to survive for many years despite protests from members of the University.

Though always controversial within the University and English religious life, the Oxford Group prospered and by the end of the 1930s it had become a worldwide movement of considerable influence. At Oxford and elsewhere Buchman and his supporters organized small groups of undergraduates within which they encouraged participants to speak freely about their most

[17] R. Loewe, 'The evolution of Jewish student feeding arrangements in Oxford and Cambridge' in D. Noy and I. Ben-Ami (eds), *Studies in the Cultural Life of the Jews in England* (Jerusalem 1975), 165–84. See also D. M. Lewis, *The Jews of Oxford* (Oxford Jewish Congregation, 1992).
[18] G. F. Allen, 'The Groups in Oxford' in R. H. S. Crossman (ed.), *Oxford and the Groups* (Oxford 1934); D. C. Belden, 'The origins and development of the Oxford Group' (Oxford DPhil thesis 1975); W. H. Clark, *The Oxford Group: Its History and Significance* (New York 1951), 37–83; *OM* 9 Nov. 1933, 170–2; 18 Jan. 1934, 338; 1 Feb. 1934, 387–9; 7 Feb. 1935, 347.

intimate concerns. The Group sought to change individual lives through a commitment to Christian living and to the pursuit of God's personal guidance by following Buchman's five Cs: confidence, confession, conviction, conversion and continuance. The Groupers, as the *Oxford Magazine* called Buchman's followers, vowed commitment to four absolutes: honesty, purity, unselfishness and love. The Group movement also organized 'house parties'. These began as short retreats held in individuals' homes and then became small conferences housed in Oxford colleges. By the mid-1930s several thousand people had attended these gatherings.[19] The Oxford Group attracted not only undergraduates but also significant senior members of the University. These included Julian Thornton-Duesbury, chaplain of Corpus Christi College and later Master of St Peter's, L. W. Grensted, Nolloth Professor of the Philosophy of the Christian Religion, and Canon B. H. Streeter, Provost of Queen's. The Oxford Group continued its activities in the University well into the 1960s but never regained the influence it had enjoyed before the war.

The protestant nonconformists, the Roman Catholics, the Jews and the Oxford Group entered a university where religion was and continued to be dominated by the Church of England. Oxford has enjoyed a more intimate relationship with the established church in the twentieth century than has Cambridge. Far more twentieth-century bishops have been educated at Oxford than at Cambridge, which can claim only two of the nine twentieth-century archbishops of Canterbury—and even they (Ramsey and Coggan) were trained at one of Oxford's theological colleges. Archbishop Carey is the first to have been educated at neither university. There can be little doubt that their common educational background established a sense of community and shared personal values among these Anglican leaders. In 1944 Oxford colleges were responsible for 504 livings and Cambridge colleges for only 263, and the population with whose spiritual welfare the two universities were charged was similarly divided. Oxford's faculty of theology also supplied many members of the various church commissions. Even in controversy and tragedy the special relationship obtained, as witnessed in 1987 by the suicide of the Reverend Gareth Bennett of New College when it was revealed that he had written the anonymous attack on Archbishop Runcie and Anglican theological liberalism in the introduction to *Crockford's Clerical Directory*.[20]

Although Oxford's Anglicans were of the same church, they were not all of the same faith. Each section of the Church of England had outposts in and

[19] G. Lean, *On the Tail of a Comet: The Life of Frank Buchman* (Colorado Springs Colo 1988), 159–62.

[20] W. D. Rubinstein, 'Education and the social origins of British élites 1880–1970', *Past and Present* no. 112 (Aug. 1986), 191; *OM* 4 May 1944, 223–4; *Observer* 13 Dec. 1987, 9; *Guardian* 17 Mar. 1988, 3.

around Oxford. Wycliffe Hall served to train evangelical clergy. Ripon Hall was associated with theological modernism, especially under the leadership of H. D. A. Major. Cuddesdon produced clergy with a high-church orientation, as did St Stephen's House. The Cowley Fathers of the Society of St John the Evangelist were also based in Oxford.

The various Anglican parties attempted to influence undergraduate religious experience. Keble College had opened in 1870 to buttress the Tractarian movement, but in the twentieth century its mission became somewhat diluted. As early as the 1930s non-Anglican students were admitted. In 1952 a constitutional revision made Keble a full college of the University and enabled fellows of any religious persuasion, or none, to join the governing body. In 1969 the wardenship became open to laymen—though the first lay warden, Christopher Ball, was not appointed until 1980. Yet despite these changes, for decade after decade until the middle of the century Keble College produced more students reading for degrees in theology than any other college. In that respect the ethos of its founders remained an abiding influence.

The second high-church institution dating from the Victorian period was Pusey House, founded in 1884 around Dr Pusey's library. Fearing that further secularization and university reform might lead to the closing of college chapels, its founders intended Pusey House to supply both a pastoral and a scholarly presence. It became a major centre for high-church apologetics and patristic scholarship. Charles Gore and Darwell Stone emerged during the first two decades of the century as defenders of Anglican orthodoxy against theological modernism. Stone was also a major Anglo-Catholic spokesman on subjects such as marriage, the eucharist and revision of the Prayer Book, and was the first editor of the *Lexicon of Patristic Greek*. F. L. Cross continued Stone's patristic scholarship and founded the important Oxford quadrennial conference on patristic studies; he also edited the *Oxford Dictionary of the Christian Church*. During Stone's principalship, between 1910 and 1926, Pusey House constructed new buildings on St Giles', including a new chapel which soon functioned as an Anglican alternative to the college chapels. More than any other institution in Oxford the chapel of Pusey House introduced a broad variety of Anglican opinion into the University. Pusey House thus exposed the University to the wider world of Anglicanism in the same manner that the nonconformist colleges opened Oxford to European and American reformed theology. Again like the nonconformist colleges, Pusey House has in recent years been short of funds.

Curiously, Anglican evangelicalism has been to Oxford religious life in the present century what the high-church movement was in the last. During the second half of the nineteenth century the churches of St Aldate, St Peter-le-Bailey and St Ebbe provided the basis for what became a determined evangelical ministry to the University.[21] In 1893 these churches helped to establish the Oxford Pastorate, which provided evangelical chaplains to supplement the work both of college chaplains and of the city churches. A. C. Christopher, rector of St Aldate's from 1859 to 1905, laid the foundations for the extraordinary later influence of that church.

In 1923 Bishop Francis Chavasse retired from the diocese of Liverpool and returned to live in Oxford, where he had previously been rector of St Peter-le-Bailey. He hoped to found an evangelical college, but it was his son Christopher Chavasse, then rector of St Aldate's who, with major financial support from Percy Warrington, actually established St Peter's College.[22] Controversy inevitably arose over whether it was advisable to establish a college representing the views of a single party within the Church of England. Keble College, of course, presented the counter-example. Convocation approved St Peter's as a permanent private hall on 29 January 1929. Evangelicals welcomed a new religious foundation, while secular academics applauded the provision of additional rooms and the reclaiming of important mid-city territory for the University. The finances of St Peter's remained uncertain until 1936, when Lord Nuffield gave the College £50,000. In 1961 it became a fully fledged college. Despite the hopes of its founders, St Peter's did not really become a citadel of evangelicalism. Its chaplains and early fellows remained of that outlook, and there were close relations between St Peter's and Wycliffe Hall; however, the character of undergraduate life and the requirement for academic freedom did not allow evangelicalism to flourish in a college setting any more than high-churchmanship had flourished at Keble.

Throughout the University the evangelicals diverged more completely from secular intellectual activity than did any other religious group. Consequently evangelical Christianity grew in Oxford primarily through the activities of groups outside the University and its colleges. Many of those groups saw themselves as being in direct competition with the values and intellectual outlook of the University's dons in general and the faculty of theology in particular. The evangelicals opposed theological liberalism no less than intellectual secularism.

The most persistent evangelical influences stemmed from the churches of St Aldate and St Ebbe (St Peter-le-Bailey having been merged with the other parishes) in conjunction with external evangelical groups. Those churches grasped better than any other religious group in Oxford the value of organization and a sense of community. During the 1960s and 1970s, for

[21] J. S. Reynolds, *The Evangelicals at Oxford 1735–1871: Record of an Unchronicled Movement with the Record Extended to 1905* (Appleford Oxon. 1975), separately paginated section entitled 'Additional comments', 52–81.
[22] E. H. F. Smith, *St. Peter's: The Founding of an Oxford College* (Gerrards Cross 1978).

example, young evangelicals gathered together for conferences at religious camps before coming to Oxford. Once they had arrived, other students attending St Aldate's made their acquaintance and saw that they came to the services. Some remained there; others went to St Ebbe's, which many evangelicals regarded as the better church for growth in the faith. The various rectors of St Aldate's did what no one else, with the exception perhaps of the Roman Catholic chaplaincy, achieved: they made religion interesting, emotionally warm and intensely personal while providing a distinct community of faith. As a result their Sunday services attracted hundreds of Oxford students, senior members and staff while the university church and the college chapels generally experienced a severe decline in attendance. Furthermore, without apology and with zestful enthusiasm the rectors of St Aldate's, most importantly Michael Green, attacked the liberal theology emerging from Oxford's faculty of theology. At the same time the evangelical emphasis on the Bible led more than one member of the faculty of theology to write books in response.[23] St Aldate's over the years also reached out to the international evangelical world; it brought the American evangelists Dwight Moody and Billy Graham to Oxford, Moody coming in 1882 and 1892 and Graham in 1954, 1955 and in the 1980s.[24]

Within the University the faculty of theology was closely tied to the Church of England and the college chaplaincies. Several of the major chairs of theology remained tied to canonries in Christ Church, which guaranteed male and Anglican occupants. Separation proved difficult, as with the ultimately successful secularization of the regius professorship of Hebrew in 1960.[25] The provision of instruction by college chaplains also presented difficulties, as their appointment reflected the concern of the colleges with pastoral care rather than theological teaching. In the early 1960s some colleges appointed non-academic chaplains for five-year terms. Henry Chadwick, then Regius Professor of Divinity, tried to get the General Board to appoint two lecturers independent of the colleges to the faculty of theology. His successor, Maurice Wiles, eventually secured three such appointments. Because they were not tied to collegiate chaplaincies, these posts were open to a significantly wider field of applicants, including women.

Non-Anglicans had been free to take the honour school in theology from its inception in 1870, but they were able to contribute directly to Oxford theology only from the First World War, when virtually all the senior members of Mansfield College and Manchester College were admitted to the faculty of theology. This nonconformist presence among the University's

---

[23] *Isis* 27 Nov. 1980, 19; M. Green (ed.), *The Truth of God Incarnate* (London 1977); D. Nineham, *The Use and Abuse of the Bible* (London 1976); J. Barr, *Fundamentalism* (London 1977); J. Barr, *Holy Scripture: Canon, Authority, Criticism* (Oxford 1983); J. Barr, *Escaping Fundamentalism* (London 1984).

[24] Green, *Religion at Oxford and Cambridge*, 357; *OM* 24 Nov. 1955, 134–5.

[25] *OM* 12 Nov. 1959, 73–4; 26 Nov. 1959, 105; 3 Dec. 1959, 117, 123–4; 28 Jan. 1960, 156.

teachers and the subsequent admission of non-Anglicans to divinity degrees (the BD and DD) represented a sharp change. During 1912 and 1913 the faculty of theology had proposed that non-Anglicans be admitted to divinity degrees and that the study of theology be brought closer to the study of religion in general. The reform failed in Convocation by a two-to-one majority because of concerns for churchmanship and fears of endangering the Christian faith in the University setting. The exclusiveness of divinity degrees was finally breached under the leadership of A. C. Headlam, Regius Professor of Divinity from 1918 to 1923. A new statute, proposed in 1919 and enacted in 1920, differed from the earlier proposal by affirming specifically that the degree was one in Christian theology. Ecumenical Christianity had triumphed over both Anglican exclusiveness and detached academic religious studies.[26] The faculty of theology and its degrees became and remained distinctly inter-denominational, but Christian.

As illustrated by its continued ties to the Church of England, by its dependence upon the college chaplains and by the events of 1912 and 1913, the twentieth-century faculty of theology lacked full independence. Interference might arise from both avowed believers and non-believers. In 1975, for example, Congregation rejected a proposal by the faculty to establish an alternative course in theology while preserving the traditional one. The new alternative would have abandoned the insistence on Greek, lessened biblical requirements and emphasized modern theology and church history. The goal was to attract more students to theology by making Greek optional. It was defeated by an alliance of Christians resisting the reduced emphasis on the Bible, non-Christians opposed to making the degree in theology more attractive, and teachers of elementary Greek.

Reflecting the lingering Anglican orientation, Oxford's syllabus in theology remained throughout the century very much directed towards scripture and the early centuries of the church. In 1917 the subjects treated in the honour school of theology included the holy scriptures, dogmatic and symbolic theology, ecclesiastical history and the fathers, the Hebrew of the Old Testament, the philosophy of religion, liturgies, archaeology and sacred criticism, and English ecclesiastical history. Neither the philosophy of religion nor the study of Hebrew were required; nor were modern theology or modern church history. By 1952 Christian ethics and the comparative study of religion had been added as possible areas of study with recommended readings from writers such as Kierkegaard, Berdyaev and Brunner—Niebuhr and Maritain being added the next year. Yet not until 1962 was even an optional paper on contemporary theology introduced. In

[26] OM 24 Apr. 1913, 280; see also OM 7 Mar. 1912, 252; 1 May 1913, 296; 28 Nov. 1919, 123, 210; R. Jasper, Arthur Cayley Headlam: Life and Letters of a Bishop (London 1960), 126–34.

1963 further modifications to the optional sections of the syllabus transformed it so that it resembled that of a religious studies department. Yet as late as 1971 Maurice Wiles, newly appointed Regius Professor of Divinity, could observe: 'while it may no longer be possible to study theology as if the world came into existence in 4004 B. C., it is still possible in Oxford—by a judicious, or rather injudicious, selection of papers which is fortunately not very common—to do so as if the world went out of existence in A. D. 461'.[27] Later revisions of the syllabus which took effect in 1976, 1979 and 1988 introduced requirements for Hebrew translations, modern church history and modern theological and ethical thought. Without these additions the programme would have more nearly resembled the study of early church history than a training in modern Christian theology.

Many twentieth-century observers criticized the honour school of theology as an academically soft alternative to the school of literae humaniores. In 1930, responding to these concerns, B. H. Streeter noted that future ordinands were warned that the school might cause them to lose their faith without at the same time providing real mental education. Recognizing that the degree in theology required less philosophical training and a lower level of attainment in both Greek and Latin, Streeter nonetheless pointed to the linguistic, historical and cultural value of the holy scriptures, and on that ground described the theological programme as 'literally a *miniature* Greats'. Although candidates in theology were admittedly weaker than those in Greats, many had read for some other honour school and the close relationship between their theological study and their vocation meant, according to Streeter, that 'the weak man who takes Theology has the spur of a keen and continuing interest in his subject'.[28] Presumably even Streeter did not confuse interest with intelligence.

Later concerns arose over whether the faculty of theology could function in a fully disinterested academic fashion. David Jenkins, then chaplain of Queen's College and later bishop of Durham, clearly articulated this dilemma in 1963 when he explained in a symposium: 'the teaching members of the faculty are acutely aware that the "justification" of their subject must lie strictly in the academic sphere, in the fact that the subject matter is important historically and culturally, whatever personal view may be taken of the Christian *faith*, and in the preservation and practice of a rigorous academic discipline, which allows no questions to be foreclosed by faith, and which requires them always to be open to all available facts and challenges.' In reality the pedagogical mission of the faculty was directed primarily to

[27] M. Wiles, *Jerusalem, Athens, and Oxford: An Inaugural Lecture Delivered before the University of Oxford on 18 May, 1971* (Oxford 1971), 21.

[28] *OM* 12 June 1930, 850–4, quotations at p. 851. There is some evidence to support the view that theology was an academically soft option. In Dr Greenstein's analysis of the data in HUD, theology appears as one of the few honour schools with a statistically significant number of fourth-class honours men.

ordinands and was academically unclear, and its result was considered
unsatisfactory. Jenkins observed that the 'present practice in the Theology
faculty at Oxford is not constructive enough for believers and not open and
relevant enough for unbelievers'.[29] The passage of time did not fully resolve
these difficulties.

As a percentage of all Oxford finalists, students reading for the honour
school of theology declined, but their absolute numbers were maintained at
more than 50 throughout the 1930s and 1950s. The high levels of the 1950s
reflect the generally friendly climate for religion in the University during
that decade. The subsequent stabilizing in overall numbers masks a change
of considerable long-term significance that is also found in other subjects:
the gradual shift, beginning in the 1960s, towards equalizing the take-up of
the subject between men and women. From only 6 per cent of theology
finalists in the 1960s, women's percentage almost doubled in each of the next
two decades, so that by the mid-1980s it had reached a quarter. Theology's
overall numbers were being kept up only by an incursion of women.[30] Up to
the 1960s finalists in theology came most often from Keble College, followed
by Jesus, Exeter, St Edmund Hall and St John's. By the middle of the
century both Oriel and St Peter's had begun to contribute significant
numbers, while Christ Church and Wadham's numbers declined.

Oxford philosophy deeply affected Oxford theology. Idealism and the
influence of literae humaniores informed theological speculation on the
incarnation and atonement. Later, logical positivism raised doubts about the
possibility of pursuing metaphysical speculation. In that regard A. J. Ayer
was as important for Oxford theology as for Oxford philosophy. By
contrast, however, formal Oxford academic theology did not touch deeply
the religious or intellectual life of the University, the Church of England, or
the wider Christian community. There was only occasional theological
controversy, as when Foundations, edited by B. H. Streeter and with
contributions from other future Anglican leaders, was published in 1912.[31]
In 1977 The Myth of God Incarnate, a collection with several Oxford
contributors, again stirred theological debate.[32] Such controversies were
rare.

Oxford's theological scholarship made little significant impact on western
theological speculation or religious observance. Kenneth Kirk's The Vision

[29] D. Jenkins, 'Oxford: the Anglican tradition' in J. Coulson (ed.), Theology and the
University (Baltimore Md 1964), 149, 159.
[30] HUD.
[31] B. H. Streeter (ed.), Foundations: A Statement of Christian Belief in Terms of Modern
Thought by Seven Oxford Men (London 1912). See T. A. Langford, In Search of Foundations:
English Theology 1900–1920 (Nashville Tenn. and New York 1969), 114–23; OM 28 Oct. 1948,
68–70.
[32] J. Hick (ed.), The Myth of God Incarnate (London 1977).

of God (1931) has been regarded as a classic study, but he had no followers. Streeter's work on the New Testament achieved international standing, as did that of several nonconformist scholars. The most important Anglican figures in the faculty were patristic scholars, such as F. L. Cross and Henry Chadwick. Although they enjoyed international reputations and produced important scholarly publications, their work did not influence Christian theology in general or the Church of England in particular. Oxford figures served on numerous commissions for the Church of England, but their service was quite specific to that church and was rarely of international significance. Furthermore, in the wake of what Leslie Houlden, formerly chaplain of Trinity College, termed 'the alienation of theology from religion', academic theology became increasingly separated from personal devotional life, the priestly vocation and the corporate life of the church.[33]

In the middle of the century Austin Farrer to some extent overcame that alienation. His career spanned the period of broad-based religious concern from the Second World War through the 1960s. The son of a Baptist minister who taught at Regent's Park College, he was converted to Anglicanism while a student at Oxford. After reading Greats at Balliol, studying theology at Cuddesdon and for a time in Germany, and serving briefly in a parish ministry, he returned to Oxford as chaplain of St Edmund Hall (1931–5) and then of Trinity College (1935–60). Thereafter till his death in 1968 he was Warden of Keble College. More than any figure of his generation in the University, Farrer embodied the highest ideal of the college chaplain-theologian. Throughout his professional life he believed that, as he had told his father in 1928, 'you cannot research profitably into the philosophy of religion . . . until you know what you are talking about and the sphere to reveal that to you is the practical life'.[34] His rootedness in the religious life first of a parish and then of colleges served to confirm that conviction. He may be regarded as an intellectual successor to C. C. J. Webb, who earlier in the century had helped to sustain the significance that many in Oxford assigned to Christian theological concerns by connecting them with the practical life.[35]

Farrer's theology and scholarship, which largely opposed the critical philosophy associated with logical positivism, were embodied in works such as *Finite and Infinite* (1943), *The Glass of Vision* (1948) and *The Freedom of the Will* (1958). He sought to reassert the relevance and legitimacy of metaphysical inquiry. He also wrote widely on biblical scholarship, where his views were regarded as eccentric. Unlike virtually every major Oxford

[33] J. L. Houlden, *Connections: The Integration of Theology and Faith* (London 1986), 21.

[34] P. Curtis, *A Hawk among Sparrows: A Biography of Austin Farrer* (London 1985), 54.

[35] J. Patrick, *The Magdalen Metaphysicals: Idealism and Orthodoxy at Oxford 1901–1945* (Mercer Ga 1985), 13–46.

theologian of his generation, he produced sermons of remarkable beauty and eloquence. He served as an example and inspiration for other Oxford theologians and philosophers—such as Basil Mitchell—who were determined to assert the continued significance of religious concerns in the face of analytical philosophy and secularism. Despite his personal presence, Farrer's influence did not extend much beyond Oxford, and was limited even within the University. Farrer declined in 1951 to be considered for the Nolloth professorship of the philosophy of the Christian religion. In 1959 however, to his great disappointment, he was passed over for the regius chair of divinity.

The single twentieth-century Oxford religious figure whose influence extended far beyond the University was Clive Staples Lewis, who was neither a member of the faculty of theology nor even a theologian.[36] Born in Belfast and reared in the Church of Ireland, Lewis went through a period of atheism in adolescence and early adulthood. As a fellow and tutor in English at Magdalen, he formed close friendships with Christians of various denominations and began a slow but steady return to Christianity. Once he had become a believing Christian he sought to communicate his faith to others and to defend it against all opponents. *Pilgrim's Regress* (1933), the first book Lewis published after his conversion, attracted only a few readers. During the 1930s, however, a group of writers known as the Inklings gathered every Thursday in his rooms at Magdalen.[37] Their chief members in addition to Lewis were Owen Barfield, J. A. W. Bennett, Nevill Coghill, Hugo Dyson, Adam Fox, J. R. R. Tolkien and Charles Williams. They were Roman Catholic and protestant laymen—not confined to any one faculty—whose novels, plays, criticism and philosophy took on a distinctly religious and Christian cast. Generally opposed to modern culture and to secularism, they were also largely indifferent to philosophical and academic theology. The group provides evidence to support the claim that the increasingly religious character of Oxford during the late 1930s and early 1940s 'was due less to the clergy than to the laity'.[38]

There matters might have remained except for the outbreak of the Second World War. Once the war began, Lewis emerged both within Oxford and outside as a major apologist for Christianity through broadcasts by the BBC, and through his remarkable series of books: *The Problem of Pain* (1940), *The Screwtape Letters* (1942), *Broadcast Talks* (1942) and *Christian Behaviour* (1943). These works grew in popularity, along with others published later, of which the most important was *Mere Christianity* (1952).

---

[36] A. N. Wilson, *C. S. Lewis: A Biography* (New York 1990).

[37] H. Carpenter, *The Inklings: C. S. Lewis, J. R. R. Tolkien, Charles Williams, and their Friends* (London 1978).

[38] A. Hastings, *A History of English Christianity, 1920–1985* (London 1986), 299.

All these books presented a spirited defence of Christianity as a faith for modern times, rejecting secularism while at the same time raising doubts about the adequacy both of fundamentalist Christianity and of philosophical theology.

Lewis also stood at the centre of the Socratic Club, the venue in the middle of the century for lively interchange between committed Christians and their philosophical detractors. Miss Stella Aldwinckle of the Oxford Pastorate founded the Club late in 1941 and prevailed on Lewis to become its president.[39] Its Monday meetings were regularly listed in the *Oxford Magazine*'s weekly calendar along with the University's major religious services. Undergraduates formed the majority of the audience, and speakers ranged across the philosophical and religious spectrum. Lewis not only led but was deeply affected by these debates. It was his encounter at the Socratic Club in 1948 with Miss G. E. M. Anscombe, herself both a Christian and a formidable analytic philosopher, that led him generally to abandon formal apologetics and to devote more of his attention to children's literature. Although the Socratic Club survived Lewis's departure to Cambridge in 1954, it was never so strong or visible again. Religious life and academic pursuits were drawing apart, and after its demise in 1972 no other single institution took its place.

The difficulty of sustaining a moderate or liberal religious group in Oxford may be illustrated by the clashes and rivalries between the two major student religious groups, the Student Christian Movement (SCM) and the Oxford Inter-Collegiate Christian Union (OICCU). Founded in the 1890s as part of the student missionary movement, the SCM had by the First World War become a major religious institution both in Britain and in Oxford. The nineteenth-century missionary impulse remained alive in the University and provided a base for the growth of the SCM.[40] The organization, guided by an adult leadership group located in London, was evangelical in its desire to draw students to the Christian faith, but quite liberal in its ecumenism, its rejection of theological dogmatism and in its social concern. For several years beginning in 1919 the SCM sponsored a 'Religion and life' week during which speakers, who were often laymen from outside Oxford, discussed topics of current political or social importance as they related to Christianity. Although some adults regarded SCM activity as a Christian alternative to contemporary secular movements, others actively resisted that image. For example in 1933 F. R. Barry of the university church wrote to Eric Fenn about the SCM's approaching national conference at Edinburgh: 'In view of a good deal that is going on here (and I suppose in

[39] W. Hooper, 'Oxford's bonny fighter' in J. T. Como (ed.), *C. S. Lewis at the Breakfast Table and Other Reminiscences* (New York 1979).

[40] R. Symonds, *Oxford and Empire: The Last Lost Cause?* (London 1986), 203–27; *OM* 4 Nov. 1937, 123–5.

other Universities) I feel rather a concern to say that I feel it awfully important at Edinburgh not to let speakers and the conference generally give the impression that we are presenting Christianity as anti-Communism. Some of our most virile Christians are becoming Communists, and the only thing that will save them from Marxism and dropping Christianity altogether is a positive affirmation of Christian communism.' Fenn replied that they should take the line 'that Christianity as a completer and truer account of human nature necessarily transcends the Communistic philosophy, at the same time doing as full justice as possible to whatever is good in Communism'.[41] Later in the decade the ideas associated with the SCM changed and became somewhat more conservative as its leaders were drawn to Reinhold Niebuhr and C. H. Dodd.

After the Second World War the SCM continued to prosper and remained actively involved in social work. Then as earlier, the students active in the SCM were also those most likely to be engaged in the various types of social work sponsored by individual colleges in the East End of London; these might involve organizing activities such as sports and recreational clubs for poor youths. Several of the people associated with the founding of Oxfam had connections with the SCM.[42] The SCM's study-groups, retreats and national and international conferences drew large numbers of students and were, in the middle of the century, probably the most important religious activities within the University. In the 1960s the SCM at Oxford and elsewhere failed to resist the pressures of renewed denominationalism.[43] Furthermore its national leadership turned in a Marxist direction and undermined the finances of the organization. Towards the end of the 1980s observers of Oxford religion could point to no change so dramatic as the eclipse of the SCM, earlier the chief vehicle for the discussion and realization of liberal Christianity.

The chief rival of the SCM was the Oxford Inter-Collegiate Christian Union, whose origins lay in the late nineteenth-century activities of the Cambridge Inter-Collegiate Christian Union, and in the twentieth century within the larger Inter-Varsity Fellowship of Evangelical Unions. In contrast to the SCM the Christian Union saw itself as non-denominational. Thoroughly evangelical in outlook, its members stressed the atonement, a moderate biblical literalism and personal conversion. The key event separating the Christian Union from the SCM occurred in 1919 during a meeting between representatives of the Cambridge sections of the two groups. The Christian Union representative asked, 'does the SCM consider

[41] Quoted in J. D. McCaughey, *Christian Obedience in the University: Studies in the Life of the Student Christian Movement of Great Britain and Ireland 1930–1950* (London 1958), 70, 71.

[42] B. Whitaker, *A Bridge of People: A Personal View of Oxfam's First Forty Years* (London 1983), 14–16.

[43] R. Pearson, 'The Collapse of the SCM', *Theology* lxxxix (1986).

the atoning blood of Jesus Christ as the central point of their message?' The reply from the SCM was 'no, not as central, although it is given a place in our teaching'.[44] Thereafter nationally the two groups went their separate ways. At Oxford, however, during the early 1920s the Oxford University Bible Union functioned as a section of the Oxford SCM rather than as a part of the national Inter-Varsity Conference. That situation changed in 1928 with the emergence of a newly organized Oxford Inter-Collegiate Christian Union which has continued to function ever since.[45]

OICCU in contrast to the SCM generally regarded itself as opposing what its members regarded as the inadequate religious witness of the college chaplains, university church, city clergy and other denominationally based Christian groups. It usually worked in close association with St Aldate's and St Ebbe's churches and became one of the most visible religious groups in the University and the city.[46] It sponsored daily prayer-meetings and also Bible-study groups. Throughout the middle years of the century its members preached weekly near the Martyrs' Memorial in St Giles'. In the second half of the century OICCU could attract several hundred students to its large public meetings on Saturday night. It also sponsored its own missions, which were separate from those associated with the university church and college chaplaincies. Intellectually many in Oxford spurned or even condemned its activities; nonetheless there was also grudging respect for this organization which had outlived the SCM.

Amid all these activities St Mary the Virgin, the university church, remained a centre for worship and religious organization. Although the Oxford Magazine routinely complained that attendance at morning services was thin and that the congregation was elderly, under the leadership of F. R. Barry (1927–33), F. A. Cockin (1933–8), T. R. Milford (1938–47), and R. S. Lee (1947–61) the university church remained a major focal point of Oxford's religious life and the chief institution for liberal Anglicanism and Anglican social concern. From the late 1920s until the late 1960s the SCM took virtual charge of the weekly Sunday evening service, which attracted large congregations. Seats were in short supply if a well-known speaker were preaching. The university church also provided a focus for the various missions to the University which may be regarded as the chief evangelistic effort of Oxford's official religious establishment. The missions were undertaken jointly by the university church and the college chaplains. The most significant mission of the early part of the century occurred in February 1931, after two years of planning. The chief missioner was

[44] F. D. Coggan (ed.), Christ and the Colleges: A History of the Inter-Varsity Fellowship of Evangelical Unions (London 1934), 17.

[45] D. Johnson, Contending for the Faith: A History of the Evangelical Movement in the Universities and Colleges (Leicester 1979), 52–6, 130, 139–42.

[46] Isis 26 Oct. 1949, 13; 24 May 1956, 25; 27 Apr. 1970, 10–11; 4 Mar. 1976, 16.

William Temple, who had recently been appointed Archbishop of York. Attendance never fell below 1,400.[47]

At the time of Temple's mission the *Oxford Magazine* observed in the University a 'vague and undefined' sense that 'Christianity is intellectually effete and therefore, as a moral sanction, a spent force'.[48] The mission sought to confront and reverse that attitude. The meetings were simple and devoid of any trappings of revivalism. In addition to the evening service, Canon Thomas Pym of Balliol held a short service and period of instruction late each afternoon. Both Temple and Pym were available for personal consultation. There were also daily celebrations of communion. Many saw Temple's mission as a turning point in the religious life of Oxford. It may be seen as the beginning of a significant increase in religious activity which was sustained through the 1930s and was to be followed by a major expansion in the fifteen years after the war. University missions continued during the 1930s, each somewhat more ecumenical than the last.[49] In 1935 St Columba's church offered counselling to Presbyterians. By 1938 services were held during the week at St Mary's, Mansfield College chapel and St Aldate's with over one thousand undergraduates attending each evening. In 1941, with the war under way, Father D'Arcy of Campion Hall held a simultaneous mission for Roman Catholics. Throughout the 1930s sermons often linked religion with discussion of the social question.

Missions were again organized after the war at three-year intervals beginning in 1947, when Stephen Neill spoke to enormous audiences night after night. The meetings were designed not to be religious services as such but rather as occasions for the audience to think about the Christian faith. For example, in 1950 the Bishop of Bristol opened the mission by stating, 'you are being asked, for one week, to consider seriously the claim of Christianity to be true, and to decide what it means for your own life'.[50] That year, as in 1947, the meetings were held in the Sheldonian Theatre. The Vice-Chancellor and senior members of the University attended the closing service. No hymn was sung at the services, so an uncommitted person could attend without feeling the least pressure to indicate any belief or to make any act of insincere conformity. Speakers drawn from across the Anglican and nonconformist spectrum held afternoon question-and-answer sessions at Regent's Park College. There were also daily meetings in each of the colleges, making it difficult for undergraduates to escape some contact with the event. Such missions continued under the guidance of the college chaplains in later decades.

[47] F. R. Barry, *Period of My Life* (London 1970), 101–4; F. A. Iremonger, *William Temple, Archbishop of Canterbury: His Life and Letters* (London 1948), 377–8.

[48] *OM* 19 Feb. 1931, 486–7.

[49] *OM* 7 Feb. 1935, 333; 27 Jan. 1938, 307–8; 17 Feb. 1938, 403–4; 6 Feb. 1941, 162; 16 June 1949, 595; *Isis* 12 Feb. 1947, 7; 8 Feb. 1950, 23; 15 Feb. 1950, 22; 10 Feb. 1960, 22.

[50] *Isis* 12 Feb. 1947, 7; *OM* 16 Feb. 1950, 308; see also *OM* 2 Feb. 1950, 270.

Although the missions were occasions for religious co-operation, a distinct rivalry existed between the college chapels and other religious organizations in and about the University. During a major appeal for St Mary's in 1946 critics feared that an enlarged staff at the university church would duplicate the efforts of the college chaplains.[51] The SCM frequently co-operated with college chaplains, but more zealous evangelical groups often saw themselves as compensating for the religious deficiency of the chaplains. Intellectually, socially and economically, Oxford organized itself around the colleges, but Anglican college chaplains could not cater fully for a pluralistic religious life in the University. More interesting preaching was likely to be found in the university church, the cathedral, Mansfield College's chapel, Pusey House, or in one of the city's churches. By the Second World War attendance at chapel had ceased to be compulsory in most, though not in all, colleges, and their captive audiences thus disappeared. Several colleges, most notably Christ Church, New College and Magdalen, employed paid choirs to provide music which may have attracted worshippers. There and elsewhere attendance grew for a few years after the war, but then generally declined. By the last quarter of the century the college chapels and chaplains had largely, though never completely, lost the struggle against religious indifference and the rival non-collegiate religious organizations.[52]

At almost any moment during the twentieth century, commentators on religion in Oxford viewed the present as a pale reflection of an earlier more reverent past. In 1911, for example, the *Oxford Magazine* pointed to the value of a special series of sermons 'even in these days when *thou shalt make him hear sermons* is no longer a necessary part of a young man's education'.[53] Most corporate recognition of religion ceased. For example, in 1931 Congregation abolished the compulsory examination in holy scripture ('divvers').[54] During the second half of the century Oxford observers continued to note signs of religious decline and indifference. In 1965 the *Oxford Magazine* commented that 'the college chapels are relatively unimportant in the total life of the University. The chaplains are extremely competent (and very cheap) welfare officers. The Theology Faculty—apart from its extraordinarily big complement of professors—is no longer a thorn in atheistical flesh.'[55] Yet this widespread dismissive attitude towards religion in Oxford served to hide remarkable religious realities—as witness the missions, the Roman Catholic chaplaincy, the SCM and OICCU, the Socratic Club and many examples of personal devotion and piety.

[51] *OM* 19 Feb. 1931, 487; 30 May 1946, 321–2.

[52] *OM* 17 Nov. 1970, 72–4, 105–6.

[53] *OM* 30 Nov. 1911, 119.

[54] *OM* 26 Nov. 1931, 230; 21 Jan. 1932, 319–20; 28 Jan. 1932, 367; 4 Feb. 1932, 396; 11 Feb. 1932, 426.

[55] *OM* 5 Nov. 1965, 86 (editorial).

Historians cannot ignore or dismiss these religious experiences and activities simply because they clash with professional academic presuppositions about the character and self-image of modern universities. The significant historical question is not why Oxford devoted less corporate attention to religion in 1975 than in 1910, but rather where and how religious thought and practice survived, and in some cases even grew and prospered. The University educated students primarily in non-religious subjects and launched most into secular careers. Yet religion persisted within that secular setting because the questions, emotions and personal needs to which it has perennially addressed itself continued to stir significant numbers of people; because the college chaplains and the faculty of theology continued to function; and because religious groups outside Oxford brought their ideas, organization and preachers to bear upon the University.

12

Medicine

CHARLES WEBSTER

The advocates of a complete medical school believed that without such a development Oxford would be starved of talented recruits to research.[1] Thereby the University would be denied the opportunity to 'become a great centre, and perhaps the centre, of medical progress'.[2] Their opponents argued that routine clinical instruction would undermine research and break with the long tradition inherited from the Victorian reformers whereby Oxford devoted itself to advanced research and to the humanistic education of the future medical élite in the fundamentals of the natural sciences relevant to medicine. This view entailed preserving the natural division of labour between Oxford and the London medical schools, where ideal conditions existed for clinical instruction. The debate over the 'lost medical school' took the best part of a century to resolve. This issue was divisive and bitterly contested because it affected fundamental questions of the self-image of the medical school and the University as a whole. The debate over the future of the medical school died down during Osler's period as Regius

[1] The fullest and most adequate reviews of this subject are contained in J. Beinart, *A History of the Nuffield Department of Anaesthetics, Oxford, 1937–1987* (Oxford 1987) and R. G. Macfarlane, *Howard Florey: The Making of a Great Scientist* (Oxford 1979). See also K. Dewhurst (ed.), *Oxford Medicine* (Sandford on Thames 1970); *A County Hospital 1920–1988* (Oxfordshire Health Authority: Oxford 1988); A. H. T. Robb-Smith, *A Short History of the Radcliffe Infirmary* (Oxford 1970). The following important and relevant studies appeared after the completion of this chapter: G. J. Fraenkel, *Hugh Cairns: First Nuffield Professor of Surgery* (Oxford 1991); I. Guest, *Dr John Radcliffe and his Trust* (London 1991); G. McLachlan, *A History of Nuffield Provincial Hospitals Trust* (London 1992). In the following notes the references to the Nuffield Committee papers are indicated as follows:

PNC   OUA Proceedings of the Nuffield Committee i–ix (1936–9)
PNCAM OUA Proceedings of the Nuffield Committee for the Advancement of Medicine
       x–lxvi (1940–59)
PCAM   OUA Proceedings of the Committee for the Advancement of Medicine i–xlvi
       (1959–74).

I am grateful for assistance and comments on earlier drafts of this chapter from Dr A. M. Cooke, Dr M. S. Dunnill, Dr J. Potter and Sir Edgar Williams.

[2] Report of visit to United States and Canada by the Regius Professor of Medicine and the Registrar, 20 May 1944, HCP 188 (1944), 125 and PNCAM xxii. 109. See also quinquennial application 1967/72, the stated aim of which was to make the United Oxford Hospitals a 'great centre for research and teaching': PCAM xix. 33.

Professor of Medicine, but after a short period it resurfaced and became a matter of central concern during the following decades.

The great Sir William Osler died in 1919 and his last years were clouded by the loss of his only son in Flanders. His successor, Sir Archibald Garrod, Regius Professor from 1920 until 1928, was a celebrated pioneer of biochemical genetics, but he was 63 on his appointment and in decline, saddened by the death of two of his sons in the First World War and the third in the influenza pandemic of 1918.[3] Of the four other professors in the medical faculty in 1918, Arthur Thomson, the Professor of Anatomy, was a reliable committee man but otherwise a minor figure who did not retire until 1933 at the age of 75. J. A. Gunn, the Professor of Pharmacology, was a respected figure in British pharmacology, but he enjoyed only a modest scientific reputation. Georges Dreyer, the Professor of Pathology, was at the height of his reputation in 1918 but, as indicated below, this reputation was soon in ruins and the development of pathology in Oxford was set back for a generation. Although Charles Sherrington, the Waynflete Professor of Physiology, was 56 upon appointment in 1913, he maintained his distinction until retirement at 77 in 1935.[4] His department enjoyed an unassailable reputation as a world centre for research in the field of neurophysiology.

By 1918 the laboratory facilities available in Oxford for the medical sciences were either antiquated, inappropriate in character or inadequate in scale, despite the fact that pathology and physiology had benefited from new building at the beginning of the century. A new department of pharmacology was opened in 1912, but this was located in the attic of the University Museum; a first priority after the war was recognized as rescuing Gunn from the 'cocklofts' of the Museum.[5]

Because medical students went to London for their clinical training, relations between the pre-clinical departments and the Radcliffe Infirmary were relatively restricted. Indeed the Radcliffe Infirmary and County Hospital was little different from its counterparts in small county towns. Before the First World War the hospital contained about 180 beds, the small medical staff comprising local general practitioners who gave their services on an honorary basis. The physicians and surgeons of the Radcliffe Infirmary were local celebrities, but they were not advanced practitioners of their arts and only rarely were they involved with clinical research.

Although both Oxford and Cambridge restricted themselves to pre-clinical studies, the Oxford school was much the smaller, during the 1920s

---

[3] Robb-Smith, 140. Osler died on 29 Dec. 1919; Garrod's appointment was announced on 1 Mar. 1920. F. G. Hopkins, 'A. E. Garrod', *ONFRS* (1936–8), 225–8.

[4] D. Denny-Brown, 'The Sherrington school of physiology', *Jl Neurophysiology* xx (1957), 543–8; J. C. Eccles, 'The Oxford laboratory of Sherrington's time', *Proc. Australian Physiological and Pharmacological Soc.* ix (1978), 69–72; E. G. T. Liddell, 'C. S. Sherrington', *ONFRS* viii (1952–3), 241–70.

[5] Medical Research Council (MRC), 1331/A, Garrod to Fletcher, 6 Jan. 1922.

being only one-third the size of Cambridge. The pre-clinical intake gradually expanded from twenty-five before the First World War to about fifty in 1930, which represented the full capacity of the laboratory-space available. Before 1923 medical students spent four years in Oxford taking their preliminary examinations in natural science and then preparing for the honour school of animal physiology. A minority stayed for a fifth year to study their pathology and pharmacology in Oxford rather than in London. There followed at least two years spent in London on clinical study, after which most students obtained their diploma as MRCS LRCP (member of the Royal College of Surgeons and licentiate of the Royal College of Physicians) which licensed them to practise medicine. The more academically inclined (about half the total) completed their medical education by taking the Oxford degree of bachelor of medicine (BM) after an average of some eight years' study and practice. A change in the General Medical Council's requirements in 1923 meant that the minimum period of clinical training was increased from two to three years. In effect this reduced the period for study in Oxford by one year, a change which was accommodated by allowing students to take their preliminary examination before coming into residence, although this proved impossible in many cases. Accordingly medical students were faced with an increasingly congested course in which they were obliged in three years to attain a decent standard in chemistry, physics, botany and zoology, followed by all the parts of the final honour school of animal physiology. It was felt that the standards of scientific attainment expected in Oxford were altogether more rigorous than in most other medical schools in Britain.[6]

To compensate for the absence of a clinical school, Osler instituted Sunday morning ward rounds which were accessible to students in the last year of the final honour school, as well as to their seniors taking 'drugs and bugs'. This tradition was continued by Garrod, but with less exuberance and success. An introduction to pathology was provided by A. G. Gibson, while senior students were able to assist the house officers of the Radcliffe Infirmary in their casualty work.[7] However, these worthy efforts at clinical instruction were amateurish when compared with the systematic provision of the London medical schools.

The end of the First World War precipitated the entire voluntary hospital system into an acute financial crisis from which it never effectively recovered. The nationalization of hospitals under the National Health Service was the eventual solution to this problem, but in the intervening thirty years the voluntary hospitals lurched from one crisis to another.[8] This

[6] E. W. Ainley Walker, 'The school of medicine', *OM* 6 Mar. 1930, 564–8.

[7] F. G. Hobson, 'Sir William Osler' in Dewhurst, *Oxford Medicine*, 89–93; R. Macbeth, 'The Radcliffe 40 years ago', ibid, 136–9.

[8] C. Webster, *Problems of Health Care: The National Health Service before 1957* (London 1988), 2–5; B. Abel-Smith, *The Hospitals 1800–1948* (London 1964), 286–430.

problem inevitably carried over into the medical schools. The whole system lacked the organization or resources for maintenance or modernization. Like many smaller provincial hospitals the Radcliffe Infirmary was not so exposed as the large London hospitals. Gradually, largely through the generosity of Lord Nuffield, the fortunes of hospitals in the Oxford area were restored, until at the outbreak of the Second World War the Oxford region was seen as the model for hospital co-ordination for the whole nation.[9]

Nuffield's involvement was also crucial for the medical school. However, he was not the first outside agent to influence events. Immediately after the war the impact of the newly founded Medical Research Council (MRC) and its energetic Secretary Sir Walter Morley Fletcher was decisive. Oxford's backwardness in biochemistry was particularly embarrassing, given Frederick Gowland Hopkins's spectacular success at Cambridge.[10] Consequently on 6 December 1919 the medicine board made an urgent appeal for a chair of biochemistry.[11] However, nothing was achieved until Fletcher intervened. Fletcher believed that massive support for the pre-clinical departments at Oxford and Cambridge held the key to the continuing ability of Britain to compete in the international field of medical research. As he explained to his correspondent in the Rockefeller Foundation: 'Their ancient endowment, and the special glamour of their reputation and of the amenities of life within them tend to draw to them the ablest brains among all classes of the community from the very poorest upwards, and from all parts of the United Kingdom.'[12] It was therefore essential that Oxford and Cambridge should be equipped to supply Britain's scientific medical élite in the future.

With these goals in mind Fletcher entered into negotiations with the Dunn trustees in Britain and Rockefeller officials in New York.[13] Although Fletcher's plans contained many facets, his firm priorities were the development of biochemistry and pathology at Oxford and Cambridge. His first preference was securing the position of Hopkins's department of biochemistry in Cambridge, and a magnificent grant of £165,000 was secured for this purpose from the Dunn trustees. The Rockefeller effort in Cambridge was deflected into pathology. In 1922 the Oxford professors submitted a brief and unconvincing memorandum on the medical sciences in Oxford. It was noted that improved facilities were needed for biochemistry,

---

[9] *A National Hospital Service: A Memorandum on the Co-ordination of Hospital Services* (Nuffield Provincial Hospitals Trust: Oxford 1941); Webster, 24–30.

[10] R. E. Kohler, *From Medical Chemistry to Biochemistry* (Cambridge 1982), 81–9.

[11] OUA FA 4/9/1/3, meeting of the board of the faculty of medicine, 6 Dec. 1919.

[12] New York, Rockefeller Archive Center, FF 250/1A, Fletcher to R. M. Pearce, 23 Oct. 1923. Fletcher expressed himself in similar terms in his memorandum of 26 Apr. 1922 on the Dunn estate: MRC 1331/A.

[13] The Dunn trustees distributed about £1m bequeathed by Sir William Dunn (1833–1912) for uses connected with religion, education and medicine.

pathology and pharmacology. In the longer term the professors envisaged the establishment of a postgraduate unit at the Radcliffe Infirmary, which they hoped would develop into a 'centre for research and advanced teaching'.[14] This arguably constitutes the first germ of the plan which eventually matured into the Nuffield benefaction.

In the short term the Oxford professors gave their highest priority to transferring Gunn's department from its inadequate accommodation, but this elicited a negative response from Fletcher. With a little further prompting the Oxford negotiators accepted Fletcher's view that the most deserving case was Dreyer. Although Dreyer already had the best accommodation, he received a grant of £100,000 to establish the Dunn School of Pathology, which was opened in 1927. Fletcher had consistently supported Dreyer and earnestly believed that Dreyer was Oxford's nearest equivalent to Hopkins. Dreyer and Fletcher aspired to make the Oxford pathology department the equivalent of the Pasteur Institute in Paris, or the State Serum Institute in Copenhagen. However, failings in Dreyer's judgement were evident from the growing débâcle over his 'diaplyte' vaccine, evolved to treat tuberculosis. Nevertheless Fletcher was determined to identify in Oxford a candidate for scientific stardom and the lot fell on Dreyer.[15] Oxford also benefited from a Rockefeller endowment of £75,000 directed to the new department of biochemistry, which was also opened in 1927. For this purpose Sherrington obtained a grant from Edward Whitley, a Liverpool businessman, to endow the chair of biochemistry. Benjamin Moore, the first incumbent, died in 1922. Consequently the first effective Professor of Biochemistry was R. A. Peters. Although less distinguished than Sherrington, Peters was considerably more effective as a teacher.[16]

New buildings for biochemistry and pathology eased pressure on the departments of physiology and pharmacology. The transmutation of the 'physiological chemistry' section of the physiology department into biochemistry created additional space for Sherrington in his department, while Dreyer's vacated department was occupied by Gunn. Once the new departments of biochemistry and pathology were opened, the initiative for change subsided. Fletcher was inclined to leave the Oxford and Cambridge structure alone, but this was not the instinct of the Rockefeller Foundation. Abraham Flexner, whose reports had provided the blueprint for the reform of medical education both in Europe and in America, urged that Oxford and Cambridge provided a better basis than the London hospitals for the development of complete medical schools. He wanted the Foundation to invite a delegation from Oxford and Cambridge to see how medical

[14] MRC 1331/A, memorandum enclosed with Garrod to Fletcher, 28 Feb. 1922.
[15] MRC 1331/A, E. For sources on Dreyer see below n. 50.
[16] Kohler, 89–91; R. H. Thompson and A. G. Ogston, 'R. A. Peters', *BMFRS* xxix (1983), 495–523.

education was organized in the most advanced American medical schools.[17] In the event a Rockefeller team visited London in the winter of 1927–8, held inconclusive discussions at the Ministry of Health and failed to locate any responsible agent in Oxford with whom confidential discussions might be held about the development of postgraduate education and research.[18] Thereby Oxford arguably lost the opportunity of securing a major Rockefeller endowment for the medical school. However, meetings in Oxford might well have been counter-productive since they would have exposed substantial resistance to changes of the kind desired by Rockefeller.

The Rockefeller visit took place at the time of an interregnum with respect to the regius professorship. Sir Farquhar Buzzard, the new incumbent, took up his appointment in 1928 and retired in 1943.[19] His period of office was perhaps the phase of most active innovation in the entire history of the medical school. In 1928 the medical school was much as H. W. Acland had left it. By 1943 the clinical professors and postgraduate departments were well established and a full undergraduate teaching programme was installed on a temporary basis. Buzzard was a Harley Street neurologist and physician to the King. Despite his conventional pedigree and manner, Buzzard proved to be a consistent ally of innovation and reform. As a skilled politician and effective communicator he was ideally placed to render reform palatable to the conservative establishment, and to mediate with the vested interests threatened by the dramatic changes taking place. As a member of the Huntercombe Golf Club Buzzard was also part of the small medical clique which cultivated Sir William Morris, Lord Nuffield from 1934. An invaluable adviser to Buzzard in university politics was Douglas Veale, who left the Ministry of Health to become Registrar of the University in August 1930. Coincidentally both Buzzard and Veale had been involved in discussions with the Rockefeller representatives in London.[20]

A minor and seemingly innocuous step towards reform was taken when it became evident that the Radcliffe Observatory and its extensive site were to be vacated. On 5 March 1930 the medicine board reported that it might be possible to use the Observatory for an institute of medical research.[21] It was hinted that support was likely to be available from 'generous individuals or corporations interested in the efforts of science to relieve human suffering and promote public health'. This was an oblique reference to Morris, who

[17] Flexner to Pearce, 21 Nov. 1927, Rockefeller Archive Center, 696/7172.

[18] D. Veale, 'The Nuffield benefaction and the Oxford medical school' in Dewhurst, *Oxford Medicine*, 143; A. M. Cooke, *Sir E. Farquhar Buzzard, Bt.* (np 1975), 26.

[19] Cooke, *Buzzard*; Robb-Smith, *Radcliffe Infirmary*, 148–9. Veale's high estimate of Buzzard is revealed in his correspondence with Sir Geoffrey Jefferson 1958–9 in the Jefferson papers (in private possession).

[20] Cooke, 26.

[21] OUA FA 4/9/1/3, meeting of the board of the faculty of medicine, 5 Mar. 1930; HCP 146 (1930), 9, resolution sent by board to the General Board and thence to Council.

8.2 Christ Church New Library: north front before and after restoration, 1962

8.3 Corpus Christi College bump supper, 1963

8.4 'A word from the proctor', June 1957

8.5 10 veteran members of University College staff with the Master, 1962

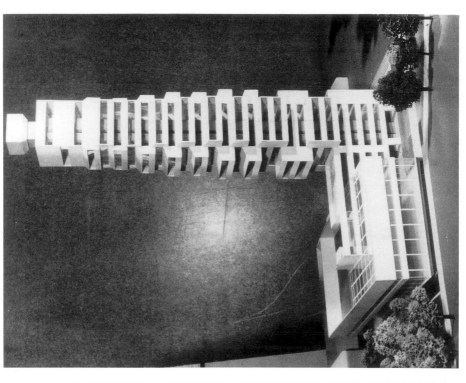

10.2 Proposed zoology department building, 1962

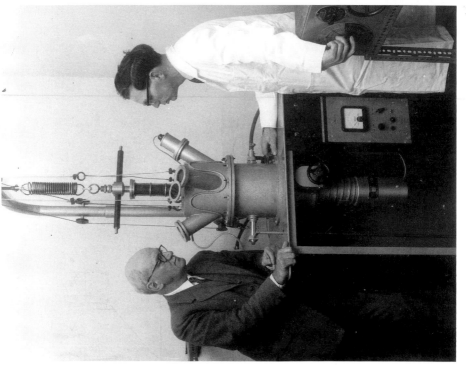

10.1 William Hume-Rothery, c. 1957

had already displayed generosity towards the Radcliffe Infirmary, and especially towards the Wingfield Morris Orthopaedic Hospital. Morris was induced to set up a trust to purchase the Observatory and its site, half of which was granted to the Radcliffe Infirmary to make way for much-needed extensions.[22] The rest, including the Observatory itself, was converted into the Nuffield Institute of Medical Research. The scheme for the Institute was not finally drawn up until Hilary term 1934, only shortly before the expiry date set by Morris. Much of the delay stemmed from the slowness of the University in guaranteeing £1,000 per annum towards the cost of the Institute.[23] The first director of the Institute was James Gunn, who transferred from his post in pharmacology. His assignment in the new Institute was experimental therapeutics, while the second main activity was x-ray cinematography. Gunn's department was also permitted to engage in medical teaching requiring reference to clinical material in the Radcliffe Infirmary.[24] The Nuffield Institute therefore represented a modest step towards establishing a postgraduate medical school. Further confirmation that this move was in the mind of Veale and Buzzard is provided by a letter from the Ministry of Health refusing to help fund the Oxford scheme for a postgraduate medical school.[25] This letter also indicates that the reformers enjoyed support from A. S. MacNalty of the Ministry of Health, who was soon to gain promotion to the post of Chief Medical Officer.

The scheme of Buzzard and his associates for a postgraduate medical school was probably supported by Nuffield, who increasingly inclined to major schemes and grand gestures. New life to this expansionist initiative came from Hugh Cairns, an Australian Rhodes scholar, son-in-law of the Master of Balliol, who had established a major reputation as a neurosurgeon at the London Hospital. He was a natural and charismatic leader who conveyed an aura of greatness and stimulated intense loyalty from those around him.[26] The precise details of Cairns's involvement are not easily established from the rival accounts of the Nuffield benefaction.[27] It seems unlikely that Cairns had decided to leave the London Hospital before his visit to America in 1935.[28] At Rockefeller instigation he took up a travelling fellowship to work with his long-standing patron Harvey Cushing at Yale. It is quite likely that the combined effect of Rockefeller propaganda and experience of the American medical schools in October 1935 brought to a head Cairns's disenchantment with the London medical schools. Perhaps

[22] Robb-Smith, 145–9, 150–1.
[23] HCP 158 (1934), pp. xci (minute 24), 211, 217; 156 (1933), pp. lxxxiv (23), 176.
[24] PNC i. 49–56, memorandum by Gunn on the future of the Nuffield Institute, 1937.
[25] OUA UR/FS/MD/13/1, Sir A. Robinson to Veale, 2 Dec. 1932.
[26] G. Jefferson, 'Memories of Hugh Cairns' in Dewhurst, Oxford Medicine, 155–73.
[27] For representative accounts see Beinart, Anaesthetics, 22–30; Cooke, 26–33; Macfarlane, Florey, 244–50; Robb-Smith, 155–64.
[28] Jefferson papers, Cairns to Alan Gregg, 25 Jan. 1933.

with Rockefeller encouragement, he conceived an ambitious plan for establishing a complete medical school at Oxford, making it clear that he wished to return to Oxford to implement his ideas. It seems unlikely that Cairns had much opportunity to propagate his ideas before December 1935, but from this date onward he produced memoranda arguing the case for a school of clinical medicine in Oxford. Experience in London and America convinced him that the presence of undergraduates was fundamental to the success of a centre for advanced teaching and research.

Central to Cairns's proposal was the establishment of departments under clinicians of outstanding ability, who would devote themselves to teaching and research, free from the burden of private practice.[29] The clinical departments would turn the Radcliffe Infirmary into a first-class hospital, and they would provide a vital link with the pre-clinical departments, thereby providing for the first time a truly organic connection between advanced research and facilities for comprehensive treatment of the entire local population. Cairns's plan was indeed ambitious. He envisaged the establishment of full-scale departments of medicine, pathology, pathological biochemistry, surgery, paediatrics, obstetrics and gynaecology—and preferably also psychiatry—and forensic medicine and public health. Essential to his scheme was the introduction of clinical training for a selected group of about twenty students, who would then proceed to a series of resident appointments for a period of six to eight years after graduation. Eventually he hoped to expand the clinical intake to between forty and sixty. At that stage he envisaged that there would be forty postgraduate students and a permanent staff of some twenty exclusively engaged in teaching and research within the Infirmary. This scheme required an initial endowment of between one and two million pounds. Cairns recognized that a project on this scale would transform the Infirmary, and constitute one of the major innovations in British medicine in the twentieth century.[30]

Initially Cairns was contemplating relying on Rockefeller support for the new school, but discussions with the Oxford expansionists soon indicated that there existed sufficient common ground for Cairns's project to be regarded as the natural continuation of the developments at the Observatory recently funded by Nuffield.[31] In that case Nuffield was a potential

[29] The relevant documents are: Jefferson papers, 'Memorandum to the regius professor of medicine on the desirability of establishing a complete school of clinical medicine at Oxford' (undated typescript, inscribed by hand *Hugh Cairns' First Memorandum. Date 1934 or early '35*, 9 pages); OUA UR/FS/MD/13/1, 'A proposal to establish a school of clinical medicine at Oxford' (undated typescript, 3 pages); Jefferson papers and OUA UR/FS/MD/13/1, 'Second memorandum from Mr. Cairns to the regius professor of medicine on the establishment of a complete school of clinical medicine at Oxford: estimates' (typescript dated March 1936, in two versions, 30 and 39 pages).   [30] Cairns, 'Proposal', 1.

[31] For the early expectation of Rockefeller support see OUA UR/FS/MD/13/1, Cairns to Florey, 8 Aug. 1936, Gregg to Cairns, 6 July 1936; OUA UR/FS/MD/13/D, Cairns to Veale, 13 Jan. 1937.

benefactor, while Rockefeller might be held in reserve for supplementary support. Indeed there was an appropriate symmetry about obtaining support from the profits of the motor industry since, as Cairns pointed out, the internal combustion engine had made it possible to centralize expert medical services in regional centres located at the foci of transport and communication.[32] In Buzzard and the orthopaedist G. R. Girdlestone, Cairns had the benefit of skilled negotiators who enjoyed the complete confidence of Nuffield.[33] The medical politicians were urged on by Veale, who was captivated by Cairns, and who was the willing advocate of reform on the broadest scale. A further valuable ally was William Goodenough, the chairman of Barclays Bank, who became the main figure among Nuffield's trustees. As treasurer of the Radcliffe Infirmary, Goodenough was relied upon to influence the governors and medical staff. Nuffield was at this point in an expansive mood, eager to purchase the neglected canal site between Carfax and the railway station, upon which he aimed to build a major academic institution to complete the ring of colleges around Carfax. His instinct for monumental expression of his philanthropy thus came together with his long-standing commitment to the advancement of medicine. Nuffield was therefore a ready convert to Cairns's proposals, which he recognized as offering an appropriate vehicle to bring his Oxford benefactions to a fitting climax.[34] Nuffield took little interest in the details of Cairns's scheme. Once assured that the clinical school was ambitious enough to be identified as a major act of philanthropy, he was willing to leave execution to the experts.[35] Accustomed as they were to long drawn-out negotiations with government bodies over funding for medicine and science, the University authorities were taken aback by Nuffield's haste to bring his benefaction to fruition.

Accounts of the Nuffield benefaction are embellished with anecdotes concerning the meeting of the British Medical Association held in Oxford between 19 and 25 July 1936. In fact Nuffield had already committed himself to support the clinical school before the meeting. Indeed the first leader in the *Times* on 18 July ended with the hint that 'the School seems to many to be destined to become a centre of postgraduate teaching. If that teaching is combined as at present with research, Oxford will achieve in the days to come a new distinction and a still more exalted usefulness.' A much broader

---

[32] Cairns, 'Proposal', 1.

[33] For Girdlestone see R. Duthie, 'Orthopaedic services in Oxford and the region: the first 100 years' in *County Hospital*, 98–109; A. D. Gardner, 'Some recollections', typescript [1960] deposited in University College, Oxford, pp. 180–91; J. Trueta, *G. R. Girdlestone* (Oxford 1971).

[34] OUA UR/FS/MD/13/1, Girdlestone's memorandum on meeting with Nuffield, 30 July 1936.

[35] Ibid. note of meeting between Cairns, Girdlestone and Nuffield, 24 July 1936.

hint was contained in Buzzard's presidential address to the British Medical Association on 21 July, where he surveyed the medical services and looked forward to a future when primary care would be delivered in advanced health centres, and hospital care would be regionally co-ordinated. He ended by appealing for greater collaboration between scientists and clinicians. The Nuffield Institute was mentioned as a model for this collaboration. He then made a thinly disguised appeal to Nuffield to support this objective by developing the Nuffield Institute into a complete postgraduate medical school, which he described as an 'ambitious dream'.[36]

Behind the scenes events moved rapidly. At a dinner on 20 July Nuffield informed the Vice-Chancellor that he would give up to £2 million for the clinical school. On 24 July Nuffield held a brief discussion with Cairns at Girdlestone's house. On 27 July the Vice-Chancellor, Buzzard and Nuffield agreed on a memorandum in which Nuffield offered £1 million immediately, with a further £1 million after one year, subject to the success of the scheme. At Congregation on 24 November 1936 Nuffield raised his gift to £2 million [plate 12.1].[37] Soon afterwards he added £200,000 as a building fund, while £300,000 was given to the Radcliffe Infirmary to raise the standard of its services up to the level of a teaching hospital.[38] In reporting these events to Florey, Cairns admitted 'we are all hypnotised into a dream-like state by this overwhelming good news'. A first leader of the *Times* welcomed the fact that Buzzard's ambitious dream 'had come true so promptly'.[39]

The remarkable speed and facility with which the huge Nuffield benefaction was settled should not disguise the many points of conflict underlying the superficial accord. Especially difficult was the question of the scope of the clinical school. The reforms initiated by Buzzard assumed that developments would be restricted to the postgraduate level, whereas Cairns was pledged to a full clinical and graduate school. Although Veale supported Cairns, the elder statesmen among the expansionists doubted whether Oxford could sustain a full medical school. Cairns argued for a rapid move towards a complete medical school, although he accepted the case for an incremental approach.[40] The letter to be sent by Nuffield to the Vice-Chancellor was therefore carefully drafted to give emphasis to the graduate medical school, while not precluding eventually, in the scope of its clinical training, 'a limited number of Oxford medical students'.[41] This sentiment

---

[36] *Times* 22 July 1936, 12; E. F. Buzzard, 'And the future', *Brit. Med. Jl* 1936, ii. 166.

[37] Nuffield to Vice-Chancellor, 10 Oct. 1936, *Gazette* lxvii (1936/7), 67–8, PNC i. 35–9 and HCP 165 (1936), 31–5. For relevant decrees etc. see PNC i (1–17); ii (1–24).

[38] PNC iii. 73–7.

[39] OUA UR/FS/MD/13/1, Cairns to Florey, 8 Aug. 1936; *Times* 16 Oct. 1936, 15.

[40] OUA UR/FS/MD/13/1, Cairns to Florey, 8 Aug. 1936, Cairns to Veale, 19 Aug. 1936, memorandum by Cairns [Aug. 1936]; OUA UR/FS/MD/13/D, Cairns to Veale, 1 Jan. 1937; OUA UR/FS/MD/13/2, Cairns to Veale, 6 Jan. 1937.

[41] Nuffield to Vice-Chancellor, 10 Oct. 1936.

THE HORN OF PLENTY

"SAY WHEN!"

[With Mr. Punch's congratulations to Lord NUFFIELD, who has increased his enormous gift to Oxford University for Medical Research by another £750,000.]

12.1   *PUNCH* 2 DEC. 1936 ON LORD NUFFIELD'S BENEFACTIONS TO OXFORD

was echoed in the deed of trust of 24 November 1936 and the decree of 1 December 1936.

The narrower focus of the clinical school permitted a smaller range of departments than would normally be found in a medical school. Initial discussions between Buzzard and Cairns suggested concentration on medicine, surgery, obstetrics and gynaecology, morbid anatomy, and perhaps biochemical pathology, while subjects like paediatrics, psychiatry, or preventive medicine and public health were proposed for a later stage. By November 1936 the main professorial departments were narrowed down to medicine, surgery and obstetrics and gynaecology. At the insistence of Nuffield, and in the face of resistance from Buzzard, Cairns and Veale, anaesthetics was elevated to the status of a professorial department.[42] Also at the request of Nuffield, his friend and fellow golfer Girdlestone was elevated to an honorary chair in orthopaedics.[43] Finally, in order to regularize his position with respect to the Nuffield professors, Gunn was appointed Professor of Therapeutics.[44]

The appointment of the initial incumbents to the four full-time professorial posts at Oxford created no particular difficulty. Cairns was the first to be appointed, to the chair of surgery, on 27 January 1937.[45] Robert R. Macintosh, Nuffield's nominee, was appointed Professor of Anaesthetics on 1 February 1937. Macintosh thereby held the first chair in his subject to be established in Britain, and one of the first in the western medical world. The appointment of John Chassar Moir as Professor of Obstetrics and Gynaecology followed in April 1937. Recruited from University College, London, Chassar Moir was a discoverer of ergometrine for the control and prevention of postpartum haemorrhage.[46] The appointment to the chair of medicine gave more difficulty. Initially Cairns could think of only two possibilities, L. J. Witts and George Pickering, both from London.[47] But objections were raised to both, and other names were canvassed before Witts was finally appointed in November 1937. The full complement of Nuffield professors was not established in Oxford until mid-1938, leaving them only one full year before the outbreak of war.

The good fortune of the four Nuffield professors in enjoying the disposal of the income from an endowment of £2 million inevitably created envy and

[42] Beinart, *Anaesthetics*, 23–9.

[43] OUA UR/FS/MD/13/1, Cairns to Veale, 29 Nov. 1936. For the unhappy consequences of this decision see Gardner, 'Some recollections', 183–8; PNC vii. 87–94; viii. 27–8, 69, 94–5. In 1939 Girdlestone stood down in favour of H. J. Seddon, who became the first full-time Professor of Orthopaedics; Seddon retired in 1948.

[44] PNC vi. 69–70.

[45] Beinart, 29–30.

[46] A. Turnbull, 'Maternity services and the Nuffield Department of Obstetrics and Gynaecology 1937–1988' in *County Hospital*, 117–32.

[47] OUA UR/FS/MD/13/1, Cairns to Florey, 8 Aug. 1936; OUA UR/FS/MD/13/2, Cairns to Veale, 23 Dec. 1936; PNC i. 20–2; iv. 31–8.

hostility among their colleagues in the Radcliffe Infirmary and in the pre-clinical departments. Instead of providing a unifying factor, the Nuffield professors risked alienating both clinicians and bio-medical scientists.[48] There was essentially no way of appeasing the senior honorary medical staff of the Radcliffe Infirmary and the first generation of National Health Service consultants who followed them. The intrusion of the Nuffield departments into the Infirmary totally undermined the independence and dominance of the existing medical staff, who now saw themselves as second-class citizens. Senior figures such as A. G. Gibson, or juniors such as A. M. Cooke, who were supportive and co-operative, were in a minority. The Nuffield endowment's generosity also highlighted the inadequacy of the funding of the pre-clinical departments. The pre-clinical professors were apprehensive about the Nuffield scheme because it seriously weakened their dominance on the medicine board. The possibility of benefit from the endowment temporarily softened their hostility, but their anger and disappointment were intensified when it emerged that they would receive only negligible reward.

This problem was exacerbated because a new generation of pre-clinical professors was taking over. In 1934 Thomson was replaced by the able comparative anatomist and authority on the evolution of primates, W. E. Le Gros Clark. When Gunn transferred to the Nuffield Institute, his successor was J. H. Burn, the Dean of the College of Pharmacy in London. In 1936 the distinguished Sherrington was replaced by John Mellanby, a lesser figure, elder brother of Sir Edward Mellanby, the successor to Fletcher as Secretary of the MRC. The most important appointment was that of Howard Florey as Professor of Pathology in 1935 following the premature death of Dreyer. Le Gros Clark, Burn and Florey made determined and successful attempts to build up their departments. John Mellanby died in 1939, when he was replaced by E. G. T. Liddell, a former assistant of Sherrington, who loyally continued the traditions of his master until retirement in 1960.[49]

Despite Gunn's competence, only one member of his department became a Fellow of the Royal Society, whereas during Burn's period in office eleven received this distinction. Florey achieved even greater success with the department of pathology and was rewarded in 1945, along with his colleague Ernst Chain, with the Nobel prize for physiology and medicine. Especially

---

[48] For the difficulties of Macintosh see Beinart, 34–5. For the 'orthopaedic imbroglio' see Gardner, 'Some recollections', 183–8. Gardner (ibid. 229) described the Nuffield and clinical staffs as 'lamentably disconnected'. The committee on the Nuffield chairs described clinical staff as 'in general unsympathetic to the new venture': PCAM xvi. 71.

[49] Lord Zuckerman, 'W. E. Le Gros Clark', BMFRS xix (1973), 217–33; E. Bülbring and J. M. Walker, 'J. H. Burn', BMFRS xxx (1984), 45–89; J. B. Leathes, 'J. Mellanby', ONFRS iii (1939–41), 173–95; PNC ix. 117 (Mellanby); H. Dale, 'F. Mellanby', BMFRS i (1955), 193–222; Macfarlane, Florey; Gardner, 199–221 (Florey); E. P. Abraham, 'H. W. Florey', BMFRS xvii (1971); C. G. Phillips, 'E. G. T. Liddell', BMFRS xxix (1983) 333–59.

during the early years of their tenure, the new pre-clinical professors were desperately short of funds. The position was especially difficult for Florey, whose department had sunk into a severely depleted condition under Dreyer. Dreyer's School of Pathology, although built as 'a monument to him after his death became a mausoleum some years before it'. In attempting at a time of extreme retrenchment to reverse the dereliction of his department, Florey experienced severe difficulties in gaining funds for his team. Even the early work on penicillin was affected by this problem and the project was rescued by funds from the Rockefeller Foundation, which constituted the first substantial grant gained by Florey since his arrival in Oxford.[50]

The Nuffield benefaction was vitally important to Florey, and his expectations were undoubtedly aroused by his friend and fellow countryman Cairns. The latter had indeed spoken of siphoning off substantial sums from the benefaction for the pre-clinical departments, partly in recompense for the new obligations on them imposed by the Nuffield departments. Cairns mentioned £250,000 and even £500,000 as an appropriate share for the pre-clinicians.[51] However, vague promises of assistance evaporated when the Nuffield scheme came into operation. The pre-clinicians were thrown back on the small 'fluid research fund', which was controlled by a committee not weighted sufficiently in their favour. Florey's attempt to secure half the £15,000 available annually for pre-clinical research met with a rebuff from the Registrar.[52] The pre-clinical professors made direct representations, expressing their 'misgivings' and seeking for the departments an annual grant of £2,500 from the benefaction.[53] This plea also fell on deaf ears. Unsurprisingly Florey complained to the Secretary of the MRC, who urged that the University risked a 'calamitous split' between the pre-clinicians and the Nuffield professors.[54]   As Simon Flexner of the Rockefeller Foundation appreciated, the position of the pre-clinicians was likely to be further threatened because other grant-giving bodies would refuse to help them on the assumption that they fell within the orbit of the Nuffield benefaction.[55] The pre-clinical departments lost their technical staff to the new Nuffield departments, which paid better wages. This was damaging because the better technical staff were essential to the success of their departments.[56] As a final indignity the pre-clinicians watched £500

[50] Macfarlane, 251–326 (quotation at 231). For Dreyer see the obituary notice [by E. W. Ainley Walker] in Jl Pathology and Bacteriology xxxix (1934), 707–23; S. R. Douglas, 'Georges Dreyer 1873–1934', ONFRS i (1932–5), 569–76; Gardner, 99–115, Macfarlane, 227–33.
[51] OUA UR/FS/MD/13/1, Cairns to Florey, 8 Aug. 1936, Cairns to Veale, 29 Nov. 1936.
[52] OUA UR/FS/MD/13/11, exchanges between Veale and Florey, 1937.
[53] PNC iii. 67–9, 29 Oct. 1937.
[54] OUA UR/FS/MD/13/11, memorandum by Sir E. Mellanby, 24 Jan. 1938, and related correspondence.
[55] OUA UR/FS/MD/13/11, Flexner to Veale, 1 June 1938.
[56] For instance Amos Chown (pathology, Radcliffe Infirmary), Jim Kent (Dunn School), H. W. Ling (pharmacology) and Richard Salt (anaesthetics).

being added to the salaries of their Nuffield colleagues to compensate them for the loss of private earnings.

From 1937 onward the major effort within the new graduate school went into developing the four Nuffield departments as quickly as circumstances permitted. Inevitably, in the limited time before the outbreak of the Second World War, only modest progress was made in providing much needed additional accommodation. New wards were made for surgery and gynaecology, and a new wing was added to the maternity home for an obstetrics ward. These schemes absorbed about half of the £200,000 set aside for new building.[57]

The other main activity was the establishment of what were seen as ancillary specialisms at an appropriate level of seniority. Morbid anatomy had been eliminated from the list of chairs, but the veteran A. G. Gibson was appointed Nuffield Reader in Morbid Anatomy and Director of Pathology to take charge of the much needed expansion in pathological services. A. H. T. Robb-Smith was recruited from St Bartholomew's Hospital as assistant director. R. L. Vollum, the experienced bacteriologist from the Dunn School, was given the post of clinical bacteriologist. The post of Reader and Director of the Department of Clinical Biochemistry went to J. R. P. O'Brien from the Department of Biochemistry. This marked the beginning of biochemical research at the Radcliffe Infirmary. This team formed the nucleus of the division of laboratories of the clinical school.[58]

A further function of growing importance was radiology. Cairns was keen to establish a chair of radiology, but in the event leadership in this field was assumed by the experienced Alfred Barclay, who joined the Nuffield Institute as honorary radiologist from 1936 after a distinguished career at Manchester and Cambridge. Barclay remained in this post until 1948, when he died at the age of 72. In 1939 F. H. Kemp was appointed Nuffield radiologist and took charge of extending radiology facilities in the hospital group until his retirement in 1976.[59]

As a relatively late development, the chair of social medicine is usually discussed in isolation. However, from the outset both Buzzard and Cairns wanted to exploit new developments in preventive medicine, including the establishment of health centres. Nuffield was under pressure from various quarters to support academic development in preventive medicine.[60] In 1938, as Chief Medical Officer to the Ministry of Health, MacNalty also pressed the University to take a major initiative in this field. But at that time

57 For details see PNC iii–ix; Robb-Smith, *Radcliffe Infirmary*, 170, 220–1.

58 PNC ii–v.

59 OUA UR/FS/MD/13/2, Cairns to Veale, 7 Aug. 1937, 21 Nov. 1937, Veale to Cairns, 18 Nov. 1937; PNC i. 49–56; viii. 115–17; J. M. Guy, 'A. E. Barclay and angiographic research', *Brit. Jl Radiology* lxi (1988), 1110–14.

60 OUA UR/FS/MD/13/1, Buzzard to Cairns, 18 Aug. 1936, Cairns to Veale, 28 Aug. 1936, 31 Oct. 1936; OUA UR/FS/MD/13/D, Veale to W. Hobbs, nd [1937].

preventive medicine and public health possessed little cohesion and a relatively poor academic image. This was changed by John A. Ryle, the distinguished clinician from Guy's Hospital who was appointed Regius Professor of Physic in Cambridge. Under the banner of the recently coined term 'social medicine', Ryle wanted the emphasis of clinical teaching shifted from the intimate causes to the ultimate causes of disease, such as poverty, crowding and unemployment. In the mood of realism and commitment to social reconstruction at the beginning of the Second World War, social medicine was identified as a major priority in medical research and teaching. With financial support from the Nuffield Provincial Hospitals Trust, Oxford established Britain's first department of social medicine. Lord Nuffield's imagination was caught by this project, which was given special significance and prestige when it emerged that Ryle was willing to abandon the regius chair to direct the social medicine experiment in Oxford.[61] This coup was sufficiently important to merit a public announcement as the centrepiece of the Harveian Oration for 1942 delivered at the Royal College of Physicians by Sir Wilson Jameson, the recently appointed Chief Medical Officer to the Ministry of Health. The scheme for the Institute of Social Medicine was announced in the medical press in June 1942. At 55, Ryle took up his appointment on 1 April 1943.[62]

The Second World War presented an unexpected chance for Oxford to make the transition to a full medical school,[63] an opportunity grasped by Buzzard and his allies. This otherwise controversial move was presented as the only responsible reaction to the demands of the wartime emergency. Dispersal of the London medical schools meant that London students needed training elsewhere, while Oxford students were denied the usual clinical facilities in London. Beginning in October 1939, Oxford admitted about fifty clinical students each year.[64] The Oxford departments lost staff to military service, but three groups of people were available to make up the shortages: elder statesmen of medicine who had migrated to Oxford;

---

[61] OUA UR/FS/MD/17 and UDC/M/41/2.

[62] E. F. Buzzard, 'Reconstruction in the practice of medicine', *Lancet* 1942, ii. 343–7, 21 Mar. 1942 (Harveian Oration to Royal College of Physicians for 1941). See also E. F. Buzzard, 'The place of social medicine in the reorganization of health services', *Brit. Med. Jl* 1942, ii. 703–4, 6 June 1942; E. F. Buzzard, 'Social medicine and the future of health services', *Canadian Medical Services Jl* Nov. 1943, 77–82. W. Jameson, 'War and the advancement of social medicine', *Lancet* 1942, ii. 475–80 (24 Oct.) (Harveian Oration, 19 Oct. 1942).

[63] For Oxford's role in emergency medical services and research in the war see Beinart, *Anaesthetics*, 45–59; C. L. Dunn (ed.), *Emergency Medical Services* (2 vols London 1952); Macfarlane, *Florey*, 294–327; Robb-Smith, 170–84. A particularly important development was the establishment of the American hospital in Britain at Headington; it was named the Churchill Hospital and at its height contained 1,800 beds: OUA UR/FS/MD/18. Because of the war, in 1943, with Nuffield's support, T. Pomfret Kilner was brought in as Professor of Plastic Surgery; this chair was discontinued at Kilner's retirement in 1956.

[64] Gardner, 'Some recollections', 201–10; Robb-Smith, 172–4; O. Wrong, letter in *Lancet* 1978, i. 724 (Apr. 1978); J. Potter, 'The Oxford clinical medical school' in *County Hospital*, 29.

refugees fleeing from Fascism; and women, who could at last assume positions of real responsibility.[65] The evident success of the temporary and improvised medical school was received with quiet satisfaction by the reformers. This experiment provided a practical demonstration that transition to a full medical school was possible without prejudicing any of the fundamental features of the Nuffield scheme.[66]

The interdepartmental inquiry into medical education initiated by the government in 1942, chaired by Sir William Goodenough, forced the University to state its long-term intentions concerning the medical school. The evidence of the University, emanating from a committee chaired by Buzzard, accepted that the improvised clinical school, although 'in the circumstances not unsatisfactory', was too unselective to be a suitable model for the future. They proposed 'to retain in a very specially modified form this bridge between pre-clinical and advanced clinical studies'. It was argued that clinical teaching could preserve the traditional humanistic spirit of pre-clinical education. The committee warned that the position of the clinical school 'must not be allowed to become unbalanced by devoting an undue portion of its resources, intellectual and financial to the service of medicine'. In the unified and restructured pre-clinical and clinical course, it was argued, Oxford would maintain a consistent scientific rather than dogmatic approach to medicine, appropriate 'to the training of leaders, teachers, and investigators'. The intake for pre-clinical studies was expected to remain at fifty, whereas the clinical school would adopt a quota of twenty-five highly qualified graduates, most of whom would be recruited from Oxford.[67]

The University committee responsible for the evidence to the Goodenough Committee performed an awkward balancing act. For the purposes of the outside world it wanted to locate Oxford in the vanguard of reform and social experiment. On the other hand, to appease internal critics it was necessary to represent reform in terms of continuity with the humanistic and élitist traditions of an ancient university. The Goodenough Committee was intrinsically friendly towards Oxford, and the experimental medical school for training the medical élite received its positive blessing.[68]

[65] Especially notable elder statesmen were Leonard Findlay, George Gask, Sir Arthur Hurst, Sir William McArthur, Sir Robert McCarrison, Sir A. S. MacNalty and Sir Max Page. The refugees included H. K. F. Blaschko and Edith Bülbring (pharmacology), Ernst Chain (Dunn School), H. G. Epstein (anaesthetics) and Josep Trueta (orthopaedics). Among the women appointed were Bülbring; Ida Mann, Reader (1942) and soon Professor of Ophthalmology; the paediatrician Victoria Smallpeice (1940); and Honor Smith (1941) who worked on pyogenic and tubercular meningitis.

[66] Cairns advertised the positive benefits for research of the wartime arrangements: PNCAM xx. 55.

[67] HCP 185 (1943), 5–20, 'Report of the committee on the future of the medical school', 3 Apr. 1943; see also PNCAM xx. 43–63 and OUA UR/FS/MD/13/C.

[68] [Sir William Goodenough, chairman] Report of the Interdepartmental Committee on Medical Schools (London 1944).

However, this support had no practical importance. Apart from some technical concerns about the status of the London medical schools, the Committee's recommendations left little mark. All attention at this time was absorbed by arrangements for the post-war reorganization of the health services. Consequently the reformers needed to convince their colleagues within the University to accept the idea of a complete medical school: an idea which had been received critically at a meeting of the medicine board in December 1941.[69] Although opposition to the scheme for a selective clinical intake gradually waned, the critics of this idea kept up a vigorous rearguard action.

In 1947 Macintosh argued that the complete undergraduate medical school would 'strangle the development of the Nuffield scheme', that the majority of the Nuffield professors, himself, Witts and Moir, were opposed to this innovation, and that it had never been wanted by Nuffield.[70] On the pre-clinical side Florey also kept up his opposition to the complete undergraduate school. Florey was a member of the Medical Advisory Committee of Council, set up in November 1938 to advise on general policy questions. In 1951 Florey asked whether the undergraduate school issue had ever been referred to this Committee. The Registrar's confirmation that the Committee had not been consulted prompted Florey's resignation from it.[71]

The leadership of the medical school weakened after Buzzard's retirement. His successor as Regius Professor, A. W. M. Ellis, although successful as director of the Medical Unit at the London Hospital, was a negligible figure at Oxford, incapable of inspiring confidence among his fellow professors.[72] Upon his retirement in 1948 the University turned to the safe pair of hands of A. D. Gardner, the local bacteriologist, who was at least an efficient committee person. Gardner was 64 on appointment and remained in office until the age of 72 in 1956.[73] He possessed the inestimable advantage that, as a non-clinician, he posed no threat to the Nuffield professors in the competition for scarce clinical resources at the Radcliffe Infirmary.

Notwithstanding uncertainty about the future, the University applied for funds from the University Grants Committee (UGC) to support the development of the clinical school, and for the financial year 1946/7 this application was successful. In March 1945 and more explicitly in May 1946, despite their qualms about lack of funding and laboratory resources, the honorary medical staff committee of the Radcliffe Infirmary, the Nuffield Committee and the medicine board resolved to continue the clinical school.[74] The relevant committees went on to consider proposals by Cairns

[69] OUA FA/4/9/1/3, minutes of the board of the faculty of medicine, 20 Dec. 1941.
[70] OUA UR/FS/MD/13/2, memorandum by Macintosh, 17 Feb. 1947.
[71] OUA UR/FS/MD/A, exchanges between Florey and Veale, 1951.
[72] Robb-Smith, *Radcliffe Infirmary*, 193.
[73] Gardner, 'Some recollections'; Macfarlane, *Florey*, 241–3.
[74] HCP 191 (1945), 5; 192 (1945), 8; 194 (1946), 73, 318; 195 (1946), 24; OUA FA 4/9/1/4,

and Robb-Smith for the long-term development of the medical school.[75] Their suggestions for an entry quota of twenty-five and a co-ordinated divisional structure of the clinical departments were acceptable, but in October 1946 the medicine board rejected their proposal for splitting the functions of the teaching hospital between a 1,000-bed hospital on the Manor Road site in Headington and a 450-bed hospital based on the Radcliffe Infirmary. The medicine board resolved that 'steps be taken to establish a medical centre together with a Clinical Medical School on the Manor Road site, Headington, as soon as possible'. After a careful review of the alternatives, this view was also adopted by the Nuffield Committee.[76]

The centre of gravity of the debate over the medical school thus switched from the question of the complete school to questions of siting, organization and control of the hospital facilities required for teaching. It was realized that the clinical departments faced very much the same difficulties over the control of hospital facilities, whether they retained the complete clinical school or reverted to the previous graduate arrangement. Under the National Health Service Act (1946) the Radcliffe Infirmary, the Churchill Hospital and certain other local hospital facilities became designated as a teaching hospital and were amalgamated under a Board of Governors. The new grouping was called the United Oxford Hospitals. Although one-fifth of the Board of Governors were nominated by the University, it was arguably a more difficult entity to influence and control than the former separate voluntary hospitals. Unlike other provincial teaching hospital groups, the teaching hospitals in the Oxford and Cambridge groups accepted responsibility for routine services of the surrounding area. The local Regional Hospital Board—which controlled all hospitals outside the United Oxford Hospitals group, including the Nuffield Orthopaedic Centre as the Wingfield Morris Hospital was now called—was vigilant about the observance of these obligations. Thus it was by no means obvious that the needs of either clinical teaching or the research departments would be automatically protected under the National Health Service; this new situation called for a positive and unambiguous University policy on the development of the teaching hospital.[77]

Clarity was not assisted when the Nuffield Committee recommended in Michaelmas term 1947 that Council should at once pronounce in favour of

minutes of the board of the faculty of medicine, 5 Mar. 1945 and FA 4/9/1/5, minutes of 15 and 25 May 1946; PNCAM xxviii. 53; A. M. Cooke, 'A clinical school at Oxford?', OM 17 May 1945, 244–5.

[75] OUA UR/FS/MD/13/11, 'A longterm plan for the undergraduate clinical school', 11 June 1946.

[76] OUA FA 4/9/1/5, minutes of the board of the faculty of medicine, 16 Oct. 1946; PNCAM xxix. 89–91.

[77] Webster, Problems of Health Care, 262–73; E. J. R. Burrough, Unity in Diversity: The Start of Life of the United Oxford Hospitals (Oxford 1978).

'(1) building a single hospital centre at Headington and designating it as a teaching hospital, and (2) preserving the Radcliffe site for hospital development until experience has been gained'.[78] This 'pronouncement'—which encouraged an *ad hoc* approach to planning, leaving open the possibility of development on the Radcliffe Infirmary, Manor Road, and indeed Churchill sites—was adopted as a line of least resistance. The ground was prepared for extravagant expenditure on facilities which were not intended for permanent use, or which would hinder rational planning. The absence of planning mechanisms within the Ministry of Health and the starvation of resources for capital development within the National Health Service tended to encourage the casual approach to planning adopted in Oxford.[79] Further complication resulted from the conflicting interests of the various parties involved in hospital development. Accord, even over minor planning issues, was difficult to obtain among the Oxford clinicians, or between the University, Board of Governors and Regional Hospital Board. Each party was inclined to blame the other for the chaos which ensued. The normally statesmanlike Veale later revealed his frustration at the Board of Governors' failure to co-operate over a report reaffirming the University's adherence to the 'pronouncement' concerning the two-site basis for immediate extension in hospital facilities: 'One thing which was clear from this report was that there was no firm control anywhere of the relations between the Board of Governors and the University: they were not, in fact, in harmony on the fundamental questions. In the next few years attempts were made to improve the administrative machinery, in the hope that such improvements might produce identity of purpose, but the efforts of the University were not met by corresponding efforts of the Board of Governors.'[80] As indicated below, Veale must have been caused much personal anguish by the damage to the reputation of the University stemming from shortcomings of the Board of Governors. In a more sanguine judgement Potter concludes that 'it is perhaps not unfair to regard the 1950s as a period of the doldrums for the clinical school, while it waited in vain for the facilities essential for confidence in itself and for evidence which would convince others that it was a well-founded enterprise'.[81]

The National Health Service placed special emphasis on first-class hospital treatment for all, and the teaching hospitals were expected to set the standards for this reform. The situation in Oxford illustrates the manifold obstacles to translating Bevan's principle of 'universalising the best' into practice.[82] Indeed, in the annals of the National Health Service Oxford's record in the 1950s came to be regarded as an unmitigated disaster.

[78] PNCAM xxxii. 66–8.   [79] Webster, 216–20.
[80] Veale, 'Nuffield benefaction', 151.
[81] Potter, 'Oxford clinical medical school', 37.
[82] C. Webster (ed.), *Aneurin Bevan on the National Health Service* (Oxford 1991).

A committee, specially convened by Council to consider the future of the medical school, deplored the inadequacy of teaching beds in the Oxford area. The war had intervened before adequate accommodation had been provided for the Nuffield departments, and subsequent developments had exposed the inadequacy of the meagre additional facilities provided at the Radcliffe Infirmary before 1939. Despite developments at the Churchill site, Oxford could not meet its commitments to undergraduates or to the research departments. An explosive situation was developing in which the University would be unable to offer accommodation to the next regius professor if an active clinician were appointed, or to the next Nuffield professor of surgery if a specialist outside the field of neurosurgery.[83] The tragic and premature death of Cairns in July 1952 resulted in the appointment of the cardiovascular specialist P. R. Allison of Leeds. The problem was exacerbated with the appointment in 1954 as regius professor of George Pickering of St Mary's Medical School,[84] the first active clinician to take up the appointment since the time of Osler. Time was purchased by the willingness of the two new incumbents to delay taking up their appointments until beds and laboratories were provided for them. This effectively meant an interregnum of two years in the case of Pickering and four years with Allison. The University regarded this delay with dismay; there was a risk that the stability of the prestigious department of surgery would be undermined.

An increasingly hysterical tone entered into the University's efforts to persuade the Board of Governors to respond to its requirements for additional teaching accommodation.[85] After failing to make any impact in Oxford, the University turned for assistance to the Ministry of Health and to the UGC, who made high-level representations on its behalf. In 1953, in extreme frustration, the University threatened to close the undergraduate medical school unless immediate steps were taken to extend teaching facilities.[86] At last in March 1954 the Board of Governors entered into discussion on the future of clinical teaching. The smooth conclusion of these discussions was not helped by an aggressive memorandum sent to the Ministry of Health setting out the University's demands. Acrimonious negotiations were held in autumn 1954 before the hospital authority and the University agreed on a joint plan to put before the Ministry of Health.[87] The

[83] HCP 207 (1950), 247–321, report of committee on medical school annexed to quinquennial application 1952/7; see too OUA UR/FS/MD/13/2.
[84] PNCAM liii. 1–4; lvii. 75–9; lxi, p. iii.
[85] The following paragraphs are derived mainly from London, PRO, T227/954. See also A. H. T. Robb-Smith, 'The swinging pendulum', Oxford Medical School Gazette xiv (1962), 61–89; Veale, 'Nuffield benefaction', 150–3.
[86] PRO, T227/954, Workman to Vetch (Treasury), 16 May 1955.
[87] HCP 217 (1954), pp. xcvii (27), 159; 219 (1954), pp. lxix (3), 159; PNCAM liii, pp. iii–xvii; Veale, 'Nuffield benefaction', 151–2.

result was an over-hasty production of a 'master plan' for comprehensive development on the Radcliffe Infirmary site, with no reference to major hospital development on either of the sites in Headington. The main aim of the new plan was to provide fifty beds each for the professors of medicine and surgery, together with improved laboratory services and adequate premises for the anaesthetics department. The plan was amended to include laboratory space for the new regius professor. In March 1955 the provisional estimate for this plan was £426,000, although the only parts accurately costed were the facilities for the department of medicine. From non-Exchequer funds, mainly derived from Nuffield sources, the University offered a contribution of £196,000, which was regarded on all sides as a generous gesture of goodwill, offering significant savings to both the Ministry of Health and the UGC.[88] The master plan was approved by the Minister of Health and given enthusiastic backing by the UGC. However, the atmosphere soured when it emerged in 1956 that more detailed estimates amounted to £815,000, while this figure had reached £1 million by January 1958.[89] The University resolutely refused to increase its contribution to the inflated costs, with the result that the entire additional burden fell on the taxpayer. Veale alludes parenthetically to 'mismanagement of the building programme which caused delays and heavy excess expenditure', which at the time was largely but not entirely held to be the responsibility of the Board of Governors.[90]

The process of realizing the master plan was accompanied by incompetence and irregularities of many kinds—so much so that the affair came under scrutiny from the parliamentary Public Accounts Committee, which criticized all the parties involved, including the University. The Radcliffe Infirmary extension seemed to exemplify the commitment of Exchequer funds without prior approval. To Labour members of the Public Accounts Committee, it seemed that the Ministry of Health was applying a double standard, favoured treatment to the University of Oxford contrasting with parsimony elsewhere in the National Health Service.[91] Fortunately for the University the Public Accounts Committee was not aware that the large sums of public money being poured into the master plan at the Radcliffe Infirmary were merely a stop-gap measure pending action on a longer-term plan likely to involve transfer of the entire medical school to Headington. However, in the shorter term the University doggedly pursued development on the Infirmary site, spurred on by the departments deprived of modern facilities as a result of escalation in costs. Especially hard hit by poor

[88] HCP 219 (1954), 215.
[89] HCP 220 (1955), p. cii (13); 222 (1955), 276.
[90] Veale, 'Nuffield benefaction', 153.
[91] *Third Report from the Committee of Public Accounts (Session 1957–58)* (PP 1957–8 iv), minutes of evidence, 163–71; *Times* 14 Aug. 1958, 4; *Economist* 23 Aug. 1958, 593.

facilities were laboratory services and the department of anaesthetics.[92]
Macintosh never ceased to complain that the difficulties of the anaesthetics
department derived from the decision to introduce undergraduate teaching.
He exploited his difficulties to demonstrate that the University had betrayed
its obligations to Lord Nuffield. The great benefactor may well have been
persuaded by Macintosh, and thereby to some extent alienated from the
medical school. Nuffield's continuing generosity to the Nuffield Orthopaedic Centre stands in marked contrast to his reticence concerning the
medical school.[93] Lord Nuffield died in 1963. Macintosh retired in 1965.
Neither lived to see the Nuffield departments accommodated along lines
envisaged in 1936. The Gibson Laboratories for housing pathology were
finished in 1964 and the block containing the anaesthetics department in
1967. Expenditure on the entire project had risen from the anticipated
£426,000 to £2 million. This was not quite the end of public investment on
the Radcliffe Infirmary site. The main addition was the medical school's first
large lecture-theatre. This left provision of a library as the main desideratum
for the future. The tower of the Radcliffe Observatory, the 'Tower of the
Winds', was designated for this purpose, but this scheme was abandoned and
proper library provision for the medical school was therefore delayed until
phase II of the John Radcliffe Hospital.

Between 1936 and 1970 the main effort to improve the Radcliffe Infirmary
was devoted to the needs of teaching and research. Service needs were
neglected. As a general hospital, the Infirmary compared unfavourably with
the better provincial general hospitals. The old buildings and the site
hindered radical improvement, with the result that ever-increasing reliance
was placed on the Churchill Hospital at Headington for incremental
developments on both the teaching and service fronts. The result was a
paradox in which the University was formally committed to relocating the
teaching hospital at Manor Road in Headington, whereas in practice most
development continued to take place at the Radcliffe Infirmary, with the
large complex of the Churchill Hospital, also in Headington, emerging as
the obvious base for relocation. Recognizing the logic of the situation, the
Regius Professor proposed that the University should abandon its resolution
favouring Manor Road.[94] This dilemma was not resolved until Sir Oliver
Franks's term as chairman of the Board of Governors (1958–63). A further
conciliatory influence was Dame Janet Vaughan, the distinguished
haematologist who became Principal of Somerville College in 1945. Vaughan
was a well-known social reformer, a pioneer of the national blood
transfusion service, a member of the Goodenough Committee, an activist

[92] Complaints from the pathologists began at least as early as 1943: PNCAM xxi. 70–84. For
later representations see PNCAM lxii. 65–8.
[93] Beinart, *Anaesthetics*, 94–103.
[94] PNCAM xlvii. 41–2.

within the Royal College of Physicians and for a short time chairman of the Oxford Regional Hospital Board. Gradually animosities between the University and the Board of Governors subsided and a sense of common purpose emerged.

Preparation of the quinquennial application for 1962/7 and the submission required in connection with the ten-year hospital plan initiated by Enoch Powell (Minister of Health, 1960–3) forced the local planning bodies to decide on the future siting of the teaching hospital. Initially neither the Regius Professor nor the Board of Governors wanted to abandon the Radcliffe Infirmary site as the main centre for the teaching hospital. They were sharply aware of obligations stemming from the 'very large physical investment of public money' at the Infirmary.[95] It was from the clinical grass roots that the pressure came to revive the idea of concentrating future development at Manor Road. The Medical Staff Council was swayed by a group known as the 'Young Turks' to support the Manor Road option by a large majority. The Manor Road site assumed ascendancy in the planning documents produced in 1961, although the Radcliffe Infirmary continued to be mentioned as 'the main teaching hospital' or 'natural headquarters' for the foreseeable future.[96] Once a joint committee of the University and the Board of Governors was established to investigate planning possibilities at Manor Road, this proposal acquired its own momentum.[97] The Manor Road scheme gradually became translated from a plan for a general hospital for routine services into the 'main, possibly the only teaching hospital'. By 1964 plans had been made for a two-phase development, phase I being a maternity hospital and a relocated Nuffield Institute for Medical Research, and phase II the 1,000-bed teaching hospital. The former was needed to relieve pressure on the obstetric beds, which had not been expanded since 1939, despite the enormous increase in demand for institutional confinement that had occurred since that date. Building work at Manor Road began in 1968. Phase I of the John Radcliffe Hospital opened in 1971 and phase II in 1979.

The siting of the teaching hospital now resolved, a new sense of buoyancy and optimism emerged within the medical faculty. This change was assisted by the rotation of senior appointments, which helped to eliminate deep-seated misunderstandings grounded on ancestral grievances. Three Nuffield professors retired in 1965 and one in 1967. The opportunity was taken to review the Nuffield benefaction, and it emerged that fundamental changes in deploying the resources were permissible.[98] However, in view of the strong

[95] PCAM v. 25–9, report of meeting, 26 Nov. 1960.
[96] PCAM vi, pp. i–ii, 25–7, 45–7; ibid. vii. 5–13.
[97] PCAM xvii. 53–4; [W. R. S. Doll, chairman] *The Development of the Clinical School: Report of a Working Party* (University of Oxford 1971), 19–20.
[98] PCAM xiv. 59–71; xvii. 71–86.

backing received for all the departments concerned, it was decided to maintain continuity. Two of the appointees—John Stallworthy (obstetrics and gynaecology) and A. Crampton Smith (anaesthetics)—were long-standing members of their respective departments.[99] A major success was achieved by the appointment to the chair of medicine of the distinguished Paul B. Beeson, Professor and chairman of the department of internal medicine at Yale.[100] The chair of orthopaedics went to R. B. Duthie, a Scot who was Professor and chairman of the department of orthopaedic surgery at Rochester University in New York state.[101]

A similar pattern of change took place in the pre-clinical departments.[102] In the biochemistry department Peters retired in 1954, to be replaced by H. A. Krebs, famous for his work in Sheffield on the tricarboxylicacid cycle. Krebs was in turn replaced by R. R. Porter in 1967. At the department of physiology Liddell was replaced by G. L. Brown in 1959. When the latter was appointed Principal of Hertford College in 1967 he was succeeded by D. Whitteridge, formerly a research worker in the department, who had become Professor of Physiology in Edinburgh. In the department of pathology Florey resigned in 1963 to become Provost of Queen's College. He was replaced by Henry Harris, a fellow Australian and future regius professor. In 1960 Burn was replaced as Professor of Pharmacology by W. D. M. Paton from University College, London. In the department of anatomy Le Gros Clark was replaced by G. W. Harris in 1962. This period also saw enlarged accommodation for the pre-clinical departments, beginning with the physiology department, which was planned before the Second World War but not completed until 1953.[103] From the appointment of Sherrington to 1970 there persisted a roughly similar pattern of appointment to chairs within the medical school. A minority of routine internal appointments created continuity. Distinction was provided by outsiders, albeit many of them with some Oxford connection, such as Rhodes scholars. The latter factor contributed to a dominance of the Commonwealth over Europe. Many distinguished European and Jewish refugees found their way to Oxford, but few ended up in chairs in the medical school.

In the 1950s the professors of social medicine, plastic surgery and ophthalmology retired and were not replaced. The 1960s witnessed a reversal of this trend. In 1964 R. G. Macfarlane was granted an *ad hominem* chair in clinical pathology, making him the first to hold a professorial

[99] Turnbull, 'Maternity services', 120–4; Beinart, 104–10.

[100] Potter, 'Oxford clinical medical school', 39–40.

[101] Duthie, 'Orthopaedic services', 111–14.

[102] H. Harris, 'Medical research in South Parks Road 1920–1987' in *County Hospital*, 58–66.

[103] F. C. MacIntosh and W. D. M. Paton, 'G. L. Brown', *BMFRS* xx (1974), 41–73; M. L. Vogt, 'G. W. Harris (1913–1970)', ibid. xviii (1972), 309–29; H. Kornberg and D. H. Williamson, 'H. A. Krebs (1900–1981)', ibid. xxx (1984), 349–85; S. W. Perry, 'R. R. Porter (1917–1985)', ibid. xxxiii (1987), 443–89. See also Phillips, 'Liddell', ibid. xxix. 353–4.

appointment in the division of laboratories.[104] Oxford was somewhat backward in recognizing psychiatry as a major medical discipline. Serious consideration of a chair of psychiatry began in 1960, but its realization was delayed by lack of accommodation. In 1967 the chair was endowed with a grant from the W. A. Handley Trust, and M. G. Gelder was appointed.[105] During the 1960s periodic efforts were made to establish chairs in geriatrics, neurology and paediatrics. In the latter half of the decade endowments were obtained for neurology and paediatrics, and also for clinical pharmacology and radiology. Reflecting the general scale of values within medicine, geriatrics was given least priority.

In keeping with the compromises worked out at the time of the Nuffield benefaction, Oxford aimed to provide clinical training for a small élite who were destined to become teachers, investigators or consultants. Any element of complacency concerning the success of the clinical school was dispelled in 1952 by the first report of S. Truelove, the director of clinical studies. The intake was below twenty before 1950, and it rose just above this level in the 1950s. The school was small because it attracted few applicants and they were not outstanding in quality. College tutors, reflecting their pre-clinical bias, were prejudiced against the Oxford school and continued to recommend their better students to London hospitals. Truelove thought that the scepticism of the pre-clinicians was justified: the school had been unadventurous, and had merely imitated London teaching patterns but at a lower standard. In the director's view, Oxford had failed in its 'attempt to graft a medical school on to a county hospital supplemented by a few specialized medical units'; the 90 per cent of teaching undertaken by clinicians without serious research interest was barely competent, while the Nuffield departments took little part in undergraduate teaching and displayed no real commitment to the undergraduate medical school.[106]

Reflecting the general revival of the medical school in the 1960s, the fortunes of the clinical school also improved. The intake increased sharply to about fifty by 1968, and was projected to rise to seventy with the opening of phase II of the John Radcliffe Hospital.[107] Quality improved as numbers increased. For most of the 1960s the pre-clinical quota was one hundred. The view was increasingly taken that the low clinical intake reflected educational mediocrity rather than élitism, because the intakes lacked the

[104] For the chair of clinical pathology 1961–4 see PCAM vii. 45–6; ix. 25–7; x. 7–9; xi, pp. vii–viii; xvi, p. ii. G. V. R. Born and D. J. Weatherall, 'R. G. Macfarlane', BMFRS xxxv (1990), 209–45.

[105] For the chair of psychiatry 1960–7 see PCAM iv. 23–6; v. 33–4; vii, pp. ii–vii; ix, 37–8; xx. 11–15; xxiv. 27–8; xxvi, pp. xi–xii.

[106] PCAM xlvii. 1–18. Cf Development of the Clinical School, 10. The report of the 1971 working party indicates a significant but uneven increase in the contribution to teaching by university personnel between 1952 and 1970: ibid. 14–15.

[107] Development of the Clinical School, 10.

minimum critical mass necessary to develop a spirit of healthy competition and emulation. In 1970 it was even admitted that an intake of fifty was 'less than the optimum for the intellectual development of the students'.[108] By the mid-1950s it had been frankly accepted that the original conception of the pre-clinical school was becoming outdated. It was recommended that clinical training of the scientific type offered in Oxford was appropriate to all classes of the medical profession, including general practitioners.[109] However, it was not until Beeson and M. S. Dunnill, as director of clinical studies, took the initiative in the late 1960s that a thorough review of the teaching programme was undertaken. In line with the recommendations of the Royal Commission on Medical Education, a completely new curriculum was introduced at both the final honour school and clinical levels.[110]

Central to the new syllabus was a bridge course designed to serve as an introduction to the scientific basis of clinical medicine. This was the first serious attempt to integrate pre-clinical with clinical studies and establish a common ethos for the whole course. Yet again in Oxford, a new initiative depended on non-Exchequer funding, in this case from the Commonwealth Fund which gave £535,000, mainly for a clinical teaching laboratory which was completed in 1970. This was the last major building of the medical school to be constructed at the Radcliffe Infirmary. The Commonwealth Fund made its grant in the belief that the University was 'embarking upon one of the most significant undertakings in British medical education in recent times'.[111] Thus in 1970, after more than a century of vacillation, Oxford had come to terms with its role as a complete medical school. It was at last recognized that the presence of large numbers of clinical students, and diversification of their subsequent employment, need not subvert Oxford's aspirations as a great centre of medical progress.

[108] PCAM xxv, quinquennial application 1972/7, 50.

[109] HCP 229 (1958), 198; PNCAM lxii. 97.

[110] PCAM xxviii. 181; xxxv. 1–3; *Report of the Royal Commission on Medical Education 1965–68* (PP 1967–8 xxv Cmnd 3569). See also General Medical Council, *Recommendations as to Basic Medical Education* (London 1967).

[111] PCAM xxii. 53–62; xxiii. 167–8; xxiv. 111–13; *Development of the Clinical School*, 12.

13

Women

JANET HOWARTH

The peculiarities of women's higher education at Oxford and Cambridge stem largely from the peculiarities of those universities themselves.* Women were latecomers to these ancient institutions, which, unlike the ancient universities of Scotland and continental Europe, are residential collegiate communities. Different again was the situation at the newer coeducational universities of provincial England, the Commonwealth and the American west, which admitted women in significant numbers from their early days. As residential single-sex societies the women's colleges of Oxford and Cambridge invite comparison with the women's foundations of the eastern United States, the oldest of which, Mount Holyoke, was founded in 1837, some decades before the opening of Girton (1869), Newnham (1872), Lady Margaret Hall and Somerville (1879). Yet the American women's college—self-contained, endowed, controlling its own curriculum, employing men as well as women as faculty members—had a closer parallel in London's Royal Holloway College. Within Great Britain London had indeed a claim to the title of pioneer in women's higher education. Women were admitted to its degrees and to the coeducational University College in 1878; by 1914 London had well over a thousand internal women students, more than both ancient universities put together, and two of its professors and four readers were women. Oxford and Cambridge were at that stage the only British universities still to deny women degrees.

The introduction of women students to Oxford had come about as a result of the work of mid-Victorian dons in university extension. Whereas Emily Davies's college at Girton was a product of the women's movement of the 1860s, the patrons of women's education at Oxford were, like Newnham's founder Henry Sidgwick, members of the university community. Many of them were husbands and fathers of women who shared their interest in providing higher education for teachers and access to the world of learning

* I am grateful to the librarians of the Oxford women's colleges and the Fawcett Library, to Mark Pottle for processing the prosopographical data, to the many graduates and colleagues who have provided material for this chapter and above all to Pauline Adams and Anne Whiteman.

for women with an aptitude for scholarship. Annie Rogers, daughter of the economic historian Thorold Rogers, was for many years Secretary to the Association for Promoting the Higher Education of Women in Oxford (AEW), formed in 1878 to provide lectures for women students. She looked back on the movement that secured Oxford women 'degrees by degrees' as one in which 'men have taken the lead, though women have throughout advised and helped'. 'It has been a domestic matter, and there has never been occasion to . . . apply pressure from outside. The women and their friends have worked out for themselves the problems of growth and adaptation to a University of ancient traditions and constant changes.'[1] The women's societies on the eve of the First World War—three residential halls situated in the suburbs of North Oxford, a fourth on the wrong side of Magdalen Bridge and the Society of Oxford Home-Students—were the product of that process of evolutionary change, by which venerable institutions acquired new functions through spontaneous adaptation and experiment, on which the English were apt to pride themselves.

The four halls, each with its own principal and staff of women tutors, were constitutionally quite unlike the men's colleges but nevertheless fairly well integrated into Oxford's academic life. They were incorporated as companies under the Board of Trade and governed by councils or committees which included men dons as well as academic wives, old students and a few of the women dons. Many men dons also took women for tutorials and all but a very few admitted them to lectures. Each of the women's societies had characteristics that linked it with a particular section of university opinion. Somerville's associations were with university liberalism and Gilbert Murray, Liberal candidate for Oxford University between 1918 and 1929, was a long-serving member of its council. Somerville was undenominational and over a third of its students in the early twentieth century were nonconformists. It had no chapel until its governing body, against some opposition from past and present students, accepted a benefaction in 1932 from a Baptist old Somervillian, Emily Kemp, to build an undenominational 'house of prayer for all peoples'.[2] Lady Margaret Hall had been the earliest venture by Anglican high churchmen into women's higher education. Founded by the Warden of Keble, Edward Talbot, and his wife Lavinia, it had its own settlement run on definite church lines in Lambeth and connections through the work of Mother Edith Langridge with the Oxford mission to Calcutta. Its principal and members of its council were required to be members of the Church of England and the same was true of St Hugh's, a hall opened in 1886 by Elizabeth Wordsworth, Principal of Lady Margaret Hall, to cater for poor students; the requirement

---

[1] A. M. A. H. Rogers, *Degrees by Degrees* (London 1938), 2.
[2] V. Farnell, *A Somervillian Looks Back* (Oxford 1948), 65.

that both principals should be Anglicans lasted until the late 1960s.[3] Both societies admitted a few non-Anglicans but St Hugh's, in particular, attracted a great many daughters of the clergy. A third Anglican foundation, St Hilda's, in 1914 the smallest of the halls, was also the only one to be founded by an initiative from outside Oxford. Opened in 1893 by Dorothea Beale, Principal of Cheltenham Ladies' College, it was incorporated with a sister-college, St Hilda's, Cheltenham, where students of the Ladies' College trained as teachers and did London external degrees. But it was run by an Oxford committee, and St Hilda's likened itself, as a college linked with a great public school, to the sister-foundations of New College and Winchester.[4]

The Society of Oxford Home-Students, for which Cambridge had no equivalent, and which also had a principal and staff of tutors, made provision for women students not attached to a hall: local residents living in their own homes, Catholic students living in the hostel at Cherwell Edge run by the nuns of the Holy Child Jesus, and others living with 'hostesses' in the city. A second hostel was opened in 1928 by the Anglican Wantage Sisters, Springfield St Mary in the Banbury Road. Some home-students were, like the men non-collegiates, too poor to afford the cost of residence in a hall. Many were foreigners, mostly American graduates or continental students taking English language courses. But the Society catered also for families who believed—like its Principal, Bertha Johnson, wife of the historian and chaplain of All Souls A. H. Johnson—that many women were better suited to home than to institutional life while pursuing their education [plate 13.1].[5] The halls also catered for a spectrum of opinion on women's education, from the moderately advanced to the moderately conservative, that characterized the Oxford of 1914. Somerville and St Hugh's had taken the name 'college' but Lady Margaret and St Hilda's retained the description 'hall', originally chosen to emphasize, by contrast with the feminist ethos of Girton, the domestic and ladylike style of Oxford's women's societies. At St Hilda's, according to Dorothea Beale's wishes, students who did not need professional qualifications were encouraged to follow non-examination courses, thus catering for those who believed that examinations were bad for women's health or character.[6]

The women's societies had a quasi-extramural relationship with the University, which was slower to grant them official recognition than to

<hr>

[3] 'The Lady Margaret Hall settlement' in G. Bailey (ed.), *Lady Margaret Hall: A Short History* (London 1923); C. Hibbert and E. Hibbert (eds), *The Encyclopaedia of Oxford* (London 1988), 213; HCP 263 (1969), 1019.

[4] *The Four Oxford Women's Colleges* (Oxford 1923), copy in Bodl. dep. c. 707, p. 14.

[5] R. F. Butler and M. H. Prichard (eds), *The Society of Oxford Home-Students: Retrospects and Recollections 1879–1921* (privately printed [1930]), 24.

[6] E. Raikes, *Dorothea Beale of Cheltenham* (London 1911), 236–7.

admit their students to lectures and examinations.[7] Between 1910 and 1920 they were brought under the supervision of a university committee, the delegacy for women students, which took over most of the functions of the AEW and on which nine women, six of them elected by the women dons and administrative staff, sat together with the vice-chancellor and proctors and nine members of Convocation. A committee of this delegacy became in 1910 the governing body of the home-students and their Principal became the first woman to receive a senior appointment from the University (although Mrs Johnson, who retained the post until 1921, was at her own insistence unpaid). After 1920 the home-students were governed, like the men non-collegiates, by a delegacy of their own.

Shortly before the war Council set up a committee to explore the suggestion in Curzon's 'scarlet letter' to the University that women should be admitted to the degree of BA. But in 1914 opinion was not in favour of admitting women to positions of influence or authority in the University. The committee proposed that women should be eligible for the BA but not the MA, which conferred membership of Congregation and Convocation.[8] Nor were women to be members of faculties or examine for the University—despite the evident distinction of such pre-war dons as Mildred Pope, Somerville's French tutor, who became in 1927 the first woman Reader at Oxford and in 1933 was elected to a chair at Manchester; Ada Elizabeth Levett, the St Hilda's historian, whose career culminated in a chair at Westfield College, London; and a future principal of Westfield, Eleanor Lodge, the tutor and Vice-Principal of Lady Margaret Hall who had already been invited to lecture to postgraduates by Oxford's modern history board in 1913/14.

Ad hoc provision for women's academic needs which nevertheless emphasized their separate status was a characteristic strategy. Oxford published women's examination results in a separate class-list; this practice continued until 1952. Both Oxford and Cambridge opened their medical examinations to women in 1916–17: Oxford's Professor of Human Anatomy, Arthur Thomson, insisted on the appointment of a woman demonstrator to look after them and on the building of a separate laboratory in his department, where women did their anatomy practicals until 1934. Whether women really belonged in an ancient university was a question that continued to trouble some dons. They were not all misogynists or college tutors who feared the distracting influence of women on their men pupils. Ernest Barker had taught such women of 'memorable ability' as Elizabeth Levett and Maude Clarke before leaving Oxford to become Principal of the coeducational King's College, London. An admirer of the American

[7] G. N. Curzon, Lord Curzon of Kedleston, *Principles and Methods of University Reform* (Oxford 1909), 193–200.

[8] Ibid. 195–7; Rogers, *Degrees by Degrees*, 94–5.

women's colleges, he remained unconvinced that women were best educated in universities where 'the women's colleges are feminine islands in a male sea, half isolated and half besieged with attentions, and the general run of studies and the course of social life is determined by masculine predominance'.[9] The unique prestige and resources of Oxford and Cambridge meant that the claims of women to share in their advantages were hard to resist: how far they could be assimilated by these masculine communities remained an open question.

The First World War shifted the balance of opinion at Oxford towards assimilation. In a University all but emptied of men undergraduates, women's fees became a crucial source of revenue, while nine of the thirty women tutors at Oxford in 1920 had lectured for the University during or immediately after the war.[10] With the opening of the degree of BM to women, a recognition of their war work, they were eligible to sit all undergraduate examinations; in 1918 the postgraduate BCL examination was also opened. Parliament's concession of votes for women in that year and the Sex Disqualification (Removal) Act of 1919 were the prelude at Oxford to a statute, introduced in Congregation on 17 February 1920 by Professor Geldart and A. D. Lindsay, which admitted women to full membership of the University. The only degrees still closed to them were the BD and DD (for which women became eligible only in 1935). Amendments designed to exclude women dons from faculty boards and examinerships were roundly defeated (108 votes to 43 and 107 votes to 35) and the statute passed in May 1920 without further opposition. 'The War had made a peaceful change in the status of women which seemed incredible six years ago', wrote Annie Rogers. Oxford's 'revolution . . . made with rose-water' was not repeated at Cambridge, however, where on 8 December 1920 the Senate rejected a proposal to admit women to full membership. In March 1923 they were made eligible instead for titular degrees which gave Cambridge's women dons no voice in university government, a position with which they had to rest content until the MA was conceded to women in 1948. At the same time a limit of five hundred was placed on the number of women in residence at Cambridge, a ratio of one to eight or nine men undergraduates.[11]

The ground had been better prepared at Oxford by committee work that resolved in private issues that were fought out at Cambridge in the Senate, which included non-resident MAs as well as dons. Girton and Newnham were, moreover, larger and more self-sufficient than the women's communities of Oxford, and less under the influence of university men. By the

[9] E. Barker, *Age and Youth* (Oxford 1953), 100.
[10] Rogers, 106.
[11] Ibid. 105, 107; R. McWilliams-Tullberg, *Women at Cambridge: A Men's University—though of a Mixed Type* (London 1975), 203–4.

1970s Oxford men had ceased to regard women's colleges as their protégés and had come to see them as rivals; that point was perhaps reached sooner at Cambridge. But whatever the cause of the Cambridge decision, endorsed by the Asquith Commission which considered it should remain 'a "men's University" though of a mixed type', the result was to increase the relative attractions of Oxford for women.[12] Numbers of resident undergraduates rose from 400 in 1918 to 751 in 1925, not far short of one woman to four men, a trend that created alarm.[13] Lewis Farnell, Vice-Chancellor from 1920 to 1923, was a supporter of the movement that in 1927 imposed a quota, albeit a more generous one than at Cambridge, on women students. According to Farnell, 'we all believed in 1920 that Cambridge, if we made the great concession which the altered circumstances of the time commended to most of us, would be certain to follow our lead. We have been detrimentally deceived. It is a law of nature that as the numbers of women indefinitely increase our young men will prefer "the other place" '.[14]

The history of women's education at Oxford in the half century after 1920 can be viewed from two different perspectives: as a story of growth and assimilation, a theme familiar in other chapters in this volume, or as one of constraints of various kinds experienced by 'women implanted into a men's society' (a phrase used by Lady Ogilvie, Principal of St Anne's from 1952 to 1966).[15] The first of these interpretations appealed to earlier historians of women at Oxford, Annie Rogers and Vera Brittain. This was a period when the 'uncompromising' view, that women's higher education ought to be assimilated to the best academic traditions developed by men, gained more ground in Britain than in the United States and became firmly entrenched at Oxford.[16] An appeal brochure issued in 1923 stated that 'all the Women's Colleges have from the first been organized as far as possible on lines parallel with those of the ancient foundations for men'.[17] Though strikingly untrue as a historical statement, that does reflect their aspirations in this half-century.

The curriculum followed by men and women students at Oxford was already very similar by 1914, although women were permitted to substitute modern for classical languages in responsions and to sit honour or pass schools without first taking all the qualifying examinations demanded of undergraduates. From 1920 the same regulations applied to both sexes, a policy supported by both the Association of Headmistresses and the

[12] *Asquith Report*, 173.
[13] HCP 132 (1925), 401; 137 (1927), 50.
[14] L. R. Farnell, *Statute on Limitation of Numbers (Women)* (12 June 1927), copy in Bodl. GA Oxon. c. 314, fo 28.
[15] Franks Commission, oral evidence xxx. 12.
[16] S. Delamont, *Knowledgeable Women* (London 1989), 102–32; B. M. Solomon, *In the Company of Educated Women* (New Haven Conn. 1985).
[17] *Four Oxford Women's Colleges*, 4.

women's colleges. It was fortunate for their students that compulsory Greek in responsions was abolished months before women were admitted to degrees. No exemption was sought from the continuing matriculation requirement for Latin, which lasted until the 1970s, despite the relatively weak tradition of classical language teaching in girls' schools. Nor was there any attempt to exempt women who had taken honour schools but not the men's full degree course including 'divvers' and 'pass mods' from jumping through those hoops before they qualified for degrees. The early 1920s saw many middle-aged women, including college tutors, taking such elementary examinations garbed in undergraduate gowns.

There was growing recognition in these years of the advantages for women of modelling their societies more closely on the men's colleges. Within the University, colleges enjoyed a recognized autonomy. Within colleges, moreover, tutors enjoyed a status as members of self-governing communities of scholars that was very different from the subordinate position of schoolmistresses in the only other kind of academic community familiar to women. The 'St Hugh's row' of 1923–4, in which a tutor, Cecilia Ady, was dismissed with less than a week's notice and no right of appeal for allegedly subverting the Principal's authority, reinforced the case for constitutional change.[18] Newnham had already led the way by obtaining a royal charter reincorporating the College under a governing body of which the Principal was chairman; its tutors became fellows and members of the governing body. The four residential societies of Oxford followed suit in 1925–6. Governing bodies continued to include outside members, mostly men dons, but over the years men became less willing to give time to running communities increasingly capable of running themselves [plate 13.2]. Between 1950 and 1955 the four colleges changed their statutes to confine membership of the governing body to the principal and fellows.

These constitutional changes involved some breaches with past tradition. There is irony in the complaint voiced by some undergraduates in the 1930s and after, that women's colleges were narrowly academic communities devoid of the traditions that gave character to the men's foundations.[19] The real problem was that the traditions of their founders did not have a continuing appeal to Oxford women. For St Hilda's, which ceased to encourage non-examination students after the war, the new charter severed its constitutional links with Cheltenham and styled it a 'college'; oral tradition recalls that a bust of Miss Beale was deposited by students in the Cherwell. At Somerville the role of old students, described by Emily Penrose as 'the children of the college', who under its deed of incorporation

[18] R. Trickett, 'The row' in P. Griffin (ed.), *St Hugh's: One Hundred Years of Women's Education in Oxford* (Basingstoke and London 1986).

[19] Marghanita Laski, reported in *Daily Telegraph* 6 Mar. 1936, 16; K. McLeod, 'Women in Oxford', *Isis* 30 May 1962, 8–14; J. Ashley, 'Women in Oxford', *Isis* 10 Oct. 1975, 6.

had recreated it periodically by electing council members, was marginalized in a way that contributed to ill feeling over the issue of the chapel.[20] The Society of Oxford Home-Students was to go furthest in repudiating tradition. Its name was changed in 1942 to St Anne's Society, after a petition from ten of its BAs to their delegacy had argued that the name 'home-student' suggested to the outside world a correspondence college, a domestic science college or a body of external students. The idea of the woman home-student had become anachronistic. The shortage of lodgings after the Second World War made it impossible to accommodate her in practice. In 1952 St Anne's received its charter as the fifth women's residential college in Oxford. It chose to retain men members on its governing body until 1959 but marked the break with tradition by dropping the Society's motto—that of Mrs Johnson's family, *faire sans dire*—in favour of the more assertive family motto of their current Principal, Eleanor Plumer, a field marshal's daughter, *consulto et audacter*.[21] St Anne's was in 1979 the first of the women's colleges to go mixed.

To Vera Brittain it seemed that the triumphant culmination of changes that brought women's colleges into line with the men's ancient foundations was their formal recognition in 1959 as full 'colleges of the university'. 'Women at Oxford had finally ceased to be a class apart. Henceforward their story would belong to the history of Oxford University, and the history of the university would be theirs.'[22] Their principals were now eligible to be vice-chancellor, and Lucy Sutherland was at once appointed pro-vice-chancellor. Acceptance of a woman in the disciplinary role of proctor took longer, and it was not until 1977 that women's colleges were incorporated in the proctorial cycle. But a 'representative of the women's colleges' was elected annually to assist the proctors from 1960 to 1963, when this officer was renamed the 'assessor' and the constituency widened to include mixed postgraduate as well as women's colleges, which elected by rota.

There was much to sustain the impression that women students were well assimilated in Oxford by the 1960s. The national press was quick to note their achievements in the Norrington table, as it had been to record their success in winning University prizes when these were opened to them in the 1920s.[23] Women and men students came increasingly from similar class backgrounds. An Oxford education, previously sought chiefly by the daughters of the middle-middle classes, now attracted rather more debutantes, while admission to the men's colleges became more meritocratic.

[20] SCA charter file, papers concerning the constitution of the Association of Senior Members (ASM) 1925–6; ASM report 1932–3.

[21] M. Reeves, *St Anne's College, Oxford: An Informal History* (Oxford 1979), 6–7, 28.

[22] V. Brittain, *The Women at Oxford* (London 1960), 238.

[23] London, Fawcett Library, press cuttings, education, Oxford. *Daily Telegraph* 11 Mar. 1930, 15 recorded that the Arnold Memorial prize for an essay on English literature had gone to a woman three times in the past decade.

It remained the case that women were recruited from a wider spread of schools, but by 1965 there was little to choose between the proportions of men and women undergraduates who came up from maintained schools (40.2 and 42.7 per cent respectively).[24] As Mary Bennett, Principal of St Hilda's from 1965 to 1980, observed, 'the men had dug further down and the girls had become much classier'.[25] Not surprisingly, moreover, Oxford's women graduates now more frequently married men graduates of Oxford. Of those women who did marry, the proportion who chose an Oxford spouse rose from 45 per cent in the 1930s to over 60 per cent in the 1960s [figures 13.1–2]. The University became, in the words of one woman graduate (St Hugh's 1946) 'a marvellous "dating agency"'.[26]

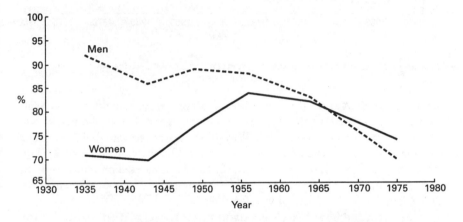

FIGURE 13.1   PERCENTAGE OF OXFORD STUDENTS, 1930–79, WHO BY 1991 HAD
MARRIED, DISTINGUISHING MEN AND WOMEN

Women dons were in some respects less well assimilated. Between the wars there were complaints that they were rarely asked to examine.[27] In the late 1950s only one of Oxford's 97 professors was a woman and there were only three among its 595 members of boards of electors to chairs. On Council women provided two out of twenty-two members, on the General Board one out of twenty-two, and they were equally under-represented on faculty boards other than English language and literature. Yet in a generation concerned 'to keep well clear of any imputation of fanatical and boring

---

[24] *Franks Report* ii. 47; cf above, 55–7 and table 3.2.
[25] SHCA tape-recording of interview by Fernanda Perrone with Mary Bennett, 29 June 1989.
[26] Where this chapter makes use of the replies to the History of the University's postal survey of matriculants 1930–79 (HUD/C/SV) respondents are identified only by their college and date of matriculation.
[27] Anonymous letter to *OM* 1 Nov. 1928, 86.

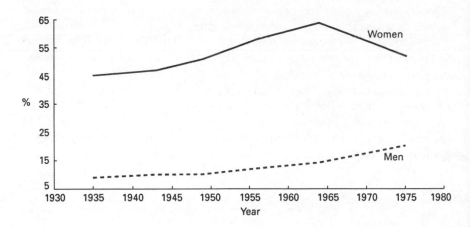

FIGURE 13.2   PERCENTAGE OF MARRIED OXFORD STUDENTS, 1930–79, WHO MARRIED
AN OXFORD SPOUSE

feminism' explanations for this state of affairs were sought not in male discrimination but in the historic disadvantages of the women's colleges—poor, short of research fellowships, distanced by their suburban location 'from that sort of casual contact, in Common Rooms or in Turl Street, where so much of one's practical business is carried on and where the normal exchange of information and opinions takes place'—or even in the choice, apathy or defeatism of women dons.[28]

Evidence of the University's goodwill towards the women's societies was provided by the decision to extend to them (even before they had become full colleges) the system of Common University Fund (CUF) appointments—crucially important in enabling poor colleges to extend their fellowships—whereby University Grants Committee (UGC) funds were channelled into the payment of college tutors while leaving to colleges the right to make appointments.[29] This system, unique to Oxford and not replicated in Cambridge's faculty-dominated system of appointments, explains the fact that the proportion of dons in the 1960s who were women (13 per cent) was slightly above the national average (10 per cent) and not far short of the proportion of women among Oxford's students (16 per cent). At Cambridge, by contrast, only 4.7 per cent of university teaching staff in 1973 were women.[30] Oxford was, moreover, a society in which successful senior

[28] 'The subjection of women', *OM* 7 Feb. 1957, 250–4; 'Where are the women?', *OM* 6 Mar. 1958, 334.

[29] On the CUF system see below, 652–6.

[30] *Franks Report* i. 51–2. *Forty Years On: the CUWAG [Cambridge University Women's Action Group] Report on the Numbers and Status of Academic Women at the University of Cambridge* (Cambridge 1988), 2.

10.3 L. R. Wager in East Greenland, summer 1953

10.4 Bureau of Animal Population field course in Wytham Woods, 1953

10.5 The Clarendon Lab's 1.2 MeV Cockcroft Walton installation, 1954

13.1 Miss Ruth Butler with some home students, 1941

13.2 The Principal of St Hugh's and four fellows studying plans for a new building, 1936

13.3   Queen Mary's visit to Oxford, 11 Mar. 1921

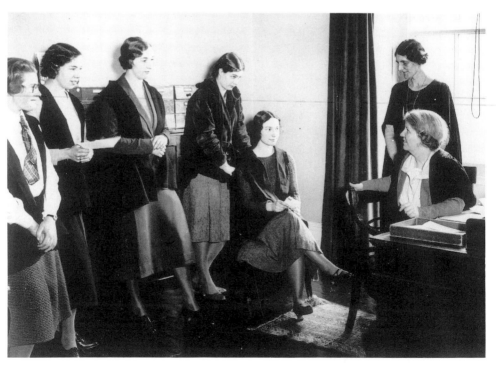

13.4   Miss Darbishire and Miss Farnell with the Somerville JCR committee, 1930 or 1931

13.6 St Hilda's College eight with their coach, 1921

13.7 Oxford University Women's Rowing Crew with their coach, 1938

13.8 A history tutorial in St Hilda's, 1952

13.9 Group photograph at St Hilda's College ball, Feb. 1955

13.10 Four principals of St Hilda's, 1981

14.1 The Oxford Union debates Victorian ideals, 1922

women were increasingly given ungrudging recognition. Lynda Grier and
Grace Hadow were on Council between the wars; Margery Perham became
in 1937 one of the first six fellows of Oxford's first mixed graduate society,
Nuffield College; Lucy Sutherland was part of the inner ring of Council
members who ran Oxford in the post-war decades; Helen Gardner gave
evidence to the Franks Commission jointly with Maurice Bowra urging the
need to free dons for research. The drift of opinion in favour of
incorporating successful women is shown by the experience of Janet
Vaughan, Principal of Somerville from 1945 to 1967 and for some years the
only scientist on Council, to which she was elected with the backing of her
friend Principal Stallybrass of Brasenose.[31] Yet he had been known before
the war as a misogynist who banned women from his lectures and was
among those who had resisted the inclusion of women in the brief of the
Appointments Committee, forcing the creation in 1936 of a separate
women's committee (not amalgamated with the men's committee until
1953).[32] Asked by the Franks Commission, 'do you think there are any sex-
linked barriers persisting in Oxford still?', Dame Janet replied, 'I would have
said none in Oxford . . . unless people imagine them'.[33]

A more pessimistic assessment of the experience of women is suggested by
the graduate (Lady Margaret Hall, 1958) who commented, 'in my days going
to Oxford as a female was like being on the "sidelines" of a giant male public
school'. Despite a modest increase in the absolute numbers of women
students they remained a small minority, less than one in five of the
undergraduate body after the mid-1920s [figure 3.1].[34] The falling proportion of women students in the two decades after the Second World War
reflected a national trend, but in other British universities in 1963 they
amounted to 28 per cent of the student population. Headmistresses
considered that the imbalance in Oxford's sex-ratio created harmful
pressures on women, and some students agreed.[35] Others, however, found
that it also 'provided a lot of fun' (St Hilda's graduate, 1967). Only after the
first men's colleges went mixed in 1974 did the sex-ratio change significantly.
Meanwhile the poverty of the women's colleges left them unable to offer
amenities and scholarships to their students or stipends to their dons on a
scale comparable with the men's colleges. Moreover the masculine and club-
like traditions of a collegiate university were not readily modified to
accommodate women, and many doors remained closed to them. They

---

[31] SCA J. Vaughan, 'Jogging along, or a doctor looks back', 128.
[32] SHCA tape-recording of interview by F. Perrone with C. Cole and B. Dodgson (Oxford
Home-Students 1925), 5 May 1989; HCP 152 (1932), 223–5.
[33] Franks Commission, oral evidence xxvii. 2.
[34] Cf above, 45–6.
[35] Franks Commission, oral evidence i. 41; McLeod, 'Women in Oxford'.

could not join the undergraduate Union until 1962 and even then the hostility of life members confined them to debating membership until the following year. Nor did women have a Union of their own; an attempt in the 1930s to provide an equivalent, known as the Pentagon Club, with rooms in the High Street, had failed for lack of funds. Membership of the Oxford University Dramatic Society was closed to women until 1964 (although the official ban on invitations to individual women undergraduates to act in its productions had been lifted in 1926). There was bitter conflict within the Alembic Club before membership was conceded to women chemistry dons in 1950.[36] The treasurers of the women's colleges were excluded until 1960 from the estates bursars' committee: an earlier request for representation was turned down on the grounds that it met over dinner.[37] Women guests were not permitted at meals in the halls of men's colleges even at the point when the first serious proposal for co-residence came under discussion at New College in 1964. A St Hugh's graduate (1956) concluded that 'the full university experience was still not really available to women in the late 50s . . . one felt women's colleges . . . were still poor relations . . . Now my daughter is at a very different Oxford I have felt when discussing it with her and with an old, old friend (born 1904) who was at Somerville that the real divide comes not between her and me (even though there was World War II) but between the 1950s Oxford and the Oxford of today'.

The principle that 'the university has a right to remain predominantly a men's university' was asserted by supporters of the statute, passed by a large house (229 votes to 164) in Congregation on 14 June 1927, which limited the number of women students in residence to 840 and prohibited the foundation of a new women's college if it would make the ratio of women to men students higher than one to four.[38] Dame Lucy Sutherland, listening to the debate from the gallery as an undergraduate, was shocked by the animosity shown towards women by some speakers and she remained convinced that the quota had had a deeply damaging effect: 'it kept the women's colleges . . . poor; it drove away able young women to less restrictive universities, and it resulted in very poor pay for their teachers'.[39] This episode, headlined in the press as 'Sex War at Oxford', was in fact the only occasion when the women's colleges took a stand on an issue that was one of principle rather than practical needs.[40] When Council first considered

---

[36] J. C. Smith, 'The development of organic chemistry at Oxford' (undated typescript available at Dyson Perrins Laboratory), 54; see also above, 151, 268.

[37] Bodl. dep. c. 687, fo 71, principals' meeting 26 Oct. 1942; dep. d. 762, principals' minute-books 1959–79, fo 11.

[38] G. B. Allen et al., To the Members of Congregation (6 June 1927), copy in Bodl. GA Oxon. c. 314, fo 26; Gazette lvii (1926/7), 646.

[39] L. S. Sutherland, 'Women in Oxford', History of the University tape-recorded seminar, Nuffield College, 5 June 1973, HUA.

[40] Oxford Chronicle 7 June 1927, 6; Daily News 18 Mar. 1927, 5.

limiting their numbers in 1925, a figure of 700 had been suggested—an actual decrease in numbers. Negotiations secured a quota that left them room to expand, while the women's colleges voluntarily passed by-laws restricting their intake. They even offered in 1927 to accept the statute without opposition if it were limited to a term of ten years. Yet they refused to acquiesce in a permanent measure that denied them the same right as other colleges to determine their own numbers and ruled out the possibility of a new women's foundation. The underlying issue was parity of esteem for women's societies within the University.[41]

Why did Congregation make a point of denying them this parity? Not, it seems, because of any general backlash of feeling against women in Oxford. The Union had, it is true, debated and passed earlier in the year a motion that 'the women's colleges should be razed to the ground', but Dame Lucy, who was guest-speaker in that debate, described it as a light-hearted affair, full of bad jokes, after which she struck up a lasting friendship with the proposer of the motion.[42] When the 'limitation statute' was mentioned in the Union there were loud cheers for an undergraduate who said 'it's just a bit of beastly selfishness on the part of the older men'. Anti-feminist speakers in Congregation—notably Principal Hazel of Jesus, who spoke of 'locking the stable door' and said that women had not been ungenerously treated, seeing that they contributed so little to the University—did not represent the views of the majority. According to Alice Bruce, Vice-Principal of Somerville, many of them were 'thoroughly ashamed, and it was amusing afterwards to hear the number of people who apologized for their votes, and gave a variety of foolish reasons for them'.[43]

The real reasons for the vote were partly to do with pressure on library and lecture space and on lodgings in crowded post-war Oxford. The view that when resources were scarce priority should be given to men still had defenders in the 1960s on the grounds that 'the return that the nation expects to get . . . is very much larger in a direct way, though perhaps not in an indirect way, from university education of men rather than of women'.[44] But in 1927 the 'fundamental question', as one friendly male don had put it, was 'feminine influence and the "monstrous regiment of women"'.[45] It was illogical, claimed Margery Fry, to blame women undergraduates for the fashion for 'unmanly' activities like dancing and taking morning coffee; yet their part in eroding the traditional masculine way of life had attracted comment, as had the prominence of women in the Labour Club and as

[41] SCA limitation of numbers file.
[42] Sutherland, 'Women in Oxford'.
[43] Quotations from *Times* 15 June 1927, 11 (Hazel); SCA limitation of numbers, Bruce to Penrose, 17 Sept. 1927.
[44] M. Shock in Franks Commission, oral evidence xxx. 3.
[45] SCA limitation of numbers, M. N. Tod to E. S. Craig, 9 Dec. 1926.

canvassers for Gilbert Murray.[46] There were anxieties—not wholly foolish ones, perhaps—about Oxford's image with parents and public schools. Annie Rogers was told that 'there is a Cambridge propaganda to get boys for themselves by representing Oxford as socialistic, weak in athletics and be-womaned, and the idea is that we should endeavour to meet this by "limitation", i.e. to give the men's College an advertisement of anti-feminism'.[47] Ill feeling had been caused, too, by the belief that there was a 'women's vote' in Congregation. This was also rebutted by Margery Fry, who claimed that her generation were 'heartily weary of the subject of sex inequalities' and that 'there was not the slightest need for a woman's party in the University'.[48] Yet circumstances had in fact led to canvassing for a women's 'slate', including Lynda Grier, Principal of Lady Margaret Hall, in the Council elections of 1926. After 1920 fewer prominent members of the University took an active interest in the women's colleges and they felt ill represented on Council when the limitation issue arose. 'Our five got in among the first seven', Annie Rogers had observed gleefully to John Myres. 'It is not very difficult to turn a council election, but don't say I said so'.[49] On that occasion at least there was a 'women's vote', and the result—according to the *Oxford Magazine*—was that 'two at least of the most valuable members of Council were unseated'.[50]

The long-term effect of the quota on the development of the women's colleges is not easy to assess. Their intake remained below 840 until 1945, when they were allowed to take in women who had served in the war—*extra numerum*. In 1948 the quota was raised to 970; a motion for adjournment, proposed in Congregation by Sir Richard Livingstone, President of Corpus, caused alarm because college finances in these inflationary years depended on student fees, but it was defeated by a massive 228 votes to 11. The fear that women would compete for scarce lodging accommodation was met by renewed efforts to house them in college, and the proportion of women in lodgings fell from about 40 per cent in 1948 to 21 per cent in 1960 (when, by contrast, about half the male students lived out of college).[51] In 1957 the quota was abolished without controversy. Yet it was not clear at that stage how far the women's colleges wanted to challenge what Dame Lucy termed 'the general proportionate arrangements' of the limitation era.[52] Pressure for university expansion, which began in the 1940s with the Barlow report on

[46] *Oxford Chronicle* 17 June 1927, 7; L. R. Farnell, *An Oxonian Looks Back* (London 1934), 295–6.
[47] SCA limitation of numbers, Rogers to Penrose, 29 Oct. 1926.
[48] *Oxford Chronicle* 17 June 1927, 7. See also A. Bruce and 'a woman member of Congregation', *OM* 23 June 1927, 619; Sutherland, 'Women in Oxford'.
[49] Bodl. MS Myres 79, fo 111.
[50] *OM* 16 June 1927, 582.
[51] HUD.
[52] SCA UGC file, Sutherland to the other principals, 3 Nov. 1956; HCP 224 (1956), 279.

scientific manpower and intensified in the 1960s, met a conservative response from the women's colleges. Expansion threatened to upset the subject-balance within colleges, already skewed for women towards the biological and medical sciences and the modern arts subjects. As the Principal of St Hilda's put it, 'the Fellows feel that if candidates coming up in future continue to choose their subjects of study as they have in the past a larger college will be overburdened in . . . History, English and Modern Languages'.[53] There was also, and despite stiff competition for places, some scepticism about the existence of a pool of able schoolgirls who could be admitted without lowering standards. Women dons surveyed by *Isis* thought that 'not many people worthy of a place were turned away'. One of them 'distinguished between intelligence and the academic potential limited to far fewer people, perhaps enough to fill one more women's college and no more'.[54] There was also the consideration that, if women could not follow the poorer men's colleges and put their students in lodgings, expansion would entail building and cost money.

It was not just the quota but lack of external funding that had kept the women's colleges poor. They had grown up, as the five principals noted in an appeal for building funds, 'without endowment, rich benefactors, or support from the State'.[55] Inter-war efforts to attract funds had very modest results. On the recommendation of the Asquith Commission the women's colleges at both Oxford and Cambridge received a grant of £4,000 a year from the UGC, earmarked for the amortization of debts and an increase in tutors' pay and pensions, but this grant was phased out in 1938–43.[56] The Asquith Commission also urged fund-raising to build up endowments. Each of the women's colleges did run appeals in the 1920s, and there were also combined appeals, the most professional of which was launched in 1922 with Cecil Percival, a well-connected professional fund-raiser and daughter-in-law of Somerville's first chairman, Bishop John Percival, employed as organizer on a percentage commission. She found that 'as long as one appeals to old students and friends of the Colleges one is met with great sympathy, but the moment I mention the Appeal Fund to the outside world, I am generally faced with absolute indifference'.[57] Virginia Woolf, after her visit to Newnham in 1928, concluded that women's colleges were poor because of 'the reprehensible poverty of our sex'.[58] But it was equally true that rich women did not regard the higher education of their sex as a particularly

[53] SCA UGC file, J. de L. Mann to the Registrar, 20 June 1946.
[54] McLeod, 'Women in Oxford', 8.
[55] *Times* 20 June 1958, 11; J. Howarth and M. C. Curthoys, 'The political economy of women's higher education', *Historical Research* lx (1987).
[56] See above, 39.
[57] SCA appeals file, appeal report for 9 Mar.–6 May 1923.
[58] V. Woolf, *A Room of One's Own* (London 1929, Glasgow 1977 edn), 22.

deserving cause. Viscountess Rhondda, who had not enjoyed her brief spell at Somerville, gave the appeal an office and acted as its honorary treasurer, but spared it little of her inherited millions.[59] A veteran of the suffrage movement wrote: '£100,000 or £200,000 to her is equal to £10 to me. I think hundreds of people feel this way, and resent her being content to be "Treasurer" of such a Fund.' Lady Bathurst wrote: 'I am of the opinion that women have completely spoilt Oxford as it is, and to build more women's colleges would achieve its ruin. I have a son there, and he is obliged to attend the lectures of 3 lady dons. I consider this ridiculous—humiliating. I wish we had sent our sons to Cambridge, where the atmosphere is still virile.'[60]

The indifference of the general public was reflected in the BBC's response to a request to give the appeal broadcasting time: 'the claims of Hospitals [were] so far more important that they are compelled to refuse'.[61] A grand bazaar and balls under aristocratic patronage in the Hyde Park Hotel in London's West End; a handsome appeal magazine, *The Heritage*, and ample press coverage for events such as a Mansion House meeting addressed by the Archbishop of York and Dean Inge; approaches to foundations and city companies, to American women's colleges and former Rhodes scholars, to women golfers and to girls' schools, which sent in the takings from their school plays and concerts; a bridge drive (sharply criticized by Somerville's education committee); lectures, concerts, jumble sales and the like put on by women dons in their spare time—all these added up to little in cash terms.[62] The major achievement of the joint appeal was a 'benefactor's scheme', in which Lady Mond gave £100 on condition that a hundred others did likewise. Queen Mary, who had been the first woman to receive an honorary degree at Oxford and had visited the women's colleges in 1921 [plate 13.3], made that scheme fashionable by contributing to it. But this joint appeal for £80,000 closed in 1925 with less than a quarter of that sum. The 1920s were, admittedly, a bad time for fund-raising in the United Kingdom. Yet it remained difficult to convey the point of women's higher education in a country where universities educated only the privileged few. Two out of three major benefactions received by Oxford's women's societies between the wars came from American women, accustomed to a system where universities were open to a wider spectrum of students.[63] In England the notion that higher education was a preparation for élite careers and wasted on women who married survived into the mid-twentieth century, while even among Oxford's women graduates there were some who suspected that

[59] M. H. Mackworth, Viscountess Rhondda, *This Was My World* (London 1933), 104–7.

[60] Somerville, appeals, Bathurst to the Lord Mayor of London, 18 Feb. [1923]; appeal report, 9 Mar.–6 May 1923.

[61] Somerville, appeals, appeal report 11 Dec. 1923.

[62] Bodl. dep. c. 706–7; SCA education committee minutes, 1923.

[63] Brittain, *Women at Oxford*, 179, 186, 219, 239.

academic training left wives and mothers with little but a burden—of discontent and guilt.[64]

For Oxford women's colleges financial aid did come in the 1950s and 1960s, both from the newer British foundations—particularly Wolfson and Nuffield—and from the UGC, which provided funds for building and furniture, and also made the somewhat embarrassing offer of a grant to supplement the stipends of the conspicuously underpaid women principals.[65] Help came too from the richer Oxford colleges. A scheme for redistributing income and capital from richer to poorer colleges, put forward in 1961, won the approval of Franks.[66] Women's colleges were not the sole beneficiaries of this scheme, which was motivated by a desire to maintain Oxford as a community of autonomous colleges whose survival was in no case over-dependent on state funding. But it brought for the first time to the Oxford women's societies endowments of their own that were not immediately swallowed up by building, and the prospect of paying tutors on a scale comparable to men dons—a goal towards which they were moving by 1970.

Relief also came over the decades from pressures of a different sort which had given the women's colleges a reputation for extreme conservatism in their rules governing interaction between the sexes.[67] Women had been admitted to lectures in the early days only on the understanding that they would not mix socially with men undergraduates; this was what Emily Penrose described to Somervillians as the 'unwritten compact' made with sympathetic men dons.[68] Behind it lay not just concern for propriety but also the concern of parents and tutors to prevent undergraduates from jeopardizing their careers by early and imprudent marriage. By 1914 this segregated regime had already begun to give way. Women sang in the Bach Choir, held occasional mixed dances and debates and attended Fabian Society meetings. In 1915 the women principals agreed after a student petition to allow the formation of mixed societies run by mixed committees provided that meetings were chaperoned by a woman tutor.[69] The number of these societies grew; tutors complained of the burden of chaperonage; men's college deans on the other hand were in some cases hostile to mixed meetings in their own colleges. In 1919 a conference of principals and deans, in which the more conservative line was taken by the men, agreed a set of

---

[64] Lois Mitchison, 'The price of educating women', *Manchester Guardian* 18 Jan. 1960, 4. See also J. Newsom, *The Education of Girls* (London 1958); *The Education and Training of Girls* (National Council of Social Service, London 1962), 8–12; E. Leach, *Culture and Nature, or La femme sauvage* (Stevenson lecture, London 1968).

[65] HCP 239 (1961), 859–69; see also below, 655.

[66] HCP 239 (1961), 537–9; *Franks Report* i. 284–95; below, 655–6.

[67] K. Briant, *Oxford Limited* (London 1937), 125–36; C. Hobhouse, *Oxford* (London 1939), 102–3. See also W. Holtby, 'Should Women go to Oxford?' *News Chronicle* 2 Feb. 1934, 8.

[68] SCA Penrose MS 2, 'The compact'.

[69] Bodl. dep. d. 759, principals' minute-books 1912–21, fos 34–5.

rules for women students that was to be described by *Isis* as 'a disgrace to Oxford'.[70] They must not, among other things, enter men's rooms nor go to the theatre with a man without their principal's permission and a chaperon approved by her, nor go to a café with a man, nor on the river, nor for walks, bicycle or motor rides unless with principalian permission and at least two women in the party. Mixed societies required permission, to be renewed annually, from the women principals as well as the proctors, and meetings in men's colleges must be chaperoned. Mixed parties in cafés were allowed only between 2.00 and 5.30 p.m. In 1924 Gerald Gardiner, President of the Union and a future Lord Chancellor, was sent down for publishing a leaflet called *The Truth about Somerville* in which these rules were lampooned; he was abetted by the future *Sunday Times* columnist Dilys Powell, who had been rusticated and deprived of her exhibition for climbing into college.[71] A more diplomatic protest came the following year from the women's junior common rooms, claiming that the rules set up 'an artificial standard of conduct . . . which does not exist either in home-life or in other Universities'.[72]

The rules were relaxed over the years, but in some cases rather slowly. Principals used discretion in waiving rules for engaged couples, yet in 1932 'the propriety or otherwise of permitting the *fiancée* of a Fellow of All Souls to visit him, although a BA, in his rooms was discussed, and such an exception felt to be undesirable'.[73] Chaperonage by a senior woman was superseded in the 1920s by the 'two women' rule; that lasted until 1935 when the general ban on tête-à-tête visits to men's rooms was dropped in favour of a proctorial rule excluding women from men's colleges after evening hall.[74] In the same year St Hilda's and Lady Margaret Hall began to allow unchaperoned visits by men to undergraduates' rooms on Sundays. One graduate (1935) recalls that at St Hugh's 'if you invited a Young Man to tea on Sunday the bed was ceremonially wheeled into the corridor'. But this was the start of the system of authorized 'men hours' that lasted, with gradual extensions, until the 1980s.[75] Similarly 'gate-hours', normally somewhat earlier than at the men's colleges, were gradually pushed back: in 1965 Somerville began the practice of allowing latch keys to late returners from evening parties.[76]

Until the age of majority was reduced to 18 in 1969 colleges acted as if they were *in loco parentis* [plate 13.4]. In earlier years their rules had 'played some part in shielding [women students] from hostile criticism' in Oxford's

[70] Ibid. fos 83–8; 'Discipline in the women's colleges', *Isis* 4 June 1924, 5.
[71] SCA discipline file.
[72] Bodl. dep. d. 760, principals' minute-books 1921–33, fo 64.
[73] Ibid. fo 136.
[74] *Proctors' Memorandum* 1935, 8.
[75] Bodl. dep. d. 761, principals' minute-books 1934–41, fos 22, 24.
[76] Bodl. dep. d. 762, principals' minute-books 1959–79, fo 49.

socially conservative community.[77] 'Men hours' also gave some protection to the generations up in the decades when contraception was relatively unreliable and the undergraduate consensus was that 'nice girls don't' (graduates of Somerville, 1951; St Anne's, 1952 and 1960). In provincial universities regulations in women's hostels were sometimes even more restrictive than they were at Oxford, and resistance to the encroachment by women on 'men's space' could be equally strong in that era of single-sex schooling. An inter-war graduate of Leeds University recalled that the sexes always sat separately in the refectory and if a woman approached the men's area they would bang their soup spoons on the tables; some of these spoons were, he observed, almost flat.[78] Rules, finally, were sometimes allowed to lapse and offences even against those that were strictly enforced, such as gate-hours, were not always severely punished, as Nina Bawden discovered when she was spotted climbing into Somerville by Helen Darbishire and told to go and have a hot bath so as not to get a chill.[79] There were colleges in the 1930s where the system of 'permissions' was largely disregarded: 'if we did our work satisfactorily and behaved like ladies—that was very important—nobody cared what you did'.[80]

One peculiar feature of student discipline at an ancient collegiate university was, however, that it raised complex issues of authority and delineation of male and female spheres. By the usages of genteel society, women were responsible for the conventions governing their own sex. Yet in becoming matriculated members of the University they came under the jurisdiction of the vice-chancellor and proctors, and within the walls of the men's colleges they were on territory governed by heads of house and deans. These men, though they usually consulted the women principals about issues affecting women, did not necessarily defer to them. The principals did not, for instance, like the soft hat which was substituted for the mortarboard in women's academic dress: it was the proctors who insisted upon it.[81] Again it was Farnell, implementing his policy of 'equality with separation', who in 1920 forbade the participation of women undergraduates in productions of the University dramatic society after the principals had tentatively agreed to it.[82] Men could call the tune. At Cambridge, where women were not under proctorial jurisdiction, students 'felt more free under the regulations of our own dons than were our counterparts at Oxford'.[83] Until 1925 the Oxford

[77] E. A. O. Whiteman, 'Women in Oxford since 1945', seminar, 11 Mar. 1986 (Brian Harrison's transcript, HUA), 5.

[78] *University of Leeds Review* xxxii (1989–90), 226. See also M. Tylecote, *The Education of Women at Manchester University 1893–1933* (Manchester 1941).

[79] A. Thwaite (ed.), *My Oxford* (London 1977), 162–3.

[80] SHCA tape-recording of interview by Doreen Forsyth with Stella Alexander (St Hilda's, 1930), 29 Jan. 1987.

[81] Rogers, *Degrees by Degrees*, 114–15.

[82] Bodl. dep. d. 759, principals' minute-books 1912–21, fos 121–2.

[83] A. Phillips (ed.), *A Newnham Anthology* (Cambridge 1979), 193.

proctors did not incorporate detailed regulations for women in the memorandum on conduct and discipline given to matriculands; instead, women were subject to inter-collegiate rules issued by their own societies, in fact sanctioned by the proctors but widely regarded as the work of the women principals. After 1925 rules on 'mixed parties' were incorporated in the proctors' memorandum and it was made clear that men as well as women undergraduates were responsible for observing them. Yet even then the system of 'permissions', though a proctorial rule, emphasized the women's colleges' special responsibility for regulating association between the sexes—and exposed them to ridicule as a puritanical 'spinster-autocracy'. The principals' sanction for mixed societies was required until 1949. As late as 1960 a head of house asked them to give a definite ruling on the times at which women should be permitted to visit men's colleges. They declined to do so.[84]

Preoccupation with ladylike behaviour and dress was, of course, a common feature of women's colleges of this period, but Oxford's rules and restrictions, attacked in the undergraduate press according to a St Anne's graduate on average at least twice a term, were influenced also by the lingering sense that 'women were still in the University on sufferance'.[85] Oxford was, moreover, unusual among universities in imposing dress-codes for formal occasions on its members of both sexes [plate 13.5]. Women's colleges therefore felt responsible not only for discouraging fashions that caused over-exposure (shorts in the 1930s, low necklines in the 1940s) but also for censoring versions of subfusc likely to cause proctorial disapproval. They drew criticism for imposing a 'lipstick limit' and a ban on black nylons, on the grounds that 'black means black, not dirty pink'.[86] Miniskirts were not permitted with subfusc, nor were trousers until the 1970s. Yet undergraduates too felt the need to maintain a college image acceptable to their male peers: most junior common rooms between the wars permitted punting only to those who had undergone instruction before breakfast by an experienced senior. Other restrictions reflected medical advice: women's eights, for instance [plates 13.6–7], were until the mid-1930s required to compete on style rather than speed and to row consecutively rather than side by side.[87]

And yet, especially for the riverside colleges Lady Margaret Hall and St

[84] Briant, *Oxford Limited*, 126; Bodl. dep. d. 762, principals' minute-books 1959–79, fo 4.

[85] Anne Bavin, 'The second-class sex', *New Statesman* 28 Apr. 1961, 669; Whiteman, 'Women in Oxford', 1. On rules and dress-codes elsewhere see Delamont, *Knowledgeable Women*, 73–101, 178–9; J. Sondheimer, *Castle Adamant in Hampstead: A History of Westfield College 1882–1982* (London 1983), 107; C. Bingham, *The History of Royal Holloway College 1886–1986* (London 1987), 156–7; Solomon, *Educated Women*, 159.

[86] Lady Julia Pakenham, 'Oxford women under discipline', *Evening Standard* 17 June 1935, 21; St Anne's graduate, 1948.

[87] Bodl. dep. c. 691, principals' correspondence 1932–8, fos 83, 263.

But I'm wearing blue stockings.

13.5 'TROG' ON DRESS REGULATIONS FOR WOMEN IN EXAMINATIONS, *OBSERVER*
5 JUNE 1966

Hilda's, set in beautiful grounds and with their own punts and canoes, the river offered above all great freedoms. In the 1930s the curators of the University Parks created a bathing place for women, commonly known as Dame's Delight, where nude bathing was forbidden only after some hesitation and on the grounds that safety required the employment of a male attendant.[88] The Oxford experience as recalled by women students up in the first half of the twentieth century includes much that was shared with the men: 'the charisma of this ancient and wonderful university town' (St Hilda's graduate, 1948), an idyllic countryside, May morning, participation in the Bach Choir, the Student Christian Movement and the Oxford Inter-Collegiate Christian Union, undergraduate theatre and journalism and the political clubs, the opportunity to form lifelong friendships with members of one's own sex and to talk late into the night over cocoa or coffee. As for the strictly educational experience of Oxford, it varied widely for students of both sexes. Interaction between tutor and pupil [plate 13.8] is recalled as building self-confidence in some, destroying it in others. Tutors might be 'schoolmarmy', remote, inadequate, drab or they might be kind and friendly, stimulating, even inspiring; elegant as the St Hilda's medievalist Beryl Smalley or as unconventional as Somerville's French tutor Enid Starkie, in her scarlet and blue trousers and jacket and French sailor's beret.

[88] Ibid. fos 103–4, 200.

For women scientists the department rather than the college was in any case the focus of academic work—zoology is remembered as a particularly friendly department—while arts undergraduates were often farmed out to men tutors and were free, like the men, to choose whether to attend lectures or to go to lectures outside their subject given by such stars as C. S. Lewis, J. R. R. Tolkien, Lord David Cecil and A. J. P. Taylor.

Despite this common ground, women's colleges continued to display a distinctive pattern of social life. Their buildings, arranged on a corridor plan but also incorporating Victorian family houses, had evolved from school and domestic models. The system of taking all meals in common in hall, not modified until the 1960s when undergraduates won the right to 'sign out' for a limited number of meals, was redolent of school. More domestic modes of behaviour lingered on, too; at St Hilda's between the wars students could request breakfast in bed if they were unwell or had an essay crisis. The pattern of demand for places in the women's colleges produced a social mix that was less varied than that of male undergraduates, and also a more general emphasis on the prior claims of work. In the late 1920s there were more than eight applicants per place at Somerville, the most popular women's college (although many candidates were not up to entrance standard in Latin).[89] In 1965 competition for entry was almost twice as severe for women as for men: 46.6 per cent of men candidates gained places at Oxford but only 24 per cent of women candidates.[90] These figures overstate the true level of competition since women retained the option of taking Cambridge as well as Oxford entrance examinations in the 1960s, while before 1963 the Oxford colleges examined in pairs or individually rather than as a group and candidates often applied to more than one college.[91] Yet it is clear that the pattern of competitive entry and meritocratic selection that became general in the men's colleges only in the 1960s was established for women much earlier. After 1914 all women students took an entrance examination, and it became usual for scholars and commoners to take the same examination. Scholars were not, as in many men's colleges, marked out as a class apart. Industry and commitment were expected of all women. The decline in the pass school was particularly marked in the women's colleges: in 1923 about 4 per cent of women finalists were pass candidates (by comparison with about 7 per cent of men) and only in one year after 1935 did the number of women pass candidates rise as high as ten.[92]

Despite the fact that fees were somewhat lower in the women's colleges, many of their students were under financial pressure between the wars.

---

[89] Somerville, education committee minutes, 8 Nov. 1922; Council minutes, 7 Feb. 1928.
[90] *Franks Report* ii. 59, 75.
[91] Franks Commission, oral evidence lviii. 2–3 gives an account of the entrance procedures of the women's group in the 1960s.   [92] HUD; see also above, 58, 76.

There were few state scholarships, and Local Education Authorities often restricted awards to those who had also won college scholarships, of which there were proportionately fewer for women than for men.[93] Other sources of finance included grants from the Board of Education for those who would pledge themselves to teach, and bursaries from secondary schools and educational trusts. Such grants might be withdrawn in case of unsatisfactory work, while many women were conscious that they were supported at Oxford by financial sacrifices that their families could ill afford. More generous state funding after the Second World War eased financial but not academic pressures. Lady Antonia Fraser (Lady Margaret Hall, 1950) recalled that girls of her generation wrote two essays a week while the men wrote only one: fifteen years later the average work-load of women and men differed less, but nevertheless perceptibly.[94]

The notion that community life was 'something which the female sex does not find rewarding or agreeable in itself' enjoyed a certain revival in the mid-twentieth century in the context of debates over co-residence.[95] Yet in earlier years the women's colleges had been small, intimate societies whose communal life had much in common with the men's foundations—although they also retained a distinctively feminine flavour, shown most positively to the outside world in forms of entertainment, the tea party and the non-alcoholic dance, that brought University men to the colleges in gatherings run by women and in accordance with their preferred conventions. Common religious observances (even at Somerville prayers were said in hall), college societies and inter-collegiate sporting competition promoted group loyalties: as a graduate of the 1930s recalled, 'one was very proud of the college and very glad that it existed'.[96] Yet as early as 1924 the Lady Margaret Hall *Brown Book* noted that 'the activities of mixed societies now tend to absorb most of that energy which formerly went into organizing Hall Societies': the Essay Club and Debating Society had died and 'Hall meeting has lost some of its old enthusiasm and excitement'. Somerville's Parliament disappeared; so did its Going Down Play in the early 1930s, when the inter-collegiate women's magazine the *Fritillary* also ceased publication. The decline in women's team sports, pursued by a falling proportion of students in the 1930s and after, was also particularly marked. It was associated in part with the rise of new fashions in games—ping-pong,

[93] Of women admitted in 1938/9 17.7 per cent won awards, as did 23.7 per cent of the men: *Franks Report* ii. 46.

[94] Ibid. 153; Thwaite, *My Oxford*, 179.

[95] P. C. Bayley, 'College life' in *Handbook* 1965, 302. See also M. Vicinus, *Independent Women: Work and Community for Single Women 1850–1920* (London 1985), 121–62, 281–92.

[96] Anne Whiteman in discussion after my talk on 'Women's higher education: the Oxford experience 1914–70', seminar, Corpus Christi College, 2 Feb. 1990 (Brian Harrison's transcript, HUA).

croquet, chess, tiddlywinks—or, in the era that started with the Campaign for Nuclear Disarmament and the War on Want lunches of the late 1950s, in student politics. Yet the major college sports for men were sustained in these years by higher levels of public interest and by resources lacking in the women's colleges. Only Lady Margaret Hall possessed its own playing field, an amenity taken for granted in the men's colleges. The income generated by the Varsity rugby and cricket matches and the boat race—used to subsidize men's sports—was not shared with the women, although the University contributed £150 a year from 1951 (increased in 1960 to £1,000) towards the cost of women's sports in which Oxford competed with Cambridge. In 1951 the University Women's Boat Club was forced to close when junior common rooms proved unwilling to cover its rising costs. It was revived in 1963 and from the following year women's eights started to row (without much success) against men's crews in Eights Week. But only with the advent of mixed colleges in the 1970s was a separate women's division started so that rowing could become a serious college sport for women.[97]

The erosion of communal life was perhaps less marked for women dons than for undergraduates. Within colleges, the life of the senior common room lost some of the cosy and hierarchical atmosphere that had put off some young dons in the 1940s: most of the eight resident academics interviewed by *Isis* twenty years later agreed with the tutor who was 'conscious of advantages of life in a women's college, not of any disadvantages'.[98] Solidarity among academic women had been encouraged by the conflicts of the 1920s—the limitation debate, the St Hugh's row (which led to a boycott organized by women tutors on the teaching of St Hugh's undergraduates)—and by financial pressures, which encouraged a degree of inter-collegiate collaboration that was unusual in Oxford. Between the wars responsibility for teaching and library provision for the sciences was shared among the five women's societies. They gave evidence jointly to the Asquith and Franks commissions and made joint approaches to funding bodies. The women principals continued to meet regularly to discuss policy.

But for undergraduates corporate life within the women's colleges, significantly larger by the 1950s, became much less vigorous. Unable to attract members to meetings even by free coffee, Somerville's junior common room was forced to reduce its quorum, while for some years the only thriving college society had been the Worcester–Somerville music

---

[97] Oxford University Registry, minutes of the curators of the University Chest, 16 Feb. 1951, p. 85; HCP 235 (1960), 105–9, 300; *Handbook 1965*, 319–41; Somerville, ASM reports 1952–3, 1960, 1963–4.

[98] P. West, 'Reminiscences of seven decades' in Griffin, *St Hugh's*, 164–5; SHCA tape-recording of interview by Jill Pellew with Sybil Crowe (fellow, 1942–75), 11 Oct. 1989; 'Women dons: an inferior type of men?', *Isis* 23 Oct. 1968, 9–11.

society.[99] A St Hilda's graduate (1948) who felt women were to be congratulated on avoiding the rowdier rituals of male college life nevertheless thought that for her generation 'there was a fundamental difference between male and female colleges and loyalties' because of 'the basic male-hunt syndrome'. 'I always found that within a group of women there was an unwritten endorsement . . . for putting "chasing your male" before anything else, so that whereas with men college could come first for women it never could.' The mannequin parade staged by Lady Deirdre Hare, the Hon. Sarah Rothschild and others (but inspired by an undergraduate of St Peter's) with a view to improving dress-sense underlined the preoccupation of Oxford women with society outside their own colleges: 'summer dresses . . . for the occasion bore such apposite titles as Tutorial Teaser, Balliol Bliss and Coxswain's Distraction' [plate 13.9].[100] There is little evidence of feminist activity among undergraduates between the demise of the women's suffrage society over which Mary Stocks had presided in the early 1920s and the University Women's Action Group formed in 1974—although the British Women's Liberation Movement chose Oxford as the venue for its first conference in 1970 and drew in many Oxford graduates, including its historian, Sheila Rowbotham (St Hilda's, 1961).[101]

The impact of Oxford and the colleges on the careers of their alumnae between 1914 and 1970 deserves fuller investigation than is possible here. Women graduates in these generations were increasingly likely to marry and the proportion of Oxford women known to have married rises sharply from 30 per cent of those up before 1914 to 71 per cent of the 1930s and 84 per cent of the 1950s cohort.[102] Graduate women were also increasingly unlikely to devote their lives exclusively to family roles or voluntary work. The Oxford evidence suggests that the Second World War greatly accelerated this trend: all but 7.3 per cent of those up in the years immediately after the war and 5.1 per cent of 1960s graduates are known to have spent some time in paid employment [table 13.1]. The lifecycles of graduates of the 1940s and 1950s commonly included a career break as full-time wife and mother, but this pattern was less marked for graduates of the 1960s [figure 13.3]. A mid-century survey of Oxford medical graduates showed that half of those who had ceased to practise for family reasons regretted it.[103] The role of housewife—though still happily, even proudly, embraced by some Oxford graduates—came into conflict with women's professional aspirations and with the need for a dual income to sustain middle-class family lifestyles. Yet

[99] SCA Somerville Students Association reports 1950, 1958.

[100] Daily Telegraph 2 Mar. 1954, 5.

[101] R. Clayton, 'Women's action', Isis 30 May 1974, 9; S. Rowbotham, The Past is Before Us: Feminism in Action since the 1960s (London 1989).

[102] On the nuptiality of early women graduates see Howarth and Curthoys, 'Political economy'; the later figures are derived from HUD.

[103] A. H. T. Robb-Smith, 'The fate of Oxford medical women', Lancet 1 Dec. 1962, 1158–61.

TABLE 13.1

CAREERS OF OXFORD WOMEN BY COHORT, 1900–1967 (%)

	1900–19	1920–39	1940–5	1946–52	1953–9	1960–7
religion	3.8	1.2	0	0.5	0.3	0.4
education	41.8	43.6	39.6	36.1	46.5	43.0
professional	2.0	6.9	4.6	9.2	6.9	8.1
social	3.2	4.2	2.9	2.1	3.6	3.6
literary/media	2.1	3.4	1.1	5.4	6.6	3.6
secretarial	3.8	3.9	7.1	6.6	3.6	2.7
library/museum	1.7	2.0	3.2	3.1	2.2	4.0
clerical/manual	1.5	0.9	2.5	3.8	0.6	1.8
research (not in-dustrial or com-mercial	0.6	3.6	6.8	7.5	8.3	11.2
government/politics (national or local)	2.3	2.6	11.4	5.2	4.2	4.9
armed forces/police	0.3	0.1	7.1	0.9	0	0
commerce/finance	0.9	2.1	3.2	3.1	2.8	2.5
industry	0.8	1.3	5.4	7.3	7.8	7.8
non-profit-making organization	0.8	1.4	0	1.4	0.6	1.1
other paid employ-ment	0	0.4	0.4	0.5	0	0.2
total	65.6	77.6	95.3	92.7	94.0	94.9
voluntary work	4.4	1.3	0	0.5	0.3	1.1
housewife	0	0	0.7	0.9	1.7	0.7
not employed	0.3	0.8	0.4	3.8	1.9	1.1
total	4.7	2.1	1.1	5.2	3.9	2.9
unknown	30.1	20.3	3.6	2.1	2.2	2.0
number in sample	665	768	280	424	361	446

Source: HUD.

even for women graduates of the 1960s career opportunities remained relatively limited. Education was still, as before 1914, their major field of employment, and one of the few that offered women both a career structure and opportunities for married 'returners'. Other 'women's profes-sions'—social, secretarial and library work, literary work and the media—in practice absorbed rather few Oxford women. Increasing numbers found posts in industry or research work immediately after graduating, but most moved out of these fields as they acquired family responsibilities or ran into barriers to promotion [table 13.2]. Openings in commerce and the

TABLE 13.2

KNOWN CAREERS OF OXFORD WOMEN, 1940–1967 ON LEAVING OXFORD AND 10, 20, 30 AND 40 YEARS THEREAFTER (%)

	on leaving	after 10 years	20 years	30 years	40 years
religion	0.3	1.0	1.1	1.4	1.3
education	42.3	34.1	45.7	49.8	25.1
professional	7.7	6.1	7.1	7.5	7.0
social	3.1	2.0	3.3	3.3	3.5
literary/media	4.5	5.5	6.4	5.9	7.0
secretarial	4.9	2.5	2.2	2.4	1.3
library/museum	3.3	2.2	3.3	2.8	1.6
clerical/manual	2.2	1.0	1.8	1.5	1.3
research (not industrial or commercial	8.9	4.7	3.3	2.8	2.5
government/politics (national or local)	6.2	4.0	3.7	3.9	1.9
armed forces/police	1.6	0.2	0.2	0.1	0
commerce/finance	2.9	2.0	3.1	3.0	2.2
industry	7.4	2.9	3.5	2.9	1.0
non-profit-making organization	0.9	1.3	1.8	2.3	1.0
other paid employment	0.3	3.9	1.6	1.5	0.6
total	96.5	73.4	88.1	91.1	57.3
voluntary work	0.5	0.6	1.0	1.3	2.9
housewife	1.0	18.9	7.7	4.4	5.4
not employed	2.0	7.0	3.2	3.4	34.6
total	3.5	26.5	11.9	9.1	42.9
number	1,475	1,420	1,345	797	315

Source: HUD.

professions (chiefly medicine and law) expanded between the wars, then levelled out. In central and local government the opportunities opened by the war contracted in peacetime.[104] How far did an education at Oxford—an élite university but one recently described as 'l'un des bastions du phallocratisme'—affect the career prospects of its women graduates?[105] Experiences differed. Many recall, often ruefully, that an Oxford degree 'opened doors' or made it easier to return to work after bringing up a family.

[104] For further analysis of the careers of women graduates see above, 73–7 and tables 3.6 and 3.7.
[105] C. Demanuelli, 'Face aux gentlemen, la bataille des femmes' in F. du Sorbier (ed.), *Oxford, 1919–1939* (Paris 1991), 177.

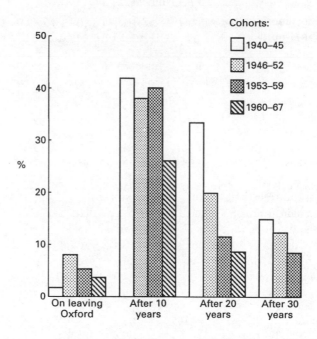

FIGURE 13.3   PERCENTAGE OF WOMEN GRADUATES WHO DESCRIBED THEMSELVES AS
HOUSEWIVES, VOLUNTARY WORKERS OR UNEMPLOYED ON LEAVING OXFORD AND
AFTER 10, 20 AND 30 YEARS

A few encountered 'anti-Oxbridge' discrimination or found themselves in milieux where it was wiser to conceal a privileged education. Some felt that the mental agility developed by the tutorial system contributed to their success in professional life. A triple blue (Somerville, 1949) found, like her male peers, that employers assumed it stood for impressive personal qualities. Instant recognition of shared affiliations with other Oxford graduates was for some a career advantage. In journalism and at the bar the 'old-boy network' sometimes produced results (graduates of St Hilda's, 1958; Lady Margaret Hall, 1960). Yet other graduates asked why that network did so little for women. A medical graduate (Somerville, 1967) was one of the few who had found support from an Oxford-based network of working women. Another Somervillian (1966) had watched with interest the rise to eminence of several male contemporaries but asked 'where are the women of that period, I wonder?' Others had found women's colleges unsympathetic towards the aspirations of married graduates. One (Lady Margaret Hall, 1961) recalled, 'my moral tutor, at my careers interview, actually said to me, "well, Miss —, we needn't worry about your career as you are getting married" '.

At one level women's colleges, by their very existence, encouraged achievement among their graduates. Students encountered a range of potential 'role-models' among senior Oxford women [plate 13.10]: the dedicated professional single woman; the married woman prominent in voluntary work, like the trio of dons' wives, Mrs H. A. Prichard, Mrs J. Wells and Mrs H. A. L. Fisher, who ran Oxford's infant welfare movement in the 1920s; or, though much more rarely, the distinguished scholar, for example Dorothy Hodgkin or Elizabeth Anscombe, who combined full-time work with raising a family. Lady Margaret Hall, Somerville and St Hilda's were among the first Oxford colleges to publish registers recording their senior members' achievements. Some dons attempted to provide careers advice: Margery Fry and Grace Hadow used their contacts to help those whose interests lay outside schoolteaching.[106] But the women's Appointments Committee—formally amalgamated with the men's Committee in 1953 but not fully integrated until 1966[107]—attracted much criticism for the narrow range of options it offered and for its conservative attitude to married 'returners' to employment. Part of the difficulty lay in the state of the labour market. But in the long-running debate on the social role of the educated woman, to which Oxford graduates had contributed since the days of the Somerville novelists and *Time and Tide*—the left-wing feminist paper founded by Viscountess Rhondda in the 1920s—women dons did not speak with one voice. Some anticipated the trend that led increasing numbers of professional women to work after marriage; others took a fatalistic view of the effects on recruitment to the higher professions (their own included) of what Lucy Sutherland termed 'the ravages of matrimony'.[108]

The 1960s were in some respects a golden age for the women's colleges, yet they also brought a crisis of identity. Encouraged to expand, freed from financial constraints and from disciplinary functions required of them in a less permissive era, they became less like schools. Permission for under-graduates to marry, previously given only in exceptional cases, was granted more readily. Married women dons with young families became more common. St Anne's and Somerville set up crèches. Yet there was no return to the *esprit de corps*, to the bonding within women's communities, that had been so marked in earlier generations. Undergraduates, influenced by the

[106] H. Deneke, *Grace Hadow* (London 1946), 118; E. H. Jones, *Margery Fry: The Essential Amateur* (London 1966), 149.

[107] Tom Snow at History of the University seminar on 'Education or Training? What they studied and where they went' (Nuffield College, 28 Nov. 1986, Brian Harrison's transcript, HUA), 12.

[108] M. H. Mackworth, Viscountess Rhondda, *Notes on the Way* (London 1937), 66–118; P. Berry and A. Bishop (eds), *Testament of a Generation* (London 1985), 45–152; S. Leonardi, *Dangerous by Degrees: Women at Oxford and the Somerville Novelists* (New Brunswick NJ 1989). Franks Commission, oral evidence xxx. 3; lxxiii. 21.

vogue for coeducation which had led the London women's colleges to go mixed, were often sharply critical of their single-sex communities; as one put it, 'there is something absurd about a community of women which one does not find in a community of men'.[109]

In academic terms women's colleges more than justified their existence after 1945, achieving a steadily higher proportion of second-class degrees than the men's colleges, and in five years between 1959 and 1973 a higher proportion of firsts [figure 3.4].[110] In the process they reinforced the case for increasing the proportion of women at Oxford. Yet only St Anne's proved willing to expand at a rate that would have met the modest Franks objective of an increase of seven hundred in the number of women undergraduates in the next fifteen to twenty years.[111] Several men's colleges considered admitting women in the 1960s: New College, Brasenose and Wadham consulted the women's colleges and were for the time being dissuaded. The motives of the women principals were open to misconstruction as mere college chauvinism; a more justified charge might be that their concern for the welfare of women at Oxford outweighed broader considerations of the need to expand women's higher education. They foresaw that the men's colleges would 'skim the cream' from the women's entry, thereby impoverishing the intellectual life of students at the women's colleges, and some doubted if women would thrive in predominantly masculine communities. Mary Bennett spoke up for the idea of the women's college: 'the one-sex college seems to me an agreeable institution, flexible, efficient and capable of inspiring a surprising degree of loyalty among its members'. She added, however, 'I do not personally attach any importance to parity of numbers between men and women in the University'.[112]

This was not a position that could be held. Some women dons publicly welcomed proposals that would create more places for women at Oxford. Newnham and Girton, despite some anxieties, did not oppose moves made by men's colleges in Cambridge to go mixed. A survey of the junior common room in 1969 showed that 90 per cent of Somervillians wanted all or some Oxford colleges to go mixed: a clear majority wanted Somerville to go mixed.[113] Suggestions were made for partnerships or mergers between men's and women's colleges to meet the demand for coeducation, but such arrangements could not meet what was felt to be a need for a substantial increase in the number of places for women. The admission of women to Brasenose, Jesus, Wadham, Hertford and St Catherine's in 1974—and its

[109] McLeod, 'Women in Oxford', 9.

[110] J. Hart, 'Women at Oxford since the advent of mixed colleges', *Oxford Review of Education* xv (1989). See also above, 62–3.

[111] Franks Commission, oral evidence xxx. 21; Bodl. dep. d. 762, Principals' minute-books 1959–79, fo 69.

[112] SCA co-residence file, Bennett to Bowra, 29 Nov. 1968.

[113] SCA, co-residence file.

sequel, the transformation of Oxford into a university of co-residential colleges in which by 1993 only St Hilda's remained single-sex—fall outside the scope of this chapter. Its consequences remain to be investigated. In the meantime it can, like much else in the history of women at Oxford, be interpreted in two ways: as 'the demise of the single-sex women's colleges', a bleak phrase used by Professor Halsey;[114] or alternatively as another stage in the continuing process of adapting Oxford to a changing world and, for women, a new kind of assimilation, opening to them for the first time the full Oxford experience.

[114] See below, 726.

14

Politics

BRIAN HARRISON

Oxford has educated 9 of twentieth-century Britain's 19 prime ministers, 14 of the 33 leaders of its three major parties, a third of the cabinet ministers appointed since 1905 and more than a fifth of MPs since 1945. Nor has this impact been narrowly based. Since 1918 Oxford has educated about a quarter of all Conservative MPs (partly because Oxford-trained Conservative MPs gravitate towards the safer seats), and a rising proportion of Labour MPs—13 per cent since 1945, as compared with the Conservatives' 23 per cent.[1] No other British university can match this record. 'Ah, how I wish that I could have had a training in this place', said Joseph Chamberlain to John Morley when visiting Oxford;[2] many ambitious twentieth-century politicians could well have said the same. As for the civil service, of the 161 permanent under-secretaries from 1920 to 1970 who reached the tertiary stage of education, 77 went to Oxford—far more than to any other British university. From 1948 to 1963, for the administrative class of the civil service and the senior branch of the foreign service, Oxford did far better by both methods of entry than any other university. The alliance between Sir Ralph Furse and Margery Perham, together with Oxford's special courses for colonial officials, ensured an equally close relationship with the colonial service. 'We are satisfied customers', said the civil service commissioners in 1964, 'and feel Oxford does as well for us as anybody else, if not better'.[3]

---

[1] Information gathered from D. and G. Butler, *British Political Facts 1900–1985* (London 1986), 1–64, 88–135, 142–3, 158. Information on MPs from J. F. S. Ross, *Elections and Electors* (London 1955), 418 (for 1945) and Nuffield election studies for all elections between 1950 and 1992; see also S. A. Walkland (ed.), *The House of Commons in the Twentieth Century* (Oxford 1979), 99, 105, 113; P. Pulzer, *Political Representation and Elections in Britain* (London 1967), 71. I gratefully acknowledge help from the following who have been kind enough to read parts of this chapter in earlier drafts: Lord Beloff, Dr D. E. Butler, Sir Alec Cairncross, Professor Hugh Clegg, Mr H. D. Hughes, Mr Roger Liddle, Mr Michael Maclagan, Dr Iain McLean, Sir Henry Phelps Brown, Professor Ben Roberts, Professor John Saville and Sir Keith Thomas. I have acted upon many of their criticisms (some of them most painstaking) but I do not of course implicate them in my interpretation.

[2] J. L. Garvin and J. Amery, *The Life of Joseph Chamberlain* (6 vols London 1932–69) i. 36.

[3] Franks Commission, oral evidence viii. 14. Statistics from W. D. Rubinstein, 'Education and the social origins of British élites 1880–1970', *Past and Present* no. 112 (Aug. 1986), 190; cf K. Theakston and G. K. Fry, 'Britain's administrative élite: permanent secretaries 1900–1986',

Given the inter-war triumph on the left of a political party which originated with working people outside parliament, Oxford's persisting twentieth-century impact on British politics is surprising. It partly reflects the fact that success breeds success. A virtuous circle operates whereby the many distinguished Oxford-educated politicians initiate their successors, so that Oxford both attracts and advances the politically aware. Out of more than 95,000 full-time students in Great Britain in 1959, about 10,000 were politically active; of these, 4,000 were students in Oxford.[4] Oxford's geography is also relevant. C. B. Fawcett, staking out the provinces of England in 1919, pointed out that Oxford and Cambridge 'belong to the nation as a whole, and not to any one region'. For him, Oxford 'as a focus of thought and opinion' was 'almost a part of the metropolis'.[5] Psychologically close to London, Oxford is on the route to important places out of London. Surrounded by rural areas long tamed by Anglicans and aristocrats, Oxford men could readily reach the many country houses where (until recently) political opinion was formed: Blenheim, Cliveden, Hughenden, Waddesdon—not to mention the smaller but significant political establishments set up nearby by the Morrells at Garsington, the Asquiths at Sutton Courtenay, the Murrays at Boars Hill, Birkenhead at Charlton. So cultural geography extends an all-party lifeline to a University located within a county all of whose seats have been captured by Conservatives since 1918, and where Labour has never matched the occasional impact that the Liberals once made.

Furthermore, until 1950 the University returned two MPs of its own, and until 1974 it also had its own city councillors, elected partly by college heads and bursars and partly by Convocation. The single transferable vote introduced in 1918 made a big change in the University constituency: whereas its MPs from 1832 to 1914 had been returned unopposed in 24 of its 30 elections and by-elections, from 1918 there were contests at every election except 1931 [table 14.1]. There were further changes. Before 1918 votes were cast in person and only by members of Convocation. After 1918 virtually all graduates were enfranchised on paying the University's registration fee. The University put them on a register, automatically afforced it with new graduates, and despatched voting papers through the post. Oxford University's electors grew quite steadily from 7,907 in 1918 to 28,865 in 1945. The balance of electoral influence therefore shifted away from dons in Oxford to their former pupils in London, so that by 1935 resident electors contributed only 3 per cent of the whole.[6]

Public Administration lxvii (1989), 132–3. For success-rates at entry see Franks Commission, written evidence iii. 11–12. For the colonial service see D. Veale, 'Colonial studies' (1969), typescript deposited in OUA.

    [4] W. T. Rodgers, 'Politics in the universities', *Political Quarterly* xxx (1959), 79, 81.
    [5] C. B. Fawcett, *The Provinces of England* (rev. edn London 1960), 156, 78.
    [6] *OM* 13 June 1935, 737.

TABLE 14.1

ELECTION RESULTS FOR OXFORD CITY AND UNIVERSITY SEAT, 1918–1970

OXFORD UNIVERSITY					OXFORD CITY			
candidate	party	1st vote	final vote	% 1st vote	candidate	party	vote	%
18 CECIL	Co C*	2771	1855	49.8	MARRIOTT	Co C	9805	70.7
PROTHERO	Co C	1716	2546	30.9	Higgins	Lib	4057	29.3
Murray	Lib	742	812	13.3				
Furniss	Lab	335	351	6.0				
19 [Prothero peerage]								
OMAN	Co C		2613	52.5				
Murray	Lib		1330	26.7				
Riley	Ind		1032	20.8				
22 CECIL	C	3185	1883	56.4	GRAY	Lib	12489	59.0
OMAN	C	1018	2170	18.0	Bourne	C	8683	41.0
Murray	Lib	1444	1594	25.6				
23 CECIL	C	3560	2712	43.8	GRAY	Lib	12311	56.1
OMAN	C	2206	2950	27.1	Bourne	C	9618	43.9
Murray	Lib	2368	2472	29.1				
ne 24					[1923 election void]			
					BOURNE	C	10079	47.8
					Fry	Lib	8237	39.1
					K. Lindsay	Lab	2769	13.1
24 CECIL	C	4320	2901	49.6	BOURNE	C	12196	57.3
OMAN	C	1738	2968	20.0	Moon	Lib	6836	32.1
Murray	Ind	2643	2832	30.4	Ludlow	Lab	2260	10.6
29 CECIL	C	6012	3822	52.4	BOURNE	C	14638	52.5
OMAN	C	2174	4112	19.0	Moon	Lib	8581	30.7
Murray	Lib	3277	3529	28.6	Etty	Lab	4694	16.8
31 CECIL	C	unopposed			BOURNE	unopposed		
OMAN	C	unopposed						
35 CECIL	C	7365	5081	48.3	BOURNE	C	16306	62.8
HERBERT	Ind	3390	5206	22.3	G. Walker	Lab	9661	37.2
Cruttwell	C	1803	3697	11.8				
Stocks	Lab	2683	—	17.6				
37 [Cecil appointed Provost of Eton]								
SALTER	Ind		7580	50.2				
Buzzard	C		3917	25.9				
Lindemann	Ind C		3608	23.9				
					[death of Bourne]			
38					HOGG	C	15797	56.1
					A. Lindsay	Ind Prog	12363	43.9

TABLE 14.1 *(cont.)*

ELECTION RESULTS FOR OXFORD CITY AND UNIVERSITY SEAT, 1918–1970

	OXFORD UNIVERSITY					OXFORD CITY			
	candidate	party	1st vote	final vote	% 1st vote	candidate	party	vote	%
1945	SALTER	Ind		6771	44.2	HOGG	C	14314	45.3
	HERBERT	Ind		5136	33.5	F. Pakenham	Lab	11451	36.2
	Cole	Lab		3414	22.3	Norman	Lib	5860	18.5
1950						HOGG	C	27508	46.9
						E. Pakenham	Lab	23902	40.7
						Tweddle	Lib	6807	11.6
						Keeling	Com	494	0.8
Nov 1950						[Hogg receives peerage]			
						TURNER	C	27583	57.5
						Lewis	Lab	20385	42.5
1951						TURNER	C	32367	56.0
						Elvin	Lab	25427	44.0
1955						TURNER	C	27708	52.3
						Elvin	Lab	19930	37.6
						Davies	Lib	5336	10.1
1959						WOODHOUSE	C	26798	51.0
						Anderton	Lab	18310	34.8
						Davies	Lib	7491	14.2
1964						WOODHOUSE	C	22212	42.9
						Luard	Lab	20783	40.1
						Davies	Lib	8797	17.0
1966						LUARD	Lab	24412	46.5
						Woodhouse	C	21987	41.8
						Peterson	Lib	6152	11.7
1970						WOODHOUSE	C	24873	47.0
						Luard	Lab	22989	43.4
						Reeves	Lib	5103	9.6

* Co C = Coalition Conservative

Sources: F. W. S. Craig, *British Parliamentary Election Results 1918–1949* (Glasgow 1969, 2nd edn Basingstoke and London 1977), 213, 670–1; F. W. S. Craig, *British Parliamentary Election Results 1950–1970* (Chichester 1971), 235. Successful candidates are in SMALL CAPITALS. Under the vote for Oxford University, column 1 indicates the first count, column 2 the final count after redistribution of preferences surplus to the quota; the percentage figure relates to the first count only. For the University seat's voting system see R. B. McCallum and A. Readman, *The British General Election of 1945* (London 1947), 216–17.

Turnout (67.4 per cent) was close to the national average (71.7 per cent), and well ahead of Cambridge (59.7 per cent).[7] Conservatives won both University seats at every election from 1832 to 1931, except for losing one of the two in 1859. Yet in the early 1920s they were privately much concerned at Gilbert Murray's rising proportion of first-preference votes, and worked hard to whip up support. In the 1930s they were divided between traditionalists within the caucus and evangelicals mobilized by Lindemann in the Oxford University Conservative Association (OUCA), a split which helped Independents to capture one seat in 1935 and both in 1937 and 1945.[8] Members of the University did not normally interfere in elections to the city seat, but six of its seven MPs between 1914 and 1970 were educated at or held posts in the University, and at the by-election of 1938 the University's intervention was memorable. Not till the 1970s did undergraduates become, as voters in the city constituency, numerically more important than the dons. *Isis* covered the general election in 1970 more fully than any previous election, but the undergraduates' immediate impact was small; Oxford city had already become a marginal seat, and in 1970 the High Court decision enabling them to vote in their place of study came too late to affect the result.

Oxford's political preoccupations were nourished by ready access to the political élite—a tight network whose members met one another by chance quite as often as the characters in Anthony Powell's novels. But many such meetings were engineered, and happened in Oxford. Colonial administrators addressed the Ralegh Club on Sunday evenings in the 1920s: H. A. L. Fisher at New College mixed undergraduates with his well-known politician-guests in the 1930s: and the Cole Group thereafter entertained Labour Party leaders such as Dalton and Citrine. Fred Jarvis, fresh from student politics in Liverpool, was impressed in the late 1940s with how easily the Labour Club attracted leading politicians, many of whom felt personally indebted to Oxford, to address its meetings. All this perhaps helped to discourage in Oxford the anti-political outlook whose inter-war influence on a few Cambridge undergraduates brought subsequent notoriety to that University. Visiting Cambridge in 1953, R. H. S. Crossman noted in his diary that in Oxford, by contrast, 'life is public affairs, not private affairs'.[9]

Contact with the political élite was all the easier in Oxford because until the Oxford University Student Union was established in the 1970s the

[7] Oxford turnout calculated from F. W. S. Craig, *British Parliamentary Election Results 1918–1949* (Glasgow 1969, 2nd edn Basingstoke and London 1977), 665–75. National figure from D. and G. Butler, *British Political Facts*, 224–6.

[8] The inside story can be pieced together from the valuable documents generously made available to me by Mr Michael Maclagan and now deposited in the Bodleian Library. These include the minute-book 1919–47 of the Oxford University Election Committee, and the minute-book 1935–54 of Oxford University Senior Conservative Association.

[9] Author's tape-recorded interview with Fred Jarvis, 18 Oct. 1988. R. H. S. Crossman, *Backbench Diaries*, ed. J. Morgan (London 1981), 228.

undergraduate's main route into a political career lay not through student politics but through a debating society: the Oxford Union [plate 14.1]. There the élite made new recruits and the recruits learned from the élite. The Union began inviting speakers down from London in 1888, a practice which eventually became rather frequent. 'It is quite noticeable', said a close observer in 1928, 'that after Mr. Lloyd George or Lord Birkenhead has paid a visit to the Union speakers attempt to adopt their mannerisms on subsequent occasions'. Sir John Simon's Union performance made Edward Heath want to speak fluently without notes: 'I've never been so impressed in my life, and I said "well, one day I must try and do that" '. R. H. S. Crossman became a brilliant and regular performer at the Union, where by the mid-1930s he was already exercising the combative talents earlier honed up in his tutorials. A reporter in 1949 thought his Union speech 'a *tour de force*. He coaxed the opposition, played with them, he waved his hands in gestures reminiscent of Max Miller and overwhelmed the house with a wealth of arguments.'[10]

Imitation sometimes produced ponderous undergraduate absurdity. In 1950 Robert Robinson ridiculed young men of 21 who strive 'to adopt the comportment, the gestures, the facial expressions, the phraseology and the inflections of old port-poisoned buffers'.[11] Yet the young men were learning more than public speaking. The Union's procedure owes much to the House of Commons, though the analogy is incomplete: its president is more ephemeral and controversial than the Speaker, for instance; the most influential debaters are invited guests, and are not necessarily members; the voters are a relatively non-partisan and shifting group, unelected, uninformed, and unrepresentative; and voting is less constrained by party, more influenced by what is said—votes are, in the technical sense, irresponsible. Nonetheless Union members unconsciously absorb parliamentary values, for this is one of many British assemblies—trade unions, rotary clubs, voluntary organizations—which foster civilized debate. Within a democratic society, said Birkenhead, the power of speech becomes 'a possession almost indispensable to every cultivated man'.[12]

By 1914 the Union was only the best-known among Oxford's many debating societies. Most were small and college-based, and some scarcely distinct from junior common rooms (JCRs). The St John's College Debating Society (whose members included Dean Rusk, Hore-Belisha and Michael Stewart) is perhaps typical of these in its half-serious tone and semi-

---

[10] F. Murthwait-How, 'The politics of the undergraduate', *Nineteenth Century* June 1928, 776; Heath on the BBC Radio 4 programme 'Desert Island Discs', 18 Dec. 1988; *Isis* 2 Feb. 1949, 29.

[11] *Isis* 22 Feb. 1950, 21.

[12] Charlton, Oxon: Birkenhead MSS, typescript headed 'The Oxford Union Society' and endorsed 'Oxford and Cambridge July 1927' (carbon copy).

recreational purpose. Self-education in speaking, not student power, was its concern, and style was at least as important as content. The political parties, too, had discussion groups and speakers' classes: his cousin Jasper told Charles Ryder that a Union career required a reputation 'outside first, at the Canning or the Chatham'.[13] Talent thus nurtured moved upwards into the Union, there silently to be urged on by the Union's monuments to the great: to Gladstone, Salisbury, Simon, Curzon, Asquith, Birkenhead. Inter-war reports of Union debates dwell heavily on style, which supplanted content entirely in Eights Week debates, whose contributions from Ronald Knox and Philip Guedalla were too memorably funny to be reportable. Nor did reporters then neglect the lesser-known late-night speakers. 'The *great* thing about the Union late at night', Max Beloff recalls, was 'a large empty hall, with half a dozen people, and you're trying to project your voice so at least they hear you'.[14]

Union orators were expected to be spontaneously and wittily responsive to their audience, lacing their speeches with drama and humour. For R. H. Bernays in 1932 the Union manner involved 'an arrogant self-assurance and a rather irritating maturity'. In its debates with Americans, first held in 1921, the Union found the transatlantic style unfamiliar because earnest, thoroughly briefed, and proceeding upon a law-court analogy. The Union's preoccupation with style was seen as frivolous by those on the left who were in a hurry to change the world, or who (like Fred Jarvis) were already practised debaters in the National Union of Students (NUS), where debates had serious consequences.[15] Such critics either did not value or did not need Oxford's pursuit of verbal facility.

The Union has always been much more than a debating society. Its library had 37,000 books by 1916 and 55,000 by 1969.[16] Its dining room opened in 1934, its bar in 1950, and its cellars opened for social functions under Michael Heseltine. By the 1950s self-education was giving way to recreation within the Union—not only from distinguished visiting speakers, but also outside the debating hall. The gulf between the politician and other types of communicator—journalists, writers, actors—has never been wide, and Oxford's links with Fleet Street have long been close. Many authors and journalists have been Union officers: Roger Fulford, Anthony Howard, Patrick Hutber, Keith Kyle, Beverley Nichols, William Rees-Mogg, Godfrey Smith, Philip Toynbee, Kenneth Tynan, Douglas Woodruff,

[13] E. A. St J. Waugh, *Brideshead Revisited: The Sacred and Profane Memories of Captain Charles Ryder* (London 1945, Harmondsworth 1986 edn), 28. See SJM UGS.V.4–5 for the Debating Society minutes 1913–53.
[14] Author's tape-recorded interview with Lord Beloff, 9 Mar. 1988.
[15] Bernays, *News Chronicle* 4 Nov. 1932, 10; interview with Fred Jarvis, 18 Oct. 1988. For Americans see C. Hollis, *The Oxford Union* (London 1965), 165–8; C. H. O. Scaife, 'The essence of debate', *Johannesburg Star* 25 Aug. 1924.
[16] *OM* 19 May 1916, 324; HCP 263 (1969), 1117–19.

Michael and Paul Foot. Already by 1935 the BBC's monthly-paid non-engineering staff of 395 included 76 Oxford graduates, as compared with 40 from Cambridge and 75 from other universities. The Ullswater Committee in that year felt the need to dismiss claims that the BBC was biased towards Oxbridge in its recruiting.[17] By the 1950s the Union had become both spectacle and recruiting-ground for the media [plate 14.2]. The BBC's Grace Wyndham Goldie scrutinized Union presidents for media talent, and the later careers of Brian Walden, Robin Day, Bryan Magee, Jeremy Isaacs and Peter Jay exemplify the Union's media connection. In 1954 the Union became the first debating society in the world to be televised, and 1967 saw the first televising (live and in colour) of an entire debate—on Catholicism.

In its visiting speakers and membership, the Union responded to shifting national power relationships. Ruskin College speakers were already contributing to debates in 1920, and in 1932 a lounge-suited Walter Citrine attacked the National Government. By 1955 Bill McCarthy had become 'the Union's cheeky chappie . . . like Mr. Max Miller . . . a fine technician and a superb showman'.[18] Women had long been invited as visiting speakers—Mrs Humphry Ward in 1912, for example—but the Union mood was facetiously anti-feminist, and would now be seen as insulting to women. After running their own separate debating societies for decades, women were at last admitted in 1963. The Union acquired its first woman president, Geraldine Jones, in 1968. A Union presidency, said Birkenhead in 1922, is 'the blue ribbon of Oxford success', and 'the first step to a conspicuous Parliamentary career'.[19] The Oxford careers of Rosebery, Attlee, Douglas-Home, Wilson, Eden and Thatcher—none of whom was active in the Union—scale down such hyperbole, but the Union did offer useful publicity, debating experience and connections. There ambition was not thought vulgar, and could be harnessed to promote the public interest. The Union's many scandals made it a good training-ground for the politics of imperfection, and the many grumbles it evoked suggest that people thought the Union mattered.

Political talent could also emerge from the parties' University branches. The Coningsby Club, founded in 1921 for all Oxford and Cambridge Conservative MPs, holds social functions in London and in both universities, and liaises with Oxford's many Conservative organizations. But it was Labour, as a new party, which needed to make special efforts with Oxford. Its working-class leaders shared R. H. Tawney's view that 'a Socialist Community cannot afford to economise on knowledge and intelligence', and spoke several times at the Union. Lansbury's 'very moving and impressive speech' in 1925 'took the House by storm', and in 1931 Morrison laid on 'an

17 Ullswater Committee on Broadcasting, PP 1935 vii (Cmd 5091), 13.
18 McCarthy, OM 3 Nov. 1955, 76; Citrine, OM 19 Oct. 1932, 15.
19 F. E. Smith, first Earl of Birkenhead, Points of View (2 vols London 1922) i. 81–2.

admirable mixture of mirth, wit, sarcasm, and serious argument'.[20] Morrison triumphed again in 1933 and 1935. Labour also recruited more directly. In the early 1930s Lansbury urged readers of the Oxford periodical *Plan* 'to come over and help us', saying that 'we need you, and you need us. Your true self-interest is to be found on our side.' Attlee's 'Letter to Oxford' of 1936 thought Oxford's receptiveness to socialism illustrated 'the way things are done in this country', with old institutions adapting to new purposes.[21] In providing the ambitious undergraduate with contacts, the Labour Club helped Oxford's political impact to survive the left's transition from Liberals to Labour.

Isis in November 1936 carried a joint letter from several Labour leaders urging readers to join the New Fabian Research Bureau, founded in 1931 by G. D. H. Cole. It channelled Oxford talent towards moulding Labour Party policy in London, eventually merged with the Fabian Society, and provided policy backing for the Attlee government of 1945. An Oxford man, John Parker, was General Secretary from 1933 to 1945, and helped many Oxford socialists into parliament.[22] Oxford's involvement with workers' education made such contacts seem natural. The Workers' Educational Association (WEA) in 1908 spoke of the 'grave loss to both Oxford and to English political life were the close association . . . between the University and the world of affairs' to be impaired by 'the accession of new classes to power'. Cole told Hugh Gaitskell that WEA tutors were the true modern missionaries, doing what the churches had once done, and it was as an extra-mural tutor in Nottingham that Gaitskell first made contact with working people.[23]

The WEA class launched many working men into politics and sent some to Oxford. Between the wars the WEA, Ruskin College, the Extra-Mural Delegacy and sympathetic tutors in the undergraduate colleges eventually built up a network to attract them. Ruskin College taught about 40 students in any one year between the wars, 110 in the 1950s and 170 in the 1970s, by which time it was sending about 20 students a year to university, 7 or 8 of them to Oxford.[24] It made a big impact on the labour movement, with students such as John Prescott, Bill McCarthy, Richard Marsh, Dennis Skinner, Eric Varley, George Woodcock, and numerous Labour candidates and MPs. The Trades Union Congress wanted the Franks Commission to recommend Oxford to place more emphasis on adult education, and when

[20] R. H. Tawney, *Education: The Socialist Policy* (London 1924), 46; *OM* 12 Mar. 1925, 371; 11 June 1931, 832.
[21] *Plan* no. 1, nd, 23; Attlee, 'Letter to Oxford', *Isis* 29 Apr. 1936, 4.
[22] *Isis* 25 Nov. 1936, 5; H. D. Hughes to author, 16 Oct. 1989.
[23] *Oxford and Working-Class Education* (Oxford 1908), 48. See also H. Gaitskell, 'At Oxford in the twenties' in A. Briggs and J. Saville (eds), *Essays in Labour History* (London 1960), 15; W. T. Rodgers (ed.), *Hugh Gaitskell 1906–1963* (London 1964), 39.
[24] Statistics compiled from Ruskin College annual reports.

this failed it is not surprising that Woodcock wrote in to express regret.[25] He, Ben Roberts and Len Murray had been PPE undergraduates at New College under Henry Phelps Brown. A hard-working ex-Communist, Murray as a post-war undergraduate was single-mindedly determined to equip himself to work in the labour movement. 'I really can't pay enough tribute to him', Murray recalls of Phelps Brown, 'because he was so sensitive to this brash . . . rough, uncultivated, uncultured young hobbledehoy'.[26]

Oxford respected the Greek ideal of a harmony between the active and the contemplative life. As a power-house of the Church of England it had long been entangled in politics, and twentieth-century Anglican paternalism could fertilize both right and left. So also could the social conscience nourished by T. H. Green, Arnold Toynbee, Alfred Milner and Samuel Barnett which drew many Oxford men into university settlements and workers' education, and inspired A. D. Lindsay in his many public causes. Four Oxford colleges made a speciality of fostering outside links: All Souls (with lawyers and politicians), Nuffield (with employers and trade unions), St Antony's (with diplomats and foreign visitors), and Christ Church (with the Church of England). 'In modern times', wrote J. C. Masterman, 'there must have been few men prominent in Church or State who had not at one time or another been entertained in Christ Church'.[27]

Social contacts of this sort fostered a practical outlook within Oxford, a distaste for theory, especially when vaguely idealistic in tone. So Oxford's first politically virtuous circle was reinforced by a second: a University with a taste for the practical was alert to governmental concerns. Oxford dons tended to choose higher-grade civil servants as the group whose salaries should be comparable to their own, and several well-known Oxford figures worked in or closely with the civil service—including A. R. W. Harrison, A. H. Smith and Lords Balogh, Franks, Crowther-Hunt, Redcliffe-Maud and Trend. When the young American scholar Samuel Beer proposed publishing his *Treasury Control* with the Clarendon Press, Kenneth Wheare as Gladstone Professor of Government and a delegate of the Press readily reassured Sir Edward Bridges (Permanent Secretary to the Treasury) of its right to veto anything Beer proposed to include; 'we are most anxious', he wrote in 1954, 'that you should not be let down on this'. The Fulton Committee on the civil service was appointed in 1966 by an Oxford-trained prime minister, and Oxford contributed five of its twelve members (including its chairman and the director of its influential Management Consultancy Group).[28] The marriage of theory with practice, already

[25] HCP 255 (1966), 65–6, 69–70.   [26] Author's interview with Lord Murray, 19 Jan. 1988.
[27] J. C. Masterman, *On the Chariot Wheel: An Autobiography* (London 1975), 127.
[28] J. E. Cronin, 'Power, secrecy and the British constitution', *Twentieth Century British History* 1992, 73, cf p. 75. For Fulton, see R. H. S. Crossman, *The Diaries of a Cabinet Minister* (3 vols London 1975–7) iii. 103. Compare Oxford's impact on the selection of a chairman for the Royal Commission on Local Government, ibid. i. 367, 400, 479, 491, 512.

14.2 An Oxford Union debating episode, Dec. 1950

14.3 Michael Stewart addressing the Vietnam teach-in, 1965

14.4 St Hilda's under-
graduates being
presented to Princess
Margaret, 1954

16.1 John Johnson, 1956

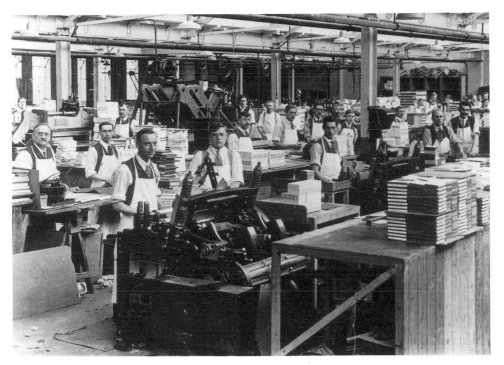

16.2 The new bindery at the Oxford University Press in the 1920s

16.3 Sir James Murray and helpers in his Scriptorium, 10 July 1915

applied successfully through the Nuffield medical benefaction, lay behind the creation of Nuffield College, an institution central to Oxford research in economics and politics. The first four wardens of Nuffield College (Butler, Clay, Loveday and Chester) all moved easily between academic life and British or international governmental bodies, and it was from an after-dinner talk there in autumn 1947 that Herbert Morrison's textbook *Government and Parliament* emerged.

All this was reflected in the undergraduate syllabus—in the governmental preoccupations of Greats and modern history, for instance, in the establishment of PPE, and in the two-year diploma in public and social administration which Oxford set up in 1936 to help train officials in local and central government. The University consulted continuously with the civil service on whether its courses met the entry requirements. It frequently adduced its courses, together with the moral impact of college life, as evidence that its undergraduates would make good civil servants. The *Oxford Magazine* before 1914 tabulated civil-service examination results in much detail, and in the mid-1920s regularly carried Scoones' advertisements offering to prepare candidates for the civil and diplomatic service examinations. Through the scholarship system's recognized meritocratic route, clever and industrious undergraduates from a modest background moved into civil-service posts and thus reinforced the political élite.[29]

From the 1930s to the 1970s new directions in Oxford's social studies brought Whitehall still closer. Keynes wanted to cure business depression through combining central control of currency and credit with collecting and disseminating ample economic data so that society could exercise 'directive intelligence' over private business. On 9 June 1937 twenty-two Oxford economists (including Harrod, Hubert Henderson and Meade) wrote to the *Times* urging the government to time its 'works of capital development' for the onset of a depression so as to smooth out economic fluctuations. As Trinity's economics tutor Robert Hall (later Lord Roberthall) wrote in 1937, '*laisser faire* is a lost cause which finds no home in Oxford'. Fully in tune with this was a recruit from Cambridge, the economist Sir Hubert Henderson, together with the many Oxford-educated 'planners' behind the Attlee government: Douglas Jay, Hugh Gaitskell, Evan Durbin, James Meade. Henderson's Economists' Research Group sought to place economic theory on a firm empirical basis by building up generalizations from the after-dinner comments made to the group by visitors with practical experience. Oxford had ample contacts of this sort; in 1958 it had educated 46 of the 148 directors of the 'Big Five' banks, 24 of the 107 directors of fourteen merchant banks or discount houses and 30 of the 149

[29] H. E. Dale, *The Higher Civil Service of Great Britain* (London 1941), 69–70, 74 is excellent on this.

directors of eight major insurance companies—surpassing all other universities in all three categories.[30]

Secondments to Whitehall brought Oxford dons all the glamour and
intellectual excitement of glimpsing government from within, all the
reassurance of public usefulness—without any need to burn academic boats.
By March 1940 Oxford's teaching strength in economics was already
seriously depleted by dons departing for Whitehall. Given that the managed
economy after 1945 brought public funding of higher education, and given
that Oxford-trained civil servants filled some of the government posts thus
created, Oxford in the 1950s and 1960s understandably went along with the
growth of central government power. Critics of the social-democratic
consensus within the economics sub-faculty were relatively isolated and
uninfluential individualists. In these years an interventionist style of
Conservatism led Robert Hall to recruit young economists (several from
Oxford) to serve in the Economic Section. The frustration of the ROBOT
scheme for a revolution in economic policy in 1952 (by Allen, Salter,
McDougall, Cherwell and Hall) illustrates the prominence of Oxford men in
Whitehall's decision-making.[31] Labour's advent in 1964 reinforced Oxford-
in-Whitehall—so much so, that what Max Beloff called the 'positive flight
into Whitehall of senior members of the Sub-Faculty of Economics' soon
confronted Oxford with serious teaching scarcities.[32] It was an Oxford
economist, Thomas Balogh, who first introduced the idea of a 'social
contract' into Labour Party thinking in 1970,[33] and economists continued to
shuttle between Oxford and Paddington until 1979.

Until the 1970s governmental concerns also dominated Oxford's approach
to Commonwealth studies, history, sociology and politics. Just as Oxford's
professors of the history of war (until Gibbs's appointment in 1953) were
sometime military men, so its professors of politics (until Berlin's
appointment in 1957) were involved (at least part-time) in public life. From
Marriott to Wheare to D. E. Butler, political studies in Oxford have been
fertilized by frequent visits to Westminster and Whitehall, or by archival
communings with the politicians of the past. The eight issues of *Political
Quarterly*, edited by W. G. S. Adams in 1914–16, are all severely practical in
their subject-matter, with articles mostly by Oxford dons on topics of
current political interest. In the 1930s, while Henderson's Economists'
Research Group was entertaining visiting businessmen, politics tutors were

[30] J. M. Keynes, 'The end of laissez faire', in his *Collected Writings* (30 vols London 1971–89)
ix. 292. Hall, *OM* 27 Jan. 1938, 316. See also T. Lupton and C. S. Wilson, 'The social
background and connections of "top decision makers" ', *Manchester School* 1959, 33–7.

[31] *The Robert Hall Diaries 1947–53*, ed. A. Cairncross (London 1989), 202–3.

[32] Beloff, *OM* 28 Jan. 1965, 171; cf 18 Feb. 1965, 226. See also *OM* 7 Mar. 1940, 247–8; HCP
175 (1940), 94, 166.

[33] W. H. Fishbein, *Wage Restraint by Consensus: Britain's Search for an Incomes Policy
Agreement, 1965–79* (London 1984), 115.

entertaining visiting non-academic speakers in their Public Administration Group.

Practical concerns also inspired the first of the Nuffield election studies in 1945: R. B. McCallum's desire to ward off from the post-war settlement of 1945 the damaging mythology that had accumulated after 1919. Thirteen British election studies later we can see that the series has not only deterred myth-makers, but has performed a fine service to British democracy by placing its understanding of elections on a firm empirical foundation. It rests on continuous private consultation with politicians in London, complemented by the seminar in Oxford to which they are often invited. A similar involvement with government at the local and national level, and a similar empiricism of outlook, could be demonstrated in Oxford's handling of sociology (or 'social studies' as Oxford called it until the 1960s), and in the so-called Oxford 'school' of industrial relations, which so deeply influenced national policy in this area during the 1960s.[34]

Oxford's parliamentarism meant that its impact was channelled through the three major parties—Conservative, Labour and Liberal—each of whose separate histories will now be considered in turn. Conservative strength at Oxford between the wars reflected the circumstances of the dons and the social class of their pupils. 'How good life seemed', wrote Virginia Woolf of a pleasant dinner among Oxford dons in 1928: 'how sweet its rewards, how trivial this grudge or that grievance'.[35] No twentieth-century Oxford college has matched Peterhouse's reputation for Conservative influence, though Christ Church's clerical connections and All Souls' involvement in empire (with three viceroys of India and Lionel Curtis among its fellows) made both colleges centres for inter-war Conservative discussion. Political discussion inevitably flourished in All Souls, given its links to the *Times*, its non-resident fellows regularly coming up from London at weekends and its tradition of scholarship in history, politics and law. In such a place, appeasement came up as naturally for debate (between supporters and opponents) as any other major topic of the day. As for Christ Church, through two of its historian fellows—Keith Feiling and Robert Blake—a single Oxford college established the history of British Conservatism as a subject for respectable academic study.

Conservatives supplied five of Oxford's six chancellors between 1914 and 1970. Quick Conservative action secured Milner's unopposed election in spring 1925, but Conservatives were less decisive later in the year. The Lord Chancellor, Viscount Cave, was elected by 987 to 441 votes only after backwoodsmen rebelled against the leading Conservatives who had backed

---

[34] I have discussed the 'school' in more detail in my 'Oxford and the labour movement', *Twentieth Century British History* 1991, 268–70.

[35] V. Woolf, *A Room of One's Own* (London 1929), 17.

Asquith. Bitterly disappointed at his defeat, Asquith blamed it on the fact that 'the sound of the tocsin was heard in the rural parsonages'.[36] Oxford Conservatives learned their lesson, and on Cave's death in 1928 Grey was elected without opposition as the consensus candidate; in 1933 Irwin (later Lord Halifax) succeeded him without fuss.

By no means all Conservative senior members welcomed undergraduates as political allies. Farnell and Wells, vice-chancellors in the 1920s, were keen to prevent Oxford undergraduates from becoming politicized in Spanish or Russian style.[37] The Conservatives' nearest approach to a Cole, a Crossman or a Lindsay was Lindemann. Yet Conservative undergraduates had certain advantages over the left: they were happier with Oxford's mood and structure and less schismatic in tendency. Their loose network of dining clubs, policy groups and debating societies catered for different tastes, and Conservatives foregathered less with the aim of scrutinizing political conviction than of celebrating it with the aid of formality, toasts and tradition. Between the wars they could often afford to celebrate well. In the 1920s two clubs were of central importance, the Canning and the Chatham, which Evelyn Waugh addressed more than once. But Oxford's Carlton Club (founded in 1919) was gaining ground, and in 1937 timed its annual dinner to coincide with coronation celebrations, 'showing both the Carlton's respect for the English Crown and its contempt for the International'.[38] In the late 1940s and early 1950s it had well over 200 members, many of them attracted more by its social facilities than by its politics. Rising costs thereafter reduced it to a dining club without premises, but during the decade of student revolution its minutes are laced with menus. Redefining its purpose in 1965, it 'accepted that political discussion remained its most important function, despite a minority view that dining was just as important'.[39]

Conservatives sometimes dined so well that they moved on for dinner-jacketed assaults on the enemy: on Roy Harrod, for example, whose rooms were wrecked in June 1919 after he denounced the Versailles Treaty. Prominent in many college dining clubs [plate 4.4] were the public-school athletes who were 'in general very Blue'. New College Prae Prandial Club's facetious minutes, stuffed with *doubles entendres*, record a raid in 1926 on one of the General Strike's leading sympathizers who, compelled to sing the

[36] Nuffield College, Cherwell MS J3, fo 1, Asquith to Lindemann, 5 July 1925. For more detail on the election see G. B. Grundy, *Fifty-Five Years at Oxford: An Unconventional Autobiography* (London 1945), 142–4 and correspondence in London, British Library, Add. MS 62492 (Cave Papers).

[37] L. R. Farnell, *An Oxonian Looks Back* (London 1934), 291; Wells, *OM* 18 Feb. 1926, 297.

[38] Bodl. MS top. Oxon. d. 472/1, Oxford Carlton Club minute-book no. 1, fo 57, 27 Jan. 1937. Waugh's contributions (on 31 Jan., 14 Feb., 30 May, 24 Oct., 14 Nov. 1923) are in the Chatham Club's minutes in Bodl. MS top. Oxon. d. 726.

[39] Bodl. MS top. Oxon. d. 922, Oxford Carlton Club minutes, 28 Jan. 1965.

national anthem, was then debagged.[40] A. J. P. Taylor's difficulties at Oriel did not compare with those of a Communist friend at Merton who within one term had his books burned twice and his wardrobe four times: as he told Taylor, 'it is easy to have a persecution complex if you are a Communist at Merton'.[41] The history of the left in Oxford is marked by collective martyrdoms, disrupted and intimidated meetings: Keir Hardie's visit to Oxford Town Hall in 1909, Lansbury's visit in May 1921, the Labour Club meeting on 4 May 1926 and the May Day procession of 1940. Not till the 1960s did the left steal the right's intimidatory clothes.

Such exploits were only semi-political in motive. Celebrating the national or college community, they were small-scale versions of what happened after boat-club dinners and Twickenham matches. Undergraduate strike-breakers in 1926 saw themselves as helping their country during an emergency in a non-political fashion, not as participating in a class war. Fascism made far less impact on Oxford than Communism. A Fascist Club existed by 1935, but never enjoyed the October Club's following; nor were Fascists in OUCA ever as influential as Communists in the Labour Club. British Union of Fascist meetings in the Town Hall ended in violence and controversy in both 1933 and 1936, and although a Corporate Club briefly surfaced in Christ Church in 1946 (evoking protests from Tony Benn), it came to naught.[42] Usually somewhat to the left of the national party, Oxford Conservative attitudes reflected the impact of the public schools and their well-intentioned left-inclined religion, the paternalism of a persisting aristocratic culture, the remoteness of the entrepreneurial struggle and the profoundly consensual impact made by two world wars.

The point can be documented by briefly surveying the Conservatives' evolution in Oxford from the 1920s to the 1960s. Oxford's post-war undergraduate radicalism soon evaporated, and in the 1920s ambitious undergraduates tended to identify with those who were socially above them as energetically as their successors in the 1930s identified with those lower down. The Oxford Union in the 1920s helped launch several Conservatives later well known: Quintin Hogg, A. T. Lennox-Boyd and Derek Walker-Smith. In 1923 the Chatham and Canning clubs for the first time entertained a prime minister, Baldwin, at a joint dinner. In 1924 the Carlton Club endorsed Baldwin's new-style liberalized Conservatism by welcoming Conservative defectors from the New Reform Club (which had been formed earlier to back the Lloyd George coalition). In the same year Feiling

---

[40] Quotation from T. Greenidge, *Degenerate Oxford?* (London 1930), 56. Harrod, *Isis* 27 May 1936, 5; NCA 14930, Prae Prandial Club minutes, 22 May 1926. Mrs C. Dalton referred me to this volume, and gave me much other help besides.

[41] A. J. P. Taylor, *A Personal History* (London 1983), 68.

[42] Benn, *Isis* 14 May 1947, 17; 22 May 1947, 35.

collaborated with Central Office in setting up OUCA to propagate the faith, and by June 1926 it had about 800 members.[43]

During the early 1930s, when articulate Oxford undergraduate opinion was moving leftward, Conservatives seldom marshalled their full strength. Not till the 1970s could general elections provide an occasion for mobilizing all undergraduates, and no eloquent Conservative emerged after John Boyd-Carpenter (President of the Union in Michaelmas term 1930) to mobilize Conservatives within the Union. *Isis* pointed out in 1927 that 'the majority of unthinking undergraduates are Conservatives', and in 1937 that 'the large majority of Conservatives in Oxford have never been inside the Union or attended any kind of political function'. This meant that the larger the turnout at Oxford Union debates, the higher the proportion of Conservatives among the undergraduates present. An informed estimate of 1935 claims that there were probably 800 socialist undergraduates, of whom 600 were active: and that there were 2,000 Conservative undergraduates, of whom less than 200 were active.[44] Yet the politically inarticulate did leave some trace behind: the prosperity of non-political bodies such as the Student Christian Movement and the university church, then flourishing under F. R. Barry. Undergraduate recollections of the early 1930s tend to dwell as much on Archbishop Temple's mission of 1931 or on controversy about the 'Oxford Group' as on overtly political activity.

In the mid-1930s Ian Harvey and Keith Steel-Maitland in OUCA revitalized latent Conservative feeling, and three presidents of OUCA— Harvey, P. J. M. Anderson and Edward Heath—became presidents of the Union. Oxford's Conservatives, like their national leaders, poached on the Liberal constituency; indeed, Frank Hardie thought they 'would anywhere else be . . . rightly described, as Liberals'.[45] Whereas, as we shall see, liberalism within the Labour Club survived (amidst controversy) through secession, in OUCA it arrived unobtrusively through annexation. OUCA battled against the more exclusive Conservative caucus of senior members because it thought Conservatism could be genuinely popular, and so had no need for conspiracy, exclusiveness or privilege. By 1935 it had 1,000 members, soon to become voters, together with 5,000 enfranchised life-members; it could claim to speak for a quarter of the University constituency's total electorate.[46]

By November 1937 Heath was the Union's 'leading defender of the National Government'. *Isis* claimed in 1939 that 'no President has done more to re-establish the prestige of the Union not only as a debating society . . .

[43] For New Reform Club see Carlton Club minute-book no. 1, 15 Jan. 1924, fos 32–3; for Feiling see Oxford University Election Committee minute-book, 17 Dec. 1924.

[44] *Isis* 9 Mar. 1927, 1; 5 May 1937, 1; D. M. Crichton (ed.), *Tory Oxford: Essays in University Conservatism* (London 1935), 98. See also *Isis* 12 Mar. 1930, 8.

[45] F. Hardie, 'Youth and politics' in A. C. Johnson (ed.), *Growing Opinions: A Symposium of British Youth Outlook* (London 1935), 183.   [46] *Daily Telegraph* 13 Mar. 1935, 14.

but also as a club' and that 'he will not be soon forgotten'.[47] By spring 1938 Heath was leading the attack on appeasement. The Union's Munich debate of October 1938 was more crowded than any since Lloyd George's visit in 1913. In attacking the Munich settlement, Heath 'was the personification of quiet reasonableness', and the motion deploring the policy of peace without honour was carried by 320 votes to 266. Conservative undergraduates like Heath collaborated enthusiastically with the government's left-wing critics in Lindsay's by-election campaign. In November, branding the government as 'nothing more nor less than an organized hypocrisy', Heath described Chamberlain's foreign policy as 'if at first you don't concede, fly, fly, fly again'. Despite Harvey's vigorous defence of the government, the motion of no confidence was carried by 203 votes to 163. Trying in December to get Churchill to speak at the Union, Heath told Churchill that 'Professor Lindemann will vouch for me as an excellent rebel Tory'.[48]

Unlike the Oxford Carlton Club, OUCA did not ward off women: Alice Johnston (from Central Office) was on the first committee of its graduate branch in 1936, and by 1949 'the queenly sway of Margaret Roberts' within post-war OUCA had become a vivid memory.[49] Elected President in Michaelmas term 1946, she moved on to enliven the executive committee of its graduate branch. It would be anachronistic to expect her in the mid-1940s to diverge from her party's centrist alignment; her distinguishing feature was rather her energy and her belief in widening her party's appeal at a time when some despaired of it. This mood informs her motion for more working-class officers within the party at the Federation of Conservative and Unionist Associations, to whose 150 representatives OUCA contributed seventeen. Equally characteristic was her resistance to the idea of disbanding OUCA's graduate branch once the University seats had gone: it should, she thought, persist as a 'ginger group'.[50]

Michael Heseltine carried forward OUCA's relatively democratic image into the 1950s. By helping to found the Blue Ribbon Club, which aimed to empower OUCA's members directly to elect its officers, he boldly challenged 'the sleepy dominance of the port-swilling socialites of the Carlton Club'. This colourful and controversial figure used recreation rather than idealism or policy to make Oxford politics interesting again. His ambition, his flair for publicity and his business sense made him President of

[47] *Isis* 25 Jan. 1939, 7; 8 Mar. 1939, 8.
[48] *OM* 20 Oct. 1938, 50; *Isis* 23 Nov. 1938, 5; Heath to Churchill, 12 Dec. 1938 in M. Gilbert, *Winston S. Churchill* (8 vols and 5 companion vols in 13 pts London 1966–88) v, companion vol, pt 3, 1309–10.
[49] *Isis* 26 Jan. 1949, 12; cf H. Young, *One of Us: A Biography of Margaret Thatcher* (London 1989), 25.
[50] For her motion see *Isis* 1 May 1946, 11. For her role in the Oxford University Senior Conservative Association see its minutes for 10 July 1947, 14 Apr. 1948, 13 Mar. and 6 May 1952, 5 July 1954.

the Union in 1954. 'Michael has all the roguish honesty, the sudden reckless humility, and the rakish charm to be the hero of a picaresque romance', wrote Anthony Howard.[51] For Heseltine as for other well-known self-made Oxford Conservatives before and after him—Birkenhead, Harvey, Heath, Thatcher, Archer, Redwood—the world was his oyster.

Conservative governments' centrism between 1951 and 1964 made it easier for the party to attract dons than it later became, and the party's influence was made manifest when—long before urban conservation became fashionable—Oxford Conservatives defeated the project for a road through Christ Church Meadow. Promoting that achievement was an alliance between Lord Cherwell (friend of Churchill and cabinet minister from 1951 to 1953), manœuvring behind the scenes, and his friend Robert Blake, who argued against the road in public. On Halifax's death in 1959, Conservatives presented the Prime Minister Harold Macmillan as the anti-establishment candidate for Chancellor. The rival candidate Lord Franks (backed by most heads of house) had been a fine college tutor, later head of house, and was a well-known administrator. Old members rushed to qualify by paying the fees for the MA degree, and nearly half the electorate turned up in person to vote. Despite a hostile *Times* leader, Macmillan secured 1,976 votes to Franks' 1,697.

When reinforced on such occasions by lay support, Oxford Conservatives could still be formidable, but within the University their mood became increasingly defensive from the late 1950s. Robert Blake might dislike the Robbins report's 'sort of sour Benthamite egalitarianism', but he acquiesced in the idea of a public inquiry into Oxford. Agreeing in 1966 to attend a Conservative dinner, John Buxton (New College's English tutor) said he was 'glad there may be a chance to dispel the notion that it is not intellectually respectable to be against Wilson, Jay, Crossman et hoc genus omne'.[52] Undergraduate Conservatism was substantial but relatively unobtrusive. When one-fifth of Oxford's male finalists were surveyed in 1961, 40 per cent said they would vote Conservative at a general election tomorrow, 24 per cent Liberal and 20 per cent Labour.[53] After 1964, as after 1945, the Oxford Union turned against the government of the day—expressing confidence in the Wilson governments with diminishing majorities in November 1964 and October 1965; in October 1966 the government lost by 642 votes to 161. But unlike their predecessors after 1945, Conservatives in the late 1960s had to share with extra-parliamentary left-wingers the benefits of disillusionment with Labour; the far left branded the Union 'along with the Proctors and American Imperialism as a tool of

[51] Quotations from *Isis* 3 Feb. 1954, 18 (J. S. Bingham); 20 Oct. 1954, 9 (Howard).

[52] R. Blake, 'The effects of Robbins on Oxford', *Oxford* May 1964, 62; Buxton's letter (25 May 1966, to Michael Maclagan) is inserted with other documents in Senior Conservative Association minute-book 1935–54.

[53] *Isis* 4 Mar. 1961, 6 (special survey number).

the bourgeoisie'. When undergraduates were polled in June 1970, 37 per cent said they were Labour, 33 per cent Conservative and 12 per cent Liberal.[54]

Oxford contributed little to 'Thatcherism' apart from its two leading exponents, Thatcher and Joseph. What at first look like anticipations of it in Oxford turn out on closer inspection to be somewhat different. The University of course fended off the state from its own affairs. Colleges tended to fortify themselves against intruders, and G. R. Y. Radcliffe was not alone among college bursars in being 'a complete master of the technique of fighting the bureaucracy';[55] in C. K. Allen, Oxford produced a scourge of delegated legislation. But this was non-political traditionalism, not radical Conservatism. The Society for Freedom in Science, founded in 1941 by two Oxford biologists—J. R. Baker and A. G. Tansley—with Karl Polanyi, then at Manchester, denounced Bernal's ideology of planning. But Baker's intemperate style of argument and failure to extend it beyond the scientific sphere show that its prime impulse was non-political, and reflected the Oxford scientist's sturdy intellectual individualism. Hayekian libertarianism does not seem to have inspired Margaret Roberts' impact on OUCA, and *The Road to Serfdom* attracted few British social scientists anywhere when published in 1944. John Jewkes had little influence in Oxford as Professor of Economic Organization between 1948 and 1969, though he helped Polanyi into a research fellowship at Merton in 1959. Heath's desire for tax cuts and distaste for incomes policies in 1970–1 won little support among members of the economic establishment at the Treasury, the National Institute, the National Economic Development Council or the Organization for Economic Co-operation and Development. The roots of 'Thatcherism' lay in universities outside Oxbridge and in pressure groups such as the Institute of Economic Affairs.[56] In February 1974 only 31 per cent of British university teachers said they would vote Conservative, and only 18 per cent by May 1987.[57] Oxford's dons, so closely tied to Conservatism in the 1920s, were now moving in very different directions.

Oxford's influence on the Labour Party has been profound, if only because the party has carried into the twentieth century that alliance between intellectuals and organized labour which inspired nineteenth-century Owenism, positivism and Fabianism. After 1914 the Labour Party in Oxford owed most to three senior members: Lindsay, Cole and Rowse. Lindsay's unsectarian socialism enabled him to combine membership of the Labour Party with the claim to have been a lifelong Liberal. For him, socialism meant applying democratic principles to industry, and this should

---

[54] Quotation from *Isis* 11 Oct. 1969, 6 (David Walter); see also 15 June 1970, 12.
[55] *Times* 20 July 1959, 8.
[56] L. Brittan, *The Economic Consequences of Democracy* (London 1977), 26.
[57] *Times Higher Education Supplement* 22 Feb. 1974, 6 (sample of 222 university teachers in

enable Liberals and Labour to collaborate. Elected to the Fabian Society's Oxford branch in 1898, he soon began giving talks and holding office, but resigned the presidency in 1914 to make way for Cole. Lindsay repeatedly helped the Labour Club in the 1920s by speaking at meetings and arbitrating in disputes, and as Master of Balliol he carried on A. L. Smith's work for the WEA; R. H. Tawney could 'never be sufficiently grateful for the inspiration of his example'. During the General Strike Lindsay backed neither side, but mobilized moderates behind the Archbishop of Canterbury's appeal for conciliation. Though denounced by the *Morning Post* for corrupting the young with his 'subtly poisonous book' on Marx, he was a resolute popularizer whose scholarship aimed at a practical purpose without ever degenerating into propaganda.[58] In the 1930s he acted for a time as the Labour Club's Senior Treasurer, and through the WEA did much for the unemployed. Roy Jenkins and Denis Healey were among the many pupils to acknowledge in writing the importance of his influence.[59]

G. D. H. Cole—the second, equally eclectic, major influence on Oxford socialism—was, in his own words, 'one of the many who as undergraduates got inspiration from' Lindsay, who 'started me off on my course as a political theorist'. Lindsay and A. L. Smith also led Cole into the WEA 'with consequences momentous to me'.[60] No Oxford positivist or Fabian could rival either the intensity or the time-span of Cole's impact on the British labour movement. It is he and Tawney who have accustomed us to the idea of the university teacher as its guide. Instinctively irreverent towards authority, Cole nonetheless expected intellectuals to be deferential within the labour movement. His first major book, *The World of Labour* (1913), grew directly out of discussions within the Fabian Society's Oxford University branch; between 1907 and 1914 it attracted at any one time about eighty members, several later famous.[61] There is a direct line of continuity between the Oxford University Socialist Society (Cole's syndicalist or Guild Socialist offshoot from the Fabians in 1915) and the Oxford University Labour Club which sprang up late in 1919.

Cole hoped trade-union-sponsored research would undermine the employers; research and education lay at the heart of his socialist programme. As with many Oxford dons in public life—Lindsay, Fisher, Murray—his scholarship merged with his practical politics. His conscientious objection during the First World War caused his extremism to be

British universities); 5 June 1987, 8 (sample of 497). I am most grateful to Professor Ivor Crewe for generous help at this point. For a fuller treatment, see my 'Mrs. Thatcher and the intellectuals', *Twentieth Century British History* 1994.

[58] *Morning Post* 12 Feb. 1926, 12.

[59] Keele University Library, A. D. Lindsay MSS, L/228, Jenkins to Lindsay, 13 June 1949; L/231, Healey to Mrs Lindsay, 20 Mar. 1952.

[60] Ibid. L/23, Cole to Mrs Lindsay, 'Thursday' 1952.

[61] Three of the branch's minute-books (1895–1916) are at Bodl. MS top. Oxon. d. 465-7.

wildly exaggerated by those (many of them in Oxford) who did not know him. A *Morning Post* correspondent in 1919 detected 'a definite attempt to gain over the educated portion of the coming generation to the forces of anarchy and to make our universities centres of political disaffection as is so often the case on the Continent'. Yet Cole's aim, like Tawney's, was to ensure a peaceful transition from the old society to the new by educating working people for power. He aimed 'to prevent any big upheaval at the present time', and told Warren he thought it 'the business of responsible people to try and convert this unrest into definite proposals and politics. As soon as that is done, it becomes far easier to deal with'. After becoming Reader in Economics in 1924, he was in a position to apply his ideas: 'I am damned well not interested in adult education', he would say: 'I am interested in workers' education'.[62]

From the mid-1920s Cole spent much time in London, but after 1926 he kept the University strike committee in existence as an informal discussion-group meeting regularly in Oxford. This was the origin of the 'Cole Group'. At its meetings Cole kept in the background, quietly clarifying issues and lacing discussion with his immense knowledge of labour history and socialist thought. His eclecticism warded off narrowness, and it became a nursery for Gaitskell, Durbin, Stewart and Meade. Harold Wilson, also in the Group, says 'it was G. D. H. Cole as much as any man who finally pointed me in the direction of the Labour Party. His social and economic theories made it intellectually respectable.' The *New Statesman* was Cole's weekly pulpit for years, and its inter-war vitality reflected the Labour Party's growing impact on intellectuals. Nor did Oxford's journalistic impact cease with Cole; Kingsley Martin (a Cambridge man) was succeeded by four Oxford editors in succession: John Freeman, Paul Johnson, R. H. S. Crossman and Anthony Howard. Yet Cole did not set out to create Labour Party careers. He was too cerebral in his pursuits to establish a permanent bond with trade-union leaders; too suspicious of parliamentarism, too hostile to bureaucracy, to be loved by Labour's leaders: too independent in outlook to build up a following. For Attlee he was a 'permanent undergraduate'.[63]

These influences caused socialism to spread among senior members, who launched their 'Socialist Dons' Luncheon Club' in 1932 with up to forty members. The Oxford University Labour Party was founded in 1933 to keep Labour activists in touch with the party while at Oxford and to win one of the University seats; it adopted J. L. Stocks as candidate in 1934. Meanwhile the Labour Club had been growing fast, with much help from its third major personality, A. L. Rowse—an energetic, popular and respected

[62] *Morning Post* 14 Aug. 1919, 8; MCA box marked 'fellows: dossiers and credentials of successful applicants c.1912–1930', Cole to Warren, 30 Mar. 1919; R. Williams, *Politics and Letters* (London 1979), 78.

[63] H. Wilson, *Memoirs: The Making of a Prime Minister 1916–64* (London 1986), 48; Attlee quoted in A. W. Wright, *G. D. H. Cole and Socialist Democracy* (Oxford 1979), 6.

figure on the left in the mid-1920s. Many political allegiances among twentieth-century undergraduates have been shaped by the social distinction between grammar and public school. Whereas Edward Heath, fresh from Chatham House Grammar School, Ramsgate, found social security through joining the Conservatives, Rowse (from St Austell County School) found his home from home in the Labour Club. As Secretary in 1924 he immediately transformed the handwriting and content of the minutes, and as a young graduate gave several talks to the Club. In October 1930 he 'reviewed the political situation from the standpoint of a Marxian' and 'considered the universal depression a tangible sign of the failure of Capitalism'. Like so many early socialists he was equivocal about the poor, whom he was eager to abolish. Walking from All Souls to St Clement's one evening in 1930, he saw 'pubs every few steps. Sordid types outside the doors . . . Twisted types limp along, harsh ugly women. And these are the people for whom . . . my New Jerusalem is intended. They'd foul the doorstep before they got into it.' Or as Christopher Mayhew put it later, 'I did not feel compassion or affection towards them, but simply unease'.[64]

Rowse's *Politics and the Younger Generation* (1931) grew out of the Labour Club's discussions just as Cole's *World of Labour* had grown out of the Fabian branch. Its hopes for the future rested on the younger generation and on an increasingly united working class, whose leaders would emerge from an increasingly meritocratic educational system. The Labour Party, 'the natural representative of the working class', would eventually win a permanent electoral majority.[65] Impressed by Soviet Russia's rapid economic growth, Rowse thought a reformed social structure would free the British economy from wasteful trades and squandered wealth. Respectfully critical of Marxist theory and owing much to Tawney, he thought class war both inefficient and unnecessary, and favoured only the gradual revolution that grows out of British political traditions. Rowse's socialism, unlike Cole's, drew upon First-World-War precedents to harness the machinery of the state. Peace would arrive through European federation and the spread of socialist governments. This programme, plausible in the context of its time, turned out to rest on entirely mistaken social and political analysis. After standing as a Labour candidate in Cornwall in 1931 and 1935, Rowse's politics changed and his priorities became the writing of history and poetry.

'In England . . . it is not to-day expected of any man of ability that he should sink with the Liberal ship when there is a chance of political rescue in another ship's boat', wrote Egon Wertheimer in 1929, discussing 'hopeful young Liberals and Conservatives' who had by then joined the Labour

[64] Bodl. MS top. Oxon. d. 298, Oxford University Labour Club minute-book no. 3 (1926–31), fo 125 (17 Oct. 1930); A. L. Rowse, *A Man of the Thirties* (London 1979), 142; C. Mayhew, *Party Games* (London 1969), 24.

[65] A. L. Rowse, *Politics and the Younger Generation* (London 1931), 77.

Party. He went on to say that 'political effectiveness in England is regarded as something of value in itself'.[66] It was in the Labour Club that many of these new recruits congregated. It had well over a hundred members in the early 1920s, and by 1926–7 its meetings were attracting an average attendance of more than a hundred. The members included A. J. P. Taylor, Evan Durbin, Reginald Bassett and Barbara Betts (later Castle), and Ruskin College students were active from the start. It was a lively body: the Red Flag was quite often sung, there were social meetings, dramatic functions, films, dancing, party games, impersonations, Sunday rambles, frequent fund-raisings for deserving labour causes and above all plenty of argument. The Club often worked closely with the city Labour Party, especially at elections. Much valued were its opportunities for meeting the opposite sex. With help from Norman Haire, the Club in Barbara Castle's time went still further, and 'blazed the trail of sex knowledge'. 'The most mentally proficient among us who bother about politics at all', claimed an *Isis* editorial in 1927, 'possess distinct Socialist leanings'.[67]

Well before the 1931 crisis, Labour was poised for further advance. The Cole Group was one source of the determined bid made in the late 1920s by Michael Stewart and Roger Wilson, backed strongly from St John's College, to push the Oxford Union into debating more serious topics. There had not been a Labour Union president since Kenneth Lindsay in 1921, but between 1929 and 1932 there were four more. Styles of Union debating began to change. Like the Fabian branch, the Labour Club occasionally attracted Ramsay MacDonald as speaker, but all this and much else came to an end in 1931. Barbara Betts and Tony Greenwood campaigned against his honorary presidency (helping to get him replaced by Cole), and also opposed him at the general election. The economic crisis directly affected undergraduate careers and funding, and made the British political system seem more vulnerable. For Frank Hardie, the long vacation of 1931 was the moment of transition: thereafter, he said, seriousness and sincerity gradually ousted flippant speaking styles.[68] 1932 was the year of *New Signatures*, the first sign that the Auden group of writers, hitherto non-political, was changing its tune. Between 1930 and 1935, wrote Orwell, 'the typical literary man ceases to be a cultured expatriate with a leaning towards the church, and becomes an eager-minded schoolboy with a leaning towards Communism'.[69]

Labour Club members soon doubled to 600, and moved left of the national leadership. Discussing a Union debate on 'the Russian experiment', an *Isis* reporter in 1932 noted that 'the old Union style is going. There is no one to-day who can stuff a speech with plummy epigrams.'[70] Energetic Club

[66] E. Wertheimer, *Portrait of the Labour Party* (London 1929), 132.
[67] Mrs Barbara Castle to author, 19 Oct. 1988; *Isis* 9 Mar. 1927, 1.
[68] Hardie, 'Youth and politics', 179; cf G. Rees, *A Chapter of Accidents* (London 1972), 97.
[69] G. Orwell, *Collected Essays, Journalism and Letters* (4 vols Harmondsworth 1966–8) i. 559.
[70] *Isis* 26 Oct. 1932, 13; cf Hardie, *Isis* 4 May 1933, 600.

chairmen of the mid-1930s—Brian Farrell, Frank Hardie, Bill Nield—were also prominent in the Union, though with the occasional protest against its rules on dress. In 1936, the year when Frank Pakenham first trod the Union boards as a socialist speaker, the Labour Club's 600 members provided a good basis for influencing the Union's 1,250 subscribing members—and this at a time when the University's male undergraduate population totalled only 3,800. By May 1937 the Labour Club was the largest undergraduate club in Oxford, and its meetings usually attracted half its 750 members. 'Behind every Oxford stone', Charles Fenby complained in 1934, 'some missionary now lurks; every undergraduate is regarded primarily as a potential convert'.[71] There were study-circles, distinguished visiting speakers, vacation forays into rural parts with open-air speaking, visits to the distressed areas, camps for the unemployed, chalking the streets for striking Oxford busmen, collaboration with Communists. The cheer-leader in 1934 who urged on the October Club's procession with the hunger marchers inspired ambiguous reactions in Barbara Pym, who nonetheless joined in: ' "1–2–3–4–Who are We For? We are For the Working Classes—Down with the Ruling Classes. Students join the Workers' struggle" etc. Still I wish them luck even if I do disapprove of much that Communism stands for.'[72]

Undergraduates remained intensely interested in politics during the 1940s, and soon after the war the three leading party clubs together included more than 60 per cent of all undergraduates. 'For about fifteen years past', wrote Orwell in 1948, 'the dominant orthodoxy, especially among the young, has been "left". The key words are "progressive", "democratic" and "revolutionary".'[73] Nonetheless in Oxford the Union's rightward shift began as early as October 1946, when (in the largest vote since the 'King and Country' debate) 424 refused to applaud the Attlee government's domestic policy and only 375 supported it. Political enthusiasm waned markedly in the late 1940s, and the Labour Club's membership halved between 1948 and 1952.[74] The 1950s saw the heyday of Oxford's special brand of analytical philosopher, eager to clarify thought by excluding all potentially emotive issues. When asked by UNESCO after the Second World War what they were doing to resist totalitarianism, the sub-faculty was unembarrassed at feeling obliged to reply that it was doing nothing.[75] Critics branded their concerns as merely trivial: 'they discussed hypothetical men on hypothetical desert islands', Liam Hudson complained, 'never real gas chambers, real Jews'.[76]

[71] Fenby, Isis 7 Feb. 1934, 5; cf L. Whistler, 31 Oct. 1934, 12; N. F. Hidden, 14 Nov. 1934, 15. For statistics see Isis 27 May 1936, 13; 20 May 1937, 5.
[72] B. Pym, A Very Private Eye, ed. H. Holt and H. Pym (London 1985), 49.
[73] Orwell, Collected Essays iv. 464; Rodgers, 'Politics in the universities', 83.
[74] Rodgers, 83 (for Labour Club membership).
[75] Author's tape-recorded interview with J. O. Urmson, 10 Aug. 1985.
[76] L. Hudson, The Cult of the Fact (New York 1972), 34.

Events in 1956 revived politics on the left from two directions: the Suez venture stirred suspicion of the Eden government and the Hungarian uprising broke up the University's Communist Party branch. This liberated Marxism for wider influence within the British left, and the *Universities and Left Review* (later *New Left Review*) was founded at Oxford in 1956. Its quest for a positive alternative to Communism linked it to three powerful trends of the day: the Campaign for Nuclear Disarmament (CND), the internationalist anti-imperialism then so prevalent on the left in Oxford, and the widespread contemporary interest in a sociological approach to literature. The *Review*'s mood was less political—even anti-political—and certainly more literary than that of the Cole Group. But it chimed in with Cole's latter-day more international socialist preoccupations, and published an article by him in its first number. Rather than pursue short-term parliamentary aims through the Labour Party, the 'New Left' (as it came to be called) sought to open out public discussion on the left. Its base soon shifted to London and its influence soon extended far beyond Oxford.[77]

The New Left revitalized debate within the Labour Club, epitomized in the lively confrontation between two products of grammar schools: Brian Walden, the Gaitskellite down-to-earth machine politician and President of the Union: and Dennis Potter, the romantic and impulsive editor of *Isis* and future playwright. 'Few presidents have exercised such an authority over the House . . .', wrote *Isis* of Walden in 1959. 'As a debater, he has become a legend among his contemporaries.'[78] Potter's undergraduate career was marked by some fine speaking in the Union and by numerous eruptions and explosions: protests at alleged corruption in Oxford Union appointments, attacks on the lack of serious debate within the Labour Club, ructions with the proprietors of *Isis*. Socialism, he argued in 1959, should seek more than merely material gains: it must 'take account of the wealth, vitality and dignity of the ensuing culture'. In a scathing article on 'Potter and Potterism', Walden denounced Potter's wrong facts, vague terminology, intolerantly protest-minded mood and distorted reasoning. Potter approached political discussion, said Walden contemptuously, 'as a useful way of defining certain attitudes, expressing psychological frustrations, and seeking temperamental affinities'.[79]

The left now began to question the debater's art: could tolerance and style be reconciled with conviction and sincerity? Early in 1958 Perry Anderson gave up trying to report Union debates: 'impossible', he wrote, 'to fill a

---

[77] This paragraph owes much to my tape-recorded interviews with Raphael Samuel, 18 Sept. and 20 Oct. 1987. See also R. Archer *et al.* (eds), *Out of Apathy: Voices of the New Left 30 Years On* (London 1989), chaps 1–3.

[78] *Isis* 4 Nov. 1959, 14.

[79] *Isis* 21 May 1959, 21 (Potter); 13 May 1959, 22 (Walden). See also D. Marquand, 'The secret people of Oxford', *New Statesman* 13 July 1957, 43, and the interesting correspondence it evoked on 20 July (p. 84) and 27 July (pp. 115–16).

column with this trash'.[80] In 1959 Union reports in *Isis* cease altogether, and attempts at revival failed. The *Oxford Magazine* followed suit in the early 1960s, though it briefly retracted later in the decade. The Union 'is now virtually boycotted by a large section of the Left', wrote Jack Waterhouse in 1962: 'significantly the section responsible for the most articulate journalism and most vital political thinking in the University'.[81] By this time, fierce dilemmas involving personal integrity were raising the temperature: squabbles with the proctors, disputes with the proprietors of *Isis*, CND's call for direct action. 'Commitment' was the vogue and study must be 'relevant'. All this reflected an important long-term leftward shift among a significant minority of undergraduates, as in the nation as a whole. Behind it lay the ending of national service, the collapse of empire, the reaction against public-school values and the growing irreverence of the media towards authority. By 1958 *Isis* had moved unblushingly leftwards, and abandoned its once-detailed sports reporting. The weekly 'Isis Idol' feature, singling out a prominent undergraduate for a biographical sketch, also died away about this time. Even within the Union, votes of no confidence in the Conservative government won large annual majorities between 1961 and 1963.

Senior members, too, were moving leftward. In the early 1950s the *Oxford Magazine*'s mood was a-political (though it published the occasional cold-war sally against Communism), but by the mid-1950s it was analysing examination statistics, worrying about the class basis of Oxford's recruitment and embracing syllabus reform. In the early 1960s it moved on to discussing how to broaden Oxford's entry and simplify its admissions system. Oxford felt vulnerable in the face of fashionably egalitarian attacks on privilege, rationalistic attacks on tradition, and educational explanations for Britain's relative industrial decline. In 1964, 52 per cent of the Oxbridge dons surveyed placed themselves on the far or moderate left, 25 per cent in the centre and only 23 per cent on the right; when asked to say which party they supported, 40 per cent saw themselves as Labour, 15 per cent Liberal, 38 per cent Conservative, and 7 per cent other or none.[82]

Comparing student politicians in 1970 with their predecessors, *Isis* journalists found it 'striking how few of these people want to go into politics. The notable student politicians of the Left are disenchanted with the whole political system and seem determined to opt out.' The Labour Club's boycott of the Union, begun in 1972, persisted until 1986. R. H. S. Crossman thought that whereas in the 1930s youthful idealists' dialogue with the political establishment was fruitful, the new generation were

[80] *Isis* 19 Feb. 1958, 31.

[81] *Isis* 24 Jan. 1962, 11. For an understanding of the climate at this time on Oxford's left, I gained much from tape-recorded interviews with Dr R. Floud on 12 Oct. 1987 and Dr. I. McLean and Mr D. Soskice on 8 Mar. 1988.

[82] A. H. Halsey and M. A. Trow, *The British Academics* (London 1971), 434; cf 400–2.

'making reform and improvement much more difficult' by 'adopting revolutionary methods but without any prospect of a revolution'.[83] The Hart Committee on relations with junior members thought that no more than twenty to twenty-five undergraduates were involved in planning radical student incidents, with between 80 and 120 attending meetings;[84] but their energy made life difficult for visiting speakers.

Douglas Jay was already coming under fire in the Labour Club by June 1965 for his 'smooth answers', especially over the Wilson government's policy on Vietnam. Police protection was needed in February 1967 for Michael Stewart, who had difficulty in making himself heard when addressing the Democratic Labour Club. Later in the year R. H. S. Crossman, after a heavily policed visit to the Union, was shocked at being unable to move freely about Oxford, and drew an analogy with Fascism in his diary.[85] A crowd of 2,000 people outside the Town Hall in January 1969 could not prevent Enoch Powell from speaking, but only because he resorted to a remarkable system of decoys and concealed entrances. In May 1970 the Foreign Secretary Michael Stewart needed physical protection when speaking on the government's foreign policy—persevering against a barrage of chanting and missile-throwing.[86]

One aspect of this narrative deserves emphasis: with Labour, as with the Conservatives, extremists and opponents of parliamentarism made little headway in Oxford. Whenever Marxists seemed likely to prevail within the Labour Club (as in 1940, 1947, 1965 and 1975), social-democratic secessions backed by the Labour Party's national leadership bequeathed the Marxists only a rump.[87] In this hard school the social-democratic loyalties of people such as Reginald Bassett, Shirley Catlin (later Williams), Evan Durbin, Christopher Mayhew, Frank Pickstock, Ben Roberts, William Rodgers, Dick Taverne and Philip Williams were tempered. Social-democratic networks of friends within the labour movement were thus created which later re-surfaced in national politics with structures such as the Campaign for Democratic Socialism in the early 1960s or the Campaign for Labour Victory in 1977, which Rodgers sees as 'basically a C. D. S. re-born'.[88] Its failures in the late 1970s led directly to the Council for Social Democracy of 1981—which enlisted (among others) David Marquand, Frank Pickstock,

[83] *Isis* 9 Feb. 1970, 8; R. H. S. Crossman, *The Role of the Volunteer in the Modern Social Service* (Sidney Ball memorial lecture, Oxford 1973), 11.

[84] [H. L. A. Hart, chairman] *Report of the Committee on Relations with Junior Members* (University of Oxford 1969), 155.

[85] *Isis* 16 June 1965, 4 (Jay); 22 Feb. 1967, 2–3 (Stewart); R. H. S. Crossman, *Diaries of a Cabinet Minister* ii. 566–7.

[86] C. Wolman, 'Revolting students', *Isis* 23 Jan. 1976, 20; *OM* 15 May 1970, 247.

[87] This discussion summarizes only briefly the material presented in my 'Oxford and the labour movement', 257–65.

[88] My discussion of 'social-democratic' links with Oxford owes much to a most helpful tape-recorded interview with the Rt Hon. W. T. Rodgers on 25 Aug. 1987.

Dick Taverne and Philip Williams—and to the 'gang of four', three of whom had once been Oxford undergraduates, who founded the Social Democratic Party. By 1985 the Liberal-Social Democratic alliance (with 37 per cent of British university teachers) had become 'the "house" party of higher education', and two years later it was to give Oxford Macmillan's successor as Chancellor.[89]

Oxford talent has of course also flowed elsewhere within the labour movement: through Benn, Castle and Foot, for example. Even within the social-democratic leadership, some major figures owe nothing to Oxford: Dalton and working-class social democrats like Bevin, Henderson, Morrison. Identifying the 1970s with the labour movement's extra-parliamentary wing, Benn played down Oxford's role in his own education, and dismissed Oxford Union types and Gaitskellite Oxbridge journalists as voices from the past. Yet Oxford's social-democratic impact on national politics has been significant. Oxford has groomed prominent social-democratic recruits through its collegiate cellular power-structure, its many incentives to ambition, its encouragement of political friendships, and its abundant contacts with practising politicians. Such contacts, says Michael Stewart, ensured that 'the theoretical approach to politics, with which most of us had started was tempered and enriched by practical knowledge'.[90] Such a climate was less congenial to Guild Socialism and the New Left. So twentieth-century Oxford's contribution to national political continuity was twofold: it reinforced parliamentary tendencies within the labour movement, thereby easing the transition from Liberals to Labour; and in so doing, it prolonged its own political impact.

To say that Oxford Conservatism and Oxford socialism were both predominantly centrist and parliamentary in tone is only another way of saying that liberalism in the broad sense retained vitality in Oxford throughout the period. The structurally polarized duel between government and opposition might prise Liberals and Labour apart at Westminster, but in Oxford they were free to collaborate in many internationalist and humanitarian causes. Besides, there is an affinity between liberalism and the scholarly mind, whose ideal is to shun the narrowness of class for a balanced, peace-loving, humane and rational outlook. Liberalism chimes in with the internationalism of modern scholarship, shares the academic passion for the open mind and attracts the rationalist who yearns for unanimity through discussion. It also attracts the idealist who lacks political sophistication: the

[89] *Times Higher Education Supplement* 18 Jan. 1985, 12.

[90] M. Stewart, *Life and Labour: An Autobiography* (London 1980), 22–3; cf. P. Foot, *The Politics of Harold Wilson* (Harmondsworth 1968), 39. For Benn, see his *Office Without Power: Diaries 1968–72* (London 1988), 82, 301–2, 345; *Against the Tide: Diaries 1973–76* (London, paperback edn 1990), 14.

type of undergraduate who is inquiring, progressive, impressionable and as yet uncommitted.

There was no rapid decline in the Liberal Party's formal structures at Oxford, though from 1920 onward they experienced the national party's bifurcating tendency. The Liberal Club was publicly launched in 1920, but D. A. Ross of New College had already seceded leftward to form the Labour Club, and Lloyd George's followers soon departed rightwards to form the New Reform Club. Yet the Liberal Club gained vitality from its President, Lloyd George, who in the early 1930s evoked among Oxford Liberal undergraduates feelings that were 'little short of hero-worship'.[91] Liberalism survived particularly well in the Oxford Union—partly because tolerant and rational debate is central to the Liberal outlook, and partly because Liberals were less worried than Labour by the Union's class image, or by its formalities of dress, speaking style and procedure. In the late 1940s the Liberals Robin Day, Jeremy Thorpe and Keith Kyle were among the Union's brightest stars [plate 14.2]. For thirty years Thorpe, a brilliant Union debater and President in 1951, lent panache to Oxford Liberalism by his regular return-visits. At a big Union debate in June 1975 Barbara Castle found him 'obviously in his element, cracking jokes and telling historical anecdotes', with his audience 'rolling in the aisles'.[92]

More importantly, Oxford liberalism flourished within the other parties. Wertheimer's comments of 1929 on Liberals who joined Labour could equally be applied to Liberals who moved rightwards: 'their distinguishing feature is a strong and often rather artificially cultivated will to power that in certain circumstances might be turned to the advantage of the oppressed and injured, but never for a lost cause'.[93] Some Liberals—Fisher, and in later life both Murray and Beloff—gravitated towards the Conservatives. 'Some form of Liberalism has become a political necessity for all parties', Fisher told Murray in 1926, 'and is in fact an essential feature of democratic civilization'. In 1955 Murray said that 'nearly all the educated people I meet are Liberal, but vote Conservative'. Among those who moved left were Michael Foot in February 1935, and (more gradually and less obtrusively) Harold Wilson later in the decade. 'Liberalism had permeated all parties', Heath told the Union in February 1938, 'and the remnants that were left were only anachronism'. This was small comfort to Warden Pember, who told Murray in 1932 that Liberalism involves 'a spirit, and a view of the world, which I confess I do not find very conspicuous in the other parties, and which I think the world cannot well do without'.[94]

[91] D. F. Karaka, The Pulse of Oxford (London 1933), 27.
[92] B. Castle, The Castle Diaries 1974–76 (London 1980), 405–6.
[93] E. Wertheimer, Labour Party, 132, cf 135.
[94] Bodl. MS Fisher 55, fo 92, Fisher to Murray, 15 Feb. 1926; A. D. Wilson, Gilbert Murray OM 1866–1957 (Oxford 1987), 391, cf 392; Heath, Isis 2 Feb. 1938, 5; Bodl. MS Gilbert Murray 62, fo 14, Pember to Murray, 7 Aug. 1932.

International issues frequently drew Liberals and Labour together. Oxford Liberals like Bryce and Murray courageously resisted First-World-War chauvinism just as liberal-minded Oxford dons in the early 1920s promoted internationalism, tried to repair cultural relations with Germany and resisted Black-and-Tan policies in Ireland. It was liberalism, too, which moulded the Oxford Union's famous debate of 9 February 1933 on the motion 'that this House will in no circumstances fight for its King and Country', which passed by 275 votes to 153. The motion originated with a Liberal, David Graham; in its unambiguous and even provocative wording it was calculated to divide the audience into two roughly equal groups, and thus to attain the liberal aim of provoking a good debate. Its supporters, by singling out for attack the emotive phrase 'King and Country', were pursuing the long-standing liberal campaign against jingoism, with all its rhetoric. And many of the votes cast were influenced, in liberal fashion, by the quality of the argument put forward in debate—not by preconceived and rigid political positions. The Union between the wars was less a forum of opinion than a training-ground for public speakers, and on this occasion responded generously to the pacifist eloquence of C. E. M. Joad.

The Union's open-minded mood emerges from the popularity at this time of the German Rhodes scholar Adolf Schlepegrell, who gave 'a sensible little speech'[95] in the debate. His anti-Fascist views did not prevent him from arguing in May 1933 (to applause) that it was 'the fault of the whole world and not merely of Germany that Hitler was now Chancellor', nor did his remarks preclude his election as Secretary of the Union in 1934. Nonetheless the political import of the 'King and Country' debate was blown up out of all proportion by the press, and damaged the Union's reputation for some years, not least with Winston Churchill, who felt that it weakened Britain abroad, and who refused to speak at the Union 'until its members acquire a sense of responsibility'.[96]

Liberals and Labour drew together again in the Oxford city by-election of 1938. In defiance of Transport House, their candidates withdrew in favour of A. D. Lindsay, the Master of Balliol, who courageously stood as an Independent Progressive against the government's Munich policy. Among Lindsay's distinguished Oxford supporters were John Austin, Beveridge, Bowra, Collingwood, Crossman, Harrod, Livingstone, Murray, Pakenham, Ryle and Sadler. The government candidate Quintin Hogg attracted Fisher, A. E. W. Hazel, A. P. Herbert, H. W. B. Joseph, Marriott, Oman, and two former Labour candidates (by then National Liberals) Kenneth Lindsay and

[95] Report by P. A. S[tockil], *Isis* 15 Feb. 1933, 7.

[96] For Schlepegrell, see *OM* 18 May 1933, 674; there is a biographical note on him in *Churchill*, ed. Gilbert v. 504–5. The 'King and Country' debate is ably and fully discussed in M. Ceadel, 'The King and Country debate, 1933: student politics, pacifism and the dictators', *Historical Jl* xxii (1979). Churchill to J. A. Brown, 22 May 1937 in *Churchill*, ed. Gilbert, v, companion vol, pt 3, 1982, 679; cf ibid. 159 and v. 456.

Lord Sanderson. Fisher publicly advocated giving 'every possible chance to the policy of international appeasement': other countries should not be led to think that significant British opinion thought war with Germany inevitable.[97] Of the 26 fellows of All Souls who speculated on the outcome, only 7 predicted that Lindsay would win, and then only by a small majority, whereas Hogg's backers were more confident.[98] Lindsay's turned out to be the largest proportion of the total votes cast that any anti-Conservative candidate for Oxford city had won since Frank Gray in 1922, but Hogg won more votes than any other candidate for the seat since 1918 with the single exception of Bourne in 1935. As late as February 1939 the Union opposed immediate peacetime conscription by 192 votes to 173, though on 27 April a packed house demanded conscription by 423 votes to 326 'amidst scenes of anger and enthusiasm'.[99]

After 1945 the Liberal–Labour alliance found new causes in humanism, famine relief and opposing nuclear weapons. The young Canadian philosopher Charles Taylor launched the Hydrogen Bomb Campaign Committee in 1954 to petition against the bomb as morally more repugnant than other weapons, and the philosopher G. E. M. Anscombe made her lonely protest in Congregation in 1956 against President Truman's honorary degree. The theoretical chemist and prominent Methodist Professor Coulson contributed to the much-publicized *Isis* H-Bomb issue (26 February 1958), which published horrific photographs of unidentified casualties. Prosecutions under the Official Secrets Act prompted a Defence Fund whose contributors included Priestley, Tynan and Lindsay Anderson. A referendum in 1958 elicited the views of 3,950 undergraduates on nuclear weapons. Only 350 supported government policy unequivocally, whereas 3,000 expressed varying degrees of hostility and 600 endorsed 'the straight "anti-bomb" ticket'.[100] CND attracted Christians, internationalists, Communists, pacifists and A. J. P. Taylor. There was much lobbying at Westminster against the nuclear weapons tests and, by 1959, conflict with the proctors on the right to organize meetings and processions.

In 1956 Hungary and Suez again drew Labour and Liberals together. Funds were raised to support Hungarian students, fifty-one of whom at different times received hospitality and guidance in the English language—some embarking upon Oxford courses. On the Suez crisis, older members of the *Oxford Magazine*'s editorial committee thought 'Oxford has not been so deeply stirred since Munich'. Beveridge opened the protest meeting in the Union three days after the news broke: there was a 'tense atmosphere' in which 'every point was greeted with roars of applause or

[97] *Times* 21 Oct. 1938, 7.
[98] All Souls College Betting Book 1920–1960, entry for Oct. 1938.
[99] *Isis* 3 May 1939, 8.
[100] *New Statesman* 22 Mar. 1958, 377.

disapproval'. A protest against the Suez venture was signed by 10 heads of house, 20 professors and readers and 235 fellows of colleges; a hundred undergraduates joined the student protest march in London.[101] At the Union's emergency debate on 8 November—less crowded than many expected, but 'stimulating, dramatic and frequently noisy'—352 opposed and only 206 supported the government.[102] But Ruskin College's demonstration encountered well-aimed tomatoes hurled by undergraduates mainly from Brasenose singing 'Rule Britannia' and the dons' counter-petition won 8 heads of house, 2 former heads, 15 professors and readers (including Gilbert Murray) and 75 fellows of colleges. On 11 November in the House of Lords, Lord Cherwell launched a blistering attack on the idea of entrusting the whole matter to the United Nations.[103]

In the 1960s much of this protesting energy was marshalled against American policy in Vietnam. Immense interest was aroused by the 'teach-in' on 16 June 1965, which involved eight hours of continuous speeches and discussion in the Oxford Union [plate 14.3]. Advised as Foreign Secretary not to go, Michael Stewart recalled that as an old Union hand he 'decided . . . that I had a good case and knew enough about Oxford student audiences to put it over', in a speech which was 'to the chagrin of the organizers . . . extremely well received, as was my subsequent answering of questions'; all agreed that the American spokesman Henry Cabot Lodge fared much worse.[104] In 1966 over 100 senior members—among them Bowra, Strawson and Dorothy Hodgkin—signed a letter opposing British policy on Vietnam, and opinion gradually shifted towards their view. An unspecified number of undergraduates polled in February 1968 showed 57 per cent favouring a total American withdrawal from South Vietnam and 40 per cent opposing it.[105]

Oxford's liberal traditions are encapsulated in the linked careers of three much-respected senior members. The career of the first, H. A. L. Fisher, seemed to Livingstone 'Greek in its completeness and manysidedness'. In 1926 Fisher was welcomed back to New College by the second, Gilbert Murray, who told him he was a loss to national politics but that he could help 'to save this appalling place from itself'.[106] Though they disagreed about Lloyd George, Murray and Fisher had been fellows of New College together, and jointly edited the Home University Library. They shared that rationalistic but broad liberal culture whose idealism was not afraid to

[101] *OM* 8 Nov. 1956, 81; *Isis* 7 Nov. 1956, 10–11. Dons who deplored the Suez venture are listed in *Oxford Mail* 5 Nov. 1956.

[102] *OM* 15 Nov. 1956, 112.

[103] *Isis* 7 Nov. 1956, 10 (Ruskin); *OM* 15 Nov. 1956, 14 and 22 Nov. 1956, 140 (pro-Suez opinion); F. W. F. Smith, second Earl of Birkenhead, *The Prof in Two Worlds: The Official Life of Professor F. A. Lindemann, Viscount Cherwell* (London 1961), 357.

[104] Stewart, *Life and Labour*, 155; but see S. Lukes in *OM* Michaelmas 1965, no. 1, 16–17.

[105] *OM* Trinity 1966, no. 8, 499 (dons); *Isis* 28 Feb. 1968, 3 (undergraduates).

[106] Bodl. MS Fisher 214, fo 163, Livingstone to Mrs Fisher, 19 Apr. 1940; MS Fisher 55, fo 90, Murray to Fisher, 14 Feb. 1926.

grapple with the real world. Both brought scholarship to bear on the world of affairs. In the late 1920s Fisher was still moving in high Liberal circles, but in June 1932—despite his free-trading views—he felt that the National Government had 'restored the credit of the Country' and was 'better than any alternative Government which is as yet in sight'. Resigning his presidency, he thought the city's Liberal Association should be disbanded and 'rebuilt from the foundations' when needed. No Liberal candidate stood for the city in 1935, in which year both Fisher and Murray endorsed the Next Five Years Group's non-party programme.[107] In 1938 Christopher Hill scorchingly reviewed Fisher's *History of Europe*: its cast of mind was 'in the worst sense of the word Whig', it exaggerated the autonomy of thought of statesmen and inventors, and it judged all periods and countries by the standards of the English gentleman.[108]

'I was in College on Tuesday', Murray told Mrs Fisher six days after her husband's death, 'and could not bear the sight of your house, thinking it would now be empty'. Fisher's influence radiated widely, as letters of condolence amply show. Bowra found him 'my ideal of the scholar and man of affairs'. Lionel Robbins, 'bruised and made cynical by the ordeals and disillusionments of war', learned from Fisher's example 'that it was still possible to believe in goodness and justice and disinterested service'.[109] In the same year Murray declined to write Fisher's biography,[110] though he wrote the *Dictionary of National Biography*'s memoir, and outlived Fisher by seventeen years. To his many inter-war Oxford admirers, Murray seemed the sage and saint of the new liberal internationalism, quietly and lucidly lighting the liberal way through diplomatic thickets and alien ideologies, epitomizing liberal values in his own person.

Isaiah Berlin, the third of Oxford's three liberal exemplars, was helped by Fisher at a crucial moment in his career and 'was absolutely devoted to him, would have done anything [sc. for him] at any time'. Fisher had set before him 'standards of life and behaviour which dwarfed those of most of his contemporaries in Oxford'. Berlin's first book (on Karl Marx) was published in the Home University Library. Steeped, like Fisher and Murray, in a rich historical understanding of European culture, Berlin was well placed to appreciate the great tragedies of human history: to know how idealists can unwittingly produce 'the worst cruelties on this earth'; to see how easy it is for ultimate values to collide.[111] On 31 October 1958 there was a huge

[107] Bodl. MS Fisher 69, fo 103, Fisher to Ald. Lewis, 21 June 1932.
[108] *Modern Quarterly* i (1938), 284.
[109] Bodl. MS Fisher 217, fo 7, Murray to Mrs Fisher, 24 Apr. 1940; MS Fisher 218, fo 112, Bowra to Mary Fisher, 18 Apr. 1940; fo 57, Robbins to Mrs Fisher, nd.
[110] Bodl. MS Fisher 133, fo 94, G. M[urray] to Mrs Fisher, 21 May 1940 (carbon copy).
[111] Bodl. MS Fisher 214, fo 174, I. Berlin to Mrs Fisher, 'Thursday' [?18 Apr. 1940]; cf MS Fisher 74, fo 82, Berlin to Fisher, 1 Feb. 1937. See also Berlin's fine statement of liberal principles in his interview published in *Isis* 17 May 1985, 8–9.

attendance for his inaugural lecture on 'Two Concepts of Liberty'—lucid yet learned, humane yet without illusions. In this and many other crowded lectures, long after the Liberal Party had lost its governmental status, Berlin continued to win new enthusiasts for the liberal ideals of tolerance, compromise and freedom of inquiry.

What can we conclude about Oxford's overall political impact between 1914 and 1970? First, that only rarely was it exercised corporately, if only because universities were seldom at the centre of political controversy. Oxford did not struggle after 1951 to regain the University seats, which had anyway been a burden for the Registry. The University did not want controversy, and was amply represented by other routes. Oxford was corporately projected into politics only spasmodically on special issues such as tithes and local roads and amenities. When G. R. Y. Radcliffe thought Oxford's interests required an amendment to the Land Valuation Bill in 1930, he told the Registrar that 'we shall, of course, have to undertake a thorough canvass of all old Oxford men in the House of Commons, paying particular attention to Liberal and Labour Members'. Similar backstage influence pervaded the controversy over the Meadow Road in the 1950s. Faced in 1969 by hostility to reducing Convocation's powers, the Vice-Chancellor briefed 130 Oxford MPs on his case.[112]

Oxford's corporate political influence could usually remain unobtrusive partly because the University's old members were so prominent within all three major political parties. The diversity of these destinations stemmed from Oxford's relish for the clash of opinion and from the frequent encounters ambition and opportunity fostered between undergraduates and practising politicians and administrators. Not only did Oxford men engage in the public rituals of party warfare; they also clashed behind the scenes. There was friction, for instance, between Oxford politicians and Oxford civil servants. In the vanguard of the attack on the Whitehall branch of the 'Establishment' during the 1960s were two former Oxford dons, Balogh and Crossman.[113] Harold Wilson when a minister under Attlee clashed with Robert Hall, the former Oxford don in the Economic Section;[114] and Wilson's eagerness to adopt the Fulton report when prime minister seems partly to reflect an Oxford meritocrat's revenge on Oxford Greats men.[115] In the highly competitive world of politics, ambition could readily disrupt Oxford connections. Jenkins's relations with Crosland in the 1960s and 1970s reveal a close Oxford bond being transformed into a wary mutual

---

[112] HCP 147 (1930), 153 (Radcliffe); HCP 262 (1969), 755–8.
[113] Crossman, *Diaries* ii. 627.
[114] *Robert Hall Diaries 1947–53*, 69, 113.
[115] P. Kellner and Lord Crowther-Hunt, *The Civil Servants: An Inquiry into Britain's Ruling Class* (London 1980), 27, 62; B. Castle, *The Castle Diaries 1964–70* (London 1984), 468.

watchfulness, and there was a distance between George Woodcock and Crossman, his former tutor; between Benn and Rodgers; between Healey and Jenkins; between Jenkins and Balogh; between Crossman and Stewart.[116]

Oxford has worked harmoniously with the two-party system, and has helped to smooth its operation by reinforcing centre tendencies in both government and opposition. So between 1914 and 1970 the University naturally took its place among the country's established institutions—conferring a doctorate on the Prince of Wales in 1921, floodlighting its buildings and lighting its bonfires for the jubilee in 1935, ceremonially strengthening bonds with the allies during the Second World War, getting the King to open the New Bodleian Library in 1946 and filling its allocation of seats at the coronation in 1953 [plate 14.4]. Yet by the 1970s Oxford's political impact was in decline. This was partly because the governments of the 1960s, in which Oxford had been so well represented, had proved such disappointments. Furthermore both Labour and Conservative parties have subsequently democratized their image, the media have broadened out political participation well beyond the tight university circles once so influential in British politics, and Oxford felt uncomfortable with the less consensual mood of national politics between 1970 and 1990. Its reputation had long ceased to rest on the social-class connections which seemed so important between the wars, yet governments after 1970 challenged the new source of status which Oxford had acquired to replace them: the contribution that a meritocratic intellectual élite can make towards framing central government policy.

What light does this analysis shed on intellectuals' role in British politics between 1914 and 1970? Some argue that intellectuals anticipate future political trends: 'if Oxford and Cambridge can be won largely for Socialism', said G. D. H. Cole in 1910, 'the conversion of the middle-classes is only a matter of time'. For Robert Blake, 'a rebellion by the intellectuals usually accompanies and probably in some measure causes a great political shift'.[117] At first sight, Oxford's history since 1914 lends some support to this: a political shift among significant sections of Oxford opinion during the 1930s anticipated the Labour victory of 1945, other groups at once began anticipating the Conservative victory of 1951, and developments on the left in Oxford between 1956 and 1964 foreshadowed the Wilson governents.

Yet after the mid-1960s the pattern broke down, and at no time did Oxford on particular issues unite behind some special political insight or

<hr/>

[116] Crossman, *Diaries* i. 397; ii. 373, 397; Benn, *Against the Tide*, 88; T. Dalyell, *Dick Crossman: A Portrait* (London 1989), 39; D. Healey, *The Time of My Life* (London 1989, pbk edn 1990), 329.

[117] G. D. H. Cole, 'Oxford socialism from within', *Socialist Rev.* Dec. 1910, 283–4; R. Blake, *The Conservative Party from Peel to Thatcher* (London 1985), 186. See also A. L. Lowell, *The Government of England* (2 vols London 1908) ii. 103–4.

foresight denied to the layman. Individual dons might sometimes more readily grasp the complexity of political situations, but on the big issues—the Russian revolution, the Munich settlement, Suez, the Vietnam war—Oxford was as divided as the rest of the country. Besides, it is important to distinguish shifts in the mood of politically aware undergraduates from the University's overall political tendency, which has if anything lagged behind national shifts in political opinion. Slow to accept Labour as leading party of the left, Oxford thereafter clung to the corporatist strategy from which (at least in the short term) it seemed to gain so much. The University's contribution to national politics lay not in any special political insight, but in nourishing parliamentarism and in channelling talent towards all the national parties. So modest a role may well not satisfy those with the highest expectations of reason's impact upon politics. Nonetheless, in drawing theory and practice into fruitful alliance, Oxford contributed significantly to the social stability and political continuity that make so much else possible.

15

Literary Culture

VALENTINE CUNNINGHAM

Without Oxford writers modern English literature would be a vastly different, indeed indifferent place. Where, for instance, would English modernism be without T. S. Eliot? Where, again, would England's literature of war be without Robert Graves, Edmund Blunden, Edward Thomas, T. E. Lawrence, Keith Douglas, Sidney Keyes, Alan Ross? As for the 'Auden generation'—W. H. Auden himself, Stephen Spender, Louis MacNeice, Cecil Day-Lewis (or Day Lewis, as he liked to be known in the radical thirties), Rex Warner, Kenneth Allott, Bernard Spencer, John Betjeman, Edgell Rickword, Montagu Slater, Randall Swingler, Ralph Fox, Richard Hughes, Graham Greene, Evelyn Waugh, Anthony Powell, Henry Green—it's a crowd of Oxford men. Just so, Oxford provided the core of fifties 'Movement' poetry—Philip Larkin, Kingsley Amis, John Wain, Elizabeth Jennings. 'Martian' poetry—Craig Raine, Christopher Reid—is Oxford poetry. Remove Aldous Huxley, L. P. Hartley, William Golding, Angus Wilson, Iris Murdoch, Kingsley Amis, Joyce Cary, Jocelyn Brooke, Brigid Brophy from mid-century English fiction and it dramatically loses importance. Take away John Fowles, D. M. Thomas, Penelope Fitzgerald, Jennifer Dawson, Penelope Lively, Margaret Forster, J. G. Farrell, Jenny Joseph, Melvyn Bragg, and there'd be considerably less wind in the sails of later twentieth-century English fiction. Without Martin Amis, Julian Barnes, Alan Hollinghurst, A. N. Wilson, Timothy Mo, William Boyd, Jonathan Keates, Caryl Phillips, Nigel Williams, or Sarah Maitland, Maggie Gee and Jeanette Winterson, the most promising younger generation of English novelists loses its promise. The same is true of Raine, David Constantine, James Fenton, Andrew Motion, Tom Paulin, Mick Imlah in relation to the rising generation of younger English poets. Again, no John Heath-Stubbs, Al Alvarez, Alan Brownjohn, Christopher Middleton, U. A. Fanthorpe, Martin Seymour-Smith, Geoffrey Hill, Anthony Thwaite, George MacBeth, John Fuller, and the crowd-scene of post-war English poetry instantly thins.[1] Take out John Buchan, Dorothy Sayers, J. I. M.

[1] Many of these poets are discussed by A. Brownjohn, 'A preference for poetry: Oxford undergraduate writing of the early 1950s', *Yearbook of English Studies* xvii (1987).

Stewart (Michael Innes), Cecil Day-Lewis (Nicholas Blake), Bruce Montgomery (Edmund Crispin), David Cornwell (John le Carré), Antonia Fraser, Simon Brett, T. J. Binyon, and the detective and crime fiction landscape looks very depleted indeed. Remove J. R. R. Tolkien, C. S. Lewis and Robertson Davies and the foundations of modern English fantasy crumble. Without Gabriel Josipovici, Christine Brooke-Rose and Ronald Frame there is really not much of an English experimental novel to boast of. And so on. The mere lists of modern Oxford writers are most impressive.

On this showing, twentieth-century Oxford appears an extraordinary matrix of English literary talent. Why should this be? Other universities, in North America as in East Anglia, would look to their MA courses in creative writing for explanation. But Oxford, though it has long encouraged undergraduates in its music school to compose, and eventually got around to bringing the Ruskin School of Drawing in from the margins and to awarding the degree of bachelor of fine art for painting and allied skills, has always eschewed incorporating creative writing into its literary courses. Other explanations have to be sought. Much, of course, must be accidental. You cannot teach people to write as you can teach them to drive a car. Clearly, though, literary talent, albeit necessarily contingent and uncovenanted, is often a branch of intelligence and talent in general, and as Oxford attracts large numbers of the talented as teachers and students from home and abroad, it would be surprising if writers did not emerge in numbers from this rather special clientele.

But not everything is left entirely to chance. The Oxford environment has been in numerous respects most friendly to writing. The atmosphere is bookish. The place is full of bookshops, booksellers, libraries, publishing houses. There may well be more books in the few square miles of central and north Oxford than in any similar sized plot on earth. 'Books': it's among books that Aldous Huxley rightly has his writing hero Anthony Beavis beginning his career at Oxford in *Eyeless in Gaza* (1936). 'The table in Anthony's room was covered with them'—De Gourmont, Dostoevsky, Byron, St John of the Cross. 'He pored voluptuously over the table, opening at random now one volume, now another.' A page of assorted quotations follows as Beavis dips into passages about beheading, happiness, cuckoldry, purgation and French mealymouthedness before settling for *The Way of Perfection of St Teresa*. This is one model, an early twentieth-century one, of a liberal Oxford education in progress.[2] Studying in Oxford is still known as *reading*.

Huxley *read* English—he achieved a first in his finals, one of only two in 1917—when the English school was still new and small (and depleted even further by the Great War). And as our century has proceeded and the

---

[2] A. Huxley, *Eyeless in Gaza* (London 1936), ch. 10.

English school has ballooned to equal the very largest arts faculties, the association between reading English and going on after Oxford to be a writer has become more and more conventional. It has not been essential to have read English literature at Oxford in order to 'write'. Many writers *read* the literature of other cultures. MacNeice, Bernard Spencer, Iris Murdoch and Peter Levi, for instance, read classics. Dorothy Sayers, Ralph Fox, Christopher Middleton, John Fowles, Edmund Crispin, John le Carré, Julian Barnes read modern languages. For their part, writers like Evelyn Waugh, Melvyn Bragg, Penelope Lively, Jennifer Dawson, Nigel Williams read history. Spender started in history and switched to philosophy, politics and economics (PPE). But reading some kind of literature, and above all in the school of English language and literature, is characteristic of the great majority, including many of the best-known names among Oxford writers: Huxley, Graves, Auden, Keith Douglas, Larkin, Amis *père* and Amis *fils*, John Wain, Geoffrey Hill, William Golding, Barbara Pym, Rex Warner (after classics 'mods'), Penelope Fitzgerald, Craig Raine, and so on. In the early days of the English school after the First World War, English often recruited exiles from other subjects, especially classics, men such as Edmund Blunden, C. S. Lewis, Richard Hughes and Rex Warner. Switches the other way, like James Fenton's from English to PPE, have been most rare among potential writers.

Reading, as English students must, steadily throughout the canonical texts of English literature, and some of the not-so-canonical ones as well, provides one with the great, but dead, literary examples. But Oxford has been generous too with living models—tutors and the spouses of tutors who write, professors of poetry who are 'name' poets, notable literary residents in the town or vicinity, distinguished writing visitors to undergraduates' associations. Writers who have taught English in various official capacities in Oxford colleges have included C. S. Lewis, J. R. R. Tolkien, John Bayley, W. W. Robson, John Wain, John Jones, Edmund Blunden, John Heath-Stubbs, J. I. M. Stewart, John Fuller, Francis Warner, Jon Stallworthy, Bernard O'Donoghue, Craig Raine, Anne Stevenson, Alan Hollinghurst, William Boyd, A. N. Wilson, Mick Imlah. Iris Murdoch taught philosophy at St Anne's, David Constantine teaches German at Queen's and T. J. Binyon Russian at Wadham. In some colleges, if you weren't getting tutorials from a writer, you might have been invited home to meet the writing spouse of your own or a friend's tutor: John Bayley and Iris Murdoch are married to each other; Craig Raine is married to an English tutor at St Anne's; Penelope Lively to a former politics don of St Peter's; Jennifer Dawson to Michael Hinton a former philosophy don, this time at Worcester; Angela Huth, novelist and short-story writer, to James Howard-Johnston, a history don at Corpus; Barbara Trapido, South African-born novelist, to Stanley Trapido, historian of Africa and fellow of

Lincoln; Susan Hill, novelist and ruralist, to Stanley Wells, who was editor of the Oxford Shakespeare and fellow of Balliol; the novelist Candia McWilliam to an English tutor at St Catherine's, Fram Dinshaw. A. N. Wilson's first wife teaches English at Somerville.

Some Oxford writers have enjoyed manifestly encouraging relationships with their tutors and tutors' spouses. The path of Robert Graves through the English school—he'd won a classical scholarship to St John's in 1913, but took up English when he actually arrived after war service in 1919—was greatly smoothed by the genial interventions of Sir Walter Raleigh, Merton Professor. This Boche-despiser and official historian of the Royal Flying Corps smiled on the strong-willed war-veteran who was not only allowed to proceed to the BLitt without actually having sat for the BA (Raleigh agreeing to supervise him on the understanding he was not to be bothered by much contact) but also to submit an already published critical volume *Poetic Unreason* in lieu of a thesis.[3] W. H. Auden, admitted to Christ Church on a natural sciences scholarship, flirted briefly with PPE, then opted for English and, Christ Church having no English tutor in 1925, was farmed out to the very supportive Nevill Coghill at Exeter—the medievalist, amateur playwright and drama producer, who was to become doyen of Oxford drama and senior pillar of the Oxford University Dramatic Society (OUDS). Auden sometimes read his own poems to Coghill during tutorials. He introduced his tutor to the poems of Eliot.[4] Coghill helped to acquaint Auden with the rhythmic potencies of Anglo-Saxon verse, which Auden then imitated in his own poetry. Auden's volume of essays *The Dyer's Hand* (1962) is dedicated to Coghill. In the Festschrift for Coghill got up by devoted pupils and assorted thespians, Auden's poetic eulogy is conspicuously warm to his old tutor's Irish tolerance ('you . . . never looked cross or sleepy / when our essays were / more about us than Chaucer').[5] In the same memorial volume the film-producer John Schlesinger (who read English at Balliol 1948–50) declares that for him and other theatrically keen ex-servicemen 'the OUDS was one of the more important reasons for . . . going to Oxford' (he got an actor's third class in finals), and the OUDS meant Coghill. In Schlesinger's first term Coghill played the drunken sea captain in the OUDS production of *The Shoemaker's Holiday*.[6] It was Coghill's offer to direct his former Exeter pupil Richard Burton that drew Burton and his then wife, Elizabeth Taylor, to play in a memorable OUDS

[3] M. Seymour-Smith, *Robert Graves: His Life and Work* (London 1982), 80.

[4] C. Osborne, *W. H. Auden: The Life of a Poet* (New York and London 1979), 39–40.

[5] W. H. Auden, 'To Professor Nevill Coghill upon his Retirement in 1966' in J. Lawlor and W. H. Auden (eds), *To Nevill Coghill from Friends* (London 1966); W. H. Auden, *Collected Poems*, ed. E. Mendelson (London 1976), 572–5.

[6] J. Schlesinger, 'Oxford theatricals, 1948' in Lawlor and Auden, *To Nevill Coghill from Friends*, 97, 98.

Doctor Faustus (1966), one consequence of which was the funding of the Burton-Taylor theatre (in rooms behind the Playhouse).

When he was English tutor at Merton, Edmund Blunden seems never to have appeared on stage for the OUDS, but he did act the part of Chronos in a production of Dryden's *Secular Masque* in which his pupil Keith Douglas 'assisted'. And he dedicatedly encouraged Douglas's poetic precocity. The fact that they were both Christ's Hospital men seems to have made Blunden's interest particularly acute. He was the *fons et origo* of *Augury: An Oxford Miscellany* that Douglas edited with Alec Hardie (1940). He read Douglas's poems in typescript with critical interest ('you will find a very few pencil markings on the pages'). He tuned Douglas into the literary world with tips about Graham Greene, wartime literary editor of the *Spectator*, T. S. Eliot at Faber, and the firm of Cape ('with Mr Hart-Davis of Cape I have an ancient friendship, and can speak to him of you and your work'). He sent Eliot Douglas's poems: 'he had a considerable reputation here alike as a writer and as an artist, so I hope you will not find it totally uninteresting to glance at what he offers'.[7] John Mulgan, the New Zealand novelist, who edited *Poems of Freedom* with Auden (1939), was another pupil of Blunden's.

Other fruitful tutor–pupil relationships have been the ones between Will Moore, French tutor at St John's, and Bruce Montgomery (Moore is said to have provided the model for Edmund Crispin's amateur detective, Gervase Fen, Oxford Professor of English Language and Literature)[8] and between John Bayley and A. N. Wilson, one of Bayley's favourite New College pupils. Wilson dedicated his first novel *Sweets of Pimlico* (1977) to Bayley and Iris Murdoch; he wrote a glowing introduction to the 1986 Oxford reprint of Bayley's novel *In Another Country* (1955) and became the official biographer of Iris Murdoch. Craig Raine taught both Martin Amis and Christopher Reid at Exeter College, the latter friendly relationship laying the foundation of the so-called Martian school of poetry of which Raine and Reid have remained the two chief exponents. As for Magdalen College, among the pupils of John Fuller and, more latterly, Bernard O'Donoghue there has been an extraordinary efflatus of writing talent: Fenton, Hollinghurst, Keates, Imlah (according to O'Donoghue, 'without John Fuller, Mick Imlah would probably not have written any poems'). Hollinghurst and Imlah have both returned to their old College at various times to assist in the English teaching. The literary relationship between Fenton and Fuller—poems written for each other, mutual respect, dedications, support—has been one of the most obvious poetic collaborations of recent times. It's not surprising that Seamus Heaney should have been associated

---

[7] *Keith Douglas: A Prose Miscellany*, ed. D. Graham (London 1985), 34 ff. Faber eventually published Douglas's *Collected Poems* in 1965.

[8] T. J. Binyon, *Murder Will Out: The Detective in Fiction* (Oxford 1989, Oxford 1990 edn), 52–3.

with Magdalen when he became Professor of Poetry in 1989. The 1994 election of James Fenton to this chair simply confirmed Magdalen as a centre of Oxford poeticity.

Encouragement of a less focused kind has come the student poet's way from some at least of the poets who have held the unonerous elective post of Professor of Poetry since 1945. Occupants of the chair in this period, when it became conventional to elect practising writers, have been Cecil Day-Lewis (1951–6), Auden (1956–61), Graves (1961–6), Blunden (1966–7), Roy Fuller (1968–73), John Wain (1973–8), John Jones (1979–84), Peter Levi (1984–9). Levi's successor Seamus Heaney and Roy Fuller are the only two non-Oxonians in the post-war list. The attempt to elect the great American poet Robert Lowell in 1966 was scuppered through the combined efforts of French fellow of Somerville Enid Starkie and Francis Warner the English tutor at St Peter's, a poet and playwright newly arrived from Cambridge who would himself stand unsuccessfully for the post on subsequent occasions. Their man Blunden was by then old and poorly, his lectures were not a success and he retired early through ill health. Not every poet has the necessary fifteen crowd-pulling lectures in him. Graves, for instance, most awkward as a public speaker, was quickly reduced to driving jeeringly through Quiller-Couch's *Oxford Book of English Verse* and to reading his own stuff—at which he was singularly bad. But still the effect was electrifying. Auden's tenure was memorable in a different way for poetically ambitious students. He was permitted to give his statutory three annual lectures in a single term each year, and shuffled about Oxford magnetically in carpet slippers, holding court in the Cadena tea-rooms and other watering-holes, showering goodwill and ready pontifical advice on the inquiring and adoring throngs. When he retired from threatening New York to Oxford in 1972 to take up residence in a grace-and-favour cottage in the grounds of his old college Christ Church, he tried to re-enact the former triumphs in St Aldate's Coffee House. But he was older, tetchier, even less inclined to listen, and his audiences were now commandeered by thrusting postgraduate students, especially North American ones, whose well schooled pushiness quite alienated the more timid natives.

In the period between these two poetic reigns Auden was also not infrequently in Oxford, invited to read his poems to student audiences. He was part of the large army of patient poets who are willing to come—in many cases to return—to Oxford in order to read to the young, not for cash but for the love of the craft and the satisfactions that attend enthusiastic audiences. In Michaelmas term 1920 Robert Graves, wishing to 'shake up' Oxford, duly achieved a sensation by inviting the Illinois poet Vachel Lindsay to read. He was 'a knockout'. 'Raleigh in returning thanks said he had never been so moved by a recitation in his life—quite like the pictures.'[9]

⁹ Seymour-Smith, *Robert Graves*, 87.

Spender calculatedly used his post as secretary to the English Club in his final year to enlarge his yearning personal acquaintance with poets. He met and enjoyed the confidences of Walter de la Mare, J. C. Squire, Humbert Wolfe and William Plomer, most of them full of wry warnings about the poetic existence. 'Generously overlooking the wrong information I had given them about the trains from London to Oxford, they delivered their sad advice on the literary life which I was now just about to enter, like ghosts in purgatory, conscious of the relative failure of their illusions, but still glowing with the effulgence of a vision.'[10]

After the Second World War undergraduate poets were apparently apter to look with less starry eyes on their poetic elders. In Michaelmas term 1949 Geoffrey Grigson, chief poetic arbiter of the thirties, was given a very rough ride by the hard-minded members of the Poetry Society.[11] But still the mutual craving for touching the hems of poets' garments and for flaunting poetic mantles went on. One of the most arresting poetic encounters recounted by the American poet Donald Hall is the hilariously sad story of his driving in 1953 with his young wife to Laugharne in order to escort the notoriously unreliable Dylan Thomas to Oxford, in an effort to make sure that the not-so-old soak should keep at least one of his appointments with the Poetry Society of which Hall was then President. This drunken encounter certainly had its troubles for everyone involved, not least the 'forty-seven leading Oxford poets' anxiously waiting to toast Thomas in sherry—perhaps the only drink he loathed. But the ritual of such meetings was, as ever, maintained.[12] It's a tradition nicely illustrated in Spender's career. 'Fifty years on' he had assumed the position of the ageing poets whom he had met in his own youth in Oxford—Walter de la Mare redivivus.[13]

On that memorable boozy occasion in 1953, Thomas had to travel some distance to meet his Oxford audience. It was not always so. Thomas and his stormy spouse camped for the whole of 1946 in Magdalen historian A. J. P. Taylor's summer-house. His drunken lack of considerateness eventually got him moved on, but only to a house in South Leigh belonging to Taylor's wife. (Characteristically Thomas failed to pay even the peppercorn rent demanded.[14]) And Thomas has not been alone among non-Oxonians in finding bookish, cultured, quiet Oxford and its surrounding area agreeable and convenient to live and write in. During the First World War Ronald Firbank lived and wrote at 66 High Street in his decadently post-nineties, black-painted rooms there. Around new year 1918 W. B. Yeats moved with

---

[10] S. Spender, *World within World: An Autobiography* (London 1951, London 1953 edn), 84.
[11] 'Grigson on spot: Oxford poets weren't satisfied', *Isis* 16 Nov. 1949, 27.
[12] D. A. Hall, *Remembering Poets: Reminiscences and Opinions* (New York 1978), 8–23.
[13] 'Spender remembers', *Isis* 9 Oct. 1980, 10–11.
[14] See C. FitzGibbon, *The Life of Dylan Thomas* (London 1965, London 1968 edn), 287 ff.

his new wife Georgie Hyde-Lees into 45 Broad Street. In October 1919 they moved to number 4. In 1921 they moved out, but only to Shillingford (April–June) and Thame (June–September). Yeats found the Bodleian Library a lovely place in which to pursue his hermetic studies: 'one can leave one's books on one's table and read them at odd moments . . . the most friendly, comfortable library in the world and I suppose the most beautiful'.[15] After the Great War John Masefield took up residence on Boars Hill. (He rented out a cottage in his garden to the undergraduate Graves who, like Blunden, had permission to live outside the proctorial three-mile limit.) Elizabeth Bowen lived in Old Headington in 1923–4 and wrote her first four novels there. After service in the Second World War Brian Aldiss, who was to become the grand old man of British science fiction, moved into digs in King Edward Street, working for the booksellers Sanders' (where a younger colleague was Roger Lancelyn Green, just down from Merton) and Parker's. He claims to have received his literary education by attending college plays. He began his literary career with the bookshop satires in the *Bookseller* that made his name when republished as *The Brightfount Diaries* (1955).[16]

Aldiss stayed on in Oxford to become literary editor of the *Oxford Mail* (for which paper Adrian Mitchell also worked as a reporter and drama critic) and a permanent, though somewhat peripatetic, resident of the area. In 1952 the poet Ruth Pitter, who had been converted to Christianity through the wireless broadcasts of C. S. Lewis, moved to Long Crendon in order, among other reasons, to be near Lewis, Professor Lord David Cecil and other Oxford friends such as John Wain.[17] In 1969, towards the end of his short life, the American science fiction writer James Blish came to England to settle near Henley in token of his affection for C. S. Lewis's works. He thought living 'in the vicinity of Oxford as equivalent to a resurrection into a new ideal of life'.[18] The marvellously macabre fictionist Ian McEwan (famous product of Malcolm Bradbury's MA course in creative writing at East Anglia) moved in the eighties into Rawlinson Road. The most famous living Indian writer resident outside India, Nirad Chaudhuri, has lived in Oxford, mainly in Kidlington, since 1970. The novelists Michael Dibdin, Haydn Middleton and P. D. James all have houses in Oxford. (The setting of Sayers's *Gaudy Night* and the home of Inspector Morse is perhaps particularly conducive to crime novelists such as Dibdin and James.)

And Oxonian writers have been perhaps even more susceptible to the attractions of residence in and about Oxford. In the seventies Barbara Pym

[15] J. M. Hone, *W. B. Yeats 1865–1939* (London 1942, 2nd edn London 1962), 308–9.
[16] See B. Aldiss, *Bury My Heart at W. H. Smith's: A Writing Life* (London 1990), *passim*.
[17] A. Russell (ed.), *Ruth Pitter: Homage to a Poet*, intr. D. Cecil (London 1966), *passim*.
[18] D. Ketterer, *Imprisoned in a Tesseract: The Life and Work of James Blish* (Kent Ohio 1987), 22 ff.

retired to a cottage in Finstock—in whose church T. S. Eliot had been baptized in 1927. Finstock was convenient for Oxford's libraries, for meeting David Cecil, Iris Murdoch and John Bayley, for the hospitals that treated the cancer Pym died of, and for dinner at St John's.[19] For much of the post-war period John Wain lived and wrote in Wolvercote, in a proximity to the city centre that greatly facilitated his functioning as fellow in creative arts at Brasenose (1971–2) and subsequently as Professor of Poetry. John Buchan, a Brasenose man, set up his 'ivory tower' at Elsfield after the First World War, driven by 'an intense craving for a country life' near the Oxford that 'claimed' him in the nineties and whose 'bonds have never been loosed'. Many of his novels were written during his Elsfield period, from 1919 to 1935.[20] Robert Bridges, Corpus man and Poet Laureate, passed the whole later part of his life (1907–30) on Boars Hill. When he was invalided out of the colonial service in 1920, Trinity man Joyce Cary settled at 12 Parks Road where he lived until his death in 1957, and wrote seven novels. John Betjeman settled near Wantage, Rex Warner in Wallingford. Evelyn Waugh's first book *Rossetti* was written in retreat at Beckley in August 1927.[21] For many years Waugh haunted the local tradesmen with whom his undergraduate accounts continued. Brian Aldiss hated Waugh's visits to Sanders' for rare books ('like some minor devil . . . a bad payer'). Aldiss much preferred giggling, warm, impoverished Betjeman, arriving from out Wantage way in his dodgy van laden with rubbishy review copies for sale ('a fiver, John?').[22] A local child—she attended the girls' High School—Elizabeth Jennings stayed on after graduation, working as a city librarian, in and out of local mental hospitals. In more recent times Sally Purcell, James Fenton, Tom Paulin and Craig Raine (long before returning to New College as an English fellow) have all set up house in the city. Staying on is clearly an Oxford convention.

Tom Harrisson, the youthful literary terrorist who was to co-found Mass Observation, sneered in the early thirties at Oxford's citizen army of writers (he was himself living on an Oxford canal barge at the time): 'the Ox district is lousy with minor poets, journalists, religious revivalists and homosexuals who have come to settle about and parasitise the tender young bodies'.[23] But the so-called parasites have mightily enhanced the host city and institution. Yeats made himself readily available to undergraduate societies and held keenly attended Monday evening At Homes for undergraduates.[24] Letters of

[19] See her letters to Larkin and diary entries from 24 Oct. 1972 onward in *A Very Private Eye: The Diaries, Letters and Notebooks of Barbara Pym*, ed. H. Holt and H. Pym (London and Basingstoke 1984), 270 ff.

[20] J. Buchan, *Memory Hold-the-Door* (London 1940), 47, 182 ff.

[21] *The Diaries of Evelyn Waugh*, ed. M. Davie (London 1976), 286–7, 295.

[22] Aldiss, 26–30.

[23] T. H. Harrisson, *Letter to Oxford* ('Reynold Bray, The Hate Press', Wyck, Glos. [1933]), 18.

[24] Hone, 331–2.

C. S. Lewis describe the puritan Ulsterman's astonished encounters in 1921 with the wild transcendentalisms and magic obsessions of Yeats ('you'll think I'm inventing all this but it's really dead, sober truth'). Lewis also found that Yeats liked 'Morris prose romances'. It's not difficult to detect signs in these encounters of the way Lewis's own writings would move.[25] And Lewis was himself to have just such magnetic effects on the young—such as John Wain—who were attracted into the Inklings ambience or drawn to one of the numerous student societies Lewis was associated with—the religio-philosophical Socratics, it might be, founded in the forties by another local poet, the formidable and cranky Stella Aldwinckle (then said to occupy some sort of pastoral office in Somerville) or the Oxford University Speculative Fiction Group which Lewis and Aldiss initiated.[26]

Out on Boars Hill—popularly known in the twenties as Parnassus because of the combined presence there of Bridges, Masefield, Graves and Blunden—John Masefield, who succeeded Bridges as Poet Laureate in 1930, sponsored the amateur company of the Hill Players in an adapted barn on his property. Characteristically of their efforts, they performed Coghill's comedy *The Tudor Touch* there in November 1930 at a festival in honour of Yeats. Dacre Balsdon recalled 'that stifling afternoon in the Barn on Boar's Hill': ' "Beautiful-voiced maidens will now recite the poems of Yeats." They did, beautifully. The trouble was that they never stopped.'[27] Masefield was so keen on recited verse that in 1923 he started the annual verse-speaking competitions in the Examination Schools that later turned into verse-speaking festivals. John Buchan was a judge in 1926. 'I lived for the Recitations', Masefield declared. His ill health brought them to an end in 1931. This did not prevent him and Coghill devising the so-called Oxford Summer Diversions—ballet, music, Christopher Hassall's *Devil's Dyke*, still more spoken verse—in New College and Rhodes House in 1937.[28]

Out at Elsfield Manor John Buchan's Sunday afternoon teas provided a mecca for undergraduates (and their seniors: T. E. Lawrence 'would turn up without warning . . . at any time of the day or night on his motor-cycle Boanerges').[29] Robert Graves, who had moved to Islip in 1921 after the failure of his wife's Boars Hill shopkeeping venture, was, it seems, another of Buchan's visitors. (Buchan was, along with Lawrence, one of Graves's referees for the chair in English literature in Cairo that Graves moved to in

[25] *They Stand Together: The Letters of C. S. Lewis to Arthur Greeves (1914–1963)*, ed. W. Hooper (London 1979), 287.

[26] W. Griffin, *C. S. Lewis: The Authentic Voice* (London 1988), 195, 220; Aldiss, 121; *C. S. Lewis and Oxford: A Guide for Visitors* (C. S. Lewis Society, Oxford 1984).

[27] D. Balsdon, 'Open letter' in Lawlor and Auden, *To Nevill Coghill from Friends*, 31–2.

[28] J. Masefield, *So Long to Learn* (London 1952), 194 ff; letters of 24 July 1926 and Jan. 1937 in *Letters of John Masefield to Florence Lamont*, ed. C. Lamont and M. Lamont (London and Basingstoke 1979), 152, 235.

[29] Buchan, 212, 221.

1925.[30]) When he was first in Oxford in 1917, invalided to a military hospital at Somerville, Graves had got to know Aldous Huxley and he passed many weekends within the pacifist literary-philosophical circle of Lady Ottoline Morrell at Garsington, where the Morrells kept up a busy coterie of intellectuals from 1915 to 1927. But Graves was no pacifist and he did not visit Garsington when he returned to Oxford after the war to study. Ottoline Morrell and her chums were much more Edmund Blunden's or Aldous Huxley's cup of tea. Through his friendship with her ladyship ('arty beyond the dreams of avarice') and his many visits to Garsington, Huxley met the likes of Eliot, Katherine Mansfield and Lytton Strachey and was taken up by D. H. Lawrence (whom Graves couldn't stand): 'my adventures here . . . always peculiar'; 'what amusements we had . . . in spite of the somewhat wet blanket of Bloomsbury'.[31]

Other undergraduates, too late for Elsfield or Garsington—or not, unlike Huxley or Harold Acton and Brian Howard, Old Etonian enough for Lady Ottoline's taste[32]—were constrained to meet heroizable authors under less glamorous circumstances, such as in the pub. At the Port Mahon in St Clement's in the later forties you could have encountered Dylan Thomas and his cronies, including MacNeice. C. S. Lewis was often to be spotted at the Bodleian readers' favourite hostelry, the King's Arms. So was John Wain. Over Wain's regular seat in a back bar of the 'KA' there hung in the early nineties a photograph of Wain and local versifier Dan McNabb (several times outsider contender for the chair of poetry). But Lewis and Tolkien might equally well have been seen in the Eastgate (plotting to foster Anglo-Saxon studies, literature dons would darkly and with reason allege: Beer and Beowulf went proverbially together) as well as in the several beery Inkling hangouts, notably the Eagle and Child or 'Bird and Baby' (Tuesday mornings till 1962, the Lamb and Flag on Mondays thereafter). One of the regular Inkling drinkers was Charles Williams. Publisher, sado-masochistic Christian, Arthurian poet and author of a number of violently minded spiritual thrillers—soul-rippers you might call them—he'd been speedily absorbed into the group and on to the depleted English faculty lecture-list during the Second World War, when the staff of the OUP's London office was evacuated to Oxford for the duration. He resided in South Parks Road. And he was only one of several writers who have made the Press into the proverbial nest of singing birds. The novelist Dan Davin (like John Mulgan, a New Zealander) worked at the Press from 1948 onward and ended up as the Academic Publisher. Jon Stallworthy was a Press editor from 1959 to 1977, when he entered the academic profession full-time at Cornell. Anne

---

[30] Seymour-Smith, *Robert Graves*, 121.

[31] *The Letters of Aldous Huxley*, ed. G. Smith (London 1969), 86, 88–9, 97, 109, 118.

[32] See M. Green, *Children of the Sun: A Narrative of 'Decadence' in England after 1918* (London 1977), ch. 4, '1918–22: Eton'.

Ridler, wife of Vivian Ridler, University Printer 1958–78, resident in Oxford ever since her husband became works manager of the Press in 1948, has been one of the city's most distinguished modern poets. Winifred Davin, wife of Dan, became a great friend of Joyce Cary, and eventually his literary executor. Nor have other supplementary university institutions been without their writers. Colin Dexter, author of the Inspector Morse stories that feature a local police detective and are usually set in the region, worked for the University delegacy of local examinations.

The presence of publishing houses in Oxford has undoubtedly stimulated Oxford writing and publishing. Traditionally, of course, the mighty OUP has greater fish to fry than undergraduate verse—its poetry list is tiny and the only fictions it publishes are canonical classics and children's stuff. But the story is very different with the other local presses. Basil Blackwell was for many years the backbone of publishing for University writers. He brought out the first published (verse) volumes of Aldous Huxley and Dorothy Sayers in 1916. He published Spender's *Twenty Poems* (1930), Rex Warner's novel *The Kite* (1936) and the anthology *Augury* (1941). Above all, Blackwell was until 1953 the publisher of the annual volumes of *Oxford Poetry*. In that year *Oxford Poetry* was taken over by non-Oxonian Oscar Mellor's Fantasy Press. Started in Mellor's Oxford digs in 1951, Fantasy flourished out at Swinford from 1951 until 1962. It was a main arm of the University Poetry Society, printing its term cards and flyers and publishing its members' work in the Fantasy Poets pamphlet series. Edward Lucie-Smith, Adrian Mitchell, Anthony Thwaite, Al Alvarez, George Steiner, Donald Hall, Elizabeth Jennings all appeared as Fantasy Poets and helped associate Fantasy decisively with The Movement. Kingsley Amis's own Fantasy pamphlet coincided with *Lucky Jim* (1954) and caused a great stir. Other Mellor ventures included the New Poems series, started in 1952 under Donald Hall's editorship, and undergraduate magazines like *Arbiter*, *Dragon*, *Gargoyle* and *Tomorrow*. Two of George MacBeth's early volumes of verse, *A Form of Words* (1954) and *Lectures to the Trainees* (1962), were published by Fantasy. Soon after returning to Oxford in 1966 as Magdalen tutor in English, John Fuller set up at his home in Benson Place the small hand-printing Sycamore Press which has published many Oxford writers, especially in its Sycamore Broadsheets: Alan Brownjohn, James Fenton, Peter Levi, W. H. Auden, Roy Fuller (father of John). A typical Sycamore Press publication is *Poems for Roy Fuller on his Seventieth Birthday* (11 February 1982), including poems by Spender, Alan Ross, Anthony Powell, Anthony Thwaite and John Fuller. In 1967, when he was a postgraduate student in English, Michael Schmidt took over the small Carcanet Press and, from Pin Farm, South Hinksey, proceeded to issue a steady stream of notable poetry pamphlets (including his own first volume of verse, *Black Buildings*, 1969), sheet-poems and the series of volumes called Fyfield

Books. Many Oxford writers, including Sally Purcell and Elizabeth Jennings, were published by Carcanet in its South Hinksey phase.

When Schmidt took over Carcanet he also took over the poetry magazine *Carcanet*, which he edited until 1970. And the plethora of magazine outlets in Oxford for embryonic writing of course plays a key part in Oxford's role as forcing house of writing. Undergraduates with writing ambitions have a vast wealth of friendly college and university training pages for their early efforts. Often over-condoning because run by chums with more momentary enthusiasm than nose for quality (Blunden referred to the 'rather too ready ways into print here' in a letter to Eliot about Keith Douglas's 'perhaps too fluent' poetry),[33] such papers succeed one another in bewildering profusion. *Carcanet* was founded in the gap left by the demise of the Mellors-sponsored magazines such as *Tomorrow*, but also in the wake of the departure for London of Michael Horovitz's *New Departures*, a paper edited from a South Hinksey cottage and committed to underground or Beat poetry and supporting the live performance of poetry and jazz in the 'Beat-den' at 4a St Clement's (Horovitz had started a BLitt on the Beat generation's obligatory hero, William Blake). For its part *New Departures* had taken up where Alan Brownjohn's *Departure* (1952–6) had left off. And Brownjohn had continued in the wake of John Waller's earlier *Bolero* and *Kingdom Come*—in which Keith Douglas had cut some of his poetic teeth. And so on. That's how things work in the small world of the student paper: there are plenty to choose from, and when one fails you move on to the next.

Some of these publications, like Horovitz's *New Departures*, enjoy a life after Oxford. John Fuller's undergraduate poem 'Morvin', for example, appeared in *Gemini* in 1959, originally an Oxford and Cambridge paper, but by then edited from London. Ian Hamilton's stern-minded journal *The Review*, consciously a successor to Geoffrey Grigson's ferocious *New Verse* of the thirties, began in 1962 in Oxford (it was to have Stephen Wall, English tutor at Keble, as well as John Fuller on its editorial board) but from 1965 to 1972 it was edited from London. The long-running national satirical paper *Private Eye* is the direct descendant of *Parson's Pleasure*, the paper that Paul Foot and Richard Ingrams edited from 1959 in Oxford. Most such Oxford papers, though, die like flies in winter. Only a handful survive any length of time. The few, though, that have persisted have functioned extraordinarily influentially as English literature's nursery slopes: in particular the annual volumes *Oxford Poetry* and Oxford's two most hardy student weeklies, *Cherwell* and *Isis*.

In the early twenties an Evelyn Waugh could contribute, it might be, to *The Oxford Broom*, edited by Harold Acton. In the twenties and thirties there was *The Oxford Outlook*, ready to receive the works of L. P. Hartley

---

[33] Letter of 10 Feb. 1941, *Douglas Miscellany*, ed. Graham, 74.

or Graham Greene or Auden, Spender, Arthur Calder-Marshall and Bernard Spencer. In the forties there was *Mandrake*, to which Larkin and Kingsley Amis contributed. But during all of this time there were also *Isis* and *Cherwell*. *Cherwell*'s pages have welcomed Greene, Powell, Auden, Spencer, Day-Lewis (as he then was, with the hyphen), MacNeice, Iris Murdoch, Sidney Keyes (who also edited the paper), John Heath-Stubbs, Betjeman, Larkin. In the depopulated Oxford of 1940 when the paper was hard-up for support, Keith Douglas not only edited it but wrote most of the articles under his own and a variety of assumed names. Generally, though, *Cherwell* was not so pressed for writers, nor was *Isis*. *Isis* was started up again after the Great War by Beverley Nichols, and its long list of impressive editors has included Claud Cockburn, Ronald Knox, Peter Fleming, Alan Brien, Robert Robinson, Dennis Potter, John Fuller and Lord Grey Gowrie. And the names crowding into the annual pages of *Oxford Poetry* have been, in aggregate, even more eye-catching.

Aldous Huxley's first Oxford publication was in *Oxford Poetry 1915*. Between the wars the pages of this extraordinary publication featured the likes of Richard Hughes, Robert Graves, Blunden, Edgell Rickword, Harold Acton, Lord David Cecil, L. P. Hartley, John Strachey, Graham Greene, Lord Longford, A. L. Rowse, Peter Quennell, T. O. Beachcroft, James Sutherland, Day-Lewis, Auden, Tom Driberg, Rex Warner, Geoffrey Tillotson, Spender, Richard Crossman, Douglas Jay, Bernard Spencer, Goronwy Rees. Great days, clearly. But the potent names go on and on. Kingsley Amis, for example, had poems in *Oxford Poetry 1948*. He edited *1949* with James Michie. Geoffrey Hill's early poems 'Pentecost', 'Saint Cuthbert on Farne Island' and 'Genesis' appeared in *1952* and *1953*. Donald Hall and Geoffrey Hill were the editors of *1953*, published now by the Fantasy Press. Contributors that year included Alvarez, Brownjohn, Jenny Joseph, Edward Lucie-Smith, George MacBeth, Adrian Mitchell, Anthony Thwaite. Thwaite was one of the editors of *1954*, Mitchell of *1955*. *1955* included poems by Peter Levi, Dennis Keene and Gabriel Pearson. *1956* had Gabriel Pearson as an editor and published work by Roger Lonsdale of Lincoln. Dennis Keene was an editor of *1957*, in which Patrick Garland, Lonsdale and Dom Moraes appeared.

What strikes us, of course, from any dip into the Oxford student journals, magazines and annuals is not just the now famous literary names but also the huge crowd of lost literary leaders. The names of the editors, the now famous reviewers of films, plays and books, and of the various 'idols' certainly have a proleptic ring to them. Here are Derek Cooper, Alan Brien, D. C. Watt, Derwent May, Colin Haycraft, W. J. Harvey, Brian Tesler, Robert Robinson, George MacBeth, George Steiner, and so on and on. Most of them are headed for the worlds of broadcasting, literary journalism, publishing, academe. Many of them would have the odd novel in them. But the highest ground of the literary future would be in other hands.

The owners of these names all had evidently high literary ambitions. Knowingly they were seeking to exploit the platform of their student journalism as a hoist to the top of the literary tree, even if it involved open truckling to the famous or indeed to anyone who looked useful in the way of literary careers. Alan Brien, for example, goes to the Biarritz film festival to interview Graham Greene for *Isis*. The *Isis* of Trinity 1950, under Robert Robinson's editorship, includes keen sucking up to Auden and an interview with Michael Innes (26 April) followed by one with Edmund Crispin (3 May). John Lehmann is roped in to judge the poetry competition (5 March 1952) and awards the prize to Christopher Driver. Notable literati— Spender it might be, or Anthony Powell, or Andrew Motion—are regularly corralled as *Isis* contributors or interviewees. In a typical *Isis* interview, Brigid Brophy reveals why she's glad she was thrown out of Oxford (9 October 1968: the literary editor that term was Michael Schmidt, assisted by Jeremy Treglown). And what the editors and writers hope for in all this touching of garment-hems and pressing of flesh is what Spender hoped for as secretary of the English Club, namely passports to where real literary jobs are, and to where the literary merit, even literary greatness is. But, plainly, what's most readily obtainable is passports rather to Grub Street, publishing, the media, front-rank positions merely among the quotidian opinion-formers of the chattering classes. The pages of Oxford's student magazines are thickly peopled by those who will go on to mastermind the culture, but as promoters, entrepreneurs, arbiters, editors, commentators, publishers and suchlike, even professors—that is, second-fiddle players, hangers-on, backers-up rather than front-line, first-team producers and creators. With a sure feel for some of the actual destinations really within reach, *Isis*'s editorial of 17 May 1967 (its literary editor was Philip Hodson, then reading English at St Peter's, a future editor of *Forum* magazine and highbrow sex-counsellor) upbraided beginning journalist Polly Toynbee (actually Mary Toynbee of St Anne's, who came up in 1966, was put off English by its Anglo-Saxon component, read some history, but left without ever taking her finals) for 'boiling down the gossip of her first term' in the *New Statesman*. Hodson also noticed the appearance of future critic and novelist and former editor of *Isis* Marina Warner in *Vogue*—'to justify the fashion ads'. It's a scene that the narrator of John Fowles's *Daniel Martin* (1977) has theories about. Why have so many of his immediate post-war Oxford generation become 'journalists, critics, media men, producers and directors'? It's because they were scared into mere 'watching and bitching' by 'the whole working-class, anti-university shift in the English theatre and the novel'. He may be right; certainly the 'failure' that preoccupies him is pervasive. 'As with Ken Tynan, so many others': when they were undergraduates 'destiny then pointed to far higher places than the ones actually achieved'.

The most glittering of prizes do, of course, seem to be held out within reach. *The Glittering Prizes* (1976) is not just the title of a novel by Frederic Raphael about successful Cambridge graduates: it's a phrase that comes aptly from Auden's poem 'Oxford'. In his diary entry for 3 December 1962 Stephen Spender meditated on what was for him Oxford's particularly glittering reward: 'Suddenly realized that I want very much that Matthew [his son] should go to Oxford. That it is an elite, that his friends are going there, and that if he doesn't he will be left behind by the best members of his generation . . . It is a thought that runs contrary to my principles and even my sympathies, but I realized that I thought my Oxford contemporaries as in some way superior beings. Going there makes me enjoy such conversation and exchange of ideas in circumstances of easy companionship and comparative leisure with the best contemporaries of one's generation during their most formative years.'[34] The syntax is confused but the sentiment is clear enough: the culturally worldly glitter that Oxford promises is indeed seductive. So much so that Oxford connections have sometimes been laid claim to quite bogusly by writers. In his autobiography *Broken Record* (1934) the South African poet Roy Campbell makes great play with having been at T. S. Eliot's old college, Merton. But the nearest Campbell got to residence there was digs in Walton Street. And rather slight Oxford experiences can, by the same token, be exaggerated. The biographical note, for example, in Jeffrey Archer's first novel *Not A Penny More Not a Penny Less* (1976) declares him to have been 'educated at Wellington College, Somerset and Brasenose College, Oxford'. He was at Brasenose only briefly on a certificate of education course (without, it appears, having graduated from any university whatsoever) but the limited association is felt to be well worth playing up.

Oxford's glittering prizes are, nonetheless, by no means inevitably the highest ones, even for the literal prizewinners (and there are many of those, winners for example of the Newdigate prize for poetry, such as John Buchan, Donald Hall, Jon Stallworthy, John Fuller, James Fenton, Alan Hollinghurst, Andrew Motion). Oxford indeed leads to places, but it's a rite of passage for would-be writers for whom life on the other side of graduation can be more hellish than at first might have seemed likely, more easily a matter of journalistic deadlines than joining Golding in the Nobel prize. As in the poem 'At the Ferry' by U. A. Fanthorpe, where punting across the Cherwell feels uncannily like crossing a river of Hell.[35] Not for nothing is Cyril Connolly's most famous book titled *Enemies of Promise* (1938). What, for example happened to the so-called Walton Street poets of 1954–7—Roger Lonsdale, Bernard Bergonzi, Gabriel Pearson, John Gross,

---

[34] S. Spender, *Journals 1939–1983*, ed. J. Goldsmith (London 1985), 245.
[35] U. A. Fanthorpe, *Selected Poems* (Harmondsworth 1986), 41.

Dennis Keene? They all ended up merely in the professoriate of literature. And so many Oxford writers have drifted ploddingly in and out of academic life. As well as those who've done pedagogic time in Oxford colleges there have been lots of others—Blunden, Graves, Auden, Spender, MacNeice, Rex Warner, Bernard Spencer, Robertson Davies, John Wain, Kingsley Amis, Geoffrey Hill, Anthony Thwaite, Francis King, Ian Hamilton, Michael Schmidt, Tom Paulin, Gay Clifford—who've taught in universities in Britain and around the world, done tours of duty for the British Council, been writers-in-residence, needily propped up their bank balances with short-term professorships especially in the USA. University teaching is a line of work that has, of course, become a standard means of survival for writers in the twentieth century, and it's one for which Oxford seems admirably to prepare you.

Oxford also provides excellent training, apparently, for that other common clutch of financial resources for the hard-up writer: being a literary hack, editing, publishing, doing literary journalism. In this respect London is helpfully near (Oxford is by no means, as Michael Innes's Doctor Johnson-quoting title of 1946 has it, *From London Far*). Several significant heavyweight literary journals have been founded and variously kept going or edited, by Oxford men—for example, T. S. Eliot's *Criterion*, Cyril Connolly's *Horizon*, Alan Ross's *London Magazine*, and *The Calendar of Modern Letters* (1925–7), one of whose editors was Edgell Rickword and which F. R. Leavis praised as the forerunner of his journal *Scrutiny*. Rickword was also an editor of the thirties socialist literary paper *Left Review*. So were Montagu Slater and Randall Swingler. On a far less intense ideological plane the weekly *Times Literary Supplement* has proved a welcoming home-from-home for very many Oxonians. Alan Pryce-Jones (whom Leavis dedicatedly opposed) went on from Oxford to edit it; so did John Gross and Jeremy Treglown. Martin Amis and Alan Hollinghurst have been assistant editors on the *TLS*. Ian Hamilton was at one much-cursed period in the sixties both poetry editor of the *TLS* and chief poetry reviewer of the *Observer*, at the same time as running *The Review*. If Hamilton didn't like your poems they were as good as dead in the water. Auden looked on the *Listener* in its mid-century heyday under the literary editorship of J. R. Ackerley as a kind of house-journal for himself and his friends. Philip Toynbee was for many years chief reviewer of the *Observer*. John Wain was a main *Observer* reviewer. Cyril Connolly, chief reviewer of the *Sunday Times*, was succeeded, while Julian Barnes was assistant literary editor, by Merton Professor John Carey. One much remarked feature of serious London newspaper and magazine reviewing from the sixties onward has been the prominent role in it of members of the Oxford English faculty—Stephen Wall, John Bayley, Peter Conrad, John Carey and so on. Poor academic salaries are one commonly touted reason.

Auberon Waugh, a ubiquitous reviewer and literary commentator, founded and edited the *Literary Review*. Derwent May, novelist and one-time lecturer on the British Council circuit, has been literary editor of a large number of journals, the *Listener*, the *Sunday Telegraph*, the *European*. A. N. Wilson has been literary editor of the *Spectator*. Anthony Thwaite was variously literary editor of the *Listener* and the *New Statesman*. Martin Amis was also literary editor of the *New Statesman*, with Julian Barnes as his assistant. Sacked by the *New Statesman*'s incoming editor, R. H. S. Crossman, Thwaite moved on to *Encounter*, undeterred by the CIA-funding scandal that led Spender to quit the paper he had helped set up. Ian Hamilton's *New Review*, successor to *The Review*, employed Craig Raine as an assistant editor. Mary-Kay Wilmers, *TLS* fiction editor, helped found and later edited the *London Review of Books*. Raine moved on to T. S. Eliot's old chair as poetry editor of Faber's, a firm with strong Oxford connections, not least through Charles Monteith, a fellow of All Souls. Andrew Motion has been poetry editor for various publishers, including Chatto & Windus, where he was preceded by Cecil Day-Lewis. One of the chief movers in television's cultural efforts in the seventies, eighties and nineties has been novelist Melvyn Bragg, ITV's Mr Big of culture, presenter, writer and commissioner of numerous TV arts programmes and bookshows, especially the *South Bank Show*. The Oxford graduates doing good cultural leg work in the BBC are so thickly massed as to defy individual naming, though mention might be made of Paul Vaughan, regular presenter of Radio Four's nightly arts programme *Kaleidoscope*.

The Oxford dominance in this scene is all too obvious. Nor has it been dinted to any significant extent by rival contingents such as the Cambridge Leavisites led by Professor Karl Miller of University College, London (literary editor of the *New Statesman*, editor of the *Listener* and then of the *London Review of Books*) and Claire Tomalin (literary editor of the *New Statesman* and then of the *Sunday Times*) who are afforced by Miller's protégé Blake Morrison (fiction editor of the *TLS*, literary editor of the *Observer* and then of the *Independent on Sunday*). When Richard Boston reported in 1989 the widely canvassed claims that 'most of the official UK poetry show' was being run by a small, closely-knit gang of self-promoting men through the prize-giving, publishing and reviewing machinery, it was noticeable that virtually all the alleged members of this mafia were, apart from Karl Miller and Blake Morrison, Oxford names—Raine, Reid, Paulin, Motion, Fuller, Fenton, Hamilton. And, even more interestingly, the most vociferous complainer to Boston against this closed shop was Michael Horovitz: one more Oxford graduate himself.[36]

Those outside this charmed and allegedly hegemonic circle naturally find complaining about its deplorable effects on the national cultural life even

[36] *Guardian* 24 June 1989, 23.

easier than does the disgruntled insider Michael Horovitz. Deploring, negative noises have been variously made by Christopher Booker (Shrewsbury and Cambridge) in *The Neophiliacs* (1969), Martin Green (a pronounced Cambridge Leavisite from Rutgers University) in *Children of the Sun* (1977) and Hugh Kenner (the Canadian critic at Johns Hopkins University) in *A Sinking Island* (1988). And nobody has been more pointedly hostile to England's 'closed literary society' than Cambridge's Mrs Leavis in her notorious *Scrutiny* review in the late thirties of books that included Connolly's *Enemies of Promise*. Her target was the whole public-school–Oxbridge clique that she saw as running England's literary show ('the public-school–University hold over literary criticism') but she was particularly angry about the Eton–Oxford axis within it that Connolly personally straddled.[37] And actual cases again and again support Mrs Leavis's angry hunches about rampant old-boyism, closed public-school–Oxford shops and clique-puffery. Lady Ottoline Morrell persuaded the editor of the *Athenaeum*, Middleton Murry, without difficulty, to take Edmund Blunden on to his staff in 1920, 'sans degree, sans examinations, sans everything'. Murry had already accepted Blunden as a contributor with delight that they were both Christ's Hospital men. The career of Old Etonian Alan Pryce-Jones took off when, rusticated from Magdalen for complete idleness and for being out of college when he was gated, he bumped into J. C. Squire, editor of the *London Mercury*, in the barber's at the National Liberal Club and was taken on to the paper as an unpaid assistant, Squire having remembered some of Pryce-Jones's schoolboy poems.[38] Some careers are open only to familiar talents, ones whose fame does circulate rather rapidly around the cousinhood that runs such things in the small island of Britain, a large number of whose members come from the small village that Oxford is.

'Craig told me that . . . the wonderful thing about Oxford is that it is like a village but has all the facilities you'd miss in a village, like bookshops and theatres.'[39] Thus Andrew Motion in an *Isis* interview talking of his chum Craig Raine. And, of course, the crossing of paths in what Auden called our tight little island and the consequent offers of helping hands are by no means as unnatural or immoral as Mrs Leavis suggested. It's certainly no surprise to find T. S. Eliot moving swiftly to get the youthful Auden and Spender on to his Faber poetry list (though it was a little more of a surprise to find Craig Raine so prompt to get his own stuff on to that list). And Cyril Connolly was, as it happened, more alert to the enclosing force of Oxford than Mrs Leavis conceded. In Trou-sur-mer on the Med in Connolly's novel *The*

[37] Q. D. Leavis, 'The background of twentieth century letters', *Scrutiny* viii (1939–40), 74–6.
[38] B. Webb, *Edmund Blunden: A Biography* (New Haven Conn. and London 1990), 116 ff; A. Pryce-Jones, *The Bonus of Laughter* (London 1987), 53.
[39] 'Student days: Andrew Motion', *Isis* 7 June 1983, 26.

Rock Pool (1936) the hero Naylor receives a letter from his old school and Oxford friend Spedding, now in the law, a missive full of Oxford gossip, the words of 'our dear tutor', and the like. 'Spedding', reflects Naylor, 'had simply exchanged the Gothic quads, dining-halls, gowns, subfusc pleasures and gregarious intolerance of Winchester and Oxford for those of the law-courts. He would never leave the quadrangle.'[40] But not all Oxonian fictions offer such satire of the perennial quadrangle-dweller. Iris Murdoch's novels are perfectly content, delighted even, to inhabit the scholarly environment provided by quadrangles and donnish enclaves such as Rawlinson Road. Her protégé A. N. Wilson might seek to effect a double-minded picture of Oxford in his novel *The Healing Art* (1980) by seeing through the eyes of two socially distinctive female cancer patients; but while his medievalist don moves well-roundedly through the learned and Anglo-Catholic world (not a million miles from Somerville) that is so obviously familiar to her author, her working-class counterpart from the council-estate milieu where the college scouts live is the Oxford equivalent of pure cockney-sparrer caricature.

By contrast Auden's poem 'Oxford' comes from the social-conscience-stricken thirties and is built on a much more aggressive and worried opposition between the enclosed interiors of 'the college garden', 'these quadrangles', and what lies 'without'—'the shops, the works, the whole green country'.[41] But still, however much the poem might protest that this 'outside' matters, it too fails to break the seductive grip of the enclosure, the magnetic hold on the imagination of a magical place, this formative Oxford matrix that remains afterwards for so many of its alumni (and alumnae), both writing and non-writing ones, a decisive and inerasable part of the self. And much the same is true of many other Oxford texts that seek to contrast Oxford University adversely with the less fortunate worlds of Oxford city, the unemployed, Welsh miners, General Strikers, ordinary folk, the Other and the others outside—as Day Lewis's novel *Starting Point* (1937), Spender's autobiography *World within World* (1951) or John Wain's novel *Hurry on Down* (1953) all try to do. Like childhood traumas and Jesuit education these memories are formative: they last, and they're likely to go on influencing behaviour and to pervade texts. As the Bombay author Dom Moraes puts it in his poem 'For Peter', a meditation on the differences between his career and those of the gentlemanly English friends he made at Oxford: 'those gardens far away, explain my lives'. As he drowns, William Golding's Pincher Martin recalls Carfax, Big Tom, a quadrangle, bare wooden stairs, 'all the bells of Oxford' invading a college room. He's in the High Street—forever. Not unlike Stephen Spender's famous poem 'The

[40] C. Connolly, *The Rock Pool* (Paris 1936), ch. 6.

[41] First version of the poem, Dec. 1937, in *The English Auden*, ed. E. Mendelson (London 1977), 229.

Express', whose phrase 'gliding like a queen' was, Spender later confessed, a subversive memorial to 'an Oxford queen called M—— gliding down the High when I was an undergraduate'. The being of such texts and characters has been inerasably inscribed by the college and streets where their authors passed their youth. These writers are spear-carriers in the Oxford stage-army who signed on young for life.[42]

'I could go through Oxford', thinks Anne Linton, the much travelling heroine of Penelope Lively's novel *The Road to Lichfield* (1977). And so many Oxonian texts do, whatever the pain or difficulty involved ('traffic-wise', her husband had said, 'you would do better not to'). Lured into making a detour to Leckford Road, Ms Linton becomes logjammed with memories. 'At this point, by this particular lamp-post, once upon a time, she would walk more slowly, prolonging the approach, because however glorious the seeing him, the being-about-to-see-him had to be savoured to the full, drawn out step by step along this enchanted street of sour brick and shabby privet hedges.' Once snagged in these potent streets, once admitted into this secret garden, the initiated cannot leave. Anne Linton was once in this place and now it's forever in her. It remains a place whose friendships and mutual succour, its secret languages and codes will go on being shared. Oxford on this reckoning continues (in the case of so many public-school pupils) or initiates (in the case of others) what amounts to a personal and cultural freemasonry. This is the social and intellectual result that Spender was celebrating in his diary entry of December 1962.

Oxford looks after its own, whoever they are. Jeffrey Archer's career as a best-selling novelist began in the cottage lent him by Noel Hall, Principal of Brasenose, when Archer was reduced to penury in the financial scam that features in *Not A Penny More Not A Penny Less*, the fortune-recouping novel that he wrote there. Oxford writers feel a family obligation to assist each other in every sort of writerly and sub-writerly matter. T. E. Lawrence cheerfully gives Graves some manuscript pages of *Seven Pillars of Wisdom* to get him out of a tight financial spot. Tom Driberg and John Sparrow regularly correct Betjeman's erratic punctuation, syntax and scansion.[43] In wartime Cairo Keith Douglas kips in Bernard Spencer's flat and, naturally, has his poems published in *Citadel*, the journal edited by David Hicks, Spencer's flatmate.[44] Auden tries, in vain, to get his old friend Spender elected Professor of Poetry in a kind of apostolic succession. Anthony Thwaite edits Larkin's sixtieth-birthday Festschrift and the posthumous

---

[42] D. Moraes, 'For Peter' in his *Collected Poems 1957–1987* (New Delhi, Harmondsworth etc 1987), 113; W. Golding, *Pincher Martin* (London 1956), chaps 6 and 12; S. Spender, *The Thirties and After: Poetry, Politics, People (1933–75)* (London 1978), 224–5.

[43] F. Wheen, *Tom Driberg: His Life and Indiscretions* (London 1990), 411, 413.

[44] *Douglas Miscellany*, ed. Graham, 91.

Collected Poems. Andrew Motion becomes Larkin's official biographer.[45] Peter Levi, who married Connolly's widow, completes Connolly's unfinished novel *Shade Those Laurels*.[46] John Wain's *Professing Poetry* (1977)—which includes Alan Hollinghurst's and Andrew Motion's Newdigate verse, poems by Avril Bruten (St Hugh's English don), Andrew Harvey and Sally Purcell, and Wain's lectures on Auden, Larkin and Edward Thomas, as well as anecdotes about Larkin, Heath-Stubbs, Jennings and Levi—is a wonderfully clear example of Oxonian writerly staunchness, the family warmth, at its most admirable.

A major outward sign of such cordial mutualities in books and texts is the way these authors dedicate poems to each other, drop each others' names, feature each other as characters, share allusions, swap private jokes. This proneness to coterie self-celebration is a well-known characteristic of thirties writing, but it's by no means limited to one period or one group.[47] Edmund Crispin's volume of detective stories *The Moving Toyshop* (1946), for instance, is not only dedicated to Larkin, but has a Larkin crop up in one of its stories ('The episode of the interrupted seminar') as a boringly scholarly and enthusiastically medievalist pupil of Gervase Fen. It's a private joke about Larkin's undergraduate contempt for such things that all his friends, at least, would have laughed satirically at. Just so, Amis and Larkin would swap quotations from each other in their published work: someone, for example, is noted 'running up to bowl' in both *Lucky Jim* and Larkin's poem 'The Whitsun Weddings'.

These incestuous moments can be more or less discreet. They're pretty well concealed in, say, the preference for mauve among the girls in 'The Whitsun Weddings', a train-poem's tribute to Louis MacNeice's earlier poem 'Train to Dublin', which has a girl in it 'preferring mauve'. But they can be utterly open as in, for example, John Fuller's volume *Epistles to Several Persons* which consists of long poems, conscious descendants of Auden's *Letter to Lord Byron*, addressed *inter alia* to James Fenton, Ian Hamilton and David Caute. Characteristically the one 'To Ian Hamilton' celebrates ten years of the financially precarious *Review* and recalls Hamilton's equally sticky efforts at running literary magazines as an undergraduate at Keble, whose authorities impounded 'stacks of *Tomorrows*' because of unpaid battels.[48] At such literary moments the closet of collective undergraduate memory is opened and it's as stacked with early literary adventures as the scouts' pantry in Keble was with Hamilton's

[45] A. Thwaite (ed.), *Larkin at Sixty* (London 1982); P. Larkin, *Collected Poems*, ed. A. Thwaite (London 1988); A. Motion, *Philip Larkin: A Writer's Life* (London 1993). See also *Selected Letters of Philip Larkin 1940–1985* (London 1992).

[46] C. Connolly, *Shade Those Laurels*, concluded by Peter Levi (London 1990).

[47] See V. Cunningham, *British Writers of the Thirties* (Oxford 1988), especially ch. 5, 'Too old at forty', for lengthy illustrations of the phenomenon.

[48] J. Fuller, *Epistles to Several Persons* (London 1973), 44.

unsold magazines—adventures that started and sealed the literary associations that have continued up to the present of the poem.

It would be wrong, however, to assume, for all this atmosphere of chummy bonhomie, friendly co-operation and what F. R. Leavis called coterie flank-rubbing, that there is any complete or completely predictable uniformity of behaviour and of literary consequences among Oxonian writers. Such is the mistaken assumption of outsiders like Mrs Leavis and Hugh Kenner. In Kenner's briskly satirical map of England's modern literary ills, Craig Raine and Andrew Motion are made to stand as representative of the eighties 'group of poets, novelists, publishers and editors which includes most of his [Motion's] Oxford friends and without whose permission nothing seems to move in British literature at the moment'. The pair—much like Roy Campbell's corporate butt of the thirties, MacSpaunday—are turned into a kind of composite Oxford writer. This figure also contrives capaciously to embrace a Betjeman, a Larkin and a Sayers ('the Oxford graduate'), as well as anyone who's served as professor of poetry or been commended in *The Oxford Companion to English Literature* or gained extensive quotation in *The Oxford Dictionary of Quotations* (Auden's seven columns particularly irk Kenner).[49]

There is, of course, enough truth in Kenner's satirical diagram of the Oxonian Hack's Progress ('How to make it in London with poetry') to make much of it stick.[50] There is indeed an Oxonian literary career path, just as there are certain shared identikit features of Oxonian writing. The Oxford voice in twentieth-century literature is as audibly distinctive as once the Oxford accent was. D. H. Lawrence, another outsider, taken as the representative outsider by Q. D. Leavis in her attack on Connolly, and the carefully selected target of some insiders (like T. S. Eliot in his lofty Arnoldian polemic in *After Strange Gods: A Primer of Modern Heresy*, 1934), made superiority precisely the essence of 'The Oxford Voice' in his poetic 'pansy' of that name. The smart, even smart-alec male knowingness of the Martian school of poetry is the very ground of its appeal to Andrew Motion and Blake Morrison, according to the introduction to their *Penguin Book of Contemporary British Poetry* (1982): 'spectacular confidence . . . outrageous simile . . . Martians' ingenuity . . . new confidence in the poetic imagination'. (The Martian poet Reid has nicely deflated this Oxonian superiority in a poem, 'Go, Little Book', about an unsuccessful working-class poet whose volume, published by a Northern Press, was destroyed by its 'only reviewer'—'an Oxford post-graduate / on the make / in "literary London"'—who 'was able to dispatch it / in two brisk sentences, / one containing a joke'. Which all too knowing text appeared with a certain grim aptness in the *TLS* for 10–16 August 1990.) But such aggressive descriptive

---

[49] H. Kenner, *A Sinking Island: The Modern English Writers* (London 1988), *passim*.
[50] Ibid. 254.

and prescriptive power is by no means new. It's what has long annoyed some readers of Graves's and Auden's poetry. And an anti-bogus, seeing-through-everything, even cynically know-it-all mind is what Louis MacNeice, in section XIII of his long poem *Autumn Journal* (1939), credits his Oxford education with producing. After Oxford:

> You can never really again
> Believe anything that anyone says and that of course is an asset
> In a world like ours.

Nor is worldly *savoir faire* restricted to poetry. It's the driving force of A. N. Wilson's or Martin Amis's or Julian Barnes's fiction. It's a knowingness manifestly grounded in knowledge, classical in the case of Graves, Rex Warner, MacNeice ('the classical student is born to the purple, his training in syntax / Is also a training in thought / And even in morals': *Autumn Journal*); philological in the fictions of Tolkien or Robertson Davies or the poems of Auden, who vexed readers of his later poems by what they thought a lazy habit of scanning the *Oxford English Dictionary* for out of the way vocables to fox his audience with. (Huxley's John Beavis in *Eyeless in Gaza* is a big contributor to the *OED*; Julian Barnes worked on the *Supplement*.) Eclectic learning is what unites the poems of John Heath-Stubbs, the novels of Iris Murdoch and those of Gabriel Josipovici or Barnes's *Flaubert's Parrot*. Such writings are never far away from being variously locked into a bookishness that approaches the stereotypically donnish. All of Iris Murdoch's fictions revel in learned chat, philosophical reference, the earnest detritus of Oxford senior common rooms. And any page of Connolly's *Shade Those Laurels* indicates how easy the well educated novelist finds it to choke his or her texts to death on a surfeit of scholarly lampreys.

What such writings seek to achieve is the sheer power and authority over readers that their knowledgeableness is expected to wield. This is just what Auden, himself a quarrelsome pedant and pedagogic tyrant, admired in Eliot: authority in, and of, the quadrangle. 'And through the quads dogmatic words rang clear.' Thus *Letter to Lord Byron*, of T. S. Eliot. And for all Auden's investment in youthful terroristic toughness—something he has in common with the early fictions of Kingsley Amis and John Wain, the Angry Young Men of the fifties, and their offspring Martin Amis and Julian Barnes, the young turks of the eighties, or, more recently, with the aggressively confident fictions and *obiter dicta* of Jeanette Winterson—this professed Oxonian classicism of Auden's was not at all immune to the conservative tendencies that Eliot preached as necessary to it. Auden's professed affection for Tolkien and what was known as the philological side of the English school —shared by U. A. Fanthorpe, whose poem 'Genesis (for J. R. R. Tolkien)' bears comparison with Auden's 'Short Ode to a Philologist', that is Tolkien — was symptomatic of the reaction latent in his early work. When Auden became a practising Anglican again after the Spanish Civil War, he was merely tying the label on the conservative package-deal that the likes of Tolkien and Coghill offered him, a set of religious, social, class and cultural values that brought together a certain kind of Englishness, Anglicanism and Anglo-Saxon studies.

The English faculty that was so notoriously conservative as to syllabus (compulsory Anglo-Saxon, nothing twentieth-century until 1970, a situation Auden admired and that twentieth-century-hating Tolkien and his allies fought to preserve)[51] was packed with unmutedly professing Christians, Roman Catholics in some number, including Tolkien, but especially Anglicans: laymen and laywomen such as C. S. Lewis and Charles Williams, of course, but also Coghill and Peter Bayley (University College) and Professor Dame Helen Gardner and her god-daughter Katherine Duncan-Jones (Somerville) and *her* former husband, A. N. Wilson, one-time tutor at St Hugh's and sometime Anglican ordinand, and Rachel Trickett, doughty opponent of Prayer Book modernizers, English tutor at St Hugh's and then its Principal, as well as a significant clutch of ordained clergymen of the Church of England—Roy Ridley (Balliol), Ralph Houghton (St Peter's), Canon Adam Fox (Dean of Divinity at Magdalen and one of John Wain's tutors), Graham Midgley (St Edmund Hall), Humphry House (Wadham, a deacon). Admittedly there was a skewed, even scallywag air about many of these male Anglicans—Lewis with his suspiciously odd ménage in Headington, Coghill with his homosexuality, Roy Ridley with a yen for sexual scandal that finally got him sacked from Balliol, Humphry House with his loss of faith that lost him his English tutorship as well as his chaplaincy at Wadham, Wilson with his abandoning of his theological studies, his wife and, finally, religion, and devoting himself to busy satire of Anglo-Catholic sexual vagaries—'spiky woofters', and so on. But for all the whiff of naughtiness, this faculty, nursery of so many articulate orthodox literary Christians—C. S. Lewis, Dorothy Sayers, Auden, Robertson Davies, Barbara Pym, and so on—was manifestly wedded to the traditional establishmentarian views of English and Englishness that all this established Christianity would imply.

For his part, Tolkien believed 'philology' to be central to his business of 'the patriotic study of English'.[52] The criticisms of English chauvinism and establishment ideology directed by the Methuen New Accents school of critics and others at Sir Walter Raleigh, Merton Professor, and by extension at Oxford English as a whole, are not undeserved.[53] Likewise, F. R. Leavis's

[51] Cf above, 121–2, 239–40.

[52] See his extraordinary argument for a reformed English syllabus, 'The Oxford English school', *OM* 29 May 1930, 778–82, in which nobody would study nineteenth-century texts and the specialist philologists would 'naturally' drop Shakespeare. Cf H. Carpenter, *The Inklings: C. S. Lewis, J. R. R. Tolkien, Charles Williams, and their Friends* (London 1978), 55, 229–30.

[53] See T. Hawkes, 'Swisser-Swatter: making a man of English letters' in his *That Shakespeherian Rag: Essays on a Critical Process* (London 1986) and C. Baldick, *The Social Mission of English Criticism 1848–1932* (Oxford 1983), 75 ff ('Confessions of a pimp'), 88–9.

lifetime of abusive strictures against the dilettantism of Professor Lord David Cecil seems only too aptly sustained when you read, say, the 1952 *Isis* interview in which Cecil attacks 'ephemeral theories'—historical, sociological, psychological—as 'temptations' and 'heresy', methods hostile to 'tradition' and 'the spirit of Oxford culture', distracting from the 'pleasure and laughter' central to literary study. Such delight, though, was not, it appears, central to the study of all literature. 'As a critic, he would not advise the study of any work after 1914.' The charm and gush of the interview are able to mask neither the intellectual emptiness nor the pompously superior iron-fistedness of a reactionary.[54] In the light of such attitudes it's small wonder that Oxford and Oxford English should have generated only a tiny handful of modernist or postmodernist writers. After Eliot—and *Prufrock* was written before he got to Oxford—there are no Oxonian experimentalists in fiction to talk of before Christine Brooke-Rose, Gabriel Josipovici, Ronald Frame, Maggie Gee and Julian Barnes came along. All of these are important enough formal innovators, but they are very few in number. What's more, the anti-modernist case was made nowhere more vigorously in Britain after the Second World War than by Philip Larkin, notably in the swingeing dismissal of Pound, Picasso and Charlie Parker in the introduction to his *All What Jazz* (1970). Nor is it surprising, given the English faculty's devotion to minor poems such as *The Owl and the Nightingale* and its prolonged resistance to the great nineteenth- and twentieth-century texts, that minor modes should have proved so much to its graduates' tastes.

Hugh Kenner finds it easy, as befits a North American, to mis-hear the tone of Larkin's blokeish grouching about the modernist arts, and to mis-read his Plain Englishman persona's utterances ('Books are a load of crap'; 'Who's Jorge Luis Borges?') as intellectually fuddled, irresponsible and auto-destructive of any significance in the face of the wider world's heavyweight modernist achievements. D. H. Lawrence knew better about the Oxford voice's establishment of superiority through self-deprecation. The no-nonsense saloon-bar debunking and vulgarity that pervade the texts of Larkin and Kingsley Amis (Larkin's 'Poem about Oxford', glad about leaving the place, sneers, for instance, at 'the arselicker who stays') would be mistakenly construed as crudely unprincipled or simply low-minded. So would Graham Greene's interest in cinema and the songs of Cole Porter, or Dennis Potter's obsession with the popular songs of the thirties and forties, or the interest in jazz sustained by Larkin, Amis and Wain. A relish for Beer and Dixieland is no more self-evidently a sign of cultural deprivation than one for, say, Beer and Beowulf. They are much more certainly signs of the hostility to pretentiousness about learning and education that the Canadian

---

[54] 'Guardian angels 15: Lord David Cecil, Goldsmith's Professor of English Literature', *Isis* 5 Mar. 1952, 26.

novelist Robertson Davies claims Oxford taught him. 'What astonished my Canadian soul was the gusto which these men [E. K. Chambers, Percy Simpson, Coghill, Roy Ridley] brought to their work. Gusto had never entered into Shakespeare studies before . . . The greatest gift that Oxford gives her sons is, I truly believe, a genial irreverence toward learning, and from that irreverence love may spring. Certainly it was so in my case.'[55]

There's a lot to be said for carrying your learning lightly, for lightness of touch, and also for the masses of light literature that Oxonians have generated. Kenner looks too thumpingly heavy-handed in bearing down on the likes of John Betjeman, both as poet and symptom of Oxford's and England's frivolity—'engulfed by public bathos'. Nonetheless it's not insignificant that Oxonians should have advocated light verse so strenuously—the old *Oxford Book of Light Verse* was edited by Auden (1938), the new one by Kingsley Amis (1978); that they've kept up the Lewis Carroll tradition so assiduously and produced and nourished critically so much literature for children (I'm thinking of C. S. Lewis, J. R. R. Tolkien, Penelope Lively, Humphrey Carpenter, Julia Briggs, Gillian Avery);[56] that they've turned into journalists and journeyman critics in such profusion (the one craft that the practice of rapidly composed weekly essays, necessarily cobbled together out of thinness and glibness, truly prepared you for, according to John Wain);[57] and above all, that they've become detective story writers in such profusion.

Detective fiction is proverbially donnish stuff; dons like G. D. H. Cole, J. C. Masterman, J. I. M. Stewart, T. J. Binyon, John Fuller write it; dons read and discuss it (Binyon's book about it, *Murder Will Out*, promises to be a standard work); dons' pupils write it, read it and enthuse about it (T. S. Eliot and W. H. Auden were renowned fans and theorists of the genre);[58] its detective heroes are commonly Oxford dons, like Edmund Crispin's Gervase Fen, or Fuller's Speedfall, or they're Oxford graduates like Dorothy Sayers's Lord Peter Wimsey and Blake's Nigel Strangeways; its murders frequently occur in Oxford and Oxford colleges (as, most famously, in Sayers's *Gaudy Night*, 1935, or in Crispin *passim*, in Masterman's *An Oxford Tragedy*, 1933, Michael Innes's *Death at the President's Lodging*, 1936, Robert Robinson's *Landscape with Dead Dons*, 1956, Antonia Fraser's *Oxford Blood*, 1985, John Fuller's *The Adventures of Speedfall*, 1985). A

[55] 'Shakespeare over the port' in *The Enthusiasms of Robertson Davies*, ed. J. S. Grant (New York 1990 edn), 293.
[56] See for example H. Carpenter and M. Prichard, *The Oxford Companion to Children's Literature* (Oxford 1984); J. Briggs, *A Woman of Passion: The Life of E. Nesbit* (London 1987); and G. Avery and J. Briggs (eds), *Children and their Books: A Celebration of the Work of Iona and Peter Opie* (Oxford 1990), whose introduction dwells on the association between Oxford and children's books.
[57] 'An author on the English school', *OM* 12 June 1958, 504–6.
[58] See T. S. Eliot's review of detective fiction, *Criterion* v (Jan. 1927), 139–43, and W. H. Auden, 'The guilty vicarage' in his *The Dyer's Hand* (New York 1962, London 1963).

flatteringly high level of cultural and literary reference (Innes's Appleby bears all his author's tutorial armoury of quotations and allusions); a taste for closed societies and inside stories from the academic *hortus inclusus*; the impressively authoritative and elegant solution of intricate little brain-teasers, a donnish feature that unites crime-solvers as disparate as Crispin's Fen and John le Carré's Smiley: it's easy to see how quintessentially Oxonian the detective story is, and also how damagingly revelatory of a collective taste that is, according to Kenner, 'middlebrow enough to crave literariness in what ought to be Tit-Bits narrative, and gullible enough to equate superfluous words with Kulchur'.[59]

These are all generalizable features of the Oxonian literary voice. But at the same time it remains the case that this voice resonates with great variations of tone and pitch. It has altered, for example, with the changes in Oxford's population in terms of class, gender and race. The twenties gang of writing Etonians gives way to the grammar-school boys of the forties and fifties. The predominant maleness characteristic of the twenties—there are no women in 'the Auden generation'—gets diluted by the increasing numbers of women writers stemming later on from Oxford. There start to appear in the publishers' lists the likes of the Indian 'poetic' novelist Vikram Seth who graduated from Corpus with a first in PPE in 1975 and produced *The Golden Gate*, hailed as 'the Great Californian Novel' in 1986, or of Caryl Phillips, the black immigrant Briton who was born in St Kitts, went to school in Birmingham and Leeds and graduated in English from Queen's College in 1979. In earlier times black writers from Oxford had been non-existent apart from the odd Commonwealth incomer such as the West Indians Stuart Hall and V. S. Naipaul or the Indian Dom Moraes (before the Second World War Oxford writers from overseas had the white faces of North Americans such as James Elroy Flecker, T. S. Eliot, Robert Penn Warren and Robertson Davies). Of course the older Oxford tones, the bourgeois English ground-bass, do have a way of rumbling on. And you can get dedicated throwbacks like A. N. Wilson, as well as the numerous writers like Penelope Lively or Andrew Motion, who go on being locked into inescapable bourgeois public-school assumptions, memories, experiences. But still a great gulf of difference does yawn between the works of Old Etonian Aldous Huxley and, say, Caryl Phillips whose racial marginality has so stoked his fiction, or indeed Philip Larkin the dedicated provincial writer from a grammar school in Coventry, or Dennis Potter the scholarship boy whose upbringing among Forest of Dean coalminers haunts all his plays, or Sarah Maitland the leading Christian-feminist novelist, or Jeanette Winter-son the lesbian feminist who seeks repeatedly in her novels to come to terms with her brashly northern fundamentalist pentecostalist upbringing, or Tom

[59] Kenner, *Sinking Island*, 177 ('Kulchur' is Ezra Pound's derisive spelling).

Paulin the Protestant Ulsterman and intensely self-conscious Northern Irish poet who came to Oxford as a postgraduate student via a Belfast grammar school and Hull University. When Jeanette Winterson writes in *The Oxford Women's Handbook 1991* that 'as women we do not inherit the grandeur that moves us or the scholarship that makes the University famous. We are not heirs, we are claimants', she is only repeating the radically subverting claims upon Oxford of half a century's various sets of new-Oxonians.

Clearly, Oxford writers are not all alike. They do not all like each other. Craig Raine quarrels venomously with Tom Paulin in the pages of the *London Review of Books*; John Wain stands against Stephen Spender for Professor of Poetry and the Oxonians of the *TLS* bitch mercilessly against him; Keith Douglas calls Spender 'that shit'; Sidney Keyes deliberately leaves Larkin out of *Eight Oxford Poets* (1941); Evelyn Waugh labels Auden a 'public bore'; Auden wages public war on John Sparrow for having the gall to criticize his poems; Robert Graves slights Auden for allegedly stealing techniques from his and Laura Riding's poems; and so on.[60] What's more, they do not all like Oxford. And Oxford did not like all of them.

It's no surprise that Potter's Nigel Barton plays for television should register the anger of their working-class hero at the cushioned privilege of the public-school products who still dominated early fifties Oxford ('it's not brains which sets the middle-classes apart from yobs like me, just privet hedges. And as for all those chinless upper-class nits in British Warms hanging about outside Trinity . . . '). No surprise, either, that these dramas are about Barton's dismay at the social displacement Oxford has effected in him, so that he's at home neither 'at home—in the village, in the working man's club, with people I went to school with', nor in college ('Latin prayers and glinting silver. Undergraduates talking about foreign cities with overwhelming familiarity. Braying accents across the quad. Horribly smug, offensively arrogant'). Oxford upsets Nigel Barton. No Anglican, nor even Anglo-Saxonist he, nor ever likely to be. For him the embrace of Alma Mater is by no means unquestionably benign. His is the authentic voice of Lucky Jim at Oxford, a fifties cliché, gracelessly discontent with the establishment that has graciously opened its doors to the eleven-plus exam successes.[61] But loud discontents are, interestingly, by no means limited to the Nigel Bartons of Oxford.

Upsetting alike for those who wish to lump all modern Oxford products

---

[60] Cunningham, *British Writers of the Thirties*, 22, 305 (Graves), 139 (Sparrow); Douglas, letter to John Hall, 10 June 1943, *Douglas Miscellany*, ed. Graham, 121; K. Amis, 'Oxford and after' in Thwaite, *Larkin at Sixty*, 27 (Larkin); J. Wain, *Professing Poetry* (London 1977), 12–13, 54 (professor of poetry election, Spender, *TLS*); E. Waugh, 'Mr Isherwood and friends', *Spectator* 24 Mar. 1939, repr. in *The Essays, Articles and Reviews of Evelyn Waugh*, ed. D. Gallagher (London 1983), 250–1.

[61] D. Potter, *Stand Up, Nigel Barton* and *Vote Vote Vote for Nigel Barton* (both 1965) in *The Nigel Barton Plays* (Penguin Modern Playwrights 5, Harmondsworth 1967).

into one undifferentiated glop—the Kenner–Leavis wish—as well as for any argument about a pervasively helpful relationship between Oxford (and its English school) and writing, is the observable case that some sort of hostility between Oxford writers and Oxford proves to be not at all uncommon. Again and again Oxford has turned out, like Mother England in Auden's *Letter to Lord Byron*, to be a harsh nurse of men, *dura virum nutrix*, especially academically. Auden may have found in Coghill 'a tutor in whom one could confide', as the dedication of *The Dyer's Hand* puts it, but the English examiners thought the budding poet worth only a third class in finals. A conspicuous number of Oxford writers have, of course, done very well academically, not least in English. Firsts in English were achieved, for example, by Philip Larkin, Kingsley Amis, John Wain, Penelope Fitzgerald, D. M. Thomas, Al Alvarez, U. A. Fanthorpe, Gay Clifford and Gabriel Josipovici; Alan Hollinghurst has a DPhil in English, Craig Raine and Gay Clifford MPhils; Andrew Motion, Maggie Gee and Tom Paulin have English MLitts. But Dom Moraes managed only a third in English finals. J. G. Farrell got a third in modern languages, Penelope Lively the same in history. In the twenties when, of course, exam success was not so highly regarded as in later more meritocratic decades, such failure was relatively normal. Rex Warner and Anthony Powell both got thirds. Evelyn Waugh's third was reported to be a very bad one. Others weren't even this successful. Betjeman cheerfully cut tutorials with C. S. Lewis—Lewis thought him an 'idle prig', 'ignorant' and 'stupid'. He failed a divinity exam, and went down without a degree. So did another Lewis pupil, Henry Green, who famously mis-spent his time at Oxford, sleeping a lot, attending the cinema every day and trying to write fiction. For his part, Jocelyn Brooke failed his law prelims at the end of his first year and then left Oxford for good. Edgell Rickword, Alan Pryce-Jones, Constantine FitzGibbon, Stephen Spender, Randall Swingler, Alan Ross, Auberon Waugh all kept up this tradition of leaving Oxford degree-less. (So did Nicholas Blake's hero Nigel Strangeways, sent down for answering exam questions, in the manner of Christopher Isherwood at Cambridge, with limericks.) Adrian Mitchell sat and failed his English finals in 1955. Edmund Blunden, mightily upset by his Great War soldiering, never settled to his English studies and had left Oxford by the end of his first year (he was granted an MA by decree in 1931 to enable him to function as Merton's English tutor). That other troubled veteran of the Great War Robert Graves never sat for his BA in English, though he did get the BLitt he was allowed to transfer to. In the case of Kingsley Amis, his BLitt in English was failed outright (for which, as his *Memoirs* reveal, Amis rather understandably never forgave Lord David Cecil, his sluggish supervisor and, eventually, slapdash examiner).[62] Ronald Frame's English DPhil thesis was granted only an MLitt. Craig Raine abandoned his DPhil work. Michael

[62] K. Amis, *Memoirs* (London 1991), especially 101–7, 'Lord David Cecil'.

Horovitz, Gabriel Josipovici, Michael Schmidt and William Boyd all left Oxford with their postgraduate theses in English incomplete. The classicist Brigid Brophy was sent down from St Hugh's in her final year (for creating 'a scene in chapel'). She spoke, perhaps, for many of Oxford's disappointed and disappointing literary examinees when she hubristically told *Isis* that the 'ideal advice to undergraduates who are subject to the writing compulsion is "come (or get sent) down at once" '.[63]

Anthony Powell revealed in *Isis* that he'd been 'rather gloomy at Oxford', and the tone of the Oxford section of his memoirs is indeed lugubriously low-key.[64] Others' unpleased reactions are far fierier. John le Carré's blurbs make a point of dismissing Oxford's importance to him: he merely 'attended the universities of Berne and Oxford' (his first class in German is never mentioned). T. S. Eliot found Oxford 'not intellectually stimulating'. He felt 'not quite alive there': 'I could never endure to live there'.[65] It was the compulsory study of Old English that many would-be writers found the particular bane of their Oxford existence. Huxley complained of the 'nauseous diet of Anglo Saxon'—'that loathsome language is a nuisance beyond all words'—and he wished 'that damned MS' of *Beowulf* had perished in the fire that only singed it.[66] Kingsley Amis and Larkin shared a violent antipathy to Old English and its texts: all 'ape's bumfodder'.[67] Amis's disrelish for 'philology' animates his nicely spry poem 'Beowulf' ('So, bored with dragons, he lay down to sleep').[68] It was his and Larkin's ill luck to have the Anglo-Saxonist Gavin Bone as their college tutor at St John's ('he set . . . an exacting standard of scholarship which refused to allow the English School to become a divan for literary dalliance' purred his *Oxford Magazine* obituarist).[69] Larkin's dislikes went further. Amis reports finding a note in Larkin's hand at the end of the college library's copy of *The Faerie Queene*: 'First I thought Troilus and Criseyde was the most *boring* poem in English. Then I thought Beowulf was. Then I thought Paradise Lost was. Now I *know* that The Faerie Queene is the *dullest thing out. Blast it*.'[70]

And the feeling does recur among such embryonic writers that the required subjects of study are a great distraction, even when they're the canonical works of English literature. They want to read precisely what's not

---

[63] B. Brophy, 'Why I'm glad I was thrown out of Oxford', *Isis* 9 Oct. 1968, 23. See also (on Brophy) S. Durrant, 'Puzzling it out', *Independent Magazine* 7 July 1990, 44–6.

[64] J. Dugdale and J. Otlet, 'Anthony Powell', *Isis* 15 June 1973, 22; A. Powell, *To Keep the Ball Rolling: The Memoirs of Anthony Powell* (4 vols London 1976–82) i *Infants of the Spring*.

[65] Letters, 14 Oct. and 31 Dec. 1914, 3 Jan. 1915, *The Letters of T. S. Eliot* i *1898–1922*, ed. V. Eliot (London 1988), 61, 74, 78.

[66] Letters, Oct. 1915, 15 Feb. 1916, 10 Mar. 1916, *Letters of Aldous Huxley*, ed. Smith, 81, 90, 92.

[67] Amis, 'Oxford and after', 25.

[68] K. Amis, *Collected Poems 1944–79* (Harmondsworth 1980), 17.

[69] J. D. M[abbott], *OM* 7 May 1942, 276–7.

[70] Amis, 'Oxford and after', 25.

required by the syllabus (W. H. Auden was introduced to *The Waste Land* by his fellow undergraduate Tom Driberg, not by his English tutor, who hadn't read it). 'They will certainly not be writing', says Alan Brownjohn of student poets, 'in a manner suggested by their studies with academic tutors'.[71] Henry Green's unhappy run with C. S. Lewis is more representative than Auden's happy time spent with Coghill. The poems and novels and plays undergraduates want to write, the magazines they want to produce, the plays they want to act in, are commonly unofficial stuff, pastimes, sidelines, and a worry to their tutors who often see them as time wasted. They may be wonderfully useful for later literary careers (like, perhaps, *Yellow Jacket*, the magazine Constantine FitzGibbon spent most of Michaelmas 1938 editing, with articles in it by Dylan Thomas, Cocteau, De Montherlant, Betjeman and T. F. Powys) but they're usually bad for academic performance (the next term FitzGibbon went down: Middle High German was getting in the way of what he really wanted to do).[72]

By contrast with many young writers' interests, official Oxford looks boring, *passé*, philistine. And often, of course, it *is* philistine. The English faculty's stout resistance to twentieth-century literature, the University's foot-dragging over an honorary DLitt for T. S. Eliot, the voting down of Robert Lowell as Professor of Poetry, the scandalously unresolved question of the Playhouse and a permanent home for serious drama in Oxford, are all witnesses to that. The great missed opportunity to act on the recommendations of the Drama Commission of 1945—with its progressive proposals for theatre- and film-study facilities as well as its plans for a permanent 700-seat auditorium, backed by generous promises of funding from the Board of Trade under Oxonian Harold Wilson—rightly grieved Coghill, who was one of the Commission's members. But this was only one moment in a long sequence of such neglects.[73] The revived plans collapsed again in 1957.[74] The career of the restored Playhouse in Beaumont Street was never financially secure. Frank Hauser, director of the Playhouse Meadow Players Company, used to complain repeatedly and bitterly in the sixties about the habitual neglect by dons and students, even those professionally concerned with literature, of his wide-ranging theatrical menu: he had only 'contempt for Oxford's provincialism and miserable self-satisfaction' that sustained an 'amused, knowing disbelief' in the value of a theatre in Oxford.[75] Some

[71] Brownjohn, 'Preference for poetry', 62.

[72] C. FitzGibbon, *Through the Minefield: An Autobiography* (London 1967), 186 ff.

[73] 'Oxford Drama Commission', *OM* 14 June 1945, 299–300; *Report of the Oxford University Drama Commission with Supplementary Architectural Report by Frederick Gibberd FRIBA, MMTPI* (Oxford 1948); N. Coghill, 'Notes on the report of the OU Drama Commission', *OM* 25 Nov. 1948, 176–83.

[74] H. Carpenter, *OUDS: A Centenary History of the Oxford University Dramatic Society 1885–1985* (Oxford 1985), 179.

[75] F. Hauser, 'The *Oresteia*, the professor and others', *OM* 30 Nov. 1961, 107–8; 'A great white wail', *OM* 21 Jan. 1965, 158.

things hadn't changed, it seems, from when Waugh complained of the lack of 'genuine culture' in Oxford—judging 'by the decoration of my tutor's rooms', the University's backwardness 'in the latest theories of aesthetics and psychology from Berlin and Paris' and 'the heartiest contempt' expressed by great numbers of undergraduates 'for everything to do with Art or intellect'.[76]

No wonder dissatisfactions of some kind animate so many Oxonian texts about Oxford. 'Frustration and ignorance' are the declared subject of James Fenton's poem 'South Parks Road'. His poem 'The Pitt-Rivers Museum, Oxford' sets the tone of its wary fascination with the black magics and other ensnaring attractions that the building houses by opening with the glum reflection that the place 'is shut / 22 hours a day and all day Sunday'. To enter there is to 'Take / Your heart in your hand'.[77] Penelope Lively's story 'At the Pitt-Rivers' in her collection *Nothing Missing but the Samovar* (1978) is a sobering tale of a schoolgirl who becomes wised up about the facts of love in this 'weird . . . really weird . . . depressing' place. Mick Imlah's poetic self climbs to his college room one midnight to find a tramp, 'raggled', 'poisonous', 'horrible', in his bed; the episode is read as an emblem of a future that promises to be haunted by such grim bedfellows.[78] In John Fowles's novel *Daniel Martin* an idyllic summer-term punting expedition up the Cherwell is disrupted for Daniel Martin and his friend Jane by the awful discovery of the corpse, 'greyish-white', of a woman who's been dumped in the river. 'Dull Bodley' haunts Larkin's 'Poem about Oxford': 'the old place hadn't much tone'. 'They were all very kind at Oxford', begins Jennifer Dawson's *The Ha Ha* (1961), a novel about a mentally disturbed Oxford graduate, but this kindness was of an ironically minimal sort. 'No one shunned me or ripped my stockings or took my bicycle on "loan".' This woman made no friends at university. Jennifer Dawson's later novel *Judasland* (1989) is built around the spurious friendliness of Sanctus Spiritus College and the rest of its Oxford kind, or unkind. Lonely women gather at the river in Anne Stevenson's poem 'By the Boat House, Oxford'. In her poem 'Temporarily in Oxford' Stevenson meditates on Oxford's damp but 'educated earth' as a possible burying place for herself.[79] In U. A. Fanthorpe's job-interview poem entitled 'You Will Be Hearing From Us Shortly' her Oxford education proves no asset; it gives her poem blackly comic pause:

> And your accent. That is the way
> You have always spoken, is it? What

[76] E. Waugh, 'Was Oxford worth while?', *Daily Mail* 21 June 1930, repr. in *Essays, Articles and Reviews*, ed. Gallagher, 82–3.

[77] J. Fenton, *Terminal Moraine* (London 1972), 13–15, 17–18.

[78] M. Imlah, 'Goldilocks' in D. Constantine (ed.), *The Poetry Book Society Anthology 1988–1989* (London 1988), 52–5.

[79] A. Stevenson, *Selected Poems 1956–1986* (Oxford 1989), 99, 103.

Of your education? We mean, of course,
Where were you educated?
                                        And how
Much of a handicap is that to you,
Would you say?[80]

But these are all fairly gentle ironizings of a widely felt Oxford plight. Some Oxford texts prefer more venomous ways of working off their dissatisfactions. Julian Barnes's novel *Flaubert's Parrot* lengthily lampoons the one-time pillar and adornment of the modern languages faculty, Dr Enid Starkie, Somerville's Reader in French Literature (she who opposed Robert Lowell). In Barnes's text she's the owner of 'an atrocious French accent' (and so becomes the emblem of Oxford's preference for treating modern languages 'as if they were dead'). She's the pedantic biographer of Flaubert who cavils needlessly at Emma Bovary's 'rainbow eyes' and then (Barnes's scholarly narrator gleefully points out) has a portrait of Louis Bouilhet by mistake for Flaubert as the frontispiece of one of her books.[81] For his part, Evelyn Waugh waged unremitting literary war on his old history tutor C. R. M. F. Cruttwell, who is said to have awaited each new Waugh novel with apprehension lest yet another shady or absurd character should bear his name.[82]

'There was a don at my college', Waugh alleges in his early travel book *Labels* (1930), 'exactly like a prominent murderer'. And Waugh's imagination turned early on to thoughts of murdering a tutor. One of his funniest contributions to *Cherwell* (13 June 1925) is a story entitled 'Edward of unique achievement: a tale of blood and alcohol in an Oxford college', in which Edward, like Waugh a reporter of Union debates, murders his tutor Curtis with a dagger while a debate at the Union is going on. His scout reports finding the corpse: 'dripping blood, sir. Quite slowly, pit-a-pat, as you might say.' Another undergraduate, the drunken Lord Poxe, is blamed for the crime and fined thirteen shillings by the Warden as punishment. 'It was an act of wanton foolishness, Lord Poxe . . . but I do not wish to be hard upon you . . . We hope and trust that it will not occur again'. Thus began Waugh's long career as a satirist and sick-humorist—in a murderous black comedy in an Oxford college. Literary revenges could scarcely come more sweetly, nor the anxiety of deplored influences be expressed more bloodily. And, of course, such violent oedipal resistances are the stock-in-trade of the most characteristic form of Oxonian fiction, the Oxford detective story: the remembered tutorial landscape of the writer's youth is simply strewn with dead dons; presidents' lodgings pullulate with cadavers; Oxford blood is spilled with curiously exuberant passion and freedom.

[80] Fanthorpe, *Selected Poems*, 64.
[81] J. Barnes, *Flaubert's Parrot* (London 1984), ch. 4, 'Emma Bovary's eyes'.
[82] See *Diaries of Evelyn Waugh*, ed. Davie, 153 n. 1.

In his introduction to the reprint of *High Table* (1931), the novel about fluttering breasts in donnish North Oxford by don's daughter Joanna Cannan, Anthony Quinton notes tellingly that Oxford features crucially in many a modern English example of the *Bildungsroman*, the novel of personal development.[83] He mentions Waugh's *Decline and Fall* (1928) and *Brideshead Revisited* (1945) and Anthony Powell's *A Question of Upbringing* (1951). And one could add to this list Larkin's *Jill* (1946), John Wain's *Hurry on Down* (1953), Fowles's *Daniel Martin*, Martin Amis's *The Rachel Papers* (1973), Robertson Davies's *What's Bred in the Bone* (1985). Certain autobiographical long poems such as Auden's *Letter to Lord Byron* and MacNeice's *Autumn Journal* might also be so classed. So, possibly, might Powell's novel *Agents and Patients* (1936). Wain's *Where the Rivers Meet* (1988) certainly should. The first part of a projected trilogy featuring a local Oxford lad who gets into Episcopus College and his brother who has jobs in various Cowley motor works, this is in some ways a deliberately *déclassé* redoing of Powell's *roman-fleuve* with Etonians, *A Dance to the Music of Time*, of which *A Question of Upbringing* is the first volume—Wain rewrites Widmerpool, so to say, as Jude the Obscure. And, noticeably, in these numerous and variously *Bildungsroman*-like texts some kind of oedipal unease or dislike or venom or working out of hostility is a recurrent trope.

Equally noticeable, though, in such fictions is that the angry prodigal sons also have a way of eventually returning home, that rebellious voices get toned down, and hates tend to dissolve into affection, and commonly sooner rather than later. It took some time for Waugh's dewy-eyed upper-class romantic vision of *Brideshead Revisited*—*Et in Arcadia ego* is the title of its first, Oxford section—to displace and make amends for 'Edward' or for *Decline and Fall*'s satirically acerbic treatment of hapless theological student Paul Pennyfeather—debagged by the rioters of the lordly philistine Bollinger Club (they 'tore up Mr. Partridge's sheets, and threw the Matisse into his water-jug'), he's sent down by a stupidly myopic governing body and compelled to continue his rake's progress at the terrible Llanabba School under Dr Augustus Fagan (named for the proprietor of the first Oxford Playhouse located in the former big-game museum opposite Somerville): 'God damn and blast them all to hell'. But some such revisionism occurs in Wain's *Hurry on Down* and Martin Amis's *The Rachel Papers* before these novels are even over.

Wain's Charles Lumley, minor-public-school boy and drop-out window-cleaning graduate, sharply hostile to the respectability Oxford tried to manacle him into, is made unwillingly to visit his old college by a girlfriend. He finds it peopled as ever with boorish undergraduates and

[83] J. Cannan, *High Table* (London 1931, Oxford 1987 edn), introduction, p. vii.

crassly ambitious young dons, but despite himself he responds to 'the breath-taking perfection' of the buildings and the late April beauty of the garden. In *The Rachel Papers* unfazable know-it-all Charles Highway, armed with sixty pages of his own clever-dick entrance interview tips ('Appearance Change Midway: 18. Jacket unbuttoned; if old turd, do up *middle* one on way in'), has his 'pageant-like' entrance exam essays surgically unpicked by an unstoppably tough pseudo-urban-guerrilla of an English don called Knowd. The satirical disrespect for this classic tutorial pomposity and ruthlessness is clearly a kind of Amis revenge for his failure to get into his father's old college of St John's and only to achieve acceptance into Exeter instead. Nevertheless Highway's sheer pleasure at being accepted by Knowd ('I'm going to take you anyway; if I don't somebody else will') is strong and not at all diminished by his professedly contemptuous refusal to be impressed either by his tutor-to-be ('I hawked richly into my handkerchief and studied its contents') or the buildings ('Oxford skylines offered spurious serenity in the form of gold stone against sharp blue, which I of course refused'). *The Rachel Papers* turns out, after all, to be a torrential tribute to the felt imperative of going to Oxford. Just so, Larkin's grousing 'Poem about Oxford' ends up admitting that the old place 'holds us', and Kingsley Amis's *Lucky Jim* reeks with nostalgia for a 'proper' university like Oxford that the Welsh one Jim Dixon is compelled to teach in fails dismally to imitate. What's more, the emotional trajectory of such texts—waylaid at the last by dreaming spires and Arnoldian nostalgias; finally ready with the flushed purple patch in praise of Oxford—imitates the very common authorial career-path, on which thirties rebels and Communists like Auden, Day-Lewis and Spender end up standing for Professor of Poetry, and one-time Angry Young Men like Larkin, Amis and Wain accept honorary fellowships at their old college from the hands of the very people whose 'donnish snivelling' (the phrase is from *Hurry on Down*) they'd once thought worthy only of a derisive jeer.

Feelings, tones, reactions are, then, mixed. And the topos of Oxford that recurs in so much Oxonian writing proves an extraordinarily variable one, tonally, rhetorically, figuratively. *A Learned City* and also 'this stagnant town';[84] harsh nurse and also full of 'all that long patience Oxford represents';[85] an ancient towered paradise 'bounded by rivers' and containing fabulous inhabitants and also a dismaying place where it always rains in Keble Road and 'along the High';[86] loved and hated; derisory and

---

[84] P. T. Toynbee, *A Learned City: The Sixth Day of the Valediction of Pantaloon* (London 1966); A. N. Wilson, *The Healing Art* (London 1980), ch. 4 ('this stagnant town').

[85] J. B. Wain, 'Green Fingers: To Elizabeth Jennings in Oxford' in his *Letters to Five Artists* (London 1969), repr. in his *Poems 1949–1979* (London and Basingstoke 1980), 105.

[86] The fabulous arcadia is the city Jeanette Winterson's northern heroine escapes to at the end of her first novel *Oranges Are Not the Only Fruit* (London 1985). Cf the verses by Dorothy

embraceable; heroically, or terrifyingly, serious and ludicrously silly: in all of its textual guises Oxford proves as variously rewritable as it is variously experienced and remembered. In Larkin's *Jill* John Kemp tries to write out his Oxford impressions for Jill, but finds that writing Oxford is hard. He keeps going wrong, keeps having to start new paragraphs, but he's still challenged by the possibilities, realizing that all textualizing of Oxford will be partial and lopsided. And he's right. No single text tells a complete story. Naturally there is distortion—catachresis—and rearrangement of parts (*bricolage*). Convenient and inconvenient fictions about the place are readily traded. Texts help themselves freely to names and places and recycle them at will as fiction, or fact, or gratuitous mixes of the two. Historians must tread warily when they mine these writings as sources of fact. Waugh's several Cruttwells are all at once Cruttwell of Hertford and not he. The Geoffrey Caston of Jeffrey Archer's *Not a Penny More* both is and is not a respected former Registrar of the University. Barnes's Enid Starkie is and also is not the woman who used in the life to 'barrel' along Walton Street in a French matelot's titfer.

'It would be idle to deny that the City and University of Oxford (*in aeternum floreat*) do actually exist, and contain a number of colleges and other buildings, some of which are mentioned by name in this book': thus the 'author's note' by Dorothy Sayers in her *Gaudy Night*. But, she goes on, 'Shrewsbury College, with its dons, students and scouts, is entirely imaginary', and she offers apologies to the University of Oxford 'for having presented it with a Chancellor and Vice-Chancellor of my own manufacture and with a college of 150 women students, in excess of the limit ordained by statute. Next, and with deep humility, to Balliol College—not only for having saddled it with so wayward an alumnus as Peter Wimsey, but also for my monstrous impertinence in having erected Shrewsbury College upon its spacious and sacred cricket-ground.' Only the professed humility is unusual here. The catachresis and the *bricolage* that are being apologized for are utterly usual in such texts. But catachresis, as all ancient rhetoricians recognized, is the essence of the distortions that texts customarily perform—it's central to the poetic function, even if it can't guarantee the quality of the poetry produced. And *bricolage*—that free spatchcocking of reordered items, familiar to all movie-goers watching a well-known place cut up and put back in unfamiliar order, or, for that matter, to television viewers familiar with Oxford who are compelled to wonder why Inspector Morse drove from Brasenose to the Examination Schools via Walton Street—*bricolage* is, according to structural anthropologists, the essence of the story-telling tactics by which tribal, archaic and other peoples construct

Sayers, 'It's O it's O for Oxford' ('With the rain on Keble Road' and 'With the rain along the High') in C. G. Heilbrun, 'Sayers, Lord Peter, and Harriet Vane at Oxford' in her *Hamlet's Mother and Other Women* (New York 1990), 255.

their belief-systems, codes and myths. Turning Oxford into fiction inevitably involves such distortions. And in this technical sense, if in no other—and of course there are others—Oxonians recycling their various Oxfords in their fictions are indeed manufacturing and purveying myth.

16

Publishing and Bookselling

R. A. DENNISTON

However controversial the impact of twentieth-century British universities on the national economy, Oxford University's impact on the local economy through the booktrade has been substantial. Indeed the twentieth-century successes of Oxford bookselling, printing and publishing have transcended their immediate environment and have added a commercial dimension to Oxford's worldwide academic reputation.[1] Take first the booksellers. Their respected role within the city was symbolized in 1937 when Basil Blackwell presided over a citizens' committee which raised over £5,000 for the University appeal. Blackwell was Oxford's leading bookseller. The firm began as a one-man shop, but during the twentieth century it became world-famous. Harry Blackwell died in 1922 and was succeeded as chairman by his son Basil. Aged 23 when he joined his father in 1913, 'the Gaffer', as he came to be known, remained chairman for forty-five years. Under him bookselling and, later, publishing developed strongly. Promotion within the firm was on merit and from within, while training was by example. Like many booksellers Blackwell was hard hit by the First World War, and thereafter staff numbers rose only modestly—from thirty-two in 1919 to forty-five by 1924. The fifteen years from 1924 to 1939 were not easy for the company. The inter-war depression is reflected in the firm's annual accounts, and slowed down growth for a full five years.[2] But in 1938 the new building in 48–51 Broad Street was completed, and thereafter the Blackwell retailing empire extended inexorably, partly through absorbing other local bookshops.

The firm's success stemmed partly from an alertness to new opportunities that its rivals did not display. Oxford's nineteenth-century preoccupation with religion had nourished several local religious publishers and booksellers—from the Church Army Press in Cowley to the Newman Bookshop in St Aldate's. Leading the field was Mowbray, co-publisher with the

[1] I am grateful to Dr Mark Pottle for much assistance with this chapter, particularly with the maps and statistics.
[2] A. L. P. Norrington, *Blackwell's 1879–1979: The History of a Family Firm* (Oxford 1983), 53, 81.

Oxford University Press (OUP) of *The English Hymnal*. Mowbray's Oxford staff had grown to 111 by 1906, but only diversification could produce substantial growth, and after the First World War Mowbray gradually declined like the church it served, and was sold to Pentos in 1987. There was decline, too, in the non-specialist trade in second-hand books—a decline that is concealed behind the fact that both in 1952 and in 1990 one-third of Oxford's booksellers dealt in second-hand and antiquarian books. The established firms of Parker, Blackwell, Sanders and Thornton all combined selling new books with second-hand. Thornton's in the Broad remained in the family till 1983, when it merged with Holdan Books. For scholarly browsers its many rambling and largely unsupervised rooms opening off two staircases made it a most important port of call—together with Sanders' at 104 High Street, which catered for topographical and antiquarian tastes—but in second-hand books the future lay only with specialization.

Refugees from Europe were quick to perceive this opportunity. The Dolphin Bookshop in Fyfield Road dealt exclusively in Spanish books, while Albi Rosenthal (originally in the Turl but now in Broad Street), a refugee from Hitler, specialized in Spanish and Portuguese literature and Judaica. He reinforced his background in the history of art with musicology, and after adding the London firm of Otto Haas to his Oxford business in 1955 he found time to play a major role in Oxford's musical life.[3] The influx of Jewish refugees fertilized Oxford bookselling in other ways too. At Parker's, Sanders' and Thorntons' several distinguished refugees served customers. In 1939 Wili Brown, who was to run the import department of Parker's—the long-established family bookseller on the corner of the Broad and the Turl—arrived in Oxford after his family had been killed in concentration camps. He and Hans Kale came from the high-German tradition of bookselling, performing a service as valuable to the academic world as the scholarly refugee editors and proofreaders at the Walton Street headquarters of the OUP.

In non-specialist academic bookselling Blackwell's gradually overtook and sometimes digested its less enterprising rivals. After 1937 Parker's was gradually drawn into the Blackwell empire. Handsomely re-housed in the 1960s, it is now Blackwell's art and poster shop. In 1966, in partnership with Trinity College, Blackwell's underground Norrington room was completed; it housed 160,000 volumes on two and a half miles of shelving in 10,000 square feet of well utilized space. Blackwell's children's bookshop opened in 1950, the art bookshop in 1966, the music shop in Holywell in 1970 and the travel shop in 1988. By 1990 there were no less than nine Blackwell's bookshops in Oxford. Blackwell's success stemmed partly from quickly

---

[3] Brian Harrison, interview with Albi and Julia Rosenthal at 9–10 Broad Street, Oxford, 28 May 1991.

appropriating ideas pioneered elsewhere. It was not Blackwell, for instance, but Johns Bookshop in St Michael's Street, that pioneered paperback sales in Oxford in the 1950s. Although the old-style moneyed undergraduate bibliophile was in decline, the mass student market was beginning to open up, and was reinforced later by the growth of the trade in remaindered books, many of which filled the Turl Cash Bookshop (now the Classics Bookshop) in the 1960s and 1970s. Yet Johns did not survive, the Turl Bookshop was incorporated into the Blackwell empire, and Robert Maxwell offered only a brief challenge in 1963 when he set up his substantial but short-lived bookshop on the Plain, complete with coffee shop and cultural facilities.

Supreme within Oxford, Blackwell was in a good position to expand worldwide. In 1960 the firm entered a successful partnership with OUP by establishing a joint venture company—University Bookshops Oxford. This bold enterprise significantly extended the core-business of academic retailing: UBO acquired majority shareholdings in some ten shops in Britain—notably Lears of Cardiff, Willshaws of Manchester, Bissets of Aberdeen, Hartley Seed of Sheffield and Godfrey's of York. The partnership ended in 1983 when Blackwell acquired the OUP's 50 per cent interest in UBO and continued alone. Another major area of growth was the mail-order business, identified by Richard Blackwell in 1949, along with education and export, as a high priority for Blackwell's business plan. By 1974 it accounted for well over half the total business.[4] To cater for the company's growing administrative needs, a purpose-built office block, Beaver House, was constructed near the railway station and opened in 1973.

The overall pattern of change in Oxford bookselling between 1910 and 1990 combines expanded custom with concentration of ownership and dispersed location (see table 16.1 and figure 16.1). Many of Oxford's smaller bookshops were becoming adjuncts of the larger, and mounting pressure on city-centre space was steadily dispersing the booktrade outwards. To that extent there was some dilution between 1914 and 1970 (subsequently reversed) in the wealth of cultural opportunity that bookshops extended to junior and senior members residing in college.

Blackwell played a major role, too, in the twentieth-century growth of Oxford publishing, with which the rest of this chapter will be concerned. Between the wars, however, the OUP was unrivalled in this sphere. The relationship between its printing division, its London business and the Clarendon Press was never clear-cut, and varied with the capabilities and interests of those in charge. Broadly speaking, the Clarendon Press was (and remains) the imprint given to scholarly books. These are individually selected for publication by the senior members of the University who

---

[4] Norrington, 140, 170.

TABLE 16.1

THE OXFORD BOOK TRADE 1910–1990: NUMBERS OF BOOK-SELLING, PRINTING AND PUBLISHING FIRMS AND THEIR LOCATIONS

	firms					locations				
	1910	1930	1952	1970	1990	1910	1930	1952	1970	1990
inner booksellers	20	13	13	11	20	21	18	18	15	26
printers	19	19	18	8	9	21	21	16	8	9
publishers	1	1	7	5	4	1	1	8	5	4
outer booksellers	3	4	7	9	19	3	4	7	12	20
printers	6	8	13	18	25	6	8	14	18	24
publishers	0	0	2	7	41	0	0	2	7	32
total booksellers	23	17	20	20	39	24	22	25	27	46
printers	25	27	31	26	34	27	29	30	26	33
publishers	1	1	9	12	45	1	1	10	12	36

Sources: *Kelly's Directory of Oxford* 1910, 1930, 1952, 1970; *Yellow Pages Oxford* 1990. These sources have their defects of detail, as anyone who studies Walton Street in figures 16.2 and 16.3 will see, but there is no reason to doubt the overall picture that they convey. The city within Folly Bridge, Magdalen Bridge, Hythe Bridge and the St Giles' war memorial is defined as 'inner' and elsewhere as 'outer'. The variously named Blackwell bookselling companies have been counted as a single firm. The change of source at 1990 may have inflated the change since 1970.

become delegates of the Press and take collective responsibility for its finances and for the quality of its products. The London business was allowed—in the hands of such capable publishers as Frowde and Milford—to publish what it liked, so long as its quality was acceptable and so long as it could subsidize the Clarendon Press's scholarly but sometimes unremunerative work. The printing division handled much of the production process for both publishing arms of the OUP, from copy-editing to binding.

As Secretary to the delegates from 1898 till his death in 1919, Charles Cannan ran all the publishing and printing operations, and combined overall responsibility for the OUP's affairs with specific responsibility for the Clarendon Press. With firsts in mods and Greats and a mind equally attuned to scholarly and business problems, he was the ideal chief executive. He found it easy to communicate with dons, and worked well with the delegates. Having won the confidence of the University, he was able to free the OUP from inhibiting controls. Formidable and silent, Cannan was a good delegator who knew how to develop the talents and harness the energies of those around him. This freed Humphrey Milford, who joined the OUP as Assistant Secretary in 1900 and became the London publisher from

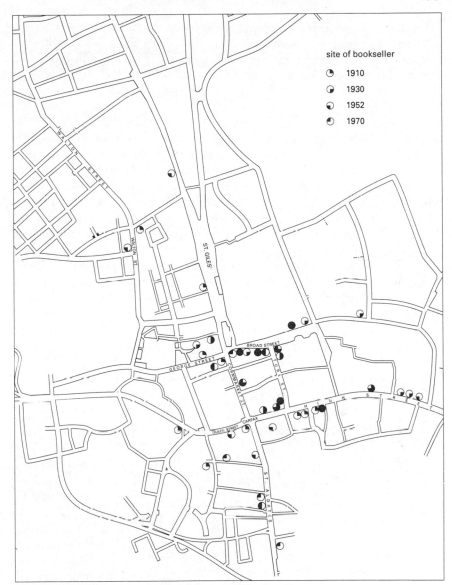

FIGURE 16.1   LOCATION OF BOOKSELLERS IN OXFORD, 1910–1970

1913 to 1946, to exercise his talent for identifying and developing good publishing ideas from whatever source, and to cater for new overseas markets. Milford worked well with Cannan's successor R. W. Chapman (Assistant Secretary from 1906) and they almost coincided in their reigns as, respectively, London publisher and Secretary to the Press. Chapman was a tall, bird-like man who somehow combined distaste for small talk with membership of many dining clubs and societies. With firsts in mods and Greats, he was well known as a Johnsonian scholar and editor of Jane Austen, 'a scholar-publisher who might just as easily have turned professor'.[5]

John Johnson [plate 16.1] who became Assistant Secretary in 1915, was the OUP's Oxford printer from 1925 to 1946; he never learned, and would probably have denied the reality of, managerial skills. With a first in mods and a second in Greats, he spent his early years on Egyptian excavations, married Cannan's daughter Margaret and learned the craft of printing on the job. Although Johnson lacked the direct experience in high-quality printing of his predecessor Horace Hart and of his successors Charles Batey and Vivian Ridler, all four were at one in their commitment to high standards of typography, design and materials—indeed to every aspect of book-printing and binding. 'An exacting man, sometimes difficult, occasionally hard', Johnson built up a unique collection of printed ephemera, sorted by subject, which was transferred to the Bodleian Library in 1968 as a permanent aid to scholarship.[6]

The strategic decisions affecting OUP were made in Oxford but the engines for its growth were in London. The first catalogue, published in 1916, assigned a quarter of its 476 pages to classics and religion, but only a twelfth to the natural sciences and medicine. Yet on science, at least, the OUP was not wildly out of line with national trends: of the 12,067 new books and pamphlets published in Britain in 1912, only 1,853 concerned science, technology or medicine.[7] During the First World War, printing the Bible for the troops became a major priority, together with producing encrypting and decrypting number-books known as 'one-time pads' for the Admiralty's burgeoning cryptographic establishment. The publishing departments also contributed to the war effort. *Why We Are at War: Great Britain's Case* was written during August 1914 by members of the modern history faculty, and was followed by an influential series of Oxford pamphlets—some instructional, some educational, some polemical. Eighty-seven had appeared by September 1915.[8] Ambitious building projects on the Oxford site followed soon after the war: the Nagel Building [plate 16.2] opened in 1921 to house the new bindery, a new Monotype Building opened in 1926 and a new warehouse was built at Neasden in 1929.

    [5] *OM* 19 May 1960, 282–3.
    [6] *OM* 8 Nov. 1956, 88; *Clarendonian* Jan. 1926, 190; June 1968, 198–201; spring-summer 1971, 29–30. For the collection see *Bodleian Library Record* viii (1967–72), 114–15, a reference kindly supplied by Ms Julie Wilson.
    [7] *Publishers' Circular* 4 Jan. 1913, 9.
    [8] Cf above, 15–16.

The OUP's inter-war achievement must be set in overall publishing context. British publishing was then centred mainly on London, where inter-war expectations of fame and fortune in the booktrade were not high. Workers were seriously underpaid, and potential editors and managers of publishing houses were discouraged by their owners' archaic business practices. Most publishing and printing firms were family-run concerns, and precarious in their finances. By contrast the scholar-managers who led the OUP, backed by the University, provided an incorruptible stability, as well as a steady flow of important work.[9] Publishing was seen as a profession suitable for only a handful of graduates in the humanities, and the many principals of the OUP who had read Greats reckoned no problem insoluble, given careful study and intelligent application. Scholar-editors continued to provide the backbone of the OUP's publishing, and indeed still do. A steady supply of such people—Cannan, Chapman, Milford, Johnson, Kenneth Sisam, Arthur Norrington, Charles Williams, Gerard Hopkins, Dan Davin—enabled the OUP to prosper at all levels, from the editing of texts to stock-control and annual accounting.

Between the wars the OUP built out effectively from its earlier strengths in religious publishing, supplementing its bibles and prayer-books with many successful liturgical and devotional publications. But it did not neglect the growing twentieth-century demand for educational literature at every level. Its learned journals catered for scholarship, and when three of Cannan's daughters came to do their voluntary war work in Walton Street, one was put in charge of the *Quarterly Journal of Medicine* and another ran the *Journal of Theological Studies*. The OUP took over Crockford's *Clerical Directory* in 1921 and *Notes and Queries* in 1939. Frowde's acquisition of the World's Classics from Grant Richards enabled Cannan and Milford to provide a wide selection of English classics for an eager public at a low price, in a market that demanded small-format cheap books. Good schoolbooks were needed at all levels, and teenage fiction with an improving tone (often given as a reward in Sunday school) sold not only in Britain but throughout the empire, especially in Africa. In London the primary-education list prospered, with Oxford continuing its somewhat haphazard programme for secondary schools. The most important inter-war development, publishing in overseas education, was in the capable hands of E. C. Parnwell, who travelled to the ends of the earth selling books and commissioning school texts, children's stories and reference books for local use, as well as writing or compiling them himself.

Publishing growth came largely from the shrewd intuitive moves of Humphrey Milford. In him the OUP had a great publisher. While the

---

[9] For an informative account of how the trade operated at the time see S. Unwin, *The Truth about Publishing* (London 1926).

editors of the Clarendon Press produced fine works of scholarship, Milford found or invented (often in partnership or by acquisition) books and series in all fields and at all levels. Such a strategy produced a shapely and appropriate growth, though in the difficult years after 1945 it needed trimming, concentrating and ordering. Milford's predecessor Frowde acquired the sixty-six volumes of the World's Classics shortly before the launching in 1906 of Dent's Everyman's Library, edited by Ernest Rhys. Milford developed the series, and by 1916 his own contribution, *Homage to Shakespeare*, had been translated into nine languages. Oxford's editorial processes were less high-minded and consistent than Dent's, and reflected the reading habits of Cannan, Milford and their successors. It was, for instance, Milford's love of Trollope which gave the World's Classics a substantial proportion of Trollope's novels which other publishers of classics then or since have failed to dislodge. It was Milford too who in 1941 acquired from Thornton Butterworth the Home University Library, reborn in 1966 as the present OPUS series of paperbacks.[10] These two series, with similar but less wide-ranging lists of classics from Nelson and Collins, led many new readers into English and other literature.

In academic publishing a major inter-war venture was *The Oxford History of England*, authorized in 1929. Its editor, G. N. Clark, commissioned the contributors, who all attended an editorial conference in 1931 to settle problems of overlap. When completed in 1965 the series brought great credit and profit to the OUP and deeply influenced the teaching of English history. In the 1920s the OUP was one of the leading publishers of works on Roman law, legal history and international law, but limited headway was made in this area between the wars. In co-operation with Hodder & Stoughton, Milford launched a medical list, much helped in Oxford by Sir William Osler, who edited *A System of Medicine* in seven volumes. A series of medical manuals began to appear, and Cunningham's *Textbook* and *Manual of Anatomy* were acquired by the joint purchase of a specialist medical list. Another Osler scheme was *The Oxford Loose-Leaf Medicine* which was published in 1920 by the New York branch; the venture lasted until 1923 when Hodders sold out to their partner. The OUP's medical programme prospered and was eventually linked to the science list in Oxford.

Even more impressive was the sudden growth, from a few items in the bible department, of music. This began in 1923 when Milford selected Hubert Foss to develop all aspects of music for the OUP. It was an inspired choice. Foss's main work with the OUP was twofold: to find and befriend all the leading British composers and edit, promote and publish their work in sheet form; and to publish books on music at all levels. He succeeded in both

---

[10] *The Periodical* autumn 1966, 310.

these endeavours. He completely dominated the field of English music, becoming the friend and publisher of many notable composers, including Ralph Vaughan Williams and William Walton (once a choral scholar and chorister at Christ Church). Of his general music publishing, his most conspicuous success was Percy Scholes's *The Oxford Companion to Music* (1938), still in steady demand despite being replaced in 1984 by Denis Arnold's *New Oxford Companion to Music*. Foss's was an astonishing achievement, yet for many years the department 'spent' (or lost) considerable sums. The Oxford principals remained bemused, perhaps nettled, by Foss's activities. There was little evidence of control, and much of the publishing was inspirational and intuitive—the backing of one man's commitment. Nevertheless the result was a list in almost all aspects of music which put OUP in the forefront of British music publishers.

Immense as Milford's contribution was, two of OUP's grandest inter-war undertakings were not his brainchild: *The Dictionary of National Biography* and *The Oxford English Dictionary*. The University was presented with the *DNB* in 1917 by the family of its founder, George Smith. Chapman suspected it might be the sort of gift that OUP could do without, since keeping the multi-volume series in print was potentially as demanding as bringing out its decennial supplements. The initial aim was to correct and update the printed volumes, but until the 1990s this seemed too expensive. The computer age came to the aid of *The Oxford English Dictionary* rather earlier [plate 16.3]. In the *OED*'s early days and before the scale of the task was fully apparent, the OUP's relations with its compilers were poor.[11] But Cannan provided the right staff and support and enabled publication to take place. In 1928, seventy years after the first decisions were taken, the last part appeared. A supplement with an introduction and bibliography appeared in 1933, and between 1972 and 1983 the major four-volume supplement was published. The triumphal declaration made by Professor George Gordon in a radio broadcast in 1928 still stands: 'it is a dictionary not merely of modern English, but of *all* English . . . the English of Chaucer, of Spenser, of Shakespeare, of the Bible, of all our writers for twelve centuries past, is revealed there.'.[12] The *OED* became the flagship of Press and University and made 'Oxford' a household word. A whole family of lucrative and well known Oxford reference books and dictionaries grew directly or indirectly out of these two projects, including *The Oxford Companion to English Literature* (1932), *The Oxford Dictionary of Quotations* (1941) and the *Oxford History of English Literature* (1945 onward). Attaching the word 'Oxford' to a series goes at least as far back as the 1820s, but in the hands of

[11] K. M. E. Murray, *Caught in the Web of Words: James A. H. Murray and the Oxford English Dictionary* (New Haven Conn. and London 1977), 215–31, 239, 252–3, 256, 261, 267–71, 283.
[12] *The Periodical* Oct. 1928, 144; I am indebted to Edmund Weiner for this reference.

16.4 'SPROD' ON THE OXFORD ENGLISH DICTIONARIES, *PUNCH* 17 AUG. 1949

the OUP the idea took on new and most profitable dimensions during the twentieth century [plate 16.4].

Publishing networks have radiated out from Oxford throughout the twentieth century, nowhere more so than with Faber, a partnership between two fellows of All Souls, Sir Geoffrey Faber (Bursar from 1923 to 1951) and Maurice Gwyer. The choice of T. S. Eliot as the firm's literary adviser was made with Charles Whibley over dinner at the College.[13] Even within Oxford, publishing between the wars was beginning to diversify beyond the OUP. Blackwell's publishing grew only modestly, and bookselling (particularly for export) remained dominant. But from 1921 onward the firm's Shakespeare Head Press produced elegant editions of classics, and Blackwell became a significant publisher when he turned to education after an exploratory visit to Eton. There he secured what turned out to be a series of lasting and long-selling history textbooks—Marten and Carter's histories. E. N. d'A. C. Andrade and Julian Huxley's *Introduction to Science* followed, and attempts were made in the 1930s to broaden the textbook range towards higher education.

The Second World War extended Oxford's links with London publishers, notably in the case of the Phaidon Press, whose creation of illustrated art books for a popular readership did not preclude lavish design. In 1938 Dr Béla Horovitz arrived in Oxford, fleeing his native Austria after the German invasion. He had founded his press, named in honour of the speaker in the Socratic dialogue on immortality, in Vienna in 1923. His early publications were all in German and were notable for superb design. The first art book appeared in 1937—W. Ehde's *Van Gogh*, still in print when the firm celebrated its diamond jubilee in 1983. In Oxford the refugee publisher was notably helped by Sir Stanley Unwin, and Phaidon remained in the city till 1946. After Horovitz's death in 1955 the company was sold to a subsidiary of Encyclopaedia Britannica, and later to the Dutch conglomerate Elsevier; it returned to Oxford when Elsevier themselves established a publishing branch there.

The OUP's links with refugee scholars were not always lucrative. Rockefeller funds had enabled it to employ about twenty refugee scholars throughout the Second World War.[14] It offered its printing and editing resources to several distinguished German academics, including Paul Jacobstahl (1880–1957), Fritz Pringsheim (1882–1967), Richard Walzer (1900–75), Stefan Weinstock (1901–71), Egon Wellesz (1885–1974) and Felix Jacoby (1876–1959); Paul Maas (1880–1964) was actually employed by the OUP as an adviser.[15] Of the refugees' vast learning and cultural distinction there was no doubt; but it was difficult to satisfy their expectations. Some who later became famous went elsewhere for their publishers. Blackwell published Wittgenstein's posthumous works, while Cambridge published many of the continental scientists. Some moved on to American campuses and many looked to continental or American publishers—though the Clarendon Press attracted the German classicists. During the Second World

[13] E. T. Williams and C. S. Nicholls (eds), *The Dictionary of National Biography 1961–70* (Oxford 1981), 341.
[14] P. H. Sutcliffe, *The Oxford University Press: an informal history* (Oxford 1978), 258–61.
[15] Information from Professor Sir Hugh Lloyd-Jones.

War government contracts enabled many printers to survive, and at OUP, as in 1914, the production of one-time pads for the needs of Bletchley Park kept machines running and machinemen in employment.[16]

The war saw the advent of paper-rationing and hence of shortened print-runs. This had some advantages, especially for the newer and smaller firms, because publishers were able to sell all that they decided to produce. After 1945 small new London firms were able to move fast and flexibly. Publishers like Collins, Heinemann, Longman, Hodder & Stoughton, and Macmillan dominated the trade, but smaller firms, normally the creation of one man, had become a feature of the later 1930s—Jonathan Cape, Hamish Hamilton, Allen & Unwin, Gollancz and especially Faber. Such businesses became market-leaders after 1945 and developed a healthy two-way traffic with their American counterparts. The OUP, by contrast, laboured to honour its distinctive ancestral commitments while pursuing a timid post-war pricing policy. Readers of Isis and the Oxford Magazine could not understand why it failed to reprint much-needed textbooks. 'Mr. Blackwell is fast becoming unofficial Printer to the University', said the Magazine, delighted when he reprinted three political texts that the University needed in a hurry.[17] It was a difficult time for the OUP, when stocks were depleted, skilled craftsmen in short supply, re-equipment an urgent necessity and undergraduate numbers mounting fast. But Charles Batey, John Johnson's successor as printer, set about improving the situation with some energy. The old-style paternalism had for some time been giving way to more formal negotiating procedures throughout British industry, and in 1948 Batey set up a joint works council to promote regular consultation between management and employees.[18] In the following year he set off for the United States to study American printing techniques, and was impressed with what he saw.[19]

In some respects the OUP was slipping behind at this time on the publishing side. Whereas London publishers commissioned work from a new generation of scholars in the humanities and the burgeoning social sciences, the Clarendon Press did not approach potential authors—a policy which by the 1950s was being vociferously criticized by some dons. After 1945 it decided not to aim for the expanding market in law publishing, which fell into the hands of Stevens, Sweet & Maxwell, and Butterworth. The delegates felt that the Press's law publishing should be concentrated mainly on jurisprudence. In 1961, however, Herbert Hart published his Concept of Law and later as a delegate edited the Clarendon Law Series in which several valuable books appeared; the law list which flourished in the 1980s therefore

---

[16] A. Hodges, Alan Turing: The Enigma of Intelligence (London 1983), 162, 164.
[17] OM 17 Oct. 1946, 10. See also OM 7 Feb. 1946, 162–3; 28 Feb. 1946, 209; 21 Nov. 1946, 99–100; Isis 6 Nov. 1946, 5.
[18] Clarendonian Mar. 1948, 3; June 1949, 60–1; Sept. 1958, 200.
[19] Ibid. Sept. 1949, 90; Mar. 1950, 11.

dates only from the 1960s. With scientific publications, too, the OUP lagged behind. Its somewhat demure publicity organ, *The Periodical*, replete with long extracts from recent literary publications, reflects (to quote a later critic) the flavour of 'a classical and literary publishing house' yet it survived from 1896 till the late 1970s.[20] The OUP was slow to include journals among its mainstream activities, and its disparate journal-lists were properly integrated into publishing programmes only in the 1980s.

Contrast Pergamon Press, the scientific publishers bought and re-named by Robert Maxwell in 1951. This thrusting firm prospered through acting as intermediary at two levels: between scholars in east and west, and between the scientist eager to get his work published quickly and his colleagues who were eager to read it. Pergamon moved to Oxford in 1960, by which time it was publishing significant works of reference and forty scientific journals, fourteen of which were translations from Russian.[21] Blackwell's journal-lists were also growing, but more slowly. Most of these emanated from Blackwell Scientific Publications, an offshoot launched in 1939 and run by Per Saugman, a Dane who had settled in Oxford. Saugman became the outstanding medical publisher of the post-war period, and in the 1950s under his guidance BSP became an important scientific, technical and medical publisher. Its first scientific periodical, the *British Journal of Haematology*, appeared in 1955, and was joined by more than fifty others during the next quarter-century.[22] It also developed an impressive list of postgraduate texts and monographs.

The fortunes of publishing houses are largely determined by their owners' individuality, ambition, energy and luck, and of no firms was this more true than of Pergamon and Blackwell. Robert Maxwell was becoming a major force in the communications industry. By 1970 Pergamon was publishing over 150 journals and had more than 3,000 titles in print. After some well publicized difficulties Maxwell bought his firm back from Leasco in 1974 and revitalized it, so that by 1977 it was employing 600 people in Oxford and producing 240 journals and 250 books a year. Maxwell's career subsequently brought him international notoriety, which was not ended by his mysterious death in 1991. This left a legacy of debt running into billions, even after the sale of the jewel in his crown, the Oxford-based Pergamon Press, to Elsevier. To both Pergamon and BSP, journals and books were of equal importance, the former providing positive cashflow in the form of advance subscriptions, the latter yielding steadily increasing, profitable and stable revenues for a world market hungry for up-to-date and accurate scientific

---

[20] [Sir Humphrey Waldock, chairman] *Report of the Committee on the University Press* (University of Oxford 1970), 55.
[21] For a very different view of Pergamon's scientific achievement see the letter from M. R. Hoare, *Independent* 18 Nov. 1992, 22.
[22] Norrington, *Blackwell's*, 166.

information. Both Pergamon and Blackwell profited by the interaction of their staff with journal editors, whereas in the 1950s and 1960s the OUP was less alert to the scientific community's needs. Cambridge University Press, whose structure was more centralized and compact, was quicker off the mark. So too was Blackwell, whose turnover between 1946 and 1979 rose from £165,000 to £27,000,000 in a steady post-war development that is closely identified with Richard, the Gaffer's elder son.[23] He correctly identified three important areas of development: export, mail-order and education. By the mid–1970s Basil Blackwell had become international academic publishers in the social sciences and humanities.

Meanwhile the OUP's achievement involved building upon existing strength, so that by the 1960s its profitable marriage of scholarship with accessibility had become a hallmark. In 1967–8 60 per cent of the Clarendon Press's profit came from reference books.[24] The Oxford Atlas (1951) and Concise Oxford Atlas (1952) conquered new territory, and the success of the Oxford histories was followed up after 1947 with volumes in the Oxford History of Modern Europe. 1965 saw a revision of Paul Harvey's Oxford Companion to English Literature, and 1972 saw the first of the OED supplements. In 1970 the OUP's London music department was the second-largest music publisher in the United Kingdom, and one of only two firms in the country publishing sheet music.[25] Particularly notable was The New English Bible, a collaborative venture with the Cambridge University Press, completed in 1970 after twenty years' gestation. C. H. Dodd, the translation's director, noted the need for a new version of the Bible which spoke to people of today in the language of today. The New Testament's in-house editor Geoffrey Hunt worked closely with his opposite number in Cambridge, and ordered a combined print-run of a million copies when it was published in 1961. It was a fine achievement, both for the scholars who re-translated the original texts and for the university presses which responded to the public's apparently insatiable demand for the product. Other translations have come and prospered, but The New English Bible, revised and republished as The Revised English Bible in 1989, filled a recognized gap with authority and confidence.

By now OUP had built up a fine worldwide network of branches: New York in 1896, Canada in 1904, Australia in 1908, India in 1912, South Africa in 1915, and after 1945 in Pakistan, Africa and the Far East. The branches did not confine themselves to distributing books from the British list, but developed lists of their own.[26] Particularly valuable were the repatriated profits from locally produced schoolbooks. A long-standing joint venture

[23] Norrington, Blackwell's, 139.
[24] Report on the University Press, 82.
[25] Ibid. 62.
[26] Ibid. 20, 88. Clarendonian Mar. 1951, 7 is informative on the New York branch.

with Hodders, whereby popular children's 'rewards' such as Gunby Hadath's school stories circulated widely at low prices through Britain and the empire, came to an end in 1952. In that year OUP decided to go it alone and back the new concept of 'quality' children's publishing initiated by John Bell. Children's books were becoming increasingly important in London publishing, and by 1969 a third of the OUP's titles in print consisted of school books.[27] The OUP regularly won the Carnegie medal for the most distinguished children's book of the year—in 1965 for the ninth time in fourteen years.

There was significant OUP achievement too in paperback publishing. The case for it had been discussed in 1954 but was pronounced 'unsound from the economic standpoint'. By 1959, however, authors and publishers were pressing for a change in policy, if only in response to the mounting student population. Better Books of Charing Cross Road were by then importing American paperbacks on a large scale, and according to an internal OUP memorandum 'Johns of Oxford now devotes nearly half his paper-back room to various U.S. series and reports that sales have gone up considerably in the last year', so that 'if we want to be in on the ground floor of quality paper-back publishing in this country we must act soon'.[28] The first six OUP paperbacks came out in autumn 1960 and within five years one hundred titles had been published.

In response to these developments both printing and publishing expanded on the Walton Street site. Large additions to the Oxford premises were begun in 1966 to accommodate the expanded litho and bindery departments. Comparison of the ground plans of 1913 and 1968 shows the editorial departments gradually spreading out from the Walton Street side of the front quadrangle down the Clarendon Street side. Yet the printing and manufacturing departments still occupied the other two sides, together with the massive factory-like extensions of the 1920s and the 1960s towards the west and south. By 1967 the printing business and the Wolvercote paper-mill were each contributing one-eighth of the turnover of the OUP (including its London business and overseas branches).[29] By then the printing department was employing about 930 people, and in the twenty years from 1949 to 1968 contributed 17 per cent of the OUP's pre-tax profits.[30] There was as yet no hint that twenty years hence the OUP would have to take a decision 'melancholy . . . for all concerned' to close down its main printing operations.[31]

[27] Report on the University Press, 51.
[28] OUP archives, file labelled 'Oxford paperback misc pkt 193', carbon copy of anonymous typescript memo headed 'Notes on paper back publishing', dated 19 Oct. 1954, and memo by A. T. G. P[ocock] dated 1 Apr. 1959 headed 'Sales of quality paper-backs'.
[29] Report on the University Press, 79.
[30] Ibid. 93, 183–4.
[31] Letter from the OUP's chief executive, Sir Roger Elliott, Times 2 Mar. 1989, 17.

Yet despite all these signs of growth, the OUP's efficiency was being called into question. The problem was partly structural, stemming from the division of labour between London and Oxford. In the twenty years from 1949 to 1968 the Oxford-based Clarendon Press accounted for an eighth of the OUP's total turnover (including printing and overseas books) and the London business nearly half.[32] Yet there was little logic to the bifurcation. Whereas the London business published much that was distinguished and sometimes unprofitable, the Clarendon Press was as ready to publish profitable items as to embark on scholarly ventures requiring cross-subsidy. Nor could OUP readily meet the growing need for specialization—under supervisory editors who could produce textbooks for students, for example, or create series in science, technology and the social sciences.

This complex situation was addressed by the Waldock Committee, which grew out of the Franks report and was appointed in 1967. The OUP could hardly escape the general zest for opening up established institutions to public scrutiny during the 1960s. Council could find few references to the Press in the University's central records, and the OUP's annual reports to Congregation in the 1960s consisted of little more than a list of titles published.[33] Waldock investigated the OUP's function, organization, operation and relationship to the University, and the report (published in 1970) aimed partly to reassure the OUP's University critics. It thought it 'essential to . . . bring the affairs of the Press . . . more openly before the University as a whole', and so condemned 'the undue reticence—not to say secrecy—which has characterized the conduct of the Press's affairs'.[34] It thought greater publicity for OUP matters 'in the best interests of the Press itself, no less than of the University' and saw it as 'a desirable goal' to give every member of the editorial staff a footing in a college, either as a fellow or as a member of the senior common room.[35]

Waldock thought the OUP's subsidies to the University (donations to University appeals, gifts of books, free publishing facilities) 'comparatively modest in relation to the size of its annual profits', but believed that any move towards increasing them must await re-equipment and increased profits.[36] The committee described the OUP's workings with admirable clarity, and provided valuable statistics, yet its conclusions lacked bite. Entrenched attitudes within the OUP seem to have muted recommendations for change. The report noted the unsatisfactory division between academic editorial staff in Oxford and marketing staff in London, for instance. But it worried about the risk to the morale of London employees if publishing

[32] *Report on the University Press*, 183–4.
[33] Ibid. 11, 119.
[34] Ibid. 121, 137, cf 18.
[35] Ibid. 14, 161.
[36] Ibid. 110, 115.

were centralized in Oxford, and feared weakening the OUP's contacts with the London publishing world, and so did not advocate giving up the London base. It recommended changes to editorial attitudes at the Clarendon Press, and noted that the sales value of all OUP science books in 1967 amounted to 'barely half' that of children's books.[37] Yet it did not recommend a strategic business plan which would weigh conflicting priorities and survey both existing initiatives and future possibilities. These could have included enhancing and integrating the journals list in Oxford, particularly within the sciences, better focused academic marketing, and more flexible arrangements for American publication. This might have entailed more centralization, but it would have given the centre more control over the periphery, so that the OUP could have moved more confidently into all central areas of contemporary academic publishing.

Some of the Waldock recommendations were adopted: more science editors were recruited and more monographs were published. By this time, though, the OUP faced stiff competition from Cambridge University Press as well as from several American and London firms. Cambridge University Press created and maintained new academic series in all the social sciences and humanities. Furthermore Pergamon, Elsevier and Academic Press were outstripping OUP in the volume of academic science published, while Penguin and Routledge catered effectively for students in the social sciences. Investment in the paper-mill at Wolvercote or even the retailing partnership with Blackwell arguably reflected neither the true aims of the Clarendon Press nor the less specific objectives of the London business. What was missing was a clear concentration on priorities: the acquisition and marketing of first-rate academic books and journals.

The place of publication now ceased to be important (if it ever had been); Harmondsworth, Minneapolis or Berkeley provided what was needed. Academic excellence seemed less concentrated on Oxford and Cambridge. Authors were more likely to be abroad than in Britain. North America accounted for over half of total sales; rising demand for academic work in English was to be found in Japan and western Europe, while the demand continued in Australia, the Far East and South Africa; Britain absorbed only about a third of the print-run. There was a mismatch between the location of the principal markets for academic books and journals and the OUP's established areas of strength—particularly in overseas education. Those in charge at Walton Street acted as house editors for particular authors, volumes or even series, and sometimes wrote or edited for publication themselves. This was admirable, but events elsewhere—at Westminster, in Europe, and above all in New York and Washington—were discovered only at second hand and were interpreted only reactively and perhaps somewhat

[37] Report on the University Press, 55.

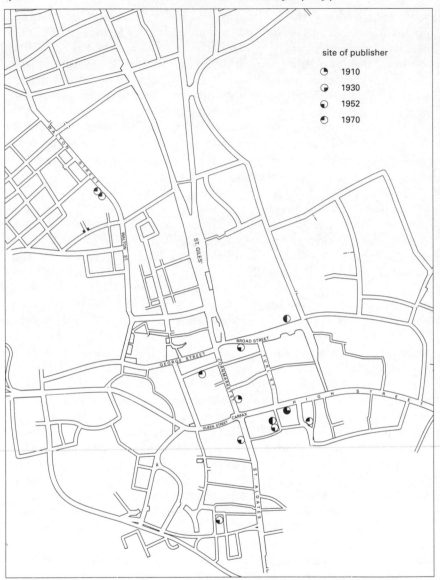

FIGURE 16.2   LOCATION OF PUBLISHERS IN OXFORD, 1910–1970

dismissively. It was now, in other words, more important that Oxford was less than an hour's drive from Heathrow than that Walton Street was within a few minutes' walk of St John's and Balliol. Yet OUP did not even make the most of this advantage, whereas editors from Faber, Routledge, Weidenfeld, Harvester and Macmillan made regular sweeps through Oxford senior

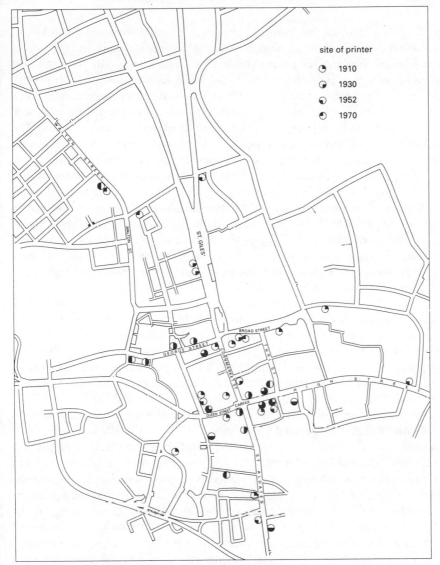

FIGURE 16.3   LOCATION OF PRINTERS IN OXFORD, 1919–1970

common rooms and rarely came away from a college dinner without a new author. It is against this background that the OUP's difficulties of the 1970s must be seen. As its chief executive from 1974 to 1988 later recalled, 'the experience . . . was traumatic; my early years were spent in what I think is called crisis management'.[38]

[38] George Richardson, *OM* Michaelmas 1988, no. 8, 10.

To sum up, for all their missed opportunities and misjudgements, Oxford publishers have mounted impressively in number since the 1940s—an entirely suburban development [table 16.1, figure 16.2]. In 1910 the city housed only two publishers, OUP and Hills & Saunders of Cornmarket Street; by 1970 there were twelve, two of them Blackwell operations. Since 1970 their number has been expanded further by the computer's explosive impact upon a city with a high concentration of authors and scholars. The suburban trend was still more marked in printing [figure 16.3]. Although between 1910 and 1970 there was a dramatic fall in the number of city-centre printing firms—from nineteen to eight—there was an equally dramatic rise in their number elsewhere in Oxford: from six to eighteen, and the trend continues. The move in part reflects the search for cheaper and improved off-centre premises (E. W. Morris, Alden & Co., and Seacourt Press). But it also reflects the demise of long-established firms (Slatter & Rose, Vincent Joseph, Phipps & Co., William E. Bridge) and the emergence of new enterprises off the Cowley and Botley roads (Classic Press, Nuffield Press, Parchment & Co., S & S Press).[39]

Oxford's twentieth-century publishing history is a story of the pursuit of success under difficulties. Just when the great movement for universal education had produced its first generation of readers, the First World War intervened. No sooner had recovery taken place than the inter-war depression hit a whole generation of potential book-buyers and bankrupted many booksellers. Recovery was hardly on the way when the Germans invaded Poland. After 1945 the OUP left to others the exploitation of scientific information-processing, particularly in nuclear physics. Others (notably Penguin) pioneered paperbacks. Still, the OUP's achievement in reference works was impressive, and the number of new OUP titles doubled between 1950 and 1970—from 810 a year to 1,624. Staff numbers rose from 1,776 to 2,905, with a significant proportion employed in the printing works. And in English literature the OUP rendered exemplary service with its critical editions of a dozen great authors and poets, its nurturing of the World's Classics through periods of doubt and difficulty, its editions of letters and its Oxford Standard Authors. So by 1970—taking all Oxford's publishers, printers and booksellers into account—the city had built up a worldwide reputation as a centre for the booktrade in its many dimensions.

[39] *Kelly's Directory of Oxford* 1910, 1930, 1952, 1970; *Yellow Pages Oxford* 1990.

17

Libraries

GILES BARBER

E. W. B. Nicholson, Bodley's Librarian from 1882 to 1912 and the thirteenth holder of that office, died on 18 February 1912, less than a week after his ill health had forced Congregation to release him from duty.[1] His dying words are reputed to have been 'don't let them break up the Bodleian', an expression of a fear which may strike later observers as unfounded and indeed incomprehensible. The late nineteenth century had seen a phenomenal growth in the Library's collections, the stock of printed books rising from some 240,000 around the middle of the century to about a million in 1914, while the number of readers had risen from a very lowly figure to some 275 a day in what had become the principal undergraduate reading room, the Radcliffe Camera, alone. Nicholson had faced these problems with selfless and untiring energy, but he was also both meticulous and difficult. The Library progressively took over the ground floor of the Schools' quadrangle, the basement of the Sheldonian Theatre and those of the old Ashmolean Museum and the new Examination Schools. The desk space available in the Radcliffe Camera was increased and part of the picture gallery in the Old Library was opened up as a reading room in 1907. Provision was made for easier access to palaeographic works, for full-scale catalogues of manuscripts and for more and better reference shelves. The opening hours were increased in the Camera, although those of the Old Library could not be altered until the introduction of electric light in 1929. The high cost of processing copyright intake dominated the Library at the expense of the purchase of foreign scholarly works, and spending on binding was erratic. Bad relations with the curators hardly helped to improve the Library's poor financial position. Space was clearly the major preoccupation. Nicholson was a man largely incapable of delegation and feared any reorganization based on the diffusion of books to autonomous sections. The

[1] This chapter draws heavily on H. H. E. Craster's admirable *History of the Bodleian Library 1845–1945* (Oxford 1952) and on P. Morgan, *Oxford Libraries outside the Bodleian* (Oxford 1973, 2nd edn Oxford 1980). I am also deeply indebted for advice to Miss G. M. Briggs and to Messrs J. B. Bamborough, S. Gillam, P. Morgan, R. J. Roberts and D. G. Vaisey (Bodley's Librarian).

underground bookstore in Radcliffe Square, opened just after his death, was seen as a long-term solution on a central site. As ever, these expectations proved to be over-optimistic.

The Bodleian Library's facilities had to be those of a treasure-house and, increasingly, of a copyright library, both serving principally the academic staff of the University and a number of visitors. In 1914 undergraduates acquired their own books, used the Taylorian, Codrington and Union libraries, and were increasingly allowed to use (and were catered for by) the libraries of their colleges. A few other libraries were also available to them, but in general it was thought necessary for the University itself to provide only the Camera. The slow rise in the number of undergraduates through the 1920s and 1930s and the escalation in the decade following the Second World War (1958 doubling the figure for 1923) coupled with the post-war boom in both postgraduate studies and that specialized and expensive field, science, were to force the University radically to alter its approach. Changing circumstances were met by adaptation and piecemeal development rather than by firm central control. The Bodleian Library therefore remained the major library in the University but it was neither the sole University library nor the official centre of an organized system.

Nicholson was succeeded as Bodley's Librarian by his senior sub-librarian, Falconer Madan (1851–1935). Known through his bibliography of *Oxford Books* (published in three volumes at Oxford in 1895, 1912 and 1931) and as the historian of local printing, Madan was also a book-collector specializing in the seventeenth century. His period of office, due to end in 1915, was extended to cover the First World War. The war claimed the lives of two of the forty-one serving members of the Library's staff but left the institution otherwise untouched and indeed able to express its patriotism by a special exhibition marking the tercentenary of Shakespeare's death.[2]

In 1919 the senior sub-librarian, Arthur Ernest Cowley (1861–1931), was appointed Bodley's Librarian, a post he held, with extension, until 1931. Cowley was an eminent Hebraist, having been appointed assistant to Adolf Neubauer, the ageing Hebraist sub-librarian, in 1895; *in extremis* Cowley was knighted, the first Oxford librarian to be so honoured. His period of office saw the future of the Bodleian Library placed very much in the centre of the Oxford stage, and the lively debates in which he naturally took a leading part were directly responsible for the main lines of the Library's development in the later twentieth century.

Cowley's initial vision for the Bodleian Library was that it should be of a decentralized nature which, although the idea had been broached as far back as 1877, would indeed have horrified Nicholson. In 1921 Cowley wrote: 'I see the Bodleian of the future as a great central library, with a number of

---

[2] 'Notes and news', *Bodleian Quarterly Record* ii (1917–19), 210.

special libraries as departments of it, housed in buildings adjacent to it but not necessarily all in the same building. Each special library should be under the charge of an expert in the subject, and the whole should be controlled by the central librarian.'³ The curators approved this policy and the first step towards it and a rationalization of provision by the University came in 1924, after the death of the Radcliffe Librarian. In 1927 an order in Chancery placed the Radcliffe Library under Bodleian management; the final stage in this development came with the completion of the extension of the renamed Radcliffe Science Library in 1934. One relic of the earlier system was the privilege, introduced in the days when the Library was in the University Museum, that its staff, then virtually the only scientific staff in the University, could take books from the Library to their departments. This was firmly maintained and is the only significant exception to the Bodleian Library's immemorial non-lending rule.

This first annexation was rapidly followed in 1927 by that of the library of the Indian Institute, so that when Rhodes House was established it was agreed that the library there would also be a 'dependent' library of the Bodleian Library, specializing in certain aspects of the history of the English-speaking British dominions and colonies, of the United States and of Africa. The library opened in 1929. This policy should logically have been extended to the library of the Taylor Institution—all the more so as from the foundation in 1845 of the Taylorian the Bodleian Library had largely withdrawn from the field of modern European literature. The Taylorian library too was overcrowded immediately after the war; moreover the study of modern languages was developing fast. However, the University had acquired adjacent land for potential development and a spirited campaign to extend the fine old building rather than move to a new one was spearheaded by the redoubtable and eccentric Professor Joseph Wright, compiler of *The English Dialect Dictionary*, and Sir Charles Firth, the Regius Professor of Modern History, whose chair had originally been responsible for the teaching of European languages. Firth's slim volume *Modern Languages at Oxford* (1928) is in fact a plea to members of Congregation to vote the site in St Giles' to modern languages rather than to the Ashmolean Museum. This was eventually achieved and the then Prince of Wales opened the extension, under the eye of his old tutor, the Professor of German, in 1932. The activity generated around the Taylorian library during this campaign may have been enough to guarantee its continued independence.

Despite these moves and the transfer to the Ashmolean Museum of certain non-book materials such as the prints in the Douce, Hope and Gibbs collections (the proposed transfer of the coins and Egyptian ostraca caused battles and was delayed) the major Bodleian problem was still one of space.

³ Craster, 251.

The bookstore in Radcliffe Square had been expected to accommodate acquisitions for some sixty years and to be extensible by a similar block to the south of the Camera. The failure, however, of the rolling bookcases to live up to expectation and the disappointing surveyors' reports on the southern site led Cowley to tell the curators in 1925 that the Library had space for only a further ten years.[4] Intense discussion followed and various solutions were propounded. First, the Library should be more selective in its accessions and should concentrate on higher studies; indeed it could even purge some of its past accretions. Secondly, it should explore the possibility of using more underground chambers. Thirdly, it should, like the library of the British Museum in 1905, establish an out-of-town repository for newspapers, directories and periodicals; there was an ideal site for this at Wolvercote. Fourthly, there were versions of the plans for extension which had been rejected in the nineteenth century: the filling of the buildings of the Schools' quadrangle, or even the quad itself, with a modern, compact stack (a solution which would leave no space for reading rooms); development on the garden of Exeter College; and the taking over of the Clarendon Building and the relocation of the University's offices in a new building on the other side of Broad Street on the 'Trinity gate to Trinity garden' site. An alternative plan, based on the advantages found in modern American libraries and calling for electric light throughout the Library and access to shelves for readers, suggested an entirely new building on the west side of the University Parks—a proposal first made in 1875. At this stage John D. Rockefeller II (1874–1960), whose charitable foundation had already financed university and other library developments, mostly in America, agreed to support a new library building. Revised plans were put forward for modernizing the old building, constructing additional storage on the north side of Broad Street, providing an out-of-town repository and revising the Library's catalogue.

The University debated these plans at some length and in March 1930 appointed a commission under Sir Henry Miers, sometime Professor of Mineralogy, then Principal of the University of London and, in 1932, President of the Library Association. In 1931 the Commission, whose visits to Europe and to the United States were funded by the Rockefeller Foundation, produced a report entitled *Library Provision in Oxford*. It rejected the construction of a totally new library but seized the opportunity of ridding the Bodleian Library of dependence on a myriad of old storage chambers, partly in the old Schools' building, partly in associated basements, some being even as far afield as the Examination Schools. The site in Broad Street was to house a large complex for storage and administration which would include study-carrels in the stacks and some rooms for teaching and

[4] Ibid. 318.

would be linked by a conveyor running through an underground tunnel to a rejuvenated old building. This, in its turn, would contain a new series of reading rooms on the two transformed upper floors, housing 100,000 volumes on open access, five times the contents of the British Museum's main reading room. This new plan was enthusiastically accepted by Congregation on 26 May 1931.[5]

It is difficult for those who have known only the system established by the implementation of these proposals to appreciate the complexity and amount of work which the use of so many miscellaneous rooms, acquired piecemeal over the years, had formerly required; it is hard now to conceive the crowded conditions of storage and the restricted reading facilities of those days or to follow sympathetically the various, sometimes apparently petty and unenlightened, debates of those years. From the 1850s onward the need for expansion had led to a series of local annexations, both within the Schools' quadrangle and adjacent to it. These moves had been made possible both by the dispersal of general university functions away from the central area and by the provision of new museum space for collections hitherto kept in the Bodleian Library. The departure of the University Press to Walton Street had freed the Clarendon Building for the University's general administrative purposes. New teaching accommodation had become available first in the lecture rooms of the Taylor Institution and later by moving the old 'Schools' away from the central Schools' quadrangle to the new Examination Schools on the site of the Angel Inn in High Street. The creation of the separate University Museum and the building up of the new Ashmolean Museum in Beaumont Street had all enabled the Bodleian Library to retain a magnificent group of central and historic buildings. Retaining these—in contrast to Cambridge, with its recent move away from the centre—nevertheless limited the options which had been open at the start of the century. Few of those who have used the Library since will regret the final decision. The Miers Commission also greatly simplified the management of the Library, though it left it with the difficulty of administering buildings on many sites. This, combined with restrictions brought in after the Second World War on the use of the new library building, was to have important effects on the development of libraries in Oxford generally.

The Commission's ambitious building aims reflected a new and active sense of purpose in the library world. The Bodleian Library's Latin statute of 1856 had been replaced in 1913 by an English version and the opportunity had been taken to increase the number of curators elected by members of Congregation from five to seven. Meanwhile, the daily management of the Library's affairs had passed to a standing committee over which Dr A. B.

Poynton, first Bursar and then Master of University College, presided for the eighteen years from 1919 to 1937. It was accepted that the Librarian would not only be present at these meetings but would even frame agenda and reports. Cowley established himself in his own separate study; he brought in the concept of departments which Jowett had thought up as far back as 1857. In 1927 the post of Keeper of Western Manuscripts was introduced, followed in 1931 by that of Keeper of Oriental Books and Manuscripts. A Secretary to the Library was appointed in 1933, a Keeper of Printed Books and a Deputy Librarian in 1938. In 1913 the age of retirement was fixed at 65 (with an optional extra five years). In 1919 the Library acquired a typewriter and a telephone. A sense of purpose was in the air and the *Staff Manual*—an invaluable annual guide to every aspect of the Library's life, started by Nicholson in 1902, which listed when and by whom the front staircase was swept, the great gate locks were oiled or the hygrometer readings in the underground bookstore were taken—informs readers in 1925 that the Library 'is now the largest University library in the world'. 'In size and importance (together) it ranks about eighth in the world, and among English-speaking people is second only to the British Museum', it states, adding 'readers are desired to bear in mind that a Library of this kind should be used for study and research, and not for trivial purposes'.

The pressures on the Bodleian Library and the growth of undergraduate schools in new subjects had caused alternative sources of library provision to arise. The model here probably lay in the German 'seminar' libraries, and some of those in Oxford indeed initially bore this name. These libraries started as collections of books used by professors and were by no means made up just of modern textbooks but also contained a fair variety of older, rarer and more obscure works. Geography (1899), philosophy (1904), forestry (1905), modern European languages (1906), modern history (1908), social anthropology (1911), agricultural economics (1913) and English (1914) can all claim to have started before the First World War and contained some remarkable books.[6] These specialist libraries were the university-based successors of the abortive attempt in the 1870s to get college libraries to specialize each in a different subject. These empires were doubtless part of the movement that Nicholson feared, thinking that they suggested a pattern for breaking up the Bodleian Library along the lines of separately housed subject-libraries. After the war, however, the movement was in general centripetal. Several college libraries also found themselves under spatial constraints. All Souls disposed of books to Belgrade in 1919, to Leeds, to Manchester and, as late as 1950, to Hull. In 1928 Balliol gave a thousand volumes to the Bodleian Library and throughout the 1930s various colleges passed older continental periodicals over to the library of the Taylor

---

[6] See Morgan, *Oxford Libraries* under each library.

Institution. The older communal library provision for the women's colleges was no longer acceptable and colleges built their own, Lady Margaret Hall in 1910, St Hugh's in 1936 and St Anne's in 1938.

There was, too, a desire to take stock of Oxford's riches. Many of those interested in libraries came together in 1922 to form the Oxford Bibliographical Society.[7] This influential body, which had strong connections with the University Press, included such librarians as Falconer Madan and Strickland Gibson and Press potentates like John Johnson and R. W. Chapman together with bibliophile academics of the calibre of P. S. Allen, Sir Walter Greg, Percy Simpson, David Nichol Smith, Gordon Duff (an Oxford bibliographical prize bears his name), J. P. R. Lyell (an annual readership perpetuates his memory) and, to end with one of the most legendary of Oxford's modern book-collectors, C. H. Wilkinson. The Society published works on or catalogues of the libraries of Worcester, Magdalen, Jesus and All Souls colleges; it studied great Oxford collectors or authors; it catalogued the Bodleian Library's outstanding collection of early English newspapers; and it published two major books on the history of the University Press. The Bodleian Library and many of Oxford's colleges participated in the compilation of Pollard and Redgrave's *Short-Title Catalogue*.[8] A start was made on a local counterpart for continental books, although this was doomed to remain purely on cards in the Bodleian Library for many years.

It was evident fairly early in the discussion about development that a large part of the money for the extension of the Bodleian Library would be available, and in the event the Rockefeller Foundation met three-fifths of the cost.[9] Normal library budgets had been a matter of considerable concern for many years. Nicholson's last year had ended with a deficit of £901 and, ill timed as it happened, Council issued an appeal on behalf of the Library in June 1914. The Library did in fact receive a notable number of substantial bequests during the next seven years and some colleges continued their previous support, but the fall in the value of money after the war left it in a very difficult situation. The Asquith Commission wanted a tenth of the state's annual grant to Oxford to be assigned to the Bodleian Library, but in the event this was progressively whittled down, particularly during the Second World War. The inter-war years saw a growth in staff (and notable compensation for war service), higher prices, new capital expenditure on shelving and wiring and higher costs of maintenance. Strict economies had to be instituted, including cuts in the provision for binding and even in opening hours.

[7] See anonymous 'Oxford Bibliographical Society, 1922–1947', *OM* 15 May 1947, 323.
[8] A. W. Pollard and G. R. Redgrave, *A Short-Title Catalogue of Books Printed in England, Scotland, and Ireland and of English Books Printed Abroad 1475–1640* (London 1926 [1927]).
[9] Craster, *Bodleian Library*, 327; cf below, p. 646.

H. H. E. (later Sir Edmund) Craster, Keeper of Western Manuscripts since 1927, succeeded Cowley as Librarian in 1931. Craster (1879–1959) has been described as 'perhaps the greatest of Sir Thomas Bodley's librarians since Dr James'.[10] Despite a strange impediment which made unbroken speech impossible, he brought to the enormous tasks of those years his experience as proctor in 1916/17, strong clear views, meticulous thoroughness and unfailing courtesy. A master of systematic planning, he presided over the change whereby the Bodleian Library became a great modern library on the national scale, an achievement recognized by his knighthood in 1945. Sir Hubert Worthington was commissioned as architect for the extension to the Radcliffe Science Library in June 1932 and the building opened in November 1934. In 1937 a University appeal was launched both to fund the balance required for the proposed new building in Broad Street and for higher studies generally. In June 1934 Sir Giles Gilbert Scott, who had just completed the new out-of-town Cambridge University Library, was appointed architect for the new building; work started on the site in December 1936. Subterranean water caused initial problems but Queen Mary was able to lay the foundation stone in June 1937 and a royal opening was envisaged for June 1940.

It was fortunate that construction had in fact been completed by the outbreak of war since this allowed for the transfer and wartime security of treasures both of the Bodleian and other libraries and of colleges. The New Library also housed numerous wartime organizations including naval intelligence departments of the Admiralty. Over fifty members of staff were away; one, captured at Dunkirk, even acted as librarian in his prisoner of war camp.[11] Despite all these activities and long hours of 'fire-watching', the Library reached the end of the war with the greater part of its stock safe, sorted and reorganized in its new accommodation, which was thought capable of holding four million volumes. (The libraries of the British Museum and of Liverpool University each lost some half million items through enemy action.) On 29 October 1946 King George VI officially opened the new Bodleian building.

Access to books by senior members had been the main academic demand in the 1930s: social studies and maps had been allocated major reading rooms and there was provision for study-carrels and desks for senior readers within the stacks. Departments of the Library, especially another new pre-war project, catalogue-revision, and a number of external academic units (the *Dictionary of National Biography*, the Victoria County History of Oxfordshire and the Oxford dictionaries of Latin and patristic Greek) were housed, together with a public exhibition room, in a belt of rooms around

[10] Note by Sir Godfrey Driver on Craster's retirement, *Bodleian Library Record* ii (1941–9), 143.
[11] 'The staff and the war', ibid. 96.

the bookstack. Among all the other post-war problems there remained, however, the task of the major internal reconstruction of the old Bodleian building. Sir Edmund Craster was succeeded in 1945 by his deputy H. R. Creswick (1902–88) who in turn was followed in 1948 by J. N. L. Myres (1902–89). It would have been difficult to find a more appropriate person than Myres, an archaeologist and Student of Christ Church, for these particular tasks. Despite the modernity of the New Library the Bodleian Library of these earlier days has been described as 'a library run by eccentrics for eccentrics'. The problems of finding space for storage had been solved for the time being but there remained the refurbishment of the Radcliffe Camera and the reconstruction of the Old Library, which would entail the complete renovation of Duke Humfrey's Library and the rediscovery of the seventeenth-century frieze in the upper reading room. All this had to be carried out at a time when resources and materials were rare and new and greater demands were being made both by senior and—increasingly—by junior members. The Librarian was constrained to note that there were now early morning queues outside the Camera, that there had been a spate of thefts of books and that it had even been necessary, from its inception in 1946, to open the new PPE reading room to undergraduates.[12]

Staff appointments, however, were inspired: the new Keeper of Western Manuscripts, Richard Hunt (1908–79), was a great scholar who not only saw to the completion of the catalogue of western manuscripts but also, with academic colleagues such as Roger Mynors and Neil Ker, made Oxford into a major centre for palaeographical studies. Similarly the Keeper of Printed Books, Lars Hanson (1907–66), formerly in the library of the British Museum, together with Professor F. P. Wilson and the new Reader in Textual Criticism, Herbert Davis, brought in the practice of postgraduates printing on a handpress in the new Library and, with it, renewed bibliographical studies. The history of bookbinding flourished but its sister, conservation, was not similarly pursued. Scholarship was kept at a high level, and there was a series of notable exhibitions, each accompanied by a suitable catalogue. It was perhaps partly as a result of this activity that major collections of books and manuscripts came in by benefaction. The second great gift of Shelley items was received in 1946. Paul Mellon and Esmond De Beer enabled both a large part of John Locke's library of printed books and his manuscripts to find a home in the Bodleian Library. In the next three decades John Johnson's extraordinary collection of printed ephemera [plate 16.1], the equally multiform collection of ballads, songs and music which W. N. H. Harding had assembled in down-town Chicago, and Albert

[12] J. N. L. Myres, 'The Bodleian Library in post-war Oxford', *Oxford* xi (1952) and the anonymous 'Some reflections on Bodleian reconstruction', *OM* 26 Jan. 1956, 208–10.

Ehrman's fabulous Broxbourne library of fine bindings also arrived and had to be assimilated. Besides all this, there were individual gifts and purchases of books and manuscripts, but still funds had to be raised for the completion of the historic restoration yet in progress. The Friends of the Bodleian, formed in 1925, were constantly active and in 1957 were reinforced by the American Friends. In the 1960s the lunch at the autumn visitation provided another platform for the Library.

The quarter of a century or so following the Second World War was largely a period of expansion. The Library's staff rose in thirty years from about one hundred and fifty to around four hundred; the proportion of women rose from 41 to 54 per cent and many new graduates arrived from universities other than Oxford. At the same time the Library was losing staff, often to prestigious posts elsewhere: R. H. Hill became librarian of the National Central Library, Stanley Gillam took charge of the London Library, K. W. Humphreys was librarian successively of Birmingham University and of the European University at Florence, E. G. W. Bill went to Lambeth Palace, P. Long to Essex University and B. J. Enright (via other posts) to Newcastle University, to name but some. The Library was nevertheless staunch in its academic stance even if staff were less active in the professional world of the Library Association (although Myres was the Association's President in 1963). The Bodleian Library sided with libraries with similar interests: it took a leading part, under Myres, in founding the Copyright Libraries Conference in 1948 and was also concerned with that of the Standing Conference of National and University Libraries in 1950.

The staff of a great national library had also to face increasing demands by the University. The number of undergraduates at Oxford more than doubled between 1913 and 1950 and increased by a further 52 per cent between 1950 and 1970. Nor was it just their number which changed: fewer took pass schools, the honours-school curricula increased in variety and complexity, and both the new student and his tutor became more library-conscious. In addition, the number of those seeking the degree of doctor of philosophy, only a happy few between the wars, increased astronomically during the 1960s, so that by the 1970s postgraduates represented nearly a quarter of the entire student body. Nor was this phenomenon characteristic of Oxford alone, for it was common to both Europe and America. The number of foreign scholars, both academics and postgraduates, visiting the Library rose sharply too. The Bodleian Library's annual admission of non-Oxford persons, or *extranei*, which stood at around five hundred in 1950, rose so fast that by 1971 it was a quarter higher than that for local matriculants. On one August afternoon in the mid–1960s the population of the upper reading room even contained an absolute majority of Frenchmen.

The Bodleian Library's restored reading rooms, planned purely for research, were expected to cope with this influx. The University's attention was concentrated, as ever, on provision for undergraduates, a problem to which the Norrington Committee addressed itself in 1958. The Committee's recommendations resulted in the strengthening of existing faculty libraries, in the creation of new ones, and in university subvention of college libraries. The colleges had continued to make provision, albeit variable, for their undergraduates. Many, including Brasenose, Christ Church, Corpus, Hertford, Pembroke and St John's, refurbished and enlarged their libraries, while New College (1939), Lady Margaret Hall (1961) and Wadham (1977) built new ones, the last with Iranian financial support. The library of Nuffield College (and to a lesser extent that of St Antony's) admitted undergraduates from other colleges to their specialized collections and thus made an important contribution to provision within the University. Unusual developments included the conversion of redundant churches by two colleges, that of St Peter in the East by St Edmund Hall (1970) and All Saints by Lincoln College (1975). New faculty libraries were established for music (1944) and for the department of the history of art (1955) while the French government's foundation of the Oxford Maison Française (1946) assisted provision in this field. The St Cross building, opened in 1964, typified the piecemeal expansion of the times by containing, in the same complex, a research library in economics and statistics, the Bodleian Library's law sections (organized for the first time for joint senior and junior use) and the basically undergraduate English faculty library. Numerous buildings in the science area (biochemistry, botany, Dyson Perrins, engineering, forestry, mathematics and metallurgy) also contained library accommodation, as did the Oriental Institute.

In 1951 Sir George Clark noted that the traditional free growth of Oxford libraries had many advantages for each small working unit, be it college or research institute, but that since it also entailed much waste, overlap and loss of opportunity, the rapid growth of modern times required much more co-ordination and co-operation.[13] A similar approach was in hand on the national level with the post-war evolution of regional library systems and that of a unified and reorganized British Library. Inter-library lending became a regular service for many, but Oxford—richer than most—was slow even to contribute to this scheme. The Franks Commission left libraries to a separate committee, of which the chairman was Robert Shackleton, Reader in French and fellow and librarian of Brasenose. The committee was directed to consider co-ordination, union catalogues, policies on acquisition, training, priorities in accommodation, methods of funding and the creation of a permanent central libraries committee. Four of the nine members were librarians of colleges; the Secretary of the Bodleian Library (I. G. Philip) and its Keeper of Printed Books were also members.

13 G. Clark, 'Libraries' in *Handbook to the University of Oxford* 1951, 189–90.

The committee toured in Europe and America and reported in 1966. It made recommendations concerning new buildings or extensions (for the Taylor Institution, social studies, the Radcliffe Science Library, geography, the Ashmolean Museum); more storage for the Bodleian Library out of town and underground (south of the Clarendon Building and south of the Camera); the creation of a central library committee requiring unified statistics; and a start on both union catalogues and library automation. However, despite a cautious note referring to the Chancellor of the Exchequer's postponement in July 1965 of certain University building contracts, little attempt was made to cost the proposals, which reflected the optimism of recent years.

Before the committee's report was complete the question of the allocation of central University buildings arose again. The Bodleian Library and the University Registry competed for the Indian Institute, of which differing structural surveys had been made. Eventually the Clarendon Building was allocated largely to the Bodleian Library, the library of the Indian Institute was transferred to new accommodation on top of the New Bodleian Library and the proscholium became the main entrance to the Bodleian Library.

In the course of the debate Myres resigned and on 26 February 1966 Robert Shackleton (1919–86) was appointed Bodley's Librarian, a post he held until 1979 when he resigned to take up the Marshal Foch chair of French. Shackleton was a well-known scholar of the Enlightenment, an authority on Montesquieu, an outstanding book-collector and a frequenter of libraries worldwide. The University Libraries Board proposed by his committee was instituted and a number of other simple recommendations were put into practice. An Anglo-American conference on the automation of library catalogues met in Brasenose and seemed set on a project linking London, Oxford and Cambridge. A specific Keeper of Catalogues was appointed in the Bodleian Library, but technical problems and a change of personnel prevented the Library from keeping up with its better funded national and American peers. The expansionist years were drawing to an end, and of the major library plans, the next few years saw the realization only of the underground extension of the Radcliffe Science Library (visited by the Queen in June 1976) and the first phase of a book-repository at Nuneham Courtenay.

The Shackleton report made many minor recommendations but was unclear as to the general lines of the library provision which the University should make. Thus the Libraries Board was, fatally, given very little real power (for example over the Bodleian Library, which retained its curatorial body presided over by the vice-chancellor); the independent development of the faculty libraries was encouraged; and little was said about funding—a particularly striking omission since the report makes much of the fact that most American university libraries had been growing much faster than their

18.1 Queuing for Professor Wind's lecture on Picasso, 1957

British counterparts. The Libraries Board did bring a welcome uniformity to the statistics of Oxford libraries—which had earlier been bedevilled by such concepts as the *notional octavo*—but it is still difficult to make sound comparisons between the periods before and after 1966, especially since the figure for the basic Bodleian holdings was recalculated, partly to meet new national norms. A twenty-year comparison based on the Shackleton Committee's figures of 1964 does, however, suggest that the annual intake of the faculty, departmental and college libraries (that is, those responsible for undergraduate provision) rose during the years 1964–84 by a greater percentage than did that of the central research libraries. The increase in seating in such libraries was even greater. Thus just at a time when the number of postgraduates was rising rapidly, all efforts to develop the libraries were directed towards the needs of undergraduates.

Academic demand in the 1930s was for access for research, a matter of importance when there was no subject-catalogue and delivery from distant stores could be slow. The New Bodleian Library appeared to provide a compromise by allowing for increased storage and access and the retention of the historic building. It was deemed that the Camera and college libraries would be ample provision for undergraduates; after all, as late as 1964 the Parry Committee produced figures which showed that Oxford had notably more books per student than any other British university. In the post-war world this belief was clearly erroneous. The restriction on access to the stack by senior members of the University and the increasing delay in delivery time naturally encouraged a college-based—and therefore undergraduate-centred—university to make extra provision, at least in the arts, in open-access faculty libraries. This depreciation of the central libraries left them unable to increase, or even to maintain, their subject-coverage; and they could not make any real progress in meeting the new demands of cataloguing, retrieval and the introduction of new media. The financial difficulties of the 1970s not only aggravated these problems but also undermined the hard-won academic excellence of the major libraries.

By the later 1980s even 'retrenchment' had shown little sign of breaking this mould and of engendering co-ordinated policies and administration. Mid-twentieth-century Oxford showed little enthusiasm for strong central control by the university, and it is open to question whether a new university library, built in the 1930s with sufficient room for expansion, would have provided an acceptable solution to the post-war problems. Automation, finally brought in—even if on the cheap—has started to unify a basic library process and to bring a greater common professionalism to Oxford's libraries. Sir George Clark observed in 1951 that 'Oxford as it now is has the distinction and the advantage, though it is also in its way a burden and a responsibility, of carrying along with it in the present an enormous heritage from the past, a living inheritance of buildings and books and possessions of many kinds'.[14] It is undoubtedly true that Oxford and its libraries have been to some extent 'prisoners of history' and that the beauty of the central buildings has hindered radical departures. The 1930s set a new plan in hand, but this was not fully carried out and new pressures after the war encouraged piecemeal development. Greater co-ordination, which was going on elsewhere in the world of libraries, was planned in the mid-1960s but coincided with financial crises. The latter also delayed automation, itself one of the most powerful incentives to co-ordinated development. Many of the numerous problems of the period under review were met by individual libraries. But in addition there was a need for general, university-wide solutions, both technical and administrative. For these, adumbrated yet again by a committee of review in the mid-1980s, the political will was still not present.

[14] G. Clark, 'Libraries' in *Handbook to the University of Oxford* 1951, 210.

18

Museums and Art Galleries

CHRISTOPHER WHITE

A visitor to Oxford at the beginning of the First World War would have found three museums.[1] The Ashmolean Museum (founded in 1683) contained the recently united collections of fine art and most of the University's archaeological collections; these had formerly been housed in the University Galleries and the old Ashmolean building, respectively. The University Museum (opened in 1860) contained the geological, mineralogical, zoological and entomological collections. The Pitt Rivers Museum (opened in 1885) was a highly original and personal assembly by its eponymous founder of works illustrating all of man's material culture; its emphasis lay on 'ordinary and typical specimens, rather than rare objects . . . so as to trace . . . the succession of ideas by which the minds of men in primitive condition of culture have progressed from the simple to the complex'.[2] At that time Cambridge offered the Fitzwilliam Museum (founded 1816), the University Museum of Archaeology and Anthropology (founded 1884) and the Museum of Classical Archaeology (also opened in 1884) which contained casts.

Museums in Oxford entered the present century in relatively good shape. In 1908 the Ashmolean Museum was statutorily united with the University

[1] The principal sources for this chapter are the annual reports of the various institutions. For a general survey see D. Piper, *The Treasures of Oxford* (New York and London 1977). For the University Museum see K. C. Davies and J. Hull, *The Zoological Collections of the Oxford University Museum* (Oxford 1976); A. Z. Smith, *A History of the Hope Entomological Collections in the University Museum Oxford* (Oxford 1986). For the Pitt Rivers Museum see B. Blackwood, *The Origin and Development of the Pitt Rivers Museum* (Oxford 1970), rev. S. Jones (Oxford 1990). For the Museum of the History of Science see A. V. Simcock, *The Ashmolean Museum and Oxford Science 1683–1983* (Oxford 1984); A. V. Simcock (ed.), *Robert T. Gunther and the Old Ashmolean* (Oxford 1985). For my talk on 'Art galleries in Oxford since 1945: the Ashmolean Museum' to the History of the University seminar in Corpus Christi College 3 Feb. 1989 see Brian Harrison's transcript in HUA. In addition I am most grateful for help and advice from the following: Dr Schuyler Jones, Director of the Pitt Rivers Museum, Mr Francis Maddison, Curator of the Museum of the History of Science, Mr Philip Powell of the University Museum, Mr R. E. Alton and my colleagues in the Ashmolean Museum, Professor Sir John Boardman, Dr Roger Moorey, Dr Michael Metcalf, Miss Mary Tregear, Mr Timothy Wilson and Mr Arthur MacGregor. Dr Nicholas Penny kindly showed me the manuscript of his introductions to the *Catalogue of European Sculpture in the Ashmolean Museum. 1540 to the Present Day* (3 vols Oxford 1992).   [2] Blackwood, *Pitt Rivers Museum* (unpaginated).

Galleries, together with the department of classical archaeology, all now housed in the Beaumont Street building as the Ashmolean Museum of Art and Archaeology. The amalgamated institution was divided into three departments: antiquities, which now housed the major part of the University's archaeological collections; fine art; and classical archaeology. Classical archaeology was the province of the then Lincoln and Merton Professor; from 1925 he was known as the Lincoln Professor, and his museum responsibility was limited to the casts of classical sculpture. In 1922 the antiquarium and the fine art galleries were renamed as the departments of antiquities and fine art respectively.

The two later developments in the Ashmolean Museum's organization were the creation of the Heberden coin room and the department of eastern art. In 1920 Convocation authorized the transfer of the University's coins and medals from the Bodleian Library, where they were ill housed and not easily accessible; they were placed under the charge of the Keeper of the Antiquarium, as he was then known. This move, which the Keeper, Arthur Evans, had in vain attempted earlier as part of a rationalization of the University's collections, later led to colleges depositing their collections in the Ashmolean. A bequest of £1,000, left for unspecified purposes to the University by Dr Heberden, was used to set up the coin room in a fortified room; it remained a section of the department of antiquities until 1961, when it became an independent department.

The oriental collections from the department of fine art in the Ashmolean, primarily the collection of Chinese porcelain, temporarily joined the Indian sculpture in the Indian Institute, where Dr William Cohn set up a museum of eastern art as a sub-department of the department of fine art in 1948. In 1956 large gifts of eastern art required more space than was available, and the Visitors had to transfer the collections to Beaumont Street. The move was finally achieved in 1962, when eastern art was established as an independent department, which led to the renaming of the old department of fine art. The collections from the Indian Institute were displayed in new galleries to the north of the main entrance previously occupied by the cast galleries.

In the area of administration, the most momentous decision affecting the Ashmolean Museum came as a result of the report the Brunt Committee submitted to Council in 1968.[3] This, the first detailed study of the Museum in its long history, thoroughly examined all aspects of its operation. The Committee began with the intellectual situation in 1967 and, according to the *Burlington Magazine*, tackled it 'with conviction and strength'. 'It is a forceful document, modern, realistic and sane.'[4] Its conclusions, which were

---

[3] [P. A. Brunt, chairman] *Report of the Committee on the Ashmolean Museum* [*Brunt Report*] (University of Oxford 1967).

[4] *Burlington Magazine* cx (1968), 375 (editorial).

largely accepted by the University, determined the Museum's future. Particular concern was expressed about the sense of isolation felt by the staff, and the two principal objects of the report were to promote greater unity within the Museum itself and closer integration between Museum and University.

The Museum had previously been run as an association of four departments and the cast gallery under the co-ordinating hand of the senior keeper, who acted as the Keeper of the Museum. The Brunt Committee argued that 'greater centralization of administration would effect economies in money and in the time of curatorial staff and . . . reduce the traditional autonomy of the departments'.[5] As a result the post of director was established and the first holder, D. T. (later Sir David) Piper, took up office in 1973. No less important were the Committee's observations on the Ashmolean Museum as an educational institution. It wanted the Museum staff to be encouraged both as curators and as teachers. Its recommendations led to the insertion of the words 'to assist in relevant teaching and research within the University' in the definition of the Museum's purpose in the University's statutes.[6]

The University Museum continued to serve as the centre for the administration of the entire science area up to 1964, and since then has remained indissolubly linked to the relevant teaching departments. But between 1914 and 1970 important changes were introduced in the care of the collections. As a result of various ambiguities in the original statute, an amendment was made in 1939 which, apart from altering the composition of the delegacy, removed from the delegates their previous right to supervise the collections. These became the exclusive responsibility of the three professors, the professor of geology in the case of the geological and mineralogical collections, the Linacre professor for the collections of zoology and comparative anatomy and the Hope professor for the entomological collections. Given that the Museum housed more than 140 individual collections, this change was unwise, and the Museum came to suffer seriously from the lack of a single responsible authority. Regrettably but understandably, the professors were concerned only with the collections they themselves used for teaching. The haphazard growth of the collections, as well as the lack of control over their display and conservation, led to losses from decay and theft. As a result a committee, chaired by Professor L. W. Grensted, was set up by Council in 1952; a further amendment to the original statute was introduced two years later. This established a committee for the scientific collections, which acted on behalf of the delegates until 1969. Thenceforward, after a further revision of the statutes, they took over

---

[5] *Brunt Report*, 23.
[6] *Statutes* 1989, 48.

in their own right. In addition a university lecturer was appointed curator, responsible to the professor, for each of the three (later four) groups of collections. The Grensted Committee's proposal for a single curator carrying the same status as the head of department did not survive the conflict between those primarily concerned with teaching and those whose prime concern was the Museum itself. As a result the Museum still lacks a permanent head, and one of the departmental curators now serves as the curator of the Museum for a period of three years.

The first curator of the Pitt Rivers Museum (founded in 1885) was Henry Balfour, who remained in office till he died in 1939. The Museum continued to grow in the size of its collections but not in space or organization. In establishing a new post of assistant curator in 1969, the University acknowledged the serious under-staffing, but the later development of the Museum, with the renaming of the curator as the director in 1990, falls outside the period under review.

In 1924 one new university museum was added to the jewels in the University's crown: the Museum of the History of Science. It anticipated by twenty years the equivalent development at Cambridge: the Whipple Museum of the History of Science. More strictly, it was a rearrangement of existing collections around an important gift set up in an old building. Lewis Evans—a brother of Arthur, who according to his half-sister Joan Evans 'could not spell, but liked blowing himself up with chemicals'[7]—donated his collection of antique scientific instruments. This was the catalyst for establishing the Museum of the History of Science in the old Ashmolean building in Broad Street, which since 1894 had lacked any museological function. The impetus for persuading the University to accept Evans's offer and for founding the new museum came from Robert T. Gunther, a fellow of Magdalen and subsequently the first curator.

Apart from bringing together scientific instruments dispersed throughout the University, Gunther's aim was to establish a university department of the history of science. This would, he thought, strengthen the role of science, and at the same time save and refurbish the old Ashmolean building. It was then being used for purposes Gunther thought unworthy—as offices for the *Oxford English Dictionary* and storage for the Bodleian Library. One of the purposes of the old Ashmolean building at its opening in 1683 had been the teaching of science.[8] Given the determined and contentious character of Gunther, the foundation occasioned much academic in-fighting and ill will. Apart from the reluctance of the *Dictionary* and the Bodleian

---

[7] J. Evans, *Time and Chance: The Story of Arthur Evans and his Forbears* (London etc. 1943), 131.

[8] See A. G. MacGregor and A. J. Turner, 'The Ashmolean Museum' in L. S. Sutherland and L. G. Mitchell (eds), *History of the University of Oxford v The Eighteenth Century* (Oxford 1986), esp. 643.

Library to give up the middle floor and basement, respectively, the Ashmolean Museum feared that Gunther would appropriate its name and set up in rivalry. In 1924 Lewis Evans's gift was installed as the Lewis Evans collection of scientific instruments on the top floor of the old Ashmolean building. It was supplemented by items drawn from the University and by gifts or loans from colleges, such as the outstanding Orrery collection at Christ Church. In 1935 the Museum of the History of Science was incorporated in the University statutes with the purpose of containing 'objects and books illustrating the History of Science, with special reference to scientific work in Oxford'.[9] Not until the 1940s was it allowed to take over the whole building; it now offers a comprehensive survey of scientific instruments, clocks, watches and microscopes and an important library of books and manuscripts.

Another new institution, although not belonging to the University, should be mentioned, since many members of the University have been involved in its affairs and it has enriched the cultural life of Oxford. Despite being called a museum, the Museum of Modern Art has only a very small permanent collection and no acquisition funds. It is primarily involved in organizing exhibitions; these have not only opened Oxford's eyes to developments in contemporary art, but have sometimes helped to stimulate national awareness. The Museum was founded in 1965 by Trevor Green, an architect and lecturer at Oxford Polytechnic (now Oxford Brookes University), and after a year in a disused warehouse in St Michael's Street it moved into what have become reasonably permanent quarters in the old brewery in Pembroke Street, rented from the city of Oxford on a long-term lease. The original idea was to build up a collection of contemporary art, but the necessary funds were never forthcoming. Its first paid director was an undergraduate at St Edmund Hall, Barry Lane, but at that stage of the Museum's history the programme of exhibitions, which became its *raison d'être*, was relatively low-key. International interest began only after two subsequent developments: the appointment in 1970 of Peter Ibsen, an artist trained at Chelsea School of Art, and the merger in 1973 with the Bear Lane Gallery, founded in 1958, and also important for enlightening Oxford about contemporary art. Since then it has gone from strength to strength, and plays a major role in Oxford's cultural life.

From their inception the basic purpose of the University museums was twofold: to provide teaching and research facilities for the University and to make their collections available to the public. Teaching and research have always played a dominant role in the collecting policy and the activities of both the University Museum and the Pitt Rivers; indeed, the curators of the University Museum are members of the departments of zoology (faculty of

[9] *Statutes* 1989, 248.

biological sciences) and earth sciences (faculty of physical sciences) while those of the Pitt Rivers are members of the faculty of anthropology and geography. In the case of the Ashmolean Museum the situation has always been less straightforward.[10] There is still no undergraduate degree in the history of art, and nearly half a century elapsed between the foundation of a chair in European archaeology and the creation of a degree course in archaeology and anthropology in 1991. Consequently the staff of the two senior departments in the Museum (like their colleagues in the Museum of the History of Science) have usually undertaken teaching only on demand, particularly since the Brunt report, which for the first time formally opened the way for them to do so. The two junior departments, the Heberden coin room and eastern art, have provided more teaching at all levels, since appropriate degree courses with relevant options have long existed.

A word should perhaps be added about the role of art history in the University. Despite the establishment of a chair in 1955, with Professor Edgar Wind as its first holder, any idea of introducing more than the most limited teaching for undergraduates has so far been firmly resisted and would now require a major benefaction to be widely effective. There has been a general view in Oxford that art history is not a serious academic subject, and that the Slade lectures—founded in 1869 and delivered once a year—provide all that is needed. Sir Maurice Bowra, one of the prime movers in establishing the chair, told the professor-elect at the time: 'It is a comfort to think that at last the young people here will be allowed to know that there is such a thing as art. They have lived too long without it.'[11] To judge from the large audiences Wind attracted in the 1950s [plate 18.1] an undergraduate degree in the history of art, the norm in most British universities today, would be immensely popular, and Oxford's failure to establish one when money was available seems somewhat narrow-minded.

Oxford was never short of ideas concerning building. Some bold schemes—one of them dazzling—were developed, at least in the mind. But relatively little was realized, and what was built does little to engage the attention of those interested in the continuity of Oxford's distinguished architectural heritage. Between 1914 and 1970 the University Museum's accommodation was not enlarged, despite frequent complaints that the building was unsuitable for housing and displaying the collections; plans for a totally new building elsewhere were mooted. The departments of zoology and experimental psychology did, however, move out of the Museum into new quarters in 1971. The Pitt Rivers was active in the late 1960s in seeking a new building on a site off the Banbury Road. An imaginative and spectacular building of reinforced concrete designed by Pier Luigi Nervi of Rome in

[10] It is discussed in detail in *Brunt Report*, 59–69.
[11] Letter dated 14 June 1955 to Professor Edgar Wind on his appointment, in the possession of Mrs Margaret Wind.

collaboration with Powell and Moya of London [plate 19.13], which would have been located off the Banbury Road, failed to find the necessary funding. In Howard Colvin's view 'the project was, perhaps, the last chance for the university to build in the twentieth century something that would take its place with the Divinity School, the Radcliffe Library and the Ashmolean Museum as a major work of European architecture'.[12] In 1986, thanks to the bequest of unrestricted funds by Henry Balfour's son, two galleries containing musical instruments and prehistoric archaeology were opened in the newly constructed Balfour building behind 60 Banbury Road.

On its constricted site the Ashmolean Museum was constantly trying to expand its accommodation. Behind the principal façade on Beaumont Street, unobtrusive piecemeal additions were made, and there was constant rearranging of the interior. From 1923 to 1928 the high gallery on the first floor of Cockerell's west wing was divided in two, and three new galleries were installed on the upper floor; these were opened to the public with a reception in June 1929. The decision, taken in 1931 amid huge feeling, that the Taylor Institution should remain on its present site led the Visitors, 'looking forward to a still greater future', to commission a plan from Messrs Stanley Hall and Easton and Robertson.[13] The model still exists, and the plan would have destroyed the existing houses and extended the Museum to the corner of St John Street, creating a major façade there. With further developments at the back of the building this would have doubled the space available. In the event, lack of funds led to a far more modest development. In 1933 the west side of the existing building was enlarged, thanks to an anonymous interest-free loan (in fact from the then Keeper of Fine Art, Kenneth Clark), by the addition of the Weldon wing. Named after a generous benefactor to the department of fine art, the new wing included a gallery on the first floor and a lecture-room on the ground floor, now the Haverfield Library.

In 1937 the death of Professor F. Ll. Griffith's widow gave effect to his substantial bequest. This created an institute for Egyptological and Near Eastern archaeological research in the north-west corner of the Ashmolean site. It incorporated Griffith's important Egyptological library, which had previously been housed elsewhere. At the same time a donation of £10,000 from the Worshipful Company of Drapers made possible the building on the north-east of the Museum to house exhibition galleries and offices for the department of antiquities. The last major development of the decade, an offshoot of the grandiose plan of 1931, took place at the beginning of the Second World War and was completed only in 1941. This was the extension on the south-west, taking in the sites of 38–40 Beaumont Street, which

---

[12] H. M. Colvin, *Unbuilt Oxford* (New Haven Conn. and London 1983), 187. See also below, 516.

[13] *Annual Report of the Ashmolean Museum*, Oxford 1931, 2.

provided enlarged gallery space for the Egyptian collections, and space on the first floor for the western art library as well as for offices for teachers and the department. Between 1945 and 1970 the single major development, only partially realized, was the building of a new cast gallery beside the Oriental Institute across the passageway to the north.[14] This freed considerable space in the main building, and allowed galleries to be created for the new department of eastern art. In 1950 the Hill music room was opened, and 1957 saw the addition of three new galleries on the ground floor, devoted to Egyptian antiquities, and three on the first, two small and one large, which connected with the Weldon gallery.

Universities often neglect and under-fund their museums, and this certainly occurred in Oxford. K. T. Parker's *cri de cœur* of 1947 for 'patience and restraint to prevail over indignation' may be taken to represent the feelings of a long line of curators.[15] At greater length and more analytically, the standing commission on museums and galleries in 1968 drew attention to the neglect of collections, especially those of natural history and geology at both Oxford and Cambridge. If collections were to be conserved and catalogued, it argued, professional curatorial staff must replace academics preoccupied by heavy teaching duties.[16] In 1973 another report drew attention to the struggle of the future when it stated that 'where university museums exist which could provide a service to the public, local authorities should be prepared to finance such services'.[17]

Whereas Oxford's new museum buildings from 1914 to 1970 were few, underfunded and unexciting, the expansion of the collections has by contrast been spectacular. Here lies the real success-story of the period. They may not be housed in ideal quarters, they may sometimes be inadequately conserved and their academic potential may not invariably be exploited to the full, but in aggregate they immeasurably enrich and extend what the University can offer the scholar as well as the serious visitor.

Growth in the collections of the University Museum often reflects the research interests of the professor in residence. In entomology the collections of African lepidoptera were substantially increased during the Hope professorships of E. B. Poulton (1893–1933) and G. Hale Carpenter (1933–48). The holdings of Oxfordshire fossils were enriched by James Parker, an amateur palaeontologist whose bequest in 1914 included the most complete skeleton in Europe of a bipedal carnivorous dinosaur, and by the

---

[14] 'And with characteristic canniness it [the University] built only two thirds of it, promising to complete the building later, which of course has never happened': J. Boardman, '100 years of classical archaeology in Oxford' in D. C. Kurtz (ed.), *Beazley and Oxford* (Oxford 1985), 51.

[15] *Annual Report of the Ashmolean Museum, Oxford* 1947, 27.

[16] *Report on the Universities in Relation to their own and other Museums* (HMSO 1968), paras 17–19.

[17] *Provincial Museums and Galleries* (Department of Education and Science 1973), para. 13.9.

purchase in 1924 of the collection of E. A. Walford. Following his death in 1915, Hugo Müller's collection of minerals was given to the Museum by his widow. O. V. Aplin's collection of bird skins and bird eggs, many from Oxfordshire, was given by his family in 1940. Molluscs came from the collections of Dr W. T. Elliott in 1938 and Alan Poole Gardiner in 1951, and jurassic specimens from the bequest in 1951 of W. J. Arkell, a world authority on the subject. And from 1921 all kinds of material came from Oxford University expeditions.

The collections in the Pitt Rivers Museum steadily increased in size and range while Henry Balfour was Curator (1891–1939) so that by 1939 the original gift of some fifteen thousand specimens had increased to well over one million. In 1932 Balfour had given his own collection of lamps and lighting equipment and after his death his son gave the Museum the remainder of the very extensive collection, built up during Balfour's travels to almost unknown parts of the world, and notable for its musical instruments and lighting and fire-making appliances. Fieldwork carried out by other members of the staff—notably by another long-serving member, Beatrice Blackwood, in the Solomon Islands, New Guinea and New Britain from 1931 to 1938—has subsequently added valuable material to the collection.

There were several other major gifts to the Pitt Rivers Museum. J. H. Hutton and J. P. Mills gave large and well documented Naga collections from Assam (1914–38). Archaeological and ethnographical material came from Sir E. B. Tylor, both during his life and after his death in 1917. Extensive holdings of Sarawak ethnography, including weapons, textiles, beadwork and carvings, were received from Charles Brooke, Raja of Sarawak, in 1923. Between 1916 and 1922 P. A. Talbot handed over large groups of carvings, pottery and musical instruments from Nigeria. Numerous other collections brought together material from such diverse places as Melanesia, India, the Cameroons, Tasmania, New Zealand, Peru and Colombia. The great expansion of the Museum's collections took place at a time when ethnographical material was relatively cheap and the collectors who enriched the Pitt Rivers Museum were often the only people in the field.

Although he ceased to be Keeper in 1908, Sir Arthur Evans remained the outstanding single benefactor to the Ashmolean archaeological collections until he died in 1941. In 1927 he donated his father's fine collection of prehistoric and later antiquities. From his own collection he contributed not only more Cretan antiquities, notably seals, but also miscellaneous antiquities of many cultures and periods. He bequeathed funds for the continuing upkeep of the Minoan room. No less remarkable were the gifts of Sir John and Lady Beazley, who gave over four hundred items between 1912 and 1966, when in a single gift they presented their entire remaining collection of over eight hundred pieces. These ranged widely among the ancient cultures of the Mediterranean world, but were outstanding for the gems and Greek vases.

The department of antiquities regularly benefited from discoveries made during excavations in Egypt and the Near East to which either it or its friends had subscribed. Material from inter-war excavations in Nubia (including the Shrine of Taharqa) was given by Professor and Mrs F. Ll. Griffith, from Kish in Iraq by Professor Stephen Langdon and from Jericho by John Garstang. After 1945 a new generation of archaeologists continued to build up the collections in this way. Outstanding among them were two graduates of Oxford, Dame Kathleen Kenyon, digging at Jericho and Jerusalem, and Sir Max Mallowan excavating Nimrud in Iraq. In the 1970s, however, changes in local laws governing the distribution of newly discovered antiquities put an end to such activities, and in recent years the only source of excavated objects to remain open to the department in this way has been the Hashemite kingdom of Jordan. After the Second World War the Museum became responsible for rescue archaeology in the Oxford area, and this has reinforced the collections with many local finds. With the creation of the county museum at Woodstock, this activity was handed over to local archaeologists and in 1966 for the first time in many years no local excavations were initiated by the Ashmolean Museum.

Gifts and bequests of collections of fine art, continuing its tradition of attracting collections, have dramatically transformed the Ashmolean Museum's holdings in these areas. One of the first benefactors, assiduously nurtured by C. F. Bell, Keeper of Fine Art from 1908 until 1931, was Mrs W. F. Weldon; her first gift was made in 1915 and her bequest of fifty pictures remaining in her possession was effected in 1936. In the intervening years she regularly purchased works of art for the Museum. Legend has it that she sometimes left them with the porter wrapped in brown paper with the words, 'this is for the keeper'. Her principal gifts were paintings, which included Claude's last work, 'Ascanius shooting the Stag of Sylvia', given in 1926; other gifts included drawings, one of which was a preparatory drawing by Claude for the painting just mentioned. Around the same period Professor Francis Pierrepont Barnard was putting together a large and excellent group of English watercolours, which were either given to the Museum in 1916 or bequeathed in 1934. In 1933 a collection of about fifteen hundred ceramics, assembled over a long period to illustrate the history of Chinese pottery and porcelain, was received as the bequest of Professor Sayce. Although the whole period from prehistoric times until the present century is covered, the wares of the Sung and early Ming dynasties are best represented.

1939 saw three very different additions which significantly broadened the scope of the collections. The brothers Alfred and Arthur Hill, both directors of the violin-making firm of W. E. Hill and Sons, assembled one of the finest collections in existence of stringed instruments—including Stradivarius's 'Messiah' of 1716, perhaps his most famous instrument. In addition to illustrating the history of stringed instruments from the sixteenth to the eighteenth century, the collection was intended to preserve for posterity examples in pristine condition by taking them out of circulation. (This collection was reinforced in 1970 by the donation of the Bate collection of European wind-instruments, housed in the music faculty building.) The Daisy Linda Ward bequest of ninety Dutch and Flemish still-life paintings was also received in 1939. The collector, a still-life painter herself, had assembled a highly specialized collection which not only greatly strengthened the meagre holdings of Netherlandish painting but also provided a rare source of study for the subject. In the same year another part of the picture collection was enriched by the bequest of part of the F. Hindley Smith collection, which was being divided among a number of museums and galleries; paintings by later nineteenth-century French and early twentieth-century French and English artists were supplemented by drawings and watercolours of the same schools and by several fine pieces of sculpture.

In 1946 the holdings of decorative arts were enriched by the bequest, through the National Art-Collections Fund, of Gaspard Oliver Farrer's collection. This included over two hundred pieces of silver plate, unrivalled in quality or quantity for its representation of English rococo silver, by immigrant Huguenot silversmiths; it included no less than forty-four examples by Paul Lameric. In addition to six old master paintings, the collection comprised some two hundred pieces of Chinese porcelain, with eighteenth-century wares outstandingly represented. In the following year the holdings in the decorative arts were further greatly augmented by the bequest of J. Francis Mallett, whose collection was described by K. T. Parker as 'the sublimated product of a lifetime devoted with almost equal enthusiasm to the accumulation of Western and Eastern objects of art'.[18] The western section, numbering over three hundred items, is notable for the medieval ivories, the Limoges enamels and European clocks and watches. The eastern section, with over double that number of items, is particularly strong in porcelains of the Ming period.

In 1950 Esther, the wife of Lucien Pissarro and the daughter-in-law of Camille, gave the first instalment of a comprehensive representation of work by various members of the Pissarro family which eventually included paintings, prints, drawings and watercolours as well as various letters and other manuscripts related to the Eragny Press, thereby establishing the Ashmolean Museum as a centre of research in this subject-area. Another

[18] *Annual Report of the Ashmolean Museum, Oxford* 1947, 28.

very different specialized collection arrived in 1957: in memory of their son killed on active service during the war, Mr and Mrs H. R. Marshall gave their remarkable assembly of Worcester porcelain, as well as their equally specialized group of English and continental glass and silver, enamel and porcelain wine labels.

In 1956 the eastern art holdings were transformed by the arrival of Sir Alan Barlow's collection of Islamic pottery, numbering 164 examples of outstanding quality, and above all by Sir Herbert Ingram's gift of some 3,700 objects, principally Chinese ceramics and bronzes; these more than doubled the then sub-department's collections. With its examples of earlier material, of which the donor was regarded as the world's leading collector, the Chinese holdings now had a serious claim to be regarded as a major collection. The founding of a separate department devoted to eastern art rightly followed in 1962; two years later it found another benefactor in Eric North who, in addition to making generous gifts of money, systematically built up the collection of Chinese lacquer.

Between 1914 and 1970 there were also a great many single acquisitions. During Kenneth Clark's brief keepership of fine art from 1931 to 1933 Piero di Cosimo's painting of the 'Forest Fire', presented by the National Art-Collections Fund, and Jörg Petel's beautiful ivory of 'Venus and Cupid' were added to the collection. But the most remarkable three decades of purchases and gifts took place during the reign of Clark's successor, K. T. (later Sir Karl) Parker. In an early annual report he said that one of his principal aims was 'to extend and develop' the collection of drawings.[19] He nobly fulfilled his promise, so that by the time he retired in 1962 he had added well over three thousand drawings to the collection. Taking advantage of the stagnant art market as well as his good relations with a number of art dealers (notably Dr James Byam Shaw of Messrs P. and D. Colnaghi) Parker was able systematically to build up a comprehensive holding of drawings, irrespective of fashion and covering all schools, from the early Renaissance up to and including the present century. His broad taste and eye for quality resulted in many acquisitions of works by greater and lesser artists, and today the Ashmolean can boast one of the great print rooms of the world, second only in importance in Britain to the British Museum.

Outside the Ashmolean Museum the largest collection of works of art is owned by Christ Church. For many years displayed in most unsatisfactory conditions in the library, the collection was moved into the new picture gallery in 1968, which through the generosity of Mr Charles (now Lord) Forte had been built by Powell and Moya in an ingeniously contrived site at the end of the Dean's garden. The new display of the paintings and the regularly changing exhibitions of drawings, made more accessible through

19 Ibid. 1938, 30.

the publication of James Byam Shaw's two catalogues, have greatly added to the University's attractions for the visitor.

The University's patronage of contemporary artists has been neither large nor perceptive, and it has been conservative in its choice of portrait painters.[20] These include most of the well-known practitioners, including Henry Lamb from an earlier generation and Graham Sutherland, William Coldstream, Carel Weight and Pietro Annigoni from a later. New College, however, bought Jacob Epstein's vast figure of Lazarus for its chapel and a bronze by Barbara Hepworth. Some of the recent foundations such as Lady Margaret Hall, St Anne's and Nuffield have received either gifts or bequests of twentieth-century British painting. The most notable act of patronage after the Second World War took place at St Catherine's, which, as well as acquiring Epstein's bust of Einstein, purchased bronzes by Henry Moore and Barbara Hepworth to decorate its grounds.

Far more enterprise and activity, particularly during the 1950s and 1960s, could be found in the junior common rooms, whose members either through a natural eye or good luck often acquired works by artists who were later to become well established and sometimes famous. The undergraduates at Worcester acquired a Henry Moore bronze and those at Pembroke the head of a man by Francis Bacon. St Edmund Hall's junior common room (now joined by the fellows) has, through an annual subscription, purchased for the Hall a fine group of works by modern British artists, starting with Mark Gertler and Stanley Spencer and moving on to John Piper, John Minton, Ivon Hitchens and L. S. Lowry; in 1957 they commissioned an altarpiece of 'Christ at Emmaus' by Ceri Richards.

Were a pre-First-World-War visitor to return to Oxford today, he would not be greatly surprised by the change in the University's physical appearance. What would undoubtedly strike him very much more forcibly, and one can surmise not entirely pleasurably, is the transformation of the daily life in Oxford's streets, especially during the summer months. Oxford's growth as an industrial and commercial centre is as nothing compared to the effects of the explosion of world tourism since the 1960s on both city and University. Phalanxes of tourists, often herded into groups both of young and old, fill the streets. Some remain only wet-weather friends of the museums, and statistics are unreliable, but today's visitors to Oxford's museums cannot be far from ten times what they were in 1914. Furthermore, museums are becoming more resourceful. No longer can curatorial staff arrange their collections to suit the intellectual interests of themselves and the needs of their students. They must now, if they are to attract the sponsorship and outside funding vital for their survival, rethink the displays

---

[20] This subject was discussed by Kenneth Garlick in his talk on 'Portraits in hall' to the History of the University seminar, Corpus Christi College, 20 Jan. 1989, Brian Harrison's transcript, HUA.

of their collections and thereby raise and update the profile of their institution. A delicate balance needs to be struck, and judgement and determination are required if a museum is to maintain its intrinsic character, rather than risk catering for the lowest common denominator by a populist descent into a theme-park.

19

Architecture

DIANE KAY

'I do not suppose any adolescent susceptible to man-made beauty can spend a large part of three years at Oxford without being profoundly moved by those grey stones.'[1] Few undergraduates have been as profoundly influenced by Oxford's architecture as James Lees-Milne, but its educational impact, often only half-recognized at the time, is considerable. The nature of that impact has altered a good deal during the twentieth century as Oxford has responded in the face of formidable pressures for change. Many colleges have built substantial additions, new colleges have sprung up, and the University's library and faculty accommodation has greatly expanded [figure 19.1]. Yet Oxford's historic townscape has survived largely intact. Throughout the period a consciousness of Oxford's historic buildings and the University's traditions have influenced and moderated new developments. How has this come about? This discussion falls into two parts, divided by the Second World War. Each begins with repairs to the historic fabric, followed by new buildings and their interiors. Post-war building conversions close the chapter.

In 1937 the University launched a public appeal for funds, and in the late 1930s it also released money from its own reserves, which it had hitherto been unwilling to spend on buildings.[2] Capital funding from the University Grants Committee (UGC) was still rare. Between the wars the repair and restoration of Oxford's historic buildings continued. Major structural repairs took place at the Sheldonian Theatre from 1935 to 1937, when Fielding Dodd strengthened much of the timberwork with steel. Badly weathered stonework was sometimes refaced. Peckwater quad in Christ Church was refaced between 1924 and 1930. However, stonework was more often patched, as at the Radcliffe Camera in the 1920s. Environmental enhancement was already a priority. Various colleges tidied up their back areas as new buildings rose to fill available space. Worthington's library for New College [plate 19.4] and its garden replaced outbuildings and back

[1] J. Lees-Milne, *Another Self* (London 1970), 93.
[2] OUA, D. Veale's memorandum on 'The building programme', 1–2.

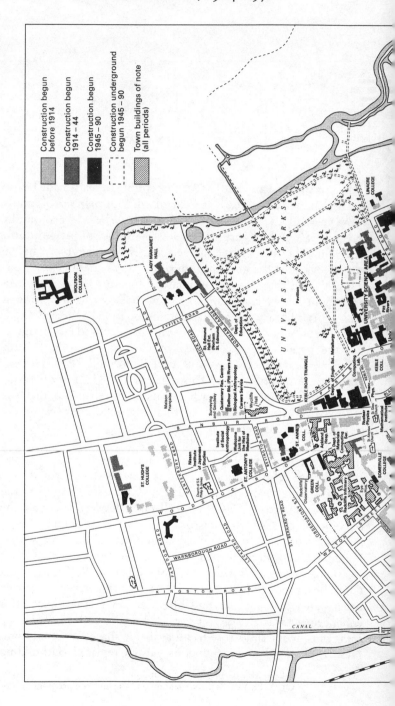

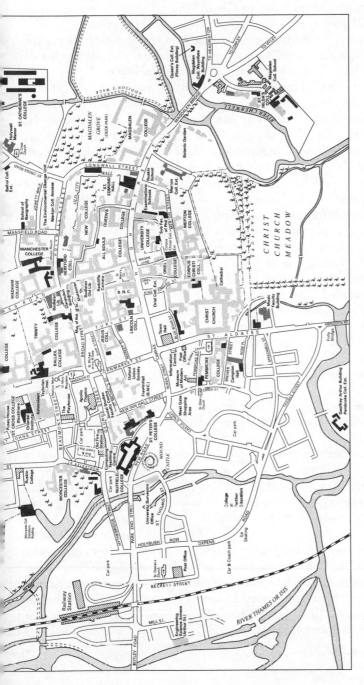

FIGURE 19.1   THE MAIN NEWLY BUILT UNIVERSITY AND COLLEGE BUILDINGS IN
OXFORD, 1914–1990

yards. Run-down buildings close to Christ Church were cleared to create the war memorial gardens, laid out by John Coleridge in 1925–6.

The use of stone was almost universal in central Oxford during the period. The durable Clipsham stone, introduced in the last century by T. G. Jackson, was popular both for repairs and for new buildings. Bladon stone rubble was also much used for new buildings. Brick was usually relegated to peripheral sites. Architects and patrons often had clear views about what was appropriate in Oxford and what was not. At Merton T. H. Hughes reclad Butterfield's Grove Building in 1930, removing the third storey, adding wings and subduing it to a mellow neo-Tudor style. Goodhart-Rendel described the result as 'something of the sort Americans expect to find at Oxford'. In 1929 the *Architects' Journal* noted the preference in Oxford for what it called 'tutor's Tudor' in contrast to the neo-Georgian favoured in Cambridge.[3] This 'Oxford style' was popular chiefly in the city centre. It was based upon late and post-medieval precedent and late nineteenth-century interpretations such as that of Bodley and Garner at Magdalen, George Gilbert Scott the younger at St John's and T. G. Jackson at Brasenose. Gables, mullioned windows and oriels were characteristic features. Inter-war examples included Giles Scott's building for Magdalen of 1928–30 and T. H. Hughes's extension of 1929 for Corpus Christi College. In the latter the detailing was simpler, many windows being wholly without drip moulds. Hubert Worthington's Besse Building for Pembroke still recalled this style in 1956. Fielding Dodd's stone rubble block of 1934 for St Edmund Hall, completing the main quad, copied more exactly the adjacent sub-medieval buildings.

Rhodes House by Herbert Baker was also nourished by this 'Oxford myth', but had a more domestic character [plate 19.1]. It was built in 1929 as the headquarters for the Rhodes scholarship system and to provide additional educational facilities for the University. The rotunda was a memorial to Lord Milner, the chairman of the trustees, who had died in 1925. Baker aimed to be 'as styleless and elementary as possible'.[4] However, the building was both complex and style-conscious—an eclectic amalgam in the arts and crafts tradition, part medieval hall, part Cotswold manor house and part Pantheon. Baker combined mullioned and transomed windows with unorthodox classical detailing in a structure which had the complexity of a public building and the roofscape of a domestic one. This fusion produced an appearance both of establishment and of accretion over time. The building had a traditional hipped stone-slated roof (since re-covered) and coursed squared Bladon rubble walls, recalling Jackson's choice at Brasenose but more roughly dressed. (This choice of material would be

---

[3] H. S. Goodhart-Rendel, *Vitruvian Nights* (London 1932), 157; 'Mr Smith', 'In Oxford and Cambridge', *Architects' Jl* 9 Jan. 1929, 96.
[4] H. Baker, *Architecture and Personalities* (London 1944), 136.

criticized by many after the war.) Yet with its plain unmoulded windows and large expanses of wall, Rhodes House had an austerity and a sculptural quality which unmistakably identified it as an inter-war building. It heralded later Oxford work, particularly that of Hubert Worthington, Morley Horder and Austen Harrison.

Campion Hall by Edwin Lutyens was built for the Society of Jesus between 1935 and 1942. The building was more urban and more collegiate than Rhodes House, hugging the streetline and forming an open quad behind. The stone rubble reflected that of the medieval town wall opposite, although in Campion Hall it was coursed and squared rather than random. The main entrance lay beneath the chapel, which dominated the street façade in place of the usual gatehouse and tower. Campion Hall was again a stylistic synthesis: gables and mullions were combined with classical entrances adorned with Lutyens's Delhi order. The same order also appeared inside the chapel [plate 19.2]. The bells which take the place of Ionic volutes in this order are said to symbolize the summons to mass. The chapel itself had Romanesque overtones although its strength and simplicity also recalled High Victorian work.

Nuffield College's architect was Austen Harrison. As built (1949–62), the College represented a culmination of the 'Oxford myth'. The original design had recalled Harrison's recent archaeological museum in Palestine, with flat roofs and pointed relieving arches, but Lord Nuffield rejected this as 'un-English' and had requested 'something on the lines of Cotswold domestic architecture'.[5] The plan was traditional, forming two linked quads with access by staircase to the students' rooms. After the war the building was heavily criticized. J. M. Richards saw it as a 'missed opportunity of a really tragic kind'; given its siting outside the city centre it might have demonstrated 'that Oxford does not live only in the past'.[6]

Classicism was by contrast more popular nationally, especially for commercial and municipal buildings and in higher education. In Oxford it was preferred for sites outside the city centre. In the science area the Dyson Perrins Laboratory of 1913–16 by Paul Waterhouse and the Sir William Dunn School of Pathology of 1926 by E. P. Warren were variations in red brick on early eighteenth-century themes; Harry Redfern's building for biochemistry (1924–7) was a stripped classical pilastered block. Classicism was also popular in the women's colleges, likewise sited on the periphery of Oxford. The 'Queen Anne' style had become associated with women's education since Basil Champneys's Newnham College in Cambridge, begun in 1874. In Oxford Lady Margaret Hall, Somerville College and St Hugh's College followed this lead. In 1914 Buckland and Haywood designed a

[5] H. M. Colvin, *Unbuilt Oxford* (New Haven Conn. and London 1983), 174.
[6] J. M. Richards, 'Recent building in Oxford and Cambridge', *Architectural Rev.* Aug. 1952, 75.

group of red-brick neo-Georgian buildings for St Hugh's; Cooper's block of 1934 for St Hilda's College was also neo-Georgian. Reginald Blomfield's buildings for Lady Margaret Hall of 1896, 1909–10 and 1915 were in a red-blooded English baroque. In 1931 Lady Margaret Hall appointed another national figure to extend the Hall. Giles Scott used a restrained but strangely proportioned neo-Georgian for his Deneke Building, this time in brown brick. Blomfield's buildings formed a series of linked pavilions in the garden, and Scott's symmetrical block avoided forming a courtyard with these. For the chapel Scott chose a simplified Byzantine manner, with transepts and a low polygonal crossing tower enclosing a dome and with circular and round-headed windows [plate 19.3]. This style gave the building religious associations while harmonizing with its classical surroundings. The chapel's massive sculptural character recalled Scott's other churches.

When classicism appeared in central Oxford it was usually in a classical context. Thus Herbert Read's rector's lodgings for Lincoln College (1929–30) were adjacent to All Saints church and T. H. Hughes's subtle extension to the Taylor Institution (1932) carried through the main cornice-line of Cockerell's adjacent block and echoed his arch motifs, while remaining visually subservient. Hughes's Regent's Park College (1938–40) was close to St John Street; Maufe's Playhouse (1938) continued the window rhythms of the adjacent Georgian houses. Hubert Worthington's block of shops for Lincoln in Turl Street (1939) emulated the self-effacing Georgian stucco-fronted houses of the area. J. Osborne Smith's library for Trinity College (1925–7) was designed under the direction of President Blakiston, who dictated the imposing neo-classical character.[7] It was not visible from the street and made its own context. Fielding Dodd's block of 1930 for St Peter's, in the style of the late seventeenth century but exceptionally of brick, was also largely concealed. In the late 1930s classicism became increasingly popular, even where the context did not demand it.

After Rhodes House, classical detailing was increasingly combined with stone rubble and sometimes with steeply pitched roofs of stone slates. One example was Morley Horder's quad of 1933 for Somerville. Hubert Worthington's building of 1936 in St Aldate's for the non-residential St Catherine's Society and W. G. Newton's block of 1939 for Worcester had followed. Other buildings by Hubert Worthington combined this architect's distinctive residual classical details with horizontal rooflines. These included the extension of 1933–4 to Jackson's Radcliffe Science Library and, in central Oxford, the Rose Lane buildings of 1939–40 for Merton, and New College's new library of 1939 [plate 19.4], both of whose walls of coursed, squared Bladon rubble were designed to fit into the context provided by the adjacent old town wall. Neither building was of urban character; each was a

---

[7] Information by courtesy of Howard Colvin.

freestanding symmetrical composition and neither formed part of a quad, unlike Horder's work at Somerville.

The eclecticism of Oxford's inter-war buildings was typical of British architecture in the period, as was the preference for simplified, massive sculptural forms. During the 1930s stylistic freedom increased, fed by growing pressure from international modernism. Modernism was gaining ground in Britain but remained controversial; given the strength of the 'Oxford myth' it is not surprising that it was shunned in Oxford. Cambridge was only slightly less conservative; the Mond laboratories (1932) and Fen court at Peterhouse (1939) by H. C. Hughes, both of brick, were simple, light designs, but were unobtrusively sited. Schemes prepared by leading modernists for both Oxford and Cambridge remained unbuilt. These included designs of 1936 by Samuel and Harding for a new dining hall and sets of rooms facing on to Broad Street at Balliol and Maxwell Fry's proposals of 1937 for an addition to All Souls.[8]

The 1930s saw a substantial expansion in the University's library accommodation. This included the New Bodleian Library, an extension to the Radcliffe Science Library and eventually also a history faculty library in Merton Street. All reflected the increasing stylistic freedom of the period, especially Giles Scott's New Bodleian Library of 1937–40. Like architects such as Herbert Rowse and Robert Atkinson, Scott sought to create an idiom which was contemporary but which, unlike modernism, could provide some of the decorative richness and monumentality associated with styles of historical revival. His Cambridge University Library (1931–4) already reflected this search and his experience there made him an obvious choice for the New Bodleian Library.

Given its site in central Oxford, the New Bodleian Library was surprisingly bold: a steel-framed structure with strong horizontal lines and curved corners, the upper floors recessed from the streetline. A tunnel connected it to the main library, carrying an automatic book-conveyor which was linked to dispatch-stations in the stack and reading rooms; internal telephone and pneumatic tubes for messages completed the system. The Rockefeller Foundation paid three-fifths of the cost of extending the Library and paid for the Librarian and architect to go on a tour of American university libraries.[9] Yet the new library's stylistic inspiration was European rather than American. Certain details recalled Dudok, such as the horizontal windows divided by upward-breaking mullions, while the rounded corners and stair tower suggested Eric Mendelsohn. However, unlike the work of these architects, the new library was neither light nor streamlined. The Bladon rubble instead ensured a massive, even monumental effect. The stone and the neo-baroque doorways were concessions to the central Oxford

[8] Colvin, *Unbuilt Oxford*, 160–6.
[9] See above, 474, 477 and below, 645–6.

context. As one journal observed, 'the elevations are designed with due respect to the traditions that produced the surrounding old buildings, but no attempt has been made to ignore modern tendencies'.[10] Scott's Hartland House for St Anne's developed the same theme in 1938. By the outbreak of war the historical straitjacket was beginning to loosen, even in central Oxford, and the use of stone remained the chief concern. In the science area Lanchester and Lodge also sought to combine modernity with monumentality. The buildings constructed for physical chemistry in 1939–40 were typical; Lodge's utilitarian brick structures were sited away from the street. For forestry and botany, fronting on to South Parks Road, Hubert Worthington was appointed instead and stone rubble was used (1947–50).

The interior detailing of the period was generally solid and simple with plenty of wood and sometimes polished stone. Rhodes House and Campion Hall had more internal decoration than most, much of it symbolic. Some interior spaces had a strongly sculptural character. At Rhodes House the rotunda and the vestibule were domed while the hall had a polygonal apse; the chapel at Campion Hall had a semicircular apse and a barrel vault [plate 19.2]. The chapel at Lady Margaret Hall also had a centralized domed space and an apse. Vault surfaces were generally left plain, emphasizing their shape. Hubert Worthington's interiors were noted for their simplified classical dignity; his Radcliffe Science and New College libraries had elegant curved staircases. In residential buildings the traditional staircase plan was sometimes used, but access by corridor was also popular. Corridors were the norm for women's colleges but were also provided for men, at Campion Hall and elsewhere. Merton's Rose Lane buildings had two-room sets with traditional staircase-access, as did Scott's block for Magdalen and Fielding Dodd's for St Peter's, but the Nuffield block at Worcester had some single rooms, while single rooms were normal in the women's colleges and at Campion Hall.

Inter-war garden design in Oxford was dominated by the influence of Gertrude Jekyll and the arts and crafts movement. Herbaceous and mixed borders were popular. A notable garden was created at St Hugh's by Annie Rogers, *custos hortulorum*, from the gardens of several houses formerly on the College's site. At Rhodes House Herbert Baker used stone-paved terraces and geometrical beds to extend the architecture into the garden. A broad herbaceous border reflected the influence of his friend Gertrude Jekyll. At Worcester the garden of the provost's lodgings was laid out by the painter-gardener Alfred Parsons with old-fashioned flowers.

The large commissions of the period were often given to architects with national reputations, such as Scott, Baker and Lutyens, Blomfield, Maufe and Cooper. Hubert Worthington and T. H. Hughes were less important

---

[10] 'Bodleian Library extension, Oxford', *Architect and Building News* 3 Aug. 1940, 143.

nationally but specialized in academic buildings and their Oxford work formed a significant part of their output. When the local architect Fielding Dodd was commissioned to design the substantial new block for St Peter's, Baker acted as consultant.

During the Second World War building work ceased, except for urgent minor works. Building licensing persisted until November 1954. In the late 1940s the post of University Surveyor was established. Jack Lankester was appointed as Deputy Surveyor in 1951 and became Surveyor in 1955. The Surveyor's office was initially responsible for repairs and minor works but was soon designing new buildings of increasing size—notably the Mathematical Institute of 1966, the local examinations delegacy of 1966–74 and the underground extension to the Radcliffe Science Library.

Capital grants from the UGC became increasingly important for the University's facilities in Oxford as in other British universities, but the UGC contributed only rarely to college projects—residential accommodation for Somerville and St Catherine's and the dining hall at St Anne's were examples. UGC funding brought with it strict constraints as to cost. Private benefactions remained important, especially to the colleges, although increases in taxation in the early post-war years reduced the flow of private benefactions.[11] The Wolfson, Rockefeller and Ford foundations and later the Sainsbury family all made major contributions. Smaller donations also played their part, especially in the Historic Buildings and St Catherine's College appeals.

By the 1950s many of Oxford's historic buildings were in a serious condition, made worse by the lack of repairs during the war. Roofs badly needed overhauling and stonework was visibly crumbling, particularly on Oxford's seventeenth- and eighteenth-century buildings, many built of poor-quality Headington freestone. The Historic Buildings Appeal was launched in June 1957. Major contributions were made by the Ford Foundation, the Historic Buildings Council (for work to colleges), the UGC (for work to the University's buildings) and by the University and the richer colleges themselves.

In the repair of stonework, aesthetic and architectural considerations often took precedence over archaeological ones (by which more original stonework might have been preserved). Refacing was now generally preferred to patching, which *Country Life* considered 'from an aesthetic point of view is almost always deplorable'.[12] One of the most dramatic refacing projects was that of the library at Christ Church from 1960 [plate 8.2]. Here Portland stone and Clipsham replaced Headington hardstone, Headington freestone and 'Burford' stone, providing an approximate

---

[11] Veale, 'Building programme', 9.
[12] A. Oswald, 'Unfamiliar faces at Oxford', *Country Life* 30 May 1963, 1239.

equivalent to the original contrast in colour, with the giant order and upper storey in white stone and the subsidiary order in cream. Clipsham stone, from Rutland, was often the preferred replacement; at Wadham a blue-vein variety was used 'to relieve the uniformity of the surface'.[13] Even where surfaces were not fully refaced, carvings were often renewed—such as those on the hall and chapel string-courses at New College. New 'emperors' heads' were sculpted by Michael Black for the Sheldonian forecourt.

Occasionally, axing back was undertaken instead of refacing, as in parts of the hall at Oriel and at Queen's for parts of the outer perimeter of the north quad (although many parts of the College were refaced). Axing back preserved more of the original fabric than refacing and produced a surface which was less susceptible to water penetration and frost damage than a pitted one; however, it had aesthetic disadvantages since it altered the relationship between architectural features—such as drip mouldings—and the wall surface. More conservative was the approach adopted in the later stages of work at Worcester, where hardly any new stone was used and the existing surfaces remained. Work on the north front and east return of the terrace building had been postponed when more urgent work was found elsewhere. When an extra grant was made, the work was confined to washing, toning down earlier cement repairs, removing loose and dangerous pieces of stone, and pointing and filling deep holes.[14] Further work is now (1993) being carried out on these surfaces.

There were some experiments in stone-cleaning. At the Bodleian Library the architect Robert Potter experimented with steam and dry sand-blasting, but the most effective method was found to be the application of a fine mist spray, generated by small electric pumps; the moisture content of the stone was monitored by bronze anodes sunk into the interior wall surfaces.[15] At Merton the two fifteenth-century statues on the north transept of the chapel were cleaned by Professor A. R. W. Baker with a lime poultice, a technique which laid the foundations for Baker's later work on the west front of Wells cathedral. Synthetic stone consolidants were not popular, since no chemical was known which would repel water without blocking the 'pores' of the stone (which could cause spalling).

Timberwork too often needed repair. Sometimes modern materials and structural techniques were used. Owing to a shortage of timber, reinforced concrete was used to re-roof the chancel of St Mary's church after the fire of 1946.[16] It was also used to repair parts of the Bodleian Library and the Sheldonian Theatre. The floor-structure of the Sheldonian arena, with its

<hr/>

[13] W. F. Oakeshott (ed.), Oxford Stone Restored: The Work of the Oxford Historic Buildings Fund 1957–1974 (Oxford 1975), 113.

[14] Ibid. 117.

[15] Ibid. 23.

[16] 'St Mary the Virgin, Oxford: new chancel roof in concrete', Builder 7 Nov. 1947, 512–13.

closely spaced and probably original oak posts, was judged by the consulting engineers to be inadequate and was replaced with a reinforced concrete floor without intermediate supports. A new meeting room was constructed in the deepened basement. At Magdalen steel beams were introduced in reconstructing the floor of the hall, and also inside the tower and elsewhere. Structural work sometimes led to hidden historic features being revealed; the thirteenth-century roof of the Warden's or Little Hall at Merton College was revealed and repaired in 1970 with advice from Cecil Hewett [plate 19.5]. Repair work of this period also indicated a changing attitude to Victorian buildings. At Worcester William Burges's alterations to the interior of the hall were removed in 1966 and Wyatt's design reinstated; however, Butterfield's Keble College was repaired from 1962 with money from the fund.[17] Arguably some of the repairs went beyond what would today be considered structurally necessary or desirable. However they surely reflected the attitudes of the period: a tremendous confidence in the future and a zeal to perpetuate Oxford's environment indefinitely. Possibly this was the same enthusiasm for 'renewal' which found an outlet elsewhere in redevelopment.

Classicism was the preferred style for early post-war buildings in Oxford, as in Maufe's Dolphin quad for St John's and Worthington's adjoining Dolphin gate for Trinity of 1948, both in ashlar; Oliver Hill's projected but unbuilt crescent for the edge of the Botanic Garden (1947) would also have been classical.[18] Later examples included Raymond Erith's subtle and restrained provost's lodgings of 1958 for Queen's, his galleried library and Wolfson West Building of red brick for Lady Margaret Hall (1959–61 and 1963–6) and buildings of 1954–5 and 1960–1 by Richardson and Houfe for St Hilda's. By the mid-1950s classicism was a minority taste in British architecture. Modernism was established both with private clients and in official circles; school building programmes and housing estates demonstrated its vitality, as did building schemes already prepared for various universities. In 1952 Hugh Casson had designed an arts faculty complex for Cambridge University and by 1959 the campus of Sussex University was being planned by Basil Spence. In Oxford the move to modernity was promoted by various individuals, notably Alic Smith as Vice-Chancellor and David Henderson as junior proctor. Henderson welcomed the end of the era 'in which too many decisions about architecture have been based on a hopelessly myopic view of what is suited to Oxford and a completely unreflective conservatism in questions of building'.[19] Goddard's stone rubble block of 1951–4 for Wadham was modern, but Pevsner thought it 'tamely handled'. The Oriental

[17] Oakeshott, 72.
[18] 'New Botanic Garden building, Oxford', *Builder* 4 July 1947, 10–11.
[19] P. D. Henderson, 'New buildings in Oxford', *Oxford* May 1958, 84.

Institute (1958–62) was also insipid and whimsical, with neo-regency decorations around the entrance. The spirit of innovation was more powerfully expressed by the placing of Epstein's 'Lazarus' in New College's chapel in 1952. The first uninhibited modern buildings were sited in the science area, away from the historic city centre. These were the Dyson Perrins lecture-theatre and the department of metallurgy, begun in 1957, both by Basil Ward. Arguably modernism was very appropriate for science buildings, related as it was to the use of new technology. However, Ward's work in the science area was not an unqualified success because his firm lacked the capacity and organization for large jobs and lacked experience in designing laboratories; the University learnt from its mistakes. The first substantial college building to be confidently modern was the 'beehive' building of 1958–60 at St John's [plate 19.6], by the Architects' Co-Partnership, who had recently extended the President's lodgings at Corpus Christi (1957–9).

Designing new college buildings for city-centre sites presented considerable problems. Thomas Sharp's report for Oxford City Council, published in 1948 as *Oxford Replanned*, already offered some guidance. Sharp identified various qualities intrinsic to the visual character of central Oxford, notably intricacy, strong architectural contrast, reticence and urbanity. These suggested a possible approach. To Sharp it was 'essential that future work should be harmonious with the old—it being understood, of course, that harmony does not lie in an imitation of *style*, but rather the choice of material and in scale'. Sharp deplored stone rubble and saw Oxford as 'essentially an ashlar city'.[20] Materials, scale and rhythm were seen to be the key. St John's 'beehive' building already offered a solution. Its plan, a web of interlocking hexagons, produced a serrated façade which broke down the scale of the block and produced a strong verticality which suited the rhythm of the surrounding neo-gothic buildings. This was comparable to Basil Spence's use of the saw-tooth plan at Coventry cathedral (1956–62) which was also designed for a gothic context.

This approach contrasted with the prevailing taste for dominant horizontals. David Roberts's block of 1961–2 for New College was an example. It was concealed from within the College by the medieval town wall but it presented a rigid horizontal façade to Longwall Street and has been criticized for this. University College's Goodhart Building of 1960–1 was also a large block although the scale was broken down by oriel windows and a ground-floor cloister. Vertical articulation could also reduce apparent scale and allied to this was a breaking away from regular geometry. Powell and Moya made an early step in their small but influential addition to Brasenose College of 1959, on a restricted 'back-yard' site [plate 19.7]. For the five-storey block,

20 T. Sharp, *Oxford Replanned* (London 1948), 172.

the architects explained, 'a rigidly rectangular plan has been rejected and an informal, serrated outline, more in keeping with the character of the surrounding buildings, allows rooms to be individually treated to make the most of the sometimes charming but restricted and oblique views'.[21] This produced a strong verticality. An early version of the design had mullioned windows but later this residual historicism was abandoned in favour of plate glass. This was the first of an important series of buildings for colleges in Oxford and Cambridge by the practice.

In a project for Cambridge Howell, Killick, Partridge and Amis also broke with regular geometry. Their acclaimed but unsuccessful entry to the competition for Churchill College (1958–9) comprised a cluster of irregular courts enclosed by chains of linked residential blocks. Aspects of the detailing and planning later informed this firm's work at St Anne's College in Oxford (planned, 1960). Here a flexible chain of six blocks was to wind around the site in an S formation, loosely enclosing the existing quad. Only two blocks were built. The 'chain' plan was also useful for sensitive central locations. In the Cripps Building for St John's, Cambridge (1964–6) and Blue Boar quad for Christ Church (1964–8) Powell and Moya developed their Brasenose idiom on a flexible chain plan, to suit the shape of the sites. Both buildings had broad stone-clad piers. At Christ Church strong vertical projections at the rear were juxtaposed with the horizontal curving surface of the rubble wall along Blue Boar Street, producing a strongly picturesque effect. As at Brasenose, the cladding was Roach Bed Portland stone, the open texture of which imparted an immediate mellow, weathered quality.

Other firms also adopted a linear plan for central sites. The Sir Thomas White Building for St John's by Philip Dowson of Arup Associates (1971–6) housed over a hundred and fifty students, many in sets. It comprised a series of three-bay blocks, linked by recessed staircase-towers to form a rough L plan [plate 19.8]. This rhythm, and the expressed structural frame, helped to break down the scale of this large scheme. The building specification was high, a white bush-hammered concrete frame contrasting with cream stone from France; its proposed lifespan was four hundred years.[22] Another linear block was the addition by Ahrends, Burton and Koralek to Keble College (1969–77). This curled up at the head to form a quad by Museum Road, while its tail swept out along Blackhall Road. A highly picturesque, almost blind elevation faced the street, with vertical projections (for kitchens and bathrooms); this was clad in honey-coloured brick, recalling the stone of central Oxford rather than the red brick of the College's original buildings by Butterfield. The internal elevation was by contrast fully glazed, like James Stirling's earlier Florey Building for Queen's College.

---

[21] Powell and Moya, 'Brasenose College, Oxford: new buildings' (undated typescript cited by courtesy of the architects).

[22] P. Dowson, 'St. John's College: Sir Thomas White building', *Arup Jl* xiv (Apr. 1979), 6.

Proposals for more assertive buildings were not unknown. In 1962 Louis Osman designed a slim 150-foot tower block for St Edmund Hall's High Street site. However, the scheme was criticized by the Royal Fine Art Commission and rejected by the city's planning committee. In September 1962 the city published guidelines on high buildings. Designs were to be considered in relation to their effect on the city centre as seen from street level and also in relation to views of the Oxford skyline from various key viewpoints.[23]

The knitting of new buildings into the city centre required ingenuity. Co-operation with shops sometimes provided an answer, as at Trinity and Wadham. Maguire and Murray provided some thirty-five sets in two quads for Trinity behind the existing structure of Blackwell's bookshop in Broad Street, as well as a large extension to the bookshop itself. Gillespie, Kidd and Coia provided accommodation for Blackwell's music shop in making an extension for Wadham in 1971. The perhaps rather unresolved façade to Holywell Street resulted from a compromise with the Royal Fine Art Commission and the city, which rejected the architects' original faceted glass design. Another ingeniously unobtrusive scheme was Powell and Moya's Christ Church picture gallery (1964–7). This was discreetly sited in a corner of the deanery garden and was reached through an existing doorway in Canterbury quad. It was visible to the public only upon entry and the roof was grass-covered to minimize its impact when viewed from above. Worcester College's Sainsbury Building by MacCormac, Jamieson and Pritchard (a commission won in competition in 1980) arguably continued the approach developed in Oxford during the 1960s. The building was carefully grafted into its spacious but sensitive lakeside site by a manipulation of scale, texture and rhythm and by the choice of materials (stone rubble to match an adjacent wall and buff brick). Harmony was achieved without resorting to the revival of historical styles.

In the design of college buildings on the periphery of the city centre there was less concern for context and considerable architectural freedom. Philip Dowson's blocks for Somerville facing Little Clarendon Street expressed their concrete frames externally, overlaying a fully glazed elevation (1958–67). These were the first of several residential blocks by Dowson's firm in Oxford and Cambridge to use this device. At St Anne's and in the hall at St Antony's [1968–70: plate 19.9] Howell, Killick, Partridge and Amis demonstrated the sculptural effect and precision which could be achieved in precast concrete. In the Florey Building in St Clement's (1968–70) Stirling also produced a sculptural effect, in fiery red tiles and glass. The building turned away from its then dilapidated surroundings and presented a fully glazed face towards the river. The Smithsons' Garden Building for St Hilda's

---

[23] City Architect and Planning Officer, *High Buildings in Oxford* (Oxford 1962).

(1968–70) also had fully glazed rooms, facing the garden. Context was not allowed to dominate in these situations, although the buildings were kept low.

Equally bold were the two newly built colleges outside the city centre, St Catherine's and Wolfson. St Catherine's, built between 1960 and 1964, confirmed triumphantly the arrival of modernism in Oxford. The Danish architect Arne Jacobsen designed the College. A scrutiny of recent British buildings had failed to yield an obvious choice of architect, so the search widened to northern Europe (as an architect with experience of a similar climate was considered desirable). In 1958 Alan Bullock, Jack Lankester, Maurice Bowra and A. L. P. Norrington visited Denmark. They were impressed by the quality of Jacobsen's work and Bullock especially by the 'human' scale of one of Jacobsen's schools.[24] Jacobsen's appointment was approved in March 1959 and received a mixed reception. One correspondent of the *Times* described it as 'the greatest slap in the face delivered to English architects since the Frenchman William of Sens was brought in to rebuild the choir of Canterbury Cathedral'.[25] Lankester was to manage the building contract.

Jacobsen took a selective approach to the Oxford tradition. On his initial trip to Oxford he visited the colleges and asked to see plans of each; New College impressed him most, because of its unusual regularity. Jacobsen's plan was formal but not severe [plate 19.10]. Its near symmetry set it apart from the collegiate tradition of 'organic' accretion and was no doubt partly a product of the relatively flat and open site in the water-meadows. Also, while the College was organized around quads, these were not fully enclosed in the traditional manner. Instead St Catherine's comprised a series of rectangular blocks which coalesced but did not touch at the corners. In this, and in its overall formality, the plan recalled Mies van der Rohe's Illinois Institute of Technology in Chicago. A sense of enclosure was achieved instead by a subtle use of covered walkways, low walls and hedges. Jacobsen's garden was very much an integral part of the architecture, which is reflected in the memorable water garden. Internally the choice of staircases rather than corridors reflected tradition, as did the provision of a hall with a high table set on a dais. (This was more formal than Gerald Banks's slightly earlier hall of 1958–60 for St Anne's which was asymmetrical and designed for self-service.) To Alan Bullock the hall was especially important in fostering a sense of community; it was therefore made unusually large.[26]

With its clean rectangular forms St Catherine's was likened in the *Times* to 'some of the best recent American architecture'.[27] However, a mellow character appropriate to Oxford was imparted by the warm buff brick and

[24] Conversation with Lord Bullock, 26 Oct. 1989.
[25] D. Braddell, 'Why not a British architect?', *Times* 28 Feb. 1959, 11.
[26] Bullock, 26 Oct. 1989.
[27] 'Designs for St Catherine's College on show', *Times* 28 Oct. 1960, 8.

bronze cladding, and an established appearance was soon achieved as Jacobsen's carefully planted garden matured. In its architectural reticence the College contrasted strongly with New Hall, Churchill and Fitzwilliam in Cambridge, each marked by a conspicuous architectural statement (a dome, barrel vaults and an arched canopy). At St Catherine's the only point of emphasis was a slim concrete bell tower. Craftsmanship and attention to detailing were everywhere apparent. The bricklaying and the concrete were of exemplary quality. Jacobsen was also an accomplished industrial designer, and filled the College with his own furniture and fittings, some especially designed (notably the remarkable high-backed chairs in the senior common room and at high table in the hall). Most of the buildings were paid for by private donations, notably from Esso, the Wolfson Foundation, Bernard Sunley and Dr Rudolph Light. The UGC paid for the study-bedrooms, which were built to a lower specification than the rest of the College as a consequence of the UGC's cost-limits and the rule that private money should not supplement that from public funds.

At Churchill College, Cambridge, by contrast, the architects were British, and likewise at Wolfson College, Oxford, built between 1969 and 1972. After a tour of recent British work the buildings committee of Wolfson College chose Powell and Moya, now well respected in Oxford and Cambridge. In contrast to St Catherine's the plan comprised an irregular cluster of quads, two fully enclosed and a third opening out towards the river and embracing a punt harbour. Although this informality recalled the additive character of the older colleges, it was generated not by urban constraints but by the riverside setting and the position of several mature trees. Concrete and glass were the main materials, used without inhibition. A graduate college, Wolfson was exceptional in Oxford because it incorporated family houses and flats. (In Cambridge the much smaller Clare Hall of 1966–9 had already provided family housing.) Unmarried students had study-bedrooms grouped into flats, an arrangement becoming increasingly popular in other British universities. Access was by corridors punctuated by frequent staircases, a compromise with tradition.

The quality of newly built student housing in Oxford was generally very high in relation to that of other British universities (and also in comparison with older accommodation in Oxford itself, which often remained extremely shabby). Private funding permitted a higher than average building specification and allowance of space—occasionally sets but mostly bedsitters. Many rooms included built-in, specially chosen or purpose-designed furniture, as at St John's, Brasenose, St Catherine's, Somerville and Keble (where interior fittings were by John Makepeace). Some architects took a great deal of trouble to provide psychological security for the occupants of rooms with large windows (though others were less considerate). At Somerville and St John's Dowson recessed the full-height windows behind a concrete frame,

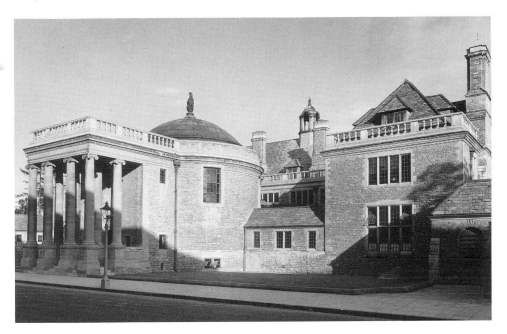

19.1 Rhodes House, north frontage

19.2 Campion Hall, interior of chapel

19.3 Lady Margaret Hall chapel

19.4 New College library

19.5 Merton College: roof of Warden's or Little Hall, after repair

19.6 St John's 'beehive' building

19.7 Brasenose Powell and Moya block, view across rooftops

19.8 St John's College: Sir Thomas White Building, view from garden

while at St Hilda's the Smithsons overlaid the glazing of their Garden Building with a timber screen. Balconies were often provided, as at St Anne's and Wolfson. At Wolfson these had glass fronts, tilted upwards to reflect the sky, giving privacy without obscuring the view. Access by staircase remained the norm, even in the new building for Keble, despite Butterfield's original corridor plan for the College. Indeed, the staircase plan was gaining popularity for student housing throughout Britain, providing a reference point for the individual and minimizing the risk of an institutional atmosphere.[28] Some new college buildings contained notable interiors. Characteristically these were austere and simple, without applied decoration; often structural materials were expressed and emphasized internally. The dining halls of St Catherine's and St Antony's [plate 19.9] were both striking and elegant, each with an exposed skeleton of finely finished concrete. Pale, polished timber cladding was also popular, as in the dining halls of St Antony's and Wolfson.

The post-war period also saw continued growth in the science area. Here functional demands and the UGC's cost-limits dictated priorities. The new buildings were uneasy neighbours. As Jack Lankester observed, 'what most scientists would like is freedom to change—to knock down, adapt, rebuild—in the same way as factories are developed'. 'This is why it is so difficult to fit science buildings into limited spaces in an urban environment where aesthetic considerations are important.'[29] Engineering (1960–3) and biochemistry (1960–2) by Basil Ward's firm were obtrusively tall and bulky and lacked architectural quality. Arup Associates' nuclear physics (from 1961) was more carefully detailed. As departments jostled for space, building high was considered. A 25-storey tower for zoology, by Chamberlin, Powell and Bon, was proposed in 1962 for a tiny site on the edge of the University Parks [plate 10.2]. It was to be slim, with a broken, tapering outline to minimize its environmental impact. However, the scheme was rejected by Congregation.[30] Zoology was finally built on a different site between 1966 and 1970. Sir Leslie Martin's highly compact low-rise design incorporated space for psychology. Martin identified servicing as a key issue in science buildings, and organized his building for zoology and psychology so that a 'tartan grid' of flexible service-zones ran between the bays of the structure (an idea simultaneously developed by Arup Associates at Birmingham University).[31] Despite its intended flexibility, however, the building today has insufficient service-capacity, and the concept was not

[28] See my thesis: D. Chablo, 'University architecture in Britain, 1950–1975' (Oxford DPhil thesis 1987), 153–4.
[29] Brian Harrison's transcript of my tape-recorded conversation with Jack Lankester, 10 July 1988.
[30] Colvin, *Unbuilt Oxford*, 184–6.
[31] Chablo, 116–20.

repeated in Oxford. Virology, by the Architects Design Partnership (1979–81), needed more sophisticated servicing (accounting for some 80 per cent of the cost) and was entirely different in design.[32]

Martin was also the architect for the St Cross Building in Manor Road (1961–5). With a grant from the Rockefeller Foundation the law library committee had visited eight American libraries. The Foundation also contributed to the building costs with the UGC and others. Facilities were provided for English, statistics and law in a compact building with interlocking accommodation, dominated by the sheer walls of the three top-lit library galleries. Martin's building was simultaneously relaxed and grand, with its low irregular massing and broad staircase [plate 19.12]. It was simply but surely detailed, internally and externally, the buff bricks and pale woodwork giving it a 'blond' Scandinavian character.

The Radcliffe Science Library required a further extension. This needed to be close by and was therefore built underneath the lawn in front of the University Museum between 1972 and 1975. Jack Lankester, as architect, took trouble to give the interior a light and spacious appearance, using slender stainless-steel columns and subtle lighting. He has compared the problem of providing 'psychological habitability' to that of designing interiors for a luxury liner.[33] One important unbuilt project (1967) was the Pitt Rivers Museum by Powell and Moya with the Italian engineer Nervi [plate 19.13]. The centrepiece was to be a glazed concrete-framed dome. Despite gaining approval from the city council, this was defeated by financial constraints.

In serving the academic purposes for which they were erected, Oxford's historic buildings have been modified over the centuries and this process has continued to the present. The creation of reading rooms in the Radcliffe Camera and the Bodleian Old Library was planned in the 1930s and completed in 1956. This has been called 'one of the greatest pieces of academic reorganization ever carried out in Oxford' and was made possible by the building of the New Bodleian Library.[34] Since the Second World War the pressure for expansion in the city centre has led various colleges to make changes in order to use their existing space more effectively. This process intensified in the 1970s as the popularity of conversions grew nationally. At New College the Oxford Architects Partnership converted the first-floor Long Room, which since the late nineteenth century had been used for bathrooms and as a place for meetings and lectures. Following a competition in 1975, Maguire and Murray modernized the kitchen facilities at Magdalen

---

[32] Lankester, 10 July 1988.

[33] Conversation with Jack Lankester during a visit to the building, 26 Oct. 1988.

[34] Anon. 'Some reflections on Bodleian reconstruction', *OM* 26 Jan. 1956, 208. See also above, 479.

and provided additional social and living accommodation, with minimal change to the medieval fabric. At Hertford, Merton, Pembroke and elsewhere bedsitters were created out of sets, while at Keble the library expanded into two ground-floor rooms by means of a new staircase.

Sometimes historic buildings were converted for radically different uses. In 1958–9 the University Surveyor established his office and works yard in a fire-damaged malthouse (a conversion symptomatic of a growing nation-wide appreciation of industrial buildings). Later the medieval church of St Peter in the East, redundant since 1968, became a library for St Edmund Hall; floors and a staircase were inserted into the tower to form a bookstack (recalling the tower of Nuffield College). The conversion of All Saints church into a library for Lincoln College by Robert Potter (early 1970s) involved more structural alterations, carried out with great sensitivity. A basement was excavated and the ground-floor level raised.

New colleges sometimes used converted buildings as a nucleus. Green College was based around the Radcliffe Observatory; new buildings on the site by Jack Lankester were neo-Georgian to match. Linacre College took over a Victorian convent and Lankester's recent residential block recalls the Queen Anne style of the earlier work. Even on fresh sites historical influence is now strong. Pembroke's new building in St Ebbe's by Maguire and Murray, built after an architectural competition of 1986, has mullioned windows and steeply pitched roofs recalling traditional forms.

Garden design in Oxford after the war moved away from herbaceous and mixed borders in the manner of Gertrude Jekyll. A balance between formality and irregularity remained important, as in the Lasker memorial rose garden of 1953, designed by Sylvia Crowe for a site between the Botanic Garden and High Street. Here formal yew and box hedges of varying heights enclose rosebeds. The department of botany, which left the buildings of the Botanic Garden in 1952, created the genetic garden on the edge of the University Parks. Its purpose was experimental, the beds being arranged to demonstrate variegation and genetically controlled breeding systems.[35] The most important new Oxford garden of the century was at St Catherine's, where Jacobsen imported his own garden-making idiom from Denmark. Hedges, walls and staggered paving provided a firm framework for the natural forms of shrubs, trees and climbers chosen for the colour and texture of their foliage as well as their shape. Jacobsen's formal moat suited this low-lying site near the river. At Nuffield, built on the site of the Oxford canal basin, a long rectangular pool provided a focus in the lower quad. Some schemes were of informal character. At Wolfson the architects 'called in the country and appropriated the landscape in true eighteenth-century fashion', creating a punt harbour and island.[36] The Sainsbury Building at Worcester

[35] M. Batey, *Oxford Gardens* (Amersham 1982), 225–6.
[36] Ibid. 232.

was also informally related to the lake. Howell, Killick, Partridge and Amis's plan of 1960 for St Anne's had included a serpentine lake with an island, but this remained unexecuted.

Within the present century Oxford's architecture has reflected massive changes of taste. Throughout the period, architects of national reputation have worked for the university and the colleges, from Giles Scott to Leslie Martin. Since the mid–1950s Oxford has shown particular flair in its patronage. Although the University has no architectural school—or perhaps because of this—many dons have taken an active interest in the choice of architects, and building committees have been keen to inform themselves about current architectural trends. Well-known architects have been employed, occasionally from abroad (Jacobsen, Nervi and even Niemeyer, who designed an abortive scheme for St Antony's). Architects then just rising to national acclaim have been commissioned—including Howell, Killick, Partridge and Amis and later Ahrends, Burton and Koralek. Some work has been especially important nationally—as at Brasenose, where Powell and Moya provided an example for all architects building in sensitive city-centre locations. Local firms have also been popular, notably Architects Design Partnership and Oxford Architects Partnership. In a century of prolific building activity, the 1960s and early 1970s have been especially notable for their architectural creativity and vitality. Their contribution to Oxford's architectural history will gain mounting recognition.

20

Sport

D. J. WENDEN*

Throughout the twentieth century sport has played a large part in the University as both an activity for students and an influence on the image Oxford presents to the outside world.[1] Oxford is renowned for the boat race and the inter-varsity rugby match. Individual sportsmen, above all Sir Roger Bannister, have achieved personal distinction. They and their University have been praised for epitomizing an ideal of high physical skill within an academic environment, educated minds in healthy bodies. This fame has been won with the minimum of effort from the university (as distinct from the colleges) which until the 1950s spent hardly a penny on sport. Oxford's story has been very different from that of some American universities which devote large sums to departments of physical education and stadiums, and where semi-professional football and basketball gladiators function outside the mainstream of academic life.

In twentieth-century Oxford there has been a mounting tension between sport and scholarship. As academic standards improved, dons became more critical of the time spent on sport. At the same time undergraduates reacted against the public-school worship of organized games, contributing to the decline of athleticism. Student radicalism in the late 1960s intensified this reaction. The world tendency towards specialization in top-level sport made it more difficult for undergraduates to retain the pre-eminent position held by their predecessors from 1920 until the late 1950s. The higher-level sport practised in university clubs rested on widespread sporting activity at a lower level within the colleges, yet after 1950 college activities were regarded less seriously by both fellows and undergraduates and became increasingly recreational 'sport for all'. Laboratory sessions and even arts tutorials in afternoons, traditionally reserved for recreation, made it harder to produce college teams. From 1944 undergraduate places qualified for automatic state

* This chapter had been completed and revised by the author at the time of his death on 7 March 1992.
[1] This chapter could have not been written without the inspiration and help of Dr Mark Pottle, who was responsible for collating and interpreting the information displayed in the tables and for other ideas and material incorporated in the text. In rowing parlance he was coach and cox to a one-man crew.

funding: tutors felt compelled to consider intellectual ability as the main criterion for admission. After 1964 college rankings in the Norrington table were more highly regarded than results on field or river. The sportsman commoner spending little time in the library virtually disappeared. His disappearance was almost unlamented. In 1912, after a written examination, V. H. Bailey (Brasenose) appeared before the admissions board. 'Mr. Bailey, if you come up what do you intend to do?' 'I'm going to row.' The whole of the august assembly burst into unseemly mirth. 'Away, away. No further questions.' He retired discomfited, but was accepted. Would he be in today, he wondered in 1963?[2]

Dons became increasingly sceptical about the value of high-level sport in a university. Nevill Coghill (Exeter) in 1938 asserted that 'great athletes are seldom great scholars'. A university should provide 'training in Thought and Learning', not aspire to form character; it is sensible to take exercise but do not imagine that 'Thought and Learning are stimulated by these activities'. Twenty years later C. N. Ward-Perkins (Pembroke), responding to press criticism of his College's decision to send down an oarsman for neglect of study, observed that 'modern sport is by no means merely taking exercise'. 'There is a real conflict of time, energy and interest, a conflict which for some is too easily resolved by skimping study.' He was unimpressed by a suggestion that 'what is needed is a positive exhortation to study, not a negative ban on taking exercise'.[3] For a long time the case for sport was taken for granted by its supporters. Dons appeared at bump suppers and on the touchline, but by the 1950s in dwindling numbers. The President of Trinity, A. L. P. Norrington, deplored the decline of undergraduate sport, of fellows' support for such activity, and above all 'the tendency of undergraduates to mooch in the afternoon instead of taking exercise'. Reliable mooching statistics were not available but he had little doubt about its increase.[4] Ironically a few years later the academic league table named after its progenitor, Norrington, encouraged the trend away from exercise and perhaps diminished also the popularity of mooching.

The controversy over the relationship between sport and study was based on limited evidence. Examination results were rarely analysed and participation in sport, except at the university level, was little recorded. It therefore seems worth analysing the academic performance of 712 blues in the six major University sports (cricket, hockey, rowing, rugby, soccer, track and field) in eleven sample years between 1920 and 1970. The academic years selected are 1920/1, 1924/5, 1929/30, 1934/5, 1938/9, 1947/8, 1951/2, 1956/7, 1961/2, 1966/7, 1969/70 (hereafter referred to by year of final examinations, 1921, 1925 and so on). Since the sample blues could have sat

[2] *Brazen Nose* 1963, 183.
[3] *OM* 16 June 1938, 764; 20 Feb. 1958, 289–90.
[4] *OM* 29 Jan. 1959, 206.

TABLE 20.1

ACADEMIC PERFORMANCE OF SAMPLE OXFORD BLUES
COMPARED WITH ALL MEN, 1920–1970; WITH ADDITIONAL
YEARS 1986 AND 1988

	1921	1925	1930	1935	1939	1948	1952
all men	65.2	63.6	64.6	65.3	65.3	66.8	66.1
blues	59.3	57.6	55.7	57.8	60.2	60.6	57.5
difference	5.9	6.0	8.9	7.5	5.1	6.2	8.6
	1957	1962	1967	1970		1986	1988
all men	65.7	67.5	71.8	72.8		78.2	78.2
blues	56.8	59.0	59.9	70.6		76.9	74.4
difference	8.9	8.5	11.9	2.2		1.3	3.8

Note: Academic years are cited by the year of final examinations: 1921 represents the
year 1920/1, and so on. Comparison of blues 1986 is with all men 1986–8,
comparison of blues 1988 is with all men 1987/9. The second class, divided in 1986
into II.i and II.ii, has been treated here as if still unified.

finals in any of three successive summers, their performance has been
compared with that of all male finalists in three-year periods: the 1921 blues
are compared with all men taking their final examination in 1921, 1922 and
1923. On the 'Norrington' basis[5] the blues performed consistently less well
than the average: the median gap was 7.5 per cent over the sample years
1921–70 [table 20:1]. This analysis points to academic under-achievement by
élite sportsmen but not on the scale suggested by their sterner critics. A
continuation of the improvement shown in 1970 is suggested by a gap in
1986 of only 1.3 per cent and in 1988 of only 3.8 per cent. The inquiry does
not reveal how the performance of the sportsmen compares with that of
students who indulged in no sport at all—nor, for that matter, with that of
undergraduate actors or politicians.

Table 20.1 relates only to the achievements of the sample blues who took
an honours degree, 72.2 per cent of the total. The next largest group were
those taking pass degrees, sometimes the soft option for sportsmen. They
accounted for 9.1 per cent of the total [table 20.2]. The pass school declined
after the mid-1920s but among the blues this decline was more dramatic than
among the male student population at large. Of the 1921–39 blues, 11.6 per
cent read for a pass degree, while in the post–1945 period only 2.7 per cent
did so; comparable figures for all men are 4.5 per cent and 0.5 per cent,

[5] For an explanation of the Norrington table, see above, 62.

TABLE 20.2

UNIVERSITY COURSE TAKEN
BY SAMPLE OXFORD BLUES,
1920–1970

course	no.	%
honours degrees	514	72.2
pass degrees	65	9.1
research degrees	26	3.7
war degrees	17	2.3
diplomas/certificates	19	2.7
others	71	10.0
total	712	100.0

Note: Although 747 blues were won
in the selected sports in the sample
years, some individuals gained
double-blues and there were 712
blue-winners. The 'others' category
includes 6.3% not proceeding to final
honours, 1.8% taking at least one
final examination but no degrees,
1.1% unknown, 0.7% taking
medicine, 0.1% whose research status
lapsed.

respectively.[6] This suggests an improved academic ambition among the blues, as does the increasing proportion taking research degrees. Before 1961 the latter proportion was insignificant—indeed in that year it was only 1.7 per cent—but it rose to 7.0 per cent in 1966 and to 16.7 per cent in 1969.

The academic performance of men in different sports varies considerably and is most noticeable if pass-school degrees are included in the Norrington calculation, each valued at nil points yet contributing four points towards the possible maximum [table 20.3]. Soccer, track and rugby blues produce significantly higher scores than blues in cricket, hockey and rowing. This is not surprising: over the whole period soccer, track and rugby drew more men from maintained as against public schools, and correspondingly a larger percentage winning scholarship awards. Both before and after the Second World War, these three sports were the most 'democratic' of the six selected [table 20.4].

It would be impossible to carry out a similar analysis for all college sportsmen, as participants' names are not regularly recorded. University and

[6] Cf above, 57–9, 92, 109–10.

TABLE 20.3

NORRINGTON SCORE OF SAMPLE OXFORD BLUES BY SPORT,
1920–1970

	cricket	hockey	rowing	rugby	soccer	track	all
honours only	56.9	57.8	60.0	59.6	61.9	61.2	59.6
including pass degrees	48.1	52.4	50.7	57.8	56.3	58.5	54.3

TABLE 20.4

SCHOOL OF ORIGIN OF SAMPLE OXFORD BLUES, 1920–1970 (%)

	cricket	hockey	rowing	rugby	soccer	track	all
1920–70							
independent	65.3	75.9	77.8	50.3	44.7	44.9	58.7
direct grant or							
maintained	14.0	10.0	8.1	20.6	47.2	23.7	21.1
overseas	20.7	13.3	14.1	27.9	1.6	29.7	18.5
unknown	—	0.8	—	1.2	6.5	1.7	1.7
pre-war							
independent	83.6	83.3	91.1	58.6	67.3	58.7	72.7
DG or maintained	5.5	7.4	4.4	10.7	18.2	4.3	8.8
overseas	10.9	7.4	4.4	30.7	3.6	37.0	16.4
unknown	—	1.9	—		10.9	—	2.1
post-war							
independent	50.0	69.7	66.7	43.3	26.5	36.1	47.6
DG or maintained	21.2	12.1	11.1	28.9	70.6	36.1	30.8
overseas	28.8	18.2	22.2	25.6	—	25.0	20.2
unknown	—	—	—	2.2	2.9	2.8	1.4

college magazines do, however, make it possible to reconstruct a picture of college sport. Between the wars an average college of between 160 and 180 members produced one or two teams for major games, two or three crews for torpids and summer eights, two lawn tennis sixes, and entries for the inter-collegiate athletics and swimming competitions. Colleges had an abundance of pitches and no ground was further than a mile and a half from its owner [figure 20.1]. Oxford had the Thames for rowing and the Cherwell for punting and canoeing, but poor facilities for swimming and water polo. Competitions were held in the cramped Merton Street baths (built in 1869) until the city opened a new pool at the distant end of the Cowley Road in 1938. No University pool has been built, despite frequent campaigns. River swimming, popular in Victorian times and up to the 1950s, was abandoned

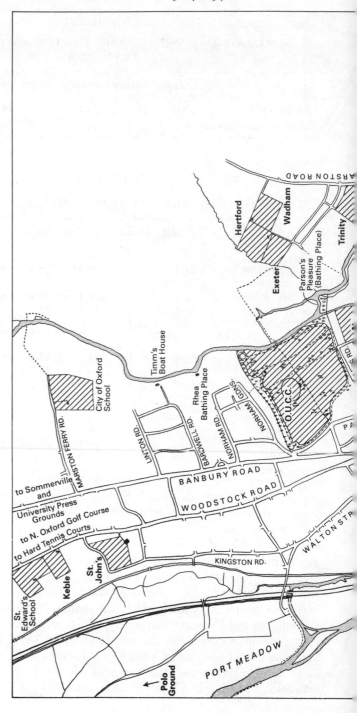

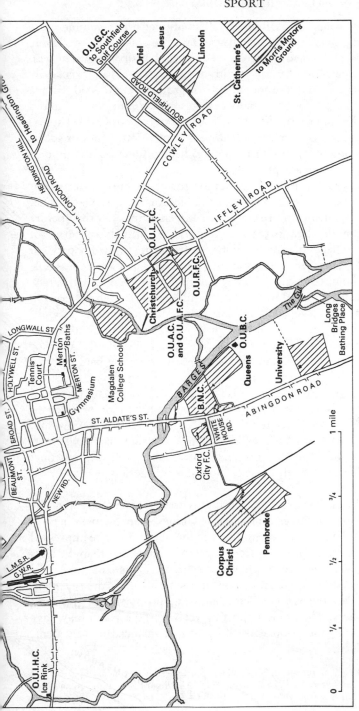

FIGURE 20.1   COLLEGE AND UNIVERSITY SPORTS GROUNDS, 1933

as insalubrious, although St Edmund Hall continued their summer race (originally from the gasworks to their barge) into the 1960s.[7] In swimming terms, Oxford was, and remains, 'a great medieval university'. Nevertheless, lack of opportunities for exercise could not be used as an excuse by Norrington moochers. A plethora of sports grounds contrasted with a shortage of indoor halls, though in many colleges squash courts were built in the 1930s. Until the Rhodes trustees (generous supporters of Oxford sport) provided the funds for a University gymnasium in 1966, other indoor sports (for example badminton, gymnastics, fencing) had to function at a modest university level in hired outside premises.

From 1922 to 1970 the number of junior members grew from under 4,500 to nearly 11,000 students. Colleges doubled or even trebled in size. However, they rarely fielded more elevens or fifteens after 1945 than before the war, and from the late 1950s often found it difficult to turn out complete sides. College magazines contain frequent condemnatory or apologetic annual reports by club captains.[8] Undergraduates were less able or willing to commit themselves to regular appearances. Until the new wave of college residential building from the mid-1960s, a high proportion of men lived outside college, making club secretaries' jobs more difficult. College and university sport was almost entirely organized for students by students, without assistance from a department of physical education or athletic union secretariat. Such coaches as existed were rarely paid and had little or no administrative role. The captaincy or secretaryship of an Oxford sports club provided a crash course in administration and improvisation. Many a future headmaster, managing director or assistant under-secretary learnt in Vincent's Club to organize and communicate, while many a visiting team suffered from the confusion that sometimes ensued. Vincent's Club was only a social centre, albeit a prestigious one; common problems could be discussed, but (like college lodges) it offered no office services.

A blue, especially in a major sport, was highly treasured. At the end of the period most college magazines still recorded blues won by members in residence. Perhaps the editors thought that old members might be impressed even if tutors were not. Employers often respected a blue more than the class of degree, especially in careers such as schoolteaching, banking and management. The respect for sport evident in the first half of the twentieth century coincided with the period when a significant proportion of graduates became schoolmasters. The modest sporting revival in the 1980s may have some connection with the popularity of careers in financial management, where a blue is valued.

---

[7] *St Edmund Hall Magazine* 1962–3, 62. For college sport, see above, 95–6, 98, 193, 202–3.
[8] For example *Brazen Nose* 1962, 134 and 1970, 111; *Oriel Record* May 1961, 46 and May 1963, 59; *St Edmund Hall Magazine* 1968–9, 9; *Wadham College Gazette* 1967–8, 5.

But how can the standing of sport within the University be measured? An examination of university magazines offers some clues. The major journals from 1919 up to 1970 were the *Isis* for undergraduates and the *Oxford Magazine* for dons. The contents of *Isis* presumably reflected undergraduate interests and values. In the 1920s nearly a quarter of its pages were devoted to sports and sportsmen. This percentage declined quickly in the early 1930s, giving way to articles on politics and the arts, and settled at little more than 10 per cent until the early 1950s, contracting rapidly to half a page out of thirty-two by 1954–5. In some issues even that half-page discussed shove-halfpenny or croquet rather than rugby or rowing. By the end of the decade, sport had disappeared as a regular feature. The *Oxford Magazine* for senior members reflected a similar trend. The issues for the 1920s devoted a surprisingly large proportion of their space to university and college sport. This faded away after 1945. College magazines are produced primarily to provide a link with old members who value, or are presumed to value, traditional activities. In them sport remains important up to 1970, although becoming overshadowed by accounts of the college's academic and building programmes after the war. All these publications suggest a sharp decline in the importance of sport from the early 1950s, a trend reflected in *Oxford*, the journal of the Oxford Society.

Some measure of the place of sportsmen in undergraduate esteem can be gauged from the 'Isis Idol', a feature of the magazine *Isis* from its birth in 1892. Each week tribute was paid to a leading personality in University life. In the first full post-war volume (1919/20) 17 of the idols were sportsmen, 5 were other undergraduates (from the Union, the Oxford University Dramatic Society and the Gridiron Club) and 2 were senior members. Until 1933/4 three-quarters of the idols were sportsmen. In that year of the 'King and Country' debate, they were equally divided between sportsmen and others (drawn from the Union, *Isis*, *Cherwell*, the film and dramatic societies). When *Isis* returned after the Second World War, only 6 of 24 idols were sportsmen. They fell to 3 in 1953, 2 a year later. Soon sports idols and sports reports disappeared altogether. Women were featured only very rarely before 1946: the pioneer in 1923/4 had rowed in the Somerville eight as well as taking a first in Greats. The shift of emphasis reflects *Isis* editorial policy, but editors presumably to some extent respond to changing taste among their readers.

All colleges made provision for sport, but some encouraged it more than others. Two colleges, Brasenose and St Edmund Hall, were notably successful in the principal inter-collegiate prizes: the headship in summer eights and the rugby cup. From 1920 to 1970 St Edmund Hall gained 17 successes (12 rugby, 5 rowing), although their first triumph was not until 1956. Brasenose scored 15 (11 rugby, 4 rowing), their last victory in 1961. Trinity was the only other college with more than 10 wins (5 rugby, 6 rowing). These three colleges account for 43 of the 88 prizes. The distribution of the sample blues also shows variation in the sporting reputation of different colleges: of the 747 blues won 46 per cent went to five colleges.

Some college sportsmen received exceptional support and encouragement from fellows of their college. This was so at Brasenose throughout a large part of the nineteenth and twentieth centuries. Sport was an important part of Brasenose life, and was much encouraged by W. T. Stallybrass ('Sonners' as he was known), fellow and Principal between 1911 and 1948. The *Brazen Nose* Magazine lists its many blues and praises even more the success of college clubs in a variety of games. For a moderately sized college—from 120 in the early 1920s to 200 in 1939—it fielded a remarkably high number of teams. On a single day in 1927 it produced two soccer and hockey elevens and three rugby fifteens. This *esprit de corps* produced 'a healthy outlook' during the General Strike 'when only eight undergraduates did not volunteer their services' with 'no distinction of race or colour or party politics'.[9] Sonners presided benignly over this healthy institution. He was a fervent touchline supporter and delighted in bump suppers. Three of the men who contributed most to sport between the wars—Sonners, Colonel Wilkinson of Worcester and Philip Landon of Trinity—were bachelors. The men who succeeded them after 1950—Greig Barr (rugby), Robin Fletcher (hockey), Arthur Selwyn (athletics) and Sir Harold Thompson (soccer)—had a greater association with university clubs and were married men who encouraged a more balanced attitude to the claims of work and play.

Brasenose's adulation of sport did not last long after Sonners's death while Vice-Chancellor in 1948. The College placed more emphasis on raising academic standards. In 1950 the College boat went down every day in torpids and other teams fell from grace. There was, however, no marked scholastic improvement relative to other colleges. An analysis of honours classifications on the Norrington scale (outlined above) shows Brasenose in the top half of the table on six occasions between 1920 and 1939 but only four under the changed regime from 1951 to 1970.

The enthusiasm and skill of the Brasenose students were matched by the College's servants. University and college servants' sports clubs had been founded in the late nineteenth century and thrived until the Second World War. Thereafter they declined and scarcely survived beyond the 1950s as the servants grew older and conferences filled the vacations. Brasenose took pride in its staff fire brigade that invariably won the annual competition between private fire brigades. Reporting success in the magazine, the president of the college servants' club emphasized that 'Brasenose had always been famous as a sporting college and the brigade members . . . hoped

[9] *Brazen Nose* May 1926, 154.

to emulate what they saw done by members of the college'.[10] No doubt a college that enjoyed a succession of bump suppers and boat burnings in the quad appreciated the advantages of having a trained fire crew on the premises. A University and College Servants' Rowing Club flourished, with an annual three-day regatta in the Easter vacation and a summer race against the Cambridge servants for which 'blues' were awarded. They sent a fraternal telegram of best wishes to the Oxford crew on each boat-race morning. Soccer, cricket, lawn tennis and bowls were also encouraged. Even before any contribution was given to undergraduate clubs, the University in 1951 made an annual grant of £150 to the servants' club in the hope that it would admit the technicians from the science area, who now wanted recreational facilities. But the marriage did not take place, and an independent university staff club appeared in Mansfield Road later.[11] Changes in college life brought separate servants' clubs, even for bowls, to an end within a few years.

Brasenose's sporting prowess over many generations was matched by St Edmund Hall for a shorter period in the 1950s and 1960s. The Hall was an ancient, modest institution. In 1920 it had only 85 undergraduates, but from 1951 it expanded under a new Principal, J. N. D. Kelly, and secured college status in 1957. It achieved great sporting successes, recruiting many outstanding sportsmen and attracting the attention of schoolmasters. By 1959 it was head of the river and holder of the rugby and soccer cups, as well as being supreme in several other activities. The *Times* congratulated the Hall on its fine record but the editor of the *Oxford Magazine* was disturbed by 'disquieting rumours' about its entrance policy: 'practically any methods were justified which get its name known, both in the schools and in the outside world'. He suggested that St Edmund Hall undergraduates were represented in only a small number of honours schools, reminiscent of one college 'which has by enormous efforts struggled out of the position of having undergraduate members who were predominantly athletes and the vast majority of whom read one school'—presumably a reference to Brasenose and law. The Principal pointed out that St Edmund Hall entered men for every school except oriental languages.[12] The class-lists in the *Oxford University Calendar* confirm this eclecticism. By then athletic success had served its purpose and the emphasis was switched to raising academic standards. In the first three years of the published Norrington table (1964–6) the Hall had averaged twenty-fifth place out of twenty-eight, but in the following three years improved to twelfth. The sporting glory lingered

[10] Ibid. Nov. 1925, 101.
[11] Minutes of the Oxford University and College Servants' Rowing Club (in private possession), 14 Nov. 1951; Oxford University Registry, minutes of the curators of the University Chest, 9 Feb. 1951, 85. See also HCP 208 (1951), 275; 227 (1957), 455.
[12] OM 11 June 1959, 454; OM 18 June 1959, 474.

on. Highlighting good examination results in 1969, the *St Edmund Hall Magazine* added: 'if anyone is tempted to infer that the Hall must be becoming a grey institution, he should reflect that the same year saw it win or retain the inter-collegiate cups for rugby, soccer, hockey, cricket, tennis and athletics'.[13] Sport had been used by the Hall to attract an academically stronger undergraduate entry.

Two other colleges have shown special features in their sporting records. Keble went head of the river for the first time in 1963 and then repeated the feat for successive summers from 1967 to 1970. This success was not reflected in any other major event. Nor in its place in the Norrington table: from 1964 to 1973 it hovered between twenty-first and bottom place, moving up thereafter. Oriel's first eight rose rapidly in the early 1930s to become head of the river from 1933 to 1937, falling back again as quickly. In 1966 it rowed head again for one year only, but maintained a leading place thereafter. The early triumphs on the river were accompanied by an improvement in schools. Oriel's tally of firsts grew from eight in 1933 to twelve, ten and thirteen in the subsequent years. The members of the 1935 eight took five firsts between them. Oriel was an established college with no need to court publicity; Keble, like St Edmund Hall, was less renowned and hoped that sporting success would strengthen its appeal to prospective undergraduates.

Women's colleges paid much less attention to sport. Oxford has never held a place in women's sport comparable to that of the men, just as nationally women's sport was until recent years the poor, and poorly regarded, relation of male athleticism. Women had to struggle to get to Oxford and then to establish a place in the University. They came in order to study. Sport was neither ladylike nor intellectual. Few women dons were willing to take sporting potential into account when assessing candidates for admission. Before 1939 many schoolgirls of outstanding athletic talent looked to teaching as a career and enrolled in women's physical education colleges.

Despite this unpromising background, sport had become established in the women's colleges before 1914. Small numbers and limited finance and facilities held back development, as with many other aspects of women's life in Oxford. After the First World War colleges continued to play the standard games—hockey, lacrosse, netball, tennis, even cricket. Blues were awarded and a reasonable proportion of women participated, but only Lady Margaret Hall, and for a brief period in the 1930s Somerville, had their own sports grounds. Although the *St Hilda's Chronicle* reported in 1926 that 'we are swollen with pride over our rowing this year' and Somerville displayed on high table cups won by junior members, sport did not have the

---

[13] *St Edmund Hall Magazine* 1968–9, 7.

significance accorded to it by the men's colleges.[14] According to Vera Brittain, 'between 1900 and 1920 games and athletic competitions between the women's colleges had taken the place of walks, but after women became members of the University they spent most of their spare time with male companions'.[15] Men and women's sport operated under an informal but very real apartheid. There was little mixing on the games field compared with the way Victorian barriers were being broken in debating, drama, musical and political clubs and even dancing.

The organization and finance of women's university clubs were improved by the formation of the Women's United Games Committee in 1937, financed by contributions from the five women's colleges. The support was modest compared with the money available to the men.[16] The general swing away from sport in the 1960s affected women; the Somerville magazine reported that it 'was not a fashionable activity for women in Oxford'.[17] But the number of women students had grown to nearly two thousand and the apartheid was broken: more sports were practised on a mixed basis, including archery, badminton, fencing and sailing. The Rhodes Trust recognized the cinderella status of the women—using pitches in the University Parks but barred from the cricket pavilion—and provided £5,000 for a women's building in the shadow of its bigger brother. With the move to mixed colleges from 1972, the variety of sports practised by women (rowing has been followed by soccer, karate and now even rugby) has expanded spectacularly. The resources of former men's colleges are now accessible, and former women's colleges, even the remaining single-sex institutions, have been persuaded to take sport more seriously. The Oxford University Women's Boat Club has produced members of British national crews, and in 1981 Susan Brown (Wadham) became the first woman to cox in the boat race, a far cry from the first female boat race when the college principals decreed that racing would be too strenuous and the contest should be decided on 'style and form'.[18]

How was college and university sport financed? Nearly thirty separate college sports grounds, boathouses or barges, and squash courts plus equipment and match expenses represented a substantial outlay, before adding more sophisticated facilities for some university clubs. High standards in sport—as in laboratories, libraries and teaching—could not be bought cheaply. In most other British universities, sports facilities were provided and maintained from central university funds. Part of the student's union fee went to the athletic union for match expenses. This system did not

[14] St Hilda's Chronicle 1926, 11.
[15] V. Brittain, The Women at Oxford (London 1960), 227–8.
[16] See above, 368.
[17] Somerville College Report 1963, 21.
[18] Isis 16 Mar. 1927, 701.

operate in Oxford, a collegiate university. The equivalent of a union fee was collected by colleges as an amalgamated clubs' subscription. This helped sustain college independence but did nothing for university clubs, which had to raise their own income from three possible sources: the participants themselves; spectators at university fixtures; and colleges that could be coaxed into passing on part of the amalgamated clubs' subscription. Television fees and commercial sponsorship had not yet arrived, and the University stepped in only as a late contributor from the mid-1950s.

Cricket, rowing and rugby attracted a substantial public following. But the boat club could not charge admission to the large crowds who lined the Thames, while the cricket club's landlord, the University, understandably forbade it to charge for admission to the Parks. The rugby club alone profited in proportion to its popularity, and the other clubs benefited from its Twickenham and Iffley Road gates. Cyril Norwood (St John's) described the university clubs as 'a troop of orphan children existing on the bounty of a devoted elder brother, the University Rugby Club'.[19] The generosity of the rugby club was remarkable, comparatively unacknowledged within the University and unchallenged by the players. Even so, every individual had to pay to win a blue in a major sport. Richard Hillary calculated that each man in the boat had to contribute two shillings for every stroke in the boat race.[20] Colleges passed on a fraction of the amalgamated clubs' subscriptions.

This makeshift system was put on a formal basis in 1930. Twelve university clubs combined to form a trust fund held by a Central Athletic Committee.[21] The rugby club supplied the largest contribution but held a controlling vote and gained a reduction in its liability to income tax. By 1945 funds were at a low ebb. Happily, strong rugby fifteens attracted large crowds, and the cricket club made a profit in 1948 from a match against Bradman's Australian tourists on Christ Church's ground. The Central Athletic Committee prospered; college clubs were asked for only modest capitation fees. However, the system began to creak. The political and social climate changed: higher education became a service funded predominantly by the state. Students expected sport to be an integral part of their course and not a privately funded activity, and could not understand why college sport was subsidized but university clubs had to be self-funding. Even if this should make sense for the sports provided at college level, many clubs now functioned only on a university basis (for example badminton, basketball, fencing, judo, lacrosse). The University took a first step by providing £4,000 towards the post-war rehabilitation of pitches.[22] In 1947 it was invited to

[19] *OM* 2 June 1938, 701.
[20] *Isis* 24 May 1939, 14.
[21] Trust deed to establish the Oxford University Central Athletic Committee, 1 Dec. 1930 (in private possession).
[22] Chest minutes, 28 June 1946, 104.

become responsible for the facilities of university sports clubs. It did not agree, but the shift was deferred for only a few years. In the late 1950s it accepted responsibility for the upkeep of the University grounds and boathouse, calculated at £2,850 a year.

The income from gates, however, diminished as spectators moved to professional sport or television. University teams were now only provincial performers of minor interest. The rugby club's surpluses fell from £5,390 in 1948/9 to £500 in 1966/7, while the number of university clubs seeking assistance increased.[23] The opening of the gymnasium funded by the Rhodes trustees produced a further crop. They functioned as university, not college, activities since they depended on central premises not provided by colleges (for example, for volleyball or the martial arts). The worst crisis of the university clubs was averted when colleges agreed to help by contributing part of the amalgamated clubs' subscriptions. The rugby club survived on income from the Twickenham gate and television fee; the boat club, too, relied heavily on its television fee—a modest £2,372 in 1969. Commercial sponsorship arrived for both clubs in the mid-1970s and with it financial independence. The University had accepted a major responsibility for sport by establishing a Sports Facilities Committee; it spent £16,500 in 1968/9, compared with the £4,554 distributed to clubs from the college levy.[24] This responsibility had been avoided for most of the period during which sport had kept the name of Oxford in the public eye. That financial contribution gave the University more right to ensure that sport should be subsidiary to and not detract from teaching and research.

In 1962 the University agreed to subscribe to the newly created British Universities Sports Federation (BUSF). Traditionally, Oxford men had entertained few sporting links with other British universities. The *Oxford University Handbook* in 1932 affirmed condescendingly: 'In most sports Oxford and Cambridge have placed themselves upon a pinnacle from which there is at present little prospect that they will have to descend. London and the modern universities cannot yet hope to compete with the older universities on equal terms, and if they play at Oxford at all, probably play one or other of the Colleges.'[25] That was only partly true in 1932 and far from true in 1962, although Oxford and Cambridge were still usually stronger in the traditional men's sports. Oxford women had been active members of the Women's Inter-Varsity Athletic Board (WIVAB) from its earliest days. The men, however, did not need BUSF for high-level fixtures and jealously guarded the status secured by being first in the field. Increasingly after 1945, however, the gap in playing standards narrowed.

[23] Minutes of the senior treasurers of university and college amalgamated clubs (in private possession), 22 May 1969.
[24] Chest minutes, Hilary term 1971, 54.
[25] *Handbook* 1932, 245.

The emergence of national championships and student national teams organized by BUSF presented Oxford and Cambridge with a dilemma. Some clubs were reluctant to embark on inter-university competition with longer and more expensive travel for fixtures less prestigious than those they already enjoyed. Such affiliation might eventually threaten Oxford's prized matches with visiting international teams in rugby and cricket, and even remove some of the magic of Twickenham, Lords and the boat race. But for many clubs—especially in basketball, fencing, hockey, soccer and volleyball—BUSF offered good competition. For Oxford to stand apart would be ungracious; the undergraduates of the 1960s were readier to identify themselves with the general student body and its youth culture. With some hesitation Oxford joined the Federation and has participated in many BUSF activities. This episode reflects the closer identification of Oxford, both at senior and junior levels, with the national university system since 1945. But in sport as in other more important areas, it has not always been an easy relationship.

In all these years the sportsmen were little concerned about—probably hardly aware of—the financial, administrative and academic background to their pastimes. They came up to enjoy sport as part of student life and most still revered the great sportsman more than the great scholar. Throughout the period, they had much to admire in Oxford and this account would not be complete without some mention of major achievements on field and river. The revival of sport in Oxford after the First World War was marked by participation in the 'Peace Regatta' at Henley in 1919 and an appearance by King George V at the rugby match in December, a gesture repeated by George VI in 1946. By 1920/1 a full programme of twenty-three contests with Cambridge was in position. The country sports characteristic of nineteenth-century Oxford revived, but although polo, point-to-point, fox-hunting and beagling continued to 1970, these activities never regained their earlier status. There were men for whom Oxford between the wars resembled an extended country weekend party punctuated by dinners at the Bullingdon Club. Tutorials and books were incidental distractions. Sir John Thomson confessed that while reading law at Magdalen from 1926 to 1929, 'I didn't work academically, but was very fully occupied. I spent all my time hunting and beagling or running point to points. I occasionally went to a tutorial—that's all you had to do.'[26] He took a third in law, went on to become chairman of Barclays Bank, a long-serving member of the University Chest, deputy high steward and an honorary DCL. But this group declined in number and importance; undergraduates or the press did not see it as representative of Oxford sport, and only two featured as Isis Idols. The undergraduate master of the Christ Church beagles in 1935

[26] Sir John Thomson, tape-recorded interview with Brian Harrison, 21 June 1990.

recalled that when Gandhi took breakfast with him at Eton 'he discussed beagling and told me very gently that he disapproved of it'.[27]

Rowing was above all *the* sport, opening in a blaze of glory. Magdalen won the Grand Challenge Cup at Henley in 1920, provided the nucleus of the British Olympic eight and took the Grand again in 1921, when Oxford college crews won four other Henley finals. But after a victory in the boat race of 1923, Oxford rowing went into what appeared at times to be a terminal decline. Between 1920 and 1970 Cambridge won thirty-three boat races to Oxford's twelve. Until the revival inspired by Daniel Topolski, with ten consecutive victories after 1976, Oxford oarsmen were often outclassed, several defeats stretching to ten lengths or more. As the regard for sport diminished and as university rowing was criticized for being a home of outdated public-school (and especially Etonian) attitudes, one might have expected rowing to become less popular. But surprisingly this socially exclusive sport went 'comprehensive'. The entries for summer eights climbed steadily from 30 in 1920, to 60 in 1936, 58 after the war and then rapidly to 84 by 1955 and 109 in 1970. The only limit appeared to be the organizers' capacity to get crews to the starting line. Rowing became Oxford's 'sport for all', taken up enthusiastically by men and later by women who had not rowed before coming up. The standard was not high; some crews were given names more appropriate to pop groups. Below the level of first and second eights, college rowing became almost a parody of the semi-religion of the inter-war traditionalists. University rowing, however, became more professional, with a squad of 30–40 oarsmen from whom the blue and Isis crews were selected. Places were no longer filled predominantly by men from traditional rowing schools. In Oxford's thirteen successive defeats between 1924 and 1936, nearly three-quarters of the blues went to oarsmen from seven public schools. In the successful years from 1976 to 1985 those seven schools netted only one-sixth of the blues, over a quarter were awarded to men from day schools with few pre-war blues, and nearly a quarter to overseas graduates. The social and intellectual composition of the Oxford University Boat Club changed radically after the 1960s.

The rugby club, usually considered the second most important, had a better record against Cambridge and until the late 1950s was equally successful nationally. But thereafter, although great individuals appeared, the sides in which they played won few matches. After the abolition of national service, undergraduate teams with an average age of 20 faced heavier and more experienced club players who now trained fiercely and were coached systematically. The blues were left with only their presumed greater intelligence, and that did not always prevail in the second row of the scrum. The teams from 1919 to 1960 included scores of men who played

---

[27] Hon. F. C. P. Wood (son of the Chancellor, Lord Halifax), *Isis* 27 Nov. 1935, 7.

international rugby while in residence or after graduation. It was an English international, of Russian parentage, Prince Obolensky, who scored the try that almost clinched victory for Oxford against the New Zealand All Blacks in 1935 before 12,000 spectators at Iffley Road. In 1949 Oxford had eleven internationals in residence. Rugby, in England pre-eminently an amateur and middle-class game, was a sport at which Oxford could for a long time compete against the best in the country.

Between the wars South Africans, all but three of them Rhodes scholars, played a role out of all proportion to their numbers, winning an eighth of the 300 rugby blues awarded. Without Oxford's Rhodes scholars, Cambridge's greater numbers would have made inter-varsity sports contests too one-sided. In each year from 1920 to 1970 an average of 68 Rhodes scholars joined over 1,800 freshmen, 4 per cent of the total. But in the sample years they won 70 (9.4 per cent) of the 747 blues on offer in the selected sports. Their impact varied from sport to sport. They secured most in rugby (27) and least in soccer (2), though proportionately their impact was greatest in track and field (almost 18 per cent). Cecil Rhodes, who favoured scholars with a 'fondness of and success in manly outdoor sports', would have been delighted.[28]

TABLE 20.5

RESULTS OF OUCC FIRST-CLASS
MATCHES, 1920–1970

	played	won	lost	drawn
1920–39	125	26 (21%)	40 (32%)	59 (47%)
1946–70	193	24 (12%)	90 (47%)	79 (41%)

Cricket was the game in which Oxford found it hardest to maintain first-class status. The decline is illustrated by the record of the University cricket club's first-class games taken from *Wisden*, shown in table 20.5. County elevens continued to visit the Parks, but after the early 1950s matches became increasingly one-sided. In 1968 the University collapsed against Surrey to five wickets down for two runs, one of which was a no-ball. The following year it was decreed that Oxford and Cambridge should no longer play their individual matches against overseas touring sides. The traditional advantage possessed by undergraduates—greater speed and enthusiasm in the field—disappeared as professional county players improved to meet the demands of limited-over competitions. Oxford's right to enjoy first-class status has been questioned since 1960. Oxford has produced fine cricketers,

[28] Quoted by S. E. Millin, *Rhodes* (London 1933), 331.

but rarely enough in one year—and even more rarely the bowlers needed to trouble professional batsmen. Blues who played full-time after going down often developed into great cricketers. Ten Oxford blues between 1919 and 1970 became captains of their country's test teams; the most notorious, Douglas Jardine of New College, displayed in the 'bodyline' dispute in Australia in 1932–3 a rigour not usually associated with cricket in the Parks.

The best-known Oxford sports feat of this era was performed on the Iffley Road track on 6 May 1954 by Roger Bannister [plate 20.1]. Coming up to Exeter College in 1946 as a 17-year-old novice Bannister perfected his running while reading for his BA in physiology. As a clinical medical student at St Mary's Hospital, London, he was in 1954 the first man to run the mile in under four minutes and was the Commonwealth and European champion in the same year. Olympic gold medals were won, and world record times set, by other Oxford athletes—T. Hampson (St Catherine's), J. E. Lovelock (Exeter), C. Chataway (Magdalen) and D. Hemery (St Catherine's). Oxford and Cambridge have track and field records superior to those of any other university in the world. Training for this sport is an individual matter that integrates with an academic programme more easily than participation in team games and rowing. But since 1970 the 'professionalization' of athletics has produced money for those who are prepared to devote themselves to the endless training needed to win at the highest level—success that the Lovelocks, Bannisters and Chataways found possible on an hour's running a day. The standing of Oxford sportsmen has been reduced not only by more stringent standards demanded by tutors, but also by the fact that top-level sport itself has moved beyond the grasp of most young people who are serious about their degree.

Soccer players faced this problem earlier. Their game turned professional before 1914. No longer could the Old Etonians expect to feature in, let alone win, the Football Association Cup. However, the professionalization was at a social and financial level that had no attraction for undergraduates. Soccer shared in Oxford's golden decade of sport from the late 1940s. Many amateur international caps were won. The range of schools from which soccer blues were drawn was broadened: Charterhouse, Repton, Shrewsbury, Winchester and Malvern were joined by a variety of maintained schools, including many in the north [table 20.4]. Soccer also established a closer relationship between town and gown. Townsmen no longer identified with undergraduate sport when the motor works replaced college service as the principal source of employment. For a few years this sense of identity was recaptured by Pegasus AFC: 'never has [sic] Town and Gown been so united'.[29] The club was the brainchild of Dr Harold ('Tommy') Thompson. He suggested that the best current and immediate past players from Oxford

---

[29] *Isis* 25 Apr. 1951, 33 (Martin Stevens).

and Cambridge should combine in a team that could enter the FA Amateur Cup. Nine months after their formation in 1948 Pegasus attracted 12,000 people to a quarter-final match at Iffley Road. They lost that game but took the cup at Wembley in 1951 and 1953 before capacity crowds. The club lingered on until 1962 but never with the same success. It came and went like a shooting star, but in its short life it shed a bright light.

Compared with the other major sports, hockey's story up to 1970 was uneventful. It retained undefiled amateur, middle-class status. A people's sport in India and Pakistan, hockey in Britain has never been a truly popular activity. After 1945 the proportion of blues from independent schools declined less than for any other major sport; indeed the sample shows that after the war, hockey was the major sport most dominated by boys from independent schools [table 20.4]. One opportunity for change was not taken: mixed hockey, popular as a diversion for club players, was rarely played at Oxford even though it was the only major sport played extensively by both sexes.

Attention has been focused on men's traditional sports, but games less familiar at English public schools were played, including basketball, with a first match against Cambridge in 1921. The first team included a South African, an American, two Etonians and a Wykehamist. The predominance of American players after 1946 made Oxford one of the strongest teams in Britain. For a few years in the early 1930s, when the city boasted a large ice-rink on the Botley Road, the University ice-hockey team (mainly Canadians) were leaders of the English league. However, when forced to travel to Richmond the team could not maintain its enthusiasm and success. The infusion of athletes from American and Commonwealth universities has been an important and innovative element in Oxford sport. Familiar with professionalized academic-based sport, they appreciate the informality and student democracy of even the most important Oxford clubs. They can also be amazed at the poverty of the system and of the facilities available to sportsmen of international standing. Their value, however, was not only as players, but also as stimulating personalities in Oxford life. They shared the lot of the average student but brought with them experience of top-level sports competition throughout the world.

The story ends in 1970 with student radicals attacking the Oxford system. They paid little attention to sport. They did not need to, because attacks on the privileged place it held in college life had already been made by senior members. Indignation that Oxford had betrayed its sporting birthright came from critics largely outside the University. Such critics were sharply rebuked by the opponents of excessive adulation for sport. In 1968 John Carey's article 'Let's scrap Twickenham' was a rejoinder to Wilfred Wooller's denunciation of 'inflexibly high academic standards which ensure that the greatest number of pimply swots enter Oxbridge' to the exclusion of 'the individual who has spread his energies at school over the wider range of activities'. Carey, accepting the need for exercise, asked 'is there any place for prestige sport in modern Oxford?'; he answered that excessive concern for high-level sport was not a sensible way of 'looking after the physical education of a college of three or four hundred busy students'. He supported the case for a swimming pool. This would provide healthy exercise for all. It should take the place of the University rugby pitch at Iffley Road.[30] Over twenty years later the issue is less hotly debated. Oxford sport has been dethroned from its cherished place in the era of Sonners, functions modestly in mixed colleges, and survives at the university level with substantial sponsorship from outside commercial interests. The swimming pool has not yet been built and rugby continues at Iffley Road.

[30] *Isis* 1 May 1968, 19.

PART FIVE
SPHERES OF INFLUENCE,
1914–1970

21

University and Locality

RICHARD WHITING

The relationship between town and university in twentieth-century Oxford has involved continuous tension. On the one hand there has been a history of economic, cultural and political participation in the local society for which there are many nineteenth-century precedents.[1] On the other hand, there have also been aspirations to segregation and exclusion. The growth from the 1920s of the motor industry at Cowley on the south-eastern edge of the town bred anxieties that it might damage the tranquil urban setting required for scholarly activity.

Two factors ensured that these parallel tendencies of segregation and involvement were fully developed. One was the self-esteem of the University. Precisely because the University enjoyed an international reputation it was willing on some occasions to ignore or override local interests, and on others to turn to them in a mood of conscious service and direction.[2] The other was the medium size of the town. Universities in great cities have had intellectual or cultural significance, but rarely political or economic influence. At the other end of the scale, in the small town completely dominated by a university, the urban setting could, for all intents and purposes, be taken for granted. Lying between these two, Oxford both encouraged involvement because influence could be exerted or direction given—and also demanded it, because the University's was not the only voice in local affairs and its wishes needed articulation and prosecution. Deliberate strategies were required either to take a leading role in town affairs or to protect the University environment from the effects of the town's growth. Add to these considerations the heterogeneity of outlook fostered by the collegiate structure, and the complexity of the town–university connection in Oxford's case can be readily appreciated.

---

[1] Anthony Howe, 'Intellect and civic responsibility: dons and citizens in nineteenth-century Oxford' in R. C. Whiting (ed.), *Oxford: Studies in the History of a University Town since 1800* (Manchester 1993), *passim*.

[2] Douglas Veale, the Registrar, told the city council in 1930 that the University wished to override local restrictions on the height of buildings in the case of the Bodleian New Library 'because of the international and not merely local significance' of the building: London, PRO, HLG 4/1730, Ministry of Health, planning schemes, Oxford, letter of 2 Dec.

The local economy contributed importantly to the balance between the town and the University. Three aspects of the interaction between the University and the local economy deserve attention: the persistence of a small-town economy in the central area near the University; the development between the wars of motor manufacture and attendant suburbs at Cowley some distance to the south-east; and the growth from the late 1960s of white-collar activity around the University.

Edwardian Oxford was a small town whose economy was dominated by the University. The professions, domestic service and small-scale craft occupations carried most weight in its occupational structure, and the University's demands greatly affected regularity of employment. The smaller printing firms often had little to do in the long vacation, whereas that was the time when the building workers were more in demand. When local unemployment among builders was a problem in 1913, the city authorities turned to the University to provide work during the winter. While the skilled workers—the printers, tailors, college servants and a small number of engineers—earned a reasonable wage (above thirty shillings per week before 1914) the unskilled were poorly paid by comparison with those in the industrial towns of the midlands, and the colleges enabled wives to supplement their husbands' meagre earnings with cleaning jobs during term-time.

Opportunities for trade-union organization, bringing some degree of independence from the University, were greatest for the skilled workers. The printers were the most heavily unionized, as were some of the higher grades on the railways, but membership was patchy among building workers and engineers. Attempts to organize the unskilled proved fruitless before 1914, and college servants were particularly slow to organize. But an even clearer demarcation between skilled and unskilled workers lay in housing, with the skilled workers living in Jericho in the west of the city in three-bedroomed houses of reasonable quality, the unskilled living in badly built cottages in St Ebbe's to the south and St Clement's to the east. North Oxford was the preserve of the professional classes, especially the dons.[3]

The growth of the motor industry between the wars brought a very significant addition to this small-town economy. It created a concentrated working-class society on the south-eastern outskirts, an entirely new development for Oxford and one which was bound to affect the older sections of the town. William Morris, a local man, progressed through bicycle repair, motor cycle production and garage ownership before moving to an old military college at Cowley, a village to the south-east which was not incorporated into Oxford until 1928.[4] Producing munitions in the First

[3] R. C. Whiting, *The View from Cowley: The Impact of Industrialization upon Oxford 1918–1939* (Oxford 1983), 11–15, 145.

[4] There is a useful short account of William Morris's life by R. J. Overy, 'William Richard Morris' in D. Jeremy (ed.), *Dictionary of Business Biography* (5 vols London 1984–6) iv. 334–41. The most complete coverage of his activities is by P. W. S. Andrews and E. Brunner, *The Life of Lord Nuffield: A Study in Benevolence and Enterprise* (Oxford 1955).

World War and a visit to America equipped and funded Morris to develop the high-output techniques a major car-producer needed in the 1920s. He was joined at Cowley in 1926 by the American firm of Pressed Steel, which made some of the first all-steel car bodies. Between the wars nearly one-third of all those employed in Oxford worked in these two factories, and this concentration of car workers persisted after 1945 when both companies became part of British Leyland. Even by the 1980s, when car production had passed its peak and a resurgence of white-collar employment had begun, the factories at Cowley employed a higher proportion of the local labour force than any British Leyland operation elsewhere.[5]

The growing labour force necessitated a major development in housing and services around what had been the villages of Headington and Cowley, which became suburbs of Oxford in 1928 [figure 21.1]. They formed a wholly different environment from the ancient heart of the city, and one whose demands for municipal spending could be used as a platform within Oxford for labour politics, otherwise without an obvious base. The conditions of large-scale production, plus the attraction to Cowley of migrants from the regions of depressed industry in Wales, the north of England and Scotland, provided conditions for significant trade-union growth; these had implications for employers in the old town economy. The car factories also offered highly paid work for those with stamina but no great skill, another novel feature for Oxford.

While the managerial element was numerically small, the arrival of business wealth was bound to affect the University, especially as Morris had a personal fortune but no heir. There were of course limits to these influences. The voice of Cowley in the council chamber was not always the loudest; college servants were happy to resist the embrace of the burgeoning Transport and General Workers' Union; and certainly for the 1930s customary patterns of transition from school to work in the poorer districts of Oxford weakened the pull of higher wages from the car factories some distance away.[6] But even between the wars the distributive trades which acted as 'feeders' for labour moving into the car factories were having to increase wages, and after 1945 Cowley's strong demand for labour affected the Oxford labour market more profoundly. Its adverse effects upon the labour supply for retailers and the public service sector (the Post Office and the bus company) were still evident in 1970.[7]

[5] 'If BL did not exist, would Britain have to invent it?', *Economist* 8 Nov. 1980, 82.

[6] On college servants and trade unions see Whiting, *View from Cowley*, 126, and 'Unionization', *OM* 14 Nov. 1946, 78; for the transition from school to work see O. Gibbs, *'Our Olive': The Autobiography of Olive Gibbs* (Oxford 1989), 75–6.

[7] J. Marschak, 'Industrial immigration', and E. Ackroyd, 'Industry', in A. F. C. Bourdillon (ed.), *A Survey of Social Services in the Oxford District* (2 vols Oxford 1938–40) i *Economics and Government of a Changing Area*, 54, 86–7, 289 (this study was produced under the auspices of Barnett House); B. Baird, 'The web of economic activities in Oxford', *Ekistics* cclxxiv (1979), 40.

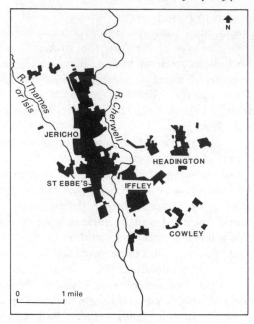

1918

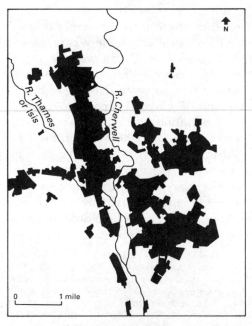

1950

FIGURE 21.1   OXFORD'S RIVER GEOGRAPHY AND THE GROWTH OF OXFORD'S BUILT-UP
AREA, 1918 AND 1950

19.9 St Antony's College: interior of dining hall

19.10 St Catherine's College from the air, 1964

19.11   St Catherine's College exterior

19.12   St Cross Building exterior

19.13 Nervi's plan for rebuilding the Pitt Rivers Museum

20.1 Roger Bannister completing the world's first four-minute mile, 6 May 1954

25.1 Students scuffling with bedels, Nov. 1968

26.1 The Franks Commission's final hearing, 17 June 1965

By the 1970s, however, foreign competition and improved technology were causing employment in the motor industry to flatten out and even contract. The growth area was now white-collar employment, either in local government or in the education and science sector. It is not just that the University grew in the 1960s (especially in the sciences) or that there was associated expansion of Oxford Polytechnic (now Oxford Brookes University); related activity in medicine, publishing and other forms of education (language schools, for example) also grew strongly in the 1970s. In this phase the University was to be a more specific attractive force for work involving research and information exchange—'quaternary functions', as one Oxford geographer has described them—than Cowley had been for the motor industry.[8] As long as car components could be easily transported from the midlands and markets easily supplied, Cowley did not require a plethora of satellite engineering companies close by. Close physical proximity, however, was seen to be an asset for the research, educational and broader professional activities for which the University was a focus. These new employees, unlike car manufacturing's satellite employees earlier, needed to be close at hand [table 21.1]. The local impact made by the University's growth emerges from University students' rising ratio of Oxford's total population: one for every 17 in 1931, one for every 14 in 1951, and one for every 10 by 1969. Compare Manchester's one in 47, Leeds' one in 57 and Bristol's one in 69 in 1969.[9]

Building to accommodate these stages of economic change was restricted by flood plains to the west and to the east of Oxford created by the rivers Isis and Cherwell. Unable therefore to follow the concentric pattern more familiar to modern urban growth, expansion kept to a north–south river-gravel terrace running south from Summertown to St Aldate's, and to gravel and chalk deposits to the east. This geological determinant, reinforced by the green belt from the mid-1950s, made it easier for Oxford to contain growth as well as to segregate the University from industrial and suburban development, but it presented the University with difficulties as soon as it too began generating employment. When it came to altering land use in the central area, what one gained, another lost. The only way out was radical relocation on the periphery—possible, perhaps, for the politically vulnerable inhabitants of St Ebbe's slums (moved to Barton on the east of the city) but not for university functions or shops. Things were not made easier by the fact that the university and colleges owned 25 per cent of land within the city boundaries, because colleges did not always wish to part with their

[8] Baird, 41; cf below, 695–6.
[9] University of Oxford, general office, returns to University Grants Committee (UGC). Figures for 1969 from S. R. Walker, 'Aspects of the concept of university centrality and external linkages of Oxford' (Oxford DPhil thesis 1974), table 1.5, 18.

TABLE 21.1

SHIFTS IN THE BALANCE OF EMPLOYMENT IN OXFORD, 1911–1971

	1911 no.	1911 %	1931 no.	1931 %	1951 no.	1951 %	1971 no.	1971 %
engineering and cars	700	3	5,524	16	18,553	31	22,590	28
paper and printing	930	4	1,810	5	2,310	4	3,720	5
building	1,970	8	2,340	7	3,510	6	4,920	6
distributive trades	2,720	11	5,480	15	8,250	14	9,300	11
national and local government	560	2	2,740	8	3,180	5	3,000	4
professional	2,160	9	4,370	12	10,570	17	19,510	24

Source: C. J. Day, 'Modern Oxford: economic history' in A. Crossley (ed.), *The City of Oxford* (History of the County of Oxford iv, Oxford 1979), 219.

houses or playing fields in order to aid university expansion. Furthermore much of this property in North Oxford was sterilized for development purposes in the 1960s by an unanticipated enthusiasm for Victoriana.

What of the social relations between town and gown? For many who lived in St Ebbe's or St Clement's, Oxford remained a 'low wage' area into the 1930s, and this local poverty stirred the conscience of University people. Violet Butler in 1912 saw the local population as 'not economically in a really satisfactory condition, but living on the whole on very friendly terms with the employing classes of the city and the University with whom it comes into contact and from whom it receives much spontaneous service'.[10] The view that intellect, social privilege and a certain amount of leisure could be converted into citizenship through social work was an inheritance from the nineteenth-century Oxford of T. H. Green and Arnold Toynbee.[11] It continued into the twentieth century with particular contributions from the wives of three heads of house: Mrs H. A. L. Fisher (New College), Mrs A. L. Smith (Balliol) and Mrs J. Wells (Wadham), together with Mrs H. A. Prichard (wife of the Professor of Moral Philosophy).

Social service—through the Charity Organization Society and the Voluntary Oxford Health Committee, which promoted infant welfare through health visiting—was the key area of activity, although Mabel

[10] C. V. Butler, *Social Conditions in Oxford* (London 1912), 246.
[11] U. Cormack, 'Oxford and early social work' in A. H. Halsey (ed.), *Traditions of Social Policy: Essays in Honour of Violet Butler* (Oxford 1976), 112–13; see also Brian Harrison, 'Miss Butler's Oxford survey', ibid. 27–72.

Prichard was particularly active in mental health and in establishing an occupational centre at Littlemore.[12] Voluntary social work within the University succumbed only slowly before public provision. Prominent in providing infant welfare at the beginning of the century, the volunteers continued to work alongside public officials.[13] The scope for discretionary intervention nevertheless decreased as officials were subject to closer supervision by government—as Provost Phelps of Oriel must have been as chairman of the Public Assistance Committee in the 1930s—and as the spread of provision superseded what had been novel or unusual. Thus Oxford City had a comparatively low infant mortality rate in the Edwardian period, but as public authorities took on more of these responsibilities in the inter-war period the outlying regions of Oxfordshire and Berkshire—beyond the University's influence—began to narrow the differences.[14]

The activities of the University élite were not necessarily welcomed by their intended beneficiaries. Much of the early voluntary effort was given with the intention of fostering religious devotion as well as offering material assistance, and this may sometimes have muted its impact.[15] The Trades Council refused to have anything to do with the Oxford Council of Social Service which was set up in 1933, and offered 'steady resistance to well meaning but patronizing persons in official positions whose "sympathy" not being prompted by knowledge or experience of working class life is sometimes obnoxious if not nauseating'.[16] Some of the college-based voluntary social work was erratic because of the inevitable turnover of individuals; in 1954 *Isis* reported that 'Wadham College a year ago sent ten people a week to the Bullingdon Youth Club. Now their interest is practically non-existent.'[17] Still, Balliol, New and Worcester colleges ran youth clubs in St Ebbe's and St Clement's, and for at least one who grew up in St Ebbe's, the inter-war Balliol Boys' Club 'catered in a way no other organization did for the recreational and leisure needs of working class boys and youths living in St Thomas's and St Ebbe's'.[18]

Nor was voluntary work of this kind confined to the old town. Trade unionists were well aware that a desirable sense of community would not spontaneously emerge in the new housing estates around the car factories. The community centres set up on the estates were therefore welcomed, and

[12] Obituary in *OM* 13 May 1965, 331. interview with Mrs Ann Spokes Symonds (city councillor since 1957 and Lord Mayor 1976–7) on 27 Jan. 1988.
[13] A. Q. Wells, W. Hyde and L. H. Witts, 'Maternity and child welfare' in Bourdillon, *Survey* ii *Local Administration in a Changing Area*, 146–9.
[14] Ibid. 95, 144–5.
[15] E. Peretz, 'Oxford University and infant welfare', seminar, Corpus Christi College, 27 Feb. 1987, Brian Harrison's transcript, HUA, p. 6.
[16] Whiting, *View from Cowley*, 135–6.
[17] Philip French, 'Social services', *Isis* 10 Nov. 1954, 12.
[18] Gibbs, *'Our Olive'*, 19.

within these the University voluntary service groups were active. Violet Butler was involved in the Rose Hill community centre, in which active and left-wing trade unionists played a significant part, and in the 1950s Oriel and St Anne's colleges also participated. The community newsletter noted in June 1954 that 'we have found to our mutual advantage how good it is to meet at games, socially and in discussion. So that this very friendly association does not falter with changes here and at the colleges each college has officially, through its senior and junior common rooms, accepted to associate in all ways possible with us here at Rose Hill.'[19]

The University's concern could also express itself through the labour movement. Members of the University tried to foster political representation before 1914, but these efforts were not wholeheartedly reciprocated, and when a local Labour Party was formed for the city in 1921 it was based on the joint energies of a national party organizer and local trade unionists.[20] Oxford trade unionists in the 1920s welcomed the support of University sympathizers, some of whom were present on Labour electoral platforms; the local party noted that 'the accession of these persons was a considerable service to the local Labour Movement'.[21] In the 1950s two historians, M. R. D. Foot and J. Steven Watson, acted as political education officers for the Labour Party, and Foot successfully campaigned in the working-class south ward in a municipal election in 1954.[22]

Within the traditional university town, Labour not surprisingly had few real strongholds. The west ward which housed printers and railway workers was the most reliable hunting ground, and became a 'safe' ward in the 1950s and 1960s.[23] When the developing suburbs of Cowley and Headington were brought into the city for local government purposes, they too helped to boost Labour's municipal presence, and here the University Labour members were able to gain a foothold. In the 1930s R. H. S. Crossman (then at New College) represented Headington, and claimed that the council was ignoring the needs of the developing periphery: controlled by 'the Conservative-Liberals' it 'paid no heed to the bitter experience of the industrial north. They allowed much the same things to happen here as happened there 100 years ago. Oxford has drifted into semi-industrialisation and the policy of drift continues today.'[24] Crossman was keen to encourage council-house building in Cowley for the car workers, but government

---

[19] Rose Hill Community Association newsletter for June 1954, copy in Oxford City Library, local history section (OCL). I am grateful to Dr Malcolm Graham and his staff for help in the preparation of this chapter. For Miss C. V. Butler and Rose Hill see Harrison, 'Butler's Oxford Survey', 69.

[20] Whiting, *View from Cowley*, 135–6.

[21] Ibid. 138 n. 38.

[22] OCL, annual reports of the Oxford City Labour Party, 1953–6.

[23] D. N. Chester, 'Oxford' in L. J. Sharpe (ed.), *Voting in Cities* (London 1967), 176–8.

[24] R. H. S. Crossman, *Labour versus the Caucus* (Oxford 1935), 4.

policy limited what could be done because it confined such activity to replacing homes demolished by slum-clearance. University Labour members took part in the rent-strikes which arose from the high cost of living on the privately built estates.[25] Frank Pakenham (later Lord Longford) was also successful for Labour in the Cowley and Iffley ward in the 1930s, and after 1948 these two were followed by Gerry Fowler (Hertford), John Briscoe (Corpus Christi) and Frank Pickstock (external studies), who represented the two wards at various times.

All this helped to put the city on a more even footing with the University, but the overall political impact should not be exaggerated. Despite the incorporation of predominantly working-class regions into the city, Labour did not gain a majority over the Conservatives until 1964. Oxford was not now governed by what Cowley wanted rather than by what the University needed. Right down to the end of our period the University remained the most powerful influence on the planning process. Furthermore, the developing south-eastern region of the city was not part of the parliamentary constituency until after 1946. The Conservative Party dominated the seat for most of the period, though Evan Luard, a fellow of St Antony's, won it for Labour in 1966.

University interest in local politics was not solely a Labour affair: the Conservatives Robert Blake (Christ Church), Peter Spokes (Bodleian Library) and Tom Meadows (laboratory technician) were frequently returned in the north and east wards, and the Conservatives were probably more united and socially more harmonious. Many Conservatives, even if they were not academics, either had been undergraduates or had family links with the University.[26] This did not ensure complete harmony; as will be shown below, some planning issues split the parties along town–university lines. However, because many local Labour politicians, unlike University Labour members, were drawn from the working class, town–gown friction was more likely on the Labour side.

A populist electoral politics which went down well with the local working class was much more the style of the idiosyncratic Liberal Frank Gray in 1922 than of Labour candidates such as Kenneth Lindsay, an ex-president of the Union, chosen in 1924 in the futile hope that he would draw support from both the University and the lower classes. A more realistic view was taken by the Labour candidate in 1929, J. L. Etty, who, for fear of alienating city voters, refused undergraduates' help in his campaign.[27] Segregation in reverse was in evidence when University interests played a decisive part in shaping the parliamentary by-election of 1938. It was University members who largely determined that A. D. Lindsay, Master of Balliol, be put

[25] Whiting, *View from Cowley*, 168.
[26] Interview with Mrs Ann Spokes Symonds.
[27] J. Parker, 'Oxford politics in the 1920s', *Political Quarterly* xlv (1974), 216.

forward as a 'peace' candidate against the Conservative Quintin Hogg and that the Liberal and Labour candidates be withdrawn. The aggrieved Labour candidate, Patrick Gordon Walker (Christ Church) claimed that this showed how University interests could dominate the town: 'the whole thing was initiated in middle class and University circles'.[28] This exaggerated the University's hold on the local Labour Party, but the election campaign was regarded as pretty much a University affair.[29] The uneasy mixture continued after the war, prompting a sympathetic observer to note in 1960 that trade unionists were a 'stabilising force in the City Party, which tends to be an uneasy *congeries* of workers, middle class socialists and academics difficult to lead and impossible to drive'.[30] Oxford was not unusual on this score; Hugh Gaitskell's experience of Leeds was that trade unionists were less mercurial in their attachment than the university lecturers in the city.[31]

However, the local Labour Party did find its University connection helpful when dealing with the colleges' rate-contribution in the 1960s, which threatened to become a serious 'town and gown' issue. The origins of the dispute went back to 1948, when the Inland Revenue took over the valuation for rates from local authorities.[32] Up to that date the colleges had negotiated their rates with the city's valuation committee instead of submitting to professional valuation, because it was difficult to estimate the replacement cost of ancient buildings. College rates before 1948 had risen in line with those of other ratepayers. Transfer to the Inland Revenue meant fresh valuation, which for the colleges brought a threefold rise in rateable value. There was a moratorium in 1955 while arguments were resolved. The controversy which followed raised two questions: should the pre-1948 sympathetic under-rating of colleges as charities be continued *de jure*; and should colleges and commercial organizations be treated alike when estimating annual value? This would have brought the colleges a double benefit: a reduced rateable value, and also a reduced proportion due from that value stemming from charitable status. Such a settlement would, the Registrar admitted, ensure that 'the citizens of Oxford would indeed suffer'.[33] In 1959 the Pritchard Committee, which had been set up in the previous year to examine the rating of charities, decided to give 50 per cent rate-relief to charities. This left Oxford particularly exposed, because the Committee excluded universities but not colleges as they were private foundations receiving no money direct from the University Grants Committee (UGC). Because of the concentration of college property in Oxford and the absence of any countervailing rate-support from either the

[28] Whiting, *View from Cowley*, 171.
[29] Gibbs, *'Our Olive'*, 95–7.
[30] A. I. Marsh, 'Industrial Oxford', *OM* 1 Dec. 1960, 129.
[31] P. Williams, *Hugh Gaitskell: A Political Biography* (London 1979), 312.
[32] HCP 244 (1963), 168, rating, memorandum by C. Cooke, Bursar of Magdalen.
[33] OUA UC/FF/229/12, file on rating, note by Registrar, 17 Sept. 1959.

county or central government, the likely loss to rates from charitable relief was greater than for any other university town. College property accounted for 1.8 per cent of effective rateable value in the city after both points went in its favour, compared to 7 per cent in the period before the changes.[34]

Because the changes had been imposed by central government, redress was sought in the form of compensation from the Treasury for loss of rates from the colleges. This moderated local antagonisms, and when discussing the issue in the House of Commons the local MP, C. M. Woodhouse, claimed that 'there need be no battle of town and gown'.[35] While the colleges had not sought reductions in their rates on both counts, one of the University members closely involved, Colin Cooke of Magdalen, warned the University in 1963 that 'the one issue which more than any other can cloud future relations between the city and the University will be questions arising out of rating'. In evidence to the Franks Commission the city council noted that the rates issue 'gives rise to intense irritation in the city and is thus inimical to complete co-operation'.[36] The Chamber of Commerce was also opposed to college rate-relief.[37]

The problem was solved not by the government providing compensation, but by the colleges' exclusion from mandatory relief in 1966. The responsibility for this lay largely with a key figure in the local Labour Party, W. E. J. (later Lord) McCarthy, a fellow of Nuffield College. The Oxford Labour Party's annual report for 1966 gives a clear picture of how this was achieved. 'During the year a great deal of effort has been put into getting Dick Crossman to redress the injustice of college rate relief. The National Executive Committee and Transport House were constantly badgered and many members of the Government including George Wigg, Anthony Crosland and Dick Crossman were continually beset by letters, telephone calls and personal approaches. The campaign was crowned with success and I must thank the chairman Bill McCarthy for the tremendous energy and enthusiasm which he brought to bear on this and certain other matters which require pressure on ministers.'[38]

The rates issue caused wider ripples: the Labour group on the council used the colleges' reduced rate-contribution to call into question the special University representation on the city council—a channel of influence separate from University members sitting for the conventional local government wards. As party majorities on the city council narrowed in the

[34] HCP 244 (1963), 170, rating; [Pritchard Committee] *Report of the Committee on the Rating of Charities and Kindred Bodies* (PP 1958–9 xix Cmd 831), 58.

[35] *HC Deb.* 30 Nov. 1960, cols 433 ff.

[36] HCP 244 (1963), 154, rating, letter to Vice-Chancellor from Bursar of Magdalen; HCP 251 (1965), memorandum submitted by Oxford City Council to the Franks Commission (1965), 277–80, para. 10.

[37] OCL, annual report of the Oxford chamber of commerce for 1965.

[38] Annual report of the Oxford City Labour Party, 1966.

1960s, the Labour interest was worried lest the University councillors should come to hold the balance between them and the Conservatives. D. N. Chester, a University councillor, reported that 'the Labour group claim, with some justification, that the University members are more inclined to support the Conservatives', even though on matters of significant political discussion such as the sale of council houses they were split evenly, three voting for, three against and three abstaining.[39]

Up to 1967 the University had twelve representatives on the city council, six 'elected' by the heads and bursars of colleges, three by Congregation, with these nine electing three aldermen. Twelve of the sixty-eight members of the council were therefore outside the named electoral process, which Gerry Fowler, a Labour councillor for Cowley and a lecturer at Hertford College, claimed was 'an anachronistic remnant of an anti-democratic system based upon class privilege'.[40] University councillors had usually justified themselves as disinterested contributors to city government, offering experience through long service but not standing for a particular University interest nor acting in concert.[41] There were some examples of long service—notably J. N. L. Baker of Jesus (1946–67), D. N. Chester of Nuffield (1953–74) and A. B. Brown of Worcester (1945–65).

Nonetheless the University councillors' very disinterestedness meant that they often appeared as a group to be of little use to anybody. In 1933 the Registrar noted that 'the University is not well served by its representatives on the council, Parliament obviously put them there to protect the special interests of the University and not, as e.g. Dr. Phelps argues, to push their own views'.[42] This rendered University representation less objectionable than it might otherwise have been. As the city council pointed out in 1965, 'the University representatives do not receive any mandate from the University, are, it is believed, rarely briefed by the University and never vote as a University block. If they did, of course, they would be even less acceptable as members of the present city council.'[43] In 1967 University representation was reduced to eight (six councillors plus two aldermen), and in 1969 the Registrar thought it 'doubtful whether there is any strong body of opinion in the University which would wish to fight for the retention of University Councillors'.[44] In the local government reforms of 1974 they were abolished.

[39] Chester, 'Oxford', 166.

[40] 'University members of the city council', OM 25 May 1961, 371.

[41] D. N. Chester, 'The University in the city' in T. Rowley (ed.), The Oxford Region (Oxford 1980), 169. See also J. Redcliffe-Maud, 'Administrative studies in Oxford 1929–1939' in Halsey, Traditions, 74–5.

[42] OUA UR/SF/CQ/3c, city questions file, Registrar to Vice-Chancellor, 17 Oct. 1933.

[43] HCP 251 (1965), memorandum to Franks Commission, para. 9.

[44] OUA UC/FF/638/2, city questions file, F. H. Sandford, 'Memorandum on University interests in the light of the Maud report', 26 Sept. 1969. University councillors themselves disputed this judgement: author's interview with Dr Geoffrey Marshall of Queen's College, 3 Feb. 1988. Dr Marshall was a city councillor 1967–74 and city sheriff 1971–2.

The failure or unwillingness of the University councillors to act as a bloc explains both their persistence and their ultimate demise. However, there were occasions when a University interest did express itself through representation on the council, and one was over the establishment of the technical college which was to become Oxford Polytechnic. In September 1950 the city council rejected the proposal to establish a college on a new site at Headington Hill, principally because of cost. K. C. Wheare, University member of the city council and of the education committee which had recommended the plan, led those who supported it. The University members voted unanimously in favour of the college but were defeated in council.[45] Wheare organized a public meeting at the town hall against the council's decision; it drew support from both the town and the University, and this gave fresh momentum to a campaign which ultimately succeeded in July 1952.

Other aspects of the University's involvement in local education were less dramatic. University figures acted as governors of local schools, much as the members of any professional groups might have done, and Council was able to nominate two members of the local education committee. This did not automatically mean that the University was able to ensure that local educational affairs were well managed. The Oxford High School for Boys catered for the children of tradesmen, the better-off industrial workers and college servants, but from the early decades of the century it was housed in very cramped buildings in the centre of the town. Proposals for a new building on the outskirts, however, came to nothing, and the Board of Education noted in 1932 that the 'story of these plans and discussions makes depressing reading for anyone who should take for granted that a City Council, certainly interested in local education questions and helped by a governing body on which eminent University lights also served, would handle such a problem with foresight, dignity and efficiency'.[46] True, the 1930s saw the building of the Southfield School for Boys and Milham Ford School for Girls; but the fact remains that at the very least a University interest in local government had failed to protect those in the state sector from severe problems of provision. Moreover, the efforts made in the 1930s to overcome these, in so far as they arose from the local political scene, derived from the extension of the city boundaries in 1928 and the changes in the personnel of the education committee which these brought about.[47] A decisive role for University members cannot be detected.

---

[45] Oxford City Council minutes, 18 Sept. 1950. K. C. Wheare was fellow of All Souls College 1944–57, Gladstone Professor of Government and Public Administration 1944–56 and Vice-Chancellor 1964–6. See also E. Henry, *Oxford Polytechnic: Genesis to Maturity 1865–1980* (Oxford 1982), 16–20.

[46] PRO, ED 53/669, Board of Education, notes on Oxford High School for Boys.

[47] Lance Jones, 'Higher education' in Bourdillon, *Survey* ii. 40.

The University taught the local population directly through its work in adult education and external studies. Cowley's growth fostered a changed emphasis in such provision.[48] Inter-war 'extension' teaching had followed conventional lines by offering some science but chiefly the more digestible forms of literature and modern history. These efforts continued after the war and attracted enthusiastic if sometimes rather small followings.[49] Attempts to encourage working-class participation in such courses (in economics, for example) were not terribly successful. Cowley's potentially enlarged audience wanted more specific applied knowledge rather than access to a bourgeois intellectual culture with a radical slant. G. D. N. Worswick, teaching economics at Cowley, found that his students from the car works wanted to discuss the theory of wages, and reported that 'the discussions have been on a high level and of considerable value to the tutor'.[50]

What the working class at Cowley really wanted was not industrial history or even economics tilted towards their concerns, but attention to the immediate problems of industrial relations. This was not so easily supplied; books and specialist teachers were scarce. Hugh Clegg's appointment as fellow of Nuffield College in 1949 was particularly useful to the department of external studies. He began teaching preparatory classes for trade unionists, so supplementing the work of F. V. Pickstock. Later, Arthur Marsh joined as a lecturer in industrial relations, McCarthy assisted as a research fellow at Nuffield, and Alan Fox also participated. All established substantial reputations in the field of industrial relations. As they noted, 'our experience confirms existing evidence that trade union students are best approached through specific studies allied to their experience'—a very different approach from adult teaching in the town, where the aim was much more to draw students into a University culture.[51]

Very few local people became undergraduates. In the two sample years 1920 and 1949, only 3 per cent of matriculants were living in Oxfordshire; in 1960 only 6 per cent came from within thirty miles of Oxford.[52] But the student body has undoubtedly affected the economic and cultural life of the town, not least because in the twentieth century nearly half the student population has lived outside the colleges. The lower middle- and working-class population who provided lodgings derived useful income from a significant number of students (1,944 in 1938/9, 4,573 in 1966/7). When

[48] Cf above, 385–6, 396–7.

[49] OUA DES/F/4/2, tutorial classes committee reports 1946–50.

[50] Ibid. report 1946–7.

[51] Ibid. report 1956–7. See also OUA UC/DES/F/4/2, trade-union policy documents collection, F. V. Pickstock, 'The teaching of industrial relations with special reference to trade union education', and Brian Harrison, 'Oxford and the labour movement', *Twentieth Century British History* (1991), 268–70.

[52] The figures for 1920 and 1949 come from an analysis by Dr Mark Pottle, to whom I am grateful. The 1960 figure is from the University's statistical return to the UGC for that year.

numbers dropped sharply, as during the First World War, the lack of income was much regretted.[53] This local service to the University was real enough. A committee of 1969, looking back over thirty years, noted how remarkable had been 'the co-operation and generosity on the part of the householders in Oxford in providing accommodation in their homes'.[54]

Student lodgings were inevitably pushed outwards to the periphery of the University area as demand grew—to Summertown in the north, Marston, Headington and to a lesser extent Cowley in the east and south-east. St Thomas's, Jericho and the area around the car factories were the chief among the few Oxford localities unaffected by student lodgings. The relationship between University and landlady was never narrowly economic, because the University tried to monitor students' behaviour in lodgings. Undergraduates could live in Oxford outside their colleges only in approved lodgings; otherwise they would default on their residence requirements.[55] Houses were approved only if they met certain standards of hygiene and if there was a resident landlady to report illness, absence overnight or even late return. Between the wars, licences were refused for lodgings where young women were employed, a survival from nineteenth-century anxieties about under-graduates meeting prostitutes.[56]

By the later 1950s the system was coming under both moral and economic pressure. Students were resident for only half the year, and even then paid rent at what were believed to be less than market rates.[57] When other customers who did not require 'supervision' were available, many landladies wanted to 'finish with students'. The feeling was mutual, since many students found supervision irksome.[58] Furthermore the colleges were largely responsible for the erosion of residential property in the centre of Oxford, which reduced the supply of lodgings.[59] In the outcome, distance between town and gown opened out in two respects: more students were housed in college halls of residence; and students not in college accommodation, diminishingly supervised, provoked a stream of complaints about noise and deterioration of properties.[60]

[53] Figures for numbers in lodgings come from returns to the UGC; the effects of the war were noted in the reports of the delegacy of lodgings held in the University Archives. I am grateful to Dr Daniel Greenstein for assistance with these.

[54] 'Report of the committee of inquiry into lodgings', Supplement No. 8 to *Gazette*, xcix (May 1969), para. 4.

[55] Ibid. para 21.

[56] T. H. Aston, 'Undergraduate lodgings in Oxford 1868–1914', seminar paper, 16 Feb. 1978, All Souls College (OUA Trevor Aston papers).

[57] HCP 228 (1957), 499, report of the secretary of the delegacy of lodgings for Michaelmas term 1957.

[58] William Miller, 'At home', *Isis* 15 May 1957, 18; report of committee of inquiry into lodgings, para. 18.

[59] The change of use of houses in Beaumont Street and St John Street is a case in point. See Oxford City Council, planning committee minutes, 20 Dec. 1957, 12 July 1960 for examples.

[60] OCL, miscellaneous documents of North Oxford Association, complaints in note of 20 Dec. 1973.

Student drinking followed a similar pattern of exclusion before 1939, followed by the intrusive exercise of freedom after 1945, without much evidence of a happy medium. Before the Second World War proctors banned students from local pubs, but after the war some became recreational outlets attached to particular colleges (Trinity and the White Horse, Wadham and the King's Arms). As a consequence 'Oxford pubs unfortunately divide into city houses and undergraduate ones, and so are more artificial than most'.[61] The Cricketers' Arms on the Iffley Road was transformed into a student pub.[62]

As with pubs, students were bound to use local shops and cafés if only to make collegiate life more bearable. In 1924 Graham Greene 'attended tutorials, drank coffee at the Cadena, wrote an essay on Thomas More'.[63] Here too was a source of friction. Students often treated shops like their colleges—running up debts without too much complaint. William Morris, in his early years of repairing bicycles, found undergraduates often slow to pay their bills. In 1925 a survey in *Cherwell* singled out some shops for 'a reprehensible habit of expecting to be paid'.[64] When Graham Greene came up, he found that 'at Blackwell's Bookshop credit seemed to a newcomer endless (though they liked a little bit sometimes on account)'.[65] After the Second World War the practice seemed to die out, at least among the conventional shops; Fred Bickerton noted in 1953 that tradesmen 'are far less inclined to give credit now than they were in my young days'.[66]

Students also influenced the town indirectly through their colleges' demands from local shops. In the 1920s the colleges provided a reasonably secure market, for the Asquith Commission noted how little advantage the colleges gained in lower prices from the size of the orders they placed.[67] By the early 1930s, however, the question had become more sensitive. The Oxford Chamber of Trade reported that 'under present conditions of cheap and rapid transport, intensive competition and urgent need for economic administration in every undertaking, trade with the University is becoming probably more difficult of attainment, certainly more difficult of retention'.[68] The deep-freeze ensured that inter-collegiate reliance on London suppliers, frowned upon in the 1920s, became more widespread forty years later.[69]

[61] For the 'policing' of students see OCL, E. F. Carritt, 'Fifty years a don', typescript (1960), 54. For pubs see 'An evening's crawl with Dennis Potter', *Isis* 12 May 1958, 14.

[62] Gibbs, 'Our Olive', 158.

[63] Graham Greene, *A Sort of Life* (Harmondsworth 1971), 103.

[64] 'A guide to the webs and parlours of commercial Oxford', *Cherwell* 28 Nov. 1925, 161. For William Morris's experiences see M. Thomas, *Out on a Wing* (London 1964), 155–6.

[65] Greene, 89.

[66] F. Bickerton, *Fred of Oxford* (London 1953), 137.

[67] *Asquith Report*, appx 1, memorandum of committee of Oxford estates bursars, 248.

[68] Bodl. Michael Sadler papers, c. 628, fo 163, 'Oxford trade and the University', memorandum of Oxford Chamber of Trade, May 1931.

[69] J. P. D. Dunbabin, 'College finances and property in the twentieth century' in Rowley, *Oxford Region*, 218.

This did not entirely exclude local traders: in the 1980s much of Wadham's food was still being bought locally, even though it would have been cheaper to buy from the bigger suppliers.[70]

In addition to its educational contribution and economic impact, the University might be expected to have had a significant cultural influence. As with education and economics, the analysis is impressionistic, but it is difficult to be precise about how to assess the cultural level of a university town. Perhaps the most specific contribution of a university would have been to support or attract cultural activity which would not have otherwise reached a medium-sized market town. The Oxford Playhouse straddled town and gown in its various premises from Woodstock Road in the 1920s to Beaumont Street in 1938 (substantially reconstructed in 1963–4). The support of St John's College and the University sustained the Playhouse when commercial returns from audiences would not have done so. It tried to bring serious drama to Oxford through its own professional company as well as providing facilities for undergraduate and town societies, and it generally contrasted with the lighter offerings at the more commercial New Theatre (now the Apollo), which had no connection with the University. In November 1946 the Playhouse offered *Antony and Cleopatra* while the New Theatre had a Frank Shelley comedy *Postman's Knock*. In November 1957 it was *Macbeth* at the Playhouse and Hugh and Margaret Williams in *Father's Match* at the New Theatre. Yet university patronage of the Playhouse was not overwhelming. Nevill Coghill pointed out in 1963 that 'not going to the theatre is an occupational disease in Oxford'.[71] This echoed the lament of the Playhouse in 1935, when the poor audience for John Masefield's *The Witch* 'has been a shock to the most optimistic supporters of the theatre'.[72]

The University also neglected fine art. The Oxford Arts Club had an even more parlous history than the Playhouse. Begun in 1920 to promote the study of fine art in Oxford, it mounted special exhibitions and lectures, but by 1930 it was reported that 'the club cannot continue except by the loyal support of all in the special campaign to increase substantially the regular membership list'.[73] The Club could not open its exhibitions to casual visitors because it could not afford to pay for an attendant. Unable to afford suitable premises, it was forced to change venue many times in the 1930s. One supporter lamented in 1935 that 'where art is concerned it [Oxford] has no sense of communal life'.[74] An important recent initiative, the Museum of Modern Art, was by the late 1980s attracting as many visitors as the

[70] *Wadham College Gazette* Jan. 1989, 51.
[71] N. Coghill, 'The University Playhouse', *OM* 2 May 1963, 297.
[72] 'Repertory in Oxford', *OM* 7 Mar. 1935, 470. Cf above, 444.
[73] Bodl. Oxford Arts Club annual reports 1930–40.
[74] Letter in *OM* 17 Oct. 1935, 17.

Ashmolean and ten times as many as Christ Church picture gallery, but it is an educational charity independent of the University.[75] The Museum tried to take art to the workers at Cowley by mounting an exhibition of modern art by Picasso, Braque, Sutherland and Hepworth in the Pressed Steel Company's works canteen, but the event failed to win a mention in the company's magazine.[76]

If fine art was left high and dry by both town and University, the cinema introduced unusual films for the University population which others could also enjoy. The programme of the Scala cinema in Walton Street was adapted to suit the special needs and tastes of a university town, yet it admitted the general public.[77] Some film showings were restricted to the University; *Housing Problems*, a product of the documentary film movement of the 1930s, was shown by the University's Labour Film Society and did not seek a wider audience. But many of the films shown by the University's Film Society were also offered to the general public at the Scala. In the 1930s Soviet films were frequently shown—*Road to Life* (1935), for example—and in the 1950s French, Swedish and Japanese films; these contrasted with the staple diet of Hollywood at the main commercial cinemas in Oxford. By the late 1950s there were signs that the gap was closing. 'A sign of growing enlightenment is that the Scala is showing *Wild Strawberries*, while the Super put on *Mon Oncle*; in the past Jacques Tati was the main stay of the Scala box office while the Super would hardly have dared touch a film with French dialogue.'[78]

Where town and gown did collaborate was in music, largely due to Hugh Percy Allen, organist of New College from 1901 and Heather Professor of Music from 1918. He brought together two amateur societies, one from the University (the Bach Choir) and the other from the town (the Oxford Choral and Philharmonic Society), to put on joint concerts and a series of festivals in 1914, 1922 and 1926.[79] So it was in the more conventional cultural activity that town–gown links flourished, rather than in the higher realms of fine art. Both could also celebrate the University's architectural display, evident in their collaboration in floodlighting and restoring college buildings. Interestingly, the magazines published by the Pressed Steel Company for its employees included studies of the University.[80]

[75] David Elliott (Director of the Museum), 'Art galleries in Oxford since 1945', seminar, Corpus Christi College, 3 Feb. 1989 (Brian Harrison's transcript, HUA), 16; cf ibid. 11 (Lucy Whitaker), 23 (Christopher White).
[76] *OM* 12 Nov. 1959, 94.
[77] Note on the Scala in *OM* 20 Oct. 1938, 42.
[78] Film reviews in *OM* 15 Oct. 1959.
[79] C. Bailey, *Hugh Percy Allen* (Oxford 1948), 40–5; see also 'The Bach Choir', *Isis* 13 Mar. 1946, 2.
[80] For city floodlighting of college buildings see MCA bursarial committee minutes, 5 June 1957; I am grateful to the College Archivist, Dr Janie Cottis, for help with these records. Pressed Steel *Pressings* Feb. 1928.

There were opportunities, too, for scholarly collaboration. H. E. Salter did much to record the history of the city, often through the Oxford Historical Society; his publications, frequently technical in character and in Latin, had only a modest circulation.[81] The growth of Cowley also gave those from the social sciences reason to be interested in their own city; the arrival of the motor industry had brought it into the forefront of interest as a case study in inter-war economic growth. Oxford was no longer idiosyncratic or 'special' because it was a university town, but rather was typical of the moderate-sized towns of the midlands and south. Barnett House's two-volume study *A Survey of Social Services in the Oxford District* (Oxford, 1938–40) was a comprehensive study of the economics and government of a changing area. A good deal of work on the migration of labour was done at the Institute of Statistics, not simply for its impact upon Oxford but rather to examine the geographical mobility of labour in response to wage incentives. This had a particular connection with the degree of migration from the depressed areas of the 1930s to growth towns like Oxford, and had direct relevance to policies concerning the regions and the location of industry.[82]

Applied social studies was the main preoccupation of Nuffield College, founded in 1937. When opinions were being canvassed about this function of the College, there was little mention of the scope in Oxford for local studies, although it was admitted that the motor industry was now making the city more representative in its economic and social conditions.[83] Peter Collison and J. M. Mogey argued in their case-study of housing and social class in Oxford that 'there seems to be no reason for assuming that this city is greatly unlike other English urban areas in the amount of residential dissimilarity and segregation'; and two more recent social-science projects used Oxford to provide material for pilot studies.[84] While sociologists were interested in what was typical about Oxford, the geographers pursued what was special. E. W. Gilbert, Professor of Geography, saw university towns as peculiar for the tension between an economically static university and a dynamic industry and for the resultant competition for 'urban space'. His successor Jean Gottmann focused on the attractive force of what he termed

[81] W. A. Pantin, 'Herbert Edmund Salter', *Proc. British Academy* xl (1954), esp. 232–3. On the Oxford Historical Society's output see Pantin's remarks in committee on financial questions, HCP 220 (1955), 142–4.

[82] G. H. Daniel, 'Some factors affecting the movement of labour', *Oxford Economic Papers* iii (1940); II. Makower, J. Marschak and H. Robinson, 'Studies in the mobility of labour', ibid. ii (1939); H. W. Robinson, 'The response of labour to economic incentives' in P. W. S. Andrews and T. Wilson (eds), *Oxford Studies in the Price Mechanism* (Oxford 1951).

[83] Nuffield College, Henry Clay papers, box 127, note by Lynda Grier, Principal of Lady Margaret Hall, 16 Aug. 1937.

[84] P. Collison and J. M. Mogey, 'Occupation, education and housing in an English city', *Amer. Jl Sociology* lxv (1960), 597; P. J. Dunleavy, *The Politics of Mass Housing in Britain 1945–75* (Oxford 1981), 388 n. 19; J. H. Goldthorpe (in collaboration with Catriona Llewellyn and Clive Payne), *Social Mobility and Class Structure in Modern Britain* (Oxford 1980), 282.

'quaternary' economic functions based on the supply and exchange of knowledge[85]—a function also investigated by Barbara Baird and Susanne Walker.[86]

In their chapter on town planning in the Barnett House *Survey*, W. O. Hart and his colleagues favoured a 'twin city' approach, dividing University from motor industry. Their views, and those of Gilbert on the clash of identity between Cowley and Oxford, lead on to the question of the physical impact of industrial growth and the political deployment of University interests within the town-planning process.[87] The colleges' independent interests made a coherent University point of view elusive, and the University's relationship with the city council and with national government was not easy. The city council admitted to the Franks Commission that it had 'to accept the fact that there is within its territory another body, the University, which is not only powerful and influential but without which Oxford would be just another town'.[88] The council's sympathy with the University was real, but rather too 'conservationist' in emphasis to accommodate University expansion flexibly from the 1950s onward. Strategies designed to protect Oxford from Cowley ended up by making it difficult for the city centre to reconcile its residential and occupational functions.

Many took the view that Oxford's character had been irreversibly changed by the arrival of the motor industry. A. H. Smith envisaged a traveller entering Oxford from Cowley in 1954 and 'as he passed the Pressed Steel and Morris Works he would have the feeling that he was in the spreading fringe of an industrial town. The long and dreary length of the Cowley Road does nothing to allay this feeling.'[89] In the same year Gilbert noted that 'industry by establishing itself at Oxford has laid its hands, not only upon the lovely countryside which formed the green setting for the grey dreaming spires, but also upon one of the fairer cities of the world'. Lord Beveridge, returning to Oxford to live in retirement on the Woodstock Road—several miles and a whole world away from the car factories—felt nonetheless that 'Oxford as a place to live in is sadly changed and damaged by Nuffield and his works and workpeople'.[90]

[85] E. W. Gilbert, *The University Town in England and West Germany* (Chicago 1961), 11, 67; J. Gottmann, 'The centrality of Oxford' in C. G. Smith and D. I. Scargill (eds), *Oxford and its Region: Geographical Essays* (Oxford 1975).

[86] B. Baird, 'Interweaving of quaternary activities' in Smith and Scargill, *Oxford and its Region*; S. R. Walker, 'External relations of Oxford', *Ekistics* cclxxiv (1979); Walker, 'University centrality and external linkages of Oxford'; cf above, 547.

[87] A. B. Emden, G. M. Harris, W. O. Hart and W. Hyde, 'Town and country planning' in Bourdillon, *Survey* ii. 438–9.

[88] HCP 251 (1965), memorandum of evidence to Franks Commission, para. 4.

[89] A. H. Smith, *Selected Essays and Addresses* (Oxford 1963), 46.

[90] E. W. Gilbert, 'The growth of the city of Oxford' in A. F. Martin and R. W. Steel (eds), *The Oxford Region: A Scientific and Historical study* (Oxford 1954), 173; J. Harris, *William Beveridge* (Oxford 1977), 467. Beveridge had favoured a strict division between the university town and Cowley in his evidence to the public inquiry of 1960 on the city development plan, 15th day, 58 ff (OCL).

The University between the wars tended to view town planning as no more than glorified sanitary inspection, and seems to have paid little attention to pleas that it should take town planning for Oxford seriously.[91] The city council drew up a planning scheme for the Ministry of Health in 1923 but the University confined its interest to demarcating a special area which protected it, and had nothing to say about the zoning of Cowley for industrial development. Yet this was the time when (in contrast to its view after 1946) the city was keen to attract industry. According to the report on the local inquiry of 1925, 'the Corporation did not want to give the impression that Oxford was merely an educational town and had no interest in industry'.[92] While Morris's had been established at Cowley before 1914, Pressed Steel did not begin producing there until 1926. Had the University objected strongly to further expansion at Cowley, Pressed Steel might not have been built.

The turn of mind which was disdainful of town planning had a more confident grasp of the rural aesthetics upon which an alternative defence of Oxford could be constructed. The English upper classes, whether of right or left, have always been keen on the countryside and they were not silent in Oxford. John Buchan, an enthusiast for the Oxford Preservation Trust, argued that 'no one can understand Oxford unless he knows the Oxford countryside. Half her beauty lies in its rural setting.'[93] When Douglas Veale, just retired as Registrar, became Secretary of the Trust in 1958, he was applauded as 'one of those amiable old-fashioned and knowledgeable persons who still finds walking in the Oxfordshire countryside one of his most cherished forms of relaxation'.[94]

Founded in 1927 and one of the most active pressure groups concerned with Oxford, the Trust's main aim was to buy land around the city to preserve open space. Its two main achievements were to purchase South Park, Headington, and to restrict Oxford's awkward spread by instituting a green belt around it in 1954. The Trust's concern with preserving green open spaces around Oxford brought it into contact with the city council which supported 'preservation' strategies, and with the major landowning colleges which frequently opposed them. The colleges had rejected the proposal put forward during the Asquith Commission's inquiries that they should

[91] M. P. Fogarty, 1 Oct. 1948: PRO, HLG 71/1388, chairs of town planning at Oxford and Cambridge universities.

[92] PRO, HLG 4/1729, report of the public inquiry of 1925; see also OUA Trevor Aston papers, notes by Douglas Veale on 'The mechanism of reform 1929–39'.

[93] Quoted in D. I. Scargill, *The Preservation of Oxford: An Account of the Work of the Preservation Trust* (Oxford 1973), 13. The initiative for forming the Trust in 1927 had come from H. A. L. Fisher (Warden of New College) and Michael Sadler (Master of University College).

[94] OCL, 31st annual report of the Oxford Preservation Trust, 1958, 12.

convert their investments from real property into equities, partly out of a wish to keep diverse portfolios, but partly because college ownership of land was the best way of ensuring the preservation of rural surroundings for the town.[95]

There is some evidence of successful collaboration between colleges and the Trust. In 1938 the Trust bought a farm from Christ Church to preserve some open space around Shotover Hill; the College promised that it would not extract a 'fancy price' and there is no evidence that it did so. It is also true that the low yields of agricultural land in Oxfordshire between the wars did not always lead to land sales. Even though the income from sales when reinvested would have been higher than rents received from land, one response was not to sell but to improve the commercial prospects of farms. Magdalen College encouraged co-operative harvesting by the smaller farms and maintained its 11,500 acres of farmland in Oxfordshire throughout these years.[96] But most of the decline in farmland in the county occurred close to Oxford, and collegiate land must have formed part of these sales—as in 1933, when Magdalen sold land near the northern bypass.[97]

Despite its earlier interest in attracting industry to Cowley, the city council emerged in the 1930s as a defender of open space in and around Oxford in a way which hampered the activities of some of the colleges and coincided with the aims of the Trust. St John's College wished to sell to Morris Motors in 1940 land near Wolvercote which it had found to be unsuitable for farming. The Trust and the city council objected to the scheme because it broke into land zoned for residential development and because they feared that the workers' housing would give rise to ribbon development. Eventually Morris's found an alternative site, and the Bursar of St John's, Ronald Hart-Synnot, told the company that 'Oxford still tends to regard itself as unchanged from what it was in the last century. Some day no doubt it will realize that the shops and small firms of which its business community mainly consists depend upon efficient factories and that Oxford and the surrounding districts cannot reasonably fail to provide its share of sites.'[98] The same tensions between the preservationist concerns of the city council and the economic interests of the colleges were evident after the war. Magdalen College unsuccessfully challenged the designation of Southfields Golf Club as permanent open space because it wanted it approved for residential development, and when the British Motor Corporation wanted

[95] Asquith Report, appx 1, memorandum of committee of Oxford estates bursars, 39.

[96] Correspondence with Christ Church noted 20 Apr. 1938 in Oxford Preservation Trust papers in Bodl. Sadler papers, c. 627; MCA estates bursar's report for 1931, 11.

[97] MCA acta 150. 12, 7 Dec. 1933; R. L. Cohen and K. A. H. Murray, 'Agriculture' in Bourdillon, Survey i. 134.

[98] Bodl. Sadler papers, Oxford Preservation Trust papers, c. 627, Bursar of St John's to Morris Motors, 21 Nov. 1940.

to build a parts department at Horspath it found that the land in question was owned by Brasenose College, which supported the project.[99]

The city's interpretation of the University's urban interests—namely the limitation and containment of growth—became more explicit and more firmly based after 1946, when the council, after discussions with the Ministry of Town and Country Planning and the Board of Trade, resolved to take all steps to 'prevent the population for which Oxford is the natural centre from increasing'. At this meeting Lewis Silkin, of the Ministry, commented that his visit to Oxford 'was made in an endeavour to safeguard one of the country's most precious heritages'.[100] Subsequent expansion by the Pressed Steel Company took place in Swindon and south Wales.

The city, in accepting the University as inextricably bound up with Oxford's identity, saw it as part of a historic heritage rather than as a source of economic growth or social change. Over some, but not all, planning questions this brought the interests of city and University together. Both were concerned to protect the traditional fabric of the town. The city council used its planning powers to restrict commercial display in High Street and Broad Street, and like the University was lukewarm towards tourists and refused to signpost places of interest. Tourism had been put forward as an alternative contributor to the local economy when the decision was made in 1946 to restrict growth at Cowley, but the main problem was seen as one of containment rather than encouragement. As early as 1933 Queen's College required tourists to be accompanied around its chapel because of the risk of damage and litter. A similarly 'non-commercial' point of view was taken when Woolworth's decided to replace the Clarendon Hotel in the Cornmarket with a department store. This was opposed, ultimately in vain, by both the city and the University because 'the Clarendon Hotel is the only secular building of architectural merit in the Cornmarket and one of the few surviving relics of Oxford's earlier existence as a county market town'.[101]

As well as limiting growth, the city council was also anxious to preserve the functions of different areas, and to uphold the housing needs of University members even at the expense of the University's institutional requirements. The research establishment of A. C. Nielsen and much other commercial enterprise was kept away from North Oxford and St Giles', and the University was consulted before the building of the Maison Française was authorized.[102] But the University could not get all it wanted out of the

[99] MCA bursarial committee minutes, 24 Apr. 1964. For the Horspath planning proposals see OCL, appx to 35th report of Oxford Preservation Trust, 1962, 19.

[100] Oxford City Council reports, town-planning committee, 25 June 1946.

[101] *OM* 26 Jan. 1933, 324 (Queen's); HCP 213 (1952), 218 (Clarendon Hotel). See Oxford City Council planning committee minutes, 9 June 1955 for the Minister's decision on the ground that the Clarendon Hotel had no economic function. For the council's attitude to tourism see Oxford City Council, planning committee minutes, 9 June 1953.

[102] For rejection of Nielsen's application see planning committee minutes, 11 Oct. 1950; for rejection of Pressed Steel's application for office space in St Giles' see ibid. 11 Apr. 1961.

planning committee, since it could not easily convert property into office space in North Oxford, nor could colleges always exploit opportunities for getting commercial tenants in areas designated for university use.[103]

Beyond the examples of individual planning decisions it is important to establish the University's impact on some of the neighbourhoods close to the city centre. University expansion seemed to threaten, both aesthetically and spatially, areas the city wished to preserve without enhancing those which required improvement. Planning decisions after 1945 had shown that even if businessmen wanted to work in the main urban area, their preferences about location had to take second place to the preservation of a stable urban pattern. The University, however, had some success in its plans to expand in the central area, even if the results showed that on aesthetic grounds it had little reason for favoured treatment. The development of the science area from the mid-1950s, and the alarm about high buildings damaging the Oxford skyline, show this.

At the outset the scientists were able to convince the city that they must expand from existing sites; when the location of research activities on the outskirts of Oxford was suggested, 'reference was made to the fact that the frontiers of knowledge were rapidly changing and that scientific subjects tended increasingly to impinge on one another'.[104] In the early stages of the growth of the science area, land had been used from the University Parks, but widespread criticism halted the encroachment in 1934. The consequent resort to the Keble Road triangle led inevitably to the planning of high buildings. Sir William Holford, the architect and town planner called in to advise on the expansion of the science area, was no zealot for high buildings. Yet he thought that 'the new engineering block holds the view quite dramatically'.[105] Not so the city council, which found the building 'quite unrelated to the landscape and out of sympathy with it both by its height and by its bulk'. Within the University Bryan Keith-Lucas thought the building 'enough to show the danger and demonstrate the rightness of the city council's resolution to prevent any more high buildings'.[106]

When plans for a 25-storey zoology building appeared in 1962 [plate 10.2], the University's search for more space seemed entirely insensitive to aesthetic considerations. Keith-Lucas had good reason to ask 'what, one may wonder, would have been the attitude of the University if similar

[103] Planning committee minutes, 13 June 1950 and 24 Feb. 1959.

[104] HCP 242 (1962), 916, note of meeting with town-planning committee. This view was opposed by R. J. P. Williams of Wadham, who argued that medicine and engineering should be located on the outskirts: R. J. P. Williams, 'The science area', *OM* 31 Jan. 1963, 148.

[105] W. Holford, 'Future requirements of the Oxford science departments', *Town Planning Rev.* xxxiv (1963), 107.

[106] The views of the city council and the city architect, Douglas Murray, are in 'High buildings in Oxford', appx 2 to planning committee minutes, 11 Sept. 1962. B. Keith-Lucas, 'Academic heights', *OM* 23 May 1963, 311.

proposals had been put forward by industrial or commercial companies?'[107] At the time when the Keble triangle was being developed, the city architect Douglas Murray drew up a report on high buildings which noted that 'Oxford already possesses a unique skyline, generally recognized as a precious national heritage'; and he claimed that any bulky high buildings in the university area would damage a fragile and spiky skyline.[108] Hence city council restrictions on high buildings in the university area.

Efforts to ease the pressure on the science area by placing some buildings in North Oxford also fell foul of the city's preservation strategies. Initially the proposal seemed likely to succeed. St John's College was willing to sell the land in question as long as the new buildings would be 'good neighbours' for what had been zoned in city plans as a residential area for private and University purposes. However, critics soon pointed out that this would extend Oxford's 'dead centre' into a residential area. Exeter College was also worried because university expansion was diminishing living space for senior academics.[109] Hence the creation of a conservation area in North Oxford to prevent significant redevelopment of a suburb in which both university and colleges had a significant stake. Calling it a 'perfectly preserved Victorian suburb . . . still redolent of an Oxford now fading away', the city architect argued that 'this area is now threatened by necessary expansions to the University and is doomed to extinction unless it can be saved by prompt action'.[110] The enthusiasm for preserving the gaunt houses of North Oxford, sustained by Conservative votes on the city council, effectively hampered the plans of the major collegiate interests—St Anne's, St John's and St Hugh's—for redeveloping their properties.

University expansion into residential areas also evoked hostility in west Oxford. Instead of the spacious layout of North Oxford, here was a densely packed working-class and lower middle-class district with some small-scale industry located within it, principally the University Press and the Eagle ironworks. In the 1950s the University saw it as a likely area of expansion for the Press and some laboratories, but the city council was hostile. So was St John's College, the major landowner, which hoped that the area would become 'a sort of Chelsea area of Oxford with mixed development of housing for all classes'.[111] The University did manage to achieve some

[107] Keith-Lucas, 'Academic heights'. A zoology building was eventually completed in 1970. Cf above, 278–9, 515.

[108] Murray, 'High buildings in Oxford', 1, 5.

[109] The criticism came from D. N. Chester, Warden of Nuffield and a university city councillor: HCP 255 (1966), 100, acquisition from St John's College of site between Banbury and Bradmore roads; Exeter College's views are in HCP 242 (1962), 150, revision of city development plan 1955, views of colleges.

[110] Quoted in HCP 256 (1967), 755, report of buildings and development committee. See also J. Briscoe, 'The north Oxford conservation area', OM 3 May 1968, 275. For a report on the approval of the area see Oxford Mail 7 May 1968.

[111] For University intentions see HCP 206 (1950), 296, report of joint committee on town planning; for St John's College see OUA UC/FF/580/3, town-planning file, note of July 1960.

expansion, but such objectives were not necessarily welcome. When Olive
Gibbs of the west ward Labour Party criticized the spread of the University
Press at a public inquiry in 1965 she was asked, 'would you not agree that the
University Press is in a rather special position in Oxford?' She replied: 'no, I
could not agree it is in any more special position than any other industry in
Oxford.'[112] Both political parties had therefore stood against university
encroachment on residential districts; only the character of the area
determined which party was involved at any particular time.

In St Clement's, the situation was very different. There the city, far from
wishing to restrain the University, wanted it to expand in order to improve
the approach to the historic centre. The city's plan in 1964 was to buy up
expensive land in this area and 'be to some extent acting as an agent for the
University in this instance' so that residential university building might
follow.[113] But the University, while agreeing to the city's intentions for the
district, did not wish to incur any obligation to build there, and only two
colleges—Magdalen and Queen's—developed any interest in St Clement's.[114]
Tempers became frayed when the development plan of 1964, which tried to
accommodate the increased student growth from the 1950s, was overtaken
by the further increase in numbers recommended by the Franks Commission. Because of a greater concentration of University population in and
around the city centre, it was feared that there would be 'a more pronounced
social difference between the populations living east and west of Magdalen
Bridge; the old idea of a "twin-city" will gain a further foothold'.[115] The city
became particularly anxious that haphazard incremental changes to the use
of buildings would alter the character of central Oxford. As it told the
Franks Commission, 'the University and colleges must accept planning
controls in the same way as other organizations in the city'.[116]

The situation was greatly complicated by the rancour which arose over
traffic and relief roads. The planning decisions of central and local
government after 1945 provided Oxford with some protection against
further encroachments of large-scale industry at Cowley, but there were still
people to deal with, and for the 1950s and 1960s this chiefly meant people
with cars. The motor car's intrusion into the University area had evoked

---

[112] Planning permission details are in planning committee minutes, 22 Feb. 1959 and 9 Feb.
1960. Cf the views of Olive Gibbs at public inquiry 1965, 18th day, 71.

[113] HCP 248 (1964), 85, revision of the town map.

[114] HCP 248 (1964), 240, report of joint committee on town planning.

[115] OCL typescript, 'Report of the city architect and planning officer on the implications of
Report of Commission of Inquiry (Franks Report)', 11 Oct. 1966, 3. The refusal of the city to
allow the conversion of some rooms in St John Street from 'residential' to 'tutorial' was seen as
evidence of mistrust of university intentions: HCP 255 (1966), 172, report of joint committee
on city questions.

[116] HCP 251 (1965), 'Evidence to Franks', para. 4.

concern before 1939 because of parking in Broad Street and the increasing use of the High. Traffic was loathed for the noise it made, and L. R. Phelps noted in 1935 that 'the roar of traffic in the main streets is in painful contrast to the peace of the old days'.[117] However, it was only after 1946, with the growing number of cars, that the University was presented with some unpalatable choices about how to protect the town.

Thomas Sharp was largely responsible for determining how this town-planning problem confronted the University. A town planner who was 'well known for combining sympathy for historic buildings with understanding of the needs of modern life', Sharp produced a widely discussed report for Oxford City Council which was published in 1948 as *Oxford Replanned*.[118] This work was a devoted celebration of Oxford's townscape, and his views influenced the council's policy on high buildings adopted in 1962. Although some of his proposals such as the relocation of the motor industry away from Oxford were regarded as foolish, his overall concern for preserving the University was welcomed by dons interested in town planning.[119]

However, Sharp's methods differed strongly from the rural aesthetic which guided many views about how to preserve Oxford. It was not that Sharp had no time for rural surroundings—he wrote extensively and warmly on the countryside—but he wanted the urban clearly demarcated from the rural, and this influenced his treatment of Oxford's traffic problem. He asked how far relief of city-centre traffic justified sacrificing open space near the University in order to build new roads. The University's response exposed divisions between the colleges and produced political problems with the city council. Even though the University was saved by another town planner, Colin Buchanan, this could not prevent a powerful institution, with routes of appeal to the highest level of central government, from falling very much on the defensive with the local authority.

Sharp stressed the key position of the High—'one of the world's great works of art, it is the backbone of university life'—and said it was the task of the town planner to remove the traffic and restore it to what it had been before, 'like a super-quad, in the middle of which aged dons could meet and argue a point of ethics'.[120] The next stage of his analysis was really the key to the conflicts over the roads issue in the pre-Buchanan 1950s and 1960s. To get traffic away from the High required a substitute road, near enough for the motorist to accept it as a convenient alternative to the High; there could be no question of compelling the motorist to take more distant routes well clear of the town. What was proposed was a road through the rural quiet and

[117] 'Traffic in Oxford', *OM* 16 Oct. 1930, 10; L. R. Phelps, 'Oxford since 1910', *OM* 9 May 1935, 568.
[118] PRO, HLG 71/1756, Oxford Preservation Trust, notes by A. R. Wagner, 20 June 1946; T. Sharp, *Oxford Replanned* (Oxford 1948).
[119] See the criticisms of the economist Henry Clay in his review of Sharp's book in *OM* 29 Apr. 1948, 378.
[120] Sharp, 21.

unspoilt beauty of Christ Church Meadow to the south of it. As Sharp told a public inquiry of 1956: 'It is the loss of quietness in the Meadow for the gain of calm in the whole University. The issue is as simple, as cruelly simple as that . . . on any side of civilized values there can be no hesitation as to which course should be taken.'[121]

There was much hesitation of course, and no such substitute road was built. It was recognized in the mid–1960s that the question had been wrongly posed. According to Denys Munby, a specialist in transport economics, 'there has never really been any conflict between peace in the High and peace in the Meadow'.[122] Sharp however had no love for the 'dank inaccessible acres' of Christ Church Meadow and preferred the more ordered beauty of the University Parks.[123] His plans required not only the road through Christ Church Meadow but also the sacrifice of Magdalen College School and the Oxford Union—the latter because the road would eventually loop northwards to carry traffic from the south of Oxford to the north, avoiding the city centre [figures 21.2 and 21.3].

Not surprisingly, the city council was reluctant to embark upon such destructive plans, arguing initially that outer ring roads and the building of a shopping and commercial centre at Cowley would ease traffic pressures. Disturbance of Christ Church Meadow was seen as a 'last resort' in 1951.[124] But over time the city council accepted that traffic conditions demanded inner roads to cater for internally generated traffic between neighbourhoods. Further encouragement came from the Minister of Housing and Local Government, Duncan Sandys, who argued in 1956 that 'the loss of quiet at the northern end of the meadow will be greatly outweighed by the gain of peace and dignity in the heart of the University'.[125] Plans for a Meadow road survived till 1966, when new views came to the fore about compulsory direction of traffic in towns.

How could such a proposal have even been contemplated? After all, the scheme for a northern relief road through the University Parks succumbed early before unanimous opposition. Part of the reason lay in the University's willingness to consider the Meadow road as a last resort. It disliked both schemes, but acknowledged that if such a road had to be built, then the Meadow road was the better.[126] Sir Patrick Abercrombie admitted at an

[121] Sharp's evidence was published as 'Oxford's roads', *Town Planning Rev.* xxvii (1956), 142.
[122] Report of debate in Congregation, *Gazette* 27 Feb. 1969. Denys Munby was Reader in Transport Economics attached to Nuffield College.
[123] In evidence to the public inquiry 1965, 15th day, 3.
[124] OCL, report on development plan by E. G. Chandler (city architect), 1956, 34.
[125] HCP 255 (1966), letter conveying Minister's decision (28 Sept.). R. Newman, *The Road and Christ Church Meadow* (Oxford 1988) examines the controversy in terms of the relations between central and local government.
[126] Debate in Congregation 29 Nov. 1955, 59. The preference, and the uncertainty about whether it was ultimately a preference, emerged during the University's evidence to the public inquiry of 1956, 2nd day, pp. 6 ff, and was pointed out by the town clerk, Harry Plowman, 9th day, 24 (OCL).

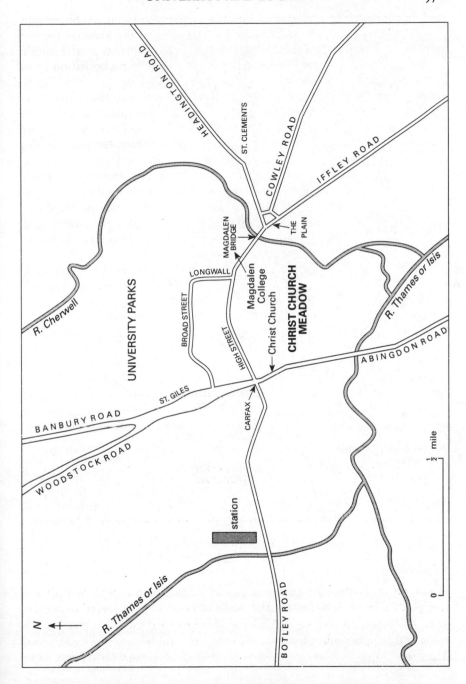

FIGURE 21.2   OXFORD'S ROAD AND RIVER GEOGRAPHY

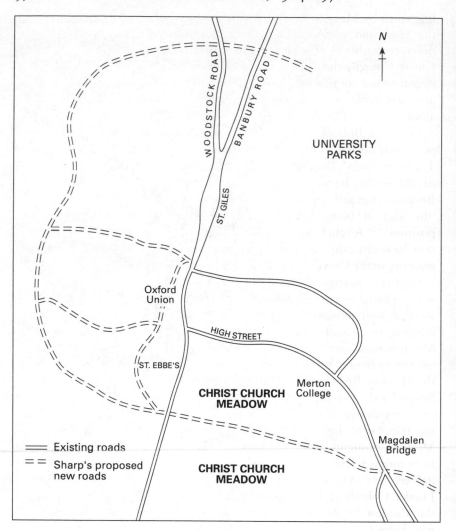

FIGURE 21.3   THOMAS SHARP'S PROPOSED NEW ROADS

inquiry in 1956 that if the need for a Meadow road was accepted, Sharp's was the best.[127] The University got the worst of both worlds: forced to express some preference, it seemed to think the Meadow road the lesser evil, but the more real the possibility became, the more forceful became the opposition. Thus the University was exposed as both in disarray and obstructive. The

[127] Public inquiry 1956, 3rd day, 13.

line taken by Maurice Bowra, Warden of Wadham College (to the north of the High and some distance from the Meadow) illustrates conciliatory pressures within the University and frustration with the line being taken by Christ Church, the College most affected. 'We must be in a position to negotiate and not rely on simply saying "no" . . . Ch[rist] Ch[urch] of course are intolerable, rude to everyone, conceited, and like the Germans as allies.'[128]

For Lord Bullock, commenting later on the roads debate, 'the turning point may appear to be the publication in 1963 of the Buchanan Report on Traffic in towns'. Instead of the motorist being offered a road he might freely decide to take, he was to be compelled to follow a more distant relief road. Buchanan himself announced at the public inquiry in Oxford in 1965 that 'the idea of being tougher with the motorist has revolutionized the position'.[129] A relief road well to the south of Christ Church Meadow could now be realistically considered, and this was supported by an overwhelming majority in the University.

Improved perceptions had to be buttressed by better tactics. Buchanan was prepared to enter the fray as an expert witness only if the University showed some solidarity of interest and fervour. 'I honestly doubt whether it is going to be sufficient for congregation to pass a resolution about the Meadow no matter how big the majority is, and then just rely on putting in the voting figures at the inquiry as evidence of the weight of opinion against the Meadow Road. I think that it has got to be demonstrated at the inquiry beyond a shadow of a doubt that a great many people and institutions do care very dearly about the Meadow.'[130] This is precisely what happened at the inquiry of 1965. Buchanan led the way with his evidence that the Meadow brought a 'sense of pastoral remoteness and simplicity, isolated from motor traffic', and that walking there was to 'experience rus in urbe at its very best'. He was followed by a string of University people—Bullock, Franks, Oakeshott, Lucy Sutherland, Wheare—all pleading the rural calm of the Meadow.'[131] As a result of the inquiry, the scheme for a Meadow road was shelved.

The University had never been keen on town planning either as something which affected Oxford or as an academic subject. After 1945 the government felt acutely the need of able town planners, but Oxford did not respond to

---

[128] Harvard University, Frankfurter MSS, Maurice Bowra to Felix Frankfurter, 23 Oct. [?1955], photocopy. I am grateful to Dr Brian Harrison for this reference.
[129] C. Buchanan, public inquiry 1964, 3rd day, 30. A. L. C. Bullock during debate in Congregation, Gazette 11 Feb. 1969. It should be noted that the University always had worries about whether Sharp's road would simply attract more traffic and so fail in its purpose: HCP 222 (1955), 98, report of committee on town planning.
[130] HCP 249 (1964), 62, revision of the town map.
[131] Public inquiry 1965, 2nd and 6th days.

initiatives from government or to an offer from Montague Burton to endow a chair for seven years.[132] The absence of any confident view about town planning—apart from the forthright views of R. M. Hare, the Balliol philosopher, in his book *Traffic: A Practical Remedy* (1948)—appears to have left the University heavily dependent on outside opinion and hesitant on tactics.

These same characteristics were evident in the aftermath of the Buchanan intervention. The University felt that relations with the city had deteriorated over the roads issue and tended to tread carefully. Bullock noted that 'there was intense suspicion of the University and its supposed influence in high places'.[133] Now that the tortuous question of the roads appeared to have been shelved, the University wished to 'avoid being drawn into the detailed problems of town planning'.[134] Such a simple solution was not possible because Buchanan's proposals required control over traffic movements and parking, and these impinged upon University interests as much as had the roads debate. When the University eventually got round to investigating its own use of the motor car, it turned out that even academics living close to the University area used cars quite heavily.[135] In earlier debates the question of traffic had been seen as an opportunity for excluding the Cowley population from the university town. Now the University had to restrict its own traffic in order to protect the environment.

It was Denys Munby's contribution to force this upon the University at a time when it wished to be circumspect and uninvolved with the city or planning questions. At the inquiry of 1965 Munby was 'very sorry that the University have not taken steps to study what might be done to reduce parking and traffic in the city centre in any detail'.[136] Munby thought it particularly scandalous that parking was allowed in Radcliffe Square. But Bullock was anxious not to press the University's views too hard upon the city. Moreover college interests were raising their heads once more. Just as Christ Church had dug in its heels over the Meadow, so Nuffield College's scope for expansion and the position of Worcester College were adversely affected by the plans for parking facilities in the centre of Oxford which emerged in the post-Buchanan period.

The University was anxious not to allow objections from individual colleges to frustrate its warm acceptance of the new proposals, which were intended to soothe the grievances which the city held from the past. It was

[132] PRO, HLG 71/1388, chairs in town planning.
[133] OUA UC/FF/638/2, city questions file, notes of meeting between Bullock and Munby, 29 Feb. 1969.
[134] HCP 248 (1964), 220, committee on relief roads.
[135] *University Travel and Parking Survey* (University of Oxford 1972), 24; this study was carried out by Munby.
[136] Public inquiry 1965, 12th day, 28.

agreed at a meeting with Buchanan 'that the University would probably not wish to support Nuffield or Worcester Colleges if they lodged formal objections to those parts of the scheme'—that is, those involving car parking in Gloucester Green—and that it would take the line with the city that 'it would welcome the report and regard objections raised by colleges as relatively minor points'.[137] Nuffield College was in the end proved right, and a grandiose car park was avoided, just as the audacious urban motorway had remained unbuilt. But for a time it looked as though conflicts about inner-city parking had merely displaced arguments about relief roads; the political problems over town planning both between University and city and within the University had not gone away.

How can the relationship between the University and the city be summarized? Any hope of the University dominating the town vanished with the advent of the motor industry. It is, of course, possible to exaggerate Cowley's disruption of Oxford life. The car factories were set many miles from the city centre, and few students need ever have seen them. 'We can persuade ourselves that it has not changed at all' was one assessment of Oxford in the 1960s.[138] But still, Cowley did administer a shock, and bred fears that Oxford's identity might be swamped by factories. The slogan 'Oxford—the home of Pressed Steel' has been repeated with unease as well as amusement. This feeling chimed in with national concerns after 1945 to contain urban growth and so fostered the protection of open spaces and the development of a 'green belt' policy. It even nourished in some the vision of the University remaining at the centre of an unchanging townscape, as a countervailing influence to the dynamism represented by industry and commerce.

Yet the University itself became a force for change, taking increased numbers of students and placing more emphasis upon the sciences. Both put pressure upon the limited space available for expansion and so altered the character of the town. Colleges too wished to exploit their assets more vigorously than protective restrictions on land use permitted. These conditions required sensitive participation by the University in local town-planning matters, which was not always forthcoming.

A more positive contribution to the development of the town, by harmonizing or reconciling collegiate ambitions with local needs, is also hard to detect. St Ebbe's languished for too long before redevelopment because of the uncertainty about the Meadow road, and collegiate building in St Clement's never met the city's ambitions for transforming that unprepossessing entrance to Oxford. Town resentments over planning matters were shared by left and right and were not easily defused either

[137] OUA UC/FF/638/2, meeting of 29 Feb. 1969.
[138] A. I. Marsh, 'Industrial Oxford', *OM* 1 Dec. 1960, 129.

through the town main political parties or through the special avenue of university representation on the city council.

Local interests were bound to feel overwhelmed by an important university operating in a small urban area. One response to the problem of harmonizing the University with the town was to argue that the University should do more to serve local interests, by taking more local students, conducting more studies on local problems, and providing more facilities for teaching and research to local institutions.[139] Such a drastic re-orientation, itself unlikely, would probably have had little effect. Students have rarely been found to be conventional, integrated members of local societies, either because college life insulates them or because they arouse resentment by monopolizing some local services and activities. All universities by their very nature have some degree of independence from their immediate environment. 'Culture' could not really provide the answer either. The fine arts were hardly more popular in the town than in the colleges. Amateur music was probably the most effective bridge, but hardly distinctive to Oxford. So the University's role, initially seen as the polar opposite to the developing motor industry on the periphery, became more complex as it responded to pressures for growth and expansion, and this was not a role which was easily fulfilled.

[139] *Oxford: A Future for Our University* (Communist Party, Oxford University branch, 1951).

22

Oxford and the British universities

A. H. HALSEY

'If a young man, talking to an educated stranger, refers to his university studies, he is asked "Oxford or Cambridge?". And if he says Aberystwyth or Nottingham, there is disappointment on the one side and embarrassment on the other. It has always been that way.'[1] Whether in the pages of eternity twentieth-century Oxford was a 'good thing' is an open question; the cultural fact of its superior image is a closed one. Not only was it a famous university but frequently the symbol of all universities. And it was more than a university. It was an integral part of an ancient establishment along with the crown and the aristocracy. So members of Council would refer to each other as the Warden (of All Souls) or the Dean (of Christ Church) with the same ceremonious attribution of dignified office as was used in the House of Lords. University College, London was seen as 'provincial' while University College, Oxford was metropolitan. Of course 'wherever two or three are gathered together' there also shall be a sociological commonplace: invidious comparisons will emerge.

The task in this chapter is to discover Oxford's position, not so much in a widening circle of British universities as in an emergent hierarchy of higher educational institutions. Its high place is beyond dispute; the changing basis of its eminence is a more intriguing story. Oxford, with Cambridge, dominated an expanding system from a numerically declining share of teachers and students throughout the period from 1914 to 1970 [figures 22.1–3]. How and why is our question. The answer will involve a narrative of Oxford's reluctant incorporation into a developing national system as the older sister of Oxbridge. Oxford remained the source of magic and moonshine that illuminated a distinctive ideal of university life. It held sway over the minds of those who selected students and appointed staff. It maintained a persistent power to place people in positions of high political and administrative office. Finally, in selecting students for academic promise and by encouraging productivity in its scientists and other scholars, it reinforced its ancient claims to status by adding merit to social connection.

[1] E. Shils, 'The intellectuals: Great Britain', *Encounter* iv (Apr. 1955), 11–12.

But first, two key words must be clarified: 'Oxbridge' and the 'system'. Insiders know that there are many Oxfords. Outsiders believe that, culturally if not geographically, Oxford and Cambridge are the same place. Surveys of opinion and official statistics commonly use the term Oxbridge—a convenient if inelegant label originating in Thackeray's *Pendennis* (1850) which came belatedly into general usage after the Second World War, when 'the system' impelled the two ancient universities to present a combined interest. The alternative construction 'Camford' has never become popular.[2] Precedence goes to longevity in the British notion of seniority. Either term in any case may serve to diminish the real differences between Oxford and Cambridge, which are so beloved of migrant dons and were elaborated for the earlier decades of the century by Ernest Barker, who studied and served in both places.[3] Oxford was more convivial, more collegiate, more oriented to classics, church and politics. Cambridge dons were more specialized, scientific and puritanical. Consultation and interchange between the Cam and the Isis grew during the period.

The word 'system', also presents difficulties. The Robbins Committee noted in 1963 that no system of higher education existed in Britain before the Committee itself was formed.[4] But this is an administrative rather than a sociological truth. From the Middle Ages there was a system in England constituted by Oxford and Cambridge, with the close connection of certain of their colleges to particular schools. The residues of that system survived into the 1970s, and Oxford and Cambridge maintained frequent, sometimes nervous consultation with each other in their responses to external pressure. But industrialization inexorably enlarged the academic circle, uniting the kingdom, connecting science and scholarship to empire, to Europe, America and the world. A new British system of higher education thus gradually appeared. As the civic universities gained recognition, Oxford and Cambridge moved from monopoly to pre-eminence. 'The other place' remained the significant other, even though its definite article increasingly and embarrassingly misrepresented the reality of a national set of institutions.

The evolution of a national system was closely linked with the relation of higher education to the state, and even here the origins of support by the state reach back to royal patronage of Oxford and Cambridge in the Middle Ages. When England and Scotland united in 1707, the crown took over the Scottish government's financial grants to the Scottish universities, and parliament paid them after 1832. Later in the century parliamentary grants

---

[2] An example is J. Rose and J. Ziman, *Camford Observed* (London 1964).
[3] E. Barker, *Age and Youth* (Oxford 1953).
[4] *Higher Education: Report of the Committee Appointed by the Prime Minister under the Chairmanship of Lord Robbins 1961–63* [*Robbins Report*] (PP 1962–3 xi–xiv Cmnd 2154), para. 14.

began to flow to the Welsh university colleges and eventually to other institutions of higher education in Britain. The University Grants Committee (UGC) was formed in 1919 and at this point a set of definable relations arguably became an official system. For in that year three bodies came into being: the UGC as the channel of state finance, the Committee of Vice-Chancellors and Principals (CVCP) as the body representing the interests of the universities, and the Association of University Teachers (AUT) as the body representing the academic staff of those institutions. Moreover a fourth body, the National Union of Students (NUS), was formed soon after, in 1921–2. Against this background Oxford may be seen to have moved from separated grandeur to incorporated stardom. And in transition Oxford remained the traditional symbol of university life—loved and loathed, extolled and condemned, as it had been down the centuries.

In terms of custom and conception the system was continuous. From the period of Victorian reform the English idea of the university gave a common stamp to universities in this country despite differences of age, size and location.[5] There were norms in British universities which reflect a more or less unified conception of higher education: an idealized representation of Oxford. Was there any alternative to the Oxford English idea? In part perhaps yes: there was the civic pride and regional need of the industrial provinces; there was the imperial invitation to make London a central examining and research metropolis; there was a growing demand for high scientific manpower in an increasingly technological economy. But these alternatives were assimilated to Oxbridge dominance. There was also a fourth possibility. The Scottish model of democratic intellectualism had made its mark on the civic universities in the shape of professorial rule and departmental organization.[6] Yet it too was assimilated and those who have tried to describe it as crushed by English hegemony or internal colonialism in the United Kingdom have written 'stirring stuff' but 'pretty poor history'.[7]

In the nineteenth century, Oxbridge met the challenge of classical industrialism and of religious nonconformity partly by reforming and expanding its own statutes and curriculum, partly by drawing in the sons of successful businessmen and partly by the movement of Oxford and

[5] On the English idea of a university see A. H. Halsey and M. Trow, *The British Academics* (London 1971); for its influence on the English new universities see M. Cross and R. G. Jobling, 'The English new universities: a preliminary enquiry', *Universities Quarterly* xxiii (1968–9).

[6] G. Davie, *The Democratic Intellect in Scotland and her Universities in the Nineteenth Century* (Edinburgh 1961, repr. Edinburgh 1982); see also his *The Crisis of the Democratic Intellect: The Problem of Generalization and Specialization in Twentieth Century Scotland* (Edinburgh 1986). For a persuasive analysis see A. McPherson, 'Selections and survivals: a sociology of the ancient Scottish universities' in R. K. Brown (ed.), *Knowledge, Education and Cultural Change* (London 1973).

[7] P. Slee, review of Davie, *Democratic Intellect* and *Crisis of the Democratic Intellect* in *Higher Education Quarterly* xli (1987), 194.

Cambridge dons to teach in the newly created universities.[8] As a result two traditions emerged. Oxford and Cambridge were national and residential federations of colleges connected with the national élites of politics, administration, business and the liberal professions. They offered a general education designed to mould character and prepare their undergraduates for a gentlemanly style of life. All the rest were provincial and, including London, aimed to meet the needs of the professional and industrial middle classes; furthermore they took most of their students from their own region. The percentage of students drawn from within thirty miles in 1908–9 was at Bristol 87 per cent, Leeds 78 per cent, Liverpool 75 per cent, Manchester 73 per cent, University College, London 66 per cent.[9] The students at civic universities were offered a utilitarian training for middle-class careers in courses typically concentrated on a single subject and directed especially towards the newer technological and professional occupations such as chemistry, electrical engineering, teaching in state grammar schools and the scientific civil service.

In the nineteenth century these two traditions existed side by side with little contact. But in the twentieth century a pyramidal structure evolved with Oxford and Cambridge at the apex and a widening array of civic and new universities and polytechnics at the base. Oxford thus occupied a commanding but numerically declining place among British universities in a period of unprecedented development of higher education. In 1900 the population numbered thirty-nine million, with 20,000 university students taught by 2,000 university teachers of whom a third were at Oxbridge. By 1964 the British academic staff was equal in number to the students at the beginning of the century. In the subsequent 'Robbins' decade further expansion raised the total of university students to over a quarter of a million and the teachers and researchers to 40,000. Of these, less than 3,000 (7.5 per cent) were resident in Oxford or Cambridge, teaching a much reduced proportion of the country's undergraduates—down from a third at the beginning of the century to less than 8 per cent by 1980. The chances of reaching a university for the members of the relevant age-group grew from 1 in 60 between the wars to 1 in 31 in the middle of the century to 1 in 5 by 1980.[10]

The two world wars stimulated growth for two reasons: they encouraged opinion favourable to reform, and to educational reform in particular, and thus increased the effective demand for university places; and they

    [8] On internal change and on recruitment see S. Rothblatt, *The Revolution of the Dons: Cambridge and Society in Victorian England* (London 1963), 86–7.
    [9] L. D. Whiteley, *The Poor Student and the University* (London 1933), 14.
    [10] For a detailed analysis by social class of chances of entry to university over the period from before the First World War to the 1960s see A. H. Halsey, A. F. Heath and J. Ridge, *Origins and Destinations* (Oxford 1980), ch. 10.

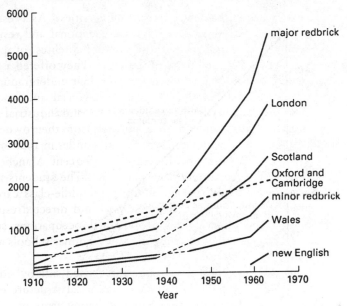

FIGURE 22.1 NUMBER OF UNIVERSITY TEACHERS IN GREAT BRITAIN BY UNIVERSITY
GROUP, 1910–1964

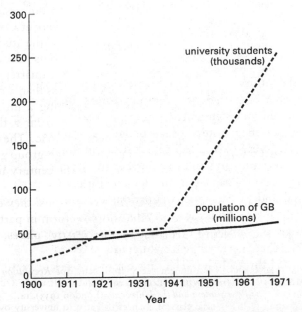

FIGURE 22.2 POPULATION OF GREAT BRITAIN AND NUMBER OF UNIVERSITY STUDENTS,
1900–1971

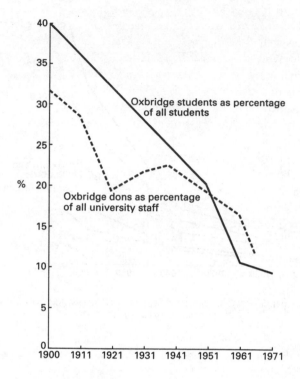

FIGURE 22.3   OXFORD AND CAMBRIDGE AS A PROPORTION OF ALL STUDENTS AND STAFF
IN UNIVERSITIES IN GREAT BRITAIN, 1900–1971

dramatized the utility of university research for military and industrial efficiency. Underlying these accelerating forces of war there was also pressure from beneath, stemming from the increasing number of grammar schools in a national system of secondary schooling after 1902. The proportion of 17-year-olds in full-time education doubled from 2 to 4 per cent between 1902 and 1938 and rose further to 15 per cent by 1962 and 20 per cent by 1970. At the same time the demand for graduates strengthened as the managerial and professional occupations expanded in government, in industry, and in the educational system itself. Managers and higher professionals grew from 4.4 to 13.6 per cent of all occupations between 1911 and 1971;[11] and they increasingly sought graduate recruits.

Expansion had three phases. The first began in the late Victorian period with the foundation of the civic universities and continued after the First

---

[11] R. Price and G. S. Bain, 'The labour force' in A. H. Halsey (ed.), *British Social Trends Since 1900* (Basingstoke and London 1988), table 4.1b.

World War until it faded during the depression years of the 1930s. At the beginning, Oxford and Cambridge were conspicuously preponderant numerically, as well as academically and socially. By the end, just before the Second World War, they had been surpassed in numbers of students and staff by the major redbrick universities and overtaken by London. Within the first decade of the century Birmingham, Bristol, Leeds, Manchester and Sheffield all gained charters as independent universities and, together with Durham and its Newcastle constituent, they began to lead the expansion of the British university system.

The second phase of growth began after 1945 and included the granting of independent charters to the former London-dominated provincial university colleges at Nottingham, Southampton, Hull, Exeter and Leicester. The last-named became independent in 1957, bringing the total number of British universities to twenty-one. In 1949 the establishment of the University College of North Staffordshire at Keele, largely under Oxford influence and without tutelage from London, anticipated the much publicized movement to found new universities with independence from the outset. The earliest of these, Sussex, admitted its first students in 1961. Subsequently East Anglia, York, Essex, Kent, Warwick and Lancaster received charters and four new Scottish universities were formed—Strathclyde (out of the Royal College of Science) in Glasgow, at Stirling, Heriot-Watt in Edinburgh and the fourth at Dundee. These new foundations contributed little to the second phase of expansion between 1947 and 1964. This mostly took place in the established universities in the industrial provincial cities, in London, in Wales and in the ancient Scottish universities as well as in Oxford and Cambridge, whose numbers gently drifted upwards.

Then came a third phase. Social and economic developments after the Second World War surpassed all previous pressures towards growth. The change in opinion about the desirable provision of university and other forms of higher education after the mid-1950s was quite unprecedented.[12] At that time only a very small minority of radical expansionists was ready to contemplate 10 per cent of the age-group being in universities. By the time the Robbins Committee reported in 1963 middle-class opinion, including academic opinion at Oxford and nationally, accepted that some 20 per cent of the age-group should be educated to this level by 1980. Behind this shift lay fundamental changes of political and social outlook: aspirations to higher education came to be taken for granted in the middle classes and began to penetrate into working-class families, especially those in which the parents

---

[12] For a graphic description of the changing climate of opinion see N. Annan, 'Higher education' in B. Crick (ed.), *Essays on Reform 1967: A Centenary Tribute* (Oxford 1967).

themselves had some experience of education beyond the minimum school-leaving age. And the old fear of industrial decline, with its invidious international comparisons and its acceptance of the theory that skill and training make the largest marginal contributions to the productivity of the economy, brought political support for the ever-growing budget of higher education.

Moreover the older class-based conceptions of education, so strongly associated with Oxbridge, were challenged after 1945. Inequality of access to the universities became an almost commonplace illustration of distributive injustice. Economic growth required the cultivation of all potential talent. The assumption that there existed a restricted 'pool of ability' came to be seen as a rationalization for preserving class privilege. The traditional ideological defence of an Oxbridge system of universities for the élite was no longer tenable and the development of higher education came to be seen more in terms of economic feasibility and a balanced regional distribution.

In the newness of their early urban beginnings the civic universities were not particularly preoccupied with matching the prestige of Oxford. There were formidable barriers to attaining the Oxford ideal. One indispensable requisite was that a university should be national rather than local. The nineteenth-century foundations in the industrial cities were creatures of a nonconformist and non-metropolitan culture, selecting their students, in the main, from the middle and lower middle classes of their own suburbs and region, while Oxford and Cambridge drew from the sons of those families who were able to use the national public schools.

Redbrick sought a different clientele. In the 1920s women took 30 per cent of the places, though their proportionate gains were halted in the slump years. In Oxford men outnumbered women by 5 to 1 and in Cambridge by 10 to 1, ratios which were to persist into the 1960s.[13] Early in that decade G. E. M. de Ste Croix led the move by New College to transform an ancient male preserve into a mixed college, but the ratio of 5 to 1 was maintained at Oxford until 1974.[14] Oxbridge influence partly explains why the position of women was less favourable in England than in Scotland and Wales, where opportunities for scholarships were more evenly divided between the sexes. Oxford and Cambridge awards were biased towards men, whereas in the nationally maintained scholarships—state scholarships and royal science scholarships—and in most local awards no such distinction was made between candidates of equal merit.

Another inter-war feature was the increased flow of students into the arts faculties. In 1930/1, while Oxford had 80 per cent, only 52 per cent of all

[13] Whiteley, *Poor Student*, 25.
[14] G. E. M. de Ste Croix, 'The admission of women to New College', *OM* 15 Oct. 1964, 4–6.

British university students were reading arts—and of these a third were prospective teachers subsidized by the Board of Education. This government subsidy was especially important for women, nearly three-quarters of whom were in the arts faculties in 1930/1 compared with 44 per cent of the men. Intending teachers also swelled the numbers registered for honours rather than ordinary or pass degrees. Scotland maintained the predominance of ordinary degrees, for in 1930/1 only 24 per cent of graduates in Scotland took honours, while 66 per cent did so in England; the percentage in Wales was 55.[15]

Postgraduate studies also made relative gains from small beginnings after the First World War. In 1919 the percentage of students engaged in research was 2. By 1930 it was 5. Of the 1,941 postgraduate students 173 were at Oxford, 237 at Cambridge, 237 in Scotland, 116 in Wales, 430 at the English provincial universities and 748 were in London. At the time it was thought that London's place 'at the heart of national and international activities' and the location of the provincial universities 'in close proximity to industrial enterprise' offered both support and incentive to research.[16]

When the UGC assessed financial assistance to university students in 1928/9 it found that 50 per cent received some form of help. Oxford's place was privileged. Between them Oxford and Cambridge had £250,000 a year to award in scholarships, which was rather more than the total cost of scholarships maintained by the nation as a whole.[17] State scholarships were keenly sought. Between 1919 and 1929 the number of applicants for the 200 available awards quadrupled. In 1931 there were 300 scholarships and 4,333 applicants, a ratio of 1 to 14. The state scholars had a decided preference for Oxford and Cambridge. In 1929/30 232 were holding their awards at Oxford and 177 at Cambridge while 115 were at London, 94 at provincial universities and 24 at the Welsh colleges.[18]

But Oxford remained difficult of access to 'the poor student'. Though nearly two-thirds of the 642 state scholars in 1929/30 were at Oxford or Cambridge, only 11 per cent had been pupils in elementary schools compared with 15.6 per cent in London, 36.1 per cent in the provincial universities and 54.7 per cent in Wales. A report presented to Nuffield College showed that 18 leading schools (9 boarding and 9 day) provided 40 per cent of the scholars and exhibitioners in the Oxford colleges between the wars. Winchester was the clear leader and also headed in the degree performance of its scholars. Only 5 of the 18 were grammar schools not in membership of the Headmasters' Conference.[19]

---

[15] Whiteley, 27.   [16] Ibid. 29.   [17] Ibid. 32–3.   [18] Ibid. 33.
[19] B. N. Clapham and E. Brunner, 'A study of Oxford undergraduates: their school and university records' (unpublished paper 1944, in Nuffield College Library).

Oxford could in principle have expanded to accommodate early twentieth-century demand for university education. Lord Curzon had included a chapter on 'The admission of poor men' in his report of 1909, noting that the question had been raised only to be dismissed by the commissioners of 1850.[20] He himself distinguished between expansion of admission to Oxford and the expansion of Oxford's extramural activities in the industrial cities. Between Pattison in the 1850s and Jowett in the 1870s the extramural had largely displaced the intramural solution. And this evasion lay behind the twentieth-century distinction between 'undergraduates' tutored by 'dons' at Oxford and 'students' taught by 'university teachers' elsewhere. The extension movement, so brilliantly led in Rochdale by R. H. Tawney, was largely displaced by the provincial university colleges after 1918, by the Open University in the 1960s, and by the polytechnics in the 1970s.

Largely displaced but not wholly, for Oxford continued to boast the largest extramural staff. The extension impulse took a new turn in the 1920s under A. D. Lindsay's enthusiasm, which led eventually to the foundation of Keele University in the Potteries. Lindsay and his friends, including Kenneth Leys, Walter Moberly, David Ross and J. L. Stocks, formed an Oxford reform committee which drew up a memorandum for the Asquith Commission. Their aim was to make Oxford more accessible by reducing the bias towards boys from the public schools, by reducing the costs of being a student at Oxford and by forging stronger and wider links with the educational system of the country as a whole. They wanted extramural work to be recognized as an essential part of the work of the University, with claims on its endowments, with extramural tutors being fellows of colleges and extramural students holding scholarships. They also sought University support for the summer schools pioneered at Balliol.[21]

Balliol did in fact change its pattern of admission in Lindsay's time. In 1906 two-thirds of the 53 entrants were from public schools, including 19 from Eton. In 1939 half of the 104 entrants were from public schools, 14 being Etonians. In 1949, when Lindsay left, the public schools contributed 28 per cent of the 109 entrants, with only one Etonian. And a further indication of Balliol's influence in the academic world beyond Oxford is that while Lindsay was Master his College provided 250 professors to universities throughout the world.[22]

The relation of Oxford to the provincial universities between the wars is epitomized in the academic biography of the Chancellor of Oxford elected to succeed Harold Macmillan in 1987, Lord Jenkins. Roy Jenkins attended

[20] G. N. Curzon, Lord Curzon of Kedleston, *Principles and Methods of University Reform* (Oxford 1909), 43.

[21] See D. Scott, *A. D. Lindsay: A Biography* (Oxford 1971), 89.

[22] Ibid. 110, 118.

the University College of Cardiff from October 1937 to May 1938, being not quite 17 years old when he started. He came with 'an indifferent Higher Certificate' from Abersychan County Grammar School, it being thought that 'if I was ever to get into Oxford I needed to be shaken out of this early staleness by some broader horizons'. His father had been at Ruskin College before the First World War and 'had conceived an almost romantic attachment for that shore'. His own 'object at Cardiff was therefore to learn some history and some French . . . to start some elementary economics and to try to prepare myself for Oxford scholarship and entrance examinations'.[23]

All this heavily underlines Oxford's tentative response to the rise of the modern universities after the First World War. Keele was exceptional in its direct institutional connection between Oxford and a new university. Oxford's initial reaction to the expansion of the university system was isolationist. Oxford neither colonized nor incorporated the civic innovations. Before 1930, though paying its subscription, Oxford had held aloof from the Universities' Bureau of the British Empire and the Committee of Vice-Chancellors and Principals. The Vice-Chancellor rarely attended in person, nor did he send a deputy when absent.[24] Instead Oxford clung more closely to Cambridge between the wars. For example Oxford agreed privately and politely with 'the other place' not to disagree publicly over the Bureau's articles of association. Both wanted to safeguard their common interest against any possible future domination of the Bureau by the University of London.[25] From 1931 Council regularly received reports of decisions of interest to Oxford taken by the CVCP, though the Vice-Chancellor still did not go to its meetings. An Oxford and Cambridge standing joint committee was formed in 1935 and met regularly twice a year to discuss such matters as saving money by avoiding unnecessary duplication of academic courses and research, the age of call-up for war service and the power of the two universities to alter the conditions on which trusts had been settled.

During the 1930s, however, it became clear that Oxford and Cambridge had to involve themselves with the CVCP, which was becoming a main channel of communication between the government and the universities. It was consequently agreed that the Registrar should attend meetings of the CVCP and in fact both the Vice-Chancellor and the Registrar normally did so. Suspicion of Oxford and Cambridge among the civic vice-chancellors declined, the Oxford and Cambridge standing joint committee became an

[23] R. Jenkins, 'Pisgah sighting' in G. Jones and M. Quinn (eds), *Fountains of Praise: University College, Cardiff, 1883–1983* (Cardiff 1983), 97–8.
[24] OUA untitled memorandum (1969) by D. Veale on the University's relations with outside bodies, fo 12.
[25] HCP 150 (1931), 5 (8 Oct.).

effective apparatus for presenting an Oxbridge common front, the other universities recognized the special position of their seniors, and the Oxbridge point of view could be transmitted to government through the CVCP without animosity. In the same period a network of alliances between Oxford and Cambridge colleges was established: the two colleges of Corpus Christi allied in 1926, Merton and Peterhouse in 1930, New College and King's in 1931, and others followed suit, in each case granting common-room rights to the fellows of the sister college.[26]

Still more important, individuals consolidated a powerful nexus. Graduates of the 1920s and 1930s moved between the two places. John Hicks in economics, Asa Briggs and John Habakkuk in history, and Frederick Dainton in chemistry are famous examples, each exemplifying interchange in research, each also playing an important part in the interactive development of the wider university system. Hicks held a chair at Manchester from 1938 to 1946, Dainton and Briggs held chairs at Leeds. Habakkuk was chairman of the CVCP, Dainton became chairman of the UGC. Habakkuk was Vice-Chancellor of Oxford, Dainton of Nottingham and Briggs of Sussex; and all collected national honours in the course of their career spirals.

All in all, Oxbridge gradually became a real entity within the British university system after 1914. This involved much more than the ritual of competitive solidarity in the annual boat-race. It was an intricate network of institutional and individual exchange, born of common interest in perpetuating the Oxbridge ideal within a growing system that might otherwise have engulfed the ancient universities.

Yet the Oxbridge ideal had to yield to modern reform of the curriculum. For example there was a national movement which aimed to bring higher technological education into the service of industry. It was inspired by fear of industrial competition from the continent, by appreciation of the industrial benefits gained by Germany, France and Switzerland from their polytechnics, and by admiration of the American land-grant colleges. This movement was naturally concentrated in the civic universities and in applied scientific courses. Oxbridge opinion was suspicious. Oxford's dons feared that technological education would lessen the spell of Newman's lectures, Pattison's essays and Jowett's teaching. 'It is not surprising, therefore, that they opposed the segregation of technological education into separate institutions. The manager-technologist must receive not only a vocational training: he must enjoy also the benefits of a liberal education; or at least he must rub shoulders with students who are studying the humanities.' On the other hand there was also opposition in the same circles to the idea that the lower middle classes needed the cultural benefits of higher education and so,

[26] S. C. Roberts, 'College alliances', *Oxford* summer 1935, 41–5.

contrarily, 'the most powerful argument for the new university colleges was one based on their utilitarian value'.[27] The utilitarian argument was less persuasive in Wales: 'in Aberystwyth and Bangor it was the idea of a university as a place for liberal education which aroused public support'.[28]

Thus technology first established itself in the civic colleges in Scotland and in London, spreading later to Oxford and Cambridge to become an integral part of the university curriculum. At the same time, however, technological and applied studies never gained the prestige accorded to them in either the separate technological institutions of Germany or France, or such American institutions as the Massachusetts Institute of Technology (MIT) or the California Institute of Technology (Cal Tech). Once established, the provincial universities tended everywhere to shift the scope and balance of their studies towards the norms of Oxford and Cambridge. But they lacked the wealth, the libraries and laboratories, the independence of cultural tradition, the social status and the political connections to offer a serious challenge to the entrenched position of the ancient foundations.[29]

Moreover Oxford was always able to raid the departments of the other universities to modernize its own research and teaching. It has been described above how Oxford science was built up after 1918, importing professors and directors of research from elsewhere.[30] For example, organic chemistry was heavily dependent on Manchester, which as a 'first-class waiting room' yielded up both Perkin and Robinson. Oxford's external relations were, to repeat, interactive. Some developments, for example in philosophy with Austin and Ayer or in chemical kinetics with Hinshelwood or in zoology with Goodrich, were indigenous. In other areas Oxford postgraduates went elsewhere to learn—at Imperial College or Leipzig or MIT. In yet other cases the Jewish exodus from the Third Reich was exploited, for example by Lindemann at Breslau or, after a long delay, with the translation of Rudolph Peierls via Birmingham to the Wykeham chair of physics in 1963.

Oxbridge also initially held aloof from the nationally organized representation of university teachers and researchers, taking no part in the foundation of the AUT in 1919 and not forming a local association until 1939. Even then, and subsequently, the proportion enrolled as members of the AUT remained relatively small. In part this was because collegiate life

[27] E. Ashby, 'On universities and the scientific revolution' in A. H. Halsey, J. Floud and C. A. Anderson (eds), *Education, Economy, and Society* (New York 1961), 473.

[28] Ibid. n. 13, citing B. E. Evans, *The University of Wales: A Historical Sketch* (Cardiff 1953).

[29] Their private endowments were modest, and by the end of the First World War were negligible by comparison with governmental grants. The income from endowments in 1919/20 was: Birmingham £7,500, Bristol £8,000, Leeds £7,100, Manchester £30,500. UGC *Returns from Universities and University Colleges in Receipt of Treasury Grant 1919/1920* (PP 1921 xxvi Cmd 1263). On libraries see Halsey and Trow, *British Academics*, 92, table 4.20.

[30] See above, 158–61, 163.

was based on the democracy of fellowship, while the modern universities were departmental monoliths ruled by professors in their senates and by laymen in their councils. A co-operative of producers has no place for a union. The staff of civic universities, because of their contrasted organization, could appropriately see vice-chancellors and senates as employers. The dons of Oxford, however, were a self-governing corporation. In the 1920s the AUT represented above all the teaching staff of the civic universities.

Oxford's influence on the AUT was nonetheless deep. As its official historian puts it, 'A.U.T. policy on university government was closer to the collegiate ideal of a community of scholars than to the civic tradition of a professorial-dominated hierarchy'.[31] A local association in Oxford had been mooted as early as 1921, and when it was formed finally in 1939 it had as its President the Warden of All Souls, Dr W. G. S. Adams, and as Vice-President Professor E. R. Dodds, a long-standing member of the AUT's executive. Perkin describes the relation aptly in reference to 1947/8: 'Oxford had only 103 and Cambridge only 18 members out of staff numbering over 800 and over 700 respectively. Their few members were very keen, and some of them, such as Professor E. R. Dodds of Oxford and Dr V. E. Cosslett of Cambridge, both sometime Presidents of the A.U.T., played a very active role in the national Association. Nevertheless, the old tension between the Oxbridge tradition of a community . . . and the professional academics elsewhere with their natural penchant for professional organization, still polarized university teachers into Oxbridge sheep and redbrick goats. One of the jibes of the former against the latter was that the A.U.T. was really a trade union, and from time to time some members of the Association who were not automatically horrified by the notion have toyed with the idea of registering, or procuring a certificate, as a trade union in order to bring the universities and through them the UGC and the Treasury to arbitration in salary matters.'[32]

Oxbridge influence was again vividly illustrated in 1961 when the submission of the AUT to the Robbins Committee argued that Oxford and Cambridge were already too big, attracted too large a share of the best arts students, and should not be allowed to expand further or to develop into universities of postgraduate students. But at the council of the AUT in December 1961 the paragraphs critical of Oxford and Cambridge were withdrawn and replaced by a statement urging the need to examine the relation between the ancient and the modern universities.[33] So despite the decline in the proportion of university teachers who were Oxbridge graduates and the increased proportion of scientists and technologists who

---

[31] H. Perkin, *Key Profession: The History of the Association of University Teachers* (London 1969), 64.
[32] Ibid. 143.   [33] Ibid. 218.

had been recruited from elsewhere, the ancient influence remained crucial in a vital expression of AUT policy.

As with the organized academic profession so also with the state. Nothing better explains the peculiar character of the UGC than the Oxbridge network of prestigious influence. The UGC's own account of its early days after 1919 refers to the concept of a 'buffer' which was advantageous to both sides. 'It relieved the government of assuming direct responsibility for the universities, and it safeguarded the universities from political interference. More positively, it was an earnest of the government's willingness to provide money for the universities "without strings", and it enabled the universities to enjoy public funds without the fear that the gift might turn out to be a Greek one.'[34] And the key to the working of the principle? 'From 1919 until 1963 the University Grants Committee was the direct concern of the Treasury. Its staff consisted of Treasury civil servants. It was always clear, and totally accepted, that once they "came to the University Grants Committee" these Civil Servants were the servants of the Committee and not of the Treasury. But they knew the Treasury, its habits, its ways of thinking; and they knew personally the individual Treasury officials with whom they were dealing on the Committee's behalf . . . The Treasury was deeply committed to the "buffer" principle, and guarded most jealously the Committee's independent status. A succession of highly paid Treasury officials, among whom the most determined was Sir Edward (now Lord) Bridges, defended with all their acumen and experience the autonomy of the universities, and of the Committee, against every attack from whatever quarter.'[35]

So, within the framework of a recently completed parliamentary democracy, Oxbridge retained its effective control of élitist institutions by like-minded members of the élite. It survived fifty years of Conservative and Labour governments because, as the Committee put it, 'it has been rooted and grounded in one indispensable element, reciprocal confidence between the bodies concerned'.[36] The tribute is more specifically to the extraordinary stability of the British system of recruitment from Oxford and Cambridge to positions of political and bureaucratic power. It is obvious that Oxford was a gateway to power. Most of those who passed through it imbibed and disseminated a set of ideas and assumptions reflecting the norms of the Oxford establishment. Of course others have been heretical; and those who have not been Oxford people may also have been either conformists or deviants. There is no mechanical processing of opinion by institutional experience. Nonetheless the Oxford impact on educational thought and policy was highly significant if only because of the concentration of Oxford

---

[34] UGC *University Development 1962–1967* (PP 1968–9 xlvii Cmnd 3820), para. 554.
[35] Ibid. paras 576–7.   [36] Ibid. para. 555.

men and women in the relevant public offices. Of the 31 political heads of the Ministry of Education between 1914 and 1978, 17 were Oxford graduates, from H. A. L. Fisher (1916) to Shirley Williams (1976); 5 were from Cambridge, 3 from other universities and 6 were not graduates at all.[37] The first chairman of the UGC, Sir William McCormick, was a Scottish graduate, but the first full-time chairman, Sir Walter Moberly, was an Oxford man. So also was Keith Murray, who became chairman in 1953 and for the next ten years presided over a crucially important period in its history.[38]

While notables in the world of academic administration and leadership frequently had their origin or early career in Oxford, migratory career-patterns suggest that Oxford assumptions were also carried to other parts of the academic system. Thus Henry Hadow left Oxford in 1909 to become the Principal of Armstrong College, Newcastle and later (1919) the Vice-Chancellor of Sheffield University. J. L. Stocks vacated his fellowship at St John's in 1924 to take the chair of philosophy at Manchester and, in 1936, the vice-chancellorship at Liverpool. The Morris brothers became vice-chancellors—Charles at Leeds, Philip at Bristol. Sir Charles Grant Robertson went from All Souls in 1920 to be Principal and later Vice-Chancellor at Birmingham. Sir Walter Moberly began as a tutorial don and ended as an academic administrator, becoming the Principal of University College, Exeter in 1924, Vice-Chancellor of Manchester in 1926 and chairman of the UGC in 1934. Ernest Barker left Oxford in 1920 to become Principal of King's College, London. William Beveridge, after Balliol and Toynbee Hall, eventually became the Director of the London School of Economics. John Fulton, another Balliol don, became Principal at Swansea in 1947 and the founding Vice-Chancellor of Sussex in 1959. A network of famous men linked Oxford to the other British universities throughout the period.

More widely, there was a secure and comprehensive connection of Oxford and Cambridge with the world of 'top' people. In 1960 115,000 graduates of these two universities (one-fifth of the total) contributed half the entry to *Who's Who*, three-quarters of graduate MPs and nearly all of those who entered the administrative class of the civil service and foreign service by method II, which includes a series of personal interviews.[39] And even where initial entry to professions, business and high scientific posts was open to all graduates, the freemasonry of school and college tended to publicize the abilities and accelerate the promotion of the public-school and Oxford or

[37] The title of the post was President of the Board of Education 1911–44, Minister of Education 1944–64, and Secretary of State for Education and Science from 1964.

[38] J. Carswell, *Government and the Universities in Britain* (Cambridge 1985), 14.

[39] Halsey and Trow, *British Academics*, 74. The total for *Who's Who* excludes bearers of inherited titles and professional soldiers and sailors.

Cambridge man. A recurrent resentment in the redbrick universities between the wars was that the civil service, the professions, and leading industrial enterprises systematically preferred graduates of Oxford and Cambridge to those of 'provincial' universities.

Moreover graduates of Oxford and Cambridge continued to dominate the Royal Society, the British Academy, the upper echelons of the civil service and the older professions, and the vice-chancellorships [tables 22.1–3]. They

TABLE 22.1

FELLOWS OF THE ROYAL SOCIETY, SPECIFYING THE UNIVERSITY GROUP WHERE LAST DEGREE QUALIFICATION WAS TAKEN, 1900–1971/81 (%)

	Oxford and Cambridge	London	others
1900	36	32	32
1920	37	33	30
1940	34	34	32
1960	39	26	35
1971-81	44	21	35

Sources: Halsey and Trow, *British Academics*, 217; and for 1971–81 H. Eisener, 'The Cambridge connection', *New Scientist* 14 Jan. 1982, 99–100.

TABLE 22.2

FELLOWS OF THE BRITISH ACADEMY, SPECIFYING THE UNIVERSITY GROUP WHERE LAST DEGREE QUALIFICATION WAS TAKEN, IN 1910, 1930 AND 1961/2 (%)

	Oxford and Cambridge	London	civic	Scotland	Wales
1910	74	8	6	12	0
1930	62	16	7	11	4
1961/2	63	24	3	7	2

Sources: Halsey and Trow, *British Academics*, 218.

TABLE 22.3

UNIVERSITY EDUCATION OF VICE-CHANCELLORS
AND PRINCIPALS IN 1935, 1967 AND 1981 (%)

	Oxford and Cambridge	London	civic	Scotland	Wales
1935	66	5	18	5	6
1967	59	nk	15	10	nk
1981	60	11	8	26	3

Sources: Halsey and Trow, *British Academics*, 163 (1935, 1967);
figures for 1981 kindly supplied by Professor W. Taylor,
Director of the London University Institute of Education.

also maintained their exchanges with the House of Commons, the House of
Lords, and the major political parties. The average size of the cabinet in the
twentieth century has been 19.5, of whom 13.5 have been graduates and no
less than 11.5 from Oxford and Cambridge. Over the same period a quarter
of all ministers (inside or outside the cabinet) came from Oxford, and nearly
a half from Oxford and Cambridge together.[40]

Student organization and sentiment mirrored that of the senior members.
As the colleges' senior common rooms had stood aside from the AUT, so
their junior common rooms were reluctant to join the NUS.[41] Provincial
students both gained and lost by national representation. There was a
stronger voice and more national publicity for student needs, but the older
universities tended to dominate NUS leadership, to patronize and mis-
represent the newer universities and to subordinate the interests of
provincial students to the political agenda of the Oxbridge junior common
rooms.[42] Even as late as the 1950s the separatist tendency of Oxford's
undergraduates was still to be found and Anthony Howard, as President of
the Oxford Union, failed to persuade his members to debate with their
redbrick counterparts.[43]

The development of governmental policy—reflected in the UGC, the
CVCP, the AUT and the NUS—promoted increasing standardization. One

[40] Calculated from D. Butler and A. Sloman, *British Political Facts 1900–1979* (London
1980), 90–128.
[41] See B. Simon, 'The student movement in England and Wales during the 1930s', *History of
Education* xvi (1987).
[42] E. Morse, 'The changing idea of a university: the universities of Bristol and Manchester,
1900–1940' (Univ. California, Berkeley, PhD thesis 1990), ch. 4.
[43] *Isis* 28 Apr. 1954, 12.

consequence was the nationalization of student entry with the formation of the Universities Central Council on Admissions (UCCA), another body which Oxford and Cambridge could bring themselves only half-heartedly to join in 1964 while preserving their separate admission procedures. Standardization through nationalization gave the system more substance and, in particular, created a national body of students. After the Anderson Committee reported in 1960, the redbrick universities were each free individually to attract students from the whole country and also from abroad. The trend was towards national and international status for every university, and so Oxbridge lost one of its major distinguishing features. State scholarships freed students from the need to earn, and encouraged them to live away from home by offering a larger grant if they did so. Moreover the new universities of the 1950s and 1960s were free to choose a model or image with a less regional colouring than was possible for their Victorian and Edwardian predecessors. The later foundations did not think of themselves as provincial, and the term itself was now less often heard in reference to any British university. All the forty-six institutions empowered to grant degrees in 1970 now had a cosmopolitan flavour.[44]

Nonetheless Oxford and Cambridge continued to choose their students from the upper strata of the hierarchy of class and status of English society. Only 13 per cent of Oxford undergraduates in the 1950s came from the families of manual workers, compared with a third at universities like Manchester, Leeds and Birmingham.[45] Oxford students had fathers who were predominantly well-to-do, southern, professional and managerial, Conservative and Church of England. Three-quarters of the entrants at that time came from public or direct-grant schools, whereas two-thirds of the redbrick entrants came from schools maintained by Local Education Authorities (LEAs).[46] Secondary schools supported the hierarchy, in that the self-respect of grammar schools was firmly tied to the annual scholarship stakes for places in Oxford and Cambridge. Moreover inquiring parents of sixth-formers soon discovered—if not from wireless and, later, television programmes from King's College chapel, then from headmasters and LEA officers—that student life at Oxford and Cambridge was blessed with much superior amenities. All Oxford undergraduates either lived in college or enjoyed common-room, library and dining rights in a college. Only a quarter of the redbrick students lived in accommodation provided by their university, and the student union was widely judged to be no substitute for civilized collegiate life. In the brave pioneering days of the civic universities local philanthropists began to provide halls of residence, for example the

[44] For instruction on how to count universities in the UK see Carswell, appx III.
[45] See the results of an inquiry commissioned by the CVCP: R. K. Kelsall, *Report on an Inquiry into Applications for Admission to Universities* (London 1957), 9.
[46] For further analysis of the educational background of students see below, 598–9, 727–8.

Wills family at Bristol. But such provision waned in the depression years after 1929. The UGC provided exhortation but little cash. The results are shown in table 22.4: outside Oxford and Cambridge the proportion of students in university residences rose to a quarter by 1930 but stagnated thereafter until the 1960s.

TABLE 22.4

TERM-TIME RESIDENCE OF FULL-TIME
UNIVERSITY STUDENTS IN GREAT
BRITAIN, 1920–1980 EXCLUDING OXFORD
AND CAMBRIDGE (%)

academic year	in colleges or halls of residence	in lodgings	at home
1920/1	10.2	37.5	52.0
1929/30	24.9	32.9	42.1
1938/9	25.1	33.2	41.7
1950/1	24.3	39.1	36.6
1960/1	27.4	50.7	21.9
1971/2	39.7	41.7	16.3
1979/80	46.4	35.0	14.6

Source: UGC returns.

Between the wars redbrick universities lived through a demoralizing period of self-criticism and low esteem, poorly regarded by the national intelligentsia. There was a series of critical appraisals from Herklots in 1928 to Truscot in 1943.[47] Truscot's principal anxiety was about the connection between redbrick and what Edward Shils later described as the Ox-ford–London–Cambridge axis. Truscot's book appeared at a time when idealism and utopian euphoria about 'post-war reconstruction' was sweep-ing through the Whitehall corridors and the Nissen huts, crew-rooms and quarterdecks. It was a best-seller by the standards of the day and had to be reprinted. Truscot argued for 'an England . . . in which there are no longer two large residential universities for those who are either well-to-do or brilliant, and nine smaller universities, mainly non-residential, for those who are neither'. He urged that there be eleven universities of approximately equal size, 'all in the main residential and each having certain schools in which each excels the rest'.[48]

[47] H. G. G. Herklots, *The New Universities: An External Examination* (London 1928); B. Truscot, *Redbrick University* (London 1943, repr. 1945, new edn Harmondsworth 1951).
[48] Truscot, 54.

This formulation retained Victorian Oxford's idea of a university as an élitist teaching institution. Truscot argued that the state should become a generous patron of what would be in effect a system of Oxfords, enlarged to educate an expanded professional élite. And there was essentially the same recipe of commensality: 'it should be an axiom that every university must have sufficient hostels to accommodate a very large proportion of its undergraduates, and every student should be compelled to reside, either within one of these hostels, or in lodgings affiliated, as it were, with the hostels, and under strict university control'.[49] The restrictive character of this notion he noted but dismissed. 'The total numbers of students at the university would probably be reduced—but that might not be a bad thing, for many think the present numbers too high. The advantages are obvious. One has only to contrast the present Redbrick University situated in (or very near to) the slums to the Redbrick University City of the future, lying well outside the municipal boundaries, with its Great Hall, its playing fields, and, above all, its Greengates, its White Gables and its Goldcrest, each creating traditions of its own and gradually endowed by the benefactions of its own former residents—the colleges, hoary with tradition, of centuries to come.'[50]

Truscot had in effect abandoned the modern urban conception of the university which had motivated John Owens in Manchester and Joseph Chamberlain in Birmingham. The result was that post-war expansion came more as a threat than as a support to the civic universities. Moreover, for all its merits, Truscot's call for reform of the structure of university studies had similar effects. Leeds, Liverpool and Sheffield were devoted to the departmentally organized, single-subject honours degree and thereby lost cachet to the new (if more anciently conceived) universities where, beneath the superficialities of competitive advertising, there were attempts to redefine university courses across the boundaries of the arts and sciences.

There was, of course, a countervailing belief: the idea that universities should provide high scientific and professional manpower for an increasingly affluent society. Yet the idea of a university was still for the most part legitimized in the public mind through its association with the magic of Oxford. Thus, though there was solemn debate about the location of universities—with arguments and counter-arguments over the availability of digs, the crowding of cities, the need to take advantage of existing civic amenities and the desirability of missionary movements to civilize new industrial centres lacking higher education—the policy that eventually emerged was a comic pattern of return to medieval symbols. York and Lancaster, Essex and Sussex, Norwich and Warwick, were resounding

[49] Ibid. 58.   [50] Ibid. 59.

names of places which might have been Oxford and Cambridge but for the minor accidents of our pre-industrial history. True, there was expansion, but the Oxford model was sufficiently powerful to ensure that the new English foundations were established in ancient or pre-industrial locations rather than, as the Victorian universities were, at the urban growth-points of population. Professor Armytage proposed a university for Scunthorpe, but in the scramble for UGC funds the cathedral town was preferred to the industrial area. Only two of the successful applicants were from the industrial north.

It seemed to some critics and reformers at the end of the 1950s that the 'ancient' and the 'modern' universities might now compete for public esteem on more level terms. A more gloomy view envisaged a meritocracy, in the sense that anticipated reform would strengthen the existing social hierarchy of learning by further legitimizing merit. On the other hand, room at the top of the professional and scientific world would clearly expand faster than the output of Oxford and Cambridge, which produced a quarter of the graduates in England and Wales in 1938 but only one-fifteenth in the 1970s.

Sir Charles Morris believed that in postgraduate studies the modern universities had already gone a long way towards establishing themselves as independently excellent—and certainly their Victorian founders favoured the training of scholars for research and the pursuit of scientific research. But the primary emphasis of expansion, no doubt properly, was on under-graduate education in science and technology, and the major burden of this training of the new white-collar classes was to be borne by the redbrick universities. Though the traditions of the modern universities might have fitted them better for postgraduate education, in 1959 Manchester, Birming-ham and Leeds combined had fewer postgraduate students (2,426) than did Oxford and Cambridge (2,842).[51]

By the 1960s the civic universities were no longer regarded as new institutions. That label was appropriate, if ever, only during the first decade of the century. Once Oxford and Cambridge were established, there could be only two aspects of newness in the idea of a university: one with respect to who should enter, the other with respect to what should be studied. In this sense the seven new English universities of the 1960s were also never new. They accepted established definitions of the conditions for entry and they chose curricula and a balance of learning between research and teaching from within the practices current in the existing western universities. A true history of novelty in the idea of the university in modern England would have two main chapters. The first would be on the incorporation of science and would therefore concentrate on the end of the nineteenth century, with its redbrick monuments in London, Manchester, Birmingham and Leeds and

51 Halsey and Trow, *British Academics*, 75.

its reform of the hitherto arts and Anglican Oxford and Cambridge. The other would examine that single and singular innovation of the twentieth century, the Open University. Thus the first chapter would refer to new learning and the second to a new vision of who might learn.

The perspective from Brighton pier in 1961 was of an expansionist future. In that year fifty students arrived to join a handful of founding dons. By 1970 the senior common room could boast over five hundred members—a growth within a decade which a redbrick university or a provincial university college dependent on London had taken half a century to attain. By all standards of previous experience the new universities moved with astonishing speed. They were optimistic, modern, youthful, democratic and eager to demonstrate high capacity for teaching and research. They depended on the established universities to supply new professors and old skills, but they would soon repay the debt with interest through a flow of able and productive graduates. Their educational inspiration drew heavily on their vice-chancellors, people like Fulton of Sussex, Sloman of Essex and James of York, products of Oxbridge who had been deeply impressed by the merits of Oxford's Greats or PPE. It was natural that their major curricular inclination was to move from the inflexibilities of the single-subject honours degree associated with redbrick towards the older traditions of the multi-subject schools in which they had themselves been nurtured at Oxford or Cambridge.

Oxford and Cambridge still represented the older social and educational ideals of the cultivated member of a governing class as opposed to the highly trained professional expert. They cultivated the ideal of an intimate relation between teacher and taught, maintained through the tutorial method, shared domestic life in a college, and the separation of the roles of teacher and examiner. They were held up as examples of democratic self-government by academics who were themselves in charge of the administration. Above all they had the dignity of antiquity, riches and architectural splendour to produce a calm assurance of secure status for intellectual life no matter what political or economic vicissitudes might assail their society.

It seemed possible in the early 1960s that a score of competing educational principalities might emerge to replace the old polarity between redbrick and Oxbridge, unleashing creative energy and stimulating change, and perhaps even subverting the relative popularity of Oxford and Cambridge.[52] Yet Oxbridge preserved its predominance, and competition for places at Oxford became still fiercer. A stern meritocracy had emerged by the 1970s: whereas the proportion of undergraduates admitted with very high grades at A-level (AAA, AAB, AAC or ABB) was stable for the British universities as a whole at about 22 per cent, in Oxford it was 58.6 per cent, and rose to 73.5 per cent

[52] Cf A. H. Halsey, 'A pyramid of prestige', *Universities Quarterly* xv (1960–1).

by 1980.[53] In 1976 university teachers were asked 'Which is the best place in your subject?'[54] The results are set out in table 22.5 as 'league tables'. The question was asked in the light of expansion and the foundation of new universities after Robbins, by reason of which it was anticipated that particular 'centres of excellence' would develop in new places.

There was clear agreement as to university excellence in Britain. Among the seventeen subjects, Cambridge led strongly in the sciences and Oxford equally strongly in the arts. Taking all votes, and not only those in the subjects tabulated, the ancient English universities secured 36 per cent of the total, with London second (27 per cent) and the major redbricks third (14 per cent).

To be sure, this was by no means the whole story. The London School of Economics had always been a strong challenger in the social sciences, and still held the highest number of votes in economics, in sociology and in government and administration. Imperial College had a possibly more remarkable prestige in the applied sciences and engineering. Moreover the solid worth of the Victorian foundations in Manchester and Birmingham, the enduring excellence of Edinburgh and Glasgow, the rise to prominence of Bristol, and the quickly established position of some departments in the new universities were all features of the university scene by the 1970s. The institutions which seem to have fared least well were the technological universities and the smaller redbricks such as Leicester, Hull and Exeter. These formerly provincial colleges of London University had fewer votes than the new universities founded in the 1960s. They were too late to acquire the solidity of such places as Manchester and Leeds, but too early to benefit from the excitement and adventure of the universities founded in the following decade.

The one-in-six sample of academic staff were also asked whether they agreed that 'Oxford and Cambridge have preserved their predominance in practically everything that counts in academic life'. There was less accord in response to this bald assertion. Just over one-third agreed, one-third disagreed with reservations, and nearly one-third disagreed strongly. The percentages shown in table 22.6 make it clear that agreement about Oxbridge predominance was strongest among those connected to the ancient institutions by study or teaching experience, among older academics and in the arts and pure sciences. Disagreement was strong among those whose careers had not taken them into the orbit of Oxford and Cambridge and among those who taught the applied, natural or social sciences. As the system widened, the Oxbridge connection narrowed, but still roughly

[53] A. H. Halsey, 'The decline of donnish dominion?', *Oxford Review of Education* viii (1982), 218.
[54] A. H. Halsey, survey of British academics, 1976, deposited in British Library.

TABLE 22.5

'WHICH IS THE BEST DEPARTMENT IN YOUR SUBJECT?'
(% OF VOTE GIVEN TO INSTITUTION IN EACH SUBJECT, 1976)

English
Oxford	35.9
Cambridge	24.6
UCL	6.3
East Anglia and York	4.2

history
Oxford	47.2
Cambridge	21.0
Edinburgh and LSE	3.7

economics
LSE	49.8
Cambridge	20.3
Oxford	7.0
Edinburgh	3.0
Warwick	2.2

law
Oxford	35.1
Cambridge	30.9
LSE	8.2
Edinburgh	4.1
King's (London)	3.1

French
Oxford	22.7
Cambridge	13.6
Manchester	10.6
Bristol	9.1
Bradford	7.6

philosophy
Oxford	89.3
UCL	2.7

geography
Cambridge	56.3
ICL	14.8
Bristol	5.9
Durham	4.4
Aberdeen and LSE	3.0

sociology
LSE	27.1
Oxford	11.2
Essex	9.8
Manchester and Cambridge	6.5

biology
Cambridge	29.1
Edinburgh	10.3
Sussex and Glasgow	5.6
Bristol and Liverpool	4.7

physics
Cambridge	43.9
Oxford	14.7
Imperial	13.7
Bristol	4.1
Birmingham and UCL	2.5

civil engineering
Imperial	40.0
Cambridge	36.2
Swansea	5.7
Leeds and UCL	3.8

government and administration
LSE	26.6
Oxford	25.2
Manchester	12.9
Essex	7.2
Birmingham	5.8

geology
Imperial	22.2
Cambridge	18.5
Oxford	17.8
Leeds	11.1
Edinburgh	6.7
Manchester	4.4

mathematics
Cambridge	36.9
Manchester	13.3
Oxford and Imperial	9.4
Edinburgh	4.0

chemistry
Cambridge	26.1
Oxford	20.1
Imperial	17.0
Bristol	7.4
Leeds	3.1

electrical engineering
Imperial	33.1
UMIST	9.6
Leeds	4.2
Birmingham, Manchester and Queen Mary (London)	3.6

physiology
Cambridge	39.0
UCL	28.0
Oxford	13.4

TABLE 22.6

PERCENTAGE OF ACADEMIC STAFF IN 1976 SAMPLE
AGREEING THAT OXFORD AND CAMBRIDGE HAVE
PRESERVED THEIR PREDOMINANCE IN
PRACTICALLY EVERYTHING THAT COUNTS IN
ACADEMIC LIFE

Oxford and Cambridge dons	54	arts dons	44
London dons	35	pure scientists	39
redbrick dons	36	applied scientists	35
Scottish universities	33	medicine	35
Welsh universities	34	social studies	32
new English universities	33		
the over-50s	39		
the under-50s	34		
all	36		

Source: Halsey, survey of British academics, 1976.

TABLE 22.7

FIRST PREFERENCE BETWEEN UNIVERSITY
POSTS AS EXPRESSED BY SAMPLE SURVEYS IN
1964 AND 1976 (%)

	1964	1976
university lecturer and fellow of a college at Cambridge	33	35
professor at Sussex	30	27
professorial head of department at Leeds	21	23
reader in the University of London	16	19

Source: A. H. Halsey, sample surveys of university teachers 1964 and 1976.

12,800 (32 per cent) of British university teachers in 1976 had studied or taught in Oxford or Cambridge at some time.

The continued importance of the ancient universities within the expanded national system of higher education is confirmed by the fact that the number of migrants to other universities was much greater than the resident members of Oxford and Cambridge. Still more telling are the replies to a further question. 'Which of the following posts would be most attractive to you personally: university lecturer and college fellow at Cambridge, professor at Sussex, professorial head of department at Leeds, or a reader in the University of London?' As may be seen from table 22.7, the Cambridge post, although lowest in salary and formally the lowest of the four in rank, attracted most first votes in both years, and in fact rose from 33 per cent in 1964 to 35 per cent in 1976; the chair at Sussex, the chair at Leeds and the readership in London followed in that order. In both years the respondents were asked whether they would prefer another university to the one in which they were presently serving. Nearly one-third wanted to move, and there was a strong preference for Oxford and Cambridge. By this measure, therefore, the attraction of Oxford and Cambridge was still very marked, if slightly reduced. Preference with respect to other groups of universities was fairly stable, the solidity of the major redbricks in Manchester, Birmingham, Bristol and Leeds again being notable. In the light of such ambitions it is not surprising that Oxbridge was the most self-recruiting of the groups—that is, its staff was most heavily drawn from its own graduates. The Robbins Committee found that in 1961/2 78 per cent of Oxbridge dons had graduated from Oxford or Cambridge, while self-recruitment in the civic universities was 40 per cent (with 26 per cent from Oxbridge).[55] The Halsey survey in 1976 showed that Oxbridge's self-recruitment had dropped to 59 per cent, while the figure of 39 per cent for civic universities was roughly where it had been in 1961/2 (with again 26 per cent from Oxbridge).

Satisfactions mirror aspirations. Compared with all other groups, Oxford and Cambridge dons were most satisfied with their present university, least interested in moving, and most contented with the standing of their departments or faculties. These satisfactions were in turn well grounded in favourable stipends, career success, library and laboratory facilities, opportunities for sabbatical leave, and the company of able and well qualified colleagues and visitors. Over 40 per cent of Oxford and Cambridge dons had already been offered a chair in a British university compared with 15 per cent of their nearest rivals in London University. They lived in a more research-minded environment than their colleagues elsewhere. Two-thirds of them were more inclined to research than to teaching, compared with barely more than one-half of university staff generally. By the various measures of research activity—books and articles—they were the leading group, though only slightly ahead of London. Among their immediate colleagues, 58 per cent held first-class degrees compared with 40 per cent in the redbricks and under a quarter in the former colleges of advanced technology.

In short, the Oxford and Cambridge dons of the 1970s retained advantages of both market and working conditions. And they had meritocratic advantages in terms of academic selection and reputation. In 1976 as in 1964 they were relatively heavily recruited from the professional

[55] *Robbins Report*, appx 3, tables 45 and 46.

and managerial classes (59 per cent compared with 49 per cent for all university staff) and the private sector of secondary education (41 per cent against 30 per cent).

Such was the grip of the ancient over the modern in all realizations of the idea of the university in England. Moreover the twentieth-century foundations became more and more like each other after Robbins. To walk through the campus at Warwick or Lancaster in 1970 was to experience the same international airport ambience that was to be found at Leicester or Exeter, or even at Birmingham if one turned one's gaze from the Aston Webb buildings across the extended campus in the Calthorpe estate. The new universities demonstrated the continued vitality of Victorian ideas, and in the process made the label they received in the 1960s meaningless.

Was Oxford the triumphant defender then of a pre-industrial, even anti-industrial tradition? Lord Curzon told the Vice-Chancellor in 1909: 'a greater injustice could not be done to modern Oxford than to represent it as the home of stationary forces or ideas. On the contrary, the spirit of reform is probably even more active inside the walls of the University than it is among the vast and scattered constituency of non-resident Oxford men. Our object accordingly should be to . . . convince the nation at large that Oxford is as capable now as ever—nay more so—of fulfilling its traditional part as the focus of the best educational activities, the highest civic aspirations, and the most advanced thought of the age.'[56] At the end of the period—after Robbins, despite Franks and before Thatcher—the question remained. From the dead, the quick had inherited architectural surroundings of exquisite beauty, libraries of fabulous amenity and standards of intellectual accomplishment to humble their achievements and inspire their dreams. The challenge now as then was to match privilege with respon-sibility in an age in which egalitarian claims, if denied, could quickly turn into ugly resentment.

In the past, Oxford had carried academic excellence in a vessel of economic and social advantage. In the future it would have to justify the claims of its scholarship and science on public academic resources. A Leeds lecturer recorded his nightmare of an Oxford with full private status and charging economic fees.[57] To others, too, this idea was repugnant because for them Oxford was a priceless national and international centre of learning. Responsibility had to be public for a public institution. The Robbins Committee nationally and the Franks Commission locally raised the same issue in the 1960s. Indeed Lord Franks discussed it publicly with Lord Robbins, who made his view clear in 1965: 'the solution to the problem

[56] Curzon, *University Reform*, 13–14.
[57] *Times Higher Education Supplement* 6 Dec. 1974, 13.

arising from excessive competition for places at Oxford and Cambridge is for the Government and private donors to see to it that other centres of learning are enabled to develop on such a scale and in such a way as to provide places which are not deemed so manifestly inferior as so many of the places provided hitherto have been. This is not something that can happen overnight. But the progress already made in some other universities, both old and new, suggests that, given a more deliberate adoption of this objective, it should not be impossible to achieve it over the next quarter of a century or so.'[58]

Robbins's idea of British higher education included a place but no monopoly for the ancient universities. He went on to criticize Oxford for the obscurity of its statistics, its grasshopper vice-chancellorship, its open scholarships (which he wanted transferred to postgraduates) and its syndicalist approach to its own government. Finally he speculated on the future of Oxford and Cambridge, opposing both great expansion and their development as exclusively postgraduate schools. Nevertheless, within the general context of a more pluralistic system of competing centres of excellence, he envisaged the substantial enlargement of postgraduate studies at Oxford beyond 20 per cent as 'something like manifest destiny.'[59] It was, however, still unclear at the end of our period how far British higher education, and Oxford within it, could follow the path which Robbins had sketched out for them.

Oxford in the 1970s remained a proud symbol and exemplar of the western university. Between the magnificent medieval masonry of the divinity school and the elegant twentieth-century concrete of Wolfson College there was a continuously evolving equilibrium of conservatism moderated by civility and of radicalism moderated by reason. From the middle of the nineteenth century, the pace of evolution had quickened as Oxford absorbed the sciences into the collegiate organization of a liberal university. After the Second World War the increasing financial intrusion of the state demanded further and faster adaptation. Oxford University had to find its place in the system of higher education as an administrative hybrid of public funding authorities and private colleges. It had to justify itself by meritocratic admission of students and election of dons and it had to negotiate competitively with government departments and quasi-governmental agencies like the UGC and the research councils. The evidence is broadly that a successful adaptation was in train.

Yet uncertainty also persisted. Meritocracy had widened the social composition of senior, middle and junior common rooms, and Oxford could be represented satirically as the best liberal arts college outside or inside

---

[58] Franks Commission, written evidence xi. 174.

[59] Ibid. 180. The proportion had in fact risen to 24 per cent by 1981: not a dramatic destiny in the event.

America. But was even a successful realization of that reputation enough to honour the past and bequeath to the future? Some thought not. Their essential notion was that the future development of the 'system of higher education' would transform the traditional arrangement of universities admitting their students directly from secondary schools. Instead they envisaged a framework of continuing education which could not be confined to a narrow age-band in full-time, state-funded study but would embrace a range of liberal or vocational studies beyond school for students of all ages. Oxford could of course ignore this possible future, which in any case would not prevent it from continuing its established teaching and research. If, however, Oxford were to respond, then its admissions, teaching methods, examinations, residence requirements and fees would all have to face drastic change. In its relationship with the British system of higher education we thus leave Oxford at yet another turning point in the ceaseless debate which has to be carried on wherever men and women pursue educational excellence.

23

A World University

J. G. DARWIN

Even in modern times Oxford's peculiar character as a university has made it unusually self-sufficient and self-preoccupied. Yet since 1914 the University has been deeply influenced by the outside world, both by its overseas connections and by its periodic and uncoordinated attempts to strengthen its position among the great universities of the world. It is tempting, then, to describe Oxford as a 'world university' if only to emphasize how misleading is the enclosed and arcadian image so often evoked in literary depictions of Oxford. But what is a world university and when did Oxford become one? Four criteria suggest themselves. The essence of a world university is an international reputation as a centre of scholarship. For this there must be sufficient funds to sustain a very substantial volume of academic activity, since even outstanding quality in one or a few branches of learning would scarcely enable a university to qualify. Thirdly, to be a world university also implies a wide range of academic interests extending far beyond a parochial concern with the local or national. In the arts and social sciences it means familiarity with and involvement in the academic activity of other cultures and societies; in the sciences, the capacity to engage in research which commands the attention of the most advanced centres elsewhere. Lastly, and perhaps most importantly, a world university must recruit a significant proportion of both its academic staff and its students on an international basis.

The international standing of Oxford and Cambridge in the nineteenth century owed much to their role as the finishing schools of a ruling élite widely regarded as the vital element in a political system renowned for its strength and stability. Even more than Cambridge, perhaps, Oxford came to be regarded at home and abroad as the main recruiting ground for politicians and officials, and as the principal forcing house for opinion-formers of all kinds—writers, journalists, theologians and social critics. As the British empire expanded, British universities staffed its elaborate bureaucracies, and foreign fascination with the academic nurseries of the 'official mind' became all the greater. With imperial expansion came the export of British educational and cultural institutions. Oxford's reputation abroad in 1914 probably owed less to its scholarly activity than to its association with the political and social élite of a great world power. From the time of the 'King and Country' debate in 1933, through the Suez crisis of 1956 to the Vietnam war 'teach-in' of 1965 [plate 14.3] there was an unspoken assumption that Young Oxford articulated the opinions of the next generation of the political class—and of the conscript subalterns of the next war.[1]

Such sources of influence have gradually become less important in the twentieth century. Instead, universities have built their reputations on scholarship which, at least in open societies, has become more and more internationalized. Of course in universities and among thinkers and artists there has always been a traffic in ideas and influences from abroad. But in the present century this tendency has become far more widespread and systematic, reflecting not only the ease of travel but also changes in the life of academic disciplines. In the natural sciences especially, access to a rapidly expanding global reservoir of knowledge required universities to maintain an international presence and, if necessary, to recruit academic staff with experience of research techniques not available locally. The social sciences with their inherently comparative and transnational bias have followed suit, and so have other more obviously culture-bound disciplines. The great legacy of the nineteenth century, the creation of a world economy and a system of world politics, has enormously increased the academic prestige attached to knowledge of foreign cultures and international processes.

There were other important changes in the academic environment at home and abroad which could hardly be ignored in Oxford. Government's spasmodic demand for expert knowledge of foreign lands and cultures was one. Another was the growing competition between universities for academic staff and students and their jostling to offer new and attractive fields of study. A third was the search for overseas funding which, especially in recent years, has made British universities eager to recruit foreign students. For twentieth-century Oxford these changes in the outside world have raised a number of contentious issues. Was the University to compete with other major institutions abroad or to preserve its late Victorian character largely intact? How far was it to modify its syllabus and its somewhat ambivalent attitude towards research? From where was the initiative for change to come in so conservative and decentralized a confederation of colleges? Would embracing new disciplines push Oxford into becoming a more specialized university? Would change reinforce its academic connections with Europe or strengthen those with the empire and the United States? In short, would Oxford have either the will or the ability to transform itself into a modern international university? And if it did, could it do so without a fundamental reconstruction of its institutions?

---

[1] For the 'King and Country' debate see OM 16 Feb. 1933, 426–7; M. Ceadel, 'The King and Country debate, 1933: student politics, pacifism and the dictators', Historical Jl xxii (1979). For Oxford reactions to Suez see Isis 7 Nov. 1956, 10–11.

Oxford in 1914 was far from parochial in its interests. The narrowness of the undergraduate syllabus, with its heavy concentration on Greats, Anglocentric modern history and English literature, belied the range of academic activity in the University. Oxford lacked the seminar system which was characteristic of German universities and was copied in the United States. Its scholarly tradition was individualistic and informal. But in late Victorian and Edwardian times it was not without academic figures of great international authority, Pollock, Holdsworth, Bryce, Tawney, Carlyle and Bradley among them. There was a scattering of appointments in exotic subjects like Sanskrit or Arabic. Some tutors like Margoliouth, Reginald Coupland or Alfred Zimmern, who earned their bread and butter as workaday classicists or ancient historians, were (or became) formidable scholars in other fields (Margoliouth in Arabic, Coupland in British imperial history, Zimmern in international relations).[2]

Oxford had also long been open to academic influences from Europe. Much of the study of classics and ancient history had been refashioned in the light of the work of German scholars especially. Theology and philosophy were strongly marked by continental opinion. In modern history York Powell, Creighton, Freeman and Fisher were all notable for the breadth of their historical interests and their freedom from a narrowly Anglocentric bias. Even that most imperialist of regius professors, James Anthony Froude, had built his academic reputation upon command of the great Spanish archives at Simancas. In the natural sciences too—underdeveloped as they were at Oxford before 1914—keen attention was paid to European research. In physics Berlin was the recognized centre of advanced research and some of the ablest young scientists in Oxford sought opportunities to study there.[3]

Nonetheless, in the Oxford of 1914 the influence of the imperial connection seemed more pervasive than the European, and contributed more to Oxford's reputation as a world university. Since 1884 Oxford had possessed an Indian Institute and a small corps of teachers in Indian history and law.[4] It also attracted a small number of Indian students, with most colleges reserving 'one or two vacancies' for them.[5] Here was the basis of a modest but significant academic diversification. But by 1914 neither Indian studies nor India had made the impact which had once appeared likely. There were various reasons for this: the difficulty of grafting an exotic new

---

[2] H. A. L. Fisher, *An Unfinished Autobiography* (London 1940), 45–6.
[3] F. W. F. Smith, second Earl of Birkenhead, *The Prof in Two Worlds: The Official Life of Professor F. A. Lindemann, Viscount Cherwell* (London 1961); R. W. Clark, *Tizard* (London 1965), 13–15.
[4] R. Symonds, *Oxford and Empire: The Last Lost Cause?* (London 1986), 108 ff.
[5] There were 70 Indian students in Oxford in Trinity term 1914: *Report on the Work of the Indian Students' Department, 1913–14* (PP 1914–16 xlviii Cd 7719), 10–11.

growth on to the old academic stock in Oxford, particularly at the undergraduate level; the tendency of the historians of India to be excessively 'official' in their outlook; and the lack of large-scale financial sponsorship to promote interest in India or to bring Indian students to Oxford in sufficient numbers.

A far stronger imperial influence was that which derived from Cecil Rhodes's notorious bequests. On Rhodes's death in 1902 his trustees had swiftly implemented his scheme to bring to Oxford some 57 students a year: 20 from the countries of the empire, 32 from the United States and 5 from Germany. The German scholarships were abolished in 1916 and only briefly revived in the 1930s.[6] These students came to read for degrees alongside their English counterparts and were admitted to the colleges on equal terms, as junior members of the University. Rhodes's scheme provided exactly what was lacking in Indian studies, or in Oxford's connections with Europe: the funds to bring a regular stream of overseas students to the University in substantial numbers, and thus to spread its reputation and academic relationships as far and as fast as the returning Rhodes scholars could carry them. The prestige which the scholarships quickly acquired, and the need to organize the selection process in the countries of the empire and in all the states of the American union helped to build up influential local lobbies whose business was to proclaim the value of an education in Oxford. The fraternal activism of returning Oxonians was an invaluable resource. Its indirect effects were greatly to benefit twentieth-century Oxford.

By accident or design, the Rhodes trustees—especially George Parkin—maximized the impact of the scholars in Oxford. By successfully negotiating acceptance of them by the colleges, Parkin prevented them from becoming a transient, segregated group, secluded in a colonial menagerie in North Oxford. Nobody proposed to create for them what the Master of University College urged on the Asquith Commission in 1920: a special college for Indian students 'with sufficiently homogeneous antecedents to secure an esprit de corps . . . comparable to the traditions of a normal college'.[7] The idea was, perhaps fortunately, stillborn. Rhodes scholars' easy social acceptance doubtless owed much to their white skins. 'No doubt', wrote Francis Wylie, the Rhodes Trust's agent in Oxford in 1916, 'we must expect an occasional coloured man from Barbados or Trinidad . . . but that can't be helped'.[8] It also helped that Rhodes had insisted on more than academic quality as a criterion for selection. Sporting prowess became almost synonymous with the Rhodes scholar. Between the wars 85 per cent

[6] C. K. Allen, *Forty Years of the Oxford Rhodes Scholarships* (Oxford 1944), 5–7; above, 4–6.

[7] Bodl. MS Asquith 140, memorandum by the Master of University College, Aug. 1920.

[8] C. W. Newbury, 'Cecil Rhodes and the South African connection: a great imperial university?' in A. Madden and D. K. Fieldhouse (eds), *Oxford and the Idea of Commonwealth* (London and Canberra 1982), 91.

of Rhodes scholars entered their college boats or other teams.[9] Nothing could have been better designed to promote social integration and extract deference from the arbiters of undergraduate society —from Boy Mulcaster (Evelyn Waugh's archetypal Christ Church hearty) and even, if for different reasons, from Anthony Blanche. But perhaps most important of all was Rhodes's use of his colonial fortune to bring Americans to Oxford in numbers greater at first than those from the countries of the empire. The imperial connection had opened the way to the transatlantic relationship. Perhaps nothing short of the dramatic scale of Rhodes's scheme, creating two scholarships for every state, could so rapidly have overcome American reservations about study in Oxford.

Of course, before 1914 the Rhodes scholarship scheme was still in its infancy and the Rhodes trustees themselves were far from taking the view that Oxford had first claim on the ample funds left over after meeting the costs of the scholarships. Under the powerful influence of Viscount Milner and Rhodes's banker Lewis Michell they concerned themselves with carrying on Rhodes's political and social projects in South Africa: subsidizing unprofitable agricultural experiments on Rhodes's estates, supporting Rhodes's old political allies and assisting English-speaking public schools.[10] 'We are inclined to think that Higher School Education in South Africa, especially of the English Public School type, has one of the first claims on us after the Scholarships themselves', wrote Milner in 1912.[11] But even before 1914, Rhodes's gift had triggered an important secondary bequest, that of Alfred Beit, who endowed a chair and a lecturership in colonial—later Commonwealth—history. Significantly, the first incumbent of the chair announced his intention to lecture on topics too recent for a modern history syllabus that then ended at 1837.[12] The early holders of the Beit lecturership, notably Lionel Curtis, quickly established a tradition of scholarly (but far from disinterested) investigation of contemporary imperial problems.[13] The seeds of what became the much larger enterprise of colonial studies had been sown.

The imperial connection thus contributed to a healthy diversification of student recruitment and, incipiently, to a widening of the range of academic interests, especially in the field of contemporary international affairs. In fact, even before 1914 Oxford was attracting a significant number of overseas students, a substantial proportion of whom appear to have been the children

[9] F. Aydelotte, *The American Rhodes Scholarships: A Review of the First Forty Years* (Princeton NJ 1946), 73.

[10] Bodl. MS Milner 468, Michell to Milner, 6 Oct. 1909.

[11] Ibid. Milner to Feetham, 6 Sept. 1912.

[12] H. E. Egerton, *The Claims of the Study of Colonial History upon the Attention of the University of Oxford* (Oxford 1906).

[13] D. Lavin, 'Lionel Curtis and the idea of Commonwealth' in Madden and Fieldhouse, *Oxford and the Idea of Commonwealth*.

of expatriate Britons, many of them no doubt in countries of the empire. Some colleges in Oxford, notably Balliol, were already distinctly cosmopolitan, although the trend was for other colleges to match or even exceed Balliol's proportion of foreign students: Worcester, Queen's, Lincoln and Merton all had more by 1911–14.[14]

Despite these outside influences, Oxford's claim to international standing in 1914 would not be sustained without major changes in the provision for natural sciences and the academic study of contemporary issues, in the arrangements for postgraduate students, in the status of research in the eyes of tutors and their colleges and in the scope of the undergraduate syllabus. Too much of Oxford's energy went into undergraduate teaching, whereas research or writing commanded less respect, as selfish preoccupations best left to professors.[15] In Balliol, as late as 1910, H. W. C. Davis had to threaten resignation in order to extract some concession to his passion for research; he was allowed to live out and his teaching was reduced to twenty hours a week.[16] Furthermore, competition between the colleges to achieve the best results in examinations built an immensely powerful vested interest in narrowing rather than widening the syllabus. The incentives to study, let alone teach, new disciplines were correspondingly reduced. The importance attached to sympathy, devotion to the college interest and the possession of examination skills necessarily reinforced the tendency for colleges to recruit tutors from within their walls and certainly from within Oxford. Such a system denied Oxford the fertilizing effects of intellectual migration, one of the characteristics of a modern world university. Moreover, there were major obstacles to widening student recruitment. The insistence upon compulsory Greek, the antipathy to vocational studies and the difficulty of providing adequate scientific facilities in a university organized as a loose confederation of colleges were all a severe check on Oxford's progress beyond a prestigious finishing school. Vested interests sprouted a luxuriant growth of principles held with theological intensity. 'To reform a university', as Chancellor Curzon ruefully remarked, 'is like reconstructing a church'.[17] Perhaps what chiefly preserved the institution from inertia in its Edwardian heyday was its social contact with the 'opinion-forming' classes and its role as a great pool through which there rushed a constant rejuvenating stream of talent. The academic activity pursued in Edwardian Oxford and Cambridge has even been described as 'unrecognizable as a co-descendant with the German universities of the great intellectual powerhouses of the Middle Ages'.[18]

[14] L. Stone, 'The size and composition of the Oxford student body 1580–1910' in L. Stone (ed.), *The University in Society* (2 vols Princeton NJ 1975) i, table 9.
[15] A. J. Engel, *From Clergyman to Don* (Oxford 1983), 231.
[16] J. Jones, *Balliol College: A History 1263–1939* (Oxford 1988), 237.
[17] Bodl. MS Selborne 10, Curzon to Selborne, 9 Aug. 1907.
[18] E. Ashby, *Universities: British, Indian, African* (London 1966), 6.

Oxford needed to transform itself in order to become a great, open, outward-looking centre where research would enjoy the prestige and facilities increasingly offered elsewhere. The First World War was, from this point of view, a moment of transition through its stimulus to scientific research. For a brief moment there had also seemed to be a prospect of closer academic ties with France and Italy, Britain's principal European allies in wartime, as well as continued interest in the European problems of nationality to which considerable attention had been given during the war.[19] In retrospect, however, we can see that the war actually checked Oxford's interest in Europe and reinforced the preference for imperial and transatlantic connections—stronger than ever with the rupture of older Anglo-German links.

Even so, the report of the Asquith Commission revealed some attempt to grapple with the dangers of academic insularity. 'It is a disaster', it remarked, 'that at a moment when we have become far more deeply involved than ever before in the affairs of countries overseas, our highest academical class is condemned through poverty to know little or nothing of life or learning outside this island'. The report also chided the University for neglect of living foreign languages, and urged it to seize the opportunity to become a centre of research and postgraduate education to a much greater extent than before.[20] Albert Mansbridge, himself a member of the Commission, wrote briskly: 'in principle, there must be open access to Oxford and Cambridge from the entire world; so only can they be universities in the highest sense'.[21] In 1930 the American scholar Abraham Flexner, the friendliest of critics, expressed a similar point of view. He was full of praise for Oxford's resistance to degrees in cooking and physical education. But he complained of an excessive preoccupation with undergraduate teaching; the inadequate provision for, and paucity of, postgraduate students; and the dominance of the colleges, with their indifference to what Flexner saw as the needs of the wider educational world.[22] But none of these critics gave much guidance on how to achieve these objectives. For that would require not only new resources but also agreement on the new areas of study to be promoted within a university that was under-funded at the centre and hampered by its decentralized decision-making machinery. If Oxford was to be transformed, or merely changed, the initiative would have to come from outside.

It was in this context that Oxford's imperial connection came to play so important a role between the wars. Before the war, as we have seen, the grandiose beginnings of Indian studies in Oxford had yielded rather

[19] See the enthusiastic welcome for new academic links with France and Italy in OM 22 Nov. 1918, 74.
[20] Asquith Report, 51, 45.
[21] A. Mansbridge, The Older Universities of England (London 1923), 241.
[22] A. Flexner, Universities: American, English, German (Oxford 1930), 268, 271, 273.

disappointing results and their impact had been relatively slight. After 1918, however, there were several attempts to strengthen interest in and sympathy for India in Oxford. The first was Lord Lothian's project for a visiting lecturership to bring distinguished Indian academics to Oxford. This was to be financed by the Rhodes Trust, of which Lothian was Secretary, and the offer was made to the University in 1932. Perhaps for administrative reasons, nothing developed.[23] The second was the more ambitious scheme floated by Lionel Curtis and Edward Thompson, then a research fellow at Oriel (and, by default, the real centre of Oxford scholarship on India) to replace the Indian Institute by an ideologically more salubrious 'Irwin House', freed from the stigma of official connections with the India Office. As the costs of this seemed substantial, Lothian, Thompson and Curtis turned for help to Thompson's own sponsor, Henry Spalding. Then, in discussion with the Vice-Chancellor, an even grander notion emerged, of an 'Asia House' where the study of the modern east would be concentrated under a sympathetic warden, and which would complement Rhodes House and its African interests.[24] But these schemes, despite their powerful sponsors, came to nothing—perhaps because, like the Indian Institute they were designed to supplant, they had too explicit a political purpose. In the early 1930s Lothian and Curtis were obsessed with Indian politics, deeply committed to Irwin's attempts as Viceroy to construct a 'moderate' centre in Indian politics, and convinced that British opinion about India required a Pauline conversion away from Churchillian reaction. Asia or Irwin House was to be the symbol of the new spirit of Anglo-Indian relations: the visiting lecturers would assault the bastions of prejudice from the bridgeheads of North Oxford. But like many such schemes these fell victim to the notoriously brief attention-span of the politician or, in Curtis's case, of the self-appointed statesman-visionary. The agenda of British politics changed. By 1935 the Indian question had been settled as an issue in British politics. New and much more urgent issues arose. Visiting lecturers from India no longer seemed a useful way to change the world. There was, however, one valuable outcome: the extension of the Rhodes scholarships to India.

Modest they might have been, but the effects of the Indian connection were far from insignificant. By the early 1920s the number of Indian students was considerable, though it gradually dwindled from a peak of 149 in 1922 to less than half that number in the mid-1930s.[25] Indian students established themselves as a distinct community with a society of their own, the Majlis, a forerunner of many later societies catering for foreign students in Oxford. Indian influence was felt particularly in left-leaning clubs and societies and at the Union. During the 1930s political controversy over Britain's policy in

[23] Symonds, *Oxford and Empire*, 117–18.
[24] Ibid.
[25] OUA UDC/M/20/1, minute-book of the delegates for oriental students 1916–44.

India was reflected in a series of debates in which Indian students figured prominently. Motions sympathetic to greater Indian self-government consistently attracted large votes and on two occasions (in 1932 and 1935) carried the day.[26] Indians were elected librarian and president of the Union. The importance of this should not be underestimated. Oxford's appeal to overseas students of high calibre depended heavily not only upon the prestige of its degrees but also on its reputation as a sophisticated, cosmopolitan environment in which students of all races could win social acceptance and aspire to social distinction. Moreover, although the plans for an Irwin House came to nothing, Indian affairs also helped to establish in Oxford the tradition of direct engagement with contemporary international problems, widely seen today as an important function of an international university. All Souls served privately and informally as the meeting place for a remarkable array of old India hands and of those with a consuming interest in its problems. Lord Curzon, Lord Chelmsford and Lord Halifax were all quondam viceroys; the other luminaries of the All Souls–India connection included Sir John Simon, Geoffrey Dawson, Sir Maurice Gwyer, Curtis, Leo Amery, Sir Reginald Coupland, Sir Sarvepalli Radhakrishnan (later first president of India) and Lord Radcliffe (who supervised the making of the partition line between India and Pakistan). A more public advertisement of the University as a reservoir of expert knowledge and practical information in international affairs was Coupland's role in the search for a wartime political settlement in India and his organization of a research project on Indian politics based at Nuffield College. Moreover, for all its defects, the old Indian Institute and the 'official history' it propagated did bear some valuable fruit. The Institute's library became one of the most important repositories of research materials on Indian history outside the subcontinent and a focus for postgraduate research, while subjects in Indian history formed the earliest and for long the largest component of third-world history available to undergraduates.

It was already clear before 1914 that Cecil Rhodes's influence on the University was likely to be much greater than that of India. By chance, and in pursuit of a quite different goal, Rhodes and his trustees had found an almost perfect method of infiltrating a new influence into the University, bypassing its administrative bottlenecks. Of course we should not exaggerate the speed with which Rhodes scholars established themselves as a characteristic part of the Oxford scene. The publication of *Oxford of Today* in 1927 as a manual-cum-brochure for intending Rhodes scholars indicates, perhaps, that advertisement was still felt necessary to widen the scholarships' appeal.[27] Nevertheless, just because of their numbers, the Rhodes scholarships were a long stride towards diversifying internationally Oxford's

[26] *OM* 5 Nov. 1931, 140–1; 19 May 1932, 700–2; 31 Jan. 1935, 314–15; 7 Dec. 1939, 123–4.
[27] L. A. Crosby, F. Aydelotte, A. C. Valentine (eds), *Oxford of Today* (Oxford 1927).

recruitment of undergraduates and postgraduate students. Between the wars the number of overseas students from foreign countries as well as the empire fluctuated between 525 and a little over 600 in any one year in a total student body of between 4,163 in 1923/4 and 5,023 in 1939.[28] If we assume, not unreasonably, that the 100 scholarships eventually available to the countries of the empire and the 96 open to Americans were normally filled, then Rhodes scholars typically made up at least one-third of Oxford's total of overseas students. Of course it is possible that Rhodes scholars took places that would otherwise have gone to other foreign students, and did not entirely represent a net gain in numbers. But it seems likely that the scale, regularity of recruitment and reputation of the Rhodes scheme made a qualitative difference to Oxford's attitude towards foreign students. It is also likely that, as the scheme became known more generally, it encouraged applications from a much wider overseas constituency than before 1914, with favourable implications for academic standards.

Indeed a striking feature of twentieth-century Oxford is the stream of academic talent which has flowed to it from the Commonwealth, sometimes though not invariably as a result of the award of a Rhodes scholarship. Kenneth Wheare, who became the leading authority on the British constitution and the constitutional workings of the Commonwealth; Robert Hall, an economist and later a senior official in the Cabinet Office; and Howard Florey, who discovered how to apply penicillin clinically: all came as Rhodes scholars from Australia and spent much of their careers in Oxford. Perhaps appropriately, Rhodes House became the home of the Ralegh Club, established in 1912 to encourage friendship among students from the countries of the empire and to promote interest in imperial—later Commonwealth—questions. It was addressed by many of the most distinguished political figures of the day, including Gandhi. A further crucial consequence of the arrival of the Rhodes scholars was the impetus they gave to the recognition of the importance of postgraduate studies and of the prestige of a postgraduate degree. Oxford's degree of doctor of philosophy, claims the historian of the American Rhodes scholars, 'was established largely in response to American demand'. Indeed in the years after 1930 some 30 per cent of American Rhodes scholars took research degrees in Oxford. And although home demand for the DPhil grew rapidly, of the 1,110 recipients of the degree in the twenty-five years after its creation in 1918, nearly half were overseas students.[29]

Before 1914, as we have seen, the Rhodes trustees had been inclined to regard Oxford as merely one among several pressing obligations. By the early 1920s, however, Oxford had risen in the Trust's priorities. The crucial step was taken to invest in the construction of Rhodes House as a home for

[28] HUD.
[29] Aydelotte, *American Rhodes Scholarships*, 57; *Gazette* lxxiv (1943/4), 43.

the growing library of books and archival material on colonial and American history and politics.[30] Moreover, the Trust became an important patron of what grew into colonial studies: it was the award of a Rhodes travelling fellowship that effectively launched Margery Perham on her career as the leading academic authority on colonial administration.[31]

By the later 1930s colonial studies was already becoming perhaps the most important influence for enlarging and diversifying the University's research interests in the arts and social studies. As early as 1925 the idea had been canvassed of Oxford's becoming a training ground for colonial civil servants (as it already was for probationers entering the Indian civil service) to take advantage of, among other things, the collection of books soon to be placed in Rhodes House.[32] In 1926 the tropical African service course was created. Oxford was already, through its school of forestry, pre-eminent for its training in colonial forestry.[33] By the 1930s it had become the main centre for the study of colonial administration, with Margery Perham as the dominating force. In 1937 the Oxford University summer school on colonial administration was started. In 1938 the programme, costing £2 10s with an extra £6 12s for accommodation in college, included discussion of 'the influence of the mandate system', 'native administration in the Sudan' and 'land problems and native administration'.[34] Upon these modest foundations a larger structure was gradually erected. In 1939 Margery Perham was appointed Reader in Colonial Administration and elected a fellow of Nuffield College. The outbreak of war provided a powerful stimulus, intellectual and to some extent financial, for research in colonial government and economics. Academic help was mobilized to ward off transatlantic schemes for internationalizing control over all colonial territories—regarded in Britain as merely a euphemism for inserting American influence in place of British.[35] Posts in colonial law, colonial administration and a chair in colonial economic affairs (endowed for a period by the United Africa Company) sprang up.[36] Of the three major research projects established in Nuffield College one was concerned with social reconstruction at home, but a second with India and the third with colonial research.

At the end of the war the Devonshire Committee, established by the government to inquire into the training of colonial officials, recommended an enlargement of the kind of course created in Oxford before the war.

[30] Newbury, 'Rhodes and the South African connection', 92.
[31] M. Perham, West African Passage (London 1983), introduction.
[32] OM 29 Jan. 1925, 224; OUA HU/DV 4, note by Douglas Veale, Apr. 1969; F. Madden, 'The Commonwealth, Commonwealth history, and Oxford, 1905–1971' in Madden and Fieldhouse, Oxford and the Idea of Commonwealth, 7–29.
[33] Veale, Apr. 1969; OM 1 Feb. 1934, 396–8.
[34] From a copy of the timetable in Alfred Zimmern's papers, Bodl. MS Zimmern 116.
[35] W. R. Louis, Imperialism at Bay (Oxford 1977), passim; Gazette lxxiv (1943/4), 39 (8 Oct. 1943).
[36] Veale, Apr. 1969; Gazette lxxv (1944/5), 30, 34.

Government funds made possible the establishment of university lecturerships in colonial administration, agriculture and economics—primarily to teach for the Devonshire courses.[37] In 1946 Margery Perham's informal empire of books and bodies was incarnated as the Institute of Colonial Studies. Seven years later, with £50,000 from the government and £100,000 from Sir Ernest Oppenheimer—another reminder of the importance of the South African connection in all this—Queen Elizabeth House was founded at the suggestion of the Colonial Office as a colonial 'centre' where trainee colonial administrators and visitors from overseas colonial territories could meet each other as well as other interested scholars, politicians and senior officials.[38]

In retrospect, we can see that this irruption of the colonial periphery into Oxford was doomed to an early demise. Only eight years after Queen Elizabeth House was established, South Africa, the major source of its endowment, left the Commonwealth. By the end of the 1960s the brief boom in Commonwealth studies had passed. But in several respects the imperial and Commonwealth connection had contributed importantly to Oxford's evolution into a university of the modern international type. Geography, forestry, agriculture, oriental studies, modern history, economics, politics and law, among others, benefited from the demand for specialized teaching in what were originally classified as colonial aspects of the subject, and from the endowment or creation of specialized posts eventually absorbed into the general body of the University's academic staff.[39] It was also colonial studies which first exemplified the modern conception of the University as a research institute for government-funded research programmes and as a training ground for practical skills of a highly specialized kind. The creation of Rhodes House [plate 19.1] with its library and archive collection endowed Oxford with a superb resource, constantly expanded, for the study of American and imperial history. Rhodes House itself was home to a variety of academic activity, notably the perennial postgraduate seminar in Commonwealth history. All this is not to say that Oxford would have failed to become a world university (on our criteria) without the colonial connection. But it seems likely that the progress would have been slower and the range and character of research interests and teaching would have been different, and perhaps considerably narrower, than they have become.

There is something ironic about the fact that a colonial fortune and an imperialist's dream should have helped establish a powerful Oxonian bridgehead in the United States. Quite apart from the worldly success of former Rhodes scholars in their chosen careers and their rise to positions of

[37] Madden, 18.
[38] Symonds, *Oxford and Empire*, 287–8.
[39] Madden, 18.

influence, the Rhodes connection was a major stimulus to the rapid growth between the wars of funds that encouraged British students and academics to visit the United States; by the Second World War the number of American Rhodes scholars was exceeded by the number of British academic visitors in the United States.[40] In this sense the Rhodes bequest helped prime the pump of academic interchange—that vital feature of the modern international university. But Oxford in particular benefited from the ripple effects of the Rhodes scholarships, for the system of selection by state committees planted in every part of the United States well-connected lobbies whose function was to advertise Oxford's existence and extol its virtues. Had Rhodes conferred no other gift on the University, this by-product of his endowment of scholarships would deserve its gratitude.

The benefits of this subtle advertising campaign were soon felt. When Frank Aydelotte, the American Secretary to the Rhodes trustees, promoted a revised plan for selecting the scholars in 1924, among those whose support he obtained were the presidents of the major educational foundations, including the Rockefeller and Carnegie foundations.[41] The twentieth-century generosity of such foundations, outstandingly Rockefeller, must owe something to the high profile that Rhodes had given Oxford in Anglo-American academic relations. Indeed the Rockefeller Foundation tried without success to give money to Oxford in the mid-1920s in order to encourage the development of clinical medicine, but had found no university body with which it could negotiate effectively.[42] But without later Rockefeller contributions towards the New Bodleian Library, the development of social studies, the creation of an Institute of Experimental Psychology (1936) and the expansion of the Dyson Perrins Laboratory (1939), the University could scarcely have strengthened its academic resources, and hence its international reputation, in a range of important fields.[43] The same might be said in the post-war years of the Ford Foundation, whose munificence culminated in the 1950s and 1960s with the gift of a million dollars to the Historic Buildings appeal (1958) and $4,500,000 in 1966 towards establishing Wolfson College.[44] The University was also exceptionally fortunate in the generosity of individual Americans, especially those who had studied in Oxford. In 1938, at the time of the University's major appeal, some 48 per cent of the American undergraduates and 52 per cent of the postgraduate students had subscribed by the middle of the year, as against only 15 per cent of the British members of the University.[45]

[40] Aydelotte, *American Rhodes Scholarships*, 109.   [41] Ibid. 32.
[42] See above, 322.
[43] *Gazette* lxiii (1932/3), 21; lxvii (1936/7), 22, 23; lxx (1939/40), 53.
[44] *Gazette* lxxxix (1958/9), 132; xcvii (1966/7), 118.
[45] Brian Harrison, 'Campaign for Oxford III: a historical perspective', *American Oxonian* lxxvii (1990), 19–32.

It was perhaps between the wars that Oxford was, if ever, the 'imperial university par excellence'—the title claimed by the University Press in 1921.[46] There never developed in Oxford between the wars the critical academic attitude towards empire that was to be found particularly at the London School of Economics. By contrast, European influences in Oxford seemed much less assertive and certainly no match for their transatlantic and imperial counterparts. Nevertheless, Oxford remained, by necessity, a European university. Though modern languages remained an unfashionable school, its teaching was reorganized in 1926 and money found for the extension of the Taylor Institution.[47] The number of finalists grew steadily after 1920 [table 23.1].

TABLE 23.1

OXFORD FINALISTS IN MODERN LANGUAGES
AT FIVE-YEAR INTERVALS, 1920–1940

5 years ending	no. finalists	as % of all finalists
1920	72	9.1
1925	252	5.7
1930	382	7.9
1935	551	9.8
1940	599	11.2

Source: HUD.

In philosophy the growing intellectual pre-eminence of logical positivism was accelerated by A. J. Ayer's visit to Vienna as a newly appointed tutor and by the widely influential *Language, Truth and Logic* (1936) which emerged from his encounter with Viennese philosophy. A strong academic interest in contemporary Europe was sustained by Humphrey Sumner at Balliol, by A. J. P. Taylor at Magdalen from the late 1930s and by Alfred Zimmern as first Montague Burton Professor of International Relations (1930–44). In ancient history the most powerful work written in Oxford between the wars, *The Roman Revolution* (1939) by Ronald Syme (a New Zealander by birth), was deeply influenced by German classical studies and tacitly by the spectacle of Fascist politics in Germany and Italy. And of course throughout the 1930s, from the 'King and Country' debate in 1933 to the famous 'appeasement' by-election in 1938, public events in Europe, far more than those in the countries of the empire or the United States, claimed the attention of dons and students alike.

[46] *Some Account of the Oxford University Press 1468–1921* (Oxford 1922), 81.
[47] *OM* 26 May 1938, 667–9.

Nevertheless, Oxford's European influences could not compete with the growing band of experts in colonial studies, the inflow of students from the empire and the United States and the presence in the University of such talented Commonwealth recruits as Wheare, Hall, Florey, the neurosurgeon Hugh Cairns and Sir Robert Macintosh, the first professor of anaesthetics in Britain. There was as yet no institutional bridgehead of 'European studies' to match the role played by Rhodes House or even the Indian Institute. No squadron of European students came each year to rival the perennial incursion of Rhodes scholars. One reason was a lack of resources. No great philanthropist appeared on the scene filled with a missionary fervour to rejuvenate Oxford's ties with the academic world in Europe, to endow scholarships or fund fellowships. Perhaps this was merely fortuitous, but other circumstances made the coming of such a benefactor unlikely. Oxford could not stand in the same relation to the universities of Europe as it still stood to the universities of much of the Commonwealth and empire; here postgraduate studies were little developed, research opportunities few and academic careers in many fields hardly established. It was not surprising that to able Canadians, Australians, New Zealanders, South Africans, Indians, British West Indians and others, Oxford served as an academic training ground for advanced studies. With no barrier of language and a common academic culture, Oxford also readily became a stage in the academic career of undergraduate students from the countries of the empire and from the United States (where, of course, postgraduate facilities were abundant). There was far less reason for students from mainland Europe to beat a path to Oxford's door. Among the 1,110 postgraduate students admitted to the degree of DPhil in the first twenty-five years after its creation, 572 came from Britain, 259 from the countries of the empire, 169 from the United States and a mere 110 from all other overseas countries.[48]

The years after 1918 had seen not a new appreciation of the importance of Britain's relations with Europe but, if anything, a stronger sense than ever of the differences in law, literature, history and politics separating the offshore island from its mainland neighbours. At the political level the lesson drawn from Britain's experience before and during the First World War was the danger inherent in close ties with any European state. It was an unpropitious moment for a 'European Rhodes', eager to promote stronger academic links as the avenue to closer political co-operation. By the mid-1930s the European scene, both politically and academically, seemed darker than ever, and the scope for a more vital European academic presence in Oxford narrower still.

Paradoxically it was precisely the catastrophe which overwhelmed so many scholars and centres of scholarship in Europe after 1933 which

[48] *Gazette* lxxiv (1943/4), 43.

prompted the most important revival of continental academic influence in Oxford between the wars. Oxford became a haven for a small but brilliant group of physicists for whom Hitler's Germany had become dangerous or intolerable. There was nothing inevitable, however, in their choice of Oxford as a refuge. It was largely due to Frederick Lindemann, later Viscount Cherwell, who had come to Oxford as Dr Lee's Professor of Experimental Philosophy in 1919. Lindemann was perfectly equipped by background, training and temperament to be a fisher of foreign physicists. Born in Baden-Baden, he was brought up in Devon but educated mainly abroad. Before 1914 he had worked as a research student under the great German physicist Nernst in Berlin and had met Einstein. His own interests lay in the field of low-temperature physics, which he actively promoted in Oxford between the wars. During the First World War Lindemann made his reputation in a different sphere—as an aeronautic expert and test pilot at Farnborough. The importance of this phase lay chiefly in the wide contacts it gave him among industrial sponsors to whom he was to turn in the 1920s and 1930s. At Oxford Lindemann maintained his interest in German physics and kept in personal touch with its major figures, including Einstein who made several visits to Christ Church as Lindemann's guest. But Lindemann's major preoccupation was promoting the claims of the natural sciences in Oxford and reviving research in physics. Thus the disaster of Nazi rule was for him a heaven-sent opportunity to recruit some of the ablest talent in German physics with funds provided by his industrial sympathizers, especially by Imperial Chemical Industries. In this way Simon, Kurti, Mendelssohn and Kuhn came to Oxford as also, briefly and unhappily, did the Nobel prizewinner Erwin Schrödinger, considered to be Max Planck's successor as the genius of German physics.[49]

Lindemann's enterprise and the grim twist of European politics reinforced the existing strengths of Oxford science in chemistry, zoology, ecology and genetics at the very moment when the national importance of basic research in the universities was about to receive fuller public recognition than ever before. Oxford's claim to be a university with broad research interests in both the arts and sciences, sustained at the highest level even if with straitened resources, was strengthened. In a modest way an older tradition of intellectual borrowing from Europe had been vindicated. But on the eve of the Second World War it remained true that it was chiefly from the empire and Commonwealth that Oxford recruited its ablest overseas teachers and researchers. It was perhaps fitting that the scientific discovery of the widest human benefit made in Oxford between the wars and in the early part of the Second World War—Florey's clinical application of antibiotics—was made

[49] On Lindemann's role see R. F. Harrod, *The Prof* (London 1959); Smith, *The Prof in Two Worlds*; above, 160–1. For Schrödinger see W. Moore, *Schrödinger: Life and Thought* (Cambridge 1989) and Smith, 102–3.

by an Australian-born pathologist who had come to Oxford as a Rhodes scholar.[50] Moreover, despite the progress made since the strictures of the Asquith report in 1922 towards transforming Oxford into a world university, it remained obstinately underdeveloped in the scale of its scientific research and teaching, in the range of its interests, especially in social studies, and in its provision for postgraduate study.

Once again the impetus for change came not from within the University but from the shock of external events and the initiative of new sponsors. Like the First World War, the second was a vector of academic change, but on a more far-reaching scale and with different consequences. Together with its bitter aftermath, it enormously enhanced the prestige of specialized knowledge of Europe's recent history and contemporary politics, and sharply raised its value in the eyes of government. Strengthening Britain's academic expertise in a number of key geographical areas now became a priority. The Scarbrough inter-departmental commission, set up by the government at the end of the war, recommended the urgent reinforcement of oriental, African, Slavonic and east European studies, and new money became available to fund teaching posts at several universities.[51] In Oxford the call to new academic duty was given a particularly urgent note. In 1947 Llewellyn Woodward, then Montague Burton Professor of International Relations, sounded the alarm at the new advance of barbarism (the Soviet variety) and the decline of civilization as Oxford knew it.[52] Warning against the onset of barbarism had become something of a tradition among the Montague Burton professors.[53] With Oxonian confidence Woodward proposed to meet this global emergency with a minor academic innovation. Citing the 'excellent provision' for colonial studies in Oxford as an example of what could be done, he urged the creation of an institute for postgraduate work in international studies modelled on the Russian Institute at Columbia University in New York.[54] Woodward did not get his institute, but his own sideways shift into the newly created professorship of modern history was intended to reflect the greater importance now attached by the University to the study of Europe.

A more original conception which also reflected a new sensitivity to Britain's relations with the European mainland was the foundation of the Maison Française in 1946. This was both a cultural centre, supported by the French government and the University of Paris, and a part of Oxford, established by university decree.[55] Formally opened in June 1948, it was

---

[50] On Florey see above, 252–3.

[51] UGC University Development: Interim Report on the Years 1947 to 1951 (PP 1951–2 xviii Cmd 8473) 4, 13; Gazette lxxix (1948/9), 72.

[52] E. Ll. Woodward, Towards a New Learning (London 1947), 7, 12.

[53] Cf A. Zimmern, The Study of International Relations: An Inaugural Lecture (Oxford 1931), 19.

[54] Woodward, 14, 17.   [55] Gazette lxxv (1944/5), 75; OM 12 May 1967, 315–17.

designed as a window on French intellectual life and also perhaps as a symbol of the special relationship between Britain and France in wartime—a relationship which had acquired added significance in the post-war world and which, like the old imperial connection, required nurturing by closer academic contact. But undoubtedly the most important instrument for widening Oxford's post-war contacts with Europe and for promoting the academic study of other regions, a number of them outside the old imperial ambit, was the foundation of a new college on the Woodstock Road.

St Antony's exemplifies the idiosyncratic, almost fortuitous, way in which so many of the most important academic developments in twentieth-century Oxford have come about. The College owed its foundation to the generosity of Antonin Besse, a wealthy businessman based in Aden, then a British colony. Besse's personal charm is captured delightfully in Evelyn Waugh's early travel book *Remote People* (1931). His original intention had been to promote closer Anglo-French relations, and his first proposal envisaged both a new college and a programme to bring a considerable number of French students to study in Oxford in a scheme reminiscent of Rhodes's.[56] The actual outcome of Besse's negotiations with the University was rather different, but still something of a novelty in Oxford. The new College was established with a small number of official fellows whose interests lay chiefly in modern Europe. Thereafter it became the academic home for a growing band of specialists in Soviet, east European, African, middle eastern and far eastern history and politics, many of them recruited from outside Oxford. In 1953 the new Rhodes chair of race relations, a post founded with an eye to contemporary events in colonial Africa, was associated with the College. In the 1960s, when the British government decided that Britain's export opportunities in Latin America would be improved by promoting Latin American studies in British universities (a mystical calculation not easy for the layman to understand), St Antony's was the obvious base for the centre to be founded in Oxford, as it was more recently for the Nissan Institute devoted to Japanese studies.

By a curious irony the special emphasis on Anglo-French relations which had been Besse's original objective did not materialize, although research in French history has been active in the College. But if Besse, like many academic founders (not least Rhodes himself), did not see the realization of his original design, in its broader contribution to Oxford's academic development there can be no doubt of the signal importance of his foundation. For St Antony's rapidly became a major centre for the study of the contemporary world and supplied Oxford with the necessary institutional concentration on what had previously been comparatively neglected academic fields. It also represented—as did Nuffield College, founded in

[56] *Gazette* lxxix (1948/9), 72–3. See also below, 653.

1937—a successful adaptation of the college system to the modern University's need for a wider research base, specific provision for postgraduate education and (especially in St Antony's case) attention to the colossal post-war expansion in area-studies in higher education. But no less important was St Antony's role in bringing to Oxford considerable numbers of foreign students and creating for them a sympathetic, cosmopolitan environment where British postgraduate students could encounter unfamiliar histories and cultures through personal contact rather than academic study alone.[57] By the early 1960s some 70 per cent of students at St Antony's were from overseas, mainly from non-Commonwealth countries.[58] In this social function, in its promotion of a range of area-studies extending far beyond the pre-war academic interest in the colonial empire and India, and in its demonstration of the vitality and adaptability of the collegiate system to new needs, Besse's College has been perhaps more significant than any other single development in Oxford's adjustment to the contemporary international academic environment, certainly in the arts and social studies.

In recent years there has been some further reinforcement of the newer disciplines which have come to be so powerfully represented in the world's major universities. Between the wars Sir Alfred Zimmern pleaded for the establishment of a postgraduate school of government, so that Oxford men could 'civilise the barbarians' and tame 'the international economic forces which mould our material existence'.[59] But nothing had come of this, despite Zimmern's efforts to show how much interest there was in contemporary international affairs. It was in the 1970s, with the arrival of Hedley Bull as Montague Burton Professor, that Oxford eventually established itself as a major centre for the study of international relations attracting high-calibre postgraduate students from all over the world. In other fields too—geography, for example—the post-war years brought significant expansion, though the proportion of oriental studies students remained small, and modern languages, after a burst of expansion between 1940 and 1965, seemed to lose momentum [table 23.2].

In terms of scale, however, it is the rapid growth in the sciences in Oxford since 1945 which has made the greatest impact on the overall shape of the University and its academic relations with the rest of the world. The Second World War was a watershed: it marked the onset of a period of more than thirty years in which public support of scientific research at British universities was recognized as a major priority of the government and indispensable to Britain's survival as a great power. Government funding of Oxford science increased rapidly. The growth in student numbers that followed at last improved the balance between the arts and social studies on

[57] *Isis* 12 June 1963, 10.
[58] HUD.
[59] Zimmern, *International Relations*, 19.

TABLE 23.2

OXFORD FINALISTS IN GEOGRAPHY,
MODERN LANGUAGES AND ORIENTAL
STUDIES AT FIVE-YEAR INTERVALS,
1945–1990

5 years ending	no. finalists			as % of all finalists		
	G	ML	OS	G	ML	OS
1945	102	738	5	3.4	24.5	0.2
1950	204	869	42	2.6	11.0	0.5
1955	259	1040	28	2.9	11.7	0.3
1960	347	1136	47	3.5	11.6	0.5
1965	351	1112	95	3.2	10.2	0.9
1970	355	1178	114	3.1	10.2	1.0
1975	338	1030	131	2.8	8.6	1.1
1980	451	1025	109	3.4	7.7	0.8
1985	427	1128	114	3.0	8.0	0.8
1990	449	1084	140	3.2	7.6	1.0

Source: HUD.

the one hand and the natural sciences on the other. By 1989 there were in Oxford five times as many postgraduate students in science as there had been in the later 1940s. Among these, postgraduate students from overseas have been an expanding group, making up by 1989 one-third of the total. This took place despite Oxford's reluctance to expand as much in the applied sciences and technology, both of which are major recruiting grounds for foreign students (especially from third-world countries) in other British universities [table 23.3]. All this reinforced the huge diversification in academic interests after 1945 and multiplied the University's overseas academic links to an extent unimaginable before 1939. The growth of new disciplines, subject-areas and academic links pulled Oxford, like Britain itself, towards Europe. Once again, however, it is worth noticing the accidental nature of this expansion, which in so many ways was a product not only of the kind of war Britain had embarked upon in 1939 but of its unexpected outcome and consequences. If founders and sponsors find that their creations soon take on a life of their own, how much more do universities find themselves merely a fly on the wheel of government and its often short-lived preoccupations.

Along with the great post-war change in the balance of disciplines and the external orientation of the University, there came an important shift in its social character in relation to students from overseas [figures 23.1 asnd 23.2]. The number of overseas students as a proportion of the total student

TABLE 23.3

OVERSEAS STUDENTS AT OXFORD IN SELECTED YEARS, 1923–1964

selected years	total students	overseas students	overseas as % of total
1923	4,163	603	14.5
1925	4,353	533	12.2
1930	4,658	539	11.6
1935	4,848	536	11.1
1938	5,023	562	11.2
1946	6,680	573	8.6
1950	7,207	736	10.2
1955	7,346	914	12.4
1960	8,975	965	10.7
1964	9,450	1,167	12.3

Source: HUD.

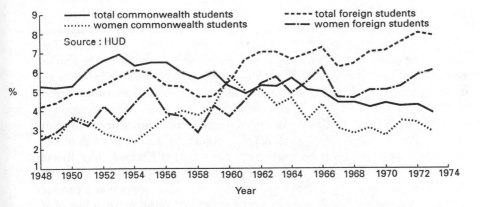

FIGURE 23.1   COUNTRY OF RESIDENCE OF JUNIOR MEMBERS, 1948–1973: PERCENTAGE OF TOTAL, AND OF WOMEN, FROM COMMONWEALTH AND FOREIGN COUNTRIES

population of the University seems to have remained roughly constant from the early years of this century up until the mid-1960s [table 23.3]. However, between 1945 and the early 1960s the proportion of women students from overseas rose significantly, and certain colleges, notably the graduate colleges, showed a strikingly high percentage of overseas students. By

TABLE 23.4

OXFORD'S JUNIOR MEMBERS WHOSE HOME RESIDENCE IS LISTED AS COMMONWEALTH OR FOREIGN: PERCENTAGE OF EACH COLLEGE'S TOTAL JUNIOR MEMBERS AT THREE-YEAR INTERVALS, 1947–1966

College/hall	Commonwealth						foreign					
	3 years beginning Michaelmas term						3 years beginning Michaelmas term					
	1947	1950	1953	1956	1959	1962*	1947	1950	1953	1956	1959	1962*
Balliol	8.6	11.5	11.6	9.3	8.8	9.9	6.0	9.8	6.3	5.6	5.6	10.7
Brasenose	4.1	7.3	8.9	6.2	3.6	5.6	4.2	4.3	4.2	4.6	4.5	4.8
Campion Hall	6.7	11.1	13.7	18.5	16.4	11.5	4.3	45.5	41.1	37.0	16.4	26.9
Christ Church	4.9	5.6	6.1	5.9	3.0	4.3	3.9	5.5	9.1	6.7	4.6	5.9
Corpus Christi	3.6	6.8	5.9	5.5	6.1	4.1	2.4	3.6	6.2	5.7	3.5	5.1
Exeter	8.2	7.9	6.0	5.1	3.6	3.2	5.0	6.7	5.2	3.5	5.6	4.0
Greyfriars					26.0	12.1					32.0	8.6
Hertford	1.9	1.6	0.8	1.2	1.1	2.8	1.3	2.3	3.1	1.6	1.1	5.6
Jesus	3.2	3.1	2.9	3.4	2.2	3.7	3.4	2.9	3.3	3.7	3.4	3.5
Keble	4.5	1.4	3.0	3.0	2.8	2.1	1.8	0.9	0.9	2.3	3.3	2.8
Linacre (M)					25.2	10.9					34.3	47.1
Lincoln	7.4	12.3	11.0	8.0	11.9	6.5	4.4	6.0	5.1	3.8	6.3	8.6
Magdalen	7.4	9.2	9.5	7.4	7.9	5.6	3.7	5.7	8.9	6.9	6.0	8.2
Mansfield				7.4	5.2	2.8				14.0	20.1	20.6
Merton	4.8	4.3	5.7	5.9	4.0	5.5	5.0	7.0	4.6	5.9	6.4	7.9
New College	3.4	5.1	14.2	5.6	5.9	4.2	3.8	5.2	2.5	6.1	4.0	6.5
Nuffield (M)					39.1	15.2					23.7	23.2

St Antony's (M)												
St Benet's Hall	6.9	6.5	16.4	9.0	3.7	4.3	13.8	13.0	8.2	10.4	11.1	18.6
St Catherine's	8.4	8.2	6.5	11.0	10.2	3.7	9.4	11.4	15.6	11.2	10.3	6.0
St Edmund Hall	2.4	2.3	2.8	5.0	3.1	3.8	2.8	3.3	2.8	2.2	3.2	5.0
St John's	7.1	5.2	5.2	3.1	3.6	5.2	3.0	3.8	5.0	1.7	5.5	4.6
St Peter's	6.8	4.7	3.8	6.0	2.9	3.8	3.9	2.6	2.1	2.7	3.0	2.9
Trinity	7.8	10.3	10.1	6.3	6.2	5.8	1.7	2.8	4.1	3.6	8.4	7.9
University	9.7	10.2	10.4	8.2	5.9	8.3	2.6	3.6	4.8	3.8	5.2	6.5
Wadham	6.4	7.5	8.9	6.4	5.6	3.1	4.3	6.4	5.8	3.2	5.4	8.0
Worcester	4.5	4.6	2.7	2.0	4.7	3.9	1.6	3.2	4.0	3.6	4.3	7.2
males	**5.8**	**6.6**	**7.3**	**6.2**	**5.2**	**5.3**	**4.1**	**5.3**	**6.2**	**5.2**	**5.6**	**7.4**
Lady Margaret Hall	2.4	3.4	3.3	7.2	6.5	5.1	2.4	5.1	4.1	3.1	4.2	6.3
Linacre (F)						10.9						14.1
Nuffield (F)					—	18.2					14.3	27.3
Somerville	2.3	4.2	2.7	4.0	4.6	6.2	3.1	3.5	4.5	4.6	4.9	5.0
St Anne's	1.7	2.8	3.0	3.0	6.1	3.0	2.3	3.2	4.6	3.4	4.8	3.6
St Antony's (F)						6.7						20.0
St Hilda's	3.3	3.9	1.9	2.6	3.6	3.9	2.8	3.7	5.1	4.0	3.8	4.8
St Hugh's	3.6	2.2	1.9	2.0	3.8	1.9	1.5	2.9	3.4	1.8	2.6	3.6
females	**2.5**	**3.3**	**2.6**	**3.8**	**5.0**	**4.3**	**2.4**	**3.7**	**4.4**	**3.4**	**4.2**	**5.7**

*Figures for the academic years 1963/4 and 1964/5 are missing: this figure aggregates figures for the years 1962/3, 1965/6 and 1966/7.

Source: HUD.

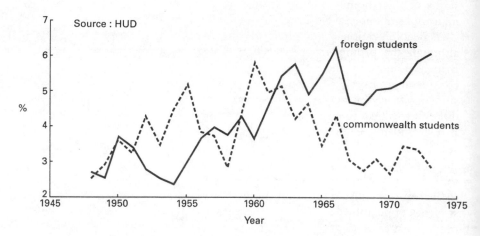

FIGURE 23.2   COUNTRY OF RESIDENCE OF WOMEN JUNIOR MEMBERS, 1948–1973:
PERCENTAGE OF WOMEN FROM COMMONWEALTH AND FOREIGN COUNTRIES

contrast in some others—Hertford, St Edmund Hall, Keble, Worcester and
the women's colleges—they were few and far between [table 23.4].

Between the wars most overseas students in Oxford, whether from
Commonwealth or foreign countries, were white. In the competitive, not to
say narcissistic, jungle of undergraduate social life a sense of social isolation
was easily felt—by Afro-Asian and Caribbean students especially. English
social attitudes were frequently interpreted as indifference shading into
hostility. G. K. Chettur, who looked back fondly from Mangalore to his
undergraduate years in Oxford and to his elegant rooms in New College,
also remembered his sense of outrage at the crude and contemptuous
portrayal of his fellow-countrymen in a play seen in the town.[60] S. W. R. D.
Bandaranaike, a future premier of Sri Lanka, and a very self-confident young
politician who revelled in the opportunity for debate at the Union, noted
that Indians in Oxford tended to cling together, while among English
students he detected an 'intense race-consciousness' and a reserve which
made social relations very difficult.[61] Another premier-to-be, Eric Williams
from Trinidad, ascribed his failure to be elected a fellow of All Souls to racial
prejudice—an explanation which, if nothing else, surely exaggerated the
predictability of that intriguing ritual.[62] Altogether it seems likely that the
social status and sense of social acceptance felt by students from Africa, Asia
and the Caribbean in some measure reflected the political and constitutional

[60] G. K. Chettur, The Last Enchantment: Recollections of Oxford (Mangalore 1934), 160,
192.
[61] S. W. R. D. Bandaranaike, 'Memoirs of Oxford' in his Speeches and Writings (Colombo
1963), 16.   [62] E. Williams, Inward Hunger (London 1969), 46.

status of their home country: to be a colonial was to feel inferior in the metropolis of imperial culture.

As decolonization spread after 1945 the delicacy of social relations eased, although the prominence of racial issues in international and domestic British politics in the 1960s and 1970s probably delayed the process considerably. Even in the mid-1960s there was still evidence that foreign students from Europe as well as non-western countries found Oxford difficult to adjust to—though the same observation could be made of many British students. Climate, food, rooms, the difficulty of meeting the opposite sex, the social dislocation of the end of term, as well as racial prejudice and the English 'shell', all figured in the survey reported in *Isis* in 1963.[63] From the early 1960s, however, the size of the overseas student community began to increase not just in absolute terms but as a proportion of the overall student population of the University. At the same time the long predominance of students from the empire and Commonwealth among the overseas contingent at last came to an end [table 23.5].

By 1989/90 overseas students made up nearly 18 per cent of the total. Increasingly, too, overseas students have tended to be predominantly postgraduate students: by 1989/90 they accounted for 40 per cent of the University's postgraduate students, reflecting Oxford's success in (and dependence on) an international 'market' for research students. The effect of this growth, together with the reduced numbers of and opportunities for British postgraduate students, has been to turn postgraduate work in many fields almost into a preserve of overseas students. At the same time the sense of social isolation still felt in the 1960s has probably diminished considerably. The establishment of more graduate colleges with a cosmopolitan atmosphere, the provision of more college accommodation for postgraduate students, the extension of self-catering, the higher proportion of overseas students enjoying the more permanent and stable society of postgraduate rather than undergraduate life and their effective 'colonization' of many subject-areas have transformed the old status of overseas students as peripheral members of an overwhelmingly home-grown University population. In the postgraduate field at least, it is British students who are likely to envy the prosperity, optimism and prospects of their overseas peers, and not the other way round. In that sense, Oxford has become a world university with a vengeance.

So far the focus of this chapter has been upon some of the ways in which Oxford has responded to the stimulus of outside influences and to the growing internationalization of higher education. It remains to examine briefly Oxford's status as a world university from the opposite point of view: Oxford's influence on the world outside the United Kingdom. It might be

[63] S. Fisher, 'The overseas student in Oxford', *Isis* 12 June 1963, 6–12.

TABLE 23.5

COUNTRY OF ORIGIN OF OXFORD'S OVERSEAS STUDENTS FOR EACH
ACADEMIC YEAR, 1973–1990

	1973/4	1974/5	1975/6	1976/7	1977/8	1978/9	1979/80	1980/1	1981/2
USA	440	464	487	477	491	478	466	437	383
Canada	149	145	134	143	163	161	145	151	140
Australia	99	110	124	109	113	117	124	106	89
South Africa	53	61	63	55	54	44	53	43	48
India	51	44	46	36	38	41	46	41	41
West Germany	26	39	43	38	44	47	49	47	42
Greece	?	?	30	29	21	28	32	31	?
Japan	26	30	27	28	27	36	30	35	30
New Zealand	31	29	30	32	33	28	28	39	37
Singapore	15	25	30	?	?	?	?	?	?
Italy	17	22	28	?	?	?	?	?	?
Iran	?	?	30	29	29	25	?	?	?
Hong Kong	?	?	?	?	19	25	38	42	50
Mexico	?	?	?	?	?	24	26	28	30
Brazil	?	?	?	?	?	?	?	?	29
others	397	467	365	464	477	408	414	417	384
overseas	1,304	1,436	1,437	1,440	1,509	1,462	1,451	1,417	1,303
all students	11,260	11,408	11,547	11,783	12,184	12,243	12,354	12,310	12,313

	1982/3	1983/4	1984/5	1985/6	1986/7	1987/8	1988/9	1989/90
USA	388	513	573	619	669	651	605	613
Canada	139	155	165	177	220	212	187	173
Australia	93	96	111	115	119	120	113	136
South Africa	52	64	65	65	56	73	66	63
India	38	43	46	58	63	70	72	81
West Germany	53	70	75	83	94	116	132	153
Greece	36	39	42	46	53	46	48	48
Japan	34	34	43	35	?	39	47	63
New Zealand	43	42	32	?	?	36	35	37
Singapore	30	41	50	58	69	81	74	69
Italy	?	?	33	41	?	42	46	58
Iran	?	?	?	?	?	?	?	?
Hong Kong	55	50	69	83	101	111	122	96
Mexico	?	?	?	?	?	?	?	?
Brazil	36	35	40	37	40	34	32	34
China	?	?	?	?	35	55	83	80
South Korea	?	?	?	?	?	27	32	?
France	?	?	?	?	?	36	43	41
Eire	?	?	?	?	?	23	37	51
Belgium	?	?	?	?	?	20	24	23
Spain	?	?	?	?	?	20	23	28
Netherlands	?	?	?	?	?	15	18	27
Denmark	?	?	?	?	?	6	13	19
Portugal	?	?	?	?	?	7	10	13
Luxembourg	?	?	?	?	?	0	3	4
Malaysia	?	?	?	?	?	?	43	48
others	383	400	462	536	648	465	459	517
overseas	1,380	1,582	1,806	1,953	2,167	2,305	2,367	2,475
all students	12,322	12,527	12,671	12,915	13,260	13,498	13,618	13,948

Source: Gazette.

supposed that a definable overseas impact was a necessary characteristic of a world university, but this rather simple notion has to be handled with caution.

The most important influence which any university can exert is through the diaspora of those who have passed through its faculties or colleges and experienced both the formal and informal side of its academic life. It is difficult to measure such influence, but the number and quality of overseas applicants reveal the continuing attractiveness of what Oxford is thought to offer its students. To Rhodes and his followers, Oxford was to be the place where a thousand secular missionaries were fired with enthusiasm for the unity of the English-speaking world. Nor was it entirely implausible to see Oxford's fame as a university resting in part on the loyalty of old members subsequently occupying positions of power and influence in every English-speaking country—though by no means every overseas student went home, like Bandaranaike, to be welcomed by a procession of elephants, loyal addresses from deferential villagers, a Boy Scout march-past and a fireworks display.[64] After the Second World War, however, doubts began to creep in about the beneficence and durability of Oxford's influence on the political ethos of the countries of the empire. 'I have tried my best, in a small way, by bringing young men from India and training them in our centres', Ernest Bevin told the Labour Party conference in 1945, explaining how Britain was assisting Indian economic development. But, he went on, 'many of the young men who came to Oxford and Cambridge and learned our bad habits, have not proved very helpful to us when they returned'.[65] By the later 1950s Harold Macmillan was gloomily predicting 'the collapse of the agreeable, educated, North Oxford society to whom we have transferred power, in the face of the dynamism of Communism'.[66] Civilization could no longer be defended by a thin blue line—or by a thin line of blues. In more recent times Cecil Rhodes's notion of a great international freemasonry of Oxford graduates exerting a direct influence in world affairs has been overshadowed even more by the enormous expansion in the educational opportunities for citizens of Commonwealth and third-world countries in western Europe and the United States. Nor was it to be expected that those like Bandaranaike—for whom a major part of Oxford's appeal lay in the chance to rub shoulders (and cross swords) with the rulers of the empire, present and future—would feel the same magnetic attraction to Oxford once that empire had passed away. Oxford's influence in the post-colonial world is better judged as part of the wider, and necessarily diffuse, impact of what is still a prestigious national culture enjoying the benefits of a universal language.

[64] Bandaranaike, 'Memoirs of Oxford', 81–2.
[65] *Report of 44th Annual Conference 1945* (Labour Party, London 1945), 118; I owe this reference to Nicholas Owen.
[66] H. Macmillan, *Riding the Storm 1956–59* (London 1971), 395.

Is so cautious a verdict justified if the focus is narrowed to the world of higher education? How much influence has Oxford exerted over the development of universities in the countries of the former British empire? At one level it was considerable. New universities in colonial and Common-wealth countries drew their academic staffs in part from graduates trained in British universities. In certain subjects, notably in history, Oxford was particularly important as a nursery for those who would return to promote the historical study of new nations. There developed in Oxford between the wars, under the influence of Douglas Veale, a commitment to promoting higher education in the colonial territories. The extramural delegacy played an active part in setting up a university system in west Africa. In 1940 an Oxford advisory committee was established to assist Makerere College in Uganda in curricular and administrative questions and to arrange for academic visitors.[67] In fact this special relationship did not last long, and the committee's functions were soon passed over to the Inter-University Council in Britain, where Veale again played a prominent role. There was also the work of Christopher Cox of New College, educational adviser to the Colonial Office between 1940 and 1961, with the task of translating into reality the recommendations of the Asquith Commission (1943–4) for an expansion of colonial higher education. Thus to some extent institutionally, but more through the work of individuals, Oxford played a role in the post-war expansion of universities overseas.

For several reasons, however, Oxford's peculiar model could not be widely replicated abroad, although many institutions, not least in the United States, found aspects of the collegiate system attractive. From as far back as the later nineteenth century, colonial universities had found affiliation with London University more appropriate to their need for a federal degree-granting body that would allow them wide local autonomy. Moreover, of all types of university, the residential and collegiate model of Oxford and Cambridge was the hardest to re-create in colonial societies where patronage tended to be intensely local, where state regulation followed state funding, where resources were limited and where the hiring of professors and their assistants came far more naturally than the establishment of self-governing corporations of teachers in the Oxbridge manner.

It may now be possible to answer the question set out at the beginning of this chapter. At the outset of the period Oxford was undoubtedly a university of global reputation which enjoyed, if only by default, the prestige of being, with Cambridge, the principal seat of learning in England. It attracted overseas students, even if their absolute number was small, and in several branches of scholarship its academic staff was of great and

[67] M. Macpherson, *They Built for the Future: A Chronicle of Makerere University College 1922–1962* (Cambridge 1964), 36.

recognized distinction. Yet, judged by the criteria of the modern international university, Oxford was also curiously underdeveloped and almost parochial. The sciences and the study of the modern world were marginal to its main academic interests; postgraduate education had hardly begun.

What has occurred since 1914 has been a remarkable transformation in an institution whose conservatism was the despair of such ruthless proconsuls as Milner and Curzon. Oxford is now a world university in the range of its academic interests, its accessibility (in all senses) to overseas students and in its ability to attract overseas scholars of the first rank—at least for a time. But the path of change has been idiosyncratic and fortuitous to a degree: unexpected (even resented) bequests; unfulfilled expectations; unintended academic consequences; the accidents of personality and war. The overwhelming importance of external stimulus, whether private philanthropy or government initiative, is very striking and suggests the close limits set to internal initiative in this period. Equally notable has been the resilience of the University's old structure, its collegiate system and decentralized and unbureaucratic government. Despite the huge expansion of interests and a major expansion in numbers, Oxford has preserved the tradition of close personal contact between teacher and taught, although the full implications of becoming to such a great extent a university of postgraduate students are only now being confronted. But whether by accident or design, and despite the speed with which some of the changes described in this chapter have come about, Oxford has escaped being taken over by new institutions or new money (a common enough fate in higher education) and has largely preserved the ideal of a balanced, non-specialized academic community that was originally set out in its development plan more than fifty years ago.[68]

[68] *A Programme of Development* (Oxford University 1938).

PART SIX

THE STRUCTURE OF THE UNIVERSITY, 1914–1970

24

Finance Since 1914

J. P. D. DUNBABIN

Before the First World War, finance was at the heart of Oxford politics, Chancellor Curzon seeing in it 'the clue to the majority of University problems, and the condition of the majority of University reforms'.[1] 1912 brought perhaps the most ambitious change ever implemented in the way the University conducts its financial business, the creation of a Board of Finance charged with: preparing comprehensive, and comprehensible, combined accounts for the university and the colleges; making recommendations for more efficient administration in both, and for the 'suitable disposal of surplus income' accruing to university institutions; considering contributions by colleges for university purposes—which might well involve proposing schemes for the diversion to university purposes of the richer colleges' 'surplus revenues'.[2]

The Board of Finance first sought central control over departmental funds. In 1913 it secured legal opinion that the university could, by altering the statutes governing any delegacy, 'determine how its surplus income and investments shall be applied'; it then pressed for action. So in March 1915 the various delegacies were asked for their reactions to a draft statute empowering Council to appropriate any funds not needed for their day-to-day working.[3] They duly submitted thirty-five pages of forthright observations. The general view was that 'as the experience of a now discarded financial system at the British Museum notoriously proved, the liability of departments to repay their balances into general funds directly encourages wasteful expenditure'. Prospective benefactors would be deterred by the knowledge that their gifts might be diverted to other purposes. University taxation of the colleges had already led to funds being established in the hands of external trustees, and 'an unpopular extension of control over the funds of the Delegacies may lead to similar organizations'. 'There will be societies of Friends of the Bodleian or the Ashmolean, just as there are of the

---

[1] G. N. Curzon, Lord Curzon of Kedleston, *Principles and Methods of University Reform* (Oxford 1909), 171.
[2] *Gazette* xlii (1911/12), 498–9 (6 Mar. 1912).
[3] HCP 100 (1915), 195–8.

Louvre and the National Gallery.' The local examination delegacy contended that were it thus fleeced, Oxford's influence 'in the Secondary Schools . . . will disappear', the delegates of the Press that the change would compromise defence of its copyright privileges and damage its financial credit. But there were hints that if the proposal were not pressed, some delegacies would voluntarily contribute what would certainly otherwise prove very difficult to extract from them. Unsurprisingly, Council decided that the draft statute presented real problems (especially for the Press) and that it would be much wiser to accept 'the sums which have been offered by certain Delegacies in the present emergency . . . without prejudice to the question of introducing [the statute] at a later date'.[4]

The failure of this attempt to establish 'rational' central financial control left Oxford highly decentralized, not only in respect of the well-known cleavage between university and colleges, but also within the university sector itself. University posts and departments have continued to be very unequally funded. Some are better endowed than others (during the 1980s, posts whose endowments covered at least 80 per cent of their costs escaped the general freezes) and some are more successful in raising external finance. Such departmental autonomy shows up in the published university accounts (those for 1953/4 run to 425 pages) and the aggregation of the departmental figures into a single consolidated account is a somewhat artificial exercise.[5] Departmental independence also has implications for university politics. As the Secretary of Faculties explained in 1955, the General Board's power was mostly 'shown in selection not initiation', in deciding 'what new posts shall be established' and 'what departments, if any, shall receive larger grants'; 'examples of proposals emanating from Council or the General Board are rare and it is usually found that they run into difficulty at the faculty board level'.[6]

After failing with the delegacies in the spring of 1915, the Board of Finance proceeded to tackle the colleges on the form of their accounts. This had, in general terms, been laid down by the Selborne Commission in 1881. But the Board established that colleges' interpretations of the requirements differed. It then submitted a schedule of the differences and asked for legislation to secure clarity and uniformity. In due course a watered-down

[4] HCP 101 (1915), pp. lv, 55 ff, 131–2, 175, 191. The issue threatened to revive in 1931 as a result of the Owen case, on which see above, 146 and below, 690. For the science professors saw, in the precautions the University then wished to take, the thin end of a wedge that might eventually deprive the head of a department of 'the power of disposing as he thinks proper of funds voted to him by Convocation': HCP 150 (1931), 48. It took over a year to work out a compromise which, though it involved funnelling all receipts through the University Chest, preserved both operational departmental banking accounts and full departmental control over surplus funds deposited with the Chest.
[5] Cf Abstracts of the Accounts of the Curators of the University Chest and of University Institutions and Departments for the Year ended 31 July 1954 (University of Oxford 1955).
[6] K. C. Turpin, 'University government: the General Board', Oxford May 1955, 90, 92.

amending statute was sent to Congregation in 1917. But the Board's chief enemy, President Case of Corpus, weighed in with a hostile letter which so shook Council that it decided instead to seek legal advice. This effectively confirmed Case's view that the original statute could not be altered without each college's consent, so Council dropped the question.[7] This second defeat cannot have done the Board of Finance's prestige any good, and in 1919–20 the Vice-Chancellor successfully moved to transfer its functions to the curators of the University Chest. These acquired a formidable position in relation to new university expenditure. But though they theoretically retained supervisory powers over the expenditure both of delegacies and of colleges, they were less anxious than the Board of Finance to use them.

As far as the colleges were concerned, the Asquith Commission greatly reduced the university's incentive to interfere. This had formerly lain in the fact that the colleges represented a possible source of new university income. The Selborne Commission, unsure as to future trends in the revenues of the colleges, had imposed on them not only a system of graduated taxation but also provisions empowering their Visitors to direct the application to university purposes of revenue which was surplus to their own reasonable requirements.[8] Only in Magdalen was there in fact any question of this. But Curzon had observed that most (though not all) colleges were now a good deal richer than in 1882 and suggested that a case could be made for greater contributions by the colleges. In 1913 the university may indeed have begun the process of pushing for them, by circulating to colleges legal opinions on questions relating to surplus revenues.[9] After the war, reformers suggested to the Asquith Commission that the university should supervise college finances and appropriate any surplus income. But this was rejected: 'the Colleges would no longer be independent bodies administering their own funds . . . with a full sense of responsibility and complete freedom of initiative, but would become dependent bodies executing the policy of the University . . . such a change would impair the vigour of College life and hamper educational development . . . the strength of the two Universities is very largely due to the existence of a number of independent Colleges acting in wholesome competition with one another, and we are convinced that it would be a grave mistake to subject them to final control by the Universities

---

[7] HCP 102 (1915), 111–24; 104 (1916), 109; 105 (1916), 9; 106 (1917), pp. xl, lxviii, lxxvii, cxi, 43 ff, 231–2, 241; 107 (1917), 247–50; 108 (1917), pp. xxiii, lxvii, 89. Cf [Lord Selborne, chairman] *University of Oxford Commission* (PP 1881 lvi C 2868). The accounting practice the draft statute sought to enforce had not been the first choice of the auditors consulted. It was, however, implemented in the 1920s as part of the reform of the Common University Fund taxation system.

[8] M. Bernard, *A Letter to the Right Hon. W. E. Gladstone on the Statutes of the University of Oxford Commission* (London 1882), 13, 43.

[9] Curzon, *University Reform*, 150–3; HCP 94 (1913), pp. xii, xiii, xxxvii [circulation of Sir John Simon's opinion of 1909, ibid. 84 (1909), 49–52]; 96 (1913), 23; Vice-Chancellor Heberden's letter of 2 Dec. 1912 to colleges, copy in Bodl. GA Oxon. c. 153.

and to deprive them of the power of initiating new policy.' Indeed, the Commission found that the colleges were already making 'the full contribution [to the university] that they can properly be asked to make out of their revenues'; instead of requiring more, it eased the university's position by recommending a state grant.[10] So the direct university interest in college finances was effectively reduced to ensuring the smooth operation of the system of taxing the colleges by means of the Common University Fund (CUF).

The Commission led to minor reforms of the CUF designed to smooth fluctuations, readjust the burden as between colleges, and slightly increase total receipts. The first year of operation (in respect of college accounts for 1927) produced a largely adventitious fall of £22,000, and by 1929 it looked as if there would be a permanent decline of £7,500 per annum. This was particularly awkward since it seemed likely to compromise the University's bid for an increase in its annual grant from the government (from £85,500 to the £110,000 recommended by the Asquith Commission). Early in 1930 the committee of estates bursars voted for an *ex gratia* payment by the colleges in respect of the 1927 shortfall, but felt it too soon to embark on another revision of CUF taxation. Instead it offered to explain the financial relations between colleges and the university to the University Grants Committee (UGC). Officially the UGC's chairman would consider representations only from the university; unofficially he suggested that the system be considered by a tripartite committee representing the University Chest, the colleges and the Treasury. It is a measure of the concern felt, and of official goodwill towards Oxford, that the Permanent Secretary of the Treasury, Sir Warren Fisher, decided to chair it himself. And 'on the assumption that the report of this committee will be followed by [early and] effective action', the UGC and the Treasury agreed to increase Oxford's government grant to £97,500. The committee in fact estimated the annual shortfall at only some £4,000–5,000, and recommended changes to meet it. Implementation was complicated by the insistence of Queen's and Magdalen on securing relief from anomalous university obligations placed on them by nineteenth-century reforms. But agreement was finally reached by the end of the year.[11]

In one direction, however, the Asquith Commission did extend supervision by the university. It was shocked by what it took to be the incompetent catering of Oxford's colleges; accordingly the curators of the Chest acquired the obligation to supervise a triennial inspection, with reports on individual colleges. After the first such exercise in 1929, the auditors agreed that the

[10] *Asquith Report*, 200, 215. The colleges of the University of London are chiefly funded (by the University Grants Committee) through the university; its recent imposition of several relocations and mergers of colleges shows that the source and independence of college incomes can be important.

[11] HCP 144 (1929), 141–53; 145 (1930), 151–3, 210–12 (index); 146 (1930), 193–4 (index); 147 (1930), 5–16, 198–9.

Asquith panacea, centralized college purchasing, was impracticable; they did, however, note that the prices paid by colleges varied considerably and recommended weekly reports to be analysed by the domestic bursars' committee. The committee instead proposed termly reports. It also lobbied for much longer intervals between inspections, which were therefore made quinquennial. Inspection was conducted in 1934 and 1939, but then fell into abeyance. In 1950 the domestic bursars' committee sought its abolition, declaring robustly that 'no useful purpose has been served by this inspection since its commencement' and that it generated much extra work. Council was more impressed by testimony that the Cambridge stewards' committee had found the reintroduction of a similar system to be worthwhile. So abolition did not come till 1963.[12] Shortly thereafter the question engaged the attention of the Franks Commission, since college charges were so much higher than board and lodging charges in other universities' halls of residence.[13] The Commission doubted whether any clear judgements were possible, given 'that colleges' educational, social, and housekeeping functions are organically related and hence that there is a large element of what economists call joint costs'. It looked therefore to the reform of college accounts as a prerequisite for making 'any useful comparisons'. It also sought to make colleges 'much more collectively self-conscious about the need for economy in domestic matters', but through self-discipline, not control by the university. 'In the past the Domestic Bursars' Committee has been little more than a post office for the clearing of information between colleges. In the future we recommend that it should actively concern itself with ensuring that colleges are run efficiently and with due regard for economy, and that it should make an annual report on these matters to the [proposed] Council of the Colleges.'[14]

But to revert to the 1920s, perhaps the most important feature of university–college relations was that, in contrast to Cambridge, Oxford's colleges continued to charge tuition-fees. Colleges had traditionally levied these in both universities. If their undergraduates needed to use university laboratories (or departmental facilities in what were then minor arts subjects), colleges had then paid these the appropriate fees; and in Cambridge payments were sometimes made to individual lecturers holding university posts. The colleges also mounted free inter-collegiate lectures, given by their fellows. These were more extensive at Oxford, where in 1920 they encompassed all disciplines other than science, modern languages and English, whereas in Cambridge they survived only for divinity and classics.

---

[12] *Asquith Report*, apps 9 and 10; HCP 144 (1929), 77–89, 166 (index); 145 (1930), 210 (index); 160 (1935), 165–70; 161 (1935), 125–6; 174 (1939), pp. xli, 36; 207 (1950), 43, 152, 210–12; 221 (1955), 185–93; 246 (1963), 229–30, 684 (index).
[13] Board and lodging in Bristol, Durham and Manchester ranged from £140 to £172 per annum, whereas in Oxford average 'receipts for students living in' were apparently £280.
[14] *Franks Report* i, paras 369–91.

The Asquith Commission found that 'at Oxford the balance of opinion is clearly in favour of retaining the system', and suggested little change. But at Cambridge it recommended 'that in all subjects alike the formal teaching should be placed on a Faculty basis, and that all fees paid for such teaching should go no longer to the Colleges or to the individual lecturers but to the Faculty Funds'.[15] At Cambridge such fees amounted to 18.9 per cent of the income the University declared to the UGC in 1925/6, but in the next year, after the change took effect, to 26.8 per cent. The comparable Oxford figures were 6.9 per cent and 6.7 per cent. Over time, Oxford University came to charge the same tuition-fees as other British universities.[16] But colleges, which remain the primary source of undergraduate teaching, continued to collect fees; and these have recently become an increasingly important part of their income.

The Asquith Commission broke new ground in recommending permanent state aid to Oxford and Cambridge, but only as 'the minimum necessary to prevent immediate decline'. For future growth it looked to private benefaction: 'here lies the real hope of prosperity and development for the Universities'.[17] The UGC initially shared this view and left British universities 'to rely for their capital transactions almost entirely on accumulated savings and the liberality of private benefactors'. After the Second World War 'an entirely new situation presented itself' as a result of 'the growing needs of the universities and the drying up of many sources of private benefaction'. So in 1947 the UGC persuaded the Treasury that 'by far the greater part' of the universities' capital needs 'would have to be found, if at all, from the Exchequer'. Up to that date, though, UGC statistics give some indication of the seriousness with which Oxford took the Asquith Commission's advice—more pungently formulated by the Canadian academic Stephen Leacock as 'capture a few millionaires [and] give them honorary degrees at a million pounds sterling apiece . . . I give Oxford warning that if this is not done the place will not last another two centuries'.[18] At first things went very slowly. From 1923/4 to 1928/9 capital benefactions to the universities of both Oxford and Cambridge totalled only £600,000 (or 11 per cent of those received by all universities in Great Britain); over the next five years benefactions paid (as distinct from promised) to Oxford were only 5 per cent of the British total, behind

[15] Asquith Report, 79–91.

[16] UGC Returns from Universities and University Colleges in Receipt of Treasury Grant 1925/1926 (HMSO 1927); UGC Returns from Universities and University Colleges in Receipt of Treasury Grant 1926/1927 (HMSO 1928). In determining its grants to universities the UGC assumed certain levels of fees; 1977/8 saw a distinct shift (now to be taken further) from grants to fees.

[17] Asquith Report, 54.

[18] UGC University Development: Interim Report on the Years 1947 to 1951 (PP 1951–2 xviii Cmnd 8473), 999; UGC University Development from 1935 to 1947 (HMSO 1948); S. Leacock, My Discovery of England (London 1922), 102–3.

Birmingham and well behind London and Cambridge. But over the whole period from 1929/30 to 1946/7 Oxford emerged with £3.9m, or 19 per cent of all benefactions paid and appreciably more than any other university.[19] It owed this chiefly to the local industrialist Lord Nuffield, whose determination to make it a centre of medical research prompted a celebrated cartoon in *Punch* [plate 12.1].

Outside benefactors might have their own views on how the University should develop, and seek to use their money to give them effect. Nuffield made his first gift, for a chair in Spanish, partly because he thought it time that Oxford paid more attention to modern studies.[20] A more ambitious attempt to nudge Oxford into reform came in connection with library expansion, which was by the later 1920s generally recognized as the University's chief need. The Rockefeller Foundation had helped build a university library at Cambridge and was thinking of establishing 'a modern science library at Oxford'. In 1929 it was lobbied by Frank Aydelotte, the President of Swarthmore College and a former Rhodes scholar, who (besides coming up with eccentric proposals for making more space by relocating the Sheldonian Theatre) served as an informal intermediary between the Foundation and the University.[21] The Foundation was formally approached in May, and its agents then plunged into the controversy on where and how to rebuild the Bodleian Library.[22] They had clear ideas of dragging Oxford into the twentieth century: 'we are certainly interested primarily in the influence the Library may have upon research at Oxford'. They thought Bodley's Librarian was interested only in 'storage space for books—he seems to have little or no conception of a modern university library with its special facilities for advanced work under the leadership of trained investigators'. They tended to view the controversy in terms of a cleavage between 'younger scholars' and 'a small group of old-timers' seeking 'to preserve the old Liberal Arts College tradition, whereas the need today is for an expansion of the work at Oxford into the field of research'.[23] Given these perceptions and the strength of local feelings, it is a tribute to the agents' tact and to the political skill of the Chancellor and successive vice-chancellors

[19] UGC *Report including Returns from Universities and University Colleges in Receipt of Treasury Grant: Academic Year 1928/29* (HMSO 1930), 12; UGC *Report for the Period 1929/30 to 1934/35 Including Returns from Universities and University Colleges in Receipt of Treasury Grant for Academic Year 1934/35* (HMSO 1936), 59 (excluding Birmingham's Henry Barber Trust); UGC *University Development 1935–47*, 91.

[20] P. W. S. Andrews and E. Brunner, *The Life of Lord Nuffield: A Study in Benevolence and Enterprise* (Oxford 1959), 273–4.

[21] This account derives chiefly from copies obtained by Dr D. I. Greenstein of material in the Rockefeller Archive Center (Pocantico Hills, North Tarrytown, New York), 1.1/401R, boxes 60–3. See for example '1932. The Oxford Library Situation. History of the Request', box 62, 474–5.

[22] See above, 474–5.

[23] J. S. van Sickle to S. M. Gunn, 2 Apr. 1931, Rockefeller Archive Center, 1.1/401R, box 61, folder 806; G. E. Vincent's diary, 19 July 1929, ibid. box 60, folder 796.

that an explosion was avoided and a compromise settlement reached in May 1931. In December the Foundation agreed to contribute up to £616,000 if the University raised £378,000.[24] During the negotiations the Foundation's agents acquired rather more sympathy with the Oxford approach and its appreciation for antiquity. But they continued to pin hopes on the way in which the new Bodleian building would be developed: it would, an appreciation maintained in 1939, 'be open to advanced workers with carrels in the stacks' and its cataloguing would provide subject-indexes.[25]

The extension of the Bodleian Library helped move inter-war Oxford towards another University appeal (to succeed that of 1907). For the Rockefeller contribution was conditional on Oxford raising £378,000. This had been done by 1933. But the University had had to promise an annual payment of £7,000, and the library's extension would, when complete, cost an extra £20,000 a year to run.[26] This would restrict the University's expenditure in other directions, and people were anxious to restore the money through a general appeal. There were also local ginger groups. Lionel Curtis of All Souls, an enthusiast for federalism, had felt that the University was in a bad way as a result of: a lack of efficient, responsible and progressive government; a self-satisfaction born of 'ignorance of its own ignorance'; the domination of old men who lacked vision and energy; the need of funds which could have been secured if only any one had had the faith and courage to ask for them; and a failure to understand the meaning of a university, namely advanced postgraduate work. At first he wanted a private study of American universities, followed by a plan for Oxford's reorganization. This idea fell out of sight—perhaps because, as the Vice-Chancellor remarked, the Asquith Commission had produced only minor changes and a self-appointed committee was unlikely to do better, especially in any time-scale relevant to the needs of the Bodleian Library. So what remained was fund-raising.[27] In late 1930 Curtis submitted a memorandum on the financial needs of the University. One consequence was the formation in 1932 of the Oxford Society. This had been meant to organize Oxford men 'to do their

[24] Ibid. box 62, folder 810.

[25] Ibid. box 62, folder 818. The non-appearance of these facilities did not alienate the Foundation. When approached in the 1950s by the Dean of the Harvard Law School, who was concerned at the state of the Bodleian law holdings, it encouraged production of 'a substantial and imaginative plan' and granted £150,000 (just over half the costs) towards 'a modern law library with ready access to materials for study and research'. 'Our grant was based on the strong feeling of your own and visiting law professors that the future of law at Oxford was severely limited by the inaccessibility of a high percentage of material in the Bodleian'. HCP 224 (1956), 293–6; 226 (1957), 399–404; 227 (1957), 589; 230 (1958), 625–6.

[26] Colleges contributed £65,000, the trustees of the University Endowment Fund £48,000 (the balance left from the 1907 appeal); £33,000 was privately raised; the university provided £99,000 (chiefly the value of the building sites) and promised to contribute £7,000 per annum. H. H. E. Craster, *History of the Bodleian Library 1845–1945* (Oxford 1952, repr. Oxford 1981), 327; *Gazette* lxiii (1932/3), 448; HCP 163 (1936), 170–1.

[27] Vincent's diary, 13 and 21 Aug. 1929.

part' in raising 'the enormous sums which Oxford needs to save what the past has given her and also maintain her position as a seat of learning'. But in indicating the Society's objects, Council 'deleted all reference to money-raising as a prime purpose';[28] and though the Society has been of considerable help to Oxford, it has never been as full-blooded as have many American associations of alumni.[29]

When Council first considered Curtis's memorandum, his ally H. A. L. Fisher (President of the Board of Education 1916–22, Warden of New College from 1925) suggested a general University appeal to the Pilgrim Trust. The Registrar, Douglas Veale, saw the Trust's Secretary informally, and was told it would not welcome an appeal 'covering many different items' with no indication of the priority attached to each; nor did it relish the uncoordinated appeals sent by individual professors and institutions of the University. So early in 1931 faculty boards were canvassed as to their needs. By the summer Council had determined on priorities, approached the Pilgrim Trust (only to be rejected), and was preparing to go public.[30] The national economic crisis that then broke constituted an unsuitable back-ground for an appeal, and for some time Oxford concentrated rather on economies (including, for the sake of public relations, a moratorium on college balls in 1932).[31] Not until late 1935 did conditions seem right to renew planning; the appeal finally went public early in 1937. It sought at least £500,000—half for the Bodleian Library, half for other needs, including 'research in social studies' and a new physical chemistry laboratory; it was launched with contributions of £100,000 each from the Rhodes trustees and from Lord Nuffield.[32]

But the situation was transformed in the summer by a further approach from Lord Nuffield offering about £1m for a college of engineering and accountancy. Vice-Chancellor Lindsay was less imaginative: using rather dubious arguments, he and Veale talked Nuffield into substituting for engineering a new £100,000 physical chemistry laboratory.[33] As for what

[28] HCP 151 (1932), 175–6 (12 Mar.); *Oxford* May 1956, 7. In the 1950s, too, Council discouraged Vice-Chancellor Smith's idea of using the Society to manage the Historic Buildings appeal in the hope that it would then develop into an American-style association that would provide the University with continuing support: W. F. Oakeshott (ed.), *Oxford Stone Restored: The Work of the Oxford Historic Buildings Fund 1957–1974* (Oxford 1975), 8–9.

[29] Less than 14% of those eligible used to join; so to compile a central register of former members of the University, the 'Campaign for Oxford' had to seek their addresses from colleges: *Gazette* cxix (1988/9), 303. See also below, 716.

[30] HCP 147 (1930), pp. lxxv–vi; 148 (1931), 7–8; 149 (1931), pp. xci, 241–2; 150 (1931), p. xi.

[31] HCP 153 (1932), pp. iv, xiv, lxxxiii. The 'Keynesian' economist Harrod tried to persuade people 'that it is unpatriotic for institutions at this time to reduce their expenditure below the normal level, except from necessity', but seems to have cut little ice save (according to oral tradition) in his own Christ Church.

[32] 'Needs of the university', *The American Oxonian* xxiv (1937), 3–9.

[33] Though Oxford had recently accepted money for a readership in engineering, Nuffield was told that 'for us to set up a rival school' would breach an agreement with Cambridge and

Nuffield meant by 'accountancy', its academic counterpart was the social studies that were so dear to Lindsay's heart and whose current funding was distinctly precarious. A 'Post-Graduate College . . . made the centre of our Modern Studies' would fulfil 'exactly what [Nuffield] really had in mind . . . in all essentials, much as it differs from it in details'.[34] Nuffield appears to have been hurt, the more so as he was to be vigorously criticized in certain University circles for patronizing the social rather than the physical sciences. But since much of his motivation had been aesthetic—'to improve the aspect of the approach to Oxford from the West'—he agreed.[35] However, when he saw a model of the building the University proposed to erect, he finally put his foot down. 'I consider the design to be un-English and out of keeping with the best tradition of Oxford architecture; as well as contrary to my expressed wishes that it should be in conformity with that tradition.'[36]

Nuffield's benefaction had thus been steered into meeting two of the appeal's chief aims, funding for social studies and physical chemistry; and the £421,000 that had been independently contributed by October 1937 more than took care of the Bodleian Library. There was some debate on whether the appeal should be taken any further, and it was eventually decided to reactivate it briefly for the general endowment of research.[37] Grants were made to several institutions in the university, and a balance was left with the trustees of the 'higher studies fund', which is still drawn on to support small research initiatives.

It had always been felt that 'once the Appeal is closed, it will be a long time before it can be reopened'.[38] What finally provoked its revival was the state of Oxford's buildings. Already by the end of the 1940s an appeal was talked of in connection with the Sheldonian Theatre; in the absence of a major programme of restoration the university could only remove the bits that looked like falling off. The question was strongly pushed by Vice-Chancellor Smith, and by 1955 the Pilgrim Trust and the chairman of the Historic Buildings Council were privately suggesting a comprehensive

wastefully duplicate its facilities. Dividing up 'some of the less important branches of knowledge' had indeed been discussed with Cambridge, but engineering was not mentioned: HCP 161 (1935), 139–40, 224–5 (index); 162 (1935), 113–14.

[34] Veale to Chancellor Halifax (and to Hobbs, Nuffield's private secretary), cited in N. Chester, *Economics, Politics and Social Studies in Oxford, 1900–85* (Basingstoke and London 1986), 64–7.

[35] Andrews and Brunner, *Nuffield*, 311–12; D. Veale, 'Lord Nuffield and the university', *OM* 5 Dec. 1963, 124. Chester (67–9) doubts whether Nuffield was disappointed at the time, arguing that he could have threatened to withdraw his offer, as he had in 1936 when the university proved reluctant to agree to a chair in anaesthetics. This perhaps underplays Nuffield's concern for the canal wharf site, stressed in the formal letter offering his gift: HCP 168 (1937), 53.

[36] H. M. Colvin, *Unbuilt Oxford* (New Haven Conn. and London 1983), 172–4; above, 325, 503.

[37] *Oxford University: A Programme of Development* (University of Oxford 1938), copy in Bodl. GA Oxon. 8. 1132 (21).

[38] HCP 168 (1937), 46.

appeal to include the colleges, several of which were considering launching their own appeals. Inclusion of the colleges proved controversial, but in 1956 it was finally decided to proceed. The head of the civil service, Sir Edward Bridges, did much to prepare the ground. In particular he had the Ministry of Works check the costs of the repairs, and he helped persuade the colleges to provide information for an external determination of the amounts each should contribute. The appeal was launched in June 1957 and by August 1958 had achieved £1.6m.[39] A follow-up was made in 1963. Together the two raised £2.4m net, exclusive of Oxford's own contribution of £0.4m. Between 1957 and 1974 the Historic Buildings Fund spent some £2.2m on repairs, whose full cost was significantly greater.[40] Oxford's appearance had been transformed. But the work never finishes. Magdalen's tower cost £900,000, while its total expenditure between 1974 and 1989 on the restoration of stonework and on internal modernization was £6.2m (three-quarters of which was covered by an appeal). The far poorer St Edmund Hall found itself in 1979 faced with £444,000 of emergency repairs, and had to spend £153,000 in 1988 on releading the roof of the former church of St Peter in the East; English Heritage (and similar public bodies) could contribute less than £30,000.

The existence of the Historic Buildings appeal inhibited the launching of others (including one by the women's colleges for which the University's sponsorship was sought in 1958). In the 1960s Oxford was politically on the defensive, its primary concern being to put itself in order and justify itself to the outside world through the Franks Commission. It is nevertheless remarkable how little consideration the Commission gave to the raising of money, even though it prescribed expansion. Later, thought did turn in this direction; and Sir Alan Bullock, whose skill at fund-raising had earlier transformed St Catherine's Society into a college, began his vice-chancellorship in 1969 by securing $750,000 from IBM. 'But my hopes that this would be the prelude to another university appeal comparable with that before the war . . . proved vain. I could not get the thing moving, and whatever chances there were did not survive the impact of the student troubles, and the lasting effect this had on the image of the University and even more of the students.'[41] Accordingly an appeal was not seriously considered until the later 1980s, the chief stimulus then being changes in government funding.

[39] £653,000 from Ford and other trusts, £420,000 from Oxford graduates, £268,000 from commerce and industry, £250,000 from the Historic Buildings Council and the UGC, and £50,000 from other sources.

[40] Oakeshott, *Oxford Stone Restored*, 7–16 and *passim*; HCP 242 (1962), 683. In the decade before the first appeal the university had spent £43,000 and the colleges £250,000 on repairing historic buildings: *Oxford Historic Buildings Appeal* [1957], copy in Bodl. GA Oxon. 4° 744.

[41] HCP 229 (1958), pp. cv–cvi, 319 ff; 230 (1958), 269–71; 258 (1967), 861 ff; 259 (1968), 103–34; 264 (1969), 730–2; A. Bullock, 'Reminiscences of a former vice-chancellor', pt 2, *OM* no. 30 (2nd week, Hilary 1988), 4.

Exchequer grants have been crucial to the late twentieth-century university, accounting for two-thirds of its income in the early 1970s. They started on an 'emergency' basis in 1919 and were made permanent as a result of the Asquith Commission. But they were at first very modest—totalling less than half of Lord Nuffield's benefactions to Oxford between the wars—though they did have the advantage of not being tied to particular projects.[42] After 1945 things changed; the Treasury accepted a UGC plea for the doubling of the general grant to universities, and in 1946 universities were invited to submit proposals for training scientists on the assumption that 'the Treasury purse was open wide'.[43] Oxford's grant had been £108,400 in 1938/9 and had stayed much the same until 1944/5; in 1945/6 it was £242,000 and by 1951/2 it had reached £971,600.[44] In real terms this last figure represented a fourfold increase on 1938/9 and a sixfold on 1944/5.

When compiling its bid for the quinquennium 1952/7, Oxford had come to reckon on ever-increasing support from the UGC. Thus it discovered, apparently with surprise, that in 1952/3 it would need an extra £212,000 simply to meet 'the full expenditure to which it is already committed'. But as the submission blandly stated, 'Council assumes that it is not called upon to justify the present scale of expenditure . . . The following notes, therefore, are directed [only] to the [proposed] expansion'.[45] In all it sought a rise of at least 57 per cent. Late 1951, however, witnessed a national financial crisis. The UGC ultimately announced a rise of only 24 per cent, to be followed by an increase of 19 per cent over the rest of the quinquennium.[46] Universities were warned not to plan on the basis that the grants for the quinquennium 1957/62 would be set at a yet higher level; but inevitably they did so, often (as we shall see) with the UGC's approval of the new expenditure. Oxford found the increase of 11.8 per cent announced in 1957 most disappointing and submitted a memorandum of protest. It began by explaining that there was very little scope for flexibility in universities' expenditure, and that 'there has grown up a tacit understanding . . . that no university shall have its grant cut so as to prevent its carrying on its existing activities unimpaired. In their quinquennial interviews with the Committee of Vice-Chancellors and Principals, Chancellors of the Exchequer have accepted this convention as basic. They have never hinted at the possibility of their not accepting the

---

[42] Treasury grants totalled £1.6m to the end of 1938/9, Nuffield's £3.8m. For Nuffield's benefactions see Andrews and Brunner, *Nuffield*, 259. For Treasury grants see UGC *Returns 1919/1920* (PP 1921 xxvi Cmd 1263) and the returns for the years from 1920/1 to 1938/9 published annually by HMSO.

[43] UGC *University Development 1935–47*, 11; HCP 194 (1946), 221.

[44] HCP 175 (1940), 82; 194 (1946), 176; 197 (1947), 172; 215 (1953), 255. The figure for 1951/2 includes grants earmarked for new developments and support for the supplementation of academic salaries, but not 'non-recurrent' grants (£17,250 in 1945/6, £76,671 in 1951/2).

[45] HCP 209 (1951), 560–1.

[46] HCP 212 (1952), 347, 350; 213 (1952), 321.

current rate of expenditure as a liability, to which they add from time to time such money for expansion as they can find.' Against this background Oxford proceeded to argue that its difficulties did not stem, as the UGC assumed, from the cavalier incurring of new expenditure late in the previous quinquennium in the hope that it would then be adopted as an 'existing commitment'; the UGC had 'expressly approved' all departures from its last application.[47]

Space will not let us follow Oxford's negotiations with the UGC. There were disappointments, but, as will be demonstrated below, the general trend was upwards. The Franks Commission repeatedly emphasized the transformations effected by the rise in state grants from £30,000 in 1922 to £5.2m in 1963/4. It took for granted 'the dependence of Oxford, like other British universities . . . on large grants from public funds' and accepted 'the degree of control' by the UGC that this 'inevitably involved'.[48] There are no signs in the Commission's report of worry either about its nature or about the security of state funding. Such concerns did not really surface until the 1980s.[49] But there had been one portent of things to come. For in 1966 the Education Secretary announced, without prior consultation, that he expected universities to charge higher fees for foreign than for home students and would adjust their funding accordingly. The sums involved were small, but the principles highly contentious. Council initially accepted the advice of the Committee of Vice-Chancellors and Principals to comply, but not so Congregation. In 1968 Cambridge gave in, and the General Board urged Oxford to do likewise; Congregation again refused. By 1969/70 the university was in deficit by about the £100,000 its opposition to the government was then costing. A privately launched 'Oxford University Independence Fund' had achieved little, and the price of defiance was expected to double. The prospect did not convince either Council or those who attended Congregation in person, and Oxford was urged to show the Dunkirk spirit by keeping up its (almost) lone resistance to the government's evil proposals. But in 1970 the newly instituted postal vote was twice invoked to insist on the introduction of differential fees. The chief argument was from financial necessity, and the Vice-Chairman of the General Board warned that 'we are now in a world in which we can no longer expect that rising costs or wage claims will automatically be covered by increased government grants'.[50]

The advent of plentiful state aid altered the balance between the university and the colleges; but few wished this to lead to the demise of Oxford's

---

[47] HCP 228 (1957), 56–7, 62, 400–1.

[48] *Franks Report* i, paras 74, 457.

[49] They had, though, between 1968 and 1976 prompted the foundation of an 'independent university' at Buckingham.

[50] HCP 259 (1968), 529–30, 587–8; 264 (1969), 440–2; *Gazette* c (1969/70), 643–4, 1292–3, 1340.

distinctive collegiate system—indeed Franks's first recommendation was that 'Oxford should develop and improve its collegiate structure'. All colleges face the problem of being ineligible for state aid. For many this has been moderated by the possession of endowments, but more recent foundations were (in Franks's words) 'insufficiently endowed to achieve the level of financial security necessary for the unfettered . . . performance of their academic tasks'.[51] Efforts to overcome this have been an important feature of Oxford's post-war history. In 1946 the Principal of St Edmund Hall, A. B. Emden, sounded out the chairman of the UGC on the prospect of grants for less well endowed colleges; he was told the UGC would deal only through the university and that it would insist on scrutinizing the accounts of the colleges in question. Emden then pressed Council, which set up a 'Committee on the Needs of the Poorer Colleges'. There followed a long process of consultation, the submission of pessimistic memoranda by the estates bursars' committee and some exchange of views with Cambridge. The UGC's decision of 1949 to provide all universities with money to improve academic salaries served to crystallize discussion. For the Vice-Chancellor felt that not even the richest colleges could afford to match the increases, and 'that only by relief on a scale far beyond anything hitherto considered can the quality of College teaching and research be maintained'. He noted that the UGC had approved a scheme whereby the University of Cambridge returned to its colleges some deductions made from the salaries of university teachers who also held substantial college appointments. And he suggested an annual university contribution of £55,000 to the salaries of college tutors by making all established college arts tutors into CUF lecturers.[52]

Since this did much to mould Oxford's subsequent evolution, the technicalities must be explained. The Common University Fund derived from taxation of the colleges and had originally supported purely university posts and purposes. But the Asquith Commission had eased the pressure on university finances by procuring state support. It had also urged that 'a number' of 'teachers' be accorded 'leisure for the specialized work of study and research in addition to their activities in College teaching, by freeing them from an excessive burden of teaching in term and from the necessity of seeking paid work in the vacation'. So Oxford decided to create, as a first charge on the CUF, fifty lecturerships (at £200 for each of ten years) for tutors who undertook to do specific research and limit their other commitments.[53] The scheme was adjudged a great success, and by 1949 the number of lecturers had risen to 106 (at £250 a year). The Vice-Chancellor

[51] *Franks Report* i. 28, 284, 411.
[52] HCP 198 (1947), 91 ff; 200 (1948), 223–4; 203 (1949), 81 ff, 113–15; 204 (1949), 63–4, 98–100; 205 (1950), pp. xxxiii–xxxiv, 44–50.
[53] *Asquith Report*, para. 92; HCP 195 (1946), 96–7.

now proposed including all 286 'inter-collegiate lecturers' and persuading the UGC to underwrite this on the ground that the public 'lecturing which was done in most Universities by persons employed by the University was, in Oxford, done by the College teachers'. In January 1950 the UGC's chairman promised that, while no grant could be provided in the current quinquennium, he would recommend it for the next. Accordingly the university went ahead, using the surplus the CUF had accumulated during the war to cover the cost for the intervening year. This proved an important step in the development of what Franks was to call 'the "collegiate university"... inhabited by a new type of academic, the "fellow-lecturer", who has double loyalties, joint functions, and composite remuneration'.[54] The grant from the UGC grew into a substantial contribution through the university towards the costs of CUF fellow-lecturers, whose posts are still mostly funded by the colleges and whose primary teaching obligations are college-based. But it was of little immediate help to the poorer colleges as the money went not to them but to their tutors; and it was by and large the richer colleges who had the most tutors to be thus benefited—particularly Christ Church, New College, Magdalen and Balliol, though also (it is pleasing to note) Somerville.[55]

Of more immediate advantage were cheap building loans from the CUF surplus. The idea had evolved in parallel with that of the extension of CUF lecturerships, and a statute was passed to enable women's colleges to participate even though they had not contributed to the Fund through university taxation. For 1950–3 over £170,000 was allocated to these loans, which were dovetailed with the benefaction by Antonin Besse for the propagation, as he later put it, 'of the ideas that are dear to me'. This gift of £1.5m—whose size occasioned a strike by his workforce in Aden—was chiefly to found a new graduate college (St Antony's), one-third of whose students should be French. But to forestall opposition, £250,000 was allocated to helping seven of the poorest men's colleges to expand (again with some preference for French applicants).[56] Faced in 1950 by yet another plea from the estates bursars' committee for the ending of CUF taxation, Council listed these and other 'alleviations of the Colleges' difficulties', and concluded that it had gone as far as was prudent, since any further readjustment of costs between the university and the colleges would raise 'issues which it would be wiser to leave alone'.[57]

[54] *Franks Report* i, para. 33.
[55] Eligible tutors are listed by college in HCP 203 (1949), 115.
[56] D. Footman, *Antonin Besse of Aden* (London 1986), chaps 26–7; see also above, 624–5. Gordonstoun School might have been a better vehicle for Besse's wish to reinforce Britain's waning pioneer virtues, but he discovered it only after making his gift to Oxford. Several recipient colleges named buildings after Besse, though French applicants were not numerous.
[57] HCP 204 (1949), 39–40, 79, 205–7, 245–50; 205 (1950), 48, 129–30; 206 (1950), pp. v, xxxi, 157, 453–6.

Some people still favoured a direct approach to the UGC on college funding. During a UGC visitation in 1952 the Vice-Chancellor expatiated on the colleges' difficulties and the need 'to avoid any cleavage arising at Oxford owing to the poverty of the colleges and the relative affluence of the University'. He was encouraged to discuss the question with Cambridge and then submit a proposal. Cambridge, always more apprehensive than Oxford about the risk to college independence, deprecated any direct aid to colleges from public funds. But it said that it had 'for many years paid the colleges for the use of lecture rooms, though the amount involved was small'.[58] Oxford eventually decided to take this route. So it was resolved, with the UGC's blessing, that in the final year of the quinquennium (1956/7) the CUF would divide £60,000 between the colleges 'for services rendered to the University' in the expectation that the UGC would then adopt it as a continuing commitment. The proposal encountered strong opposition from Brasenose and Corpus, which objected to Council's thus taking upon itself to strike deals on a matter 'which touches the foundations of the independence and finance of the colleges'. But, unlike the earlier institution of CUF lecturerships, it proved of little long-run importance, since payments to colleges did not greatly expand in later years. Nor, as they were general and linked to rateable values, did they do much for the poorer colleges: Christ Church and New College got most, St Anne's and St Edmund Hall least.[59]

So the issue of aid from the UGC to the colleges remained live. In the later 1950s it was linked with the problems of increasing numbers and of providing rooms in college. In 1958 less than half the male undergraduates were said to be so accommodated, a ratio below both the target recently recommended by a sub-committee of the UGC and that achieved by several other universities. A committee was set up to consider asking the UGC for 'financial help for college accommodation'. But in May 1959 Council turned the idea down, partly in response to the UGC's coolness. The chairman had initially been encouraging, but in 1959 suggested that the residential needs of 'the older civic universities' were more urgent. Also any such grant would have to come out of Oxford's general allocation for capital works, and the university was afraid this would squeeze out its own projects. Instead it decided on some expansion of the 2 per cent CUF building loans to colleges.[60]

By now, improved income from their endowments was easing the financial position of most colleges, but the problem of the 'poorer' colleges was being increasingly pressed. All the women's colleges fell into this

---

[58] HCP 212 (1952), 9–10, 117–19.

[59] HCP 212 (1952), 413 ff; 213 (1952), 263–4; 215 (1953), pp. cv, 195–6, 267–71, 357–8; 216 (1953), pp. lxxxii, 19; 217 (1954), 212–14, 311–15; 218 (1954), pp. cxxvi–cxxvii, 35–8, 109, 291–2, 319–20.

[60] HCP 230 (1958), 77–82, 373–9; 232 (1959), 287–91; 233 (1959), pp. lxix–lxxi, 221–3.

category. The UGC was well disposed, and had provided money (through the university) for projects like the new dining hall at St Anne's.[61] Then in 1960 its chairman indicated a readiness to contribute towards their principals' stipends, at 'the rate paid to wardens of halls of residence at other universities'. This rather embarrassed the principals and it attracted the jealousy of the poorer men's colleges. St Edmund Hall grumbled that 'it is common knowledge that the endowment position of certain men's colleges is no better, and possibly worse, than that of the women's colleges'. It would have been foolish to reject the offer, which was accepted in 1962, but that November it was also agreed to pay Hertford, Keble, St Edmund Hall and St Peter's a similar sum (£2,000) each year from the CUF.[62]

This proved the thin end of quite a large wedge. Council had, since 1960, been considering 'the relationship between the University and the Colleges'; for another current issue, that of 'entitlement' to college fellowships, could be resolved only with the goodwill of the colleges. By 1961 the richer colleges were also contemplating inter-collegiate financial assistance, though in the event they could not agree on its details. And in 1964 Council put forward a scheme that, though temporarily retaining the income grants, laid more stress on raising endowment and proposed annual capital grants to the poorer colleges from the CUF. It was generally well received; but Trinity observed that it would increase the recipients' annual incomes by a mere £150–300; University College went further, suggesting that the CUF 'become a fund whose primary purpose would be the redistribution of wealth between colleges'.[63] In 1965 the Vice-Chancellor persuaded colleges to forgo various loopholes that had reduced their CUF tax-liability, promising to devote the extra income to increased aid to the poorer colleges. The Franks Commission saw such aid as vital to the proper development of the collegiate system, and described the wide acceptance of this view as 'one of the most notable changes of opinion that has occurred in Oxford in recent years'. Accordingly it recommended a new system of CUF contributions whose 'principal object' should be 'to bring the statutory endowment income of all colleges up to £40,000 a year'—whereas in 1964 the poorest, St Peter's, had had only £6,364. The recommendation was broadly accepted and payments began in 1967/8. Before they had finished, the combination of runaway inflation and the need to control the level of college fees prompted a review that led to their extension. So by 1978/9 some £5m had been distributed in endowment grants. These grants had been envisaged as a

---

[61] Such help was facilitated by the fact that (like St Catherine's, also a UGC beneficiary) the women's colleges were not in the 1950s financially fully independent of the university. But it continued for some years when they were. By Michaelmas 1964 building grants totalled £191,000, exclusive of payments for site-assembly and so on: HCP 249 (1964), 317.

[62] HCP 238 (1961), 229–31; 239 (1961), pp. clxvii–clxix, cxcix–ccii, 597–8, 859–69; 240 (1961), 51–4; 246 (1963), 632–3.

[63] HCP 241 (1962), 541–3; 246 (1963), 618, 632–8; 247 (1964), 253–63.

once-for-all measure to enable every college to stand on its own feet. But the question was revived in the mid-1980s by colleges that had been just too rich to benefit. The cuts in the university's UGC grant imposed in 1986 provided a further catalyst, for to offset them colleges took on a greater share of the costs of their CUF lecturers. 1988 saw both this readjustment and the start of the distribution of a further £7m of (inflation-proofed) inter-collegiate endowment grants.[64]

We must now turn from the perspective of the university to that of the colleges. For in 1920 the university's income was little more than a third that of the colleges collectively; it did not overtake them until the early 1950s. Even in 1987/8 the colleges' income was equivalent to 57 per cent of the university's. Colleges have always varied considerably both in endowment and in their dependence on 'internal' income—that is, on money derived from their students. From the mid-nineteenth century they were free to sell land and so vary their investment policy; some were better placed than others to compensate for agricultural depression by moving into house property. So it is perhaps surprising that their individual fortunes have not varied more. But no single college in Oxford has ever become financially as dominant as Trinity at Cambridge; rich colleges have tended to remain fairly rich and only a few colleges have moved far up the scale of relative wealth. Testing this proposition is not easy, since there are several possible definitions of wealth, and since college accounts have varied over time in their comprehensiveness, but table 24.1 may constitute a rough guide. There are indeed changes, some perhaps significant. Thus a former bursar has compared Magdalen's relative decline from a peak early this century to that of the British empire, both being lulled by good fortune into easy-going complaisance; and at the lower end of the table several colleges have risen through prudence and abstemiousness. Among the graduate colleges Nuffield conducted a far more successful investment policy than did St Antony's, and has increased the number of its junior members much less. But the overall picture is of comparative stability, if also of some convergence (accentuated by CUF taxation). Its features can perhaps be best brought out by briefly discussing the changing sources of college incomes.

Traditionally the colleges' incomes had been based on land. Although this was increasingly being supplemented by houses, in 1913 land and tithes still accounted for nearly two-thirds of the colleges' gross external income. The First World War was good for arable farming. But neither Oxford nor

---

[64] *Franks Report* i. 283–95; [Sir Rex Richards, chairman] *Report to the Conference of Colleges [Richards Report]* (University of Oxford 1976), 1, 8 ff; J. P. D. Dunbabin, 'College finances and property in the twentieth century' in T. Rowley (ed.), *The Oxford Region* (Oxford 1980), 216; *Gazette* cxvii (1986/7), 58; cxviii (1987/8), 508, 586; cxix (1988/9), 177. Franks had in fact recommended the discontinuance of all payments to the university from CUF taxation of the colleges, but this was resisted and did not come about until 1973.

TABLE 24.1

OXFORD COLLEGES' INCOME OR EXPENDITURE AND (IN BOLD)
INCOME OR EXPENDITURE PER RESIDENT UNDERGRADUATE OR
STUDENT AS A MULTIPLE OF PEMBROKE'S IN SELECTED YEARS
FROM THE 1660S TO 1987/8

Colleges/halls	1660s	1871		1920		1954		1970/1		1987/8	
Christ Church	20	5.2	**2.3**	4.0	**1.9**	3.4	**2.0**	2.3	**1.8**	2.1	**1.8**
Magdalen	12	4.2	**3.0**	4.7	**3.7**	2.4	**1.8**	1.9	**1.8**	1.6	**1.4**
New	10	2.9	**2.5**	2.5	**1.4**	2.1	**1.4**	1.8	**1.5**	1.7	**1.3**
All Souls	5	1.8	—	1.4	—	1.1	—	1.2	—	1.3	—
Corpus Christi	5	1.6	**1.7**	1.2	**2.2**	1.0	**1.5**	1.0	**1.6**	1.1	**1.6**
Merton	4	1.9	**2.2**	1.9	**2.6**	1.6	**1.5**	1.6	**1.9**	1.5	**1.7**
St John's	4	1.6	**1.6**	2.2	**1.8**	1.7	**1.6**	1.6	**1.6**	2.3	**2.0**
Brasenose	3	1.7	**0.9**	1.9	**1.7**	1.6	**1.1**	1.5	**1.3**	1.3	**1.3**
Queen's	2.5	1.7	**1.0**	2.4	**1.5**	1.8	**1.4**	1.5	**1.7**	1.5	**1.7**
Exeter	2	2.0	**0.7**	1.5	**1.3**	0.9	**0.7**	1.0	**1.2**	1.1	**1.2**
Oriel	2	1.4	**1.9**	1.5	**1.3**	1.4	**1.2**	1.1	**1.3**	1.1	**1.2**
Trinity	2	0.6	**0.5**	1.3	**1.4**	1.1	**1.1**	1.1	**1.6**	1.1	**1.4**
Lincoln	1.3	1.0	**1.3**	1.1	**1.0**	1.0	**0.8**	1.0	**1.2**	1.2	**1.4**
University	1	1.6	**1.2**	1.7	**1.5**	1.5	**1.0**	1.4	**1.3**	1.7	**1.4**
Balliol	1	1.4	**0.6**	2.5	**1.4**	2.3	**1.3**	1.6	**1.1**	1.6	**1.3**
Jesus	1	1.6	**2.3**	1.3	**1.2**	1.3	**1.1**	1.1	**1.1**	1.3	**1.3**
Wadham	1	1.4	**1.7**	0.9	**0.9**	1.2	**0.8**	1.1	**1.6**	1.9	**1.0**
Pembroke	1	1.0	**1.0**	1.0	**1.0**	1.0	**1.0**	1.0	**1.0**	1.0	**1.0**
Worcester	—	1.0	**1.0**	1.0	**1.2**	1.1	**0.9**	1.2	**1.2**	1.2	**1.2**
Hertford	—	—	—	0.7	**0.9**	0.7	**0.7**	0.7	**0.9**	1.0	**1.0**
Keble	—	—	—	—	—	1.2	**0.8**	1.2	**1.1**	1.3	**1.4**
St Edmund Hall	—	—	—	—	—	0.9	**0.7**	1.3	**1.1**	1.3	**1.2**
St Peter's	—	—	—	—	—	0.7	**0.8**	0.8	**1.0**	0.8	**1.1**
St Antony's	—	—	—	—	—	1.0	**5.1**	1.2	**5.0**	1.0	**1.7**
Lady Margaret Hall	—	—	—	—	—	—	**1.0**	1.1	**1.1**	1.2	**1.2**
Somerville	—	—	—	—	—	—	**0.9**	1.1	**1.0**	1.2	**1.2**
St Hugh's	—	—	—	—	—	—	**1.0**	1.0	**1.0**	1.2	**1.1**
St Hilda's	—	—	—	—	—	—	**0.8**	1.0	**1.1**	1.0	**1.0**
St Anne's	—	—	—	—	—	—	**0.8**	1.1	**0.9**	1.2	**1.2**
Nuffield	—	—	—	—	—	—	—	1.6	**9.9**	1.1	**6.8**
St Catherine's	—	—	—	—	—	—	—	1.4	**1.1**	1.4	**1.1**
Wolfson	—	—	—	—	—	—	—	—	—	0.9	**1.0**
Linacre	—	—	—	—	—	—	—	—	—	0.3	**0.7**

This table measures income or expenditure. Other rankings of colleges often reflect
'endowment income' only, both as a proxy for wealth and capital gains and because,
unlike fees and charges on junior members, it entails few internal costs; such rankings
show less convergence and boost the position of colleges like All Souls and Nuffield.
Christ Church's position would appear less advantageous if expenditure for the
chapter fund were deducted as being for university or extraneous purposes (reducing
the figure for expenditure per undergraduate in 1920 to 1.4 that of Pembroke).

TABLE 24.1 (cont.)

Sources:

1660s: Assessment for rates of 'old rents': see J. P. D. Dunbabin, 'College estates and wealth 1660–1815' in L. S. Sutherland and L. G. Mitchell (eds), *The Eighteenth Century* (History of the University of Oxford v, Oxford 1986), 272–3.

1871: Net income from [Duke of Cleveland, chairman] *Report of the Commissioners appointed to inquire into the Property and Income of the Universities of Oxford and Cambridge and the Colleges and Hall therein [Cleveland Report]* (3 pts PP 1873 xxxvii C856), pt 1, 200–2. Trinity's income was about to rise sharply with the falling in of beneficial leases; that of some other colleges, notably Christ Church, was inflated by the treatment as income of borrowing to run out such leases.

1920: Net income less expenditure for university purposes: *Asquith Report*, appx 16. Allowance is made for augmentation of benefices by Christ Church and New College and for Magdalen's expenditure on schools. Hertford also received significant sums from external trustees.

1954: HCP 222 (1955), 301–16, synopsis of college accounts. For men's colleges the figures represent net income less contributions and donations for university purposes; for women's colleges expenditure on 'education and research' in 1953/4 per resident junior member as a multiple of Pembroke's.

1970/1 and 1987/8: *Accounts of the Colleges*[65], expenditure for colleges' own purposes.

Cambridge raised their rents: Oxford's rented corporate agricultural estates produced some £181,000 gross in 1913 and £187,000 in 1918, Cambridge's £107,000 and £109,000, a considerable fall in real terms. The Asquith Commission felt there was a general bias towards leaving rents on the low side, perhaps reinforced by 'the war and the desire to encourage food production'; and it implied that, because colleges were 'not fully qualified to estimate the market value of the land', they had sometimes fallen for the rent-increases volunteered by tenants.[66] But it was not only colleges which found it hard to raise rents in line with agriculture's improved fortunes, and many landlords preferred instead to sell, especially as tenants could now afford unprecedented purchase prices. It was said at the time that a quarter of England changed hands in the years after the war. Seven Oxford and twelve Cambridge colleges, and the university of Cambridge, took the opportunity to sell land, Oxford raising over £332,000 and Cambridge more than £525,000. The Asquith Commission calculated that by reinvesting the

[65] The *Accounts of the Colleges* are published annually by the University (the exact title varying from time to time).
[66] *Asquith Report*, 221 and appx 19, pp. 354, 363.

proceeds at 5 per cent they had more than doubled their net receipts; Oriel, Oxford's most active college, believed that it had tripled them.[67]

The Oxford estates bursars found the Asquith Commission's interest alarming and feared it would insist on sales. So they contended that 'the Colleges can find no investment likely, in the long run, to be more remunerative than land'; had they sold out in Queen Elizabeth's reign and taken perpetual rent-charges, these would now be worth only a twentieth of the current value of the land in question. 'There is also the element of appreciation in value, and "windfalls" of various kinds . . . Probably all the richest Colleges have benefited largely by the development of building land, . . . which would not have affected the selling price of their estates 100 years ago'. Moreover, if their endowments consisted only of 'stocks and securities', it 'would be argued that the Colleges were, in effect . . . glorified hostels . . . that they ought to be put under the central management of some University Delegacy . . . and that the Tutors and Lecturers of the Colleges should become Recognised Teachers of the University and be appointed thereby. The College system would thus be destroyed . . . It may also be remarked, that confiscation of Stocks and Securities is a simpler matter than that of lands.'[68]

The Asquith Commission was not wholly convinced, but it did accept 'that the retention of some land is a useful asset in the corporate life of a College, and should afford that training in practical affairs which is particularly valuable to an educational body'. While it saw no advantage in the central management of college estates, whether by an expert board for each university or by the Ministry of Agriculture, it did suggest that since the state was now supplementing college contributions to the two universities it had a direct interest in maximizing the colleges' incomes. Nothing, however, came of its proposal that the Ministry of Agriculture should therefore be empowered to commission expert reports on ways of doing this (like building, quarrying, rent-increases or sales of land) and to enforce their recommendations. And though it commended sale and reinvestment, it pressed this particularly on colleges too poor to employ a full-time bursar or a professional land-agent. In any case, by the time the Commission reported, agricultural depression was returning and the scope for profitable land-sales was being correspondingly reduced. The Commission felt that 'limited opportunities still exist', but the burden of its message was retrospective: the last two and a half years had seen 'an exceptional combination' of excellent prices for agricultural land and unusually high

[67] Ibid. appx 19, pp. 358, 366. The sales enabled Oriel to appoint three new fellows; but by the 1980s it was ruefully noting the increase in land values it had forgone by selling (one farm sold for £4,650 in 1921 fetched over £1m in 1987). E. Vallis, 'Oriel's estates and interests in land, 1324–1991', *Oriel College Record* 1991, 32–57.

[68] Ibid. appx 1.ii.d (pp. 38–9), memorandum by the committee of Oxford estates bursars.

TABLE 24.2

COMPONENTS OF OXFORD COLLEGE INCOMES IN SELECTED YEARS, 1913–1970/1 (£)

(a) historic colleges[a]

	1913	%	1920	%	1926	%	1938	%	1948	%	1954	%	1964	%	1970/1	%
lands, rent-charges etc.	184,250	47	207,484	44	183,643	35	183,115[b]	30	274,825	37	326,749	34	569,416	33	929,454[c]	27
tithes	47,086	12	68,094	14	70,366	13										
	231,336	59	275,578	59	254,009	48										
houses at rack-rent	56,137		61,483		75,166		119,879		197,296		300,465		478,531			
houses on long or beneficial leases	72,745		75,522		83,521		115,697		114,048		111,060		107,945			
leaseholds	—		—	23			16,283		21,347		36,285		40,914			
	128,882	33	137,005	29	158,710	30	251,859	42	332,691	45	447,810	46	627,390	36	1,050,645[d]	30
dividends and interest	29,784	8	58,308	12	117,354	22	165,771	28	129,171	18	200,397	21	534,354	31	1,513,143	43
gross external receipts	390,002	100	470,891	100	530,073	100	600,745	100	736,687	100	974,956	100	1,731,160	100	3,493,242	100
less external payments	167,575		188,996		188,906		209,535		310,862		393,753		562,847		1,079,265	
	222,427		281,895		341,167		391,210		425,825		581,203		1,168,313		2,413,977	
from trust and special funds	36,648		51,051		44,495		91,835		160,128		142,375		286,108		included above
net external and trust	259,075	65	332,662	62	385,662	64	483,045	65	585,953	51	723,578	53	1,454,421	54	2,413,977	54
as 1920 £s													731,496		878,738	
internal income[e]	140,542	35	207,998	38	215,992	36	255,374	35	563,268	49	640,521	47	1,231,178	46		

Calendar.

b Net receipts to 'dividends and interest'.

c Agricultural land.

d Non-agricultural land.

e Including income from fees but not catering account charges.

Sources: *Accounts of the Colleges*, revenue accounts for 1913–64, statement II for 1970/1.

(b) all colleges

	1970–1	%	1980–1	%	1987–8	%
i) gross income managed (not all for college purposes)						
agricultural land, timber and minerals	935,000	21	3,355,000	22	5,689,000	17
non-agricultural land	1,235,000	28	4,493,000	29	10,090,000	30
houses occupied by fellows or students	99,000	2	154,000	1	119,000	
interest and dividends	2,142,000	48	7,540,000	48	17,175,000	51
miscellaneous	13,000		58,000		351,000	1
	4,424,000	100	15,600,000	100	33,425,000	100
less expenses of obtaining income	1,079,000		3,884,000		6,809,000	
	3,345,000		11,716,000		26,616,000	
ii) income for college purposes from:						
endowments and other funds (including external trustees)	3,370,000	39	11,657,000	31	26,422,000	38
fees, dues and charges	5,090,000	59	25,848,000	68	42,260,000	60
grants, donations, other (excluding receipts from university or other colleges)	170,000	2	655,000	2	1,489,000	2
in current £s	8,630,000	100	38,161,000	100	70,171,000	100
in 1920 £s	3,142,000		3,800,000		4,764,000	

Sources: *Accounts of the Colleges*, statements I–III of men's and women's undergraduate colleges, All Souls, Nuffield and St Antony's 1970–1, with addition of Wolfson 1980–1 and Wolfson and Linacre 1987–8.

interest rates. Some colleges had 'largely profited by the advantageous opportunity', and more could have done so.[69]

Be this as it may, post-war sales did reduce Oxford's dependence on agricultural land. Table 24.2 suggests that such land (and the various incidents that went with it) provided some 47 per cent of the gross corporate external receipts of the historic men's colleges in 1913, but only 35 per cent in 1926. Subsequently things were more stable, and the proportion was still 33 per cent in 1964. There may have been some slippage later in the 1960s, but the apparent drop to 27 per cent in 1970/1 is exaggerated by a change in the form of the accounts. In the 1970s agricultural income again held its own, though the 1980s saw a decline in its relative importance.

These shifts, of course, represent not only general trends but also sales (sometimes involuntary) and purchases by individual colleges. The needs of colleges differ—some of the sales were to finance new buildings—but so do their policies. Balliol sold all its agricultural land in the late 1960s and now holds only the ruins, gifted by a former member in 1984, of the Galloway castle where its original statutes were sealed; Nuffield sold almost all its land at the end of the 1970s but made new purchases in the early 1980s; Merton's overall acreage has been remarkably stable, but was higher in 1988 than in 1900. The process can to some extent be followed through the published accounts of capital transactions, but unfortunately these do not always distinguish between different types of property. A cursory survey of nine rich colleges suggests that sales of real estate (both agricultural and urban) considerably exceeded purchases in the early 1920s. In the second half of the decade there was a rough equilibrium. The early 1930s saw substantial net sales, followed by a swing back later in the decade and significant net purchases in the 1940s. The tide then turned again; and later trends seem to have been away from real property, though not always as fast as in the decade after 1955.[70] But we are on firm ground only in comparing specific years. As table 24.3 and figures 24.1–3 show, there has been a fall in overall acreage and a limited shift towards agriculturally more favoured counties. But there has always been a considerable concentration on the Oxford region, and the tendency between 1871 and 1920 was to increase it; similarly 30 per cent of Cambridge's (smaller) acreage lay in Cambridgeshire in 1920.[71] However, Oxford has never been in a very dynamic agricultural area (though recent growth in population has made building 'windfalls' quite likely). So since 1920 there has been a modest move towards better farming districts like Lincolnshire. It is surprising that it has not gone further.

---

[69] *Asquith Report*, 219–24. See also above, 24, 36.

[70] Dunbabin, 'College finances and property', 205–6.

[71] On the concentration of college estates in the Oxford region before 1500 see T. A. R. Evans and R. J. Faith, 'College estates and university finances 1350–1500' in J. I. Catto and R. Evans (eds), *Late Medieval Oxford* (History of the University of Oxford ii, Oxford 1992), 655–6 and map 4.

Scotland was completely ignored in both 1871 and 1920; one college now has land in Banff, a satisfactory but isolated and recent purchase.

As table 24.4 shows, in 1920 Oxford also held 'tithe rent-charges' notionally worth £70,000 a year, these being especially important to Christ Church. Their actual yield had previously varied from this 'par' value according to a formula based on wheat prices in past years. So tithes rose with the wartime boom until capped in 1918 at 9.2 per cent above par. The cap was due to end in 1926, and the Asquith Commission anticipated that tithe would then rise by 20 per cent 'unless legislation again intervenes'. In 1925 parliament stepped in to fix tithe at 105 per cent of par value for ever. The Oxbridge colleges most affected lobbied in vain against this, urging either a return to the pre-war system or a scheme for compulsory commutation drawn up by the Bursar of King's College, Cambridge, J. M. Keynes. Further trouble came with the depression of the early 1930s, when tithe-collection encountered vocal and organized, if sporadic, resistance. Oxford colleges took their traditional line: they would accommodate individuals in genuine financial difficulties but would not make across-the-board reductions. They told the Royal Commission on Tithe Rent-Charge that in 1933 87 per cent of their tithes were paid in full, 5 per cent withheld without good reason and the remainder adjusted to meet cases of hardship. The Commission recommended the reduction of tithe to 8.44 per cent below par and subsequent commutation on terms that further disadvantaged 'lay impropriators' like colleges. In 1936 this was carried into effect, despite further lobbying from Oxford. Gilt-edged stock thus replaced a long-standing link with the fortunes of agriculture.[72]

Before the First World War the fastest growing sector of Oxford's income had been that from 'houses', and more especially building leases. The war checked this. For inflation eroded the real value of ground-rents, and, according to the Asquith Commission, 'some difficulty was experienced' in collecting ordinary rents without abatement. The Commission indeed anticipated no subsequent improvement. In fact building boomed between the wars, and in 1938 the historic colleges' income from 'houses' was nearly twice as high in money, or three times in real, terms as in 1920. Both rack-rents (which could be readjusted periodically) and ground-rents had contributed. But after the Second World War, though receipts from rack-rents continued to grow, ground-rents did not, even in money terms. It was, however, possible to look to the falling in of the original nineteenth-century

---

[72] *Asquith Report*, 219; material relating to Oxford, Cambridge and the tithe bill of 1925 (copies of 3 printed memoranda and a letter to the *Times*) in Bodl. 1229 d. 11; *Report of the Royal Commission on Tithe Rentcharge in England and Wales* (PP 1935–6 xiv Cmd 5095), 865 ff and *Minutes of Evidence taken before the Royal Commission on Tithe Rentcharge* (20 pts and appx HMSO 1934–6), esp. 523, 533; R. Hart-Synnot, 'The passing of tithes', *OM* 21 May 1936, 600–1; Tithe Act 1936.

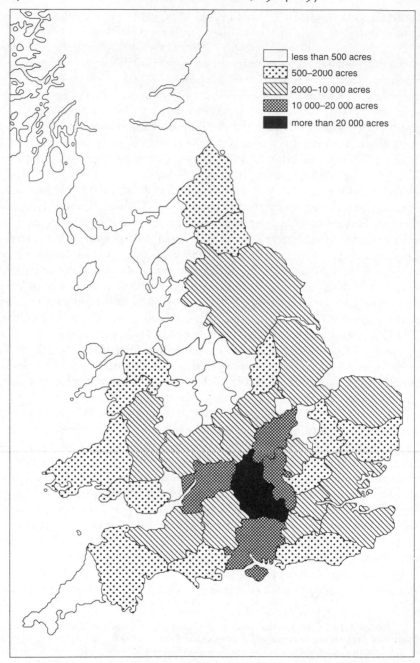

FIGURE 24.1   OXFORD'S HOLDINGS OF AGRICULTURAL LAND AND WOODLAND
(ACRES) IN 1871

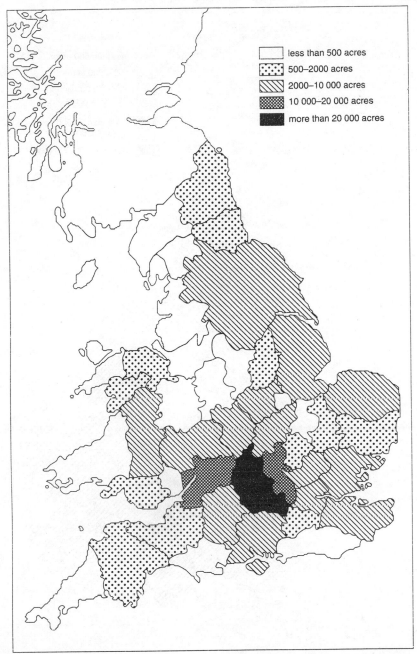

FIGURE 24.2 OXFORD'S HOLDINGS OF AGRICULTURAL LAND AND WOODLAND
(ACRES) IN 1920

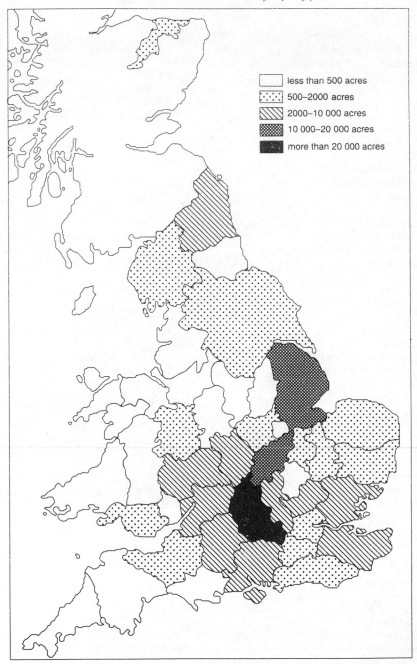

FIGURE 24.3   OXFORD'S HOLDINGS OF AGRICULTURAL LAND AND WOODLAND
(ACRES) IN 1988/9

TABLE 24.3

OXFORD COLLEGE AND UNIVERSITY HOLDINGS OF
AGRICULTURAL LAND AND WOODLAND (ACRES) BY COUNTY
IN 1871, 1920 AND 1988–9, SHOWING % OF TOTAL HOLDINGS
WITHIN EACH COUNTY

	1871	1920	1988/9	1871 %	1920 %	1988/9 %
Anglesey	242	270	—	0.13	0.15	—
Banff	—	—	845	—	—	0.66
Bedfordshire	2,113	1,986	—	1.10	1.13	—
Buckinghamshire	11,644	14,375	5,870	6.05	8.17	4.60
Cambridgeshire	1,026	1,338	1,818	0.53	0.76	1.42
Clwyd	588	674	19	0.31	0.38	0.01
Cornwall	—	1	—	—	0.00	—
Cumbria	350	—	526	0.18	—	0.41
Derbyshire	41	—	—	0.02	—	—
Devon	1,115	762	—	0.58	0.43	—
Dorset	1,080	5	428	0.56	0.00	0.34
Durham	1,535	1,058	—	0.80	0.60	—
Dyfed	952	381	—	0.49	0.22	—
Essex	7,340	5,167	2,397	3.81	2.94	1.88
Glamorgan	1,674	1,436	1,080	0.87	0.82	0.85
Gloucestershire	10,464	10,819	4,113	5.44	6.15	3.22
Hampshire & Isle of Wight	12,380	6,094	2,364	6.43	3.47	1.85
Hereford & Worcester	2,847	2,470	3,128	1.48	1.40	2.45
Hertfordshire	1,316	2,749	3,915	0.68	1.56	3.07
Huntingdonshire	417	420	1,151	0.22	0.24	0.90
Kent	9,331	9,831	7,511	4.85	5.59	5.88
Lancashire & Cheshire	86	22	487	0.04	0.01	0.38
Leicestershire	2,839	3,220	1,846	1.47	1.83	1.45
Lincolnshire	4,258	3,629	17,986	2.21	2.06	14.09
Merioneth	965	869	—	0.50	0.49	—
London & Middlesex	3,008	2,320	600	1.56	1.32	0.47
Monmouthshire	257	236	8	0.13	0.13	0.01
Norfolk	4,087	4,051	1,881	2.12	2.31	1.47
Northamptonshire	14,468	9,673	11,651	7.52	5.50	9.12
Northumberland	850	1,020	3,543	0.44	0.58	2.77
Nottinghamshire	664	651	—	0.34	0.37	—
Oxfordshire & Berkshire	62,370	60,579	37,983	32.40	34.45	29.75
Powys	3,159	3,254	—	1.64	1.85	—
Shropshire	365	—	1,994	0.19	—	1.56
Somerset	2,315	1,979	1,608	1.20	1.13	1.26
Staffordshire	250	217	240	0.13	0.12	0.19
Suffolk	1,359	897	518	0.71	0.51	0.41
Surrey	2,409	1,780	1,423	1.25	1.01	1.11
Sussex	538	84	671	0.28	0.05	0.53
Warwickshire	8,064	8,050	3,761	4.19	4.58	2.95
Wiltshire	7,185	7,989	4,361	3.73	4.54	3.42
Yorkshire	6,563	5,499	1,964	3.31	3.13	1.54
TOTAL	192,514	175,855	127,690	100	100	100

TABLE 24.3 (*cont.*)

Note: Some counties have been grouped together to reduce sensitivity to boundary changes or by way of consolidation where Oxford's property was small. Roundings up prevent columns 4–6 from totalling exactly 100.

Sources:
1871: Computer-based analysis of property (other than leaseholds held by colleges and the like) managed by Oxford halls, colleges and university, as listed by the *Cleveland Report*, pt 2.
1920: *Asquith Report*, appx 19, pp. 356–7.
1988/9: Information from bursars and land agents; amenity land like the University Parks and Shotover is excluded.

99-year leases, and thought was beginning to be given to the redevelopment of north Oxford. This prospect was clouded by the passage of the Leasehold Reform Act, 1967. Much of the colleges' property was above the rateable value there specified, and so not directly involved; but fears that this value would be raised, and of the unpopularity that the running out of leases would generate, led St John's in particular to sell off the freeholds and seek less exposed investments instead.[73] Even so there has been, as table 24.5 shows, a very strong concentration on Oxfordshire and little geographical change: in 1871 Oxfordshire, Middlesex and Hampshire together accounted for 83 per cent of the rental value of Oxford's 'house' property, in 1920 for at least 80 per cent of its tenancies, and in the late 1980s for 74 per cent of income from commercially rented buildings and 'non-agricultural land'.

In 1913 'dividends and interest' provided some 8 per cent of the historic colleges' gross corporate external receipts, in 1987/8 51 per cent of the gross external income managed by the colleges. Such income grew steadily between 1913 and 1938, and its share was enhanced by the commutation of tithe. But in 1948 it was down even in nominal terms, presumably reflecting both purchases of real estate and the post-war economic difficulties of colleges. By 1954 it had risen somewhat, and by 1964 its share had grown considerably [table 24.2]. For the 1950s saw not only higher interest rates but also Oxford's move into equities. As estates bursars had reminded the Asquith Commission, 'Colleges, when investing the proceeds of sales of their lands, are restricted to the comparatively narrow range of strict Trustee investments' (with results that had appalled Cecil Rhodes). In 1931 R. B. McCallum was complaining that it was impossible to invest in equities,

[73] See also T. Hinchcliffe, *North Oxford* (New Haven Conn. and London 1992), ch. 8.

TABLE 24.4

OXFORD COLLEGE AND UNIVERSITY HOLDINGS
OF TITHE ['PAR' OR 'GROSS AWARDED' VALUE
(£)] IN 1871 AND 1920

	1871	1920
Essex	9,904	11,054
Yorkshire	6,817	6,238
Cheshire	6,640	6,801
Hampshire & Isle of Wight	6,259	1,259
Oxfordshire	6,031	6,414
Northumberland	5,612	5,401
Lancashire	4,814	4,047
Kent	4,489	3,432
Gloucestershire	4,011	3,959
Berkshire	3,790	1,744
Montgomeryshire	2,494	2,464
Wiltshire	2,430	2,180
Sussex	2,389	348
Anglesey	1,533	1,098
Bedfordshire	1,405	1,509
Shropshire	1,371	1,380
Warwickshire	1,291	704
Buckinghamshire	1,244	780
Cornwall	1,017	872
London & Middlesex	996	442
Devon	945	1,018
Hertfordshire	832	492
Cambridgeshire	822	951
Herefordshire & Worcestershire	773	780
Somerset	762	824
Cumbria	686	590
Norfolk	479	543
Dorset	478	518
Carmarthenshire	467	511
Northamptonshire	381	403
Surrey	243	12
Lincolnshire	90	90
Cardiganshire	—	871
total	81,495	69,729

Sources: As for table 24.3.

though he felt this too skilled a task for 'bursars and curators' and advocated
a co-operative investment trust. And Keynes's celebrated transformation for
King's of £30,000 into £410,000 between 1924 and 1946 was done with a
fund to which, untypically, such investment restrictions did not apply.[74]

[74] *Asquith Report*, appx 1.ii.d, p. 38; R. B. McCallum, 'Oxford and the financial crisis', *OM*
15 Oct. 1931, 13; R. F. Harrod, *The Life of John Maynard Keynes* (London 1951), 368.

TABLE 24.5

INCOME OF OXFORD COLLEGES AND UNIVERSITY
FROM 'HOUSES' AND 'NON-AGRICULTURAL LAND':
DISTRIBUTION BY COUNTY OR GROUPS OF COUNTIES
(%)

	1871	1920	1988/9
Ayrshire	—	—	1.1
Cumbria, Lancs, Ches, Northumb, Durham, Yorks	1.0	1.2	1.4
Staffs, Shropshire, War, Herefs, Worcs	0.3	0.6	1.7
Lincs, Notts, Derby, Leics, Rutland, Northants	0.9	0.9	0.1
Beds, Bucks, Herts	0.1	1.2	5.0
Norfolk, Suffolk, Cambs, Hunts, Essex	0.6	1.1	2.6
London, Middlesex	15.1	38.9	14.7
Kent	—	2.1	3.2
Surrey, Sussex	12.7	7.2	4.2
Oxon, Berks	49.5	41.5	50.7
Hants, Isle of Wight	17.0	0.3	11.7
Wilts, Dorset, Devon, Cornwall	0.1	0.2	1.4
Glos, Somerset	2.2	2.8	1.6
Wales (including Mon)	0.3	1.6	0.4

1871: Percentages (by area) of estimated annual value of property on
beneficial lease, reserved rent of property on long lease and gross rent of
property at rack-rent.

1920: Percentages of the total number of tenancies. The number of
tenancies is however an indifferent guide to their value (especially in
Hampshire).

1988/9: Percentages of gross income (excluding that from houses in
Oxford for students and staff). Geographical distribution is sensitive to
the sequence of rent-reviews.

Sources: As for table 24.3.

These restrictions were eased by the University and Colleges (Trusts) Act of
1943, which permitted the establishment of trust pools with powers of
investment to be approved by the Privy Council. There was some doubt
whether such powers could legally extend to investment in equities. But
Queen's consulted counsel and, with Keynes's assistance, elaborated a
scheme permitting such investment that was approved in December 1945.[75]

[75] Investment was only to be in companies which were listed on the stock exchange, were
capitalized at over £0.5m and had paid dividends of at least 4% for the last five years: HCP 195
(1946), 251–4.

1945 also saw All Souls' first purchases of shares, and in 1948 Christ Church bought £66,738 worth of 'industrials'. Next year the university passed a statute to give itself most of the powers of the Queen's scheme. This encouraged colleges to follow suit (women's colleges being among the more adventurous). In 1950 Nuffield forecast that equities would yield 4.94 per cent, considerably more than the 2.3 per cent it expected from agricultural property in general, let alone the Wytham estate in which the university had placed some £76,000 of Nuffield's money, and it pressed the university to give it a mixture of saleable land and equities instead.[76] Soon such views were not uncommon.

Oxford's entry into equities was followed by an increase in the number of bodies with full collegiate status. Together these two developments altered the colleges' investment profile. In 1987/8 there were thirteen colleges with no income from agricultural land, of which Balliol and Hertford were the only old ones. Eight of these colleges also figured among the ten that derived less than £10,000 from non-agricultural land, and of the others only Balliol had substantial investment property beyond its curtilage. Equally of the newer foundations only Nuffield, by far the wealthiest, approximates to the traditional investment pattern of a college. 'Dividends and interest' therefore represent the bulk of the external income of the newer and of the poorer Oxford colleges, but also the chief component in that of most of the others. Each college manages its own. There have been suggestions that this could be better done centrally. But the nearest approach to this was the unit trust Nuffield operated in the late 1960s and early 1970s to allow other colleges to share in its success. Unfortunately the trust's performance proved disappointing and it was abandoned as a failure; and although in the long run Nuffield's own investments have done very well, they were heavily geared and were therefore hit particularly hard by the collapse of the market in the mid-1970s. Indeed, whereas for the colleges as a whole gross dividends fell only marginally in money terms in 1975/6 and then resumed their rise, those of Nuffield declined by a quarter, with a further 10 per cent fall the following year; a number of Nuffield's internal economies date from this period. Interest, however, is only one facet of investment. The other is capital growth. Here college accounts are completely silent.[77] But, from the early nineteenth century onward, would-be reformers have been free with their conjectures. One such estimate, of the wealth of the richer colleges as at December 1988, produced a reply from the Vice-Chancellor that probably

[76] *Gazette* lxxix (1948/9), 547; *Accounts of the Colleges*; HCP 206 (1950), 419–31. Wytham had originally been acquired for reasons of conservation as well as investment; Nuffield money had been used as a convenient source of funding, but in 1948 the University's general fund had offered to buy out the Nuffield trustees.

[77] Their pre-Franks format was designed with a view to CUF taxation of external endowment income; Franks was chiefly concerned with the clear portrayal and allocation of current expenditure.

tells us as much as we are likely to learn. 'Informal inquiries of four colleges listed by you suggest that their endowments have been overvalued by at least 50%. If the same over-estimation occurred in the case of the other colleges, your £900m "conservative estimate" of the value of college endowments may be £300m too high.'[78]

We must now turn from the external to the internal income of the colleges. Here too difficulties arise from the form of accounts. But it would seem that for the historic colleges, internal income (mostly fees and charges) provided just over a third of corporate income both in 1913 and between the wars. After the Second World War it jumped to just under a half, and had fallen back only slightly by 1964. The change was no doubt caused by greater numbers of students and the sluggishness of other forms of income in the 1940s. But it also reflected the far greater availability of help to meet such charges after the war. In 1935/6 50 per cent of Oxford students were assisted by sources other than their own families, in 1948/9 82 per cent received such support. The increase owed much to the further education and training scheme for ex-servicemen; and as this was phased out, the proportion of 'assisted students' fell back to 71 per cent in 1953/4. But by 1960/1 it had risen to 84 per cent, as Local Education Authorities became steadily more ready to support anybody who had gained a university place.[79] In 1962 such support was made mandatory. It involved payment of 'approved fees' plus a maintenance grant on a means-tested but fairly generous basis. Although the colleges were still barred from direct receipt of public money, they thus benefited indirectly from state support of university students, and their finances became sensitive to changes in its administration.

It had always been possible to run a college with very limited endowments, albeit at the price of sub-standard facilities and numbers or stipends of fellows, as Keble and the women's colleges had shown. One commentator, writing in the *Oxford Magazine* under the pseudonym 'Overdraft', noted that in 1947 and 1948 colleges' deficits were positively correlated with their wealth and consequent CUF payments. The women's

---

[78] *Economist* 8 July 1989, 25–6 and 29 July 1989, 6. University investments (mostly held for tied funds and endowments) had a market value of £200m in July 1989: *Gazette* cxx (1989/90), 505.

[79] HCP 165 (1936), 9; 204 (1936), 61; 219 (1954), pp. lix, 30; 240 (1961), 183, 355; UGC *Returns from Universities and University Colleges in receipt of Treasury Grant: Academic Year 1948/49* (HMSO 1950); UGC *Returns from Universities and University Colleges in Receipt of Treasury Grant: Academic Year 1953/1954* (PP 1955–6 xxx Cmd 9477); UGC *Returns from Universities and University Colleges in Receipt of Treasury Grant: Academic Year 1960/1961* (PP 1962–3 xxvi Cmnd 1855). Inter-collegiate competition for good undergraduates prevented a corresponding reduction in awards by colleges. Franks drew attention to the £135,000 thus spent to little useful purpose and urged cuts: *Franks Report* i, paras 185–9. But, until the reform of the entrance examination in 1985, such savings as did materialize came chiefly through the erosion of the awards by inflation.

colleges made a profit or broke even as a result of their receipts from conferences, and St Edmund Hall 'made a comfortable surplus . . . by the simple method of paying nothing to the Fellows except from the tuition fund'.[80] In the 1950s, the then Principal notes, St Edmund Hall 'silently abandoned the role, adopted since the eighteenth century . . . of providing a full Oxford education at more economical rates than the colleges. This had been on the way out in the immediate post-war quinquennium, but had been made obsolete (as Keble, St Catherine's and St Peter's were also quick to perceive) by the public funding of student grants and university lecturerships.'[81] An important corollary was that a large student body could prove an economic asset. Since 1945, there has been no shortage of applicants and this must have been of some importance in encouraging the gradual increase in the size of colleges that began in the later 1950s. There was, however, one drawback: the most profitable students were those living out, but pressure from various quarters to increase the proportion housed by colleges compelled the periodic construction of new buildings whose capital costs could not be met from charges to students. This helps to explain the proliferation of college appeals from the 1960s. Other factors were the success of the Historic Buildings appeal, and of Balliol's appeal in 1963 for the then noteworthy sum of £1m. Most previous college appeals had either marked centenaries or reflected special circumstances. Indeed, in 1938 the Treasurer of Christ Church could write that it 'had never been the custom for the Colleges to appeal to their former members for financial assistance', though his counterpart at Lincoln would have known better.

Tuition-fees became regulated after the war by the new inter-collegiate senior tutors' committee; colleges then adjusted other fees to bridge the gap between their projections of overall revenue and expenditure. The result was a general, if imperfect, correlation between college 'poverty' and high fees, though until the 1970s this was obscured by the absence of a uniform fee structure. In 1970 the Bursar of University College circulated a paper arguing that college fees had recently lagged behind inflation and recommending increases, and in 1971 similar recommendations were made by a new inter-collegiate committee on fees which he chaired. 1972 brought a national prices and incomes policy, and the committee on fees now assumed the role of advising colleges on the appropriate response. Their percentage increases came accordingly to move more and more in parallel. The process was completed when the Department of Education and Science insisted on negotiating, with representatives of the colleges of Oxford and Cambridge,

---

[80] 'Overdraft', 'University and college finances', *OM* 4 Nov. 1948, 96 and 'The college accounts for 1948', *OM* 20 Oct. 1949, 36.

[81] J. N. D. Kelly, *St Edmund Hall: Almost Seven Hundred Years* (Oxford 1989), 130. In the 1940s public maintenance grants for students at St Edmund Hall had been lower than for those at ordinary colleges.

overall annual changes for each university with effect from 1977/8. There remained the problem of constraining colleges to keep within these guidelines. In the mid-1970s this occasioned a review of college finances and a substantial increase in the endowment grants paid to the poorer colleges from CUF taxation. The grants were originally suggested as a prelude to the adoption of a common level of fees by all colleges; but it was eventually agreed that the existing pattern of college fees should be frozen, with changes only to be permitted (in exceptional circumstances) by the Conference of Colleges. The system has worked surprisingly smoothly and without visible intrusion on the exercise of college autonomy. But the payment of fees to colleges as well as to the university can seem anomalous if viewed in isolation from the general pattern of Oxford's finances.[82] In 1986 the UGC deducted from its grant to the university half the fees paid to colleges from public funds. In response Oxford volunteered a cut of a third, and in 1987/8 the UGC settled on 42 per cent.[83] Then in 1992 the government decided that college fees should be progressively squeezed in real terms. This engendered alarm as to many colleges' long-term financial viability, and was one of the causes of the commissioning in 1994 of a new internal inquiry into the University's general operation.

By contrast with fees each college sets its own charges for the meals and accommodation of students. Until the 1970s these were determined unilaterally, but since then undergraduates have increasingly insisted on prior discussion. For this they are briefed with growing sophistication by the Oxford University Student Union, and nationally determined trends in student maintenance grants (and eligibility for social security) loom large. Governing bodies then make the final decisions, which (despite occasional rent strikes) were, before the 1990s, seldom very seriously contested, though there have been rent-strikes. But the decline in the importance of charges on junior members relative to college income both from fees and from conferences suggests that junior members are not ineffective bargainers.[84]

It remains to draw the threads together by offering some picture of the changes in Oxford's finances over time. Unfortunately it is not easy to allow for inflation. No single measure is ideal, if only because some payments (including, over long periods, college awards) are fixed in money terms and the effect of inflation is felt by the recipients, not by the institution. Setting this aside, much depends on the choice of index: thus the *Economist*

---

[82] *Richards Report*, ch. 5; cf below, 763–4.

[83] *Gazette* cxvii (1986/7), 58; cxviii (1987/8), 381–2. College fees for postgraduate students (whose supervision is a responsibility of the university) pose a special problem, as research councils tend to question the justification of such fees and forget that their own income has been adjusted to meet them.

[84] The relationship of income from fees, charges to members and charges to conferences and the like was 40:53:8 in 1970/1, 53:40:7 in 1980/1 and 51:38:11 in 1988/9.

calculated that university income had grown by 54 per cent 'in real terms' between 1976/7 and 1987/8 whereas the Vice-Chancellor, using the 'university pay and prices index', put the gain at only 24.8 per cent. Costs in service industries, of which universities are one, tend to rise faster than prices in general. And it can be argued that by using the retail price index—largely for historiographical convenience, but also because it provides a more neutral measure of opportunity cost—the calculations that follow give too rosy a picture. With this caveat, it will be convenient to turn first to the colleges. Table 24.2 gave their incomes, and table 24.6 lists their internal expenditure.

Both world wars brought major setbacks, as income (and therefore expenditure) fell behind rising prices. That occasioned by the First World War was by far the sharper, but recovery was slower after the second. We have already noted the gloomy memorandum of 1947 of the estates bursars' committee: 'All indications point to a danger of net external revenues being reduced. The reduction in the rate of interest on trustee securities, the loss of income on the redemption of tithe, the effects of the blitz, the fall of site values . . . in the City of London, and above all the whole trend of modern legislation in depriving the landowner of any form of increment, are all exercising a depressing effect, which forthcoming legislation is likely to intensify, while outgoings of all kinds, particularly repairs and rates, are soaring.' The bursars were agitating for a cut in university taxation to leave room for inter-collegiate aid. There was much support in the *Oxford Magazine*, 'Overdraft' suggesting that it would be easier for the university than for the colleges to make economies. But he later noted that 'the College results which have got steadily worse over the whole period 1946–50 took a small turn for the better in 1951'.[85] And, as the Richards Committee noted in 1976, at the time of the Franks Commission most colleges seemed comfortably placed: endowment income had grown rapidly 'for several years, reflecting increased dividend distribution, the first phase of the urban development boom, and the unfreezing of agricultural rents'; the Historic Buildings appeal had relieved a major worry; there was no real 'consciousness of the potential limitations of fee income'; 'nor was the ability and willingness of junior members to pay increasing board and lodging charges in question'.[86] Since then there have inevitably been setbacks (especially in 1974/5 when an overall college surplus of £240,000 was turned into a deficit of £350,000) but overall income (in constant prices) has been on a rising trend. In per capita terms, though, progress has been less marked. For, at face value, the level of real expenditure per undergraduate of 1913 was not attained again until the later 1980s (and then on the basis of markedly more comprehensive accounts). This is impressive evidence for the view of

[85] HCP 198 (1947), 101 (cf above, 653–4); 'Overdraft', 'University and college finances', 96 and 'College accounts for 1948', 36; 'Overdraft', 'The turn in the curve?', *OM* 12 Feb. 1953, 191–2.   [86] *Richards Report*, 2–3.

TABLE 24.6

INTERNAL EXPENDITURES OF OXFORD COLLEGES (IN CURRENT £s, CONSTANT £s, AND CONSTANT £s PER RESIDENT STUDENT)

colleges	£*	1913	1920	1926	1938	1949	1954	1964	1970/1	1980/1	1987/8
men's colleges	a	344,000	477,000	545,000	688,000	1,118,000	1,267,000	2,847,000			
(University–Hertford)	b	831,000	477,000	790,000	1,079,000	982,000	865,000	1,432,000			
	c	323	138	NA	NA	189	177	236			
men's colleges	a						1,627,000	3,723,000			
(University–Keble,	b						1,110,000	1,873,000			
SEH, St Peter's plus											
St Antony's and the											
women's colleges	c						168	228			
as above plus St	a							4,059,000	8,267,000	35,922,000	66,381,000
Catherine's, Nuffield,	b							2,041,000	3,009,000	3,577,000	4,507,000
Wolfson (from 1980/1)											
and Linacre (1987/8											
only	c							237	289	305	347

Sources:

* *a* current £; *b* 1920 £; *c* 1920 £ per resident undergraduate/student

1913–64: Synopses of college accounts in HCP; to make the 1953/4 figures for women's colleges more comparable with the less inclusive accounts for the men's colleges, 'food' has been omitted.

1970/1 to 1987/8: Accounts of the Colleges, expenditure for the colleges' own purposes, excluding CUF contributions and donations for university objects.

Edwardian upper-class comfort as an Indian summer. But it should not be taken too far, for modern colleges are indisputably warmer and better plumbed than their counterparts of 1913 (with poorer colleges often leading the way because they need income from conferences), their catering is more cost-effective and they probably also enjoy economies of scale.

For the university, the era before 1914 was one of financial strain, albeit chiefly deriving from the recognition of new needs. Thanks partly to the annual 'government emergency grant' of £30,000, it did not emerge from the war in too bad shape. Net money-income had risen from £119,000 in 1913 to £217,000 in 1920; but in real terms this represented a fall of about a quarter, and the University pleaded poverty to the Asquith Commission.[87] The Commission concluded that Oxford could not survive without state aid. Its recommendations were accepted only in part. But between 1920 and 1925/6 the university's income nearly doubled: only 27 per cent of this improvement came from the enhancement of the Treasury grant; and endowments, other government departments, fees and 'other' income all contributed considerably. By 1929/30 the university's income was slightly down in money, though perhaps up in real, terms. In the 1930s there was an improvement of about a third, due chiefly to the rise in endowment income. After 1945, as we have seen, the scale of UGC funding was transformed, and grants, which had accounted for a quarter of the university's income in 1938/9, provided just over a half ten years later. By 1953/4 the proportion was two-thirds, where it remained until 1970/1, falling back to 53.5 per cent in 1980/1 and 46.3 per cent in 1987/8. On the basis of the retail price index, total recurrent university income grew more than sixfold between 1948/9 and 1987/8, with the fastest rises in the 1950s and 1960s. In the 1970s growth was slower but still clearly positive, as was not the case with Cambridge, whose absolute decline left Oxford, for the first time in our period, the richer university.[88] In 1977/8 income from research grants and contracts, which had been declining in real terms, turned up sharply and continuously; by 1987/8 they accounted for almost a third of all university income. But though total income was buoyant in the 1980s, the true picture was much more variegated. For specific income from research contracts cannot readily support such other basic university activities as libraries, teaching and the arts generally; and in 1981 and 1986 cuts were announced in the

---

[87] For 1913 see HCP 99 (1914), 65 (excluding income-tax repayments, a contribution from capital for loan repayments, and external expenditure); for 1920 see *Asquith Report*, 196–7.

[88] Cambridge's recurrent university income was, as a multiple of Oxford's, 1.17 in 1920, 1.41 in 1929/30, 1.36 in 1938/9, 1.25 in 1948/9, 1.09 in 1963/4, 1.18 in 1970/1, 0.89 in 1980/1, 0.87 in 1987/8. For 1920 see *Asquith Report*. For the other years see UGC *Returns from Universities and University Colleges in Receipt of Treasury Grant (sub anno)*; Department of Education and Science, *Statistics of Education 1971* (6 vols HMSO 1974) vi; UGC *Universities* (1970–1); UGC *University Statistics 1980* (3 vols Universities' Statistical Record 1982) iii (finance 1980–1); UGC *University Statistics 1987/88* (3 vols Universities' Statistical Record 1988–9) iii (finance).

government's funding (Exchequer grants plus home-students' fees) from which these had chiefly been financed.[89] These cuts have so far (1990) proved smaller than was feared; but they have brought programmes of retrenchment aimed at cutting or freezing over 15 per cent of the posts on the academic establishment of 1981, and turned the University to external fund-raising to limit the damage.[90]

If one were to look at the UGC returns, one would conclude that Oxford is rather a poor university. Its real position can be computed only by including the colleges, which (since they never receive UGC money) do not figure in its statistics. Unfortunately it is hard to reduce their accounts to the UGC format since they cover much housekeeping activity that other universities either do not conduct or relegate to separate non-UGC accounts. Moreover, apportioning college expenditure is difficult.[91] Judgements are periodically made of what constitutes 'education and research'; the historian has to use them, but they have varied over time and are clearly rather arbitrary. Table 24.7 attempts to meld college and UGC figures to provide some comparison between Oxford and other British universities (excluding Cambridge, where college incomes present many of the same problems as at Oxford). Its comparisons are, however, based on income or expenditure per student, while some costs are largely independent of student numbers. (Oxford contends that the allocation of grants by the UGC in 1986, the first to seek uniformity of treatment as between universities, did not allow sufficiently for the costs of maintaining museums and libraries of national importance.) Also, of course, since some academic disciplines cost more than others, Oxford's large (if diminishing) arts profile will have been financially advantageous.

The gap is no longer as wide as in the 1920s. But Oxford's income per student (in areas covered by the UGC returns) has been consistently above the average of British universities, and in all but one of the years chosen also above that of relatively well funded Birmingham. This owes much to endowments. Their importance has diminished over time—with a recovery in the 1980s—but for most of our period they have sustained Oxford in the face of below-average grants of public money. Oxford's income from grants, indeed, is still below average. If one takes grants and fees together (though

[89] Campaign for Oxford (University of Oxford [1989]), 7, 30.

[90] As converted by the RPI, UGC grants plus home-student fees stood slightly lower in 1987/8 than in 1980/1, but slightly higher in 1988/9 (albeit partly because of the subvention of early retirement and so on). If the fees of overseas students are added there has been a definite, though modest, improvement. (Furthermore, endowments benefited from the stock-market boom, but these are mostly tied to specific purposes.)

[91] Since St Edmund Hall had really only one machine, photocopying for this chapter featured in its accounts not as an academic item but under 'office expenses'. On a less parochial level, college teaching was thought in 1951 to have 'saved' the UGC between a tenth and a quarter (depending on the assumptions made) of its total grant to Oxford: HCP 209 (1951), 126–30. Smaller savings stemmed from the provision by colleges of academic rooms and administration.

SOME COMPARISONS OF OXFORD UNIVERSITY AND COLLEGE FINANCES WITH THE EQUIVALENTS FOR 'ALL UNIVERSITIES IN GREAT BRITAIN' (£) (PRINCIPAL ITEMS ONLY)

	income				expenditure			
	total[a]	endowment	grants	fees	total	administration	departmental maintenance	maintenance of premises
1925/6								
Oxford: university colleges[b]	420,000	125,000	137,000	114,000	393,000	18,000	226,000	24,000
	492,000[c]	399,000	—	94,000	385,000[c]	NA	352,000[e]	33,000[f]
	913,000	524,000	137,000	207,000	779,000		578,000	57,000
per full-time student	210 (268)	120	31	48	179		133	13
all universities in Great Britain	4,826,000	752,000	2,358,000	1,430,000	3,893,000	381,000	2,529,000	470,000
per full-time student	116	18	57	34	93		61	11
1953/4								
Oxford: university colleges[b]	2,020,000	317,000	1,383,000	206,000	2,030,000	86,000	1,593,000	204,000
	1,053,000[c]	705,000	—	348,000	774,000[g]		774,000[g]	
	3,073,000	1,022,000	1,383,000	554,000	2,804,000		2,367,000	
per full-time student	437(298)	145	197	79	398		336	
all universities	31,112,000	1,829,000	23,094,000	3,725,000	30,260,000	2,210,000	21,006,000	3,827,000
per full-time student	386	23	286	46	375		261	

[a] Figures in brackets are in 1920 £s.

[b] In 1925/6 the colleges are the men's colleges from University College to Keble; in addition St Edmund Hall, St Peter's, St Antony's and the women's colleges have been included for 1953/4.

[c] Endowment and tuition fees only.

[d] 'General', tuition, buildings.

[e] General academical and tuition.

[f] College buildings.

[g] Education and research only.

Sources: Oxford and other universities: UGC returns; 'endowment' includes 'donations and subscriptions' and, for Oxford, college contributions; 'all universities in Great Britain' includes Cambridge University but not the colleges of Oxford or Cambridge. Oxford colleges: the figures for 1925/6 are those for 1920 as reworked for the Asquith commission, *Asquith Report*, appx 16, since the published accounts cannot be reduced to the UGC's format; those for 1953/4 are from HCP 222 (1955), 301–16.

TABLE 24.7 (cont.)

SOME COMPARISONS OF OXFORD UNIVERSITY AND COLLEGE FINANC[...]
WITH THE EQUIVALENTS FOR 'ALL UNIVERSITIES IN GREAT BRITAIN'
(£) (PRINCIPAL ITEMS ONLY)

	income				
	endowments	grants	fees	payments for research and other	total recurrer[...]
1963/4					
Oxford: university	447,000	4,233,000	408,000	1,276,000	6,3[...]
colleges[b]	1,547,000	—	680,000	73,000	2,3[...]
	1,994,000	4,233,000	1,088,000	1,349,000	8,6[...]
per full-time student	222	472	121	151	967
all universities in Great Britain	2,709,000	76,322,000	9,157,000	15,453,000	104,44
per full-time student	21	604	72	122	
1970/1					
Oxford: university	897,000	9,071,000	553,000	3,455,000	13,9[...]
colleges[b]	3,370,000	—	2,005,000	170,000[c]	5,5[...]
	4,267,000	9,071,000	2,558,000	3,625,000	19,5[...]
per full-time student	385	819	231	327	1,76
all universities	4,664,000	235,389,000	20,010,000	55,500,000	315,5[...]
per full-time student	20	1,032	88	243	
1980/1					
Oxford: university	3,974,000	33,734,000	10,383,000	15,022,000	63,1
colleges[b]	11,657,000	—	10,953,000	655,000[c]	23,2[...]
	15,631,000	33,734,000	21,336,000	15,677,000	86,3.
per full-time equivalent (FTE) student load	1,218	2,628	1,662	1,221	6,73[...]
all universities	14,661,000	993,463,000	265,839,000	289,071,000	1,563,0
per FTE student load	47	3,184	852	927	
1987/8					
Oxford: university	6,582,000	53,237,000	14,294,000	40,828,000	114,9[...]
colleges[b]	26,422,000	—	17,788,000	1,489,000[c]	45,6[...]
	33,004,000	53,237,000	32,082,000	42,317,000	160,6
per FTE student load	2,430	3,919	2,362	3,115	11,82
all universities	36,430,000	1,512,154,000	355,261,000	803,953,000	2,707,79
per FTE student load	114	4,748	1,115	2,524	

[a] Figures in brackets are in 1920 £s.

[b] In 1953/4 the colleges are the men's colleges from University College to Keble plus St Edm[...] Hall and St Peter's, the women's colleges, and St Antony's; from 1963/4 Nuffield and St Catherine's are also included, as are Wolfson from 1980/1 and Linacre in 1987/8.

[c] Grants, donations, other.

ne		recurrent expenditure			
rent	non-educational college fees	total	adminis-tration	academic departments and services	maintenance of premises
904,000	—	6,162,000	272,000	4,853,000	578,000
—	662,000	2,375,000	337,000	1,085,000	669,000
904,000	662,000	8,537,000	609,000	5,938,000	1,247,000
101	74	952	68	663	139
296,000	—	102,302,000	6,878,000	73,743,000	14,287,000
342	—	809	54	583	113
74,000	—	13,636,000	622,000	10,755,000	1,180,000
—	856,000	4,346,000	373,000	2,753,000	742,000
74,000	856,000	17,982,000	995,000	13,508,000	1,922,000
142	77	1,624	90	1,220	174
63,000	—	313,797,000	21,303,000	219,982,000	43,520,000
359	—	1,376	93	964	191
76,000	—	62,574,000	2,974,000	48,696,000	6,785,000
—	4,724,000	17,802,000	1,975,000	10,710,000	3,490,000
76,000	4,724,000	80,376,000	4,949,000	59,406,000	10,275,000
247	368	6,262	386	4,628	801
34,000	—	1,555,551,000	95,129,000	1,102,726,000	252,605,000
332	—	4,986	305	3,535	810
32,000	—	116,351,000	4,941,000	90,947,000	12,544,000
—	6,985,000	34,049,000	3,498,000	19,684,000	6,637,000
32,000	6,985,000	150,400,000	8,439,000	110,631,000	19,181,000
393	514	11,073	622	8,145	1,412
07,000	—	2,721,909,000	153,763,000	1,958,910,000	374,549,000
396	—	8,546	483	6,151	1,176

es: Oxford and other universities: UGC returns; 'endowment' includes 'donations
ubscriptions' and, for Oxford, college contributions; 'all universities in Great
in' includes Cambridge University but not the colleges of Oxford or Cambridge.
rd colleges: *Franks Report* i. 157 and UGC returns (1963/4); *Accounts of the
ges* (1970/1 onward).

not all fees come from the public purse) Oxford was below average as late as 1963/4, when the Franks Commission calculated that 'half its endowment income is used to meet academic costs which would otherwise fall on the public purse'.[92] This was, however, no longer the case in 1970/1, and by 1980/1 Oxford had overtaken Birmingham. 'Payments for research and other income' is harder to categorize. But here too Oxford's receipts have been high, and by 1980/1 they contributed more money than did endowments, though probably less net profit. Two other categories lie outside the main UGC accounts: 'non-recurrent' grants (where Oxford has generally done rather badly) and its unusual receipt of 'approved fees' applicable to colleges' domestic expenditure (which seem to have overtaken non-recurrent grants by 1980/1).

Overall Oxford has always been a rich university by British (if not American) standards. But there have been richer. No doubt the London and Manchester business schools (with their large contract incomes), the Welsh National School of Medicine and (in 1963/4) the infant University of East Anglia are special cases. However the Manchester College of Science and Technology (until 1963/4) and Reading University (in 1953/4 and 1963/4) also appear to have had higher incomes per student. Since 1953/4 so has London University taken as a whole—partly, no doubt, because of its location, but also because scientific institutions like Imperial College do not come cheap.[93]

We should, however, conclude on a more domestic note. Twentieth-century Oxford has grown in size and income, and indeed in income per student, probably faster than ever before. But then it needs to. For though money is a very imperfect guide to academic performance, a modern university would not get far on the fifty-two shillings a year of the award that in 1214 launched Oxford on its corporate existence.

[92] *Franks Report* i, paras 362, 366.

[93] 1925/6 Manchester College of Science and Technology £434, Oxford £210, London £146; 1953/4 Reading £546, London £520, MCST £460, Oxford £437; 1963/4 London £1,161, Reading £1,047, MCST £1,033, Oxford £967, Birmingham £963; 1970/1 London £2,089, Oxford £1,763. See the UGC returns for these years.

25

Government and Administration,
1914–1964

BRIAN HARRISON

Lord Franks used the phrase 'quiet revolution' to describe how Council during the twentieth century gradually and unobtrusively came to co-ordinate and formulate University policy. In a University composed of autonomous colleges this was a major change, but the phrase can also be used to describe a related but wider revolution: the growth in the University's central direction and administration that stemmed from its mounting size and complexity and from its tightening relations with outside bodies. Like Beveridge's scheme for a revolution in public welfare, this was 'a natural development from the past . . . a British revolution'.[1]

The University's structure is not illuminated by what Kenneth Wheare called Oxford's 'delusions of Westminster' and 'illusions of Downing Street':[2] by its taste for drawing analogies with the British or even the American constitution. It can best be clarified by describing how it worked within three consecutive periods: the *ancien régime* from 1914 up to the early 1930s; 'Veale's Oxford', the years when Sir Douglas Veale was Registrar from then until the mid-1950s; and 'the age of reform' that lasted from then till the mid-1970s. However important the world wars may be as signposts in national history, and even for some aspects of Oxford's history, they are mere interruptions in the history of the University's constitution. Within each period, the discussion will move down the University's hierarchy: from chancellor to vice-chancellor to Council to General Board to Congregation and junior-member representation. Each section will conclude by discussing the central administration, which has to handle the consequences of interaction between the first four and the last two.

---

[1] *Franks Report* i. 198; [Beveridge] *Report on Social Insurance and Allied Services* (PP 1942–3 vi Cmnd 6404), 17. I acknowledge here most helpful comments on earlier drafts by the former Bursar of St John's, Harry Kidd, and by Sir Keith Thomas.

[2] K. C. Wheare, 'The government of the University 1947–67', History of the University seminar, 13 Feb. 1973, typescript in HUA, p. 5. See also C. H. Wilson's lecture, *OM* 16 May 1946, 285.

The phrase *ancien régime* is of course relative only to what followed. In its research, in the growth of its science, in its responsiveness to outside reforming pressure and in its broadening international links, Edwardian Oxford was far from stagnant, and First-World-War Oxford responded notably to national needs. Nor was the period between 1914 and 1930 uniform in its mood: the war years were a hiatus in Oxford's history, and the University in 1918 was bristling with reforming pressures which the Asquith Commission moderated only gradually in the early 1920s. Looking back from the 1990s, however, or even from the 1950s, Oxford's political and administrative structure between 1914 and 1930 seems remote indeed. Almost all initiatives then came from the colleges, whence also came most of Oxford's revenue (from fees and endowments). Without the colleges, said the University's official *Handbook* in 1932, the university 'is only an empty conception and a row of monuments'.[3]

In 1925 the *Times* thought Oxford men wanted a chancellor who would combine 'eminence in public life' with 'a certain academic distinction', the difficulty being 'to find the two in combination'.[4] Chancellors, elected for life by Convocation, filled a remote and largely ceremonial role. Curzon's activism as Chancellor was unusual, and Oxford did not yearn for a repeat performance. Those who wanted the old and frail Alfred Milner to stand in 1925 frequently emphasized the lightness of the duties, and Lord Cave was told that a 'position . . . almost the most splendid attainable by an Englishman' entailed 'scarcely any labour' and brought 'nothing but honour and pleasure'.[5] Chancellors left day-to-day administration to the vice-chancellors whom they chose by convention from heads of house in order of appointment as head, for one year in the first instance. Normally re-appointed three times by the chancellor, vice-chancellors thus chosen were imbued with collegiate values, and between 1906 and 1941 they entered office at a median age of 56.[6]

The vice-chancellor enjoyed wide discretion but, like the prime minister, had only unwritten tradition as guide. He lacked both the time for all his duties and reliable indicators of University opinion, yet his doings were jealously scrutinized and he had no strong administration behind him. On assuming the post in 1906, President Warren acquired from his predecessor some useless items of bric-à-brac, a few letters about quite recent events and a handsome walking stick, but no correspondence or records of policy, no office, no secretary; as he put it, he inherited 'a stick, but no staff'.[7] He

    3 *Handbook* 1932, 80.
    4 *Times* 25 Mar. 1925, 14.
    5 BL Add. MS 62492 (Cave Papers), fo 23, undated note from 'G', reporting conversation with 'C. L.'. See also Bodl. MS Milner Dep. 54/76, Crawford of Balcarres to Milner, 3 Apr. 1925.
    6 For age at accession see *OM* 17 Oct. 1957, 1; 31 Oct. 1957, 57.
    7 Asquith Commission, oral evidence, Bodl. MS top. Oxon. b. 104, fos 210–11.

introduced improvements, and under Strong in 1916 the duties of the Bedel of Arts became largely secretarial. But L. R. Farnell's conscientious and busy but indiscreet activism, critical of the colleges, weakened the case for making the post of vice-chancellor permanent. When contaminated chocolates, sent to him as a prank, were at first interpreted as a murder attempt and then discovered to contain only toothpaste, Farnell's stout and courageous defence of traditional values in a threatening post-war world was touched by farce. When senior members petitioned against his renewal, Farnell was subjected by Curzon, his Chancellor, to 'a three-hours' talk without grace or hospitality'.[8] The Asquith Commission curtailed the vice-chancellor's term from four years to three, and Farnell's more cautious successors Wells (1923–6) and Pember (1926–9) interpreted their role less strenuously. By corresponding frequently with his vice-chancellors, the conscientious and approachable Lord Cave, Curzon's successor as Chancellor (1925–8), helped to repair relationships at the highest level.

Council, with 23 members, resembled the cabinet only in its size. Like cabinet ministers, its members broke their façade of unity with only the occasional judicious leak. Yet the analogy with the cabinet was misleading. Council's nominal chairman (the chancellor) did not attend, and the vice-chancellor could not hire or fire any of his 21 colleagues. And if Oxford's acting prime minister was not 'primus', neither were his colleagues on council 'pares'. Three (two proctors and either the previous or future vice-chancellor) attended by virtue of their office, and until the Asquith Commission's reforms, the eighteen elected members had to include three heads of house, six professors and nine members of Convocation. Thereafter the eighteen were elected by Congregation for a six-year term in biennial batches of six. Council was as much advisory as executive, and few of its members had any personal or continuous 'ministerial' responsibility. They could, at least in theory, oppose Council's proposals both in Congregation and within their colleges. Council offered no legislative programme to its electors, who therefore voted for personalities not policies. Indeed, much resentment was felt when the women were thought to have mobilized their voting power at Council elections during 1926.[9]

At no stage did Council operate within a unitary state. The University in the 1920s was confederal, and Council members (including the vice-chancellor) were only temporary refugees from their colleges. It was the college that provided the vice-chancellor with accommodation and such secretarial facilities as there were. College views were reinforced in Council by the presence of two proctors, projected by their colleges into full-time university administration for one year only. Many acquired a taste for

---

[8] L. R. Farnell, *An Oxonian Looks Back* (London 1934), 315.
[9] See above, 356–8.

university administration; of the 141 elected members of Council between 1914 and 1970, 43 had at some time been proctor. Council lacked overall financial control, which was fragmented between university and colleges, given that the Asquith Commission rejected what the Labour Party regarded as 'an obvious and important reform': the centralized administration of college and university property. Control was also fragmented at the university level in the 1920s, given that 'real power lay with' the Chest, whose sharing of power with Council was seen in 1932 as 'one of the most striking features of the government of Oxford'. Council had to consult the Chest on the financial aspect of any change it was contemplating. A smaller body than Council, and formed in 1920 from amalgamating the old Chest with the Board of Finance, it 'had a reputation for special sagacity and strength of purpose' and employed methods which 'bordered upon the obscure'.[10]

In 1930 Council's 18 elected members filled 53 committee places, yet it is symbolic of Oxford's diffused power-structure that many heads of house have never been on Council, and that even so prominent an Oxford administrator as Lord Franks was on for only two years.[11] On the other hand, a college fellow such as A. S. L. Farquharson of University College was on Council for 14 years and P. A. Landon of Trinity for 18. Forty-eight of the 141 elected members between 1914 and 1970 were elected as heads of house, and 10 as professors, but only 18 were at any time members of the Ashmolean Club, Oxford's élite dining club, which drew together some of the University's leading administrators, heads of house and science professors. Co-opted and all-male in membership, unofficial in status and combining business with sociability—the Club was characteristic of Oxford's approach to government. Maximum membership gradually increased during the period from 18 to 27, and members toasted one another on winning knighthoods or Royal Society medals, drank silently in memory of the departed, and were interested enough in their past to publish a centenary history in 1969.[12]

From 1913 Council was complemented by a General Board of the Faculties. Its subject-based structure cut across Oxford's multi-disciplinary collegiate organization. Wearing their faculty hats, the teaching fellows of colleges mingled with professors and other university appointees in their subject-area; together they organized the faculty's university-wide ac-

[10] Quotations from *Asquith Report*, appx vol., 62; D. Veale, 'The mechanics of reform 1922 to 1939', History of University seminar, 1 May 1973, typescript in HUA, p. 6; *Handbook* 1932, 81; Veale, 6.

[11] *The Government of Oxford* (London 1931), 46–7; membership of Hebdomadal Council is to be found in successive annual volumes of the *Calendar*.

[12] See the anonymous *A Hundred Years of the Ashmolean Club 1869–1969* (Oxford [1969]); Bodl. MSS top. Oxon. f. 64, minutes of the Ashmolean Club 1869–1930, and f. 81, minutes 1930–77.

tivities. The eight faculties, each with its (plenary) faculty meeting and its (executive) faculty board, dispatched a total of twenty representatives (half elected by the boards and half by the faculties) to the General Board, where they were united with the vice-chancellor (chairman) and the two proctors. The Board was better placed than Council to encourage research, yet it belied the Asquith Commission's hopes that it would transcend the fragmented subject-based concerns of its faculty representatives. Its membership was eventually cut to fifteen, three of the elected ones chosen by Council, the other nine by the faculties. Nor did the Commission's Common University Fund (CUF) lecturerships, originally designed to free college tutors for research, weaken college control over tutorial appointments. On arriving in Oxford, Veale found the General Board enjoying little prestige, largely preoccupied with routine matters, unable to make academic policy and far less powerful than the Chest.[13]

Oxford's executive arm was weak by comparison with the vigour of its many parliaments: Convocation, Congregation and the governing bodies of its colleges, whose fellows administered the colleges' property, fiercely upheld college autonomy, and used Congregation as their weapon at the centre. Convocation was in theory made up from all masters of arts and doctors of divinity, medicine or civil law who had paid their university dues and kept their names on the college books. Its membership rose steadily, and during the 1920s averaged at 7,691, but few of its members ever turned up, its powers had long been waning, and it met rarely.[14] In practice, Convocation's meetings attracted the same people as Congregation, a university legislature whose membership was one-tenth as large and much more professional in composition, made up from those who taught within or helped to run the university or colleges.

In *ancien régime* Oxford many senior members genuinely believed in direct democracy and had the leisure to make it a reality. There was no postal vote, and snap votes were thought fair because Congregation was seen as a live assembly whose decisions should be moulded by its debates. It suffered from 'delusions of Westminster', perhaps because its membership was then comparable in size. Yet the analogy stopped there: most Council members were elected directly, whereas cabinet ministers are selected from the legislature. Council members and Curators of the Chest felt obliged to attend if only in self-defence, which ensured that attendance in the 1920s seldom fell below 30, but others had little incentive even to turn up regularly, let alone vote responsibly. The demands of research and administration were growing, and in all three of his orations as Vice-Chancellor, Wells complained that the young were coming less often.

[13] Veale's comments during the discussion after his paper on 1 May 1973, HUA tape-recording.
[14] Convocation statistics collated from the *Calendar*.

Frequently no more than 50 attended from a total membership of over 600.[15] So organized groups—men hostile to women, arts dons hostile to science—could unobtrusively prevail, though on an important issue a flurry of fly-sheets could tempt hundreds out of their colleges. Congregation could not be disciplined through whips or appeals to party loyalty, nor was its debating chamber bifurcated between 'government' and 'opposition'. It was more like an electorate, free to conduct periodic referenda on the executive's proposals. To Oxford's central administration, whose initiatives Congregation restrained, the assembly seemed a dangerous and unpredictable creature.

Undergraduate opinion was not centrally represented, though shortly after the First World War there was a brief foretaste of things to come. Leslie Hore-Belisha in 1919 thought junior members should influence syllabuses and wanted Congregation complemented by an assembly of resident undergraduates. 'The time has come', he wrote, 'for the brute vote of Convocation to be vitalised by the living voice of the undergraduate'. Nothing came of his schemes, and the Asquith Commission ignored A. E. Zimmern's proposal for a student representative council. *Isis* revived the idea early in 1922 in the midst of the undergraduates' free-speech battles with Farnell, and junior common room (JCR) presidents met to consider it.[16] But undergraduates, like their seniors, wanted a return to pre-war normality, and most were content to play the disciplinary game by the proctors' very flexible rules; 'only a dour and ill-balanced nature considers itself outraged by this discipline', wrote C. K. Allen in 1932.[17] With undergraduates' corporate consciousness as with employees' trade-union loyalty, the collegiate structure's impact was fragmenting. Besides, within the colleges junior members were largely self-governing through their junior common rooms, and could sometimes (as at St John's in 1919) gain direct influence over colleges' domestic policy.[18]

In so far as order needed to emerge from the peaceful anarchy of *ancien régime* Oxford, the responsibility lay largely with a small group of academic statesmen, many of them heads of house, backed up by the small staff of full-time professional administrators. The University's constitution, said the *Handbook* in 1932, 'is legislative rather than administrative'. Administration was not assigned to a separate part of the constitution, but was entrusted to committees of senior members and to a few paid officers; Oxford's committees typically consisted of a 'combination of official, co-opted, and

[15] Attendance figures from *OM* 27 Apr. 1944, 214; *Government of Oxford*, 4.
[16] *Oxford Outlook* June 1919, 71–2. Asquith Commission, oral evidence, Bodl. MS top. Oxon. b. 104, fos. 252–62 (Zimmern). See also *Isis* 8 Feb. 1922, 1; CCCA, college meeting [JCR] minute-book, 12 Mar. 1922.
[17] *Handbook* 1932, 114.
[18] SJM governing body minutes, 6 Mar. 1919; *Isis* 8 Mar. 1922, 5.

elected members'.[19] A relatively small university, made up from a network of club-like colleges whose fellows frequently dined together, could do much of its collective business informally, and private conclaves could pre-empt public controversy. Personal networks ensured that even relationships with Westminster and Whitehall were relatively informal. The *ancien régime* did not need the mountains of paper or the elaborate bureaucratic structures that later generations were to see. In 1914 the Registry's staff of five occupied only three rooms in the Clarendon Building.

This could not last for long. Soon after the war, growing undergraduate numbers, a widening university franchise, government grants and the full incorporation of women undergraduates all increased the Registry's work-load. The Asquith Commission recommended 'a centralized University Secretariat' and a permanent head with enhanced power. Yet this new world was slow to arrive. Until 1925 the Registry rarely used typewriters, and shorthand not at all. It kept no subject-files and no diary of dates when recurring action was required. 'Everything depended', Veale recalled, 'on someone—generally the registrar's secretary—happening to remember'. Veale used to illustrate Council's capacity for 'not rising to the occasion' by citing its failure to respond in any way to the planning application of 1923 which caused the motor works to be built at Cowley. Employed at that time as Neville Chamberlain's private secretary, he thought that if the University had objected, his Minister could have blocked the scheme.[20] Science impinged only slowly. Leading scientists might grumble about Oxford's 'Gilbertian' administration and about colleges' indifference, yet rarely did they venture into the University's central structure, so the mysteries of university accounting could in effect be unobtrusively deployed to their detriment. Heads of department administered their funds in direct com-munication with the Chest, which on Veale's arrival in 1930 still viewed the science departments 'in much the same way as a High Church clergyman would have regarded a collection of dissenting Chapels in his parish'.[21] Nor were donors energetically pursued: the Rockefeller Foundation, eager to fund postgraduate medical research in Oxford in 1927–8, found no point of contact at the heart of Oxford, so the benefaction went to Hammersmith.[22]

From 1906 the former mathematics tutor Charles Leudesdorf was Registrar. An unmarried Senior Fellow of Pembroke, he was efficient and exact—'always nervously anxious not to act foolishly or hastily, yet absolutely unswerving in devotion to duty'. His cello and piano helped him to relax. Also a mathematician was E. S. Craig, the Assistant Registrar from Ulster who succeeded him in 1924—fond of sport, notable for his quiet humour and good manners, and popular in Magdalen, his College. Farnell

[19] *Handbook* 1932, 81, 89.
[20] *Asquith Report*, 68; Veale, 'Mechanics of reform', 3, 10. See also above, 563.
[21] *OM* 20 Feb. 1920, 233; Veale, 7.
[22] Veale, 8; D. Veale, 'Medical school', typescript in HUA.

thought him 'the best university official that I ever worked with, wise, tactful and devoted'. A Secretary of Faculties was appointed in 1925 to look after General Board and faculty business: H. M. Margoliouth, editor of Marvell and Blake. Holding the post for twenty-six years, he was respected for knowledge of precedent and grasp of detail, popular for his wide interests, humanity and quick sense of humour.[23]

Into this relatively peaceful world there exploded the Owen case, which was still reverberating in Oxford's administrative folk-memory decades later. It exposed the University's financial administration as utterly inadequate. B. J. Owen was Director of the Institute for Research in Agricultural Engineering from 1924 to 1931, and in the name of the University sold patents for extracting sugar from beet which turned out to be worthless. After his exposure in 1931 his victims claimed £750,000 from the University. He had been able to wield a personal endorsement from the Vice-Chancellor, and the Chest had done nothing to curtail his career.[24] The Asquith Commission's moment had come: the registrar must work unobtrusively towards clipping the wings of the Chest. Several other pressures worked in the same direction. By 1922, funding by the University Grants Committee (UGC) was already pushing Oxford into standardizing its accounting year and the form of its statistical returns, and the mounting needs of Oxford science required new university accounting procedures.

'Veale's Oxford', then—the second of Oxford's three administrative phases—sprang from a close match between the man and his times. The phrase 'Veale's Oxford' is in one respect misleading, because Veale kept carefully in the background. Yet he took so industrious and constructive a view of his role that he acquired considerable influence. Furthermore, while academic administrators came and went, Veale held a key post for 28 years.

As chancellors, Lords Grey (1928–33) and Halifax (1933–59) kept their distance. Despite the Asquith Commission's hopes, vice-chancellors were still drawn from heads of house in order of seniority. Veale thought F. Homes Dudden (1929–32) changed for good 'the conception of what a V[ice] C[hancellor] in Oxford really ought to be'. The 'Dudden revolution' established the model of a vice-chancellor who combined gifted and efficient chairmanship with giving the University a lead. Homes Dudden's skilful co-ordination of Oxford opinion safeguarded Rockefeller's offer of £500,000 for Bodleian library funding.[25] Reinforcing both Veale and Homes Dudden

[23] For Leudesdorf see E. B. E[lliott?] in *OM* 23 Oct. 1924, 33. For Craig see Farnell, *Oxonian Looks Back*, 310; *OM* 13 Nov. 1924, 100; 29 May 1930, 774; 25 Jan. 1940, 153. For Margoliouth see *OM* 7 Nov. 1946, 61; 11 June 1959, 460.

[24] D. Veale, 'Communication to Lord Franks, 1965', typescript, 8 Apr. 1965, in HUA, pp. 2–4; 'Some consequences of the Owen case', typescript in HUA, Mar. 1969, pp. 1–3.

[25] Veale, 'Mechanics of reform', 14; discussion after Veale's paper, 1 May 1973, HUA tape-recording; for McCallum's obituary of Homes Dudden see *OM* 13 Oct. 1955, 12.

as reformers were the associates of Lionel Curtis, whose recent failure to get funding for African studies prompted the discussions summarized in a short book on *The Government of Oxford* (1931). Veale thought vice-chancellors of the 1930s gave 'not less than two-thirds of a heavy day to the University' in all but twelve weeks of the year.[26]

Arguing in 1934 that the vice-chancellor's three-year term was 'a direct encouragement to the short view, the unco-ordinated advance', R. W. Livingstone said the post should be permanent and filled by merit, not seniority, but in 1936–7 he and Farquhar Buzzard failed to get the procedure changed.[27] By then A. D. Lindsay's actions as Vice-Chancellor (1935–8) were undermining Livingstone's case. The powerful partnership between Lindsay and Veale made much progress with resolving disputes about allocating space within the science area, diverted unused university funds to laboratory building, launched Lord Nuffield's scheme for promoting clinical medical research in Oxford, and built a similar bridge between theory and practice in social studies by setting up Nuffield College. Lindsay thought a permanent vice-chancellor would weaken college influence, though he wanted vice-chancellors chosen by election rather than by seniority, and thought they should be initiated into university business well before taking office.[28] Nor was Livingstone's case helped by G. S. Gordon (1938–41), who gave the University a notable lead early in the war.

Vice-chancellors gradually delegated many of their committee responsibilities to deputies, and in 1951–4 Bowra demonstrated the continuing importance of the ceremonial role which Homes Dudden had performed so well. *Oxford* saw his tenure as 'triumphant' in its wit and hospitality, and the *Oxford Magazine* emphasized his capacity for rising to a great occasion; the Rhodes scholars' jubilee in the Sheldonian inspired him to 'grave and moving eloquence'.[29] The office declined under A. H. Smith (1954–7), however, because of his controversial opinions on Oxford roads and his serious illness. His successor J. C. Masterman (1957–8) got the vice-chancellor's term curtailed from three years to two, and selection confined to those whose term would be complete before reaching 65.[30]

---

[26] Franks Commission, written evidence xi. 202. For Curtis see A. F. Madden and D. K. Fieldhouse (eds), *Oxford and the Idea of Commonwealth* (London and Canberra 1982), 115; *Government of Oxford*, 61, 79.

[27] *OM* 15 Nov. 1934, 151; Buzzard, *OM* 22 Nov. 1934, 187. The idea was not new: see Asquith Commission, oral evidence, Bodl. MS top. Oxon. b. 104, fo 120 (R. W. Macan, 1920). For Livingstone's defeat see *OM* 22 Oct. 1936, 46; 11 Feb. 1937, 367.

[28] D. Scott, *A. D. Lindsay: A Biography* (Oxford 1971), 221, 224, 226, 228–9, 231–4; see also Lindsay's 'Nuffield College', *OM* 2 Dec. 1937, 246. For his views on the Vice-Chancellor see *Oxford* winter 1938, 63.

[29] *Oxford* xiii (1954), 15; *OM* 17 June 1954, 393.

[30] J. C. Masterman, *On the Chariot Wheel: An Autobiography* (London 1975), 284, 286; Wheare, 'Government of the University', 3–4. For the roads issue, see above, 568–75.

Council in Veale's Oxford gradually assumed overall direction of university policy and became 'a busy, active, initiating and deciding body'. It did not need to consult Congregation on many of the decisions arising from Oxford's tightening links with outside bodies (especially with government), and access to UGC funds helped it erode the Chest's autonomy. Postal voting after 1933 enhanced its moral authority by increasing the turnout in the election of its members. Nonetheless Council's was 'the influence of a leader in a free community, who remains a leader only as long as anyone chooses to follow'.[31]

Veale used to describe the door between the offices of registrar and secretary of faculties (an unobtrusive official of mounting importance) as the Clarendon Building's most important door—symbolic of Council's collaboration with the General Board.[32] During the 1930s the Board's role in educational policy was enhanced when it was assigned a block grant, and Margoliouth claimed that his work-load as Secretary of Faculties doubled between 1925 and 1937. In the same period the Board's papers trebled in bulk and its membership grew twice (in 1937 and 1947) to include more scientists.[33] By 1960 it again attained its membership of 1913: twenty-three. Yet in Veale's day the Board never developed much corporate sense: its aggregation of distinct faculty interests tended (especially in the arts) to reflect college tutors' priorities.

Unlike more famous legislatures, Congregation lacked the discipline supplied by party loyalty, personal ambition, electoral commitment or governmental necessity. It lacked a cabinet to discipline its policy and proceedings, and like all large assemblies was liable to pass contradictory motions.[34] Nor was attendance regular, given that no procedural change could make Congregation really exciting; there could be no House-of-Commons clash between government and opposition. Members of Council (acting on false cabinet analogies) refrained from publicizing their conflicting views, and felt a diminishing obligation to attend—as did college tutors, who felt a growing commitment to research and college-based teaching and administration. When they did turn up, distance had not lent enchantment to their view of the University's men of business.

Convocation's membership rose from 8,816 in 1934 to 15,186 in 1954, but it was too large and dispersed to acquire any corporate sense. Congregation's membership rose in the same period from 740 to 1,161, and was distributed unequally between the colleges: whereas in 1937 Magdalen contributed 9 per cent of its members and Christ Church 8 per cent, only 2 per cent came from

[31] Veale's address to the Oxford University Lunch Club, 8 June 1950, *OM* 12 Oct. 1950, 8.
[32] Author's tape-recorded interview with Mr D. M. Hawke, 5 Sept. 1988.
[33] Veale, 'Mechanics of reform', 11–12; HCP 168 (1937), 114–15.
[34] See for example the amazing 'Arithmetical afterthoughts on the Latin vote' of 'Congregationalist' in *OM* 14 May 1959, 388.

Worcester and Pembroke. Tutorial fellows accounted for a quarter of its membership in that year, professors for 11 per cent, women for 9 per cent, heads of house for 3 per cent.[35] Yet Congregation could never be ignored: in January 1948, for instance, when about 250 turned up to vote on whether to enlarge the quota of women undergraduates, it 'for once presented the appearance of a democratic assembly'. A small turnout could be still more alarming. In 1950 Veale thought the presence of even a dozen members unusual 'and generally ominous' because likely to be irreverent in mood and better informed than Council. 'The general disposition of Congregation . . .', he wrote, 'is to put its money on the opposition'.[36] After he and Council had curbed the Chest in the early 1930s, and had thus made financial discussion more public, Congregation's unpredictability exposed delicate and complex funding negotiations with outside bodies to yet another hazard.

Policy formation in Veale's Oxford was, however, spared another complication: central representation of the undergraduates. In Oxford's turbulent year 1973, Max Beloff recalled undergraduate attitudes of the 1930s: 'the whole thing was *there*, to be taken for granted, like the geography of the country'. There might be disputes within college about domestic issues, but these could be resolved through direct and informal consultation. At the university level however, Veale's early years saw a resurgence among a vociferous minority of the undergraduate agitation that Farnell had provoked in the early 1920s. Even the youthful Beloff told the Union that the debate had converted him to student self-government.[37] In both periods—the early 1920s and the 1930s—the motive for restiveness was the same: concern at alleged proctorial infringements of free speech and assembly. JCR presidents resisted ideas for an undergraduates' council 'democratically elected by the whole University', and the conflict between centralized and collegiate approaches to junior-member representation complicated the issue for the next three decades.[38]

Out of this episode came the most sustained attempt at central undergraduate representation to occur before the 1960s. Early in 1939 influential undergraduates including Edward Heath backed the Peace Council's inquiry into undergraduate life. Its 4,000 questionnaires evoked 758 who supported and only 349 who opposed the idea of an undergraduate representative council. Encouraged by the Vice-Chancellor, meetings of JCR presidents in the summer set up a JCR-based Undergraduate

[35] M. C. Curthoys and M. Heimann, 'The Oxford academic community 1937–8', copy in HUA, pp. 3–4.

[36] *OM* 29 Jan. 1948, 238; 12 Oct. 1950, 9–10.

[37] M. Beloff, 'Oxford in the thirties', History of the University seminar, 12 June 1973, HUA tape-recording; cf *OM* 7 Feb. 1935, 352.

[38] *Isis* 22 Feb. 1934, 6.

Representative Council (URC), which soon immersed itself in war-work.[39] Undergraduates did not then attain their majority until 21, could not vote in parliamentary elections and usually shared the class background of the dons, so the 'generation gap' was even less of a reality for them than for others in their age-group. Proposals to strengthen links with the National Union of Students (NUS)—highly politicized under Brian Simon's Marxist presidency in 1940—always foundered, and in 1941 JCRs rejected the idea of merging the Council with the Oxford Union to form a central student union. Thereafter the Council led a rather shadowy existence. Denied proctorial recognition and shunned by Merton JCR, it renamed itself the 'Joint JCR Committee' on its deathbed and died away during 1947. 'It cannot be said ever to have flourished', the *Oxford Magazine* pronounced. 'The fact is that most undergraduates are not inter-collegiately minded.' Undergraduates, reviving the cause in 1961, did not even know they had predecessors until unexpectedly presented with their minute-books.[40]

UGC funding was by now loading the central administration with new duties. Yet in some ways (at least in the short term) it strengthened the colleges against the university because it subsidized college-based teaching. After 1950 tutorial fellows received CUF lecturerships from their second year of tenure until retirement; thenceforward their pay came routinely from two separate sources. During the 1950s and 1960s the colleges were sucked further into receiving university subsidy when they accepted university payment for such educational services as providing lecture-rooms and libraries.[41] Closer government supervision was the longer-term price that Oxford paid for these short-term financial gains. Although Veale could still say in 1954 that 'any shoulder must be ready to be applied to any one of the many wheels, large and small, which revolve within the Clarendon Building', government funding required mounting administrative expertise at Oxford's centre. The heads of science departments were 'semi-independent potentates' negotiating with the university 'from their several Pentagons in the Parks', and the growth of research everywhere spawned institutes, committees and delegacies which were nourished from the centre rather than by the colleges.[42]

Although some of the administrators' commitments declined during Veale's time—maintaining the electoral register, for instance, or monitoring

[39] *OM* 8 June 1939, 699–700; 16 Nov. 1939, 74.

[40] *OM* 14 Feb. 1946, 175; Professor Hugh Stephenson to author, 26 Oct. 1989. I am most grateful to Professor Stephenson for giving me the URC's two minute-books for 1939–47 (on which the above account is based) for eventual deposit in OUA.

[41] For CUFs see H. H. Keen in Franks Commission, written evidence ii. 31–2; cf *OM* 2 Nov. 1950, 81–2; HCP 209 (1951), 119, and see above, 652–4. For subsidies to colleges see *Franks Report* i. 296.

[42] D. Veale, 'The organisation of the Registry', *OM* 11 Nov. 1954, 78; editorial, *OM* 29 Nov. 1956, 149.

undergraduate conduct—their work-load steadily grew, undulating after 1945 with the quinquennial upheaval that co-ordinated Oxford's requests for government funding. This required the University further to co-ordinate its structures and conform to procedures developed elsewhere. Standardization was occurring at two levels: between British universities, thus denying Oxford some of its distinctiveness; and between Oxford colleges, whose foibles and peculiarities irritated outsiders. Standardized statistics had to be collected centrally, accounts had to be simplified, and forward planning became essential; Margoliouth had pointed out as early as 1932 that Oxford needed 'an organ for long-range and deliberate consideration of its needs and future development'.[43] Veale's staff were now guiding dons through the complexities of government intervention and scrutiny, and defending them in negotiation with outside bodies. In its administration, as in other respects—in scholarly research, for example, or in undergraduate recreation—Oxford was edging itself slowly from decentralized amateurism towards centralized professionalism.

The university staff were becoming affiliated to national professional structures. By 1928 the annual conference of university finance officers had been established. 1939 saw the first joint conference of university appointments board officers. By 1954 university registrars were meeting annually, and by the late 1950s annual gatherings of university finance officers were being held. In 1959 Jack Lankester got the university surveyors thenceforth to organize annual meetings.[44] By then the scholar-bibliophile, that earlier speciality of the Bodleian Library, was giving ground to the professional librarian who had as much in common with librarians elsewhere as with the Library's readers. The books, too, were being sucked into a national structure: Bodley's Librarian set up the annual conference of copyright libraries in 1948, and by the 1960s Bodley was buttressing the British Library's Lending Division.

The teaching staff, too, were throwing out lines to form a national system. The number of readers, lecturers and demonstrators in Oxford's science departments rose from 21 in 1900 to 78 in 1920 to 120 in 1940, many with no college connection.[45] The fellow of a college might not see himself as an employee, but teachers working standard office-hours in hierarchical and non-residential research institutes and laboratories inevitably drew analogies with industry and commerce and joined the Association of University Teachers. Nonetheless with only 145 members in 1961, Oxford's branch membership was proportionately the lowest within any British university. To quote the *Oxford Magazine*, 'many Oxford dons never think of

[43] HCP 151 (1932), 3.
[44] I am most grateful to Adrian Allan, Assistant Archivist of Liverpool University, for help on these points.
[45] See the valuable table in HCP 175 (1940), 18–22.

themselves as "university teachers" at all'. Like their pupils they only slowly drew towards their peers elsewhere.[46]

The non-academic staff were readier for national structures. By 1951 the science departments were employing 353 full-time and twelve part-time technicians.[47] Oxford's pay-levels for laboratory staff now had to respond to pay-levels developed elsewhere: in Cowley and at other universities. Outside bodies (professional associations, trade unions, civil servants) were gradually eroding Oxford's financial autonomy, and were simultaneously complicating the task of its managers. Heads of science departments, keen for better technicians, worked from within to improve their wages; trade unions independently reinforced them from without. By the mid-1940s Oxford's administrators were standardizing grades of pay and then assigning people to the categories created. To this burden were now added all the complexities of trade-union negotiation. Collective self-help through unionization gradually ousted the individual self-help that had been nourished in the science area for so long. A branch of the Union of Scientific Workers had been founded in 1920 amid some controversy. When the University formed a Joint Consultative Committee with its employees in 1947, the Association of Scientific Workers claimed it was already the sole negotiating body, and prevailed in 1954. By 1970 Arthur Dent thought non-union staff committees 'as anachronistic as the penny farthing'. Younger University employees, he said, were 'not easily persuaded by the old type of paternalistic employer'.[48] In the colleges, though, the flexibility of working patterns and the intimacy of face-to-face relationships prolonged the life of more traditional attitudes.

All this created an abundance of administrators both within the colleges and at the centre. Whereas the Registry had only eight employees in 1930, by 1958 there were forty. In 1937 Veale's administrators found they needed an inter-office telephone, and Margoliouth thought things were all becoming too impersonal: 'the wheels run more smoothly', he wrote, 'when officials have time to think of people as individuals and not as names'.[49] By the late 1930s the Clarendon Building's accommodation had begun to seem mean, and it later sprouted into out-stations. In 1961 the Chest's expansion caused it to anticipate the larger administrative migration of the 1970s when it moved out to Wellington Square. To judge from their self-mocking unofficial periodical *Panic*, the Registry staff in the 1950s saw themselves as continuously fending off incipient chaos with improvisation and humour,

[46] *OM* 2 Feb. 1961, 183.
[47] HCP 209 (1951), 6.
[48] Dent, 'Oxford and trade unions', *OM* 5 June 1970, 288; see also *OM* 6 Nov. 1947, 85.
[49] HCP 168 (1937), 116. See also *Panic* supplement to no. 5 (Mar. 1958), souvenir number to celebrate Veale's retirement. I am most grateful to Miss Dorothy Avery for donating several numbers of this periodical to HUA. R. Clifford's 'Room and the Registry', *OM* 19 Nov. 1962, 99–100 is also valuable.

and sought relief in the office parties and hoaxes at which C. H. Paterson, the Secretary of Faculties, was so adept.[50]

What sort of man presided over this complex administrative world? Despite a CBE for his work in the civil service, Veale at 39 was understandably not the University's first choice as registrar in 1930. The preferred candidate was the 55-year-old H. E. Dale, another civil servant, but some on the appointing committee favoured the internal candidate Margoliouth, whose relations with Veale were at first difficult. Veale many years later credited Warden Smith of New College (another former civil servant) with being 'almost solely responsible for my coming here'.[51] Fears that Veale would be a centralizer soon disappeared. He believed in patiently inducing people to work together, and knew that Oxford could be shifted in no other way. He gave a lifelong loyalty to his own College, Corpus, whose governing body meetings he never missed. He understood, valued and publicly defended a collegiate structure whose academic staff were in firm control. Paterson facetiously labelled Oxford's central administrators 'black men', employed to serve their white (academic) masters.[52] Veale did not envisage administrators as taking decisions, but as creating the climate within which decisions were taken by others, and concentrated on promoting the University's two main concerns: teaching and study.

Yet Veale implemented the Asquith Commission's aim of giving Oxford an efficient central administration. According to Lord Chelmsford, the Commission had envisaged a further inquiry into Oxford once its reforms had generated the necessary evidence, but the authorities were pleasantly surprised to find that by 1933 the University had begun to reform itself.[53] So Veale helped defend Oxford from the disruption involved in outside inquiry for what was (by nineteenth-century standards) a long period, while unobtrusively securing for it many of the outside inquiry's reforming benefits. He loved the University, and did more than any other individual during his lifetime to ensure its prosperity.

How was it done? Veale's unusual combination of determination, industry and tact soon commanded respect. He was a Victorian in outlook, without introspection or self-doubt: a man who enjoyed twenty-mile walks on Sundays, retained his incisive memory well into old age, walked at a brisk pace even in his 80s and played a vigorous game of tennis at 82. He 'had the great gift of looking you straight in the eye', said Wheare, 'particularly when

[50] For interviews which illuminated the Registry's mood at this time (as well as the personality of Sir Douglas Veale) I am most grateful to Miss Dorothy Avery (27 Oct. 1989), Mrs Rosalind Brain (27 July 1989) and Miss Margery Shearer (2 Aug. 1989). I alone am responsible for the interpretation of Veale which results.

[51] NCA 14763, Veale to Alic Smith, 3 July 1958; see also HCP 145 (1930), 169–70.

[52] D. M. Hawke in History of the University seminar discussion on 2 Mar. 1990 (Brian Harrison's transcript, OUA).

[53] Veale, 'Mechanics of reform', 14.

he was telling you something, which he thought you might be reluctant to accept'. Yet, rather unusually, he combined this directness and energy with a discretion all the stronger for being rooted in conviction. The civil servant, he wrote in 1931, 'needs common sense and the power quickly to assimilate facts and see the relations between them. He must be resolute but not obstinate, and sceptical but open to conviction. He must know his own mind, but be ready to carry out loyally decisions of his superiors which he feels to be wrong. Above all, he must have tact.'[54]

Nowhere was tact more needed than in sorting out the Owen case. Not only was it a major embarrassment in itself: it greatly complicated the University's financial planning and delayed the launching of a public appeal. Yet in some ways it helped Veale by enabling him to demonstrate his mettle—thus strengthening his hand against the body least within his control: the Chest. With Council's support he courageously decided to reject the advice of the University's lawyers—in effect a plea for mercy—and conduct the University's case himself. His eleven-hour exposition got the University's liability reduced from the then huge sum of £750,000 to a mere £70,000.

'If the University does not voluntarily reform the system', he wrote in 1931, 'reform will be imposed upon it'. In 1931 Council by a majority rejected the idea of amalgamating the Chest and the Registry under the Registrar, but Veale was given the right to communicate directly with the University's solicitor instead of having to go through the Chest, and won the right to attend meetings of the Chest's curators.[55] Closely collaborating in the early 1930s with W. M. Goodenough, then a local director of Barclays Bank, Veale as Registrar (speaking in the name of the Vice-Chancellor and the General Board) gradually eroded the Chest's autonomy. Council steadily gained influence over the appointment of its curators, a procedure for jointly preparing a University budget was developed, financial decisions became more public, and the General Board's financial discretion was extended. There was still an undercurrent of friction in the 1950s between Veale and H. H. Keen (Secretary to the Chest from 1946 to 1964), and it was not till the 1970s that an integrated filing system for the entire University administration was set up—but Veale had won the essential battle soon after his arrival.[56]

Veale's brief was to introduce Whitehall methods into the Clarendon Building. Wheare saw him as 'a master of the art of silence', deliberately inscrutable in Council. Once he had prepared the papers and briefed the

[54] K.C. Wheare's address at Veale's memorial service on 3 Nov. 1973, *Pelican* Jan. 1974, 79; *OM* 15 Oct. 1931, 18.

[55] HCP 149 (1931), 154, cf 145–7.

[56] For the 1930s see Veale, 'Communication to Lord Franks, 1965', 7, 10–11; D. Veale, 'Appeals', typescript, 1970, in HUA, p. 2. For Keen see author's tape-recorded interviews with D. M. Hawke, 5 Sept. 1988 and with Mr B. G. Campbell, 22 Aug. 1988.

vice-chancellor, Veale felt that he had had his say. The preparation was thorough. For about five hours after lunch on the Saturday before Monday's Council meetings, Veale closeted himself with his private secretary, a typist and a trolley-load of files, and went through the agenda so thoroughly as to feel able to write out the minutes in advance. 'No good civil servant in Whitehall', he said, 'would think of going into a meeting without having settled his draft minutes beforehand'.[57] His remark should not be misinterpreted. Members of Council were not puppets in Veale's hands: he briefed himself and others upon the issues so thoroughly that it saved him time thus to predict what Council would decide. He would meet crucial people informally over a meal in Corpus, and frequently went down to Whitehall to exploit his civil-service connections. He made a point of getting on well with key people: the Secretary of the UGC, Oxford's Town Clerk Harry Plowman, the Secretary of the Medical Research Council and the solicitor acting for the philanthropist Antonin Besse. He thus became midwife to the University's many large benefactions during his time—especially in his favourite areas of clinical medicine and Commonwealth studies—and did much to advise the founders of the new Commonwealth universities.

Underlying all this was a pronounced capacity for winning the loyalty of his staff and welding them into a team. Veale hated wasting time and expected subordinates to appear as soon as he rang the bell. He began dictating to his shorthand typists as soon as they entered the room, and they scribbled in their notepads while hurrying into a seat. He was inconsiderate about keeping subordinates after hours, and exhausted them with his passion for purging drafts of ambiguity. Yet when they made mistakes, they would find themselves fiercely defended against outside critics, and thrice a year Veale took the trouble personally to choose a book for his private secretary as a gift. His paternalism was never fussy: it entailed insistence on high standards, but it also sometimes led him to take great trouble in sorting out his subordinates' personal difficulties. He set a tireless example of hard work, yet was accessible, keen on new projects and broad in his approach to any question.

Many Oxford observers saw Veale as permanent secretary to the vice-chancellor or as cabinet secretary to Council. 'In him', said Wheare, 'we had, in Whitehall terms, and largely on the Whitehall model, the Head of our civil service, the Secretary of our Cabinet, the Permanent Secretary of our Prime Minister's Department, and our Deputy Prime Minister all rolled into one'. Wheare saw 1948 as the year of Veale's apotheosis: the unexpected death of Stallybrass left the University temporarily without a vice-chancellor, and 'Veale was magnificent. For a few days he was, in practice, the authority of

[57] Wheare's address at Veale's memorial service on 3 Nov. 1973, Oxford May 1974, 64 and Wheare, 'Government of the University', 2.

the University'.[58] Thereafter the mounting demands of the state—and, from the late 1950s, the mounting restiveness of junior members—threatened Veale's Oxford simultaneously from above and below. Between May 1951 and December 1956 the number of the Registry's current files rose by more than 50 per cent and the number of letters entering policy-files almost doubled.[59] Oxford's reputation with the UGC and other universities suffered seriously from its inaccurate estimate of expenditure in the quinquennium of 1952/7, and one close observer thought Veale's mounting work-load in his last years made him 'very very tetchy indeed'.[60]

Veale's retirement coincided with the onset of an 'age of reform' whose sustained momentum and long-term impact was paralleled only in Edwardian Oxford. In both periods, national and Oxford reforms inter-acted—with all their paraphernalia of inquiries, reports, surveys, question-naires and hopes for the future. Oxford's age of reform sought a structure better able to handle the twin pressures from government and junior members. Veale's Oxford had also been an age of reform, but of so unobtrusive and gradual a variety that the label would be unsuitable. Nor were internal self-doubt or external criticism powerful enough in Veale's day to require the University publicly to vindicate itself.

Macmillan's election as Chancellor in 1960 confirmed the ceremonial interpretation of the office, not simply because Macmillan was then Prime Minister but because the defeat of his rival Lord Franks owed something to Oxford's fear of cancellarial activism.[61] Nor did activism come easily to vice-chancellors. Rescued by Masterman's reform from the weakness of old age, their reign was too short to formulate policy. With steadily mounting responsibilities they, like American presidents, lacked a powerful party machine to overcome the system's many checks and balances. Under A. L. P. Norrington (1960–2), however, the vice-chancellor began to develop the resources and even the will needed for a more positive role. He acquired a room in the Clarendon Building, a competent secretary and ready access to the registrar.[62] In handling admissions reform, Norrington's decisive leadership got the colleges to agree on an important decision. Yet the vice-chancellor's balancing act as spokesman simultaneously for the university and for the colleges was always precarious. In 1965 when Lord Franks floated the idea of the vice-chancellor chairing the proposed council of colleges, Wheare (Vice-Chancellor in 1964–6) saw him rather as represent-

[58] Wheare, Pelican Jan. 1974, 79–80.
[59] HCP 226 (1957), 115.
[60] Interview with B. G. Campbell, 22 Aug. 1988. For the quinquennium see Franks Commission, oral evidence iv. 4 (Lord Heyworth, 20 Oct. 1964); oral evidence xxix. 3 (Lord Murray, 19 Nov. 1964).
[61] See for example J. C. Masterman in Times 3 Mar. 1960, 13.
[62] Sir Folliott Sandford to author, 16 June [1986].

ing the university than the collectivity of colleges. 'He is in both camps, is he not?' said Franks. 'Yes', said Wheare, 'he is, but people do not always believe it'.[63]

The vice-cancellarial mood tended to be somewhat disillusioned even after the Franks Commission had extended the term to four years. The post's very limited scope fitted admirably with the pawkily pragmatic outlook and sceptical, dry tone of Kenneth Wheare, whose oral evidence to the Franks Commission reflected a shrewd and homely wisdom. To the idea of setting up a sub-committee of Council for forward planning, Wheare replied: 'I must say that I think that the first meeting would be a very entertaining occasion'. Enthusiasts for planning ahead, he said, 'seem to fail to appreciate the fact that, to start with, we are in the middle of life'. Would he, then, favour a sequence of expedients? 'I think that a great part of government is concerned with the policy of expedients. Some will admit it, and some do not.' In retrospect, he saw his period of office as being spent largely 'swimming against the stream'.[64] No delusions of grandeur could have survived a poll in 1968 of 1,000 Oxford undergraduates: asked to name the Vice-Chancellor, only 53.4 per cent said Turpin, whereas 46.6 per cent did not know, gave a wrong name, or did not reply.[65]

Oxford's age of reform saw Council still unobtrusively extending its role as co-ordinator of university policy, though it did not yet wholly control either the Chest or the General Board. Bowra thought Council dealt 'with everything in the world which is not thought of in advance, which has not been covered by statutes in the past, notably external relations, but a great deal more, and a great deal of internal stuff such as building'.[66] The University's increasing interaction with outside bodies meant that more and more things had not been 'thought of in advance'. Mounting UGC funding required Council to decide where expansion should occur, and its Building and Development Committee organized the architectural consequences. The Committee was almost the sole university body that, through sheer force of necessity, looked more than five years ahead. Yet the Franks Commission thought Council 'had been behaving like shock troops rushing from emergency to emergency', and wanted something less wasteful of effort. The decision to set up the Commission itself shows Council exceeding its statutory powers, strictly interpreted. The Commission wanted Council's enhanced role confirmed: it must become 'the chief administrative body of the University'.[67]

[63] Franks Commission, oral evidence ci. 45.
[64] Ibid. lxxx. 48–9; Wheare, 'Government of the University', 6.
[65] *Isis* 19 June 1968, 17. The response-rate seems to have been high; although no figures are given for this question, the 'no reply' percentage for three preceding questions was 4.3, 5.8 and 1.1, respectively.
[66] *Franks Report* i. 201–2.
[67] Ibid. i. 228, 222.

The General Board, hitherto a low-status body, gradually accumulated influence during Oxford's age of reform. Meeting five times a term and once in the long vacation, it was by the 1960s chaired (in the absence of the vice-chancellor) by an increasingly influential and annually-elected vice-chairman. The need to prepare the University's quinquennial grant-application enhanced its importance by tightening its links with the faculties and forcing it into forward planning, as did its involvement in the building ventures of the 1950s and 1960s. The resulting joint committees with Council strengthened the links between the two bodies. Two further developments enhanced the Board's role. Whereas in the early 1920s it was the college which acted as sole paymaster for most of Oxford's teaching staff, the age of reform was dominated by the fellow-lecturer with a dual loyalty. To this was added the impact made on the Board's Committee for Advanced Studies by the growth of postgraduate studies and the associated burgeoning of faculty centres, which were designed to be for the arts what laboratories were for the sciences.

Despite all this, the Board concentrated on allocating the funds: it was no power-house of academic policy-making. Its outlook remained fragmented, just as its aim remained to cater for interest-groups fuelled by the college tutors. Critics saw it as 'a needy collection of axe-grinders'—still subordinating postgraduate to undergraduate studies, small and growing subjects to large and traditional ones. In 1965 its Vice-Chairman, J. B. Bamborough, did not see the Board as stirring things up like a swizzle stick: its situation was 'more like sitting on the lid of a boiling kettle', because so many initiatives came up from faculty boards and meetings.[68] The Secretaries of Faculties K. C. Turpin (1946–57) and C. H. Paterson (1957–70) were (and needed to be) men thoroughly versed in Oxford's college-based power-structure, Turpin himself eventually becoming Provost of Oriel.

Congregation in Oxford's age of reform remained unpredictable as ever in attendance and mood. Attendance did not grow concomitantly with membership, which rose to 1,620 in 1964 and 2,043 in 1974. When 500 of Congregation's members were polled in 1968, 1 per cent said they attended regularly, 25 per cent fairly often, 63 per cent rarely and 11 per cent never. In 1968 an attendance of 180 was thought good, and nobody could predict when the beast would spring to life. So Congregation did not provide Oxford's executive with a reliable sounding board for opinion. The Oxford roads issue in the 1950s showed how easily Oxford's reputation could be endangered when Council and Congregation got out of step.[69]

[68] J. N. L. Myres, quoted by Lord Blake, in History of the University seminar, Nuffield College, 7 Mar. 1986, (Brian Harrison's transcript, HUA); Franks Commission, oral evidence lxxx. 55 (Bamborough); cf L. R. Palmer, ibid. iii. 3, 9.

[69] For the poll see *Isis* 12 June 1968, 17; on attendance see D. C. M. Yardley, *OM* Trinity 1966, no. 3, 391; Congregation figures from *Gazette*. For the roads issue, see above, 568–75.

Furthermore, Congregation almost relished such situations. It retained its 'country party' spirit—suspicious of the executive, and periodically humiliating Council by throwing out its proposals. There were few incentives to attend and many counter-attractions, so those present were likely to be well-informed people with axes to grind. The Franks Commission thought Congregation was in danger of going the same way as Convocation and 'ceasing to be a dignified or useful part of the present constitution': its size 'prevents coherence, though it is an ideal theatre for the sort of controversy which attracts public attention detrimental to Oxford's reputation as a centre of learning and instruction'. An assembly with diminishing knowledge of the University's overall working was difficult to handle; 'what has gone', said Bowra, 'is the feeling that everybody is responsible for everything'. Nonetheless Council knew that Congregation could not be ignored: 'the democracy may be latent', said the Vice-Chancellor in 1961, 'but it is the reality, not the pretence. Consent may usually be silent, but it is none the less consent'.[70] The Franks Commission hoped to revive it through procedural reform. Yet Oxford in its age of reform experienced a dilemma: a rejuvenated Congregation would become a useful forum of opinion, but it might risk the University's reputation by unduly complicating its government.

In the outcome, the reputation of Oxford (as of other universities) was most seriously and unexpectedly threatened in the 1960s from another quarter. Congregation's democracy operated on the Athenian model: it excluded a significant group within the local community. By the late 1950s a close observer of the undergraduate press found that 'radicalism is associated with a fair amount of wild talk and rancorousness . . . In general there is a suggestion that rudeness is an indispensable proof of integrity and seriousness'. Oxford's student radicalism did not begin in the mid-1960s with attempts to mimic Berkeley; it began with national developments in the late 1950s, and with local difficulties in the early 1960s.[71] The latter reflect the fact that Oxford's rules adjusted only slowly to Oxford's broadened intake and to changing attitudes among the young. 1961 saw the proctors banning reviews of university lectures in *Isis* and St Hilda's expelling an undergraduate found with a man in her room; in 1962 the proctors censored *Isis* for discussing sexual relations; in 1964 they ran into further trouble over censorship and protests against apartheid. In the summer, angry undergraduates pioneered an unsavoury tactic by telephoning proctors in their homes.

[70] *Franks Report* i. 235; cf ibid. 308 and Lucy Sutherland in Franks Commission, oral evidence lxxvii. 17; Bowra, ibid. lxxviii. 6 (26 Apr. 1965); *Gazette* 5 Oct. 1961, 121.
[71] See the anonymous and penetrating article entitled 'A brief guide to the undergraduate press', *OM* 13 Mar. 1958, 378; cf 'Isis and the Isis', *Spectator* 20 June 1958, 799, and above, 204–5.

Unlike other themes in this chapter, the story of undergraduate representation must be carried beyond 1964 because it lay outside the debate associated with the Franks Commission (discussed in Chapter 26). The Student Representative Council (SRC), set up in spring 1961 in the wake of the controversy about lectures, concentrated at first on preparing very detailed reports about aspects of junior members' life—lodgings, proctorial regulations, sporting facilities. In 1965 it gave some well-presented evidence to the Franks Commission, whose terms of reference did not force student representation on to its agenda. The Council was widely dismissed as unrepresentative, and in 1966 the proctors thought it staffed by 'the non-college man and to some degree by a new form of careerist'. Experience elsewhere, however, rapidly revealed the need for lightning conductors, and the authorities soon changed their line; the Council moved into premises in Wellington Square early in 1966.[72] *Isis* first discussed the American student revolt on 23 January 1965 and in February 1967 events at the London School of Economics inspired it to urge its readers to organize criticism of Oxford's syllabus. Oxford undergraduates had hitherto prided themselves on rejecting the label 'student'; for them the term 'undergraduate' had denoted not subordination to Oxford authorities, but superiority to students elsewhere. Both senior and junior members were realizing only slowly that Oxford was now involved in a 'system' of higher education. By 1970 the Senior Proctor R. J. Elliott could pronounce the term 'student' useful—not just because the junior members themselves used the term, but 'as a collective noun for undergraduates and graduate students', the term 'junior member' (a survival from Latin usage) being 'not always convenient'.[73]

When the Franks Commission failed to recommend student representation, a future minister for higher education was among those who petitioned the Privy Council in 1967 against the new statutes. The University prevaricated lengthily and legalistically: central representation seems to have been thought good enough for senior members but not for junior. Dramatic events outside Oxford soon changed everything. In March 1968 seven senior members privately pressed Council to take an initiative because 'it seems to us unwise to continue to think that "it cannot happen here" '.[74] In June 1968 the proctors, mobbed in their premises, gave up trying to curb undergraduates' distribution of political leaflets. Senior members who had been radical in their day were now either admiring or aghast at successors who

[72] HCP 254 (1966), 662. There is a good summary of the SRC's evolution in [H. L. A. Hart, chairman] *Report of the Committee on Relations with Junior Members* [*Hart Report*] (University of Oxford 1969), 128–9.

[73] Elliott, 'Relations with junior members before Hart and after', *Oxford* Dec. 1970, 65. For earlier undergraduates repudiating the label 'student' see R. Pares, 'The National Union of Students', *Cherwell* 1 Dec. 1923, 118 and A. D. G[ardner] in *University College Record* 1967, 114.

[74] HCP 259 (1968), 593.

drew such immediate and practical implications from their democratic objectives. Hitherto unfamiliar phrases such as 'double jeopardy' and 'natural justice' were now heard, and University ceremonies were disrupted [plate 25.1]. In October 1968 Tariq Ali, a prominent Oxford radical only three years before, found it 'fantastic how things have changed': in his time, proctors punished much milder offences far more fiercely. Oxford's first 'sit-in', in the Clarendon Building, occurred in spring 1970.[75]

In retrospect, junior and senior members' response to all this seems surprisingly mild. This was partly because of the national political climate, which favoured representation and participation. The Wilson government cut the age-qualification for the vote in 1969 from 21 to 18, the UGC pressed universities to put students on their councils, and precedents were set by Ruskin College and the Oxford Polytechnic for Oxford colleges' subsequent moves towards junior-member representation.[76] Besides, in a University which emphasized the role reason should play in argument and the close relation between tutor and taught, the firm assertion of authority seemed something of a betrayal, especially when authority's critics were intelligent and plausible. After each breach of the rules, senior members could always be found who would discover extenuating circumstances for individual offenders, or who argued plausibly that firmness would reactivate trouble-makers now dormant. So when 500 senior members were asked in 1968 whether undergraduates should as a matter of course sit on committees discussing matters that concerned them, 8 per cent did not reply, 73 per cent said yes and only 20 per cent said no. And when asked whether they favoured a student council, 8 per cent did not reply, 60 per cent said yes and only 32 per cent said no.[77]

Still, there was some resistance. Merton undergraduates tried to convince the Franks Commission that at least some undergraduates were contented, and after the demonstration of June 1968, 1,211 junior members petitioned the proctors against what they saw as unrepresentative and aggressive student demonstrations.[78] Conservatives (and others) derived quiet enjoyment when the *Spectator* published the anonymously satirical letters of 'Mercurius Oxoniensis'—anti-Catholic, anti-Balliol, and very knowledgeable about Christ Church and all matters historical. The letters impugn the motives of the reformer, who is seen as perennially afraid of falling out of fashion and ever subject to false hopes and delusions—especially when articulated by the new discipline of 'sociology'. 'That whole coll. is now little

[75] *Isis* 16 Oct. 1968, 15 (Tariq Ali). For a convenient chronology of the 'student revolution' up to 1970 see *Isis* 11 Oct. 1970, 16–17. See also below, 744–6.
[76] 'Lesson from the Tech' (editorial), *Isis* 28 May 1969, 3; Ruskin College *Report* 1968–9, 3–4; 1969–70, 3.
[77] *Isis* 12 June 1968, 17.
[78] For Merton see Franks Commission, written evidence iv. 118 ff; x. 122–30; xi. 67, 70–2, 86, 183–4; for the petition see *Hart Report*, 202.

other than an extroverted privy-house', Mercurius grumbled in November 1968 of the revolutionary graffiti that now adorned Balliol's walls: 'the scribblings which there, through shame, are writ inwardly being here shamelessly publish'd to the world'.[79]

Central undergraduate representation now seemed a generally acceptable middle way, and in 1968 a committee on relations with junior members was set up. From the start its chairman H. L. A. Hart, Professor of Jurisprudence since 1952, thought the present proctorial system indefensible.[80] In its report published in 1969, his Committee did not go all the way with the radical students, of whose outlook it offered an astute critique. It questioned their representativeness and denied that democratic principles can apply indiscriminately within universities.[81] Its recommendations involved creating an abundance of committees: a Rules Committee, composed equally from junior and senior members; a Disciplinary Court to replace the Appeals Committee and deal with major university offences, and composed from a panel of ten compiled by the Rules Committee; joint committees with senior members in all the faculties and major libraries, leaving senior members with ultimate authority on how their subject was taught; and joint committees with Council and the General Board (whose junior members would be supplied by the Student Council) to consider matters of concern to junior members.

As for central junior-member representation, the Committee dismissed two devices: the radical option of creating a 'junior Congregation' to parallel the senior body, and the conservative option of working through a council of JCR presidents. But it thought junior members could 'play a constructive and valuable role' in the University's central government; it sketched out a procedure for lending official recognition to the Student Council, which would be federal in structure and constituted by junior and middle common rooms, and it dismissed the idea (much-discussed at the time) for merging the Council with the Oxford Union. The Committee's report and the debate it evoked probably helped to defuse trouble for the time being, and even Mercurius expressed himself 'truly . . . almost in love with' Hart's 'Socratique rationality', though he feared that Hart 'errs in presuming all men to be as rationall as he'.[82]

It was the administrators—in the colleges and in the central university offices—who bore the brunt of this age of reform. During the 1960s established British institutions were blamed for national problems whose roots a later generation uncovered at a deeper level—in the workings of the economy and in society's attitudes to it. Furthermore, from the late 1950s

[79] *The Letters of Mercurius Oxoniensis* (London 1970), 2.
[80] Tape-recorded interview by M. G. Brock and the author with Professor H. L. A. Hart, 19 May 1988.
[81] *Hart Report*, 22, 88–9, 92–3.
[82] Ibid. 123, cf 126–7, 130; *Letters of Mercurius*, 81.

the administrators' work was further complicated by governmental zeal for accountability, by pressure to expand numbers (especially in science), by the resulting need to forecast the University's size and shape, and by national policies on incomes and employment. The Contracts of Employment Act of 1963 launched a sequence of interventionist legislation which culminated in the Employment Protection Act of 1974 and formalized still further the relations between employer and employee. Pressure to standardize procedures and pay structures between universities imposed further strains.

The University's participatory structure generated mountains of paper. 'When I came here I was appalled at the amount of paper', Sir Folliott Sandford (Veale's successor as Registrar in 1958) recalled; 'it was quite beyond my conception as a civil servant'. Norrington thought Council's documentation had doubled between 1955 and 1965.[83] Embarrassments inevitably resulted: Oxford was slower than other universities in forecasting its expenditure, and by the late 1950s this was becoming awkward—Oxford's delays even sometimes led to missed chances of government funding; it was difficult to plan the science area so as to accommodate both the planning requirements of the city and the ambitions of incoming professors as forceful as the zoologist J. W. S. Pringle; and there was indecision on whether to enter the national system of university admissions.[84] Building operations from the mid-1950s became so complicated and extensive that the Surveyor's Department eventually moved into separate premises.

In some respects the University was deliberately inefficient. Until 1969 its *Calendar* irritated its busier readers by listing colleges in order of foundation or recognition instead of alphabetically. Not till the mid-1950s did the Registry cease rendering into Latin the first names of male (though not female) candidates at degree ceremonies; and not till 1963 did the proctors favour a source of authority 'less picturesque' than the Latin statute of 1636. The University's *Statutes* were a strange mélange of Latin and English published annually; not till 1969 was the Latin confined to ceremonial detail.[85] When it was proposed in 1965 to substitute English for Latin in all University ceremonial, the 114 who voted the change through Congregation encountered 58 opponents, and found their motion successfully amended to preserve Latin at degree ceremonies, matriculation and Encaenia. The debate gave rise to a memorable speech from W. A. Pantin, Keeper of the Archives. Extolling the use of Latin as a reminder of the University's long history and

---

[83] Franks Commission, oral evidence ci. 52 (Sandford, 10 June 1965), cf Franks, ibid. 50; for Norrington see ibid. 57.

[84] *Franks Report* i. 261; for Pringle see HCP 242 (1962), 749; 246 (1963), 680; for missed funding see Franks Commission, oral evidence iv. 3 (Lord Heyworth, 20 Oct. 1964); for indecision on building see ibid. xxix. 17 (Lord Murray, 19 Nov. 1964).

[85] For proctors see HCP 246 (1963), 615–16; for Latinizing of names, HCP 216 (1953), 61–2; for Englishing of statutes, HCP 244 (1963), 393–4.

international status, he thought English understatement ill-suited to ceremonial. How could any vice-chancellor address the pop singer (no doubt the future recipient of honours) as 'O top-most of the Pops, delight of teenagers'? Infinitely preferable would be 'Cantorum popularium culmen et fastigium adolescentium deliciae'.[86]

Administrative problems often bring their own solutions. In 1958 H. H. Keen predicted crisis within five or ten years unless Oxford's administration found larger quarters. The move to a purpose-built administrative building in Wellington Square was not the only remedy considered. Rejected schemes for central sites vacated by the empire—the Indian Institute Building or Rhodes House—gave way to a decision in 1968 for the solution eventually adopted.[87] A second improvement was more gradual: the tightening of the University's internal communications. The idea of co-ordinating the separate college messengers into a college messenger-service occurred to Cecil Head (scout and part-time messenger at New College) in the late 1940s. A semi-official network was then set up, using his pantry at New College and later at St John's as a postal room, and by the 1980s it had colonized almost all the colleges. It was complemented by a separate university messenger service whose annual deliveries of letters between university departments rose from 70,000 to 359,000 between 1951 and 1969.[88] From the 1950s, technical improvements made it possible to create a university-wide internal telephone network—beginning with the science area and then gradually incorporating the university administration and the colleges. During the 1960s it became possible directly to dial anybody in the system and also to dial out into the Post Office network. During the 1980s it at last became possible to dial into the University's network from outside.[89]

In the late 1960s there was also some administrative streamlining—enhancing the roles of vice-chancellor and General Board and extending the registrar's control over the Chest. For Lord Franks the separation between Council and Chest was 'a dying diarchy', though duplicated paperwork between the Chest and the Registry persisted well into the 1970s.[90] Here as elsewhere, the Franks Commission identified,

[86] *OM* 18 Feb. 1965, 225.

[87] HCP 230 (1958), 110 (Keen); *OM* 19 Oct. 1961, 1 (Rhodes House); R. Symonds, *Oxford and Empire* (London 1986), 119–20 (Indian Institute).

[88] Statistics from W. R. Skinner, 'University messenger service' typescript, 1973, in HUA, p. 2. On the history of the university messenger service I am most grateful for a tape-recorded interview with Mr A. C. Packford on 10 Feb. 1990; see also plate 25.1. Tape-recorded interviews with Mrs Beatrice Beament (14 Feb. 1990) and Mr Cecil Head (13 Feb. 1990) explained to me how the college messenger service evolved.

[89] Telephones were illuminated for me by tape-recorded interviews with Dr Rupert Cecil (13 Feb. 1990) and with Mrs Croft and Mr Simon Sessions (17 Feb. 1990).

[90] Franks Commission, oral evidence lxxxix. 12 (Franks, 25 May 1965); tape-recorded interview by M. G. Brock and the author with Mr Geoffrey Caston, 25 Aug. 1986.

endorsed and sought to legitimate recent trends: it felt that an efficient and integrated central administration, far from threatening college autonomy and academic control over the administrators, would clarify the location of power and thus reduce the dons' administrative burden.[91]

In the eye of Oxford's administrative storm during its age of reform was Folliott Sandford, deputy under-secretary in the Air Ministry from 1947 to 1958 and thereafter Registrar until he retired in 1972. His background equipped him admirably for playing cabinet secretary to the vice-chancellor's prime minister—unobtrusively providing expertise and continuity while his masters came and went. Like Veale he was a loyal college man (to New College), and set the example of intensely hard work that he expected from his subordinates. He was a fine draughtsman—Alan Bullock thought that some of his papers were 'classic accounts of university affairs'—and he was the driving force behind University policy on sites and buildings, a subject he relished. In his remarkable grasp of detail Sandford was (unlike Veale) a filing-system in himself, and talked a lot in Council. His stacks of files, always to hand, invariably produced the answers. But with his virtues there came defects: he lacked Veale's vision and sense of proportion, and so his stringent demands sometimes irritated subordinates. He seemed a lesser man than Veale, whose shadow he understandably found somewhat oppressive. In the 1960s, a decade peculiarly difficult for Oxford, such a man could not do for the University what Veale had done in the 1930s.[92]

Oxford between 1914 and 1970 saw a quiet revolution in its political and administrative structure. Moulding that revolution were two forces in tension: on the one hand, the centralized administration required by efficiency and by increased interaction with outside bodies; on the other hand, the continuing belief in collegiate self-government. The colleges' strong instinct for survival ensured that crises drew them together and resolved this tension. Although they have never seriously considered centralized management of their property, they have helped to fund the centre by taxing themselves differentially according to wealth—a scheme which later evolved into a system for redistributing wealth from rich colleges to poor. The world wars saw college chapels and kitchens readily collaborating as undergraduate numbers fell and government departments moved in. The Second World War saw the pooling of fees for accommodation and rents for requisitioned buildings, and heads of house met regularly

[91] *Franks Report* i. 241.
[92] Lord Bullock to author, 20 June 1986. For tape-recorded interviews which helped on Sandford as Registrar I am most grateful to Mrs R. Brain (27 July 1989), Mr B. G. Campbell (22 Aug. 1988), Mr G. Caston (25 Aug. 1986) and Mr Jack Lankester (28 June 1989), but none of these should be blamed for my interpretation. For Sandford's obituary see *Times* 8 July 1986, 14.

to co-ordinate their colleges' policies. Relative poverty and special interests brought the women's colleges continuously together through joint examinations and meetings of heads, and at a meeting summoned by the Vice-Chancellor in 1962, college heads and senior tutors at last co-ordinated Oxford's admissions policy.[93]

Inter-collegiate committees of college officers carried collaboration further down. The continuous existence of the estates bursars' committee seems to date from 1908–9, when the colleges were seeking tax concessions; it became a regular forum for sharing news and problems.[94] By the 1960s the domestic bursars had a similar committee—useful, though less influential. By the 1930s college deans were meeting regularly. The senior tutors' committee emerged in 1946 to standardize piece-rates for tutorial teaching, and became a useful though rather unambitious co-ordinating body on teaching and syllabus matters. College librarians were slower to get together, thus prolonging Oxford's wastefully duplicated book purchases and delay in producing a union catalogue. In 1966, however, they at last decided to meet regularly with a chairman and secretary.[95] Some saw these inter-collegiate committees as natural sub-committees for the council of colleges which the Franks Commission proposed as instrument and symbol of the collegiate university it thought Oxford had now become.[96]

Reinforcing this structure were many less formal inter-collegiate relationships—lunching and dining clubs, research groups and alliances. Tutorial liaisons grew up spontaneously to meet specific and temporary needs just as inter-collegiate lectures had emerged earlier. College tutors, who at first ran their college entrance examinations in mutual isolation, eventually set up enough groups to form a co-ordinated inter-collegiate admissions network—at first for admitting award-holders and much later for commoners. In the mid–1960s some colleges felt that college autonomy had actually advanced amidst all this collaboration since 1945—given their broadened powers of investment and the abolition of the quota on women undergraduates.[97]

Decentralized management brings delay, short-term views, parochial perspectives, and apparent inefficiency. Oxford's elaborate central examination structure enforced a relatively conservative and rigid pattern of study, and required a distracting and complex (because decentralized) administration which enmeshed senior members in cross-cutting faculty and college loyalties. In 1964 a fifth of Oxford's academic staff held a college office of

[93] Franks Commission, oral evidence xxi. 21 (Wheare, 29 Apr. 1965, on admissions); ibid. lxxxviii. 16 (Sutherland, 25 May 1965, on women's colleges).

[94] Ibid. c. 2.

[95] *OM* Hilary 1966, no. 4, 250.

[96] HCP 254 (1966), 779.

[97] See for example Trinity in Franks Commission, written evidence xiii. 72.

some sort, and another two-fifths belonged to university and inter-collegiate committees which met regularly.[98] Yet such a system brought compensations which in the longer term perhaps made for efficiency. By complementing their one-man-one-vote with committees, democracies ensure that policy is moulded collectively. Oxford's participatory structures, whether their decisions were right or wrong, harnessed diverse energies, strengthened commitment and ensured that academic priorities governed administrative decisions. Regular rotation of college and university posts, together with the annual succession of proctors, distributed administrative experience widely and ensured exchange of collegiate and university-based expertise. For the Franks Commission, 'the intimate democracy of the college underpins the democracy of the University. It gives to a member of Congregation . . . the strength which comes from membership of a vigorous group', and the college fellow 'approaches university problems not as an outsider nor as a subordinate member of a team, but as one accustomed to dealing with such matters at a practical level and with authority'.[99]

In 1918 the *Oxford Magazine* thought Oxford's structure ensured that university did not dominate colleges and don did not dominate undergraduates, and that 'from this material freedom comes a freedom of the spirit; truth is valued for its own sake, not as the road to material gain; all ideas, all opinions, if honestly held, are welcomed; and men develop their own peculiar excellences'. At the other end of the period the Franks Commission saw 'the idea of a republic of equals, the spread of initiative and responsibility over all who teach or research' as 'one of Oxford's qualities'.[100] College autonomy sometimes also had the major academic virtue of protecting minority opinions or approaches: Corpus was F. C. S. Schiller's base for the pragmatist school in philosophy just as Exeter nurtured social anthropology as a young discipline. For junior as well as senior members, and in recreation as well as in study, the college was a small arena within which initiatives could be taken with minimal risk. As J. B. Bamborough told the Franks Commission, in Oxford 'initiative in academic matters may come from anywhere, and go almost anywhere . . . Ideas are darting about all over the machine'.[101]

Suspicion of professional administrators, at college or university level, was Oxford's mood, and dons at any level were wary of 'planning'. For them, academic initiatives should spring up spontaneously from below and reflect the researcher's shifting interests or the student's changing priorities. 'What the University dislikes is being kept in the dark about what the administrators are doing', said Veale: 'Of course it often imagines that it is in

[98] *Franks Report* ii. 327–8.
[99] Ibid. i. 28.
[100] *OM* 15 Nov. 1918, 60; *Franks Report* i. 235.
[101] Franks Commission, oral evidence lxxx. 52 (6 May 1965).

the dark because it obstinately keeps its eyes shut. But its tendency to do that is a fact which the administrator must reckon with.' Hence twentieth-century Oxford's mounting tide of paper, fed ever more generously by typewriter and duplicating machine. Far from initiating claims on resources, Oxford's professional administrators focused on adjudicating between the claimants. 'The ferment . . . starts at the bottom of the saucepan', said Keen in 1965, 'the bubbles rise to the surface, and what the cook has to do is to see that it does not boil over'.[102]

The four examples which follow can illustrate Oxford's decentralizing mood. From the 1920s onwards the bursars dismissed ideas of centralizing the management of college property for fear of stifling college initiative and aiding grasping governments. In 1933 the colleges scotched F. J. Lys's proposal to speed up urgent decisions by afforcing the vice-chancellor with college representatives during the long vacation. From 1962 college admissions were co-ordinated, not by the central administration, but by the Oxford Colleges Admissions Office, a body responsible directly to the colleges. And in the 1960s book-borrowing facilities were improved, not by co-ordinating college libraries, but by subsidizing them and extending the faculty library system as an intermediate level of provision between the college library and the Bodleian Library.[103]

Up to the 1960s this complex system was made workable partly by the overlapping and duplicated efforts of individuals—'by the fact that everybody wears two hats' through the tutors' dual membership of college and faculty.[104] Informal structures—clubs or personal networks—complemented the formal. Overlapping membership linked Oxford lunching and dining clubs. Academic dynasties were less important for their integrating role in Oxford than in Cambridge, but intermarriage linked the Lindsays and the Powickes with Richard Pares, the H. H. Keens with the G. N. Clarks, the McCallums with the Veales, and family connection lent prominence to the Sidgwicks, the Hodgkins and the many Oxford links of A. L. Smith's seven daughters. As for the central committees, their overlapping membership did duty for a party system and provided such political organization as Oxford possessed. In the 1950s and 1960s a small group of dedicated academic statesmen—Bowra, Wheare, Norrington, Sutherland, Oakeshott—worked continuously with the professional administrators, and acted in effect as the University's general purposes committee. 'I used to think as they emerged from their Colleges and met in the Broad', Lord Franks recalled, '[that] they informally decided on the

[102] *OM* 12 Oct. 1950, 10 (Veale); 4 Mar. 1965, 260 (Keen).
[103] Lys's cyclostyled letter is pasted in CCCA college minutes, 4 Nov. 1933, 247. For libraries see [R. Shackleton, chairman] *Report of the Committee on University Libraries* (University of Oxford 1966), 16.
[104] Franks Commission, oral evidence lxii. 62, 11 (Franks, 11 Feb. 1965).

direction of University policy and went off to work in their several committees to win acceptance'.[105]

By the 1960s, however, Oxford's complexities were producing serious strains. Not only were there now more colleges: research was gaining over administration among the senior member's priorities. That Oxford's complex administrative structure worked at all was, for Bowra, 'a miracle of good temper, goodwill and all that'. The Franks Commission thought Oxford's machinery had been speeded up since 1945 'by heroic efforts', but that 'it is a bizarre achievement to show great skill in avoiding obstacles of one's own creation'.[106] To the problems of rigid syllabuses, wasted resources and collegiate parochialism were now added several new problems that seemed soluble only through streamlining Oxford's structure. Three of these were particularly serious: entitlement to college fellowships; Oxford's unsympathetic public image; and its widening distance from the lay public. Each deserves brief discussion in conclusion.

The entitlement problem flowed directly from the dominance in Oxford of the great undergraduate schools, and of 'mainline' subjects within them. Whereas the colleges' short-term interest lay in making 'mainline' teaching appointments, research (of mounting importance in all universities) often specially flourished on the academic frontiers.[107] After 1914 new specialisms prospered, especially in the natural and social sciences: biochemistry, geography, psychology, economics. No university of international standing could ignore these, but in Oxford a college fellowship was the route to status. How could the colleges be induced to house the newcomers, sometimes doubly distant from college life because themselves educated in non-collegiate universities?

The non fellow professors (62 of them by 1925) presented what seemed a big entitlement problem in the 1920s, but the statutory commissioners got the chairs allocated to colleges, and thus ensured automatic fellowships for future appointees.[108] The entitlement problem in its later guise developed only slowly because the established arts schools were so powerful and because Oxford's scientists readily exported their young talent instead of accumulating it in Oxford-based empires. Furthermore the non-fellows were fragmented between subjects, and lacked self-confidence. Non-fellows were most numerous in Oxford's lower academic ranks and in smaller and newer subjects such as engineering, geology, forestry, social studies, modern and oriental languages—scarcer in the large teaching schools such as

[105] Lord Franks, in History of the University seminar, Nuffield College, 31 Jan. 1986, (Brian Harrison's transcript, HUA).

[106] Franks Commission, oral evidence xcvi. 38 (Bowra, 3 June 1965); *Franks Report* i. 31.

[107] See the bitter complaints of L. R. Palmer (Professor of Comparative Philology) in Franks Commission, oral evidence xxxiii. 4 (26 Nov. 1964), and of the archaeologist C. F. C. Hawkes, written evidence xi. 60.

[108] HCP 131 (1925), 146.

chemistry, classics, law, physics and physiology. If Oxford was to retain talent in the smaller and newer subjects, and if it was to remain a collegiate university, fellowships must be spread more widely. Furthermore by 1962 the non-fellows were both numerous and in a position to bring pressure to bear, because they made up 43 per cent of Congregation's members.[109]

In Oxford there was widespread prejudice against science, or at least against some of its concomitants, and smaller subjects posed genuine difficulties to colleges preoccupied with undergraduate teaching. Bowra's private letters do not mince matters. The non-entitled, he wrote in 1963, 'have indeed a case—their wives complain of social inferiority, they don[']t get free meals, they lack status. But it is hard to take them all in. Some are no good, others are bright but impossible, most of them do subjects which are more or less useless to Colleges, everyone of them living in means an undergraduate living out, and of course they will talk their heads off at College meetings, with the happy knowledge that they have really no responsibility to see that things are properly run.' Much consideration was given to the Cambridge solution of creating a very large university-based college, or some diluted version of it, which would provide collegiate facilities for all non-fellows. 'The right solution', wrote Bowra, 'is to gather all of them that can read and write (some can[']t) into a graduate college and to turn over a large wad of graduates to them'; Rhodes House, largely now redundant, was his preferred ghetto.[110]

Yet neither this option, nor the Franks Commission's modest nod towards the idea of colleges specializing by subject,[111] was taken up. After several inquiries and much discussion in the 1960s the solution was seen to be tripartite: existing colleges should absorb those entitled people most likely to fit in with their needs; specially-founded colleges must absorb the rest; and all future appointments of fellowship status should be joint between the university and the colleges. This last remedy, so obvious to the outsider, had been urged by several of the Asquith Commission's witnesses decades before. As events turned out, the colleges' customary instinct for survival caused some of the richer ones to help fund the new institutions now known as St Cross, Linacre and Wolfson colleges. As with their predecessors St Catherine's, Nuffield and St Antony's colleges—Council lent its support, supplementary outside funding was attracted, and many academic waifs and strays were gradually absorbed into colleges new and old. The price of doing this was to reduce the colleges' autonomy and

[109] *OM* 31 Jan. 1963, 146. For good statistics on the non-entitled see *OM* 3 Mar. 1955, 242; 23 Jan. 1964, 139; HCP 227 (1957), 161; 243 (1962), 346–7. For a useful chronology of the entitlement issue see *OM* 4 May 1973, 3–4.

[110] Washington, Library of Congress, Felix Frankfurter MSS, Bowra to Frankfurter, 1 Feb. 1963 (xerox copy). For discussion on the Cambridge solution see HCP 243 (1962), 361; 246 (1963), 629–32.

[111] *Franks Report* i. 112.

corporate sense, but not yet to overthrow it. By 1970 the central difficulty lying behind the 'entitlement problem'—college sovereignty in choosing its own fellows - had not yet been surmounted.[112]

Oxford's second serious problem concerned its image. As at some earlier moments in its history, the University was accused of failing to keep up with the times. Whereas in later decades all universities felt under attack, in the 1960s hostility was specially directed at Oxford and Cambridge. The media tended to dwell upon aspects of Oxford that were untypical or trivial or that did not spring from its considered policy: the extravagant or eccentric but newsworthy conduct of individual undergraduates and dons, for example. In the mid–1960s all established institutions with restricted entry (the monarchy, parliament, the independent schools, clubs and trade unions) found themselves on the defensive with populist media. As the Franks Commission put it: 'Oxford is now in a world that believes that the only reason for withholding information is that it is discreditable. It is also in a competitive world.'[113]

Oxford's image problem stemmed partly from the University's complex structure. Outsiders found the University difficult to understand: its financial and admissions procedures were obscure, and on the roads and entitlement issues it seemed to be fighting within itself. Referring to Oxford and Cambridge, the Robbins Committee on British higher education (echoing the UGC) spoke of 'the general obscurity in which so many of their administrative and financial arrangements are shrouded'. Better public presentation might help, and the Franks Commission welcomed Council's idea of appointing a University information officer.[114] The Commission also tackled the problem at a deeper level by clarifying Oxford's practices, explaining them to a wider public and arranging for their regular compilation in future. But the most important of its streamlining devices came to nought: its scheme for co-ordinating college opinion through a council of colleges. 'The colleges are part of a federal union', it wrote, 'and not simply of a confederation. They cannot nullify the actions of the central authority without reducing the University and themselves to impotence in a world increasingly impatient of such behaviour.'[115]

Accentuating Oxford's image problem was a third and longer-term difficulty: its widening distance from the lay public. In all universities twentieth-century professionalization has caused the scholar to encroach on

---

[112] See for example Asquith Commission, oral evidence, Bodl. MS top. Oxon. b. 109, fo 459 (G. C. Bourne); b. 104, fo 146 (L. R. Phelps). For later developments on this front, see below, 742–4.

[113] *Franks Report* i. 274.

[114] *Higher Education: Report of the Committee Appointed by the Prime Minister under the Chairmanship of Lord Robbins 1961–63 [Robbins Report]* (PP 1962–3 xi–xiv Cmnd 2154), 224; cf *Franks Report* i. 19.

[115] *Franks Report* i. 222, and see below, 740–1.

the amateur, the meritocrat on the privileged, the secular on the clerical, the young on the old. But universities dependent on state funding could not ultimately neglect the layman. By the 1960s Oxford's quinquennial application to the UGC for funds had become 'the master-plan which governs the life of the University',[116] and the layman was not yet alerted to his power. Unobtrusive discussions with civil servants and politicians (often former pupils) usually ensured adequate funding. The student protest movements of the late 1960s changed all this, and politicians felt obliged to respond to constituents' concern. The layman's power was enhanced still further by the move away from state funding in the 1980s. By then it was discovered that Oxford's circle of friends had not broadened concurrently with its needs.

So Oxford in the 1980s had to resume its unfinished business of the 1930s: that is, its systematic search for private funding. In retrospect the Oxford Society (Oxford's organization for its old members launched in 1931) could have done more to strengthen Oxford's lay connections. Inspired by Lionel Curtis, who had himself experienced Oxford's defective fund-raising structure, it owed much to the college precedent set by the Balliol Society, whose manager Kenneth Bell advised the University on organizational aspects.[117] In its early years the Oxford Society found colleges wary of poachers on their preserves, and there was friction with the Appointments Committee. Nonetheless by October 1933 the Society had over 200 local branches world-wide, and by May 1939 it had 11,400 members.[118]

The Society did not fulfil its early promise as a source of guidance on careers. Its fund-raising potential was revealed both in the appeal of 1937 (to which one in four of its members responded, but only one in ten of all Oxford graduates) and in its special efforts for the Historic Buildings appeal in the 1950s.[119] But its growth-rate lagged conspicuously behind University membership: between the late 1940s and the mid–1960s the Society's numbers stagnated at about 14,000, and by the late 1970s had reached only 16,000. In 1958 the Society briefly toyed with the idea, adopted thirty years later, of enrolling all graduands automatically, leaving the University to keep up its address-list and distribute its periodical—but nothing came of it.[120] Government funding from the 1940s to the 1980s relieved the University of any strong fund-raising reason for collectively mobilizing its old members, and this partly explains why it did not involve them elsewhere in its affairs.

---

[116] Ibid. 233.

[117] HCP 148 (1931), 45; 149 (1931), 159; D. Veale, 'The founding of the Oxford Society', *Oxford* May 1964, 77–8.

[118] For college fears see Veale, in *Oxford* May 1964, 84; for the Appointments Committee see Lord Kilmaine, 'The Oxford Society in the 1930's', *Oxford* May 1966, 81; statistics from *OM* 19 Oct. 1933, 48; 25 May 1939, 648.

[119] *OM* 25 May 1939, 646; *Oxford* May 1958, 11–12.

[120] HCP 230 (1958), 94; 232 (1959), 43–4.

The colleges, with their gaudies and their periodic appeals for funds, were more alert to the layman's importance—though few laymen became heads of house. Of the 48 heads elected between 1914 and 1945, 41 were Oxford dons; of the 55 elected between 1946 and 1970, 42 were Oxford dons and 7 more had once been university teachers. Non-resident fellows had once kept colleges in contact with the world of affairs. Warren suggested their revival to the Asquith Commission and even floated the idea that old members should join governing bodies or help elect heads of house—but in vain.[121] The left's dalliance with the idea of boosting lay influence did not come to much. The Labour Party, Tawney and the Workers' Educational Association wanted lay representation on university bodies, and Mansbridge wanted outsiders in Convocation. But Asquith's sceptical intellect got to work: outsiders would not attend regularly, said the Commission, and would therefore contribute little of value even when present.[122] Nothing came of A. L. Smith's suggestion for raising funds through 'some small body of first-rate business men', on the model of an American board of trustees.[123] So although links with Barclays Bank through the Goodenough family unobtrusively brought lay influence to bear on the University Chest, twentieth-century Oxford has lacked the highly visible participation of laymen in its government that is familiar in academic institutions elsewhere.

The Robbins Committee revived the issue of lay participation in university government. 'It is in general neither practicable nor justifiable', it pronounced, 'that the spending of university funds should be wholly in the hands of the users'; lay members should make up a majority within university courts or councils, whereas (as Lord Robbins told the Franks Commission) Oxford and Cambridge 'are syndicalist organizations—pure examples of producer's democracy'. He and Lord Murray thought laymen could contribute much, as arbiters removed from the academic fray and as sources of wisdom and experience.[124] Nonetheless Asquithian counter-arguments once more prevailed: Oxford's procedures were open, said the Franks Commission, and Oxford's informal consultation with lay people was already extensive. It did no more than urge colleges to extend hospitality to those outside academic life who wanted to 'take stock of their ideas in an academic atmosphere'.[125]

Lay involvement elsewhere in Oxford went into marked decline from the 1940s to the 1970s. Meritocratic admissions policy and the gradual decline of

[121] Asquith Commission, oral evidence, Bodl. MS top. Oxon. b. 104, fo 205 (Warren).

[122] *Asquith Report*, appx vol., 63, 68–9; Bodl. MS Asquith 139, fo 159 (Mansbridge); Asquith Commission, oral evidence, Bodl. MS top. Oxon. b. 109, fos 530, 532 (Asquith); *Asquith Report*, 72–4.

[123] Asquith Commission, oral evidence, Bodl. MS top. Oxon. b. 104, fo 188.

[124] *Robbins Report*, 218; Franks Commission, written evidence xi. 178 (Robbins), cf oral evidence xl. 8; oral evidence xxxix. 22 (Murray).

[125] *Franks Report* i. 224, cf 131; Franks Commission, oral evidence lxxx. 39.

private funding weakened old members' college links. Non-resident members wielded appreciable power on governing body only in All Souls, which itself felt pressed towards academic professionalism. 'Fewer and fewer young candidates', wrote John Sparrow in 1969, 'regard All Souls as a spring-board from which to take off for the outer world'.[126] When Nuffield College from the 1950s involved laymen in its social life, the aim was less to give them control over policy than to reinforce the College's scholarly expertise with relevant outside knowledge in a highly professional academic context.

The growing number of electors in the University seat caused London-based laymen steadily to gain in electoral influence over Oxford-based dons. At no election between the wars did the turnout for the University seat fall below 60 per cent in a scattered electorate that grew steadily from 7,907 in 1918 to 28,865 in 1945.[127] But direct university representation in parliament ceased in 1950, and the *Oxford Magazine* regretted the consequent weakening of contact with old members: 'to cast one's vote was a very pleasant link with the University'.[128] The role of the old members declined even in a private club such as the Oxford Union. In the 1920s Lord Birkenhead would stroll casually in to participate in debates as an ordinary member, and in 1927 Evelyn Waugh (who had gone down in 1924) wrote parts of his book on Rossetti in the Union library, 'all very quiet and nice without all those gawky young men'. There was 'the liveliest opposition' when Roy Jenkins tried to get life members of the Union disfranchised in 1941 and life-members were powerful enough in the early 1960s seriously to hold up women's admission. Discussing the 1930s in 1985, the long-serving Union library clerk recalled how the day began with an army of senior members 'dashing in for the *Times* crossword . . . and . . . country parsons . . . writing their sermons in the theology section'. Yet by then this seemed a long-lost world.[129]

As for Convocation, Congregation's nineteenth-century encroachment on its powers proceeded apace. R. W. Macan stressed to the Asquith Commission 'the importance for a purely academic society of having a large body of witnesses to whom it may have to justify its actions', and the Commission rejected the idea of abolishing or altering Convocation's composition. The participation of old members in Convocation, it said, 'tends to strengthen the bond which all must wish to see maintained between non-resident graduates and the University to which they belong'.[130] Yet the

126 J. Sparrow, 'All Souls 1929 and 1969', *Oxford* Dec. 1969, 71.

127 F. W. S. Craig, *British Parliamentary Election Results 1918–1949* (Glasgow 1969, 2nd edn Basingstoke and London 1977), 670–1.   128 *OM* 5 Nov. 1953, 58.

129 E. Waugh, *Diaries*, ed. M. Davie (Harmondsworth 1976), 287; *OM* 13 Mar. 1941, 250; *Isis* 22 Feb. 1985, 6.

130 Asquith Commission, oral evidence, Bodl. MS top. Oxon. b. 109, fo 520 (Macan); *Asquith Report*, 63. For a good summary of Congregation's advance over Convocation see I. G. Philip, 'A note on the history of Convocation', *Oxford* Dec. 1968, 63 ff.

Commission further curbed Convocation's powers. In 1966 the Franks Commission recommended abolition of its remaining powers, except for election of the chancellor, but a committee set up in 1967 under Jossleyn Hennessy petitioned the Privy Council against the change. It was in Oxford's interest, the committee argued, 'to maintain a body of alumni, established by statute, who were interested in Oxford and who wished to play a part in the life of the University'. Yet since the abolition of the university franchise no list of Convocation's members had been maintained, and to judge from their turnout at elections for the chancellor or the professor of poetry, laymen were loath to participate. The Vice-Chancellor felt that 'the responsibility of governing the University should rest with those who have to live with the results of the decisions taken'. He therefore briefed 130 MPs connected with Oxford and got the reform enacted.[131]

Here, as so often elsewhere, the Franks Commission did far more than merely give the appearance of responding to Oxford's critics from without. It seized the opportunity they had created to promote reform from within—with the aid of Oxford-based reformers whose aims Oxford's outside critics did not necessarily share. The Commission's achievement was less to introduce new ideas and approaches, more to focus and publicize ideas that Oxford's age of reform had generated internally since the late 1950s. But the Commission's overall impact must now be considered in more detail.

[131] HCP 258 (1967), 315; 262 (1969), 757, cf *Franks Report* i. 221. For Hennessy's campaign and its outcome see HCP 258 (1967), 117–19, 315–20; 259 (1968), 86; 262 (1969), 757.

26

The Franks Commission

A. H. HALSEY

Oxford before Franks could be described as a central redoubt of what Henry Fairlie had dubbed 'the establishment', encircled by a complex of admiration, envy and hostility.[1] The Robbins report of 1963 triggered expression of these mixed emotions.[2] Oxford was challenged to explain itself to the outside world while responding internally to the many tensions resulting from its enlarging scale and modified shape. There was not a simple opposition of left and right. Oxford's critics attacked from all quarters. From the left the thrust was against a traditional bastion of privileged inequality. But the *Times* and *Encounter* also carried the views of a wider group who felt that Oxford was not responding adequately to the meritocratic requirements of the scientific and managerial professions.

Antipathy towards Oxford's role as a nursery of the ruling class, old or new, was merged with complaint from the right about the anti-industrial ethos of the ancient colleges. Criticism from the left, much of which was made respectable by Anthony Crosland, condemned the narrow basis of recruitment of the nation's leading administrators, politicians and businessmen through the private (that is, 'public') schools and the ancient universities.[3] Oxford seemed to be failing to meet both the social and economic needs of modern Britain—to be obstructing the national aspiration towards wealth and equality. She became a scapegoat for critics from every quarter of the political circumference who sought either to explain or to rescue Britain from its fading position of imperial power, its faltering industrial competitiveness and its stubbornly persistent class-inequality.

Such critics ignored much of what Oxford had already achieved by way of piecemeal adaptation to the changing demand for its graduates and its research: the development of science and engineering, the search for talented

---

[1] Fairlie contributed to H. Thomas (ed.), *The Establishment* (London 1959).

[2] *Higher Education: Report of the Committee Appointed by the Prime Minister under the Chairmanship of Lord Robbins 1961–63* [*Robbins Report*] (PP 1962–3 xi–xiv Cmnd 2154).

[3] W. L. Guttsman, *The British Political Elite* (New York 1963); H. Thomas (ed.), *Crisis in the Civil Service* (London 1968); C. A. R. Crosland, *The Future of Socialism* (London 1956) and *The Conservative Enemy* (London 1962).

recruits as staff and students, the reform of syllabuses, the gradual modernization of an Anglican collectivity of undergraduate colleges into a collegiate university of secular scholars and scientists. She was stereotyped by her critics, both intramural and extramural, as the bearer of outmoded culture and the perpetuator of anti-modern principles and practices.

In reality, of course, both Oxford and the wider world of higher education had been changing rapidly. 'Doubling in a decade' had emerged in the later 1950s as the slogan of higher-education policy among the countries of the 'first world' and was powerfully expressed in the endless conferences and reports of the Organization for Economic Co-operation and Development.[4] Investment in human capital was believed to be the key to economic growth and, coupled with the continuing clamour for more equal social opportunity, gave compelling impetus to plans for the expansion of universities. There had been commissions in Sweden, France and Germany. The California Master Plan was widely regarded as a model for appropriate tertiary education in a modern country. The report of the Robbins Committee was enthusiastically accepted as the British version of a wider drive towards economic efficiency and popular opportunity.

Oxford had to adapt to these events. It had expanded over the previous forty years from its 4,000 students and 350 academic staff of the 1920s to 9,500 students and 1,127 academic staff in 1964/5. Its academic shape had also shifted significantly towards science and postgraduate study. In the forty years from 1923 to 1963, while student numbers had more than doubled, the proportion of undergraduates had dropped from nine-tenths to four-fifths, and the proportion reading arts and social studies from four-fifths to two-thirds. Concomitant shifts in the relation between the university and the colleges, between research and teaching, and between private and public funding, were changing the anatomy as well as the face of Oxford. Yet Oxford had not been thoroughly investigated since the 1870s. Since that time there had emerged what Robbins explicitly recognized as a national system of higher education.[5] Oxford needed a defined place within this system.

The Franks Commission was consequence not cause of these transformations. The question in this chapter is how effectively the chosen method of internal appraisal succeeded in turning piecemeal adaptations into a planned and purposive programme. Was it an effective diagnosis of ills and prescription of cure? Was it, as was suggested at the time, a 'lightning conductor' of external storm?[6] Or was it a more fundamental renovation of ancient establishment into modern function? Was Oxford essentially different after Franks because of Franks, or irrespective of Franks?

[4] The Organization for Economic Co-operation and Development was set up to renew the economy of western Europe after the Marshall Plan of 1948.

[5] On which see above, 578–84.

[6] J. Vaizey, *OM* 3 June 1965, 373.

When Robbins reported in October 1963, Harold Macmillan had relinquished the premiership to Sir Alec Douglas Home, Oliver Franks (made a life peer in 1962) was Provost of Worcester College and Walter Oakeshott was Vice-Chancellor. Oakeshott brought the Robbins challenge before Council in November, and specifically its recommendation that Oxford and Cambridge either solve the problems of their inability to reach rapid decisions, their obscurity of financial and administrative arrangements, their over-payment of staff and their narrow social recruitment of students within a reasonable time, or be the subject of an independent inquiry.[7] Over the following three months the Oxford–Cambridge–London axis was hyperactive. A royal commission? A statement replying to Robbins? A motion in Congregation? A letter to the *Times*?

Change, then, seemed inevitable in the Oxford of the early 1960s. Its winds blew gustily in Africa. Externalities generated new challenge for the imperial nation. As Prime Minister (1957–63) Macmillan had sought a post-imperial role for Britain: yet as Chancellor of Oxford (from 1960) he was less inclined to bend. The University was after all much older than the United Kingdom: it had eight centuries of successful survival behind it and retained an enviable eminence among the world's leading centres of learning. Such conservative figures as Robert (later Lord) Blake agreed with Macmillan and instinctively resisted a proposal for either a new royal commission or an internal inquiry in response to Robbins.[8]

Blake later changed his mind.[9] But, in any case, the external pressures were too strong. The compromise was an internal appraisal. The central circle of Council and General Board members believed that without it, another external commission was highly likely. In 1963 R. H. S. Crossman, the shadow Minister of Education, was vigorously and ominously interested in reform of a kind unlikely to be friendly to Oxford and Cambridge, and a general election was impending.[10] In any case, some dons in both Oxford and Cambridge wanted a royal commission in order to facilitate reform and to clarify the position of the ancient universities in the emerging national system of universities. But R. A. Butler and some of his Cambridge friends were unconvinced.

In the end an external commission was blocked by Cambridge's caution, Macmillan's opposition and governmental unresponsiveness. Lesser responses were judged inadequate, and Council decided to ask a small committee—Lord Franks, Kenneth Wheare, Rector of Exeter College, and

[7] *Robbins Report*, para. 687.
[8] Lord Annan outlines parallel developments through the Bridges syndicate in Cambridge in his 'The Franks report from the nearside', *Universities Quarterly* xx (1965–6).
[9] R. Blake, 'The structure and government of the university since 1945', History of the University seminar, Nuffield College, 7 Mar. 1986 (Brian Harrison's transcript, HUA), 1.
[10] *Observer* 26 Jan. 1964, 10.

Professor Sir Lindor Brown, fellow of Magdalen College and Waynflete Professor of Physiology—to review Robbins's criticisms of Oxford and, if they found them justified, to propose terms of reference for a larger committee. The committee did so and promptly recommended a commission of inquiry to report upon Oxford's present and future role in the United Kingdom's system of higher education, having regard to its position as both a national and an international university. Further detailed questions were to be considered, covering virtually every aspect of Oxford's funding, admission of students, teaching, research and administration and the relation of the university to the colleges.[11]

Council adopted this recommendation and on 18 March 1964 appointed Lord Franks, with his wide experience of the political and business world and his skill as an investigator, to be chairman. The other members were Sir Lindor Brown; Mrs J. Floud, sociologist and fellow of Nuffield College; Sir Robert Hall, economist and visiting fellow of Nuffield College, Principal-elect of Hertford College; Miss M. G. Ord, fellow, tutor and Dean of Lady Margaret Hall, university lecturer in biochemistry; Mr M. Shock, fellow, tutor and Estates Bursar of University College; and Mr J. Steven Watson, Student and tutor in history at Christ Church. Mr B. G. Campbell, fellow of Merton College, a deputy registrar of the University, was seconded to be secretary to the Commission [plate 26.1].

Response to Robbins had to be immediate. Reform for modernity had to be long-term. The problem was to state the essential nature of Oxford in twentieth- or even twenty-first-century terms, because both organization and minds needed transformation and because particular piecemeal changes were already in train through the committees of the early 1960s, including Hardie on admission (1962), Harrison (1962) and Norrington (1964) on entitlement and Kneale on syllabus (1965).[12] Franks and these committees paralleled the Bridges syndicate and other reform mechanisms in Cambridge.[13] Franks conceived of his task as an integrating process of collective reorientation. He thus followed a method of open hearings, maximal involvement of dons in their senior common rooms, college governing bodies and departmental laboratories as well as in the formal university assemblies of sub-faculty, faculty, General Board, Council and Congregation. There was a mounting drama of internal debate. Franks and

---

[11] For details see *Franks Report* i. 12–13.

[12] [W. F. R. Hardie, chairman] *Admissions to Colleges: Report of a Working Party on Admissions* (University of Oxford 1962); [A. R. W. Harrison, chairman] *Report on the Closer Integration of University Teaching and Research with the College System* (University of Oxford 1962); [A. L. P. Norrington, chairman] *Further Report on the Closer Integration of University Teaching and Research with the College System* (University of Oxford 1964); [W. C. Kneale, chairman] *Report of the Committee on the Structure of the First and Second Public Examinations* (University of Oxford 1965).

[13] See Annan, 'Franks report'.

his colleagues became a seminar of continuing education. From the chair he was adept at masterly summaries of inarticulate witness.

Whether the method was adequate to the task remained a disputed question. A shrewd editorial in the *Lancet* insisted on its weaknesses. The tone of the report was 'ineffably bland'. 'It [was] almost as if the insiders were aware that unless they flattered their audience—the teaching masters of arts in Congregation—they would be unlikely to push through the real changes to which they were committed. One suspects that Lord Franks was instinctively aware of this and that his insistence on hearing all the evidence in public was a way of bringing home the facts to the University, well in advance of the report itself.' The *Lancet* concluded that the internal commission 'must have postponed any serious consideration of many matters by an external and broadly constituted outside body'.[14] Sir Hans Krebs also thought that open hearings inhibited internal witnesses, especially those with embarrassing knowledge of Oxford's 'financial and administrative obscurities'.[15]

The distinction between inside and outside pressure in the dynamics of the inquiry is perhaps unreal, given that Oxford graduates held positions of power and influence throughout the nation as well as in Oxford itself. Crossman, Crosland, Macmillan and Blake were all, after all, Oxonians. Besides, Lord Franks repeatedly distanced himself from the University's daily practices and made himself the embodiment of an outside view. He sought criticism and suggestion from outside—from Lord Heyworth and the University Grants Committee (UGC), from Lord Robbins and the progressives of higher-education policy—and he delighted in the ensuing intellectual exchanges. A million words of written evidence were collected and published, a million and a half words of oral exchange were recorded and a compendium of numbers on teaching and research in Oxford was compiled. Twice a week through the three terms of the academic year 1964/5 Franks presided as a regal, puritanical and earnest commissioner over public hearings to discuss the written submissions. He was, in Sir Maurice Shock's phrase, 'both the mechanism and the lubricant'. As Franks himself told Congregation, Oxford was aroused 'to a reflective and constructive dialogue within itself' while the voices from outside were widely heard.[16]

Method apart, we cannot expect any human inquiry to be omniscient. Two spectacular developments in the immediate aftermath of the Franks Commission illustrated its limited vision. One was the 'student troubles'. The Commission noticed the Williams Committee on the disciplinary powers of the vice-chancellor and proctors and hoped that one of its results would be 'the more effectual ventilation of grievances of the student body'.[17]

---

[14] *Lancet* 21 May 1966, 1141–3.

[15] Franks Commission, written evidence xi. 69.

[16] *Gazette* xciv (1963/4), 1203. Sir Maurice's comment was made orally to the author in 1990.

[17] *Franks Report* i, para. 639; cf *Gazette* xcvi (1965/6), annual report 1964–5, 42–3; [E. T. Williams, chairman] *Report of the Committee on the Disciplinary Powers of the Vice-Chancellor and Proctors* (University of Oxford 1965).

But Franks went no further, despite evidence received from the Student Representative Council: its grievances had to be dealt with in 1969 by the Hart Committee.[18] The demise of the single-sex women's colleges was also unforeseen, despite the wish expressed by New College in 1964 to become mixed and the presence of two women on the Commission.[19] The decision not to discuss the second issue was deliberate.[20] Though a clear lead on mixed colleges might have averted later confusion, it seems that the Commission was influenced by the principals of the women's colleges—Dame Lucy Sutherland, Dame Janet Vaughan and Lady Ogilvie—none of whom attached 'great importance to the value of shared residence in a collegiate society in a small city like Oxford'.[21]

The report itself was in two volumes. The first comprises a reasoned statement of recommendations, the second is a digest of the relevant statistics: the whole constitutes perhaps the best sociological account of the working of a single university in this century. As Oxford's riposte to the charges of obscurity and inwardness it must be judged a distinguished success. No royal commission could have been more thorough or better informed. As a reform movement by collective self-education and sustained seminar, it reflected the personality of its chairman as a man of stern principle, worldly practicality and mandarin resolve to incorporate criticism into conserved tradition. The attendant publicity certainly offered weapons to Oxford's foes but also reassured its friends. It removed all excuse from the decision-making bodies if they failed to act, because it gave them comprehensive information and unambiguous if general guidelines. Perhaps Franks's gift for synthesis and generalization left too much detailed interpretation for subsequent internal administrative decision. But the bold outline of a future Oxford was admirably clear.

Ancient Oxford was to modernize its collegiate glories. It selected its students carefully, though still disproportionately from the type of school and social background which had hitherto maintained the established life and character of the University; it offered them not merely training but education in a small-scale residential community affording close contact of teachers with taught, a shared domestic life and individualized teaching. The collegiate university, as Franks understood that phrase, was a rare form of organized higher education. Indeed, it was arguably unique despite its superficial resemblance to Durham, Harvard, Claremont, London, Wales or

---

[18] Cf [H. L. A. Hart, chairman] *Report of the Committee on Relations with Junior Members* (University of Oxford 1969).
[19] On New College see G. E. M. de Ste Croix, 'The admission of women to New College', *OM* 15 Oct. 1964, 4–7.
[20] HCP 249 (1964), 353.
[21] Dame Janet Vaughan, Franks Commission, written evidence iv. 173; Lady Ogilvie, ibid. 140; Dame Lucy Sutherland, ibid. 17.

even Cambridge. The departmentally segmented and hierarchically controlled monolith was the dominant form in Germany, France, the United States and in all countries which had inherited the European medieval university. The starting-point for Franks was Oxford's distinctiveness.

Nevertheless, modern conditions meant that collegiate ideals had to be reinterpreted. The colleges would have to change in response to the growth of the natural sciences and new methods of scientific research, the increasing presence of postgraduate students and new demands for wider educational opportunity. And given that the riches of the colleges (though not all colleges were rich) had been increasingly augmented by state funds channelled through the university, greater public accountability for collegiate expenditure would also be required. Franks took the problem of attaining socially fair and academically meritocratic admission of undergraduates with methodical seriousness. On the basis of careful inquiry the Commission recommended that Oxford should work towards reform within the emerging national system. This would require a single entrance examination, a streamlined admissions office for the colleges, the abolition of scholarships and clear criteria for open awards on entry.[22]

There was an organic connection between the Oxford and Cambridge colleges and the 'public' schools. Earlier in the century these schools had dominated admission to the colleges. For example, of the men entering Oxford as undergraduates in 1938/9, 55.2 per cent came from boarding schools of the Headmasters' Conference. The direct-grant schools contributed 12.6 per cent and the private sector as a whole 74.6 per cent, leaving only 19.2 per cent for boys from maintained schools in the United Kingdom and a small recruitment from overseas. Among women the private sector was less closely connected but still dominant, 63.9 per cent being recruited from it, 32.6 per cent from the maintained schools and 3.5 per cent from elsewhere. The continuing improvement of the state secondary schools after the 1944 Education Act, against the background of increasing pressure towards meritocratic selection, led to changes in these proportions. By 1965/6 the maintained schools had increased their share to 40.2 per cent of the men's and 42.7 per cent of the women's places. The fact that the maintained schools in 1963/4 had produced 64 per cent of the men and 72 per cent of the women who intended going on to British universities clearly raised the question of how far places in the Oxford and Cambridge colleges were being allocated on merit and how far there was a selective bias in favour of the private sector.

The Franks Commission concluded from the evidence that the qualifications of men entrants from the maintained schools had been better on

---

[22] *Franks Report* i. 116–98; ii. 44–108; recommendations ibid. i. 412–13.

average than those of entrants from independent boarding schools. Moreover the independent boarding schools had provided the lowest proportion of firsts and the highest proportion of thirds in degree classification among men entering from the different types of school. The independent day and direct-grant schools had contributed the highest proportion of firsts, and the maintained schools the lowest proportion of thirds. Thus the traditional public schools were suspect in this crucial test of meritocracy at a time when Anthony Crosland was introducing a new initiative on the public schools question. We cannot know how far the sensitivity fostered by Franks or the formal reforms introduced after Franks were the cause of subsequent change. But we do know that in the 1970s Oxford made dramatic progress towards meritocratic entry as measured by 'A-level' performance. She attracted the aspirations of less than 5 per cent of university applicants, but admitted a high and rising proportion of those with high A-level attainment. The universities collectively admitted 21.4 per cent with grades AAA, AAB, AAC or ABB in 1970. The Oxford figure was 58.6 per cent. But by 1980, while the figure for all universities (22.5 per cent) had hardly moved, the Oxford figure shot up to 73.5 per cent. Thus Oxford's admissions progressed markedly in the 1970s towards severe selection on academic criteria.

The recruitment of senior members was also seen by Franks as in need of adaptation. While Oxford remained the collegiate university *par excellence*, the inherently divergent tendencies of modern teaching and research—which had elsewhere produced the 'multiversity'[23]—were beginning to make it difficult for colleges to maintain their high teaching standards and their attractive careers for the college tutor. Accordingly the Commission's highly self-conscious effort to modernize a federation of colleges into a strong collegiate university carried proposals which were just as fundamental for the academic staff as for the students. The central core of Victorian Oxford had been a group of working tutorial fellows to which the growth of the University added professors, readers and lecturers. The modernized collegiate conception would produce further convergence of the older structure of academic staff with the hierarchy of ranks which characterizes the Scottish and the English redbrick universities. Before Franks the Oxford academic staff were divided between the colleges and the university, with most wearing two hats—either as university staff with college fellowships or as college men and women with part-time university posts.[24] Under the new proposals two hats were to become standard issue.

The Commission's scheme for fellow-lecturers, which was essential to the full participation of colleges in expanded postgraduate work, involved the

[23] See C. Kerr, *The Uses of the University* (Cambridge Mass. 1963), ch. 1.
[24] That is, with statutory obligations to lecture in the university (typically sixteen lectures a year) as CUF lecturers paid from a Common University Fund supplied by the UGC. Cf above, 652–3.

proposal that all appointments should be advertised and then made jointly by the university and a college. In effect it was to propose greater university control over the internal affairs of colleges. A version of it was instituted in the 1970s. Likewise faculty centres for the arts and social studies, which were seen by the Commission as essential to the development of collegiate participation in postgraduate teaching and research, were provided in the course of the following decade. There was, in short, some marginal shift of the academic centre of gravity away from the colleges towards the university.

The Commission envisaged a medium-sized university for the future and its proposals on size and shape were approved. Oxford would grow in the 1970s and 1980s to accommodate 13,000 students, including 3,500 to 4,000 postgraduates. These targets were in fact reached by 1986/7, when there were 13,260 matriculated students of whom 3,530 were postgraduates. In the course of expansion greater emphasis was to be placed on the applied sciences, engineering, clinical medicine and social studies. More generally the natural and social sciences were to be encouraged—with 'compensating contractions', presumably in the arts. The Commission noticed that the expansion of Harvard and other leading American universities had involved the creation of large postgraduate schools and research centres, more or less separated from undergraduate schools. In rejecting this strategy of expansion the Commission may have misconceived the academic staffing of American universities as a two-tier profession of postgraduate and undergraduate teachers; but they correctly anticipated college opinion in Oxford. 'Our reasons', Franks told Congregation, 'were that we thought, first, that if [separate postgraduate schools] came into being in Oxford, undergraduate education would almost certainly be devalued. Secondly, it leads to a division in the academic staff between those who do research and teach graduates, and those who teach undergraduates. We believe that this would be a bad thing in that society of equals to which Oxford aspires.' It was feared that the development of postgraduate schools would drive the colleges into a secondary place in Oxford, 'but since it was our purpose to preserve the life, the enterprise, the initiative, and the responsibility of the colleges, we therefore turned away from separate great graduate schools'.[25]

The commissioners therefore set out to produce a plan in which new developments would be made to fit into or revolve around a modernized college system. They recognized all the contemporary threats to the viability of collegiate organization, not least the plight of the poorer colleges which had generated discreet unease inside the walls. They sought solutions making Oxford safe for commensality. The postgraduate student was to be incorporated, and income was to be redistributed from the richer to the

[25] *Gazette* xcvi (1965/6), 1487.

poorer colleges. The university would support and integrate the work of the federated colleges, would streamline its own administration and government, and explain itself more quickly and more clearly to the UGC and the outer world by better statistical services. Oxford would justify itself to an egalitarian age by a reformed procedure for admission, the abolition of closed scholarships, the encouragement of more women students and the rationalization of dons' incomes. At the same time the claim to international standing was plainly asserted. 'Oxford', noted Franks, 'is an international university with a higher than average concentration of talent, and . . . it is reasonable that this should be reflected in a higher than average salary, age for age, than is to be found in British universities taken as a whole'.[26]

How, then, could increased numbers be fitted into the colleges? The commissioners saw that 'in the collegiate university those who are not fully brought into college life inevitably suffer'. They therefore contemplated the creation of one or two new colleges. But how far could postgraduate students be integrated into the existing colleges? Given that many were married, and all were in pursuit of academic excellence, it was argued that they would best fit into departments. Witnesses to this effect included the students themselves as represented by the Student Representative Council, the economists as represented by their sub-faculty, and some natural scientists who also wanted undergraduate teaching transferred from college to university. Rudolf Peierls thought that the tutorial system for scientists was 'highly wasteful of the time and energy of the staff' and doubted its benefits to undergraduates.[27]

The nub of this problem was to ensure a proper distribution of students and staff between colleges. The number of postgraduate students was increasing, and they needed specialist dons. Yet all dons must be involved with both postgraduate and undergraduate studies, for research scholars might gain more status than those who taught only undergraduates. The commissioners did not exaggerate when they said that 'if postgraduate training is to be brought into the system of college education and made part of the balance of life of the fellow-lecturer, the consequence will be a fundamental change in the nature of Oxford, and the magnitude of this change should not be underestimated'.[28] For the undergraduate, or at least for the arts undergraduate, the educational advantages of the traditional college were widely held to remain immense. However, these colleges had hitherto made no serious attempt to take over the university's responsibility for postgraduates and, with a few recent exceptions, had done little to offer them social amenities. If postgraduate teaching, a responsibility of the university, was now to be offered in colleges, at least one of the arguments

[26] *Franks Report* i, para. 430.
[27] Franks Commission, written evidence iii. 77 (SRC), 70 (economics); iv. 140 (Peierls).
[28] *Franks Report* i, para. 256.

for the traditional college had to be abandoned. Except in very small schools, the 'college-department' would tend either to be too big or to fail to meet the requirement that a college is a microcosm of a wide range of studies.

There was, and still remains, no obvious way out of this dilemma. The Roberts report, discussing in 1987 the relevant section of the Franks report, was saddened to see, on re-reading the selection of evidence provided, how little things appeared to have changed in twenty years.[29] Here, then, was an area where the Commission failed to provide sufficiently detailed guidance on how its aspirations could be realized. It left postgraduate admissions in the hands of the university but also proposed to leave the general organization of studies to the faculties and recommended the setting up of faculty centres to fulfil the same functions for postgraduate studies in arts as did the science departments for science subjects. It regarded 'the establishment of these centres as essential'. It was no more than tentative in its recommendation of specialization between colleges, despite the fame of Nuffield College as a model of specialized postgraduate study. In fact most postgraduate students continued to belong to the traditional undergraduate colleges. The Commission contented itself with advising that no college be allowed to admit a postgraduate unless someone in the college could look after him academically. Specialization was recommended but its extent was to be confined within the limits compatible with manageable size in what remained all-subject, undergraduate-centred colleges. Oxford was therefore left with awkward problems of duplication in the larger subjects and co-operation between colleges in the smaller and more specialized fields. In these respects very little collegiate progress was to be made in the next decade.

The report came before Congregation on 31 May 1966 as a resolution to take note of the Commission's findings and as a signal that a process of legislating changes in the statutes of the University would now begin. In the following two years Congregation approved new statutes arising out of the report. Congregation, like the Commission, was mindful of the criticism made by the Robbins Committee of 'the difficulty Oxford has in reaching rapid decisions on matters of policy with its present constitutional arrangements, and the general obscurity in which so many of its administrative and financial arrangements are shrouded'. The need for administrative reform was generally accepted. Despite protests organized in London by Jossleyn Hennessy (which were much discussed by Council) all the powers of Convocation were abolished, with the exception of its power to elect the chancellor and the professor of poetry.[30] Council became

---

[29] [J. M. Roberts, chairman] *Report of the Committee of Inquiry into Provision for Graduate Students* (University of Oxford 1987), 7; cf *Franks Report* ii, paras 662–78.

[30] For the protests see HCP 258 (1967), 117–19, 738–44; 261 (1968), 29–43, 249–54; 262 (1969), 755–8.

established by statute as the chief administrative body of the University. The central administrative services were unified under the registrar, and additional statistical information and liaison services on a professional basis were established. And, most important, a four-year vice-chancellorship was instituted, beginning with the tenure of Alan Bullock, the Master of St Catherine's, in 1969. The vice-chancellor henceforth was to be elected by Congregation (on the nomination of a committee consisting of the chancellor or vice-chancellor and representatives of Council, Congregation and the colleges) from among the members of Congregation.

These administrative changes had been proposed by the Franks Commission in order to arrive at an optimal combination of democracy with decision. Yet on this crucial issue there were difficulties: Oxford dons were jealous of their ancient and established forms of democratic academic government. Over the centuries they had resisted or escaped control from without—from popes and prime ministers, bishops and bureaucrats, kings and capitalists. Were they to be defeated at last by a drive towards internal hierarchical efficiency?

In the event, the Commission's plan was seen as too radical, and was accordingly defeated at two crucial points. First, Congregation refused to empower Council to make decrees. Instead Congregation retained the power to annul, amend or repeal decrees and regulations made by Council. It reserved its right to pass resolutions which, if carried with at least seventy-five members voting in favour, would require Council to promote legislation giving effect to them. Academic democracy was thus preserved, but it was made more effective: henceforth any decision taken on a division at a meeting of Congregation could be submitted, if Council so decided or if at least fifty members of Congregation so required, to a postal vote of all the members of Congregation. This procedure was followed for the first time in 1969, when opposition to setting up a new degree in human sciences was rejected by 153 to 122 votes and was finally overcome through a postal vote by 540 to 491.

Second, the Commission was keen to make the General Board more effective. It proposed to group the existing sixteen faculties into five 'super faculties' with up to eight sub-faculties under each faculty board. Professor Beloff argued before Congregation that the super-faculties would find it impossible to draft a sensible agenda. Lord Franks argued in reply that 'seventeen bodies reporting to the General Board . . . is an administrative nonsense, as much of a nonsense as thirty-one colleges being in correspondence with the Hebdomadal Council'. But Beloff's nonsense was preferred by both Council and the General Board 'mainly because it seemed to them that the new faculty boards would have no clear function to perform and that the new sub-faculty boards (up to forty in number) would fragment academic administration too greatly'.[31] They advised rejection, which was

[31] *Gazette* xcviii (1967/8), annual report 1966–7, 52–3.

carried by 179 votes to 115. Franks had hoped for a streamlined academic senate of no more than fourteen. But the super-faculties never came, and in 1966/7 there were twenty-four members of General Board.

Thus the Commission did not fully persuade Oxford of the need for administrative reform of the University's central bodies, though both the vice-chancellorship and the Registry were strengthened and, despite the vice-chancellor's non-attendance, the General Board became a more powerful mechanism of academic policy and resource allocation. Looking back as retiring Vice-Chancellor in October 1985, Sir Geoffrey Warnock thought the criticism that Oxford was slow and cumbrous in her operations had somewhat died away. 'We have found ways', he asserted, 'while remaining an essentially federal and inevitably rather complex system, of speaking with one voice when necessary and of acting when necessary with respectable decisiveness and celerity; we have found ways of presenting ourselves, to Government and the UGC, and particularly perhaps to schools, as one university, and not a disorderly crowd'.[32] Warnock's is the authentic and informed voice of collegiate Oxford two decades after Franks.

In presenting the report of the Commission to Congregation Lord Franks was explicit about two principles which had guided him and his colleagues: 'our democratic form of government, whereby academics govern themselves, and the college system'.[33] Franks's notion of democracy was Schumpeterian (the electorate chooses between competing élites) whereas dons were natural children of Rousseau (the 'town meeting' of citizens). True, the Commission's scheme for internal taxation—aimed at redistributing income between the richer and the poorer colleges—was accepted, along with a series of proposals for rationalizing the keeping of college accounts. Nevertheless, both before and after Franks, defence of college autonomy had been probably the most strongly held interest in Oxford.

Under the Commission's recommendations a council of colleges would have been set up, under a statute of the University, having power to bind colleges by the votes of a majority of its members. Franks believed, and continued to believe,[34] that the council of colleges would strengthen the democratic influence of colleges in the University and that the alternative was anarchy. Opponents saw it as a major constitutional change in the relationship between the university and the colleges, moving the balance of power still further towards the centre. Congregation would not have it, and set up a conference of colleges which met for the first time in November 1966; it had no formal powers but provided a forum for the exchange of

---

[32] Ibid., cxvi (1985/6), 60–1.
[33] Ibid., xcvi (1965/6), 1486.
[34] See his 'The Franks report in retrospect' (Brian Harrison's transcript of History of the University seminar at Nuffield College, 31 Jan. 1986).

information and opinions. From the Commission's point of view this outcome was a disaster: anarchy or fragmented democracy precluded purposive decision and clear policy. Far from strengthening the colleges, a 'conference' as distinct from a 'council' actually weakened college power by denying it a collective voice. Many dons subsequently dismissed the conference of over sixty representatives as a useless body. It was Oxford's equivalent of the North American Indian's league of the Iroquois, which shied away from the binding collective decision that would have held back the White Peril.

Must we then conclude that the Franks Commission failed to bring about a decisive shift of democratic power in Oxford? In retrospect it certainly seems that continuity rather than change ruled the transition. But we must ask 'power for what?' before delivering a verdict. The Commission was primarily concerned with enabling the central bodies to make decisions. Yet this was surely too narrow a view of where the important decisions in Oxford are in fact made: they are made in the college common rooms, the laboratories and lecture-halls as well as in the statutory committees of the university. To put the matter perhaps too simply, the coterie, the private lunch in a fellow's rooms, the informal seminar, were the vehicles of charisma, the college was the custodian of custom and tradition, and the academic post the bearer of expertise. Each offered a base for innovation. Informal exchanges and *ad hoc* committees have always been the fertile seedbed of change whether in practice or in statute. They have been the hidden multiple motors of Oxford's recurrent versatility.

Only within this pluralistic nexus of influence can we ask the narrower question of where power lay before and after Franks. Did the power of the vice-chancellor increase? Probably not, though it came slightly closer to resembling the presidency of an American university. Though acquiring no substantial financial power, the office until the 1980s remained one of considerable influence but largely ceremonial authority. Until the 1960s it had rotated among the heads of colleges, each either refusing or taking a two- or three-year term. Franks made it an elected four-year term as part of a plan to give central direction to the collegiate university, strengthening its foreign relations while a streamlined university administration would ensure internal integration. Was, then, effective power put into the hands of the full-time university administrative officers headed by the registrar and the secretary of faculties? Certainly not. These officials had no formal power at all. They were conceived, and conceived of themselves, in classical civil-service terms—serving, that is, the elected dons in their several offices just as Whitehall civil servants served their ministers, though also influencing the composition of committees and sub-committees within the framework of Council and General Board.

Were, then, the heads of house the power élite? Again no. Colleges continued to be run by their governing bodies, comprising the fellows, each of whom had a vote. The head of house was selected by the fellows and controlled by them, and was unlikely to be a currently charismatic or expert leader in the teaching or research life of Oxford. If from outside, the head might become an important lay influence on Council, but only through competitive election by the dons' ensemble—Congregation. Must we, then, look to the professors? At the time of the Franks inquiry there were 120 of them among the 1,400 dons. Each had convinced an electoral board that he or she possessed high expert distinction or exceptional promise. In the sciences especially, the professor could enjoy the considerable baronial power which is familiar on the American campus. But professors in arts and social studies could be, and quite often were, without influence. Franks did nothing to change the fact that their access to faculty boards, or the supreme General Board or Council, depended on election.

In simple constitutional terms, Congregation continued to rule. Council or the General Board might propose, but the assembled dons disposed. Congregation could, and occasionally did, say *non placet* to the wishes of those it had elected to the formal heights of university authority. The ancient syndicalist arrangement survived and the central university bodies could still, justly if satirically, be described as the 'executive committee of the collegiate class'. Franks left the public life of Oxford as he found it, quietly led and controlled by the private life of its colleges.

The Commission's claim that Oxford should receive special consideration as a university of international standing was heard with much misgiving and some hostility by academics in other institutions. One of the more articulate voices was that of Charles Carter, Vice-Chancellor of the new University of Lancaster: 'Certainly we must not level the universities down to a dull mediocrity. But, before we can allow Oxford to get away with the argument, there are some awkward questions to be answered—to which the report gives no attention at all. What is meant by calling Oxford an "international university"? Taking a broad view of her activities, is she contributing more (per head of staff) to civilization than Manchester, or (dare we say it) Sussex? There are subjects to which Oxford, though apparently having a "higher than average concentration of talent", is contributing little. There are important areas of study which Oxford has neglected. If the state is to be asked to use public money to maintain, say, two privileged centres of excellence, does it follow that the two should be sited at Oxford and Cambridge?' Carter argued that the 'centres of excellence' argument was itself suspect: 'The activities of a university grow, not like a single tree, but like a forest, with some fine and vigorous specimens and others stunted or in decay. It is not reasonable to expect that all will be vigorous at once, and a given sum of money may be better used in encouraging vigour where it is found in the university system, rather than in trying to raise the average quality of the single university.'[35]

Here was an ultra-modern voice, speaking in terms not of separate universities but of a national system—with the implication that some form of central planning was desirable which would treat faculties, departments or even smaller teaching and research groups as its units. The logic of this view was that there had to be one national university or (better) one university system, on the grounds that 'in the contemporary and coming world no university or institution of higher education of any other kind can be looked upon as an independent unit. Each and every one of them must be regarded as belonging to a network, a national network for the most part but one which has increasing connections and extensions abroad.'[36] Future developments were to afford a comment on Charles Carter's view. The UGC in 1986, the Universities Funding Council in 1989, and unofficial surveys of national academic opinion in 1976 and 1989, produced rankings of university departments which gave overwhelming evidence of Oxford's and Cambridge's continuing dominance.[37] As a modern research university, Oxford emphatically confirmed its repute among the world's leading institutions.

There was no Franks revolution. The Commission had staged an impressive performance of advanced organizational analysis and had met the Robbins challenges on external coherence and administrative dispatch. There were two years of absorbing drama. Franks had magnificently redesigned the collegiate ideal in contemporary costume. But the electric electoral atmosphere of 1964 passed, the acrimony of 'outside' criticism moved towards blandness, and Oxford's conservative champions were already growing in self-confidence during 1965.[38] Drama momentarily became farce in the Commission's confrontation with All Souls. Could this venerable institution find a justified role in twentieth-century Oxford? This College without undergraduates, pilloried as suffering from infirmity of purpose, after wobbling between deciding to take in postgraduate students and merging itself with St Antony's now introduced a visiting fellowship scheme for academics from other institutions in Britain and overseas. In 1966/7 sixteen visitors came into residence. By 1988 well over three hundred foreign academics had experienced Oxford in this way. Yet, for better or for worse, the ancient anatomy was essentially undisturbed. When an Oxonian, senior or junior, made a new acquaintance inside or outside the University he or she could expect the same old inquiry: 'and which college are you from?'

[35] C. F. Carter, 'The Franks report from the outside', *Universities Quarterly* xx (1965–6).
[36] Ibid. 384.
[37] See A. H. Halsey, *Decline of Donnish Dominion. The British Academic Professions in the Twentieth Century* (Oxford 1992).
[38] See J. Griffin, 'A neglected moral function of the university', *OM* Hilary 1966, no. 2, 220.

PART SEVEN
EPILOGUE

27

The University since 1970

MICHAEL BROCK

Oxford has changed greatly since 1970.* As always, the process has been cumulative: like the rest of the volume, this epilogue depicts change without the appearance of change. The first part of it is concerned with administrative adjustments. Where these resulted, directly or indirectly, from the Franks report the details given are no more than a supplement to the last chapter. In the long central section which follows, some account is provided of Oxford's response to the developing social and educational scene, and to the policies and requirements of successive governments. The last section is an attempt to summarize how these twenty years affected Oxford's standing and what they revealed about its changing style. A commentary such as this has to be written from a central stance. Being based largely on official papers and publications, it is bound to reflect the views emanating at the time from Council and the university offices. The reader is asked to keep in mind what was said in the last chapter about 'informal exchanges'.[1] Many of the most important meetings of these two decades were of the kind where no minutes were taken.

The members of Council received their copies of the Franks report on 11 May 1966. Their review of the recommendations where a decision was required of them began on 23 May, continued through a hot July and ended on 3 October. The first of the new statutes was promulgated in Congregation on 14 February 1967; and this part of the business was completed on 13 June. The effects of this speedy process were not apparent at once. The vice-chancellorship had been modernized, but the first vice-chancellor to be elected under the new system, the Master of St Catherine's (Lord Bullock as he later became) would have been nominated under the old, and it was not until 1989 that someone other than a head of house became vice-chancellor. The integration of the university offices had been decreed; but the detailed planning for achieving this, and the committee

---

* The members of the University who have helped with this epilogue are too many to name. Its author is most grateful to them all. He bears the responsibility for its faults.

[1] See above, 734.

system to correspond to it, had to await the arrival of the new Registrar (G. K. Caston) in 1972.[2]

By the time that the Franks report was ten years old, however, no one disputed the benefits which enacting the new statutes had brought. The four-year vice-chancellorship enhanced Oxford's standing in the university world. During 1976/7, Sir John Habakkuk's fourth year as Vice-Chancellor, he was chairman of the Vice-Chancellors' Committee, the first Oxford incumbent of that post. The rise in the inflation-rate towards the end of the 1960s had done something to upset the Commission's plans for bringing the neediest colleges to a minimum level of endowment; but by the mid-1970s the inter-college transfer of resources had become very substantial. The burdens were falling as intended: four-fifths of the payments had come from the seven best-endowed colleges, Christ Church, St John's, All Souls, Merton, Magdalen, Nuffield and Queen's. In the event, the redistribution scheme, originally intended to end when 'the Franks objectives' had been met, was continued throughout the period.

Behind the recommendations of a royal commission lurks the authority of the government. Lord Franks and his colleagues commanded no such sanction; but large changes were engendered by their report, even where its recommendations were not followed. As was recounted in the previous chapter, the 'super-faculties' and the council of colleges were set aside;[3] but neither story ended there. The defeat of the 'super-faculty' proposal was taken as a signal that the General Board was to remain a large body representing every faculty; and in May 1967 its vice-chairman proposed a reform on this basis which would have taken its membership from twenty-four to thirty. Lord Franks and his colleagues were not the only people, however, who wanted to reduce the size, and increase the authority, of the Board. Congregation was persuaded to reduce the membership to twenty-one. Eight would be drawn from arts and social studies and eight from science and medicine, all sixteen being elected by Congregation as a whole. This stands out as an important decision. Thanks to the Franks Commission the vice-chairmanship of the General Board was to become a full-time post like the vice-chancellorship.[4] The Board now acquired members who served long enough to know the business and who were not delegates from narrow constituencies. By the end of the 1970s the gibe terming it 'a needy collection of axe-grinders' was no more than a memory.

Council saw consultation with the colleges as essential to the launching of the new statutes. All colleges were promptly invited to send two representatives to meet the Vice-Chancellor and to discuss 'effective machinery for inter-college consultation and for consultation between the

---

[2] HCP 275 (1973), 346–62, 417–19; *Gazette* ciii (1972/3), 1132, 1137; civ (1973/4), 346–7.
[3] See above, 732–4.
[4] In 1990 this officer became the chairman of the General Board.

colleges and the central bodies of the University on the recommendations in the Report'.[5] At this meeting on 27 June 1966 'there was general agreement that it would be useful without prejudice to future arrangements, and in particular to the question of the establishment of a Council of Colleges on the Franks pattern, to have a conference of colleges meeting during the next twelve months'.[6] The conference, which met for the first time on 3 November 1966, was not abolished when the new statutes had been adopted. By March 1970 it was well enough established for the Rector of Exeter, Sir Kenneth Wheare, to give notice of moving 'that the standing committee should be asked to consider the possibility of drawing up proposals . . . for amending the constitution so as to bring the Conference nearer to the Council of Colleges recommended by the Franks Commission; and in particular to consider a procedure whereby, subject to all necessary safeguards, the Conference would be able in some matters at any rate to make resolutions binding on its members'.[7] Sir Kenneth had been both Vice-Chancellor and chairman of the conference. He was thus uniquely qualified to make this move; but even his authority could not give the proposal life. At the next meeting, in May 1970, he had to report that his College 'did not wish to proceed' with it.[8] In student admissions a procedure had been established in January 1969 whereby the colleges' representatives could declare a proposition supported by a majority vote to represent 'a formal decision of the associated colleges' to which all should adhere.[9] This apart, the failure of the council of colleges scheme meant that any crisis arising from the absence of unanimity among the colleges would continue to call techniques of 'crisis management' into play.

The Franks Commission was clearly right to object to a system whereby Council, 'faced with a problem concerning the colleges as a whole', sought the views of each college by letter, and received some thirty uncoordinated replies.[10] In more than one of the episodes with which this epilogue is concerned, conference discussions and 'straw votes' gave the vice-chancellor of the time much-needed information about the balance of feeling in the colleges. To hope for more than this was perhaps a little romantic. It was generally assumed in Oxford that in the face of an external threat the colleges would unite with the university and each other, and that no part of college independence need be surrendered in the meantime: crisis management would be the answer in a crisis. Lord Franks and his colleagues were thought to have exaggerated the need for inter-college uniformity on such matters as college housing arrangements. Moreover the basis for united action by the colleges did

[5] HCP 254 (1966), 409.
[6] Ibid. 779.
[7] University of Oxford, conference minutes, 19 Mar. 1970, minute 4. iii, 26 Feb. 1971.
[8] Ibid. 28 May, minute 4.
[9] 30 Jan. 1969: see records, Oxford Colleges Admissions Office, MC/800 26 Feb. 1971.
[10] Franks Report i. 262.

not exist. The disparities between them in numbers, resources and function were considerable. By 1966 the time when all of them had been concerned with undergraduate tuition was long past. Each college had something to fear from decisions by a majority of the others. Each could rely on the others to repel encroachments by the university. Each preferred allowing the university to decide to being subjected to a combination of other colleges.

The 'entitlement problem' of the 1960s, and the fellow-lecturer proposal which the Franks Commission produced to solve it, have been described above.[11] The General Board were suspicious of that proposal; and in May 1968 the senior tutors' committee voted against it by 19 to 5. Over the next few years the General Board's own proposal for joint appointments was hammered out. Approved by Council and circulated to colleges in November 1973, it came into effect on 1 January 1974, ironically a few weeks before a moratorium on new appointments had to be announced. Under this arrangement, which held the field for fifteen years, intending applicants were given the prospect, but not the certainty, of a fellowship. The chosen college's right to decline was underlined by the formula in the advertisement: 'the appointment may be accompanied by a fellowship'.

The General Board had ensured that 'the entitlement problem' would not grow rapidly with each year's appointments; but the University was left with a band of university lecturers to whom it had promised fellowships which it had no power to procure. The prospect of the new colleges absorbing the remaining non-fellows had vanished. In an inspired moment Iffley College had invited Sir Isaiah Berlin to be its head. By securing large grants from the Wolfson and Ford foundations he had put Wolfson College (as it soon became) on the road to chartered independence and had thus ended any prospect of prolonging its entitlement obligations beyond 1970. It would have been impossibly invidious to keep St Cross in chains when Wolfson had been set free. By 1970, moreover, the climate had changed. Student unrest had produced a reaction against the universities, and the prospect of further new colleges had receded. Now that the 'non-fellows' had shrunk to a band of fifty or so, the 'problem of entitlement' looked less menacing to the colleges.[12] All had increased their number of fellows, and some were feeling the financial strain of having done so. None felt a special responsibility for helping to abolish the list of 'non-fellows'.

A flurry of further entitlement reports followed. Writing to Rhodes scholars of many generations for Christmas 1972, the Warden of Rhodes House commented: 'Since the problem is insoluble men of goodwill continue to feel that it cannot be beyond the bounds of human ingenuity to

   [11] See above, 713–15, 728–9.
   [12] The phrase is taken from [J. H. E. Griffiths, chairman] *Report of the Committee on the Long-Term Problem of Entitlement* (University of Oxford 1970). The 'non-fellows' figure given here includes those who were not yet (but soon would be) entitled.

discover a solution, whereas men of good sense find this blinkered buoyancy increasingly exasperating.' In February 1971 the Conference of Colleges had resolved by 19 to 11 that the entitlement statute should be repealed, the interests of those already in post being preserved. In May the preamble to a statute to this effect was rejected by Congregation on a postal vote by a majority of 99. In 1972 a committee recommended the creation of a collegiate society for the entitled. Council's resolution on these lines was defeated in Congregation itself in May 1973, but given a majority of 28 in a postal vote of 950.[13] This 'Southgate College' would inherit the Linacre College building in St Aldate's when Linacre moved to Cherwell Edge. It was to be held to its purpose of providing for non-fellows and given no prospect of independent status. When the statute came forward in December, Lord Franks opposed it with devastating force, declaring that any new Oxford society must be given 'the hope of becoming a college'. A later speaker suggested that as very few non-fellows were likely to accept fellowships of Southgate, it might be renamed 'the College of the Holy Sepulchre'.[14] The preamble was rejected in the house by 112 to 30, and the postal vote confirmed this by 535 to 240. In June 1974 the Conference of Colleges voted again (this time by 17 to 7) for the repeal of entitlement. There was, however, nothing Council could do. Congregation was unwilling either to repeal the statute or to take the only feasible course for bringing it fully into effect. To found a new society with a prospect of independent status, but with little hope of endowment except from the bounty of the colleges, was judged to be no solution.

Matters rested there until a group of non-fellows asked a question in Congregation in June 1984. They met Council's entitlement committee in the following February and intimated that they had sought a legal opinion about their position: it had led them to the view that, where they were concerned, the University was 'vulnerable'. When the Vice-Chancellor said that the University 'had not sought expert legal advice on the matter', it was suggested that to do so might constitute the essential prelude to 'persuading' the colleges to provide the fellowships required.[15] Council took informal advice and received immediate confirmation of the University's vulnerability at law. The key passage ran: 'every time the University appoints a lecturer for whom there is no college fellowship it commits a breach of contract and the breach continues for as long as no college association can be arranged'.[16]

In September the Vice-Chancellor met heads of colleges and asked for their co-operation in removing the danger which threatened. A backlist of some forty non-fellows had to be found fellowships. It was still more

---

[13] On the same day that the resolution was defeated in Congregation a proposal, supported by Lord Franks, that no 'entitlement post' might be filled unless a fellowship had been offered with it was defeated by 88 to 47.   [14] *Gazette* civ (1973/4), 373–4 (Franks), 375 (Kenny).
[15] HCP 311 (1985), 100–1.   [16] Ibid. 105–7.

important to devise a means of ensuring that 'the entitlement problem' would not recur: the guarantee of a long-term solution was indeed the prerequisite for receiving the colleges' co-operation in overcoming the immediate difficulty. The method to be adopted had to ensure, on the one hand, that in future no one would be appointed to a university post carrying entitlement without also securing a fellowship; on the other hand there had to be an equally firm assurance that the university would be left with sufficient freedom in making such appointments, and that the ultimate autonomy of the colleges would remain intact.

The challenge was daunting. An outline scheme was put tentatively to the colleges in March 1986. A period of consultation and discussion followed while firm proposals were hammered out: this involved Council, the General Board and each college individually. By July the Vice-Chancellor was able to assure colleges that never again would there be any 'new, entitled, non-fellows'. In March 1987 he announced that agreement had been reached between all the parties on a fully formulated scheme for dealing with any joint appointment which gave rise to difficulties of entitlement. To meet such a case a 'rota' of colleges would be invoked, the college at the top of the list having the duty of association with a post for which no college had made a voluntary bid; once that duty had been discharged it would move to the bottom of the list.

The forty non-fellows had then to be allocated to colleges. Council had decided a year earlier that, when the right stage had been reached, three 'wise men' should be asked to undertake this delicate and demanding task. The colleges welcomed the proposal; Lord Franks, Lord Bullock and Sir John Habakkuk accepted the job. The non-fellows were duly distributed and elected. Three colleges accepted two each and so gained places at the foot of the rota mentioned above. The opportunity was taken to improve the entitlement statute by enacting that the offer of a fellowship discharged the University's obligation. The last piece was inserted into the jigsaw in 1990, when the director and academic staff of the department for external studies became the president and fellows of a new collegiate society.[17] The settlement was a notable effort of crisis management which removed one large item from the crisis list.

The earlier phase of student unrest in Oxford has been described above.[18] Legislation implementing the recommendations of the Hart Committee came before Congregation in March 1970. Council's principal spokesman, the Provost of Oriel, K. C. Turpin, faced an unusually difficult task. On 11 February students occupying the offices of Warwick University had

[17] See *Gazette* cxx (1989/90), 518. The presidency and fellowships were conferred by the Chancellor at a ceremony in Rewley House on 11 May.
[18] See above, 703–6; cf [H. L. A. Hart, chairman] *Report of the Committee on Relations with Junior Members* (University of Oxford 1969).

discovered in the files evidence, as they thought, of political discrimination in undergraduate admissions by that University's staff affecting students and an applicant. There were several press reports of the incident. On 13 February a dinner in the Garden House Hotel in Cambridge was disrupted by students in protest against repression in Greece. Much damage was caused and a proctor and a police officer each received serious injuries. From 24 February to 1 March a group of Oxford students occupied the delegates' room in the Clarendon Building in a foredoomed search for incriminating files. On 27 February the vice-chancellors met the National Union of Students and agreed 'that details of a student's academic records would, in future, be open to that student'.[19] Shortly after this, when Oxford's Vice-Chancellor met a deputation of students, he was told by one of them to 'shut up' and dismissed the deputation.[20]

This was not the best time at which to introduce conciliatory measures. Council's position had one great strength however: it was under attack from both sides. In the 1970s and 1980s the image of Oxford's academics as foot-dragging diehards bore little relation to the facts. In so far as the administration of the University could be characterized in political terms, it was in 1970, as it had long been, a regime of the centre. Despite all the disruptive incidents the centre held throughout the Hart discussions.[21] The Provost, and J. D. Davies who spoke for Council on the legal questions, were confronted with twenty-nine amendments. They accepted a few, including one sponsored by Professor Hart; but all except two of those which they opposed at all seriously were defeated. The Privy Council assented to the new statute on discipline on 30 April 1971.

There were 'sit-ins' at Cambridge in February 1972 and February 1973; and in November 1973 Oxford's Examination Schools were occupied for a week. By now, however, direct action was losing its popularity almost everywhere; and the decline of militancy was particularly marked in Oxford. The dispersal of power, and the relatively close relations between young and old characteristic of a collegiate university and of the tutorial system, had begun to have their effect; and the determination of Oxford's senior members to meet all reasonable suggestions had been put beyond doubt. The demand for a central students' union, which had provided the ostensible reason for occupying the Examination Schools, was seen as a manœuvre to undermine the moderates who had gained control of the Student Representative Council; and a referendum which followed the sit-in at the Examination Schools showed the latter to have the support of the majority of Oxford's students. By the end of 1973 the harassment to which not merely the university police but other members of the university staff were being subjected was causing great resentment. On 13 February 1974 some fifty intruders attempting to occupy the Indian Institute building were expelled by members of the administrative staff whose abilities in the scrum revealed their sound training in the Rugby game. On 4 March a violent attack on the new university offices in Wellington Square was repulsed by the University police and staff. The latest of the new statutes to be enacted was now brought into effect. Eighteen students were charged before the University's disciplinary court. After many attempts at disruption, all were found guilty and sentenced to be suspended for a year. Thirteen cases were taken to the University's appeal court. One sentence was reduced, the other appeals being dismissed. There was no recurrence of such troubles during the period under review, though Oxford had a small share in the threats to 'free speech on the campus' which engaged parliamentary and departmental attention during the 1980s.[22]

The social and educational changes of these twenty years led not merely to many alterations in the University's work and life but to a radical shift in its composition. In September 1974 no Oxford college admitting under-graduates contained fellows or students of both sexes. By October 1985 none was confined to men and only two (Somerville and St Hilda's) were confined to women. The Franks Commission's decision not to report on the possibility of mixed colleges has been described above.[23] A letter from Lord Franks in response to the approach by New College was published in the *Gazette* in March 1965. New College's proposal to admit women came, he wrote, under the general rule that changes should not be held up until the Commission had reported. He added the warning that 'if New College decided to proceed with the proposal and, in so doing, set a fashion which several other men's colleges would wish quickly to follow' it would be important to ensure that the women's colleges were not damaged by these changes.[24] This warning was echoed throughout the early discussions. None of the women's colleges was well endowed. Of recent years their contribution to Oxford had been recognized by perceptive donors, notably the late Sir Isaac Wolfson. Shortly before Lord Franks wrote his letter, St Anne's had moved into its Wolfson building and had received benefactions

---

[22] For precautions against disruption of meetings see Education (no. 2) Act, 1986, section 43; and the University's code of practice (11 June 1987) in *Statutes* 1989, 679–85. In 1987 a Department of Education and Science committee of three, with Sir Albert Sloman as chairman, reported after complaints about a boycott by the students from a former member of the staff of Ruskin College, one of the University's associated institutions. Its recommendations were promptly adopted by the College, and the complainant received damages and costs in an out-of-court settlement. See *Times* 17 Nov. 1988, 24.

[23] See above, 726.

[24] *Gazette* xcv (1964/5), 782.

from the Max Rayne Foundation and from two Oxford men's colleges. Nonetheless, such help could not match the long-standing endowments of the better endowed men's colleges.

An inter-college committee representing the women's colleges and those men's colleges contemplating 'co-residence' met from December 1970. At its core was 'the group of ten'. This consisted of the five women's colleges and the five which wanted to admit women undergraduates—Brasenose, Hertford, St Catherine's, Jesus and Wadham. By May 1972 Council's scheme was ready to be put to Congregation. The total number of women to be admitted annually by the five colleges was restricted to a hundred. A five-year pause was to follow, the effects of the 'experiment' being due for review in 1977. Until the results of the review became available 'the University', Council's explanatory note continued, 'should withhold its consent to the alteration of the statutes of any other men's colleges designed to permit the admission of women'.[25] The scheme exemplified Council's new-found confidence. Its legal basis was doubtful. In Cambridge the university did not interfere with the colleges' applications to the Privy Council to be allowed to admit women. Council's interference, Lord Bullock recorded, 'nearly led the Master and Fellows of Balliol to want to take the Vice-Chancellor of the day and myself to the Privy Council'.[26]

The Provost of Queen's (Lord Blake, as he later became) spoke for Council in the debate in Congregation on 30 May 1972. His conservative views, allied to his high standing and popularity, made him eminently suitable for the task. Council was again appealing successfully to the centre. Opposition to the change was defeated in the house by 200 votes to 66 and in the postal vote by 690 to 259. Those assaulting from the other side, who objected to the delaying procedure, were repulsed by majorities less massive than this, but still very substantial. The Principal of St Hugh's, speaking for the women's colleges in the debate, asked: 'Why do we not counter all this by going mixed ourselves? The answer is, of course, that quite apart from the fact that the ostensible object of this exercise is to increase the number of women at Oxford, we should get the dregs. Only men who failed to make the grade at a man's college would try to creep in this way; and only a man who saw no hope of getting a fellowship elsewhere would accept one at a college where it would require an effluxion of time of some thirty years before petticoat government disappeared.'[27]

These remarks underestimated the speed with which a change in patterns of schooling was producing a similar change throughout British higher

[25] Ibid. cii (1971/2), 760.
[26] Lord Bullock in discussion after Lord Blake's talk on 'The structure and government of the University since 1945', seminar, Nuffield College, 7 Mar. 1986 (Brian Harrison's transcript, HUA), p. 17.
[27] Gazette cii (1971/2), 1059.

education. The switch to comprehensive schools had made the mixed
secondary school the norm. By January 1973 more than 70 per cent of
'public sector' secondary schools in the United Kingdom were mixed.
Despite the Principal's words, some fellows in the women's colleges were
already considering the possible advantages of 'going mixed'. The accelera-
tion of events originated, however, not in Oxford but in Westminster. The
government's consultative paper entitled *Equal Opportunities for Men and
Women* came before Council and the Conference of Colleges in 1973; and
when Labour returned to office in the following year it became clear that a
comprehensive enactment would soon follow.

The Rhodes Trust was the first Oxford institution to take advantage of the
Sex Discrimination Bill. While it was in the Lords the trustees secured an
amendment enabling them to open their scholarships to women. They had
long wanted to do this, but had been told that they could not use the Trust's
money for this purpose since the testator had restricted his scholarships to
men and this restriction did not make his scheme unworkable. The
amendment allowed an educational institution to apply to the Secretary of
State for Education and Science to remove a single-sex limitation from any
gift or bequest more than twenty-five years old. The order about the Rhodes
scholarships was signed and laid before parliament in October 1976 and
came into effect in the following month.

The Sex Discrimination Act reached the statute-book in the last days of
1975. By the time that the review was held, fears about injury to the
women's colleges had receded. No evidence was found that the new element
of competition had presented them with serious difficulties; and it was
known that several of them were in any case likely to admit men. The
reviewing committee reported: 'We have concluded that any attempt by the
University to impose on the colleges a further "controlled experiment"
would give rise to many problems . . . While there is a need for some
restraint, such restraint must be voluntary and its limits agreed amongst the
colleges themselves . . . It is our view that candidates applying to Oxford
should continue to have a choice between single-sex and mixed colleges; and
we hope that colleges will bear this in mind in their discussions.'[28]

In March 1977 approval of the report was carried in Congregation by only
88 votes to 85, but in the postal vote by 744 votes to 355. The speed with
which the remaining men's colleges then applied to admit women did not
show notable signs of 'restraint'; and the committee's hope that young men
applying to Oxford would be left with the choice of single-sex colleges was
quickly belied. The men's colleges, long hailed as the protectors of choice
and variety, changed in this matter in just over ten years from one kind of
uniformity to the other. The explanation for this lay in their competitive

[28] *Gazette*, cvii (1976/7), 462.

outlook. Each college wanted to compete for academic talent, whether for senior or junior members, wherever that could be found. It is mistaken to suppose that the 'independence' of colleges necessarily sustains their diversity.

Between 1973/4 and 1984/5 the percentage of women nearly doubled among Oxford's undergraduates, and rose by half among postgraduate students. In the tenured academic staff the increases were much smaller—from 13 to 14 per cent among fellows, and from 3 to 5 per cent in the professoriate. The women on college governing bodies elected many men to fellowships: the men elected few women. The men offered fellowships by the other sex did not fear 'petticoat government' and would have been foolish had they done so. When honorary, emeriti and research fellows have been excluded, Lady Margaret Hall had twenty-four fellows in 1977, all of them women: by 1989 this figure had grown to forty-four, of whom twenty-seven were men. Mr Duncan Stewart had been Principal since 1979.

The small proportion of women in Oxford's academic staff has commonly been attributed to male prejudice. 'Like women in other professions', a recent Hansard Society report suggests, 'women at Oxbridge are subject to "taken for granted" assumptions and disparaging stereotypes . . . selectors tend to assume that women's primary interests and responsibilities lie elsewhere, and thus often do not see them as potential . . . professors'.[29] While this factor may well have been operative, a rather different one was far more obtrusive. Where, as in Oxford during this period, the competition for academic staff appointments was extremely keen, almost any interruption to scholarly work could doom a candidate to be placed second in the listing. It could have had just enough effect on the quality or quantity of research output to prevent success; and women academics were far more subject than men to interruptions when establishing their careers. Thus, while complaints that the University remained a male-dominated society continued in full force, they rang much more truly for senior than for junior Oxford. In the summer of 1990 nine presidents of junior common rooms and sixty of the 207 Rhodes scholars were women; and in the Oxford Union elections women won both the presidency and the secretaryship. In the Oxford University Student Union (OUSU, successor to the Student Representative Council) the presidency went to a woman four times running from 1987 to 1991. The full effects of this revivifying transformation of Oxford's colleges cannot yet be estimated. As table 27.1 shows, it neither disturbed the balance between undergraduates and postgraduates nor prevented a welcome shift towards mathematics and science.

[29] *Report of the Hansard Society Commission on Women at the Top* (Jan. 1990), 67. See too *Oxford Review of Education* xv (1989), 213–303; J. Hornsby, N. Lacey, S. Lovibond, J. Pallot and J. Stapleton, 'How long, O Lord . . . : permanent Oxford posts for women', *OM* Hilary 1987, no. 4, 2–6.

TABLE 27.1

NUMBERS OF FULL-TIME OXFORD STUDENTS IN
SELECTED CATEGORIES IN 1968/9 AND 1988/9

	1968/9		1988/9	
	no.	%	no.	%
men	8,505	81.1	8,414	61.8
women	1,977	18.9	5,204	38.2
undergraduates	7,643	72.9	10,005	73.5
postgraduates	2,839	27.1	3,613	26.5
arts & social studies	6,540	62.4	8,021	58.9
maths & science	3,942	37.6	5,597	41.1
total	10,482		13,618	

Note: All mixed courses with a scientific component are here counted as science. The shift to science was more pronounced among undergraduates than among postgraduate students.

Source: *Gazette Supplements* 4 June 1969, 1235–42; 10 July 1989, 995–1003; *Statistics of Education, 1986* (HMSO 1970), 6. 48.

In 1970 Oxford's women undergraduates were better qualified academically than the men. More than 56 per cent of the women admitted held three A-level passes with grades of AAC/ABB or better, against fewer than 52 per cent of the men. An increase in the proportion of women undergraduates was thus likely to entail some raising of the standard. Table 27.2 indicates how it rose during these years. The table does not suggest that the change to mixed colleges impaired the academic performance of either women or men. All five of the colleges which had been confined to women in 1970 improved their performance; there was little to choose in the extent of this improvement between those which had become mixed and those which had not. Table 27.3 compares the performance in 1969 with that in 1989 for each of the five. Two men's colleges have been introduced for purposes of comparison: Corpus, which headed the 'Norrington table' in both years, and Balliol, which was said in press comment to have lost some of its pre-eminence by the later 1980s.[30] The experience of Balliol in the 1970s and 1980s reproduced what had happened many times in Oxford's history. One college took the lead and, after some years, the others followed, and even overtook it.

[30] *Times* 30 July 1987, 13. For a powerful criticism of the Norrington table see *OM* Trinity 1991, no. 4, 1–2 (editorial). For a survey of British university degree results during the 1980s see *Journal of Further and Higher Education* 16 (1992), 60–70 (B. Macfarlane). In December 1991 a resolution against specifying candidates' colleges in class lists was carried on a postal vote by 664 to 579. It was to apply to 'a trial period of five years.'

TABLE 27.2

CLASSIFIED HONOURS: MEN AND WOMEN
IN OXFORD FINALS, 1969 AND 1989 (%)

class	men		women				all	
	1969	1989	1969	1989			1969	1989
				a	b	c		
I	11.57	19.57	9.24	12.11	10.35	11.78	11.13	16.41
II	68.24	74.03	76.44	83.22	83.74	83.32	69.78	77.73
III	20.19	6.40	14.32	4.67	5.91	4.90	19.09	5.86

a in mixed colleges   b in women's colleges   c all.

Note: Since 1986 the second class has been divided; the two divisions (2i and 2ii) have been aggregated here for ease of comparison. The figures for the decades 1967–76 and 1977–86 are given in Oxford Review of Education xv (1989), 219. In this and the following tables concerned with honours finals the BCL is excluded.

Source: Gazette Supplement 5 Sept. 1969, 1533–56; Calendar 1989/90, 386–411. The total entry percentages in Gazette cxx (1989–90), 240, are not quite correct.

The fact that more than 94 per cent of those who gained classified honours in 1989 were in the first class or the second is striking; but the evidence of greatly improved performance provided by table 27.2 should be treated with some reserve. The improvement was not the result of the second class being divided. In 1985, the last year before the division, firsts and seconds already accounted for more than 91 per cent of the class-lists. Still less is it a result of dealing with the class-lists only and of excluding those who failed to be classed for honours. Those who failed, or received an aegrotat or a pass degree only, were very few by 1969 and still fewer twenty years later. By 1992 there were external examiners in all of Oxford's principal honour schools; and apart from this, since a college tutor, when examining, was debarred from the viva voce and from decisions on classes where his or her own candidates were concerned, all Oxford examining had an 'external' flavour. It is thus very improbable that any great relaxation of standards occurred during the twenty years; they met the criteria normal for British universities. Nonetheless there can be no certainty that they remained constant for two decades. The testimony on this point from the handful of people who examined for finals at the start of the period and again at the end of it is conflicting.[31] It may be

---

[31] See Sir Keith Thomas in discussion at seminar on 'Oxford since 1970', Corpus Christi College, 20 Feb. 1987 (Brian Harrison's transcript, HUA), 20. During this period the percentage of firsts was higher in mathematics/science than in arts/social studies. The proportionate growth of mathematics/science may therefore have helped to raise the figure for firsts in table 27.2. For the proportion of firsts in other universities (1989) see University Statistics 1989–90 (Universities' Statistical Record 1991) i. 60.

TABLE 27.3

NORRINGTON TABLE
PERFORMANCES ATTAINED BY
SELECTED OXFORD COLLEGES
IN 1969 AND 1989 (%)

	1969	1989
Corpus Christi	73.5	76.7
Balliol	69.3	72.7
St Hilda's	64.7	68.0
St Anne's	64.3	70.0
St Hugh's	64.3	67.0
Somerville	64.0	68.9
Lady Margaret Hall	63.3	70.9

Note: In the Norrington table a first = 3,
a second = 2, a third = 1. A score of
100% would be achieved if all in a
college's list were awarded firsts. The
figures for 1989 have been adjusted for
the division of the second class, all
seconds being aggregated.

permissible to conclude that undergraduate academic performance in Oxford rose sharply during these years, though not necessarily as sharply as the figures would indicate.

This improved performance in finals reflected a greatly improved entry, in which the larger proportion of women entrants had been a contributing factor. In 1969/70 20 per cent of those admitted had achieved three A grades in A-levels; and nearly 53 per cent had AAC/ABB or better. In 1989/90 the corresponding percentages in the post-A-level entrants were 55 per cent and 90 per cent; and more than 95 per cent of conditional offers were dependent on the candidates gaining A-levels at grades no worse than AAC/ABB.[32] The entry from independent schools improved most of all.[33] Table 27.4 shows how this was reflected in finals performance.

[32] In 1969/70 36% of the post-A-level candidates accepted also held S-level distinctions. In 1989/90 21% of the corresponding cohort had achieved more than three A grades at A-level, in some cases by a combination of A- and AS-levels. In the figure referring to conditional offers in 1989/90, the cases where the candidates were so strong that no grade was specified have been disregarded.

[33] The Universities Central Council on Admissions did not distinguish between types of school in the figures for the A-level performance of university entrants until 1983. Between that year and 1990 the numbers from the LEA-maintained schools who had achieved grades of AAC/ABB or better rose by 15.8%, those from the independent schools by 37.7%. These figures relate to England and Wales only.

TABLE 27.4

PERFORMANCE IN OXFORD 'FINALS' IN 1961/2, 1982 AND
1988 BY TYPE OF SCHOOL (% OF LIST IN CLASSES I AND II)

	1961 & 1962		1982		1988	
	I	II	I	II	I	II
independent schools	8	50	12.22	76.01	14.62	75.61
direct-grant schools	11	56				
maintained sector	8	61	12.23	76.78	14.35	75.22

Note: The outcomes in particular subjects may have differed materially
from the one in this aggregated summary. For instance, entrance
examining for PPE, where performance in sixth-form work may be a
particularly poor predictor, has been found to give a different result:
see P. Collier and C. P. Mayer, 'An investigation of university selection
procedures', *Economic Jl* xcvi (1986), supplement, 163–70. For the
performance of men and women from each type of school see *OM*
Trinity 1991, no. 8, 16–17 (McCrum); Michaelmas 1991, no. 0, 10
(Treisman).

Sources: Figures for 1961 and 1962 are from *Franks Report* ii. 90–1
(one-in-two samples): those for 1982 from *Dover Report*, 34; those for
1988 from USR/UCCA. The treatment of aegrotats and passes may not
have been identical in all three cases, but the consequent distortions
would not be great.

The 'amiable, well-connected, public school dunce' mentioned above
faded out in these years.[34] The independent schools contrived to erase the
stigma from 'swotting' and to use their academic advantages to effect in the
competition for places at Oxford. Their pupils realized that they could
expect no favours from those operating the Oxford admissions system, and
that a second in finals had become as necessary for them as for anyone else.
As the gap in performance mentioned in the last chapter between those from
the independent schools and the others disappeared, undergraduate Oxford
became not more solemn but more serious.[35]

The improvement in the entry from the independent schools increased
concern about attracting a strong entry from the sixth forms in the
maintained sector. As table 27.4 shows, it could not be held in the early
1980s that applicants from the maintained schools were being unfairly

[34] See above, 193.
[35] See above, 727–8.

treated: the difficulty was that their sixth-formers found the admissions system so deterrent that they did not apply. To be judged free of class bias the Oxford admissions tutors had to do more than behave fairly and perceptively to applicants: they needed to adopt a system which would encourage applications from everyone possessing the attributes needed. Sir Kenneth Berrill told one of the vice-chancellor's seminars of 1970/1 that 'no institution changes from within unless it is threatened from outside'.[36] Though this pronouncement came from the then chairman of the University Grants Committee (UGC) it needed qualification perhaps where Oxford was concerned. In a collegiate university, a college's pressure from within could be a powerful propellant. Both of the recent reforms in Oxford's undergraduate admissions system originated in the need to bring the initiative of a college (or of a small group of colleges) under control. In the case of the Hardie report on admissions (1962) the adventurous college was Balliol; the Dover report (1983) was precipitated by the notification of a change from Keble.[37]

It was not the task of Sir Kenneth Dover's committee on undergraduate admissions simply to devise a just system and to record it on tablets of stone. Any system which it recommended, while fair to each type of school, and especially to the LEA-maintained schools, had to be acceptable to all the colleges. The basic fact confronting the Dover Committee was that, whereas many in the independent schools took GCE O-levels (precursors of GCSE) at fifteen, in the maintained schools it was a 'sixteen plus' exam. The Committee's stance was more radical than that of the Franks Commission detailed in the last chapter.[38] It concluded that no entrance examination which could be taken by both pre- and post-A-level applicants would ever be seen as fair by the former. They therefore recommended that Oxford's entrance examination should not be available to any post-A-level applicant and that entrance scholarships and exhibitions should be abolished. The two recommendations hung together, since entrance scholarships had been outside the reach of many maintained-school applicants who could not spend a seventh term in the sixth form: they were therefore seen as a sign that the pre-A-level applicants were not being taken very seriously. Under the system adopted on the Dover Committee's recommendation the pre-A-level candidate could choose whether to sit the entrance exam, or to try, on the basis of record and interview, for an offer conditional on A-level

[36] 'Oxford discussions on higher education', *Minerva* x (1972), 317.

[37] [W. F. R. Hardie, chairman] *Admissions to Colleges: Report of a Working Party on Admissions* (University of Oxford 1962); [Sir Kenneth Dover, chairman] *Report of the Committee on Undergraduate Admissions* (Oxford Colleges Admissions Office 1983).

[38] See above, 727–8.

performance; the post-A-level candidate had to rely on record and interview. Table 27.5 shows the outcome in 1989.

TABLE 27.5

METHOD OF ADMISSION OF OXFORD HOME UNDER-
GRADUATES 1988/9 BY TYPE OF SCHOOL

	on entrance exam	on record and interview a	b	total	%
LEA-maintained schools	907	467	83	1,457	46.1
independent schools	1,118	197	148	1,463	46.2
others	46	74	124	244	7.7
total	2,071	738	355	3,164	100.0

a conditional on performance at A-level   b post-A-level applicants

Note: Of the 3,164 offered places, 2,715 were applying to enter in Oct. 1989, the remaining 449 in Oct. 1990.

Source: *Gazette Supplement* 30 Oct. 1989, 229.

A few years had put beyond doubt the popularity of the conditional-offer route of entry with the maintained schools. The Committee had never expected to eliminate all complaints about Oxford's selection of undergraduates. 'It must also be recognized that no selection procedure can ever expect to be entirely immune to charges of unfairness. When people have competed unsuccessfully for something which they greatly desire, it contributes to their self-esteem to believe that their rejection was unfair.'[39] The more the independent schools put forth their strength, the harder it became during the 1980s to reconcile the correct predictions about degree course performance illustrated in table 27.4 with the effort to prevent the maintained schools' proportion of the entry from shrinking. Moving upwards on the down escalator proved impossible, as table 27.6 shows.

Not surprisingly, a group of powerful Cambridge colleges had decided by the end of 1990 on an experiment in 'positive discrimination'. In a more general view of admissions problems, it is too early yet to assess the side-effects of the post-Dover changes. Many students benefit from a break between A-levels and university; but that hardly makes a case for a seventh term in the sixth form. The argument for entrance awards was that they spread talent between the colleges and enabled the less eligible colleges to attract some 'fliers'. Even in 1982/3, when by a new rule an applicant could choose a place at his or her first-choice college in preference to a scholarship

[39] *Report on Undergraduate Admissions*, 9.

TABLE 27.6

ADMISSIONS OF OXFORD HOME UNDER-GRADUATES BY TYPE OF SCHOOL IN 1969/70, 1979/80 AND 1989/90 (%)

	1969/70	1979/80	1989/90
Maintained schools	43.5	49.0	44.5
direct-grant schools	17.3	—	—
independent schools	38.2	48.2	48.0
others	1.0	2.8	7.5

Source: Gazette Supplements 5 Aug. 1970, 1407, 1412;
25 Sept. 1980, 23; 10 Dec. 1990, 467.

elsewhere, over a hundred applicants had won awards which took them away from their first-choice colleges. The longer-term effects of abolishing this talent-spreading device are not yet known.[40]

TABLE 27.7

NUMBER OF OXFORD FINALISTS IN SINGLE-SUBJECT AND MULTI-SUBJECT COURSES IN 1969 AND 1989

	1969	1989
single-subject honours	1,856	2,037
bipartite and multi-subject honours	444	691
total	2,300	2,728

Note: Aegrotats, overstanding for honours,
'unclassified honours', pass, and fail are
excluded. In 1989 98.8% of the entry obtained
classified honours; only nine candidates failed.

Source: Gazette c (1969/70), 129; cxx (1989/90),
240, and as for Table 27.2.

The pattern of undergraduate studies changed greatly in these years with the expansion of bipartite and multi-subject honours courses [table 27.7].

[40] In 1988/9 nearly 19% of successful applicants accepted places at colleges other than their first choices, as compared with less than 14% in 1969/70; but the 19% consisted of the more marginal acceptances. As far as the admissions tutors could judge, it was not the highest talent which was being spread by 1988/9.

Thus, while those gaining single-subject honours had increased by less than 10 per cent, the increase in the bipartite and multi-subject schools exceeded 55 per cent. Fourteen such schools had been created since 1969; and five of these spanned the arts/science divide. Engineering, economics and management, and human sciences—to name only the two largest of the five—had become well established courses. These developments followed a trend discernible in the schools in the 1960s where the 'mixed group' of A-levels had been the fastest growing. Oxford's new mixed courses attracted their full share of high ability [table 27.8].

TABLE 27.8

1989 OXFORD DEGREE RESULTS BY TYPE OF HONOURS SCHOOL (%)

	I	II.i	II.ii	III
single honours	16.5	51.6	24.8	5.7
older mixed courses	12.5	50.6	28.9	6.7
newer mixed courses	20.9	51.9	22.1	4.1

Source: As for table 27.7. Percentages correspond to the figures used for that table.

The radical reconstruction of undergraduate courses proposed by the Kneale Committee in 1965 found no favour; but one of that Committee's aims—to facilitate 'new combinations of subjects'—came near to being attained by more piecemeal methods.[41] A further increase in Oxford's mixed courses may be expected to follow the reform of the 'eighteen plus' exams promised for 1994. By 1990 this prospect had increased anxieties about proper preparation for work for research degrees and had brought into discussion an increase in the number of Oxford's taught postgraduate courses.

The period was marked by much revision of honours courses, many of which must remain unmentioned in this short narrative. Bipartite options were introduced in the school of philosophy, politics and economics (PPE) in 1970. A 'literature option' in Greats, and a variant of 'classical mods' for those starting Greek at the University, were both launched in the early 1970s. These changes in PPE and Greats led to some numerical decline in undergraduate philosophy; among those taking honours in 1989 it had not been studied by more than half the Greats list and by more than a third of the list in PPE. The modern history syllabus underwent a thorough overhaul during the 1980s; and in 1990 the year abroad during the modern languages

---

[41] [W. C. Kneale, chairman] *Report of the Committee on the Structure of the First and Second Public Examinations* (University of Oxford 1965), 34, 48.

course became compulsory. The changes were equally substantial in science. Agriculture and forestry were combined into a single course in 1971; but in January 1982 Congregation decided, by a large majority on the postal vote, to accept the UGC's advice and to phase out the school of agriculture and forest sciences. Maintaining so specialized and expensive a course for small numbers could not be justified when funds were short. It was replaced by honours in pure and applied biology. A much larger step towards a broader course was taken at the end of the period. It was decided that the 1990 intake would read for honours in biology. They would be allowed, but not obliged, to specialize in zoology or botany; the separate honours schools in those two subjects would disappear. This decision was echoed by the creation of a preliminary examination in physical sciences to replace honour moderations in physics and 'prelims' in chemistry, metallurgy and science of materials, and geology. The four-year, single-subject engineering course was examined for the first time in 1991, and by a decision of December 1992 this became the route to the new degree of master of engineering. A new first degree, that of bachelor of fine art, was established in 1977. With this and new premises, the Ruskin School of Drawing and Fine Art was given the chance of making its mark in the modern era.

The plea in the Franks report for an end to the abuse whereby tutorials at Oxford had been multiplied in order to 'cover the course' has been mentioned above.[42] The Commission recommended that no undergraduate should have more than one tutorial a week. This recommendation had little or no effect and the strain on the tutorial system was felt throughout the period.[43] J. I. M. Stewart included these remarks in *A Memorial Service* (1976): ' "College tutors, unhappily, are subject nowadays to a great deal of distraction. They carry novel administrative burdens. They are many of them in demand by an enlarged and extramural public through . . . the media. They often feel obliged, through a supposed professional exigency, to make constant, diffuse, and even supererogatory contributions to the scholarship of their subject." . . . "And as a consequence . . . they neglect their pupils?" "Far from it. They are in general a most conscientious body of men [sic]. But they have let their syllabuses—the mass of mere information which students are expected to acquire in pursuit of a first degree—proliferate at the expense of any absorbing and satisfying intellectual discipline . . . It's up to the tutor to generate and sustain that intense

---

[42] See above, 230.
[43] Lord Franks, 'The Franks report in retrospect', seminar, Nuffield College, 31 Jan. 1986 (Brian Harrison's transcript, HUA), 8–9; Blake, 'Structure and government', 7–8; *OM* Trinity 1986, no. 8, 6–7 (Lucas); *OM* Hilary 1991, no. 8, 2–3 (Crouch and Innes), 8–9 (Holmes); *OM* Trinity 1991, no. 0, 4–5 (Johnson); *OM* Trinity 1991, no. 4, 12, 13, 16 (Harrison); *OM* Trinity 1991, no. 8, 21–3 (Briggs).

intellectual excitement which you and I know to be the finer breath of all knowledge." [44] Table 27.9 gives an idea of how far the funding cuts of the later 1980s increased these strains. The figures include only those holding 'university-funded teaching posts'. Towards the end of the period the cuts induced some colleges to elect to 'five-year fellowships' where no university-funded post was involved. The Oxford ratio was thus a little more favourable in 1988/9 than is apparent in table 27.9.

TABLE 27.9

UK AND OXFORD STAFF/STUDENT RATIOS IN 1968/9 AND 1988/9

	United Kingdom		Oxford	
	1968/9	1988/9	1968/9	1988/9
student load	227,562	349,644	10,810	13,727
full-time teaching staff	26,654	30,621	1,121	1,195
staff/student ratio	1:8.5	1:11.4	1:9.6	1:11.5

Note: The published figures for 1968/9 give numbers, not 'load', for postgraduate students. The part-time numbers have been halved to give an approximation there for 'load'.

Source: *Statistics of Education* (UGC/HMSO) 1968, vi. 84; 1969, vi. 149; *University Statistics* 1988/9 (UFC/USR), iii. 61.

Substantial changes were made in the pattern of postgraduate studies. When the period began, Oxford was the only British university giving a bachelor's degree for a thesis by postgraduate students in science. In 1971 the BSc was retitled MSc; and a new-style MSc, based on an examination supported by a short dissertation, replaced a number of diplomas. In 1979 the BLitt was similarly retitled, as was the BPhil in all subjects except philosophy itself. By this date it had been agreed that a student who had taken an MPhil should be allowed to 'develop' his MPhil thesis for doctoral purposes. The fact that the Oxford MA was obtained by the passage of time and payment of a fee meant, however, that the University still had no MA courses. The MPhil was clearly too exacting to remain the only mastership degree in arts subjects, and the mastership of studies was introduced in 1983.

The Swinnerton-Dyer report (published in April 1982) highlighted a national problem of long-delayed completion of doctoral theses and low completion rates among those holding postgraduate awards, especially in

[44] J. I. M. Stewart, *A Memorial Service* (London 1976), 179–80. Dr Stewart was a Student of Christ Church 1949–73 and Reader in English Literature 1969–73.

social studies.[45] This posed particular problems for Oxford where it had long been the practice, in both history and social studies, to blur the distinction between 'research training' and the completion of a young scholar's first book. Indeed shortly before the report appeared, a single Oxford University Press list in politics had included six books consisting of theses by recent students of Nuffield College. In 1986 the 'research training' aspect of doctoral work was emphasized by a note in the *Examination Decrees*. All examiners of theses were 'asked to bear in mind that their judgement of the substantial significance of the thesis should be based on what might reasonably be expected of a diligent and competent student after three, or at most four, years of full-time study'.[46] At the same time supervision of postgraduate students was included in the stated duties of newly appointed university lecturers.

Postgraduate students and 'post-doctorals' gained from the establishment of the faculty centres and from the growth during this period of the graduate colleges. Wolfson occupied its buildings in 1974; they included flats and 'terraced housing' for married students. Linacre moved to Cherwell Edge in 1977, enlarged its accommodation, and in 1986 obtained its charter. St Cross moved from temporary premises to Pusey House in 1981. A new graduate college was established in 1977 primarily to encourage the development of clinical medicine. It became Green College almost at once, on receiving an endowment from Cecil and Ida Green of Dallas. The percentage of Oxford's postgraduate students who were members of the graduate colleges rose during these years from 12.5 to 28.4. It was not, however, until the end of the period under review that Oxford grappled vigorously with the problems of postgraduate study described in the last chapter.[47] The Roberts report (October 1987) underlined how acute these were in a collegiate university long famous for its first-degree work.[48] Directors of postgraduate studies were then appointed by each faculty board; and a working party on postgraduate provision presented its report in October 1990. By that time the possibility of the Oxford DPhil ceasing to be recognized throughout the world as a doctorate of the highest standing had appeared on the horizon. Heavy tutorial work hindered some tutors from giving enough attention to postgraduate seminars and supervisions. Given that colleges competed against each other, each cherishing its independence, undergraduates were sometimes allowed to neglect lectures and classes and to look on the tutorials

---

[45] [Sir Peter Swinnerton-Dyer, chairman] *Report of the Working Party on Postgraduate Education* (Advisory Board for the Research Councils 1982).

[46] In May 1991 the note was incorporated into the text of the decree, the words 'take into account' replacing 'be based on'.

[47] See above, 731–2.

[48] [J. M. Roberts, chairman] *Report of the Committee of Inquiry into Provision for Graduate Students* (University of Oxford 1987). The Committee's main recommendations on 'admission and transfer' were brought into effect by decree in May 1991.

provided by the college as their sole means of instruction. The overloading of tutors to which this misuse of tutorials led was perceived not merely as distorting undergraduate courses but as an impediment to the strengthening of postgraduate programmes.

Modern Oxford has been principally concerned with the teaching of young, full-time students, and with research in the main academic disciplines; yet it contains important institutions which lie wholly or partly outside these central interests, and which may not fit without some contrivance into the collegiate pattern. These met with varying fortunes during the 1970s and 1980s. The department for external studies and the department of social and administrative studies fared well. The former, brought under the aegis of the General Board in 1971, as the Habakkuk Committee had recommended, obtained a further grant from the Kellogg Foundation in 1982 and added substantially to its buildings. In 1988/9 external studies enrolled some 9,300 students, nearly 40 per cent of whom attended residential courses; by then the department's summer schools had an enrolment of over a thousand. This scale of operation represented an expansion over the twenty years of some 50 per cent.[49] After working closely for some years with the Open University, the department entered in 1988/9 into an agreement with the Council for National Academic Awards to participate in the CNAA scheme for credit accumulation and transfer. The research output of the department of social and administrative studies was well regarded, and at the end of the period the MSc in applied social studies became the first Oxford degree obtainable by part-time study.

The department of educational studies was less fortunate. Until the final years of the period it remained the only such department in a British university to lack a professor. Until 1984 its staff tutors were the University's only tenured staff in charge of resident students who were not entitled to fellowships. When Oxford's bachelor of education degree was established in 1966, the University had a responsibility, by the terms of the Area Training Organization (founded in 1951), for four colleges of education—Culham, Milton Keynes, Lady Spencer-Churchill, and Westminster. This BEd had been in operation for no more than a few years when changes were announced in the national pattern which posed a problem for Oxford. Under these, the pass course for the degree would last for three years; and, as it would necessarily include substantial periods of teaching practice, only a part of it could be devoted to academic study. A joint committee of Council and the General Board, set up in 1973 to study the

---

[49] In 1975 the department transferred its responsibilities in Kent and East Sussex to the universities of Kent and Sussex. There had been annual enrolments of more than a thousand in these areas during the early 1970s. The expansion in Berkshire, Buckinghamshire and Oxfordshire was of the order of 70%. The 'load' in 1988/9 was the equivalent of more than 600 full-time students.

new situation, recommended that the Oxford BEd should be phased out.[50] Its members were influenced by three considerations. First, now that teaching was to become an all-graduate profession, Oxford would not be able to cope with the numbers involved. Secondly, whereas in 1966 it had been an Oxford degree or nothing, there was by now the alternative of degree validation by the CNAA. Finally, as no one expected Oxford to validate the three-year pass BEd, University responsibility for the four-year honours degree would involve the colleges of education in the impracticalities of 'split validation'.[51] When these arguments were put to Congregation, they were rejected on a postal vote by 359 to 308. Syllabuses were then prepared by the education colleges and put to the faculties concerned, the majority of which reported willingness to tackle validation. The General Board therefore decided to support an Oxford honours BEd; but Council, suspicious of external degrees, remained opposed. This process took two years, at the end of which the University rejected validation on a second postal vote by 648 to 329.

In the circumstances of the 1970s this decision was almost certainly right; but it could scarcely have been made in a more damaging way. The committee's report had been unanimous, and it carried the signatures of both the Vice-Chancellor and Vice-Chancellor elect, besides those of the Vice-Chairman of the General Board and the director designate of educational studies. A recommendation with such backing was likely to prevail in the end. Yet the colleges of education could not be blamed for trying their luck among all the uncertainties of votes in Congregation. They knew the department of educational studies to be split on the question. Validation by the University would have enhanced their attractions to potential student applicants: they could not pass up the chance of securing such an advantage. In the event, their struggle to secure it harmed them and the department (though in 1992 Westminster College, a survivor from another world, secured Oxford validation for the BEd and other degrees). The most fervent supporter of the democracy of the dons does not claim it to be a governmental system ideally suited to every situation.

Early in the 1960s the University declined to bid for one of the management schools then in prospect.[52] At least one very distinguished and influential member of the economics sub-faculty pronounced such schools to impart no more than a smattering of economics, improperly mixed with odds and ends from other disciplines. As always, the objection to them was not that they were vocational, but that their studies might not be pursued with depth and rigour. In July 1965 an enthusiastic Oxford group,

[50] [A. L. C. Bullock, chairman] *Report of the Joint Committee on Teacher Education* (University of Oxford 1973).
[51] Ibid. 10.
[52] See Lord Franks, *British Business Schools* (British Institute of Management 1963).

generously supported by a London businessman, Clifford Barclay, founded the Oxford Centre for Management Studies, as a company limited by guarantee, and obtained an ample site for it near the southern edge of the city. It was to pursue 'studies of interest to management in industry, commerce, finance or public administration'.[53] BPhil and certificate courses in management studies were instituted in the following year. The Centre developed a research capability and important executive programmes, and took a large part in developing the engineering, economics and management course mentioned earlier. In 1983 it received a substantial benefaction from Sir John Templeton; a year later it was granted a limited right to matriculate postgraduate students and became Templeton College. In 1987 a committee was set up under the Warden of Wadham, Sir Claus Moser, to recommend on the part the University should play in management studies. By then the fund-raising 'Campaign for Oxford' was being planned. Oxford's facilities for expanding these studies, whether at undergraduate or postgraduate level, were exceptionally good: to leave in doubt how far the university and colleges intended to be involved in them was no longer possible. In March 1988 the Moser Committee recommended that 'Oxford should make an important, fresh contribution to the needed developments in Management education . . . as speedily as possible'.[54] On 11 December 1990 Congregation accepted that there should be a new school of management studies on the Templeton site. This important initiative was to be based on a two-year course for the master's degree in business administration which would have an intake of 150 a year.

The entitlement question was not the only one which called for crisis management during these years. There was some irony about the first occasion in the 1970s when a governmental decision made a sharp impact on the University. In July 1976 the Labour government announced a decision which accorded with the views of a large majority of Oxford dons, but confronted its colleges with an acute difficulty. They introduced a change (short-lived in the event) to raise university fees to a level which would eliminate fee discrimination between home and overseas students.[55] To make the change electorally acceptable, fees (as opposed to maintenance payments) were to be exempted from the parental means test. Thus college fees, if they remained uncontrolled, would represent, as the Minister of State wrote, 'an open-ended commitment of public funds'. 'This open-endedness', he added, 'will be more exposed to adverse criticism when the extent of government liability for student awards in higher education increases this

[53] [Sir Claus Moser, chairman] *Report on the Future of Management Studies* (University of Oxford 1988), 32.

[54] Ibid. 11.

[55] At the lowest point in this period, 1981/2, overseas students formed 10.6% of the student body. By 1988/9 they formed 17.4%. Students from the European Community are included in both figures.

year as a result of substantial increases in tuition fees generally'.[56] The fee increases applied to both undergraduates and postgraduates: the postgraduate increase was indeed slightly the greater.

The vice-chancellors of Oxford and Cambridge met the Minister of State and were assured that his object 'was to close the open-ended commitment and not to reduce the total income of colleges' from fees.[57] The crucial point was simply that the total must not increase from one year to the next by more than an appropriate allowance for inflation. An inter-college agreement was then hammered out in the Conference of Colleges; and in March 1978 the colleges' fees committee was authorized to negotiate with the Department of Education and Science (DES) and to determine each college's fees annually on the basis of an agreed formula. In broad terms, the annual increase in the total of college fees was negotiated thereafter between the DES and the committee. The division of the total between colleges was then determined by the Conference on the advice of the committee, the DES not being concerned with the fact that, in the main, the poorer colleges were charging higher fees than the richer. By perpetuating the system largely as it had been in 1976, this arrangement entailed some rough justice to those poorer colleges which had succeeded in keeping their fees low; but it worked acceptably over the twelve years to the end of the period covered by this epilogue.

The quinquennial system of university financing collapsed in the 1970s, and from 1981 onward substantial cuts in grant were imposed. Sir David Phillips calculated that, allowing for changes in staff numbers, the recurrent budgets of the Oxford science departments had been halved between 1966 and 1990.[58] An account of all this belongs, not to this epilogue, but to a history of higher education in Britain; and it will be some years before the effect of these cuts can be properly assessed.[59] In 1985 the UGC announced that its long-established system of deficit funding would be succeeded by formula funding; and the funding levels planned for 1989/90 were announced in the following year. Although the University had already made all the reductions it could short of disrupting research and teaching, it was running a deficit in 1985/6 of £1.1 million. A programme of further reductions was devised. The period covered was deliberately made longer than the UGC's to reduce disruption: expenditure was to be brought some

[56] HCP 287 (1977), 109. This was one of several occasions during the period when the research councils expressed disquiet at being obliged to pay college fees for postgraduate students in the sciences: HCP 286 (1977), p. xxix.

[57] HCP 287 (1977), 110.

[58] For the 1970s see UGC *Annual Survey 1975–6* (PP 1976–7 viii Cmnd 6750), 5. For Sir David Phillips's views see *Independent* 6 Aug. 1990, 13; Sir David had lately become the first full-time chairman of the Advisory Board for the Research Councils.

[59] Many cuts in grant have not been announced as such. Whenever the inflation allowance has been inadequate a cut has been made, not merely in one year's grant but in the base-line from which the next year's may be calculated.

11 per cent below the 1985/6 level by 1990/1, after which, as was hoped, a period of level funding would enable the University to rebuild its reserves. The colleges' share of Common University Fund (CUF) lecturership costs was increased, the redistribution of college endowment income being stepped up to enable the poorer colleges to cope with this increase.

Against this background it was decided to launch a Campaign for Oxford, with the aim of raising £220 million for the University in five years. The boldness of the decision matched anything in Oxford's past. Many years of deficit funding by the UGC had implanted the notion that, while gifts to colleges were to be encouraged, giving to the university itself simply relieved the government from meeting its proper obligations.[60] Oxford's refusal of an honorary degree to the Prime Minister, Margaret Thatcher, in January 1985 had angered some potential donors. However, the boldness proved justified: before the launch in October 1988 £51 million had been raised.[61] By July 1990, nine months after the start of the Campaign across the Atlantic, the total stood at £117 million. When all allowance has been made for the inclusion in these figures of some research grant money not directly attributable to campaigning activity, the Campaign represents financial self-help on a scale, and of a professionalism, not previously seen in Oxford.[62]

The change in the balance of Oxford's funding over these two decades was striking. Throughout the period, the University received recurrent income from public funds (payments for services apart) in three principal ways: in the UGC/UFC block grant, as university fees and as research council grants. In 1968/9 these items accounted for 82 per cent of recurrent income, in 1988/9 for less than 62 per cent.[63] By 1987/8 the percentage of the University's income from research grants and contracts was 46 per cent above the average for the British universities, and the percentage from Exchequer grants more than nine per cent below the average.[64]

The 1980s ended in uncertainty, the Universities Funding Council (UFC) having decided 'to base funding on competitive bidding for numbers of

[60] Campaign donors could earmark their gifts for a particular college.

[61] The Campaign for the Bodleian Library was opened some weeks earlier. The Prince of Wales attended a dinner in the Radcliffe Camera on 5 July 1988.

[62] By July 1990 the amount raised was more than four times as much as the total produced by the Higher Studies Appeal of the 1930s, and more than six times that of the Historic Buildings Appeal of the later 1950s, when the receipts from those two appeals are shown at 1989 values.

[63] The 1988/9 'home fees' total has been treated as if all of it had come from British taxpayers and ratepayers. In fact a small fraction of it related to students from other countries of the European Community.

[64] Research grants and contracts rose between 1968/9 and 1988/9 from 18% to nearly 31% of university revenue. These percentages relate to all subjects; but nearly all the grants were scientific (a substantial proportion of those in social studies being made not to the university but to Nuffield College). Research training grants have been excluded. During the 1980s university-funded academic and research staff fell from 1,441 to 1,435 (by 0.4%); grant-supported staff in these grades increased from 589 to 1,151 (by 95%). There was no corresponding increase in grant-supported technical and clerical staff.

TABLE 27.10

LOSS AND GAIN OF ESTABLISHED ACADEMIC POSTS IN OXFORD,
1981–1990

i *posts abolished*[1]

	arts and social studies	mathematics and science[2]	total
abolished by 31 Mar. 1990	69	58	127
to be abolished	41.5	25.5	67
	110.5	83.5	194

ii *posts created by 31 Mar. 1990*[3]

	arts and social studies	mathematics and science	total
1 'new blood' posts 1983–5	4	32	36
2 information technology	—	9	9
3 engineering and technology programme	—	18	18
4 oriental studies ('Parker posts')	5	—	5
5 clinical medicine (earmarked UFC funding)	—	3	3
6 earth sciences (including two professors)	—	5	5
7 other rationalizations: Slavonic and east European studies, archaeology, linguistics (including one professor)	7	—	7
8 NHS funded	—	17	17
9 endowed posts 1981–8 (before the launch of the Campaign for Oxford)	6	2	8
total	22	86	108

iii *posts funded or partly funded by the Campaign for Oxford to 31 Mar. 1990*[4]

	funding[5]	arts and social studies	mathematics and science	total
professorships	a	3	2	5
	b	4	1	5
	c	1	—	1
	d	8	—	8
readerships	b	2	—	2
	d	—	1	1

TABLE 27.10 (*cont.*)

	funding[5]	arts and social studies	mathematics and science	total
university lecturers	*a*	2	—	2
	d	5	2	7
faculty and CUF lecturers (university duties not full-time)	*a*	4	—	4
	d	1	—	1
totals	*a*	9	2	11
	b	6	1	7
	c	1	—	1
	d	14	3	17
total		30	6	36

[1] At 1 Mar. 1990 44 posts had been not abolished but 'suspended'; 37 of these had become vacant, while 7 were due to become vacant on the resignation or retirement of the holder.

[2] Anthropology and geography are counted under mathematics and science.

[3] Item 1 was Oxford's share in a government scheme intended to ensure that recruitment of young talent continued while universities were cutting their expenditure. Items 2–5 resulted from governmental concern about particular fields of study. Items 6 and 7 resulted from UGC schemes for concentrating much of the work in certain subjects in designated universities. In item 6 there were three posts to be filled; in the other two cases, and in all of item 7, people moved from other institutions to Oxford. The total of 108 in section ii excludes 11 posts in iii. *a* below. Item 9 comprises a university lecturership in chemical pathology (E. P. Abraham research fund, 1981), the Nissan professorship and 2 university lecturerships in modern Japanese studies (1982/3), the Khalid bin Abdullah al Saud professorship for Study of the Contemporary Arab World (1984), the Andrew W. Mellon professorship of American Government (1985), the Soudavar professorship of Persian Studies (1986) and the professorship of Clinical Oncology (Imperial Cancer Research Fund, 1988 but not part of the Campaign).

[4] By 31 Mar. 1990 the Campaign also had secured full or partial funding for many posts in the Bodleian Library, for one in the Ashmolean Museum and for one in the Pitt Rivers Museum. The Campaign was designed not merely to maintain the University's establishment but to encourage new initiatives. The 11 posts in iii.*a* were new creations.

[5] *a* fully endowed; *b* funded as to not less than two-thirds of endowment or brought to full endowment; *c* partly endowed; *d* funded in whole or part for a term of years.

students'. Decisions about the allocation of funded student numbers, the Council announced, were 'to favour (other things being equal) universities who submitted low bids'.[65] One point had been clarified, however. 'We will not abate public support', the Secretary of State told vice-chancellors in 1987, 'if universities succeed in raising more private funds'.[66] Under the Education Reform Act of 1988 the UFC was instructed to 'have regard to the desirability of not discouraging any university . . . from maintaining or developing its funding from other sources'.[67]

The effects of the changes since 1981 on the shape of the University's academic staff are summarized in table 27.10. The effect of cuts in public funding during the 1980s was to reduce Oxford's strength in both arts and science. This was offset quite substantially by new governmental initiatives in mathematics and science, and by support from the National Health Service in clinical medicine; in arts and social studies the offsetting was slight. While the effects of the Campaign for Oxford cannot yet be estimated, they are likely to be considerable, especially in strengthening arts and social studies.[68] The figures for fully endowed posts [table 27.10, iii.*a*] tell their own story.

Hard times not only stimulated new initiatives: they drew attention to the constraints and inequities of Oxford's collegiate system. 'The only bulwark against external pressures', said the Warden of All Souls, Sir Patrick Neill, in his valedictory oration as Vice-Chancellor in October 1989, 'will be a united University. The colleges and the central university will have to work together more closely than ever before. This may mean touching the untouchable questions and looking again at some of the lingering inequalities which survive.'[69]

Table 27.11 suggests how one of these 'inequalities' persisted during the period. It shows the benefits conferred on two colleges through the CUF lecturer scheme. This scheme of part-time university lecturerships was extended in 1950 to virtually all college tutors in arts and social studies, primarily in order to help colleges with their teaching obligations.[70] College A's endowments were among the largest, College B's among the smallest. Proportionately to its student numbers, College A gained more from the university in CUF lecturerships than College B; and although in this

---

[65] *Gazette* cxx (1989/90), 297. It was announced in October 1990 that the bidding system would not be used to allocate numbers for 1991/2.

[66] 30 Oct. 1987: speech to the Committee of Vice-Chancellors and Principals. This confirmed assurances given in UGC circular 10/82 and circular 12/85, 9 May 1985, annex 3. 5j: see HCP 311 (1985), 142.

[67] Section 131 (7).

[68] For an assessment of the less tangible effects of this fund-raising see Lord Jenkins, *An Oxford View of Cambridge* (Cambridge 1988), 17–20.

[69] *Gazette* cxx (1989/90), 299.

[70] Cf above, 653.

particular case the discrepancy diminished during the period, it was still substantial in 1988/9.[71] A correction of this imbalance would have entailed 'touching the untouchable question', namely the independence of colleges.

TABLE 27.11

RATIO OF TUTORS HOLDING CUF LECTURERSHIPS IN
ARTS AND SOCIAL STUDIES IN TWO OXFORD
COLLEGES IN 1968/9 AND 1988/9

	1968/9			1988/9		
	1	2	3	1	2	3
College A	193	16	12.06	221	18	12.27
College B	137	5	27.40	154	9	17.11

1 relevant honours students
2 tutors holding CUF lecturerships
3 ratio of 1 to 2

Within these constraints, Oxford's particular combination of managerial control and 'college independence' achieved notable successes in these years. In 1973/4 there were just under 4,300 students for whom neither the colleges nor the university provided accommodation, and the inroads made by students on Oxford's housing stock were causing concern in the city. By 1987/8, while the student total had grown by nearly 20 per cent, the number in private accommodation had fallen to 3,926. It may be doubted whether any centralized institution could have matched that achievement of construction and adaptation. Much of the new building added notably to Oxford's beauties. In 1975, when the University won a Civic Trust award in European Architectural Heritage Year, the citation stated: 'University and colleges have together mounted and brought to impressive conclusion a massive programme of major restoration . . . No less impressive is the conviction and panache with which essential new college building has been undertaken over the past fifteen years. University and colleges are to be congratulated on their decision to build in the manner of the day, rather than resort to period pastiche, and on their choice of architects capable of designing the new buildings, often in congested sites, with exemplary sensitivity and skill.'[72]

These achievements did not alter the University's image as it was projected in television and the popular press. The successful television series based on

[71] For the resentment which this caused in the poorer colleges during the early 1960s see the comments of G. D. Ramsay at seminar on 'The Franks commission and its aftermath', Corpus Christi College, 26 Jan. 1990 (Brian Harrison's transcript, HUA), 8–9.

[72] This was one of the 'Special Heritage Year Awards' for 'continuing effort over a number of years'. The Duke of Edinburgh presented it to the Vice-Chancellor.

Evelyn Waugh's *Brideshead Revisited* depicted Oxford undergraduates as rich and decadent. This picture seemed to be confirmed in June 1986 when an undergraduate died from a lethal combination of heroin and alcohol. Olivia Channon's father was a cabinet minister and the tragedy attracted enormous publicity. It was easily overlooked that, as Waugh had been writing of the 1920s, his Oxford had disappeared long ago, and that, while three people were sent to prison in the aftermath of Olivia Channon's death, none of them was a student of the University.

Among serious observers, by contrast, Oxford's reputation rose during these years. To a considerable degree this resulted from extraneous factors, though the appointment of an information officer in 1970 had a significant effect. Some of yesterday's critics had come under attack in their turn: the insurgents of the 1960s had no wish twenty years later to snipe at a potential ally. In May 1988 it was Oxford's Chancellor Lord Jenkins who, by defeating the government in the Lords, had inserted the definition of academic freedom into the Education Reform Bill.[73] In 1963 the Robbins Committee had pronounced three features of Oxford and Cambridge not to be 'compatible with a situation in which they . . . were largely dependent on public funds'. The first of these three was simply 'the number of times when it is necessary to except Oxford and Cambridge from general statements about British universities'.[74] In 1990, by contrast, the *Times Higher Education Supplement* was reproaching the DES for failing to 'protect the international competitiveness of the best British universities'.[75]

Moreover the university climate of the late 1980s, in which assessment and appraisal recurred regularly amid much publicity, favoured Oxford. In 1985 500 employers of graduates, responding to a survey, put it at the top of the British university system.[76] When the UGC assessed research in 1985/6 33 of the University's 42 'subject areas' were judged to be 'outstanding', only one being pronounced 'below average'. A more elaborate research survey in 1988–9, prepared by sixty specialist committees, awarded 32 of Oxford's 46 'units of assessment' the highest point on a five-point scale, only one falling below the median for the British universities. A. H. Halsey had meanwhile conducted a survey which was not confined to research, by asking his respondents: 'where are the best three departments in your subject?'[77] In the aggregated results Oxford was placed first, just ahead of Cambridge. Oxford

[73] Section 202 (2). See *HL Deb.* 19 May 1988, 444–62. Lord Jenkins had been elected as the University's Chancellor in succession to the late Earl of Stockton on 14 Mar. 1987.
[74] *Higher Education: Report of the Committee Appointed by the Prime Minister under the Chairmanship of Lord Robbins 1961–63* (PP 1962–3 xi–xiv Cmnd 2154), 224.
[75] *Times Higher Education Supplement* 8 June 1990, 48.
[76] HCP 314 (1986), 220.
[77] *Times Higher Education Supplement* 2 Feb. 1990, 17. For these surveys see above, 600–3 and n. 36 on p. 592 above. See also Edward Tapper and Brian Salter, *Oxford, Cambridge and the Changing Idea of the University* (1992).

gained the top place in social studies and shared the lead with Cambridge in arts, coming second to Cambridge in science and to London in medicine. An international survey in 1988–9 by the *Asian Wall Street Journal* had the following rankings: '1. Harvard; 2. Cambridge/Oxford; 3. Stanford; 4. Berkeley'.[78] During the three years from 1986 to 1988 Oxford academics won, among international awards, a Fields medal in mathematics, two Wolf prizes in science, the newly founded Agnelli prize for the study of ethical questions, and the Balzan prize for medieval history. In 1988 the University had forty-six successes in the final selection board for the civil service, Cambridge being the nearest rival with fourteen. Ten Oxford people (six men and four women) joined the Foreign Office in that year out of a total recruitment of twenty-three. In April 1990 the University computing laboratory, in conjunction with a micro-electronics firm, won a Queen's Award for Technological Achievement.

During these twenty years Oxford adapted in all kinds of ways to new features of the scene. The students gained the right to speak in Congregation and to have their representatives attending Council. A resolution against 'top-up' loans for students was passed *nem. con.* by Congregation in November 1989 after an Oxford University Student Union flysheet about it had been circulated with the *University Gazette*. By that date OUSU had three sabbatical officers, a fourth—its Women's Officer—being added in 1990. By then it included one of the largest student publishing organizations in the country.[79] Isis Innovation Ltd was established to exploit the patents obtainable from scientific work where the University owned the intellectual property. Not all the initiatives came from the centre. St Catherine's College laid plans for an institute in Kobe, Japan, which would provide bridging courses to postgraduate work for Japanese students. At the edge of the University the Postgraduate Hebrew Studies Centre was founded in 1972, the Institute for Energy Studies in 1982 and the Oxford Centre for Islamic Studies in St Cross College in 1985. Swimming against the tide was judged an unacceptable indulgence: Oxford abandoned its old stance as the only university which left the second class undivided and required a pass in Latin for matriculation. The colleges accepted that each of them could not do everything: the need for such a central facility as the University counselling service, founded in 1972, was quickly established. The Union Society and the sports clubs accepted sponsorship. The call for an enlargement of 'continuing education' was heeded. In 1989 Manchester College was licensed as a permanent private hall intended specifically for mature students.[80] In

---

[78] *OM* Hilary 1989, no. 8, 6–7.
[79] The OUSU succeeded the Student Representative Council, gaining a new name and constitution, on 1 Jan, 1974. From September 1990 the *Gazette* appeared in a new and attractive format.
[80] The decree limited the mature students there to 60.

1990 the Brundin Committee on continuing education policy recommended that the University should offer part-time postgraduate degree courses 'in many areas'.[81]

There were false starts and delays. A promising inter-collegiate scheme for helping colleges with modest investment portfolios (OXCUT) foundered in the 'stag-flation' of the 1970s. When the *Oxford Magazine*, the only University-wide periodical for informal debate among senior members, died in 1970 it was fifteen years before the University and the Oxford University Press revived it.[82] Any idea, however, that Oxford was held back by its traditions in these years would be mistaken. A less tradition-bound institution would have been hard to find. The refusal of an honorary degree for Margaret Thatcher and the nomination of Lord Blake for the university chancellorship two years later had only one feature in common: both defied precedent. It was unknown for an Oxford prime minister to be refused the degree or for a serving academic to be nominated for the chancellorship.[83] College independence was defended, not in deference to tradition, but in the belief that the balance between initiative and control, between the small units at the circumference and the large one at the centre, had to be maintained, since without this Oxford would lose its unique quality and its effectiveness. These years did nothing to weaken the conviction that the quality of life in Oxford depended on its collegiate character. The strength of college loyalties, to which almost all college appeals for money gave eloquent testimony, was held to establish beyond reasonable doubt that human relations were best where the units were small and where each could maintain its own character. This was doubtless a convenient belief for academics who wanted to be more than the university's employees; but these two decades did not show their convictions to run counter to the general interest.

Any assessment made during this century of Oxford's performance in the 1970s and 1980s must be provisional. The Oxford students of those years are unlikely to reach the peak of their influence until the next century: the full

[81] *Report of the Committee on Continuing Education Policy* (University of Oxford 1990). The chairman, Dr C. L. Brundin, then Vice-Chancellor of the University of Warwick, had formerly been a fellow of Jesus College and vice-chairman of the General Board.

[82] There was a short-lived revival in 1972/3. By 1987 the commercial success of the OUP made possible the transfer of some of its funds for the direct support of the University's primary activities.

[83] For the honorary degree see H. L. A. Hart in *New York Review of Books*, 28 Mar. 1985, 7 and Brian Harrison, 'Mrs. Thatcher and the intellectuals', *Twentieth Century British History* v (1994). For a proposal in 1979 that honorary degrees should no longer be conferred on 'eminent public figures' see HCP 294 (1979), pp. lix, 139–41, 215–16. An earlier dispute, after Mrs Thatcher had been elected FRS, is discussed in *Times* 25 Feb. 1984, 9. When Lord Franks (as he later became) was nominated for the University's chancellorship in 1960 he was chairman of Lloyds Bank. He had been Provost of Queen's and in 1962 he became Provost of Worcester College. Lord Blake, who was Provost of Queen's when nominated, came second in the chancellorship voting.

impact of the research done in the later 1980s will not be measurable for some years. Even when the historical inquest is held, an agreed verdict is unlikely. Neither in this period nor in any other during the last hundred years did the University enjoy easy relations with other universities and with the wider world. It provided a role model for many British academics: yet its most characteristic institutions could not be reproduced elsewhere. It constituted a resource for every government and yet harboured shoals of each government's critics. Its achievements were substantial: so were its resources. To have failed to produce improved first-degree results when the entry had improved would have been culpable. Much of the record of these years was impressive; and yet, during a large part of them, a substantial group of the academic staff were deprived of their legal rights. There is no great paradox here. Both the good and the bad side of the coin betoken a degree of ascendancy and a collegiate structure. A university less eligible than Oxford would not have been allowed by its employees to overlook such an injustice. If the institutions electing to fellowships had been large and impersonal they would have been brought quickly to account; but that anyone should force his way into a small community seemed unthinkable.

In the post-Franks era the Oxford system imposed heavy demands on those who managed it. More and more was expected of vice-chancellors. Yet they commanded no 'leverage'. Comparatively few professors and fellows were seeking promotion; fewer still stood in need of a vice-chancellor's goodwill. When the Warden of All Souls stepped down he described his vice-chancellorship (1985–9) as 'a fairly unrelenting struggle to sustain what is best in Oxford'.[84] This struggle demanded administrators in the university offices of exceptional quality, and a willingness among the academic staff to concede and co-operate. These attributes were as much in evidence at the end of the period as they had been when it began. The determination to retain a leading role in research and in undergraduate and postgraduate studies had if anything become even firmer. No one doubted the extreme difficulty of this triple assignment.

No university is wholly the master of its fate. Each depends on the school system, and on decisions by the government of the day. It is misleading to view any one university in isolation. In this brief survey of two decades, Oxford's peculiarities have received some attention. These are considerable: no other modern university consists entirely of endowed colleges all of which contain fewer than a thousand students and possess, or will soon gain, 'chartered independence'. But it should not be inferred from this that Oxford represents one of the few eccentricities in Britain's 'post-compulsory' education system, which conforms elsewhere to some international norm. In its principal features the whole British system differs sharply and

[84] *Gazette* cxx (1989/90), 297.

eccentrically from the others. The contrasts which characterize it are not found in any other country. By international standards Britain's numbers in higher education are small; yet in the 1980s its output of graduates and 'higher diplomates' (seen as a proportion of the relevant age-group) exceeded that of West Germany, France or the Netherlands.[85] While British first-degree courses are admired everywhere, the rest of Britain's 'post-compulsory' performance is still woefully inadequate by comparison with what is achieved elsewhere.

Oxford represents a unique feature in a system which is itself unique. Britain has not suffered for more than three centuries from revolution, civil war, invasion or defeat in any war near home; and it was the first country to be industrialized. The peculiarities of the British higher education system result from the country's peculiar history. Oxford has been moulded by a long development and has itself been something of a moulder. An educational institution can best be maintained and improved by those who understand how it came to be what it is. These volumes have been produced in the hope of contributing to this understanding.

[85] *Higher Education: Meeting the Challenge* (HMSO 1987), 4, Fig. C.

Index of persons

This index and the General Index which follows were prepared by the editor with the aid of the computer package MACREX5. Page references in **Bold** are the most important references for the heading under which they appear. In preparing the index, the editor acknowledges the help he received from Joshua Mandel of Corpus Christi College in improving the entries relating to Chapter 14. He also received a generous response from several college secretaries and college archivists who were asked at a late stage for missing details.

Abercrombie, Sir (Leslie) Patrick (1879–1957), town planner 570, 572

Abraham, Sir Edward (Penley) (1913–), Professor of Chemical Pathology 159, 253, 283

Ackerley, J.R. 429

Acland, Sir Henry Wentworth (1815–1900), Regius Professor of Medicine 322

Acton, Sir Harold (Mario Mitchell) (1904–), author 99, 423, 425, 426

Adams, William George Stewart (1874–1966), Warden of All Souls:
  and Asquith Commission 32, 33–4, 43
  and public policy 83, 186, 388, 590

Ady, Cecilia Mary (1881–1958), historian xv, 351

Aeschylus (525/4–456/5 BC), dramatist 134

Ainley-Walker, Ernest William (1871–1955), Reader in Pathology xi

Alcibiades (c.450–404 BC), Athenian politician and military commander 287

Aldiss, Brian Wilson (1925–), writer 420, 421, 422

Aldwinckle, Elia Estelle ('Stella') 311, 422

Ali, Tariq (1943–), author 705

Allen, Sir Carleton Kemp (1877–1966), Warden of Rhodes House 94, 110, 194, 200, 395, 688

Allen, Sir Hugh Percy (1869–1946), musician 118, 560

Allen, Percy Stafford (1869–1933), President of Corpus Christi College, Oxford 82, 83, 477

Allen, Thomas William (1862–1950), classical scholar 135

Allen, William Maurice (1918–88), economist 388

Allison, Philip Rowland (1907–74), Nuffield Professor of Surgery 337

Allott, Kenneth Cyril Bruce (1912–73), Professor of English Literature, Liverpool 413

Alvarez, Alfred (1929–), poet and author 413, 424, 426, 442

Amery, Leopold Charles Maurice Stennett (1873–1955), Conservative politician 615

Amis, Kingsley (1922–), author 224, 413, 415, 426, 436, 439
  and Larkin 434, 438, 443
  Lucky Jim 424, 448

Amis, Martin Louis (1949–), author 413, 415, 417, 429
  academic career 429, 442
  fiction of 436, 447–8

Anderson, Sir Hugh Kerr (1865–1928), Master of Caius College 31, 32, 34, 42
  and Asquith Commission 36, 39, 40

Anderson, John Stuart (1908–91), Professor of Inorganic Chemistry 269

Anderson, Linsday (Gordon) (1923–), film and theatre director 407

Anderson, Maisie, daughter of H. K. Anderson 32

Anderson, Patrick John McAlister (?–1979), Worcester College undergraduate xii, 392

Anderson, Francis Rory Peregrine ('Perry') (1938–), author 401

Anderton, Leslie N., Labour candidate 380

Andrade, E.N.d'A.C. 461

Angel, Andrea (1877–1917), chemist 139, 157

Annan, Nöel Gilroy, Baron (1916–), historian 244

Annigoni, Pietro (1910–88), painter 497

Anscombe, Gertrude Elizabeth Margaret (1919–), Fellow of Somerville College 311, 373, 407

Aplin, Oliver V. (1858–1940), solicitor and naturalist 493

Applebey, Malcolm Percival (1884–1957), Fellow of St John's College, Oxford 140

Apuleius, Lucius (c.124–?), author 134

Archer, Jeffrey Howard (1940–), politician and author 394, 428, 433, 449

Aristophanes (c.450–c.388 BC), Greek dramatist 134

Aristotle (384–322 BC), Greek philosopher 115, 122, 134, 137, 233

Arkell, William Joscelyn (1904–58), geologist 150, 493

Arms, Henry Shull (1914–), Rhodes scholar 182

Armytage, Walter Harry Green (1915–), Professor of Education, Sheffield 598

Arnold, Denis 459

Arnold, Matthew (1822–88), poet and critic 127–8

Asquith, Herbert Henry (1852–1928), Liberal prime minister 17, 31, 42, 107, 383, 717
  attitude to Oxford 27, 40, 41, 107
  stands as Chancellor 43, 390

Asvaghosha (?80–150), Indian poet 134

Atiyah, Sir Michael (Francis) (1929–), Savilian Professor of Geometry 263, 270

Atkinson, Christopher Thomas (1874–1964), military historian 93, 136

Atkinson, Robert (1883–1952), architect 505

Attlee, Clement Richard, Earl (1883–1967), Labour prime minister 384–5, 397

Auden, Wystan Hugh (1907–73), poet 413, 417, 427, 429, 434, 439
  and chair of poetry 418, 433
  and the English school 415, 416, 436–7, 442, 444
  his poetry cited 428, 432, 436, 447, 448
  his publishers 424, 426, 431

Austen, Jane (1775–1817), novelist 134, 135, 456

Austin, John Langshaw (1911–60), White's Professor of Moral Philosophy 233, 243, 406, 589

Avery, Gillian Elise [Mrs. A.O.J. Cockshut] (1926–), 439

Aydelotte, Frank (1880–1956), American Secretary to the Rhodes Trustees 4, 619, 645

Ayer, Sir Alfred (Jules) (1910–89), philosopher 90, 138, 243, 308, 589, 620

Bacon, Francis (1909–92), artist 497

Badger, Richard McLean (1896–?), Professor of Physical Chemistry, Caltech 163

Baeyer, Adolf von (1835–1917), Professor of Chemistry, Munich 158

Bailey, Vivian Horsman (1894–1988), Brasenose undergraduate 520

Baird, Barbara 562

Baker, A. R. W. 508

Baker, Sir Herbert (1862–1946), architect 502, 506, 507

Baker, Herbert Brereton (1862–1935), chemist 40

Baker, John Norman Leonard (1893–1971), geographer 135, 280, 554

Baker, John Randal (1900–84), Reader in Cytology 148, 150, 395
  research of 155, 278, 280

Baldwin, James Mark (1861–1934), psychologist 150

Baldwin, Stanley, Earl (1867–1947), Conservative prime minister 391

Balfour, Gerald William, Earl of Balfour (1853–1945), politician 31, 39, 40

Balfour, Henry (1863–1939), Curator of the Pitt Rivers Museum 488, 493

Balfour, Lewis, bullion broker, son of Henry 491, 493

Ball, Sir Christopher (John Elinger) (1935–), Warden of Keble College 303

Ball, Sidney (1857–1918), Fellow of St John's College, Oxford 7, 125

Balogh, Thomas, Baron (1905–85), economist 185, 386, 388, 410, 411

Balsdon, John Percy Vyvian Dacre (1901–77), Fellow of Exeter College 93, 135, 422

Bamborough, John Bernard (1921–), Principal of Linacre College 702, 711

Bandaranaike, Solomon West Ridgeway Dias (1899–1959), Prime Minister of Sri Lanka 630, 634

Banks, Gerald, architect 513

Bannister, Sir Roger (Gilbert) (1929–), Master of Pembroke College xix, 519, **537**

Barber, Eric Arthur (1888–1965), Rector of Exeter College 134

Barclay, Alfred Ernest (1876–1949), Consulting Radiologist to Radcliffe Infirmary 331

Barclay, Clifford Henry (1907–92), businessman 763

Barfield, Owen 310

Barker, Sir Ernest (1874–1960), scholar 15, 348, 578, 592
  and PPE's origins 113, 115, 122–3

Barker, Thomas Vipond (1881–1931), Reader in Chemical Crystallography 148, 151, 163

Barlow, Sir (James) Alan (Noel) (1881–1968), public servant 496

Barnard, Francis Pierrepont (1854–1931), numismatist and historian 494

Barnes, Mgr. Arthur Stapylton (1861–1936), Catholic chaplain 299

Barnes, Julian (Patrick) (1946–), novelist 413, 415, 429, 430 his fiction 436, 438, 446, 449

Barnett, Samuel Augustus (1844–1913), social reformer 386

Barr, William Greig (1917–), Rector of Exeter College 528

Barry, Frank Russell (1890–1976), Vicar of St Mary's (University) Church 293, 311, 313, 392

Barthélemy, Joseph (1874–1945), political scientist 114–15, 117

Bassett, Reginald (1901–62), Professor, London School of Economics 399, 403

Bateson, Frederick Noel Wilse (1901–78), Fellow of Corpus Christi College, Oxford 240

Batey, Charles, Printer to the University 456, 462

Bathurst, Lady 360

Bawden, Nina Mary (1925–), novelist 363

Bayley, John Oliver (1925–), Warton Professor of English Literature 415, 417, 421, 429

Bayley, Peter Charles (1921–), Fellow of University College 206, 437

Beachcroft, Thomas Owen (1902–88), author 426

Beale, Dorothea (1831–1906), Principal of Cheltenham Ladies' College 347, 351

Beazley, Sir John Davidson (1885–1970), classical archaeologist 133, 493

Beer, Samuel H., political scientist 386

Beeson, Paul Bruce (1908–), Nuffield Professor of Clinical Medicine 341, 343

Beit, Alfred (1853–1906), financier and benefactor 611

Bell, Charles Francis (1871–1966), Keeper of Fine Art, Ashmolean Museum 494

Bell, Arthur Clive Heward (1881–1964), art critic 17

Bell, Sir (Harold) Idris (1879–1967), papyrologist 133

Bell, John 465

Bell, John (1890–1958), Fellow of Queen's College, Oxford 93

Bell, Revd. Kenneth Norman (1884–1951), historian 93, 130, 716

Bell, Ronald Percy (1907–), Fellow of Balliol College 157

Beloff, Max, Baron (1913–), historian 130, 383, 388, 405, 693, 732
  and the Oxford Union 383

Benn, Anthony Wedgewood ('Tony') (1925–), Labour politician 391, 404, 411

Bennett, Revd. Gareth Vaughan (1929–87), Fellow of New College 302

Bennett, Jack Arthur Walter (1911–81), Fellow of Magdalen College 310

Bennett, Mary Letitia Somerville (1913–), Principal of St Hilda's College xvi, 353, 374

Berdyaev, Nikolay Aleksandrovich (1874–1948), religious thinker 306

Bergonzi, Bernard (1929–), Professor of English 428

Bergson, Henri (1859–1941), French philosopher 298

Berlin, Sir Isaiah (1909–), Fellow of All Souls College 182, 231, 248, 388, 609
  as head of house 742
  as political theorist 243, 409–10
  publications 137, 409

Bernal, (John) Desmond (1901–71), physicist 151, 280, 395

Bernays, Robert Hamilton (1902–45), politician 383

Berners, Sir Gerald Hugh Tyrwhitt-Wilson, Baron (1883–1950), musician and author 93, 182

Bernstorff, Count Albrecht Theodor von 4, 5

Béroul (fl. 1150–1200), poet 134

Berrill, Sir Kenneth (1920–), Chairman, University Grants Committee 754

Besse, Antonin (1877–1951), businessman and philanthropist 223, 624, 653, 699

Bethmann-Hollweg, Friedrich von, son of German Chancellor 4, 5

Betjeman, Sir John (1906–84), author 413, 426, 433, 435, 439, 444
  sells off review copies 421
  undergraduate career 98, 442

Beveridge, William Henry, Baron (1879–1963), Master of University College 87, 136, 406, 407–8, 562, 592
  early career 185
  as head of house 83, 84, 105
  in Second World War 183, 185–6

Bevin, Ernest (1881–1951), trade-union leader and politician 183, 404, 634

Bickerton, Fred (1879–1955), Head Porter of University College 558

Bill, Edward Geoffrey Watson (1924–), Librarian, Lambeth Palace 480

Binnie, Alfred Maurice (1901–86), demonstrator in engineering science 145

Binyon, Timothy John (1936–), Fellow of Wadham College 414, 415, 439

Birkenhead, Frederick Edwin Smith, Earl of (1872–1930), Conservative politician 378, 394
  and the Oxford Union 382, 383, 384, 718

Birley, Sir Robert (1903–82), headmaster 128

Black, Michael, sculptor 508
Blackman, Aylward Manley (1883–1956),
    Egyptologist 133
Blackman, Geoffrey Emett (1902–80),
    Sibthorpian Professor of Rural
    Economy 275, 281
Blackwell, Sir Basil Henry (1889–1984),
    Chairman of Blackwell's 424, 451
Blackwell, Donald Eustace (1921–), Savilian
    Professor of Astronomy 271, 272
Blackwell, Richard (1918–80), Chairman of
    Basil Blackwell Publisher Ltd. 453, 464
Blackwood, Beatrice Mary (1889–1975),
    social anthropologist 135, 493
Blake, Robert Norman William, Baron
    (1916–), historian 394, 723, 725, 747,
    772
  in local politics 551
  and Meadow road 394
  on the tutorial 196, 389
Blake, William (1757–1827), poet and
    painter 425, 690
Blakeway, Alan Albert Antisdel (1898–1936),
    archaeologist 116
Blakiston, Herbert Edward Douglas
    (1862–1942), President of Trinity
    College, Oxford 83, 504
Blaschko, 'Hugh' (Hermann Karl Felix)
    (1900–93), Reader in Biochemical
    Pharmacology 285, 333
Bleaney, Brebis (1915–), Dr Lee's Professor
    of Experimental Philosophy 266, 267
Blish, James Benjamin (1921–75), American
    science fiction writer 420
Blomfield, Sir Reginald Theodore
    (1856–1942), architect 504, 506
Blunden, Edmund Charles (1896–1974), poet
    and author 420, 422, 423, 425, 426,
    431
  and First World War 23, 168, 413, 442
  poetry professor 418
  teaching career 415, 417, 429
Bodley, George Frederick (1827–1907),
    architect 502
Bone, Gavin David (1902–42), Fellow of St
    John's College, Oxford 443
Booker, Christopher John Penrice (1937–),
    author 431
Boothby, Robert (1900–86), Conservative
    politician 130
Borges, Jorge Luis (1899–), Argentinian
    author 438
Boston, Richard (1938–), writer 430
Bourne, Ray (1889–1948), demonstrator in
    forestry 147
Bourne, Robert Croft (1888–1938),
    Conservative politician 379, 407

Bowen, Edmund John (1898–1980),
    chemist xi, 157
Bowen, Elizabeth Dorothea Cole
    (1899–1973), writer 420
Bowman, Thomas (1853–1945), Warden of
    Merton College 83, 84
Bowman, Herbert Lister (1874–1942),
    Professor of Mineralogy 150–1
Bowra, Sir (Cecil) Maurice (1898–1971) 129,
    409, 513, 701, 712, 713
  attitudes to:
    entitlement 714
    history of art 490
    Meadow road 573
    politics 406, 408
    undergraduate life 193, 203, 209
  as head of house 83, 199
  on Lord Normanbrook 96
  salon of 87
  in Second World War 173, 181, 287
  as vice-chancellor 691
Boyd, William Andrew Murray (1952–),
    author 413, 415, 443
Boyd-Carpenter, John Archibald, Baron
    (1908–), Conservative politician 392
Bradbury, Malcolm Stanley (1932–),
    author 420
Bradley, Francis Herbert (1846–1924),
    philosopher 609
Bragg, Melvyn (1939–), writer and
    broadcaster 413, 415, 430
Bragg, Sir William Lawrence (1890–1971),
    physicist 266
  and Asquith Commission 32, 33, 37, 39,
    40, 41
Braque, Georges (1882–1963), French
    artist 560
Braudel, Fernand (1902–85), French
    historian 236
Brett, Simon (Anthony Lee) (1945–), crime
    novelist 414
Brett-Smith, Herbert Francis Brett
    (1884–1951), Goldsmith's Reader in
    English 121, 134
Brewer, Frederick Mason (1902–63), Reader
    in Chemistry 268
Bridges, Edward Ettingdene, Baron
    (1892–1969), public servant 386, 591,
    649
Bridges, Robert Seymour (1844–1930), Poet
    Laureate 6, 421, 422
Brien, Alan (1925–), novelist and
    journalist 426, 427
Briggs, Asa, Baron (1921–), historian 227,
    237, 588
Briggs, Julia Ruth (1943–), Fellow of
    Hertford College 439

Briscoe, John, Reader in Latin, Manchester
University 551
Brittain, Vera Mary (1893–1970), feminist and
author 12, 350, 352, 531
Brook, Norman Craven, Baron Normanbrook
(1902–67), civil servant 96
Brooke, Sir Charles Vyner (1874–1963), Raja
of Sarawak 493
Brooke, (Bernard) Jocelyn (1908–66),
author 413, 442
Brooke, Rupert Chawner (1887–1915),
poet 12, 25
Brooke-Rose, Christine (1926–), novelist and
critic 414, 438
Brophy, Brigid (Antonia), (Lady Levey)
(1929–), author and playwright 413,
427, 443
Brown, Alan Brock (1911–80), Fellow of
Worcester College 554
Brown, Sir (George) Lindor (1903–71),
Principal of Hertford College xix,
341, 724
Brown, Susan, (1958–), Wadham
undergraduate 531
Brown, Wili (of Parker's bookshop) 452
Brown, William (1881–1952),
psychologist 143, 279
Brownjohn, Alan Charles (1931–), poet 413,
424, 425, 426, 444
Bruce, Hon. Alice Moore (1867–1951), Vice-
Principal of Somerville College 357
Brunet, Peter Cameron Jamieson (1921–91),
Fellow of Jesus College 281
Brunner, (Heinrich) Emil (1889–1966), Swiss
theologian 306
Brunt, Peter Astbury (1917–), Camden
Professor of Ancient History 486–7
Bruten, Avril Gilchrist (1940–), Fellow of St
Hugh's College 434
Bryan Brown, Armitage Noel (1900–68),
Fellow of Worcester College xi
Bryce, James, Viscount (1838–1922), Liberal
politician 406, 609
Buchan, John, Baron Tweedsmuir
(1875–1940), author 413, 421, 422,
428, 563
Buchanan, Sir Colin (Douglas) (1907–), town
planner 569, 573, 575
Buchman, Frank (1868–1961), founder of
Moral Re-Armament 301–2
Bülbring, Edith (1903–90), Professor of
Pharmacology 285, 333
Bull, Hedley Norman (1932–85), Montague
Burton Professor of International
Relations 625
Bullock, Alan Louis Charles, Baron (1914–),
historian 235, 709, 744

as head of house 513, 649
on Meadow road 573, 574
as vice-chancellor 649, 740, 745, 747
Burges, William (1827–81), architect 509
Burke, (Ulick) Peter (1937–), historian
237
Burn, Joshua Harold (1892–1981), Professor
of Pharmacology 285, 329, 341
Burnett, Sir John (1922–), Sibthorpian
Professor of Rural Economy 276
Burney, Revd. Charles Fox (1868–1925),
theologian 135
Burton, Sir Montague Maurice (1885–1952),
multiple tailor 574
Burton, Richard (1925–84), actor 176, 416
Butler, David Edgeworth (1924–), Fellow of
Nuffield College 388
Butler, Sir Harold Beresford (1883–1951),
Warden of Nuffield College 387
Butler, Harold Edgeworth (1878–1951),
classical scholar 134
Butler, Richard Austen, Baron Butler of
Saffron Walden (1902–82),
Conservative politician 186, 723
Butler, Ruth Florence (1881–1982), Fellow of
St Anne's College xv
Butler, (Christina) Violet (1884–1982),
pioneer of social-work training 548,
550
Butterfield, William (1814–1900),
architect 502, 509, 511, 515
Buxton, John (1912–89), Fellow of New
College 394
Buzzard, Sir (Edward) Farquhar (1871–1945),
Regius Professor of Medicine 322,
334, 379, 691
helps create postgraduate medical
school 323–8, 331, 332, 333

Cadbury, Paul Strangman (1895–1984),
businessman 185
Cadoux, Cecil John (1883–1947), Mackennal
Professor of Church History 296
Caird, Revd. George Bradford (1917–84),
Dean Ireland's Professor of Exegesis of
Holy Scripture 296
Cairns, Sir Hugh William Bell (1896–1952),
neurosurgeon 182, 337, 621
and postgraduate medical school 323–8,
330, 331, 335
Calder-Marshall, Arthur (1908–92),
author 426
Callaghan, (Leonard) James, Baron (1912–),
Labour prime minister 482
Campbell, Brian Guy (1928–), Bursar of
Corpus Christi College 724
Campbell, Roy, poet 428, 435

Camus, Albert (1913–60), French author 248
Cannan, Charles (1858–1919), secretary to
  OUP delegates 454–5, 457, 458, 459
Cannan, Joanna (?–1961), novelist 447
Carey, George Leonard (1935–), Archbishop
  of Canterbury 302
Carey, John (1934–), Merton Professor of
  English Literature 429, 538–9
Carlyle, Alexander James (1861–1943),
  political philosopher 609
Carpenter, Geoffrey Douglas Hale
  (1882–1953), Hope Professor of
  Zoology 154–5, 492
Carpenter, Humphrey William Bouverie
  (1946–), author 439
Carr, Edward Hallett (1892–1982),
  historian 221, 224–5
Carr-Saunders, Sir Alexander Morris
  (1886–1966), biologist and
  sociologist 154–5
Carritt, Edgar Frederick (1876–1964),
  philosopher xi, 137
Carroll, Lewis [pseud. for Charles Lutwidge
  Dodgson] (1832–98), Student of Christ
  Church 439
Carter, Sir Charles (Frederick) (1919–), Vice-
  Chancellor, University of
  Lancaster 735–6
Cary, Arthur Joyce Lunel (1888–1957),
  author 413, 421, 424
Case, Thomas (1844–1925), President of
  Corpus Christi College, Oxford 83,
  84, 111, 641
Casson, Stanley (1889–1944), Hellenist 9, 133
Castle, Barbara (Anne) (1910–), Labour
  politician 399, 404, 405
Caston, Geoffrey Kemp (1926–),
  Registrar 740
Catiline (Lucius Sergius Catilina) (108–62
  BC), Roman conspirator 221
Caute, (John) David (1936–), writer 434
Cave, George, Viscount (1856–1928),
  Conservative politician 389–90, 685
Cecil, Lord (Edward Christian) David
  (Gascoyne) (1902–86), Goldsmiths'
  Professor of English Literature 225,
  240, 420, 421, 426
  criticized 438, 442
  his lectures 366
Cecil, Lord Hugh Richard Heathcote
  Gascoyne-, Baron Quickswood
  (1869–1956), politician 97, 379
Chadwick, Henry (1920–), Regius Professor
  of Divinity 305, 309
Chain, Sir Ernst Boris (1906–79), biochemist
  and Nobel prizewinner 182, 253, 262,
  329, 333

Chalmers, Robert, Baron Chalmers
  (1858–1938), civil servant 32, 39, 40,
  41, 43
Chamberlain, Joseph (1836–1914), Liberal,
  then Liberal Unionist, politician 376,
  597
Chamberlain, (Arthur) Neville (1869–1940),
  Conservative prime minister 168, 393,
  689
Chambers, Sir Edmund Kercheinver
  (1866–1954), historian and civil
  servant 135, 439
Champernowne, Francis Gawayne
  (1866–1921), Bursar of Keble 93
Champion, Sir Harry George (1891–1979),
  Professor of Forestry 277
Champneys, Basil (1842–1935), architect 503
Channon, Olivia Gwendolen Violet
  (1964–86), St Hilda's College
  undergraduate 770
Chaplin, Sir Charles Spencer (1889–1977),
  film actor and director 233
Chapman, David Leonard (1869–1958),
  chemist 157
Chapman, Robert William (1881–1960),
  publisher 134, 455–6, 457, 459, 477
Charles, Robert Henry (1855–1931), biblical
  scholar 134
Chataway, Christopher John (1931–),
  businessman 537
Chattaway, Frederick Daniel (1860–1944),
  chemist 157
Chaudhuri, Nirad Chandra (1897–), author
  and broadcaster 420
Chavasse, Christopher Maude (1884–1962),
  Bishop of Rochester 304
Chavasse, Francis James (1846–1928), Bishop
  of Liverpool 304
Cheeseman, George Leonard (1884–1915),
  archaeologist 135
Chelmsford, Frederic Augustus Thesiger,
  Viscount (1868–1933), Viceroy of
  India 42–3, 615, 697
Cherwell, Frederick Alexander Lindemann,
  Viscount (1886–1957), physicist:
  attitudes to:
    college laboratories 88
    engineering 273
    Meadow road 394
    Radcliffe Observatory 153
    science's status in Oxford 252, 286–7, 288
  in First World War 622
  impact on Clarendon Laboratory 160–1, 163
  in national politics 388, 408
  in Oxford politics 379, 381, 390, 393
  recruits refugees 160–1, 252, 589, 622
  research in physics 160, 266

in Second World War 173, 181–3, 251, 252

Cheshire, Geoffrey Chevalier (1886–1978), academic lawyer 137

Chester, Sir (Daniel) Norman (1907–86), Warden of Nuffield College 387, 554, 567

Chettur, Gorinda Krishna, author 630

Chilver, Guy Edward Farquhar (1910–), ancient historian 225

Chomsky, (Avram) Noam (1928–), Professor of Modern Languages and Linguistics, MIT 245

Christopher, A.C. 304

Chrystal, Robert Neil (1891–1956), entomologist 147

Church, Arthur Harry (1865–1937), botanist 148, 152

Churchill, Sir Winston Leonard Spencer-(1874–1965), statesman 87, 220
and Oxford Union 167, 393, 406
in Second World War 173, 174, 181–3

Cicero, Marcus Tullius (106–43 BC), Roman statesman and author 116, 131, 134

Citrine, Walter McLennan, Baron (1887–1983), TUC General Secretary 381, 384

Clapham, Arthur Roy (1904–90), demonstrator and lecturer in botany 152

Clark, Albert Curtis (1859–1937), classical scholar 134

Clark, Sir George Norman (1890–1979), Provost of Oriel 136, 169, 458, 712
and libraries 481, 483

Clark, Kenneth Mackenzie, Baron (1903–83), Keeper of Fine Art, Ashmolean Museum 491, 496

Clark, Sir Wilfrid Edward Le Gros (1895–1971), Dr Lee's Professor of Anatomy 329, 341

Clarke, Maude Violet (1892–1935), historian 135, 348

Claude Lorrain (1600–82), French artist 494

Claudian (Claudius Claudianus) (370–404), Latin poet 134

Clay, Sir Henry (1883–1954), Warden of Nuffield College 387

Clegg, Hugh Armstrong (1920–), Professor of Industrial Relations, University of Warwick 556

Clifford, Gay Allis Rose (1943–), academic 429, 442

Clodius Publius (c.93–52 BC), Roman politician 221

Clough, Blanche Athena (1861–1960), Principal of Newnham College 32, 34, 37

Cobb, H. M., employee of Clutton's 32, 35

Cockburn, (Francis) Claud (1904–81), author and journalist 426

Cockerell, Charles Robert (1788–1863), architect 504

Cockin, Frederic Arthur (1888–1969), Vicar of St Mary's and Bishop of Bristol 313, 314

Cocteau, Jean (1889–1963), French author and artist 444

Coggan, (Frederick) Donald, Baron (1909–), Archbishop of Canterbury 302

Coghill, Nevil Henry Kendal Aylmer (1899–1980), Fellow of Exeter College 422, 520, 559
as English tutor 416, 437, 439, 442, 444
and OUDS 180, 310, 416

Cohn, William (1881–1961), scholar and museum official 486

Coldstream, Sir William (Menzies) (1908–87), painter 497

Cole, George Douglas Howard (1889–1959), socialist and author xi, 25, 185–6
and adult education 385, 396, 397
as Fellow of University College 84
in First World War 396
and General Strike 397
and Nuffield College 220
and political theory 103
and PPE 242
publications 136, 137, 439
and reconstruction survey 184–5
as socialist 16, 380, 385, 411
and undergraduate politics 381, 390, 395–9

Coleridge, John, landscape gardener 502

Coleridge, Samuel Taylor (1772–1834), poet 135

Collingwood, Robin George (1889–1943), philosopher and historian 248, 406
autobiography 130, 221
in First World War 9, 86, 99
publications 135, 137, 221

Collison, Peter Cheeseborough (1925–), sociologist 561

Connolly, Cyril Vernon (1903–74), author and journalist 428, 429, 431, 434, 435, 436

Conrad, Peter John (1948–), Student of Christ Church 429

Constant, Benjamin (1767–1830), Franco-Swiss writer 134

Constantine, David John (1944–), Fellow of Queen's College 413, 416

Cook, Douglas, Physical Chemistry Laboratory technician 281

Cooke, Alexander Macdougall (1899–), Fellow of Merton College 329

Cooke, Colin Arthur (1903–), Bursar of
Magdalen College 553
Cooke, George Albert (1865–1939), Canon of
Christ Church 134
Cooper, Derek Macdonald (1925–),
broadcaster and journalist 426
Cooper, Sir (Thomas) Edwin, architect 504,
506
Cooper, John Phillips (1920–78),
historian 237
Cornwell, David John Moore ('John Le
Carré') (1931–), writer 414, 415, 440,
443
Cosslett, Vernon Ellis (1908–), Cambridge
physicist 590
Coulson, Charles Alfred (1910–74), Rouse
Ball Professor of Mathematics 270,
407
Coupland, Sir Reginald (1884–1952),
historian 609, 615
Cowley, Sir Arthur Ernest (1861–1931),
orientalist and Bodley's Librarian 133,
472, 474, 476, 645
Cox, Sir Christopher William Machell
(1899–1982), Fellow of New
College 93, 635
Cox, Harold Henry (1903–74), Fellow of
Lincoln College 85
Craig, Edwin Stewart (1865–1939),
Registrar 689
Craster, Sir (Herbert Henry) Edmund
(1879–1959), Bodley's Librarian 101,
478
Creighton, Mandell (1843–1901), Bishop of
London 609
Creswick, Harry Richardson (1902–88),
Bodley's Librarian 479
Crombie, Alistair Cameron (1915–), Lecturer
in the History of Science 288
Crombie, J.E., benefactor 162
Crosland, (Charles) Anthony (Raven)
(1918–77), Labour politician 410–11,
553, 651, 721, 725, 728
Cross, Revd. Frank Leslie (1900–68), Lady
Margaret Professor of Divinity 303,
309
Cross, Mr., Jesus College servant 103
Cross, P.J., Corpus Christi College
servant 105
Crossman, Richard Howard Stafford
(1907–74), Labour politician 426, 430,
725
    hostility to 394, 403, 411
    in national politics 397, 406, 410, 723
    and Oxford local politics 550, 553
    in the Oxford Union 382
    in Second World War 183

and university politics 381, 390, 403
as university teacher 25, 90, 136, 138
Crowe, Dame Sylvia (1901–), landscape
architect 517
Crowther-Hunt, Norman Crowther, Baron
(1920–87), Rector of Exeter
College 386
Cruttwell, Charles Robert Mowbray Fraser
(1887–1941), historian 42, 136, 379
    Waugh snipes at 446, 449
Curtis, Lionel George (1872–1955), public
servant 389, 611, 614, 615, 646, 691,
716
Curzon, George Nathaniel, Marquess
Curzon of Kedleston (1859–1925) xv,
107, 383, 586, 604, 615
    as Chancellor 27–8, 612, 636, 639, 641,
684, 685
    in First World War 18
    and science 28
    and women in Oxford 28, 348
Cushing, Harvey Williams (1869–1939),
Professor of Neurology, Yale
University 323

Dahrendorf, Ralf, Baron (1929–),
sociologist 245
Dainton, Frederick Sydney, Baron (1914–),
Chancellor of Sheffield University 588
Dale, Harold Edward (1875–1954), civil
servant 697
Dalton, (Edward) Hugh (John Neale)
(1887–1962), Labour politician 381,
404
Dante Alighieri (1265–1321), Italian
Renaissance poet 134, 141
Danton, Georges (-Jacques) (1759–94),
French revolutionary leader 130
Darbishire, Helen (1881–1961), Principal of
Somerville College xv, 363
D'Arcy, Father Martin Cyril (1888–1976),
Jesuit provincial 299–300, 314
Darlington, Cyril Dean (1903–81), Sherardian
Professor of Botany 276
Darwin, Charles Robert (1809–82),
naturalist 287
Darwin, Sir Horace (1851–1928), civil
engineer 32, 34, 37
Davidge, Cecil Vere (1901–81), Fellow of
Keble College 193–4, 198
Davidson, Randall Thomas, Baron
(1848–1930), Archbishop of
Canterbury 396
Davies, (Sarah) Emily (1830–1921), pioneer
feminist 345
Davies, Ivor R.M., Liberal candidate 380

Davies, John Derek (1931–), Tutor in Law, St Catherine's College 745

Davies, (William) Robertson (1913–), Canadian novelist/playwright
his career 429, 437, 438–9, 440
his fiction 414, 436, 447

Davin, Daniel Marcus ('Dan') (1913–90), publisher 423–4, 457

Davin, Winifred Kathleen, wife of Dan 424

Davis, Henry William Carless (1874–1928), historian 15, 133, 136, 612

Davis, Herbert John (1783–67), Reader in Textual Criticism 479

Dawkins, Richard MacGillivray (1871–1955), Professor of Byzantine and modern Greek 87

Dawson, Sir (George) Geoffrey (1874–1944), Editor of *The Times* 615

Dawson, Jennifer (1929–), novelist 413, 415, 445

Day, Sir Robin (1923–), television and radio journalist 384, 405

Day-Lewis, Cecil ('Nicholas Blake') (1904–72), poet laureate 413, 426, 430
and chair of poetry 418, 448
crime fiction of 414, 439
Oxford in his fiction 432, 439, 442

De Beer, Esmond Samuel (1895–1990), historian 479

De Beer, Sir Gavin Rylands (1899–1972), zoologist 140, 150, 154–5

De la Mare, Walter John (1873–1956), poet 419

De Madariaga, Salvador (1886–1978), Professor of Spanish 136

De Montherlant, Henri (-Marie-Joseph-Millon) (1896–1972), French novelist and dramatist 444

de Ste Croix, Geoffrey Ernest Maurice (1910–), Fellow of New College 584

Deakin, Sir (Frederick) William (Dampier) (1913–), Warden of St Antony's College 182

Demosthenes (?–413 BC), Athenian statesman 116, 135, 221

Denholm-Young, Noel (1904–75), historian 135

Denniston, John Dewar (1887–1949), classical scholar 134

Dent, Arthur William (1912–84), Chief Technician, Department of Human Anatomy 696

Descartes, René (1596–1650), French mathematician and philosopher 120

Dexter, Colin (1930–), crime writer 424

Dibdin, Michael (1947–), crime novelist 420

Diesgardt, Baron G. G. A. von 3

Dillwyn, Colin Lewis (1913–40), Student of Christ Church 181

Dinshaw, Fram Eduljee (1954–), Fellow of St Catherine's College, Oxford 416

Dobson, Gordon Miller Bourne (1889–1976), physicist and meteorologist 160–1, 260

Dodd, Charles Harold (1884–1973), biblical scholar 134, 135, 296, 312, 464

Dodd, Fielding 499, 502, 504, 507

Dodds, Eric Robertson (1893–1979), classical scholar 590

Douglas, Claude Gordon (1882–1963), physiologist 14–15

Douglas, James Archibald (1884–1978), geologist 150, 251, 274–5, 282, 433

Douglas, Keith Castellain (1920–44), war poet 415, 417, 425, 426, 441
his war poetry 181, 413

Douglas-Home, Alexander Frederick ('Alec'), Baron (1903–), Conservative prime minister 384

Dover, Sir Kenneth James (1920–), President of Corpus Christi College, Oxford 754

Dowson, Sir Philip (Manning) (1924–), Founder Partner, Arup Associates 511, 512, 515

Dreyer, Georges (1873–1934), Professor of Pathology 14, 318, 321, 329–30

Driberg, Thomas Edward Neill, Baron Bradwell ('Tom') (1905–76), Labour politician 426, 433, 444

Driver, Christopher Prout (1932–), writer and broadcaster 427

Driver, Sir Godfrey Rolles (1892–1975), Professor of Semitic Philology 225

Driver, Samuel Rolles (1846–1914), Canon of Christ Church 134, 135, 298

Drumm, Walter, Catholic chaplain 301

Duckworth, Revd. Henry Thomas Forbes, head of Trinity College, Toronto 5

Dudden, Revd. Frederick Homes (1874–1955), Master of Pembroke College 171, 690–1

Dudok, Willem Marinus (1884–1974), architect 505

Duff, Gordon 477

Duncan-Jones, Katherine Dorothea, Fellow of Somerville College 416, 437

Dundas, Robert Hamilton (1884–1960), Student of Christ Church 93, 201

Dunnill, Michael Simpson (1928–), Director of Clinical Studies 343

Durbin, Evan Frank Mottram (1906–48), Labour politician 185, 387, 397, 399, 403

Duthie, Robert Buchan (1925–), Nuffield Professor of Orthopaedic Surgery 341

Dutt, (Rajani) Palme (1896–1974), British
    Communist leader 9, 17
Dyson, Henry Victor Dyson ('Hugo'), Fellow
    of Merton College 310
Dyson Perrins, Charles William (1864–1958),
    manufacturer 37, 158, 162

Eden, (Robert) Anthony, Earl of Avon
    (1897–1977), Conservative prime
    minister 384
Edward VIII, King, later Duke of Windsor
    (1894–1972), as Prince of Wales 106,
    411, 473
Edwards, Sir (John) Goronwy (1891–1976),
    historian 134
Egerton, Sir Alfred Charles Glyn (1886–1959),
    Reader in Thermodynamics 140, 160
Ehrman, Albert (1890–1969), diamond
    merchant and book collector 479
Einstein, Albert (1879–1955), physicist 497,
    622
Eliot, Thomas Stearns (1888–1965), poet and
    critic 413, 421, 428, 436, 438, 440
    and Auden 416
    and crime fiction 439
    his criticism 435
    his literary connections 417, 423, 429, 430,
        431, 460–1
    and Oxford 443, 444
Elizabeth II, Queen (1926–) 482
Elliott, (Sir) Roger (James) (1918–), Professor
    of Physics 704
Elliott, William Thomas (1855–1938),
    dentist 493
Ellis, Sir Arthur William Mickle (1883–1966),
    Regius Professor of Medicine 334
Elton, Charles Sutherland (1900–91), Reader in
    Animal Ecology 285
    research of xiv, 148, 154–5, 163, 253, 278
Elton, Godfrey, Baron (1892–1973),
    historian 124
Elvin, George H., trade unionist 380
Elwes, Valentine (1896–1966), Catholic
    chaplain 300
Emden, Alfred Brotherston (1888–1979),
    Principal of St Edmund Hall 199, 652
Enright, Brian James (1929–90), Librarian,
    Newcastle University 480
Ensor, Sir Robert Charles Kirkwood
    (1877–1958), Fellow of Corpus Christi
    College, Oxford 136, 221
Epstein, Hans Georg (1909–), First Assistant,
    Department of Anaesthetics 333
Epstein, Sir Jacob (1880–1959), sculptor 497,
    510
Erith, Raymond Charles (1904–73),
    architect 509

Ernle, Baron see Prothero
Etty, J.L., Ruskin College lecturer 379, 551
Euripides (484–406 BC) Greek tragic
    dramatist 134
Evans, Sir Arthur John (1851–1941),
    archaeologist 133, 486, 493
Evans, Lewis (1853–1930), collector of
    scientific instruments 488–9
Evans-Pritchard, Sir Edward Evan (1902–73),
    social anthropologist 135, 242, 248
Ewert, Alfred (1891–1969), Professor of the
    Romance languages 134

Faber, Sir Geoffrey Cust (1889–1961),
    publisher 87, 460
Fagan, James Bernard (1873–1933),
    dramatist 447
Fairbairn, Andrew Martin (1838–1912),
    Congregationalist scholar 296
Fairlie, Henry (1924–90), political
    journalist 721
Fanthorpe, Ursula Askham (1929–),
    poet 413, 428, 436, 442, 445
Farnell, Lewis Richard (1856–1934), classical
    scholar xv, 16, 131, 134, 689–90, 693
    and Asquith Commission 40
    and Lit.Hum. 116
    as vice-chancellor 101, 390, 685, 688
    and women at Oxford 350, 363
Farquharson, Arthur Spenser Loat
    (1871–1942), Fellow of University
    College, Oxford xi, 686
Farrell, Brian Anthony (1912–), Fellow of
    Corpus Christi College, Oxford 400
Farrell, James Gordon (1935–79),
    novelist 413, 442
Farrer, Austin Marsden (1904–68), Warden of
    Keble College 309–10
Farrer, Gaspard Oliver (1861–1946),
    collector 495
Fawcett, Charles Bungay (1883–1952),
    geographer 378
Fedorov, Evgraf Stepanowich (1853–1919),
    Director, Imperial School of Mines, St
    Petersburg 151
Feiling, Sir Keith Grahame (1884–1977),
    historian 136, 389, 391–2
Fenby, Charles (1905–74), journalist 400
Fenn, Eric 311–12
Fenton, James Martin (1949–), poet 413, 417,
    421, 424, 434, 445
    literary connections 430
    undergraduate career 415, 428
Fiedler, Hermann Georg (1862–1945),
    Professor of German 16, 119, 473
Findlay, Leonard (1878–1947), Consulting
    Physician to Radcliffe Infirmary 333

Firbank, Arthur Annesley Ronald (1886–1926), author 419

Firth, Sir Charles Harding (1857–1936), historian 132, 473

Fisher, Herbert Albert Laurens (1865–1940), Warden of New College 34, 221, 396, 563, 647
and by-election (1938) 406–7
as cabinet minister 17, 592
forms Asquith Commission 31–3
as head of house 82–3, 381
as historian 409, 609
influences Asquith Commission 34
moves rightwards (1930s) 405, 409
as Oxford reformer 29
and schoolteaching 29
and science 30
at Sheffield 29
and working men 29

Fisher, Lettice, founder of the Society for the Unmarried Mother and her Child 373, 409, 548

Fisher, Sir (Norman Fenwick) Warren (1879–1948), head of the civil service 642

Fisher, William (brother of H.A.L.) 29

Fitzgerald, Penelope Mary (Mrs. Desmond Fitzgerald) (1916–), writer 413, 415, 442

FitzGibbon, (Robert Louis) Constantine (Lee-Dillon) (1919–83), writer 442, 444

Flaubert, Gustave (1821–80), French novelist 446

Flecker, (Herman) James Elroy (1884–1915), playwright/poet 440

Fleming, Sir Alexander (1881–1955), bacteriologist 252–3

Fleming, (Robert) Peter (1907–71), writer and traveller 426

Fletcher, Charles Robert Leslie (1857–1934), historian 15

Fletcher, Robin Anthony (1922–), Fellow of Trinity College 528

Fletcher, Sir Walter Morley (1873–1933), Secretary, Medical Research Council 31, 32, 34, 320–1

Flexner, Abraham (1866–1959), Director of the Institute for Advanced Study, Princeton 321, 613

Flexner, Simon (1863–1946), Director, Rockefeller Institute for Medical Research 330

Florey, Howard Walter, Baron (1898–1968), experimental pathologist 341, 616, 621, 622–3
research of 182, 253, 262, 329–30, 334

Floud, Jean Esther (1915–), sociologist xix, 724

Foligno, Cesare (1878–1963), Professor of Italian 119

Foot, Michael (1913–), Labour politician 384, 404, 405

Foot, Michael Richard Daniell (1919–), historian 550

Foot, Paul Mackintosh (1937–), journalist 384, 425

Ford, Edmund Brisco (1901–88), Professor of Ecological Genetics 148, 150, 154, 155, 278, 280

Forster, Margaret (1938–), author 413

Forte, Charles, Baron (1908–), Chairman, Trusthouse Forte PLC 496

Foss, Hubert James (1899–1953), head of OUP music department 458

Fotheringham, John Knight (1874–1936), Reader in Ancient Astronomy 148, 153

Fowler, Alfred (1868–1940), astrophysicist 163

Fowler, Gerald Teasdale (1935–93), Labour politician 551, 554

Fowler, Henry Watson (1858–1933), lexicographer 133

Fowles, John (1926–), writer 413, 415, 427, 445, 447

Fox, Revd. Adam (1902–77), Fellow of Magdalen College 310, 437

Fox, Alan (1920–), sociologist 556

Fox, Leslie (1918–92), Professor of Numerical Analysis 270

Fox, Ralph Winston Winter (1900–36), novelist and critic 415

Frame, Ronald William Sutherland (1953–), novelist 414, 438, 442

Francis, Elizabeth Annie (1895–1979), Fellow and Tutor in French, St Hugh's College xv

Frank, Sir Howard (1871–1932), partner in Knight, Frank and Rutley 32

Franks, Oliver Shewell (1905–93), Provost of Worcester College xix, 83, 712–13, 725
and 'entitlement' 743, 744
as Fellow of Queen's 86
as head of house 686
and Meadow road 573
and Oxford hospitals 339
in Second World War 183, 386
stands for chancellorship 394, 700, 772
view of democracy 733

Fraser, Lady Antonia (1932–), writer 367, 414, 439

Freeman, Edward Augustus (1823–92), historian 609

Freeman, John (1915–), Labour politician 397

Frisch, Otto Robert (1904–79), physicist 182
Froude, James Anthony (1818–94),
    historian 609
Frowde, Henry (1841–1927), publisher 454,
    458
Fry, Charles Burgess (1872–1956),
    sportsman 379
Fry, Sara Margery (1874–1958), Principal of
    Somerville College 357, 358, 373
Fry, (Edwin) Maxwell (1899–1987),
    architect 505
Fry, Roger Eliot (1866–1934), art critic 92
Fulford, Sir Roger Thomas Baldwin
    (1902–83), Liberal politician and
    author 383
Fuller, John Leopold (1937–), Fellow of
    Magdalen College 413, 426, 428
  his poetry 424
  as publisher/reviewer 424, 425, 430
  as tutor 415
  writes detective fiction 439
Fuller, Roy Broadbent (1912–91), poet and
    author 418, 424
Fulton, John Scott, Baron (1902–86), Vice-
    Chancellor, University of Sussex 592,
    599
Furniss, Henry Sanderson, Baron Sanderson
    (1868–1939), Principal of Ruskin
    College 379, 407
Furse, Sir Ralph Dolignon (1887–1973), civil
    servant 377

Gaitskell, Hugh Todd Naylor (1906–63),
    Labour politician 385, 387, 397, 552
Gandhi, Mohandas Karamchand (1869–1948),
    Indian political leader 535, 616
Gardiner, Alan Poole (1871–1951), science
    master, Bradfield College 493
Gardiner, Gerald Austin, Baron (1900–),
    Lord Chancellor 362
Gardner, Arthur Duncan (1884–1978), Regius
    Professor of Medicine xi, 334
Gardner, Dame Helen (Louise) (1908–86),
    Professor of English Literature 225,
    355, 437
Gardner, Percy (1846–1937), archaeologist
    and numismatist 14
Garland, Patrick Ewart (1935–), writer and
    producer 426
Garner, Thomas (1839–1906), architect 502
Garrod, Sir Archibald Edward (1857–1936),
    physician and biochemist 42, 318,
    319
Garrod, Heathcote William (1878–1960),
    Fellow of Merton College 93
Garstang, John (1876–1956),
    archaeologist 494

Gask, George Ernest (1875–1951),
    surgeon 333
Geddes, Sir Auckland Campbell, Baron
    (1879–1954), public servant 33
Gee, Margaret May ('Maggie') (1948–),
    novelist 413, 438, 442
Geldart, William Martin (1870–1922),
    Vinerian Professor of English
    Law 114–15, 349
Gelder, Michael Graham (1929–), Professor
    of Psychiatry 342
George V, King (1865–1936) 534
George VI, King (1895–1952) 82, 99, 411,
    478, 534
Gertler, Mark (1891–1939), painter 497
Gibbon, Edward (1737–94), historian 236
Gibbs, Norman Henry (1910–90), Chichele
    Professor of the History of War 388
Gibbs, Olive (1918–), Oxford Labour
    councillor 568
Gibson, Alexander George (1875–1950),
    Consulting Physician, Radcliffe
    Infirmary 319, 329, 331
Gibson, Strickland (1877–1958), sub-
    librarian, Bodleian Library 477
Gilbert, Edmund William (1900–73),
    Professor of Geography 280,
    561–2
Giles, Peter (1860–1935), philologist 35
Gillam, Stanley George (1915–), Librarian,
    The London Library 480
Girdlestone, Gathorne Robert (1881–1950),
    orthopaedic surgeon 9, 325
Gladstone, William Ewart (1809–98), Liberal
    prime minister 383
Goddard, Henry, architect 509
Goldie, Bruce Morton (1869–1959), academic
    coach 132
Goldie, Grace Wyndham (1900–86), Head of
    Talks and Current Affairs, BBC
    TV 384
Golding, Sir William (1911–93), author 413,
    415, 428, 432
Gollancz, Sir Victor (1893–1967),
    publisher 180
Goodenough, Sir William Macnamara
    (1899–1951), Chairman, Barclays
    Bank 325, 333, 698, 717
Goodhart, Arthur Lehman (1891–1978),
    Master of University College xi, xiv,
    137, 178, 199, 241
Goodhart-Rendel, Harry Stuart (1887–1959),
    architect 502
Goodrich, Edwin Stephen (1868–1946),
    zoologist 154, 163, 277, 589
Gordon, Edward Duff (1863–1924), writer on
    bibliographical matters 477

Gordon, George Stuart (1881–1942), President
of Magdalen College 152, 459
as head of house 83, 95, 97, 102, 106
in Second World War 169, 173, 691
Gordon Walker, Patrick Chrestien, Baron
Gordon-Walker (1907–80), Labour
politician 25, 379, 552
Gore, Charles (1853–1932), bishop 16, 17,
33, 34, 303
as Oxford reformer 27, 29
Gottmann, Jean (1915–), Professor of
Geography 280, 561–2
Gowrie, Alexander Patrick Gresteil Hore-
Ruthven ('Grey') (1939–),
politician 426
Graham, David Maurice (1911–),
broadcaster 406
Graham, William (1887–1932), Labour
politician 32
Graham, William Franklin ('Billy') (1918–),
American evangelist 305
Graves, Robert Ranke (1895–1985),
author 422, 423, 426, 429, 436, 441
and First World War 23, 168, 413
as junior member 415, 416, 418, 420, 442
and poetry chair 418
T.E.Lawrence assists 433
Gray, Frank (1880–1935), Liberal
politician 379, 407, 551
Green, Cecil (1900–) and Ida (1903–86),
benefactors 760
Green, Henry [pseud for Henry Vincent
Yorke] (1905–73), 413, 442, 444
Green, Martin, critic and literary
historian 431
Green, Rev. (Edward) Michael (Bankes)
(1930–), Rector of St Aldate's 305
Green, Roger (Gilbert) Lancelyn (1918–),
author 420
Green, Thomas Hill (1836–82),
philosopher 386, 548
Green, Trevor, founder of the Museum of
Modern Art 489
Greene, Graham (1904–91), novelist 413,
417, 426, 427, 438, 558
Greenwood, Arthur William James ('Tony'),
Baron (1911–82), Labour
politician 399
Greg, Sir Walter Wilson (1875–1959), scholar
and bibliographer 477
Grensted, Revd. Canon Laurence William
(1884–1964), Nolloth Professor of the
Philosophy of the Christian
Religion 302, 487
Grey, Sir Edward, Viscount Grey of Falloden
(1862–1933), Liberal politician 4, 249
as Chancellor 390, 645–6, 690

Grier, (Mary) Lynda (Dorothea) (1880–1967),
Principal of Lady Margaret Hall 355,
358
Griffith, Francis Llewellyn (1862–1934),
Egyptologist 491–2, 494
Griffith, Nora Christina Cobban
(1870–1937), Egyptologist 491–2
Grigson, Geoffrey Edward Harvey
(1905–85), poet and man of
letters 419, 425
Gross, John Jacob (1935–), author 428,
429
Grundy, George Beardoe (1861–1948),
ancient historian 134–5
Guedalla, Philip (1889–1944), author 383
Gullick, Charles Francis William Rowley
(1907–81), Fellow of St Edmund
Hall 193
Gunn, James Andrew (1882–1958), Professor
of Pharmacology 318, 321, 323, 328
Gunther, Robert William Theodore
(1869–1940), zoologist 148, 149,
488–9
Gwyer, Barbara Elizabeth (1881–1974),
Principal of St Hugh's College xv
Gwyer, Sir Maurice (1878–1952), lawyer and
civil servant 460, 615

Haakon VII (1872–1957), King of
Norway 178
Habakkuk, Sir John (Hrothgar) (1915–),
Principal of Jesus College 204, 588,
740, 744
Haber, Fritz (1868–1934), Director, Kaiser
Wilhelm Institute of Physical
Chemistry, Berlin 163
Hadath, Gunby (–1954), writer for
children 465
Hadow, Grace Eleanor (1875–1940),
Principal, Society of Oxford Home-
Students 171, 355, 373
Hadow, Sir (William) Henry (1859–1937),
Vice-Chancellor, Sheffield
University 592
Hailsham, Lord see Hogg, Quintin
Haire, Norman (1892–1952), sexologist 99, 399
Halifax, Edward Frederick Lindley Wood,
Earl of (1881–1959), Conservative
politician 168, 390, 394, 615, 690
Hall, Donald Andrew (1928–),
poet/critic 419, 424, 426, 428
Hall, Edward Thomas (1924–), Professor,
Research Laboratory for Archaeology
and the History of Art 283, 288
Hall, Sir Noel (Frederick) (1902–83),
Principal of Brasenose College,
Oxford 433

Hall, Robert Lowe, Baron Roberthall
 (1901–88), economist xix, 616, 621,
 724
 advises government 388, 410
 as economist 137, 183, 387
Hall, Stuart McPhail (1932–), Professor of
 Sociology, The Open University 440
Halsey, Albert Henry (1923–), Professor of
 Social and Administrative
 Studies 770–1
Hamilton, Ian (1938–), poet 425, 429, 434
Hampshire, Sir Stuart (Newton) (1914–),
 philosopher 181
Hampson, Thomas (1907–), Olympic
 athlete 537
Hanbury, Harold Greville (1898–1993),
 Vinerian Professor of English Law 137
Hancock, Esra (–1914), head porter of Balliol
 College 93
Hanson, Laurance William (1907–66), Keeper
 of Printed Books, Bodleian Library 479
Harcourt, (Augustus George) Vernon
 (1834–1919), chemist 40
Hardie, Alexander MacKenzie ('Alic') (1918–),
 New Zealand novelist 417
Hardie, (William) Francis Ross ('Frank')
 (1902–90), President of Corpus Christi
 College, Oxford xiii, 138
 report on admissions (1962) 194, 724
Hardie, Frank Martin (1911–89), businessman
 and historian 392, 399
Hardie, (James) Keir (1856–1915), Labour
 politician 391
Harding, Walter Newton Henry (1883–1973),
 musician and collector 479
Hardy, Sir Alister Clavering (1896–1985),
 zoologist 139, 150, **278**, 297
Hardy, Godfrey Harold (1877–1947),
 mathematician 140, **155–6**
Hare, Deirdre Freda Mary, Lady (1935–) 369
Hare, Richard Mervyn (1919–),
 philosopher 574
Hargreaves, Eric Lyde (1898–1984),
 economist 137
Harman, Sir Charles Eustace (1894–1970),
 judge 260
Harris, Geoffrey Wingfield (1913–71), Dr Lee's
 Professor of Anatomy 341
Harris, Henry (1925–), Regius Professor of
 Medicine 341
Harrison, Alick Robin Walsham (1900–69),
 Warden of Merton College 386,
 724
Harrison, Austen St Barbe (1891–1976),
 architect 503
Harrisson, Thomas Harnett ('Tom') (1911–76),
 social anthropologist 421

Harrod, Sir (Henry) Roy (Forbes) (1900–78),
 economist 183, 390
 on economics 137, 387, 647
 and Munich 406
 on tutorials 196
Hart, Herbert Lionel Adolphus (1907–92),
 Principal of Brasenose College 231,
 241, 462
Hart, Horace (–1916), Printer to the
 University 456
Hart, Sir William Ogden (1903–77), Fellow of
 Wadham College 562
Hart-Synnot, Ronald Victor Oakes
 (1879–1976), Bursar of St John's
 College, Oxford 564
Harte, Walter James (1866–1954),
 historian 134
Hartley, Sir Harold Brewer (1878–1972),
 physical chemist 9, 139, 140, 157
Hartley, Leslie Poles (1895–1972), novelist and
 critic 413, 425, 426
Harvey, Andrew Charles (1952–), poet 434
Harvey, Ian Douglas (1913–87), Conservative
 politician 392, 393, 394
Harvey, Paul 464
Harvey, W.J. (–1967), Professor of English,
 Belfast 426
Hassall, Arthur (1853–1930), historian 15
Hassall, Christopher Vernon (1912–63),
 author 422
Hauser, Frank Ivor (1922–), stage director 444
Haverfield, Francis John (1860–1919),
 archaeologist 135
Haycraft, Colin Berry (1929–), publisher 426
Hayek, Friedrich August (von) (1899–1992),
 economist 395
Hazel, Alfred Ernest William (1869–1944),
 Principal of Jesus College, Oxford 16,
 357, 406
Head, Cecil George (1916–), college scout and
 part-time messenger 708
Headlam, Arthur Cayley (1862–1947), Regius
 Professor of Divinity 306
Healey, Denis Winston (1917–), Labour
 politician 396, 411
Heaney, Seamus (1939–), poet 417–8
Heath, Edward Richard George (1916–),
 Conservative prime minister 205, 394,
 395, 398, 693
 and the Oxford Union 167–8, 382, **392–3**,
 405
Heath-Stubbs, John (Francis Alexander)
 (1918–), poet 413, 415, 426, 434, 436
Heberden, Charles Buller (1849–1922),
 Principal of Brasenose College 486
Hemery, David Peter (1944–), Olympic gold
 medallist 537

Henderson, Arthur (1863–1935), Labour
 politician 28, 32, 404
Henderson, Bernard William (1871–1929),
 ancient historian 135
Henderson, (Patrick) David (1927–),
 economist 509
Henderson, Sir Hubert Douglas (1890–1952),
 economist 184, 387
Hennessy, Jossleyn Michael Stephen Philip
 (1902–?) 719, 731
Hepworth, Dame (Jocelyn) Barbara
 (1903–75), sculptor 497, 560
Herbert, Sir Alan Patrick (1890–1971), author
 and wit 379–80, 406
Herbertson, Andrew John (–1914),
 geographer 117
Herklots, Rev. Hugh Gerard Gibson
 (1903–71), Moderator of the Church
 colleges of education 596
Heseltine, Michael (Ray Dibdin) (1933–),
 Conservative politician 383, 393–4
Hewett, Cecil, architectural historian 509
Heyworth, Geoffrey, Baron (1894–1974),
 industrialist 725
Hicks, David 433
Hicks, Sir John (Richard) (1904–89),
 Drummond Professor of Political
 Economy 588
Higgins, G.H., Liberal candidate 379
Higman, Graham (1917–), Waynflete
 Professor of Pure Mathematics 270
Hill, Alfred (1860–1939) and Arthur
 (1862–1940), collectors and dealers in
 musical instruments 494–5
Hill, (John Edward) Christopher (1912–),
 Master of Balliol College xvii, 200,
 236, 409
Hill, Geoffrey (William) (1932–), 413, 415,
 426, 429
Hill, Oliver (1887–1968), architect 509
Hill, Reginald Harrison (1894–1976),
 librarian 480
Hill, Susan Elizabeth (Mrs Stanley Wells)
 (1942–), novelist 416
Hillary, Richard Hope (1919–43), Battle of
 Britain pilot xiii, 168, 181, 532
Hindley Smith, F. (–1939), collector 495
Hinshelwood, Sir Cyril Norman
 (1897–1967), physical chemist and
 biochemist 269, 273, 288
 a college man 141
 in First World War 139
 research of 157–8, 163, 262, 589
Hinton, John Michael (1948–), Fellow of
 Worcester College 415
Hitchens (Sydney) Ivon (1893–1979),
 painter 497

Hitler, Adolf (1889–1945), German Nazi
 leader 5, 25, 167, 172, 174, 406
Hobbes, Thomas (1588–1679),
 philosopher 115
Hobhouse, Emily (1860–1926),
 humanitarian 17
Hobhouse, Henry (1854–1937), pioneer in local
 government 17
Hobhouse, Margaret Heyworth (1854–1921),
 sister of B. Webb 17
Hobhouse, Stephen (1881–1961), Quaker and
 pacifist 17–18
Hodgkin, Dorothy Mary Crowfoot (1910–94),
 Nobel laureate in chemistry 151, 163,
 262, 268, 373, 408
Hodgkin, Robert Howard (1877–1951),
 Provost of Queen's College,
 Oxford 136
Hodson, Phillip Ian (1946–), editor 427
Hogarth, David George (1862–1927),
 scholar 42
Hogg, Quintin McGarel, Baron Hailsham of St
 Marylebone (1907–), Conservative
 politician
 Munich by-election (1938) 168, 267, 380,
 406–7, 552
 as undergraduate 391
Holder, Douglas William (1923–77), Professor
 of Engineering Science 274
Holdsworth, Sir William Searle (1871–1944),
 lawyer 87–8, 137, 609
Holford, William Graham, Baron (1907–75),
 town planner 566
Hollinghurst, Alan James Graves (1954–),
 novelist 413, 417, 429, 434
 as junior member 428, 442
 teaching career 415
Hollings, Rev. Michael Richard (1921–),
 Catholic chaplain 300
Hollis, Father (Roger Francis) Crispian (1936–
 ), Catholic chaplain 301
Holmes, Rev. Samuel (1858–1918), lecturer in
 theology, Jesus College, Oxford 134
Holmes, William (1917–85), Fellow of St John's
 College, Oxford xiii
Homer, Greek epic poet 135
Honoré, Antony Maurice (1921–), Regius
 Professor of Civil Law 241
Hopkins, Sir Frederick Gowland (1861–1947),
 biochemist 320, 321
Hopkins, Gerard Walter Sturgis (1892–1961),
 OUP editorial adviser 457
Horder, Percy (Richard) Morley (1870–1944),
 architect 503, 504–5
Hore-Belisha, (Isaac) Leslie, Baron
 (1893–1957), Conservative
 politician 382, 688

Horovitz, Béla, publisher 461

Horovitz, Michael (1935–), poet and critic 425, 430–1, 443

Houghton, Ralph Edward Cunliffe (1896–1990), Tutor of St Peter's College 134, 437

Houlden, Rev. Canon James Leslie (1929–), Chaplain-Fellow of Trinity College, Oxford 309

House, (Arthur) Humphry (1908–55), scholar 437

Howard, Anthony Michell (1934–), political journalist 383, 394, 397, 594

Howard, Brian Christian de Claiborne (1905–58), poet and man of letters 423

Howard-Johnston, James Douglas (1942–), Fellow of Corpus Christi College, Oxford 415

Hudson, Liam (1933–), psychologist 400

Hugh-Jones, Edward Maurice (1903–), economist 136–7

Hughes, Hugh C. (1893–1976), architect 505

Hughes, Richard Arthur Warren (1900–76), novelist and poet 413, 415, 426

Hughes, Professor T. Harold (1887–1949) architect 502, 504, 506

Humboldt, Alexander von (1769–1859), German naturalist and explorer 287

Hume-Rothery, William (1899–1968), Professor of Metallurgy xiv, **159–60**, 163, 272

Humphrey, George (1889–1966), Professor of Psychology 279

Humphreys, Kenneth William (1916–), Librarian, European University, Florence 480

Hunt, Geoffrey 464

Hunt, Richard William (1908–79), Keeper of Western MSS, Bodleian Library 479

Hurnard, Naomi (1908–86), historian 124

Hurst, Sir Arthur Frederick (1879–1944), physician 9, 333

Hutber, Patrick (1928–80), journalist 383

Huth, Angela Maureen (1938–), author 415

Hutton, John Henry (1885–1968), Professor of Anthropology, Cambridge 493

Huxley, Aldous Leonard (1894–1963), man of letters 413, 423, 426, 440
  his fiction cited 414, 436
  as undergraduate 414, 443

Huxley, Sir Julian Sorell (1887–1975), zoologist 154–5, 461

Ibsen, Peter, artist 489

Imlah, Michael Ogilvie ('Mick') (1956–), poet 413, 415, 417, 445

Inge, William Ralph (1860–1954), Dean of St Paul's 360

Ingram, Sir Herbert (1876–1958), collector 496

Ingrams, Richard Reid (1937–), journalist 425

Isaacs, Jeremy Israel (1932–), television producer xii, 384

Isherwood, Christopher (William Bradshaw) (1904–86), novelist and playwright 442

Jacks, Lawrence Pearsall (1860–1955), Principal of Manchester College 297

Jackson, Derek Ainslie (1906–82), physicist 160–1

Jackson, Robert Victor (1946–), Conservative politician 704

Jackson, Sir Thomas Graham (1835–1924), architect 502

Jacobsen, Arne (1902–71), Danish architect 513–14, 517

Jacobstahl, Paul Ferdinand (1880–1957), Student of Christ Church 461

Jacoby, Felix (1876–1959), classical scholar 461

James, Eric (1909–92), Vice-Chancellor, University of York 599

James, Rev. Herbert Armitage (1844–1931), President of St John's College, Oxford 82

James, Montague Rhodes (1862–1936), scholar 32, 34

James, Phyllis Dorothy (1920–), crime novelist 420

James, William (1842–1910), psychologist 298

James, William Owen (1900–78), plant physiologist 152, 253, 276

Jameson, Sir (William) Wilson (1885–1962), Chief Medical Officer, Ministry of Health 332

Jardine, Douglas Robert (1900–58), cricketer 537

Jarvis, Frederick Frank ('Fred') (1924–), General Secretary, National Union of Teachers 381, 383

Jay, Douglas Patrick Thomas, Baron (1907–), Labour politician 183, 387, 394, 403, 426

Jay, Hon. Peter (1937–), writer and broadcaster 384

Jekyll, Gertrude (1843–1932), garden designer 506, 517

Jenkin, Charles Frewen (1869–1940), Professor of Engineering Science144

Jenkins, David Edward (1925–), Fellow of Queen's College, Oxford 307

Jenkins, Roy Harris, Baron (1920–), Labour, then SDP, then Liberal Democrat politician 410, 411
  as Chancellor 770

and SDP 404
  as undergraduate 396, 586–7, 718
Jenkinson, John Wilfred (1871–1915), Fellow
  of Exeter College 139, 154
Jennings, Elizabeth (Joan) (1926–),
  author 413, 421, 424, 425, 434
Jewkes, John (1902–88), economist 395
Joad, Cyril Edwin Mitchinson (1891–1953),
  philosopher 406
Johnson, Rev. Arthur Henry (1845–1927),
  Chaplain of All Souls College 347
Johnson, Bertha Jane (1846–1927), Principal
  of the Society of Oxford Home-
  Students xv, 348, 352
Johnson, Charles (1870–1961), historian 134
Johnson, John de Monins (1882–1956),
  Printer to the University xvii, 456,
  457, 477, 479
Johnson, Paul (Bede) (1928–), author 397
Johnson, Samuel (1709–84),
  lexicographer 94, 456
Johnston, Alice Crawford (1902–76),
  Conservative Party worker 393
Johnston, Edward Hamilton (1885–1942),
  Boden Professor of Sanskrit 134
Jolowicz, Herbert Felix (1890–1954),
  academic lawyer 137
Jones, Sir Ewart (Ray Herbert) (1911–),
  Waynflete Professor of Chemistry 269
Jones, Geraldine (later, Greineder) (1946–),
  President of the Union 384
Jones, (Henry) John (Franklin) (1924–),
  Fellow of Merton College 415, 418
Jonson, Ben (1573?–1637), dramatist 134
Joseph, Horace William Brindley
  (1867–1943), philosopher 137–8, 406
Joseph, Jenny (1932–), poet 413, 426
Joseph, Keith Sinjohn, Baron (1918–),
  Conservative politician 395
Josipovici, Gabriel David (1940–),
  novelist/playwright 414, 436, 438,
  442, 443
Jourdain, Eleanor Frances (1863–1924),
  Principal, St Hugh's College xv, 351
Jowett, Benjamin (1817–93), Master of Balliol
  College 218, 286, 476, 586, 588
  as head of house 83
Jowett, Frederick William (1864–1944),
  socialist 17

Kaiser, the [William II] (1859–1941),
  Emperor of Germany 3, 4
Kaldor, Nicholas, Baron (1908–86),
  economist 185
Kale, Hans (of Parker's bookshop) 452
Kaye, John Marsh (1931–), Fellow of
  Queen's College, Oxford 226

Keates, Jonathan (Basil) (1946–), critic and
  novelist 413, 417
Keats, John (1795–1821), poet 135
Keeble, Sir Frederick William (1870–1952),
  botanist 140, 152
Keeley, Thomas Clews (1894–1988),
  physicist 161
Keeling, E., car worker 380
Keen, Harold Hugh (1902–74), Secretary to
  the University Chest 698, 708, 712
Keene, Dennis, poet 426, 429
Keir, Sir David Lindsay (1895–1973), Master
  of Balliol College xi, 189
Keith-Lucas, Bryan (1912–), Fellow of
  Nuffield College 273, 566–7
Kelly, Revd. John Norman Davidson (1909–
  ), Principal, St Edmund Hall 529
Kemp, Emily Georgiana (1860–1939),
  author 346
Kemp, Frederick Harold (1912–76),
  Chairman, X-ray Department,
  Radcliffe Infirmary 331
Kennard, Canon Charles Henry (–1920),
  Catholic chaplain 298
Kenner, (William) Hugh (1923–), literary
  critic/historian 431, 435, 438, 439, 442
Kenny, Sir Anthony John Patrick (1931–),
  Master of Balliol College 743
Kenyon, Dame Kathleen Mary (1906–78),
  archaeologist 494, 747
Ker, Neil Ripley (1908–82),
  palaeographer 479
Keyes, Sidney Arthur Kilworth (1922–43),
  poet/playwright 413, 426, 441
Keynes, John Maynard, Baron (1883–1946),
  economist 184, 387, 670
  and Beveridge 185
  as bursar 663, 669
Kierkegaard, Søren (1813–55), Danish
  philosopher 306
Kilner, Thomas Pomfret (1890–1964),
  Nuffield Professor of Plastic
  Surgery 332, 341
King, Cyril (1899–1955), head porter, Balliol
  College 93, 104
King, Edmund Jesse (1872–1963),
  groundsman, Brasenose College 207
King, Francis Henry (1923–), author 429
King, Joseph (1860–1943), Liberal MP 18
Kirk, Kenneth Escott (1886–1954), Bishop of
  Oxford 308–9
Knox, Ronald Arbuthnott (1888–1957),
  Catholic chaplain 299, 383, 426
Knox-Shaw, Harold (1885–1970), Radcliffe
  Observer 153
Kolkhorst, George Alfred (1897–1958),
  Hispanist 87

Krebs, Sir Hans Adolf (1900–81), Whitley
    Professor of Biochemistry 279, 281,
    341, 725
Kuhn, Heinrich Gerhard (1904–94), Reader in
    Physics 161, 163, 182, 622
Kurti, Nicholas (1908–), Professor of
    Physics 161, 182, 266, 622
Kyle, (John) Keith (1925–) xvii, 383, 405

Lack, David Lambert (1910–73), Director,
    Edward Grey Institute 285
Lamb, Henry Taylor (1883–1960),
    painter xv, 497
Lamb, Willis Eugene, Wykeham Professor of
    Physics 266
Lambert, Bertram (1881–1963), chemistry
    tutor 9
Lamerie, Paul de (1688–1751),
    silversmith 495
Lammasch, Heinrich, Austrian jurist 3
Landon, Philip Aislabie (1888–1961), Fellow
    of Trinity College, Oxford 137, 528,
    686
Lane, Barry John (1944–), first paid Director
    of the Museum of Modern Art 489
Lang, (William) Cosmo Gordon (1864–1945),
    Archbishop of York, then of
    Canterbury 360
Langdon, Stephen Herbert (1876–1937),
    Assyriologist 133, 494
Langridge, Edith (1864–1959), Mother
    Superior, Oxford Mission Sisterhood
    of the Epiphany 346
Lankester, Jack (1921–), University
    Surveyor 507, 513, 515, 516, 517, 695
Lansbury, George (1859–1940), Labour
    politician 384–5, 391
Larkin, Philip Arthur (1922–85), poet 413,
    426, 435, 440, 445
    criticized 438, 441
    Jill cited 96, 174, 179, 447, 449
    and poetry chair 448
    as undergraduate 415, 442, 443
Lascelles, Mary Madge (1900–), Fellow of
    Somerville College 135
Last, Hugh Macilwain (1894–1957), Roman
    historian 287
Latham, Richard Thomas Edwin (1909–43),
    Fellow of All Souls College 174
Lawrence, David Herbert (1885–1930),
    novelist 423, 435, 438
Lawrence, Thomas Edward (1888–1935) of
    Arabia 9, 413, 422, 433
Lawson, Frederick Henry (1897–1983),
    Professor of Comparative Law 115, 137
Lea, Kathleen Marguerite (1903–), Fellow of
    Lady Margaret Hall 133, 135

Leacock, Stephen Butler (1869–1944),
    Canadian author 644
Leavis, Frank Raymond (1895–1978), Reader
    in English, Cambridge 239–40, 429,
    435, 437–8, 442
Leavis, Queenie Dorothy (1906–81),
    critic 431, 435
Lee, Robert Warden (1868–1958), Professor
    of Roman-Dutch Law 137
Lee, Revd. Roy Stuart (1899–1981), Vicar of
    St Mary's 201, 313
Lees-Milne, James (1908–), author 102, 499
Legg, Leopold George Wickham
    (1877–1963), historian 15, 133
Lehmann, John Frederick (1907–),
    author 427
Lennox-Boyd, Alan Tindal, Viscount
    (1904–83), Conservative politician 391
Leudesdorf, Charles (1853–1924),
    Registrar 689
Levett, Ada Elizabeth (1881–1932),
    historian 348
Levi, Peter Chad Tigar (1931–), Fellow of St
    Catherine's College, Oxford 415, 418,
    424, 426, 434
Lévi-Strauss, Claude (1908–), social
    anthropologist 245
Lewis, Clive Staples (1898–1963), Fellow of
    Magdalen College 366, 415, 422, 423,
    437
    publications 135, 239–40, 414, 415, 439
    religious impact 310–11, 420, 437
    in Second World War 180, 184
    as tutor 442, 444
Lewis, S.K., Labour candidate 380
Leys, Agnes Moncrieff (née Sandys)
    (1890–1952), historian 135
Leys, Kenneth King Munsie (1876–1950),
    Fellow of University College 92, 586
Lichnowsky, Prince Karl Max Furst von,
    German ambassador 3
Liddell, Edward George Tandy (1895–1981),
    Waynflete Professor of
    Physiology 329, 341
Light, Rudolph Alvin (1909–70), surgeon and
    philanthropist 514
Lightfoot, Robert Henry (1883–1953),
    Ireland Professor of Exegesis of Holy
    Scripture 298
Lindemann see Cherwell
Lindsay, Alexander Dunlop, Baron Lindsay
    of Birker (1879–1952), Master of
    Balliol College 349, 712
    attitudes to:
    General Strike 396
    Labour Party 395–6
    research 89

science 141
social reform 386
WEA 396
as head of house 83, 137, 141
and Keele 586
and Nuffield College 144, 647–8, 691
parliamentary candidate (1938) 379, **406–7**, 551–2
as political theorist 103
and PPE 120
in Second World War 169
and undergraduate politics 390
as vice-chancellor 691
Lindsay, Kenneth Martin (1897–1991), politician 379, 399, 406, 551
Lindsay, (Nicholas) Vachel (1879–1931), poet 418
Little, Ian Malcolm David (1918–), Professor of Economics of Underdeveloped Countries 243
Lively, Penelope Margaret (1933–), writer 413, 439, 440
fiction cited 433, 445
as undergraduate 415, 442
Livingstone, Sir Richard Winn (1880–1960), President of Corpus 138, 358, 406, 408, 691
Lloyd George, David, Earl Lloyd George of Dwyfor (1863–1945) 29, 408
political impact in Oxford 382, 393, **405**
Lloyd-Jones, Sir (Peter) Hugh (Jefferd) (1922–), Regius Professor of Greek 233
Lobel, Edgar (1888–1982), papyrologist 133
Locke, John (1632–1704), philosopher 479
Lodge, Eleanor Constance (1869–1936), Principal of Westfield College, London 348
Lodge, Henry Cabot (1902–85), senator 408
Loewe, Herbert Martin James (1882–1940), Lecturer in Rabbinic Hebrew 301
London, Heinz (1907–70), physicist 161
Long, Philip (1918–78), Librarian, Essex University 480
Lonsdale, Roger Harrison (1934–), Fellow of Balliol College 426, 428
Loreburn, Robert Threshie Reid, Earl (1846–1923), Lord Chancellor 107
Lothian, Philip Henry Kerr, Marquess of (1882–1940), Secretary to the Rhodes Trustees 614
Love, Augustus Edward Hough (1863–1940), mathematician and geo-physicist 160
Loveday, Alexander (1888–1962), Warden of Nuffield College 387
Lovelock, John Edward (1910–49), Olympic medallist 537

Lovett, Sir (Harrington) Verney (1864–1945), Reader in Indian history 136
Lowell, Robert (Traill Spence) (1917–77), poet and playwright 418, 444, 446
Lowry, Laurence Stephen (1887–1976), painter 497
Luard, (David) Evan (Trant) (1926–91), Labour politician 380, 551
Lucas, John Randolph (1929–), philosopher 286
Lucie-Smith, (John) Edward (McKenzie) (1933–), poet and art critic 424, 426
Lutyens, Sir Edwin Landseer (1869–1944), architect 300, 503, 506
Lyell, James Patrick Ronaldson (1871–1949), lawyer and collector 477
Lys, Revd. Francis John (1863–1947), Provost of Worcester College xi, 42, 83, 712

Maas, Paul (1880–1964), classical scholar 461
Mabbott, John David (1898–1988), philosopher 187
Macan, Reginald Walter (1848–1941), Master of University College 610, 691, 718
McArthur, Sir William Porter (1884–1964), Director-General of the Army Medical Services 333
Macartney, Carlile Aylmer (1895–1978), historian 87
Macaulay, Thomas Babington (1800–59), historian 236
MacBeth, George Mann (1932–92), writer 413, 424, 426
McCallum, Robert Buchanan (1898–1973), Master of Pembroke College, Oxford 117, 124, 131, 168, 224, 668–9
family connections 712
research of 389
McCarrison, Sir Robert (1878–1960), medical scientist 333
McCarthy, William Edward John ('Bill'), Baron (1925–), Fellow of Nuffield College 384, 385, 553, 556
McCormick, Sir William Symington (1859–1930), Chairman of UGC 592
MacDonald, (James) Ramsay (1836–1937), Labour prime minister 399
MacDougall, Sir (George) Donald (Alastair) (1912–), economist 388
MacDougall, William (1871–1938), psychologist 139, 140, 143
McEwan, Ian Russell (1948–), author 420
McFarlane, (Kenneth) Bruce (1903–66), historian 197
Macfarlane, Robert Gwyn (1907–87), Professor of Clinical Pathology 341

McGowan, Harry Duncan, Baron (1874–1961), businessman 162

Macgregor, David Hutchison (1877–1953), Professor of Political Economy 137

Macintosh, Sir Robert (Reynolds) (1897–1989), Nuffield Professor of Anaesthetics 182, 328, 329, 334, 339, 621

Mackinder, Sir Halford John (1861–1947), geographer 135

McKisack, May (1900–81), Fellow of Somerville College 136

Macmillan, (Maurice) Harold (1894–1986), prime minister 97, 634, 725
  as Chancellor 394, 723
  and First World War 24, 81

McNabb, Dan, candidate for chair of poetry 423

MacNalty, Sir Arthur Salusbury (1880–1969), expert on public health 323, 331, 333

MacNeice, (Frederick) Louis (1907–63), poet 413, 423, 426, 434
  his poems cited 436, 447
  teaching career 429
  as undergraduate 92, 415

McWilliam, Candia Frances Juliet (1955–), novelist 416

Madan, Falconer (1851–1935), Bodley's Librarian 472, 477

Magee, Bryan (1930–), author and politician 384

Magrath, Rev. John Richard (1839–1930), Provost of Queen's College, Oxford 84

Mailer, Norman (1923–), author 248

Maine, Sir Henry James Sumner (1822–88), jurist 115

Maitland, Sarah (Louise) (1950–), novelist 413, 440

Major, Rev. Henry Dewsbury Alves (1871–1961), Principal of Ripon Hall 303

Major, Kathleen (1906–), Principal of St Hilda's College xvi

Makepeace, John (1939–), designer 514

Mallet, Mr., Worcester College servant 105

Mallett, John Francis (1875–1947), fine art dealer and collector 495

Mallowan, Sir Max Edgar Lucien (1904–78), archaeologist 494

Manley, John Job (–1946), Fellow of Magdalen College 157

Mann, Dame Ida (Caroline) (1893–1983), Professor of Opthalmology 333

Mann, Julia de Lacy (1891–1985), Principal of St Hilda's College xvi, xvii, 359

Manning, Charles Anthony Woodward (1894–1978), Professor of international relations 136

Mansbridge, Albert (1876–1952), founder of WEA 613, 717
  and Asquith Commission 32, 33, 34, 37, 41–2
  and Statutory Commission 42

Mansfield, Katherine [pseud. for Kathleen Murry] (1888–1923), writer 423

Marchant, Edgar Cardew (1864–1960), classical scholar 134

Marett, Robert Ranulph (1866–1943), social anthropologist 132, 135

Margaret, Princess (1930–) xvii

Margoliouth, David Samuel (1858–1940), orientalist 134, 609

Margoliouth, Herschel Maurice (1887–1959), Secretary of Faculties 690, 692, 695, 697

Maritain, Jacques (1882–1973), French philosopher 306

Marquand, David (Ian) (1934–), Labour, then Liberal Democrat politician 403

Marriott, Sir John Arthur Ransome (1859–1945), Conservative politician 136, 379, 388, 406

Marsh, Arthur (1922–), Fellow of St Edmund Hall 556

Marsh, Richard William, Baron (1928–), Labour politician 385

Marshall, Geoffrey (1929–), Provost of Queen's College, Oxford 554

Marshall, Henry Rissitz (1891–1959), collector 496

Marsland, Kenneth Thomas (1932–) 282

Marsland, Thomas Arthur (1905–) 282

Martin Clarke, Daisy Emily, Fellow of St Hugh's College 134

Martin, (Basil) Kingsley (1896–1969), journalist 397

Martin, Sir (John) Leslie (1908–), architect 515–16, 518

Marvell, Andrew (1621–78), poet 690

Marx, Karl (1818–83), economist and revolutionary
  influences Oxford study 236
  and PPE syllabus 245
  study in Oxford on 137, 396, 409

Mary, Queen (1867–1953) xv, 360, 478

Masefield, John Edward (1878–1967), poet laureate 93, 420, 422, 559

Mason, Kenneth (1887–1976), Professor of Geography 279–80

Mason, Timothy Wright (1940–90), historian 237–8

Massey, Raymond (1896–1983), actor 130

Masterman, Charles Frederick Gurney (1874–1927), politician and journalist 15, 439

Masterman, Sir John Cecil (1891–1977), Provost of Worcester College 181, 386, 691

Matheson, Percy Ewing (1859–1946), Fellow of New College 42, 115–16

Maturin, Father Basil William (1847–1915), Roman Catholic chaplain 299

Maud, John Primatt Redcliffe, Baron Redcliffe-Maud (1906–82), Master of University College xi, 136, 386

Maufe, Sir Edward Brantwood (1883–1974), architect 504, 506, 509

Maxwell, (Ian) Robert (1923–91), businessman 285, 453, 463–4

May, Derwent, novelist/editor 426, 430

Mayhew, Christopher Paget (1915–), Labour, then Liberal politician 398, 403

Meade, James Edward (1907–), economist 387, 397

Meadows, Tom, laboratory technician 551

Medawar, Sir Peter (Brian) (1915–87), Fellow of Magdalen College 155

Meiggs, Russell (1902–89), ancient historian 195

Melchett, Henry Mond, second Baron (1898–1949), merchant banker 185

Mellanby, Sir Edward (1884–1955), Secretary of the Medical Research Council 329

Mellanby, John (1878–1939), Waynflete Professor of Physiology 329

Mellon, Paul (1907–), philanthropist 479

Mellor, Oscar, publisher 424, 425

Mendelsohn, Eric (1887–1953), architect 505

Mendelssohn, Kurt Alfred Georg (1906–80), Reader in Physics 160–1, 163, 622

'Mercurius Oxoniensis' 278–9, 705, 706

Merton, Sir Thomas Ralph (1888–1969), physicist 160

Michell, Sir Lewis Loyd (1842–1928), South African banker and politician 611

Michie, James 426

Micklem, Nathaniel (1888–1976), theologian 296

Middleton, Christopher, poet 413, 415

Middleton, Haydn Keith (1955–), novelist 420

Midgley, Revd. Edward Graham (1923–), Fellow of St Edmund Hall 437

Miers, Sir Henry Alexander (1858–1942), mineralogist 32, 33, 37, 40, 474–5

Mies van der Rohe, Ludwig (1886–1969), architect 513

Milford, Sir Humphrey Sumner (1877–1952), publisher 454–6, 457–9

Milford, Theodore Richard ('Dick') (1895–1987), Vicar of St Mary's 313

Mill, John Stuart (1806–73), philosopher 115, 245

Miller, Karl Fergus Connor (1931–), Professor of Modern English Literature, University College, London 430

Miller, Max (1894–1963), comedian 382, 384

Mills, James Philip (1890–1960), colonial administrator and anthropologist 493

Milne, Edward Arthur (1896–1950), mathematician 155–6, 163, 251, 271

Milne, Joseph Grafton (1867–1951), numismatologist 133

Milner, Alfred, Viscount (1854–1925), imperialist and statesman 386, 389, 636
  as Chancellor 684
  and the Rhodes Trust 4, 17, 502, 611

Minton, Francis John (1917–57), artist 497

Mitchell, Adrian (1932–), writer 420, 424, 426, 442

Mitchell, Basil George (1917–), Nolloth Professor of the Philosophy of the Christian Religion 310

Mitchell, Frank W. 86

Mitteis, Ludwig (1859–1921), German classical scholar 3

Mo, Timothy Peter (1950–), writer 413

Moberly, Sir Walter Hamilton (1881–1974), university administrator 586, 592

Mogey, John McFarland (1915–), sociologist 561

Moir, John Chassar (1900–77), Professor of Obstetrics and Gynaecology 328, 334

Mond, Lady 360

Monteith, Charles Montgomery (1921–), publisher 430

Montgomery, (Robert) Bruce ('Edmund Crispin') (1921–78), writer 414, 415, 417, 427, 434, 439–40

Moody, Dwight Lyman (1837–99), American evangelist 305

Moon, Robert Oswald (1865–1953), consulting physician 379

Moorbath, Stephen Erwin (1929–), Reader in Geology 275

Moore, Benjamin (1867–1922), Whitley Professor of Biochemistry 321

Moore, Henry (1898–1986), sculptor 497

Moore, (Georgina) Mary (1930–), Principal of St Hilda's College xvi

Moore, Will Grayburn (1905–78), Fellow of St John's College, Oxford 135, 417

Moraes, Dom (1938–), Indian poet and author 426, 432, 440, 442

Morazé, Charles Constant C., historian 236

Morley, John, Viscount, of Blackburn (1838–1923), Liberal politician 376

Morrell family 93

Morrell, Lady Ottoline Violet Anne
(1873–1978), literary patron 423, 431

Morris, John Bayard (1903–92),
schoolmaster 115

Morris, Charles Richard, Baron (1898–1990),
Fellow of Balliol College 137, 592, 598

Morris, John Humphrey Carlile (1910–84),
Fellow of Magdalen College 196–7

Morris, Sir Philip Robert (1901–79), Vice-
Chancellor, Bristol University 592

Morrison, (Philip) Blake (1950–),
author 430, 435

Morrison, Herbert Stanley, Baron, of
Lambeth (1888–1965), Labour
politician 384–5, 387, 404

'Morse, Inspector' 420, 424, 449

Moseley, Henry Gwyn Jeffreys (1887–1915),
physicist 139

Moser, Sir Claus (Adolf) (1922–), Warden of
Wadham College 763

Motion, Andrew (1952–), poet and
critic 413, 427, 431, 434, 435, 440
  as junior member 428, 442
  literary connections 430

Motz, Hans (1909–87), Professor of Electrical
Engineering 273

Moullin, Eric Balliol (1893–1963), Professor
of Electrical Engineering 144, 145, 251

Moy-Thomas, James Alan (1909–44),
demonstrator in zoology 155

Moya, (John) Hidalgo (1920–),
architect xviii, xix

Muhassin ibn Ali 134

Mulgan, John Alan Edward (?–1945),
novelist 417, 423

Müller, Hugo (1833–1915), research
chemist 493

Mun, Thomas (1571–1641), economic
writer 123

Munby, Denys Lawrence (1919–76), Reader
in Transport Economics 570, 574

Munro, John Arthur Ruskin (1864–1944),
Rector of Lincoln College 83

Murdoch, Dame (Jean) Iris (1919–), novelist
and philosopher 413, 417, 421, 426
  her fiction 432, 436
  as undergraduate 415

Murphy, Neville Richard (1890–1971),
Principal of Hertford College 199

Murray, Douglas, Oxford city architect 567

Murray, (George) Gilbert (Aimé)
(1866–1957), Hellenist 31, 93, 99, 116,
396, 408–9
  and First World War 15, 17
  and international issues 406, 408
  and Liberalism 379, 381, 405

research of 134
in Second World War 174
and women 346, 358

Murray, Sir James Augustus Henry
(1837–1915), lexicographer xvii

Murray, Keith Anderson Hope, Baron
(1903–93), Rector of Lincoln
College 137, 190, 199, 286, 592, 717

Murray, Lionel, Baron, of Epping Forest
(1924–), General Secretary, TUC 386

Murry, John Middleton (1889–1957),
author 431

Mynors, Sir Roger (Aubrey Baskerville)
(1903–89), Corpus Christi Professor of
Latin Language and Literature 479

Myres, Sir John Linton (1869–1954),
archaeologist and historian 9, 358

Myres, John Nowell Linton (1902–89),
Bodley's Librarian
  on General Board 702, 740
  and the Library 479, 480, 482
  publications 135

Naipaul, (V. S.) Sir Vidiadhan Surajprasad
(1932–), novelist 440

Namier, Sir Lewis Bernstein (1888–1960),
historian 16, 130, 236

Neale, Sir John Ernest (1890–1975),
historian 221

Neill, Sir (Francis) Patrick (1926–), Warden
of All Souls College 672, 674–5, 744,
768, 773

Neill, Stephen Charles (1900–84), church
historian and ecumenical worker 314

Nelson, Edward, head scout, Balliol
College 206

Nernst, Hermann Walther (1864–1941),
Professor of Physical Chemistry,
Berlin 160, 622

Nervi, Pier Luigi (1891–1979), Italian
architect xix, 490–1, 516

Neubauer, Adolf (1832–1907), Reader in
Rabbinical Literature 472

Newman, John Henry (1801–90),
Cardinal 588

Newton, Guy 283

Newton, William Godfrey (1885–1949),
architect 504

Nichols, (John) Beverley (1898–1983),
author xvi, 87, 97, 383, 426

Nicholson, Edward Max (1904–)
ornithologist and conservationist 149

Nicholson, Edward William Byron
(1849–1912), Bodley's Librarian 471,
476

Niebuhr, Reinhold (1892–1971), American
theologian 298, 306, 312

Nield, Sir William (Alan) ('Bill') (1913–), civil
servant 400
Niemeyer, Oscar (1907–), architect 518
Norman, Wing Commander A.C.W., Liberal
candidate 380
Norrington, Sir Arthur Lionel Pugh
(1899–1982), President of Trinity
College, Oxford 513, 520, 707, 712,
724
and Blackwell's 452
invents table 64
and OUP 457
as vice-chancellor 700, 703
North, Eric (1891–1979), solicitor and
collector 496
Norwood, Sir Cyril (1875–1956), President of
St John's College, Oxford 82, 180,
186, 532
Nuffield, William Richard Morris, Viscount
(1877–1963), motor manufacturer and
philanthropist
builds up motor business 544–5, 558
buys Radcliffe Observatory site 153, 322–4
funds research in:
medicine 186: 1936 benefaction xiv,
321, **323–9**, 691: its later history 334,
338, 339
modern languages 645
natural science 144, 158, 162, 261
social medicine 332
social sciences 223
funds Worcester's Nuffield block 504, 506
impact on local hospitals 320, 323
medical network round 322, 325
and Nuffield College 144, 186, 325, 503,
647–8
political views 184
and St Peter's College 304
scale of his Oxford donations 650
University appeal backed (1937) 647

Oakeshott, Walter Fraser (1903–87), Rector
of Lincoln College xix, 573, 712, 723
Oakley, Sir John Hubert (1867–1946),
surveyor 32, 35
Obolensky, Sir Dimitri (1918–), Professor of
Russian and Balkan history 536
O'Brien, John Richard Percival (1906–),
Reader in Clinical Biochemistry 331
Odling, William (1829–1921), Professor of
Chemistry 40
O'Donoghue, (James) Bernard (1945–),
lecturer, Magdalen College 415
Oelsner, Hermann (1871–1923), Professor of
the Romance languages 134
Ogg, David (1887–1965), Fellow of New
College 136

Ogilvie, Mary Helen, Lady (1900–90),
Principal of St Anne's College 350, 726
Oldfield, Richard Charles (1909–72),
Professor of Psychology 279
Oliphant, John Ninian (1887–1960), Director
of Imperial Forestry Institute 147, 148
Olivier, Laurence Kerr, Baron (1907–89),
actor 221
Ollard, Revd. Sidney Leslie (1875–1949),
historian 134
Oman, Sir Charles William Chadwick
(1860–1946), historian
attitudes to:
history syllabus 123
research 89
teaching methods 131
political career 379, 406
publications 133, 135
Onions, Charles Talbut (1873–1965),
lexicographer 133
Oppenheimer, Sir Ernest (1880–1957), South
African financier 618
Ord, Margery Grace (1927–), Fellow of Lady
Margaret Hall xix, 724
Orwell, George [pseud. for Eric Arthur Blair]
(1903–50), author 399, 400
Orwin, Charles Stewart (1876–1955),
agricultural economist 137, 146
Osborn, Theodore George Bentley
(1887–1973), Sherardian Professor of
Botany 152, 276
Osler, Sir William (1849–1919), Regius
Professor of Medicine 6, 9, 317–8,
319, 337, 458
Osman, Louis (1914–), artist and
architect 512
Owen, Arthur Synge (1871–1940), Fellow of
Keble College 129, 134
Owen, Brynar James, Director,
Agricultural Engineering Research
Institute **146**, 640, 690, 698
Owen, Wilfred (1893–1918), poet 25
Owens, John (1790–1846), Manchester
merchant 597

Packford, Alfred Cyril (1921–), bedel xix
Page, Sir Denys Lionel (1908–78), classical
scholar 135, 181
Page, Sir (Charles) Max (1882–1963),
surgeon 333
Pakenham, Elizabeth, Countess of Longford
(1906–), 380
Pakenham, Francis Aungier ('Frank'), 7th
Earl of Longford (1905–), Labour
politician 136, 380, 400, 406, 426, 551
Pantin, William Abel (1902–73), Fellow of
Oriel College 707–8

Pares, Richard (1902–58), Fellow of All Souls College 712

Parker, Charlie (1920–55), American jazz musician 438

Parker, Henry Michael Denne (1894–1971), ancient historian 135

Parker, James (1833–1912), bookseller and publisher 492

Parker, John (1906–87), Labour politician 385

Parker, Sir Karl (Theodore) (1895–1992), Keeper of the Ashmolean Museum 492, 495, 496

Parkin, George Robert (1846–1922), educationist and imperialist 4, 610

Parnwell, E.C. 457

Parratt, Sir Walter (1821–1924), organist and composer 118

Parsons, Alfred William (1847–1920), painter and gardener 506

Paterson, Colin Harcourt (1913–80), Secretary of Faculties 697, 702

Paton, Herbert James (1887–1969), philosopher 113

Paton, Sir William (Drummond Macdonald) D.M. (1917–93), Professor of Pharmacology 341

Pattison, Mark (1813–84), Rector of Lincoln College 586, 588

Paulin, Tom (1949–), poet/critic 413, 421, 429, 430, 440–1, 442

Payne, Humfrey Gilbert Garth (1902–36), archaeologist 116

Peacock, Thomas Love (1785–1866), novelist 134

Pearson, Gabriel (1933–), Professor of Literature 426, 428

Peel, Sir Sidney Cornwallis (1870–1938), barrister 42

Peierls, Sir Rudolf (Ernst) (1907–), physicist 182, 266, 589, 730

Pember, Francis William (1862–1954), Warden of All Souls College xv, 42, 43, 405, 685

Penrose, Dame Emily (1858–1942), Principal of Somerville College 32, 33, 37, 42, 351, 361

Penson, Sir (Thomas) Henry (1864–1955), economist 113

Percival, Cecil, professional fund-raiser 359

Percival, John (1834–1918), Bishop of Hereford 359

Perham, Dame Margery Freda (1895–1982), Fellow of Nuffield College 355, 377, 617–18

Perkin, William Henry (1860–1929), Waynflete Professor of Chemistry xii, 589

First World War and 28, 139
research under 157, **158–9**, 163

Petel, Jörg (1601/2–1634), sculptor 496

Peters, Sir Rudolph Albert (1889–1982), Whitley Professor of Biochemistry 321

Peterson, Alexander Duncan Campbell ('Alec') (1908–88), Director of Department of Education 380

Pevsner, Sir Nikolaus Bernhard Leon (1902–83), architectural historian 509

Phelps Brown, Sir (Ernest) Henry (1906–), economist 86, 386

Phelps, Lancelot Ridley (1853–1936), Provost of Oriel College 93, 549, 554, 569

Philip, Ian Gilbert (1911–85), Keeper of Printed Books, Bodleian Library 481

Phillips, Caryl Osric Kurt (1958–), novelist/playwright 413, 440

Phillips, Sir David (Chilton) (1924–), Professor of Molecular Biophysics 259, 764

Picasso, Pablo (1881–1973), Spanish painter 438, 560

Pickard-Cambridge, Sir Arthur Wallace (1873–1952), classical scholar 135

Pickard-Cambridge, William Adair (1879–1957), Fellow of Worcester College xi

Pickering, Sir George White (1904–80), Master of Pembroke College, Oxford 202, 328, 337, 340

Pickstock, Francis Vincent ('Frank'), Deputy Director, Dept for External Studies 403, 551, 556

Piero di Cosimo (1462–1521), Italian Renaissance painter 496

Pindar (518/22-c. 438 BC), Greek lyric poet 134

Piper, Sir David Towry (1918–91), first Director of the Ashmolean Museum 487

Piper, John Egerton Christmas (1903–), painter 497

Pissarro, Esther, neé Bensusan (?-1951), widow of Lucien 495

Pitter, Ruth (1897–), poet 420

Planck, Max (1858–1947), German physicist 622

Plaskett, Harry Hemley (1893–1980), Savilian Professor of Astronomy 153–4, 156, 163, 271, 272

Platnauer, Maurice (1887–1974), Principal of Brasenose 87, 134

Plato (c.428 BC–348/47 BC), Greek philosopher 137–8

Plomer, William Charles Franklyn (1903–73), writer 419

Plowman, Harry, Town Clerk of Oxford 699

Plumer, Hon. Eleanor Mary (1885–1967), Principal of St Anne's College 178, 352

Polanyi, Michael (1891–1976), physical chemist and philosopher 280, 395

Pollock, Sir (John) Donald (1868–1962), industrialist 144, 162

Pollock, Sir Frederick (1845–1937), jurist 609

Pope, the 298

Pope, Mildred Katherine (1872–1956), philologist 134, 348

Porter, Cole (1893–1964), lyricist 438

Porter, Rodney Robert (1917–85), Whitley Professor of Biochemistry 261, 262, 341

Postgate, Raymond William (1896–1971), journalist/historian 9

Potter, Dennis (Christopher George) (1935–), playwright 401, 426, 438, 440, 441

Potter, Robert (1909–), architect 517

Poulton, Sir Edward Bagnall (1856–1943), entomologist 150, 154, 155, 162, 492

Pound, Ezra (1885–1972), American poet 438

Powell, Anthony Dymoke (1905–), author 413, 424
    his novels 381, 447
    undergraduate career 442, 443
    and undergraduate periodicals 426, 427

Powell, (Elizabeth) Dilys (1901–), film critic 362

Powell, (John) Enoch (1912–), Conservative politician 340, 403

Powell, Frederick York (1850–1904), Regius Professor of Modern History 609

Powell, Herbert Marcus (1906–91), Professor of Chemical Crystallography 151, 163, 268

Powell, Sir Philip (1921–), architect xviii, xix

Powicke, Sir Frederick (Maurice) (1879–1963), historian 235, 712
    and history syllabus 123
    and postgraduate study 127
    research published 134, 136

Powys, Theodore Francis (-1953), author 444

Poynton, Arthur Blackburne (1867–1944), Master of University College xi, 84, 476

Prescott, John Leslie (1938–), Labour politician 385

Prestwich, John Oswald (1914–), Fellow of Queen's College, Oxford 131

Prestwich, Menna (1917–90), Fellow of St Hilda's College xvi

Price, Henry Habberley (1899–1984), philosopher 137

Price, Langford Lovell F.R. (1862–1950), economist 113

Prichard, Mabel (1875–1965), wife of the White's Professor 373, 548–9

Priestley, John Boynton (1894–1984), author 407

Pringle, John William Sutton (1912–82), Linacre Professor of Zoology
    his tower 278–9, 707
    research of 278

Pringsheim, Fritz (1882–1967), 461

Procter, Evelyn Emma Stephanos (1897–1980), history tutor xv

Propertius Sextus (55/43–?), Latin elegiac poet 134

Prothero, Rowland Edmund, Baron Ernle (1851–1937), minister of agriculture 32, 35, 36, 40, 379

Proudfoot, Mary (1911–), Fellow of Somerville College xv

Proust, Marcel (1871–1922), French novelist 240

Pryce, Maurice Henry Lecorney (1913–), Wykeham Professor of Physics 266

Pryce-Jones, Alan Payan (1908–), author 429, 431, 442

Purcell, Sally (Anne Jane) (1944–), poet 421, 425, 434

Pym, Barbara Mary Crampton, (1913–80), novelist 101, 400, 415, 421, 437

Pym, Revd. Thomas Wentworth (1885–1945), Fellow-Chaplain of Balliol College 314

Quennell, Peter (1905–93), author 426

Radcliffe, Cyril John, Viscount (1899–1977), lawyer and public servant 615

Radcliffe, Geoffrey Reynolds Yonge (1886–1959), Fellow of New College 395, 410

Radcliffe-Brown, Alfred Reginald (1881–1955), social anthropologist 135

Radhakrishnan, Sir Sarvepalli (1888–1975), President of India 615

Radice, Edward Albert (1907–), economist 137

Raine, Craig Anthony (1944–), poet 413, 421, 431, 441
    attacked 430, 435
    his marriage 415
    as postgraduate 442

Raine, Craig Anthony (*cont.*)
as tutor 417
Raleigh, Sir Walter Alexander (1861–1922),
critic and essayist 136, 416, 418, 437
Ramsey, Arthur Michael, Baron (1904–88),
Archbishop of Canterbury 302
Raper, Robert William (1842–1915), Fellow
of Trinity College, Oxford 93
Raphael, Frederic Michael (1931–),
author 428
Rayleigh, third Baron (1842–1919),
mathematician and physicist 35
Read, Herbert (1893–1968), critic and
poet 504
Redcliffe-Maud *see* Maud
Redfern, Harry (1861–1950), architect 503
Redwood, John Alan (1951–), Conservative
politician 394
Rees, (Morgan) Goronwy (1909–79),
author 426
Rees-Mogg, William (1928–), Editor of *The
Times* xvii, 383
Reeves, Peter H. (1922–), Liberal
candidate 380
Reid, Christopher John (1949–), poet 413,
417, 430, 435
Rhodes, Cecil John (1852–1902), imperialist
and philanthropist 4, 536, 615
internationalist aims 3, 634
will 3, 5, 610
Rhondda, Margaret Haig Thomas, Viscountess
(1883–1958), feminist 360, 373
Rhys, Ernest Percival (1859–1946), author
and editor 458
Richards, Ceri Giraldus (1903–71), artist 497
Richards, Sir James (Maude) (1907–92),
architectural writer 503
Richards, Owain Westmacott (1901–84),
entomologist 150
Richards, Sir Rex (Edward) (1922–), Warden
of Merton College 256
research by 257, 259, 269, 284
Richards, Theodore William (1868–1928),
Professor of Chemistry, Harvard 157
Richardson, Eleanor (1892–1982),
landlady 192
Richardson, George Barclay (1924–), Warden
of Keble College 469
Rickword, (John) Edgell (1898–1982),
critic 413, 426, 429, 442
Riding, Laura [later Laura (Riding) Jackson]
(1901–), writer 441
Ridler, Anne (Barbara) (1912–), author 424
Ridler, Vivian Hughes (1913–),
publisher 424, 456
Ridley, Maurice Roy (1890–1969), Fellow of
Balliol College 135, 437, 439

Riley, Dennis Parker (1916–?) 151
Riley, J.A.L. 379
Rilke, Rainer Maria (1875–1926), Austro-
German poet 134
Robb-Smith, Alastair Hamish Tearloch
(1908–), Nuffield Reader in
Pathology 331, 335
Robbins, Lionel Charles, Baron (1898–1984),
economist 409, 725
Roberts, Benjamin Charles (1917–),
Professor of Industrial Relations,
London School of Economics 386,
403
Roberts, David Wyn (1911–82), architect 510
Roberts, John Morris (1928–), Warden of
Merton College 731, 760
Roberts, Margaret *see* Thatcher
Roberts, Paul Ernest (1873–1949),
historian xi
Robertson, Sir Charles Grant (1869–1948),
historian 87, 592
Robinson, Henry Wheeler (1872–1945), Old
Testament scholar 297
Robinson, Sir Robert (1886–1975), chemist
and Nobel prizewinner 151, 268–9,
589
research under 157, 159, 163, 282
in Second World War 251, 262
Robinson, Robert (1927–), writer and
broadcaster 382, 426, 427, 439
Robson, William Wallace (1923–93), Fellow
of Lincoln College 415
Rockefeller, John Davison, II (1874–1960),
philanthropist 474
Rodgers, William Thomas, Baron (1928–),
Labour, then SDP, then Liberal
Democrat politician 403, 411
Rogers, Annie Mary Anne Henley
(1856–1937), tutor, St Hugh's
College 346, 349, 350, 358, 506
Rogers, James Edwin Thorold (1823–90),
economist 346
Roosevelt, Franklin Delano (1882–1945),
American president 178
Rosebery, Archibald Philip Primrose, Earl of
(1847–1929), statesman and author 4,
384
Rosenthal, Albi, bookseller 452
Ross, Alan John Brackenridge (1922–),
author and editor 413, 424, 429, 442
Ross, Sir (William) David (1877–1971),
philosopher 134, 586
Ross, David Amyas (1900–?), New College
undergraduate 405
Roth, Cecil (1899–1970), Reader in Jewish
Studies 301
Rothschild, Hon. Sarah (1934–) 369

Rouse Ball, Walter William (1850–1925),
     Fellow of Trinity College,
     Cambridge 162
Rousseau, Jean-Jacques (1712–78), French
     philosopher 733
Rowbotham, Sheila (1943–), feminist
     author 369
Rowe, Sir Reginald Percy Pfeiffer
     (1868–1945) barrister 102
Rowse, Alfred Leslie (1903–),
     historian 177–8, 426
   at Christ Church 96, 128
   in Labour Club 397–8
Rowse, Herbert James (-1963), architect 505
Rudler, Gustave (1872–1957), Professor of
     French literature 134
Runcie, Robert Alexander Kennedy (1921–),
     Archbishop of Canterbury 302
Rusk, Dean (1909–), Professor of
     International Law, University of
     Georgia 382
Russell, Alec Smith (1888–1972), chemist 157
Russell, Bertrand Arthur William, Earl
     (1872–1970), philosopher 92, 155
Ryle, Gilbert (1900–76), philosopher 181,
     406
Ryle, John Alfred (1889–1950), Professor of
     Social Medicine 332, 341

Sadler, Sir Michael Ernest (1861–1943),
     Master of University College 406, 563
   as head of house xi, 82, 83
Sainsbury family 507, 512, 517–18
St John-Stevas, Norman Antony Francis,
     Baron St John of Fawsley (1929–),
     Conservative politician xvii
Salazar, António de Oliveira (1889–1970),
     prime minister of Portugal 178
Salisbury, Robert Arthur Talbot Gascoyne-,
     Marquess of (1830–1903),
     Conservative prime minister 383
Salter, (James) Arthur, Baron (1881–1975),
     politician 136, 379–80, 388
Salter, Herbert Edward (1863–1951),
     historian 561
'Samgrass, Mr' 92
Sandford, Sir Folliott Herbert (1906–86),
     Registrar 707, 709
Sandford, Kenneth Stuart (1899–1971),
     geologist 133
Sandys, Duncan Edwin, Baron Duncan-
     Sandys (1908–87), Conservative
     politician 570
Sankey, John, Viscount (1866–1948), Lord
     Chancellor 33
Sassoon, Siegfried Loraine (1886–1967),
     poet 10, 168

Saugman, Per Gotfred (1925–),
     publisher 463
Sayce, Archibald Henry (1845–1933),
     orientalist and comparative
     philologist 494
Sayers, Dorothy Leigh (1893–1957),
     writer 413, 424, 435, 437
   her detective fiction 420, 439, 449
   as undergraduate 415
Sayers, Richard Sidney (1908–89),
     economist 137
Schiebold, Ernst (1894–?), Professor of
     Mineralogy, Leipzig 151
Schiller, Ferdinand Canning Scott
     (1864–1937), philosopher 86, 137, 711
Schlepegrell, Adolf (1912–), German Rhodes
     Scholar 102, 406
Schlesinger, John Richard (1926–), film
     director 416
Schlich, Sir William (1840–1925), forester 147
Schmidt, Michael Norton (1947–),
     publisher 424, 427, 429, 443
Scholes, Percy Alfred (1877–1958), musical
     writer and encyclopedist 459
Schrödinger, Erwin (1887–1961), Fellow of
     Magdalen College 622
Schumacher, Ernst Friedrich (1911–77),
     economist and conservationist 185
Schumpeter, Joseph A(lois) (1883–1950),
     American sociologist and
     economist 733
Schuster, Sir Arthur (1851–1934),
     physicist 32, 34, 37
Schweitzer, Albert (1875–1965), German
     theologian and philosopher 298
Sciama, Dennis William Siahou (1926–),
     Fellow of All Souls College 271
Scott, George Gilbert the Younger (1839–97),
     architect 502
Scott, Sir Giles Gilbert (1880–1960),
     architect 478, 502, 504, 505–6, 518
Seddon, Sir Herbert (John) (1903–77),
     Nuffield Professor of Orthopaedic
     Surgery 328
Selbie, William Boothby (1862–1944),
     Congregationalist scholar 296
Selbourne, David Maurice (1937–), writer
     and former Ruskin College
     lecturer 746
Selwyn, Arthur Wakefield (1916–88),
     Assistant Secretary, OU
     Appointments Committee 528
Seth, Vikram (1952–), novelist 440
Seymour-Smith, Martin Roger (1928–)
     poet/critic 413
Shackleton, Robert (1919–86), Bodley's
     Librarian 481, 482

Shakespeare, William (1564–1616),
    dramatist 121, 122
  exhibition on 472
  publishers and 458
  research on 134, 135, 439
Sharp, Thomas Wilfred (1901–78), town
    planner 510, 569–70, 571, 572
Shaw, James Byam (1903–92), art historian and
    fine art dealer 496, 497
Shelley, Percy Bysshe (1792–1822), poet 479
Sherrington, Sir Charles Scott (1857–1952),
    Waynflete Professor of Physiology 318,
    321
Sherwin-White, Adrian Nicholas, (1911–93),
    ancient historian 135
Shils, Edward Benjamin (1915–), American
    sociologist 596
Shock, Sir Maurice (1926–), Rector of Lincoln
    College xix, 357, 724, 725
Sidgwick family 712
Sidgwick, Henry (1838–1900), philosopher 345
Sidgwick, Nevil Vincent (1873–1952), Professor
    of Chemistry 157
Silkin, Lewis, Baron (1889–1972), Minister of
    Town and Country Planning 565
Simon, Brian (1915–), Professor of Education,
    Leicester 694
Simon, Sir Francis (Franz) Eugen (1893–1956),
    physicist 224, 272, 622
  research 160–1, 163, 182, 266, 267
  in Second World War 252
  on the status of science 285, 287
Simon, John Allsebrook, Viscount
    (1873–1954), statesman 32, 41, 382, 383,
    615
Simpson, Rev. David Capell (1883–1955),
    biblical scholar 135
Simpson, Percy (1865–1962), scholar 134, 439,
    477
Singer, Charles (1876–1960), historian of
    science 149–50
Sisam, Kenneth (1887–1971), Secretary to the
    delegates of the OUP 457
Skinner, Dennis Edward (1932–), Labour
    politician 385
Slade, Edwin (1903–89), Fellow of St John's
    College, Oxford 198
Slater, (Charles) Montagu (1902–) 413, 429
Sloman, Sir Albert (Edward) (1921–), Vice-
    Chancellor, Essex University 599, 746
Small, Leonard, zoology department
    technician 281
Smalley, Beryl (1905–84), Fellow of St Hilda's
    College 365
Smallpeice, Victoria, paediatrician 333
Smith, Adam (1723–90), political
    economist 123

Smith, Alexander Crampton (1917–),
    Nuffield Professor of
    Anaesthetics 341
Smith, Alic Halford (1883–1958), Warden of
    New College 647, 697
  and the environment 509, 562, 648, 691
  and natural science 273, 386
  as vice-chancellor 691
Smith, Arthur Lionel (1850–1924), Master of
    Balliol College xv, 83, 396, 712, 717
Smith, David Nichol (1875–1962), Merton
    Professor of English Literature 477
Smith, Geoffrey Watkins (1881–1916), Fellow
    of New College 139, 154
Smith, George (1824–1901), founder of the
    Dictionary of National Biography 459
Smith, Godfrey, journalist xvii, 383
Smith, Hon. Honor Mildred Vivian, May
    Reader in Medicine 333
Smith, John Alexander (1863–1939),
    philosopher 112
Smith, J.Osborne 504
Smith, Mary Florence (1855–1946), wife of
    A.L.Smith 548
Smithson, Alison Margaret (1928–93),
    architect 512, 515
Smithson, Peter Denham (1923–),
    architect 512, 515
Smuts, Jan Christiaan (1870–1950), South
    African statesman 17
Snow, Sir Charles Percy, Baron (1905–80),
    author 219, 224, 287
Soddy, Frederick (1877–1956), Dr. Lee's
    Professor of Chemistry 157
Sollas, William Johnson (1849–1936),
    geologist 150
Southern, Sir Richard (William) (1912–),
    historian 237, 248
Southwell, Sir Richard Vynne (1888–1970),
    Professor of Engineering Science 144,
    163, 251, 274
Southwood, Sir (Thomas) Richard (Edmund)
    (1931–), Linacre Professor of
    Zoology 279
Spalding, Henry Norman (1877–1953),
    philanthropist 614
Sparrow, John Hanbury Angus (1906–92),
    Warden of All Souls College 433, 441,
    718
Spence, Sir Basil Urwin (1907–76),
    architect 509, 510
Spencer, Charles Bernard (1909–63), 413, 415,
    426, 429, 433
Spencer, Sir Stanley (1891–1959), artist 497
Spender, Sir Stephen (Harold) (1909–), poet
    and critic 413, 419, 428, 441, 448
  autobiography 432

literary connections 430
teaching career 429
undergraduate career 415, 427, 433, 442
where poems published 424, 426, 431
Spens, Janet (1876–1963), Fellow of Lady
    Margaret Hall 133, 135
Spiller, Reginald Charles (1886–1953), Reader
    in Mineralogy 151
Spokes, Peter (1893–1976), on Bodleian
    staff 551
Squire, Sir John Collings (1884–1958), poet
    and man of letters 419, 431
Stahl, Ernest Ludwig (1902–92), Professor of
    German 134
Stallworthy, Sir John (Arthur) (1906–93),
    Professor of Obstetrics and
    Gynaecology 341
Stallworthy, Jon Howie (1935–), Fellow of
    Wolfson College 415, 423, 428
Stallybrass, William Teulon Swan
    (1883–1948), Principal of Brasenose
    College 194, 286, 355, 528, 699
as head of house 83, 199, 212
Stanley, Arthur Penrhyn (1815–81), Dean of
    Westminster 35
Starkie, Enid Mary (1897–1970), Fellow of
    Somerville College xiii, 135, 365, 418,
    446, 449
Steel-Maitland, Sir Keith Richard Felix
    (1912–65), Balliol undergraduate 392
Steiner, George (1929–), author 424, 426
Stevenson, Anne (1933–), poet/critic 415,
    445
Stevenson, George Hope (1880–1952),
    ancient historian xi, 135
Stewart, Duncan Montgomery (1930–),
    Principal of Lady Margaret Hall 749
Stewart, John Innes Mackintosh ('Michael
    Innes') (1906–), novelist and Student
    of Christ Church 427, 429, 758–9
his detective fiction 413–4, 439–40
as tutor 415
Stewart, (Robert) Michael (Maitland)
    (1906–90), Labour politician
as debater xvii, 106, 382, 408, 411
and Oxford socialism 397, 399, 404
police protection for 403
Stirling, James Frazer (1926–), architect 511,
    512
Stocker, William Nelson (1851–1949),
    physicist 86, 198
Stocks, Charles Lancelot (1878–1975), civil
    servant, then headmaster 36
Stocks, John Leofric (1882–1937),
    philosopher 379, 397, 586, 592
Stocks, Mary Danvers (1891–1975),
    feminist 369

Stokes, John (1915–), Australian
    schoolteacher 173
Stone, Darwell (1859–1941), Anglo-Catholic
    theologian 303
Stone, Lawrence (1919–), historian 226, 236
Strachey, (Evelyn) John (St Loe) (1901–63),
    politician and writer 426
Strachey, (Giles) Lytton (1880–1932), critic and
    biographer 423
Stradivarius (1644?–1737), Italian violin
    maker 495
Strange, Father (Charles) Roderick, Roman
    Catholic chaplain 299, 301
Strauss, Richard (1864–1949), German
    composer 3
Strawson, Sir Peter (Frederick) (1919–),
    philosopher 408
Streeten, Paul Patrick (1917–), economist 248
Streeter, Burnett Hillman (1874–1937), Provost
    of Queen's College, Oxford 307
as head of house 83
and Moral Re-Armament 302
as scholar 135, 298, 308, 309
Stretton, Hugh (1924–) historian 193
Strong, Thomas Banks (1861–1944), Dean of
    Christ Church 118, 132, 685
and Asquith Commission 32, 34, 36, 39, 40,
    41
in First World War 8
and Statutory Commission 42
Strutt, Hon. Edward (Gerald) (1854–1930),
    land agent 32, 35
Stuart, Charles Harborne (1920–91), Tutor in
    Modern History, Christ Church 745
Stuart-Jones, Sir Henry (1867–1939), classical
    scholar 133–4
Sullivan, John Patrick (1930–93), Fellow of
    Lincoln College 234
Sumner, Benedict Humphrey (1893–1951),
    Warden of All Souls College 83, 620
Sunley, Bernard (1910–64), Chairman of
    Blackwood Hodge Ltd 514
Sutherland, Graham Vivian (1903–80), painter
    and print-maker 497, 560
Sutherland, James Runcieman (1900–),
    Professor of English Literature 426
Sutherland, Dame Lucy Stuart (1903–80),
    historian
and Meadow road 573
and mixed colleges 726
publications 136
university career 352, 355, 712
and women in Oxford 356, 357, 358, 373
Swingler, Randall Carline (1909–), author and
    editor 413, 429, 442
Swinton, Sir Ernest Dunlop (1868–1951),
    Professor of Military History 9

Syme, Sir Ronald (1903–89), ancient historian 135, 620–1

Talbot, Edward Stuart (1844–1934), Warden of Keble College 346
Talbot, Lavinia, wife of the Warden of Keble 346
Talbot, Percy Amaury (1877–1945), colonial administrator 493
Talleyrand-Périgord, Count Hélie 3
Tansley, Sir Arthur George (1871–1955), plant ecologist 152, 163, 280, 395
Tati, Jacques (1908–), French film actor 560
Taverne, Dick (1928–), Labour, then Liberal Democrat politician 403–4
Tawney, Richard Henry (1880–1962), historian 185, 396, 397, 398, 586, 609
and Asquith Commission 38, 717
Taylor, Alan John Percivale (1906–90), historian 235, 419
as undergraduate 391, 399
as Fellow of Magdalen 92
as lecturer 366
and Second World War 172, 183, 221
research of 620
political views 407
criticized 236–7
Taylor, Charles Margrave (1931–), Professor of Political Science 407
Taylor, Elizabeth (1932–), film actress 416
Taylor, Frank Sherwood (1897–1956), historian of science 288
Temple, George Frederick James (1901–92), Sedleian Professor of Natural Philosophy 270
Temple, William (1881–1944), Archbishop of Canterbury 314, 392
Templeton, Sir John (Marks) (1912–), businessman and benefactor 763
Tesler, Brian (1929–), television producer 426
Thatcher, Margaret (Hilda), Baroness (1925–), Conservative prime minister
honorary degree refused 765, 772
as undergraduate 384, **393**, 394, 395
Thom, Alexander (1894–1985), Professor of Engineering Science 274
Thomas, Donald Michael (1935–), poet and novelist 413, 442
Thomas, Dylan Marlais (1914–53), poet 419, 423, 444
Thomas, Edward (1878–1917), poet 413, 434
Thomas, Sir Keith (Vivian) (1933–), historian 236
Thompson, Edward John (1886–1946), Research Fellow in Indian History, Oriel College 614

Thompson, Sir Harold Warris (1908–83), physical chemist 163, 528, 537
Thompson, Reginald Campbell (1876–1941), Assyriologist 133
Thomson, Arthur (1858–1935), Professor of Anatomy 318, 329, 348
Thomson, Sir John (1908–), banker 534
Thornton-Duesbery, Julian Percy (1906–88), Master of St Peter's College 302
Thorpe, (John) Jeremy (1929–), Liberal politician xvii, 405
Thwaite, Anthony Simon (1930–), poet 413, 424, 426, 429, 430, 433–4
Tillotson, Geoffrey (1905–69), Professor of English Literature 426
Tinbergen, Nikolaas (1907–88), Reader in Animal Behaviour 262, 278, 285
Titchmarsh, Edward Charles (1899–1963), mathematician 156
Tizard, Sir Henry Thomas (1855–1959), scientist and President of Magdalen College 9, 139, 140, 141
Todd, Alexander Robertus (1907–), Master of Christ's College, Cambridge 159
Todd, Joseph Derwent (1923–), Fellow of St Edmund Hall 274
Tolkien, John Ronald Reuel (1892–1973), author and philologist 423
and the English school 121–2, 423, 436–7
fiction of 414, 415, 436, 439
and Inklings 310, 423
as lecturer 366
and reconstruction 184
research of 134
Tomalin, Claire (1933–), writer 430
Topolski, Daniel (1945–), rowing coach 535
Toulmin, Stephen Edelston (1922–), University Lecturer in the Philosophy of Science 288
Towle, Arthur Edward (1878–1948), hotel manager 38
Townsend, Sir John Sealy Edward (1868–1957), physicist 160, 266
Toynbee, Arnold (1852–83), economist 386, 548
Toynbee, Arnold Joseph (1889–1975), historian 15–16
Toynbee, Mary ('Polly') (1946–), journalist 427
Toynbee, (Theodore) Philip (1916–81), author and critic 383, 429
Trapido, Barbara (1941–), novelist 415
Trapido, Stanley (1933–), Fellow of Lincoln College 415
Treglown, Jeremy Dickinson (1946–), author 427, 429

Trend, Burke St John, Baron, of Greenwich (1914–87), Secretary of the Cabinet 386

Trevelyan, George Macaulay (1876–1962), historian 32, 34, 39

Trevor-Roper, Hugh Redwald, Baron Dacre of Glanton (1914–), historian 181, 236

Trickett, (Mabel) Rachel (1923–), Principal of St Hugh's College 437

Trollope, Anthony (1815–82), novelist 458

Trotman, Percy, zoology department technician 281

Trott zu Solz, (Friedrich) Adam von (1909–44), Rhodes scholar at Balliol 5–6

Troup, Robert Scott (1874–1939), Professor of Forestry 147–8

Truelove, Sidney Charles, Director of Clinical Studies 342

Trueta, Josep Anthony (1897–1977), Nuffield Professor of Orthopaedic Surgery 333

Truman, Harry S. (1884–1972), President of the United States 407

Truscot, Bruce [pseud. for Edgar Allison Peers] (1891–1952), Hispanist 596–7

Tucker, Bernard William (1901–50), ornithologist 149, 155

Turner, Henry Frederic Lawrence (1908–77), Conservative politician 380

Turner, Herbert Hall (1861–1930), astronomer 153

Turpin, Kenneth Charlton (1915–), Provost of Oriel College 640, 701, 702, 744–5

Tweddle, D.W., Liberal candidate 380

Tylor, Sir Edward Burnett (1832–1917), anthropologist 493

Tynan, Kenneth Peacock (1927–80), theatre critic 93–4, 383, 407, 427

Unwin, Sir Stanley (1884–1968), publisher 461

Urquhart, Francis Fortescue (1868–1934), Fellow of Balliol College 93, 299

Varley, Eric Graham (1932–), Labour politician 385

Vaughan, Dame Janet (Maria) (1899–1993) Principal of Somerville College 339, 355, 726

Vaughan Williams, Ralph (1872–1958), composer 459

Veale, Sir Douglas (1891–1973), Registrar 85, 174, 338, 647, 709, 712
  how appointed 697
  methods 690, 697–700, 711–12
  policy on:
    city questions 552, 554, 563, 689, 699

Commonwealth universities 635, 699
  medical research 322–3, 325, 326, 330, 336, 699
  Nuffield College 144, 647–8
  Owen case 146, 698
  science area 152, 543
  relations with:
    Chest 687, 690
    Congregation 693

Veblen, Oswald (1880–1960), Professor of Mathematics, Princeton 156

Vincent, Ewart Albert (1919–), Professor of Geology 275

Vinogradoff, Pavel Gavrilovich (1854–1925), historian 132

Virgil (Publius Vergilius Maro) (70–19 BC), Latin poet 232

Vollum, Roy Lars (1899–1970), Demonstrator in Pathology 331

Wager, Lawrence Rickard (1904–65), geologist xiv, 275

Wain, John Barrington (1925–94), novelist 413, 420, 423, 434, 436, 447
  his novels 432
  honorary fellowship for 448
  interest in jazz 438
  and Oxford religious/literary affinities 180, 295, 422, 437
  and poetry chair 418, 421, 441
  teaching career 429
  as undergraduate 176, 415, 432, 442

Waismann, Friedrich (1896–1959), Austrian-British philosopher 288

Walden, (Alastair) Brian (1932–), television presenter and journalist 384, 401

Wales, Charles, Prince of (1948–) 765

Walford, Edwin A. (1847–1924), Banbury bookseller 493

Walker, Revd. Edward Mewburn (1857–1941), Provost of Queen's College, Oxford 83, 125

Walker Smith, Derek Colclough (1910–), Conservative politician 391

Wall, Stephen de Rocfort (1931–), Fellow of Keble College 425, 429

Waller, Sir John Stanier (1917–), author 425

Walton, Sir William Turner (1902–83), composer 459

Walzer, Richard Rudolf (1900–75), Reader in Arabic and Greek philosophy 461

Ward, Basil Robert (1902–76), architect 510, 515

Ward, Daisy Linda (1883–1937), artist and collector 495

Ward, Mary Augusta (Mrs Humphry) (1851–1920), author 384

Ward-Perkins, Charles Neville (1917–60), economist 520

Wardale, Edith Elizabeth (1863–1943), Fellow of St Hugh's College xv

Warner, Francis (Robert Le Plastrier) (1937–), Fellow of St Peter's College 415, 418

Warner, Marina Sarah [Mrs John Dewe Mathews] (1946–), writer and critic 427

Warner, Rex (1905–88), author 413, 421, 436
his publishers 424, 426
teaching career 429
undergraduate career 415, 442

Warnock, Sir Geoffrey (James) (1923–),
  · Principal of Hertford College 733

Warren, Edward Prioleau (1856–1937), architect 503

Warren, Robert Penn (1905–89), American writer 440

Warren, Sir Thomas Herbert (1853–1930), President of Magdalen College xv, 397, 684
as head of house 82–3, 102, 717

Warrington, Percy Ewart (1889–1961), founder of public schools 304

Waterhouse family 158

Waterhouse, Jack 402

Waterhouse, Paul (1861–1924), architect 503

Watson, Sir James Anderson Scott (1889–1966), Professor of Rural Economy 145

Watson, (John) Steven (1916–86), Student of Christ Church xix, 194, 550, 724

Watt, Donald Cameron (1928–), Professor of International History, London University 426

Watts, Mrs Hugh, philanthropist 143, 162

Waugh, Arthur (1866–1943), author 131

Waugh, Auberon Alexander (1939–), author 430, 442

Waugh, Evelyn Arthur St John (1903–66), author 413, 421, 441, 445, 447, 624
Brideshead Revisited cited 92, 99, 102, 293, 383, 611
Brideshead Revisited and Oxford's image 770
and Catholicism 293, 299
and Oxford Union 718
as undergraduate 390, 415, 425, 442, 446, 449

Weaver, John Reginald Homer (1882–1965), President of Trinity College, Oxford 84

Webb, Clement Charles Julian (1865–1954), theologian, philosopher and historian 309

Weber, Max (1864–1920), German sociologist 245

Weeks, Sir Ronald Morce, Baron (1890–1960), industrialist and soldier 194

Weight, Carel Victor Morlais (1908–), painter 497

Weir, Sir Cecil McAlpine (1890–1960), industrialist and public servant 185

Weiskrantz, Lawrence (1926–), Professor of Psychology 279

Weldon, Florence (?–1936), collector and benefactor 491

Weldon, Thomas Dewar (1896–1958), Fellow of Magdalen College 84, 243

Wellesz, Egon Joseph (1885–1974), music scholar 461

Wells, Frances Mary (?–1925), Wife of the Warden of Wadham College 373, 548

Wells, Joseph (1855–1929), Warden of Wadham College 6, 390, 685, 687

Wells, Stanley William (1930–), Fellow of Balliol College 416

Wenden, David John ('Charles') (1923–92), Bursar of All Souls College xix

Wertheimer, Egon, German journalist 398–9, 405

Whale, Rev. John Seldon (1896–), Mackennal Professor of Church History 296

Wheare, Sir Kenneth Clinton (1907–79), Rector of Exeter College 87, 386, 621, 683, 712
and the Conference of Colleges 741
on Douglas Veale 697, 698, 699–700
and Franks Commission 723–4
and Meadow road 573
in Oxford local politics 555, 573
as scholar 136, 388, 616
as vice-chancellor 700–1

Wheatley, Frederick Ivor ('Fred') (1913–85), Steward of St Antony's College 206

Whibley, Charles (1859–1930), writer 461

White, Very Rev. Henry Julian (1859–1934), Dean of Christ Church xv

Whitehead, John Henry Constantine (1904–60), Waynflete Professor of Pure Mathematics 156, 270

Whitley, Edward (1879–1945), Liverpool businessman 321

Whittaker, Eric James William (1921–), Reader in Mineralogy 281

Whitteridge, David (1912–94), Waynflete Professor of Physiology 341

Wigg, George Edward Cecil, Baron (1900–83), Labour politician 553

Wild, Very Rev. John Herbert Severn (1904–92), Master of University College xi

Wilde, Henry (1833–1919), scientist and philanthropist 143

Wiles, Rev. Maurice Frank (1923–), Regius Professor of Divinity 305, 307

Wilhelmina, Helena Pauline Maria (1880–1962), Queen of the Netherlands 178

Wilkins, William Henry (1885–1966), demonstrator in botany 152

Wilkinson, Cyril Hackett (1888–1960), Fellow of Worcester College xi, xii, xiii, 477, 528

Wilkinson, Sir Denys (Haigh) (1922–), Professor of Experimental Physics 267, 281

William of Sens, French master mason 513

Williams, Alwyn Terrell Petre (1888–1968), Dean of Christ Church 82

Williams, Charles Walter Stansby (1886–1945), author and scholar 180, 184, 310, 423, 437, 457

Williams, Sir Edgar (Trevor) (1912–), Warden of Rhodes House 725, 742–3

Williams, Eric (Eustace) (1911–81), Prime Minister of Trinidad and Tobago 630

Williams, Ivy (1877–1966), barrister 137

Williams, Nigel (1948–), novelist/playwright 413, 415

Williams, Philip Maynard (1920–84), Fellow of Nuffield College 403–4

Williams, Robert Joseph Paton (1926–), biochemist 259, 265

Williams, Shirley Vivien Teresa Brittain (1930–), Labour, then SDP, then Liberal Democrat politician 403, 592

Willmer, (Edward) Nevill (1902–) Professor of Histology 155

Willoughby, Leonard Ashley (1885–1977), scholar in German 135

Wilmers, Mary-Kay 430

Wilson, Andrew Norman (1950–), author 413, 416, 417, 430, 440
his fiction 432, 436
teaching career 415, 437

Wilson, Sir Angus (Frank Johnstone–) (1913–91), writer and critic 413

Wilson, Frank Percy (1889–1963), Merton Professor of English Literature 479

Wilson, (James) Harold, Baron Wilson of Rievaulx (1916–), Labour prime minister 244, 386, 394, 405, 410, 444
in Second World War 183
undergraduate career 94, 384, 397

Wilson, John Cook (1849–1915), philosopher 137

Wilson, Roger Cowan (1906–91), Professor of Education, Bristol 399

Wilson, Thomas Woodrow (1856–1919), American President 34

Wind, Edgar (1900–71), Professor of the History of Art xviii, 490

Winterson, Jeanette (1959–), novelist 413, 436, 440–1, 448

Wittgenstein, Ludwig Josef Johann (1889–1951), philosopher 461

Witts, Leslie John (1898–1982), Nuffield Professor of Clinical Medicine 328, 334

Wolfe, Humbert [formerly Umberto Wolff] (1886–1940), poet and civil servant 419

Wood, Sir Martin (Francis) (1927–), founder of Oxford Instrument Company 283

Woodcock, George (1904–79), TUC General Secretary 385–6, 411

Woodhouse, Hon. (Christopher) Montague (1917–), Conservative politician 380, 553

Woodroffe, Sir John George (1865–1936), Reader in Indian law 134

Woodruff, (John) Douglas (1897–1978), Catholic journalist 383

Woodward, Sir (Ernest) Llewellyn (1890–1971), historian 87, 136, 623

Woolf, (Adeline) Virginia (1882–1941), author 359, 389

Wooller, William 538

Wordsworth, Dame Elizabeth (1840–1932), Principal of Lady Margaret Hall 346

Worswick, (George) David (Norman) (1916–), economist 556

Worthington, Sir Hubert (1886–1963), architect 503
Besse Building, Pembroke 502
Dolphin Gate, Trinity 509
New College Library xviii, 499, 506
Radcliffe Science Library 478, 506
St Catherine's Society building 504

Wright, Joseph (1855–1930), Corpus Christi Professor of Comparative Philology 473

Wyatt, James (1746–1813), architect 509

Wyatt, Justine (1954–), Chaplain of Mansfield College 296

Wylie, Sir Francis (1865–1952), Secretary of Rhodes Trust 4, 610

Xenophon (431–? BC), Greek historian 134

Yeats, William Butler (1865–1939), Irish poet and playwright 419–20, 421, 421–2

Young, John Zachary (1907–), biologist 150, 154, 155

Zaharoff, Sir Basil (1850–1936), philanthropist and banker 6

Zimmern, Sir Alfred Eckhard (1879–1957), scholar 16, 136, 169, 609, 620, 625, 688

Zuckerman, Solly, Baron (1904–93), anatomist 150

Zulueta, Father Alfonso De (–1980), Catholic chaplain 299

Zweig, Ferdynand (1896–1988), sociologist 248

General Index

Page references in **bold** are the most important references for the heading in which they appear. Place names have been located in the counties as they were before the local government reform of 1974.

Aberdeen, Scotland 453, 601
Abersychan County Grammar School 587
Aberystwyth 589
Abu Shahrain (Eridu), Iraq 133
Academic Assistance Council 173
Academic Press 467
accountants 56, 68–9, 72, 647
acting 383, 444
  in college 94, 203, 367, 420
  in Oxford City 180
  women and 356, 363
  see also Oxford University Dramatic
    Society; individual theatres
Aden 624, 653
The Admiralty 9, 181, 251, 456, 478
admission to Oxford
  Cambridge's rivalry 350, 358, 755
  categories admitted:
    alumni offspring 102, 192, 193–4, 213,
      428, 433, 718
    by region 50–2, 556, 595
    by schooling 52–5: inter-war 94–6, 585;
      1945–70 193, 204, 213, 595; since
      1970 752–6
    by social class 56–8; before 1914 586;
      inter-war 38, 47–8, 94–6; 1945–70
      48–9, 192–5, 595; since 1970 753–5
    ex-servicemen 49, 57
    Indians 6, 97, 609–10, 614, 630, 634
    women 54–5, 352–3
  and the colleges:
    admissions groups 62, 84, 194, 710, 741
    college supremacy over 712, 745, 754
    entrance awards distribute talent
      between 755–6
    head of house's role 83, 84, 193, 199
  criteria:
    A-level performance 599, 728, 750, 752
    academic promise 194, 227–8, 359
    character 193–5
    intellect 91, 194
    sporting prowess 193–4, 520, 529, 530,
      610–11
  examinations:

    criticized 35, 214, 224, 755
    in fiction 448
    how organized 34, 91, **193–4**, 366, 745
    reformed (1963) 64, 194, 227, 700, 710,
      712
  investigations of:
    Chilver (1960) 225
    Dover (1983) 754–5
    Hardie (1962) 194, 724, 754
  meritocratic tendency 64, 71, 193–4, 411,
    599, 605
    Asquith Commission fosters 38
    Franks Commission fosters 727–8
    women's colleges pioneer 352, 366
  pressure to get in:
    modest inter-war 46, 47, 91, 100
    increases in 1940s 188, **192–3**
    intense by 1970 247, 773
  subjects examined:
    classical languages 55
    Greek 29, 37, 110–11, 612
    Latin; restricts inter-war entry 47, 55,
      59, 110, 351; phased out as
      requirement **225**, 233–4, 771
    modern languages 350
  and UCCA 595, 707
  of women 350–1, 584, 727: calibre 62–3,
    366, 750; women's colleges and 62,
    366
  see also Responsions
adult education 556
  see also delegacies; Workers' Educational
    Association
Advanced Studies, Committee for 15
aeronautics 139
'aesthetes' 92, 96, **98–9**, 168
aesthetics 137, 445
Africa 473, 493, 617, 635
  publishing in 457, 464
  study of 623, 624, 691
age of majority 362, 694, 705
Agnelli prize 771
Agricultural Economics Research
    Institute 145–6, 476

Agricultural Engineering Research
    Institute 145, **146**, 690
Agricultural Research Council (ARC) 145,
    149, 261, 262, 275
agriculture 162, 618, 758
    and the colleges 143, 271, 275, 564
    and forestry 264, 277, 758
    becomes honours school 145, 264
    postgraduate numbers 140
    quality of entry 145, 275
    research in 137, 145, **275–6**, 281
    undergraduate numbers **142**, **254**, 275, 276
Agriculture, Board of, *see* ministries
Ahrends, Burton and Koralek, architectural
    practice 511, 518
air raids:
    First World War 12
    Second World War 169, 171, **174–5**, 251
Alberta, Canada 5
Albright and Wilson 144
Alembic Club 151, 157, 268, 356
aliens 173–4, 181–2
All Saints church 191, 481, 517
All Souls College 20, 42, 87, 220, 389, 505
    finances 657, 671, 740
    and Franks Commission 208, 736
    influences:
        appeasement 389, 407
        Commonwealth 389, 615, 630
        publishing 460–1
    outside connections 386, 718
    and St Antony's College 215, 736
    visiting fellowships 215, 736
    see also Codrington Library
All Souls Group 186
Allen and Unwin, publishers 462
alumni 103, 202–3, 208, 423–4
    attitudes to:
        clubs 103
        co-residence 209
        college sport 526–7
        student radicalism 213
    careers:
        election successes 94, 107
        honours 94, 212
        Oxford monitors 94, 212
    college attitudes to:
        pride in 81, 94, 102, 212
        servants recognize 103
        tutors' after-care 93, 102
    fund-raising from 100, 102, 193, 212–3,
        619, 649, 716–7
    marry in chapel 102
    offspring admitted 102, 192, 193–4, 213,
        428, 433, 718
    societies for 102, 212; *see also* Oxford
        Society

and women's colleges 346, 351–2
amalgamated clubs 532
America, United States of 10, 29, 283, 440, 560,
    617
    academic subjects influenced by:
        biochemistry 253, 284
        chemistry 157, 158
        law 516
        mathematics 156;
        medicine 182, 320, 321–5, 330, 332, 341
        metallurgy 272
        modern history 235
        philology 241
        physics 163, 260
        theology 296, 298
    civic universities influenced by 588
    college system imitated by 81, 635
    criticized 223, 229
    DPhil designed for 6, 125, 616
    fund-raising from 360, 619, 717
    influences Oxford:
        laboratory power-structure 266
        libraries 88, 473, **474–5**, 480, 516, **645–6**
        motor manufacture 544–5
        radical protest 704
        religion/theology 296, 298, 301, 305
        research 88, 89, 253, 272, 645
        sport 538
    junior members from 6, 51–2, 209, 347,
        632–3
        postgraduate numbers 126, 418, 616
        Rhodes scholars 610–11, 616
    and OUP 458, 464, 467
    and Oxford Union 383
    refugees to (1940) 174
    research in Oxford on 136–7
    in Second World War 182, **252–3**, 617
    tutors visiting 196, 619
    USA universities:
        contrasts with Oxford 519, 538, 589, 609,
            647, 727
        women at 345, 349, 350
    see also Rockefeller Foundation; Vietnam
American Friends of the Bodleian 480
anaesthetics 328, 339, 341, 648
anatomy, human 14, 262, 271, 329, 341
anatomy, morbid 328, 331
ancient history 132, 221, 232, 238
    Germany influences 609, 620
    in Literae Humaniores 90, 234
Anderson Committee on grants to students
    (1960) 595
Angel Inn, High Street, Oxford 475
Anglo-Iranian Oil Company 282
Anglo-Saxon 239–40, 416, 423, 427, 436–7, 443
Angry Young Men 436
antibiotics 283

apartheid 703
Apollo (formerly New) Theatre 180, 559
appeals:
    for Bodleian Library 477, 765
    by colleges 39, 649, 673, 772: women's
        college xv, xvi, 39, **359–60**, 649
    Historic Buildings 507, 619, **648–9**, 673,
        675, 765
        and Oxford Society 647, 716
        visual impact xiii, 191
    OUP donations to 466, 772
    student radicalism damages 649
    University (1907) 646
    University (1937) 451, 499, **646–8**, 698,
        716, 765
        and Bodleian Library 478
        and social studies 220
    University (1988, 'Campaign for
        Oxford') 647, 649, 763, 765–8
    see also alumni
appeasement, see Munich
Appointments Committee 72, 201, 695,
    716
    origins 70, 93
    inter-war growth 70–1
    women and 71, 77, 355, 373
Arabic 609, 767
archaeology 133, 222, 223, 236, 490
    benefits Ashmolean Museum 486, 491, 493,
        494
    in Lit.Hum. 116, 233
    no first degree in 89, 221, 246
    see also Ashmolean Museum; Egypt;
        Literae Humaniores
Archaeometry 288
Archery Club, St John's College, Oxford xii,
    95
Architects' Co-Partnership 510
Architects Design Partnership 516, 518
architecture:
    cleaned xiii, 191
    college contrasts in 106
    college expansion in 1960s 191
    European influences on Oxford 490–1,
        513–14, 516, 518
    floodlit 560
    height-limits 273, 512, 515, 543
    interior detailing 506, 514
    laboratories 158, 256, 503, 506, **515–16**
        must be adaptable 261, 515
    Oxford lacks school of 518
    quality of Oxford patronage 518, 769
    restored/renovated:
        Bodleian Library 479, 480, 508
        Merton College xviii, 502, 509
        Oriel 508
        Queen's 508

Worcester 508
    and Second World War 171, 507
    styles of Oxford 502–5, 509–16
    traffic's impact on 106
    undergraduates affected by 103, 448, 499
    women's colleges xv, 104, 366, 503, 506,
        507
Oxford's new buildings since 1914
    Balliol College dining hall (plans,
        1937) 505
    Beaver House 453
    Besse Building, Pembroke 502
    Blackwell's bookshop 452
    Blackwell's music shop 512
    Blackwell's Norrington Room 512
    Blue Boar Quad, Christ Church 511
    Brasenose extension (Powell &
        Moya) xviii, 510–11
    Campion Hall xviii, 300, 503, 506
    Christ Church picture gallery 496–7,
        512
    Deneke Building, Lady Margaret
        Hall 504
    Dolphin Gate, Trinity 509
    Dolphin Quad, St John's 509
    Dunn School of Pathology 503
    Dyson Perrins Laboratory 503
    Dyson Perrins lecture-theatre 510
    Florey Building, Queen's 511, 512
    Goodhart Building, University
        College 510
    Grove Building, Merton 502
    Hartland House, St Anne's 506
    History Faculty Library 505
    Keble College quad 511, 515
    Lady Margaret Hall chapel xviii, 506
    Local Examinations Delegacy 507
    Mathematical Institute 507
    Metallurgy Department 510
    Nagel Building 456
    New Bodleian Library 88, 411, **474–5**,
        477, **478**, 505–6, 645–6
    New College library xviii, 499, 504, 506
    nuclear physics department 515
    Nuffield College 325, 503, 648
    Oriental Institute 510
    Parker's bookshop 452
    Pitt Rivers Museum (projected) xix, 516
    Playhouse 504, 559
    President's Lodgings, Corpus 510
    psychology/zoology building 515
    Queen's, Provost's lodgings 509
    Radcliffe Science Library
        extensions 478, 504, 505, 516
    Regent's Park College 504
    Rhodes House xviii, 502–3, 506
    Rose Lane buildings, Merton 504, 506

architecture: Oxford's new buildings since
    1914 (*cont.*):
  Sainsbury Building, Worcester 512
  St Anne's dining hall 507, 655
  St Anne's residential blocks 511
  St Antony's College dining hall xix, 512,
    515
  St Catherine's College (1936) 504
  St Catherine's College (1964) xix, 507,
    513–14, 515
  St Cross Building xix, 481, 516
  St Edmund Hall (projected) tower
    block 512
  St Hilda's Garden Building 512–13, 515
  St John's, 'bee-hive' building xviii, 510
  St John's, Sir Thomas White
    Building xviii, 511
  Somerville front quad 504, 505
  Somerville graduate block 512
  Taylor Institution extension 504
  Trinity College library 504
  virology laboratory 516
  Wolfson College 514, 515
  zoology tower xiv, **278–9**, 515
  see also appeals
aristocrats 91, 227, 298
  as undergraduates 3, 55, 67, 92
  see also landowners
Arlosh Hall, Oxford 209
armed services 67–9, 74–5, 91, 370–1
  see also army
armistice day 25, 81
Armourers and Braziers Company 159
army 56–7, 67, 68, 136, 190, 208
  see also armed services
Arnold Memorial prize 352
art 204, 414, 461, 489
  Bachelor of Fine Art (BFA) degree 414, 758
  history of xviii, 133, 236, 237, 481
  and Lit.Hum. 116
  no first degree 89
  Oxford's indifference to 445, 497, 559–60
  research laboratory on 223, 283–4, **288**
  see also 'aesthetes'; Ashmolean Museum; fine
    arts; Museum of Modern Art; sculpture
Arup Associates 511, 515
Ashmolean Building, Old, Broad Street 149,
    471, 485, 488–9
Ashmolean Club 686
Ashmolean Museum 475, 485, 639
  academic role 149, 487, 490
  chronology:
    before 1914 485–6
    in Second World War 170
    Campaign for Oxford creates posts 767
  collections:
    books 482

Chinese works of art 486, 494, 495, 496
  coins 133, 473, 486, 490
  decorative arts 494–5
  drawings 496
  musical instruments 492, 494–5
  oriental 486, 490, 492, 496
  paintings 494–6
  silver plate 495
  management structure 486–7
  numbers visiting 497, 560
  premises 473, 491–2
Asia 134, 614
Asquith Commission 31, 131, 368
  pre-history 27–30
  terms of reference 35
  origins 30–1
  organization:
    chairman's role 32, 36, 38, 39, **41**
    composition 31–2
    procedure 35–6
    women on 33, 34, 37
  influences on from:
    H.A.L.Fisher 34
    Labour Party 31, 35, 717; admission to
      Oxford **37–9**, 41, 101–2; college
      property 36, 686
    Oxford Reform Committee 35, 586, 641
    religion 33, 34
  attitudes 36–41
    Bodleian Library 477
    college catering 558, 642–3
    college laboratories 156–7
    college/university relations **39–42**, 108,
      641–2
    entitlement to fellowships 714
    faculty centres 88
    finance 663, 677: college costs 35–9;
      college property management 563–4,
      641–2, 658–9, 662, 686
    General Board of the Faculties 37, 43, 687
    Hebdomadal Council 685
    laymen's role 37, 717, 718
    modern languages 613
    private funding 644
    professors 41, 43
    redistribution of college wealth 361
    research 36, 37, 88, 89, 613, 652
    science 31, 37, 41, 43, 88
    state funding 650
    undergraduate representation 688
    university administration 689, 690, 697
    vice-chancellors 685, 690
    women 31, **39**, 350, 359
Statutory Commission **42–3**, 108, 713
  impact:
    on college system 107–8, 156, 641, 652–3,
      659

in other areas 102, 646, 684
  evaluated 41–2
Asquith Commission on higher education in
    the colonies (1943–4) 635
assessors 352
Assistant Registrar 8
Association of Headmasters 35
Association of Headmistresses 35, 350
Association for the Higher Education of
    Women in Oxford (AEW) 346, 348
Association of Scientific Workers 155,
    696
Association of University Teachers
    (AUT) 579, 589–90, 695
Assyrian 109
Assyriology 133, 134, 494
astrography 154
astronomy 153, 156, 271–2
  and the colleges 148, 271
  history of 148, 153
astrophysics 156, 163, 271
Athenaeum 431
athletics, *see* sport
atomic bomb 182, 252
Atomic Energy Research Establishment 259
Australia:
  junior-member numbers from 632–3
  OUP and 464, 467
  Rhodes scholars from 6, 323, 330, 341, 616,
    622–3
  and sport 532, 537
Austria, Oxford links with 3, 6, 106, 221
automation, *see* computers
awards, *see* scholarships and exhibitions

Bach Choir 361, 365, 560
bachelors 199, 528
  holding salons 87, 93
  as junior research fellows 200
  living in college 85, **86**, 91, 103, 197–8, 213
bacteriology 252–3
Bagley Wood, Oxon. 277
Bahamas the 5
Balliol College:
  academic aspects:
    admissions 193, 586, 754
    adult education summer schools 586
    arts/science balance 141
    attitude to research 612
    examination performance 105–6, 213,
      750, 752
    intellectual ambitions 92
    passmen rare 92
    undergraduates without degree 58–9
  appeal (1963) 673
  architecture 505
  criticized 705–6

facilities:
  chamber pots 104
  college servants 93
  expanded accommodation 191
  library 263, 476
  portraits 107
  tea 204
fellows 85
finances 11–12, 653, 657, 662, 671
in First World War xi, 7, 8, 9, 11–12, 22–3
influence:
  on the British left 395–6
  through colonizing fellowships 106, 586
junior members:
  clubs 102
  from overseas 628
  increasingly cosmopolitan 612
  Indians 97
  indiscipline 91
  JCR 205
  politics 106, 205, 705–6
  Rhodes scholars 214
  vendetta with Trinity 100
  women 209–10, 747
in Second World War 170, 178
size 190
traffic's impact 106
youth club 549
Balliol Society 102, 716
Balliol-Trinity Laboratory 40, 88, **157–8**, 263
  closed 157, 260
balls:
  at women's colleges xvi
  commem 97, 204, 647
Balzan prize 771
banalisation de la guerre 10
Banff, Scotland 663
Bangor 589
banking 72, 387–8
  see also Barclays Bank
Baptists 297, 346
Barbados 5, 610
Barclays Bank 325, 534, 717
barges, college 104
Barlow report on scientific manpower
    (1946) 49, 187, 358
Barnett House 242, 561, 562
Barton, Oxon. 547
Bate collection of wind instruments 495
baths 11, 96, 191, 202, 677
battels 100
BCL degree, *see* degrees, postgraduate
beagling 534, 534–5
Bear Lane Gallery, Oxford 489
Beaumont Street, Oxford 557
Beaver House, Hythe Bridge Street,
    Oxford 453

Beckley, Oxon. 421
bed-sitting rooms 38, 104, 190–1, 192, 506,
　　514, 517
Bedel of Arts 685
Belgian Club 7
Belgium 6–7, 633
Belgrade 476
bells 13, 103, 293, 432
Benedictines 298
Beowulf 239
Berkeley, California, U.S.A. 467, 703
Better Books, Charing Cross Road 465
betting 87
Beveridge report 183, 185, 683
Bible 464
biochemistry 271, 276, 320, 481
　accommodation for 261, 503, 515
　funds for 262, 321
　in postgraduate medical school 324, 331
　research in 281, 285
　undergraduate numbers 142, 254
　undergraduate school established 264
　see also careers
biology 150, 163, 279, 601, 758
Birmingham 295
Birmingham University 27, 480, 583, 592,
　　595, 597
　Arup Associates build at 515
　finances 644–5, 678, 682
　physics at 252, 589
　postgraduates in 598
　reputation 600–1, 603
birth-rate 49, 91
Bissets bookshop, Aberdeen 453
Blackfriars, Oxford 298–9, 300
Blackhall Road, Oxford 191, 511
blackouts, wartime 12, 171
Blackwell's:
　bookselling:
　　its history to 1939 451
　　expands after 1945 452, 512
　　forms UBO with OUP 453, 467
　　mail-order business grows 453, 464
　　credit offered 558
　publishing/printing 461, 462, 463–4, 470
　Scientific Publications 463
Bladon (Oxon.) rubble stone 502, 504, 505
Blenheim Palace, Woodstock, Oxon. 378
Bletchley Park 181, 462
BLitt degree, see degrees, postgraduate
blitz 174–5
Bloomsbury 423
Blue Boar Street, Oxford 511
Blue Ribbon Club 393
'blues' 526, 536, 537, 634
　and academic attainment 520–3
　for college servants 103, 529

public-school hold over 535, 538
　for women 530
Board of Agriculture, see ministries
Board of Education, see ministries
Board of Finance 27, 42, 639, 641, 686
Boars Hill, Oxford 93, 378, 420, 421, 422
boat race:
　for college servants 529
　for junior members 531, 534, 535
Bodleian Library 101, 420
　buildings:
　　accommodation expanded 471, 475, 483,
　　　516
　　Clarendon Building acquired 482
　　Indian Institute Building sought 482
　　New Bodleian extension 88, 411, **474–5**,
　　　477, 483, 505–6
　　Nuneham Courtenay bookstack 482
　　Old Ashmolean Building 149, 488–9
　　proscholium becomes main entrance 482
　　renovated 479, 480, 508
　　underground bookstores 472, 474, 482,
　　　507, 516
　and dependent libraries:
　　faculty libraries 712
　　Indian Institute 473
　　Radcliffe Science 153, 473
　　Rhodes House 473
　external influences:
　　other British libraries 480, 482, 695
　　U.S.A. 88, **474–5**, 480, 516. **645–6**
　facilities:
　　catalogue 471, 474, 477, 479, 482, 483
　　exhibitions 472, 479
　　loans to other libraries 481, 695
　　loans to senior members 473
　　research on printing 479
　finances 477, 483
　　appeal 477, 765
　　bequests/donations 477, 479, **645–7**
　　Campaign for Oxford 767
　　purchasing policy 471
　in First World War 472
　holdings:
　　college library deposits 476
　　John Johnson collection xvii, 456, 479
　　non-book material moved out 473, 475,
　　　486
　management problems:
　　burden of history 483–4
　　confusing statistics 483
　　decentralization 471, 472–3
　　delayed automation 482, 484
　　diverse aims 472
　　structure 475–6, 482
　　theft 479
　pressures on from:

increased research emphasis 645
longer opening hours 471, 477
more scholar-visitors 472
mounting stocks 471, 483
postgraduates 480, 483
reader numbers 471, 480
undergraduate demand 472, 479, 480
in Second World War 170, 475, 478
staff:
  conditions 476
  move elsewhere 480
  numbers 480
  professionalize 695
see also Radcliffe Science Library
bookshops in Oxford, 414, 420, 421, 451–5,
  see also Blackwell's
Botanic Garden, Oxford 152, 509, 517
botany 60, 253, 481, 517, 758
accommodation for **152–3**, 256, 259, 261,
  276, 506
and the colleges 148, 197, 271, 276
and related subjects:
  biochemistry 276
  genetics 276
  mathematics 152
  medicine 319
research in **152**, 163, **276–7**
undergraduate numbers reading 142, 254,
  276
Botley Road ice-rink 538
BPhil degree, *see* degrees, postgraduate
Bradford University 601
Brasenose College 83, 86, 189, 199, 287, 421
alumni 212
architecture:
  expanded accommodation 191
  interior decoration 514
  new buildings xviii, 502, 510, 511, 518
examination results 750
finances 654, 657
in First World War 10, 20
junior members:
  clubs 95
  from overseas 628
  gate keys issued 202
  library usage 195, 481
  numbers 190
  politics 205, 408, 528
  sport 106, 194, 520, **527–9**
  women 374, 747
and rural conservation 565
St Hugh's College alliance 210
Brazen Nose 212, 528
Brazil 632–3
breakfast, *see* meals
Breslau 160–1, 163, 589
Brideshead Revisited, *see* Waugh

Bristol University 27, 583, 592, 596
finances 589, 643
and the local community 547, 580
reputation 600–1, 603
British Academy, Fellows of 82, 88, 593
British Broadcasting Corporation 360, 384,
  430
British Council 429, 430
British Dyes Ltd. 139
British Empire Forestry Conference 147
British Guiana 5
British Journal of Haematology 463
British Leyland 545
British Library 481, 695
British Medical Association 325–6
British Motor Corporation 564–5
British Museum 474, 475, 476, 478, 496,
  639
British Ornithological Trust 149
British Oxygen Company 144, 162
British Restaurants 207
British School of Archaeology at Athens 116
British Universities Sports Federation 533,
  533–4
Broad Street, Oxford 565
Broadway, Glos. 7
Brundin committee on continuing education
  policy (1990) 772
Brunt Committee on the Ashmolean Museum
  (1967) 486–7, 490
Buckland and Haywood, architectural
  practice 503
Building Research Station 144
buildings, *see* architecture
Buittle Castle, Galloway 662
Bulkley-Johnson Building, Balliol
  College 191
Bullingdon Club 534
Bullingdon Youth Club 549
bump suppers xii, xiii, 96, 100–1, 202, 528,
  529
Bunce's Hall (Corpus Christi) 103
Bureau of Animal Population xiv, **148–9**,
  163, 278
Burford stone 507
Burnham Committee 71
bursars 85, 93, 190, 395
heads of house as 83, 199
resist centralized property
  management 686, 712
see also domestic bursars' committee;
  estates bursars' committee
bus trips 101
business studies 88, 144, 757, **762–3**
Butterworth, publishers 462
by-election, Oxford City (1938) 168, 381,
  393, **406–7**, 551–2

cabinet, the:
    analogy with Council 685, 692
    ministers 378, 594
Cadena tea-rooms 418, 558
cadets, Second World War 48, 54, 57, 175,
        266
Cairo, Egypt 422, 433
Calcutta 346
The Calendar of Modern Letters 429
California Institute of Technology 163, 589
California, U.S.A. 722
Cambridge City 335
Cambridge Inter-Collegiate Christian
        Union 312
Cambridge University:
    architecture:
        modernist building 505, 509, 511, 512,
            514
        other references 502, 503
    Bridges Syndicate 723–4
    characteristics:
        close public-school links 27, 584
        less political than Oxford 381
        national not local 580
        relative university size 580
        reputation for science 141, 255, 264
        self-recruiting in teaching staff 603
    colleges 40, 81, 97–8, 588, 643, 654; see also
            individual colleges
    extra-mural classes 31
    finance:
        college 31, 643–5, 658, 662
        government funding 30, 39, 651, 654
        Oxford the richer university (1970s) 677
    and First World War 19, 155
    influence:
        literary/cultural 384, 430
        political 389, 607
    library 475, 478, 505, 645
    M.P.s for 381
    museums and galleries 485, 488
    novels on 428
    and outside bodies:
        Asquith Commission 31, 359
        AUT 590
        civic universities 27, 533–4, 580
        Labour Party 35
        Robbins committee 723, 770
    and Oxford:
        Cambridge's ideas appropriated on:
            catering 643; economics 244;
            engineering 273; English 240; mixed
            colleges 374; science 163; tripos
            system 231
        college/university funding 654
        compared: on admissions 350, 755; in
            biochemistry 320; contrasts 89, 347,

        381, 578, 643, 712; on FRSs 262; in
            mathematics 156; similarities 27
    competition in: admissions 350, 358,
        755; college servants' boat-race 529;
        economics 244; modern
        languages 119; physics 160;
        sport 533–6; see also boat race
    mutual consultation extends 578, 587–8,
        654
    Oxford's ideas rejected 239–40, 714
    staff gains from Oxford 311
    staff losses to Oxford in:
        astrophysics 271; biology 278;
        economics 387, 588; engineering 144;
        English 418; medicine 332; modern
        history 224–5; physics 267;
        zoology 278
    studies mutually demarcated 59, 587,
        647–8
    postgraduates at 585, 588
    power structure 27, 31
        college/university power 40–1, 141,
            643–4
        faculty power 39–40
        lay influence 717
        legislative process 27
        senate composition 349
        senate powers 37
    religion at 293, 298, 302
    reputation 537, 600–4, 715, 770–1
    scientists' status at 28, 37, 40, 141, 264, 286,
        600
    and Second World War 172, 183
    state scholarships to 585
    subjects studied:
        biochemistry 320
        engineering 141, 647–8
        Greek 29, 37
        history of science 289
        mathematics 156
        medicine 318, 348
        modern languages 119
        pathology 320
        philosophy of science 289
        theology 296
    undergraduates at:
        careers 384
        social class 607
        student violence (1970) 745
    and women 31, 345, 347, 348, 354, 363
        delayed integration 14, 39, 349
        gender balance 39, 350, 584
        mixed colleges arrive 747
    see also individual colleges
Cambridge University Press 461, 464, 467
Campaign for Democratic Socialism 403
Campaign for Labour Victory 403

Campaign for Nuclear Disarmament
(CND) 368, 401, 402, 407
Campaign for Oxford 647, 649, 763, 765–8
Campion Hall 298, **299–300**, 628
architecture xviii, 300, 503, 506
Canada 5, 174, 178, 440, 464, 538
junior members from 5, 6, 52, 632–3
Canning Club 390, 391
Canterbury, Archbishops of 302
Canterbury cathedral 513
Canterbury Quad, Christ Church 94,
512
carbon dating 288
Carcanet Press 424, 424–5
Cardiff 453, 587
careers:
aids to:
degree result **72–3**, 275
Oxford connection 592–3
Oxford Union 383–4
sporting success 526
student journalism 424–7
curriculum and 115–16
non-vocational aspects 60, 70–1, 90,
147, 218, 612
in family firms 70–71, 91
of German undergraduates 4
guidance on from:
alumni 433–4
heads of house 373
Oxford Society 716
tutors 70–71, 93
see also Appointments Committee:
Second World War's impact on 179, 369
subject-specific in:
agriculture 275
biochemistry 282
chemistry 268, 282
economics 244
engineering 282
metallurgy 282
natural science 60, **69–72**
pathology 282
pharmacology 282
physics 282
undergraduates' individual 66–77:
accountancy 68–9, 72; armed
services 67–9; banking 72, 387–8;
business/industry 66–71; civil service
66–72, 223, 387; colonial/empire 67–70;
estate management 67, 275; forestry 67;
insurance 387–8; journalism 383–4,
424–7; law 66–72, 241; local
government 47, 68–9, 71, 387;
media xvii, 223, **383–4**, **427**;
medicine 66–71; professions 47, **66–76**,
223, 582; publishing 424–31, 457;

religion 66–71, 301, 302;
schoolteaching 66, 68–71, 119; social
work 68–9; university teaching 49–50,
67–76, 429
women undergraduates':
gender contrasts 76
increasing take-up 369
individual: accountancy 74–5; armed
forces/police 370–1; armed
services 74–5;
business/industry 73–6; clerical
work 73–5; clerical/manual 370–1;
commerce/finance 370–1;
government/politics 370–1;
industry 370–1; law 73–6;
literary/media 370–1; local
government 74–5; medicine 73–6,
369; professions **73–7**, 370–1; public
administration 73–6, 370–1;
religion 74–5, 370–1;
schoolteaching 13, 58, **73–6**, 347,
370–1, 530, 585; for scientists 76;
secretarial 370–1; social work 74–5,
370–1; university teaching 74–5
marriage's impact 76–7, 370–2
Oxford's impact on 369–73
poor networking for 372
role-models for 373
Carlton Club, Oxford 390, 391, 393
Carnegie Corporation 149
Carnegie Foundation 619
Carnegie Trust 33
cars, undergraduates' 101
see also Oxford city and region
catering, *see* meals
Cathedral, the 315
Catholics, *see* Roman Catholics
Cavendish Laboratory, Cambridge 160
Central Athletic Committee 532
cephalosporin 268, 283
certificates, school 64
certificates, Oxford 47, 49, 55
chamber pots 104
Chamberlin, Powell and Bon, architectural
practice 515
chancellors:
conduct in office 684–5, 690, 770
elections of 389–90, 394, 700, 719, 770
chapels:
college:
attendance no longer compulsory 201,
315
facilities provided: bells 103;
memorials 22; music 315; weddings
for alumni 102
individual: Campion Hall xviii; Lady
Margaret Hall xviii; Somerville 346

chapels: college (*cont.*):
    and religion outside college: Catholic
        chaplaincy 300–1; OICCU 313; Pusey
        House 303; University Church 315;
        University missions 313–4
    scholars' role in 91
    tourists damage 565
    unifying college 99
    in wartime 709
    presbyterian 97
chaperonage 361–2
chaplains, college:
    in First World War 19
    loss of faith among 437
    and non-collegiate religion 313–4, 315
    as student counsellors 201, 305, 315
    theologians as 85, 309
    women as 296, 305
charges, college 94, 105, 661, **672–4**, 675
Charity Organization Society 548
Charlton, Banbury, Oxon. 378
Charterhouse School 47, 537
Chatham Club 390, 391
Chatham House 170, 178, 182
Chatto and Windus, publishers 430
Cheltenham Ladies' College 347, 351
chemistry:
    accommodation for 258, 267
    chronology:
        in First World War 9, 14–15, 139
        in Second World War 251
        after 1945 260–1
    and the colleges 90, 159, 271
        college laboratories 40, 89, 157
    funding:
        from government 30
        from industry 159, **162**
    and industry
        personal links with 70, 144, 268, 282
        research and 15, 28, 30
        see also Imperial Chemical Industries
    laboratories 40, 89, 157, 281, *see also* Balliol-
        Trinity; Dyson Perrins; Physical
        Chemistry
    outside influences:
        foreign 158, 622
        Manchester 158–9, 163, 589
    and related disciplines:
        medicine 319
        metallurgy 272
    reputation of Oxford 157, 601
    research xii, 40, **156–9**, 163, **268–9**, 270
        Part II course 15, 47, 70, 159, 267, 272
    staffing levels for 267
    undergraduate numbers reading **141–2**, 156,
        254, 267
    see also careers

Cherwell 425–6, 527
Cherwell Edge 347
Cherwell, River 547
Chest, University 534, 696, 717
    Asquith Commission and 37, 43
    autonomy dwindles 686, 692, 693, 698, 708
    and the Owen case 146, 690, **698**
    relations with:
        Board of Finance 641, 686
        Congregation 687, 693
        Council 686, 693, 698, 701
        departments 640, 689
        Registrar 687, 693, **698**, 708
        UGC 642, 690, 700, 707
Chicago, U.S.A. 272, 479, 513
children's literature 439, 457, 465
Chilver Committee on admissions
    (1960) 225–6
China 633
    artistic collections from 486, 494, 495, 496
choirs 315
Christ Church 85, 87, 92, 418, 564, 573
    academic aspects:
        admissions policy 194
        examination performance 213
        laboratory 40, 157
        quite a lot of passmen 92
        theology 308
    architecture:
        cleaned xiii, 507
        expands accommodation 191
        Great Tom 12
        memorial gardens 23, 502
        new buildings 511
        restored 499
    facilities:
        choir 315, 459
        library xiii, 481
        Orrery collection 489
        picture gallery 496–7, 512, 560
    finances 647, 653, 654, 663:
        appeals not mounted 673
        moves into equities (1948) 671
        relative wealth 657–8, 740
    in First World War 8, 9, 10, 20, 23
    influence with:
        Church of England 305, 386, 389
        Congregation 692
        Conservative Party 389
    junior members:
        discipline 100
        from overseas 628
        intimidation among 96, 390
        social-class aspects 94, 106
    politics within:
        Conservative historiography 389
        Oxford Union ambitions 106–7

undergraduate politics 391
and public schools 94–5, 214
in Second World War 170, 189
see also Meadow road
Christ's Hospital 417, 431
chromatography 269
Church Army Press 451
Church of England 302, 306, 386
and the colleges:
  Christ Church 305, 386, 389
  Lady Margaret Hall 55, 346–7
  St Hugh's 55, 346–7
and heads of house 82
high-church tradition 303, 346, 437
and junior members 56, 595
see also chapels, chaplains; evangelicalism
Churchill College, Cambridge 511, 514
Churchill Hospital, Headington 332, 335,
  336, 339
cinemas 93, 97, 101, 180, 203, **560**
see also individual cinemas
civic universities 64, 229, 578–9, 585, 593
administrators form professional
  bodies 695
AUT strongest in 589–90
characteristics:
  becoming a higher-education
    'system' 578–80, 704, 722, 736
  endowments small 589, 595–6
  increasingly similar 604
  less internal recruitment 603
  low inter-war self-esteem 596
  overseas influences on 588
and the new universities (1960s) 598–602
and Oxbridge:
  contrasts with 27, 345, 514, 579–80, 590,
    626
  Oxbridge's strong influence 577, 580–2,
    589, 592, 594, 597–9
  talent unduly concentrated in
    Oxbridge 604–5
and Oxford:
  civic universities criticize 219, 226, 593,
    735–6
  competing with 227
  costs and expenditure compared 679–82
  how civic universities evaluate 600–4,
    736
  librarians from 480
  mounting numbers relative to 577,
    580–2, 598
  Oxford stands apart 587
  sporting links 533–4
  talent exported to 713
  talent imported from 589, 713
student body:
  accommodation for 596–7

arts/science balance 584–5, 626
class background 595
facilities poorer than Oxbridge's 595
industrial background 57
locally recruited 51, 580, 595
numbers at 187, 580–1
postgraduates 585, 598
school background 595
women 345, 363, 584
syllabus:
  adult education 586, 761
  applied science stressed 30, 588–9, 626
see also individual universities
civil service 56, 410
administrative class recruitment 377, 592,
  592–3, 771
civil-service examinations 28, 33, 71, 117,
  387
curriculum and 71, 116, 387, 617
Oxford linkages of 24, 699
pay 72, 386
senior members seconded:
  in Second World War 170–1, 182–3, 221,
    388
  in 1960s 244, 388
see also careers; examinations
Clare Hall, Cambridge 514
Claremont University, California 726
Clarendon Building:
  administrators in 475, 689
  administrators move out 696, 708
  and Bodleian Library 474, 482
  sit-in (1970) at 705, 745
  vice-chancellor moves in 700
Clarendon Hotel, Cornmarket, Oxford 565
Clarendon Laboratory xiv, 259
  new building (1939) 261
  refugees' impact 160
  research at 260, 266
  in Second World War 181–2, 186, **252**
Clarendon Press, see Oxford University Press
  (OUP)
'Clarendon' schools 47
class, see social class
classes, as mode of teaching 131–2, 230, 238,
  263
Classic Press, printers, Oxford 470
Classical Association 288
classical studies:
  admissions impact 57, 59, 110, **225**, 233–4,
    771; see also admission
  Corpus Christi College and 88, 89
  and creative writing 415
  implications for empire 232
  European influences on 233, 461, 609
  examinations, impact on 128, 219
  in First World War 9

classical studies (*cont.*):
   German influences on 233, 461, 609
   heads of house engage in 82
   prestige of 110, 233–4, 287
   within public schools 28, 128
   publishers of 461
   refugees' impact on 233, 461
   and related subjects
      English 114, 121, 122
      philosophy **111–12**, 233
      theology 89, 307
   research in 133–4
   in Responsions 110
   in Second World War 221
   teaching methods 132
   vocational features 232
   women and 350–1
   see also Greek; Latin; Literae Humaniores
clergymen, as Oxford parents 55, 56, 106, 347
climatology 280
climbing in 101, 201–2, 363
clinical pharmacology 342
Clipsham stone, Rutland 502, 507, 507–8
Cliveden, Bucks. 378
clothing, *see* dress
clubs, amalgamated 532
clubs and societies:
   alumni taste for 103
   chance to meet the famous 385, 404, 418–9
   oil Oxford's complex machinery 710, 712
   scientists form 268, 270
   in sport 526
   women join mixed 361–2, 364, 367
   see also colleges; politics; individual societies
Co-operative Union 35
co-residence, *see* mixed colleges
coaches:
   academic 92, 129–30
   rowing 93, 535
   sporting 526
Codrington Library 13, 472, 476, 477
Cole Group 381, **397**, 399
collections 263
college registers 373, 647
colleges of education 761–2
colleges, Oxford:
   academic role:
      collections 263
      collective control over admissions 712,
         745
      inter-collegiate teaching alliances 89, 221,
         710
      narrowing impact on syllabus 612, 710
      Norrington Table preoccupies 520
      protect minority opinion 711
      and research **87–8**, 90, 195, 217, 612, 694,
         713

   specialize by subject 714, 731
   tuition responsibilities 39, 90, **127–32**,
      230
   undergraduate tutorials central to **89–93**,
      126, 247
accommodation for junior members:
   Asquith Commission and 38
   bed-sitters 38, 104, 190–1, 192, 506, 514,
      517
   expands 49, 190, 557, 769
   gradations of 94
   see also lodgings
and alumni 81, 94, 100, 102, **212–3**, 716–7
buildings:
   cost of maintaining 679, 681
   impact made by 103, 499
   see also architecture
characteristics:
   autonomous 189, 199, 215, 641, 710,
      741–2
   competitive 108: in examination
      results 129, 196, 760–1; in sport 106,
      202, 214, **527–30**; for talent at
      admission 194, 748–9, 754; *see also*
      Norrington table
   conscious of seniority 707
   flexible 285
   in loco parentis 362–3
   increasingly uniform 57, 77, 107, 213
   inspire loyalty 98, 106, 212–3, 772
   instinct for survival 709, 714
   intimate 85, 189
   launching-pads for young and old 711
   overseas students' proportion
      varies 628–9
   proud of old members 81, 94, 102
   regional affinities 106
   resilient 107–8, 214–5, 636
   size 93, **190**, 213, 673
   sources of innovation 754, 772
clubs within 203, 367
   dinners of 95, 203
   dons attend 93
   regalia xii, 95, 100
   traditions 99
   women at 95, 210
   see also junior common rooms; senior
      common rooms; individual colleges
contrasts between 105–7, 213–4, 652–5,
   742, 768–9
corporate sense:
   ceremonial 81–2, 99, 100–1
   threatened 47, 101, 108, **214**
divisions within about:
   discipline (1960s) 205
   money 674
   nationality 96–7, 610–11

politics 107
social class 94, 96, 208–9, 441
sport 98–9
facilities:
 general improvement in 105, 677
 relatively comfortable 208
 ale 95
 art collections 497
 baths 11, 96, 191, 202, 677
 bed-making 207
 catering **38–9**, 86, 104, **642–3**: *see also*
  meals
 central heating 191
 chamber pots 104
 coal fires 191, 207
 gardens 506
 gas fires 207
 laboratories 40, 88, 157, 256, 267
 laundering 207
 lavatories 96, 191
 magazines 198, 212, 526–7
 messenger service 708
 plate 82, 171, 193
 prizes 94
 registers 373, 647
 running water 105, 191, 207
 shoe-cleaning 207
 other possessions 171
 see also libraries
governing bodies:
 agenda 199
 head of house's role 734–5
 inter-war mood 85
 laymen on 717
 minutes 84
 size 190, 197, 212
 students invade 205
 undergraduates influence 204, 205, 674,
  688, 705
impact of outside events:
 First World War **11–12**, 20, 108, 663,
  675, 709
 General Strike 82, 83, 85, 100, 390, 528
 Second World War 99, 103, 170, 186,
  189, 675: bombing precautions 171,
  175; co-operation extends 170, 221,
  709
income 656–8
 compared with university 211, 651–2
 university subsidy 481, 654, 694
 alumni 100, 102, 212–3
 appeals 39, 649, 673, 772
 benefactions 82, 507, 644
 bequests 102
 charges 94, 105, 661, **672–4**, 675
 conferences 105, 191, 208, 673, 674, 677
 dividends 660–1, 668, 710

dues 212, 661
endowments 38, 656, 660–1, 675, 678,
 682
estates 36, 547, 564, 656, **658–70**, 671–2,
 675
postgraduate fees 48, 276–7, 674
state 39, **652–3**
tithes 660, 668, 675
tuition fees 643–4, **672–4**, 679–80, 763–4
 see also fees
influence:
 on American universities 81, 635
 through church patronage 302
 on new Commonwealth universities 635
 on political theory 103
 on public schools 99–100
internal structure:
 administration 83–6, 190
 heads of house 82–4
 hierarchies 100, 205
 integrating influences 99–101
 participatory 711
 statutes 42
 see also bursars, deans, senior tutors
and outside bodies:
 Cambridge colleges (alliances with) 588
 central student bodies 205, 688, 693–4
 the city **552–3**, 557
 Conference of Colleges 740–2
 Congregation 687, 692–3, 711, 735
 OUP 466
 Oxford Society 716
 the state 36, **652–3**
 trade unions 103, 688, 696
 UGC 507, 642, 652, 654
 the university: before 1939 27, **39–41**,
  83, 640–1, 684; after 1939 125, 768;
  CUF lecturerships and 89, 90, 190,
  211, **652–4**, 687, 702
 see also National Union of Students
pecking order between:
 academic 92, **105–6**, **213**, 528: *see also*
  Norrington table; pass school
 architectural 106
 fashion 89, 91
 political 106–7
 social 91, 105–6
 sport 102, 106, 213, **527–30**
 wealth 105, **656–7**
postgraduates 89, 126–7, **210–11**, 214, 277,
 674, 729–31
recreations within:
 acting 94, 203, 367, 420
 concerts 93
 discussion groups 99
 drinking 87, 92, 95, 98
 rowing xii, 102, 106, 202, **535**

Colleges, Oxford (*cont.*):
   recreations within *see also* undergraduates
   and science 143, 162, 265, 286:
      Asquith Commission's views 40–1,
         59–60
      awards distribution hinders 59–60, 62, 264
      distinction sometimes ignored 148, 285
      lectures gravitate to science area 263
      mutual distance 197, 211–12, 276–7,
         284–7
      problems for small (often new)
         subjects 148, 212, 271, 276, 713
      and subject-balance within science 90,
         141, 271
      see also 'entitlement problem'
   social alliances between 210, 374
   sport:
      college zeal declines in 1950s 519, 526
      encouraged by 93, 95, 99, 193, 202–3,
         527–8
      helps get a college known 529
      helps integrate college 98
      lavish outdoor facilities for 98, 523–5
      in Second World War 98
      some sports neglected 533
   subjects studied 197, 308
      agriculture 271, 275
      astronomy 271
      biochemistry 271
      botany 148, 197, 271, 276
      chemistry 90, 159, 267–8, 271
      classics 132
      engineering 143, 144, 271, 274
      English literature 89, 197
      entomology 271
      forestry 143, 271
      geography 89
      geology 148, 271, 274
      human anatomy 271
      law 197, 241
      mathematics 156, 269
      medicine 90
      modern languages 61, 89, 119, 132, 197
      pharmacology 271
      physics 90, 269, 271
      physiology 90, 271
      PPP 197
      theology 308
      zoology 90, 148, 197, 271
   threats to 214
      from entitlement 212
      from government funding 654, 673–4
      from living out 192
      from specialization 218
      from the university 211
      from wider subject-spread 197
   wives' role 85, **86**, 92, 197–8, 200, 209, 346

   see also admission; chapels; finance;
      graduate colleges; heads of house;
      junior common rooms; mixed colleges;
      senior common rooms; servants;
      women's colleges; individual colleges
Collins, publishers 458, 462
Colombia 493
Colonial Office, *see* ministries
colonies, *see* Commonwealth
Combined University Fund, *see* CUF
commem balls 97, 204, 647
Committee for Advanced Studies 15, 125,
   126, 702
Committee on Imperial Forestry
   Education 147
Committee of Oxford Heads and Fellows 35
Committee of Vice-Chancellors and
      Principals:
   origins 24, 579
   Oxford and 587–8, 740
   and university funding 650–1
Committee of Younger Cambridge
      Graduates 35
Common University Fund (CUF) 228, 642
   origins 652
   Asquith Commission reforms 642, 652
   fellow/lecturer system introduced
      (1950) 653, 694, 702
   and 1980s cuts 765, 768–9
   and the colleges 89, 90, 190, 211, **652–4**,
      687
   and women 354
Commonwealth:
   All Souls' College's links with 389, 615,
      630
   anti-imperialism in Oxford 401, 620
   civil-service courses in Oxford 617–18, 634
   Communism subverts 634
   and First World War 613
   impact on disciplines:
      agriculture 145, 618
      classical studies 232
      economics 617, 618
      entomology 155
      forestry 147–8, 262, 277, 617, 618
      geography 241, 618
      law 617, 618
      literature 440
      medicine 323, 341, 621
      modern history 235, 611, 618
      modern studies 613–15, 618
      oriental studies 618
      politics 136, 388, 618
      social anthropology 242
   junior members from:
      college distribution 628–9
      lonely 630, 631

numbers **51–2**, 96, 626–30, 632–3
  women 627–30
library for 473
OUP and 464–5
Oxford's influence on 218
research boosted by 616, 618, 621
research in Oxford on 136, 388, 614, 617, 618
and Second World War 617
and sport 538, 634
undergraduate careers in 67–9
universities in:
  Oxford fosters 635, 699
  Oxford staffs 635
  women at 345
see also Ralegh Club; Rhodes scholars; individual countries
Commonwealth Forestry Bureau 277
Commonwealth Forestry Institute, see Imperial Forestry Institute
Commonwealth Fund 343
Communism:
  attacked in 1950s 402
  in the Labour Club 400–3
  and the New Left 401
  and nuclear weapons 407
  persecuted 391
  prospers in 1930s 391
  religion versus 312
  subverts Commonwealth 634
computers:
  and Oxford libraries 482, 483
  philologists don't use 241
  and publishing/printing 459, 470
  and science research 261
computing laboratory 270, 771
computing service 270
Conference of Colleges:
  pre-history 214
  origins 733, 740–2
  role 674
  and 'entitlement' 743
  and tuition fees 763–4
conferences in colleges 105, 191, 208, 673, 674, 677
Congregation:
  Cambridge arrangements compared 27, 31
  characteristics:
    attendance rate 687–8, 692, 693, 702
    direct democracy 687, 703, 733
    House of Commons analogy 687–8, 692
    irresponsible 687–8, 693, 703
    size 687, 702, 703
    unexciting 692
    unpredictable 688, 692, 702
  composition:
    by college 687, 692–3, 711

heads of house 693
  non-fellows 714
  professors 693
  women 14, 348, 358, 685, 693
Curzon reforms 27–8
Franks Commission on 703, 711, 731, 732, 735
and issues:
  B.Ed. degree 762
  'entitlement' 743
  forestry/agriculture school 758
  human sciences degree 732
  loans to students (1989) 771
  Meadow road 702
  mixed colleges 747–8
  modern history syllabus (1939) 124
  overseas student fees 651
  quota for women 357–8, 693
  zoology tower 278–9, 515
postal vote for 687, 692, 732
relations with:
  colleges 687, 692–3, 711, 735
  Convocation 27
  General Board 740
  Hebdomadal Council 685, 687–8, 692, 693, 702, 703, 732
  junior members: junior equivalents proposed 382, 706; right to speak in xix, 771
  University Chest 687, 693
  Vice-Chancellor 732
Congregationalists 295
Coningsby Club 384
conscientious objectors, see conscription
conscription:
  in First World War 3, 16, **17–18**, 25, 396–7
  Oxford Union opposes 407
  in Second World War 60, 167, 168, 169, 175, 176
Conseil Européen pour la Recherche Nucléaire (CERN) 267
conservation:
  of books 479
  rural 563–5
  urban 548, 562
Conservative Party:
  national:
    Cambridge's influence 389
    Christ Church and 389
    Coningsby Club 384
    leaders 377
    Oxford-educated M.P.s 377, 411
    in Second World War 184, 185
    senior-member opinion 395, 402
    undergraduate opinion 394–5
  local:
    on city council 554, 567

Conservative Party: local (*cont.*):
  and Meadow road 394
  success in City seat 381, 551
  see also Oxford University Conservative
    Association; Oxford University M.P.s
  university:
    captures chancellorship 389–90, 394
    centrist tone 391, 404, 411
    chronology: prospers in 1920s 391; splits
      in 1930s 381, 392; on defensive from
      1950s 394; dinners important 390; and
      the Liberals 391, **392**, 405, 409; parental
      influence on undergraduates 595; slow
      to mobilize full strength 392; and
      women 393
contraceptives 204
Contracts of Employment Act (1963) 707
conversation 87, 88, 99, 270, *see also* wit
Convocation:
  Asquith Commission and 37, 43
  chancellorship elections 389–90, 684
  composition 687, 692–3
    laymen 717, 719
    non-residents 27, 37
    women 348
  Franks Commission and 703, 719
  and M.P.s for Oxford University 378
  powers reduced 410, 719, 731
  relations with; Congregation 27;
    Hebdomadal Council 685
Copyright Libraries Conference 480, 695
coronations:
  (1937) 82, 99, 390
  (1953) 411
Corporate Club 391
Corpus Christi College:
  academic aspects: classical studies 88, 89;
    examination performance 105, 213, 750,
    752; intellectual ambitions 92; passmen
    rare 92; protects philosophical
    pragmatism 711
  buildings 502, 510
  characteristics: fends off university 640, 654;
    public-school intake 19; size 213–4
  and Corpus Cambridge 588
  facilities: expanded accommodation 191;
    library 481
  finances 657
  in First World War 9, 19, 20
  junior members: bump suppers xiii, 100–1;
    clubs 95; proportion from
    overseas 628; religion 302;
    urination 95
  in Second World War 189, 220
  other references 82, 210, 697
Corpus Christi College, Cambridge 588
corridors 366, 506, 514, 515

Council, *see* Hebdomadal Council
Council for National Academic Awards
  (CNAA) 761, 762
Council for Social Democracy 403
counselling, student 201, 771, *see also*
  chaplains
country houses 378
Coventry, Warwickshire 510
Cowley 451, 547, 570, 574
  adult education in 556
  critics of 543, 562, 575
  First World War and 10, 544–5
  Labour sympathies in 545, 550–1
  lodgings for students in 557
  motor industry grows up in 544–5, 548
  planners restrict growth 565
  prises town from gown 537
  raises wage-levels 103, 105, 207, 545, 696
  Second World War and 174, 178, 182
  sociologists study 561
  swimming pool 523
  'twin city' concept 562, 658
  University fails to prevent growth 563, 689
  University insulated from 543, 575
Cowley Fathers of the Society of St John the
  Evangelist 303
crèches 373
cricket, *see* sport
Cricketers' Arms, public house, Iffley Road,
  Oxford 558
crime fiction 414, 420, **439–40**, 446
The Criterion 429
Crockford's *Clerical Directory* 302, 457
crystallography 151, 261, 268, 274
Cuddesdon theological college 303, 309
Culham, Oxon. 259, 260, 761
cultural anthropology 485, 490, 493, *see also*
  Pitt Rivers Museum
curriculum, Oxford's:
  chronology: Second World War 223;
    reforming mood of late 1950s 224–6;
    undergraduate reforming pressure
    (1960s) 227, 245–6
  civil service and 71, 116, 387, 617
  criticisms: Anglocentric 218, 237–8, 609;
    college system narrows 612, 710;
    creativity not nourished by 414; non-
    vocational 60, 70–1, 90, 147, 218, 612;
    unspecialized 90, 242–3
  and industry 116
cytology 276, 278
Czechoslovakia 178

Dafydd ap Gwilym Society 97
Dame's Delight 365
dances 98, 101, 361, 367, *see also* balls
deans 84, 201–2, 206, 361

meetings between 88, 214, 361, 710
must live in college 85–6
punishments inflicted by 95, 202
debagging 96, 391, 447
debating societies 99, 390
JCRs as 95, 382
within colleges 203, **382–3**
see also discussion groups; Union Society
debts 558
degree classification 129, 442
careers helped by 72–3, 275
changing pattern of 63–4
fourths abolished 64, 248
gender contrasts 61–2
long-term improved performance 64
passmen and 57
seconds divided 63, 71, 771
degrees, undergraduate:
Bachelor of Fine Art (BFA) 414, 758
BEd 49, 761–2
BM 319, 349
BMus 49, 109, 118
combined-subject 88, 90, 228, 238, 264,
274, 289
fees for 11
multi-subject increasing 756–7
switching between 227, 228
uncompleted **58–9**, 101
see also war degrees
degrees, postgraduate:
more of them 49–50
reputation of 730–1, 760, 774
role in academic career 90
BCL 241, 349
BD 109, 306, 349
BLitt
in English 126–7, 416, 442
introduced 124
numbers taking 109, 124
re-titled MLitt 759
relation to DPhil 125–6
supervision for 124–7, 442
BPhil
introduced 49, 222
re-named M.Phil. 759
succeeds 225, 243
in economics 222
in philosophy 222, 759
in sociology 245
BSc becomes MSc 759
DD 109, 306, 349
DLitt 109, 125, 444
DMus 109
DPhil
Americans, designed for 6, 125, 616
Americans take 52, 621
Commonwealth students for 621

criticized 152, 218, 223
introduced 15, 52, 89, 125
numbers taking 47, 72, 126, 480
qualification for 125
relation to BLitt 125, 126
reputation of 760
subjects studied for: agriculture 140;
chemistry 158; medicine 140;
science 140–1; social studies 140
supervision for 125–6
MA 102, 212, 442, 759
MEng 758
MLitt replaces BLitt 759
MPhil replaces BPhil 759
MSc 759, 761
MStud 759
see also certificates; diplomas; postgraduates
degrees, honorary:
and fund-raising 644
recipients (or not)
Germans (1914) 3, 5
Queen Mary (1921) xv, 360
allies in Second World War 178
Mrs.Thatcher (1985) 765, 772
delegacies:
Extra-mural Studies 385, 635, 744, **761**
Local Examinations 507, 509, 640
Military Instruction 8
Women Students 348
Democratic Labour Club 403
Denmark 158, 513, 517, 633
Dent, publishers 458
Department of Education and Science, see
ministries
Department of Scientific and Industrial
Research (DSIR) 24, 28, 162
departmental committees 265–6
departments, Oxford, see under individual
subjects
Development Commission 145
Devonshire Committee 617–18
dictionaries xviii, **133–4**, 435, 436, 459
Dictionary of National Biography 82, 133,
409, 459, 478
dinner, see meals
diplomas:
career implications 70–1
local government and 71
MSc replaces some 759
numbers taking 47
overseas students and 4, 7, 47
social class of those taking 55
subjects of:
archaeology 222
biology 71
economics and political science 4, 7, 47,
109, 112

diplomas: subjects of (*cont.*):
  education 47
  geography 109, 117
  social anthropology 109, 222
discipline, *see* deans; proctors;
  undergraduates
discussion groups 99
divinity, *see* theology
divorce 92
'divvers' 110, 111, 315, 351
DLitt degree, *see* degrees, postgraduate
doctors 56, *see also* individual hospitals;
  medicine
Dolphin Bookshop, Fyfield Road 452
domestic bursars' committee 643, 710
dons, *see* Fellows
DPhil degree, *see* degrees, postgraduate
Drama Commission (1945) 444
Drapers, Worshipful Company of 491
dress:
  college regalia 100
  college rules on 101
  for dinner 206
  for examinations xv
  senior members' 198
  undergraduates':
    inter-war xi, 94
    in 1950s xiii, xviii, 205
    regulations relaxed in 1960s 201, 205
    for clubs 95, 203
    in Oxford Union 400, 405
    public school 208–9
    scouts' attitudes 104
    for sport xi, 94
  women undergraduates' xv, xvi, xvii,
    363–5, 369
drinking 87, 92, 95, 98, *see also* public houses
drugs 770
Dundee University 583
Dunn, Sir William, trustees 34, 320
Dunn School of Pathology, *see* pathology
Durham University 601, 643, 726
dyes 15, 139
Dyson Perrins Laboratory 15, 37, 481, 503,
  619
  organic chemistry research in 157, 267, 268

Eagle and Child, public house, Oxford 423
Eagle Ironworks, Oxford 567
earth sciences, *see* geology
East Anglia, University of 420, 583, 597, 601,
  682
Eastgate, public house, Oxford 423
ecology 148–9, 152, **154–5**, 276, 278, 622
economic history 236
Economic Section 388, 410
economics 120–1, 128, 481, 556

BPhil in 222
chronology of:
  inter-war empiricism 241
  in Second World War 183–4, 388
  expands after 1945 222
  refugees fertilize 173–4, 185
  new careers in, from 1950s 244, 249
  non-Thatcherite after 1960s 395
Commonwealth connections 617, 618
Oxford's governmental priorities 387–8
no first degree in 109, 244
and related subjects:
  business studies 757, 762–3
  engineering 244, **254**, 264, 274, 757
  mathematics 120, 123
  modern history 123, 124
  philosophy 112
  statistics 120
Oxford's reputation 600, 601
research in Oxford on 137
economics, agricultural, *see* agriculture
economics and political science, diploma in 4,
  7, 47, 109, 112
Economists' Research Group 387, 388
ecumenism 296, 306, 311, 346
Edinburgh University 600–1
education:
  certificates 47
  diplomas 47, 49
  see also secondary schools; schoolteaching
Education Acts:
  (1902) 27, 46
  (1918) 29
  (1944) 49, 71, **186**, 188
  (1986, No.2) 746
  (1988) 768, 770
Education, Department of, Oxford 210,
  761–2
Edward Grey Institute of Field
  Ornithology 149, 162, 278
Egypt 133, 473, 491–2, 494
Eights Week xii, 97, 104
  debates 299, 383
Eire 406, 633
elections:
  general:
    alumni successes in 94
    bets on 87
    study of 389
  local, university supports Labour 550–1
  see also by-elections; politics
Electra Cinema, Queen Street 180
Elsevier, publishers 461, 463, 467
Elsfield, Oxon. 421, 423
embryology 154
empire, *see* Commonwealth
Employment Protection Act (1974) 707

Encaenia 707
Encounter 430
Encyclopaedia Brittanica 461
'endowed' schools 47
endowments:
    college contrasts in 656
    and college scholarships 38
    as component of college income 660–1
    and First World War 24
    inter-university comparison 678–82
    long-term trends in college 675
    see also finance
engineering:
    accommodation for 256, 258–9, 261, 515,
        566
    at Cambridge 141
    chronology:
        Nuffield funds diverted from 647–8
        inter-war research output 144, 163
        in Second World War 251
        expands in 1950s 273, 282–3
        grows in 1980s 766
        four-year course from 1991 758
    and the colleges 143, 144, 271, 274
    hostility to 144
    industrial contacts 144, 274, 283, 284
    library for 481
    quality of intake 144
    and related subjects:
        economics 244, **254**, 264, 274, 757
        management 757, 763
        mathematics 274
        physics 260, 274
    reputation of Oxford 601
    undergraduate numbers reading **142**, 144,
        254, 274
English Club 419, 427
English Faculty Board 121, 353
English Heritage 649
English literature, Oxford's course 41, 415
    and adjacent subjects:
        classical languages 114, 121, 122
        modern history 122
        modern languages 114, 121, 122
    and Anglo-Saxon 239–40, 416, 423, 427,
        436–7, 443
    BLitt degree 126–7, 416, 442
    characteristics:
        anti-modernist 438, 444
        anti-pretension 438–9
        patriotic/chauvinist 437
        philological emphasis 114, 121–2, 218,
            239–40, 245, 436, 437
        religious influences 180, 184, 310, 437
        role of criticism 239–40
        taste for light verse 439
    examinations:

    first public 121, 122
    second public 129, 239
    Oxford authors' results 442
    hostility to degree in 89
    influence on:
        children's fiction 439
        creative writing 414–38, 443–4
        crime fiction 439–40
        publishing 424–7, 458, 459, 461, 470
        reviewing 429
    library for 476, 481, 516
    numbers reading 110, **142**, 197, 240
    reputation 601
    and Second World War 223
    syllabus 109, **114**, **121–2**, **239–40**, 245, 246,
        436–7
    teaching methods 133, 439, 643
    women reading 61, 89, 110, 116, 359
Eno's Salt 87
enteric fever 14
'entitlement problem' 761, 773
    of professors solved in 1920s 713
    science area first accumulates 695
    early attempts to solve 211, 215, 655
    Cambridge (ghetto-college) solution
        rejected 714
    solved 742–4
    anti-science influences on 286, 714
    college system threatened by 212, 285, 714
    harms Oxford's image 715
    reports on 724
    small science subjects harmed most 271,
        285, 713
Entomological Society 155
entomology:
    and the colleges 271
    and forestry 147, 154–5
    funding 162
    museum collections 487, 492
    research in 150
Enzyme Group 257, 259, 268, 284
Eragny Press 495
ergometrine 328
essays, *see* tutorials
Essays in Criticism 240
Essex University 480, 583, 597, 601
Esso 514
estates bursars' committee 88, 214, 653, 659,
        675, 710
    excludes women 356
Eton College 47, 461, 535
    alumni at Oxford 99, 299, 431
    classical studies at 128
    college affinities 95, 586
Europe 6, 222, 345
    books on 473
    First World War and links with 6, 613, 621

Europe (*cont.*):
　impact in Oxford on:
　　aesthetic ideas 445
　　architecture 490–1, 513–14, 516, 518
　　art collections 494–6
　　chemistry 158
　　classical studies 233, 461, 609
　　films 560
　　legal studies 137
　　medicine 341
　　modern history 136, 235–7, 609, 624
　　music 3
　　philosophy 90, 609, 620
　　physics 160, 163, 252, 589, 609, 622
　　publishing 467
　　student politics 390, 397
　　theology 296, 298, 609
　junior-member numbers from 51, 632–3
　Second World War and links with 623, 626
　see also individual countries; modern
　　　languages; refugees; St Antony's College
'European Greats' 222, 227, 228
European University, Florence 480
evacuees (1940):
　from Oxford 174
　to Oxford 170, 171, 177
evangelicalism 303–5, *see also* St Peter's
　　College
Everyman's Library 458
Examination Schools 278, 475
　books in 471, 474
　in First World War 10
　in Second World War 170
　occupied (1973) 745
examinations:
　boycotted 16
　centralized in Oxford 88, 92
　civil service 28, 33, 71, 117, 387
　classics as influence on 128, 219
　college collections 263
　dress for xv
　entrance, *see* admission to Oxford
　fees 13–14
　first public 90, 132
　　Cambridge ideas influence 231
　　chemistry 273, 758
　　engineering 269, 273, 274
　　English 121, 122
　　geology 758
　　law 57, 111, 117
　　mathematics 269, 273, 287
　　medicine 319
　　metallurgy 273, 758
　　modern history 117, 122–4
　　music 118
　　physical sciences 758
　　physics 269, 273, 274, 758

　　in science 264
　　in First World War 12
　　improving performance 751–2, 773
　　not taken **58–9**, 92, 101, 442
　　school impact on performance 728, 753
　　second public 129
　　　English 129, 442
　　　modern history 13
　　women and xv, 76, 348, 350
　　see also admission; coaches; degree
　　　　classification; degrees; examiners; pass
　　　　moderations; war degrees
examiners:
　external 751
　women as 349, 353
excavations 133
Exeter College 85, 567
　accommodation expanded 191
　Bodleian extension in 474
　and coronation (1937) 99
　spurns council of colleges 741
　finances 657
　in First World War 20
　junior members:
　　clubs 99
　　proportion from overseas 628
　　urinating 95
　rectors 84
　in Second World War 170
　social anthropology and 88, 711
　theology and 308
Exeter University 583, 600
exhibitions:
　of art 559–60
　in Bodleian Library 472, 479
exhibitions, entrance, *see* scholarships
extra-mural classes 28, 33, 38, 586
　Cambridge and 31
　summer schools 586, 761
　see also delegacies; Ruskin College;
　　　Workers' Educational Association

Faber and Faber, publishers 417, 430, 460–1,
　　462, 468
Fabian Society (Oxford branch) 361, 385,
　　395–6, 398, 399
faculties
　and General Board 686–7
　growing influence 218
　Oxford/Cambridge contrasts 643–4
　undergraduate influence within 227, **237–9**,
　　245, 706
　weak in Oxford 217
　see also General Board of the Faculties;
　　　individual subjects
faculty boards:

and General Board 269, 640, 686–7, 707,
    732–3
and professors 735
women on 349, 353
faculty centres 760
    Asquith Commission and 88
    Franks Commission and 230, 729, 731
    and General Board 640, 702
    see also libraries
faculty libraries, see libraries
faculty meetings 687
Family Reform Act (1969) 202
Fantasy Press 424, 426
Faringdon, Berks. 93
farming 13, 564, 658, 662, 664–8
Fascism 391, 403, 406, 620
Federation of Conservative and Unionist
    Associations 393
fees:
    degree 11
    examination 13–14
    matriculation 11
    for overseas students 52, 651, 678
    for postgraduates 276–7
    for scientists 59
    tuition 643–4, **672–4**, 679–80, 763–4
    for women 349, 366
Fellows of colleges:
    activities:
        betting 87
        book collecting 482
        commissioning artists 497
        drinking xi, 198
        eating 198: see also meals
        entertaining junior members 200
        holding college offices 711
        managing estates 659
        managing investments 668–9, 710
        policy-making over meals 86, 710, 712,
            734
        doing research (or not) **87–8**, 198, 603, 612
        resigning 92, 437
        sitting in committees 710–12, 734
        upholding discipline 100–1: see also
            deans
        walking 563, 697
        watching sport 93, 102, 520, 528
    characteristics:
        age 9, 86
        eccentric 88, 103, 219, 280, 479
        individualist 86, 219
        often unmarried 85, 86, 528
        place of residence 86, 567
        political views 389, 394, 395, 402, 404
        sarcastic 100
        schooling 604
        self-image as self-employed 590, 695

social class 100, 603–4, 694
    wary of planning 711
    work-pattern 90
conditions of employment:
    college contrasts 105, 214
    entertainment allowances 200
    overseas leave 90
    pay 11–12, 36, 103, 386, 652
    pensions 36
    retirement age 86
    sabbatical leave 88, 196
    in First World War 8, 9, 11–12
    how appointed 85, 90, 106, **195–6**, 211
        from within Oxford 85, 141, 603
    numbers 190, 722
    relationships with:
        colleagues 85, 197
        head of house 83–4, 199
research:
    Asquith Commission and 36, 37, **87–8**,
        90
    inter-war 85, **132–8**, 162–3
    since 1945 198, 603
    in Second World War 170–1, 181–4
types of:
    junior research 200, 212
    life 86
    visiting 215, 736
university posts for 40–1, 85
wives of 85, **86**, 92, 197–8, 200, 209, 346
see also life fellows; senior common rooms;
    tutorials; tutors
feminism, Cambridge attitudes 39
feminism, Oxford attitudes:
    anti-feminism before 1914 28, 348
    First World War's impact 14, 348
    women's full admission 14, 31, 34
    inter-war anti-feminism 348, **356–8**
    Second World War's impact 14
    anti-feminism in 1950s 353–4, 355, 356,
        360–1
    Oxford Union's anti-feminism 384, 718
    see also women
fertilizers 152
fever, enteric 14
Fields medal 771
Film Society 560
finance:
    college:
        accounts format 656, 662, 675, 678:
            attempted reform (1915–17) 640–1;
            and Franks Commission 643, 671, 733
        centralized management resisted 641,
            686, 712
        chronology: First World War 24, 663,
            675; Asquith Commission 36, 39,
            563–4; Second World War 170, 675;

finance: college: chronology (*cont.*):
    collaborative investment (OXCUT)
        fails 671, 772; fees conformity advances
        (1970s) 673; long-term expenditure
        trends 675–7
    cost of living **38–9**, 41, 47, 91, 673,
        675
    inter-college contrasts 105, 653, **656–7**,
        673, 768–9
    investment constraints 668–70, 710
    and rates 552–3
    redistribution of wealth between: helps
        women's colleges 361; through CUF
        system 652–6; through graduated self-
        taxing 31, 675, 709, 740, 765
    UGC aloof from 507, 642, 652, 654
    and university: colleges assist 639, 641–2,
        656, 675; colleges get building
        loans 653–5; colleges subsidized
        by 481, 654, 694
    see also appeals; colleges, income
university:
    chronology: First World War 11–12, 24,
        677; Asquith Commission 35–9, 43,
        563–4, **641–2**; Cambridge outpaced in
        1970s 677; cuts in 1980s 656, 674,
        677–8, **759**, **764–8**; research-grant
        income rises in 1980s 677, 682, 765;
        long-term trends 677–82
    inter-university comparison 678
    internal administration: attempt (1913–15)
        to control departments 639–40; Owen
        case **146**, 640; colleges in relative
        decline 211; administrative overload in
        1950s 700, 707; colleges recover 656;
        departmental autonomy persists 640,
        689; OUP finances 466, 476, 772; UGC
        wants procedures standardized 690
    private funding: inter-war
        benefactions 644–5; wanes after
        1930s 717; student radicalism
        harms 649; grows fast in 1980s 764–8
    state funds: beginning 30; Asquith
        Commission confirms 37, 39, **641–2**;
        UGC inter-war subventions 642;
        generous in mid-1940s 222, 650;
        growing fast in 1950s and 1960s 677;
        slows down in 1970s and 1980s 677,
        759; ease inter-war college/university
        relations 642; for overseas
        students 651; *see also* University Grants
        Committee
    see also appeals; Chest; endowments;
        University Finance Board
fine arts, *see* art
Finstock, Oxon. 421
fire brigades 528–9

Fitzwilliam College, Cambridge 38, 514
Fitzwilliam Museum, Cambridge 485
Fleet Street, *see* journalism
food, *see* meals
football, *see* sport
Football Association 537
Ford Foundation 507, 619, 649, 742
Ford lectures 221
Foreign Office, *see* ministries
forensic medicine 324
forestry:
    academic status of 147, 264
    accommodation for 261
    chronology:
        arrives in Oxford 147
        becomes honours school 147
        joins agriculture in combined school
            (1971) 758
        phased out as undergraduate school
            (from 1982) 758
    funding 162
    quality of entry 57, **147**, 277
    and related subjects:
        agriculture 264, 277, 758
        entomology 147, 154–5
    relations with:
        colleges 143, 271
        Commonwealth 147–8, 262, 277, 617,
            618
    undergraduate numbers reading 142, 254,
        277
    see also Imperial Forestry Institute
Forestry Commission 147, 162
The Fornicator 98
Forum Restaurant 209
four-minute mile xix, 537
fox-hunting 534
France 722, 774
    Besse wants Oxford students from 624,
        653
    films from 560
    First World War and links with 613
    gives applied science more status 589
    and historical study 236, 624
    junior members from 633
    paintings collected from 494–5
    polytechnics influence British
        curriculum 588
    its universities contrast with Oxford
        727
    see also Maison Française; St Antony's
        College
Franciscans 298
Franks Commission xix, 34, 682
    pre-history 186, 222, 227–8, 721–3
    set up 701, 724
    methods of inquiry 724–5

evidence surveyed 228–9
individual submissions:
  M.Atiyah 263
  C.M.Bowra 193, 203, 355, 701, 703, 713
  civil service commissioners 377
  C.D.Darlington 276–7
  economics sub-faculty 730
  English faculty 240
  H.Gardner 355
  Lord Heyworth 725
  junior members 201, 202, 704, 705, 726,
    730
  NUS 192, 200, 214
  Oxford City Council 553, 562, 568
  L.Robbins 725
  M.Shock 357
  TUC 385
  UGC 725
  Janet Vaughan 355
  K.C.Wheare 700–1
  women's colleges 368
topics discussed:
  admission arrangements 672, 727–8, 754
  applied science research 284
  arts/science balance 230, 729
  college accounts 643, 671, 733
  college subject-specialization 714, 731
  college/university relations 215, 652–3,
    715, **728–9**
  Congregation 703, 711, 731, 732, 735
  Convocation 410, 703, 719, 731
  council of colleges 214, 643, 700–1, 710,
    715, 733–4, **740–2**
  departmental committees 265
  domestic bursars' committee 643
  faculty centres 230, 729
  General Board 732–3, 740
  Hebdomadal Council 701, 708, 732
  humanities research 230–1, 355
  lay participation 717
  postgraduate study 229, 230, 231, 729–31
  professors' role 735
  public accountability 604, 727
  redistributing college wealth 361, 652,
    655, 729–30, 733, 740
  reputation of Oxford 715
  Robbins report 229
  senior members' work-load 229
  size and shape of Oxford 729
  tutorials 196, 229, 230, 758–9
  undergraduate representation 704
  University Chest 708
  university government 713
  University Press 466–7
  vice-chancellorship 199, 732, 734, 739,
    740
  women's admission 374, 726, 746

legislation on the report 731–4, 739
impact on:
  college finances 656
  libraries 481
  postgraduate education 731
  private fund-raising 649
  reputation of Oxford 715
  research and teaching 231, 758
  university government 732–3
assessed: assumes state funding 651
  illuminates Oxford's workings 726
  mixed-colleges issue sidelined 726
  political climate moulds outcome 736
  postgraduate problems not solved 231–2,
    730–1
  pursues irreconcileable aims 231–2
  structural remedies imprecise 726, 731
  student participation neglected 726
  wards off outside inquiry 723, 725
  works with the grain 708–9, 719, 723
free churches, see Mansfield College;
    nonconformists; Regent's Park College
French language:
  chair established in 6
  in the English syllabus 114, 122
  numbers studying 119
  reputation of Oxford in 601
  research in 134–5
  syllabus criticized 240
freshers:
  arrival at college 96, 104, 208
  'blind' 95
  boarding school prepares for Oxford 101,
    208
  recruited for sport 96
freshmen, see freshers
Friends of the Bodleian 480, 639
Friends of the Old Ashmolean 149
friendships 92, 95, 403–4 see also
    undergraduates
Frilford, Berks. 101
The Fritillary 367
fuel shortages 12
Fulton Committee on the civil service (1966–8)
    386, 410
furniture:
  architect-designed 514
  damaged in war 10
  in JCRs 96
  in SCRs 86
  vandalized 34, 96
Further Education and Training Scheme 48–9,
    57, 186
Garden House Hotel, Cambridge 742
gardeners 103
gardens:
  commemorative 23, 502

gardens (*cont.*):
    food from 104
    genetic 517
    Botanic 152, 509, 517
    Rhodes House 506
    St Catherine's 513–14, 517
    St Hugh's 506
    St John's 106
    Wolfson 517
    Worcester 506
Garsington, Oxon. 93, 378, 423
gas masks 253
gas warfare 9, 14–15, 16
gaudies 102, 193, **212**, 717
General Board of the Faculties:
    Asquith Commission and 37, 43, 687
    attitudes to:
        'entitlement' 742
        postgraduate degrees 127
        preliminary examinations 121, 124
    characteristics:
        fragmented 687, 692, 702
        initiatives taken elsewhere 702
        slow to gain status 687, 702, 708
    committees:
        advanced studies 15, 125, 126, 702
        articulating undergraduate views 706
        teacher education 761–2
    composition:
        reformed (1967) 740
        scientists 284, 692, 740
        women 353
    Franks Commission and 732–3, 740
    relations with:
        Congregation 740
        Council 687, 692, 702
        extra-mural studies 761
        faculty boards 269, 640, 686–7, 702, 707,
            732–3
        Registrar 692
        science professors 265
    vice-chairman's influence extends 702,
        740
general elections, *see* elections; politics
General Electric Company 283
General Medical Council 319
General Strike 432
    and colleges 83, 85, 100, 390, 528
    A.D.Lindsay in 396
    and Oxford socialism 397
    strike-breaking in 100, 391, 528
    and University College 82, 83
'generation gap' 694
genetics 276, 622
'gentlemen':
    as classification 55
    offspring of at Oxford 55, 57

undergraduates' destination as 68–9
geochemistry 275
geography:
    chronology:
        no first degree in 109
        diploma 109, 117
        first degree launched 117
        Second World War 253
        in the human sciences degree 279
    and the colleges 89
    Commonwealth impact on 241, 618
    library provision for 476, 478, 482
    reputation of Oxford 601
    research in 135
    and science 117
    syllabus criticized 241, 280
    undergraduate numbers reading 142, 254,
        280, 625–6
geology xiv, 758, 766
    and the colleges 148, 271, 274
    and mineralogy 274
    museum collections 487
    reputation of Oxford 601
    research in 150–1, 274–5
    undergraduate numbers reading **142**, 150,
        254, 274
    and University Museum 490
geomorphology 280
geriatrics 342
German language 119, 135
Germany 722, 774
    academic influence on:
        ancient history 609, 620
        chemistry 158
        classics 233, 461, 609
        physics 160, 163, 252, 589, 609
        theology 296, 298, 309
    academic rivalry with 6, 30, 125
    atrocities by 16
    bookselling in 452
    and college system 81, 108
    economic rivalry with 28, 588
    honorary degrees for 3, 5
    hostility to 6, 16, 174, 286
    its universities contrast with Oxford 609,
        727
    junior members from 632–3; Rhodes
        scholars 3, 4, 5, 6, 102, 610
    reconciliation with (1920) 6, 406
    and science 284, 589
    war casualties of 5, 21, 22–3
    see also refugees
Gerrans Mathematical Library 263
Gibson Laboratories 339
Gillespie, Kidd and Coia, architectural
    practice 512
Girton College, Cambridge 345, 349, 374

Glasgow University 600–1
Godfrey's bookshop, York 453
Goldsmiths' Company 149
Gollancz, publishers 462
Goodenough Committee on medical schools
(1942–4) 333–4, 339
Gordon Warren research fund 159–60
Gordonstoun School 653
Gordouli song 100
gowns, see dress
grace 91, 103, 205, 293
graduate colleges:
accommodation at 514, 760
and 'entitlement' 211, 714
foster the research idea 624–5
late start 89
postgraduates prefer 210
proliferate from 1960s 211, 215, 760
success of 214–5, 760
see also also individual colleges
graduate common rooms, see middle common
rooms
graduates, see alumni; postgraduates
grammar schools, see schools
grammar-schoolboys at Oxford:
how funded 47–8
persecuted 96
political views 96, 398
and sport 98, 537
as war cadets 54
work-pattern 92
gramophones 101
Grandpont House, Oxford 300
Grant Richards, publishers 457
Great Tom 12
'Greats', see Literae Humaniores
Greece 632–3, 745
Greek culture, research in 133
Greek language:
at Cambridge 29, 37
in degree courses:
English 114, 122
theology 306, 307
dictionaries 478
in examinations:
admissions 612
'divvers' 110
pass mods 111
Responsions 29, 37, 110, 351
Mods for the Greekless introduced
757
research in 133–5
schools hostile to 111
women and 350
see also classical studies
Greek Defence Committee 111, 112
Green College 517, 760

Grensted Committee on University Museum
(1952) 487–8
Greyfriars 298, 628
Gridiron Club 527
Griffith Institute 133, 491–2
Guild Socialism 16, 396, 404
Gulbenkian Foundation 223
Gunner's (Magdalen) 103
gymnasium 526, 533
gynaecology 324, 328, 331

Habakkuk Committee on extra-mural studies
(1970) 761
Hadow report on local government officers
(1934) 47
Halifax House 285
halls, private 20
Hamish Hamilton, publishers 462
Hammersmith, London 689
W.A. Handley Trust 342
Harmondsworth, Middx. 467
Harrow School 47, 97
Hart Committee on relations with junior
members (1969) 403, 706, 726, **744–5**
Hartley Seed, Sheffield bookshop 453
Harvard University 81, 163, 726, 729
harvester, combine 146
Harvester Press 468
Harwell, Berks. 259, 267
Hastings scholarships 106
The Hávamál 134
Haverfield, Francis John (1860–1919),
archaeologist 135
Headington, Oxford:
becomes suburb 545
freestone from 507
hospitals at 332, **335–40**
Labour support in 545, 550
literary associations 420, 437
lodgings for students in 557
South Park bought 563
headmasters 35, 82
Headmasters' Conference 35, 47, 111, 119, 585
heads of house:
attempts to oust 83
characteristics: academic background 28,
82; administrative ability 83–4, 199;
age 82; lay/academic 717; marital
state 199; religion 82; schooling 82;
symbolize the college 83, 199
competition to become 85
lodgings: dwindle in size between the
wars 84, 191, 199; Corpus Christi
College (1957–9) 510; Lincoln College
(1929–30) 504; New College inter-
war 82–3; Queen's College
(1958) 509; Worcester College 506

heads of house (*cont.*):
  meetings between 709–10
  Munich (1938) divides 168
  paintings of 497
  pay 361, 655
  power declining 84, 199
  roles: diminishingly diverse 107;
    admissions 83, 84, 193, 199;
    bursarial 83, 199; career-
    guidance 373; Congregation 693;
    Council 37, 82, 685, 686, 735;
    entertaining 82–3, 200; fostering
    sport 102; fund-raising 199; vice-
    chancellor 82, 199, 684, 690; within
    SCR 198
  selection process 717
  see also women dons
Hebdomadal Council:
  Asquith Commission and 43
  characteristics:
    area of concern 701
    centrist outlook 745, 747
    limited scope for initiative 640
    mounting influence (since 1914) 683,
      692, 701, 732
    mounting paperwork 707
    not like the cabinet 685, 692
  committees of:
    building and development 701
    medical advisory 334
    representing undergraduate views 706
    teacher education 761–2
  composition: college representation 685
    elections to 37
    heads of house 37, 82, 685, 686, 735
    proctors 685
    professors 37, 685, 686
    scientists 284
    women 353, 355, 358
  Franks Commission on 701, 708, 732
  and mixed colleges 747
  relations with:
    chancellor 685
    Congregation 685, 687–8, 692, 693, 702,
      703, 732
    Convocation 685
    General Board 687, 701–2
    Registrar 698–9, 709
    University Chest 686, 693, 698, 701
    vice-chancellor 685
    size 685, 692
Heberden coin room 486, 490
Hebrew 301, 305, 306, 307, 472, 771
Heinemann, publishers 462
Henley, Oxon. 534, 535
Heriot-Watt University, Edinburgh 583
The Heritage 360

Hertford College:
  administration 199
  buildings 517
  examination performance 213, 749
  finances 655, 657, 657–8, 671
  in First World War 8, 20
  and geography 89
  junior members from overseas 628, 630
  library 481
  admits women 374, 747
Hibbert Journal 397
The High 106, 565, 569
'high table' 100, 513
Higher Studies Fund 88, 220, 648
The Hill Players 422
Hillel Foundation 301
Hills & Saunders, printers, Oxford 470
Hinksey, Oxon. 424–5
Historic Buildings Appeal, *see* appeals
Historic Buildings Council 507
history, *see* modern history
history of science:
  as arts/science bridge 288–9
  and the colleges 148
  and modern history syllabus 237
  in 'science Greats' scheme 143, 228
  see also Museum of the History of Science
hoaxes 91
hockey, *see* sport
Hodder and Stoughton, publishers 458, 462,
  465
Holdan Books 452
Home University Library 408, 409, 458
Home-Students, Society of, *see* St Anne's
  College
Homer, Greek epic poet 135
homosexuality 421
  among senior members 198, 200–1, 437
  among undergraduates 98, 99, 433
Hong Kong 5, 632–3
honorary degrees, *see* degrees
Hooke Library 263
Hope Museum 155
Horizon 429
Horspath, Oxford 565
hospitals 10, 13 *see also* medicine; Radcliffe
  Infirmary
House of Commons:
  and Congregation 687–8, 692
  and Oxford Union 382
  Oxford's representation in 377, 410, 592, 719
Howell, Killick, Partridge and Amis,
  architectural practice 511, 512, 518
Hughenden Manor, Bucks. 378
Hull, Yorks. 100, 476, 583, 600
human anatomy, *see* anatomy
human sciences degree 279, 732, 757

Hungary 401, 407
Huntercombe Golf Club 322
hunting 534
Huntley and Palmer, biscuit
    manufacturers 162
Hyde Park Hotel, London 360
Hydrogen Bomb Campaign Committee 407

ice-hockey 538
Icelandic 221
idealism:
    and Oxford philosophy 241
    and Oxford sociology 244
    and Oxford theology 308
Iffley College, see Wolfson College
Imperial Chemical Industries 140, 162
    and botany 152
    and chemistry 144, 151, 268, 282–3
    and ecology 149
    and First World War 28
    and physics 161, 622
Imperial College, London:
    costs of 682
    high standing of 600–1
    science in Oxford influenced by 163, 589
    staff moves from Oxford to 145, 160
Imperial Forestry Institute
    building 506
    and forestry school 147–8
    funds for 262
    library 260, 277, 476, 481
    renamed (1961) 277
    research in 260
incomes policies 673, 707
independent schools, see public schools
India:
    and All Souls College 389, 615
    'Asia House' scheme 614
    forestry and 147
    hockey in 538
    junior members from 97, 609–10, 614, 630,
        634
        numbers 632–3
        Rhodes scholars 6, 614
        segregation rejected 96–7, 610
    Majlis 97, 614
    museum collections from 486, 493
    OUP in 464
    research in Oxford on 136, 609–10,
        613–15, 617
    sculpture of 486
    writers from 420, 432, 440
India Office 97
Indian Institute 486, 609
    building 482, 708, 746
    library 473, 482, 615
Indian School of Forestry 147

industrial relations 389, 556
industry 31
    and academic subjects
        botany 140
        chemistry: ICI supports 144, 151, 268,
            282–3; personal links 70, 144, 268,
            282; research 15, 28, 30, 140
        engineering 144, 274, 283, 284
        metallurgy 272, 282
        physics 161, 622
    colleges invest in 668–71
    family firms and Oxford 70–71, 91
    and First World War 28
    junior members' background in 55–7
    Oxford City Council encourages 563
    Oxford's curriculum and 116
    science in Oxford funded by 141, 144, 158,
        162, 261, 272, see also Imperial
        Chemical Industries
    universities allegedly strengthen 584
    see also careers
infant welfare 548–9
information officer, Oxford University 715,
    770
'Inklings' 184, 310, 422
inoculation 14
Institute of Agricultural Economics 137
Institute of Chemistry 70
Institute of Colonial Studies 618
Institute of Economic Affairs 395
Institute for Energy Studies 771
Institute of Experimental Psychology 279, 619
Institute of Social Medicine 269, 332
Institute of Statistics:
    accommodation for 516
    library 481
    permanently established 242
    refugees at 173–4, 185
    research at 137, 185–6, 561
    in Second World War 173, 183, 220
Institute for the Study of Metals
    (Chicago) 272
insulin 268
insurance 387–8
intelligence:
    in First World War 9
    in Second World War 181, 462
Inter-University Council 635
Inter-Varsity Fellowship of Evangelical
    Unions 312
International Business Machines (IBM) 649
International Ozone Commission 260
international relations, study of 136, 609,
    623, 625
internationalism 405–9
Iran 481, 632–3
Ireland 406, 633

Isis:
  disputes involving 401–2
  fosters creative writing 425–6
  idols 94, 402, **527**, 534
  and nuclear weapons 407
  and OUP 462
  and the Oxford Union 402, 527
  reviews lectures 226, 703, 704
  sex discussion censored 703
  sports reporting 527
  vehicle of ambition 427
Isis Innovation Ltd 771
Isis, River 547
Islip, Oxon. 422
Italian language 6, 114, 119
Italy 613, 632–3

Japan 467, 560, 624, 632–3, 767, 771
JCR, *see* junior common rooms
Jericho, Oxford 544, 557
Jericho, Palestine 494
Jerusalem 494
Jesuits, 298–300 *see also* Campion Hall
Jesus College, Oxford:
  accommodation expanded 191
  examination performance 105, 750
  finances 657
  in First World War 8, 19, 20
  junior members:
    from overseas 628
    participatory trend 204
    passmen rare 92
    women admitted 374, 747
  laboratory 40, 157, 260
  library 477
  Principals of 84
  subjects studied within:
    chemistry 89, 268
    geography 89, 286
    theology 308
  tea at 103
Jewish Society 301
Jews:
  and medicine 341
  Oxford Union and 180
  refugee scientists 589
  study of 452
  worship in Oxford 301
  see also Hebrew
John Radcliffe Hospital, Headington 339–40
John Wesley Society 209
Johns bookshop, Oxford 453, 465
joint (college/university) appointments 211
Joint European Torus (JET) 260
Jonathan Cape, publishers 417, 462
Jordan, Kingdom of 494
Journal of Ecology 152

Journal of Theological Studies 457
journalism:
  college magazines 198, 212, 526–7
  and creative writing 424–7
  and Oxford Union 383
  see also individual newspapers
jubilee, royal (1935) 411
junior common rooms (JCRs):
  activities:
    debating societies 95, 382
    meetings **95–6**, 204
    political arena 204
  facilities:
    art collections 204, 497
    beer cellars 205
    meals 104, 204
    newspapers 204
    premises 95
    radio 99
    television 204
    washing machines 207
    wine cellars 95
  government of:
    presidents 95, 688, 693, 706, 749
    public-school influence 95
  protest from women's 362
  records of 96
  tone:
    ribald 96
    rituals 95–6
    wary of outsiders 95–6, 693–4
  see also undergraduates
junior research fellows 200, 212
jurisprudence, *see* law

Keble College 198, 434
  academic aspects:
    examination results 530
    initiates admission reform 754
    passmen more common in 92
    theology 89, 303, 308
  buildings 106, 509, 511, 514, 515, 517
    bed-sits 104
    extended 191
    library extended 517
  characteristics:
    Anglican role 303, 304
    diminishingly distinct 107, 303
    size 190
  finances 657, 672, 673
  in First World War 20, 81
  junior members:
    concerts 93
    from overseas 628, 630
    history society 203
    Rhodes scholars 214
    rowing 193, 530

in Second World War 170
'Keble Road triangle' 140, 144, 256, **258**, 273, 566–7
Keele, University of 583, 586, 587
Kellogg Foundation 761
Kent, University of 583, 761
Kidlington, Oxon. 420
'King and Country' debate, *see* Union Society
kings, *see* monarchy
King's Arms, public house, Oxford 423, 558
King's College, Cambridge 588, 595, 663, 669
King's College, London 348, 601
Kish, Iraq 494
Kneale Committee on the structure of the first and second public examinations (1965) 228, 231, 238, 287, 724, 757
Kobe, Japan 771
Kosovo Day 7

laboratories:
    administrators in 282
    in colleges, *see* colleges
    power devolved within 265–6
    risks taken in 280–1
    social life within 265, 285
    trade unions in 282
    see also architecture; science; individual subjects
Labour Club:
    origins 396, 405
    activities inter-war 399, 400
    contacts made through 385, 404
    grammar-schoolboys in 96, 398
    intimidated 391
    and Liberals 392, 395–6, 405
    numbers joining 392, 399–400
    opposite sex met through 101
    Oxford Union boycotted 402
    prominent visitors 381
    and Ruskin College 399
    social democrats versus Marxists 403–4
    sympathetic senior members **395–8**
    women in 357–8
Labour Film Society 560
Labour Party:
    attitude to:
        Cambridge 35
        Liberals 392, 395–6; **404–7**
        New Left 401
        Oxford admissions 28, 101–2
    leaders 377
    and local politics 550–4, 568
    and Oxford Union 384–5
    Oxford-educated M.P.s 377, 411
    senior-member support 402, 550–1
    undergraduate opinion 394–5, 399
    weak in the Oxford region 378

    see also Asquith Commission; Labour Club; politics
Lady Margaret Hall 7, 345, 497
    Anglican tone 39, 55, 346–7
    architecture xviii, 503, 504, 506, 509
    examination performance 63, 76, 752
    finances 657
    junior members:
        clubs 367
        from overseas 629
        not taking degree 59
        rules on men 362
    Lambeth settlement 346
    library 477, 481
    mixed colleges' impact 63, 749
    register compiled 373
    state funding for 39
Lady Spencer-Churchill College 761
Lamb and Flag, public house, Oxford 423
Lambeth, London 346
Lancaster, University of 583, 597
Lanchester and Lodge, architectural practice 506
Land Valuation Bill (1930) 410
landladies 98, 192
landowners, and Oxford **55–7**, 67, 68–9
language schools 547
languages, modern, *see* modern languages
Lankester Room 263–4
Lasker memorial rose garden 517
Latin:
    ceremonial use 233, 707–8
    in degree courses:
        English 122
        theology 307
    dictionaries of 478
    for entrance exam:
        restricts Oxford entry 47, 55, 59, 110, 351
        phased out as requirement **225**, 233–4, 771
    for grace 103
    in pass mods 111
    for recording undergraduate offences 91
    research in 134
    women and 350, 366
    see also classical studies
Latin America 260, 624
law:
    and the colleges 197, 241
        All Souls 389
        college clubs 203
        law entrenched 41
    Commonwealth impact on 618
    examinations:
        moderations 117
        preliminary 57, 111, 117

law (*cont.*):
　honorary degrees in 3
　and modern history 117
　OUP and 458
　and philosophy 241
　postgraduates in 109
　reputation of Oxford 601
　research in Oxford on 87–8, 137, 241, 646
　syllabus 109, 241, 246
　undergraduates reading:
　　calibre 57, 193, 529, 534
　　numbers 110, 116, **141–2**, 197
　　societies for 102
　　student-tutor ratio 241
　　women 61, 116
　vocational aspects 241
　see also careers
Law Library xviii, 516, 646
law-moots 203
lawyers, as Oxford parents 56
L'Chaim Society 301
League of Nations 24
Lears bookshop, Cardiff 453
Leasco 463
Leasehold Reform Act (1967) 668
Leckford Road, Oxford 433
lectures xiii, 106
　assignations at 101
　in Cambridge 643–4
　college/university responsibility for 39,
　　643, 710
　criticized 41, 131, 212, 225, 226
　distinct from tutorials 130, 230
　Franks Commission on 230
　of individuals:
　　Berlin 410
　　Wind xviii
　Isis reviews 226, 703, 704
　professors' role in 131
　quality of 131
　in science area 263
　subject-areas:
　　classics 132
　　history of art xviii, 490
　　mathematics 263
　　modern history 221
　university pays colleges for 654, 694
　women at 361
Leeds University 476, 592
　endowment income 589
　origins 27, 583
　postgraduates in 598
　reputation 600–3
　staff moves to Oxford from 337
　students at 547, 595
Left Review 429
Leicester University 583, 600

Leipzig 163, 589
Letcombe Laboratory 276
Lewis Evans collection 149
Lexicon of Patristic Greek 303
Liberal Club 405
Liberal Party:
　national:
　　in the Oxford region 378, 409
　　undergraduate opinion 394–5
　senior-member opinion 402, 404–7
　university:
　　and Oxford Conservatism 391, **392**, 405
　　and Oxford Labour Party 392, 395–6,
　　　404–7
　　University seat 379–81
librarians
　exported from Oxford 480
　historians as college 85
　increasingly professionalized 695
　women as 370–1, 480
libraries:
　college:
　　individual: All Souls 477; Balliol 263, 476;
　　　Brasenose 195, 481; Christ Church xiii,
　　　481, 507; Corpus Christi 481;
　　　Hertford 481; Jesus 477; Keble 517;
　　　Lady Margaret Hall 477, 481;
　　　Lincoln 481, 517; Magdalen 263, 477;
　　　Manchester 297; New xviii, 481, 499,
　　　504, 506; Nuffield 481, 517;
　　　Pembroke 481; St Anne's 477; St
　　　Antony's 481; St Edmund Hall 191,
　　　481, 517; St Hugh's 477; St John's 481;
　　　Trinity 263, 504; Wadham 481;
　　　Worcester 477
　　general points: deposits in Bodleian
　　　Library 476, 478; duplication
　　　wasteful 710; fail to specialize 476;
　　　memorial 23; undergraduates
　　　increasingly use 101, 195, 472;
　　　university subvents 481, 694, 712;
　　　women's colleges collaborate 368, 477
　departmental science 263, 278, 280, 481
　faculty 476, 481, 482, 483, 712
　　English 476, 481, 516
　　geography 476, 478, 482
　　history of art 481
　　law xix, 516, 646
　　modern history 476, 505
　　modern languages 473, 476
　　music 481
　　philosophy 476
　　theology 297
　medical 339
　other:
　　Cambridge University 475, 478, 505, 645
　　Gerrans Mathematical 263

Hooke 263
Imperial Forestry Institute 260, 277, 476, 481
Indian Institute 473, 482, 615
Institute of Statistics 481
Oxford Union 383
Rhodes House 473, 617, 618
general comments:
  American influences 88, 473, **474–5**, 480, 516, **645–6**
  influence creative writing 414
  Oxford bibliographers study 477
  research library concept 645–6
  slow start on integrated catalogue 482
  UGC subsidy inadequate 678
  undergraduate representation 706
  undergraduate social life in 101, 192
  wasteful expenditure on 481
see also Bodleian Library; Radcliffe Science Library
Libraries Board 482–3, 710
Library Association 480
life fellows 86
life sciences 60, 254–5, 278–9
Linacre College 279, 628–9
  founded 215, 714
  gets charter (1986) 760
  admits women 210
  finances 657
  head of house's role 199
Lincoln College:
  administration 190
  buildings 504, 517
  expands after 1945 191
  Fellows 86
  finances 657, 673
  in First World War 8, 20
  library 481, 517
  middle common room 211
  overseas intake 612, 628
  public schools and 94
  Rectors of 84, 199
  in Second World War 170
linguistics, see philology
The Listener 429, 430
Literae Humaniores (Lit.Hum.):
  careers growing out of 457
  characteristics:
    fragmenting tendency 234
    governmental preoccupation 387
    strong in colleges 41, 232
    unspecialized 90, 116
    well endowed/staffed 232
  chronology:
    Second World War 221, 223
    PPE counter-attracts from 244, 249
    waning influence 116, 233–4, 244

literature option introduced (1970s) 757
  Mods for the Greekless introduced (1970s) 757
civic universities influenced by 599
Corpus Christi College and 89
criticized 410
examination performance in 232
impact on related subjects:
  ancient history 90, 234
  archaeology 116, 222–3, 233
  art 116
  English 114, 121
  philosophy 90, 111, 132, 233–4, 757
  psychology 143
  social anthropology 222–3
  theology 89, 307, 308
numbers reading 110, 115–16, **142**, 233–4
prestige of 110, 111, 115, 217, 323
syllabus 109, 116, **233–4**
teaching methods 132, 234
women studying 110, 116
see also ancient history; classical studies; philosophy
Literae Humaniores Board 120
Literary Review 430
Little Clarendon Street, Oxford 512
Littlemore, Oxford 549
Liverpool University 27, 381, 478, 580, 592, 601
Local Education Authorities, awards by 38, 46, **47–9**, 101, 367, 584, 672
local government 56, 136, 547–8
  courses relevant to 47, 71, 387
  studied in Oxford 561
  see also careers
lodging houses 98
lodgings:
  for American soldiers (1918) 10
  for Belgian refugees 6–7
  in civic universities 596, 654
  increasingly dispersed 557
  for undergraduates:
    in 1920s 357
    between the wars 47, **98**
    in 1940s 192
    in 1950s 654
    in 1960s 192, 556–7, 704
    after 1960s 769
    inter-college contrasts 195
    proportion in 47, 105, 192, 769
    university supervision of 192
  for women 352, 358–9
logic, in pass mods 111
London:
  city gilds fund research 149, 159, 491
  colleges' income from 675
  and OUP **453–4**, 466–7

London (*cont.*):
  Oxford's influence in the city 387–8
  Oxford's literary interaction 429
  Oxford's relationship to 378
  publishing in 457
London Hospital 323, 334
London Library 480
London Magazine 429
London Mercury 431
London Review of Books 430
London School of Economics 600, 620, 704
London University:
  applied science stressed 589
  as background of vice-chancellors 594
  and Commonwealth new universities 635
  and the CVCP 587
  FBAs from 593
  finances 644–5, 682
  FRSs from 593
  governmental structure 642, 726
  medical schools 317, 318, 319, 321, 323, 342, 771
  numbers at 583
  postgraduates at 585
  reputation 500–3, 771
  research at 603
  schools sending students to 585
  staff exchanges with Oxford:
    gained from 145, 149–50
    lost to 323, 328, 329, **332–3**, 334
  teacher training at 347
  women in 345, 347, 374
  see also individual colleges
Long Crendon, Bucks. 420
Longman, publishers 462
Longwall Street, Oxford 510
Louvain, University of 6
Louvre, Paris 640
lunch, *see* meals
Luxembourg 633

MA degree, *see* degrees, postgraduate
MacCormac, Jamieson and Pritchard, architectural practice 512
Macmillan, publishers 462, 468
Magdalen College 85, 102, 106, 141, 564
  buildings 502, 506, 509, 516–17, 649
  critics of 102
  examination performance 105, 106, 213
  facilities:
    accommodation expanded 191, 568
    choir 315
    gardens 104
    kitchens 104
    laboratory 40, 157
    library 263, 477

living conditions 105
  lodgings 192
  finances 564, 641, 642, 653, **656–7**, 657–8, 740
  in First World War 8, 9, 20, 22
  influence in Congregation 692
  junior members:
    hearties v aesthetes 98
    Indians 97
    JCR 95
    proportion from overseas 628
    public-school intake 95
    rowing 102, 535
  poetry emanating from 417–8
  in Second World War 179
  see also Warren
Magdalen College School 570
Maguire and Murray, architectural practice 512, 516, 517
Maison Française 481, 565, 623, 623–4
Majlis 97, 614
Makerere College, Uganda 52, 635
Malaysia 633
Malta 9
Malvern College 537
management studies, *see* business studies
Manchester City 453, 547
Manchester College, Oxford 278, **296–7**, 305, 771
Manchester College of Science and Technology 682
Manchester University 476, 583
  and chemistry in Oxford 158–9, 163, 268, 589
  early history 27, 597
  finances 589, 643
  postgraduates in 598
  reputation 600–1, 603
  in Second World War 183
  students in 580, 595
Mansfield College:
  and Congregationalism 295–6, 314, 315
  junior members from overseas 628
  and Regent's Park College 297
  and theology faculty 305
  woman chaplain in 296
marriage:
  of alumni 102, 212
  college life and 86, 92, 198
  impact on women's careers 76–7, **371–3**
  of junior members:
    a higher priority for women 369
    parents fear imprudent 361
    permission needed 373
    trend to intermarriage 77
  of senior members 85, **86**, 92, 197–8, 200, 209, 346

Marston, Oxford 557
Martyrs' Memorial 313
Marxism, *see* Communism
Masonic Hall 10
Mass Observation 421
Massachusetts Institute of Technology 144, 589
Mathematical Association 270
Mathematical Institute 156, **269**, 507
mathematics:
　accommodation for 261
　characteristics:
　　reputation 270, 601, 771
　　somewhat inbred 156
　　strong in the colleges 269
　　teaching methods 128, 263
　library for 481
　numbers reading 141–2, 155, **254**, 269
　in pass mods 111, 120
　and related subjects:
　　astronomy 156
　　botany 152
　　chemistry 270
　　economics 120, 123
　　engineering 274
　　philosophy 264, 288, 289
　　physics 89, 141, 260, 269–70
　research in 269–70, 285
　schools, contacts with 270
matriculation 11, 45, 707, 771, *see also* admission
mature students 771–2
Max Rayne Foundation 747
Meadow Buildings, Christ Church 94
Meadow road 569–75, 702, 715
　Conservative attitudes 394
　university political support mobilized 410
meals:
　for alumni 212 *see also* gaudies
　junior members':
　　breakfasts: in bed in St Hilda's 366;
　　　centralized in University College 105
　　morning coffee 101, 357
　　lunches: lunch parties 93, 104; War on Want 204
　　tea 93, 101, 103, 104, 204, 367: at Elsfield Manor 422
　　dinners: college club 93, 95;
　　　Conservative 390, 391; dress for 205;
　　　shortened halls 96
　　location: all in hall 207; with heads of house 82; JCRs 104, 204; own room 98, 104; Oxford Union 383; with senior members 83
　　other aspects: Eights Week 104; Second World War 179; self-catering 94, 631; self-service 513

senior members': breakfasts, Sunday in All Souls 87
　lunch: Bodleian autumn visitation 480; communal college meal 198; in Halifax House 285; for socialists 397
　dinners: Alembic Club annual 268; Ashmolean Club 686; college business done informally at 689; dessert after xi, 86, 198; for economists 387; estates bursars' committee 356; increasingly for residents 198; Saturday in All Souls 87
shared aspects:
　bells summon for 103
　business settled informally at 86, 710, 712, 734
　dinners once the sole communal meal 86
　formal halls 99, 100, 205–6
　sociability and science 268, 270, 285
　women's colleges eat in hall 366
　see also grace; servants
media
　attitudes to Oxford 411, 715, 770
　careers in the xvii, 223, 383–4, 426–7
　information officer appointed 715
　irreverent in 1960s 402
　and Oxford Union xvii, **383–4**
　senior members and 758
Medical Research Council (MRC) 261, 262, 320, 330, 699
medicine:
　in Cambridge 318
　chronology:
　　in First World War 9, 14
　　refugees fertilize 333, 341
　　in Second World War 182, 252–3, 332–5
　　impact of 1980s cuts 766, 768
　disputes within 328–30, 334, 336–7
　examinations 319
　funding:
　　government 30
　　patents 283
　　Rockefeller Foundation 320–5, 330, 619, 689
　　see also Nuffield, William Richard Morris
　history of 289
　laboratories 318, 343
　and London medical schools 317, 318, 319, 321, 323, 342, 771
　OUP and 456, 458
　overseas influences on Oxford:
　　Commonwealth 323, 341, 621
　　Denmark 321
　　France 321
　　USA 182, 320, 321–2, 330, 332, 341
　postgraduates:
　　calibre 342–3
　　numbers 140, 332, 342–3

medicine: postgraduates (*cont.*):
    syllabus 324, 343
  professors ensure continuity 341
  recruits from:
    Cambridge 332
    London 323, 328, 329, 331, **332–3**, 334
  and related disciplines 319
  syllabus 319, 343
  number of tutorial fellows in 90
  undergraduate numbers:
    before 1914 319
    in First World War 13
    inter-war 319
    in Second World War 176–7
  women in 13, 33, 348, 349, 359
  see also careers; Nuffield; physiology
Meir (Cusae), Egypt 133
Melanesia 493
Merton College 428
  fabric:
    accommodation expanded 191, 517
    new buildings 504, 506
    repairs/refurbishment xviii, 502, 508, 509
  finances 657, 662, 740
  in First World War 9, 10, 20
  junior members:
    clubs xii, 95
    examination performance 105, 213
    insist they're contented 705
    JCR versus URC 694
    living conditions (late 1930s) 105
    overseas intake 612
    persecution among 391
    proportion from overseas 628
    sports ground 256, 279
  and Peterhouse, Cambridge 588
  in Second World War 170, 175, 220
  wardens 83, 84
Merton Street baths 523
messenger service 708
metal detectors 284
Metal Industries 144
metallurgy 256, 261, 758
  accommodation for 261, 272–3, 510
  and chemistry 272
  and industry 272, 282
  library for 481
  research in xiv, **159–60**, 163, **272**
  undergraduate numbers reading 142, 254, 273
  undergraduate school established 264
  see also careers
meteorology 260
Methodism 270
Mexico 632–3
MI5 170, 181
middle common rooms 211
Milham Ford School for Girls 555

military history 388
Milton Keynes, Bucks. 761
mineralogy:
  and the colleges 148
  foreign influences on 163
  museum collections 487, 493
  numbers reading 150–1
  research in 150–1, 274–5
ministries and boards:
  Agriculture 36, **145–6**, 162, 659
  Colonial 147, 162, 377, 635
  Education 367, 592, 673
    criticized 770
    grants for teachers 367, 585
    and mixed colleges 748
    modern subjects and 54
    overseas student fees 651
    and Oxford schools 555
    postgraduates funded by 49
    and tuition fees (1976–8) 763–4
    see also state studentships
  Food 170
  Foreign xvii, 16, 170, 182, 771
  Health 322, 323, 336, 337–8, 563
  Home Security 170
  Housing and Local Government 570
  India Office 614
  Information 183
  Labour 170
  Overseas Development 262
  Supply 183, 251
  Town Planning 565
  Trade 346, 444, 565
  Transport 170
  Treasury 184, 185, 395, 642
  War:
    in First World War 10, 12, 14, 17
    in Second World War 167, 170, 173
  Works 649
Minneapolis, U.S.A. 467
missionaries 311, 346
missions to the University 313–5, 392
Mitre Hotel 191
mixed colleges:
  pre-history 210, 356, 374, 584
  initiated 45, 210, 746–9
  comprehensive schools fit well with 748
  change gender-balance 355
  and degree results 62–3, 750–1
  revive college life 210
  and women's colleges 352, 374
  and women's sport 531
  see also Nuffield College
'Modern Greats', *see* PPE
modern history:
  and adjacent subjects:
    ancient history 238

archaeology 236
economics 123, 124, 236, 238
English literature 122
law 117, 236
modern languages 123, 238, 473
political science 115, 120, 123, 234, 242
PPE 89, 112–13, 120, 122–3, 236, 244:
    students lost to, since 1950s 244, 249
psychology 236
social anthropology 236, 237
social sciences 236, 249
careers related to 116, 235–7
characteristics:
    diverse aims 235
    documentary emphasis 123, 235
    governmental preoccupation 387
    little historiography 236, 237
    medieval history prominent 235, 771
    moralistic 235–6
    political emphasis 238
and the colleges:
    All Souls 389
    Christ Church 389
    college societies 203
    entrance awards 264
    historians as college librarians 85
    strong in colleges 41
and creative writing 415
disputes within 124, **237–9**
European influences on 136, 235–7, 609, 624
    'European Greats' project 222, 228
examinations 12, 13
    moderations 124
    pass mods 111, 123
    preliminary examination 117, **122–4**
in First World War 15, 456
library 476, 505
numbers studying 110, **141–2**, 234
postgraduate degrees 127
publishers and 458, 461, 464
reputation of Oxford 601, 771
research in **134–6**, 235, 236, 409
in Second World War 221, 223
syllabus 109, **122–4**, **234–9**, 246, 757
syllabus criticized:
    as Anglocentric 218, 237–8
    as narrow 236
    as philistine 236
    by junior members 227, 235, 237, 239
teaching methods:
    classes 238
    increasingly relativist 236, 237
    lectures 131
    tutorials xvi, 92, 128, 130
types of:
    American 235
    art xviii, 133, 236, 237, 481, 490

Commonwealth 235, 611, 615, 618, 635
    economic 236
    European 620, 623
    military 388
    women reading 61, 110, 116, 117, 359
see also ancient history; history of science
modern languages:
    adjacent subjects:
        English 114, 121, 122
        modern history 123, 238, 473
        PPE 121
    admissions and 350
    Ashmolean Museum competes for space 473
    Asquith Commission backs 613
    benefactions to 645
    careers emerging from 119
    chronology:
        in First World War 6, 613
        inter-war syllabus reform 118–19
        prime minister's inquiry (1918) 118
        in Second World War 223
        posts lost/gained in 1980s 766
    and the colleges 61, 89, 119, 132, 197
    and creative writing 415
    'European Greats' resisted 222
    examinations:
        pass groups 110
        pass mods 111
    hostility to degree in 89
    libraries for 473, 476
    numbers reading 110, 116, 118–19, **142**, 197,
        620, **625–6**
    philological emphasis 240
    research in Oxford on 134–5
    syllabus criticized 240–1
    teaching methods:
        classes 131–2
        lectures 643
    tutorials influenced by 128
    university control over 41, 61
    women reading 60–1, 89, 110, 116, 118–19,
        359
Modern Languages Board 121
monarchy 411 see also individual monarchs
Moral Re-Armament 301–2, 392
'moral tutors' 200–1
Morning Post 396, 397
Morris Motors, Cowley 182, 562, 564, see also
    Cowley
Moser report on the future of management
    studies (1988) 763
Mount Holyoke College, U.S.A. 345
Munich agreement (1938) 407
    All Souls and 389, 407
    Oxford opinion on 167–8, **406–7**, 412
    Oxford Union and 393
munitions manufacture 13, 15, 28, 139

Museum of the History of Science 149–50,
     288, 488–9
Museum of Modern Art 489, 559
Museum Road, Oxford 191, 511
music 3, 481
   BMus introduced 49
   and the colleges 197, 203
   musical instruments collected in:
      Ashmolean Museum 492, 494–5
      Pitt Rivers Museum 491, 493
   numbers reading 109, 118, **142**
   OUP and 458–9, 464
   syllabus 118, 414
   town/gown collaboration 452, 560, 576
   see also choirs
mycology 152, 276
Myrmidons, Merton College xii, 95

National Aeronautics and Space
     Administration 260
National Art-Collections Fund 495, 496
National Central Library 480
National Economic Development
     Council 395
National Gallery, London 640
National Health Service 319–20, 335–8
National Health Service Act (1946) 335
National Institute for Economic and Social
     Research 395
National Research Development
     Corporation 283
national service:
   ends 49, 65, 190, 204, 402, 535
   student numbers and 48, 190
National Union of Students (NUS) 383
   origins 579
   and JCRs 204
   opinions:
      hostile to college system 214
      on junior-senior member relations
         200
      on student accommodation 192
   Oxford lukewarm about 594, 694
   and student unrest (1970) 745
National Union of Teachers 35
natural science moderations 90, 143
navy 190
Nazism 232
Neasden, London 456
Nelson, publishers 458
Netherlands 278, 495, 633, 774
neurology 342
neurophysiology 318
'new blood' appointments 766–7
New Bodleian Library, *see* Bodleian Library
New Cinema, Headington 180
New College 85, 381, 422, 708, 709

academic aspects:
   examination performance 105
   intellectual ambitions 92
   passmen rare 92
accoutrements:
   choir 315
   coronation celebrations (1937) 82
   Epstein's Lazarus 497, 510
   youth club 549
buildings 191, 508, 510, 516
   library xviii, 481, 499, 504, 506
fashionable image 106
finances 653, 654, 657–8
in First World War 8, 10, 20, 22
influence:
   architectural 513
   political 107, 386, **408–9**
   trade-union 386
junior members:
   clubs 390–1
   discipline 100
   from overseas 628
   JCR 95, 104
   mixed colleges pioneered 210, 356, 374,
      584, 726, 746
   and King's Cambridge 588
   wardens 84
   and Winchester College 94, 347
The New English Bible 464
New Fabian Research Bureau 385
New Guinea 493
New Hall, Cambridge 514
New Left 401, 404
New Left Review 401
New Reform Club 391, 405
New Review 430
New Road Baptist church 297
New Signatures 399
New Statesman 397, 427, 430
New (subsequently, Apollo) Theatre 180,
      559
New York Zoological Society 149
New Zealand 6, 493, 536, 620, 632–3
Newcastle University 480, 592
Newdigate prize 428
Newman Bookshop 451
Newnham College, Cambridge 345, 349,
      351, 359, 374, 503
Next Five Years Group 409
Nielsen, A.C., marketing researchers 565
Nimrud, Iraq 494
Nissan Institute 624
Nobel prizes for:
   chemistry 151, 157, 262, 268
   literature 428
   medicine 253, 262, 329
   physics 622

physiology 262, 278
zoology 155
non-collegiate students:
 and Asquith Commission 38, **107**
 in First World War 20
 number of 107
 postgraduates 125, 126
 see also St Catherine's College
nonconformists:
 and civic universities 584
 financial difficulties of colleges 297
 in the theology faculty 297–8, 305–6
 in women's colleges 346
 see also Manchester, Mansfield, Regent's
  Park colleges
Norrington Committee on libraries (1958) 481
'Norrington scores':
 of inter-war colleges 92, **105–6**
 of colleges after 1945 213, 528–30
 arts/science 61–2
 explained 62
 men/women 61–2
Norrington table 196
 criticized 750
 damages sport 520
 explained 62
 invented 64
 suspended 750
 women and 352, 374
North Oxford 93, 346, 634
 college property in 668
 conservation pressures 548, 565–7
Northfield Farm, Wytham 275
Northwest Territories, Canada 5
Notes and Queries 457
Nottingham 385, 583
novels:
 anti-university tendency 427
 Cambridge 428
 Oxford:
  cited 87, 96, 420, 439–40, 445–9
  misleading 449–50
  nostalgic 97–8, 102, 448
  written by Oxford people 413
nuclear magnetic resonance 269, 283, 284
nuclear physics laboratory 261, 281–2, 284
Nuffield College 497
 architecture 503
 becomes a college 214
 exemplar for postgraduate study 731, 760
 finances **656–7**, 662, 671, 740
 garden 517
 junior members from overseas 628–9
 library 481
 mixed college 210, 355
 and Lord Nuffield 144, 186, 325, 503,
  647–8

origins 143–4, 220, 325, **647–8**
 and research ideal in Oxford 624–5
 research on:
  Commonwealth studies 615, 617
  economics 617
  election studies 389
  reconstruction survey 184–5
  social studies 242–4, 561, 765
 in Second World War 220
 seminars at 88
 theory/practice united in 387
 and town planning in Oxford 574–5
 trade-union/employer links 386, 718
 wardens of 387
 woman chaplain in 296
Nuffield Foundation 361
Nuffield Institute of Medical Research 323,
  326, 328–31, 340, 387
Nuffield Orthopaedic Centre 323, 339
Nuffield Press, Oxford 470
numismatology 133
Nuneham Courtenay, Oxon. 482
nuns 347
nurses, college 201
nursing, in First World War 13

'oaks' 91
Observer 429, 430
obstetrics 324, 328, 340–1
October Club 391, 400
Officer Training Corps (OTC) 8
Official Secrets Act 407
Old Palace, Rose Place, Oxford 299
Old Persian 109
Oliver and Gurdens (cake factory) 179, 207
Olympic medals 535, 537
Open University 586, 599, 761
ophthalmology 333, 341
Opus Dei 300
Orange Free State 5
Organization for Economic Co-operation
  and Development (OECD) 395, 722
Oriel College 391, 550
 architecture 508
 examination performance 213, 530
 finances 657, 659
 in First World War 8, 10, 20
 governing body invaded (1970) 205
 junior members from overseas 628
 passmen rare at 92
 in Second World War 170
 sport at 530
 theology at 308
Oriental Institute 481, 510
oriental studies 109, 197, 618
 numbers reading 110, 142, 625–6
ornithology 149

orthopaedics 328
Osney, Oxford 259
Owenism 395
'Oxbridge' 578, 588
OXCUT 671, 772
OXFAM 312
Oxford 527
Oxford Architects Partnership 516, 518
Oxford Arts Club 559
Oxford Atlas 464
Oxford Bibliographical Society 477
Oxford Bird Census 149
Oxford Book of Light Verse 439
Oxford Brookes University 204, 489, 547,
     555, 705
Oxford Centre for Islamic Studies 771
Oxford Centre for Management Studies, *see*
     Templeton College
Oxford Chamber of Trade 558
Oxford Choral and Philharmonic
     Society 560
Oxford city council:
   boundary changes 544, 550, 551, 555
   and building regulation 273, 562, 564–6
   and education 555
   and industry inter-war 563
   and rates 553
   tourists, lukewarm towards 565
   university influence within 378, **553–5**, 576
Oxford City Home Guard 251
Oxford city and region:
   characteristics:
     class contrasts 398
     diminishingly distinctive 561
     literary connections 419–23
     skyline 273, 278–9, 512, 515, 543, 566,
        569
     unionization pattern 544–5
   and First World War 10, 12, 451, 557
   geography:
     of printing/publishing 453–4, 468–70
     of religion 294
     of roads and rivers 546–7, 572
     of science 256, 258
     of sport 523–6
     inter-war migration to Oxford 545, 561
     suburbanization 547
   medical aspects:
     health visiting 548
     hospitals at Headington 332, 335
     hospitals improved 320, 323–4, 332
     infant welfare 548–9
     mental health 549
   M.P.s for 279–81
     Conservatives dominate 381
     undergraduates don't vote 381
   planning of 510, 562–76

'green belt' 563–4, 575
   recreation within:
     cinemas 93, 180, **560**
     dances 98
     Museum of Modern Art 489
     music 560
     pubs 558
     sport 98, 524–5, 537, 538, 564
     theatres 180
     walking 87, 563
   in Second World War:
     foreign troops 178
     not bombed 174
     refugees 177–8
   shops 504, 512, 558
   transport changes:
     benefit local hospitals 325
     employees 544, 545, 550
     generate more visitors 101
     harm environment 106
     increase noise **102–3**, 293, 569
     parking problems 574–5
     see also Meadow road
   and the University:
     academic impact through:
        archaeology 494; geography 280, 561;
        local applicants getting places 51,
        556–7; sociology 561
     economic impact: Cowley
        diminishes 544–5; books 451, 544,
        547; building 544, 548; food 558–9;
        house owning 668;
        landownership 662; lodgings 98, 192,
        556–7; tithe-holding 669;
        tourism 497; undergraduate
        debts 558; white-collar employment
        (1960s) 547
     educational impact, on local schools 555:
        see also adult education; Oxford
        Brookes University
     planning issues: competition for
        space 191, 547, 561, 562, 567, 575;
        rural conservation 564; science
        area 566–7; urban conservation 562,
        563–7
     political impact: on city council 378,
        553–5, 569, 576; rating
        question 552–3; through Conservative
        Party 551; through Labour
        Party 550–1, 552
     social impact: social conscience 543;
        youth work 549
   see also bookshops; by-elections; Cowley;
        elections; individual political parties;
        lodgings; North Oxford; publishing;
        science area
Oxford Colleges Admissions Office 712

Oxford Companion to English Literature 435, 459, 464
Oxford Council of Social Service 549
Oxford Dictionary of the Christian Church 303
Oxford Dictionary of Quotations 435, 459
Oxford English Dictionary xvii, xviii, 133, 436, **459–60**, 464, 488
Oxford Exploration Club 149
Oxford Group Movement, *see* Moral Re-Armament
Oxford High School for Boys 555
Oxford Historic Buildings, *see* appeals
Oxford Historical Society 561
Oxford History of England 136, 458
Oxford History of English Literature 459
Oxford History of Modern Europe 464
Oxford Instrument Company 259, **283**
Oxford Inter-Collegiate Christian Union (OICCU) 311, 313, 315, 365
Oxford Jewish Centre 301
Oxford Magazine:
  alumni careers reported 94
  and examination results 64, 402
  examinations criticized 129
  moving left from 1950s 402
  and OUP 462
  and Oxford Union 402
  scientists not salient in 284
  sports reporting 527
  and Suez crisis 407
  survival in doubt 173
  temporarily dies 772
Oxford Mail 420
Oxford Ornithological Society 149
The Oxford Outlook 425–6
Oxford Pastorate 304, 311
Oxford Poetry 424, 425, 426
Oxford Polytechnic, *see* Oxford Brookes University
Oxford Preservation Trust 563–4
Oxford Psychological Society 279
Oxford Reform Committee 35, 586
Oxford Regional Hospital Board 335, 336, 340
Oxford Revolutionary Socialist Students xix
Oxford Society 646–7, 716 *see also* alumni
'Oxford Standard Authors' 470
Oxford Summer Diversions 422
Oxford University:
  administration:
    accommodation expands 696
    characteristics: academics control 599, 688, 697, 711, 712, 734; complex and time-consuming 707, 710; difficult to plan ahead 701, 707, 711; mood of

    restrained panic 696–7; re-located 474, 475, 482, 708; University elections work-load 378, 694
    external pressures: expertise required by government funding 694, 695; standardization forced by 690, 695, 707; tighter links with outside bodies 692, 695, 701, 709
    internal pressures: Joint Consultative Committee formed 696; staff relations 146, 529, **696**, 707; surveyor's department grows 507, 517, 707; vice-chancellor's staff grows 684–5, 699
    trends: administrators professionalize 695; increasingly impersonal 696; messengers and telephones improve 708; overstrain by late 1950s 700, 707; paperwork steadily mounts 689, 692, 700, 707, 708, 712; power gravitates to centre 683; quinquennial pulsations after 1945 695, 702, 716; slow integration 708, 739–40
    see also finance
  characteristics:
    active/contemplative life combination admired 386, 396, 408–9
    ambition fostered 93–4, 382–4, 404, 410, 427
    anti-theoretical outlook 386, 388, 404
    bookish atmosphere 414, 436
    change comes from without 143, 162, 636
    civic universities, aloofness from 27, 533, 587
    crisis-management required 709, 741
    democracy's limited relevance 706
    direct democracy favoured 733, 762
    government linkages close 386, 412
    increasingly meritocratic 411, 599–600
    indifferent to town planning 563, 573–4, 689
    inefficient, sometimes deliberately 707
    internally recruited 85, 141, 603
    knowing 435–6
    lifelong freemasonry operated 433–4
    literary elite merged with 418–9, 427–8
    metropolitan outlook 378, 429
    national not local 580, 584
    non-vocational bias 60, 70–1, 90, 147, 218, 612
    not tradition-bound 772
    peculiar, like the British system 773
    political elite merged with 381, 404
    politicized 378, 607–8
    potential for going private 604

Oxford University: characteristics (*cont.*):
  public-school linkages close 584
  reform is difficult 612, 636
  responsibility/initiative diffused 686–7,
    711, 754, 772
  Second-World-War flexibility 187
  social-democratic tendency 404
  tourists meet indifference 565
  criticisms of:
    aloof from the locality 543, 576
    causes economic decline 219, 402, 721
    elitist 430–1, 435, 584, 715
    entrance system defective 219, 226
    fails to explain itself 605, 715, 723, 731
    fragmented 569, 572–3, 605, 702, 715
    inbred teaching appointments 603
    indecisive 723, 731
    inefficient 646, 689
    insufficient lay participation 717
    not conforming administratively 770
    parochial 226
    philistine 444–5, 559
    privileged 227, 402, 441, 554, 721,
      770
    research neglected 612–13, 645–6
    self-satisfied 646
    too strong in civil service 593
    unduly influential 574
  critics: AUT 590
    Sir Charles Carter 735
    city opinion 552–4, 574
    civic universities 219, 226
    Lionel Curtis 646
    evangelicals 304
    industrialists 219, 224
    patriots 406
    scientists 219, 689
    see also Robbins report
  governmental structure:
    centralizing trend 683
    centrist mood 745
    college/university relations 27, **39–41**,
      211–12, 684
    family links not significant 712
    laymen's role 37, 87, **715–19**: *see also*
      alumni
    mealtime informality lubricates 86, 710,
      712, 734
    more decisive by 1980s 733
    OUP connection 466, 640
    statutes 707
    Whitehall/Westminster analogies 683,
      685, 687, 692
    see also Congregation; General Board;
      Hebdomadal Council; vice-chancellors
  influence:
    architectural 518

    on AUT 590
    on civic universities 577, 580–2, 589,
      592, 594, 597–9
    on Commonwealth universities 635
    fragmented 410–11, 435, 441–7
    literary 413–4, 429–31
    local, *see* Oxford city and region
    on new universities (1960s) 597–8
    on NUS 594
    political 17–18, **377–8**, 410–12, 591–2,
      594
    on school curricula 219
  internal (collegiate) impulses to reform 754
  mood shifts:
    reforming attempts before 1914 27, 604
    reforming enthusiasm from 1918 14
    reforming mood wanes in 1920s 43,
      107–8
    conservative in 1940s 222–3, 411
    reforming mood from late 1950s 224–6,
      411, 466, 700, 721–4
    defensive mood in 1960s 245, 649, 715
  M.P.s for:
    election results 379–81
    electoral arrangements 378, 694
    electoral turnout 381, 718, 719
    number of voters 378
    party organization 381, 392, 397
    terminated 410
  relations with outside bodies:
    AUT 589–90
    central government 24, **30**, 388
    NUS 594, 694
    public schools 27, 47
    Rockefeller Foundation 322
    UCCA 595, 707
    UGC 591–2
    see also civil service; industry; political
      parties
  reputation:
    bogus affiliations claimed 428
    with civic universities 577, 600–4, 736
    class component dwindles 411, 607–8
    Congregation risks 703
    fragmentation damages 702
    improves after 1960s 770–1
    information officer appointed 715
    international not local 543
    media distort 715, 770
    modern studies and 70
    OUP promotes 459
    for pacifism 167, 406
    with parents 358
    philosophy boosts 222
    with public schools 357–8
    in Second World War 173, 221
    sport affects 519

Oxford University: reputation (*cont.*):
  world university status claimed 607–8,
    635–6, 730, 735, 771
Oxford University Bible Union 313
Oxford University Boat Club 535
Oxford University Calendar 707
Oxford University Conservative Association
  (OUCA) 381, 391–2, 393
Oxford University Dramatic Society
  (OUDS) 7, 94, 179–80, 527
  women and 356, 363
  see also Coghill
Oxford University Gazette 252, 771
Oxford University Handbook 111, 115
Oxford University History Society 237
Oxford University Independence Fund 651
Oxford University Jewish Society 301
Oxford University Labour Party 397
Oxford University Poetry Society 424
Oxford University Press (OUP):
  categories of publication:
    children's books 457, 465
    classical studies 456
    dictionaries xviii, **133–4**, 435, 436, 459
    English literature 458, 459, 470
    history of science 149
    Home University Library 458
    law 458, 462–3
    medicine 456, 458
    modern history 458, 464
    music 458–9, 464
    periodicals 457, 463, 467, 772
    poetry 424
    religion 452, 456, 457
    school textbooks 457, 464–5
    science 284–5, 456, **463–4**, 467, 470
    World's Classics 457
  chronology:
    First World War 15
    Second World War 169, 452, 461–2
    refugees' impact 452, **461**
    Waldock report (1970) on 466–7
  commercial aspects:
    employee relations 462
    overseas sales 457
    printing operations closed 465
    staff numbers 470
    University Bookshops Oxford
      (UBO) 453, 467
  criticized:
    fails to approach authors 462, 468–9
    secretive 466
    slow in science publishing 464, 470
    slow to publish paperbacks 465, 470
    undergraduate textbooks neglected 462
  donations to University 466, 476, 772
  geographical spread:

Commonwealth 464–5
  London **453–4**, 466–7
  United States 458, 464, 467
governmental affinity 386
historical study of 477
literary connections 423–4, 477
praised:
  for children's books 464–5
  for distribution network 464–5
  for mounting scale of operations after
    1945 470
  for reference works 464, 470
premises xvii, 456, 465, 475, 567–8
research promoted by 133
University control over 466, 640
Oxford University Socialist Society 396
Oxford University Speculative Fiction
  Group 422
Oxford University Student Union 381, 674,
  705, 706, 749, 771
Oxford University Women's Boat Club 531
Oxford and Working-Class Education 34
Oxfordshire and Buckinghamshire Light
  Infantry 10
ozone research 260

pacifism 25, **167–8**, **406–8**, 423
paediatrics 324, 328, 342
Pakistan 464, 538
palaeography 471, 479
palaeontology 150
Palestine 503
Panic 696
paperbacks 453, 465
papyrology 88, 133
paratyphoid fever 14
Parchment & Co., printers, Oxford 470
Parents' Association 119
Paris University 623
Parker's bookshop 420, 452
Parks, University:
  Bodleian Library threatens 474
  cricket in 531, 532, 536
  road planned near 272, 570
  science area and 37, 42–3, 140, 256, 566
Parry Committee on Latin American studies
  (1964) 483
Parson's Pleasure 425
party leaders 377
pass moderations 90, 111, 120, 121–2, 132
  and modern history 123
  and women 351
  see also coaches, academic
pass school:
  careers of those taking 67
  coaches for 92
  colleges discourage 129

pass school (*cont.*):
    decline **57–9**, 92, 109–10, 248, 480, 751
    incidence
        by college 92
        by gender 58, 76, 116, 366
        by school 53–4
    quality of entry for 92
    sporting men less keen to take 521–2
    statistics 53–4, 116
    subjects in: agriculture 145; forestry 147
    see also coaches
Pasteur Institute, Paris 321
patents 282, 283, 690, 771
pathology 319, 320–1, 341
    in Cambridge 320
    college connections 271
    Georges Dreyer and 318, 330
    Gibson Laboratories built (1964) 339
    and industry 282
    in the postgraduate medical school 324,
        328, 329–30
    Sir William Dunn School 253, 268, 321,
        330, 503
patriotism 167–8
patristic studies 303, 309
patronage, college 302
Peckwater Quad, Christ Church 97, 106,
        499
Pegasus AFC 537–8
Pembroke College, Oxford 105, 106, 170,
        481, 692–3
    accommodation 191, 502, 517
    finances 657
    in First World War 8, 9, 20
    junior members 92, 497, 520, 628
Penguin Books 467, 470
penicillin:
    crystallographic study of 268
    first obtained pure 182, **252–3**, 622–3
    Rockefeller Foundation funds research 330
    USA mass-produces 284
    USA patents on 283
pensions 11, 36
Pentagon Club 356
Pentos 452
Pergamon Press 463–4, 467
The Periodical 463
Peripheral Nerve Injuries Centre 253
permanent under-secretaries 378
Persia 150
Persian 767
Peru 274, 493
Peterhouse, Cambridge 389, 505, 588
petrology 275
Phaidon Press 461
pharmaceuticals 28
pharmacology 271, 285, 318, 341

philology 241 *see also* English literature;
        modern languages
philosophy:
    and adjacent subjects:
        classical studies **111–12**, 233
        economics 112
        law 241
        mathematics 264, 288, 289
        physics 264, 289
        political science 112
        political theory 119–20
        psychology 143
        social sciences 241–3
        theology 308, 311
    Aristotle's influence 137
    BPhil in 222, 759
    and conversation 87
    and 'European Greats' 222
    European influence on 90, 609, 620
    impact on religion 311
    library for 476
    in Lit.Hum. 90, 111, 132, 234, 757
    moral collapse ascribed to 221
    and natural science 112, 287
    numbers studying 757
    politically indifferent (1940s) 400
    PPE and 111–15, 119–20, 241, 757
    prestige of 111–12, 601
    research in Oxford on **137–8**, 218
    schools of:
        idealism 241, 244, 308
        pragmatism 711
    teaching methods 132
philosophy of science 288–9
Phipps & Co., printers, Oxford 470
Phoenix Club, Brasenose College 95
photocopiers 712
Physical Chemistry Laboratory 267, 281
    architecture 506
    college laboratories and 88
    fund-raising for 647
    Lord Nuffield helps fund 144, 158
    opens 158, 260
physics:
    Cambridge rivalry 160
    and the colleges 90, 269, 271
    laboratories 37, 160–1, 261
    publishing in 470
    refugees' contribution 160–1, 163, **181–2**,
        252, 589, 622
    and related subjects:
        engineering 260, 274
        mathematics 89, 141, 260, 269–70
        medicine 319
        philosophy 264, 289
    reputation of Oxford 601
    research in **160–1**, 163, 266, 274

nuclear 259, 260, 470: in Second World
War 182, 252; grows fast in 1960s 261,
266, 515; elaborate equipment
required xiv, 281–2; strains college
system 284
in Second World War **181–2**, 186, 252, 266
syllabus reform (1991) 758
undergraduate numbers reading 142, 254,
266
women reading 60, 254
see also careers
physiology:
accommodation for 261, 341
Asquith on 31, 42
and the colleges 90, 271
reputation of Oxford 601
in Second World War 253
number of tutorial fellows in 90
undergraduate numbers 142, 254
Pilgrim Trust 647, 648–9
pilgrimage of prayer 13
Piltdown forgery 288
Pitt Rivers Museum 445, 485, 488, 493, 767
academic role 489, 490
Nervi's design for xix, 490–1, 516
planning 184, 244, 280, 387, 395, 562–76
plastic surgery 332
plate, college 82, 171, 193
Playhouse Theatre 180, 278, 417, 444, 504, 559
playing fields:
college buildings encroach upon 191
lavish provision for men 191, 202
scarce for women 368
poetry 413–22
Poetry Society 419
Poland 178
Political Quarterly 388
political theory:
Isaiah Berlin and 243
and modern history 115, 234, 244
in PPE 119–20
politics:
senior members':
Conservative inter-war 389
moving left from 1950s 394, 402
strongly anti-Conservative by 1970s 395
SDP sympathies in 1980s 404
Labour sympathizers 402, 550–1
local-government activism 550–6
rarely exercised corporately 410, 719
SCRs don't discuss 87
see also by-elections; elections; individual
political parties; Oxford University
M.P.s
undergraduate:
college: college rivalries at 106–7; and the
opposite sex 101; participatory trend

since 1960s 204, 205, 674, 771;
persecution for 96; within JCRs 204
national: vice-chancellors discourage in
1920s 390; Labour sympathies in
1930s 394–5, 399; highly politicized in
1940s 400; reduced interest in
1950s 393, 400; student radicalism in
1960s 394–5, **402–3**, **703–6**, 716;
apartheid stirs feeling (1960s) 703; not
voters till 1970 381, 392; opinion
surveys 394
university: central representation
pioneered 688, 693–4; student
radicalism launched (1960s) 703–4;
violent tactics xix, 403, **745–6**; militant
numbers 403; university funding
suffers 716, 749; college system
moderates pressures 205, 745; student
radicalism criticized 649, 705, 716, 742;
participation since 1960s 674, 771; *see
also* Oxford City Council;
Undergraduate Representative Council;
individual political parties
politics sub-faculty 119
politics as subject of study:
and All Souls 389
BPhil in 222
governmental priorities 388–9
and modern history 115, 120, 123, 234,
242
no first degree in 109
and philosophy 112, 119–20
reputation of Oxford 601
research:
at Nuffield College 760
Commonwealth aspects 136, 618
on elections 389
on international relations 136
within PPE 120, 757
see also political theory
Politics, Philosophy, Economics, *see* PPE
(Politics, Philosophy, Economics)
polytechnics 586, 588
pop concerts 203
the Pope 298
Port Mahon, St. Clement's, public house 423
Portland stone 507, 511
Portugal 452, 633
positivism 395, 396
Post Office 545
Postgraduate Hebrew Studies Centre 771
postgraduates:
characteristics:
getting younger 65
neglected 210–11, 636, 760
non-collegiate 126
proportion in graduate colleges 760

postgraduates: characteristics (*cont.*):
  reading for second undergraduate
    degree 89, 236
  Rhodes scholars 616
  sporting attainment 522
  teaching by 90
 in civic universities 598
 completion rates 759–60
 facilities for:
  accommodation 514, 760
  library space 472, 483
  prizes 48
  scholarships 48, 674
  training 89, 124, 126
 fees 48, 276–7, 674, 763–4
 Franks Commission on 230
 funding for:
  from DSIR 162
  from Ministry of Education 48, 49,
    72
  from prizes 150
 industry and 52
 numbers:
  before 1914 9, 109; inter-war **47, 89**,
    124–5, 210, 218, 585
  growing after 1945 49, 210, 218, 225
  booming in 1960s 480, 547, 605
  declining in 1980s 72, 729
 origins:
  America 126
  Cambridge 588
  Commonwealth 627–30
  overseas 626–31, 651, 763
 part-time 761, 772
 subjects studied 126, 140
  arts/science balance 255–6
  chemistry 15, 158
  English 126
  law 109, 126, 349
  physics 267
 supervision 125–7, 225, 230, 760
 undergraduates tending to become 49–50
 women:
  eligible to be 349
  from overseas 627–30
  gender balance 749–50
  numbers 125, 126
 see also colleges; degrees, postgraduate;
  graduate colleges
Poulton fund 150
Powell & Moya, architects xviii, xix, 491,
  496, 510, 511, 512, 514, 516, 518
PPE (Politics, Philosophy, Economics) 117,
  599
 and adjacent subjects:
  law 114–15
  Lit.Hum. 244, 249

 modern history 89, 112–13, 120, 122–3,
  236, 244
 modern languages 121
 and the BPhil degree 243, 245
 careers related to 116
 characteristics:
  fragmenting tendency 197, 226, **243**, 244,
    246
  governmental preoccupation 387
  quality of intake 57, 113
  teaching methods 132
 chronology:
  origins 33, 70, **111–15**, 143
  inter-war reform 120
  in Second World War 223
  gains new staff in 1950s 244
  reforming mood of 1960s 244–6
  goes bipartite in 1970 757
 criticized:
  embraces incompatibles 113–14
  no literary content 114
  politically quietist 245
  unspecialized 90
 library accommodation 479
 numbers reading 116, 119, **141–2**
 schooling and examination performance 753
 subjects within:
  economics 120–1
  philosophy 111–15, 119–20, 241, 757
  politics 120, 757
  sociology 245
 women reading 116
PPP (Philosophy, Psychology, Physiology):
 launched 222, 242, 264, 279
 undergraduate numbers reading 142, 197,
  254
prayer, in First World War 13
'prelims', *see* examinations, first public
presbyterianism 97, 314
Press, *see* Oxford University Press (OUP)
Pressed Steel Company 560, 565
 in Cowley 545, 562, 563, 575
 funds metallurgy 272, 282
the press, *see* journalism
prime ministers 377
Princeton 156, 228
*Principles and Methods of University
  Reform* 27, 348
printers 544, 550
printing in Oxford:
 in Bodleian Library 479
 geography of 469–70
 history of 472
 in the local economy 544, 548
 in OUP 456, 465, 470
Pritchard Committee on the rating of charities
  (1958–9) 552

Private Eye 425
'private hour' *see* tutorials
Privy Council 670, 704, 719, 747
prizes:
  academic career helped by 90, 94, 150
  by subject:
    bibliography 477
    classics 232
    geology 150
    poetry 428
  in First World War 11
  foster ambition 94
  for postgraduates 48
  women undergraduates and 352
proctors:
  criticized 227, 402, 704–6
  issues:
    central student representation 694, 704
    CND meetings 407
    discipline xiii, 101, 688
    free-speech 688, 693
    Isis censored 703
    lecture reviews banned 226, 703, 704
    pacifism 25
    the 'troubles' (1960s) 703–6
    Union debates censored 180
  roles:
    on Council 685–6
    on General Board 687
    monitoring pubs 558
    in participatory democracy 711
    revised statute for 707
    vis-a-vis women junior members 364
  women as 352
professions:
  administrators in Oxford
      professionalize 695
  curriculum and 71
  jobs in Oxford 548
  as parental influence 55, 57, 595
  want graduates 582
  women from Oxford in 73–7, 370–1
  see also careers
professors:
  appointment of 41
  Asquith Commission and 27, 41, 43, 713
  colleges and 88
  in First World War 11
  numbers 735, 766
  roles:
    in Ashmolean Club 686
    in the BLitt 125
    in Congregation 693
    on Council 37, 735
    in the DPhil 125, 126
    as industrial consultants 282
    lecturing 131

in natural science 141, 159, 255–6, 686,
    694, 735
  with postgraduate students 89, 126
subjects of:
  archaeology 222, 486
  chemistry 267
  clinical oncology 767
  clinical pharmacology 342
  contemporary Arab world 767
  education 761
  entomology 487
  French 6
  geology 487
  geriatrics 342
  history of science 289
  Italian 6
  Japanese studies 767
  medicine 341
  neurology 342
  oriental studies 222
  paediatrics 342
  Persian studies 767
  poetry 418, 433, 448: laymen help
      elect 719, 731; Robert Lowell
      defeated 444; Wain and 421, 441
  psychiatry 342
  radiology 342
  science subjects 141, 255–6, **265**
  thermodynamics 266
  zoology 487
  women as 353
prostitutes 97, 98, 171, 557
Provincial Hospitals Trust 332
psychiatry 324, 328, **342**
Psychological Studies, Faculty of 279
psychology:
  accommodation for 261, 279, 515
  and adjacent subjects:
    modern history 236
    philosophy 143
    sociology 244
  chronology:
    First World War 139
    launched in Oxford (1936) 143, 279
    professor appointed (1947) 279
    experimental psychology an honours
        school (1970) 279
    in the human sciences degree 279
  funds for 143, 162, 619
  humane ethos of 242
  obstacles to 88, 143, 279
  of religion 297
  research in 248–9
  see also PPP
Public Accounts Committee 338
Public Administration Group 389
Public Assistance Committee 549

public health, in medicine 324, 328, 331–2
public houses
　closed to undergraduates 95, 98, 558
　compete with college clubs 203
　as meeting places 423
　opened to undergraduates 201, 558
　see also individual pubs
public schoolboys at Oxford:
　characteristics:
　　active in sport 92, **522–3**, 535, 537,
　　　538
　　culturally prominent 94–5
　　dress 208–9
　　drinking 92, 390–1
　　religion 300
　　work-patterns 92
　exam record improves 753
　numbers 52–5, 226
　　inter-war 94–5
　　after 1945 195
　　admissions exam favours 27, 193
　　college contrasts 19, 214
　　from Clarendon schools 47
　types of:
　　'aesthetes' 92, 168
　　passmen 54
public schools:
　close Oxbridge links 584, 585, 727
　college scholarships and 47–8, 754
　and Conservative politics 391
　discipline in 100, 101
　and First World War 19
　friendships from 95
　and heads of house 82
　hostility to 402, 519
　house system 99–100
　number of 54
　reunions at Oxford for 95
　science and 52–4, 264
　senior members from 604
　in South Africa 611
　sports encouraged at 522–3, 535
　subjects studied at:
　　classics 28, 128
　　modern studies 54
　University wants to conciliate 358
　see also admission; individual schools
publishing
　careers in 424–31, 457
　in London, tutors effect introductions 417
　in London inter-war 457
　in Oxford:
　　fosters creative writing 414, 424–8
　　its geography 468, 470
　　wars' impact (1940s) 221, 462, 470
　see also Blackwell's; Oxford University Press
　　(OUP); Pergamon

punting 364–5, 445, 514, 517
Pusey House, Oxford 303, 315, 760

Quarterly Journal of Medicine 457
Queen Elizabeth House 618
Queen Mary College, London 601
Queen's award for technological
　achievement 771
Queen's College, Oxford 7, 85, 214
　academic aspects:
　　examination results 105, 213
　　Hastings scholarships 106
　　laboratory 40, 157
　　papyrology in 88
　buildings 508, 509, 511, 512;
　　accommodation expanded 191, 568
　finances 642, 657, 670, 740
　in First World War 8, 20, 81
　JCR committee (1948) at 208
　junior members from overseas 612, 629
　provosts' role 83
　St Edmund Hall escapes from 107
　in Second World War 170
　and tourists 565
　trumpet sounds in 103

radar 181, 252
Radcliffe Camera:
　building work in 499, 516
　fund-raising dinner in 765
　osculation observed in 101
　undergraduate readers in 471, 472, 479,
　　483
Radcliffe Infirmary:
　in First World War 10
　Lord Nuffield and 323
　in Second World War 253
　split site with Headington 335–40
　teaching laboratory built (1970) at 343
　biochemistry in 331
　facilities in 318, 339
　and the medical school 318–21, **324–6**, 329,
　　334
　NHS's impact 335
Radcliffe Observatory 339, 517
　re-located 153–4, 322–3
　and University Observatory 153
Radcliffe Science Library:
　1960s holdings 263
　architecture 504, 505, 506, 507
　extensions 263–4, 473, 478, 482, 516
　incorporated into Bodleian Library 153,
　　473
　mathematics and 156, 269
Radcliffe Square, Oxford 472, 474, 574
Radcliffe trustees 153
radio 99, 101

radioactivity 281
radiology 331, 342
Ralegh Club 381, 616
Randolph Hotel, Oxford 268
rates 552–3, 675
rationing 179, 207
The Rattler 10
readers:
  in First World War 11
  impact of 1980s cuts 766
  role in graduate supervision 126, 148
  role in science departments 265
  subjects of:
    bibliography 477
    crystallography 151
    mineralogy 151
    zoology 148
    women as 348
reading parties 93, 200
Reading University 260, 682
Red Cross Club 178
'redbrick' universities, *see* civic universities
refugees:
  academic impact on:
    the book trade 452, 461
    classical studies 233, 461
    economics 173–4, 185
    the humanities 221
    mathematics 156
    medicine 182, 333, 341
    music 452
    physics 160, 163, 252, 589, 622
  JCRs help fund 204
  in Second World War 177–8
  types of:
    Basque child 96
    Belgian 6
    German 156, 160, 173
    Hungarian 407
    Londoners (1917–18) 12
    Serbian 7
  women undergraduates (1914–18) and 13
Regal Cinema, Cowley Road 180
Regent's Park College 297, 314, 504, 629
registers:
  college 373, 647
  electoral 378, 694
registrars:
  before Veale 689–90
  attend CVCP 587
  curb Chest 690, 708
  growing power 689, 732
  meet other registrars 695
  relations with:
    Council 698–9, 709
    General Board 692
    vice-chancellor 690, 699, 709

see also Assistant Registrar; individual
    registrars
Registry
  and the Chest 698
  and elections of university MPs 378, 410
  Latinizing names 707
  size of 689, 696
  see also Assistant Registrar; Oxford
    University, administration; registrars
religion at Cambridge 293, 298, 302
religion at Oxford:
  characteristics:
    geography of 294
    increasingly pluralist 295
    intellectually on the defensive 308, 314,
      315
    not discussed in SCRs 87
    Oxford provides generously for 293
  chronology:
    First World War 7, 13, 15, 16, 19
    prospers in 1930s and 1940s 314
    in Second World War 180, 184
  and the colleges:
    college patronage 302
    churches secularized for 191, 481
    Keble 303
    St Peter's 304
    tithes 660, 663, 668–9, 673
    women's colleges 55, **346–7**, 367
    see also chaplains; chapels
  ecumenism 296, 306, 311, 346
  influences on from:
    laymen 310
    philosophy 308, 311
    Scotland 298
    secularization 219
    USA 296, 298, 301, 305
  interaction with:
    Asquith Commission 33, 34
    book trade 451–2, 456, 457, 464
    literature 310, 437
    Oxford Union 180
    psychology 297
    science 270, 278, **286–7**
    social work 549
    theology 308, 309, 315
  as qualification for fellowships 92
  theological colleges 302
  and undergraduates:
    impact of state funding 39
    social-class implications 300
    strong influence on 209, 295
    surveys of observance 295
    their religious background 57
  see also careers; individual denominations;
    war
Religious Experience Research Unit 278, 297

rent strikes 674
Repton School 537
Research Laboratory for Archaeology and the
     History of Art 223, 288
research in Oxford:
     becomes more widespread 603
     civic universities' influence 158–9, 163, 589
     weakens Congregation's attendance 687, 692
     increasingly international 608
     inter-war 132–8
     nourishes university rather than colleges 694
     obstacles to 89, 90, 612–13, 645–6
     promoted by:
         Americans 88, 89, 253, 272, 645
         Asquith Commission 613, 652
         Commonwealth 618, 621
         CUF system 88, 89, 652, 687
         graduate colleges 624–5
     see also colleges; Fellows of colleges;
         postgraduates; professors; tutors;
         individual subjects
respirators 9, 14, 253
Responsions:
     classics in 110
     Greek for 29, 37, 351
     not a major hurdle 91
     school certificate exempts from 64–5
     Statutory Commission and 43
     women and 350, 351
     see also coaches
restaurants 12, 179
retail price index 675
The Review 429–30, 434–5
The Revised English Bible (1989) 464
Revue des deux mondes 12
Rewley House, see delegacies
Rhodes chair of race relations 624
Rhodes Estate Act (1916) 5
Rhodes House:
     buildings xviii, **502–3**, 506
     gardens 506
     library 473, 617, 618
     proposed new roles 708, 714
     social facilities 97, 178, 422, 616
Rhodes scholars:
     broaden out Oxford's world
         contacts 615–16
     chronology:
         First World War 5, 19
         Second World War 5
         jubilee (1954) 691
     distribution by college 214
     fund-raising from 360
     how selected 3, 610, 619
     and medicine 323, 341, 622–3
     numbers 616
     promote postgraduate study 616

     publicize Oxford in USA 610, 619
     sporting prowess 98, 536, 610–11
     women become 748, 749
     origin:
         Australia 6, 323, 330, 341, 616, 622–3
         the Bahamas 5
         Barbados 5, 610
         British Guiana 5
         Canada 5, 6
         Germany 3, 4, 5, 6, 102, 610
         Hong Kong 5
         India 6, 614
         Orange Free State 5
         South Africa 5, 6
         Transvaal 5
         Trinidad 5, 610
         USA 6, 610–11, 616
         West Indies 6
Rhodes Trust 610
     helps to fund:
         American history 235
         Commonwealth studies 617
         engineering 144
         science research 162
         sport 526, 531, 533, **536**
         University appeal (1937) 647
         non-Oxford causes 611, 616
Richards Committee on college contributions
     (1976) 675
Richardson and Houfe, architectural
     practice 509
Richmond Road synagogue 301
Richmond, Surrey 538
Ripon Hall 303
Ritz Cinema, Gloucester Green 180
Robbins report (1963) 578, 590, 604,
     721
     criticisms of Oxford 603–5, 723
         administratively anomalous 770
         entrance system 219, 226
         inbred appointments 603
         indecisive 731
         lay participation weak 717
         unable to explain itself 715
     encourages expansion 49, 583
     and Franks Commission 229, 722–4
     Oxford criticizes 394
Roberts report on provision for graduate
     students (1987) 731, 760
ROBOT scheme 388
Rochdale, Lancs. 586
Rockefeller Foundation 34, 619
     helps to fund:
         buildings 507
         libraries: Bodleian 474, 477, 505, 619,
             645–6, 690; Law Library 516
         refugees 461

research in: biochemistry 321;
  economics 137; medicine 320–5, 330,
  619; psychology 619; science 162, 619;
  social studies 619
Oxford neglects overture from (1927–8) 322,
  619, 689
rodent control 253
roll of service, First World War 18
Rolls-Royce 283
Roman Catholics 314, 347, 384
  chaplaincy 209, 298–301
  religious orders 298–9
  return to Oxford 298
  segregate women 299, 300
  and theology 299
  Waugh and 293, 299
room charges 94
Rose Hill community centre 550
Rose Lane, Oxford 504, 506
Routledge, publishers 467, 468
rowing, see bump suppers; Eights Week;
  sport
Royal Air Force 14
Royal College of Physicians 340
royal commissions:
  Local Government (1966–9) 386
  Medical Education (1965–8) 343
  Oxford (1850–2) 35, 586
  Oxford (1877–82) 640, 641
  tithe rentcharge (1935–6) 663
  see also Asquith Commission
Royal Fine Art Commission 512
Royal Flying Corps 10, 14
Royal Historical Society 134
Royal Holloway College, Egham 345
Royal Signals 48
Royal Society:
  and ecology 149
  Fellows of:
    college fellowships sometimes elude 148
    as heads of house 82
    Oxbridge strong among 593
    Oxford and Cambridge compared 262
    by subject
      biology 150
      medicine 329
      metallurgy 159–60
      zoology 148
  and science funding 149, 159–60,
    262
rugby football see sport
Rugby School 47
rural economy see agriculture
Ruskin College, Oxford 6, 587, 746
  and economics 112
  numbers at 385
  and the Oxford Union 384

political impact:
  nationally 107, 385–6
  on Oxford 399, 705
  in Suez crisis 408
undergraduate attitudes to 204, 209, 408
Ruskin School of Drawing 414, 758
Russia:
  films from 560
  hostility to 623
  and Oxford (1939–45) 178
  political styles in 390
  revolution in 34, 412
  and science publishing 463
  socialism in Oxford influenced by 398
Russian language 119, 222
Russian orthodox church 7
Rutherford Laboratory 259, 267

S&S Press, printers, Oxford 470
sabbatical leave:
  Franks Commission on 230
  more often taken 88, 196
  relatively generous in Oxford 603
St Aldate's:
  church 303, 304–5, 313, 314
  coffee house 418
St Aloysius church 300
St Anne's College xv, 107, 374, 497
  becomes a college 107, 214, 352
  buildings 506, 511, 512, 513, 515, 655, 746
  crèche in 373
  examination performance 105, 752
  finances 654, 655, 657
  garden 518
  junior members:
    doing voluntary social service 550
    from overseas 629
    not taking degrees 59
    their origins 347
  library 477
  men admitted 352
  men's role in governing body 352
  motto 352
  planning restrictions hinder 567
  turns away from its own traditions 352
St Antony's College 199, 236, 386, 481, 625,
  629
  origins 285, 624, 653
  becomes a college 214
  admits women 210
  finances 656–7
  new buildings xviii, 515, 518
  possible All Souls alliance 215, 736
St Benet's Hall 298, 629
St Catherine's College 89, 199, 297, 497,
  771
  architecture 202, 513, 514, 517

St Catherine's College: architecture (*cont.*):
  new buildings (1936) 107
  new buildings (1964) xix, 507, 513–14, 515
  becomes a college 107, 214
  examination performance 105, 750
  finances 507, 514, 649, 655, 657, 673
  junior members 213–4, 374, 629, 747
  see also non-collegiate students
St Clement's, Oxford 398, 512, 548, 549, 568, 575
St Columba's church 314
St Cross Building (1964) xix, 481, 516
St Cross College 211, 215, 714, 742, 760, 771
St Ebbe's 547, 548, 549, 575
  church 303, 304–5, 313
St Edmund Hall 20, 107, 199, 210
  buildings 502, 512
    library occupies church 191, 481, 517, 649
  examination performance 105, 529–30
  finances 654–5, 657, 673
  junior members 105, 497, 629–30
  sport 214, 526, 527, **529–30**
  subjects studied:
    engineering 274, 286
    geography 89
    theology 308
St Edmund's Old Hall, Herts. 299
St Hilda's College, Cheltenham 347
St Hilda's College, Oxford 59, 105, 347, 351, 373, 752
  finances xvi, 657
  junior members xvi, xvii, 530, 629
  new buildings xvii, 509, 512, 515
  remains single-sex 375, 746
  rules on men 362, 703
St Hugh's College xv, 59, 210, 567
  Anglican tone 39, 55, 346–7
  architecture 503, 504
  examination performance 76, 752
  finances 39, 657
  gardens 506
  junior members from overseas 629
  library 477
  'row' 351, 368
  in Second World War 170, 182
St John Street, Oxford 557, 568
St John's College, Cambridge 511
St John's College, Oxford 448, 559, 708
  academic aspects:
    English at 443
    examination performance 105
    theology at 308
  architecture:
    expands accommodation 191
    gardens 106
    interior decoration 514

  new buildings xviii, 509, 510, 511, 514–15
  finances 657, 740
    battels payment in 100
    North Oxford development 567, 668
    planning restrictions weaken 567
    sells land to other colleges 191
  in First World War 7, 8, 9, 20
  library 481
  in Second World War 170, 176
  undergraduate life:
    archery club xii, 95
    clubs 95
    college loyalty 106
    debating society 382–3
    Essay Society 99
    grammar-schoolboys in 96
    living conditions 105
    political awareness 399
    power within college 688
    proportion from overseas 629
St Mary's (University) church 305, **313–5**, 508
St Paul's School 47
St Peter in the East 191, 481, 517, 649
St Peter-le-Bailey church 303, 304
St Peter's College:
  founded 304
  in Second World War 189
  becomes a college (1961) 214
  buildings 504, 506, 507
  finances 655, 657, 673
  junior members from overseas 629
  theology in 308
St Petersburg 163
St Stephen's House 6, 303
St Thomas's, Oxford 549, 557
salons 87, 93
Samuel and Harding, architectural practice 505
Sanders bookshop 420, 452
Sanders of the River 97
Sanskrit 109, 609
Sarawak 493
Saskatchewan, Canada 5
Saunders, printers, Oxford 470
Saxe-Coburg and Gotha, Duke of 3
Scala Cinema, Walton Street 180, 560
Scarbrough Commission (1945–6) 623
scholarships and exhibitions, college:
  abolished as entrance awards 754
  awarding process 83, 91, **193–4**, 710
  classics pressed on holders of 111
  colleges compete through 672
  criticized 38, 605
  data on 60
  examination-results of holders 91, 110

financially important 46
Hastings scholarships 106
implications for social life:
  privileges attached 91
  in women's colleges 366
number of 110
postgraduates rarely get inter-war 48
prestige of 91, 100
social-class implications:
  aids to social mobility 70, 91, 387
  public-school uptake 47–8, 264
  for working class 38, 48
for specific subjects
  classics 110, 232
  mathematics 156
  science **59–60**, 62, 264
for unfashionable subjects 89
waning significance in undergraduate
  life 77, 194, 247
as war memorial 23
war-service by holders of 9
for women 55, 366
see also admission
scholarships and exhibitions, school 101
schools:
  for Belgian refugees 7
  in Oxford 555
  see also public schools; secondary schools
schoolteachers:
  and admissions process 83
  becoming Fellows of colleges 92
  inter-war tutors resemble 92, 201
  offspring go to Oxford 56
  and Oxford science 264
schoolteaching:
  examination qualifications 76
  H.A.L.Fisher and 29
  and modern languages 119
  Oxford curriculum and 71, 119
  status of 71–2
  training in Oxford for 761–2
  for women 13, 58, **73–6**, 347, 370–1, 530
  see also careers; diplomas
science:
  accommodation for 256–61 *see also* science
    area
  and arts subjects:
    geography 117
    history of art 223, 288
    philosophy 112; research concept
     boosted by 289
    science within arts courses 228–9, **287–9**
    scientists' interest in 141, 288
  arts/science contrasts 53–4, 68–9, 74–7,
    248, 263
    courses attempting to transcend 757
  and Asquith Commission 31, 37, 41, 43, 88

Cambridge status of 28, 37, 40, 141, 264,
  286, 600
characteristics:
  change comes from without 143, 162
  improvisation and individualism 151,
    280, 281, 395
  inactive in Oxford's government 284,
    285, 689
  international collaboration 259–60, 271
  multi-disciplinary research 257, 259, 566
  non-vocational 273
  small but distinguished 144, 273, 274,
    280
  social class aspects 70, 73
  somewhat inbred 141, 156, 259
  team-work 251, 281
  wary of applied study 143–4, 272, 284,
    588, 626
chronology:
  in First World War 9, 14, 19, 28, 29, 60
  in Second World War: physics and the
    war effort 181–2, 252: raises
    proportion reading science 60, 252
  after 1945 253–7, 625
and colleges:
  admissions awards scarce 59–60, 62, 264
  college labs 40, 88, 157, 256, 267
  hostility to 211–12, 276–7
  scientists not heads of house **82**
degree results 61–2, 751
funding from:
  city gilds 149, 159
  DSIR 162, 181–2, 261
  government 162, 261, **764–8**
  industry 141, 144, 158, **162**, 261, 272: *see*
    also Imperial Chemical Industries
  patents 282, 283, 690, 771
  Rockefeller Foundation 137, 162, 320–5,
    330, 619
  Royal Society 149, 159–60, 262
  scientists' altruism 155, 160, 161, 279
  UGC 162, 261, 515
hostility to 141, 284, **286–7**
and industry:
  personal movements between 140, 144,
    282–3
  scientists' needs not met 284
  in Second World War 253
  staff lost to 282, 696
  other references 31, 265, 274
  see also Oxford Instrument Company;
    science, funding
library accommodation 263–4, 472–3, 478,
  482, 504–7, 516
mounting numbers employed in 695
overseas influences 158, 160–1, 163, *see also*
  refugees

science (*cont.*):
    periodicals published 152, 268–9, 277, 288,
        463, 467
    postgraduate numbers 140–1, 255–6, 625–6
    professors' role 141, 159, 255–6, **265–6**, 686,
        694, 735
    public schools and 52–4, 264
    publishing in Oxford 284–5, 456, **463–4**,
        467, 470
    staffing:
        difficult to recruit 265, 696
        mounting numbers 263, 267, 271, **281–2**,
            696
        new technology requires expert 265, 281
        sports facilities for 529
        wages and grading 282, 696
    status of:
        rises in First World War 28, 31
        more salient inter-war 37, 139–40
        rises in Second World War 252
        after 1945 262, 771
        lower for applied 589, 600–1
    syllabus reform 264
    teaching methods:
        classes 263
        lectures 263, 643
        libraries 263–4
        practicals 267
        tutorials 89–90, 263, 277, 730
    undergraduate numbers reading:
        before 1914 109
        inter-war 43, **59–61**, 217
        in Second World War 60, 176–7, 252
        since 1945 60–2, 218, **253–5**
    women in **59–61**, 76, **254–5**, 268
    see also careers; history of science; individual
        subjects
science area:
    centrifugal tendency 259
    centripetal tendency 256–9
    chronology:
        in First World War 14
        inter-war growth 108
        inter-war pressures on space 147, 691
        in Second World War 251
        space scarce after 1945 272, 278, 356–9,
            515
    conservation constraints 566–7
    height limits 273, 515, 566
    and individual subjects, astronomy 272
    lectures gravitate to 263
    Parks and 37, 42–3, 140, 256, 566
    second campus ideas 259, 566
    sociability within 268, 270, 285
    and specific subjects:
        astronomy 272
        biochemistry 321

    botany 152–3, 276
    forestry 147
    mathematics 156
    medicine 321
    physiology 341
    see also architecture
science fiction 420
'science Greats' 143, 228, 287
Science Reorganization Committee (1916) 28
Science Research Council 259, 261, 271
sconcing 101
Scoones 387
Scotland:
    colleges don't buy land in 662–3
    FBAs drawn from 593
    postgraduate numbers in 585
    religious influence of 298
    undergraduates from 51, 97
    universities in:
        distinctive 579, 585
        reputation 600–2
        stress applied science 589
        women at 345, 584
    vice-chancellors educated in 594
scouts *see* servants
SCR *see* senior common rooms
Scrutiny 429, 431
sculpture 133, 486, 495, 508
Scunthorpe, Lincs. 598
Seacourt Press, printers, Oxford 470
secondary schools:
    awards to undergraduates by 101
    categories of 52, 54
        comprehensive 748
        endowed 47
        girls' 351
        grammar: increasing number of 582; Latin
            and 47; Oxbridge awards important
            for 595; recruits to science from 70;
            sports encouraged at 522–3; women at
            Oxford from 54; *see also* grammar-
            schoolboys at Oxford
    co-education advances in 748
    curricula influenced by Oxford 219
    examination results vary between types of 752
    growing number of 27, 29, 582
    growing numbers at 46
    links with individual colleges 94, 347
    publishing for 457, 461
    subjects taught:
        classics 110, 351
        mathematics 270
    see also public schools
Secretary of Faculties 690, 692, 702
seismology 153, 154, 162
seminars 609
    criticized 229

early Oxford history of 88
Franks Commission on 230
subjects of:
  chemistry 268
  Commonwealth history 618
  politics 389
senior common rooms (SCRs):
  butlers 103
  conversation in xi, 87, 436
  head of house's role 198
  mood 86-7
  wives and 209
  in women's colleges 368
senior tutors:
  administrative arrangements for 84
  meetings between 88, 214, 221, 673, 710, 742
  rarely scientists 221
separation allowances 9
Serbia 7
sermons 23, 83
servants, college:
  attitudes:
    dons 103
    motor manufacturing 103, 105, 207
    proud of Oxford 103
    sporting enthusiasm 103, 528-9
    trade unions 103, 544-5, 688, 696
    traditionalist 206
    undergraduates 93, 104-5
  categories of 103
    cleaner 103, 207, 544
    head porter 103, 206
    lodge porter 93, 104
    scout xiv, 98, 103, 104-5, 206
    scout's boy 104, 105, 207
    SCR butler 103, 206
  characteristics:
    alumni recognized 103, 206-7
    hierarchical 103
    long-serving xiv, 206-7
    often scholarly 103
    patience 103
    tact 103, 206
  commemorated 103
  diminished service from 205-8
  in First World War 8-9, 22
  increasingly recruited from women 207
  organizations for 103, 528-9
  pay 8-9, 11, 103
  tips to 104
Sex Discrimination Act (1975) 748
Sex Disqualification (Removal) Act
  (1919) 349
Shackleton Committee on libraries (1965-6)
  481
Shakespeare Head Press 461
Sheffield City 453

Sheffield University 27, 29, 583
Sheldonian Theatre:
  books in basement 471
  missions in 314
  relocation proposal 645
  restored 499, 508, 648
Shell 144, 150, 162
shell-shock 9, 139, 222
Shillingford, Oxon. 420
Shotover Hill, Oxon. 564
Shrewsbury School 47, 537
silver plate 495
Simancas, Spain 609
Singapore 632-3
Sinister Street cited 104
'sit-ins' 705, 745
sixth forms 224, 225
Slade School of Fine Art 170
slang 95
Slatter and Rose, printers, Oxford 470
'smalls' *see* Responsions
soccer *see* sport
Social and Administrative Studies,
  Department of 761
social anthropology 242, 249
  diploma 109, 222
  Exeter College and 88, 711
  library for 476
  no first degree in 89, 109, 246
  and related subjects:
    archaeology 222-3, 490
    human sciences 279
    modern history 236
    sociology 244
  research in 135
  see also cultural anthropology; Pitt Rivers
    Museum
social class:
  in 1960s 226
  elite educated in Oxford 194, 218, 224,
    287, 607
    in literature 428-31
    in medicine 317, 320, 333, 342
  guilt about working class 432
  of junior members 51-8, 595
    inter-war 94-5, 100, 694
    broadens out 71, 73, 208-9, 219, 411
    moulds choice of sport 522, 535
  and local politics 551-2, 554, 568
  Oxford prestige depends less on 411
  Second World War's impact 175-6, 179,
    187
social mobility:
  difficulties involved in 441
  of lab technicians 281, 696
  Oxford encourages 208
  scholarships help 70, 91

social class: social mobility (*cont.*):
    through Conservatism 394
    and the theatre 427
    university employees and 529, 544
    women and **52–8**, 76–7, 352
    see also admission; careers; servants; trade
        unions; working class
Social Democratic Party 404
social medicine 331–2
social studies 647, 761
    Board 120
    Library 482
    see also sociology
social work 244, 373, 548–50, *see also* Barnett
        House; careers; sociology
socialism, *see* Guild Socialism; Labour Party
Socialist Dons' Luncheon Club 397
Society for Freedom in Science 280, 395
Society of Oxford Home-Students, *see* St
        Anne's College
sociology:
    at the LSE 600
    careers in 249
    characteristics:
        governmental outlook 389
        humanistic view of in Oxford 242
        suffers from idealism's decline 244
    and the local community 561
    name for 389
    opposition to 88, 244, 705
    reaches Oxford late 241–2, **245**
    and related subjects:
        human sciences 279
        literature 401
        modern history 236, 237
        philosophy 241
        psychology 244
        social anthropology 244
    reputation of Oxford 601
    Second World War boosts 220
    see also PPE
Socratic Club 311, 315
soldiers *see* army
Solomon Islands 493
Somerville College 345, 360
    academic aspects:
        competition for places 366
        examination performance 63, 76, 105,
            752
    alumni role in 351–2
    buildings 503, 504–5, 507, 512, 514–15
        furnishings 514
    characteristics:
        liberal affinities 346
        religion 55, 346, 352
        social class 55
    Corpus alliance 210

facilities:
    crèche 373
    register 373
finances 657
    appeals 39
    CUF system 653
    UGC assists 507
in First World War 10, 12–13
and mixed colleges:
    persists as single-sex 375, 746
    their impact 63
    undergraduates want 374
undergraduate life:
    clubs/societies 367, 368–9;
    gate keys issued 202, 362
    JCR xv, 368
    overseas intake 629
    rowing 527
    rules about men 362
    sport 530–1
South Africa:
    astronomy in 153
    funds from 618
    junior members from 632–3
        Rhodes scholars 5, 6, 536
        sporting prowess 536
    OUP in 464
    religion in 301
    Rhodes Trust work in 611
South America, *see* Latin America
South Korea 633
Southampton University 583
Southfield School for Boys 555
Southfields Golf Club 564
'Southgate College' 743
Spain 390, 452, 609, 633
Spanish language 119, 645
Special Operations Executive (SOE) 182
Spectator 417, 430, 705
spectroscopy 267, 269, 288
spies 13, 381
Spitzbergen 274
sponsorship of sport 532–3, 771
sport:
    and academic attainment 520–3, 528–30
        pass school 521–2
        tension between 519–20, 538
        varies between sports 522–3
    in admission process 193, 194, 520, 529,
        530, 610–11
    civic-university links extend 533–4
    class contrasts in sports taken up 522–3
    clothing for xi, 94, 100
    college servants and 103, 528–9
    colleges:
        attach prestige to 95, 100
        compete in 106, 202, 214, **527–30**

get known through success in 529–30
heads of house encourage 102
integrating impact on 98, 611
Commonwealth and 98, 536, 538, 610–11,
634
facilities:
lavish outdoors 98, 523–6
poor indoors 526
funding 368, **531–3**
from commercial sponsors 532
from the sportsmen themselves 532
from university 519, 531–3
for women 531
geography of 524–5
lawyers often active in 193, 529
mixed colleges' impact 531
pressure to participate 96
sex-segregation declines 531
specialization's impact 519, 535, 536–7,
695
timetable for 195
and town/gown relations 537
undergraduate journalists and 402, 527, 534
for women 530–1
relatively under-funded 368, 530
rowing xvi, 364, 368, 527, 531
team games decline 367–8
see also bump suppers; playing fields
types of:
archery xii, 95, 531
athletics xix, 522–3, 528, 536, **537**
badminton 526, 531, 532
basketball 532, 534, 538
bowls 529
cricket 522–3, 529, 530, 531, 532, **536**, 536
fencing 526, 531, 532, 534
field sports 534–5
football 522–3, 528, 529, 531, 534, 536,
537–8
golf 101, 322
gymnastics 526
hockey 522–3, 528, 530, 534, 538
ice-hockey 538
judo 532
karate 531
lacrosse 530, 532
netball 530
polo 534
punting 364–5, 445
rowing: and academic attainment 193,
522–3; by college servants 529; captain's
books 98; colleges prominent
for 527–30; dons' interest in 93, 102,
520, 528; 'goes comprehensive' 535;
how funded 532
rugby football 522–3, 527–33, 535–6,
539

sailing 531
squash 526
swimming 523, 526, 539
tennis 523, 529, 530
volleyball 533, 534
water polo 523
Sports Facilities Committee 533
Spring Hill College 295
squash 526
Sri Lanka 630
staircases 98, 506, 513, 515
Standing Conference of National and
University Libraries 480
State Serum Institute, Copenhagen 321
state studentships/scholarships 38, 46–7
statistical study:
accommodation for 516
in agriculture 145
in economics 120
in the human sciences degree 279
Statutory Commission, see Asquith
Commission
Staverton Road, Oxford 191
Stevens, publishers 462
Stirling, University of 583
Strathclyde University 583
Stubbs Society 237
Student Christian Movement (SCM) **311–13**,
315, 365, 392
student counselling 201, 771 see also chaplains
Student Representative Council (SRC) 227,
704, 730, 745, 771
'students' as designation 204–5, 704 see also
undergraduates
students' union, central 210, 694, 745
submarines 29
Suez crisis (1956) 401, **407–8**, 412,
608
suggestions books 96, 204
suicides 201, 302
Summertown, Oxford 557
Super Cinema, Magdalen Street 180, 560
surgery 337
in First World War 9
in the postgraduate medical school 324, 328,
331
Surveyor, University 507, 517, 695, 707
Sussex University:
architecture 509
founded 583, 597–8
Oxford feels threatened by 226–7
Oxford influences on 599, 761
reputation 601–3
Sutton Courtenay, Berks. 378
Swansea, University College 601
Sweden 560, 722
Sweet and Maxwell, publishers 462

swimming, *see* sport
Swinford, Berks. 424
Swinnerton-Dyer report on postgraduate
　　education (1982) 759
Switzerland 588
Sycamore Press 424
Sydney, University of 163
syllabus *see* curriculum; examinations;
　　individual subjects
synagogue, Richmond Road 301
syndicalism 396

Taharqa 494
tanks 9
Tasmania 493
Taylor Institution:
　　extension 504
　　library 472, 473, 475, 476–7, 482
tea *see* meals
tea-shops 101
teach-in (1965) xvii, 408
teaching *see* schoolteaching
teaching methods *see* classes; lectures;
　　tutorials
telephones 476, 696, 703, 708
television 204, 384, 533
Templeton College 763
Tenmantale, Keble College 203
Tetrahedron 269
Thame, Oxon. 101, 420
theatre 427, 559 *see also* acting; individual
　　theatres
theology:
　　Anglicans monopolize divinity degrees 306
　　calibre of candidates for 307
　　and the colleges
　　　　colleges strong in 41
　　　　Christ Church 308
　　　　Exeter 308
　　　　Jesus 308
　　　　Keble 89, 303, 308
　　　　Manchester 305
　　　　Mansfield 305
　　　　Oriel 308
　　　　St Catherine's 89
　　　　St Edmund Hall 308
　　　　St John's 308
　　　　St Peter's 308
　　　　Wadham 308
　　in entrance exam 110
　　evangelical attacks on liberal 305
　　examinations in 110
　　in First World War 7, 15
　　in Germany 15
　　libraries for 297
　　numbers reading 110, 116, **142**, 308

overseas influences on 296, 298, 309, 609
and related subjects:
　　classics 89, 307
　　philosophy 308, 311
and religious practice:
　　impact on belief 308, 309, 315
　　chaplains from 85, 309
　　nonconformity 297–8, 305–6
　　Roman Catholicism 299
reputation of Oxford 309, 310
research in Oxford on 134–5
syllabus 109, 306–7
women reading 116, 308
Thornton Butterworth, publishers 458
Thornton's bookshop 452
The Times 101, 389
Times Literary Supplement 429, 441
tips 104
tithes 660, 663, 668–9, 673
Tom Quad, Christ Church 94, 106
topology 156, 269–70
Toronto University 174
tourists 497, 565
trade unions in Oxford:
　　and adult education 556
　　college system weakens 688
　　influence on:
　　　　college servants 103, 544
　　　　lab staff 282, 696
　　　　Nuffield College 386
　　　　senior members 590
　　and Labour Party 550, 552
　　overall recruitment pattern 544
　　and social policy 549, 550
　　studied 389, 556
Trades Union Congress 385–6
Transport and General Workers' Union 545
Transvaal 5
Trinidad 5, 610, 630
Trinity College, Cambridge 105, 155, 656
Trinity College, Oxford:
　　building:
　　　　accommodation expanded 191
　　　　collaboration with Blackwell's 452, 512
　　　　library 263, 504
　　　　new buildings 504, 509
　　bursarial arrangements 83
　　examination performance 105
　　finances 657–8
　　in First World War 20
　　junior members:
　　　　advised on careers 93
　　　　class relations 209, 441
　　　　drinking 558
　　　　from overseas 629
　　　　rowing xii
　　　　sporting prowess 106, 527

urinating 95
vendetta with Balliol 100
in Second World War 170
see also Balliol-Trinity Laboratory
trust funds 11, 587, 710
trust pools 670
'tube alloys' 182, **252**
tuberculosis 321
Turin shroud 288
Turl Cash Bookshop, Oxford 453
Turl Street, Oxford 191, 354, 504
'tutorial hour' 132
tutorials:
  colleges and: central to college's
    role 89–90, 760–1; send pupils
    out 197
  criticized 130, 225, 263, 277, 439, 730
  descriptive term for 89, 132
  in English literature 133
  Franks Commission and 196, 229, 230,
    758–9
  frequency 195, 196
  how conducted xvi, **127–32**, 230
    'covering the ground' 230, 758, 760–1
    distinct from lectures 130, 230
    dress 205
    opportunity for moral guidance 92
    reading-lists 196
    relationship to conversation 87
    sexes mixed 362
    skills inculcated 197
  investigated 226
  postgraduates give 90
  praised 41, 229, 247
  scientists and 89–90, 263, 277, 730
  Second World War and 223
  tone down friction in 1960s 705, 745
  women's 365
tutors:
  activities:
    after-care of pupils 93, 198
    creative writing 415
    moral responsibilities dwindle 202
    outwitting finals examiners 92, **129–30**,
      599, 751
    supervising postgraduates 760
    visiting USA 196
    wielding college power 351
    work-pattern 90, 195
  characteristics:
    accessible 93
    age 86
    friendly with pupils 90, 92, 93
    helpful on careers 70–1, 93, 201
    imitated by pupils 197
    increasingly professional 195–6, 214,
      247, 695

less like schoolteachers 201
    unspecialized 90, 228
    versatile 92
  coach superseded by 92, 129–30
  how appointed 39, 40, 41, **195–6**, 612
  murdered fictionally 446
  pay 39, 710
  research by:
    inessential before 1960s 195, 217, 218,
      247, 612
    abundant by 1960s 229, 247
    Franks Commission on 230–1
    erodes attendance at Congregation 687,
      692
    in tension with teaching 90, 224, 229,
      242–3, 758
  schoolteachers as 92
  staff/student ratio 759
  work-load:
    Asquith Commission and 36
    inter-war 129–30, 132
    falls after 1945 196
    in 1960s 226, 229
    in 1980s 759
    colleges diverge on 214
  see also coaches; Fellows of colleges; senior
    tutors
Twickenham, Middx. 391, 532, 534, 538
typewriters 476, 689, 712
typhoid 14

Uganda 52, 635
Ullswater Committee on Broadcasting
  (1935) 384
Undergraduate Representative Council 98,
  693–4, 694
undergraduates:
  activities:
    being counselled 201, 305, 771
    book-buying 453
    climbing in 101, 201–2, 363
    conducting vendettas 100
    criticising syllabuses 227
    damaging furniture 34, 96
    debagging 96, 391, 447
    drinking 87, 92, 95–6, 99, 203, 558
    entertaining senior members 200
    hoaxes 91, 100
    imitating tutors 197
    increasingly using libraries 472, 479, 480
    inventing ritual 99, 101
    journalism 99, 424–7, 434–5, 444, 703
    persecuting contemporaries 95, 96, 390
    relieving unemployment 96, 400
    rent strikes 674
    room-renting 192
    room-sharing 98

undergraduates: activities (*cont.*):
    room-wrecking 390–1
    running up debts 558
    sconcing 101
    sex 98, 202, 209
    strike-breaking 100, 391
    suicide 201
    taking drugs 770
    urinating 95
    versifying 424–6
    receiving visitors 101
    volunteering for war service 8, 9, 19, 167
    youth work 549
  background:
    American 6, **51–2**, 95, 209
    Belgian 7
    Commonwealth 612
    ex-servicemen: First World War 23, 45, 187; Second World War **48–9**, 57, 187, 201, 208, 222, 672
    German 3
    Indian 97, 609–10, 614
    overseas 51–2, 616, 627: inter-war 96–7, 630–1; since 1945 628–30, 631; in 1960s 48; fees issue 52, 651, 678
    Serbian 7
    see also admission; social class
  characteristics:
    ability range **90–1**, 773
    academic calibre rising 773
    accent 94
    affluent, relatively 102, 770
    age **64–5**, 98, 100, 208, 222, 362
    anti-academic 248
    architecture influences 103, 448, 499
    arts/science balance **59–62**, 177, 722, 749
    competitive 93–4
    dress 94
    embracing academic ideals 248
    getting into debt 558
    hierarchical 100
    homosexual 98, 99
    idle 3-4, 38, 431, 442, 534
    immature 91
    increasingly alike 77
    internationalist 406–8
    less aloof from civic universities 534, 594, 704
    less segregated by gender 62, 77, 101, **201–2, 210**, 531, 538
    loyal to college 98, 100, 212, 215
    lukewarm on NUS 594, 694
    marriage patterns 77, 97
    mental illness 201
    patriotic 24–5
    peer-group influence 93, 200, 204, 214, 534

politics national not local 688, 693
    provoke town/gown friction 557, 576
    race prejudice 630–1
    ribald 96
    turn away from sport 520, 538
    see also social class
  discipline of:
    not easy in 1960s 227, 705
    relaxed in 1960s 205, 214
    firm but flexible inter-war 100–1
    battels payment 100
    compulsory chapel 201
    on dress 201
    gating hours 97, **201–2**, 210
    Hart Committee procedure 706, 745–6
    in lodgings 98, 557
    marriage needs permission 373
    roll-calls 97
    rules for men on women 97, 201–2, 210, **361–4**
    rules for women on men 703
  friendships with:
    college servants 93, 206
    contemporaries 92, 97, 209
    tutors 92, 93, 198, 200
  funding of:
    by schools 101
    by the state: before 1939 45, **46**, 585; in 1945–60 48, 54, 187, 672–3; in 1960s 49, 672, 673, 716; since 1960s 674
    privately 47–8, 100; proportion subsidized **48–9**, 101, 672
  influence:
    appeal prevented (1960s) 649, 716
    syllabus reform (1960s) 245–6
    within colleges 204, 205, 674, 688
  name changes (1960s) 204–5, 704
  numbers 526, 547, 722
    in First World War 9, 10, 12, 14, 19
    inter-war 45–6
    in Second World War 48, 175–7
    after Second World War 48, 49, 187, 190, 480
    in 1980s 729
  in Second World War:
    austere life-style 179
    getting younger 65, 175
    Rhodes scholars 5
    social class shifts 175–6, 179
    social life 179–80
    sport 98
    subject-balance 169
  working habits:
    not completing degree **58–9**, 92, 101, 442
    scientists 197, 263
    work timetable 195
    working harder 203

see also careers; colleges; junior common
   rooms; national service; women
   undergraduates
unemployment:
   Beveridge and 185–6
   Lindsay and 396
   Oxford guilt about 432
   syllabus reflects 115
   undergraduates help relieve 96, 400
UNESCO 400
Union of Scientific Workers 696
Union Society:
   and careers:
      ambition fostered 383, 384
      media connections xvii, 383–4
   characteristics:
      anti-feminist tone 356–7, 384
      college loyalties 106–7
      House of Commons analogy 382
   criticized 167, 393, 401–2, 404
   debates:
      with Americans 383
      with civic universities 594
      dress for 400, 405
      Eights week 299, 383
      on international issues 406–8
      'King and Country' 24–5, 167–8, 400,
         406, 608, 620
      learning to speak in 382–3
      religion in 180
      speaking style 383, 399, 401
      teach-in (1965) xvii, 408
      televised 384
      working-class speakers 384
   facilities:
      bar 383
      dining room 383
      library 383, 472
      social life in cellars 383
   Isis and 402, 527
   membership:
      alumni 718
      Indians 614–15, 630
      life members 718
      women xvii, 356, 384, 718, 749
   and the parties:
      Conservatives 391–4, 400
      Labour 167, 384–5, **399–402**
      Liberals 405–8
   premises 570
   in Second World War 180
   sponsorship accepted 771
   student union option rejected 694, 706
Unitarianism 297 *see also* Manchester
   College
United Africa Company 617
United Nations 408

United Nations Food and Agriculture
   Organization (FAO) 282
United Oxford Hospitals 335
Universities' Bureau of the British
   Empire 587
Universities' Catholic Education Board 298
Universities Central Council on Admissions
   (UCCA) 595, 707
Universities and Colleges (Emergency
   Powers) Act (1915) 11
Universities Funding Council 736, 765–6,
   770
University Air Squadron 168, 175
University Bookshops Oxford 453
University Chest, *see* Chest
University College, London 345, 580
   departures from Oxford for 149–50
   reputation 601
   women at 345
University College, Oxford
   buildings 191, 510
   college servants xiv, 207
   finances 657
   in First World War 8, 9, 10, 12, 20
   General Strike and 82, 83
   junior members from overseas 629
   living conditions in 105
   Masters of 84
   SCR life in xi, 87
   size 190
   traffic's impact 106
University and College Servants' Rowing
   Club 529
University and Colleges (Trusts) Act
   (1943) 670
University Finance Board, *see* Board of
   Finance
University Galleries 485
University Grants Committee (UGC) 146,
   226, 552, 725
   origins 24, 579, 591
   Oxford's influence over 591–2
   administrative impact:
      moulds Oxford's timetable 716
      sours relations in 1950s 700, 707
      standardizes procedures 690, 695
   funding chronology:
      increases Oxford's grant (1930) 642
      private funding dominant inter-war
         644
      endorses government funding
         (1940s) 644
      postwar expansion (1945) 49, 650, 677
      raises academic salaries (1949) 652
      slows down grant increases (1950s) 650
      assesses Oxford in 1980s 736, 770
      cuts (1980s) 656, 674, 677–8, **759**, **764–8**

University Grants Committee (UGC) (*cont.*):
policies on:
funding building 499, 507, 514, 515, 516, 654
funding colleges 507, 642, 652, 654
funding women's colleges 359, 361, 655
medicine 334, 337–8
museums and libraries 678
science 162, 261, 515
student participation (1960s) 705
University Museum 264, 475, 485, 516
jubilee (1910) 40
management structure 437
pressure on space 490
in Second World War 251
subjects studied within:
chemistry 157, 267
mineralogy 274
pharmacology 318
zoology 278
teaching role 489–90
University Observatory 153
University Peace Council 25, 693
university settlements 312, 346, 386
university teachers:
numbers in Britain 581
sending offspring to Oxford 56
University Women's Action Group 369
University Women's Boat Club 368

vacations 91, 175 *see also* conferences
Van de Graaf generator 281
Varsity 16
Vatican Council, Second 300
vendettas 100
Versailles Treaty 390
vice-chancellors:
educational background 592, 594, 599
Oxford:
administrative backing for 684, 699, 700
age 684, 691, 700
difficulties experienced 684
eligibility 732: heads of house 82, 199, 684, 690; women 352
Franks Commission on 199, 732–3
how appointed 684, 691, 732
limited powers 700–1, 773
relations with: Chancellor 684–5;
colleges 684–5, 700, 712; Conference of Colleges 741; Congregation 732;
Council 685; CVCP 587, 740
roles: ceremonial 691, 707–8; fund-raising 649; leadership increasingly required 690–1, 700, 708, 734
term of office 605, 685, 691, 701, 732, 734, 740

undergraduates cannot name 701
work-load 691, 773
Vickers, armaments manufacturers 13
Victoria County History of Oxfordshire 478
Vienna 90, 461, 620
Vienna University 6
Vietnam war xvii, 403, **408**, 412
Vincent Joseph, printers, Oxford 470
Vincent's Club 526
virology 516
Vogue 427
Voluntary Oxford Health Committee 548–9
vomit 104

Waddesdon Manor, Bucks. 378
Wadham College:
Bowra and 83, 199
buildings 191, 508, 509, 512
finances 657
in First World War 8, 9, 20
junior members:
doing social work 549
examination performance 105, 213, 750
from overseas 629
library 481
and Meadow road 573
theology in 308
women at 374, 747
Waldock report on University Press (1970) 466–7
Wales:
FBAs from 593
labour migration to Oxford 545
Oxford colleges and
Jesus College links 106
landholding in 667
tithe holding in 663, 669
Oxford undergraduates from 51, 97
University of:
degrees at 585
postgraduates in 585
reputation 600–2
resembles Oxford 589, 726
schools sending students to 585
state scholarships to 585
women at 584
vice-chancellors educated in 594
Wantage Sisters 347
War, First World 3–25
academic impact on:
chemistry 9, 14–15
classical studies 9
degree classification 64
libraries 472
links with Europe 613, 621
literature 414
medicine 13

modern languages 6, 613
  publishing 470
and Belgium 6–7
bombing 12
breaks out 8
casualties 5, 6, 81, 318
  foster conscientious objection 17
  German 5, 10, **18–19**, 23
  'lost generation' 18, 21, 23, 91, 181
  number of xi, **18–23**, 181
  treated in Oxford 10
chauvinism opposed 406
college servants serve in 8–9, 22
commemorated 12, **22–3**, 25
financial impact
  on city 557
  on university 11, 24, 658, 663, 675
food in 12
fuel in 12
historical research on 136, 416
horror at 10–11
hostility to 9, 16, 155, 423
intelligence in 9
junior members in residence during 9, 10,
    12, 557
  numbers increase after 45, 48
  Rhodes scholars 10
  women 10, 12–13, 349
legacy of 18, 24–5, 391, **406**, 683
  raises colleges' prestige 81, 108
  university growth 580, 582
memoirs on 23
propaganda from Oxford in 8, 15–16, 456
recruitment in 8, 19
refugees in 6
and religion
  anti-war feeling 16
  chaplains 19
  ecumenical effect 296
  OUP and 456
  theological aspects 15
  and women 13
respirators in 9, 14
and science
  boosts its numbers 60, 62, 64
  boosts its prestige 287, 613
  its contribution to war effort 9, 28, 29, **139**
senior members serving in 8, 9
separation allowances in 9
and Serbia 7–8
support for 8
termination celebrated 81, 534
veterans of 23–4
see also individual colleges; munitions;
    Oxford city and region
War, Second World
  academic impact

boosts Commonwealth studies 617
boosts European studies 623
boosts social sciences 220, 388
on degree performance 64
hinders and helps humanities research 220
on individual subjects: classical
    studies 221; geography 253;
    geology 274–5; medicine 332, 332–5
restricts publishing 221, 462
small on curriculum 223
through science: boosts war effort 43,
    251–3; and nuclear weapons 181–2, 252;
    numbers grow 60, 62, 176, 186; science
    prestige grows 220, 287; teamwork
    research encouraged 251
aliens in 173–4
blackout 171
boosts publishing in Oxford 461
buildings requisitioned 170
cadet courses during 48
impact on Cambridge 14
casualties in xiii, 180–1
censorship during 251–2
colleges collaborate in 170, 221, 709
commemorated 189
conscription in 60, 167, 168, 169, 175, 176
financial impact 675
governments in exile 178
home guard 251
honorary degrees for the allies 178, 411
intelligence operations 181
invasion of Britain threatened 87, 173
junior members during
  austere life-style 179
  numbers increase after 48, 49
  numbers resident 169, **176–7**
  Oxford Union 180
  Rhodes scholars 5
  social class impact 179
  sport 98, 179
  subject-balance 169
  younger 65
legacy of
  on admission criteria 176, 188
  architectural 507
  financial 653
  political 188, 391
  on state funding 187–8
  on university structure 683
morale boosted by Oxford during 169,
    183–4, 221
national identity in 221
reconstruction survey 184–5
recruitment
  conscription 60, 167, 168, 169, 175
  volunteers 167, 169
religion in 180, 184

War, Second World: (*cont.*):
  senior members during
    pay 103
    war service 170–1, 388
  stimulates university growth 580, 582
  women undergraduates
    gender balance 169, 176
    war service 176
war degrees:
  in First World War 23, 45–6, 49, 118
  in Second World War 49, **171–2**; courses
    for Canadians 178; short
    courses 175–6; women and 176
  and sporting attainment 522
War on Want 204, 368
Warneford Hospital 201
Warwick, University of 583, 597, 601, 744–5
washing machines 207
Wasps, Corpus Christi College 95
Weed Research Organization 275–6
Weidenfeld and Nicolson, publishers 468
Welch scholarship 150
Wellcome Unit for the History of
    Medicine 289
Wellington House 15–16
Wellington Square, Oxford 696, 704, 708,
    746
Wells cathedral, Somerset 508
Welsh National School of Medicine 682
West Indies 6
Westminster College, Harcourt Hill 761–2
Westminster School 47, 94
Westminster, Statute of (1931) 218
Whipple Museum of the History of Science,
    Cambridge 488
White Horse, public house, Oxford 558
William of Sens, French master mason 513
Willshaws bookshop, Manchester 453
Winchester College 47, 94, 347, 537, 585
Wingfield Morris Hospital *see* Nuffield
    Orthopaedic Centre
wireless, *see* radio
Wirral Grammar School 94
wit in Oxford 87, 99, 233
Wolf prize 771
Wolfson College:
  buildings 514, 515, 517, 760
  and 'entitlement' 742
  finances 657
  founded 211, 215, 619, 714
Wolfson Foundation 361, 507, 514, 742, 746
Wolvercote, Oxon. 421, 465, 467, 474, 564
Wolverhampton Grammar School 96
women:
  admitted as full university members
    (1920) 14, 31, 34, **348–9**
  attitudes to women from:

Asquith Commission 31, 33, 34, 37, **39**,
    350, 359
  Curzon 28
  male SCRs don't discuss 87
honorary degrees for xv, 360
mixed colleges' impact on
    opportunities 749
and religion at Oxford 299, 300
roles:
  assessors 352
  chaplains 296, 305
  college servants 207
  in Congregation 14, 348, 358, 685
  on Council 353
  CUF lecturers 354
  electing to chairs 353
  estates bursars 356
  examiners 349, 353
  on faculty boards 349, 353
  on General Board 353
  in Labour Club 357–8
  landladies 557
  librarians 370–1, 480
  missionaries 346
  in OUDS 356, 363
  OUSU women's officer 771
  proctors 352
  professors 353
  in science **59–61**, 76, **254–5**, 268
  social work 373, 548–50
  vice-chancellor 352
  winning prizes 352
  wives of fellows 85, **86**, 92, 197–8, 200,
    209, 346
  writers on Oxford 440
  see also careers
votes for 14, 349
see also Asquith Commission;
    feminism; gynaecology
women dons:
  assimilated only slowly 353–4
  careers interrupted 749
  examiners 349, 353
  having young families (1960s) 373
  as head of house 361
  pay 39, **354**, 356, 359, 361
  as proportion of teaching staff 354
  proving themselves 62
  university committees exclude 356
women postgraduates, *see* postgraduates
women undergraduates:
  academic calibre 13, 366
  in examinations **61–2**, 76, 366, 751
  higher at admission 62, 63, **366**, 750
  and mixed colleges 751
  not taking degree 59
  pass school 58, 76, 116

at Cambridge 14
background:
  American 347
  Commonwealth 627–30
  overseas 627–30
  regional 51–2
  religion 55
  schools **54**, 353, 727
  social class **52–8**, 76–7, 97, 352
characteristics:
  less interested in sport 531
  little sign of feminism 369
  more prone to marry 369
contrasts with men **53–7**, 60–1, 65, **76–7,
    366–7**
in First World War 10, 12–13, 14, 45
funding 367
join men's colleges 45 *see also* mixed colleges
lodgings for 352, 358–9
numbers **45–6**, 97, 350, 355, 374, 584
  gender-balance 750
  mixed colleges' impact 749–50
  quota 39, 45, 62, 350, **356–8**, 693, 710
roles:
  JCR presidents 749
  OUSU presidents 749
  Oxford Union officers 749
in Second World War:
  gender-balance 169, **176–7**
  war service 175, 176, 178–9
segregation:
  at mealtimes 356
  clubs gradually relax 361–2, 364
  declines over time 62, 77, 101
  marriage more likely 77
  in politics 393, 718
  rarely *Isis* idols 527
  in religion 299, 300
  rules enforcing 97, 361–4
  in sport 531, 538
  in tuition 347–9
undergraduates as spouses 77, 353
subjects read:
  arts/science balance 59–62
  agriculture 254
  biochemistry 254
  botany 60, 254
  chemistry 254
  classical studies 350–1
  engineering 254
  English 61, 89, 110, 116, 359
  forestry 254
  geography 254–5
  geology 254
  law 61, 116
  life sciences 60, 254–5
  Lit. Hum. 110, 116

  mathematics 254
  medicine 13, 33, 348, 349, 359
  metallurgy 254
  modern history 61, 110, 116, 117, 359
  modern languages 60–1, 89, 110, 116,
    118–19, 359
  physics 60, 254
  physiology 254
  PPE 116
  PPP 254
  science subjects 59–61, 76, 254–5
  theology 116, 308
  zoology 60, 254, 366
  see also careers; mixed colleges; sport
women's colleges:
  1960s a golden age 373
  academic aspects:
    admission 62, 366, 530
    calibre of entry 359
    discourage pass school 366
    examinations 347, 351
    links with schools 347
    outclass the men 374
    shared library provision 368
    subject-balance 359
  architecture xv, 503
    bed-sits 104, 506
    corridors 366
    UGC funds 507, 655
  characteristics:
    decreasingly distinct from men's 107, 351
    hard work stressed 366, 367
    modelled on school/home 366, 373
    mutual collaboration 368, 710
    proportion from overseas 630
    relatively poor 354, 355, 356, 359, 746
    traditions rejected 351, 352
  distinctive at Oxbridge 345
  finances 39, 368
    adventurous in equities 671
    appeals xv, xvi, 39, **359–60,**
      649
    benefactions from men's colleges 747
    building loans from university 653
    CUF system 653
    dependent on fees 358, 672
    UGC subsidizes principals' salaries 655
  in First World War 12–13
  formally recognized as full colleges 352
  government of 346–8, 351–2
    alumni role 346, 351–2
    men's role 346, 351
  and mixed colleges:
    reluctant to admit men 374
    unenthusiastic 747
    see also mixed colleges
  registers compiled 373

women's colleges (*cont.*):
  religion in 55 **346–7**, 367
  rivals to men's 350
  SCRs 368
  in Second World War 171
  shared library facilities 477
  subjects studied:
    English literature 89
    modern languages at 61, 89
  titles of 347, 351–2
  undergraduate life:
    community life declines 367–9, 373–4
    dances xvi, 101, 367
    proportion from overseas 629
    proportion in lodgings 358
    rules about men 97, **361–4**
    sport 364, 367–8, 530
  and the university:
    CUF system 354
    long financially dependent 655
Women's Inter-Varsity Athletic Board 533
Women's Liberation Movement 369
Women's United Games Committee 531
Woodstock, Oxon. 494
Woolworth's 565
Worcester College:
  buildings:
    accommodation expanded 191
    chapel restored 509
    distinctive features 106
    Nuffield Building 504, 506
    restoration work 508
    Sainsbury Building 512
  bursarial arrangements 83
  finances 657
  in First World War 9, 20
  gardens 506
  influence in Congregation 692–3
  junior members xi, xiii, 612
    bump supper xii
    clubs 368–9
    JCR art patronage 497
    proportion from overseas 629–30
    youth club 549
  library 477
  and Oxford town planning 574–5
  SCR (*c.*1936) xi

Worcester porcelain 496
Workers' Educational Association
  (WEA) 28, 33, 34, 35, 396, 717
  and Labour Party in Oxford **385–6**, 385
working class:
  Asquith Commission and 35, **38–9**, 41
  choice of degree-course 223
  civic universities attract 595
  difficult to get into Oxford 586
  difficulties as undergraduates 441
  proportion of total undergraduates 55, 102
  scholarships won by 38, 48
  Second World War and Oxford
    admission 176
  special college for 28
  undergraduates mimic 209
  work-pattern as undergraduates 102
The World's Classics 457, 457–8, 470
Wycliffe Hall 7, 303, 304
Wytham estate 259, 275, 277, 671

x-ray cinematography 323

Yale University 174
York 453, 583, 597, 601
Younger Society (Balliol) 102
youth clubs 549
Ypres 16
Yugoslavia 182

Zeppelin raids on London 12
zoology:
  accommodation
    plans for tower xiv, **278–9**, 515–16, 566–7
    zoology/psychology building (1970)
      261, 490
  and the colleges 90, 148, 197, 271
  First World War and 14, 139
  funds for 262
  overseas influences on 622
  and related subjects
    biology 758
    medicine 319
  research in **148–9**, 154–5, 259, 278, 281
  undergraduate numbers **142**, 148, **254**, 278
  and University Museum 487, 489, 493
  women reading 60, **254**, 366